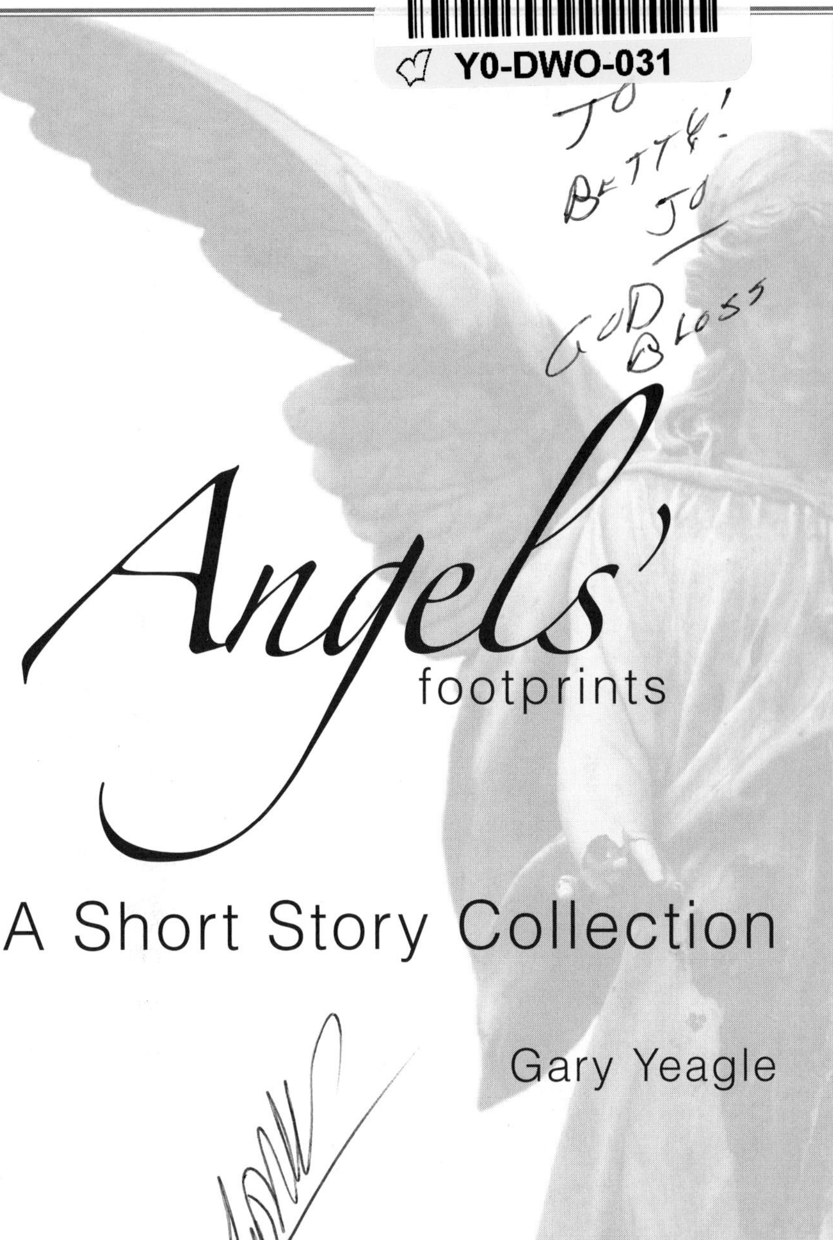

Angels' footprints

A Short Story Collection

Gary Yeagle

Publisher: Goose Creek Publishers, Inc.
4227 Vermont Avenue
Louisville, KY 40211
502-384-5109
goosecreekpublishers.com

ISBN: Trade Casebound 1-59633-011-2 $24.95

Printed in the USA

10 9 8 7 6 5 4 3 2 1

Available in retail stores.

Contents

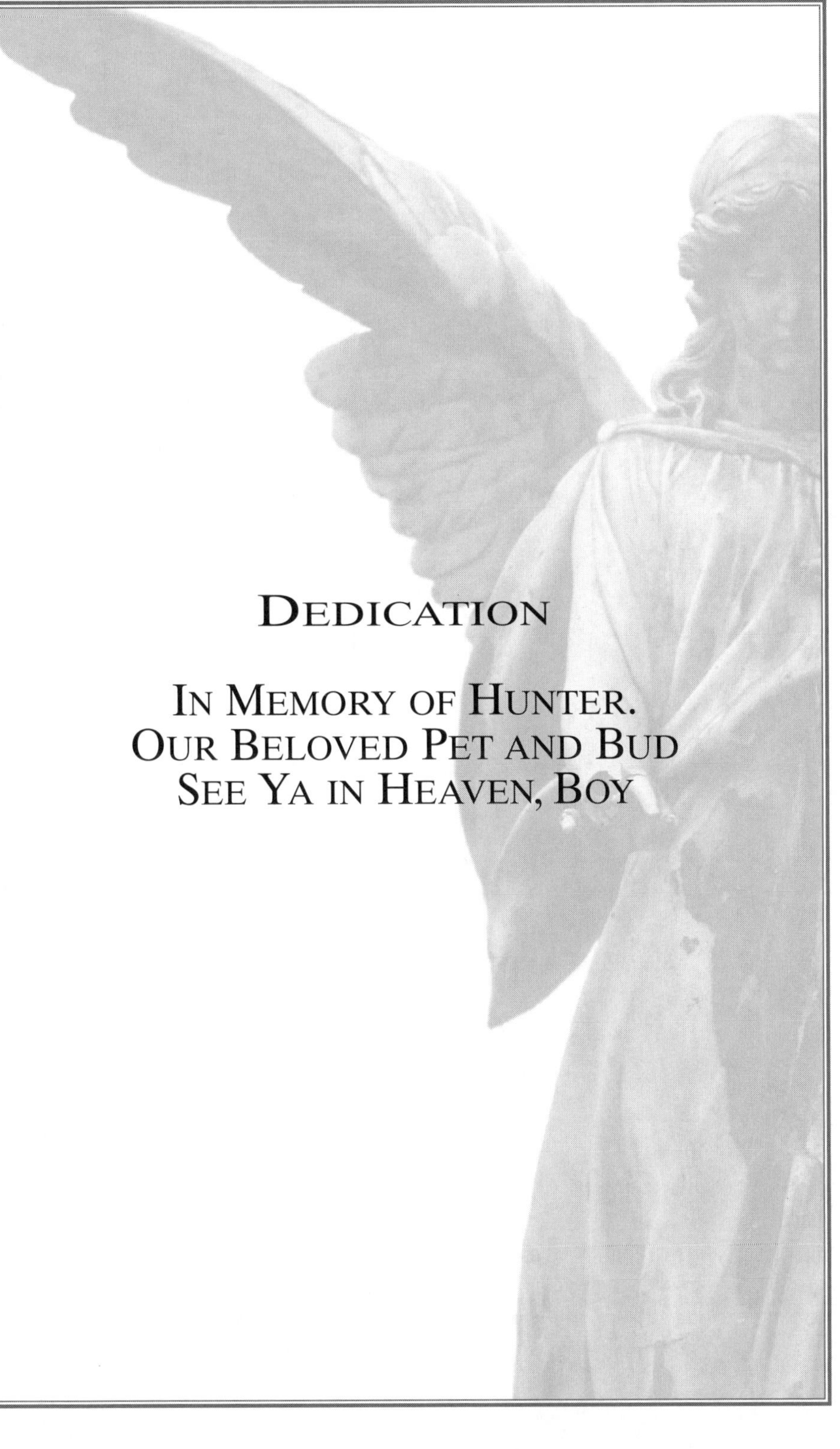

Dedication

In Memory of Hunter.
Our Beloved Pet and Bud
See Ya in Heaven, Boy

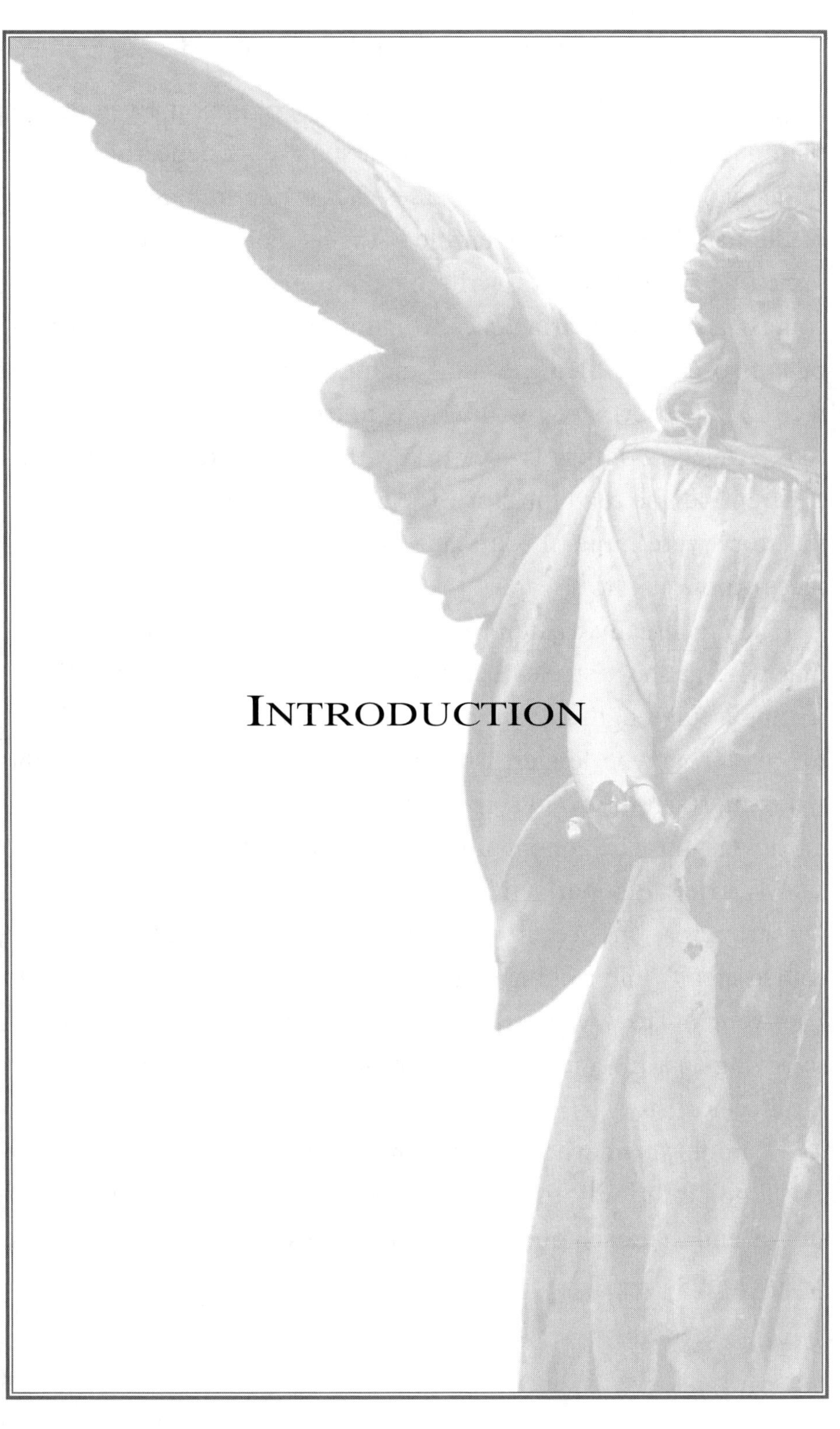

INTRODUCTION

Angels' Footprints

Angels' Footprints is a short story collection of fiction. Even though fictitious, each story is based on a personal experience of mine or someone I have know. In some cases, the stories are based on events of the past. The first story entitled Angels' Footprints which is the same title as the book was written by me years ago for a short story contest. After not hearing back from those who decide what is good or not so good, I filed the short manuscript away in a file cabinet feeling that short story writing was not my talent. Months later, I took Angels' Footprints to work with me one day and had ten different people read the story. The comments that I received about the story were quite encouraging and that I should write more of these types of stories.

Having already written a self-help book and two novels I found that writing short stories takes a different breed of writer. When writing a full length novel one must marry the characters and plot for a year, maybe longer, whereas when writing short stories the writer must get the point across, but with fewer words, plus he or she must constantly be coming up with new ideas to write about.

My wife said it perfectly one day as she was proofreading one of my short creations. According to her a full length novel is like a full course meal while a short story is more along the lines of a snack. She went on to say that if a snack was tasty it could be just as satisfying as a full meal. That being said, I feel that there is a need for the short story.

A book agent who reviewed my work told me that with the world going the way that it is that there is a need for "feel good" stories and that each one of these stories gives the reader a specific lesson in life.

Angels' Footprints

It is my prayer that as you read the following stories the Lord will bless you with each lesson, and that possibly something that I have written may change the way you think about life.

God Bless You,
Gary Yeagle

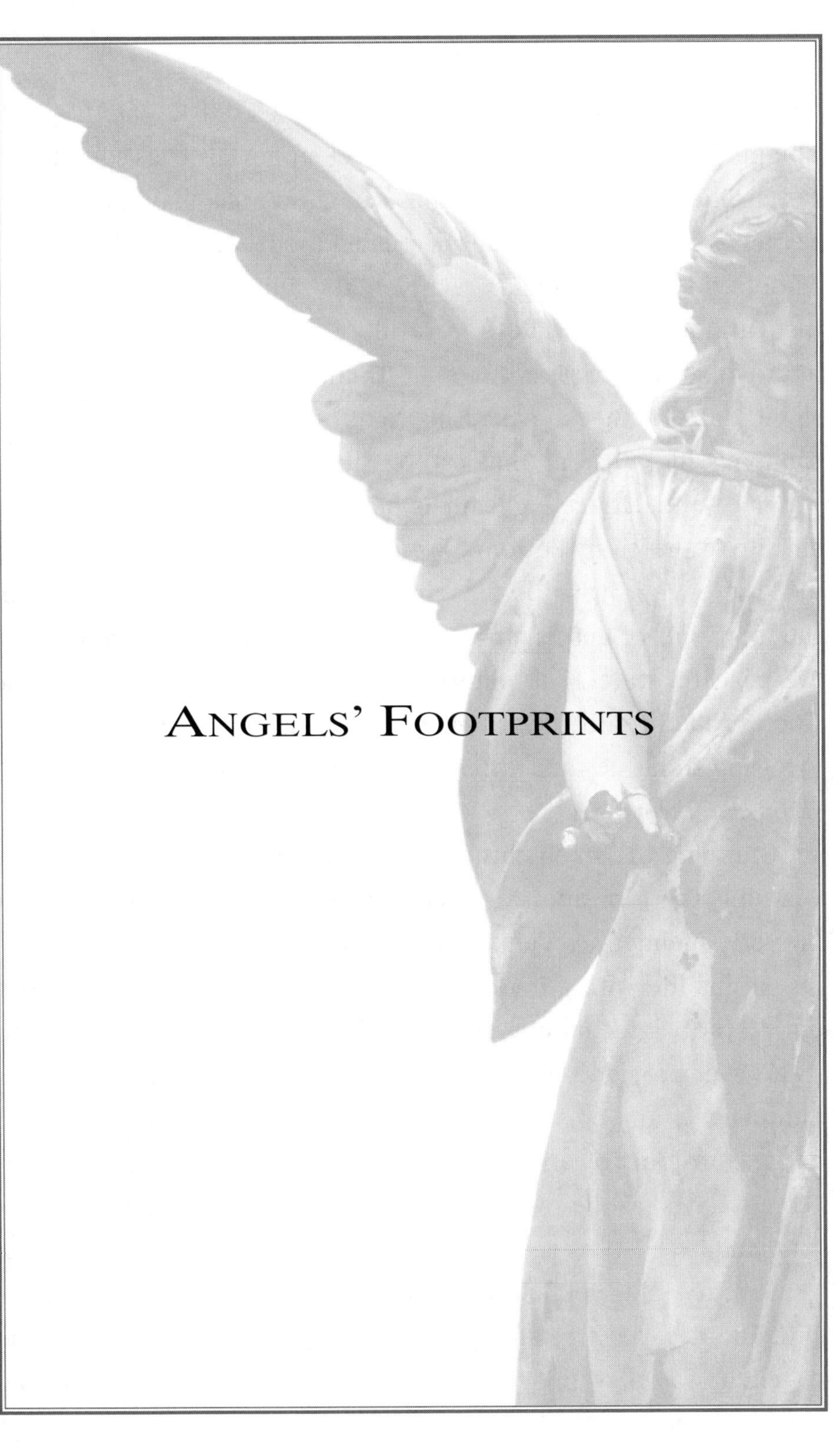

Angels' Footprints

Angels' Footprints

THE FINEST PERFORMANCE COULD ONLY BE obtained by the selection of the perfect stone. His eyes squinted in the brilliant afternoon sunlight searching the slate-gray rocks scattered on the bank. The projectile had to be contoured just right: smooth, somewhat circular, relatively flat. Flipping the rock over in his calloused hand, Pete carefully inspected it, then smiled approvingly. Placing it between his thumb and index finger, he bent slightly at the knees, cocked his right arm, and released the rock, snapping his wrist at the last possible moment. The flat stone skimmed the surface eight times before losing its momentum and sinking to the sandy bottom.

The ever-growing perfect circles always made him think about the footprints of unseen angels as they softly made their way across the peaceful water. His watery reflection became distorted as the ripples rolled gently toward the bank. Searching for another perfect throwing stone, he thought: *fifty years old and still the premier rock skipper in the county.*

Climbing the steep cliff seemed as easy as it had the previous year, but the torn and shattered ligaments of long ago had never properly mended. A Viet Cong grenade had branded him for the rest of his life with a noticeable limp, accompanied by sharp pain during the winter months. The familiar indentations in the jagged stone wall provided him ample foot and handholds as he hoisted himself over the crest of the first level. Turning slowly, he leaned back against the towering rock wall, a long, deep breath escaping his aching lungs as he wiped the beads of perspiration from his forehead.

Seventy-four feet below, the creek snaked its way lazily past the cliff. The decayed tree stump was still there, sticking up out of the water; it was a rotting tombstone where once a great tree had proudly stood. A quick movement just to the left of the stump disturbed the water as a rock trout plucked an unsuspecting water bug from the surface. The spry October wind forced its way through the thick pine boughs creating a powerful sweeping sound as if a mammoth vacuum was stirring the forest: God's way of cleaning up nature.

The golden yellow and rust-colored leaves were just beginning to release their summer grip from branches of elms and maples, the abandoned foliage gliding quietly to the creek far below, landing without the slightest sound, then slowly carried around the bend to the river miles away.

Looking to his left, he knew they would still be there. They had remained inscribed in the stone for forty years. They would be there forever: two sets of initials, a memory of childhood friends engraved in rock by young hands.

He traced his fingers over the crude markings: ES and PW. He was four when he first met Ellis Scott. Ellis, age five, whom everyone referred to as "Jake" was the new kid on the block. Mr. Scott, his wife and son had been transplanted from the Midwest with his company. They bought the house next door, and the two boys became instant companions.

The youngsters were inseparable, practically raised as brothers. Jake excelled at everything: he could throw a ball farther, run faster, achieve higher grades, and could remember the names of every ballplayer in both the American and National Leagues. The single thing he couldn't seem to grasp was how to skip a stone. After three summers, countless rocks, and excessive training from his best friend, his rock-skipping abilities left quite a bit to be desired.

Thinking about Jake always brought a wide smile to Pete's face. He ran his fingers across the rough initials once again as he remembered that first day when they had discovered the cliff: the day before Pete's tenth birthday. They had ventured into the forest further than usual. To Pete, it was like discovering King Solomon's Mines, but instead of gold, the ground was strewn with thousands of perfect skipping rocks.

They played that entire afternoon, swimming, skipping stones, and eventually climbing the cliff. Relaxing in the setting sun, they talked about the distant future. What would it be like to be fifty years old? It had been difficult to ponder. That was forty years away. They had finally arrived at the conclusion that trying to picture their future wives or kids or what kind of house they would live in was ridiculous. The sole thing they had agreed on was that they would remain the best of friends forever. To seal their pact, they carved their initials in the rock and then became blood brothers.

The method was basic: after gently slicing open their right-hand thumbs utilizing Pete's pocketknife, they pressed their bleeding skin together, vowing that they would not only remain lifelong companions, but would return to "initial rock" every year until their death.

The ceremony complete, they began to walk back home. Jake, who loved to whittle, borrowed Pete's knife as he fashioned a crude spear from a four-foot twig he found on the dirt path. He stumbled, rolling down a steep embankment to the creek, the knife flying from his hand and disappearing into the water. Pete didn't relish the thought of losing his prize treasure, but the look of astonishment on Jake's face as he slithered into the water caused uncontrollable laughter from both boys. They searched for what seemed like hours, but the knife was lost. It had been a gift to Pete from his grandfather. Jake felt bad, but Pete said it wasn't any big deal.

They parted ways once on Bell Street, with Jake running ahead saying "goodbye" and that he would see Pete tomorrow at the party. That was the last time he'd ever see Jake again, at least alive. The gentle knock at his bedroom door and the sadness in his mother's voice, "We should talk," was just the beginning of the shroud of devastation that would cover his small world.

The birthday fiesta was cancelled. The ice cream melted and the chocolate cake remained untouched. Jake, his hero, his pal, his kindred spirit, was gone. A drunken driver had put an end to Jake's life, crushing him beneath a speeding Lincoln.

The gravity of the unbearable pain at the viewing as Pete stared into the coffin was overwhelming. His legs buckling, he curled into a ball on the floor and cried until his face hurt. His father took him to a private room where he cried himself to sleep.

One week after the burial, Mrs. Scott dropped by the house, asking to see Pete. In her hands she held a small, poorly wrapped package: Pete's birthday present. Jake had picked it out the night of the accident and had said that he wanted to wrap it himself. Jake would have wanted Pete to have it.

Pete stared blankly at the small gift and only accepted it after a nod of approval from his mother. He took the gift to his room. He wanted, needed, to be alone. He carefully unwrapped the paper, opening the small cardboard box. The gift was wrapped in a handwritten note:

Sorry about the knife. Blood brothers forever.

You're the best rock skipper I ever saw. Your pal always.

Jake.

Forty years had gone by and he still carried that precious gift. Removing the knife from his pants pocket he clutched it to his heart, a tear in his eye as he thought: *Well, Ellis…I made it. Fifty years old today.* It had been close to impossible when he was ten to try and imagine what he would look like when he was fifty years old. Arriving at the half-century mark, it was arduous to think back to when he was ten. Too much had changed. The world was too complicated for things to remain childhood simple. He had gone off to war, killed the enemy, struggled through a nasty divorce, and even battled the bottle for a number of years.

Descending the cliff, he realized that the one factor in his life that had remained constant, and never changed, was this place. He had returned here every year on his birthday, skipped rocks, climbed the cliff, and thought about ol' Jake, his blood brother. As far as he could see, this unique spot had remained unscathed by the progress of the world. There were no sounds of a semi from a distant highway, only the birds and the wind. There were no neon signs or gaudy billboards, only the glorious color of the fall leaves and the deep green pines.

Near the creek's edge, he selected his final toss of the day. He hesitated, knowing this would be the finale of this year's visit. He skillfully flipped the rock toward the water. Following nine evenly spaced skips, the stone disappeared. The angels' footprints formed and grew, then slowly disappeared from sight. Maybe that unseen angel was Jake. No one could have convinced Pete that it wasn't. He had lived up to his end of the pact. He was sure God would allow Jake to return each year, too.

He turned and slowly walked up the trail toward the lofty pines, but then stopped and looked back at the peaceful creek. The water was calm now. The heavenly footprints were gone. He'd be back next year, just like always. In another forty years, he'd be…let's see; ninety years old. Would God allow him to return then? To skip a rock and to see Jake walk on the water?

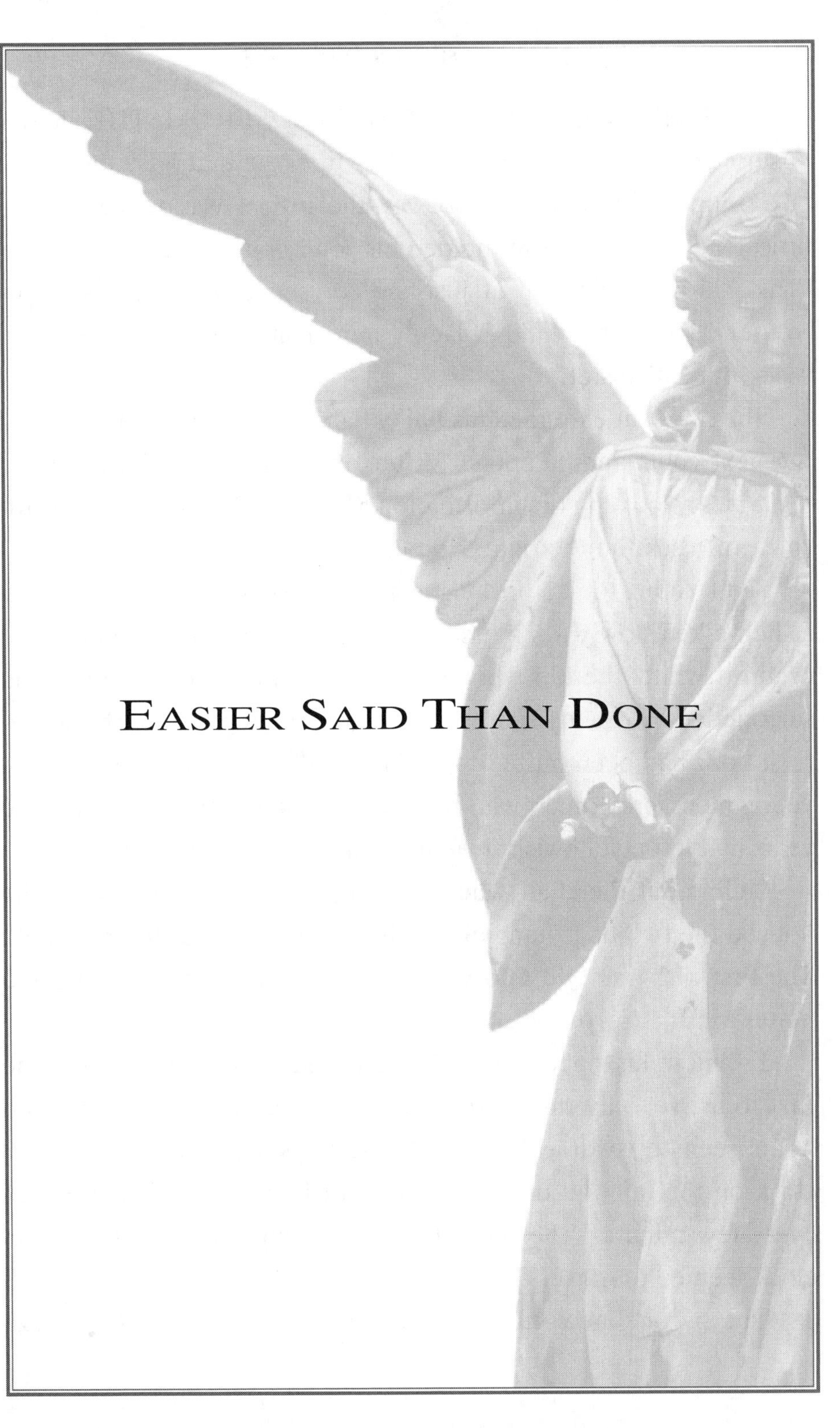

Easier Said Than Done

"NEXT!" THE STERN COMMAND FROM THE MAN positioned in the hall conveyed a clear message that once the young boy stepped through the doorway the ordeal was to begin. The officer's pressed uniform molded his solid body perfectly: starched khaki shirt, tie hanging at just the correct length, creases in his trousers like knife blades, black patent leather shoes shined to a "see-yourself" luster.

The sergeant extended his bulky hand as his harsh voice barked the next command, "Papers!" After opening the manila envelope and quickly locating the information he required, he ordered, "Third row...fifth seat on the right. No talking!"

Scott Young took a prolonged gander around the spacious room as he walked slowly to his assigned seat. The walls were painted in a drab off white, the old wooden tables placed in lines of precision surrounded by exactly spaced, faded gray folding chairs. The white-tiled floor had been buffed to a brilliant gloss, but the thousands of young men and women who had traveled across the floor over the years had left a yellowish tinge just beneath the wax finish.

Pulling out the chair where he was to spend the afternoon, he noticed the two flags hanging neatly in the middle of the rear wall. The first flag was Old Glory itself; the second that of the United States Marine Corps.

Taking in his surroundings he surmised, that he was one of the first to arrive; only three other seats were occupied. The next two hours seemed to drag by in a deliberate sluggishness, the round clock on the far wall directly in front of him gaining his attention every few minutes. The more he noticed the time, the slower the clock seemed to move.

One by one, new recruits of every imaginable shape and size

filed through the door, handed over their papers, then, like robots, walked to their designated seats. For the most part, everyone except three muscular types at the end of the first table observed the no-talking rule. Following a degrading beratement from one of the Marine officers seated at the front of the room, the threesome buttoned their lips for the remainder of the afternoon.

A tall, slender black youth took a seat directly across from Scott. His head was completely shaved and he had the biggest hands Scott had ever seen. Maybe a basketball player, he thought. The seat on his left remained empty, while the chair on the right was occupied by a short, white fellow sporting a crew cut and a friendly smile. Another hour ticked by as he thought about what a long day it was turning out to be. Following an early morning breakfast with his folks, they had driven Scott to the local recruiting office and said their goodbyes. The recruiter then drove he and two others to the county airport where they boarded a commuter over to New York, then took a regularly scheduled flight that stopped in both Philadelphia and Baltimore to pick up more recruits before their final destination in Charleston, South Carolina.

The large basement room at the airport was to be their last glimpse of civilized life as they knew it. Soon they would be herded onto a small convoy of commercial buses that would transport them to Paris Island, South Carolina.

Just after five o'clock the door was shut. For the next hour, they were informed by the trio of enlisted Marines what to expect over the next thirteen weeks of basic training. The orientation complete, they were fed a final meal of sandwiches, chips and soda. Next, any contraband, as they referred to it: lighters, food, drugs, candy, cigarettes, jewelry and the like had to be handed over until their training was complete.

Shortly after midnight, the order to file out of the room was given, each group of tables assigned to a bus, which would be waiting outside. The three-bus convoy pulled away from the airport, the Marine guides suggesting that the recruits try and get some sleep as the next few days were going to be a sleepless, nonstop hell.

The seating arrangements in the bus corresponded with the assigned seating from the airport basement, thus Scott found himself seated next to the crew-cut, ever-smiling boy. The boy offered his hand in friendship as he introduced himself, "Name's Ezra Barnes. My friends call me E. Z., but it usually turns out to be Easy."

Scott returned the handshake, "Scott Young."

Scott would have just as soon dozed off, but Ezra was full of questions about his new-found friend. Scott lived in upstate New York, just a twenty-minute drive from the Canadian border. His mother was from Vancouver, British Columbia, and his father hailed from a small seaside community in Maine.

Both of his parents were successful physicians, their combined income reaching a level that allowed his family a very comfortable lifestyle. Scott's parents were not folks that one could refer to as rich, but rather more in the category of "very well off." They were not the type of people who flaunted their wealth or possessions in front of others, but were actually quite conservative, donating a large portion of their income to a number of deserving charities in the surrounding area.

They had met in medical school, became engaged two years later, then the following year got married. They were extremely goal-orientated, investing their money wisely in stocks and bonds and in the purchase of a few prospering local businesses in town.

Scott had a sister who was two years his senior. The Youngs had raised their two children with the same success-driven ambitions as their own. Both Scott and his sister, Aubrey, had made the decision to enter the medical profession.

Aubrey was already attending her second year of medical school and well on her way to becoming an oral surgeon. Scott had surprised his parents when he informed them just prior to entering high school that he was interested in combining a medical career with that of the military. It was his intention to become a Naval doctor and, at some point in the future, retire from military service and then start a practice of his own.

The local high school offered an R.O.T.C. program for the Marines, but nothing for the Navy. He soon found that the Marines had a long-standing relationship with the Navy, whereas, the Marine Corps had no medical staff, but relied on the Navy for their medical needs. The Marine major at the high school told Scott that he could attend four years of R.O.T.C. training and still join the Navy.

Scott breezed through his high school years, eventually gaining the honor of commander of his R.O.T.C. unit his senior year. He was active in sports, community activities and extra curricular projects at school. He was the perfect example of the phrase, born leader.

There was just something about the way he handled himself and the problems that he was confronted with. He possessed a knack for taking over situations in a natural sort of way. He really never ordered anyone to do anything, but had a unique method of suggesting how and when things should be accomplished. People around him always seemed to rise to the occasion. He had a way of getting along with people.

Easy Barnes had been asking questions about his past life for over an hour. Just when it seemed like the smiling youngster was going to wind down, following a long yawn that Scott hoped would lead to the remainder of the trip being one of rest, Easy went into a long rendition of his own background.

He had been born and raised on the Kentucky-Tennessee border, his house just two-hundred yards from the Volunteer State. He had three brothers, all older than he, and two younger sisters, the youngest being a toddler of only eight months. Their nine-room farmhouse was located at the base of a mountain and had been in the Barnes family since way back before the Civil War. His great-grandfather had been a sergeant in the Confederate Army and had been killed at the Battle of Perryville, Kentucky.

He and his family lived in what was referred to as the Appalachian Region. He was not the least bit ashamed to admit that he had grown up in the poorest section of the country. He said that folks there had always been poor and most likely would continue to live in the same way for years to come.

His daddy worked in the city, which was about a two-hour drive one way. He had a good job up there. Good paying jobs were not to be found in or around Appalachia. The reason that he was joining the Marines was to escape the destitute way of life that hung like a dark shroud over his hometown. He saw what the day in and day out struggle with poverty had done to his father and wanted to offer his future family something more to live for.

Despite his father's efforts to earn a decent living, between feeding a large family and the gas expense of driving back and forth from the city, it was an unending battle to keep the family's head above water. If there would have been some sort of work that his mother could have done to create additional income, she would surely have taken it on, but taking care of the younger children in itself was full-time work.

When he was just about nine years old, he had developed a habit of wandering off alone into the woods. After a year of exploring every inch of the mountain for miles, he decided to get up early and hike not only all the way to the top, but down the other side deep into Tennessee.

At the foot of the mountain on the opposite side, he discovered a super highway being built through the wilderness. Hiding behind a huge boulder, he watched in amazement as earthmovers and gigantic trucks with tires as big as a house plowed their way through the deep forest.

His folks never questioned him as to where he had spent the day as long as he was seated at the supper table each night. The evening meal was always served late due to Mr. Barnes' long drive home after work.

He returned to the construction site every day, except on Sundays, which was a day of worship around the Barnes' house. Church started early in the morning and by the time it ended, it was close to noon. Mama always prepared a big dinner and usually surprised everyone with two or three of her blueberry or peach pies. He always said, "If mama would have had enough fixins' she could have made a fortune sellin' those pies."

One particular Saturday morning, one of the construction workers spotted Easy peering around a tall tree. With a little coaxing, he and another man got him to come out of the woods. Before the day was over, Ezra Barnes had found some new friends. Most of the men were from New York City or Jersey. Ezra was amazed at their funny way of talking, but figured they were probably amazed at his Kentucky twang also.

The men got to calling him the Mountain Boy and were always willing to share their lunch with the poor kid from the other side of the mountain. That summer was a sizzler, the temperature rising and then stalling in the nineties for three straight weeks. The men were always complaining about how thirsty they were. They had coolers containing iced tea and cold water, but the local water wasn't very tasty to begin with.

After listening to the constant bickering of the men, Easy showed up bright and early one morning toting two one-gallon jugs of fresh spring water from the Kentucky side of the mountain. After tasting the water, one of the men commented that it was surely the nectar of the gods. Before long, Easy had a small prospering business going, the men offering him a dollar a jug.

On Wednesdays, he'd always bring two homemade pies and on Fridays, a big basket full of fried chicken and biscuits for which the men gladly paid. Easy gave all the money from the construction workers to his mother. By the end of the summer, Easy had contributed over two hundred dollars toward helping the family's financial problems. His mother said that he could keep all the money. After all, toting the jugs of water and the baskets of food over the mountain had been no small task for someone his age. They could deposit the money in the bank for his future.

Easy told his mom that if she wanted to put the money in the bank that was okay, but he wasn't all that interested in the money for himself. He knew they needed it for food and the like. She finally agreed, but also insisted that he at least keep half the money from each trip over the mountain.

That fall school was back in session. The men missed seeing the mountain boy who was now only able to visit them on Saturdays. The following summer, Easy had to walk further as the workers had moved a few miles down the road to continue a new section.

Besides being paid for his daily cargo, he was allowed to ride along on the equipment. He was always full of questions and before long understood how each piece of equipment operated just from his observations.

Toward the end of the second summer of crossing the mountain to be with his construction friends, he and the men sat under the cover of a stand of trees as the pouring rain prevented them from making any progress. From previous conversations, the men realized that their little friend from over in Kentucky was dirt poor. One of the men told Easy that he had come from a large family in the city. He had twelve brothers and sisters. He had joined the Marines after high school and, thanks to ol' Uncle Sam, learned to operate heavy equipment. After leaving the service, he landed a great paying job that enabled him to never again experience poverty.

The third year of construction, a new crew of men was assigned to the highway project and stationed too far down the road for Easy to reach in a day's time. He still crossed the mountain every day and sat and thought about his friends from New York. He never forgot what the man had said about the Marines. The thing that bothered him was the man had said that in order to join you had to graduate from high school.

This presented Easy with a problem. Graduating from high school in the Appalachian Region was something that a lot of kids never got to experience. Most of the kids dropped out early to find work in order to help their families. Since most of the parents hadn't had much of an education themselves, the children didn't seem to get too motivated about finishing school either.

Easy had never been too much on setting goals. There wasn't any reason to. You were raised in poverty, usually wound up meeting some local girl from school, getting married and surviving much the same way as your folks had. It was a struggle for Easy, but the burning desire to break away from his current lifestyle drove him to study hard, eventually resulting in his graduating from high school. Two weeks before graduation, he had borrowed a friend's pickup truck, drove up to Lexington, located a recruiting office and joined the Marines. On graduation day at the supper table, he announced to the family that he was joining the service. His mother thought it was an excellent choice, but his father strongly objected.

Mr. Barnes, during his youth, had dropped out of school and joined the Marines. In those days, a high school education was not a requirement. After completing only nine weeks of school, he lied about his age and became a Marine.

His objection to Ezra, or for that matter, any of his children joining the service, stemmed from the result of a military accident that left him partially disabled. He received an honorable discharge, but the Marine Corps, upon bidding him farewell, hadn't offered him much in the way of financial restitution. He had given of himself to defend his country and in doing so had become injured. The Marines, as far as he was concerned, had turned their backs on him, leaving him scarred for life with little to show for his patriotic efforts.

Just outside Beaufort, South Carolina, Scott's eyelids could no longer defy the need for sleep. He drifted off thinking about how he and Ezra seemed to be exact opposites. He came from a background of well-to-do parents, he was a goal setter, very aggressive, and had breezed through high school. Ezra Barnes had grown up surrounded by poverty, and the only goal he seemed to have ever accomplished was completing high school. He had a laid-back attitude about life that couldn't possibly be categorized as aggressive.

Scott hadn't been asleep for more than fifteen minutes when the bus stopped at the main gates of Paris Island. The Marines back at the Charleston Airport hadn't been too far off the mark when they stated that the thirteen weeks of pure hell would start as soon as they arrived.

The next twenty-four hours were a nonstop nightmare, the young recruits constantly being shoved and shouted at as they received their 782 gear and war belt. Then there were haircuts, medical examinations and paying a visit to the base dentist. Finally separated into companies, the recruits were assigned a squad bay where they collapsed in their racks. Scott and Easy wound up in the same company. The last thing Scott remembered that night before nodding off was looking over at Ezra. Despite the total exhaustion they had all experienced, Easy had that big grin on his face as if nothing in the world could have phased him.

Two weeks later in a steady downpour, Scott's company trudged through ankle-deep mud on a five-mile run. At the end of the exercise, the squad stopped for a short pause near a dense swamp. Scott's fatiques were soaked clear through, not simply because of the rain, but from the perspiration created by the eighty-eight percent humidity. Taking a long, refreshing swallow from his canteen, he noticed the salt rings staining the armpits of his camouflaged tee shirt. At the moment, he felt so drained that he didn't think he had another drop of sweat in his system.

Scott's previous R.O.T.C. training had landed him the appointment of squad leader and it had been explained to him that he was responsible to help any recruits in his company who seemed to be falling behind in their training. Walking to the end of the line, he stopped next to Ezra who was sipping at his canteen.

"Easy, how goes it?"

Removing the canteen from his mouth, Easy produced one of those wide smiles as he responded, "Great! This rain reminds me o' some o' the summer storms back home."

Scott screwed the lid back on his canteen as he wiped the rain from his face.

"Easy, I've got to tell you as your squad leader that things aren't that great…as you seem to put it."

Easy's face wrinkled in confusion. "What're ya talkin' `bout?"

"You just don't seem to get the idea of this training we've been going through. Like today…you came in last during the run."

"Well," said Easy, "really didn't look at it like no race. I mean…I got here jus' like the rest o' the fellas. What's the big deal?"

"The deal," said Scott, "is that you have to start picking up the pace. You don't seem to be too concerned about what we're trying to accomplish here. You have to show more aggressiveness or they're going to kick you out of the corps."

"They cain't do that! I haven't done nothin' wrong. I've done everythin' they asked me to."

"That's not good enough. You have to show them that you are willing to go the extra mile…ya know…beyond the call of duty. Look, I like you, Easy. I know how important it is for you to be a Marine." Scott looked out across the dismal swamp, then continued as he turned back to Easy. "I heard the drill instructors talking the other night before we hit the rack. If you don't start showing some improvement, they're going to force you out."

"They cain't make me quit…I…I won't do it!"

"Easy, you don't understand. It's their job! If you can't take the pressure of rising to the task here at boot camp, how will you react in a combat situation?"

"I'll do jus' fine. I don't care what they do ta me. I won't quit!"
"There's an easier way to do this," commented Scott. "Just try to turn things up a notch. Be more concerned…more aggressive. I

know you have it in you."

"Cain't do it," said Easy.

"Why not?"

"Well, let's jus' say that it's easier said than done."

"What on earth does that mean?"

"Jus' what I said. It's easy fer ya ta tell me ta speed up the way I do things, but it ain't that easy fer me ta do it."

"Man, you've lost me, Ezra."

"It's like this. It's the way I was raised. Back home we have a diff'rent way o' lookin' at things. Things kinda git done when they git done. There's no rush. I've always managed to git by not worryin' too much `bout things in the past so why should the present or even my future be any diff`rent?"

The next three weeks seemed to drag by in the stifling heat. August was hotter than usual and there wasn't a day that passed where someone didn't go down from heat exhaustion. Scott excelled in everything that he was assigned and would most likely receive the honor of carrying the company flag on graduation day. Easy continued to do things at his own pace, always coming in last, but always on his feet, that great smile, which ticked off the D.I.s to no end, always plastered across his face.

Three other recruits who couldn't seem to keep up the rigorous training finally dropped out and were shipped back home. Ezra, because of his perceived rebellious attitude of not being overly concerned about things, had been a dropout candidate by the instructors from the beginning, but no matter what they threw at him, he refused to buckle under and quit.

As the hot summer rolled along, it seemed that rather than the drill sergeants wearing him down, he was grinding them to a pulp.

They found it hard to believe that he could withstand the abuse they doled out specifically at him. On one particular occasion, the instructor's patience had finally come to an end. Ezra, as usual, finished last in a five-mile run. The entire company was punished for his last-place finish by having to run the course a second time. Ezra came in last again, except for six recruits who dropped from total exhaustion along the way.

The drill instructor was determined to put an end to Easy's military career, excusing the rest of the company and making Ezra run the course a third time. He finished on his feet, smiled, and asked the sergeant if he wanted him to run it again. The instructor not only made him run again, but forced him to run harder. The energy level inside Easy's body had been worn to a frazzle and despite the fact that he seemed to fall in the mud every few steps he always got back up, smiled, said, "Sorry, sir," then continued to stumble on.

Ezra stood outside that night in the pouring rain, his full gear still attached to his body, with two recruits assigned to stand guard over him, not permitting him any sleep. The next morning there was ol' Easy standing at attention, soaked to the skin. Following breakfast, the D.I. approached Ezra, who smiled and asked him if he was ready for an early morning run. That was the first and only time Scott had ever seen one of the instructors smile. From that moment on, the instructors backed off, feeling that if the kid could take everything they had thrown at him and still keep kicking, then he was good enough to be a Marine.

Weeks later, on graduation day, Scott carried the company flag as his company marched in perfect step out onto the paved parade deck, all those present prepared to become United States Marines. Following the ceremony, Scott met with his parents and sister. He looked for Ezra in the crowd, wanting to introduce him to his folks. As far as he was concerned, his friend from Kentucky was the toughest recruit in the camp. Easy was nowhere in sight.

Hours later, packing his gear for the trip back home to New York, Scott noticed that Easy's rack was empty. Asking some of the others if they had seen him, one of the guys said that he had just come in, packed and left without even saying much of anything. Piling inside the family station wagon, Scott suggested a quick stop at the PX before leaving the base. He knew his folks, especially his sister, would be interested in picking up some souvenirs.

Scanning a shelf of coffee mugs, Scott spotted Easy paying for a sweatshirt at the sales counter. Putting down the coffee mug in his hand, he intercepted his friend as he was heading for the door. "Easy…hold on!"

Ezra turned, the permanent smile on his face gone for the moment.

Scott placed his hand on Easy's shoulder. "What's going on. I looked for you right after the ceremony. You just disappeared. I wanted to introduce you to my family. I was sort of looking forward to meeting your folks, too."

Easy placed his duffel bag next to the door, then smiled. "I'm sorry…It's jus' that I sort o' feel bad `cause I'm prob'ly the only guy on the base whose parents didn't show. I was kinda hopin' they'd be here, but with the way my father feels `bout the military I guess I knew all `long that I was on my own. My mother would've liked to be here, but with Pa bein' the breadwinner an' all, she has ta support his decisions. I really wanted ta say goodbye ta ya, but I was jus' too embarrassed."

"Are you going home now?" asked Scott.

"Don't think so. I've been assigned to a division out in San

Diego. Guess I'll jus' catch a bus an' spend a week or so on the beach `fore reportin'. Never seen the ocean."

"Look," said Scott. "I've got a great idea. I don't have to report to Philly for almost two weeks. Why don't you come up to New York with my family? We've got plenty of room. We can take a day or two and drive down to Niagara Falls, and well, the ocean isn't more than a few hours away. Whadda ya say?"

It took nearly fifteen minutes of coaxing from Scott, but finally Ezra agreed to spend the next few days with the Youngs. Scott's family lived a life that was completely out of sync with Ezra's upbringing. The sprawling six-bedroom creekstone house was snugly nestled in a grove of large maple trees, the grass surrounding the house cut to perfection. The paved driveway was lined with two stone walls, fronted by endless rows of begonias and other colorful flowers.

A three-tier water fountain was centered in a circular grass section encircled by a round drive in front of the three-story house, a mammoth vine-covered stone chimney adding a touch of warmth to the residence. The interior was decorated with antiques dating back to the Revolutionary War. Climbing the spiral staircase to the second floor was like stepping back in time. Ezra's room was enormous, a spectacular view of the mountain range just outside the large double windows.

That first evening, Ezra sat next to Scott, with Aubrey and Mrs. Young opposite them and Mr. Young at the head of the table. Easy's eyes fell on the feast before him–Yankee pot roast, new potatoes and baby carrots, Caesar salad, hot rolls and a relish tray.

As Mr. Young reached for the meat platter, Ezra spoke up, "It was really nice o' you folks ta invite me up here. If it's a`right I'd like ta say the blessin.'"

Mr. Young gave Scott a quick look, then asked his son, "I guess you did not explain to Ezra the way we feel about religion?"

Scott, realizing that he should have forewarned his friend about his parent's beliefs stumbled, "I…ah,…well, no."

Mrs. Young, wanting to avoid an awkward moment interrupted, "Easy, let me explain. We don't believe in God, so therefore we don't bless our food. We're what's more commonly referred to as atheists. We have raised both Aubrey and Scott as such, bearing in mind that when they no longer live under our roof they can decide for themselves in the possibility of the existence of a Supreme Being."

"That's right," chimed in Scott's father, "and I hope we haven't embarrassed you in any way. We are of the opinion that everyone has the right to their own beliefs. We have never taken the stand of criticizing those who profess to be Christians and we certainly wouldn't think of depriving you of the right to bless your meal. We only ask that you say your prayer in silence. In this way, we can both respect each other's beliefs."

Ezra wasn't about to touch food without thanking the Good Lord. He bowed his head and silently prayed while the Young's waited patiently. Surprisingly, after the meal was served, Mr. Young brought up the subject of religion, asking what faith Ezra practiced.

Easy explained that he had been brought up in a nondenominational church and that he had really never met anyone who didn't believe in God. Up until just a few moments ago, he had always been under the impression that everyone believed in God.

As the conversation rolled along, he told the Youngs that back home religion was a big part of their life. They attended church every Sunday morning and on Wednesday night. They read the Bible every evening after supper and thanked the Lord for what they had. While dessert was being dished out, Mr. Young commented that if Ezra didn't try to convince them that there truly was a God, then they wouldn't try to push him in the direction of believing that the Creator didn't exist. Easy stabbed a thick slice of chocolate cake as he smiled in agreement.

As promised, days later, Scott got Ezra to the ocean. Following a day of lying on the beach and swimming in the rolling waves, they went out for a relaxing dinner at a renowned seafood restaurant just up the coast, famous for its Maine lobster. Scott claimed that until you sank your teeth into a lobster from Maine, then you really hadn't experienced real lobster.

After ordering their meals, Easy ordered a beer and a glass of wine, pulling a pack of cigarettes from his coat pocket, removed one, lit up and sat back as he forced a long stream of bluish smoke toward the ceiling. Looking across the table, he saw the absolute look of amazement on Scott's face.

At first, Scott was speechless, but finally asked, "When did you start smoking…and drinking?"

Shrugging as if it were no big deal, Easy took another long drag, then a sip of beer. "Ta tell ya the truth…I guess since I was `bout seven."

Scott leaned forward, not believing what he had just heard. "How can that be? You didn't smoke at the airport when we first met. You didn't smoke at my house. You refused wine when my father offered it to you. You didn't smoke on the beach."

"The reason I didn't smoke or drink durin' that time was `cause I thought the time spent durin' basic trainin' would be a good time fer me ta stop. I've been given' it a lot o' thought, but I've been at it too long ta quit."

Scott sat back in his chair. "Let's back up here a minute. You say you've been drinking and smoking since you were seven…that's what you said…seven?"

"Yep, that's right."

"So, all those years while you were growing up, your folks never knew?"

Easy flicked ashes into a glass ash tray following another swallow. "Never said they didn't know."

"So what you're telling me is that this is and has been okay with your parents?"

"Yeah, it is. It's diff'rent where I come from. A lot o' youngins' smoke. As fer as drinkin' goes, we don't have beer or wine. We drink shine. Our neighbor jus' up the road brews the stuff. Out in the woods `hind his barn. Down home, we drink it like it was water."

"I'm confused," said Scott. "You said that you came from a nondenominational church background. What does that mean? What exactly is a nondenominational church?"

"It's a church where you don't have to belong to any particular religion. Actually, it's a church where folks from diff`rent religions can worship together."

Scott held up his hands in wonder as he stated, "You said that religion is a big part of growing up back home…where you're from. If this is true, how can parents allow their children to drink and smoke at such a young age?"

Easy stubbed out his cigarette as he twirled the beer glass in his hands. "You make it sound like we're some kind o' heathens. Mebbe the youngins smoke an' drink, but even though we don't have the luxuries ya'll do up north here, the crime rate where I come from is way below what yer faced with here. I've never been drunk an' I don't believe jus' `cause I smoke that the Good Lord is goin' ta deny me entrance ta heaven."

Scott looked out the front window and then back to Ezra. "With the way that I was raised, I can't say for sure whether there is a heaven or not. But if there is, that has nothing to do with your health while you're alive. Drinking and smoking since you have been seven means that you have been mistreating your liver, your lungs…your entire body for what…almost ten, eleven years. You may have already caused serious damage to yourself. I know I'm a long way off from being an actual doctor, but I've got to tell you that if you don't quit, or at least cut back, you could wind up cutting your life short by ten, maybe twenty years. It's not too late. I've done a lot of reading on this stuff. If you stop now, you can start to reverse the damage that may have already occurred."

"Cain't do it," said Easy.

"What do you mean you can't? Who says you can't change the way things are? Who's holding you back?"

"The way I was raised is what's holdin' me back. Quittin' is well…easier said than done."

Scott looked at Easy in bewilderment. "You said the same thing back down on Paris Island when we talked about you becoming more aggressive. It's like some kind of pat answer you have for the things in your life that you need to change."

"That's only yer opinion," Ezra pointed out. "You was the one who decided that I needed ta be more aggressive…not me. I didn't change the way I did things in basic training an' I made it through jus' like the rest o' the guys. I cain't see how stoppin' habits I've been practicin' since I was a kid change my life either."

Dinner finally arrived and the conversation continued. Scott was totally baffled about his friend's bad habits and Easy was not the least bit concerned over his future health matters. Two weeks later, Ezra hopped a flight to the West Coast and Scott drove down to

Philadelphia, their military careers were about to take shape. They agreed to stay in touch, updating each other on their progress.

Easy arrived in San Diego, the West Coast version of Paris Island, where a new training center for heavy equipment operators was making its debut. The operation was in full swing by the time Easy arrived and was assigned. The first three months were on the boring side as he and fifteen other young Marines sat in a classroom and reviewed schematics and diagrams of engine parts, drive trains and the inner working mechanisms of dozers, dump trucks, backhoes and a host of equipment he had never seen before.

The technical aspect of their training finally at an end, they spent what seemed like endless weeks on a two-hundred acre stretch of beach where they moved mounds of sand and dirt from one area to another. Easy was right at home, sitting atop a huge bulldozer, operating the numerous handles and gauges as he recalled his days watching and riding with the men from New York as they worked on the Tennessee highway back when he was a youngster.

Their training now complete, the unit was flown over to Saudi Arabia where they would be stationed for the next two years as they assisted the local government in constructing a new airport. Easy was well-liked by the rest of the crew, although he stuck pretty much to himself when it came to social activities. Even though he was still drinking, he didn't like to go out on a drunk, which seemed to be the thing to do during free time. His time alone was spent taking long walks out into the surrounding desert or maybe going into town for a few drinks, dinner and a good movie.

He wrote Scott on a monthly basis, letting him know that he finally did go back to Kentucky to visit his folks. His father still disapproved of his joining the military, but he found that if the subject wasn't brought up, they got along just fine. Scott was stationed at a military hospital situated next to a naval depot in Philly. His schooling had started right after he had reported for active duty. Between his daily instructions at the hospital, he spent four hours each day attending classes at a local university. He didn't have much time for any type of social life, but he did write that he had become a Phillies fan, going to the games whenever he had an opportunity.

It wasn't until three years later, when Easy returned to the states and was assigned to a unit in Wilmington, Delaware, that they were able to spend some time together. The three years of separation that had cut into their friendship were now being replaced with an opportunity to hook up at least two to three times a month as they were only an hour's drive apart.

Their first meeting occurred when Easy drove up to Philly just two weeks after he returned to the states. He picked Scott up at the hospital and off they went for a night on the town. Easy looked the same, that ol' smiling face beaming as always. Scott had grown a few inches taller and was now sporting a short mustache.

Following a great dinner at a barbeque rib joint, they set out for a local club. During dinner, Easy had downed three beers and smoked two cigarettes. Scott felt like saying something, but thought better of it. He hadn't seen his old pal in three years. Why stir things up by getting into a conversation that could only result in an argument based on medical facts versus how Easy had been raised?

The club turned out to be a neighborhood bar that offered live music and special prices on drinks as it just happened to be ladies' night. Scott and Easy took a corner table and settled back for a relaxing evening, Easy knocking down three beers in the time it took Scott to drink his first.

Scott had always been known as a ladies' man while in high

school, his good looks and outgoing personality always netting him an attractive female on his arm. He had gone out on a few scattered dates since arriving in Philadelphia, but his demanding study schedule limited the time he had to pursue any type of serious relationship with the opposite sex.

Spotting two good-looking females on the other side of the room, Scott scooted his chair back, stood and announced that he was going to see if he could get them to come over for a drink. Five minutes later, Scott returned flanked by a tall blond and her brunette friend. Introductions complete, Easy found himself sitting next to a brown-haired, green-eyed beauty by the name of Erika.

After a round of drinks, Scott asked the blond if she wanted to dance. Easy and Erika remained at the table. Twenty minutes later, Scott's plan of spending the evening with the girls fell apart as the blond commented that they had to get going.

Following the departure of the girls, Scott ordered his third drink, stating that three was his limit. Easy stuffed three pretzels in the side of his mouth as he finished his beer and reached for another.

"What was wrong with that girl that you were with?" asked Scott.

"Don't imagine there was anythin' wrong with her," answered Easy.

"Well you could have fooled me. You didn't even offer to buy her a drink; you didn't ask her to dance. I don't think you said more than ten words to her the whole time we were sitting here."

Easy took a long drink. "She seemed real nice."

"You amaze me," said Scott. "Do you have the slightest inclination as to why they left?"

"Well...I guess they had somewheres else ta go."

"It's only nine-fifteen. They walked in just a few minutes after we got here. The reason they left is because you treated the one you were with…like, well…as if she didn't exist."

Easy smiled. "Didn't realize that I was with one o' `em. I thought we was all jus' kinda sittin' here havin' a good time."

Scott picked up his beer, started to take a drink, but then hesitated, asking, "You almost acted as if you were afraid to speak to her. Don't people down in Kentucky date or what?"

"I never did."

"You never went on a date?"

"That's right…not when I was in school, or fer that matter since I've been in the service. I've always been on the shy side when it comes ta gals."

"I can't believe you've never been on a date."

"Well, there was that one time. I took my cousin Celia ta the prom. She was only fourteen at the time. Wore her mama's weddin' gown. She looked right pretty as I recall."

"Thank God," said Scott. "So it's just a matter of your being shy. For a while there I thought you were just being rude to that girl. We can solve this. I can give you some dance lessons, tell you what to say when you're around girls. You've got to get out there and meet someone."

"Nah…don't think that'll be necessary. You'd be a wastin' yer time. 'Sides that…I cain't do it…I mean start dancin'an' talkin' with womenfolk an' all that."

"Why not."

Before Easy even answered, Scott sat back in his chair. "Don't even say it. You're getting that look on your face. I just know you're going to say that it's easier said than done."

"Took the words right outta my mouth," laughed Easy. "Never

had no use fer girls when I was growin' up. Ain't goin' out an' lookin' fer one neither. If one crosses my path that catches my fancy, I'll worry `bout it then."

Over the next five years, Scott's plans seemed to fall right in place. He graduated from medical school and was just starting to pay back Uncle Sam for his financial support by serving as a medical doctor in the United States Navy.

Easy left the Marines after his four years of service had expired. He moved back home to Kentucky for three months, then drove up to Louisville where he landed a foreman's job with a large construction firm. Scott's parents purchased a beachside condo in Bar Harbor, Maine. The first summer following Easy's departure from the service, Scott invited him up over the July 4th holiday. The next year the same invitation was offered, which Easy accepted. After that, it became a yearly tradition to get together at the seaside getaway.

Scott was surprised beyond description when on the fifth anniversary of the annual July Fourth get-together, Easy showed up with his new bride of only two months. Old Ezra was no longer the backwoods kid from Appalachia. He owned one of the largest construction companies in the state of Kentucky and had found himself one beautiful little lady to marry. Easy had met Betty at a church social and things sort of progressed from there. Scott was still among the single crowd and, at the present time, not the least bit interested in tying the knot.

The last evening before Easy and his wife were to head back home, Easy and Scott wandered off down the beach, where they built a small fire and sat on the sand, the gentle waves creating a soothing rhythm along the shoreline. Easy looked up into the star-dotted sky as he ripped a can of beer out of the six-pack holder.

Empting half the can in four successive swallows, Easy spoke, "Ya know, there's somethin' that's been botherin' me fer a number o' years."

"What's that?" asked Scott.

"I never fergot that conversation `bout religion that first time I was at yer house. I remember yer mother sayin' that when ya was no longer livin' under her roof that ya could make up yer own mind `bout the Lord."

Scott, not grasping the gist of the conversation, held out his hands. "And?"

"Well, I been wonderin' all these years what conclusion ya've come to?"

"If you're asking me whether I believe in God or not, I just don't know."

"Ya said somethin' back a few years ago that got me ta thinkin'", said Easy. "Remember when we was in that club when you thought I was rude ta that girl…think `er name was Erika. Well, anyways, when ya found out that it was jus' a matter of me bein' shy, ya said, `Thank God.' If ya don't believe in the Almighty, why would ya say somethin' like that?"

"Easy, I've been struggling with this is-there or isn't-there-a-God issue for years…even before I left home. There isn't anything that you or anyone else can say that I haven't heard…I mean things that people say in order to prove that God does exist. Look at those stars up there in the sky. Listen to the ocean. I guess our roles are reversed now. You could very easily tell me that it's not too late for me to believe. It's sort of like me telling you that it's not too late to stop drinking and smoking. Now, it's me telling you that it's easier said than done. For years now you've been explaining to me why you couldn't change things because of the way you were raised. It's the same with me. I was raised to believe that God does not exist. I can't just say that now I believe if I'm not really sure."

Easy stood, brushing the sand off his pants. "I ain't no preacher, but I believe that the Good Lord `ill give everyone a shot at makin' a decision ta believe. Don't really know when yer chance `ill come along ...but it will."

Another decade came and went, Scott had by now left the service and had started a practice with three other physicians. He had met a lawyer from Philadelphia and they got hitched, two years later they had their first child, Cynthia. Aubrey moved to Denver where she had a flourishing medical practice. She had never gotten married and most likely never would. Mrs. Young retired and stayed at home while Dr. Young continued his medical profession. Easy and Betty never had children, since she was examined and told that it would be too difficult for her to give birth.

The year that both Scott and Easy turned thirty-eight, the Youngs spent Independence Day at the shore by themselves. Betty had called saying that Ezra was down with a severe cold and that they would not be able to attend. She apologized, saying that she and Ezra looked forward each year to coming up.

Three weeks later, Scott received a call from Betty. Easy had never recovered from the cold. After two weeks of constant prodding, she had managed to get Ezra to go to the doctor. The doctor sent Ezra to the hospital overnight for tests, then phoned Betty the next day informing her that there were some serious complications that the doctor needed to discuss with her.

The results of the examinations proved beyond any doubt that Ezra's body had been overtaken with cancer. It was spreading at a rate that left the medical staff with no other option than to pump him full of drugs to lower the level of pain her husband was feeling.

If he made it through the month, it would be a miracle. An hour following the call, Scott was on a flight headed for Kentucky.

When Scott entered the hospital room, it was all he could do to restrain the tears. Easy's short, muscular frame had been replaced with a frail, pallid-looking body; he couldn't have weighed in at more than a hundred pounds. The years of nicotine and alcohol had eaten away at his old friend. Despite the sunken eyes and the pale lips, when Easy saw Scott walk through the door, that old familiar smile managed to fight its way through the intense pain. The smile on the haggard face was almost like a hand that reached out and gripped at Scott's heart. As much as he wanted to remain composed, the tears rolled down his cheeks.

Betty, sitting beside the bed, got up slowly, placed her hand on Scott's shoulder and whispered, "I'm going to step outside so you two can have some time together."

Scott sat in the chair as he watched Betty leave and close the door. Turning his face to his friend, he tried his best to compose himself. He had always thought of himself as a doctor who possessed a good "bedside manner," but as his eyes looked at Easy's face, he lowered his head, his attempt at holding back his emotions failing as he wept silently.

"C'mon pal," mumbled Easy. "I'm the one who supposed ta be in pain." Reaching out slowly, he tapped Scott's hand as he went on, "How `bout givin' me a sip o' that water over there on the table?"

Scott held the glass just beneath Easy's chin, the straw brushing his thin lips. Following two short swallows. Easy let out a gentle laugh, "Reminds me o' that time down in boot camp when we was out on a run. We was drinkin' water when ya first told me that I had ta be more aggressive. If I remember right, that's the first time I used that phrase ya always hated…easier said than done. Seems like ya was always after me ta change. I never did. But you know that. Now, I can see that ya was right. All that smokin' an' drinkin' caught up ta me. I was thinkin' that with you bein a doctor an' all, mebbe ya could save me."

Scott wiped his tear-filled eyes with a kerchief. "I've seen your charts, Easy,…and I know you'd want me to be honest with you…"

"No need ta explain," interrupted Ezra. "I know it's too late fer me. You could tell me that savin' my life is easier said than done…but that's not yer style. That's the way I lived my life, always comin' up with some excuse why I couldn't change things. You on the other hand have always been willin' ta change. You've got a great career, wife an' family…an' most important o' all—yer health. Don't get me wrong. I've managed ta git some things done. I made it all the way through high school, toughed out boot camp, got me a great little wife an' my own business. Thing is…most folks tend ta be on the sad side when their time is up. That's not fer me. I've been smilin' ever since I was a youngin' an' I ain't `bout ta start frownin' now. I know I ain't no perfect person…an' I guess as fer as walkin' the path ta heaven, I've got off the trail a few times, but I never stopped believin' in the Good Lord. Ta me…gittin' ta heaven is `bout the greatest thing ya can accomplish…and soon, I'll be on my way."

Scott took Easy's hands as he stammered for the right words. "Look, Easy, I…I don't know…what to say. I feel weak…like I didn't have the ability to keep after you. If I would have said the right things…done something different…maybe this would have never happened."

"Don't think so, Scott. You gave me plenty o' good advice o' the years. I was jus' too hard-headed ta see what ya was sayin'. I…don't want ya ta make the same mistake."

The confused look on Scott's face caused Easy to continue. "Ya been givin' me advice fer years `bout how my bad habits would wind up killin' me `fore my time. I didn't heed the warnin' an' now, jus' like ya said…I'm gonna kick the bucket pretty early in life. What I'm tryin' ta say…is that ya have ta come ta grips with this business o' God's existence. Remember what I tol' ya on the beach a few years back? He gives everybody a chance ta believe. Everthin' happens fer a reason. I figure…it's my time ta move on, but `fore I go I need ta let ya know that God does exist…He always has. Do me a favor. Sometime soon…git to a church, go inside an' have a seat. The Lord `ill be there. Ask him ta clear this up fer ya."

Ezra's face wrinkled in pain, but then the smile returned as tears dribbled down his hollow cheeks. "Scott, git my wife."

Ten minutes later, Scott felt a strange sense of relief as he stared through the glass partition. Betty's head sank as she lowered herself to a chair. A doctor and two nurses rushed into the room, but it was to no avail.

It was an hour later that Betty met Scott in the waiting room. After they embraced, she looked directly into his eyes. "Easy really liked you, Scott. There was hardly a day that passed that he didn't talk about you. One of the last things he said was to tell you goodbye. The doctor said it was the strangest thing he had ever seen. Easy died with a big grin on his face."

A half hour later, Scott had said his goodbyes to Betty, telling her that if she needed anything to just call. Sitting in the rental that he had picked up at the airport, he noticed his tear-streaked face in the rearview mirror. He smiled to himself as he turned the ignition key. Next stop—the first church he came to.

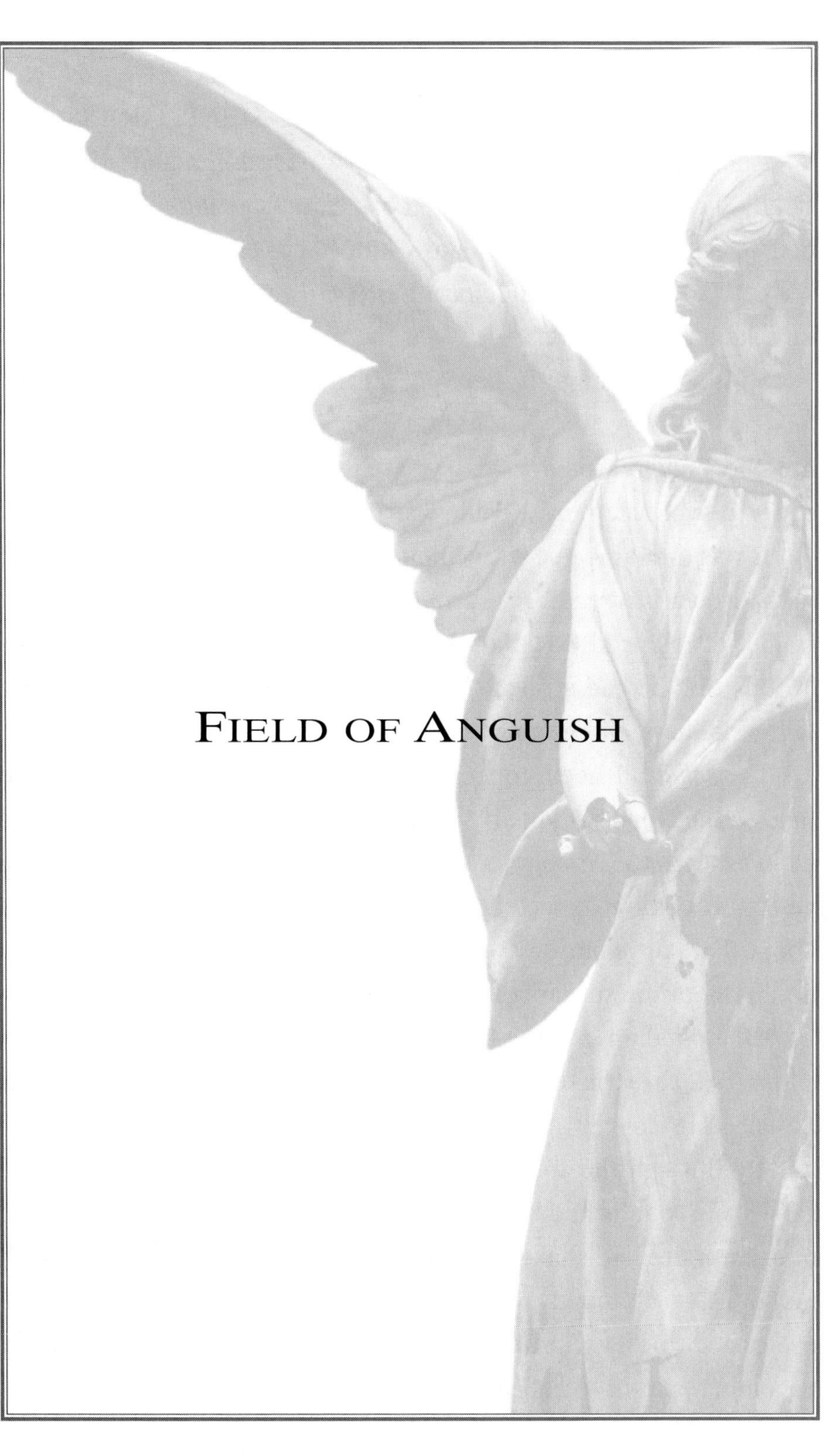

Field of Anguish

STEPPING OUT INTO THE KNEE-DEEP GRASS, ELI left the shade of the trees behind, wavered momentarily, then steadied his frame with his trusted oak cane as he looked up into the ball of sun. Removing a clean, white handkerchief from his coat pocket, he mopped his perspiring brow. It felt hotter than the first time he had been here.

Shifting his weight to his right leg, he thought about the stifling heat again. July was always humid. The blazing rays of sunlight were not the only reason for his sweating. There was also the innate concern over whether he could walk all the way across the vast field.

It was the same gut-wrenching feeling he had experienced when he had been here before. Turning, balancing his fragile 140-pound frame, he glanced back at the trees. It was there, in Spangler's Woods, that he had crouched down on his haunches next to friends, fellow soldiers, and in many cases, heros.

They had all been concerned about getting across that horrid field to the stone wall nearly a mile away. As an enlisted man, there hadn't been too much to say about the decision. Orders were given—you were expected to carry them out. The strange feeling about that particular day was that even the officers expressed some doubt about the success of the assault.

He looked up into the fullness of the towering trees and drew in a long, deep breath, the savory fragrance of the countryside filled his nostrils. He concentrated on the sounds: a slight breeze gliding quietly through the trees, the chirping of the birds. Back then, the smells and sounds had been much different. The continuous barrage of cannon fire had shaken the very ground where he had knelt with his musket clutched firmly in his hands, and the deafening, prolonged blasts vibrated every bone in his body, eventually becoming painful to his ears.

Field of Anguish

At first, the endless explosions were spaced. As the minutes dragged by, they seemed to cleave together creating a foreboding, evil ringing. There were no birds chirping that day. In a way, the winged creatures had been favored, for the God-given blessing of flight enabled them to fly off to a safe distance. He remembered pondering that day about how helpless he felt. As intelligent as human beings were, unlike the birds, he nor any of his division could escape the nightmare of the moment. The stench of death hung in the steamy, humid air. The procedure of normal breathing had become an effort in itself, with the air thick with grayish-black sulphur smoke and the abrasive smell of gunpowder.

A lieutenant walking directly behind them had suggested they try and relax. He recalled looking at Jesse Simcox. His childhood friend was shaking so badly that the wooden stock of his musket was banging against his canteen. He had shouted at his friend that day, "Jesse…Jesse!" but the boy just stared straight ahead as if hypnotized by the pounding of the constant cannonade.

What had the army expected of him and Jesse? They were just boys, twenty years of age. They had missed the opening year of the war. During the second year after joining up, they had done little more than get up each morning, then march all day until the sun sank in the west in the evening. At night, they sat around peaceful campfires and talked about the war, the general suspicion being that they were winning the affair and that it would be over soon. It had lasted longer than most folks had thought.

Aside from minor training in the beginning, he had only fired at the enemy on two occasions, the opposing soldiers too distant for him to know if he had done any damage.

The second summer of the war had placed him squarely in the center of a heated battle. Some of the boys claimed it would decide the war. That had been a pleasant thought, providing he could survive the day.

He had hidden in the shelter of the dense forest, thinking that perhaps the foe would not respond or that they were remaining patient during the non stop artillery attack. His way of thinking had changed rapidly as an explosion twenty feet to his left had ripped a tall oak from its roots. The enemy was responding. Their patience had come to an end.

Another blast, farther up the tree line, had caused him to cringe as he lowered his head, unable to bridle his fear. Five soldiers were catapulted in every direction like rag dolls. When the smoke finally cleared, three were dead, two wounded, one man screaming as he stared blankly at a bloody stump where seconds earlier his right arm had been attached to his body. It was, at that horrifying moment, that he realized that getting across the field was becoming less important. He might die right there in the woods without even seeing the enemy.

Ike, his older brother and an experienced veteran of three years of combat, was by his side, instructing him to stay down. He belonged to a different division and they hadn't discovered that they were in the same camp until the previous night. Ike told him they would be moving out soon and that he had to get back to his own regiment.

Turning back toward the long field, he leaned on the cane, his leg was growing tired. A grey hawk circled high above in search of a field mouse or some other small animal. He was sweating profusely. He removed his spectacles, wiped his face, and then placed the fragile glasses back on the bridge of his nose.

He smiled as he thought about Ike again. Reaching into his coat pocket, he withdrew the tiny silver cross. He thought back to the moment when his brother had handed it to him, folding his palm over it, he told him that if he didn't do anything else, just pray.

He inspected the cross closely. It had become tarnished over the years but the inscription on the back could still be read: To Amelia Faith in God Jacob. Jacob was his great-grandfather, and, as time had passed, the religious article had been passed down through the family. Ma had given the momento to Ike when he had boarded the train to join the Army. He flipped the cross over in his hand as the sun reflected off the tiny object. The first time he had marched across this field the Almighty had been with him. If he had any remote chance of making it on this second attempt, the Lord's presence would be required again.

He looked to his right, then to the left. It was just about this far out from the stand of trees that the soldiers had been ordered to form up. Despite the eminent fear of death, he had felt an odd sense of pride as he and thousands of other men stepped into the field. It was a strange army. Everyone was dressed somewhat differently, but in some ways they looked the same. Prior to the war, they had been farmers, shopkeepers, tailors, blacksmiths, teachers, and, in many cases, boys who had never held a job. Now they stood as mature veterans. Along with his sense of pride, a feeling of being ashamed crept into his thought process. Did he deserve to march next to these brave men, many who would not survive the day?

The line of soldiers had taken on the appearance of long snakes stretched as far as he could see in both directions. Then he had noticed Ike, just ten yards away, his old battered fishing hat balanced on the end of his bayonet as he signaled widely. He admired his older brother. He was a true soldier. He had killed eight, or maybe it was seven men, he couldn't remember. Three had been in hand-to-hand combat. Ike didn't brag about it or even like to discuss it. He said it was just his duty. The night prior to the forced attack, Ike had told him that he hoped he never had to take another man's life, but if the time came, he'd know what to do.

Ike's statement was something he didn't entirely understand. How could you possibly know when the time came to kill another man? If it was something that came naturally, then he had to consider himself as abnormal. Maybe it was some sort of insanity invading the body, causing you to pull the trigger at just the precise moment.

His thoughts were briefly interrupted as three playful squirrels raced from the trees a few feet out into the field, suddenly stopped, then darted back toward the woods, scampering up the trunk of a thick elm.

His mind returned to the peaceful solitude of the afternoon. If it wasn't for the blistering heat, it would have been perfect. It was so quiet. It reminded him of how silent it had become after everyone was in formation that day. The cannons on both sides had subsided, and no one was talking or shouting. The general galloped by, followed by his staff. He rode erect in his polished leather saddle, his magnificent horse prancing in front of the formations.

It had been hard to fathom how quiet it had become—thousands of men standing at attention, no rattling equipment, not even so much as a cough. It was like being in church as a youngster and knowing that if you made a sound during prayer it would be entirely inappropriate.

How many soldiers had prayed as they stood shoulder to shoulder? At that exact moment, those who were not in deep prayer were probably few and far between. Many held their faces toward heaven, others bowing their heads to their chests, and still others staring straight ahead. He held no doubt that there had been men present who had never walked with the Lord or attended a church anywhere.

He recalled thinking that God just might be looking down on the battlefield as he beamed with pride. Men of different religious outlooks and beliefs: Baptists, Protestants, Methodists, Lutherans, some who didn't believe at all, were somehow bound together as they all silently made the same request of the Almighty: *Please get me through this day.*

He thought about how rigidly he had prayed that day as he stood in formation. He had clutched the cross in his hand, closed his eyes, and prayed as he wondered if he had done a good stint as a Christian? If this was to be his final day on earth, had he lived a life that would ensure him entrance to Heaven?

The sound of the drums had brought him out of prayer. A team of six horses raced by, pulling a caisson that bounced up into the air, landed on one wheel, righted itself, and clattered down the line.

Pulling his watch from his pocket, he glanced at the glass face. Time to get moving. The day wasn't getting any cooler, and just standing there wasn't getting him any closer to the stone wall. Leaning on the cane, he took his first step, the second, and then the third into the field.

It was difficult walking with the cane, but he knew it would become even more of a burden when he reached the deeper grass and weeds in the uneven section of the field further on. Looking out across the field, he strained his eyes. His eyesight wasn't what it used to be. The wall was out there—he just couldn't make it out. It wasn't much different than before. The cannon smoke had started to drift off, but had been too thick to allow any of the men to see the wall.

As he doggedly continued onward, cane, then a step, cane, then a step, his mind pictured how he had marched that dreadful day. The long ranks of men wavered back and forth, officers at the rear keeping men from lagging behind or losing heart and retreating back to the trees. As far as he knew, not a man had retreated. Some may have pondered the thought, but nonetheless, kept moving forward. He had tried his best to remain in step with those to his right and left. Most of the soldiers moved forward in unison with a few out of step, but it wasn't an issue.

Surely, the enemy fortified behind the safety of the stone wall had prepared themselves for the unknown. They could only guess at the magnitude of the force advancing in their direction, with officers peering through field glasses, and the sultry heat and lack of any type of breeze hampering the smoke-filled air from clearing.

He'd been walking for ten minutes according to his old timepiece. He stopped, his hands moist from his sweating pores. At the rate of his miserable progress, if he did manage to make it all the way across, it was going to take much longer than his previous attempt.

He started again as he gripped the cane tightly, the cross still held in his right hand. If he remembered correctly, it had been somewhere around this point in the advance that their progress had seemed easy. It was like being in the eye of a storm—they were safe for the moment. Their own artillery had started another continuous barrage of the distant wall. The enemy cannon was firing well over their heads, the short-range guns silent as they were still out of range. No muskets were being fired. They were still too far off.

Thoughts of marching along safely had been obtuse. Each step had taken him and the others toward a variety of horrors. For some, death, probably swift and painless. For others, death would arrive slowly as they lay helpless, their very lifeblood flowing from their bodies as they suffered great pain. Others would only be wounded, many serious, and still, some others just slightly, in which case they would continue onward. If a soldier somehow managed to miraculously remain unscathed by cannon or musket fire, he still had to focus on getting to that wall, at the same time dealing with the inevitable carnage surrounding him. There were no pleasantries in the midst of battle.

Fifteen minutes passed. It seemed like he was stopping every four or five minutes, each moment taking longer to regain a pattern of normal breathing. Looking up toward the sun, he calculated that in a few more minutes he'd be in the area of the field where enemy short-range guns had started to find the mark. He wiped his brow with his coat sleeve, then started his journey once again.

Six minutes later, he stopped at the top of a small rise. In the distance, he could barely make out the famous stone wall. The cannons were still there, pointed ominously over the field. They were silent now—exhibits of death. The day he first viewed the wall, the big guns were anything but silent. He remembered witnessing the smoke blasting from the long barrels, the sight more frightening than the loud booming. At first the shells had hit forty to fifty yards in front of the lines, huge divots of grass and earth exploding into the air.

There had been nothing any of the men could have done to protect themselves that horrid day while moving forward, with the soldiers in each regiment packed together like sardines. As the enemy cannon began to find its range, large gaping holes were blown in the lines, with men, body parts, and equipment flying in every direction. The remaining standing soldiers plugged the holes and continued forward knowing their lives could come to an end abruptly.

Time to stop again for a short rest. The battlefield looked different now. The sea of gently swaying grass had covered the scarred earth of years past. Mother Nature had performed a magnificent job of healing the field. The wall was still a fair distance off. There was no one there now. Back then, enemy soldiers had sheltered themselves behind the stone barricade and waited nervously for the attack. The enemy couldn't have been that much different. They were men with different ideas about the war. They were men who wore a different color uniform. But when it came right down to it, they were just men who bowed their heads and prayed to the same God. What a frightening view it must have been from the other side of the wall! Upwards of 11,000 men, over a mile in length, slowly closing the break between themselves and the protection of the wall.

War was such an intricate subject, he thought. Soldiers on both sides praying to God for the blessing of His staying hand. Whose side was God on? How did He decide who lived or who was to die? He placed the cane firmly in the tall grass and stepped forward, his next goal the wooden fence.

As he approached the fence, it looked like it had been rebuilt. That made sense. The original fence had been destroyed by short-range cannon fire. Four feet from the fence, he remembered how his emotions had started to change. An explosion just to his left had knocked him off his feet. Six soldiers lay dead or wounded. There was Jesse, face down, his right arm twisted at a grotesque angle, blood spilling from the two-inch hole under his right armpit. He reached out to his close friend, but there was no time for farewells as an officer hoisted him to his feet and ordered him forward.

There had been no tears—just an empty sensation deep in the pit of his stomach. He looked back at Jesse for a transitory second as a mounted soldier rode over top of his friend, the horse's front hooves landing squarely on the dead boy's back. The horse lurched to the left, but the rider pulled stern on the reins, jerking the animal's head to correct the fall. His emotions had taken over and he remembered wondering if the tears running down his face were noticed by the others.

Another explosion on his left had made him flinch as he shielded his face from sections of dislodged flying grass and dirt. An officer was knocked form his stallion, both rider and animal thudding heavily to the ground. It was so vivid in his mind, as if it had just happened, not years ago, but just now! He could envision the brave officer, half his chest torn away as he slowly crawled to the wildly thrashing horse who was suffering great pain. The vibrant soldier withdrew his pistol, shot his trusted steed in the head, ending its misery. The man dropped the revolver to his side, leaned back against his horse, drew his last breath, and died. He remembered the compassion of the soldier's concern for his horse in the middle of the bloody debacle.

He leaned on the fence for a short breather, then stepped through and squinted toward the wall. Looking down the fence line he pondered how peaceful it appeared. It could have been a picture postcard. When he was here before he hadn't been faced with the dilemma of getting over the fence. He had simply sprinted through an opening where splintered railings and posts were scattered across the blood-soaked ground, the end result of a well-placed answer from an enemy cannon.

That day, many a man had not only run through the fence, but had quickly climbed over the top, and many soldiers died instantly, not even realizing they had been shot. The uniform lines started to break up, each man advancing at his own pace. Officers ran back and forth, trying desperately to reform the men into an organized charge.

He looked across the field at the wall. He was so tired. He felt like sitting down but knew that if he did he might not be able to get back up. As long as he remained standing, he'd get there. He walked cane in hand, for ten minutes, rested for five, then pushed on another ten before stopping.

The wall was now only forty yards away. He was exhausted. He'd make it if he had to crawl, he thought. All he had to do was concentrate. It wasn't as simple as it sounded. Normal walking for him was impossible.

Concentration hadn't been that easy before, either. Looking back, it had been difficult to reason how he had gotten himself into such a hellish situation. At this point, the enemy had flanked them, not only annihilating them from the front, but both sides. The enemy soldiers didn't even take time to aim their muskets. They simply loaded, fired into the advancing swarm of humanity, then reloaded, fired again, and on and on. Everywhere he looked, men were falling to the ground, many times on top of one another. He recalled how he had still been holding his own musket in a marching position.

He looked down at his open hand. Just to the right of the cross he noticed the dark scars where he had clutched the object so tightly that it had become imbedded in his skin, blood dripping down his arm. He had cried then, and he was crying now. He recalled stopping, almost as if he were frozen, just twenty yards from the wall. The enemy soldiers were draped over the stone barricade, with others loading their weapons as fast as humanly possible. The next few minutes had remained with him over the years, that horrible moment of time never to be forgotten.

Ike, his brother, the fearless soldier, the man who displayed no apparent fear had come to his side, shouting, "Good God, Eli, don't just stand there. Keep movin'!"

He had turned to look for Ike following the warning. Enemy musket balls had torn at his brother's body, his left ear blown from the side of his head, both legs wounded and then the fatal shot in his right eye. Blood poured from his grimaced lips as he dropped to his knees, then forward onto his face.

Eli stopped to calm his erratic breathing. Here he was, twenty yards out from the wall. This is where he had been stopped before. He had thought about returning to the battlefield many times over the years, but could never quite muster up the courage until just recently. During the week-long journey from Georgia, he had wondered if he would be able to remember how he had felt when he had been at the wall before. Now that he was standing just twenty yards away, it seemed like he had never left.

He would have thought that the many years of civilian life would erase the horror he had experienced here. He remembered a sermon Pastor Thorne had given at church years before the war. He had only been ten years of age at the time. Ol' Thorne had a reputation for spewing out more fire and brimstone than anyone in the county. That particular sermon—*What Will Hell Be Like*, had probed his ten-year-old brain and planted itself there firmly. Pastor Thorne stated Hell was the worst imaginable unending suffering you could possibly think of.

As time passed, he had attempted to imagine what unending suffering was like. He hadn't experienced much pain in his life previous to the war. Oh, there had been instances. How about when Gramps died, or when Luke, his favorite hound, had passed on from old age? Then there was the worst pain of all when Rebecca Nettleton, his first love, had up and moved west with her family. At the time, he thought he'd never get over those tragic situations. Mama, in her ever-present wisdom, had said, "Time is the best medicine. Eventually, it can heal anything." As time passed, the difficult loss of Gramps, Luke, and even Becky had subsided.

When it came to the horrifying event of this battlefield, Mama's wisdom seemed to miss the mark. The pain of what had transpired here had shrouded his very being like a disease for decades. Her remedy of "time curing anything" was long overdue.

He found himself cleaning his face with the already sweatsoaked handkerchief. His old woolen uniform was saturated with perspiration like before. What a moment in hell that had been! It was the closest thing in his life that resembled Pastor Thorne's description of Hell. It seemed so real in his mind that it could have been yesterday. Jesse had died, Ike was dead. Many others that he knew and some he didn't had taken their last step.

He stared intently at the stone barrier and remembered the blueclad, bearded enemy who had looked directly into his eyes, raised the rifle and drew a bead on him, his sole intention to put an end to Eli's life. In that second, Eli had thought that he was dead. There was no time to move, no time to level his own weapon at the enemy. For him, time had run out. The deadly musket ball never left the barrel of the gun as the soldier's left cheek disappeared in a flash of bloody skin and bone. The man slumped over the wall, twitched, and died.

Another enemy soldier withdrew the ramrod from the deadly barrel of a cannon, took a stray bullet in the back, stumbled a few feet, and collapsed. The cannon was then turned by three soldiers in Eli's general direction. Before he could react, the white-gray smoke from the cannon was immediately followed by a whoosh of forced air picking him up and pushing him back ten yards.

He hadn't been sure how much time had passed. He had been dazed, but was sitting up, his musket at his side. A badly wounded soldier, laying across his legs rose to his feet, blood gushing from both ears, and a severe hole in his neck as he attempted to run back across the field. A bullet in the back of his head ended his break from the front line.

He recalled the dizziness disappearing, and then being replaced with rushing pain. He looked at his left leg. It was missing from the knee down—blood vessels, muscle and shattered bone dangling from the severed limb. He tried to scream, but no sound escaped his aching lungs.

Still somewhat dazed, a flash of metal caught his attention. It was getting closer. The pointed bayonet attached to the enemy musket looked five feet long. The soldier wielding the deadly weapon yelled at the top of his lungs as he attacked. Ike's advice of knowing what to do when the time came erased the pain of his missing leg. Without the slightest hesitation, he grabbed his musket, positioned it across his left arm, aimed quickly and squeezed the trigger. The musket ball stopped the blue soldier dead in his tracks, his eyes rolling back in his head, a small bloody red hole appearing just above his right eye. He stood there for two seconds staring at Eli, then fell to his knees and over onto his side. The last thing Eli remembered was the butt end of a musket colliding with his chin. It had been a telling blow.

He felt his teeth move inside his mouth, tasted blood, and then fell forward unconscious.

How long he had laid there he couldn't recall. When he did finally come around, it was by means of a slow shaking of his head as he returned to reality. His eyes had opened quickly as an intense wave of pain from his mangled leg shot through his body. A realm of clear blue sky poked a hole in the thick smoke of the battle. It would have been wonderful to just levitate right up through the smoke and clouds to the azure sky above.

An enemy soldier standing above him aimed a musket at his chest. Seconds passed. The man, not much older than he, was terrified, frozen in deep thought. Finally, he pulled his gun up and moved off. Another soldier leveled his blood-stained bayonet at Eli, then backed off and ran to the left. Eli supported himself with his left elbow as he surveyed the still-raging battle. The cannonnade was now only sporadic, the smoke starting slowly to drift off. Most of the fighting was now hand-to-hand on either side of the wall.

Four more enemy soldiers stopped, gave him a confused look, but then moved away. Why had he been spared that day? Had it been because he had been so pathetic looking? He had no weapon—evidently someone had picked it up. He was of no harm to anyone. He was just a boy laying in a pool of blood with only one leg, tears streaming down his face. Why waste a bullet or even your time on a soldier who was incapable of retaliation? Maybe they were saving their ammunition and efforts for those who were still armed and capable of killing.

No one was paying him any attention. Would he just be left there to bleed to death? He was getting weaker as blood continued to flow freely from his mangled leg. Painfully, he rolled over onto his stomach and started to drag his body back across the field. It was a decision that seemed ridiculous. Inch by inch, he crawled in retreat. There was no way humanly possible he would be able to get back to the trees on his own. If he wasn't carried back, he would die soon.

He thought once again about Pastor Thorne. *What is Hell going to be like?* Wallowing amongst countless dead or wounded men had to come close. In some areas, the ground had been soaked with blood, while many men were piled two or three high where they had met their Maker. Some men had died with their eyes and mouths wide open, their faces frozen in dread. Others lay quietly bleeding to death, while others screamed in pain. One man had reached out to him pleading for help—a bayonet had slashed his face from his mouth to above his right ear.

The last moment he remembered that day was dragging himself over a dead horse, then rolling onto his side. The cross was still held in his bleeding hand. His eyes closed slowly. Was this it? Was he dying? As he was drifting off, he asked the Lord to forgive him for the soldier he had killed, and then he went blank.

He came to hours later, staring up into the filthy rafters of a barn. A man with a pair of eyeglasses perched on the end of his short nose was looking down at him, his thin body covered in a bloodsoaked apron. The Union doctor explained that they had taken six inches off his damaged leg in order to prevent infection. It was for the best if he rest for the next few days. There was a good chance that he'd be shipped out to a prisoner-of-war camp.

He had spent the remainder of the war, just two years, as a prisoner. When the war finally came to an end, he was sent back home to Virginia. The South had lost the war. Some folks claimed the three days at Gettysburg had been the turning point.

There wasn't too much work opportunity for a one-legged man. Eli struggled for five years following the war, moving from one job to the next. In the fall of 1870, he found employment working on a small farm in Lynchburg owned by a local preacher. The minister had lost both of his sons in the War Between the States and his spouse to a fight with pneumonia. He took a shining to Eli, treating him like his own son. In 1873, he passed away, leaving the farm, the church, and all his earthly belongings to Eli. The old preacher had been a proper mentor. Eli took a stab at preaching himself.

As time slowly ticked by, Eli became one of the most influential preachers in Virginia. Folks said that for a one-legged man, he possessed more energy than most men with both limbs. He wasn't certain how many folks he had turned to the Almighty. In his early years of spreading the gospel, he had kept count but eventually arrived at the conclusion that he really didn't need to know The Almighty would keep a running total.

His thoughts finally snapped back to his current situation. He stood on one leg, the cane wavering back and forth. He was soaked from the tenacious heat. He was more exhausted now than the first time he had marched across the field.

He looked at the cross clutched in his hand as he took his first step, tears streaming down his hollow cheeks. He wasn't weeping because he was in pain. He was crying because of the horrid memories. Through the tears, he managed a slight smile. He was crying because this time he was going to make it all the way to the wall. He would not stop to rest until his hands were touching the stones.

Fifteen yards to go. Familiar voices rang out from the opposite side of the wall. "Come on, Gramps…you can make it! Keep walking…just a few more yards."

Ten more yards. His breathing was labored, his heart

pounding—a warning sign that he should stop and rest. His two sons, their wives, and a total of eight grandchildren stood waving, cheering, urging him on. People he didn't even know, probably battlefield visitors, joined in on the encouragement.

At five yards, he stumbled to the left, tried his utmost to stop the fall, but fell with a heavy thud on his left arm, a signal of pain shooting through his upper torso. A number of people started over the wall to help the old soldier. Eli raised his cane and pleaded, "No, I need to do this on my own!" The visitors backed away, climbing back over the wall.

Eli drew in a deep breath, gritted his teeth, bent his leg under his body, and pushed with the cane. He slowly raised up, hesitated as if he would collapse, but then suddenly stood, weaving back and forth like a newborn foal not quite sure of its legs. Everyone was clapping and shouting. He stood as erect as his arthritis would allow, squeezing the cross in his hand as he thought, *Just five more feet, Lord.* On his next step, he went down, harder than the first time. There was complete silence as his family and the others looked on with deep concern and respect. Using the same method as before, he struggled to get to his feet, but quickly crumpled back to the ground. He wanted desperately to walk to the wall but his body was refusing to cooperate.

He wiped his eyes with the handkerchief as he looked down at the cross. A smile slowly came across his wrinkled face as he remembered the many times he had preached on Christ's journey to Calvary, eventually leading to the crucifixion. Jesus had fallen three times, suffered great pain, but nonetheless, walked on. How many Sunday mornings had he stood before a congregation and preached about bearing up under the weight of the crosses in life that we all must carry?

Suddenly, a gruff, unfamiliar voice invaded his thoughts, "Hey, Johnny Reb! You can make it!" An old man dressed in a baggy, faded, Union-blue uniform stood just on the other side of the wall. He held out his right hand, the forefinger and thumb missing. "C'mon…you've got ta make it fer both o' us."

Eli coughed twice, took a deep breath of air, and then started to drag himself forward as he thought, *Just five feet.* His intention at the outset of the morning had been to walk the entire distance. Now, that was not plausible. He couldn't even stand on his own, let alone walk. Crawling toward the wall wasn't that terrible. After all, when he was here before, he had dragged himself away from the wall. He was not on his feet, but he was getting closer to his goal.

Not a single sound came from his family or those watching. With only three feet remaining, the small crowd started to clap in unison, almost creating a peculiar cadence. His heart felt like it was going to explode, popping right through his chest, and landing on the ground.

Two more feet. They were chanting his name now: "Eli! Eli! Eli!" With only one foot separating him from the wall, he thought that if he died right then and there, he had done his best. He would be joining the ranks of many a Confederate soldier who had died at the wall that day at Pickett's Charge. Thousands of men from the South had perished that grim day. The North, even though they had held the wall, had suffered significant losses of their own.

The old Union soldier bent down slowly as he ordered the rest of the people, "Please…git back. Give this southern soldier some room. He's comin' over."

As everyone took a step back, Eli's left hand clasped around one of the rocks at the base of the wall. With his last hint of strength, he pulled himself up into a sitting position as he looked back across the field he had just crossed.

The Union soldier lowered himself next to Eli, spat out a stream of tobacco juice, wiped his lips, then said, "Name's Clement Anstadt. I was here in `63. Served with the 71st Pennsylvania." He held out his hand, displaying the missing fingers, then commented, "One o' yer boys got me with a bayonet. I gather you was here, too?"

Eli removed his spectacles as he wiped his face with the back of his arm, then smiled. "Yep, I was with Garnett's boys, under Pickett. Lost my brother and a lot of good friends in this field. I was twenty years old back then. This is my first time back."

Clement twisted his mouth as he rubbed his calloused hand over a shaggy gray beard. "Well, now…let's see. T'wuz seventy-three years back. Makes ya…`bout ninety-three. I'm ninety-two myself. I've been coming back here ever since the war ended." He looked across the endless field. "All the fightin's long gone…but in my mind, I'm still fightin' the war." He looked at Eli's leg, then asked, "You lose that here?"

"'Bout twenty yards out, she come right off," answered Eli. "You boys stopped me dead in my tracks." As he looked into Clement's eyes, he went on, "I suppose I've been fighting this war all this time, too. That's why I finally had to come back. Had to march across the field and get to this here wall. At my age, I kinda figured this was my last chance."

"This'll be my final year," Clement said. "Doctor says I got me a case o' the cancer. Gave me 'bout two months, and that's stretchin' it. Looks like I'll be takin' the war right ta the grave with me."

"Maybe not, Billy Yank!" Eli spoke. Using the combination of the wall and the cane, he forced himself to stand as he extended his hand. "Let's help each other over this God-forsaken wall so we can both put this war to rest."

Clement clutched Eli's hand and stood as he nodded his

approval, then replied, "Agreed!"

The two old veterans saluted each other, then arm in arm stepped over the wall.

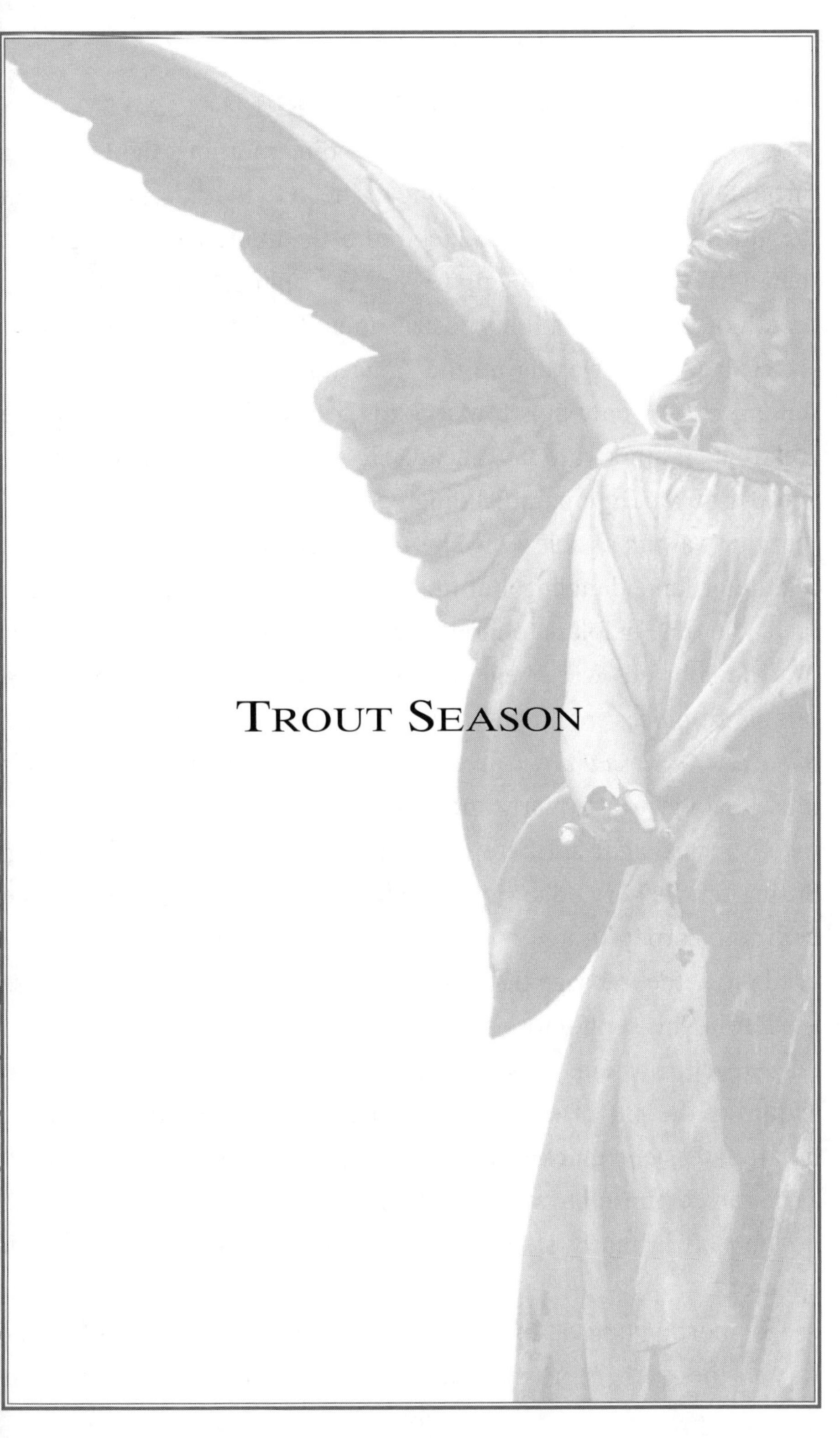

Trout Season

ANGELS' FOOTPRINTS

HE SAT SLOWLY, ALMOST RELUCTANTLY, HIS drowsy eyes not yet focused in the dim morning light drifting through the white curtains. Rolling his head to the side, he peered at the glowing red face on the clock radio, the numerals nothing more than a hazy blur. Glancing up toward the ceiling, he allowed a deep breath of fresh air to fill his nostrils then flood down into his lungs.

He had been waking up the same way for as long as he could remember. It would be a few seconds before his brain accepted the fact that another day lay ahead. He considered interrupting the process of waking up and sliding back into a deep sleep, but knew that this was impossible. Once his eyes were open, he was trapped in middle ground, dangling, but not able to reverse the process, yet at the same time helpless to move forward into the world of the alert.

The cobwebs were beginning to vanish from his subconscious, bits and pieces of reality seeping into his thought pattern: *Saturday…a special day…need some coffee.* Stretching carefully, his muscles objected to early morning activity as a shot of soreness raced up his right side, stopping at his shoulders, then subsiding. Sitting on the very edge of the bed, he placed his bare feet on the bedroom carpet. In a minute he would be capable of standing, but not before the message of being awake was transported to his legs.

During his sophomore year in high school, he had read a report on Albert Einstein. It seems that he attributed his success to acquiring the gift of sleeping only four hours a day, thus allowing him to fall asleep quickly, remain asleep and awake alert. He smiled as he forced himself to stand. Two out of three wasn't bad. He always nodded off instantly, slept deeply, but never woke up alert—even coherent.

Supporting himself by means of the hallway wall, he shuffled his way to the kitchen, crossed the cold marble-tiled floor, stopped at the counter and prepared his first coffee. It was a mindless routine. He had set the timer on the coffeemaker the evening before, the morning elixir was already brewing, its fresh aroma elevating him to the next level of awareness. All he had to add was creamer and sugar after pouring himself a mugfull.

Taking his first sip, he pulled back the lace curtains above the sink, which normally presented a panoramic view of the Pennsylvania mountains. The picturesque blue sky and rolling green mountains had been erased by a dreary, rain-swept morning.

He gulped another shot of coffee as he wiped the sleep from his eyes. This was supposed to have been a special day, the first day of trout season. He had been going fishing on opening day ever since he had been four years old with his father. In two months, he'd be sixty-three.

He sat at the antique kitchen table and thought about how he had been fishing for nearly six decades. He was, without a doubt, an avid fisherman. He had cast his line in rivers, lakes and streams from one end of the country to the other, the only two states he hadn't fished in being California and New Mexico. He'd caught fish in the Atlantic, the Pacific, and even the Gulf. He'd even gone ice fishing up in northern Canada. He looked out the window at the rain dripping from the leaking gutter. He'd have to get that repaired. The inclement weather was of no great concern. He'd gone fishing in the rain more times than he could recall.

Aside from the fact that it was the first glorious day of trout season and also a tradition, there was a second reason for the special day. It was an event he had been planning on for years, an occurrence that would only arrive once in his lifetime. It was the first day of his retirement. Thursday afternoon, just yesterday, was the final time he'd walked through the gates at the mill.

Over the years, he had heard people talk about retirement as a time to kick back, relax, and enjoy life. He had more than enough money tucked away in the bank, no bills to speak of, and his house was paid for. He was now able to fish whenever and for as long as he liked.

He had had such great plans for this day, such anticipation, but at the moment felt more alone than he could ever remember. His last year of work had been especially difficult. A year prior to his retirement, his loving wife of thirty-nine blessed years had passed on, leaving him alone. Well, not completely. He still had ol' Shep. Even though the seventeen-year-old collie was up in years, she had still been able to get around quite well.

The Mrs. had been closer to the dog. When Estelle died, the poor animal scowled around the house searching for her master, refusing to eat, whining and eventually curling up on Estelle's side of the bed and dying. Just one month after placing Estelle in the ground, he had to bury Shep also. The vet said that Shep probably died of a broken heart. Pushing his cup to the side, he thought about his son. He hadn't seen the boy in two years. He was married now, had graduated from college and had a son himself.

A clap of thunder nearby caught his attention as the rain started to pulse against the window. The day was turning out to be a bust, the bleak weather matching his own feelings of failure. He had been a good husband, but yet, had no wife. He, indeed, had been a father, but the bitterness that had developed between him and his son had prevented any chance of reconciliation. He was a grandfather, but to date had never seen his own grandson. His last bastion against loneliness had been work. The days of working side by side with his pals over at the plant, eating lunch together and joking around had finally come to an end. He was retired.

If Estelle were still around, she would have set him straight. She had always been quick to advise him when he allowed negative thinking to creep into his life. He got up. There was no sense in sitting there filled with self-pity. He was going fishing as planned. He capped off his dented thermos with hot coffee, made two egg salad sandwiches, walked out into the disorganized garage, grabbed his old fishing hat, pole, tackle box, waders, pipe and tobacco pouch, and then stepped out into the rain.

Just before entering the narrow path that led into the forest, he stopped, looking back at the house. The two metal clothesline posts stood like rusted statues in the backyard. Estelle had always hung their wash out to dry. His work clothing had always smelled so fresh. The garden in the corner, now overgrown with weeds, had been tended by her dainty hands. She had grown some of the best radishes and carrots he had ever tasted. He didn't hang the wash on the line or bother much with the abandoned garden. It would have been too painful.

He turned and started into the woods, the dense trees swallowing him from view. It was a good mile to the stream. He'd walked the path hundreds of times. He could have traveled the path blindfolded, the location of every rock, tree root and indentation filed away deep in his memory.

Halfway to his goal, he hesitated, the only noticeable sound the drops of water falling from the saturated leaves above. A young deer foraging for berries, looked directly at him, ears raised in warning. He stood perfectly silent, until finally, the doe bolted off into the trees, and then disappeared.

On his way once again, he thought about his past work career. He had worked forty-four years at the steel mill. In all that time, he hadn't been late or missed one day of work. He had been the model employee, even going as far as reporting for work when he had been sick. In a strange way, it was comical that he had remained at the mill all that time. When he had started working there, he had no intention of making it a lifelong occupation.

He had been a football star in high school. They said he was the most talented running back in the state to come along in over twenty-five years. During his junior year, he had been contacted by fourteen different universities offering full athletic scholarships.

His dreams of eventually playing professional ball were smashed to pieces during homecoming his senior year, a nasty hit from an opposing lineman rendering him unconscious. Waking up later in the hospital, he was told he had suffered a broken shoulder, collarbone and fractured hip. He would be out for the reminder of the season. After considerable surgery and therapy, he was able to walk, even run again, but his days of eluding guards and tackles on the gridiron had met with a roadblock. His bones had not healed correctly, leaving him unable to return to football.

He had been extremely angry about not being able to play football any longer. At that time, he had been playing the game since he was six. He'd been playing football for twelve years, nearly fifty percent of his young life. After offering his athletic services to some college for four years, he had planned on playing professional ball for fifteen, maybe twenty years, then retire and fish for the rest of his life.

His parents had suggested that he forge ahead and attend college despite the fact that he would not be getting a football scholarship. They said that they could raise the needed funds. This would have placed a substantial financial burden on his folks. Besides that, he had no desire to attend an institute of higher learning. He had no interest in acquiring a degree in business or becoming a physician or lawyer. He wasn't even sure that he could get into a school. He didn't have the best of grades. He had been counting on his football skills to balance out his average grades to render him an education.

That first fall after graduation, Estelle headed up to school in New Hampshire and by the time Thanksgiving rolled around, he was bored to death. The steel mill was hiring and he needed work, so he hired on. Sixty days later, he joined the union. Rather than wearing a football helmet, shoulder pads and spikes, he was donning a dented yellow hardhat, heavy-duty work clothes and steel-toed boots.

He started out as a laborer stacking sheet steel on the shearing line, with working conditions far from ideal. He froze during the winter months and sweated his backside off in the summer, but the weekly paychecks were considerably larger than most places in town paid.

A year and a half later, he bid on a shearer's position and got it, but just three months later was drafted into military service. After what seemed like endless days of pure agony in boot camp, he was shipped off to Vietnam. His life as a soldier only lasted three months. During a routine patrol in an early morning downpour, his platoon was ambushed by the enemy.

Before he had time to react, six bullets from an automatic weapon ripped into his body, sending him thudding to the ground. Painfully, he had crawled away into the dense underbrush and watched in horror as the other platoon members were gunned to death. He was the sole man in the group to survive the attack.

The next morning he was discovered by American troops, taken out of action and flown back to the states. People in town said that he was a hero, although he really didn't quite see it that way. Being labeled as a hero didn't seem right. He hadn't even fired his weapon.

He returned to work after four months of rehabilitation. It was as if he had never left to go off to war. He was back on the shearing line, laughing and joking with the guys. That was the year that he and Estelle tied the knot, bought the house and settled into the life of a typical married couple.

A year later, the combination of his old football injuries and his war wounds began to act up. It got to the point where he couldn't lift the sheet stock by himself. He discussed his predicament with the shop steward who in turn arranged with the union to have him assigned to another position at the plant.

For the next forty-three years, he was a combination security and gate guard, locking the same doors, switching off the same lights and walking the same route. He knew every corner of the mill. He was sure going to miss the place, the guys, the noise, the smells. He had been active on the company safety committee and had been a board member of the credit union.

The boys had thrown him a big party on his last day. They carted in a catered buffet and a giant sheet cake. They had even chipped in and bought him a new fishing pole. They slapped him on the back and said they'd see him around. He knew they meant well, but saying you'd see somebody around who was on the verge of retirement was just words.

He had said the very same thing to those who had retired before him. For the most part, he never saw them again, except for an occasional moment when he ran into one of them in town or at the grocery store. When asked how they were doing, the answer was always the same. "Fine…just fine." He could always tell from the look on their face that they were anything but fine.

It seemed like a lot of the boys, after retirement, just sort of started to go downhill. Why, in just the last two years, three men had died shortly after giving up employment. Now, he was retired. He trudged on through the forest, his fishing pole over his shoulder.

Minutes later, rounding the final curve in the trail, Steigman's Creek rippled peacefully over moss-covered rocks. Twenty feet to the left, he stopped, placed his gear on the wet ground and sat on a large, flat slab of rock, supporting his back with the aid of a tall pine.

Removing a small pinch of tobacco from his worn pouch, he pushed the damp mixture down into the bowl of his pipe with his thumb. After tamping down the tobacco, he added a second pinch, then lit up. Four quick puffs, followed by a long pull ensured that the pipe was in full working order, the sweet fragrance of spiced apples wafting up into the moist air. Leaning back against the tree again, he gazed out across the babbling water.

If he had his choice of fishing anywhere in the world, he had no doubt that it would be the very place where he was now sitting. Over the years, he had grown to feel that this was his private fishing hole. He was only the imaginary owner since the land was the sole property of the State Forest Commission. Still, he'd never run across any other fishermen at the stream. There was no road leading to this particular spot and the only walkable trail started in his own backyard.

On a number of occasions, he had done some fishing close to town, but it just wasn't the same. On opening day, at exactly six o'clock, a line of fishermen would march out into the water, their poles aimed like bayoneted rifles. Shoulder to shoulder, the men would stand for hours upon hours. That wasn't for him. He enjoyed the solitude of the forest, the yellow and white wild flowers, the smell of the pines and the sound of the cascading water from the falls just downstream.

He baited his hook, then cast the line, the lead sinker plunking into the quiet water. He thought about his son again. It was the same type of thinking that he had mulled over in his mind countless times in the past. Where had he gone wrong with the boy? If he had to do it all over again, he just couldn't imagine what he could have done differently. It wasn't that they hadn't gotten along. They just didn't seem to share anything in common.

He'd taken the young boy fishing on many a morning, just like his father had done for him, but the youngster hated the sport. He didn't want anything to do with worms, fish, the great outdoors—none of it. He had no desire to play catch with him or be involved with any type of sports activities. During his junior year in high school, he announced to the family that he was taking up golf, claiming it was a game of balance and physics.

This definition of the sport of golf was of no great surprise to anyone. Everything he did evolved around science, physics, chemistry or mathematics. He always had his nose stuck in some technical book. He logged an excessive amount of time working on science projects and pouring over intricate facts, figures and formulas on the computer that appeared as hieroglyphics to the rest of the family.

High school complete, his 4.0 grade-point average garnered him a full academic scholarship to a major university in Philadelphia. When his years of study were completed, he would graduate as a chemical engineer, no doubt enabling him to command a lofty position with some Fortune 500 company.

During his third year at school, he wrote home saying that he had met a wonderful girl in one of his classes. She was from a suburb of the city and was studying for the dental profession. She rode horses, played tennis and golf and was an accomplished waterskier.

Her mother was the principal of a local high school and her father a thriving real-estate investor who was also a member of the city's board of directors.

They had been dating for four months and had gotten engaged. He was bringing her home for Christmas so they could meet her. Estelle accepted the situation more readily than he had. As a father, he couldn't fathom why on earth his son would consider becoming engaged just after seeing this young woman for a few months. Estelle said that their son was his own man and had every right to make that decision on his own without involving them.

Christmas season rolled around. He went out just like always and cut down a fresh tree, strung lights on the porch and placed the plastic nativity scene in the front yard. It turned out to be the worst Christmas he had ever experienced.

His son, just like promised brought his bride-to-be home to meet the folks. When they walked in the front door yelling, "Merry Christmas," his emotions were wrenched out of kilter and had never returned to what he considered normal. His son's fiancee' was black.

Estelle, if she even had mixed feelings, didn't waver to hug the girl and welcome her to the family. She seemed nice enough to him, but the matter just wouldn't subside.

That particular yuletide weekend was the most awkward three days he ever encountered as a father. The tense feeling that hung over the house was apparent, not only to Estelle, but to his son and wife-to-be as well.

Seated at the candlelit table during their Christmas dinner, he glanced over at the girl. She was a beautiful young woman and came off as quite intelligent. He kept telling himself he had no grounds whatsoever to feel uncomfortable with her or the situation. She was in college, highly educated. He was only a high school graduate. Her father probably made ten times the money that he was earning. He didn't think he had a prejudiced bone in his body. He had played softball with blacks. He had worked side by side with black men, even gone fishing with some. As hard as he tried to shake his feelings toward the girl, they wouldn't release their ugly grip.

Tuesday morning on the back porch, he had stumbled across his son staring out into the snowy forest as he nursed a tall glass of juice. He had opened the conversation making some comments about the amount of snow expected during the remaining winter months, but there was no sidestepping what was really on their minds. His son cut right to the chase asking why he didn't approve of Monica.

He tried to explain that he had nothing against the girl. It was just the shock. It was so unexpected. His son should have told them more about Monica before bringing her home. They had been taken off-guard, unprepared. His son pointed out that if she had been white, there would have been no shock as he put it. He went on to say that they were getting married in April and that Monica was pregnant. They were happy together. Her parents had accepted him.

The controversy soon elevated into an argument, his son storming back into the house saying that he should have expected as much. His father had never been much of a dad, never supporting him in anything he had ever done. He and Monica were leaving immediately. As far as he was concerned, his father's presence at the impending wedding would not be required or even welcome. After all, there would be black people at the ceremony. He most certainly didn't want to make his white father, who spent the better part of his working life in a dirty steel mill, feel out of place.

During the next few months, Estelle tried her best to heal the wounds between her husband and son, but their heated words had cut deeply and neither was about to back down. As a wife, over the years she had always been supportive of her spouse, but there was no way she was going to miss her only son's wedding. When she returned from Philadelphia, she had said that the ceremony was wonderful and that Monica's parents were delightful and gracious. He could not have cared less.

After that, Estelle's spirit seemed to have been broken. Things just weren't the same around the house. Then, the cancer came, swift and brutal. Two months later, she laid in the hospital, a frail and feeble woman. Taking her final breath, she held her husband's hand, pleading with him to mend his relationship with their son. She said that she loved him and that she was sorry that she was leaving him. She softly closed her eyes and passed on peacefully.

He had never realized how deeply the piercing edge of the tongue could cut. He thought that Estelle's death would surely tear down the wall of hatred between him and his son. But, it was not to be. His son declined to attend the viewing at the same time as his father and stood at a distance at the funeral. Weeks later in a short letter, he informed his father that his grandson would be born in four weeks. He would not be allowed to see the boy. He didn't deserve to. He blamed him for Estelle's death. She hadn't gotten to see her grandbaby and neither would his father. Any hope of fulfilling Estelle's last wish seemed dim.

His pipe had fizzled out. He lit it again as he noticed that the rain had stopped. The gray clouds were drifting off, the rosy morning sun starting to poke its way through. A family of cardinals darted in and out of the trees on the opposite bank. The sunlight shimmered off the water. It was turning out to be a glorious day.

Even though the drab clouds and rain had slipped away, his feelings of loneliness remained deeply imbedded in his heart. His fishing line became taut, a trout tugging at the bait just beneath the surface. Reeling in the line, the trout broke loose, swimming to safety toward the middle of the creek. It was, at that moment, that he suddenly realized the very thing he loved, fishing, was a stanch example of how his life was going.

The trout that had slipped away represented all of the important things in his life that had vanished—Estelle, his son, his grandson, even working at the mill. Here it was the first day of trout season, his first day of retirement, and he felt like a lonely, bitter old man. He laid his pipe on the ground as his head sank in shame. How in the world was he going to deal with the day after day loneliness that lay ahead?

For some reason, God suddenly came to mind. He wasn't sure why. His parents had never taken him to church. Estelle had attended every Sunday for as long as he could remember. He had only gone with her on that one occasion. It was the only sermon he had heard in his life. What was it that the minister had said? The secrets to all of life's problems can be answered through prayer. Just ask the Lord for the answer and it will come. It may not arrive when or even how wc think it will, but, nonetheless, the answer will be revealed.

Getting up, he walked to the water and knelt, his knees sinking deeply into the mud. His eyes filled with tears of frustration as he silently requested that the Lord show him how to go to his son for forgiveness.

A voice sounded behind him, "Dad."

He turned, seeing his son standing at the edge of the water a few yards downstream. Holding tightly onto his hand stood a little black boy dressed in a yellow sweat suit, a funny-looking fishing hat perched on his head, a play fishing pole clutched in his right hand.

"Dad, this is your grandson. His name is Benjamin. We knew this was your first day of retirement. Knew you'd be down here alone. Ben here, well he's a bit too young to fish, but I thought maybe we could just sit on the bank and talk for awhile."

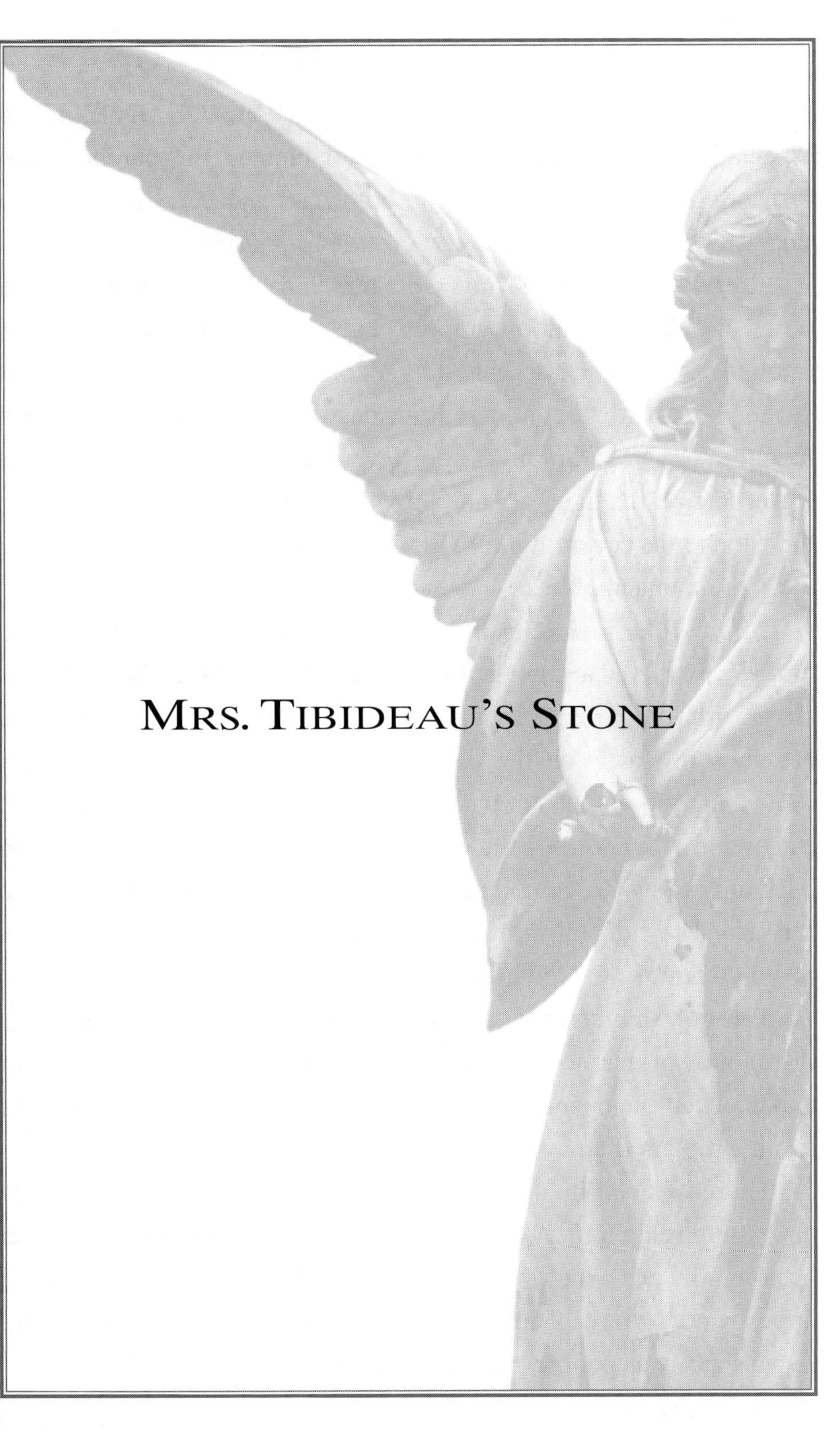

Mrs. Tibideau's Stone

ANGELS' FOOTPRINTS

EL PASO HAD TO BE THE HOTTEST PLACE ON EARTH, especially in mid-August. God had not blessed the parched land with rain for almost four months, both man and beast moving at a sluggish pace more conducive with the blazing sun.

An odd mixture of farmers, drifters and locals sat lazily on the porch of Gillman's Saloon, sipping glasses of beer and cleaning their foreheads with sweat-drenched handkerchiefs. Womenfolk browsed at the general store, conducted business at the bank, or spoke with neighbors while fanning themselves with sunbonnets. Horses tethered to hitching posts gulped water from old wooden troughs, their long tails constantly moving, swishing back and forth swatting away the menacing flies.

A lone rider pulled his black horse to a sudden stop at the edge of town, extracted a small leather pouch from his faded flannel shirt, along with some rolling paper, and started to prepare a fresh smoke. He drew in slowly on the hand-rolled tobacco as he squinted his eyes at the red ball of sun in the west, then glanced at his timepiece. Barring anything out of the ordinary, in ten minutes he'd be riding back out of town. A gentle nudge signaled the black stallion to move forward. The rider dismounted and threw the reins loosely over a post in front of the feed mill.

The tall, thin stranger started up the street, each step sending tiny clouds of dust from beneath his worn boots. He pulled his gun and checked the cylinder—six shells. He'd only need one—carrying a gun with less than a full load was dangerous.

There was no one on the street now. They were all safely inside and would remain there until it was over. It was always the same: an occasional door would be carefully cracked open, a face would appear and then the door would close. Curtains in windows would move slightly as people tried to get a look at the stranger.

Mrs. Tibideau's Stone

There wasn't anything fancy about Jack Tibideau. He looked like any number of ranch hands that might stray into town: weathered face, three-day beard and hair that needed to be cut. His boots were filthy, his shirt and pants wrinkled, his black hat faded from years of riding in the hot sun. To look at the man, one wouldn't have thought that he was in the business of killing.

Most of the men he had gunned down were gunfighters like himself or those who were generally looked upon as troublemakers. For the most part, no one had mourned the death of the men he had killed, except maybe an occasional wife or disgruntled relative. Jack realized that if he died at the hands of another gunman, no one would mourn his death, either. His folks had long since passed away. He had never married, so there was no wife or children to leave behind.

Many a man had drawn his last breath of air shortly after underestimating Jack Tibideau. His laid-back demeanor and simple style of dress were deceptive. He could have passed for an average citizen wearing a gun. His quickness and accuracy in handling a six-gun permitted him to survive forty-two face-downs.

His career spanned twenty-one years, which was longer than most men who lived by the gun. He was well-known, but not famous, making every effort to live a low-profile life. Typical gunfighters lived for the day, very few having plans for the future. Most accepted the fact that they would probably pass from life in the same way as their victims. They bragged about how fast they were, who they had killed, who they wanted to kill and hung with the wrong crowd and spread their money around like there was no tomorrow.

Jack had no intentions of dying in a pool of blood in some dusty street in a no-name town. He had been raised on a farm, understood ranching, and planned to spend the autumn of his life basking in the sun on a small spread far away from the life of gunfighting.

For the past ten years, each spring, he had ridden up toward the northern border of Montana and crossed over into Canada, placing cash in a bank in a small, sleepy-eyed town where folks didn't know or care who he was. Following six years of salting his money away, he purchased a plot of land that was to be his future home. Every year he'd spend a good month on his parcel of land, clearing it for a cabin and barn. His property backed up against a pine-covered mountain, a freshwater stream flowed and rippled near its base, the earth was fertile, and there was plenty of game.

Jack slowly made the turn onto the main street of El Paso. The place was empty of horses and people, except for one man standing in the middle of the dusty street: T. L. McDade. Jack had heard his name mentioned a few times over the past year—a man who carried a reputation as a loudmouth and was regarded as quite the ladies' man. Nobody seemed to know how old he was, but it was thought that he was in his twenties.

Standing just thirty yards away, McDade appeared as nothing more than a young boy, but Jack had no compassion for the young man. The boy had called him out, no doubt searching to make a bigger name for himself. If he was old enough to brandish a gun and brag about it, then he'd have to deal with the consequences—possible death.

Jack dropped his unfinished smoke to the street, took a relaxing breath, then his first stride toward McDade. As he got closer to T. L., he studied the man: clean shaven, except for a well-trimmed mustache, long, blond wavy hair, black hat with silver-beaded band, white shirt, tailored black leather vest and pants that fit snugly. His boots were shined to a high luster, complete with silver spurs. His gun hand low on his right hip, its pearl handle just one inch from the palm of his right hand. He looked organized, neat and confident. To many a man, he probably gave an appearance of intimidation.

Jack never allowed the way a man looked to influence his way of thinking. There was a vast difference in looking confident and being confident. Jack possessed a level of confidence that tipped the scales of logic. When two men, both trained gunmen, faced each other, it was always a fifty-fifty situation: one would live, one would die. Jack had a knack of mentally picturing an adversary taking one of his bullets in the chest, then dropping to the ground dead, affording him no opportunity to draw his weapon.

He was twenty yards away. Close enough. He stopped, then slowly examined McDade's face. He definitely had the look: cold eyes, uncaring eyes, eyes that had watched men die. Dark eyes that were focused on killing. McDade stood perfectly still, almost a statue.

Jack assumed his natural stance, his hands dangling at his side. He would remain frozen until his instinct to draw and fire took over. McDade was fast, or so it was said. One of the quickest to come along in quite some time. Jack respected speed, but knew a quick draw was only one half of being the party that survived. Timing was the other ingredient. On many such occasions, he had beat other men who were thought to be faster then he. His timing was flawless. Knowing what the other man was going to do just a split second before it happened always offered him the upper hand.

Every gunfighter did something just prior to making his move. Some spit, some twitched. Jack wondered what McDade's mistake would be. The two men stood, feet planted firmly, eyes locked on each other's face, relaxed, but yet, each was like a tightly wound spring ready to uncoil at the slightest touch. The hot sun beat down on the street, causing both men to perspire profusely. A dab of sweat made its way slowly down Jack's left cheek. He ignored it. Something as simple as wiping sweat from your face could send a man to an early grave. Another droplet of sweat ran down his neck. It was a game of waiting. Who was the most patient? Who had the most savvy?

In the next two seconds, it was over. McDade smiled. Jack's eyes fell from the youth's face to his right hand. The index finger moved slightly. Jack drew and fired, McDade stood frozen, the smile disappearing from his boyish face, his eyes filled with the reality that he was on the very edge of death. His gun fell from his hand, landing softly in the dusty street.

Jack holstered his revolver as McDade fell to his knees, a crimson red hole appearing just above his heart, the crisp white shirt rapidly changing to a murky red. Before Jack even turned to start back up the street, citizens were venturing out the front doors of buildings. People gave him a wide berth as he slowly walked away from McDade.

He watched those he passed carefully. He looked into their eyes, at their hands, searching for the smallest indication that someone meant him harm. Most of the townsfolk stared at him, but looked quickly away as his eyes met theirs. From behind him, he heard the same remarks and statements that always trailed the end of a gunfight.

"Is he dead?"

"Who is he?"

"Right smack dab in the heart!"

Jack mounted his horse, rolled another smoke and rode slowly out into the desert. He felt at ease. It was finally over. McDade was to be his final victim. It was time to get out. Earlier in the year, a gunman by the name of Jared Cates had been his forty-second kill, but not before wounding Jack in his left shoulder. It had only been a minor wound, but that was not the issue. He had never been hit before. He considered the wound a warning. He was getting older now—forty-four to be exact. His eyesight couldn't possibly be as keen as it had been in his twenties. His reflexes, his reaction time, had to be slowing down. He was still good, but why push one's luck?

He rode until sundown, stopped near the base of a huge rock formation, and made camp for the night. He watered his horse, pouring water from his spare canteen, and using his hat as a means for the animal to drink. He unsaddled the horse, gave him a handful of oats, then went about preparing some chow.

He had chosen a life of being a loner. In his business, it wasn't smart to get too close to anyone. His life was one of walking on the edge of the cliff. One wrong move, a slight slip, and over the side, down into the murky depths of death you went. It was unwise and hard to trust anyone.

It was a clear night, millions of stars, a bright moon. He rested his head on his bedroll, his hands folded across his chest. At times, being alone was the height of pleasure. He breathed deeply, the aroma of hot coffee, bacon and beans tantalizing his sense of smell. In the morning, he'd be up early, on his way to Montana.

He had one brief stop to make on the way at Enterprise, Kansas. If the weather held, he'd arrive there in about a week. Traveling there would carry him nearly a hundred miles out of his way. It was a long way to ride, considering he might only be there for an hour or so.

He wasn't even sure that she would be there. There had been plenty of time in the past when he could have asked for her hand in marriage, but the day-after-day, looking-over-your-shoulder life of a gunfighter wasn't exactly what every woman dreamed about.

When Beth Slocum was seven, the blond-haired, green-eyed little girl, her parents, and eight other families left Ohio by wagon train. Their goal was the wonderful opportunities and vast land of the great West.

Months later, the train of westbound covered wagons was attacked by Indians. The attack was swift and brutal. All of the men and women were massacred as the children looked on in horror. All sixteen children were carried off to be raised as Indians. Beth had always been a bullheaded little thing, not accepting change readily, and much to the amazement of the Indians wasn't about to change.

The tribe didn't have a set method for transforming white children over to their rough way of life. It was a matter of survival. The children had witnessed their parents being butchered and the realization that they would not be coming to take them home was all too obvious. The older the children were, the longer it took them to accept the ghastly truth of the situation.

Beth was the exception. She resisted the *Indian custom* tooth and nail. For three consecutive days and nights, she sat with her back to a tree, her fists clenched. She refused to eat, baring her teeth and snarling at the Indian women who approached her. Finally, the squaws had had enough of the defiant white child. Three women held her down, while two others pried her hands open. A small stone, circular, flat, and two inches in diameter, dropped from her hand. She lunged for the stone but was held back. After inspecting the stone, one of the women threw it to the side, deciding that it was of no value. When they released her, Beth pounced on the stone as if it were a precious gem.

Eventually, the unruly little blond girl from Ohio gave in. She had to eat because she had to keep herself alive. She lived with the tribe for seven long years, ate their food, participated in their ceremonial customs, learned their language, wore their clothing, but never accepted them in her heart.

Despite the fact that she cooperated with the tribe, her attitude toward them stated quite plainly, "I'll do what you say, but I don't like it!" On many an occasion, especially her first two months in the village, her defiant demeanor caused hatred from the Indian children. It seemed like a day didn't pass when one of the tribe's children didn't challenge her. They'd make fun of her blond hair and make brazen comments she didn't understand. She'd always try to ignore them, until the point when they physically pushed her. This always resulted in the same ending.

She still had the round stone, which she now wore around her neck by means of a leather strap. She'd always hold the stone up in front of the aggressive child, then proceed to give them the whipping of their life. After a period of time, it seemed like she had tangled with every child in the camp. She always strutted away, sometimes bleeding, clothes ripped or some hair missing, but always the champion. There was just something about that stone. The squaws said that she was crazy.

The chief had two sons who were a few years older than Beth. The eldest son walked in the ways of his father, adhering to the application of wisdom and logic in all circumstances, while the younger leaned toward the use of force, asking questions later. The younger brave had a few followers, but his older brother was destined to command the tribe after their father passed on.

The young brave looked with favor upon the blond-haired white girl who wore the stone. By the time Beth turned twelve, she was just starting to develop into womanhood. The rebellious son thought he shared common interests with the white girl. She seemed to possess a similar style of solving problems. She said little, but defeated all comers with the use of violence. He had approached her on two different occasions, but she ignored his advances. Months later, he made yet another attempt at conquering the yellow-haired maiden. It was a hot July morning as Beth stripped naked and walked slowly into the cool, deep river a mile from camp.

The brave followed her, aware of her routine of bathing. Hiding in the brush, he watched her bathe, the morning sunlight dancing about her long hair. As she came out of the water and reached for her clothing, he made his move, coming at her from behind. She struggled and tried to scream, but his left hand was tightly clamped over her lips as his other hand groped at her. When it became apparent that she was not going to willingly accept him, he threw her to the ground, followed by three swift kicks. He was so intent on overpowering Beth as he pounced on her that he never saw or felt the knife being removed from his sheath.

Beth relented only long enough for the lust-filled Indian to let his guard down. Seconds later, the chief's youngest son lay dead, his throat slit. Beth, naked, her chest covered in blood, stood over the dead youth, the stone in her hand held high. Four other women from the tribe who had gone unnoticed on the opposite bank had watched the assault and subsequent killing.

The death of the brave caused quite a stir among the tribe. Many felt that the white woman should be killed, while others claimed she had done no less than defend herself. A council was held, the chief himself having the final say. He was greatly saddened by his youngest son's death, but also took into consideration the youth's lack of respect for following the ways of the tribe. He told the people of the tribe that he could not allow his thoughts to be altered by the fact that the brave had been his own son. He had to consider the situation, not those involved. His son had chosen death by going against tribal customs. The white woman, or any of the women of the tribe, had the right to reject any man, and also to defend herself if attacked.

He went on to say that the woman who carried the stone did not deserve to die, at least by their hands. His final statement was that the woman had never accepted the tribe in her heart and would continue to remain as such.

She was escorted by four warriors on a three-day ride out into the vast desert, stripped and left to fend for herself. She would walk for days, but eventually die. As the Indians rode off, they shook their heads in amazement. The white woman had to be crazy, just like the squaws said. Standing in the blazing desert heat, stark naked, no food or water, she held the stone high, aiming it in their direction.

Six days later, she was discovered four miles east of Enterprise by the local preacher and his wife who had been paying their respects to a woman who had lost her husband to the fever. Beth, dehydrated, sunburned, unconscious, hanging on the very edge of death, was delivered in the back of a buckboard to Doc Wheeler, the town physician.

Two hours later, she came around. People in town, especially the church folk, were concerned over who she was. She had to be someone's daughter. She was much too young to be on her own. Doc notified the preacher's wife that the girl was going to recover. What she now required was a couple of days' rest. For the moment, she was too weak to answer any questions.

Sunday, following service, three church families accompanied the preacher's wife to Doc Wheeler's. The doctor said that she was eating well, drinking plenty of water, but it would be a few weeks before her sunburn would completely heal.

Beth sat upright in bed, smiling as she accepted a donation from the church of a dress and pair of shoes. She answered all their questions as she spoke of living in Ohio, traveling west, being attacked by Indians, and living with the tribe for seven years. The women were appalled when they found out how she had been left to die in the desert.

Beth's honesty about her past life with the Indians didn't exactly inspire most of the locals to offer a helping hand. Sure, they felt bad. It was an unfortunate thing, but the fact remained that she had lived with savages for all those years. The usual, and accepted opinion in regards to white women who had spent time with Indians, was that they were tainted. The church didn't side with this pagan way of thinking. Indians were children of God, just like the whites. Beth was just a child herself. Someone had to look after her and take the responsibility for providing her needs.

The individual who came forward, offering her help, was probably the least one expected. Ana Mae Kruger, proprietor of the Desert Star Saloon and Hotel, agreed to supply Beth with room and board. In return for this ample hospitality, Beth would be required to clean up around the establishment, sweeping, mopping, washing dishes, making beds and a host of other duties.

Ana Mae and her husband, Rolfe, had moved to America from Germany and worked their way to Kansas. Shortly after arriving in Enterprise, the owner of the "Star" died from a stray bullet during a harsh disagreement in the saloon. Rolfe and Ana Mae were the only couple in town with enough money to keep the place going, so they purchased the business.

With a few changes, it became the center of attraction in Enterprise. It was the best place to get a good home-cooked meal, a drink or a comfortable room with a bath. Rolfe tended bar and Ana Mae cooked and cleaned. Just three years after moving to

Enterprise, Rolfe passed away from a severe case of pneumonia.

Ana Mae had run the Desert Star by herself for eight years. She was known as a tough ol' bird who didn't take grief from anyone. She didn't put up with drunks or fighting in her place. There was many a night she had run some drunken cowboy out the front door with nothing more than a broom.

The one activity she did allow, which the church was drastically opposed to, was the presence of saloon girls. They served up alcohol, played cards, danced and joked with the men and, on many an occasion, were available to supply a method of entertainment for the local male population. As long as the men treated Ana's girls with respect, there would be no problem. It was understood that if you beat on one of the girls, you ended up the wrong end of Ana Mae's shotgun.

After much discussion, the church decided to permit Beth to stay at the Desert Star. It was agreed that she had to attend both school and church. Beth vaguely remembered going to church back in Ohio and attending campfire services with families from the wagon train, but years spent with the Indians had erased much of the strict religious doctrine her parents had taught her.

Even though she despised the Indians for killing her parents, she had grown to understand why they revolted against the white man. They were being pushed off the land they had lived on for decades. They were simply protecting their homes, their land and their way of life.

During the time spent with the tribe, she came to the realization that the Indians were not the demons white people claimed them to be. Actually, as a people they seemed more religious than whites. They worshiped a God, and she had no doubt that it was the very same God white men prayed to. They referred to the Almighty as the Great Spirit. Their very existence hinged on their relationship with the "Spirit." They prayed for rain, good hunting, long lives—many of the identical things she had heard her parents pray for.

Beth owned two dresses—one for church and school, the other for work. Wearing her best dress and sunbonnet, she'd sit at the back of the church and listen intently to the preacher, the numerous biblical stories fascinating her. After attending church for three months, she asked the pastor for a bible. At first, it was impossible for her to read. She'd only attended one year of school prior to departing Ohio, hence, her capacity for reading was quite low.

Her teacher, Mrs. Blanton, was a regular at church. She was more than pleased at Beth's request for her to read to her from the Lord's book each day following school. Beth would sit silently and listen as Mrs. Blanton read five pages each day. It took a year and a half, but together they got all the way through the thick Bible.

Beth's first few days at school were anything but easy. Her fellow classmates, mostly the boys, taunted her, calling her white trash and Indian squaw. The numerous insults came to an abrupt halt on a Friday afternoon. Clem Newton, a fourteen-year-old farm boy who bullied everyone he could overpower, tripped Beth on purpose, knocking her to the school steps, held her face in the mud and called her a dirty red Indian squaw. She fought her way to her feet, held the stone in front of his face and then proceeded to beat him until he begged for mercy.

The boy's folks were incensed, saying that they couldn't believe the town was going to stand by and allow some Indian orphan to attack their son. Nothing ever came of the incident as the other children, along with Mrs, Blanton, explained what really happened. It was rather comical around Enterprise about how the strapping young farm boy had gotten whipped by Beth.

At the start of her second year in school, she could read quite well, considering the late start she had received. Beth was now capable of reading the Bible on her own. By the time she turned seventeen, she had been working for Ana Mae for three years. She was not regarded as attractive by the men who frequented the saloon, but looked upon more as wholesome. She still wore her blond hair long, dressed very modestly, her dress always fastened up to the very top button. The stone, still supported by the leather strap, hung from her neck.

The men didn't bother much with Beth when it came to enjoying a great time. The other girls dressed provocatively, drank and danced with the men, usually winding up in a second-floor room. Beth minded her own business and went about her chores.

The Desert Star was packed to the walls on that rainy Saturday night, the saloon filled with gaiety, with the smell of cigar smoke and beer. The piano player sat on his wooden stool and banged out one spirited tune after another as locals danced with the girls. Men sat around tables playing cards, talking about the weather or the price of beef as they drank away the night.

The festive atmosphere was rudely interrupted by the entrance of three buffalo hunters. They were hungry, thirsty, and looking for action. They had been on a "hunt" for nearly two months and now it was time to cut loose. Their leader, a man referred to as Pierre, weighed in at close to three hundred pounds and towered in height at six-foot, five inches. Buffalo hunters, as a general rule. were not a welcome sight. They were usually cruel and vile men who didn't care what folks thought of them. These three most definitely fit into the design of what people expected of their kind. Between their foul language, filthy clothing and the smell of dead meat and buffalo hides, the gay attitude of the saloon changed rapidly. For awhile, it didn't seem too bad as they purchased two bottles of whiskey and grabbed a corner table. Ana Mae kept close watch on the three, her shotgun just under the bar.

As the evening wore on, the whiskey flowed as the hunters bought three more bottles. They had grown increasingly louder and had become a nuisance to everyone in the saloon. One of the hunters grabbed hold of one of the girls as she walked by carrying a tray of drinks. As he held her close, she wrinkled her nose at the fetid odor emanating from his body. The drinks fell from the tray as he dragged her toward the dance floor, throwing her about like a rag doll as he made a wobbly attempt at dancing. She looked around desperately for help as the man pulled her in close, giving her a wet, slimy kiss. Some of the men ventured the thought of helping the young girl out of her plight, but so far, it seemed harmless enough; the hunters just wanted to have some fun. The dancing man's friends shouted with drunken laughter as they slapped their knees and stomped their feet to the piano music.

The big man, Pierre, grabbed Beth by the arm as she made her way through the crowd to the bar. She quickly yanked her arm from his tight grip and stared directly into the filthy bearded face. The man displayed a wide grin, half of his teeth missing and the remaining ones a yellowish-brown. "They tell me yer an Indian," he bellowed loudly.

Beth turned to walk away and he slapped her on her backside. She thought it best to ignore his brazen manners as she continued walking toward the bar.

"Hey," he yelled. "No Indian squaw walks away from me! Git yer hide back o' here!" Beth just kept walking.

For his size, the big man was surprisingly fast on his feet as he sprung from his chair, knocking it to the floor. He grabbed a handful of Beth's hair and jerked her back as he wrapped a muscular arm around her, his beefy hand reaching for her breast. "Had me plenty o' squaws," he barked.

"They's the best kind ta have!"

Beth jammed the heel of her shoe down on the man's foot, twisted free, turned and raked her nails over his face, four dark red streaks quickly appearing just above his right eye. He wiped the blood, then backhanded Beth, sending her reeling across the room, her head colliding with the piano.

Ana Mae was just starting to bring the shotgun up from behind the bar when the huge mirror behind her shattered into a hundred slivers. Pierre's two friends stood at the table, their long rifles leveled at Ana Mae, twirling gray smoke from the rifle that had been fired slowly rising toward the ceiling. The man who had fired spit a stream of tobacco saliva to the wooden floor, then stated firmly, "Next one `ill be right `tween yer eyes."

Pierre displayed his long-barreled revolver and turned in a wide circle. "I'm takin' this here lil' Indian squaw upstairs. Any objections?"

Plenty of the men objected, but none stood to voice their disapproval. It wasn't right, but no one desired to lose his life over the matter. Pierre staggered toward Beth, took her by the hair and started to drag her across the floor. Most of the locals present hung their heads in shame as Beth was pulled up the stairs, her head banging on the edge of each step. One of the other buffalo men hollered, "I'll be next when yer finished up with `er."

Halfway up the stairs, Beth made her move, reaching up, removing the twelve-inch butcher knife from Pierre's boot-length moccasin. She drove the sharp blade clean up to the hilt into the back of the big man's leg at the same time twisting the handle.

Pierre let out a high-pitched scream of pain as he instantly released his grip on her hair. Beth scrambled up the steps, kicked him in the groin and pushed him backwards down the stairs. Pierre rolled once on the floor. Beth threw herself on the giant man and skillfully drew the razor sharp edge of the blade across his throat. She then raised the stone from around her neck high enough for all to see, then stuck the knife deep into Pierre's leg. There was no scream of agony this time, just a gurgling sound as blood gushed from the gaping wound in the hunter's neck.

Beth, who weighed no more than a hundred and ten pounds grasped the big man by his long, greasy hair and started to drag him across the floor, leaving a trail of blood behind. The weight was too much for Beth to pull. After just two feet, she fell to the floor in exhaustion, but then stood and removed the knife from the leg.

What happened next was the climax to that rainy night that would be talked about for years to come. Beth, drenched with sweat, her dress completely ripped from her left arm, her chest covered in blood, walked over and stood directly in front of the remaining hunters. Both of their guns were aimed straight at her heart. She picked up the chair that Pierre had knocked over, placed her right foot on it and stuck the bloody knife in the center of the table, the blade gyrating back and forth. The rifles were only inches from her chest. She placed her hands on her hips and snapped, "Git!"

Both men smiled, then smirked.

She stepped closer to the guns. "Ya hard o' hearin'? Go on git!"

Her strength in the presence of death itself inspired action from those watching. Every man in the saloon stood, their pistols and rifles leveled at the buffalo hunters. Ana Mae cocked the hammer of the shotgun as she commanded, "You heard the little girl…git!"

Both men reluctantly lowered their rifles, turned and walked out into the pouring rain, leaving Pierre lying in the middle of the saloon floor. There was a brief moment of stillness as everyone just stood there looking at one another in amazement. It was over. Beth picked up her broom and went back to work. From the corner the piano player began to pound out an upbeat tune as everyone sat back down to their card games and drinks.

Ana Mae requested that two men standing near the bar drag the dead buffalo hunter out the front door. Aside from Ana, no one said a word to Beth about the incident that night. From that moment on, Beth commanded a new level of respect. People claimed that she was either extremely brave or just plain loco.

Later that same year, Jack Tibideau rode into Enterprise for the first time. From the first time he laid eyes on Beth, something clicked. He paid Enterprise two, maybe three visits each year. Everyone knew who he was and that he had left a trail of dead men behind. He had never caused any trouble in their town. He usually only stayed the evening, then moved on. He seemed like a rather tranquil man, nonetheless, considered dangerous.

After three or four trips up to Enterprise, people in town claimed that Beth was Tibideau's woman. When he came to town, her entire personality seemed to change. She smiled, which was a drastic change from the normal deadpan stare that she always wore. As far as everyone knew, they had never been intimate. Their relationship consisted of casual buggy rides out into the desert, pleasant conversation, or an occasional meal together.

Jack was more nervous than he could ever recall as he walked into the Desert Star. He had faced down many a ruthless killer and had always maintained a calm, collected demeanor. Now, he was about to face a five-foot, two-inch woman who had him shaking in his boots.

Sitting at a vacant table, he scanned the interior of the saloon for her presence. She was nowhere in sight, but then, she suddenly walked through a back doorway. Her tired eyes lit up like sparklers when she noticed Jack. Ana Mae had always sensed the bond between the two. Motioning toward Jack's table, she told Beth to put up her mop and bucket and go sit and talk for a spell.

Ten minutes later, the conversation ended and so were Jack's worries about being nervous. She accepted his marriage proposal without the slightest hesitation. Her remark of why he hadn't asked before threw him off balance. She said she'd thought he'd never ask.

That very afternoon, they pulled out of Enterprise. Jack bought a used buckboard and a team of horses, his black stallion tied to the back. They purchased plenty of supplies to get them started on their journey, said goodbye to Ana Mae, and headed out for Montana, not letting a soul know where they were going.

The ex-gunfighter and the saloon girl were on the brink of their new life together. Most folks in Enterprise were of the opinion that the relationship would never hold. Jack was in his mid-forties, Beth only twenty-four—young enough to be his daughter.

They arrived in Montana and crossed over the Canadian border two months later. Their first order of business was to get married. Following the ceremony at the local church, they spent their first night as a married couple at the town motel. In the morning, they devoured a hearty breakfast and then set out for Jack's place. Beth fell in love with the property. It was even more magnificent than Jack had described. It took nearly that first year to complete the construction of the cabin and barn. The first few months were on the rough side as they had to sleep and eat in temporary shelter that

Jack had previously built.

The Tibideaus were a popular couple in and around the small town that was eight miles off to the south. They became members of the church, Beth joined the choir. They got started with a small herd of six cattle and a milking cow. The rest of the animals on the small farm consisted of fourteen laying hens, a rooster, barn cat and a stray dog that wandered onto the place.

Most of their needs were supplied by the land itself. Beth tended a large garden and Jack fished and hunted whenever meat was needed. He was regarded as an honest, hard working sort of fellow who was always willing to assist his neighbors. He was usually the first person who volunteered to help in rebuilding a barn that had burned down or ride off into the countyside to round up someone's cattle that had escaped their pen.

Their second year in Canada brought two exciting occasions. Beth gave birth to a baby girl whom they named Cora, after Beth's mother, and Jack was asked to sit on the town council. Before long, Cora was approaching ten years of age and the Tibideaus had resided in Canada for twelve years.

It was late fall and the Tibideaus had driven their buckboard into town for monthly provisions. Jack drove the wagon over to the feed mill after dropping Beth and Cora at the general store to look at material for some new curtains for the cabin. Jack was throwing the last sack of grain into the wagon as Samuel Pendleton, the town constable, a rotund, jovial type who never carried a gun, came storming across the street.

"Jack, gotta telegram for ya."

As Sam presented the wrinkled paper to Jack, he rambled on, "The news is already all over town. You know how ol' Benjamin down at the telegraph office is. Anything important comes in across the line…ten minutes later every soul in town knows of it."

Jack took the telegram and before he could even begin to read the scrawled writing, Sam went on, "Folks are wonderin' what in the world is goin' on. That message says that some man by the name of Ty Bodin is comin' here…ta our town…ta kill ya. Well, he didn't use those exact words. Said he was callin' ya out ta the town square, right in front of the hotel. I think…if I recall, it reads a week from yesterday. Says ya have ta be there at ten in the mornin' or he'll come out ta yer place and kill ya where ya stand." He stopped because he was out of breath. His eyes searched Jack's face for some type of logical explanation.

Jack thought quickly, searching his mind for anyone in his past by the name of Bodin. His lack of a response prodded Sam to probe further. "Jack, who in God's name would want ta kill a descent man like you? I mean…it don't make no sense. Do ya know this man?"

"No," answered Jack. "I don't know who he is."

"What are ya goin' ta do`bout this?" Sam asked.

Jack climbed up into the wagon, whistled, then snapped the reins and the team moved forward.

As the wagon started up the street, he looked back. "It's just a telegram, Sam. Don't go gittin' so riled up."

For the next two days, Jack wanted to say something to Beth, but he had no reasonable explanation of who Ty Bodin was or why he wanted to kill him. On Saturday morning, Beth was baking up some biscuits as she glanced out the front window. She turned to Jack who was stacking up some firewood next to the hearth. "Looks like Sam ridin' up. Wonder what he wants. He hasn't been out here for ages."

As Sam dismounted, Jack walked out the front door across the yard to a large rain barrel. "How `bout a drink, Sam. It's a long ride out this way from town. What brings ya out here?"

Sam placed his backside on a tree stump as he accepted the tin of cold water. "I did me some checkin'. Sent out some telegrams `bout this Bodin. Turns out, he's a gunman. Makes his livin' killin' other folks. But it still don't add up. Why would someone want you killed?"

Jack took a swallow of water, then spit on the ground. There was no way to get around the truth, or what he thought the truth might be. "Sam, I'll be honest with you. I'm not the man folks seem to think I am."

Sam looked puzzled. "I don't get yer drift."

"Before me and Beth moved up here I was a gunfighter. Spent a big part of my life in the profession—twenty-one years to be exact. After I retired, me and Beth come up here to get away from all that."

"Ya killed people?"

"Yes, I did."

"How many?"

"Don't make a difference, Sam. You steal a dollar, you're a thief. You steal a thousand dollars, you're a thief. It's the same with killin'. You kill one…or fifty…it doesn't matter; you're a killer."

"But why does this Bodin want ta kill you?"

"I've asked myself the same question as least a hundred times in the past few days. I made a lot of enemies in the past. He can't be coming up here because he'll benefit from killing me as far as his future fame goes. I'm too old now. Most folks have probably forgotten who I am. Most likely, it's somebody trying to settle an old score."

"Look," Sam said. "You've been a good citizen `round here. The past is the past. I'm sure we can get the folks in town ta back ya."

"We'll have none of that," Jack objected. "You don't understand how these kind of men operate. If somebody steps in their way and gets killed, this gunman won't bat an eye. I don't want anyone involved. I appreciate the offer, but it's just too dangerous."

"Well…maybe you could just leave," Sam suggested.

"Can't do that. I spent twenty-one years of my life looking over my shoulder, night after night of restless sleep wondering if someone in the dark would come up on me. Wondering if the next day just might be my last. No, I can't run. I have a wife and daughter now. This is my home, Sam. Nobody's gonna run me off. Besides that, he'd just hunt me until his next chance came up."

Sam looked off toward the mountain, then whispered as if he was speaking secretly. "Couldn't ya just shoot `em in the back? I couldn't do it. But you, well, ya said ya killed men…."

Jack cut him off. "That's not the way it works. Gunfighters have a code…believe it or not. If you're called out, you get one of two choices. You can run, or you show. Running brands you as a coward. I've never run from a face-down yet and I'm not about to start now. I'll have to face this Bodin. I have to protect my family, my home…thc folks in town."

"Maybe I could run `im outta town when he rides in," Sam said.

Jack smiled. "Don't think so. You don't even carry a gun. Most of the folks in town know nothing about guns…except for hunting. He hasn't done anything wrong. All the man did was send a telegram."

"But Jack, you've gotta be what? Somewheres in yer fifties. Can ya still shoot?"

"Yeah, I have no doubt I can still shoot. Now, hittin' what I'm aimin' at…that's the problem. Look, Sam, I appreciate you comin' out here and I appreciate your concern, but there's no other way out of this than for me than to face this man. Now, go on home and let me figure this out."

That evening after Cora was sent to bed, Jack told Beth what the chat with the sheriff had been all about. They stayed up late into the night discussing the dilemma. Jack couldn't see any reason in racking his brain over who Ty Bodin might be. He was coming and that was that. Beth told him that if he wanted to pull up stakes and move on, then so be it. No one would think any the less of him. On the other hand, if he decided to face the man, then he had her support. He had to do what was right in his own mind. Jack found it awkward to smile about the upcoming showdown, but Beth seemed at ease as she stated that she was going to pray about it. The Good Lord would provide the answer to their problem.

Jack only had two days before Tuesday rolled around. He unpacked his old gun and box of ammunition from a cedar chest stored up in the rafters and rode up into the mountains. He practiced both days. The basics came back to him instantly. He was surprised. He was still relatively fast, but his accuracy left quite a bit to be desired. His only chance would be to catch Bodin by surprise and maybe get off two or three quick shots. The chance of that happening was slim. He wasn't going up against some amateur. He was being challenged by a trained, focused, and what sounded like, a very determined gunman.

People in town were at a loss for the remedy. Most folks thought that the Tibideaus should just move away until the whole thing blew over. They'd take care of the farm until they returned. Jack wouldn't hear of it. It was clear that the man was coming because of something that he had done in his past life slinging a six-gun. The reason the man was coming was because of him. He couldn't run out and leave the good people in town, his neighbors, to brave Bodin. It just didn't sit well.

Monday evening, Beth held her husband's hand tightly as they knelt by the stream and prayed that the Lord would deliver them from the devil coming to town. Sunday at church, the entire congregation had joined in prayer that the Lord would somehow intercede.

Tuesday morning, Beth was up and out the door before her husband was even awake. The apple pie she had baked the night before bounced up and down on the oak seat as the buckboard slowly made its way down the dirt road toward town.

She arrived in town at nine-o-five, just fifty-five minutes before the planned showdown. She pulled the team to a halt in front of the saloon, took one last deep breath, then stepped down, walked to the saloon door and entered.

Lem, the barkeep, almost dropped the glass he was cleaning when he saw her. Of all the people to walk in first thing in the morning, Beth Tibideau sure wasn't who he expected. There she proudly stood in her Sunday-go-to-meeting dress and sunbonnet, her dainty hands holding a pie and a knife for cutting.

"Mornin' Lem," she said.

Lem was at a loss for words, but finally sputtered, "Morn, morn...mornin'."

Beth took four steps into the bar and then stopped. "Is there a Mr. Bodin stayin' here?"

"Ya...yes," stammered Lem. "Ba...ba...but he ain't in his room right now."

Beth followed the bartender's wide eyes to a corner table. Lem didn't have to say another word. His face said it all. She was looking at Ty Bodin.

As she approached the table, she sized the man up. He was propped back in a chair, his right leg relaxing on the table supporting his leaning frame. He wore a gray derby hat, matching gray pin-striped suit, black string tie, and expensive snakeskin boots. Balanced on the very edge of his stubby nose was the thickest pair of eyeglasses Beth had ever seen. He was smoking a well-used corncob pipe and whittling on a piece of wood, a small pile of shavings on the floor.

Beth stopped just short of the table as she boldly stated, "I'm lookin' for Ty Bodin. Would that be you sir?"

The man removed the pipe from his mouth and politely responded, "It is."

Beth motioned toward an empty chair. "May I?"

Bodin remained quiet, but nodded yes.

Beth laid the pie and the knife down on the table, sat down, removed her sunbonnet, then unfastened the top button of her dress.

"My name is Beth Tibideau. I'm Jack's wife. I came to talk with you before my husband comes walking down the street out there."

Next, she reached in the neck of her dress producing the rumpled telegram. She placed it in the middle of the table, smoothed out the edges, then slowly reached for the knife and drove it with conviction into the square piece of paper. Bodin didn't seem impressed. He just watched the knife waver back and forth, then looked directly into Beth's eyes.

Beth pushed the hair from her eyes, then spoke softly, "Jack and I received your telegram. My husband doesn't know who you are or why you want to kill him. Now, why is that, Mr. Bodin?"

Bodin enjoyed two puffs on the pipe, then answered, "Your husband doesn't know me `cause when he killed my pa I was just a youngin'."

"My husband claims he never tangled with any Bodins."

"Pa's name wasn't Bodin. His name was William Lightner. Jack knows who he is `cause he gunned him down in Abilene. Let's see…that's been `bout twenty-three years back."

"Was it a fair fight?" asked Beth.

Bodin smiled. "Not hardly, Ma'am. My pa wasn't what you would call the best of men. Some people said he was nothing but a drunk, but he was still my father. Your husband was passin' through Abilene. Everyone knew he was in town. Pa got drunk that night and walked over to the hotel where Jack was havin' supper. Said he was going to tell Tibideau that his kind wasn't welcome in Abilene. He walked right up to Jack's table, pulled out his gun, and pointed it right at him, then commenced to give him a piece of his mind. Folks claim your husband just sat there and never so much as blinked an eye. Guess that got my pa's dander up. He fired and splattered Jack's supper all over the place. Jack just looked up and told him to leave while he still could. Pa just laughed and fired again, this time the shell busted a water glass. Your husband stood, drew, and shot my ol' man right through the heart."

Beth shook her head. "Sounds like self-defense to me."

"That's what the sheriff and everybody else said, too. My pa wasn't no killer. Your husband could have walked outta there and left it be. Pappy wouldn't a shot `im. The point is, my life was changed, and not for the better, because of that night."

"How's that?" Beth asked.

"After they buried pa, my mother ran off with the local blacksmith. I didn't have nowhere to go. The preacher and his wife took me in. That man was an individual that didn't deserve to live. On Sundays, he preached on the wages of sin, then turned around and the rest of the week beat on me and his wife. He treated me like a stray dog. After a few years, I couldn't take no more. He was the first man that I killed, and I've been killin' ever since."

"And you blame my husband for this?" Beth commented.

"I do…I do indeed."

"You think killing Jack is going to make everything all right?"

"That's right…I do. That's why I came up here."

Beth reached for the knife discreetly, then the pie. "When's the last time you had a good slice of pie, Mr Bodin?"

Bodin laid his whittlin' knife and piece of wood on the table. "Well, to tell you the truth, I've never been much on sweets. I can't recollect the last time I had pie."

Cutting a thick slice, she removed it from the pan and pushed it across the table with the knife, then cut a small piece for herself. She took a tiny bite, then looked at Bodin. "Go on, try it. It ain't poisoned if that's what you're thinking."

Bodin reached out and cut off a bite with his knife then took it to his mouth. He chewed, then swallowed. "Right tasty if I do say so myself."

Beth unfastened the stone from its leather strap and laid it in the middle of the table. She patted the stone gently, then inquired, "You know much about the Bible, Mr. Bodin?"

He took another bite of pie as he answered, "Never opened one."

"There's a lot of interesting stories in there. One of my favorites is a story about a stone…just like this one. Seems there was a war between two nations, so to speak. One was called the Philistines, the other the Israelites. There was a young boy by the name of David who was too young to fight. His father ordered him to take some supplies to his older brothers at the site of the battle. It so happened that the Philistines had a great warrior named Goliath who stood over nine-feet tall. The Israelites were terrified of this giant of a man. To make a long story short, David, with nothing more than a slingshot and a stone like this one, right here, defeated Goliath. David had great faith in the Lord."

Bodin smiled then asked, "And what's all this have to do with me…or your husband?"

"My mother," said Beth, "gave me this stone when I was just six. She told me that in life there would be many people, even situations that I would be confronted with that would appear overwhelming or too formidable to deal with. She referred to these people and situations as giants.She said that if I held this stone on high, I would always be delivered from evil. You…Mr, Bodin, are one of those giants that she spoke of. You are one of those situations that seems insurmountable. I have prayed diligently that the Lord would show me the way to prevent you from killing my husband."

Bodin reached across the table and picked up the stone. He held it in his left hand, as he drew his gun, balancing in his right. "This is all very interestin', Mrs Tibideau, but the fact is that this stone is not goin' to save your husband's life. This gun *will* take his life."

He cast the stone back onto the table. Before it came to a stop, Beth picked it up and flung it with all her strength toward his face. The stone hit the rim of his glasses knocking them from his nose. The surprise move caught Bodin off balance and the chair he was reclining in fell back onto the floor. The gunman went over backwards, rolled once and stopped on his back.

In an instant Beth, had him pinned to the floor, the pie knife at his throat, his thick eyeglasses in her free hand. Bodin's gun lay on the floor just beyond his reach. He looked at Beth, to the gun, then back to Beth.

"Go on," she said. "Reach for it. I'll cut you from ear to ear before you get your finger on the trigger. A smile slowly came to

Bodin's face, then he commented, "Kill me if that's what you came here for. I'm not afraid to die."

"Neither am I, Mr Bodin. I'm going to let you get to your feet in the next couple of seconds. I'm going to back up a few paces, then we'll talk."

"If you're gonna use that knife, you better get to it. Once I get on my feet and get my gun…you're dead!"

Beth rose slowly to her feet and backed away, then quickly turned and threw the knife, its blade sinking deeply into the wooden side of the bar. Bodin shook his head in amazement as he picked up his gun and got to his feet. He dusted himself off, picked up his hat, which he centered on his head, then picked up the chair. He had plenty of time to kill this fool of a woman. He put his hand on his hip then aimed his revolver directly at Beth's heart. "Seems like a shame to kill a women with so much…well, spunk. Looks like I'm gonna kill me two Tibideaus today."

"Hold on, Mr Bodin. There's a decision you have to make before you pull that trigger." She raised both of her hands. In the right hand, she held his glasses, in the other the stone. "Just after one of those bullets from your gun pierces my heart, with my final ounce of strength, I'll destroy your glasses. From where I'm standing, the way you're squinting, I kinda gather the idea that without them you can't see all that well. The thing is…without your glasses you'll have to face my husband. He might be fifty-six years of age and rather rusty when it comes to gunplay, but his eyes work quite well. There's a fair chance he'll kill you. The only other option you have is to ride out in the next few minutes. Either way…my husband lives."

Bodin pursed his lips as if he were in deep thought. "Maybe I have an extra pair. Maybe you'll die for nothin'."

"Maybe you're bluffing, Mr.Bodin. If you have another pair,

then pull that trigger. You get to face a Tibideau today, but for the moment it's not the one you came to see."

Beth carefully approached Bodin, then stopped less than a foot away from the aimed revolver. She reached out ever so carefully and hung the glasses on the end of the deadly barrel, then spoke, "Here's the trade. I'm giving you your life back. You don't have to face my husband without your glasses. I'm asking you, Mr. Bodin, please give Jack his life back. I'm asking you to ride out."

Beth walked back to the table and scooped up her sunbonnet. She tied the stone back inside its leather strap, buttoned the top of her dress, then walked to the door. She turned and smiled. "God bless you, Mr. Bodin. One last thing—keep the pie, I baked it just for you." She walked out the door, climbed into the buckboard and drove away up the street.

Jack dismounted at the edge of town. He checked his gun one last time just like he had done so many times in the past. His old black stallion had been put to pasture, but it only seemed fitting that he ride the horse that had been with him all those years of living by the gun.

He started down the street after rolling a smoke. He wasn't very proficient at rolling tobacco any more. There was a time when he had been able to accomplish the task with only the use of one hand. Now, he could hardly get the job done with both.

Just like always, people were looking out doors and windows trying to get a quick glance at the gunfighter. He looked back toward his horse. The chance that he'd never see his loyal animal again popped into his mind. He knew that Beth would take good care of him.

His gun hung low on his hip. It felt strange and out of place, like it didn't belong there. It was difficult to believe that his life was to end this way. He had thought that this was all behind him. He was a farmer now, not a trained gunman. Maybe this was just God's way. He had lived by the gun for a long time in the past. Maybe this was how he was supposed to go out.

The confidence he had experienced years ago was completely gone. He recalled everything that he needed to do, but his reaction time, his reflexes and his timing; everything a man needed to survive a gun contest were totally out of sync. Even though he still had the skill, the feeling that a man had to have about killing another had vanished. He had no hate inside any more. He was now a man of kindness and compassion, characteristic traits that had no place in a gunfight.

The street was empty, except for a lone rider heading in his direction. The man rode closer and reined the horse to a stop. He was a stranger in town, a man Jack had never seen before. The man looked down from his hose and asked, "You Tibideau?"

Jack noticed the gun strapped to the man's hip. He looked into the man's face, then replied, "I am."

The man removed his derby hat and mopped his brow as he squinted into the hot morning sun. He placed the hat back on his head and introduced himself, "My name's Bodin. We don't have any business today, or for the matter, any time in the future. I'm ridin' out."

Jack reached up, grabbing the reins. "But why? Thought you came here to kill me. What changed your mind? I don't understand."

Bodin patted his saddle bag, "Well…let's just say that…your wife makes the best apple pie I've ever tasted. Good day to you, sir." Jack watched the stranger ride out of town until he finally disappeared in the distance.

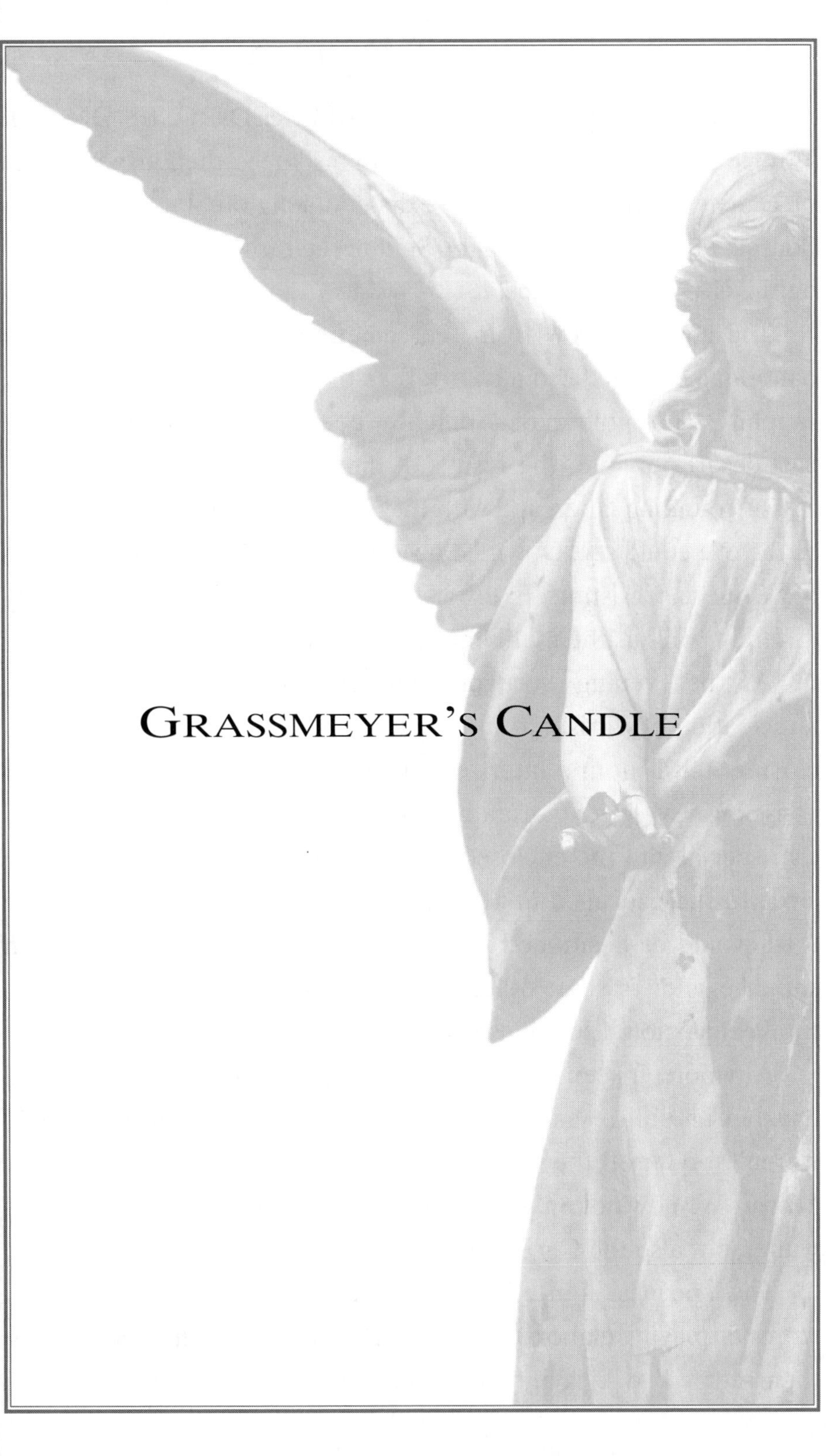

Grassmeyer's Candle

YELLOW ROSES ON THE RIGHT, RED ROSES ON THE left. He stood, brushed the snow from his knees, then inspected the placement of the flowers as he exhaled a long breath, the warm air floating off into the frigid night. Smiling, he turned and looked down on the city in the distance.

The elevated view from the cemetery was nothing short of a panorama of lights, as if a colorful sea of precious gems—diamonds, sapphires and rubies had—somehow been magically imbedded in a vast desert of white. The results of the all-day snow had blanketed the surrounding landscape with five fresh inches of whiteness as far as the eye could see. Down below on the peaceful tree-lined streets of Seymore, Christmas Eve was being celebrated in about as many different ways as the number of families in town.

As the evening wore on, children would be tucked in, the anticipation of Christmas morning preventing their little eyes from closing until hours later when sleep finally overcame their consciousness. Parents, usually dad, would be struggling to assemble that special gift, the enclosed instructions not resembling anything close to the packaged nuts, bolts, screws and assorted parts. Some folks would be positioned in front of roaring fireplaces, sipping on spiked eggnog or some other festive concoction as they collapsed in total exhaustion, Christmas just a few hours away.

Anymore, it seemed like Christmas wasn't just that one special day, but an entire season and, as far as he was concerned, people weren't too far off the mark when they referred to it as the *Holiday Season.* We now not only had the seasons of summer, spring, fall and winter, but also the Christmas season.

The craziness started shortly after Halloween, all the retail stores displaying elaborate aisles stocked with gifts and decorations, then seemed to kick into high gear on Thanksgiving Day as we stretched our poor stomach to the limit with more food than it could possibly hold. The following day folks ventured from the safety of their homes to battle the bumper-to-bumper traffic and hordes of consumers on the biggest shopping day of the year.

During the next few weeks leading up to the big day, people decorated their houses, put up the tree, baked cookies, sent out Christmas cards and, in general, ran themselves ragged, all the while thinking that there just wasn't enough time to get it all done. Then, to top things off, when Christmas came to an end, it was far from over.

The next week was sort of a seven-day period of withdrawal. By this time, between Thanksgiving and Christmas, folks had probably gained ten pounds and in just a few days would be stuffing themselves again on New Year's Day as they sat in front of the television viewing one football game after another. The final act of the holiday season started on January 2nd as most people were faced with two main obstacles—paying off all the Christmas bills and struggling to adhere to whatever New Year's resolution they had made.

Pulling the collar of his jacket up around his neck, he stomped his feet, trying to generate some warmth in his cold toes as he spotted the giant Blue Spruce almost dead- center of the downtown section. The towering tree had been standing there proudly in front of City Hall long before he or his parents had been born. The tree's domineering presence always took precedence on the town square, but during Christmas it stood out like a winter version of an inland lighthouse, its mammoth, brightly lit rotating star perched atop the tall evergreen stabbing out into the night, below, thousands of colorful lights nestled in the thick boughs.

Stretching for two blocks in either direction, the ten-foot

illuminated candy canes attached to light poles guarded Main Street as if they were soldiers assigned to specific evenly spaced positions. To the east stood the high school, the second-floor windows decorated with alternating red and green lights fashioned as four-foot wreaths.

On the very western edge of town, a dazzling glow emanated up through the darkness creating a brilliant conglomeration of lights that made the rest of the town's light seem insignificant. A good half-mile from the last street, the glow penetrated the dark fields then diminished as if swallowed from sight, the only visible lights coming from a few scattered farms.

The miniature Las Vegas section of lights below was the four-street neighborhood where I had grown up and still live. At one time, some thirty years ago, I had known the last names of every family in the one hundred-and-twenty-five-house area. For three straight years between the ages of eleven and fourteen I hiked the neighborhood delivering the local newspaper to the residents. The daily routine of supplying the news had enabled me to not only know their last names, but where they worked, what kind of car they drove, the names of their children and what kind of pet they had, if any. Like most neighborhoods, as time passed a lot of folks moved on. I'm lucky if I know twenty of the families who live there now.

According to my father, the tradition of decorating the entire neighborhood at Christmas had started back when he was in high school. In those days, there were only a few families who decorated and even then it was on the conservative side—a strand of lights spanning a front porch, a few strings of lights intertwined in a small tree or maybe some wreaths in the windows or on the front door.

Cadmus Terhune, an old codger who had to be in his late eighties, lived in the largest house in the neighborhood, which was situated at the corner of Bragg and Wilcox Streets. He was the sole owner of Terhune Construction Company, putting in no less than ten hours a day at the office. His doctor claimed that Cadmus was in great physical condition for his ripe old age, all of his major body parts functioning as if he were years younger. It almost seemed that somehow he had defied the process of aging.

The only thing that seemed to be failing him was his sight. He was able to read with the aid of reading glasses, but driving was out of the question. Despite the fact that he was told not to drive, he went ahead and guided his old black Lincoln back and forth to work six days a week.

He had been pulled over by the police and warned on numerous occasions that if he did not refrain from operating an automobile, he would be arrested, fined and his vehicle impounded. The day that the patience of the police came to an end in regard to Cadmus being a safety hazard turned out to be quite comical. Shortly after being pulled over, Cadmus climbed out of the lengthy Lincoln, snatched the ticket from the officer's hand, unlocked the trunk, removed a bicycle, mounted it and pedaled off, leaving the policeman standing alone shaking his head in amazement.

Needless to say, Cadmus had more money than he knew what to do with. The Lincoln was picked up by a crew of his men, hauled back to his place of business, spray painted gold and then suspended by means of a towering crane directly in front of the main gate of the construction company. This was by no means the end of his driving career. It was not uncommon for the elderly fellow to climb aboard a bulldozer or forklift and speed around the construction yard, at times plowing into piles of equipment or knocking signs over.

The summer following the demise of his driving days on public roads, Cadmus flew up to Canada for two weeks of peaceful lakeside fishing. His second day on the lake, while talking with some local fishermen, he caught wind of an auction that was to take place in two weeks at a warehouse up in Quebec called The Christmas Barn. Cadmus extended his vacation, showed up the night prior to the auction, located the owner and offered him a sizable amount of cash not only for the contents, but the building as well.

One month later, the building sold off, two tractor-trailer loads of every imaginable type of Christmas decoration known to mankind pulled into Terhune Construction. The two rigs were unloaded, the cargo stored in a back storage building. That Christmas, Cadmus Terhune's corner house was a sight to behold. There wasn't a single square foot surrounding the two-story stone home that was not ablaze with brightly lit decorations. The house itself was said to be covered with thousands of lights outlining the doors, windows, roof, chimney and two-car garage.

To the right of the house, he had positioned a life-size nativity scene, complete with a wooden manger and P.A. system blaring out Yuletide music. On the opposite side of the front yard stood an animated choir unlike people had ever seen. The original set included four carolers, but Cadmus had combined ten sets formed in a semi-circle in three rows, each higher than the next for a total of forty, three-foot tall Dickensville characters.

The sidewalk leading up to the front door was guarded by brightly lit toy soldiers, the driveway flanked on either side by alternating snowmen and elves. The roof of the house was topped off with a dazzling light display of Santa positioned in his toy-filled sleigh, guiding his familiar team of reindeer, Rudolph's red nose twinkling on and off.

The following year, Cadmus decided to hold an auction on his warehouse load of Christmas decorations as he had no more room left on his corner lot to squeeze anything else in. The auction was advertised in the local paper and held the week following the Fourth of July holiday. It seemed strange watching people drive away, their cars filled with Christmas items, the temperature in the low nineties.

Over the next eight years, Terhune's two truckloads of Canadian Christmas decorations could be seen at practically every house in the four-block neighborhood. At first, there were only a few houses on each street that were as elaborate as Cadmus' place, but as the years passed, folks just sort of got caught up in the decorating frenzy, everyone seemingly trying their best to outdo their next-door neighbors.

It finally got to the point where each one of the four streets tried to out decorate the other streets, each group of families holding separate meetings in the middle of the summer to determine what the theme of their street was going to be.

The four connecting streets became a family tradition, folks not only from the other neighborhoods in town paying a yearly visit, but people from as far away as a hundred miles out traveling to Seymore to slowly drive or walk through the most dynamic light display in the Midwest.

Eventually, all four streets came to the conclusion that they should all throw in together. Committees were formed to organize each and every facet of the Christmas operation. There was a group that was responsible for all of the lighting, another for the carpentry work, people who were assigned to work on the elaborate entrance and the street lights; even a group designated to conduct bake sales and flea markets to raise funds for additional lighting and displays.

My parents' house was no exception. The week prior to Thanksgiving my father and I were assigned the task by Mom of starting to decorate the outside of their home. My father never got overly excited about the yearly project, but to not decorate one's house was a sure-fire method of getting oneself ostracized by the surrounding neighbors.

Ol' dad had a liking for smoking a brand of cigars that gave off one of the foulest odors that could invade the sense of smell. He was absolutely forbidden by mom to smoke in the house, car or in her presence. Hence, my father had remained in rather good physical condition from his evening or morning "smoke walks" around the local streets. Despite the fact that he did not enjoy decorating the exterior of the house, he was content to sit on the roof, climb up and down the extension ladder and organize everything in the front yard, all the while puffing away to his heart's content on one of his nasty cigars.

The other reason my father and I were only in charge of the outside of the house was due to the fact that Mom and my sister tackled the inside. Decorating the nine-foot artificial mountain pine centered in the front picture window was nothing short of a science as far as the womenfolk of the family were concerned. Each and every light was painstakingly positioned on the fire-retardant branches, which allowed the assorted balls, bells, angels and tinsel to create a picture-perfect tree that caused passers by to hesitate on the front sidewalk as they pointed and stared at the glorious wonder of Mom's handiwork. The four-street Seymore Christmas extravaganza officially started the day after Thanksgiving, as soon as darkness set in, lines of cars and countless pedestrians passing slowly by each residence.

Possessing the privilege of being the local newsboy, for the most part, was something I had always viewed as a pain in the butt. Forcing myself out of my warm bed at the crack of dawn, I hoisted the heavy sack of papers onto my back and headed out into the dark neighborhood to brave whatever weather conditions Mother Nature had in store for me. Then, to add insult to injury, I had to trudge off to school, the teachers expecting me to be just as alert as the other kids who I always looked at as having *normal* lives.

As soon as I got home from school, the four stacks of evening papers would be waiting for me in the front yard, the morning process repeating itself. It didn't seem right. I was up delivering the morning paper before most folks were even out of bed, spent the better part of the day at school, then made sure everyone received the evening news. Their workday was at an end—but I was still at it.

The only time of the year that I truly enjoyed delivering the papers was during the Christmas season. During the morning, most of the neighborhood decorations were turned off. But at night, I had the wonderful experience of walking by each and every house, all the while thinking how lucky I was to live in such a great section of town.

The best nights were when it was snowing, the whiteness adding a special touch to the decorations. I had a special house on each street that I liked the best. The Blake's white split-level just down from my own house was always decorated in blue, the entire house wrapped up like a giant gift, a huge three-foot wide blue ribbon stretching from the left side of the house across the roof and down the back, a large blue bow centered on top of the building. The trees, every door and window on the property were dotted with thousands of blue lights.

The Webster sisters, who were in their sixties and had never been married, had to have the largest collection of animated Christmas figures that existed in the world. They not only had a large bow window displaying their collection, but had built a glassed-in porch that spanned half the length of the house filled with movable figurines, highlighted by a sophisticated lighting system. There had been many a cold winter night that I had stood in their front yard mesmerized by the various movements of Santa loading his sleigh, elves building toys, singing angels, dancing bears and on and on.

Clive Johnson's house was completely centered on trains, a large downscaled operating steam engine pulling three passenger cars not only circling his house, but chugging along the tracks, then down and back the length of his massive backyard, Along the way there were numerous displays, which were all operational and manned by two-foot elves.

Another house that always caught my attention and that of the many visitors was the Paradowski house. The family was from Poland, both mom and dad working daily at their small butcher shop located downtown. They had what seemed like an unending supply of kids, ranging from toddlers to high-school age.

Their two-story home advertised without a doubt that the theme of their home was Christ-centered. A huge illuminated sign encircled by strands of white lights reminded those who passed by that THE KING HAS BEEN BORN. Needless to say, the three churches located within the town limits were more than glad to participate in assisting the Paradowski's message of the Christ child, thus a live nativity scene was put on each year in their front yard.

The local hardware store supplied all of the lumber needed for the construction of the manger, a nursery donating all of the straw, members from the churches and the Paradowski's older children portraying the shepherds and the Three Wise Men. Mr. and Mrs. Paradowski acted the parts of Joseph and Mary, an actual baby used as the Christ child, weather permitting.

Live sheep and cattle were delivered and then taken back to a farm a few miles outside of town. One of the biggest attractions of the neighborhood was Delilah, the female camel that the surrounding families had shipped in and purchased from the St. Louis Zoo. During the year, she resided at Harry Pike's farm, but during Christmas she added a touch of realism to the nativity that could only be described as unequaled. The authenticity of live animals and participants was enhanced by homemade sandals and attire applicable to biblical times. The elevated twelve-foot wire star gracing the top of the manger was outlined by hundreds of white lights and could virtually be seen for miles.

If there would have been a chart designating my most popular house to the least popular, Mr. Grassmeyer's place fell to the bottom. Grassmeyer was said to be well up in his years; nobody was certain how far, but it was estimated to be somewhere in the late eighties. His wife had passed on years earlier and now he lived in the three-story house by himself. He hardly ever came out of the house and if someone did happen to see him, he did his best to ignore the neighbors.

The only decoration on the entire house was a single candle centered in the tiny front attic window. It was on twenty-four hours a day, every day of the year. The house itself was an eyesore, the siding chipped, delaminated and faded, most of the shutters hanging on for dear life as if they would become unhinged and fall to their death in an instant. The gutters had in numerous places rusted causing the roof to appear as small waterfalls following a steady rain. The front porch had settled and gave the house a catty-wampus effect. The sidewalk had heaved up and was infested with grass and weed-filled cracks. The grass, what there was of it, was nothing more than sporadic patches, leaving one with the impression that a herd of raging cattle had just recently stampeded across the front yard.

A group of women from the Christmas committee had at one time paid Grassmeyer a visit, suggesting that in the interest of the entire neighborhood maybe he would consider decorating the house. The women, already aware of the old man's dismal financial condition were prepared to fund any decorations required to bring the house into line with the rest of the neighborhood.

Mr. Grassmeyer lived up to his reputation, as the meeting with the local females ended after just a few short minutes as he ran them off his front porch stating that besides not having the funds himself, all of this decorating business was a waste of time, energy and money.

The following summer some of the people in the surrounding houses had joined forces and contacted the city about Grassmeyer's place saying that it was not only unsafe to be inhabited, but also an eyesore. The city inspected the house; the results nothing more than an official statement that aside from the front sidewalk and the loose shutters, the house was indeed safe and livable. Reluctantly, Grassmeyer had the shutters repaired and the front walk leveled.

Unfortunately, of all the people on our street, it seemed like I had the most contact with the cantankerous old man. I was of the opinion that he never slept. The morning and evening papers would no more than land on his porch when out the door he'd come complaining about where the paper had landed or the fact that the local news cost too much and that there was nothing but bad news in there anyway. I tried my best to ignore him and just move on to the next house until finally he would disappear back inside.

My mother was always very quick to dole out my services to the surrounding neighbors who were in need of some sort of assistance. It was not uncommon for me to pick up groceries for the Webster sisters or mow the grass at the church. She could always tell from the look on my face that there was something else that I would much rather be doing. Her explanation of helping others who could use a hand was that in the long run the time that I spent investing my efforts would be a benefit to me.

The number of times that I was awakened from a sound sleep by my mother to climb out of bed and go over to Mr. Grassmeyer's and shovel snow off his walk seemed endless. During the "shoveling years" as I always referred to them, we had adopted a stray St. Bernard, which we wound up naming Thor. He always slept on an old rug in front of the stove. Thor was always up for accompanying me on all sorts of adventures, but for some reason he never budged when it came to getting up at four in the morning and going outside to shovel sidewalks. Mom always said that he wasn't as dumb as we thought he was.

I always tried my best to remain as quiet as possible while shoveling the old man's walk. At night the house didn't look that bad, and the single candle centered in the third floor window was always there burning like some sort of eternal light. I usually got about halfway finished when the familiar sound of the front door would pierce through the solitude of the early morning as Mr. Grassmeyer would appear on the porch, his flashlight stabbing at the darkness followed by his caustic voice, "Oh, it's just you! Well, don't expect me to pay you anything. I didn't ask you to come over here this morning." With that, he'd grunt and stomp back inside the house.

My mother would have warm oatmeal and hot chocolate waiting for me when I got back home. Her question of "How did it go" was always answered by my rendition of how mean Mr. Grassmeyer was and why in the world would anyone in their right mind want to continue being nice to someone who wasn't the least bit interested in returning anything remotely close to kindness.

She would remind me that being old was kind of like being an infant. What she meant was that there were certain things that seemed to be okay depending on one's age. When you were a baby, it was appropriate to slobber, allowing food to run down your chin and over your clothes, just as it was acceptable when a person got old. The same thing was true of virtues like patience and understanding. Infants did not comprehend these qualities, and at times, some people who were up in their years tended to forget things like compassion and kindness.

According to her, it was the responsibility of adults, which included even teenagers, to be cognizant of the inability of infants and the elderly to function in this manner. She always reminded me that at one time I had been an infant and would no doubt live to arrive at an age where I would have to depend on those who understood my behavior as a senior citizen. Her advice to me was to continue to treat Mr. Grassmeyer with the utmost respect and consideration.

My mom's words of wisdom must have taken hold as I always felt sorry for the old man. Most evenings when I passed his house following my deliveries, I could see him sitting in his living room on a raggedy sofa in front of a fireplace that was never burning. He reminded me of the Norman Rockwell paintings that I had seen hanging in the doctor's office. Mr. Grassmeyer just sat there, an afghan wrapped around his thin body, earmuffs positioned on his head, the paper held in his shaking hands.

Every two weeks, I had to make the rounds of the neighborhood for the newspaper collections. Some folks would write a check for the paper, while others forked over cash. I dreaded going to Grassmeyer's house as he would always instruct me to step inside.

I'd never venture any further than a few feet inside the front door. Everything that I could see looked dusty.

The walls of the hallway were lined with black-and-white framed photographs of distant relatives. There was a rickety nightstand holding a wicker basket filled with plastic fruit and a frayed throw rug centered on the wooden flooring. After complaining about the fact that he couldn't afford the paper, he'd slowly walk out to the kitchen, open the oven and remove the appropriate amount of funds for the paper from a Mason jar. He always gave me exact change.

One particular Christmas during collections I asked Grassmeyer about the single candle in the third-floor window. When I look back now I think it was the only time that I can recall the old fellow being on the civil side. He went on to explain that the candle had been placed there in the window by his wife. She had been of the opinion that all of the decorating that went on in the surrounding houses was too extravagant, and that if everyone lit just one candle, the world would be a lot brighter and that everyone should live simply so that others may simply live. The single candle represented what she stood for and, despite the fact that he was poor as a church mouse, the memory of his wonderful wife always made him feel rich.

It was just a few weeks later after noticing old man Grassmeyer sitting on his couch in front of the "never-used" fireplace that I got an idea. He had told me at one time that the reason he never used the fireplace was that he couldn't afford firewood. I'll never forget the night following supper that Thor and I slipped out of the house, paying a visit to a number of homes in the neighborhood who had fireplaces.

The task took nearly three hours, but commandeering one or two logs from what seemed like an abundant fuel supply from each family was a slow process, my weight capacity at three to four logs.

Thor proudly followed me up the alley toting one small log. Finally finished, after numerous trips, we stood there and admired the neatly stacked wood on Grassmeyer's back porch.

A few days later, I not only noticed a swirling wisp of continuous smoke drifting from the brick chimney, but casually looking through the front window viewed Mr. Grassmeyer sitting in front of a peaceful fire, the paper in his hands, his body minus the familiar afghan and earmuffs. From that point on, every few days Thor and I had to repeat our wood withdrawals from the neighbors.

On one occasion, we almost got caught as Thor and I hid behind a woodpile as Mr. Fields and his two young sons surprised us pushing their wheelbarrow across the yard. Loading up, Mr. Fields made the comment that the pile seemed to be going down faster than the previous year. It was at that moment as I stared at Thor, praying that he wouldn't make a sound that I realized what I had thought was simply a good deed might just be looked upon as stealing in the eyes of the neighbors. We never did get caught in the act and, as far as I know, the topic of missing firewood was never discussed between the folks in the area.

A few weeks after nearly getting nabbed borrowing wood from the Field's backyard, I had another disturbing thought as I passed Grassmeyer's place, the ever-present smoking chimney evidence of the logs I had conveniently collected warming the old man as he sat on his couch reading the paper. Since the fireplace hadn't been used in who knew how long, what if the chimney wasn't in working order and set fire to the house? What if Mom was right and old people just couldn't comprehend things the way that they did when they were younger?

Maybe Grassmeyer didn't give a thought to cleaning out the chimney of years of old soot. If by some chance the house did burn down, I could add yet another random act to my crime spree as the local newsboy. Now I was not only the "firewood thief," but possibly bordering on being an arsonist. Fortunately, the house never did catch fire.

During the spring of my last year delivering papers on a rainy Friday night, Grassmeyer, after picking up the folded news, signaled me to come to the foot of the porch. Standing there in a driving rainstorm, I listened as he informed me that he was canceling the paper. It cost too much and there was nothing but bad news from the front to the back. He wanted the deliveries stopped immediately and hoped that he didn't have to tell me a second time.

That evening as I sat next to the stove in our kitchen sipping an orange soda, Thor munching on a milk bone, I thought about what Grassmeyer had said. It wasn't hard to believe that he might not be able to afford the paper. I mean—he didn't have the money for firewood and it was thought for years by neighbors that he was poor. His statement about the paper being filled with bad news didn't quite hold water as I had witnessed him countless nights on that old couch reading the paper.

Saturday morning I phoned the downtown newspaper office and cancelled Grassmeyer's paper, but also informed them that my parents wanted a second paper delivered to our house. This request was never discovered by either my father or mother and that second paper was delivered to Mr. Grassmeyer's but was now being paid for out of my meager newsboy salary.

That following Monday when the morning paper landed on Grassmeyer's porch, his craggy voice accompanied by that stabbing beam from his flashlight got the week off to a rocky start. I can still hear him saying, "Boy, I thought I made myself pretty clear about canceling the paper. I told you I can't afford the dang thing. Now if you can't follow some simple instructions I'll just have to call the paper myself and lodge a complaint."

After I informed the old man that it wouldn't do any good because I had indeed cancelled his subscription, but someone in the neighborhood had elected to purchase a second paper and have it delivered to his house, he just stood there staring at me as if he was at a loss for words. Staring up the street, he yelled at me as I started toward the next house saying that he wasn't going to read the paper. My response was that if someone wanted to pay for his paper, it was my duty to deliver it. It was entirely up to him what he did with it.

It was just about three months later that things just didn't seem right. Grassmeyer hadn't popped out of his door early in the morning to give me a piece of his mind. After seeing him in the exact same position for three nights in a row in front of the fireplace, which hadn't been lit in days, I told my father I thought something might be wrong. Dad, after peering in the window of the old house called the police. Minutes later, they arrived and after knocking on the door, the old man not budging an inch, they broke in. Old Mr. Grassmeyer had passed away on the couch, the paper folded across his chest.

The county coroner said that the old fellow had just simply passed away from a heart attack. According to his professional opinion, it had probably been rather swift and short-lived as far as any pain was concerned. The nearest relative that could be contacted was a sister who lived in a nursing home on the outskirts of Chicago. She was a few years younger than Mr. Grassmeyer had been and was in surprisingly good health. She informed the local authorities that Herman, which happened to be Grassmeyer's first name not only had a will, but instructions for his burial in a safety deposit box right there in the bank in town.

The sister, accompanied by a cousin flew down to Seymore to make all of the final arrangements. Despite the fact that Grassmeyer was dirt poor, he had managed to salt enough money away to ensure a modest casket, viewing and burial. Mom said that we had to go. After all, he had been a neighbor for as long as she could remember.

The evening of the viewing, I recall looking out the rear window of our station wagon as we passed the Grassmeyer place. The house had always been on the gloomy side, but now with the absence of its owner it seemed so sad. Even though the ol' coot had treated me badly, I was sure going to miss him. But then, I noticed the candle in the third-floor window. It was shining brightly just like always. *A sign of simplicity*, I thought to myself.

It wasn't exactly standing-room only at the funeral parlor. Besides me, my sister and parents, Grassmeyer's sister and cousin were present, along with the Paradowskis, the pastor from the church and a stranger in a three-piece pin-striped suit who didn't resemble anything close to a small town resident.

As I was returning from kneeling at the casket following a short prayer, the expensively dressed man approached my mother asking if he could have a word with our family. My mom, always eager to please, agreed as she rounded up Dad who was outside finishing up one of his cigars.

The man introduced himself as Baxter Detweiler, an attorney from Chicago. He suggested that we seat ourselves on a couch in an adjoining room. Positioning himself on a lone chair directly across from our family, he removed an envelope from his coat pocket as he looked at me, then asked Mother if I was indeed Arthur Crain—their son. My father remained silent as my mother answered, "Yes, Arthur is our son."

Sitting back and crossing his legs, Detweiler went on, "The envelope that I have in my hand was mailed to me a few months ago. The contents is unknown and only to be opened and read after Herman's death. The instructions that he sent along with the envelope designate that the letter inside must be read to Arthur in the presence of not only his parents, but myself. Furthermore, it is to be opened by Mrs. Crain and read to those in attendance."

Receiving the envelope from the attorney, my mother looked at us all as she shrugged, opened the seal, unfolded the paper and proceeded to read:

Dear Arthur,

Unfortunately, it is not possible for one to attend their own viewing so I won't be present to see the look on your face as your mother reads on. Let me start by just saying that you are without a doubt the most industrious young man I have ever met. The patience and kindness that you extended toward me, despite the fact that I treated you with what must have seemed to you a total lack of respect was nothing personal. You were simply the recipient of what I had grown to be—a selfish old man waiting to die. I knew all along that it was you and Thor who supplied me with firewood and that it was you who made it a point to purchase a paper for me when I indicated that I could no longer afford it. If it wouldn't have been for your early morning energy in shoveling my sidewalk, I'm not so sure that anyone else would have made the effort.

I have a two-part offer for you, Arthur, the first part being that I am turning over my property—the house, land and everything inside the home to you. You may be of the opinion that the old place isn't worth much,but everything is not always what it seems. The only thing that I ask is that you allow my sister to pick out a few things that she may want. The rest is yours. The second part of my offer is this. My wife always favored yellow roses, I tended to lean toward red myself. If you will agree to place a dozen roses on my wife's grave each and every year on the date of this letter as long as you live, I have something to give you in return that will benefit your life to a great extent. Before I divulge this second gift you must sign on the following line to agree with the yellow rose request. If you decline, the house is still yours, but the rest of the offer will remain a secret forever.

At this point, Detweiler spoke up, "Arthur, if you do not want to sign it's perfectly alright. Your mother will turn the letter back over to me and it will be destroyed on the spot. If you sign, then we'll continue the reading."

Sitting there in silence for close to fifteen seconds, Mom finally prodded, "Arthur?"

As if coming out of some sort of a hypnotic trance, I raised my hands in wonder and said, "Somebody give me a pen."

The document signed, the attorney signaled my mother to continue. Clearing her voice as if this was to be the most important piece of paper she was to read in her entire life she started:

As I stated earlier—everything is not what it may seem to be. If you will look behind the paneling and the drywall beneath the candle on the third floor you should discover more than enough funds to handle my flower request and to get you through whatever college you may choose. I was never really too fond of banks. Mr. Detweiler is more than qualified to assist you in any and all legal matters that should arise in regard to our transaction. The best of luck to you, young man. I have no doubt that you will succeed at whatever you may desire.

Respectfully,
Herman Grassmeyer

It was close to ten o'clock that night that I accompanied my dad, his trusty toolbox in hand, and Mr. Detweiler on our way down the street to Grassmeyer's. Once we got past my safety zone of the hallway, I was starting to get the strangest feeling. Looking into the front room, the sofa now sat empty in front of the fireplace. Passing the kitchen, I saw the stove where Grassmeyer kept his newspaper money. The ancient stove reminded me of a combination appliance/bank.

I guess the feeling that I was having was that we were invading the old man's privacy. The bed upstairs was unmade. The toilet was running and continued to do so despite my father jiggling the chrome handle. Finally on the third floor, we stood in front of the single candle that cast a dim glow around the room. The light switch on the wall was not working, but the flashlight in Detweiler's hand threw a circle of light on the wall beneath the candle.

As my dad removed a small section of paneling and then went to work on the drywall, he made the comment that he just couldn't understand why anyone would hide money in the walls. Looking past the candle out the small rectangular window, I glanced down on the street below. The amount of times that I had passed the house and looked up at the candle seemed countless. To be inside the house looking out the window was something that I couldn't have imagined.

My daydreaming was put to an end as my dad extracted a heavy leather-strapped case from in between the wall studs. Blowing a thick layer of dust and cobwebs away from the lid, he opened it, the light from the flashlight exposing stacks of money secured by large rubber bands. My father, running his hands through the musty bills, sat back against the wall as he closed his toolbox, shaking his head in amazement. "There must be thousands in here!"

My father's estimation was a little off. After transferring the case to our house, the following morning we met with the president of the bank explaining that I had a deposit to make to my account, which at the time had a balance of a whopping one hundred and thirteen dollars. Two bank employees were brought in to count the stacks of bills. The final tally was one million seven hundred thousand and forty-five dollars. I remember my dad placing his arm around me as he commented that I was probably the only millionaire paperboy in the world. By the time all of the legal red tape was complete and the government received its rightful share, I netted around nine hundred thousand dollars.

That was quite a few years ago, my forty-second birthday sneaking up on me just this past year. Grassmeyer's sister only wanted a few pieces of antique furniture and some assorted photographs. The remaining contents of the house were sold off during a yard sale. Dad and I spent three years remodeling the old house and finally rented it out to a young couple the fall that I left for college. Four years later, I had my own landscaping business right here in Seymore, got married and was looking forward to raising a family of my own. The year that my wife announced that she was pregnant with our first child, we moved into the Grassmeyer place ourselves.

I've been walking up the hill to this cemetery now for almost twenty-eight years, each and every month toting two dozen roses—yellow for Mrs. Grassmeyer, red for Herman. The old neighborhood has changed hands, a lot of folks moving away, new families taking up residence, but the four-street Christmas decoration display is larger than ever. The Paradowski's THE KING HAS BEEN BORN sign is still there right along with the live nativity. The Webster sisters had both passed away, but one of the neighbors had moved in and the tradition of the animated figurines has been there every year. The Blakes' house was no longer a giant gift, but the present family opted to decorate by means of a small Santa's village manned by local children dressed as elves serving hot beverages and homemade cookies.

Taking one final look down over Seymore, it was time for me to be heading back. Turning and inspecting the flowers one last time, I smiled to myself as I thought about the old days when Grassmeyer's house had been the laughingstock of the neighborhood. Now, the house is one of the most attractive residences in the area with its white siding and black shutters, the front porch supported by thick white columns, the chimney refaced with expensive creekstone.

During the holiday season, the old house looks very stately, the candle on the third floor now joined by a single candle in each and every window. My youngest son, age twelve is now delivering the papers just like I did in the past. At times, the boy complains about getting up so early in the morning and having to work harder than his friends, but I always remind him that things are not always what they may seem.

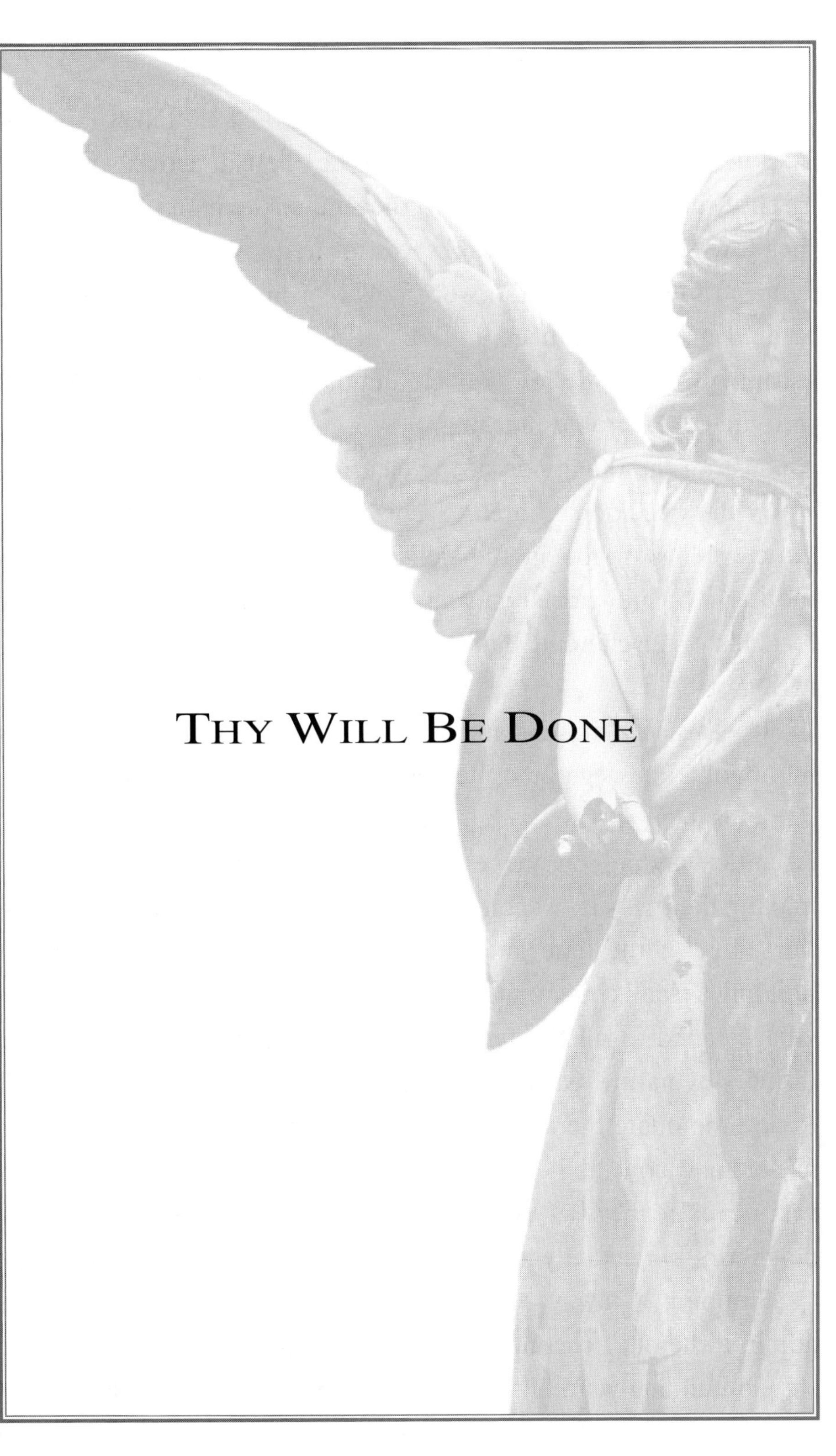

Thy Will Be Done

EMERGING FROM THE STAND OF TALL PINES, HIRAM Zeckner hesitated at the very edge of the one-half acre clearing. The steep three-quarter mile trail up the side of the mountain from the meadow below where his cabin was located taxed his eighty-three-year-old lungs. Pulling the worn collar of his frayed wool coat up around his exposed neck, he let out a long breath, the warm air escaping from inside his body creating a light vapor that drifted off into the cold October morning.

Just on the other side of the clearing nestled in the tall maples stood the one-room church. According to Hiram's estimation, the structure had to be in the neighborhood of 240 years old. His mother, who had passed on years ago had been dubbed as quite the local historian, claiming that the church had been constructed in the spring of 1756.

It was said that a distant relative by the name of Nels Zeckner had booked passage on a merchant vessel, leading to not only the Zeckner clan but six other families from Germany across the Atlantic, landing on the east coast of America and eventually making their way by wagons to the vast mountains of Virginia. Nels, thirty-five at the time and his young wife, Marta, had visions of building a small community. But their dreams of an actual mountain village faded as all the families who had made the journey were farmers by nature, each family carving out acre after acre of forest to accommodate the fields necessary for raising crops. When it was all said and done, the only building that was a part of the town that was never to be was the church. All the locals were considered neighbors, but actually lived miles apart.

Stopping a few yards from the church, Hiram smiled as he admired the old structure. It had indeed stood the test of time. The simple building was still supported by thick logs that had been cut from surrounding pines, the wood now weathered from two-and-a-half centuries of Mother Nature wielding her scorching summer heat, torrential downpours and winter mountain snowfalls. Aside from some occasional tar patching on the roof and new mortar placed in between the log walls, everything stood as it had in the mid-seventeen-hundreds.

The folks who attended the church nowadays weren't that much different than the German settlers who had first built and attended the tiny house of worship. Their mode of transportation was the automobile rather than the family horse and wagon. They enjoyed, for the most part, the conveniences of modern-day living, were more plugged into what was going on in the rest of the world, but somehow still pigeonholed into the category of "country folk," many of the locals still deeply entrenched in the day-in-day-out business of farming, while others simply chose to live away from the hassle of the city.

The closest city was located forty-three miles to the north, five different churches dotting the community, most of the families opting to worship close to their homes. The other deciding factor, aside from making the long drive up into the mountains, was due to the fact that the last sixteen miles of road slowly deteriorated from state-maintained macadam to one-lane gravel and eventually dirt, the numerous ruts and holes less than advantageous to any type of vehicle that was not equipped with four-wheel drive.

Those who were not regular members of the congregation soon found after the dusty, bumpy ride out into the wilderness, that worshiping at the small church was far from what one would refer to as "modern religion." The interior of the building was as rustic and original as its exterior. The slat floors resembled nothing even close to level as the wood had reacted over the years to the variation in temperature with the changing of the seasons.

The side of the log walls facing the inside of the church had not succumbed to the weather nearly as badly but did seem to inject every corner of the interior with a musty odor that was not really offensive to the nose, but instead left one with a sense of being in the presence of a time long past.

There were six pews situated on either side of the aisle, each capable of seating up to four people, the church's maximum capacity somewhere in the vicinity of fifty. Two windows had been placed on either side wall, framed by a pair of movable wooden shutters. It had only been about thirty years ago that the parishioners had decided to put glass in the windows. The ceiling was constructed of rough hand-hewn beams forming the apex of the roof. There was a wooden altar, an elevated pulpit for the preacher and a huge cross cut from the trunks of thick pines that had been embedded into the rear wall.

Climbing the three wooden steps up unto the small porch of the church, Hiram turned and looked down into the valley far below, the early morning fog covering any trace of the only area resembling a gathering of civilization. Jeb's Corners was just a little over thirteen miles to the southeast.

There wasn't a map anywhere that indicated Jeb's Corners as an official town. It was simply a dirt crossroads bordered by three buildings and an open field. On the north side of the intersection stood the combination gas station, general store and post office where you could gas up, mail a letter, purchase a loaf of bread or enjoy a cold root beer from an ice-filled barrel on the front porch on a hot summer afternoon.

Directly across the dirt road sat the old feed mill and tractor supply business that had been in operation since the turn of the century, a fenced-in yard next to the building displaying a collection of rusted farm machinery. It never failed. Whenever paying a visit to the general store, customers could rest assured that they would be paid a visit by the three old hounds who spent their entire lives on the porch of the mill as they would make their way slowly across the dusty road in search of a part of a Twinkie or a pretzel.

The third building situated at the "Corners" was an old dilapidated two-story barn that had seen its better day and had survived well beyond the point of remaining in an upright position. The gray boards were encased with thick climbing vines, the double doors hanging loose on their rusted hinges, the roof caved in and the entire structure leaning precariously to the south.

The field, bordering the barn and the general store, was a good six acres surrounded by barbed wire and overgrown with tall weeds, home to numerous abandoned automobiles and a small mountain of old tires.

Jeb's Corners had derived its name from the fact that during the Civil War the famous calvary officer, General Jeb Stuart, had on a number of occasions led his troops up through Virginia on his way to raids into the north. The dirt crossroads had been a favorite campsite for the general and his mounted confederates. After the war, the field and the dirt intersection retained the general's name, a stake supporting a hand-painted sign designating it as Jeb's Corners placed at the north side of the old barn.

Pushing open the heavy door of the church, Hiram stepped inside, the familiar aroma of aged wood invading his sense of smell. He drew in a long breath, then smiled as he made his way toward the second pew on the right. The inside of the church was still on the dark side as the morning sun had not fought its way through the low fog, the only means of light was the lantern swinging gently in Hiram's left hand.

Strangers would have been of the opinion that it would have been much easier and more convenient to just simply turn on the light switch. This was not possible as electricity had never been run to the church since the nearest line was located seven miles away at the nearest farm. Modern-day plumbing was also something that was not to be found at the country church. Two outhouses, one for the men and the other for the ladies, had been constructed thirty yards back in the woods. Worshiping by means of lantern or candlelight and hiking out into the woods to relieve oneself truly gave folks the experience of attending church as the settlers had done in the past years.

Hiram took his familiar seat in the second row, third seat over—the same place he had been sitting for eighty-three years. His mother had first brought him to the church when he was just two days old and continued to bring him, not only on Sundays, but each and every day as she sat in deep prayer for at least an hour. As Hiram grew, he continued to accompany his mother to the church for daily prayer and eventually accepted the Lord as his Savior when he turned nine. After that, the custom of going to church on a daily basis was no longer a habit, but a refreshing time of the day that he always looked forward to.

Hiram glanced at the walls, then the ceiling. His eyes, over the years, had inspected every scratch and defect in the old wood. He was sure going to miss worshiping the Good Lord in the familiar surroundings. This special building held more precious memories than he could recall. He had not only become a Christian here; he had been baptized in the creek just over the hill, he had married his wife, given his two daughters away in marriage and just a few years ago had put his wife of sixty-one years to rest in the old church.

A tear slowly made its way down his left cheek as he looked

down at the pew where he was seated. This was to be the last day that he would get to come to the church for his daily prayer time. Today was the day that the old church was scheduled to be destroyed. It had all started eight months ago when the state had informed all the residents in the area that a major powerline was going to be constructed through the mountains, and the valley was the only obvious and cost-effective route that could be considered. There was little that the members of the church could do as the land actually belonged to the state. At some point in the past, it had been discovered that no will had ever been drawn up designating the land initially owned by Nels Zeckner to be passed down to family, hence, the state of Virginia owned the acreage.

The state was not without a heart as a representative met with the parishioners at the church, first suggesting that they allow the state to physically move the church to another loacation. The idea seemed reasonable enough as the state would be picking up the tab, but after inspecting the church, it was decided that the old structure, even though standing after two hundred years, if moved would no doubt fall to pieces. Disassembling the church, moving it to another location and reassembling it was ruled out.

The state finally agreed to construct a brand new church at their cost to be located at Jeb's Corners. Two weeks ago, the new building had been completed. Hiram had never been to the new building, but had been told that it was a fine church: fieldstone walls, stained-glass windows, huge oak front doors, carpeted floors, handmade walnut pews shipped in from Iowa, glass chandeliers, ceiling fans, a fully operational kitchen, basement, playground for the kids and paved parking lot, not to mention, electricity and indoor bathrooms.

Activity at Jeb's Corners had changed, especially on Sundays. You could still sit on the porch of the general store enjoying one of those great root beers, occasionally throw a morsel of food to the feed mill hounds and discuss how many more years the old barn had left before it completely collapsed. Now the paved parking lot of the new church was crammed with "churchgoers," some of the folks from further out now coming in to attend.

The barbed wire had been pulled down, the field excavated and leveled, the old cars and tires hauled off miles away to a junkyard. During the next six-month period of construction, the general store enjoyed quite an increase in business, the numerous heavy equipment operators, brick masons, plumbers and electricians walking across the dirt road for a quart of milk or a soda along with a bag of chips to accompany their bagged lunches.

Hiram stood, walked out into the aisle and proceeded to the altar where he placed the lantern on the floor, the light dancing off the sixteen-foot wooden cross towering above him. Slowly lowering himself to the wooden floor, he placed his folded hands on the top rail of the altar as he bowed his head. The mathematics of figuring how many days he had knelt at the altar was beyond his comprehension. It seemed simple enough: three hundred sixty-five days per year times eighty-three years. Without a piece of paper and a pencil, the multiplication of the two figures was too difficult. It had to be well over thirty-some thousand days.

He had shared just about every human emotion he was capable of while kneeling before the Lord. He had shed many a tear during those times in his life when things or situations had not fallen in his favor. He had smiled oftentimes, thanking the Almighty for his countless blessings. He had sought direction, asked for help, searched for answers, but never asked the Lord to fix anything—so to speak. He had lived for over eight decades by simply asking that the Lord's will be done and that's exactly the way that he would end his final prayer at the small church. He was indeed thankful that the Lord had provided them with a new church where they could continue to worship and had no intention of asking Him to save the old church. He ended his prayer as usual— "Thy will be done."

Rising from the altar, he picked up the lantern as he heard the sound from deep in the valley. Turning and making his way back down the aisle, Hiram knew precisely the cause of the unwelcome noise. Pushing open the front door, he stepped to the very edge of the wooden porch slats as he peered down into the distant trees. The fog was starting to burn off, the morning sun now bringing the forest to life.

Four miles below where the mountain road crossed the stone bridge at Copper Creek, a trail of brown dust led all the way back down the steep incline where the oncoming machine had disturbed the normally quiet dirt road. Hiram tracked the continuing dust cloud for a full minute when the flatbed truck appeared for a second as it lumbered past a break in the trees.

The last mile of the road was the steepest grade, the diesel engine beneath the hood of the sixteen-wheeler sending its message of power out into the surrounding forest as the driver downshifted to a lower gear, the pounding cylinders creating a sound the local wildlife was not accustomed to hearing. Once again, the long truck appeared in a cut in the trees for the last time before its final stop at the church clearing.

The driver downshifted the truck one last time as the nose of the huge vehicle edged its way out of the pines and into the clearing where it came to a complete stop just ten yards from the church, the trailing dust floating off to the east. The cab of the truck was a dirty reddish-brown, the grill, headlights and bent front bumper reminding Hiram of some sort of distorted evil face. Attached to the cab, a rusted bulldozer that at one time had been a bright yellow, evidenced by a few traces of its original paint here and there, sat chained to a forty-foot mud-caked flatbed.

The door opened with an abrasive grinding as the driver stepped to the ground. The man had to be well over six-foot, his feet encased in heavy-duty work boots, his left boot ripped at the toe, the marred protective metal peeking through the worn leather. The remainder of his attire consisted of a faded pair of overalls and an old cut-off flannel shirt that displayed muscular arms covered with various tattoos. The man's face hadn't seen a razor for a week, his eyes tired from long hours of driving. A dingy yellow baseball cap, its bill bent from years of wear, sporting the advertisement CAT, was centered neatly on the square head.

The man spit on the ground after removing a well-chewed stogie from his thick lips. Following a deep kneebend, he cracked his knuckles, then spoke, "Mornin'."

Hiram returned the salutation with a greeting of his own. "Good morning to you."

The driver pulled a pair of sweat-stained work gloves from his rear pocket as he continued the conversation. "You the welcomin' committee?"

"No," answered Hiram, "just one of the members of the church."

Forcing the filthy gloves onto his massive hands, the man placed the ragged cigar back in his mouth. "Didn't they build you folks a new church around here somewheres?"

Hiram's response was simple, "They did."

The man motioned as he turned and walked toward the rear of the truck, speaking at the same time, "You best be gettin' off that porch. I've got to doze this building under and I only have about an hour and a half. If I don't get this done today, it'll be weeks before I can get back up in here."

Reaching up and grabbing a short lever, the driver released the hydraulic system that began to lower a metal ramp, which slowly made its way to the ground where it sent up a small cloud of dust. The driver walked up the ramp and began to unfasten the rusted chains securing the dozer as he went on, "This here machine has been with me almost nineteen years now. Never let me down. I know she don't look like much, but she runs like a top. Her name's Satan." He patted the rear of the dozer. "Used to have her name painted on the back here, but it's kind of faded off."

Climbing up into the cracked vinyl seat, the man turned the ignition key, the machine came to life instantly, black smoke shooting out of the rusted exhaust pipe. Backing the dozer carefully down the ramp, he placed it in neutral, then removed a small oil can from the floor, climbed down and began to lubricate all of the movable parts on the front blade.

Back in the seat again, the driver placed the dozer in reverse, backed up, then moved forward, finally in a complete circle, raising the blade up and down. Satisfied at the operation of his dozer, he pulled up even with the front tires of the truck. Looking at the church, the man informed Hiram, "Me and ol' Satan here have dozed more buildings than I can remember. This one here is probably one of the smallest we've ever tackled. Shouldn't be too much of a problem. In about an hour or so, she'll just be a pile of sticks...won't even be able to tell that it was a church."

Hiram stepped off the porch, removed his old bible from inside his coat and laid it in the dirt three feet in front of the dozer. Moving off to the side, he leaned up against one of the tall maples.

The driver took the cigar from his mouth as he sarcastically asked, "What's all this?"

Hiram looked at the church then back to the man. "This church has stood here for well over two hundred years. It has survived everything that has come along. It just doesn't seem right that it should be destroyed. I just can't stand by and do nothing. I've been coming here for eighty-three years."

The man gunned the engine, black smoke filling the air just above the dozer. Smiling, he shook his head in amazement. "Look, I don't have time for this nonsense. I've got a job to do. I don't have time for silly games. Now…you best move that Bible cause I sure ain't gonna climb down and move it out of the way."

Hiram folded his arms across his chest. He had nothing else to say.

With that, the operator put the dozer in gear, the rusted machine slowly inching forward, the heavy metal treads digging deeply into the ground. Six inches from the Bible, the dozer stalled—then stopped. The driver, who up to this point seemed rather pleasant, almost business-like, jerked the cigar from his lips and tossed it to the ground as he cursed. He turned the ignition once again, the dozer firing up instantly. The interior mechanism of the dozer placed the machine in forward—it stalled again.

The man cursed again as he climbed down from the seat, flipped up a dented side panel and proceeded to inspect the engine, gently tugging on wires and checking connections. Satisfied that everything looked in order, he climbed back up and started the dozer for the third time. It started, but then stalled when placed in forward gear.

Now, it seemed like every other word spewing from the man's mouth was foul as he placed the dozer in reverse and slammed his foot on the gas pedal, the machine responding by backing up, the treads throwing large chunks of thick dirt up onto the church porch. Stopping, the driver placed the dozer in neutral, gunned the engine, then jammed the gears into forward, the machine jumping forward at its top speed, a smile now forming on the man's face. The look of confidence quickly disappeared as the dozer came to a jolting halt just short of the Bible.

The man was now more determined than ever as he put the dozer in reverse, turned the machine completely around and backed it toward the church. At the Bible, the dozer stopped dead, started once again, but then stopped and would not restart. The man jumped down from the seat, cursed again and walked toward Hiram, stopping just a few inches from his face. "I can't believe this! I've had this dozer for nineteen years. She's never let me down. You don't seem to understand. I'm on a tight schedule. I'm already behind. First, I had to drive up this God-forsaken mountain and now my equipment doesn't work."

The man kicked at the dirt as he returned to the dozer, climbed back up and turned the ignition. It started. He pulled forward, stopped, turned the machine around and once again moved toward the church, the machine stopping just short of the Bible. "That's it!" The man backed the dozer to the rear of the flatbed, then drove the rusted machine up onto the truck where he climbed off and started to secure the piece of equipment with the heavy chains.

After checking to ensure that the load was safe, he raised the hydraulic ramp, walked to the cab, looked at Hiram one last time, then climbed up and started the truck. Lighting up a fresh cigar, he blew a long stream of smoke out the open window, then commented, "This has got to be the weirdest place I've ever been. I won't be coming back. They'll have to get somebody else to do *this* job."

Following some downright fancy maneuvering, the driver skillfully guided the big rig across the clearing, the dozer and the back end of the truck finally being swallowed from sight in the tall pines. Hiram walked to the edge of the clearing, his eyes following the trail of dust all the way back down the road, getting the last glimpse of the truck at the Copper Creek Bridge.

It seemed like almost thirty minutes had passed before every trace of the truck's existence had vanished. The dust was gone, the forest had returned to a state of peacefulness. Hiram walked back and picked up his old Bible as he noticed the deep tread marks left in the dirt; a sign that evil had been there but had been defeated.

Walking back across the clearing, he stopped at the beginning of the steep trail, turned and looked back at the tiny church. It was still standing and tomorrow morning he'd be back to spend yet another day in the second pew on the left, third seat over.

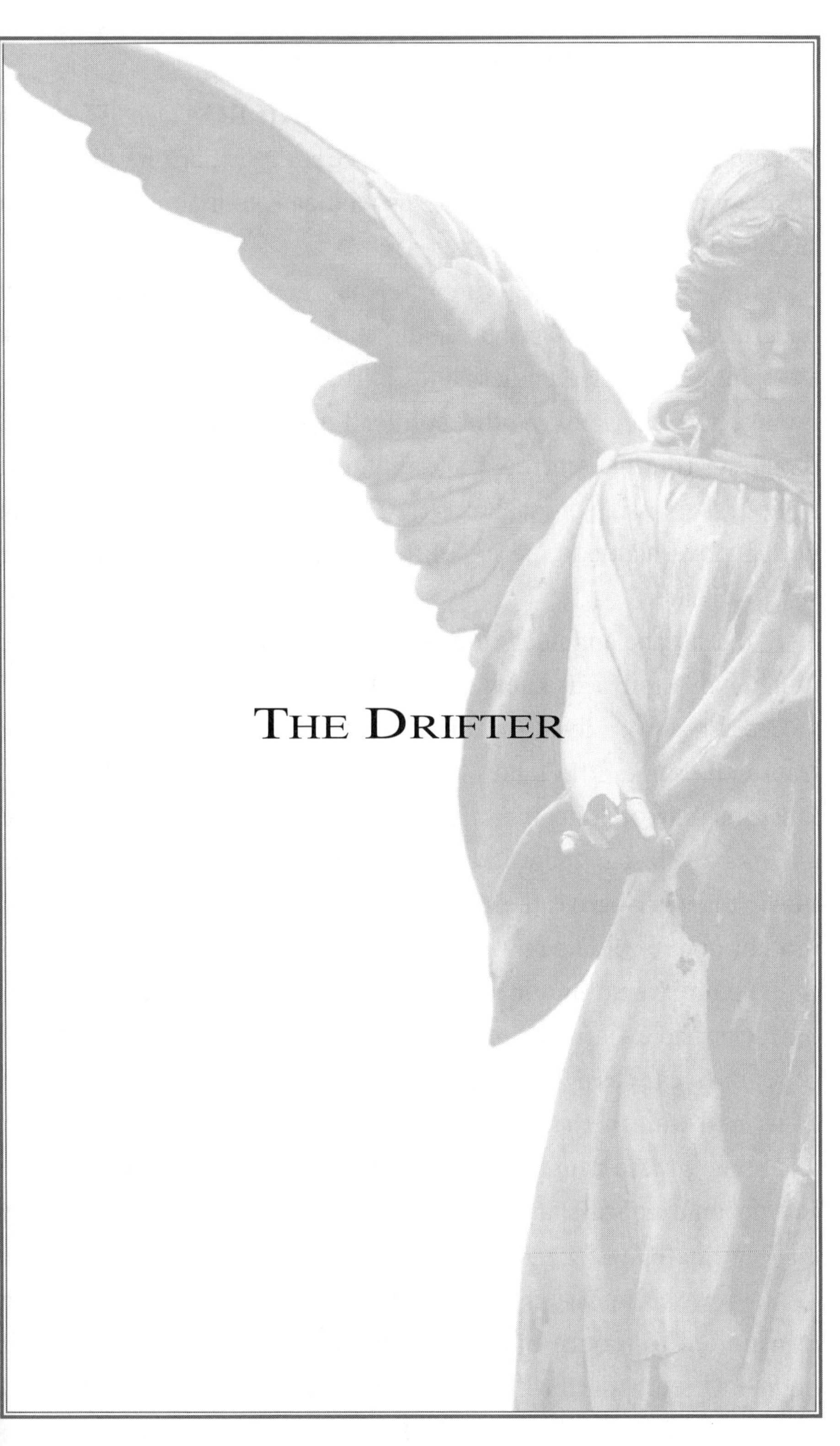

THE DRIFTER

RETIRING FROM THE RAILROAD WASN'T something Josh Ditmar desired. The Great Northern had not only been a major part of his life, but also a means of making a living for twenty-three straight years.

How many times as a youngster had he sat at the very edge of his grandfather's 130-acre farm and stared in awe as the huge black steam engines pulled endless lines of freight cars up Echo Hill? The young boy, perched on the split-rail gate, a long weed always dangling from his scarred, but smiling face was always a welcome sight to the passing engineers as they returned his enthusiastic salute with a glove-handed greeting of their own, followed by a tug on the steam whistle.

Not only the engineers, but practically everyone employed at the Duncanville railyards knew of little Joshua Ditmar. He was the six-year-old boy who lived on Pine Street just across from the freight tracks, the same little fellow who always clambered over the chain link fence surrounding the safety of his backyard. The youngster had always been fascinated with the trains and an afternoon of exploring the boxcars just across the street erased the many warnings from his mother about not leaving the yard.

The boy went unnoticed as he walked across the street, four sets of tracks, and eventually up some wooden crates into an abandoned boxcar. A carelessly discarded cigarette by a passing brakeman combined with the heat of the day, a small pile of spilled fertilizer, and some grease caused the fire that morning. The weathered and rotting pine board slats ignited instantly, and the car was quickly engulfed in flames.

Josh woke up in the hospital the following day. He had been transported to a burn unit in Columbus, with thirty percent of his body covered with third-degree burns. He would carry the mark of scarred skin tissue on the left of his face, arm, stomach, and leg for the rest of his life.

He was told that a drifter, a man who wasn't supposed to be near the yards, had fortunately rescued him from the burning car. Somebody had said that the man's name was John. He had experienced a few minor burns, refused any treatment and simply moved on. The hobo who had saved little Joshua evidently hadn't expected a thing for his heroic act.

Josh didn't let the awful experience in the burning car affect his deep interest with steam engines. During the summer of his fourteenth birthday, Josh experienced his first ride on one of the immense steamers. The Great Northern scheduled a special passenger excursion running from Duncanville all the way to Sanders for the County Fair. It was the perfect Saturday morning as Josh, his younger sister, parents and grandpa stepped up into one of the antique passenger cars for a day at the fair.

Following the ten-mile trip through the Colorado countryside, the train came to a stop in the tiny rural community of Sanders. Josh was surprised beyond belief when Gramps led him up to the engine. Grampa Ditmar, it turned out, was an old drinking buddy with the engineer and had made arrangements for Josh to ride in the cab for the two miles up to Peterson where the engine would turn around for the return trip.

It was at that precise moment, as Josh climbed the steel ladder, sat down in the worn leather seat and wrapped his hand around the throttle, that he realized he was destined to be a railroad engineer. This eye-opening experience turned out to be his first and only ride on steam. His fantasy of becoming an engineer did come true, but by the time he was of age to work on the railroad, the steamers had reluctantly given way to the more energy-efficient diesels.

Still, sitting up in the cab of a powerful diesel prior to a run was a thrill that never quite became mediocre to Josh. Every time he pulled out of the East Yards it was almost as if he had somehow stepped out of his adult life and had slipped back into childhood. It was hard to believe he was being paid to do something he enjoyed so much. It just didn't seem like a job.

There wasn't any part of the year he didn't enjoy from his vista up in the diesels. After the long glacial winter, spring brought new life to the rolling hills and fields. Gramps always referred to it as "greening up." First, came the glorious yellow forsythia bushes, then the pink and white dogwoods followed by the lilacs.

The hot summer air was transformed into a warm breeze high up in the cab. There was nothing that could quite compare with the solitude of speeding through the dark night, the raindrops from a summer storm racing across the probing head lamps as he poured hot coffee from his dented thermos into his favorite mug.

Fall was a special season, the trees taking on shades of yellow, red, and gold as the countryside splashed with stirring color. Mother Nature was preparing for winter.

As nippy as it always seemed to get, the winter months had a way of providing a panoramic scene of its own. The early morning sunlight reflected off ice-covered branches, massive icicles hanging from the cliffs at Snake Gorge, a snow squall, so thick it was like entering a pure white void.

The sights, smells, and activity of the railroad had changed from reality to nothing more than past memories. It had been just over two years since the derailment at Buffalo Flats. Why Josh's train jumped the tracks that Wednesday morning was still an unsolved situation, and an extensive investigation by railroad authorities had left them with no cognant explanation. The tracks and the engine were reported in great working order and Josh had been exonerated of any negligence.

It had taken nearly two weeks of around-the-clock work crews to clean up the forty-seven car pileup. Josh spent four months in the hospital, finally released with a gimpy leg and the loss of sight in his right eye.

The union stated that his fifty-percent eye loss would prohibit him from continuing his engineer career. Josh's record prior to the unfortunate accident had been flawless. The board offered him a job in the main yard tower, but Josh declined, claiming that sitting day after day on his backside flipping switches would never compare with taking a long freight across the steel and wood roadbed of the countryside. He decided to take an extended vacation up to Canada, which would give him some time to be alone and sort things out.

He had only been married for a short year after graduating high school. The marriage came to an abrupt end with his wife demanding that he be at home in the evenings, but the position of engineer dictated that he spend many nights on the road. Since he had no wife or children to support, he had done an admirable job of saving his money. It was not imperative that he find gainful employment immediately.

Josh was amazed how quickly he became accustomed to having only one eye. In the past, he hadn't given much thought to the God given blessing of sight. Sitting in the freshly mowed lawn on the Canadian side of Niagara Falls, he sensed that with only fifty percent of his sight he was actually seeing one hundred percent more of life. Millions of gallons of water spilled over the precipice of the falls and then tumbled swiftly in a thunderous roar to the rocks below. At the same time, a rainbow appeared, rising up out of the mist, eventually disappearing into the blue sky above. It was the perfect combination of God's power and beauty in complete agreement. He smiled. He knew what he was going to do with the rest of his life.

The following Thursday he was standing on Front Street, next to the East Yards, staring at the old dining car. The abandoned car had been on a set of rust-covered tracks for years, longer than he could remember.

The railroad was receptive to selling not only the car, but the track it was on and a three-acre lot to Josh. Over the years it had grown to nothing more than an eyesore. With an investment of a little under $10,000 and four months of handy work, the vintage car was refurbished into a nostalgic railroad diner. A small shed was added to the rear of the car to house a kitchen and storage area. The car itself was restored to its original styling, with old pictures and other railroad paraphernalia hung on the walls to create a historic aura.

Everyone in the yards always complained that there was no place to eat unless you drove into town. The diner was an immediate success, with Josh serving what he called "stick-to-your-ribs meals." He was open for business by five in the morning and soon after, the car was filled with railroad workers stuffing themselves with pancakes, sausage and biscuits, scrambled eggs, and the best coffee in town. Lunch and dinner consisted of deli sandwiches and blue-plate specials. The diner closed down at seven, and he was usually on his way home by eight. He was open six days, closed on Sundays. The sixteen-hour days were long, but Josh enjoyed operating the dining car. It was as if he were still on the railroad.

It was a typical Tuesday morning, and at 9:37 the breakfast crowd was thinning out. Soon it would be ten and Josh would have an hour to recoup before the "lunch bunch" hit. Spreading a handful of sliced onions into a frying pan of hash, he waved the steam away from his face as he gazed out the front window. A slow westbound freight was crawling into the yards, five tracks away. Following two grimy-black diesels came the long string of boxcars—Union Pacific, AT&SF, Illinois Central. He knew every road name; he'd seen them all. Each passing car seemed to have a distinct racket all its own as unoiled or rusted parts rubbed and grated against each other.

Pouring a second cup of coffee for old Charley Miller, Josh noticed a boxcar nosing its way past the maintenance shack, the car's road name practically gone from years of heat, rain and sleet, all its metal parts, ladders, braking gear, couplers, and handrail, were pitted with an orangish-brown rust. Most of the paint had peeled off the wooden sides, revealing chipped and rotted pine boards. The car should have been retired from service years ago.

Josh noticed a man standing framed in the half-open door of the car as he looked across the tracks. The train was laboring to a stop, but still moving as the man lowered to a sitting position, then jumped carefully to the cinders below. He turned, removing a filthy tan duffel bag from inside the car, slung it over his thin shoulder, twisted the upper portion of his body as if he were stretching, then started across the tracks toward the diner.

At the last set of tracks, he hesitated and then made a left, walking to the chain-link fence surrounding the elementary school. Josh wondered why the man stopped and leaned on the barrier as he watched the children play until they ran back into the school at the sound of a bell indicating the end of recess. The man continued to gaze at the play area; the only remaining proof that children had been present was a still-rolling kick ball and swings that continued to move back and forth, eventually coming to a silent halt.

The man switched the bag to his other shoulder and crossed Front Street, his eyes glued on the diner. Josh watched as he approached and thought to himself that the man would have been a superb candidate for "hobo of the month"—four or five-day stubble, weathered face, tired eyes, raggedy hat, dirty coat, baggy shirt, wrinkled pants, and shabby work boots.

The man pushed open the screen door, its regular screeching interrupting a Hank Williams tune coming out of the jukebox. The hobo shuffled slowly to the counter, deposited the duffel bag at his feet and sat on one of the vintage stools, folded his hands patiently, and looked up at the menu board.

Josh approached, the coffee pot in his hand. Looking directly into the haggard face, he asked, "What can we do for ya, Mac?"

In a barely audible voice came the reply, "Coffee…please."

Pulling a mug from beneath the counter, Josh began to pour. The man searched his coat, then shirt pocket, and eventually located a quarter, which he laid gently on the laminated counter. Leaving the coffee untouched, he began to pat his pants pockets. Finally, he reached down, opened the drawstrings on the duffel bag and removed a small, apparently well-used Bible, its cover curled and half torn away from the binding. He opened the book to a spot marked with a piece of folded newspaper where he located a second quarter, which he placed next to the first.

Josh returned the coffee pot to its assigned place on the burner as he watched the hobo pour a single spoon of sugar, then creamer, into the steaming cup. The two quarters that had been placed on the counter were probably all the money the poor soul had to his name.

Josh thought to himself, *What the hey*, as he walked back to the man, "You hungry, mister? When's the last time ya had a bite?"

The man didn't respond as he humbly lowered his eyes and pursed his chapped lips. Josh understood the attitude most railroad drifters held. Most of these men weren't looking for a handout.

Accepting charity didn't sit right with most hobos. They had chosen a life of riding the rails, drifting from one town to the next. People on the railroad and a great number of Duncanville citizens considered these down-and-out men as nothing more than typical bums.

Josh held a different doctrine. He never forgot the mysterious man named John who had saved him from the burning boxcar thirty-nine years earlier. Over time, the people in town, even his parents forgot about the drifter. Josh never did. How many times had he given his lunch or a few dollars to one of these homeless men?

The man still had his eyes lowered to his lap. Josh wondered if he had embarrassed the poor fellow. Suddenly, he had a thought. He reached out, gently touching the man on the shoulder, "Must be your lucky day! You're my one-hundredth customer this week. That, my dear friend, entitles you to a free meal. Starts out with a big bowl of my homemade potato soup and some cornbread. Then, ya get salad, a nice slice of meatloaf, peas and mashed taters. Matter of fact, it's all ya can eat."

The drifter slowly raised his head. There was no evidence of a smile, but there was a slight twinkle in his weary eyes.

"Right back with that soup," said Josh.

As Josh moved down the counter, Miller leaned forward whispering, "One-hundredth customer of the week…right! Boy…if you don't beat all."

Josh displayed a wide grin as he winked.

Just as he poured a large portion of soup into a bowl, the train across the tracks stopped, the chain reaction of each car bracing to a halt banging past the diner up the line. Josh placed the soup and cornbread in front of the man, then backed away, not wishing to make his "one-hundredth customer" nervous. The drifter bowed his head in prayer for what seemed like a full minute, then opened the old Bible again and started to read silently as he dumped some pepper into the soup. He ate slowly, almost methodically, savoring every bite as he ran his skinny finger down over verse after verse.

Josh was in the middle of slicing a thick wedge of meatloaf onto a plate when he heard the ear splitting blast. Following a blinding flash, the windows of the diner exploded, sending projectiles of slivered glass over Josh, Charley and the stranger.

By the time Josh got himself up from the floor, the drifter was through the screen door and sprinting with the mastery of an Olympic runner across Front Street. Josh stared in amazement as the old hobo hurdled the fence, raced across the playground, and disappeared inside the flaming school building.

Josh's attention was grabbed by Charley's terror-stricken voice, "Come on…we gotta get over there! All those kids!"

Josh quickly trailed Charley across Front Street as he stared in disbelief at the flaming inferno that seconds before had been an elementary school. There wasn't a single door or window where orangish-red flames were not licking at the air, the flames reaching seventeen feet above the second floor as black smoke billowed high into the sky before floating off over the rail yards.

From around the corner of the structure, Josh noticed the school principal, Bill McClarren, stumbling, finally collapsing onto a pile of bricks. Charley helped him to his feet as he bellowed, "Bill…Bill, what happened?"

Through a bleeding and soot-covered face, he replied, "My God, I think the whole building blew up. I gotta get back in there!" He tried to break away, but was restrained by both Josh and Charley.

"You can't go in there," Josh yelled. "It's too late. You'd be killed!"

"You don't understand," Bill pleaded. "Most of the teachers and kids got out the back. Mrs. Cogan's third grade class is in the front of the building, None of `em came out!"

Josh shook Bill. "It's too late! Look at those flames No one could survive in there."

Instantly, the look on the principal's face changed as he stared past Josh. In an almost slow motion movement, the drifter appeared in the flaming doorway, a small boy cradled in his arms. He ran out into the safety of the playground, deposited the child who was charred and bleeding, but still alive on the ground, turned and disappeared in the flames again.

Sirens sounded in the distance as people from town were starting to gather in front of the school. Mr. Sarbo, who ran an antique shop just up the street, ran to the child, picked him up and moved him away from the building.

"Look," Charley said as he tugged on Josh's arm. The drifter appeared in the flames once again, another small child tucked safely in his arms. The little girl was badly burned, quiet, probably in shock, but still alive. The hobo placed the child quietly on the ground and ventured into the wall of fire a third time.

A woman raced from the crowd, scooping up the second child as an explosion ripped at the rear of the building, catapulting bricks, glass, sections of wood and plasterboard out into the freight yards. The flames reached out to the crowd, but quickly retreated back to the building. Josh and Charley backed away; the heat was intense.

Two firetrucks trailed by a police cruiser pulled in. Four firemen climbed from the back of the first truck, one unloading a section of hose, another grabbing a ladder, the others placing a heavy wrench on the fire hydrant across the street.

Almost in unison, the crowd let out a gasp, many pointing at the school. The drifter emerged from the flames again, this time a child beneath each arm. His face and hands were black, his clothes smoking. He handed the children to some women who ran to help, then turned and jumped into the flames a fourth time.

Josh noticed that the back of the man's coat was on fire. "He's not going to make it back out again!"

Hank Snowden, the fire chief, moved in between Charley and Josh. "Boys…I'm afraid you're gonna have to move behind that fence. Too dangerous."

"But there's still a man in there," Josh objected. "He's tryin' to get the rest of the kids out."

The chief gave Josh a somber look. "If there's someone in there now…they ain't comin' out. Now…move back please. My boys will see things out from here."

Charley obeyed the chief's orders, but Josh remained frozen as he stared at the flame-filled structure. He knew Snowden was right about no one being able to endure the inferno, but he couldn't bring himself to accept that the drifter would perish.

"Come on," said Hank, pulling Josh by his shoulder. He relented and began to back up, but then stopped, his eyes wide with disbelief. The drifter suddenly appeared through the flames, almost as an apparition. He was carrying four children, two under each arm. Despite the hobo's effort to move through the flaming doorway, the fire seemed to wrap around his frame like red-hot tentacles trying to pull him back. There didn't seem to be a section of his clothing that was not burning. A twisted and charred roof brace broke loose and slammed down on the drifter's left shoulder sending him to his knees. The man tried to stand but his energy was gone.

"God!" Josh cried. "He's going to die right in front of us."

An explosion from somewhere deep inside the building sent a wave of forced air through the front of the structure, throwing the drifter out onto the playground. He slowly stood, still carrying the four children. He was toting them like sacks of potatoes. He was rescuing every child that he could.

His face, arms and hands were utterly black, his bright eyes and gritted teeth giving the impression of a traveling minstrel of years past. He turned painfully and started for the building again. Before he got three steps, Hank and two firemen tackled the drifter, bringing him to the ground. The man tried to resist but was too weak to overpower the three. Before they even hit the ground, a powerful stream of directed water soaked the foursome.

Josh had to work the remainder of the day cleaning up the disarray at the diner, but was open as usual the following morning, the only evidence that the dining car had been affected being boarded-up windows. The broken glass could not be replaced until the next day.

The diner was crowded, not only with regulars, but also curiousity seekers and those working on cleaning up what was left of the school. A single firetruck stood watch, dousing smoldering sections of debris as two bulldozers pushed the remains into large piles.

The only topic inside the diner was the sorrowful explosion, the paper stating that a boiler in the supply room had blown. At the time of the blast, eighty-three children and six teachers had been present. Not everyone had escaped—there had been fatalities. All the teachers had managed to get out, but seven kids were burnt to death.

The big news was the heroism of the stranger who had saved

eight children. Following the fire, the drifter had been wrapped in a blanket, administered oxygen and water, then rushed to the hospital. Mr. Dalhgreen, who resided three houses down the street from the school, had been doing some work in his front yard when he had first noticed the man disembark from the train, stop at the school, enter the diner, and eventually run into the burning building. He suggested the police talk with Josh.

The police told Josh that the man had sustained some minor burns and hair loss, but actually seemed to be unscathed. The stranger was turning out to be a lot more than just a typical railroad bum. He was a hero, a man who had single-handedly saved eight children. People in town wanted to know his name and where he was from. They wanted to reach out and help this man, who had, if nothing else, miraculously wandered into Duncanville at just the right time.

Officer O'Roark said that at the scene of the blast, the man had sat there with a blanket wrapped around him. He just stared straight ahead, tears streaming down his face. They had asked the fellow what his name was, but he remained quiet.

The attending doctor said that he wanted to keep the stranger at the hospital for a few days. His staring and inability to communicate indicated that he still might not be out of the woods. Josh gave the police the man's duffel bag. They searched everything inside the bag, which included two pairs of underwear, a flannel shirt, faded pants, a pair of woolen socks, pack of matches, a worn road atlas, two candles, and a Bible. There was no indication whatsoever of who the man was or where he was from.

Following four days of observation, the doctor gave the drifter a clean slate. His blood pressure was fine, his heart healthy, and all bodily functions operating normally. He ate everything he was offered, seemed to rest amply, and never asked any questions or answered inquires from the police or hospital staff. His room was crammed with flowers from the grateful citizens of Duncanville.

Saturday morning at the diner there was talk that a town meeting was going to be held at the high school gymnasium. Usually, the town meetings were attended by the city council members, a few businessmen, and occasionally interested citizens. The mayor stated that his office was being flooded with calls with an outcry of help for the stranger. Folks didn't feel right about just sending the man on his way. He had performed a great service to the town and they were deeply indebted.

That night Josh attended the meeting. It was standing room only. A haze of cigarette smoke hung over the crowd as they stood around in little groups drinking coffee or iced tea, smoking and discussing the terrible fire.

The mayor gave a short speech, then opened the floor for general comments. By the time everything was over, it was agreed that a group of ten people, the honorable mayor, four pastors from local churches, the police chief, one fireman, and three business people, would pay the stranger a visit.

The drifter was propped up in bed as the committee arrived. The mayor started things off, explaining that a spacious room at Mrs. Spivley's boarding house would be made available for six months at no charge. A list of possible work opportunities was read aloud, including a position at the diner for washing dishes and general cleanup.

Their mission finally complete, the mayor asked, "How's all this sound?" The man's eyes filled with tears as he reached for the paper listing the jobs, at the same time signaling to Josh. He placed his finger on the dishwashing job and handed the list to Josh.

Josh smiled. "Looks like I just got me a brand-new employee."

The drifter turned out to be the ideal employee. He got up each and every morning at four, left the boarding house, and walked the two blocks to the diner, always waiting for Josh to show up. He swept up, washed dishes, burned trash, cleared tables, and did just about anything else that needed to be done. He labored the entire day and only left after Josh locked up for the night.

Josh paid the drifter an honest wage and following two months of silence came to the conclusion that his new employee was not going to say anything to anybody. Josh knew he could talk. After all, hadn't he asked for coffee the first day he had come into town?

Five months passed—there were only two more weeks until Thanksgiving. The elementary school had been completely dozed down and transformed into a lovely park in memory of the children who had died there. At first, the diner was jam-packed with people who wanted to gain a look at the stranger who had saved eight kids, but as time passed matters returned to normal.

Josh's headlights fell on the parking area for the diner at 4:30 a.m. There was the drifter, as usual, waiting to get the day under way. As Josh climbed out of his car, he noticed something different about the man. His worn duffel bag lay at his feet, and the raggedy hat, which he hadn't worn since the first day he arrived in town, was centered squarely on his head.

Josh stopped as he searched his trousers for the diner keys. The drifter stuck out his calloused left hand. At that moment, Josh realized the man was ready to leave, but he couldn't bring himself to take his hand.

The drifter seemed to sense Josh's hesitance as he spoke softly, "It's time for me to move on Joshua."

"But why?" Josh uttered. "We…the folks in town…I …I haven't even gotten a chance to know you."

The drifter reached into his pocket, removing his old Bible from which he extracted a white envelope and gave it to Josh. "I want you to do me a favor. Most of the money you paid me is in there. I want you to purchase some shade trees and have them planted in the park in remembrance of the kids that didn't get out."

The man reached out, took Josh's hand and shook it as he smiled. He started to walk away, but then stopped and turned back. "One more thing," he said. "You do know me. We've met before. Name's John…John Meshach." He raised up the Bible. "Daniel, chapter three, verse twenty-eight. Thanks for everything." He turned and walked across the tracks toward a departing freight train. All Josh could do was stare at the envelope, then the drifter. John stopped at a boxcar, pitched the duffel sack into the open door, turned and waved one last time, then disappeared inside.

The winter was unusually hard that year, and the residents of Duncanville were welcoming spring with open arms. Charley Miller and two other engineers sat near a corner table in the diner, nursing coffee and devouring pancakes. As Josh approached, coffee pot in hand, Charley shuffled through the rumpled morning paper. His cup halfway to his lips, he hesitated, read for a moment, then spoke to Josh. "Look at this. Didn't you say that guy who saved the kids was John something or other?"

"Yeah," Josh answered. "Why?"

Charley held the paper out to him. "His picture is on the front page, Says in here a stranger by the name of John saved six kids from a burning building over in Michigan. That is him…ain't it?"

Josh reached for the paper as he put down the coffee. Looking at the photograph, he took an empty seat and read the article. The long and short of it was that a drifter known only as John had rolled into town, saved six children from a grisly fire, then afterward just left town without a word.

Josh thought to himself: *John Meshach!*

He stood and topped off Charley's cup, then headed for the counter.

"Josh," Charley said. "Doesn't that seem sorta strange? The same stranger who came here and saved our eight kids, does practically the same thing in Michigan?"

"Strange…no…not at all," Josh answered, a broad smile coming to his face as he glanced at the embroidered plaque centered over the counter: *Praise be to the God of Shadrach, Meshach and Abednego, who had sent his angel and rescued his servants! Daniel 3:28.* He looked out the front window as a backhoe poked holes in the lush green grass at the new park. Seventy-seven children, each holding a pine sapling, stood in line patiently awaiting their turn to plant a tree.

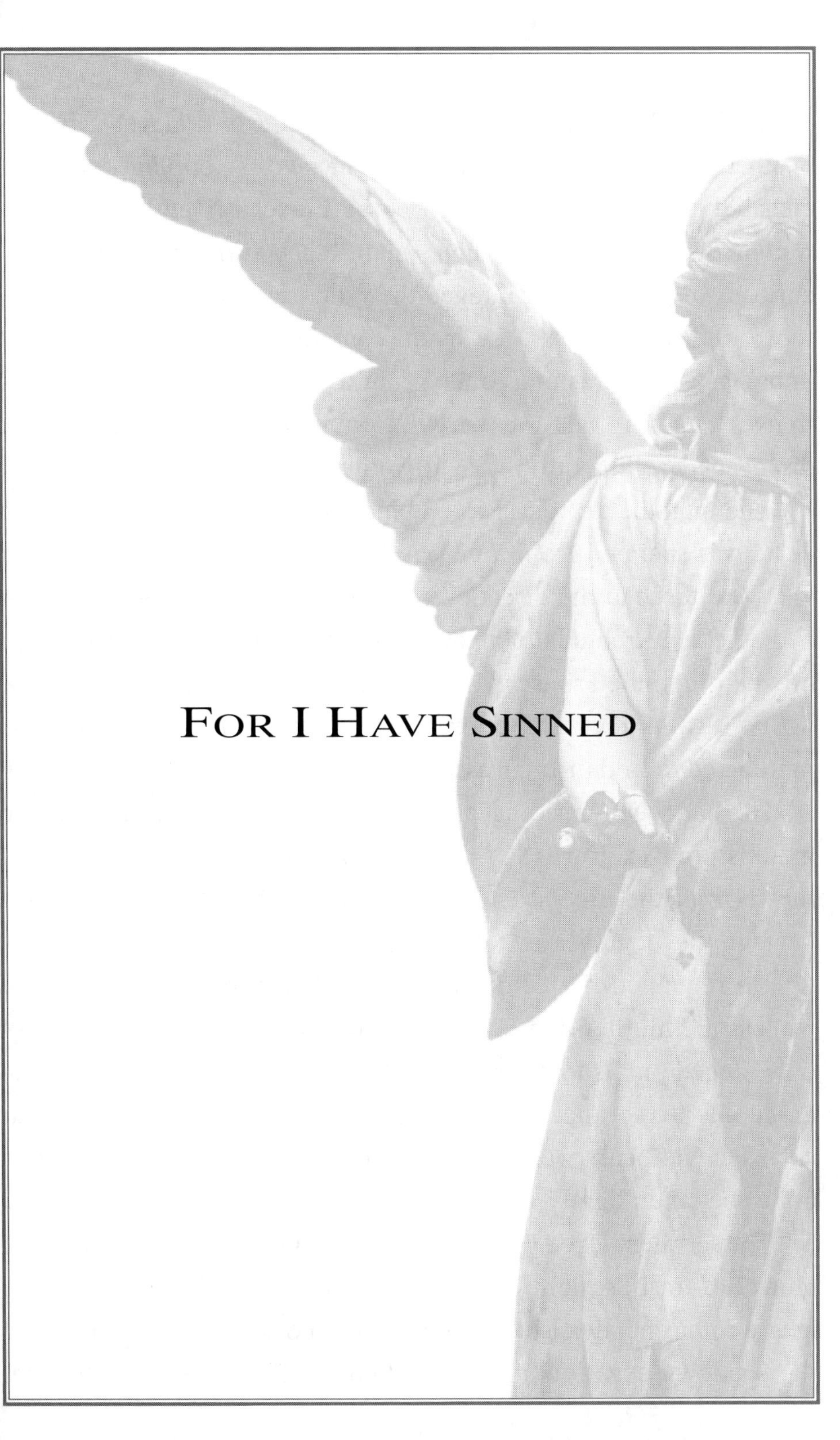

For I Have Sinned

THE GALVANIZED TRASH CAN HAD BEEN instinctively pushed to within four inches of toppling from the elevated wooden platform above the gravel driveway. Two cubs waited obediently below, their small, black furry heads raised in curiosity as the she bear nudged the cylindrical can past the edge of the rotted deck boards, the metal container reaching the point of imbalance, then crashing to the ground. The can bounced, hurling a tinny clang through the early morning fog as the lid became disengaged, rolling into the nearby unkempt grass.

The metallic clattering resembled an astute slap across the face as he was snapped from a peaceful slumber into a state of instant and total focus in the direction of the sudden disturbance. The cubs had quickly retreated up the driveway, the spinning lid chasing them off, their ingrained sense of adventure returning once the silver disc was at rest. As they drew close to the scattered trash, their mother pawed and rooted through assorted dented cans and smashed boxes.

He had been residing at the secluded cabin for almost two months now. The owner of the rental agency in town and some of the folks at the grocery store had claimed that sightings of black bears in the vicinity were very common.

He remained perfectly still, feeling privileged at being able to witness the mother and her young. His emotion of repose was not only hinged on his total amazement at the wonder of it all, but also based on the fact that he had been warned to keep away from bear cubs. Female bears were severely protective of their offspring and not to be taken lightly.

The seconds ticked by, the mother systematically inspecting each morsel of trash. A light breeze floated gently across the porch, the heavy round head raising suddenly, the moist nose twitching, then the shadowy eyes looking at the human sitting just fifteen yards away.

Any enjoyment at viewing one of nature's families in the routine of going about their daily life was replaced with an instant sense of immediate danger. Standing on her back feet, the 350 pound bear raised her massive front paws in defense as she gave out a deep bellow.

His initial thought was to stand up and run. But to where? The screen door leading to the inside of the cabin was between him and his hungry visitors. His only other option of vacating the porch quickly would be to slowly get up, jump over the wooden railing, then sprint up the driveway into the trees. This idea was soon categorized as stupid as he recalled what the advice of the locals had been: *Don't run. Remain calm. It may not seem too comfortable or even like the sensible thing to do but any sudden movement could trigger fear in the animal of harm, at which point one could become the recipient of snapping teeth and well-aimed claws attached to sure feet capable of rendering one helpless within seconds.*

The huge bear took a calculated step forward, another guttural warning escaping her broad mouth as she sliced at the air with a savage swipe in his direction. He inched ever so carefully as far across the porch swing as possible, all the while thinking how ridiculous the situation seemed. Had he survived to the ripe old age of seventy-six, only to be mauled to death by a female black bear to whom he meant absolutely no harm? As a human being, he considered himself not much of a threat at his age. He was simply a harmless senior citizen. The problem as he saw it was that the bear didn't grasp it quite the same way. Just as quickly as the unexpected dilemma had invaded his quiet style of life, it ended. Mom went down on all fours and scooted both cubs up the dirt road, the trio disappearing into the dense pines.

Letting out a long sigh of relief, he placed his right hand over his thumping chest, his pounding heart pressing against his damp skin as if the lifegiving muscle were going to explode at any second. The bear and her young were gone but the stress of the experience remained, his body tight as a span of wire stretched beyond its capability to hold, ready to break in a fraction of a second. His hand still clutched at his heart, he tried to relax as he lowered his head and whispered a frail attempt at prayer, *"Please Lord…don't take me just yet…at least not until this afternoon. Give me a chance to set things right."*

The morning sun had only been evident for about an hour, its powerful rays not yet completely penetrating the deep forest. It was a lovely morning, beams of directed sunlight poking their way down through the pines, wild flowers slowly beginning the process of opening their pedals to accept the morning sunshine, many species of birdlife joining together, their high-pitched chirps and whistles propagating an early morning symphony. It had remained in the nineties for the past week and the day ahead had been forecast as yet another scorcher.

The pain in his heart was subsiding. *Just another false alarm*, he thought. *If I can just get through this afternoon.* The chest pains had started nearly two years ago and had become more frequent and severe as the months passed. An examination by a physician in Ft. Worth had established that he hadn't suffered any heart attacks or strokes, but the pains *could* be warning signs.

After explaining that he was retired, possessed plenty of savings and really didn't have that much to be concerned about, the doctor stated that as long as he avoided any stressful situations he should be just fine. His comment of not being overly concerned about anything was a falsehood, a deep-rooted lie of which the truth had to remain concealed. There was no one that could be trusted to harbor his secret. Once the true data about his involvement was revealed, one of the greatest unresolved cases of the twentieth century would begin to finally take shape.

It had been over three decades now that he had endured the daily stressful memories of that lamentable day in his past. Last night had been yet another evening of fear. Standing slowly, he looked back up the dirt road half expecting to see a vehicle break from the trees through the low mist, and inside the car, those who were searching for him.

Walking to the edge of the covered porch, he pulled the afghan wrapped around his thin shoulders closer to his body. Looking back at the swing, he couldn't remember falling asleep on the porch. Then, he saw the empty glass next to the railing. It was all coming back now.

He recalled crawling in bed beneath the clean fresh sheets just after the eleven o'clock news, his final thoughts of consciousness drifting around the possibility of moving again. He had been staying at the cabin far too long.

Sometime during the night, it had happened again. The dream had been replayed one more time and it had affected him the same horrible way it always did. He had been catapulted up into a sitting position, almost as if a giant spring had been attached to the underside of the mattress. There he had sat, rigid, shivering, a cold sweat saturating his startled body, his eyes open wide staring into the darkness searching for those he knew would come to kill him.

He would have thought that by now he would have grown accustomed to the repeated dream, but once he was awakened by the dramatic memory there was no returning to sleep. The scene was so clear, so real. He could hear the sounds, feel the tenseness. The smells, feeling, the noise—the confusion came back to him exactly as it had happened thirty-four years in the past. The amount of nights that he had to finally get up and watch TV or read until the wee hours outnumbered nights of peaceful slumber by a vast margin.

Last night was no exception. The dream had returned again to rob him of a good night's sleep. Following a lukewarm shower to remove the perspiration from his skin, he had poured a glass of iced tea, wrapped the afghan around himself and stepped out onto the porch. At some point during the night, he must have nodded off on the swing.

After ten years of experiencing the recurring nightmare, he had reluctantly gone to a psychiatrist about his ongoing plight of interrupted sleep. His refusal to confide in the doctor and divulge the essence of the dream resulted in the physician explaining that unless he could openly discuss the dream, she would be unable to help. That had been twenty-two years gone by and he was still grappling with the dark, lingering memories of his past.

He had no one to blame but himself. He had made the decision to exchange a life of normalcy for one of financial independence. He had been compensated well for his part in the assigned task. He could go wherever he pleased, do whatever he wanted; money was not a problem.

He had planned things carefully, realizing that they could not afford to allow him to live. He knew far too much. He could name important people, persons who certainly wouldn't entertain the thought of being publicly exposed.

He had kept on the move, never living anywhere for more than a few weeks. He was always careful not to allow himself to get into any level of routine, whereas, he would be noticed. He'd missed out on so much—marriage, a permanent home, a family. He traveled alone, lived alone, ate alone.

Glancing down at the garbage, he grinned sarcastically, thinking about the female bear and her young. Their life seemed very simple. Probably just a matter of survival—food and shelter. But still, they were a family.

The last time he had been part of a family had been almost sixty years past. Even back then, he had been a loner. The absence of any brothers or sisters had always dictated that he be rather creative in entertaining himself. The farm was located miles from town or any of the other farms in the county. Aside from not having any siblings, his young life had been minus childhood friends.

His folks had been peculiarly religious, his mother a practicing Catholic, his father, a stern Baptist, neither one displaying the slightest interest in converting to their spouse's faith. As a youngster, he was juggled every other week between the two churches, at times becoming confused in the conflicting ways of belief.

Eventually, his mother, who was more strong-willed, won the battle over the direction of his faith. During the summer of 1926 at the tender age of six, he was well on his way to becoming a full-fledged Catholic. His father really never had too much to say about the matter. As long as his son believed in God and went to church, he'd go along with his mother's plan to raise him Catholic.

As a young lad, he had never been faced with accepting his loneliness on the rural farm. It was just the way it was. At some point, he actually started to enjoy being alone. He never had to agree with any other children about how his day should be spent, never had to divide his time or his possessions with anyone.

Following his daily chores, he amused himself near the swimming hole, climbing the stately oak positioned on the bank of the creek, then standing on the highest branch that would accommodate his weight, propel his body out over the deep water, contorting his lanky frame into all sorts of positions, all the while thinking he was performing Olympic-style diving techniques. These athletic efforts always resulted in the same ending—a resounding splat as he belly-flopped or landed on his side sending erratic waves in every direction.

Another activity the creek offered was a satisfying afternoon of quiet fishing. His father was so deeply involved with fishing that he would have been a great candidate for The Great American Fisherman. He had a collection of some of the most expensive rods and reels available to anglers. He made his own flies and had a spare room housing shelves of fishing trophies and a rather large library of information on the sport.

He didn't share his father's enthusiasm for fishing. He was just satisfied to sit by the calm creek, his bamboo pole, basic hook, line and sinker and whatever worm was available dangling into the peaceful water. He didn't like the idea of catching any of the swimming creatures below, and on limited occasions that he did manage to snag a bite, he'd always apologize to the flopping fish, carefully eradicate the hook and pitch the fortunate fish back to safety. He deplored the killing of anything. He was of the opinion that humans and animals alike deserved to live as long as possible.

His father also enjoyed hunting, not to the extent of his desire for fishing but nonetheless, delighted to traipse off into the woods oftentimes returning with a rabbit, squirrel or some other small defenseless animal whose existence had come to an end at the expense of his father's need to shoot something.

His parents, even though religious, didn't seem to hold the same idea of long life for animals as he did. Just about everything that was alive on the family farm eventually wound up on the dinner table, be it a turkey at Thanksgiving, a chicken for Sunday dinner or an occasional hog. Whenever one of the farm creatures fell victim to his parents' craving for meat, he always conveniently disappeared. After a number of years of what seemed to be a senseless slaughter, he started to acquire a dislike for meat. This is where his folks had drawn the line. If he didn't choose to be around when the animals were killed—fine. But, whatever was placed on the supper table in front of him—he'd eat.

His favorite and most often-practiced pastime was hiking the six-mile trail through the State Game Lands to Nechomie Hills. The hills, actually a series of sheer cliffs towered four hundred feet above the interstate far below in the valley. The hills had been named after Chief Nechomie who had been the powerful chief of the local Indian tribe prior to the invasion of the white man.

Historians and the local townfolk, who for the most part didn't know squat about the tribe, felt that there was an elaborate system of caves and connecting passages deep within the confines of the cliffs. Supposedly, the tribe elders, after much debate arrived at the conclusion that the defense of their land against the whites was futile. To avoid being killed or moved to some uninhabitable reservation, they retreated inside the caves. Some folks claim that they never came back out, while others said that the tribe had survived inside the caves for years, only venturing out at night for game or water.

The remnants of the surviving Indians were long gone now. No one had ever found the way inside the cliffs. It was believed that inside the connecting network of caves and varied rock formations there was a veritable collection of ancient Indian artifacts and treasures.

Over the years, he had carefully surveyed every square foot of the cliff face and the surrounding forest searching for the concealed entrance. During his last year of high school, a team of archaeologists from a university back east had spent the entire summer and fall scientifically probing the cliffs in hope of solving the conundrum of Nechomie Hills. Toward the end of September that year, the team packed up and started back home—empty-handed. After that, he discontinued his private search. If professionals, with all their sophisticated equipment and broad knowledge were unable to locate the entrance, then his chances were rather slim, probably impossible.

A day at Nechomie Hills was not only enjoyed by himself, but by campers, hikers, rock climbers, even couples who parked by the overlook on cool summer evenings, thus a great number of trails and roads led to the rocky attraction. By the age of nine, he had been visiting and exploring the cliffs for two years.

It had been a summer day, the first day of summer vacation, that he cut away from the main trail as he fought his way through the deep underbrush. Ten minutes later, after what seemed like an endless maze of briars and thickets, he found himself standing at the edge of a section of the cliffs that he had never seen before.

Returning the next afternoon with a long length of rope that he had found in the barn, he tied off to a large tree, then lowered himself twenty feet to a projecting ledge below where he discovered a small cave. The tiny rock indentation, only nine feet deep and four feet wide was adopted as his *special place*. He kept an old sleeping bag, extra cans of food, matches, candles and other varied prized possessions in his new hideout.

When he turned twelve, his father presented him with a B-B gun on his birthday, no doubt hoping to rally some interest in his son for the art of hunting. He thanked his father for the gun, but stated very clearly that he was only going to use it for target practice. He had no intention of shooting anything that was alive.

He was constantly collecting old cans and bottles, which by means of an old knapsack were hauled to Nechomie where he would position them on a log and practice his aim. After months of regimented practice, he was convinced that he was a lousy marksman. He kept mental records of his shooting efforts. At first, he couldn't hit anything, eventually arriving at the level, whereas, ten shots only equaled two to three hits.

It was a year later, while helping his mother clean up the attic, that he found an old rifle scope at the bottom of a dusty trunk. The wood casing was cracked, the glass lens broken. After inspecting the scope, his mother said that the thing was worthless and to pitch it in the trash with the rest of the junk they had found.

That evening, he fished through the trash, took the scope to his father and asked if he could have it. His father had no objections, claiming that he had used it years ago while hunting until he had dropped his rifle and ruined the scope.

Using thick rubber bands, he attached the scope to the barrel of his B-B gun. The broken scope was worthless to a seasoned hunter, but to him it was a great addition to his rifle. Months later, he was capable of taking out seven to eight cans in a practice round of ten shots.

Spending hour after hour in the cave tended to allow his mind to wander. Lying at the very edge of the rock ledge supporting his unloaded gun by four stacked flat stones, he pretended that he was a highly paid assassin as he focused in on the vehicles speeding past on the freeway far below. The scope, even though cracked, brought the occupants of car, trucks and busses into a magnified setting. As the cross hairs fell on the drivers, he would make the decision who was to die. He never pulled the trigger on anyone who appeared to be normal, hardworking family types. He especially disliked people who wore suits. For some reason, he didn't care much for politicians, lawyers, insurance salesmen; men who always seemed to take advantage of regular folks.

He'd wait patiently, sometimes sweat rolling down his face and neck during the sweltering summer months, at times bracing the frigid and cold winter weather, but always remained calm, sighting in on the passing motorists until his target sped by on the freeway. "Ah…ha," he'd silently whisper. "Expensive car…three-piece suit…flashy necktie…big cigar." He'd always allow the sight to fall on the back of the target's head, front of the neck or maybe the ear. He was in total control. He had a few seconds to determine how he would take out his assigned target. Taking a deep breath, then holding it, he squeezed the trigger, the unloaded rifle's interior mechanism snapping sharply, followed by his final words: "You're dead, pal."

The heat of the day was setting in fast. He walked across the porch, stopping at the rusted metal thermometer dangling by a single nail at the right of the front of the screen door. The thin red line of mercury was nearing the seventy-degree mark and it wasn't even eight o'clock yet. Opening the patched screen door, he threw the afghan on the sagging couch and crossed the room to the small one-stall redwood shower at the rear of the cabin.

The initial surge of water was ice cold, but then slowly changed from cool to tepid, eventually hot. Following some minor adjustments, he leaned against the wall as the soothing shower cleansed his clammy skin. Reaching for the misshapen bar of soap, his thoughts once again returned to his days of loneliness as a teenager.

In high school, he had segregated himself from the other students and was generally looked upon as just some stupid farm kid. He never skipped a day, was always punctual, completed all of his homework and only answered questions or spoke up when called on by teachers. Being involved with girls, sports or being popular held no interest to him. Acquiring good grades came easy as his above average retention level enabled him to remember most of what he heard or read. He didn't have to study very hard in order to just get by; being an A-student wasn't a priority in his young life.

He landed a full-time position at a local gas station and during his four-year high school stint became quite efficient as a mechanic. His uncle, a regular at the station, told him about an old Ford Coupe over in the next county hidden under a pile of rusted farm equipment. The farmer said that he'd take a hundred bucks for the thing. All it was doing was taking up space. Uncle Bill was a "car nut" and claimed that with a couple thousand dollars and some old-fashioned handiwork, the rusted vehicle could easily be refurbished into a classic street rod.

He paid his uncle the hundred dollars and the following week the rust-covered form of an automobile was delivered to the garage on the back of Bill's stake-body Chevy. The owner of the garage agreed that the heap of junk could be stored out in a spare shed in the back.

The old car was nothing more than a filthy-brown, pitted, rusted shape of an automobile. No tires, steering wheel, seats, windows; nothing. He and his uncle worked on the Ford every free moment they had. After two years, the car had been transformed into a 17-coat, hand-rubbed sunny yellow, complete with classic chrome-plated custom engine, rolled and tucked leather interior and special rims. When the finished result was finally rolled out onto Main Street, Uncle Bill informed him that he could keep the Ford for himself as a pre-graduation present.

His senior year, the bright yellow street rod propelled him into the world of the most popular around school. It wasn't so much that he was now considered great looking or even cool. It was just simply that the popular females wanted to be seen being chauffeured about in the hottest set of wheels in town. Despite all of the newfounded attention, he retained his "loner" status, not having any remote desire to be involved with those who were considered "in."

His involvement with the opposite sex was eventually prompted by a rough young girl by the name of Lucille Bender. Lucille, or "Ace" as she was referred to, wasn't too popular with the in crowd. She rode a motorcycle, smoked like a fiend, had about the foulest mouth he had ever heard and knew as much about the working mechanisms of an engine as he did.

They went out a few times, but just when the relationship seemed to be on the verge of becoming serious, Ace, without any warning, quit school and joined the Army. It wasn't until a few days prior to graduation that he received a letter from Germany. Lucille had written that she was sorry for leaving without saying adios, but she felt like things were stacking up against her. She needed to get out on her own and get her life together. According to her, the service was just the ticket. He never saw her again. She probably married some guy, raised a family, and now, if she was still alive, was more than likely somebody's great-grandmother.

Following graduation, he continued to work at the garage. When fall came on the scene, he decided that he was tired of dragging himself home every night covered with grease and oil from crawling under cars and trucks, adjusting and repairing unclean valves, busted hoses and engine parts. Maybe Ace was right about the military. In his case, it wasn't that he felt a desire to get his life together as much as a need to be more than a grease monkey working for someone else.

He didn't enjoy flying so the Air Force was out. He had no longing to stand on the bow of a ship surrounded by thousands of miles of salt water, so the Navy bit the dust. The officer who talked with him at the Army recruiting unit treated him like he was just another "wet-behind-the-ears high school kid," looking for a free ride, while the Marine recruiter displayed a genuine and sincere interest in his future.

Two months later, he found himself standing at rigid attention in ankle-deep mud, stripped to the waist, the steamy South Carolina sun pelting his spent body as a drill sergeant was just finishing a long-winded list of obscenities leveled at the brand new recruits. He had signed on under an open-ended M.O.S. as he hadn't been able to decide on any particular military occupation. He had informed the recruiter that he was an accomplished mechanic but that he wasn't interested in that field or for that matter even being around anything that had wheels or a motor. That's why he had joined the Marines in the first place. He was looking for a dramatic change in his life.

The discipline of the service taught him quickly that continuing his style of being a lone wolf was a grave mistake. During his second week of boot camp, after some of the most harsh treatment he had ever been exposed to, he acquiesced to the eye-opening fact that in order to survive the remaining weeks of training he'd have to become a team player.

In comparison to the other recruits, he fell into the category of average except for one select area; the rifle range. The DI's said he was the finest marksman they'd seen in years. He didn't think it was any big deal. It was simple: the M-1 rifle was his old B-B gun. The circled target across the field represented those men in three-piece business suits speeding along the freeway. Nechomie Hills was back.

Because of his outstanding shooting ability and the fact that he had not been given a specific military assignment, immediately following graduation, he was shipped off to Georgia where he joined a Recon unit. By the time his four years of service to the corps expired, he had gained the status of a highly skilled Marine sniper. His talent went far beyond his competence with a rifle or handgun, including lethal hand-to-hand and knife combat. He reenlisted for two consecutive four-year stints, bringing his accumulated military service to twelve years.

Following a weeklong vacation on the Rhode Island coast, he decided against re-upping for a fourth time. It was too frustrating to ponder about the fact that he had been a trained killer for well over a decade and had never been called on to put his deadly skills to the test. He had never been involved in actual combat. There had been the occasional war games, but to date, he still had no documented kills.

It was as if he had been waiting in the wings—backstage, ready and willing to do his duty. The call never came. It was becoming increasingly difficult to train day after day, for months, for years, trying to maintain his edge. The twelve years spent in the corps had been good. He had saved quite a bit of money, had traveled all over the country and Europe, but his enthusiasm was gone. It was time to infuse a new cycle in his life. What—he wasn't sure.

Stepping out of the shower, he caught a haggard glimpse of

himself in the full-length door mirror as he reached for a fresh off-white towel draped over the bedpost. The nude body that reflected back at him was nothing remotely close to the well-toned physique he had possessed when he had left the corps.

Back then, even at the age of thirty, he had been in better shape than most eighteen-year-olds. He could run a mile in under six minutes and his 182-pound muscular frame could press twice his normal weight. Over the years, his military training had stayed with him. He ran a few miles each day, followed a regimented diet, avoided smoking and excessive drinking and was sternly determined to remain in superb physical condition.

He'd been of the opinion that he had made a splendid attempt, but by the time he turned sixty, the dreaded process of old age had started to slowly eat away at his muscular body. Now, sixteen years down the road, regardless of what he consumed, he was lucky to weigh in at 130 pounds, his overall appearance that of a skeletal frame draped in pale oversized skin.

Seated near the edge of the bed, he dried his thinning hair as his thoughts picked up where they had left off in the shower. Returning to civilian life, he had interviewed with the local sheriff's office back home and even the state police. He was told that he was more than qualified to be an officer of the law, but they were really seeking younger men. Tossing the wet towel back on the bed, he thought to himself that that sort of practice would never be tolerated in today's business world. Back then, discrimination in the workplace was not an issue.

Disappointed, he had pushed his old yellow street rod out of the barn, got it running, said goodbye to his folks for the last time and headed for California. Arriving on the West Coast a week later, he positioned his coupe on a long stretch of sandy beach next to two other custom rods. Sipping a cold beer and staring out into the Pacific, he was approached by the owner of the "29" Buick parked next to his car. The man appeared to be in his late fifties, resembling a laid-back beach type; sandals, bleached grayish hair, great tan. Following some short introductions, they strolled back to their cars where a long conversation about restoring old discarded relics went on for nearly two hours.

It turned out the beach bum owned "Ronny's Custom Shop," and was in dire need of a good mechanic and combination body man. He had more work than he and his two current employees could handle. The stranger in the yellow Ford was offered a job starting the very next day.

He never imagined that he would return to the mechanic field, but Ronny's offer was attractive, and besides that, building and restoring old cars was quite different than working on late-model automobiles that always seemed to suffer at the hands of the average owner.

Being a former Marine sniper had labeled him as one of the elite marksmen in the country. Even though he had served his country to the best of his ability, retired military snipers were individuals the government preferred to keep tabs on. Every few months, some Pentagon official was at his door seeking information about his personal life: current address, phone number, marital status, plan for the upcoming year.

He had been employed at Ronny's just shy of a year when he first met Marvin. Everyone at the White Sands Beach Bar assumed that Marvin did indeed have a last name, but no one possessed enough nerve to ask him what it was. The regular patrons at the White Sands were not only leery of asking him his last name, but just plain talking with him at all.

For I Have Sinned

Marvin was a tad bit intimidating: six-foot-seven, three-hundred-twenty pounds, long blond hair fashioned in a dangling ponytail, his muscular arms covered with assorted tattoos. His black, chrome-plated chopper always parked near the front of the bar coupled with the sewn moniker "Beach Demons", emblazoned on the back of his sleeveless, frayed jean jacket was a rather obvious clue that he was a member of the notorious biker gang, hence, he was left alone.

Seated quietly on his usual stool at the end of the rustic bar, he was completely taken off guard as Marvin approached and asked very politely if he cared to engage in a friendly game of pool. He was so surprised that his voice couldn't seem to return a yes or no; he simply replied with an affirmative nod.

Marvin proceeded to rack the balls, then informed him that he should break, which resulted in none of the solid or striped pool balls dropping into any of the six pockets. Selecting a cue, Marvin rapidly cleared the table of low-numbered balls within two minutes. Smacking the eight ball into the side pocket, Marvin smiled, then offered to buy him a drink.

As the evening wore on, Marvin turned out to be quite different than his dangerous appearance hinted. He was easy to talk to, seemed to be attentive and intelligent. The truth that they had both served in Recon units in the Marines led to a second pitcher of draft beer. When the fact was made known that he was a military sniper, Marvin just couldn't believe that he was working at a garage.

Marvin agreed that acquiring a job when in your thirties, whereas your past military skills were of any use, was a waste of time in most cases. He, too, had been viewed as "over the hill" following being employed by Uncle Sam for twenty years.

Three o'clock rolled around and the bar closed for the night as they continued to swap war stories at an all-night restaurant just off the expressway. During breakfast, Marvin had taken on a serious tone, carefully explaining that there were those who required the skills of men who could kill. He had been employed by these people in the past and was on the verge of once again working for them. As of last week, they were still in need of, and actively seeking, seven more qualified men. The trade was dangerous, about as legal as anything else nowadays, depending on how one viewed matters, and paid extremely well. If he was interested, Marvin could probably get him an interview.

During the short drive back to his apartment that evening after telling Marvin that he was genuinely interested, he couldn't help but wonder what he was getting into. He returned to the White Sands every night for the next three weeks. Marvin never showed again. Just when he thought the previous conversation with Marvin was going to equal a big fat zero, he found a written note struck to his apartment door saying that they should meet at the diner for a late-night breakfast at one o'clock sharp.

In between swallows of ham and eggs, hash browns and coffee, Marvin was all business. The short briefing was as fresh in his seventy-six-year-old brain as the night it had transpired. "I can only assume that you're still interested because you're here," said Marvin. "The reason for the lapse of time since our initial contact is because the decision makers needed some time to verify your credentials. They're very interested, but need more time before a commitment can be made."

The following Thursday, per Marvin's instructions, he was parked on a remote beach at exactly 3:45 a.m. At four o'clock, Marvin and a tall, slender, distinguished-looking older gentleman suddenly appeared from out of the darkness. Marvin introduced the man as General Smith. After shaking hands, the general explained that the meeting would only last a few minutes. He went on to say that they had gone to great lengths to check every aspect of his background. His previous life as a civilian, as well as his years of military service, had been scrutinized and they had arrived at the conclusion that he fit their criteria.

Three weeks later, after informing Ronny that he was taking an extended leave of absence, he found himself standing in the midst of his new home. The remote sixty-acre compound was not only surrounded by dense trees, but well-guarded by both armed members and five vicious Dobermans.

There was a total of six unpainted cinder-block buildings: three bunk houses, sleeping ten men each, the general's headquarters, a mess hall and a supply shed containing two trucks and four jeeps. The retired general had formed the elite group of mercenaries three years prior. They offered their expert and secretive services to those who were in need of a specific category of work and who were willing to pay excruciatingly high prices for results.

For the next six years, he became a soldier of fortune, training side by side with Marvin and twenty-eight other weathered ex-military men. Assignments were doled out as they came in, the general performing all of the negotiating and planning. In most cases, no one ever knew who funded the group. At times, they traveled in pairs to different regions of the country, while on other assignments they traveled in small groups or even the entire command. Many times they were sent overseas to a foreign nation to assist in overthrowing a disruptive force or instruct local guerilla groups for combat. His competence as a sniper had pigeon-holed him for singular assignments. He had been involved in a few outfit maneuvers, but mostly traveled alone.

His first kill had been a thriving Texas rancher who had

manipulated some government contracts in his favor. He was a miserly character who didn't seem to care for anyone or anything unless it was of benefit to his own personal bank account. Andrew Decker was seated by his gargantuan swimming pool, drinking his morning coffee when he had been picked off, shot between the eyes at a little over three hundred yards.

It took him almost four weeks to get over taking out Decker, but after that he became ruthless and callous in his assignments. In his six-year career as a mercenary sniper, he had accumulated a total of fifteen kills. As far as he was concerned, all of the targets he had taken out deserved to die. As a youngster, lying near the edge of Nechomie Hills, he hadn't been too far off the mark in his opinion of individuals who took advantage of normal folks. All he had done was vanquish the world of some downright greedy and despicable people, his last kill being an American diplomat who had been getting rich selling U.S. secret information to the Soviets. A week later, the general's group was disbanded, all of the men saying their goodbyes and going their own ways.

That same month during Christmas week, he moved into a four-room condominium overlooking a long sandy beach in Hawaii. He was now retired, at forty-two, had ample cash and was in great health. He spent his days walking on the endless beach or gliding across the clear-blue water in his twenty-foot sailboat.

He had taken up gardening and over the next few years had become quite proficient at creating some absolutely beautiful water gardens surrounded by colorful shrubs and flowers. It had finally arrived at the point where every available square foot of his half-acre plot was packed with foliage. He just couldn't stand sitting around looking at his wonderful creations—he had to get his hands in the dirt. Two months later, he started his own landscape business.

Business was slow for the first year, a few scattered jobs trickling in from time to time. While picking up a fruit tree at a local nursery, he happened to overhear a conversation between a middle-aged well-dressed lady and the owner. She was in need of some professional landscaping and was interested in some creative ideas.

Placing the tree near the register, he politely entered the discussion as he introduced himself, adding that he was a landscaper. After answering a few standard questions about gardening, he agreed to drop by her place later in the afternoon.

The property turned out to be a two-story mansion, surrounded by a sprawling fourteen-acre rolling grass lot, complete with a sparkling stream and lake. The woman's spouse, who had been a wealthy industrialist, had passed on leaving her with the valuable property and a few million to boot. Over herb tea and cherry cheesecake, she laid out some of her ideas and was quite impressed with his input.

No expense was spared, her unlimited bank account readily available to fund whatever was required to create her floral desires. The job was finally complete following five months of daily work, the grounds surrounding the magnificent house transformed into nothing short of a botanical garden. The woman was extremely pleased with the colorful results, inviting the island newspaper over for some photos for their garden section. Between the article in the paper and the fact that she was a long-time member of the country club, he soon had more work than he could handle, most of it coming from her wealthy friends.

The following summer the most devastating hurricane in Hawaii's history swept across the islands leaving behind a path of destruction unlike the locals had ever experienced. The tourist trade fell to an all-time low, some of the island's most picturesque points reduced to looking like a combat zone. Landscaping was not a priority in the minds of residents. People were forced to being concerned with basic requirements: replacing doors, windows, roofs, entire homes. He quickly realized that breathtaking shrubs and flower arrangements in yards were a luxury that folks were just not interested in at the moment. He had suffered right along with the others, his condo and adjoining equipment shed flattened to a pile of useless rubble. Six months later after rebuilding his beachside house, he found himself just barely getting by.

Hawaii was an expensive place to live and just mowing a few lawns a week wasn't going to equal his cost of living. Sitting on the beach a few hundred yards down from the condo, he looked at the rolling waves as they intersected with the blue sky. He only had a couple of hundred dollars left in the bank. His meager income meant that within two months he'd be completely broke.

He could always acquire a job as a mechanic, but he had been away from the field for so long he wasn't sure if he was still qualified. He could sell his condo, snatch a flight back to the States and start over. It was so beautiful living on the beach that he hated the thought of leaving Hawaii.

A familiar voice behind him interrupted his thoughts, "Hey there, Marine. How goes it?" Marvin bent down, picked up a broken seashell, inspected it, then tossed it toward the ocean. "You are one hard dude to locate. I've been looking for you for nearly three months."

He stood, grasping Marv's big hand. "God, it's great to see you. Have you seen any of the other guys?"

"Nah, not really," answered Marvin. "I guess they're spread out all over the place. Did see the general though."

"He's still kickin' then?"

"He's doing fine…actually that's why I'm here. He wants to talk with you."

"About what?"

"I'm not privy to that. All I know is that he's got an assignment…a big one. He wanted me to find you and bring you in. All he told me was that the job paid more money than you could probably spend. You take on the assignment…you're set for life. He wants you. Says you're the man for the job."

Opening the closet, he removed a navy blue suit from a wooden hanger, then placed it on the bed next to a starched white shirt and burgundy-colored tie. Five minutes later, he inspected himself in the mirror over the oak dresser. *Not bad for an ol' coot.* The suit had been tailor-made for his feeble body and seemed to shield his flimsy-looking frame beneath the fine woolen fabric. As a general rule, he never wore suits. Over the years, he had no need for one. He hadn't attended any weddings, funerals, graduations or other social functions that required "the look."

It was imperative that he look his best when the moment arrived. He wasn't even sure that they'd believe him. He was a professional. If he expected them to take him seriously, he must look professional. Gazing down at his new black dress shoes, he thought about the meeting with the general many years past.

The many years of military life had remained with General Smith, his message concise and to the point. After explaining the target, he wavered from his "no punches pulled," style of communicating and apologized, saying that he was contrite for having offered him the target due to the fact that now that he was cognizant of the dilemma and the hoped-for results, he could be considered dangerous to their plans if he didn't accept the mission.

The general had been banking on his professionalism and the fact that he would be paid an amount of money that the average individual could only dream about to sway his decision in their favor.

The conversation had ended with the general giving him three days to make his decision and also reminding him that if his decision was to remain uninvolved, as long as information did not leak out he would be safe. He also made it clear that others were involved in the planning who were aware of their meeting. It would definitely behoove him to sanction the assignment, take the money, then retire in luxury for the rest of his life.

That night, he was to get no rest. He sat on the edge of the bed and thought about the early-morning flight he had taken from Hawaii, then following an hour layover, settled in for a two-hour flight to New York where he checked in at a predetermined hotel location where he met with the general. After discussing the general's plan and the target, he told the general he needed at least a day to think it over. He laid back on the bed and placed his hands behind his head and closed his eyelids, but the subject of the earlier meeting kept his eyes from shutting.

The same questions kept replaying in his mind like some sort of recording: *Should I accept the assignment? Do I have any other choice?* The general had made it rather obvious that if he didn't choose to be involved it could wind up being dangerous. It seemed like he was being roped in.

He remembered getting up and splashing water on his sweat-soaked face, then took a long look at himself in the mirror above the sink. The amount of money being offered was indeed the answer to the conundrum of being nearly broke. On the other hand, if he refused to become involved, he could wind up dead. The general hadn't used that specific term, but the meaning had been quite clear. It would be extremely difficult to live with what he was about to agree to, but he felt as if he really didn't have a choice. Early the next morning, he had phoned the general and agreed to the assignment.

For the next three months, all of his expenses had been covered as he remained at the hotel. Within two weeks, his condo had been sold for cash with no involvement on his part. Someone powerful was pulling some strings. He had been introduced to three other men and, along with the general, they went over the itinerary day after day; everything had to be timed to the second.

The day prior to the task arrived, he was paid his generous payment, then reviewed the plan one last time. That evening the general bid him farewell stating that he'd probably never see him again. The following day he took out his target, escaped in all of the confusion and went about his own plan for survival.

Picking up the paper-wrapped article near the foot of the bed, he inspected himself one last time, then walked out onto the porch and around the side of the cabin to the Jeep. He laid the article on the passenger seat, turned the ignition key, looked back at the cabin for a brief second, then placed the vehicle in gear and drove down the dusty road disappearing into the forest.

Seven minutes later, he turned off of the dirt road onto the two-lane paved highway that led to town fifteen miles west. In less than twenty minutes, he'd be arriving at the first of two stops that he had to make. The idea of avoiding both destinations by driving right on through town crept into his mind, but he had had enough of running. It was time to face up to what he had done.

His decision to set matters right had been long overdue in

coming to the surface. His health was grinding down rapidly and the thought of dying without confessing his sin had bothered him for the past six years. He couldn't live with it any longer. People deserved to know the truth.

The small Catholic church appeared on the right just at the edge of town. He pulled into a parking spot directly in front of the vine-covered stone building, took a deep breath, slowly climbed out of the Jeep, and then started up the cement steps to the large wooden doors.

He had timed things perfectly. Earlier in the week, he had found out when confessions were heard. He looked at his watch. Nine minutes left. He took a seat in the polished pew four rows from the back and waited until the last person, an older lady, exited the confessional, said her brief penance, then left the church.

He stared at the massive crucifix at the back of the church just behind the marble altar. He was well aware of the fact that the Lord knew of his past evil deed. As a young boy living on the farm, his mother had always instilled in him that it was never too late to turn to the Lord.

After leaving home years in the past, he had slowly drifted away from the church. He couldn't even recall the last time he had been in the House of God. He had asked the Lord to forgive him numerous times for what he had done, but had never been completely convinced that he had been sincere. His actions, years ago, without any doubt would net him a quick trip to the depths of Hell once he passed on. If he was going to set things right, he saw it as a two-phased operation. Coming to the church was phase one. He stood slowly, turned and walked to the right of the pew where he genuflected, followed by the sign of the cross. Walking toward the confessional at the rear of the church, his footsteps echoed all the way up to the altar. He hesitated at the last row of pews, first staring at the confessional door, then at the exit to the outside of the church. He was standing at a crossroads; a time for decisions. For once in his life he would do what was right. He walked to the confessional, opened the door and entered.

The interior of the black cubical reminded him of the confessional back home when he was a kid. He knelt on the padded kneeler and waited. Only a few seconds passed when the twelve-inch square partition was slid open, a fine screening preventing him from seeing the priest. He stammered as he started, "Bless…bless me…Father, for…I have sinned…."

Seconds later, his sin was confessed. The priest remained silent, which wasn't any surprise. He had expected it. The weight of his particular confession had to astonish even the most devout. He wondered what the priest could be thinking. Finally, after silence that seemed too long, he asked, "My penance, Father, what's my penance?"

The voice from behind the screening sounded like that of an older man, a priest who had probably been hearing confessions for years. "If what you have confessed to me is true…well, let me just state, that it's not even up to me to decide if what is confessed is actually true. In all my years as a priest, I have never been puzzled about how many Hail Marys or Our Fathers I should assign to various sins confessed. In this case, I can honestly say that I am not sure. You have already taken the all-important step of not only confessing your sin, but also in asking God's forgiveness. Perhaps, your penance should be to inform those who need to know what it is that you have done."

Sitting once again in the Jeep, he felt a sense of peace, a refreshing feeling of finally being free of the recurring nightmare.

No matter what they did to him now, he had confessed to The Almighty. There was no way possible that he would have been able to rally the strength to turn himself in without turning to God first.

He drove away from the church, knowing that the priest inside had to be tugging with a level of doubt that he had never experienced. The priest had just been told something that had perplexed the modern world for over three decades. In a way, it didn't seem right. The information the priest now possessed was invaluable. The man's vow of not divulging a confession would surely be put to the test.

Two blocks down the street, he stopped at the police station. It looked quaint for a building that housed the local law enforcement agency, but it did blend in with the straight rows of ranch homes that bordered the tree-lined street. The station itself was a white stucco structure fronted by a well-manicured garden of lustrous red begonias and dazzling, silver Dusty Millers. Turning off the Jeep, the reality of his actions was starting to take hold. This could very well be the last time he ever drove a vehicle, the last time he ever got to enjoy the sight of flowers.

Staring at the double doors of the station, he knew that once he entered and spoke to someone a kind of instant fame would descend on the small community. The information he had would put the town on the map. In the future, people from all over the world would visit the town on their vacation just to see the building where the truth had finally come to light. The officer inside that he was about to approach would become famous, maybe even a celebrity. Because of what he had done years ago this particular individual, whom he hadn't even met, would gain the golden opportunity for success. There would be offers to appear on talk shows, maybe even a book deal.

Maybe they wouldn't even believe him. Wouldn't that be a kicker! What if they just simply excused him and his unbelievable story as some nut trying to gain the attention of the world. Picking up the wrapped package, he got out of the jeep, took a final look around the town, then climbed the three steps to the doors.

Opening the door on the right, he wondered what they would do to him. If they decided to listen to what he had to say, there would be an investigation. If it came out that they believed him, what type of punishment would be appropriate? If they sentenced him to life in prison, it really wouldn't be all that bad. His age of seventy-six, combined with his poor health, meant that he only had a few years left anyway. Maybe they'd give him the death penalty. He didn't think so—he seemed too old for that. Possibly, they might just put him away in some insane asylum for the remainder of his years.

The older officer behind the elevated oak desk looked very ordinary: balding head, bushy eyebrows, his tranquil blue eyes peering over the top of reading glasses. Looking down at the visitor, he inquired, "What can we do for you, sir?"

Laying the paper-wrapped article onto the top of the desk, the answer came: "I'd like to report a murder."

The officer squinted as he leaned forward. "A murder you say?"

"Yes sir. If you'll kindly unwrap that paper there you'll find the murder weapon."

Removing the two thick rubber bands, the officer slowly unrolled the paper, then stared at the polished rifle in his hands.

The man standing in front of the desk spoke again, "That, sir, is one of the rifles that killed John F. Kennedy…and I'm the person who pulled the trigger."

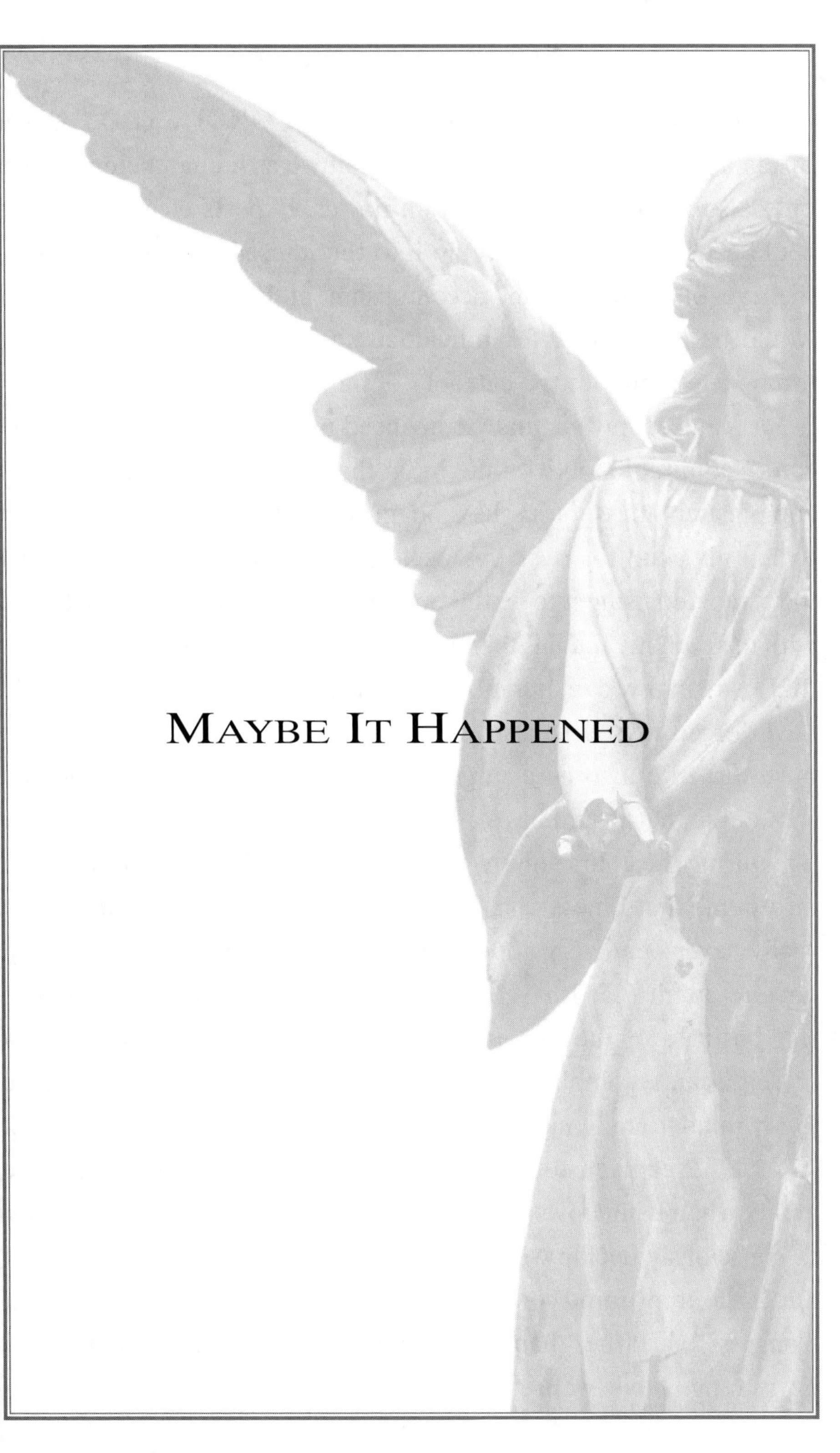

MAYBE IT HAPPENED

BASED ON EXTENSIVE STUDIES CONDUCTED DOWN through the years it has been stated that we as human beings utilize only a small portion of our brain power. Experts claim that if we could ever discover how to tap into the unused part of our minds, the level of knowledge and accomplishment that we could elevate to would be unfathomable. Individuals that are considered geniuses today might fall into the category of imbeciles in the future.

At times, I have actually convinced myself that I have not done a very admirable job with the brain that God blessed me with. This complicated mass of tissue and gray matter has been confined within my skull for over five decades now, and yet it seems as if I have avoided using it to its full potential. It's not that I'm dissatisfied with the path my life has taken or even unhappy with the occupation that I am involved in, but more along the lines that maybe if I would have forced myself to a greater level of brain application I might have turned out to be a surgeon, chemist or maybe even invented something that would have a dramatic change in the world.

During the course of my past life, I have had a number of people inform me that I have what they refer to as a vivid imagination. I've really never been very good at patting myself on the back, but I do have to admit that I have done a fairly good job when it comes to this business of the imagination. In a strange sort of way, I view myself as an accomplished artist with the talent to paint any picture in my mind, to take myself anywhere in the world or even beyond.

I've never been to places like China or Russia, yet I have the ability when lying down for the night or even sitting in my easy chair to consciously decide where I want to go and before long—there I am. It's as if my mind contains more information than the Library of Congress, but rather than row upon row of books my brain has filed everything I have ever read, heard or seen and can be pulled up with little ease. If my destination happens to be China, I can recall articles I have read about the country or movies I have seen about this foreign land. Before long—there I am standing in the streets of Hong Kong or reclining in one of those rickshaws I have always wanted to ride in.

I've never been skiing, but I have skied in the Alps. I don't have the remotest concept of how to fly a 747, and yet I have sat at the elaborate controls of one of these gigantic steel monsters, flown to all sort of exotic places and landed in some of the world's largest airports. I have climbed Mt. Everest, pitched a perfect game in the final game of the World Series and have even gone back in time to places like Little Big Horn or the parting of the Red Sea.

There have been a number of times when I have come out of one of these mental vacations that I have actually struggled with the difference between imagination and reality. Sometimes the things that we imagine can seem so real that we briefly question whether we created the situation in our mind or if it may have really occurred. One such incident has plagued me for nearly forty years.

Back in the mid-sixties after I had graduated from high school, I made the decision to attend a trade school. I had no interest in going to college or acquiring a career in the military, so a trade seemed like a good option. Halfway through my technical training, I accepted a position with a company in western New York as an offset lithographer.

I was engaged to a young lady who was to remain in central Pennsylvania while I traveled back and forth on the weekends. It was approximately a two-and-a-half hour drive up through the Pennsylvania mountains, which eventually led to the rolling hills of the Southern part of New York state.

The two-lane road that wound its way up through the mountains was well-travelled and always kept in good condition, with the speed limit back at that time posted at fifty-five miles per hour. There were a great many sections along the way where the speed limit had been reduced to thirty-five due to the curves in the road that would not allow the typical driver to maintain control of his vehicle. The repetition of driving back and forth every week eventually gained me the ability to drive the entire trip at fifty-five as I skillfully anticipated and guided my car around the dangerous curves.

On one particular occasion, I was returning from New York on a Friday evening. That morning I had packed for the trip home. As soon as I punched out for the day, I'd be on my way. As I can recall, it must have been late fall as it was dark by the time I hit the Pennsylvania border. I was excited about spending some quality time with my fianceé as I cruised down the winding road, my radio tuned to one of my favorite stations, two cheeseburgers, an order of fries and a chocolate milkshake balanced on my lap.

As a rule, the number of vehicles that passed me were few and far between. Once in a great while, someone would blast by me, no doubt discontent with the speed at which I was traveling and probably of the opinion that I was cutting into his precious time. About an hour away from my destination, it happened.

A set of headlights, on high beams no less, suddenly pierced through the rear window blinding me. I immediately adjusted the rearview mirror to counter the invasion of stabbing light, but it was to no avail. It seemed like my car was filled with the blazing headlights of the trailing motorist.

Coming out of a long curve, I backed off the accelerator reducing my speed to forty, which would allow the car behind me to pass. For some reason, the driver opted not to pass, his car still right on my bumper. Before I realized it, we were coming to another curve. Back at fifty, the car stayed right with me. At the next section of road where passing was permitted, I slowed down once again, but this time backed off to thirty-five, flashed my lights and stuck my hand out the window signaling the driver that he had plenty of time to go around. He backed off, copying my exact speed, the high beams still penetrating my rear window.

At the next section that was a straight stretch, I jacked my speed up to seventy thinking that I would just leave the trailing car behind. Not so. The driver remained right on my back end duplicating my increased level of speed, those high beams still probing at the back of my head. I made two more attempts of first slowing down and then speeding up, but it made no difference. At speeds as low as twenty-five and as high as ninety, the car stayed right behind me as if it were an extention of my bumper.

Now I was becoming concerned. Who was driving the car? Maybe there was a group of people in the car who meant me harm. It couldn't have been the highway patrol or some local officer as they would have pulled me over by this time. Pulling off to the side and stopping was quickly ruled out. As long as I was moving, I would be safe.

Turning off the radio and checking my seat belt, I decided that I would give my friend in the car behind me a run for his money. My '67 Chevy was equipped with a 327 high-performance motor, complete with a heavy-duty, four-speed transmission that would allow the car to reach speeds in excess of 120 miles per hour. On top of that—I knew how to drive the Chevy at high speeds on curves. The truck stop was just up the road about ten miles. I'd leave the driver behind me in the dust, then pull over at the truck stop where there were plenty of lights and people. I would be safe there.

Gently applying the brakes just enough for my brake lights to come on, I downshifted back into third gear, stomped the gas pedal and jammed the gearshift back into fourth, the car fishtailing slightly, straightening out, then blasting up the road. Glancing in the rearview mirror to see the results of my driving savvy, I witnessed a large ball of red flame—like an explosion—and the headlights were gone. In the next second, I was surrounded by darkness as I negotiated a curve by reducing my speed.

In the following seconds, my mind started to analyze the situation: *Had I caused an accident? Where had the car behind me gone? Had I killed someone? Were they lying on the side of the road injured?*

Back in my late teens and early twenties if I would have had to describe my attitude toward individuals who looked for trouble, the definition of my outlook would have been "caustic." I was generally known as a peaceful sort of guy and always tried my best to avoid ugly confrontations.

To this day, I have never fired a gun, took a swing at another person or victimized another with vulgar language. If pushed—I always walked away. My position on the incident on the dark highway was the same. I had applied every option aside from pulling over, but rather than walking away from the problem, I drove away. As I wheeled into the truck stop my thoughts were centered on, *If the driver who had dogged my butt up the road had crashed—it was of his own doing. He had been searching for trouble—it had come, and now, he or she or whoever it might be, had to suffer the consequences of his actions.*

Standing next to my car, I braved the stiff wind as I stared back up the road half hoping to see the car speed by. In the next five minutes, three cars and a tractor trailer, all abiding the state speed limit, passed by. If one of the three cars had been the car that had tailed me, I wouldn't have been able to identify it as its high beams had prevented me from seeing what type of auto or color it was.

Deciding on a cup of coffee, I made my way across the sprawling parking lot, the facts—as I knew them to be—not adding up. Following the apparent explosion or whatever it was, how could the vehicles that had passed the truck stop drive by the flaming incident just a few miles back up the road without stopping? Sure, there was the possibility that they had entered the highway from one of the side roads. If I remembered correctly, there were only two between the truck stop and where the ball of flame had been. Both roads were dirt and not what I considered to be main roads. I had never noticed any mailboxes indicating a residence. They probably just led up into the surrounding mountains to remote hunting lodges. But what about the eighteen-wheeler? The truck had to have come by the same route I had taken, the side roads not even capable of providing enough room for the big rig.

Sitting once again in my car, I sipped at the coffee as I realized how tired I was. Pulling back onto the road, I fought the urge to make a left and head back up the road where I had last seen the strange car. My callous outlook on those who chose to break the laws of the road, in this case—the mysterious tailgater—erased any thoughts of returning to the scene. I turned right and headed for home.

Further down the road, I struggled with my concept of those who chose to break the laws of driving. Was I any better than anyone else? After all, I had chosen to drive at fifty-five for the past few months when the limit was fifty. I had also taken the lower posted curves at a high rate of speed. Were these two infractions acceptable according to my standards while tailgating was considered a more serious offense? For the remaining sixty-two miles, I listened to the radio, just knowing that some newsman was going to inform listeners about the fatal wreck back up the road. The news did indeed come—but no mention of the accident occurred.

At my fiancee's parents' house, my future wife commented that I seemed to be acting strange sitting in the kitchen as I pushed a slice of homemade apple pie around on a plate. I told her that it had been a long day and that I was very tired. I refrained from telling her about my episode on the highway and finally said goodnight as I headed for my folks' place on the other side of town.

My mother was out in the kitchen finishing up sorting through her recipe book, my dad sitting in his easy chair, the late night news just about to flash on the TV. The familiar newsteam positioned behind their circular desk kicked things off as they announced the top story of the day: *A truck hauling a number of beef cattle has overturned and the state police and local citizens are in the process of rounding up the small herd, which has blocked traffic in both directions.*

Despite the fact that I was extremely tired, sleep did not come easily that night. Lying in bed staring out at the street light just outside my bedroom window, I mulled the incident on the highway over and over in my mind. Throughout grade school, junior high and, finally, high school, I had spent many a night lying in my bed looking out at that street light. Over the years, the oval light on the opposite side of the street had become a silent friend, always there, coming to life as soon as darkness descended on the neighborhood. Even through the heavy snow of winter or the downpours of spring, its light pierced the weather sending a warm glow into my room.

Many a problem had been resolved during my years of school as I stared out the upstairs window. The possibility that the highway incident had never occurred in the first place was slowly beginning to form. My thoughts drifted back to when I had pulled out of the truck stop and how tired I realized I was. Maybe I had simply experienced one of those driver trances I had heard people talk about where a person could actually drive for a period of time totally unaware of where he was. It was said that an individual could stop at lights, pass other cars, make turns and all of the other normal functions all the while without being cognizant of what he was doing.

The strangest thing about the whole dilemma was my lack of guilt. I didn't consider the supposed accident as my immediate fault, but still, there was the possibility that I had been involved and ignored my civic duty as a law-abiding citizen to stop and assist in any way that I possibly could.

The weekend flew by quickly and soon I was headed back up to New York. I had decided to leave a little earlier than usual in order to give myself some additional time to investigate the road a few miles above the truck stop. If the accident had indeed happened, the media seemed to be keeping a lid on things, which didn't make any sense at all. So far, the morning paper and the local television and radio stations seemed to be unaware of the accident a few miles north of the truck stop.

Since the surrounding landscape was more visible during daylight, I gave myself a two-mile leeway in either direction of where I thought the tailgating incident had occurred. I must have spent close to two hours driving back and forth over the five-mile stretch of highway, at times pulling over, getting out and looking down over the side of the road off into the trees. As evening set in, I continued my journey back to New York more convinced than ever that the whole thing had been nothing more than my imagination. There had been no signs of any sort of accident: no dented guardrails, skid marks, glass, remnants of a car or any area displaying signs of a recent fire along the road. As much as I wanted to believe that it had been my imagination, the remaining fact that it had all seemed so real was still puzzling.

Back in New York, I purchased a paper, listened to the local news and watched television for any information on the supposed accident. The media in New York had reacted to the incident in the same fashion as Pennsylvania had—nothing.

Weeks, then months passed by as I continued to drive back and forth on the weekends. Each and every time that I drove through the tailgating area, I searched for signs that it had actually happened.

Eventually, I did get married. My new wife and I set up housekeeping in Ithaca. Years later, I moved to Ohio after getting divorced. I suppose my life over the past forty years has been about as normal as anybody else's. I have held a number of different jobs, my second marriage failed and I really didn't get serious about the future until I arrived in my mid-forties. I entered into marriage a third time and, finally, settled into the life of a typical citizen, purchasing a house, planting flowers in the front yard, cleaning out the gutters every fall and all the other seasonal, even symbolic tasks that normal people seem to do to occupy their time.

It's been over forty years since I resided in New York. Every year the wife and I drive up to Pennsylvania for a week's vacation, but it wasn't until about a year ago that we ventured up into New York to spend a couple of days traveling through the Finger Lakes. For the most part, the incident of the tailgater had eventually slipped my mind and was filed away in the recesses of my brain. There were only a few occasions where the strange circumstances of that fall evening in the past came to mind, and even then it seemed like time itself had erased how real it had been.

I'll never forget that afternoon following our Finger Lakes vacation that we headed down to Pennsylvania to my mother's house. We wound up taking the same route that I had driven while working in Ithaca. The thought of the past accident nearly forty years in the past came to mind as I entered the curve where my first encounter with the mysterious driver had started. I kept looking in the rearview mirror, half expecting the car to appear. I was constantly glancing back and forth across the road in search of the exact area where the ball of fire had appeared. My wife, noticing my strange behavior, asked me what was wrong.

For the remaining trip home, I explained to her what had happened that night in the past and what great lengths I had gone to to discover if it had really ever happened or not. By the time that we pulled up in my mother's driveway, my wife was of the opinion, based on what I had told her, that it probably had been nothing but my imagination.

As it stands today and has for years, I am ninety-nine percent sure that the incident never occurred. There have been times when I have considered contacting the state police and having them dig up old records to investigate the possibility of an accident, but have refrained from doing so. Why waste someone's time on something that most likely never happened?

These days, and for a number of years, I have established a much stronger walk with the Good Lord than I had when I was a younger man. In prayer, I have asked God to forgive me for things I have unknowingly done that may have hurt others. The mystery of that night long ago on that dark highway may never be solved until I'm standing at the gates of Heaven. I, like everyone else who stands before the Almighty will have to stand in judgment for the way in which I have lived my life.

You would think that being ninety-nine percent sure that the accident did not happen would be a comforting thought. But still from time to time, my mind takes me back to that night long ago while driving home. That remaining one percent still remains and represents the possibility that—maybe it happened?

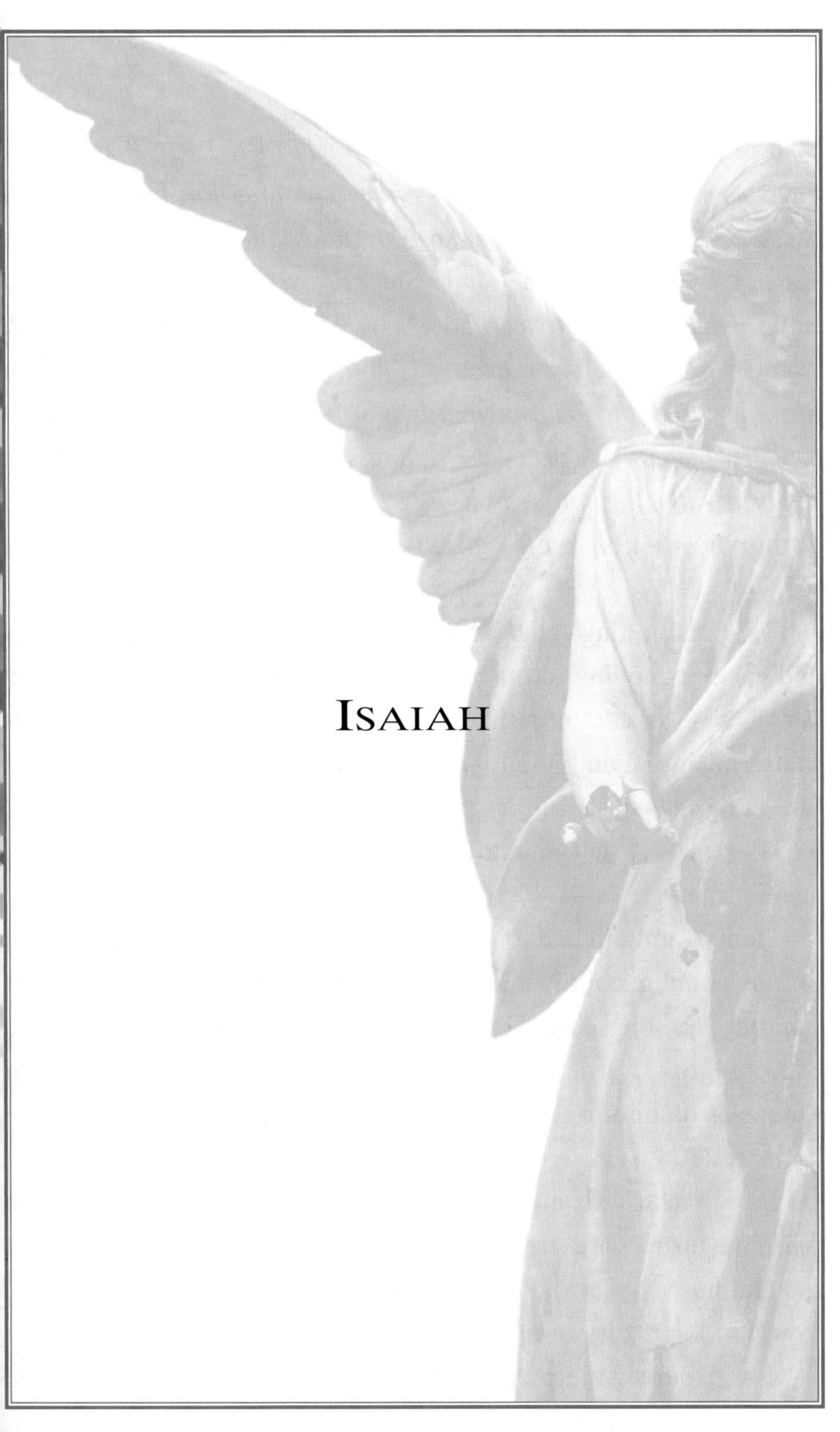

Isaiah

ROSE,

I'M SORRY THAT I HAVEN'T WRITTEN PRIOR BUT WE have been on the move for weeks now. The food has been less than acceptable, but by Army standards, I guess it'll do. The shoes I was issued were tight, but they have started to loosen up some. Heard some fellahs talking a few days back. Seems this whole thing will come to an end before it even gets under way. The enemy has been forming across the field since early morning. I've been assigned to an artillery battery. We've been trading blasts with the boys on the opposite ridge for hours. It's a frightening thought that a shell from a cannon nearly a mile off can kill or maim an enemy soldier. I best be….

The Union long-range shell collided with the ground, the grass and earth exploding into a mass of deadly debris. The iron cannon barrel was tossed into the smoke-filled air, the spoked wheels shattering into flying splinters, the surrounding Confederate soldiers breathing their last. The unfinished blood-stained letter floated off into the trees, Rose Canfield never to hear from her loving husband again.

Henry Canfield had joined the Southern army at the very outset of the coming conflict. The day he left his wife and daughter standing on the porch of his Southern Virginia farm, he had expected to return home in just a few months. The Battle of Manassas had not only taken his life, but that of many a soldier in both armies.

It took nearly six months for the news of her husband's death to reach the farm. Rose's remorse was deep, but the remaining fact that she and her six-year-old daughter Millie had to continue to survive slowly took priority over the death of Henry.

The experts—the politicians, those who understood the horrid workings of war—had been inaccurate. The thing, as they referred to it—the war—had not come to a matter of just a few weeks or months but had been raging for two long years and the state of Virginia was one of the main focal points of the invading Union Army.

Rose thanked the Lord each and every day that even though the war was entering its twenty-fifth month, the fighting in or around her small eleven-acre farm had been non-existent. She had heard distant cannon fire on occasion, but to date, no Union soldier had stepped a foot onto her rural property.

There had been numerous times when friendly Confederate troops had stopped by the farm, at which point Rose offered what she could spare and they had moved on. The whole country was in a state of turmoil, but the Canfields managed to squeeze out a meager living on the farm, the animal residents consisting of a horse, milking cow, two hogs and nine laying hens.

Out behind the barn, Rose tended a two-acre garden, which occupied a great deal of her time. She also possessed a knack for baking some of the most mouthwatering bread and biscuits in her small corner oven. Every other Monday morning, she and Millie would hitch up their horse and wagon, then load up with vegetables and baked goods and make the four-mile journey to town where they would sell their wares. Hours later, they'd return, the next two weeks' supplies stacked neatly in the back of the wagon.

The afternoon that the Canfield farm was finally invaded by the Union Army was a stifling hot day. The trees stood like green statues, not a single leaf moving. Mother Nature refused to bless the countryside with a cool breeze. Millie, now eight, was making her way slowly across the dusty yard, a wooden bucket of water balanced in each hand.

Placing her bare foot on the first step of the porch, she heard the disturbance up the lane. Turning, she saw a group of riders emerging from the trees. She had never seen a Union soldier but could tell by the Union flag flapping in the air that they were considered the enemy. Dropping both buckets, the water running over her feet and soaking into the dry earth, she warned her mother, "Momma… Yankees comin'…Momma, Yankees!"

As the small band of riders reined to a halt in front of the modest farmhouse, Rose stepped out the door, the family shotgun at her side. Quickly sizing up the unwelcome visitors, she counted nine men with a string of five tethered horses at the rear. The riders formed a sloppy semi-circle around one of the men who guided his white stallion forward, stopping just short of the porch. The slow-moving cloud of dust from the lane had now caught up with the men as it floated past the house, the dirty air clinging to their sweat-soaked skin and filthy uniforms.

The man who had assumed the position of authority removed a plumed hat from his head and slapped it on his thigh twice, dust rising from his pant leg, but then settling back in place. The eight men behind him coughed and hacked, some stretching, while others mopped at their perspiring foreheads with their dirty sleeves.

Rose's eyes fell back on the apparent leader. His hair was a light grey, so closely cropped that it appeared to be painted on his skin. He was a short man, lean-boned, his face partially covered with a neatly trimmed beard. His uniform gave the impression of normally being pristine, but for the moment was covered with several layers of road dirt.

He bowed slightly in the saddle, politely introducing himself, his verbiage and manner displaying the results of proper upbringing and formal education: "Good afternoon, Madam. My name is

Colonal William Baxter of the Army of the Potomac. Might I venture the family name?"

Rose raised the shotgun slightly as she placed her free arm around Millie, then answered, "Canfield."

The man smiled graciously as he inquired further, "Is there a Mr. Canfield about the farm?"

"No…my husband was killed at the Battle of Manassas. I run this place and whatever business you have in mind will have to be conducted through me."

The colonel's apology seemed genuine as he smiled placing the hat back on his head. "I am truly sorry about your loss. Lost a brother myself at Kernstown." Rubbing his hand over his face, he coughed twice then went on, "If I may get to the point for our visit today. You can rest assured that we mean no harm to you or your property. We have been ordered by General Joseph Hooker, commander of the Union forces, to commandeer all horses in the surrounding counties for service in the United States Army."

Millie moved closer to her mother as she pleaded, "No, Momma, don't let them take Isaiah…please, Momma!"

The colonel's education had apparently been coupled with some religion as he commented, "Isaiah…one of the great prophets of biblical times. Truly a man of God. Good name for a horse." With that being said, he turned, signaling to two of the closest riders, "Go to the barn and collect the animal."

Rose raised the shotgun, leveling it directly at the colonel's chest as she spoke calmly, "Those men make one move toward that barn and you'll be joining your brother in the Great Beyond." All eight riders drew and aimed their revolvers at Rose, Millie's scream piercing the air. Rose was torn between consoling her frightened daughter and keeping the family weapon trained on Colonel Baxter.

The colonel raised both his hands as he ordered, "Hold on…just hold on!"

Rose stepped to the very edge of the porch, the shotgun now aimed at Baxter's head. "You won't be taking our horse. Isaiah belongs to my daughter. She raised him from a colt. Besides that, he's our only means of getting to town."

Baxter leaned forward, the leather saddle beneath his frame cracking. Carefully lowering his hands, he remarked, "Mrs. Canfield, if I were an artist I would surely consider painting this moment. There you stand…daughter at your side, apron around your waist, flour smeared on your face and arms, that shotgun directed at what you consider to be the enemy. What a contrast in behavior you embody. Gentle, dainty hands that bake bread, but yet, hands that could end my life with just one squeeze of that trigger. You surely do bespeak of a proud woman. Your husband, God bless his soul was truly a lucky man."

He straightened in the saddle as he went on, "I am generally known as a patient man…more patient than most I am told. It has been said that war is not for the patient." Glancing back at his men, he then returned his attention once again to Rose. "It is difficult, to say the least, to control men who are tired, hungry and, pushed to their limits. Perhaps, I have not made myself clear as to our intentions. We have come for your horse…not your cow, hogs, chickens, food or water. If I should die at your hand this hot afternoon, I have no doubt that my men will spare no mercy on you or your farm. Many civilians on both sides of this war have lost their possessions and, in some cases, their lives. I can only hope at this point that my comments have made a magnetic influence on your thoughts and actions in favor of giving up your horse in lieu of devastating ramifications."

When Rose lowered the gun, Millie realized what decision her mother had made. The two soldiers previously ordered to the barn spurred their mounts forward as Millie pleaded with Rose, "No, Momma, please…don't let them take him…please!"

Leaning the gun against the front door, Rose placed her arm around her daughter as she knelt, trying her best to console the child, all the while aware that there were no words of wisdom that could ease Millie's pain. Isaiah was led from the barn and quickly added to the string of stolen horses. Baxter gently nodded his approval, the chestnut horse standing taller than the other five. Rose could see the fear in Isaiah's eyes as he reared up in objection, one of the men yelling, "He's a feisty one!"

Millie hugged her mother as she buried her face in Rose's dress. "I can't look, Momma…I can't look!"

Caressing Millie's long blond hair, she spoke calmly, "It'll be alright, child. Isaiah will be fine."

Baxter prodded his horse closer to the porch, leaned over and tipped his hat. "God bless you, Mrs. Canfield. You and your daughter will be in my prayers. I am aware that our visit to your quiet farm has been painful, especially for your young one there. I admire you as you have displayed the wherewithal to make the most judicious decision considering the circumstances. Good day to you, ma'am."

One of the riders lingered behind, finally urging his mount forward to the porch. Removing his filthy hat from his head, long locks of dark brown hair fell across his tired face. Rose estimated his age at no more than eighteen—maybe nineteen. The young lad pushed his thick hair from his eyes, tears slowly making their way down his dusty cheeks. "Sorry we stole yer horse. Don't know what else ta say." Seconds later, at a full gallop, he caught up with the small command at the end of the lane.

Millie broke away from Rose as she raced down the dirt road all the while yelling, "Isaiah…Isaiah!" Rose caught up to her where the road turned to the left before crossing the bridge at the creek. Millie sat dead center in the road, her face buried in her hands. Between coughing from the road dust and gasping for breath, she couldn't answer her mother's question, "Are you alright?"

Millie's inability to respond to her mother went far beyond her exhaustion from running down the long lane. She remained speechless for the rest of the day as she sat in Isaiah's empty stall. Despite Rose's effort to persuade her daughter to eat, she refused food. It wasn't until four days after the unwelcome visit that she finally ate.

The crying had stopped, the reality that Isaiah was truly gone and not to return setting in. She went about her daily chores in silence, spending her free time out in the barn or walking in Isaiah's pasture.

Two weeks to the day that Baxter and his men had come to the farm, Rose sat on the porch as she watched the fireflies dot the darkness of the surrounding fields. Millie had finally fallen asleep. Midnight would soon be upon the land, another day of frustration lay ahead.

Walking to the barn, a lantern leading the way, Rose entered Isaiah's stall. She felt so helpless as she lowered herself to the straw-covered floor, tears of anger and pain finally overcoming the strength she had previously displayed. The war had taken her husband, her daughter hadn't uttered a single word since the theft of Isaiah and they had no means aside from walking to get to town. How would they survive?

Looking around the stall, she thought about what Colonel Baxter had said about Isaiah's name: *One of the great prophets—*

truly a man of God. She felt ashamed as she hadn't given the Lord much of a thought the past few days. Maybe it was just because she just couldn't bring herself to pray. She had been tested and her anger caused her mind to question God's reasons for the war, the loss of Henry, Millie's silence, the theft of Isaiah. Kneeling in the straw, she had a difficult time weighing the difference between man's free will and the will of God.

As a young girl, she had been raised by her grandparents, her folks dying before she was even three years old. Her grandfather had been a man of deep faith and had taught her the ways of the Lord. One of the topics he had always been so adamant about was that God had given man free will to do whatever he decided was right, but that God's will would always prevail despite what mankind chose to do. Grandfather always said that if there was a giant scale that could weigh right against wrong or even love against hate, man's actions would always tilt the scales in favor of old Satan.

A clap of distant thunder sounded as raindrops started to pelt the roof of the barn. Standing, Rose picked up the lantern. The few moments she had spent on her knees hadn't answered all her questions or relieved her grief, but she was no longer angry at God. He hadn't caused the war. It was simply one of those disagreements mankind could not resolve, the scales once again tipping toward the death and destruction that the war had brought on the land.

The following morning the rain was still falling as Rose was busy at the oven mixing up her last batch of flour from the cupboard. A tug on her dress followed by Millie's pointing finger let her know that someone was outside.

Reaching for the shotgun over the wash basin, she thought to herself: More Yankees! Slowly opening the wooden door, Rose smiled, the previous night's prayer of how she was going to survive answered, at least for the present. There sat Clifton Webb and his wife Helen in their horse-drawn buckboard.

The Webbs were up in their years, pressing the mid-seventies. Clifton was a jack-of-all-trades individual. Aside from operating the town's general store with his wife, he was also the local preacher and medical doctor. There was another doctor in the next town over; a younger man who had been assigned a surgeon's position in the Confederate Army.

Putting the gun down, Rose walked to the wagon, helping Helen to the ground as she spoke, "My lands,...you'll catch your death out here in this rain. Come on in. I'll put some coffee on."

As Clifton stepped down into the mud, he signaled for Millie; "Come on over here, Child, and give me a hand with these here supplies." Rose couldn't believe it: four sacks of flour, a sack of sugar and coffee, a slab of bacon, matches and three candles. Millie sat quietly in the corner, the two sweet sticks Helen had given to her of no interest.

Removing his rainslicker, Clifton explained that the Yankees had swept the countryside stealing every horse in the county and beyond. He had been out on a house-call during the day-long invasion and had somehow unknowingly managed to avoid the numerous groups of roving Union calvary sent for the horses. Thus, he had the only horse for miles around.

He was of the opinion that the Union horse rustling was just the beginning of the coming horde of blue soldiers that were to descend upon their very lives. He had heard all the horrifying tales from northern Virginia. Union troops thick as locusts invading towns and farms, burning and looting, leaving the local citizens with little to nothing to live on. He and the Mrs. had been concerned about her and Millie, and since they hadn't been to town in close to three weeks, they thought they'd drop by with some supplies.

Rose told the Webbs about the blue riders who had taken Isaiah and how it had affected Millie's ability to speak. Clifton, who carried his worn black medical bag with him wherever he went, gave Millie an overall examination, finally stating that her ability to talk had not been impaired. The shock of losing her horse and the manner in which it had occurred had probably caused the child to refuse to speak. His advice was to remain patient, treating Millie in a normal fashion. Closing his bag, he said that in time she would speak again—when she decided to do so.

The war kept its ugly grip on the country for the next two years, the Southern army, ill-clothed and equipped, somehow managing to barely hold onto their dream of victory. The Union Army had been led by a number of generals who just couldn't seem to slam the door on Robert E. Lee, the sly fox, as he was known by many of his men.

It was about a year following the Webbs' initial visit that Clifton passed away, Helen moving to Charlestown to live with her sister. During the winter of the fourth year of the war, two divisions of Northern infantry swept across southern Virginia. The small town a few miles from the Canfields' farm suffered at the hands of the invading soldiers. Houses were ransacked, livestock was butchered, and the local bank was relieved of all monies. Abraham Lincoln had assigned General Ulysses S. Grant as the new and, what the North hoped was, the last general in command of the northern forces. In the South, Grant was known as a short, cigar-smoking tyrant who was determined to put an end to the war, regardless of the suffering of the civilian population.

Rose Canfleld and her daughter didn't wander too far from the farm and, miraculously, the Yankees never came again. The fact that they had been spared from the Union Army, aside from Baxter and his riders, was indeed a blessing. Rose had considered walking to town for supplies, but had been informed by passing neighbors that the town had been devastated, most of the townfolk moving further south.

Rose finally butchered the hogs and killed six of the nine laying hens. The cow had either been stolen or wandered off, and if it hadn't been for the garden out behind the barn, they surely would have starved. Rose had given up on Millie ever speaking again. The young girl had remained silent, her grief over the theft of Isaiah lingering in her heart.

April 10, 1865 turned out to be the first day in a long string of cloudy days where rain had not fallen in southern Virginia. Rose longed for the Virginia summer to finally break through the gloom of the previous winter. Spring would deliver new life to the surrounding landscape, the trees budding, then blooming forth, and the fields yielding a sea of lush grass. God willing, the coming summer would be the final stage of what seemed like a never-ending war. The news was that for the past two months Lee was held up in Richmond; his army near starvation and severely outnumbered, on the brink of surrender.

Rose, like many a southern woman, had been opposed to the war from the very beginning. Lincoln had put an end to slavery in the South, and the continued effusion of blood on both sides was reason enough for peace to finally settle upon the land.

Standing at the well dipping the dented tin into the hanging bucket, Rose noticed a lone rider and horse galloping up the lane. Bringing the horse to a sudden stop, the rider, a man she had never seen before, waved his hat in the air as he shouted, "War's over! Lee surrendered to Grant at some place called Appomattox Courthouse yesterday." Reining his horse to the right, the unknown rider slapped his hat on the horse's flank urging him up the dirt lane. In the distance, Rose could faintly hear the church bell from the town ringing in celebration.

The following Sunday, Millie sat in Isaiah's pasture as she watched the wispy clouds drift slowly by, a doe and two of her young standing at the edge of the trees. Her mother had told her about the war coming to an end and that soon their lives would be without the constant worry of Yankees and the fear that went with it. Rose was well aware of the fact that her daughter had never really had any great concern over the war. She probably hated what the war had brought to their farm—the death of her father and the loss of Isaiah. It was approaching three years since the child had spoken and Rose had long since given up on her ever speaking again.

Millie tossed a small pebble from her right hand to her left as a movement at the edge of the trees caught her attention; a man leading a limping horse down the lane. She looked back at the clouds above as the man was of no concern. A number of Southern soldiers on foot, as well as on horseback, had stopped by the farm in the past few days on their way back to their homes. Most of the men were more than glad to swap a few strips of bacon or some mashed corn for a cool drink from the well.

Five fence posts from the yard, Millie stood, her eyes wide, her mouth open in astonishment. Slowly walking toward the fence, she pointed, the words forming in her voice box trying to force their way through: "I…I…Isaiah." At first, it was just a whisper, but then on the third attempt, the sound of her voice raced across the field the yard and into the kitchen: "Isaiah…Momma…Isaiah's home…Momma!" Rose dropped the heavy skillet to the floor at the sound of Millie's voice.

Once out on the porch, she saw a man handing the horse's reins to Millie as they approached the front of the house. Millie had a wide grin on her tear-streaked face as she spoke, "Look, Momma…Isaiah."

Stepping off the porch, Rose addressed the young men standing before her. "Who might you be and how in the world did you know to bring this horse here?"

The young man removed his battered Yankee calvary hat and, as his long hair fell across his smiling face, she recognized the youngster who two years past had apologized for stealing their horse. "Name's Edward Miller," the young man said. "Didn't know if ya'd remember me or not?"

"Yes, I remember you," answered Rose. "You look older…you must be what…in your early twenties?"

"Twenty-three next week. Feel like I'm in my forties. I've been through a lot these the past four years." Removing a canteen and bedroll from the horn of the saddle, which he laid on the ground, he proceeded to loosen the straps. "That day we took Isaiah…well, let's just say that I sort of traded horses. Things were so muddled up that they never knew the difference. I promised myself that I'd do everything I could to keep him alive. After a few weeks, I didn't give it much thought as I wasn't sure if I was going to get through this nightmare myself."

Taking the bit from Isaiah's mouth, he slid the saddle to the ground, removed the Army-issued blanket, folded it and placed it next to the saddle. Patting the horse gently on the shoulder, he went on, "He's got a limp…probably be with him the rest of his life. He's been shot once and run through with a saber twice. He'll be just fine now that he's back home where he belongs."

"Is that where you're heading…home?" Rose asked.

"Yes, home. Has nice ring to it…home."

Rose smiled. "Where is home?"

"Small town in western Connecticut. Got me a girl up there been waitin' for me all these years. Gonna get hitched soon's I get back." Edward leaned down, picked up the canteen and bedroll, then stood. "You can keep the saddle. I have no need for it. I best be movin' along. Got a long hike ahead of me." Turning to Millie, he smiled approvingly. "Take good care of him now. He deserves some comfort."

As he turned to start down the lane, Isaiah nudged him in the back, pushing him forward. Sadly, Millie offered the reins to Edward as the tears ran down her face. "Here, he favors you. You need to take him."

Placing the bedroll on the ground, Edward went down on his haunches, his eyes looking up at Millie. "No, that's just his way of sayin' goodbye. He needs to be here…on this farm where he was raised. There was many a night when we rode together through the freezing rain, days when we went without food or water. Isaiah saved my life back about three months ago down in Tennessee. Got shot right outta the saddle in the middle of a rain-swollen river. I managed to grab onto Isaiah's tail and he swam me out to the safety of the bank. I would have surely drown if it wouldn't have been for him."

Looking out across the field, he continued, "He needs to graze out in that pasture and know that he's safe from harm. Needs to feel the warm sun on his face and wind blowin' through his mane; needs to have a warm place to lay down in the barn with plenty of oats and water. He's been through more battles than I have time to tell you about. He's as brave as any man who ever stepped on a battlefield. He needs to go home just like we all do. Now, listen to me. Just because he's been gone for a time doesn't mean he's forgotten, you Millie. Why, you shoulda seen him when we turned up the lane by the bridge. He was snortin' and prancin'. It was all I could do to hold him. He'll warm up to ya. He just needs some time…we all do. You take good care of him…he's special. Not too many horses have survived this war. Baxter was right when he said that Isaiah was a good name for a horse. The Good Lord surely had his staying hand on this fine animal." Standing, he patted the horse's head. "You're home now…you're safe… I'm at peace. Goodbye, fellah."

Edward picked up the bedroll, turned and started up the lane, Isaiah walking the fence line all the way to the trees, stopping at the intersecting fence, then watching his Union companion disappear in the trees. Standing for nearly a minute, he bolted across the field, circled twice then returned to the house, stopping in the yard next to the porch where he nuzzled Millie who sat in tears, feeling that things would never be the same. Reaching up, she caressed his wet nose. "You're home now." Rose stood in the open door, the aroma of baked bread floating across the porch. Raising her eyes toward Heaven, she thought: *Grandfather was right. God's will would always prevail.*

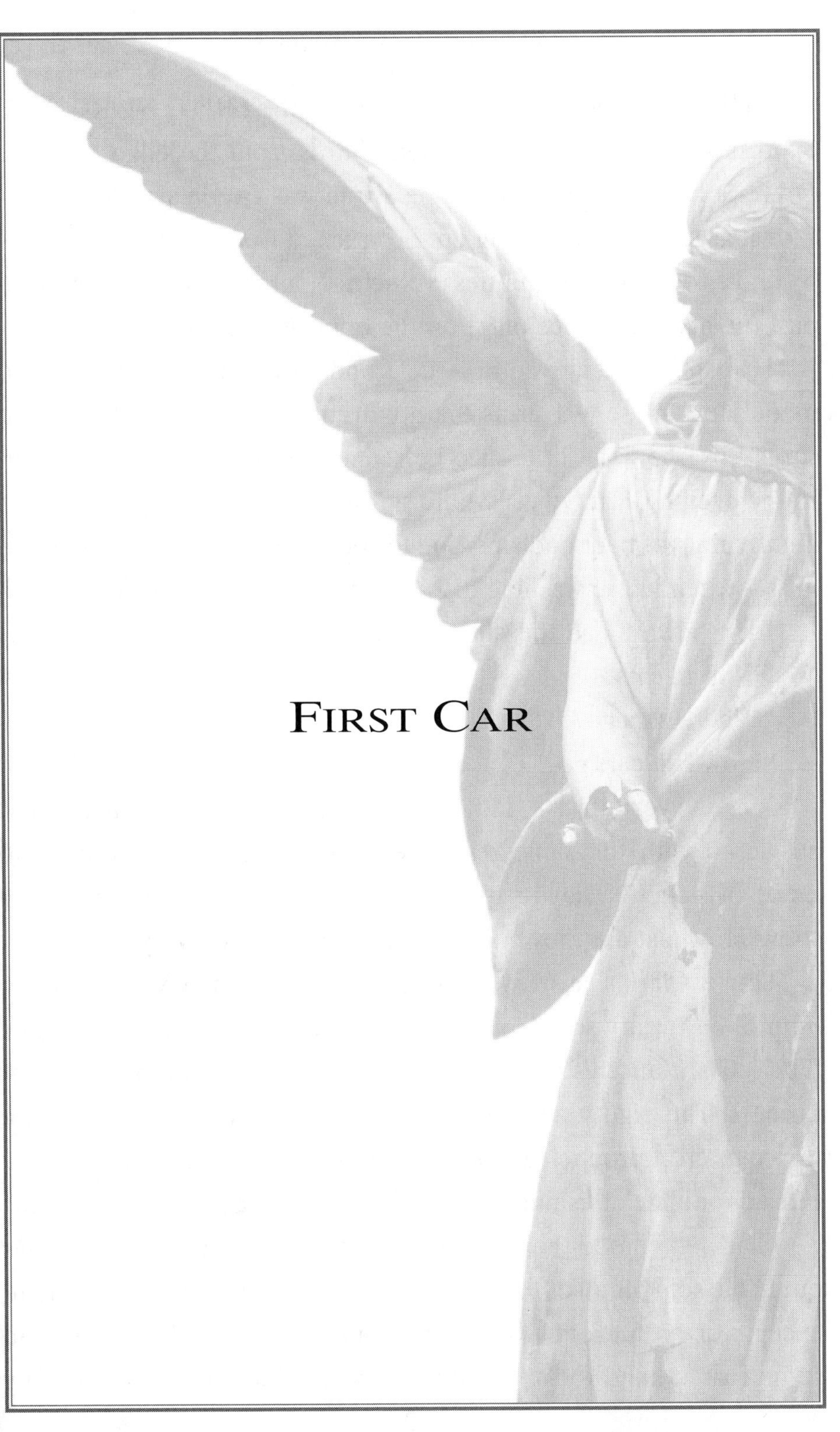

FIRST CAR

THE CONCRETE SHOULDER OF THE FOUR-LANE expressway was located just fifteen yards from the edge of Ernie Dwyer's front porch. By the time Ernie was five years old, he had grown accustomed to sitting on the cracked wooden steps for hours on end as he watched countless vehicles of all shapes and sizes speed past the abandoned ice plant on the opposite side of the highway.

He especially enjoyed the trucks and buses; they were larger and made more noise. As far as the hundreds of thousands of cars that surged by, the only difference he seemed to notice was their color. In the evening, Mr. Dwyer would sit on the porch swing enjoying his nightly mug of beer and smoking his polished walnut pipe while the missus attended to washing dishes and putting up leftovers.

Ernie always had the same questions for his father:

"Who in cars?"

"Where cars go?"

"How fast cars go?"

Mr. Dwyer always laughed at the boy's persistence, then answered with the same responses. "Secretaries, businessmen; all kinds of people. They're going home or out for dinner, maybe a show. How fast are they going? Well, let's just say…very fast!"

Uncle Clark's farm was located down the highway about an hour, then twenty some miles out into the flat Indiana countryside. Uncle Clark and his wife, Jessica, were a far cry from being actual farmers. The eighty acres they lived on had, at one time, been a thriving, crop-producing operation until the farmer and his wife retired for a life of fishing and basking in the warm Florida sunshine.

Clark purchased the farm "Lock, stock and barrel," as he always put it. He sold off all of the animals and most of the farm equipment, except for an ancient tractor that hadn't been used in years and some rusted hand tools. The two-story wooden barn was now only used to house his Cadillac, Jeep, and new stake-body truck. The only animal that had survived the auction block was an old bull by the name of Diablo. The crusty old bull had served the farmer for nine years, but was now too old to do much of anything but roam the seven acres of fenced-in pasture out behind the three-story stone farmhouse. Clark had resided on the farm for almost ten years, which meant Diablo had to be nearing the twenty-year bracket. With each season that passed, the solitary farm creature seemed to get more cantankerous.

Ernie's favorite pastime when visiting Clark and his wife was to sit in a rusted `49 Ford that had become permanently imbedded in the loose soil next to a neighboring cornfield. Aunt Jessie always explained to Ernie that it would be beneficial to walk around the fenced-in pasture. The past few years, Diablo had become rather territorial and not exactly neighborly when it came to intruders.

Ernie assured his aunt that he would most definitely walk around the fence, but his impatience of going out of his way caused him to always cut directly through the fenced field. No one, as far as he knew, ever watched to see which route he took. Besides that, he enjoyed the adventure.

The old bull always stationed himself at the northeast corner of the pasture. Ernie would always climb over the seventh top rail down from the corner. Diablo never paid the young boy much attention until he stepped down into the field. Immediately following this invasion, the massive animal would stop chewing on the clumpy grass, raise his heavy head, and snort.

At this point, the game began. Ernie had the bull's routine down to a science. Somewhere between the tenth and twelfth step across the field old Diablo would snort a second time, but louder, turn slowly, line himself up, then bolt in Ernie's direction, slowly at first, but with each step gaining speed.

This was the signal. Ernie would run as fast as his stubby legs could go as he jumped over manure piles and thick patches of grass. He always managed to arrive at the protection of the fence next to the old car, Daiblo never getting closer than ten yards.

One Thanksgiving, he tripped and fell, enabling the large approaching bull to come within four feet of running him over. Ever since that frightening day, Ernie moved down to the tenth top rail, giving himself a little bit more leeway. Ten yards had been okay, but four feet was definitely too close.

Once over the wooden fence, Ernie would always turn and greet the great animal: "Hello, there, Diablo!" Despite the massive animal's attempt to flatten him beneath his large hooves, Ernie considered the bull his friend. He wasn't quite sure if Diablo shared the same feelings.

Playing in the old car wasn't quite as exciting as racing across Diablo's field, but did make for some interesting Sunday afternoons on the farm. Nothing on the aged vehicle worked, but as far as Ernie was concerned, the car was in perfect operating condition. One moment he would be leading the pack at the Indianapolis 500, the next, a big city detective pursuing a carload of criminals in a high-speed chase. As Diablo stared through the wooden fence, Ernie turned the steering wheel, moved the gearshift up and down and pushed buttons. On occasion, he'd have Aunt Jessie pack him a lunch in case he decided to drive all the way across the country.

Ernie's incessant questions about cars were not exclusive to the front porch. Safely strapped in the back seat of the family station wagon, the youngster constantly talked, making it difficult for anyone else to get a word in. He never thought too much about the answers his parents responded with until one Monday on the way to the grocery when he inquired, "How much do cars cost?"

His father's answer, "Thousands of dollars...depending on whether the car is old or new," caused Ernie to sit in complete silence for a full minute. During this brief period of unusual solitude, Mr. Dwyer looked over at his wife, shrugging his shoulders. Could this be the six-year-old's final question about cars?

Not so. Ernie went into an endless analysis about how did people ever buy cars. He was currently receiving a one-dollar-a-week allowance. If he was lucky, maybe he'd be able to get a car when he turned fifty! Good old dad came to the rescue, explaining down payments, installments and automoblile loans. Still, owning a car seemed like an impossibility to young Ernie.

By the time Ernie turned fifteen, he thought he'd done an admirable job of saving his money. Between his allowance, which had esculated to a whopping five dollars a week, and a meager, even sporadic, income from tackling odd jobs around the neighborhood, his banking account seemed pathetic, topping out at $834.43.

As he sat on the edge of his bed, the bank book in his hand, he couldn't recall where the forty-three cents had come from. It didn't make any difference. The amount of savings he had managed to accumulate seemed rather paltry considering how frugal he had been the past years. He'd passed up many a burger and drink after school. And let's not forget Friday night football games, limiting himself to a single hot dog and small Coke. He scratched his head. Why had he put himself through all this misery? His first car—that's why!

He had lots of time to devour all the food he fancied in the future. You only got your first car one time. Ernie stacked this life experience right up there with other lifetime moments of importance: turning twenty-one or graduating from high school.

The fact that he had only managed to save little more than eight hundred dollars was only half of his frustration. The second factor, and the worst of the matter, was that his parents had informed him right from the very beginning that he could only utilize half of his money toward the purchase of an automobile. Four hundred and seventeen dollars. What kind of a car could he acquire for what seemed like "peanuts?"

Dad put his mind as ease. After he got his learner's permit, he could start practicing his driving skills in their family car. Mr. Dywer felt that getting Ernie a car of his own was a necessity. Splitting the use of the family's station wagon between himself, the missus and Ernie wasn't an option.

Mr. Dwyer was good friends with a man who owned a used car lot. After spending two hours scouring the seventy-three cars on the gravel lot, Ernie and his father agreed on a `59 two-tone Turbo-Glide Chevrolet. The car was already ten years old, but was in better condition and a better value than most of the later models. The car had been owned by an older woman who used the car to get around town, the only serious use being two trips a year to Florida.

The four hundred and seventeen dollars in Ernie's jeans was more than enough to cover the down payment. Two months later, Ernie passed his driver's exam, then said goodbye to his dad as he sat in the Chevy for the first time by himself.

He drove to the park, located a shady spot, and parked. He rubbed his fingers over the padded dash and vinyl seats. The old woman had taken great care of the car and he had every intention of continuing the habit. It wasn't what most of his friends referred to as a "fast car," but it would get him where he wanted to go. There was plenty of time to get a new car later on.

He looked out across the silver-gray hood at the symbolic

ornament on the front. His life would now be making a significant change. When he got home, he was going to hang his old bike up in the garage, retiring it from use forever. Over the years, he must have logged thousands of miles on that bike. Now things had changed. No more arriving at his friend's house bathed in sweat from muggy summer days of peddling his buttocks off. Now he would arrive there faster and in air-conditioned comfort.

No more freezing on cold winter days walking around town. Now it was just a simple matter of flipping on the heater. He didn't have to concern himself with getting drenched to the skin on rainy days. Now he had a roof over his head. How many times had he been racing along on his bike, hitting a pothole or crack, causing him to lose his station on his earphones? That was over. Now he could just push buttons with the touch of his finger without having to stop.

The greatest gain to having his own car was that wonderful feeling of independence. Going where he wanted, when he wanted. He had a job now. It was just flipping burgers, but he earned enough cash to make car payments, pay for gas, oil and insurance. He even managed to save a few bucks on a weekly basis.

Things were changing quickly for Ernie. After only three months at work, he was promoted to assistant shift manager. The new position required more hours, but also gained him a higher rate of pay. In no time at all, his savings had climbed back to the eight-hundred-dollar level.

He never quite made it to the one grand mark. An event that he hadn't planned on began eating away at his life savings. Her name was Breta. He met her at work and one thing led to another. A few movies and some excursions to the ice cream parlor and soon Ernie found himself going steady.

One evening at dinner, Ernie mentioned that it was rather

expensive to have a girlfriend. Mr. Dwyer laughed, then stated, "You think this is bad. Wait until you marry up with one!" After a dinner roll thrown by Ernie's mother bounced off his father's forehead, all three broke into laughter.

During his last two years of high school, Ernie experienced many things for the first time in the two-tone Chevy. He sat in the front seat at the drive-in and coughed and gagged trying to smoke his first cigarette. Wiping tears from his eyes, he just couldn't bring himself to understand what the big deal was about smoking. The white tobacco-filled cylinders certainly didn't taste all that great,and all that smoke being sucked into your lungs couldn't possibly improve one's health.

As Ernie tossed the half-smoked butt out the open window, little did he realize that four months later he would be up to a pack a day. He had grown accustomed to the taste, but the real reason for smoking was that it seemed to be the "accepted" cool thing to do.

Once again at the drive-in, he had his first sample of alcohol. The heavy taste of beer didn't seem to be much better than that first cigarette. He hoped his first drink of beer wasn't going to result in purchasing a case of weekly brew. Even though drinking was another one of those accepted social practices by a lot of his fellow classmates, Ernie steered away from drinking. During his first year in high school, three students had been killed in a tragic car accident linked to drinking and driving.

He encountered his initial sexual experience in the Chevy. He and Breta, after months of discussion and denial, finally gave in to their desires for each other. It had only been by the grace of God that she hadn't become pregnant.

During a short break-up with Breta their senior year, Ernie had his second sexual-related episode with a woman—an older woman.

After it was over, he vowed to never again spend time with a strange woman. Driving home that night he prayed that he hadn't contracted some type of social disease.

His last year of high school was indeed the pits. He and Breta eventually got back together, but it seemed that every other day they were breaking up again. By the time the senior prom rolled around, it was inevitable that their relationship was nearing an end. At the end of the summer, they would be going their separate ways. He had been accepted at Ohio State; Breta, an art major in Texas. They couldn't sustain the relationship living in the same city; living in different states would be the final nail in the coffin.

On a brisk, cloudy, mid-September morning, Ernie slammed the trunk of the Turbo-Glide, said goodbye to his parents, and drove off into the direction of Columbus, Ohio, and his freshman year at school. If everything went according to plan, in four years he'd be graduating with a degree in accounting.

Turning toward the on-ramp, to the expressway, he lit his first cigarette of the day. The rain was starting to pick up. He turned the wipers on high and made himself comfortable for the long drive. It was the first time he was leaving home for any great period of time. He wasn't concerned about not having his parents around, but not having Breta to talk with or go places with. The thought of no longer being with her saddened him. She had left for Texas just two days prior to his own departure. He had dropped her off at the terminal, they kissed goodbye, then she boarded the plane. She claimed she'd be seeing him around, but he knew it would never be the same. He had sat in his car at the airport parking lot and cried for five minutes after her plane disappeared in the distance. It was almost as if his old car was a close friend.

He took a long drag on the cigarette as he looked around the interior of the car. He wasn't as alone as he thought. He and the Chevy had been through quite a bit together. How about that time he had been cruising down Route 9 and finally realized that he was driving fifteen miles over the speed limit?

Unfortunately, at the same time he noticed that he was speeding, so did the state trooper on the opposite side of the highway. He kept a close watch on the trooper in the rearview mirror. Sure enough, a half mile down the road the patrol car cut directly across the grass-covered median strip. He'd never been in trouble with the law before. He had an unblemished driving record: no parking tickets, no speeding tickets, an impeccable career behind the wheel. He floored the gas pedal. His record was going to remain untarnished. He'd outrun the law! The next exit was only one mile up the road.

Ernie glanced in the mirror, the cruiser's red and blue lights flashing. Looking down at the speedometer he noticed that the old Turbo-Glide was sailing smoothly along at ninety-seven miles per hour. He wondered if the previous owner had ever driven the car at that speed. Probably not. It was most likely the first time the `59 Chevy had ever gone that fast.

As he sped up the off ramp, he noted that the cop was gaining rapidly. Ernie coasted through the stop sign, made a sharp left, and headed for the first side street he saw, his gas gauge resting on the big red E. What if he ran out of gas? If he got caught now, he would not only receive a ticket for speeding, but also reckless driving, failing to stop at an intersection, and who knew what else. He motored up and down a number of streets, finally coasting to an abrupt stop behind a Methodist Church. He was not only out of gas, but also out of breath. He stayed behind the church for an hour before retrieving his gas can from the trunk and walking four blocks for fuel. His old friend, the Turbo-Glide, had saved his hide that day.

Then there was the night of December 14th, that first winter he had the car. He and about seventy other motorists had become stranded out on Route 70 during a violent blizzard. Work crews were unable to get into the area until the following morning. He dozed on and off in the car that night, smoking cigarettes until he ran out. He'd turn on the lights occasionally, only to witness the blinding snowfall. The high winds were causing drifting that made walking out impossible. He could feel the car move from the force of the wind, but the Turbo-Glide held its ground, keeping him safe and warm.

His sophomore year was nearing an end. Ernie adjusted well to the swing of college life, except for the fact that he wasn't into skipping classes and staying out until the wee hours of the morning. He studied diligently, held an acceptable grade average, but was far from free of bad habits. He was now up to smoking two packs of cigarettes a day, swore like a veteran sailor, and was what he called a social drinker. He couldn't see any sense in drinking himself into oblivion like many of his friends. Two beers were always his limit.

Three months after his third year at college kicked off, a friend suggested that if he wasn't doing anything serious the following Sunday, maybe he'd like to help some friends of his move some furniture. Afterwards, there was to be a small picnic and maybe some horseshoes and volleyball. Ernie had no plans—he accepted the offer.

The eight people involved in the afternoon project turned out to be a youth group from a nearby church. Their assignment of mercy was to move a mother, her four small children, and all of their belongings out of a house that had been condemned. The mother only worked part time and the children were in need of clothing and medical care. The family had nowhere to go. The church was putting them up in some temporary housing until a more suitable solution could be found.

The young people of the group were Ernie's age and also college students. It didn't take Ernie long to realize, shortly after introductions, that he was going to be spending Sunday afternoon with what he had always referred to as "Bible Thumpers." It really didn't turn out to be as bad as he thought it would be. It wasn't so much what the group did but how they actually handled themselves. No one dragged him off to the side, informing him that he must repent or "see the light." No one even asked him if he was a Christian or attended church.

No one was smoking, swearing, drinking alcohol, or sharing crude jokes. He wasn't accustomed to associating with this genre of people and soon found himself conducting his behavior very carefully. His pack of cigarettes remained in his back pocket and he bit his tongue a number of times when tempted to curse. When accepting a glass of frosty lemonade from a girl by the name of Veronica, he didn't embarrass himself by asking if they had any beer.

When the tasks for the day were complete, the group retired to a local park for fried chicken and other picnic goodies. Ernie finished his fourth piece of chicken, then walked to a grove of trees. He was dying for a smoke. He had no sooner taken his first wonderful shot of nicotine when a voice interrupted his moment of pleasure, "Get enough to eat?"

Veronica smiled, then took a sip of lemonade.

Ernie cursed under his breath. Of all the people there to catch him sneaking a smoke. During the course of the day, she had talked with him quite a bit. Ernie found her rather attractive: long brown hair fashioned in a ponytail, hazel eyes, tall—probably around five-foot-nine.

Ernie never did get around to horseshoes or volleyball. He felt content to sit and talk with Veronica for hours. She possessed a pleasant, soothing disposition. She was one year behind Ernie in school and her area of interest was sociology. She enjoyed sports, loved Chinese food, and felt her main purpose in life was to reach out and help others.

The day finally came to an end. Ernie wanted the afternoon under the trees to continue forever. Somewhere during their long conversation the subject of cars had come up. She had a brand-new Mustang that she wasn't all that fond of, but her father had insisted that she drive a car to school that was dependable.

When Ernie told her about his `59 Chevy Turbo-Glide, she said she'd just as soon own an old car. Just before Ernie and his friend left the park, Veronica asked if he would like to come to their next youth gathering, which was the following Wednesday. He accepted. On the way home, he felt guilty. He wasn't going to attend the gathering because he had any remote interest in learning about the Lord. He simply wanted to spend more time with Veronica.

Weeks passed and Ernie showed up every Wednesday, as he sat through Bible readings and conversations in the church basement. Finally, he got the nerve to ask Veronica out on a date. They went out for a nice dinner, then miniature golf and ice cream. She loved the Turbo-Glide.

It took some time, but Ernie began to sense a change in himself. After dating Veronica for four months, he felt "religious." He had cut down on smoking to less than a pack a day, his cursing was limited to just a few incidental moments of impatience, rather than a diction of language, and he hadn't drunk a beer in...well, he couldn't remember. The girl definitely had an effect on his behavior.

That summer was the longest three-month reprieve from college he had ever experienced. Veronica had accepted a full-time summer position at a youth camp in Canada and Ernie returned to his previous job at Dixieland, home of the one-half-pound Mega Burger. They wrote each other, keeping each other abreast of their summer activities. Ernie couldn't wait until the fall term started. She had become an important and integral part of his life.

Being apart from her for three months was something Ernie viewed as a test. She had been so instrumental in assisting him to curb his smoking and swearing. Her ever-present words of confidence would not be available when he needed to hear them. She had presented him with a small poster, which he fastened to the sun visor in the Chevy. Whenever he was tempted to fire up a cigarette, he'd just look up at the words of wisdom: *You can make it...just be patient and wait on the Lord!*

Finally, his last year at school was to get underway. He smiled as the Turbo-Glide crossed the Ohio state line. In just a few hours, he'd be back at school. It was going to be a great year. He'd be graduating and with any luck he'd be a lot closer to Veronica.

That first night back on campus they met as planned at their favorite coffee shop. Ernie didn't have much to say about his boring summer of flipping burgers and going to picture shows by himself, but Veronica was extremely excited about her new interest. She had taken up running and was determined to participate in a marathon by the end of the school year. She had been running on a daily schedule and was now up to ten miles a day.

The fall and winter months of that year were the most fulfilling times Ernie had ever experienced. He and Veronica gathered warm coats for the needy at the mission. They stood for hours at the local soup kitchen on Saturday nights and organized groups to help feed unfortunate families at both Thanksgiving and Christmas. Ernie was now a regular at church. On three different occasions, he had teetered on the verge of taking the walk to the altar to accept the Lord, but he just couldn't seem to get up out of the pew. Veronica assured him that it was okay. When it was time for him to go up front, the Lord would supply him with the strength.

They fell in love and Veronica accepted his proposal on New Years' Day. The plan was that they would wait until one year after she graduated. This would give them two full years to save up enough money for a small house and the basic needs of newlyweds.

Veronica trained hard for her marathon goal and soon it was time for her to embark on the twenty-six mile journey. The race was held at Virginia Beach and sponsored by a Christian foundation that was raising money for the homeless. Veronica had convinced many of her classmates that she could run the distance. She had accumulated pledges of over $1200.00.

The course started on the beach, went for eight miles, then went directly through the city, out into the countryside, then back again on the beach. It was the last week of May—especially hot and humid. There were hundreds of runners of all shapes and sizes milling around on the flat length of sand. At the sound of the starter's gun, the mob of runners slowly ran up the beach. A few of the contestants, no doubt professionals, bolted into the lead instantly and left the bulk of the other participants far behind.

Ernie pedaled along the course on a rented ten-speed, keeping watch for Veronica. He finally spotted her at the seven-mile marker. At the ten-mile mark, she grabbed a styrofoam cup of water and a section of orange. She was well back in the pack, but holding her own. She wasn't required to win the race—just finish.

At the halfway turn around, she looked worn out. She had slowed down considerably, but was still plodding along. Ernie arrived at every mile marker before Veronica did and yelled words of encouragement as she passed by. At the twenty-one mile point, a rescue bus was picking up runners left and right. People were breaking down from exhaustion. Some runners had elected to walk the remainder of the way, while others just simply gave up.

With three miles to go, Veronica was alone. There was no one else in sight. Most of the runners who were going to complete the race had already crossed the finish line. She was barely on her feet when the final mile came into sight. She was wobbling side to side with her hands dangling as if they were heavy anchors.

The glow on her face had disappeared and was now replaced with a haggard, painful stare up the endless sandy beach. Suddenly, she stumbled and fell, landing on the sand with a thud. Ernie had to do something—and fast. Veronica needed more than just a few prodding words. As Ernie knelt in the sand, a Red Cross representative carrying a jug of water came to her aid, "Miss...are you alright?"

Veronica raised up on all fours, drew a deep breath of air, then stated, "If I...ever...suggest...doing this...ever again...just shoot me...on the spot. It can't...be...any worse...than this!"

She started to raise up, but fell back to the sand. "Miss...I'm not so sure that you should continue on," said the volunteer.

"Wait!" Ernie said. He held up the little poster from the Chevy and gave it to her. *You can make it...just be patient and wait on the Lord!* "If I can quit smoking, you can go one more lousy mile. There's a lot of people depending on you." Veronica never said a word as she handed back the poster, forced herself to her feet, and continued up the beach. It wasn't what you would call a good stride, but at least she was placing one foot in front of the other.

Ernie quickly mounted the bike and made for the finish line. He had to be there for her. At the one hundred-yard mark, she fell, rolling over onto her back, placing her hands on her forehead as if she were going to faint. She had to make it—one way or another. Rolling back onto her stomach, she tried to get up, but had no energy to do so. Tears streamed down not only Ernie's face, but the faces of everyone else watching as Veronica crawled the rest of the way to the finish line.

It was nearly a month after the race that Veronica collected all of her pledges. The twenty-six mile marathon had taken every ounce of strength that she had, but it was worth it. Her effort had netted a grand total of $1,250.00. On their way to the mission to deliver the cash, Veronica jotted down a short note, which she placed with the money in an envelope.

"What's that?" asked Ernie.

"Just a brief message," said Veronica.

Ernie reached across the seat. "Let me read it."

She removed the note from the envelope and handed it to him.

Unfolding the paper he read her words out loud, *"If this money helps just one person to get back on his feet, then my effort, has been worthwhile. If this small donation helps just one poor soul to pull himself up by the bootstraps, then it was worth the pain."*

Ernie pulled the Chevy into the parking lot as he handed the paper back. "I thought we'd stop and grab a quick lunch before stopping at the mission."

The truck stop along Route 70 was one of their favorite places to eat. They made one of the best western omelets in the area and you could get one twenty-four hours a day. Veronica placed the note back in the envelope, opened the glove compartment, and placed it in a slit in the material inside the compartment. The tear in the material had been there ever since Ernie owned the car. He never got around to repairing the rip. Actually, it had become sort of a joke, Veronica saying it was their special hiding place for secret items. She closed the compartment, Ernie locked the car, and they walked to the diner.

Fifteen minutes later, Ernie was taking the first delicious bite out of his omelet, when four young men burst through the front door, wildly waving three revolvers and a shotgun in every direction. It was one of those things that you see on television or hear about on the radio. It always happened to someone else.

At that moment, Ernie wished he hadn't stopped at the truck stop. This was real—not on television—not on the radio, but real. He had placed both himself and Veronica in danger by stopping. The boys were yelling for everyone to get their hands up. One of the four stuck a gun in the face of the cook demanding that he open the register.

The gang was nervous and far from being professional thieves. Their age and lack of authority were not convincing folks to cooperate. One of the boys shattered the front of the jukebox, thinking that he could make his point. The shot startled everyone in the restaurant. Veronica jerked, knocking hot coffee on her lap. She jumped up instantly, the hot liquid soaking through her cotton dress onto her leg. The boy near the door turned and fired, thinking she meant him harm. The shot caught Veronica square in the chest, knocking her across the aisle and beneath a table. The four boys lost what little control they had. They hadn't anticipated killing anyone, just robbing the place. In a state of fear, they ran out the front door, hopped in a waiting car and sped off.

Ernie was surrounded by customers as he clutched Veronica in his arms. He realized she was dead, but he just couldn't let her go. The paramedics finally pried his hands from around her blood-soaked body.

At the viewing and the funeral, Ernie couldn't even stand. He had to be led to the casket and the grave. He was now beyond crying. He was so weak from the pain of her death that he couldn't sleep or eat. He had been heavily sedated to soothe him as much as possible. After Veronica was buried, Ernie returned home and remained up in his room, except for long walks or an occasional bite. Finally, it was decided that he would not finish school that year. He needed some time off to allow his deep remorse to fade.

The `59 Chevy sat out in the backyard, but he couldn't bring himself to even get in the car. He new that he'd look across the front seat and remember that just prior to going in the truck stop, she had been in the car. It was one of those things that he just wasn't ready to handle yet. His mother was concerned about his health. He wasn't eating properly and getting very little excercize. He just sat in his room. Mr. Dwyer suggested that they just leave their son alone. He'd be fine. He just needed some time.

September rolled around and Ernie made the decision to return to Ohio State and complete his senior year. He finally realized that he had to put his life back together. He packed his bags, threw them in the back seat, and climbed in the Turbo-Glide. He hadn't driven his old car for nearly four months. As he pulled out onto the freeway, he smiled. It was the first time he had smiled in months. It was the first time that he didn't feel alone. His old friend, the Chevy, had been there waiting for him in the backyard. Surprisingly, he found he was able to glance across the seat where Veronica had last sat. The smile disappeared from his face, but he knew he was going to make it.

The decision to return to school turned out to be a drastic mistake. There were just too many memories of Veronica: the places they had gone together, the walks in the park, and the church they had attended. He couldn't seem to keep his mind on his schoolwork. The youth group urged him to become involved in church activities, but the loss of Veronica was just too much for him to deal with.

As the months passed, he found that he was spending most of his time alone. He avoided conversations in class, remained in his room and went for long drives in the Chevy. Everywhere he looked it seemed he couldn't get her off his mind.

During the long drives, he had nothing to do but sit and envision how well everything had been going. Now he was smoking again: he had thrown the poster from Veronica away. It was just another painful reminder. He was almost back up to two packs of smokes a day. He was starting to drink. He had never considered himself a heavy drinker, but it seemed that after partaking of five or six beers he could not only sweep Veronica from his mind, but his own frustrations of loneliness as well.

He drove to strange towns, located the local bar, and sat and smoked and drank until he could barely make it back to his car. There had been many a night he had fallen asleep in the back seat of the Chevy, waking up later, only to discover he had missed his classes for the day.

It wasn't long before the alcohol diversions became a necessity. When he sobered up, the memories of Veronica came back. The only way to erase her from his mind and experience a level of peace was drinking himself into a state of drunkenness. It finally got to the point where beer was no longer suitable. He needed something stronger. He became a regular customer at the liquor outlet, whiskey now the means of escape.

His grades were slipping quickly. He was not only missing class, but falling asleep during the day. One of his professors suggested that he see a guidance counselor, but Ernie knew that would only lead to some psychological garbage about accepting Veronica's death and getting on with his life. He wasn't interested in someone else's opinion of how he needed to handle himself.

A week later, he was summoned to the dean's office and told that the staff thought it best if he took some time off. It was obvious he wasn't quite ready to return to school. Ernie didn't accept the suggestion, saying he only had a few months to go before graduating. The dean explained that the school was trying to be tactful. At the rate his grades were falling, he wouldn't be graduating as planned. He had missed too many classes. The teachers and the college understood his grief, but still, they could not allow a student in the classroom who was constantly under the influence.

Ernie stormed out of the office, slamming the door so fiercely the glass panel shattered and fell to the floor. He heard the dean shout to his secretary, "Call security!" Ernie dashed out of the building, hopped in the Turbo-Glide, and sped away from the campus. Once on the freeway, he smiled. The old Chevy had saved him from another scrape.

He drove until he found himself south of Pittsburgh. He stopped, gassed up, grabbed a cellophane-wrapped cheeseburger from a deli case, and then continued on past Erie and drove toward Buffalo. He pulled over at a roadside rest, finally deciding to spend the night in the car. A sign located by the restrooms read: NO OVERNIGHT SLEEPING. He didn't care what the sign said. He was just too tired to continue on.

He felt like a bum when he woke up the following morning. He was hungry, stiff, and needed a shower, but most of all, he required a drink. He stopped at a corner market and purchased a twelve-pack. Driving in the opposite direction that he had been heading, that night he pulled into St. Louis. He was still hungry, stiff, lethargic and dirty, but none of that mattered much. The alcohol had taken its effect. At the moment, he was drifting off to sleep as his eyes glazed over. Thoughts of Veronica, and of leaving school had faded away.

He drove the Chevy for two straight weeks, drinking his daily, habitual portion of beer as he traveled along. He had also added a bottle of whiskey to his routine intake. He couldn't even remember most of the places he had been.

Soaked with perspiration, he woke up sprawled out in the back seat of the Turbo-Glide. He opened the door and tried to step out, but stumbled to the ground. Using the rear bumper as support, he managed to get to his feet, leaning on the car as he took in his new surroundings. For miles in every direction there was nothing but dirty sand. He had no earthly idea where he was, but from the looks of the barren landscape he had to be in a desert somewhere.

Getting back inside the car he checked his wrinkled clothing. He hadn't had a bath since leaving Columbus. Needless to say he smelled so foul he could hardly stand himself. The front and back seats were strewn with empty beer cans and whiskey bottles. No more, he thought. He decided to push on to the next town, call his parents, and at least let them know that he was okay. Then he'd get cleaned up, get something to eat, and maybe get a room to rest up for a couple of days. Then he could decide what to do.

An hour later, he rolled into Las Vegas, pulled into a motel near the outskirts of the city, got a room, and went about the task of allowing the warm soapy water from the shower to wash away the stench from his body. He phoned his parents and talked with his mother, explaining that he just couldn't deal with school any more. He told her where he was and that he was alright. He wasn't certain what he was going to do. He'd be in touch.

He was hungry, but his overwhelming fatigue overruled his desire for food as he fell asleep on the king-size bed, sleeping through the night, and into the next morning when he was awakened by a loud knock. He opened the door without even asking who was on the other side. A policeman stood framed in the late-morning sunlight. Looking down at a small pad the officer was holding, he politely asked, "Are you Mr. Ernest Dwyer?"

Ernie answered slowly, "Ah…yes…I'm Mr. Dwyer. Is there some sort of problem?"

"I guess you could say that. Do you own a 1959 Chevy, Indiana tags?"

"Yes, I do…why?"

"I'm sorry, but I'm afraid your car has been stolen."

Before Ernie could react to what had been said, the officer went on, "There were a total of five cars stolen from the parking lot last night. One of them happened to be yours. We've had a string of these types of thefts this summer. We're sure it's a ring working the city. On a couple of occasions, we've been able to recover the cars, but for the most part, they just seem to disappear. We think they're being shipped to other cities, then sold."

Ernie was speechless as he stared down at the macadam lot where his car had been parked for the night. He walked out to the railing, placed his hands on his hips, then asked, "What am I supposed to do now?"

The officer apologized, "I'm sorry for the inconvenience…there really isn't much we can do but continue the investigation. I'll report the make and model of your vehicle, your name, address, and phone number. If your car turns up, we'll notify you."

After the officer left, Ernie sat on a plastic chair on the veranda and looked out across the endless desert. He felt violated. His car had been stolen. He felt sick to his stomach. He had taken such great care of the Chevy, and now a stranger somewhere was driving it to another state. He felt helpless. Would the thieves strip the car or maybe change the color? It was almost as if part of his life had been yanked away from him.

Suddenly, a feeling of bitterness flooded his thinking. The loss of Veronica had been a tremendous blow to his emotions. The Turbo-Glide had always been there for him. Now, his last fragment of emotion had been snatched away. He needed a drink. He walked to a small taproom across the street.

Ernie awoke to the pungent odor of rotted food. He focused his weary eyes, at the same time shielding his face from the bright morning sun with his right hand. He sat up painfully as he wiped a half-eaten tomato from his left knee. Directly across the narrow alley, there was a two-story brick wall, the backside of a building. A door opened a few yards down the passageway. A woman wearing a dirty apron stepped out, pitched a bucketful of filthy, soapy water into the alley, glanced at Ernie briefly, and then closed the door.

A raspy voice, almost giving the impression that the speaker had laryngitis, startled Ernie, "Had a rough one…huh?" The sickly voice came from a short man sitting on an overturned trash can. He had the most pallid skin Ernie had ever seen. The man's hair was a tangled mass of grey and black, and his eyes sunk deeply into a haggard face. His clothing consisted of a long, grubby trench coat, no shirt, baggy trousers with both knees ripped out, a set of shoes that didn't match, and no socks, He held out a bottle of brown liquid to

Ernie. "Here...better have a shot. Looks like ya could use one."

Ernie's mouth felt like dry paste. He tried to spit, but he almost gagged. He took the bottle and following a long swig of cheap whiskey cleared his constricted throat. "Where am I?" he asked.

"From the looks of ya," said the man, "I'd say yer'r in the same place I am. Hell on Earth!" The man stood as he took a long pull on the liquor. "C'mon, I can see yer'r new at this. Now me, I been at it fer years. I know a place where we can git some breakfast."

Ernie slid open the heavy wooden door of the boxcar as he looked into the driving rain. As the long freight train slowly came to a jolting halt, he stepped down and pulled the collar of his tattered coat up around his neck. He wrapped his arms around his stomach. He couldn't stop shaking. He was cold, sick, hungry—but most of all, he was thirsty. He hadn't had a good drink in three days. He couldn't even remember the last time he had had anything to eat. He felt like he was on the verge of death. If he could just find a warm place to lie down, then in the morning he could get himself straightened out.

He staggered across four sets of tracks, the November wind blowing his long dirty hair in his face. Stepping across the last set of tracks, he slipped, rolling down the gravel roadbed, finally stopping at the bottom of a rotted wooden fence. He crawled through a hole, and, using the fence as support, Ernie elevated himself to his feet as he wavered back and forth. From the scattered spotlights, he guessed that he was in a junkyard that appeared to go on indefinitely. There were giant piles of tires, engines, and bumpers surrounded by row after row of rusted, abandoned automobiles.

Minutes later, he had worked his way between the endless rows of junk cars to the very back row. When he discovered that he couldn't walk any further, he opened the back door of the closest car, crawled in the back, curled up and shivered for two hours before he fell asleep from exhaustion.

It was still raining when he woke in the morning. The sky was a dark gray and cast a cloak of dreariness over the sprawling graveyard of autos. His body heat had finally overcome the shivering. For the moment, he was warm, but he knew the relief was only temporary. He recalled his thoughts of the previous night about finding a dry place to get warm and then getting himself together in the morning. He had made that very promise to himself more times than he cared to remember. It was always the same. Any effort on his part to reach a point of being sober was always replaced with his desperate need for alcohol. It gauged his life, and it dictated his every move and thought. He was well aware of the reality that he was in need of help, but was mired too deeply in the depths of alcoholism to do anything about the dire situation.

He thought about the past nine years of his life after waking up in that Las Vegas alley. He had learned the rules of the road quickly. He had held a few jobs in the beginning, but eventually learned to live by his wits. He couldn't keep a job and any money he earned went toward the purchase of liquor. He had spent just under a decade drifting around the country, literally drinking himself to death. It was not an easy thing; this living on the road. He didn't consider himself as tough, but rather pathetic.

He sat up slowly and got a brief glimpse of himself in the small, cracked rearview mirror. The gaunt face that stared back was shrouded with the countenance of an old man; a man who hadn't taken care of himself, a man who looked sixty-something, not thirty-one. He wasn't the least bit pleased with the sickly looking face that peered back at him.

The warmth was starting to wear off as he began to shiver.

FIRST CAR

Looking through the rain-streaked windshield, he took notice of the small, pointed hood ornament, then looked beyond the ornament across the junkyard. The rain, which normally had a method of cleansing the earth, did little to change the filthy condition of his surroundings. His attention drifted back to the ornament. Something about the rusted object seemed to stick in the back of his mind somewhere.

He ran his eyes over the rusted hood. It had a familiar shape to it. He'd seen it somewhere before. He was starting to get the oddest feeling as he looked around the interior of the abandoned automobile. The steering wheel was bent at an angle. He ran his fingers over the ribbed edge. It felt as if he had touched the wheel before. There was something strangely reminiscent about the ripped seats, the dashboard, and the sun visors. Then, it hit him. It couldn't be! It was all his imagination—his liquor-soaked brain playing tricks on him. He scanned the interior of the car, then the hood once again. There didn't seem to be any doubt about it. He was sitting in a 1959 Turbo-Glide Chevrolet.

The coating of rust prevented him from distinguishing what color the car had been at one time. Then he noticed something that caused him to sit up straight, and his mouth opened in wonder. There was a two-inch tear in the passenger seat. His Turbo-Glide had the exact tear in the same place. He had noticed it the day he bought the car. He had never bothered to get the flaw repaired.

What he was thinking couldn't possibly be true. The tear had to be a coincidence. Then he remembered something—something that would put an end to his ridiculous thinking. Crawling out of the car in the steady rain, he lowered himself down into the mud, and looked beneath the Chevy.

He painfully pulled his weak body under the rusted frame and slowly worked his way to where he could reach up and feel the underside of the muffler. Running his hands over the pitted metal, he stopped as his fingers wrapped around a small two-inch metal case.

His short journey under the car had not only rendered him being cold, but muddy and soaked. Back inside the car, he shivered as he tried to open the small container with his numb fingers. It finally popped open, revealing his spare Turbo-Glide key he had placed there for an emergency years in the past. He sat back in amazement. He was in his own car! Somehow, after it had been stolen in Vegas, it had come to rest in this Los Angeles junkyard.

He gazed around the inside of the car as he thought of the irony of it all. As the years had passed by, the old Chevy hadn't fared any better than he had. The car was no longer in working order. He lowered his head. As far as he was concerned, he was no longer in working condition, either. The car had been put to rest in this rusted graveyard, its capability to perform vehicular functions coming to an end. He was still walking around, but he knew that he was also reaching his own end.

He looked at the square section in the dashboard where the radio had been located. How many times had he listened to one of his favorite tunes? He tried to think of any of the old songs that he had liked. He couldn't remember a single song. He couldn't even think of any of the newer songs. He'd heard plenty of music over the past few years, but he was usually too drunk to pay any attention.

He looked down at the console and remembered where he had always kept his cigarettes and his spare change. He had taken such great care of the car—and look at it now. He looked at his face in the mirror again. He hadn't taken care of himself.

He was shivering more violently than he had in some time. He was in need of a drink and a cigarette. He looked at the old glove compartment where he noticed something. A small sliver of paper was sticking out of the torn fabric inside the open cubical. He reached over, tugging on the edge of the paper. Continuing to pull the paper from the fabric he finally noticed that it was an old envelope. Holding it in his unsteady hands, he peeled back the flap, revealing a small stack of old musty bills. This was too good to be true—money! He slowly counted the money. Twelve one-hundred-dollar bills! He looked all around the outside of the car in every direction to see if anyone was watching him. It was still pouring rain. Realizing that he was indeed alone, he clutched the money to his shivering chest as he thought, How can this be? Then, it hit him! Twelve hundred dollars—the exact amount that Veronica had raised during her run for charity years in the past. The money had never been discovered. It had remained hidden in the slit in the fabric—their secret hiding place that they always joked about. Since the tragedy at the truck stop—all those years—the money had been forgotten by him. Staring down into the envelope, he noticed a small folded piece of paper. Removing the paper, he slowly unfolded it and read it out loud, *"If this money helps just one person get back on his feet, then my efforts have been worthwhile. If this small donation helps just one poor soul to pull himself up by the bootstraps, then it was worth the pain."*

Ernie wiped tears away from his cheeks as he read the note again. Life had stolen both Veronica and his car away from him. Now he had been reunited in a strange sort of way, and in a peculiar turn of events, Veronica had entered his life once again. It wasn't so much that she was back, but what she had stood for and what she had accomplished was back.

Ernie felt the corners of his mouth form into a smile. He hadn't smiled in a long time. He looked at the money in his hand. His old friend, the Turbo-Glide had come to his rescue once again. He had experienced so many things in the car for the first time. He shook his head in amazement as he thought about how miraculous it was that he was going to be the poor soul that would pull himself up by the bootstraps due to Veronica's efforts. Placing the money and the note back into the envelope, he opened the door and stepped out into the driving rain. He knew what he had to do.

He took a few steps in the mud, then stopped and glanced back at the Turbo-Glide; a corroded shell of an automobile left to die in the endless rows of junk. He smiled again, turned, and started up the mud-filled road.

Ten minutes later, he located what had to be the main office of the yard. It was hardly what one referred to as an office, but better described as an oversized shack. The small structure was constructed of a number of different types of lumber, two unmatched windows, an uneven corrugated roof, and a warped front door, with a storm door that was barely hanging by its rusted hinges. It reminded Ernie of something a group of kids would put together as a neighborhood clubhouse.

The inside of the building was equal to its shabby exterior, the wooden walls covered with assorted hubcaps and license plates. A makeshift table of pine boards was supported by two stacks of tires piled four high in the corner under one of the dirty windows. A pot-bellied stove sat in the opposite corner, the smell of burning firewood filling the room. Centered in the front of the back wall was an old scarred wooden desk, leaning at a slight angle due to the absence of the left front leg.

A man, who was too large for a swivel chair he had somehow squeezed himself into, looked up from the newspaper he had been reading prior to Ernie's entrance. A Doberman lay on the floor at the right of the desk on a circular frayed rug. He looked up at Ernie but then slowly lowered his head and closed his eyes. He certainly didn't remind Ernie of the typical junkyard dog he had always heard about.

The man took an oversized bite out of a sausage-and-egg sandwich, wiped the crumbs from his mouth, then picked up a smoldering cigar as he asked, "What can we do for ya?"

Ernie came right to the point as he pulled the envelope from his coat and removed the wad of bills. "You have a car out there next to the back row that I would like to purchase."

The man inspected Ernie from his soaked hair to his faded shoes. Normally, he probably wouldn't have considered a bum who had strolled into his office a customer, but the cash gripped in his hand inspired him to continue the conversation. "And what car might that be?"

"It's a `59 Chevy Turbo-Glide," said Ernie. "It was stolen from me a few years back. Somehow it wound up here."

"Can't give ya a price unless I know which one it is. It's pourin' out there right now. Maybe ya can come back later when this rain clears. If it's in the back, believe me, it ain't goin' nowheres."

Ernie walked to the desk and put a twenty on a pile of magazines next to a broken ashtray. "I'd like to make the deal right now. That twenty's just for walking out there in the rain with me and taking a look at it."

The man rubbed a dirty hand over his five-day beard, then smiled through cavity-riddled teeth. He blew a stream of cigar smoke toward the ceiling, then leaned over the desk with great effort and spoke to the dog, "Looks like we have ourselves a payin' customer here, Buck." The dog got up, turned in a circle, but then went back to its original sleeping position.

"Let me grab my jacket," said the man, "then we'll take a stroll out back and you can point `er out."

Thirty minutes later, Ernie walked through the front gate of the junkyard, the cigar-smoking junk dealer and the Doberman standing in the rain. The man held fifty dollars in his hand. As he watched the hobo who had purchased the car crawl up the embankment, then cross the tracks, he knew that he'd return for the car just like he said.

Ernie checked in at a rundown hotel next to the rail yards, took a long hot shower, until the water turned cold, then forced himself to eat a good lunch at a small diner. He purchased some new clothes at a local Army-Navy outlet, then went on a long walk. He had a lot of thinking to do. More than that, he had a lot of work to do. The climb back to a normal path of life wasn't going to be easy. Veronica had gone through pure Hell running that race to raise that money. It had been her intention that somehow it would help some poor soul renew himself. Satan, through the means of alcohol, surely had him by the sleeve. Trying to picture himself as sober, clean, not hungry, and holding a job seemed dubious. Just one day at a time, he thought. Just one day at a time.

The first week was difficult. He had paid for a week in advance at the hotel. Sitting in the barely furnished room was too hard. He tried to concentrate on just getting through the day without needing a drink. He had a little over a thousand dollars in his pocket. It would be so easy to just walk to the local liquor store or bar and get his fill. He took long walks through the rail yards and visited the Turbo-Glide on a daily basis.

He ate one good meal every day and also purchased a bottle of vitamins. He couldn't believe how sickly he had become over time.

During his second week at the hotel, he got a job unloading bundles of flour from boxcars from a notice that had been posted near the hotel. Most of the workers, except for the foreman, were drifters or bums just like Ernie.

The foreman took a liking to Ernie. Unlike the rest, Ernie was always punctual, never missed a day of work, and worked harder than the others. The minimum-wage paycheck he received paid for his room and meals. After a month, the foreman offered Ernie a full-time position driving a forklift. Ernie accepted the offer.

As long as he was at work, it seemed much easier to deal with his drinking problem. Going to the junkyard and sitting in his old Chevy always motivated him to go on for another day. The full-time position paid more, and he had opened a savings account at a bank just up the street.

Ernie joined a support group of folks with the same illness that he had. He attended meetings twice a week, listened and talked with others. Eventually he had saved enough money to obtain a place of his own. It was small and simply furnished, but had a garage. He rented a truck, drove to the junkyard, and piece by piece, his old friend, the Chevy, was hauled in the back. The rusted pile of metal sitting in the corner of the garage didn't resemble anything remotely close to a car, but that was all right. A few months ago he hadn't resembled anything close to a normal human being. He wasn't completely out of the woods yet, but he was sober, had gained weight, and was holding a steady job.

Ernie smiled as he walked across the church parking lot. It had been seven years since that cold rain-swept night at the junkyard. He was married now. Alice, a woman he had met at one of his support meetings, had screwed her life up just about as badly as he had. Together they had kicked the devil squarely in the head and now marched amongst the ranks of the sober. Ernie had a good job with the railroad, while Alice remained at home, looking after their two children. Ernie Jr. had just turned five, and the baby was seven months.

The Turbo-Glide had been restored again to its original two-tone color, every inch of the car refurbished to its former styling. Alice and the baby sat in the back of the Chevy. Little Ernie liked to sit up front next to Dad.

Ernie looked both ways before turning out of the church parking lot to the street. Little Ernie tugged at his father's sleeve as he spoke, "Dad, know what?"

"No...what, Ernie."

The five-year-old smiled broadly as he ran his small hand across the dashboard. "I can't wait till I get my *first car.*"

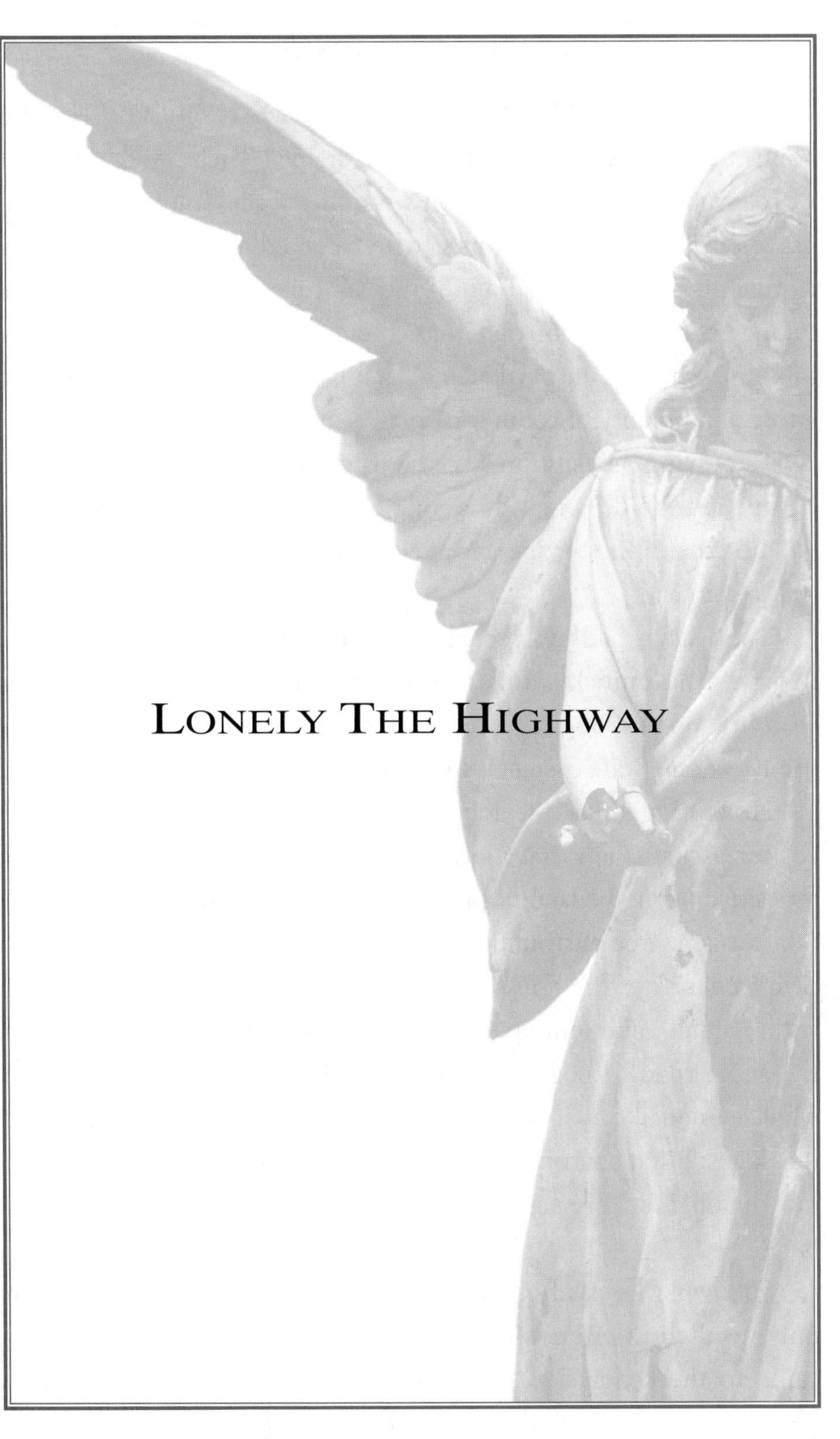

Lonely The Highway

ANGELS' FOOTPRINTS

"DO YOU HAVE ANY IDEA HOW MANY PEOPLE ARE going to stop by because they need help?" These were the first words out of Holis Fagan's son's mouth as they pulled up in the gravel driveway. Jana, Holis's, wife, seemed to ignore her son's comments as she climbed out of the car, turned in a complete circle taking in her new surroundings, then started for the front door talking to no one in particular, "This is perfect. Fireplace, two-car garage and plenty of room for Fritz."

Removing the ignition keys, Holis gaffed off his son's remark as he opened the driver's side door. "I don't think that many people will bother us. Maybe one once in a while but I don't think it'll be all that often."

The Fagans had just recently moved from upstate Pennsylvania to northern Kentucky, Holis transferring with his employer, residing with his son and dog for two months while Jana remained back in the Keystone State assigned the task of selling the family home.

Holis didn't like the idea of being apart from Jana, but the realtor assured him that a quick sale seemed rather evident, their attractive three-bedroom ranch sitting at an angle on a three-quarter-acre tree-surrounded lot just off a peaceful country road. Two weeks after the house went on the market, three other homes within a half mile went up for sale. There were only seven houses on the short road to begin with, the four FOR SALE signs stuck in what seemed like every other yard sending out a number of negative messages: What's wrong with this neighborhood? Why is everyone moving out? Is there a major highway coming through? Is the water bad?

Following week after week of OPEN HOUSE Sundays, which only resulted in offers that teetered on the brink of farcical, Holis came to the conclusion that Jana should move out, leaving their current real estate quagmire in the competent hands of the realtor. Jana agreed, as they couldn't afford another house until their present home was sold.

Holis's son's opinion of large numbers of people stopping by the rental house was based on the location of the property. Positioned just short of a quarter-mile from the off-ramp of the city's four-lane bypass, the two-story brick residence would surely attract countless motorists with all sorts of mechanical problems associated with automobile travel. It was a month to the day that they had first occupied the house. A family barbecue was in full swing in the back yard, as Holis informed his son that his prognostication of passing motorists paying them numerous visits had not come to pass.

Derek, his son, taking his first bite out of a juicy burger looked up at the driveway, then smiled as he wiped ketchup from the side of his mouth as he spoke through a mouthful of beef and bun. "The first of many has just arrived."

Following Derek's stare, Holis noticed the faded red Jeep creeping slowly up the drive, a steady stream of smoke escaping the hood. Finally rolling to a stop, the vehicle's operator climbed out, walked to the front and released the hood. Carefully turning the radiator cap, the man quickly jumped back avoiding the small eruption of fluid that spewed upward, sending a shower of hot water over the engine. Ten minutes later, the driver having sampled a tall glass of Jana's sun-brewed tea, backed the Jeep out the driveway, the radiator once again filled with cool water.

The following Wednesday they received a short visit by a local TV repairman who had been blessed with a flat, had made it to the off ramp and was in desperate need of a phone. Two days later, an older couple from Wisconsin pulled up in the driveway requiring directions to Rt. 65 South. They were on their way to visit their kids in Nashville and had somehow managed to get lost.

A week later, Holis, after an extremely hard day at work, stopped at the mailbox as he noticed the dilapidated two-tone Saab parked in the grass next to the maple tree in the front yard. Jana, meeting him on the porch explained that the owner lived on the other side of town. He wasn't exactly sure what was wrong with the car but it was on its last leg anyway. He had borrowed the phone to call his sister to come and pick him up and assured Jana that he would return the next day to retrieve the crippled automobile.

The next week netted only one troubled visitor, the following week three and the week after that another couple looking for directions. Holis was on the verge of believing that his son had been correct in his statement of the smoking Jeep of weeks ago as "the first of many."

Over the course of the next two months, there was only one seven-day period when their privacy had not been invaded by some stranger in need of their help. With each person who drove up the driveway or walked across the adjacent field to knock on their door, Holis's level of patience seemed to deteriorate. During the July 4th weekend, Jana realized just how negative her husband had become in regard to lending a helping hand as he waved sarcastically at a lady whose tire he had just changed. Turning to Jana, he stated that maybe the house had been occupied previously by some individual who had passed on, leaving the house now possessed due to the fact that during the person's lifetime they had passed many a motorist who had broken down and never stopped to offered any help. Therefore anyone who lived in the house now was punished by an unending parade of helpless motorists.

The only other possibility, according to Holis, was that there must be some sort of magnetic force field stretching two to three miles in either direction of the off ramp that caused passing vehicles to run out of gas, their engines to overheat and perfectly normal tires to lose air. And let's not forget the memory loss of the drivers themselves who started out knowing exactly where they were going but suddenly got lost.

Holis and Jana, having experienced a little over twenty-three years of wedded bliss normally agreed on just about everything. The number of times that they had disagreed on family situations could be counted on one hand. This business of countless numbers of visitors stopping by the house definitely fell into the category of two differing opinions on the matter.

It wasn't that Holis didn't want to help people—it was just so inconvenient. Jana tried to make light of the subject by comically remarking that maybe his work schedule was posted on a blinking sign along the highway or possibly those who were in need of help hid along the bypass in the nearby woods across the field as they peered through binoculars until he arrived home, at which point the decision would be made to approach the house for assistance.

Holis didn't appreciate Jana's attempt at humor. As far as he was concerned the number of times that he had been interrupted by strangers when he had just arrived home and had sat down at the dinner table or was ready to crawl into bed was no laughing matter. He just couldn't comprehend how his wife always remained so calm.

There wasn't the slightest hesitation on her part when a complete stranger rang the bell. She'd open the door without even looking out the front window. Then before the visitors could even utter a word, she'd greet them with a "Hello" or "How are you today?" After listening to whatever problem they had been plagued with, she'd invite them inside to use the phone, get out of the heat or enjoy a refreshing beverage.

Holis was more skeptical of people. The few times he had been home alone when motorists came to call, he would always peer out the front window curtains, then exit by the back door and approach the visitor from the side of the house. He never used a pleasant tone of voice, wanting to leave the impression on whoever stood on his doorstep that if their intention was anything less than honest or if they were of the mind to steal or harm—that they had indeed come to the wrong house. They were never allowed to step inside. If they required the use of the phone, he'd ask for the number and make the call while they remained outdoors.

Jana claimed that he was just too suspicious of folks and that he needed to lighten up. She did admit that there were less than desirable individuals who traveled the bypass, but the Good Lord would protect their home from evil and destruction. She was of the opinion that Holis was just viewing the situation the wrong way. Maybe they had been visited by angels or possibly the Lord had guided them to live at the house in order to help others.

This religious outlook on motorists who required help combined with their own views on faith in God was one of the topics in their lives that they bumped heads on. Jana was a devout believer, while Holis seemed to travel the road to faith with his parking brake on. Jana possessed an unquestioning belief that did not require proof or evidence, Holis always searching for an absolute answer—a sign that indicated his exact direction. Jana held a steadfast devotion to support or help others, Holis leaning toward thinking the worst of people first—that they were out to take advantage of most situations.

It was a Holloween night, and Holis had arrived home from work early. The ceramic pumpkin filled to the brim with assorted candy sat by the front door ready for the onslaught of trick or treaters from the houses up the road. Holis was out back trying his best to rake the thousands upon thousands of leaves that had fallen from the four maple trees in the yard, but the blustery wind was not about to let him experience a lawn free of leaves.

Holis noticed his wife at the kitchen window as she held up a steaming pot—a signal that dinner was about to be put on the table. Rounding up their feisty pup, Holis stepped inside the back door, removed his windbreaker and washed up for supper.

Seated at the dining room table, Holis inspected the evening meal: fish sticks, macaroni and cheese, broccoli on the side. He smiled—one of his favorites. This particular combination of food had been at the top of his cuisine list ever since he had been a young lad. Of course back in those days, broccoli or any other green vegetable for that matter, had not been part of the simplistic feast until years later.

Jana poured two glasses of iced tea, then reached for Holis's hand as she blessed the meal, adding a thank you for their many blessings. Holis was just stabbing his first fish stick when the familiar sound of the doorbell reverberated through the house.

Jana, as usual, opened the door not having the remotest idea of who stood on the front porch. From his angle in the dining room, Holis could see the two callers framed in the open door; an elderly woman with dazzling white hair, her thin body wrapped in a long light gray coat trimmed in gold. Clutching onto her right hand stood a young girl, probably about five years of age dressed in an angel's outfit complete with polyester silver wings and a golden halo.

Just trick or treaters, thought Holis. It seemed too early as the clock on the kitchen wall displayed 6:05. The man at the market down the road had told him that most parents didn't start delivering their costumed offspring until around seven or so.

The fish stick was halfway to his mouth as Jana entered the dining room flanked by the woman and child as she explained. "This is Mrs. Starr and her granddaughter. They were on their way to a church party for the children when their car suffered a flat down on the freeway. Her husband has a heart condition and can't change the tire, so she walked up here to see if she could use the phone to call her son so he can drive out and give them a hand."

The fish stick became disengaged from the fork and commenced to fall into the macaroni with a resounding plop. As Jana led them to the kitchen, she asked them if they cared for something to drink. The little girl remained behind as she stood near the far corner of the table, an innocent smile taking the edge off the bitterness that was quickly invading Holis's mind, his supper once again ruined by another stranger from the highway.

The child wasn't as shy as she appeared as she stared at the platter of three-inch strips of fish. "Fish sticks are my second favorite," she said. "Fried chicken is my most favorite...that's what we're having at the party tonight."

"Oh…I see," responded Holis.

Suddenly, Jana was at his side, her hand on his shoulder. "Mrs. Starr's son isn't at home. Do you think we could give her a hand?"

Holis answered, "Sure, no problem," but his thought pattern was not agreeing with the words coming from his mouth, his brain delivering a message of *What's this we business? I'm the one who has to make the trip down to the freeway while my macaroni and cheese is slowly changing from a palatable delicacy into a congealed glob not fit for human consumption.*

Moments later, the windbreaker once again buttoned up to his neck, the lug wrench from the trunk of his car grasped in his hand he made his way to the edge of the field, Fritz now tied in the backyard barking his disapproval at strangers infringing on his small dominion. Mrs. Starr and the little girl walked right next to Holis apologizing for interrupting his supper, the child's flimsy wings fluttering in the wind.

The grandmother was full of questions: "How long have you lived here? Do you like the area? Are you from here?"

Holis's answers were short but polite: "A few months. I guess. No."

The disabled car finally came into sight—a long white Cadillac. The car must have recently been washed as its white paint gleamed in the setting sun. A tall man, obviously Mr. Starr, dressed in a powder blue three-piece suit stepped out of the lengthy car as the trio approached. After some brief introductions, the gray-haired man walked to the rear of the car explaining that the spare was in the trunk.

The operation of changing a tire had become routine to Holis as over the past few months he had performed the now commonplace motions of tire changing more than the local auto centre at the mall. Removing the spare from the trunk, he went to work setting the jack, extracting the tire from the rim, placing the new tire back on, then finally tightening the lugs.

"Well, that should do it," Holis said as he stood and turned. The sun had assumed one of those daily blinding positions low in the sky, the blaring ball of light stabbing at his squinting eyes. He could barely make out Mr. and Mrs. Starr and their granddaughter. Framed in the intense brightness, their bodies appeared to be opaque, outlined by the sunlight.

The sudden warmth flooded over his body as he placed the flat in the trunk. Mr. Starr approached, his hand extended in gratitude.

Holis looked directly into the man's face. Mr. Starr's eyes were so penetrating, yet soothing.

Placing both of his hands over Holis's right hand he spoke, "Mr. Fagan, thank you so much for walking down here to help us. When we first stopped, we saw your home and hoped that whoever lived there was of a good nature. You're a lucky man to live so close to the freeway. You must get a lot of opportunities to help people. I have always been of the opinion that every time an individual helps someone out, he's building his treasures in heaven. Some folks go through their entire life, not getting many chances to help other people, but you have been blessed with countless times to reach out." With that, his handshake became firm sending a tingling sensation up Holis's arm to his shoulder.

The little angel stepped forward, a square white box held in her dainty hands. Holding the carton out at arm's length, she offered, "We're sorry for coming to your house during your dinner. Please…take this cake."

"I couldn't do that," Holis objected. "I mean…it's not necessary."

Mrs. Starr took the cake from the child and placed it in Holis's hands as she explained, "This is a special cake… and besides that, we insist."

"God bless you," Mr. Starr said as the three walked to the Cadillac, climbed in and drove off. Holis had the strangest feeling, the bright sun penetrating his skin down to his very bones as he watched the car pull away, the little angel in the rear window waving goodbye. Just as the car was out of what he considered readable range, he noticed the license plate: HEVN BND.

Crossing the field, the cake box and lug wrench balanced in his hands, something occurred to him. Mr. Starr had addressed him as

Mr. Fagan. If he remembered, Mrs. Starr had introduced him as Holis, not Mr. Fagan. He couldn't recall the woman mentioning his last name. How could her husband possibly know it? Maybe she had referred to him by his last name and he just hadn't been paying attention. His thoughts were interrupted as he stepped from the field onto the edge of his front lawn.

Looking up, he saw Jana walking across the grass to meet him, a steaming cup of coffee in her right hand. Fritz was now untied, barking up a storm as he raced across the yard in pursuit of a stray leaf. Accepting the white box, Jana asked, "What's this?"

"It's a cake," Holis answered. "They insisted that I take it. I really didn't want to, but for some strange reason I couldn't say no." Leading her husband by the arm, Jana suggested that they could enjoy the cake for dessert; his dinner was in the oven.

Dinner complete, Holis prepared a small plate for Fritz who had been waiting patiently for some table scraps. Sitting back, Holis looked at his wife. "Listen," he said. "I can't explain why I feel differently at this moment about the constant flow of highway visitors, but I guess I'm not bitter about it anymore. Maybe you were right about angels stopping by and about the Lord having us live here so that we can help others. It has dawned on me that He's going to keep right on sending folks until I get the idea."

Jana patted Holis on the shoulder as she reached for the white box. "I'm glad you feel better about it. Let's have some dessert." Lifting the lid, she smiled. "You're not going to believe this…angel food cake."

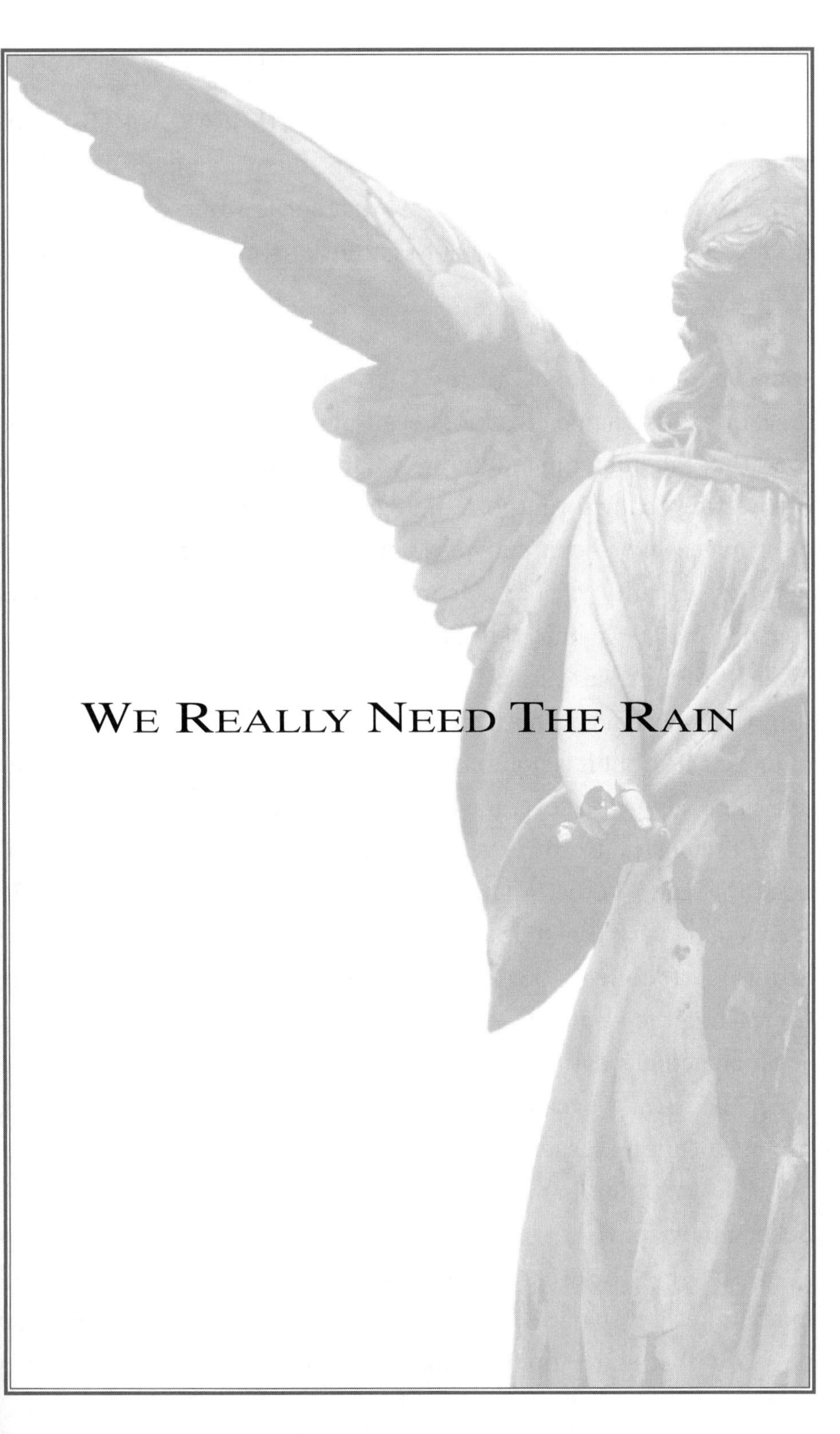

We Really Need The Rain

ANGELS' FOOTPRINTS

I'VE NEVER BEEN BIG ON CLICHÉS. AS A RULE OF thumb, whenever I hear somebody speaking emphatically about those two birds that were killed by that single stone, or the famous rolling stone that never seems to gather any moss, I always have a tendency to roll my eyes.

Thinking back, it seems to me that a few decades past, somewhere in the midst of my twelve years of basic education, a teacher, whose name I cannot recall at the moment, informed the class that the human mind knows what it is that we are going to say before we vocally form those thoughts into words.

I have never been convinced that this scientific phenomenom pertains to nifty clichés. Over the years, I have come to the conclusion that we blurt out these dainty little phrases without much thought on our part at all. I'm sorry, but I guess you'll just have to forgive me. I thought that I could start this story off without the use of any clichés, but it is not to be. So, if after reading the next line, you feel like rolling your eyes, go right ahead. I'll understand.

If I had a quarter for every time I have heard it said, "We really need the rain," I'd be financially independent—a wealthy fellow. It seems that every Tom, Dick and Harry that comes down the pike has acquired a college degree in meteorology and is skillful at forecasting the weather.

If an actual weatherman, or even a local farmer, declares that we need the rain, we can pretty well stand on the fact that their prognostication is true. On the other hand, if the bus driver or the teller down at the bank makes the same statement, what level of belief can we have?

Discussing the weather just seems like the thing to do. How many times have you received or maybe even mailed off a letter or postcard that starts off reading, "The weather here is just fine."

Perhaps, we talk about the weather at times due to the fact that we can't think of anything else to say at the moment.

I recall one particular incident in the past where talking about rain was a temporary solution to an awkward situation. It was my second year at college. I had, for some unknown reason, allowed myself to be hornswoggled into a blind date. There I was, sitting in a corner booth at Stein's Café, trying to envision the approaching evening. Would this girl be so attractive that I couldn't possibly imagine her wanting to go out with me, or would she stand a better than average chance of starring in a B-grade monster flick? I recall drinking my Irish coffee and saying a silent prayer: *God, please just let her be normal!*

My prayer was answered. Greta, who eventually became my wonderful wife, was indeed normal. Pleasant smile, nice hair, great-looking sundress and fashionable sandals.

Following a transitory introduction by my roommate and his date, we were left alone, sitting at a table, our faces a mere twenty-four inches apart. Greta appeared to be rather outgoing, and I have never been at a loss for words in any situation. I really didn't understand why we were both burdened with silence for ten seconds, which believe me, seemed like an eternity.

Greta made the first move, turning toward the front window and commenting, "Looks like rain out there."

I looked out the window, then chimed right in, with I might add, a touch of conviction, "Yeah, we really need the rain." At the time I wasn't looking toward her so I'm not sure if she rolled her eyes or not.

Most people probably don't dwell that much on the natural wonder of rainfall. That is, until we receive too much or not enough. There isn't much we can do about controlling the rain—we just have to deal with it. On the flip side of the coin, the rain can, at times, control us; what we do and where we go.

As children, it can be the dominating factor determining whether we can go outside and play or become trapped inside the house for the entire day. But then, there are also those delightful moments when Mom permits us to run back and forth yelling and screaming in a summer downpour.

As we get older, a poorly timed downpour can cancel our softball game or afternoon of golf. But even as adults, a steady rain can seem like a blessing, After an all-night storm, we discover in the morning that the ground is too soaked for us to mow the one-and-a-half acres of grass surrounding our house. Maybe we curl up with a good book and a pot of European-blended coffee, or maybe a movie and buttered popcorn later that afternoon at the mall. The delight of a leisure-filled day can be short-lived. It rains for days and the grass is now machete height. It will now take twice as long in the eighty-five-degree sun to manicure the lawn back to a state of acceptability.

In the summer of 1952, the rain touched my life in a way I never could have imagined. The train ride from Ohio to Missouri, according to my mother, would take the whole day. Having just graduated from the fifth grade, I considered myself quite fair when it came to mathematics. To me, the whole day meant just that—the whole day, twenty-four hours. Ma said, that with layovers it would take about fourteen hours to get there. When questioning her why she said the entire day when she really meant fourteen hours, she said that it was just a way of saying the better part of the day. Back then, there were a lot of things adults said that I didn't understand.

That was the first year I traveled to Grandpa Slater's place by myself. The two previous summers he and Grandma had driven from Missouri, stayed for a week, then took me back to their farm for the remainder of the summer.

Good old Mom had packed me ample food—enough to supply a small army. We weren't even an hour outside of the station when I found myself devouring a banana, a bag of salted peanuts and a bologna sandwich, while I reviewed my list of handwritten instructions: *"Don't lose your phone number or Grandpa's either, stay on the train...no matter what! If you have to use the bathroom, use the facility on the train. Do not...I repeat, do not get off the train until you arrive in Ralston. Don't talk to strangers. Mind your own business. If you have a problem, see the conductor."*

We had just crossed over the Indiana line when I first noticed the rain. It was just a light sprinkling, but nonetheless rain, which according to one of the men sitting in front of me, we really needed. Two passengers, who looked to be businessmen wearing dress suits and shiny shoes and with briefcases at their feet, rambled on about the rain. One of the men who was from Oklahoma said that four years ago during a two-month drought down home, the members of his church, the entire congregation, had dropped to their knees at the direction of their pastor and prayed to God that He would send rain.

The man laughed as he puffed on a big black cigar and went on to say that the following year they got more rain than they had bargained for. The congregation, the very same folks were once again on bended knees, but this time requesting the Almighty to put a stop to the precipitation.

I never forgot that conversation, and over the years, I've thought about it many times. It's as if we stumble through life searching for a happy medium in almost everything we do. Why should the weather be any different? Just the right amount of rain seemed rational, rather than too much or not enough.

I remember gazing at the tiny raindrops as they collected on the window pane. They looked harmless enough. It was hard to imagine enough of these tiny droplets of water could join together creating too much rain.

It was just a little after nine that night when the train rolled into Ralston, the rain still pouring down, but now much harder. I no sooner stepped down onto the wooden platform when I saw Gramps and Gram Slater standing near the side of the one-room station next to their old pickup. Hank, their blue-tick hound who had to be at least a hundred years old, sat proudly in the back. My grandparents were exactly the same age: seventy-two. They looked like old people—or at least what I thought old people should look like.

Gram was on the pudgy side. She was always saying she was going to lose weight, but never did seem to slim down. She made all of her own clothing. I can't ever remember seeing her in anything but a dress. I don't think she owned a swimsuit or a pair of jeans. She had the same old hairdo: blackish-gray locks pulled back in a tight bun, piled on top of her round face. Gramps said that when she let it down it fell clean to the floor.

Gramps was skinny and didn't eat enough to feed a bird. Despite his disinterest in nourishment, he was fit as an ox according to the doctor, who he paid a regular visit every spring for his annual checkup. He always looked like he had just stepped out of a field: baggy bib overalls, straw hat that should have been pitched years ago, and heavy-duty work boots that were always caked with mud or manure.

Gramps had four definitely distinctive characteristics: he was always smiling through his unkempt mustache, he managed the farm like a military installation, he did everything in harmony with the Good Book, and he loved to chew tobacco.

Gram was always on his case, scolding him, saying that for a religious man, she just couldn't fathom why in the world he had to stuff that terrible chew into his mouth. As far as she was concerned, it was an abomination.

Grampa Slater was a patient man. He never became upset when his wife of fifty-three years vocally attacked his only bad habit. He'd just spit on the ground, smile through tobacco-stained teeth and remark that we are all entitled to at least one vice. She'd always give him a look of disgust as she stomped off, looking toward heaven, her hands hiked high. "Save it for the Lord, Lester!" she'd shout. "God knows you'll probably be chewin' away when you're at the gate to Heaven!"

Aside from the tobacco habit, which I didn't think was any big deal, Grandpa Lester was an upstanding Christian in the community. He never gossiped, swore, drank, cheated or any of the other things people seemed to do. He sang in the church choir and helped with the collection on Sunday. Gram said that he couldn't hold a tune if his life depended on it, but maybe his effort to lift his voice in praise would offset the tobacco business in the eyes of the Lord.

Summers on Lester's farm required a different degree of religion than I was accustomed to back home in Ohio. Mom didn't attend church, so of course, neither did my brother Carl and I. We never questioned her reasons for not going. She was an adult—we were kids. It wasn't our place to pry.

Grandma Staler explained it to me once, telling me that my father had been a pilot in the Navy. During a mission, he was shot down behind what Gram referred to as enemy lines. After that, her daughter, my mother, seemed to reject faith. She just sort of drew a circle around herself. No one was allowed inside—including the Lord. I had seen my father's picture on the nightstand next to her bed many times. She didn't discuss him much. I guess it was just too difficult. She did say he had been an honest and hardworking man.

Every summer the eight-week vacation on the farm was a religious transformation. We attended church not only on Sunday morning, but Sunday night as well. Work on the farm came to a complete halt on Sundays. The Sabbath was a holy day and Lester said it was laid aside for rest and worship. Grandma always prepared a special meal on Sunday. My favorite was pot roast with corn on the cob, followed by her famous deep-dish blueberry pie.

Sunday was not the only day on the farm when Lester wielded his religious rules. We attended Wednesday evening service at the church and read the Bible every night following supper. Of course, I had to take my turn. I stumbled through countless thees, thous and thys. And, let's not forget those strange names in the Bible. Aside from John, James, Peter, Luke, Benjamin and a few others, no one alive today had those names. No wonder: who could pronounce them! I could be wrong, but I never heard of anyone with the name Jehoshaphat, Nebuchadnezzar, or Bathsheba.

To make things even worse, Gramps named every animal on the farm after some biblical character. He had a crazy old bull named Samson, Saul, the rooster; Moses, the barn cat, and a herd of cattle, sporting for the most part, unpronounceable names. During the summer of the great rain, Lester had seven new calves. He told me their names, but the only one I remembered was Noah.

His military routine of running the farm stemmed from his twenty-year hitch in the Army. Gram once told me that Lester had seen plenty of action and had been an officer the last eight years he was in. I asked her if he had ever killed an enemy soldier. She gave me a strange look, then reluctantly told me that he had only done his duty—he was a good man. From her answer, I kind of gathered, even though she never did say, that he had killed a man, especially the way she ended our conversation. She had said that I was never to ask him about it because he didn't like to discuss it.

Two decades of serving Uncle Sam had labeled Lester as a "lifer," and the discipline and regimentation of military life did not come to an end when he received his discharge. All the farm equipment had to be lined up perfectly at the end of the work day, and the hand tools hung in exact order in the barn and cleaned whenever used. Work activities were always put into motion the same time each day. I was always confused about what time it was. I could never figure how two o'clock was actually 1400 hours.

That first night I fell asleep quickly, the long train ride taking its toll. My room was on the second floor of the two-story stone house in the front right corner. I considered my room to be "really neat": rough-sawn walls, which always had the deep aroma of cedar, a massive green and brown oriental throw rug centered on the polished oak floor, and a big walk-in closet that would have passed for a room in itself. There was an antique rocker next to the window, a maple dresser, and a king-size bed with one of Gram's prize-winning quilts. I had my own small black-and-white TV and private bathroom. I was indeed a king!

My head sank deeply into the comfy feathered pillow as I snuggled beneath the quilt, the rain outside the window drumming away at the corrugated metal roof over the front porch. There was nothing quite like the sound of the rain at night.

The next morning I was jerked out of a deep sleep by a loud clap of thunder, the rain outside the bedroom window falling harder than

I could ever remember. It rained the whole week, slowing down at times, but never stopping.

The rainy weather never seemed to bother Gramps, who kept everything going according to his daily military system. Despite the rain, the animals had to be fed, the barn and stalls had to be cleaned and the equipment had to be oiled. The only difference was that we were soaked to the skin from early morning until that evening at supper.

That first Sunday at church turned out to be a royal disaster. The summer bazaar, which had been in the planning stages for weeks, was kicked off immediately following the morning service. Pastor Meirs apologized for the weeklong rain and said that they'd just have to make the best of things.

Activities were scheduled to get underway at a small clearing next to Hanson's Creek, but that was an impossibility as the normally tranquil stream had overflowed its banks, turning the clearing into a sizable lake, which meant that everything had to be moved to the church basement. Every type of imaginable home-cooked food was lined up on old card tables. Placing two deviled eggs next to a scoop of potato salad and a hamburger, I remember thinking that we had more food in the basement than some countries eat in a year.

People stood or sat shoulder to shoulder, balancing paper plates brimming with fried chicken, corn on the cob, spiced apples, and salad, as children of all ages darted in and out of the hungry crowd. Many of the men, covering their lunch as best they could, made a sudden dash to the covered pavilion out behind the church next to the ball field. I grabbed my second slice of peach crumb pie and followed, not wishing to be left behind with the women and other children.

The small, normally quiet stream running just south of the field had turned into a version of a raging river, the squalid water swirling and splashing as it carried assorted barrels, tires, logs and other debris downstream. Many of the men, as soon as they reached the protection of the shelter, lit up pipes, cigars or cigarettes, but Lester was satisfied to chew on his favorite brand of tobacco. As the thunder, lightning and torrential rain continued to scourge the countryside, I sat silently and listened to the various conversations:

"The fields are saturated! If the rain stops in the next coupla days it might drain off."

"Weather bureau says there's another big storm followin' this'n."

"My fields can't stand another week of rain. I'll lose my whole crop."

A man near the back of the pavilion blew a long stream of bluish smoke toward the rafters as he commented, "We can't handle much more. The creeks are way up now. That's just the beginning of it. They're sayin' that the river will probably crest on Wednesday. When she goes…we've had it!"

The storm conversations carried on for nearly two hours with the men discussing the consequences of a possible flood: the destruction, the cleanup and the possibility of death. Long after the men returned to the church basement to put away tables and chairs while the women cleaned up, I stayed outside in the shelter and thought about what the men had said. I sat on one of the wooden picnic tables and observed the local ants making a feast out of the pie crumbs at my feet as I stared at the creek, which appeared to have risen higher just in the last hour.

Later, on the way back to the farm, Gram remarked about how the rain was causing havoc. Back then, I had no idea what havoc meant, but just from the dismal look on her face, combined with the way she said it, I figured it couldn't be anything good.

The rain continued through the night and by Monday morning slowed to a drizzle, the sun starting to peek through the clouds. Eating hot cakes and sausage in the rustic country kitchen, I figured it was over, but then a phone call expelled any thoughts of sunny days on the farm. Hanging up, Lester informed us that another large front, larger than the last was heading our way. A meeting was being called at the fire hall. The river was rising faster than estimated. It looked like it might crest on Tuesday rather than on Wednesday.

The storm had picked up considerably as Lester and I pulled into the fire hall. The dirt parking lot, which had turned into a sea of muddy tire tracks, was crammed with cars, pickup trucks and county vehicles. Both firetrucks had been pulled into a huge pole barn behind the hall in order to accommodate all of the concerned citizens. The main room was packed as folks stood around in groups or sat on folding chairs drinking coffee or smoking, a large ventilator working hard to carry the cloud of cigarette smoke from the hall. Surprisingly, I was the only kid in attendance. Lester bought me a soda from a vending machine and told me to sit in the corner.

There was a broad representation of townfolk standing around the room: the fire chief, police captain, members of various churches, and also the Jaycees. Fleck Nelson, who wore a patch over his right eye, ran the local filling station. He was there with Bob Tetherton, president of the bank.

Gramps weaved in and out of the crowd, shaking hands and waving at people. It seemed like he knew everyone there. Mike Edwards, the city manager, started the meeting off by banging a hammer on a water pipe. Flashes of lightning lit up the windows as Ralston citizens laid out their plan for defense. At times the rain pounded so hard on the roof, it was difficult to hear what was being said.

Later that afternoon, I found myself, along with everyone else in town and the surrounding county, down on the banks near the river. The city snow removal equipment was not adequate for the chore at hand so the local farmers drove their tractors and backhoes into town where an organized motor pool was set up.

Trucks of sand and dirt were hauled in along with endless stacks of empty heavy-duty burlap sacks. Teenagers, both male and female alike, filled the sacks, then pitched them onto hay wagons that were transported to the river where rows of men stacked the sacks six high.

Hinkleman's Construction Company donated three bulldozers, which were hauled to the river where they were used to move tons of dirt toward the river's edge. The women operated food tents in a nearby park where my job, along with a host of other youngsters, was to deliver hot coffee and sandwiches to the workers. After my tenth trip up the steep, muddy embankment hauling coolers of sandwiches and thermos after thermos of coffee, I lost count.

Sloshing through three-inch mud, wearing a dingy yellow raincoat that was two sizes too large, I started wondering about my brother at Uncle Clay's farm in upstate New York. He was probably lying in the warm afternoon sun, his fishing line gently bobbing in the pond water out behind the barn near the meadow. Lucky bum!

Just when I thought it wasn't possible for the rain to come down any harder, it did just that. Grandma said that the man-made fortification near the bank of the river would only gain us about two extra days before the water would flood the town. I didn't get to bed until one in the morning. I think it was the quickest I had ever gone to sleep. I had always heard people talk of falling asleep as soon as their head hit the pillow, but this was the first time I had ever experienced it.

Gramps was up and gone by the time I awoke the next morning. Gram made me a great breakfast, and then we left for the river; another day of delivering soggy sandwiches and hot coffee in the pouring rain.

The rain had slowed down, but was still methodical. It had grown colder for some reason. Seated on an old tire on the mud floor in the corner of the tent, I wrapped my hands around a mug of hot cocoa. The chocolate really wasn't that warm, but my love for the dark liquid was overshadowed by my chattering teeth as I asked Gram if I could try some coffee.

"Ever had coffee?" she asked.

"No," I replied, "but if it's hot, that's all I care about."

I never did get to experience the coffee sample that day. As I brought the metal cup of steaming brown java to my lips, the tent suddenly gave way from the weight of the excessive rain that had collected on the canvas roof. The coffee spilled on my lap, but the burning sensation quickly vanished as I was pounded to the muddy ground by a deluge of cold rain water.

The first thing I saw was Grandma Slater sitting spread-eagled in the mud, her eyeglasses cocked sideways on her face and a loaf of now soggy bread clutched in her hand. It was the first and only time I ever heard the women curse. Her temporary use of foul language ended abruptly as she noticed my stare. Then, she did the oddest thing. She slapped her knee, smiled, and started to laugh. "You okay, boy?"

She laughed harder and started to cough when I held up my mug and asked, "Could I please have a refill?"

An hour later, an empty forty-foot tractor trailer pulled in. A second tent had collapsed and the other two looked like they could go at any minute. The inside of the trailer became our new command post for sandwiches and coffee, while the heavy downpour continued pounding the metal roof and sides of the forty-foot cubical, making it nearly impossible to hear anything but the rain.

Wednesday morning brought more rain with a hard line of thunderstorms reported to hit around one in the afternoon. The work at the river had been halted. The sandbags had been stacked up to a point where they were starting to collapse in spots.

There was no way to impede the river from flowing over its banks now. The fact that a flood would occur was inevitable. Now, the issue was how to deal with it. Prevention was no longer discussed since the goal now centered on survival. The radio was jammed with weather warnings. The familiar Country and Western music and the local farm report were not to be heard. The National Weather Bureau was strongly suggesting that, unless it was absolutely necessary to remain in the surrounding area, residents should consider evacuating.

People who chose to leave moved everything of value to the second floor, provided they had one, packed the kids and the family pets in the car and drove to the nearest relatives. Most of the people who stayed behind did so in order to be of assistance.

Gramps and I drove Grandma up to the local high school, which sat at the very top of Knoll's Hill. The gymnasium and classrooms had been prepared as temporary shelter for those who had nowhere to go. I wasn't in the best of moods. My summer vacation in Ralston had come to an immediate halt. Mom had called and wanted me on the first train back home. On the way to the station, Gramps said that it was for the best and not to get upset with her.

I was concerned about Grandma. Gramps told me she would be

fine on the hill. If the water got that high it would be the second coming of the Lord! He went on to explain that that couldn't happen because the Bible said the next time the world was destroyed it was to be by fire.

We had to drive adjacent to the river for about a half mile on the way to the station. The muddy river was a sight, the water already starting to splash down the sloping embankment as trees, tires and even an occasional building floated by. A small group of people had gathered at the base of the embankment, looking up at the sandbag wall, which was straining to withhold the tons of water.

"Why are those people standing so close?" I asked.

Lester popped a wad of tobacco inside his mouth. "They're waiting to watch the flood."

"But that doesn't make any sense," I said.

He made a strange-looking face at me as he stated. "I guess it's God's way of eliminating the stupid."

I must have given him an odd stare as the look on his face suddenly turned to one of great concern. "If you ever tell Gram what I said, I'll tan your hide."

We had just passed the gate of the farm as Gramps was telling me that next year I could visit longer than usual, when the newscaster on the radio suddenly changed his tone of voice, *"We have just received word that a thirty-foot section of the river bank has collapsed with three other sections about to give way. Anyone…I repeat, anyone residing east or south of the river must move to the second floor immediately or drive north."*

Another reporter broke in, *"Bob…the whole east side embankment has deteriorated. There's a wall of water moving down Poplar Street. From up here in the copter, you can see that it's wiping out everything in its path!"*

We Really Need The Rain

Gramps made a wide U-turn in the field, mowing down row after row of cornstalks as the `49 flatbed Chevy truck bounced back toward the dirt road. "Hold on, boy!" he yelled. "Hanson's Creek will never be able to hold all that water. It'll be here in less than five minutes. We've got to get back to Knoll's Hill...pronto!"

I looked out the side window up the road. Somewhere out there in the dismal void of the driving rain there was a wall of muddy water. The front end of the truck bounced high off the ground, landed on the road, then stalled.

Gramps turned the key and slammed his foot down on the gas pedal at the same time. The engine started instantly and the old truck lurched forward only to sputter to a stop again. The radio died out just as the reporter said something about devastating.

I looked across the road at the herd of cattle standing near the double-decker barn. "Gramps!" I shouted, "What about the herd?"

He shouted back as he desperately tried to start the truck. "We were suppose to truck them up to Ralph Fox's place after I dropped you off. Too late now."

Suddenly, Gramps had a look of disbelief on his face, the likes of which I had never seen before. I turned, looking down the road. There it was! The creek had turned into a wall of brown water, pushing tall trees, earth, fence posts and everything else in its path of destruction out of the way.

Gramps grabbed me by the shoulders as he ordered. "Listen to me. We have to get out of the truck. If we stay in here, we'll drown. When that water hits, this truck will be rolling down the road and probably shattered to bits. Won't be safe to be near it. When you get out, run around the front end and grab hold of me. We'll just have to try and swim out of this." The last thing I heard him say was something about the Lord.

The floodwater was roaring down the lane faster than Gramps had anticipated. I no sooner got the door closed when I was slammed into the side of the truck by the force of the foremost edge of the water. As the truck rolled, I was swept forward over the top of the roof. I could sense the water all around me, filling my nose, ears, mouth and eyes. I clamped my eyes tightly as I tumbled across the road. Swimming crossed my mind but the thought was out of the question. The speeding water was taking everything in its deadly swath.

At first, I didn't even realize I had been holding my breath. I knew I could hold my breath for two minutes. I had tested myself in the pool at school during swimming lessons. But that was different. When I got to the point where I needed air, I simply stood up. There was no danger of drowning. My lungs were already screaming for air and I had only been under a few seconds. I hadn't really had an opportunity to take a deep breath before the water had overtaken me.

My body was suddenly stopped! Something was blocking my forward motion as the water rushed by. I felt my body being propelled up the front of an object, then my head broke the surface of the water as I gasped for air. A tree that somehow had remained rooted had prevented me from being carried away further. I wrapped myself around the trunk and looked in every direction. There was a sea of muddy water as far as I could see. The truck was nowhere in sight—Gramps was gone. There were no buildings that could be seen—parts of the barn were drifting by.

Then, I saw the cattle. The entire herd had been swept down the road. A few of the frightened animals were making an instinctive attempt at swimming, but the current was rapidly overpowering their efforts. Most of the cattle floated by, already dead. Tears came to my eyes as I saw two dead calves, the water sweeping them away.

Another calf was swept by, his head bobbing up and down in the swift current. He was making a terrible bawling sound, his eyes wide with fear. To this day, I've never been able to figure out what possessed me to leave the protection of that tree and swim after that calf, but that's exactly what I did.

I was trying my best to cut through the water smoothly, at the same time keeping my eyes on the helpless calf. The distance separating us didn't seem to be getting any less. The calf kept going down, but then would suddenly come up again.

Just as I was gaining ground, he went under, but didn't return to the surface. I can't ever remember being more upset at anything in my life than I was at that moment. I had gotten so close—he couldn't die. I had been so close to rescuing the little fellow.

The next thing I knew, he popped to the surface right in front of me. I grabbed him, wrapping my arms around his belly. There we were floating along at over twenty miles per hour. Another tree was coming up. I reached up, grabbing a two-inch thick limb. The calf was still in a state of panic, jerking back and forth, making my efforts to hold him and at the same time work my way toward the trunk next to impossible.

For a brief moment, I thought I was going to lose my grip. At the tender age of ten, I had never been faced with making major decisions in my life. Now, it was either my life or the calf's. I looked past the tree. There was only the sea of muddy brown, murky water in the distance. Nothing appeared that would offer a method to stop myself. If I let go of the calf, he would eventually die.

My arm was wrapped around him so tightly I couldn't have released him if I had wanted to. Inch by inch, I made my way up the limb, which was moving fiercely up and down and back and forth from the force of the raging water.

The calf was starting to calm down, possibly from fatigue. I got far enough along until I managed to lift him up into a Y-shaped bough in the trunk. I climbed to another branch higher up, reached down lifting the calf, pressing him to my chest.

There we sat, just two feet below us the water rushing by, small waves splashing upwards, almost as if they were liquid fingers trying to drag us back down. To the west, the sky was pitch black, evidence of yet more bad weather.

The calf seemed to be breathing normally again, his eyes no longer filled with fear. He licked my hand and gave me a soulful look, probably wondering where his mother was. What had happened to his normally simplistic life of grazing in the lavish grass and frolicking with the other young ones?

The rain was coming down in sheets, the wind was picking up, and the raindrops were like tiny ice picks pricking my face, arms, legs and hands. I noticed that one of my sneakers had been sucked from my foot. I pressed the calf closer to me as I started to shiver, the cold air turning my drenched body into an ice cube.

An hour passed as I wondered what had happened to Gramps. Was he even alive? Had any of the other cattle survived? The water had risen another foot. I turned my face into the rain as I glanced at the top of the tree. It rose another good twenty feet straight up toward the gray sky, but there was only three feet that was climbable or capable of supporting the combined weight of myself and the soggy calf.

It seemed like another hour had gone by, the water was now at my waist. I slowly made my way up to the last possible branch that could hold us, leaving the rushing water three feet below. I wondered what the time was. It had to be four…maybe five o'clock.

The wind had died down, but I was still cold. The calf seemed content as I balanced him across my left knee. I felt like my arms were going to fall off. In the distance, I could hear the sounds of a helicopter. The aircraft never came into sight and the sound of the beating blades slowly vanished.

The blackness of the sky had been replaced with a combination of light and dark gray, the rain slowed down, but still steady. I lost track of time, but had eventually come to the realization that it was close to nightfall. Suddenly, the rain stopped—the sky was clear. The moon was shining brilliantly casting an eerie pale light over the cold water surrounding me. There were a million stars scattered in the vast sky. I located the big dipper, then the little one. The water had risen another foot.

Then. I noticed something—something very large—very strange, as it floated silently on the surface of the water thirty yards away. I strained my eyes until the huge object became clear. A house—a small house, but nonetheless, someone's house, bobbing along as if it were nothing more than a harmless log. The one-story home was tilted at an angle, its front porch pointed toward the dark sky. As the structure came closer, it reminded me of a capsized ocean liner on its way to the obscure depths of the sea.

It was at that very moment that I realized that the building was going to collide with the tree. I looked down at the water. It was no longer a brown muddy color, but had taken on an inky black shade from the darkness of the coming night. The house was now only twenty yards away, floating silent, but deadly.

My mind was racing. If the tree was knocked over, would the calf and I be able to survive? Maybe I could jump onto the house at the last moment before it hit the tree. Maybe I would be able to swim up to the house and hold on to the porch.

The main section of the building moved toward the left of the tree. It appeared that the only part that was going to hit the tree was a seven-foot section of the porch. As the structure bobbed by in the moonlight, the wooden railing gently bumped the tree just below my feet, then floated away. Suddenly, my face was encircled with a ray of light, followed by a voice, "Hey…there's somebody in that tree!"

I couldn't believe what I was seeing. A man, woman, two young children and a cat sat at the very top of the slanted roof. A flashlight was aimed in my direction. The voice came again, "Are you alright? Are you injured?"

For some reason, I didn't quite know how to answer. If I wasn't alright or if I had been injured, they were in no position to rescue me from the tree. The only words that seemed to make any sense were, "Send help!"

The voice, now disappearing in the darkness, came back, "We will, we will!"

Long after the house had moved on, the rain came again and with it excessive winds. Somewhere in the middle of the long night I was awakened from a brief nap by a stinging sensation on my arms and face like hundreds of bee stings. The hail was the size of marbles. I looked down at the calf as the tiny ice balls bounced from his thick hair. He was licking my hand again and appeared to be surviving the hail much better than I. I clutched him to my chest and lowered my head. After a few minutes, the storm subsided, followed by a soft rain.

The water had risen to my knees and, by morning light, I was colder than I think I've ever been in my life. The rain had stopped and the sun was shining in the east. I looked west wondering what had happened to the family on the roof of their house.

It was about an hour later that I heard the distinctive sound of a copter. I wasn't going to get my hopes too high. I had heard that sound before, but it hadn't come for me. In the distance I saw the aircraft, and as it continued to grow in size, I realized that it would pass nearby. Seconds later, the copter flew over and continued east as my head sank in dismay. My negative thinking was quickly altered as the copter banked to the right and then returned, stopped and hovered twenty feet above the tree, the rotating blades whipping the water in a wide circular frenzy.

A man appeared in the side door of the copter and yelled through a bullhorn, "Put the calf in the water. We'll drop a line down. Grab hold…we'll bring you up."

I shook my head as I tried to raise the calf, then shouted, "No, the calf goes first…then me!"

The man repeated his orders. I shook my head again indicating I wasn't going to cooperate. Moments later, a U-shaped harness was lowered. It took me a few seconds, but I finally managed to unlock my arms from around the calf, then worked him into the straps. Once he was secured, I waved at the copter. The calf was slowly hoisted up into the air. He was dripping wet looking down at me, but would be safe in a few seconds. Minutes later, I was being lifted toward the copter. As I spun in a slow circle, I gazed in wonder at the vast expanse of brown water that seemed to stretch as far as I could see. I took one last look at the tree that had been my salvation. It looked more like a small bush sticking up out of the ocean of water below.

They tell me that I slept for an entire day, finally waking up requesting something to eat, then asking for seconds. Gramps and Gram walked into the hospital room as I was finishing up my second grilled cheese sandwich and third glass of lemonade.

I was glad to see that they were all right. Gramps said Mom was flying in and would be along later that evening. Ralston had been destroyed—the water was starting to recede. I had been air-lifted to Edgemont, the closest hospital to the flood. The farm had been swept away by the floodwaters. Gram seemed worried about their loss, but Gramps shrugged his shoulders saying that their flood insurance would cover everything. It was going to be a lot of work, but they'd put the farm back together.

Then, I remembered: The calf!

"Gramps…what about the calf…the one that was with me in the tree?"

Gramps grinned. "Funny you should ask," he said. "There isn't any doubt about it, son. You saved that little critter's life. Doctor says that he might have saved yours, too. He says there's a good chance that the calf's body heat kept you from severe hypothermia. He's the only one out of the herd that survived. It's kind of ironic. I think this is the first time that I've ever had an animal on the farm who lived up to his name.

"What are you talking about, Gramps?" I asked.

"Calf's name is Noah. You remember Noah. We just read about him a couple of days back. He and his family were the only people on earth to survive the great flood. And, from Noah, the entire world started all over again. From that one little calf I'll rebuild the whole herd."

That was thirty years ago. Noah has long since passed away. Grandpa did rebuild the herd…and the farm. When he requested me to take the farm over in '82, he had the largest herd in the state. Gram died peacefully of old age the year after we moved onto the farm. I remember the day she passed on. We were all there in the room. Grandpa was sitting next to her, holding her hand long after she had breathed her last. When I look back now, I can't think of any other time I saw the man cry. He looked right at me as tears ran down his wrinkled and weather-beaten face. I guess he knew I'd understand what he was about to say. He cleared his throat and spoke, "She told me she'd wait for me at the gates of Heaven and that she was going to speak to the Lord about my tobacco chewin'."

Gramps died two years later, sitting on the front porch, his tobacco pouch in one hand, his frayed Bible in the other. We buried him right next to Grandma and I have no doubt he's up there with her now.

I can't tell you how many times I've walked across the field and climbed this old tree. As the years pass and I grow older, it gets increasingly more difficult to climb to this branch. but somehow I always seem to manage. The crude markings that I carved on the branch two years following the flood are still there. A straight line indicating the height of the water with the inscription: *The Ark*.

It's hard to imagine what things had been like that dismal night I spent in the tree holding old Noah. Looking across the field now, one can see acre after acre of lush farmland. Just a mile away, I can see the barn, the house and the cattle grazing peacefully in the eastern pasture, the new calves chasing each other. I guess I'm not that much different than Gramps. I run a pretty tight ship. The Good Book is still read in the evenings and all the animals on the farm have those unpronounceable biblical names. I'm sure Gram is smiling down from up above. I've never gotten into the habit of chewing.

Well…I best be climbing back down this old tree and be heading back to the house. Supper will be on the table soon and if I'm late Greta will be in a tizzy. Besides that, looks like there's a storm brewin' in the west. I'll most likely be soaked to the skin by the time I get back, But, what the heck. We really need the rain.

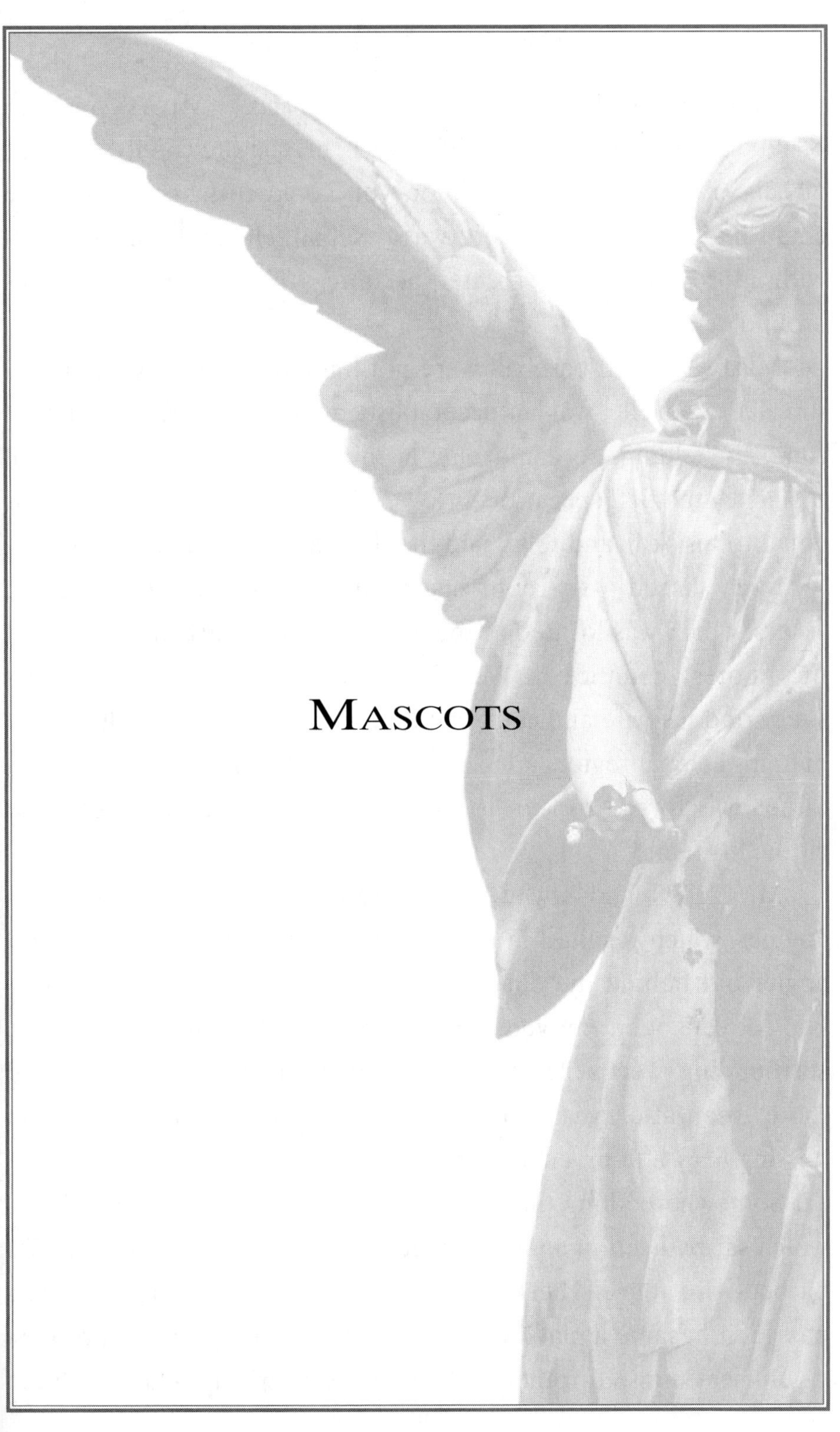

Mascots

THERE WERE TWO THINGS THAT MICA SANDS could do better thank anybody in town, maybe the county. If it had wheels, moving parts or a motor, you could rest assured that he could fix it. His second talent was baseball. He could throw a ball with more speed and greater accuracy than anyone for miles around.

Mica's skills in baseball were not limited to pitching. He could run like a gazelle, was an accomplished switch-hitter, and when it came to fielding, he could play all nine positions with a level of efficiency that left spectators in awe. His knowledge of the game was equal to his skill, and folks said that he was a walking rule book.

Mica shared a six-room shack with his five brothers and two sisters, which was located at the end of a rutted dirt road in one of the poorest counties in West Virginia. Mr. Sands had for years supported his wife and eight children as a coal miner, but like most men in the coal region, after the mines had been played out, Mica's father was forced to turn to other methods in order to feed and clothe his family.

Mr. Sands had always possessed a knack for fiddling with engines, which resulted in nine or ten old cars parked at different angles out behind the dilapidated barn. Some of the old vehicles had never been moved and were now hemmed in by the surrounding weeds. They were simply utilized for parts, parked there, year after year, some up on cinderblocks, most of them missing tires, a door, engine or transmission.

Somewhere along the line, he had picked up an old school bus, which sat by itself in an abandoned field just on the other side of a barbed-wire fence. The kids had taken it over, and, as the years passed, it became a playhouse on wheels. One of the older brothers would seat himself in the cracked and torn driver's seat, while the others sat in the back as they drove to far away places like China or England. How many times had the old bus been attacked by Indians as the boys aimed crude stick rifles out the windows? The bus had also made many a trip to the bottom of the sea as a submarine in search of lost treasure.

Whenever neighbors needed their cars tuned up, oil changed, or any type of mechanical work, they brought it to the Sands' place. Mica's father labored long days out in the old barn working on cars, mowers, farm machinery, and anything that came his way. Mrs. Sands canned string beans, tomatoes, and corn from a one-half acre garden, which not only helped to nourish the family, but was also a means of payment for their various needs.

There wasn't much money in the town of Anthracite. At one time, during the coal boom, the community had been famous for its abundance of coal. The coal was all gone now, but the town retained its odd name. Folks in the surrounding counties or those who happened to pass through town drove away with the consensus that time had just sort of stood still in Anthracite. Except for a few scattered buildings like the gasoline station, post office, or general store, most of the citizens still owned outhouses. Indoor plumbing was considered a luxury, just about everyone grew their own food and some families farther out didn't even have electricity.

It was a largely religious community, with a small nondenominational church on the edge of town. Folks didn't really consider themselves poor: it was just a way of life. They didn't have much, but were thankful for their meager possessions. If you happened to own a car that was in running condition and was in need of gas, and if you were short on cash, a couple of homemade pies or a basket of ripe tomatoes would cover the bill. If you couldn't afford to purchase a new wheelbarrow or shovel, there was always a friendly neighbor willing to lend you theirs in return for mending his fence or tilling his garden.

By the time Mica was six, he had grown tired of the fantasy trips in the old bus. Spending day after day with his father in the barn, he'd perch up in the hayloft next to Zed, their old hound, and watch his father at work. Every square inch of the barn was crammed with broken-down lawnmowers, empty paint buckets, stacks of bald tires, and every imaginable automobile part in existence. The only uncluttered area was just inside the large barn doors where a huge chain device used for pulling engine blocks hung from the rafters.

On occasion, Mr. Sands would give Mica little chores like pouring oil in an engine or pounding out a dented fender. As Mica grew older, he began to ask questions from his desire to be involved in more complicated repairs. By the time he was twelve, he was quite the mechanic.

During the summer of his eighth birthday, Uncle Lutey came to visit as usual. Lutey, at one time, had lived in Anthracite. When the mines pulled out, he did likewise, stating that he was heading for the big-city life. He finally wound up in Cincinnati where he acquired a position as a used-car salesman, with his outgoing personality and country-twang style of talking winning the hearts of many a customer. Before long, he was making more money than he knew what to do with. Eventually, he bought out the owner and purchased two more lots. If you wanted a great deal on a quality used automobile in the Cincinnati area, Lutey Dunbaugh was the man to see.

Just like clockwork, Lutey dropped by every June for a few days. He'd drive up in his long Cadillac—he had a new one every year. The kids would always try and guess what color the new car would be. The back seat was always brimming with gifts for Ma and the kids. It was a custom that every summer one of the kids would get to spend two months with Lutey in Cincinnati. The summer of `64 was Mica's turn.

Sitting in the gleaming white Cadillac, a battered suitcase in the back seat, Mica waved goodbye to the family and left Anthracite behind for the summer. Mica had never been out of the county before. He felt like he was in heaven, the Caddy speeding down the turnpike, top down, radio blaring as he sipped on a large pineapple milkshake.

Lutey lived on the Kentucky side of the Ohio River, just across from Cincinnati. He had a huge glass-and-stone house that was built into the side of the mountain. From the glassed-in porch, the view below was nothing less than spectacular. The tall buildings were something that Mica couldn't seem to take his eyes off. Back home, the tallest building he could recall was just four levels high. The river looked like a long brown ribbon as it snaked its way beneath the bridge leading into the city and then around the bend. At night, the city was transformed into a sparkling panorama of lights and color.

Lutey and his wife, Selma, had two sons of their own, Matt and Mark, ages nine and ten. Following a hefty breakfast his first morning at Lutey's, the two boys carted Mica off for a day at the local park. After some short introductions, Mica found himself playing right field in a pickup baseball game. His first day on the ball field turned out to be pathetic. He didn't have the slightest clue what he was supposed to do. Matt, the oldest, tried his best to explain the game. At first, it seemed to be too much for Mica, but toward the end of the week he started to grasp the drift for the basic rules.

The weekend rolled around and with it a big surprise. Lutey had season box seats for all of the Reds' games. It was Saturday night at the park, with sodas, hot dogs, peanuts, and a program. Matt and

Mark disposed of their programs, but to Mica the nine-page flier was a prized possession that contained the names of all the players, complete with photographs and positions played. Sitting inside the massive stadium was beyond Mica's comprehension. From his box seat, he could almost reach out and touch the players. The fans in the very top level looked like ants. It was the biggest crowd he had ever witnessed in one place at the same time.

Mica didn't shut up from the first pitch until the final out and then all the way home. "What's a bunt? What's a curve ball? Why do the players rub their hands in the dirt? How many runs are ya allowed ta git?" His questions were endless. Matt became frustrated, finally telling him to just pay attention. That night Lutey had a brief conversation with his two sons, explaining that Mica had been brought up differently and that they needed to show some patience.

As the long summer passed, Mica played ball every single day and was upset when darkness set in. He, Lutey, and his two boys attended every home game during the two-month vacation. The last week before Mica was to go back home, Lutey made arrangements for the three boys to meet Tadd Nichols, Cincinnati's top pitcher. After receiving an autograph on a brand-new baseball, Mica looked up into the chiseled face of the tall pitcher and with great sincerity stated, "Someday I'm gonna be a big leaguer jus' like you."

Reaching down, Nichols ruffled the boy's shaggy blond hair as he smiled. "I bet you will, son."

By the end of the summer, Mica had conquered the general concept of the game. He could throw the ball harder than the other boys, but it never seemed to go in the direction he intended. His hitting improved, but he couldn't hit the ball out past the infield. Surprisingly, he could field and catch better than anyone at the park. He also had the ability to run, his speed amazing the other kids.

Mica waved goodbye to Uncle Lutey. He'd never forget that summer. He had no intention of forgetting anything about Cincinnati or about the game of baseball. This was just the beginning for him. His excessive desire to conquer the game had prompted Lutey to send him home with a new bat, glove, Reds' hat, eight balls, and a manual entitled, "How to Play the Game."

On his first night back in Anthracite, Mica announced to the rest of the family at the supper table that he was going to become a baseball star when he was old enough. His mother, who thought the comment was nothing more than cute, just smiled. The kids all laughed, hooted and hollered until Dad ordered everyone to settle. After the table interruption calmed down, Mica flopped a helping of mashed potatoes on his plate as he politely stated, "Ya'll see…jus' wait."

The next morning in the barn, Mica finished tightening a lug nut on a piece of machinery, then walked slowly toward his father who was sawing a piece of rusted tailpipe off a muffler.

"Pa…kin we talk?"

Mr. Sands laid an old hacksaw on the dirt floor, then responded, "What's on yer mind, boy?"

Mica seated himself on some old tires as he began. "I meant what I said las' night at supper… bout bein' a ballplayer. I figure you an' the others think I'm crazy…but it's what I wanna do."

"Look," Mr. Sands said. "Do you have any idea how many kids wanna be a ballplayer, or fer that matter, tennis stars, or even astronauts? Everyone dreams o' fame an' fortune. Life ain't fair, Mica. Very few people git ta be stars at anythin'. It requires years o' practice an' trainin'. Don't git me wrong. I ain't sayin' ya cain't do it. It's jus' hard fer someone like you ta pull it off."

The confused look on Mica's face alerted his father that more of an explanation was needed. "Mica, it's like this. Bein' born an' raised in this part o' West Virginia ain't `xactly a stroke o' luck. It's like bein' in a foot race, but ev'rybody else gits a head start. Fer ya ta win, ya have ta try twice as hard. It ain't right, but that be how it stacks up."

"I don't care," Mica snapped. "I'll practice ev`ryday from sunup `til sundown. I'll learn ev`ry rule, how ta play ev`ry position, how ta throw, hit, catch...."

Mr. Sands reached out touching Mica on his thin shoulders. "Tell ya what. If ya wanna learn the game that's fine with me. Ya kin practice all ya want, but `member one thing: chores an' schoolin' comes first. After that...ya kin work on bein' that ball star."

Mica's face lit up like a Christmas tree, "Thanks, Pa!"

For the next year, Mica practiced with the regimentation of a boy possessed. He practiced before and after school and in between chores even if at times it was only for a few minutes. During the summer with school out and his chores complete, he'd practice for hours on end until it was too dark to see his hand in front of his face.

His brothers and sisters carried little interest in baseball, but were willing to lend a hand with some coaxing from Mica. He drilled a hole in one of the balls and placed a thick, nine-foot section of rope through the center, the end secured by a knot. He fashioned a crude home plate out of a slab of stone he found down by the creek, using some old white paint to create a batter's box. One of his siblings would position himself out nine feet from the stone and spin the ball in a wide arch. At first, the ball was nearly impossible to hit, but after months of daily practice, Mica could hit any ball that passed over or near the stone. His eyes became schooled to exactly where the strike zone was located. Even after he became an expert at hitting the ball, he continued the procedure.

There was an old cinder block wall six-feet high and twenty-four feet wide where Mr. Sands at one time had intentions of building a small garage. Due to a lack of funds, the idea was scrapped. The wall was perfect for yet another method of practice. Every day, rain or shine, and even on a few occasions when it snowed, you could find Mica standing in front of the wall fielding ground balls. It made no difference to Mica whether it was 102 degrees or ten below zero. In spring, summer, fall, and winter he'd throw nine hundred pitches at the block wall—three hundred to the left, then the right, and finally straight on.

He also suspended an old tire from a tree. Using a tree root as the pitcher's mound, he'd fire five hundred pitches a day at the tire. He kept records of his performance in an old notebook his Ma said she had no use for. He tracked how many times he missed the center of the tire or how many ground balls he bobbled. No matter how well he'd do, the following day he'd set a new goal for playing at a higher level.

Out on the back field, he measured off an actual ball diamond according to Big League standards, using stones and spray paint for the bases and foul lines. He practiced running the base paths, setting up mock situations for himself: "Okay…yer'r on second. There's one out, and the bunt sign is on. Whadda ya do? How big o' a lead should ya take?" He mastered each and every position and what should be done in every conceivable play.

During the summer of Mica's twelfth year, Mr. Sands announced he was driving the family to the state fair. The forecast was for clear skies and a high of eighty-two degrees. The plan was to get up early, eat a good breakfast, and be on the road by 6:00 a.m. It was a three-hour trip over to the fairgrounds. Mr. Sands would do all the driving, while his wife sat in the passenger seat, her time engaged with reading and knitting. The eight kids were all seated around the edges of the back of the pickup, with three large coolers jammed with sandwiches, pies, fruit, and a chocolate cake stacked neatly against the cab.

At nine-thirty, they arrived at the fairgrounds, paid the parking fee, and positioned the truck under a large shade tree. After Ma laid out the rules for the day, everyone went his own way. Ma and the two girls were interested in the fruit and vegetable displays and also the quilt section, while Mr.Sands and the boys headed for the tractor and livestock barns. Mica split off on his own. His desire: the ball fields.

Lunch was to be served back at the truck at noon, then dinner at six. Everyone was to report back to the truck at those times. All the kids had saved what money they could, knowing the fair was a rare and special treat.

Mica took a seat close to the top of the faded wooden bleachers as he placed his old glove at his bare feet. He had heard about the ballgames at the fair. Teams from every county in the state would participate for prize money and trophies.

He had no interests in anything else at the fair; not the rides, the animals, or the food—just baseball. He watched two games in a row, constantly talking to himself as he noticed the incorrect things some of the players did. He ran back to the truck for a quick bite at noon, then returned to the fields. Sipping water at a fountain next to the dugout, Mica overheard the conversation between two players on one of the teams for the next game.

"Well, if this don't beat all. We drive all the way up here and now we have to forfeit."

"That's crazy. Can't somebody else pitch?"

"Sure, we can put one of the other guys on the mound, but we'll get blown out. Without Rusty's pitching we're as good as dead. I told him to lay off all the beer. He can't even stand up."

"I guess you're right. If we go out there without a good pitcher, we'll just wind up making fools of ourselves."

"'Scuse me," Mica said, "I kin pitch fer ya."

Both players turned, remained silent, then one laughed as he repeated, "I kin pitch fer ya!" He looked Mica up and down then spit on the ground as he commented, "Boy, you ain't even got shoes on."

Mica took a big bite from a large red apple he had been carrying as he stepped forward. "Don't need no shoes. Got this." He held up his right arm.

"Got what?" asked the other man.

"My arm," Mica answered. "Ya need a pitcher…don't cha?"

One of the men shook his head in wonder, then stated, "Look, son, you need to go ride the merry-go-round or eat some cotton candy. This is a man's game."

Both men walked toward the dugout. When they were the exact distance off, Mica bent down and picked up a ball near the fence. "Hey!" he yelled.

Both men turned. Mica assumed the customary pitcher's stance. He wound up and released the ball—his target the tallest man who had a glove. The man had no chance but to raise the glove to catch the ball in order to keep from getting hit square in the chest. The ball slapped into the leather of the glove causing the man to lurch backwards.

The man cursed, looked at his friend, then at Mica in amazement, who at the moment was chewing away calmly on the apple.

The man who had caught the ball walked toward Mica. "Where'd you learn to throw like that?"

"Learnt myself," Mica said.

The man gave the ball back to Mica as he asked, "Can you throw a curve?"

"Shoot…that's easy," Mica laughed. "I kin throw a curve, forkball, slider. You name it…I kin toss it."

The two men took Mica off to the edge of the field. Following a brief demonstration of his dazzling pitching ability, it was decided that he would be their pitcher. Ten minutes later, the game was started and Mica found himself standing on the pitcher's mound. The lanky umpire took one look at the boy on the mound and signaled the coach for the team to home plate.

Pete Wilcox sauntered up to the umpire already aware of what the concern was all about. "What's the problem, ump?"

The umpire removed a sweaty hat from his head, then stated, "Two things: Your pitcher is too young and he ain't got no shoes on. Can't use `im."

"Hold on," Pete said. "I already checked the rule book. Says in there the minimum age is twelve, which he is. We'll fetch a pair of spikes for the boy."

The umpire smirked as he glanced at Mica. "All right then…but speed it up. We got a lot of ball to play today."

A pair of spikes was delivered promptly to the mound. Mica knelt down and placed the shoes on his bare feet. Some of the fans in the stands were laughing and pointing at the spectacle. "Don't let them bother you," Pete said. "You just throw like you did over by the dugout and you'll be fine."

"Play ball!" bellowed the umpire.

The lead-off batter for the opposing team was well over six-feet tall, his muscular forearms bulging beneath his jersey. He slowly adjusted his hat as he glared out at the young pitcher, a slim twelve-year-old wearing baggy bib overalls, no shirt, and a shaggy Reds' hat. The big man turned to the umpire as he laughed, "This game's gonna be a joke."

The man stood in the batter's box as he awaited the first pitch. Mica looked around the bleachers. There had to be two hundred people watching. He had thrown hundreds of thousands of pitches at the worn tire hanging in the tree. This was different. No one had ever sat and watched him before. He felt nervous, beads of sweat starting to break out on his forehead.

"Hey, boy," shouted the umpire. "You gonna get this game started or what?" The fans and the opposing team broke out in loud laughter.

Without further hesitation, Mica went into his windup and released the ball, which sailed over the top of the backstop. Now the crowd was in a state of hysteria, laughing loudly, slapping their knees, pointing at Mica as the umpire hollered, "Ball one!" The players on Mica's team lowered their heads—they had made a grave mistake.

The catcher tossed the ball back to Mica then walked back to the plate. Mica looked around at the laughing spectators. He looked in at the catcher, then relaxed as he thought to himself, *Jus' member the tire. Throw the ball through the tire.*

The catcher was taken by surprise when the ball slammed into the leather of his glove knocking him onto his butt. "Strike one," yelled the umpire. The batter wore a look of confusion on his face as he stared back at Mica. The very next pitch curved toward the batter and trimmed the inside corner as the huge man backed off to avoid getting hit. "Strike two," commanded the umpire.

The third pitch was a riser—the batter missed it by a foot. The umpire showed a wide grin on his face as he hollered, "Strike three, you're out!"

The next two batters went down swinging. The apple-eating boy had struck out the side. By the end of the sixth inning, the word had slipped out and the crowd had doubled in size. Some kid was throwing a no-hitter over at the fields. Eighteen straight men had struck out. There wasn't even so much as a foul ball. This youngster, whoever he was, was just mowin' `em down left and right.

Besides his remarkable pitching, Mica connected for a single and a long double, stole two bases, and scored twice. As the ninth inning rolled around, the stands were packed to capacity. Mica struck the first two batters out with what appeared to be hardly an effort. With each pitch, the fans were cheering him on. His teammates were poised on the edge of the dugout waiting to run onto the field after the final out.

An outside fastball and a high curve combined for the first two strikes on what Mica figured as the last batter. For his last pitch, he decided on a change-up. He hadn't thrown one yet. No one would be expecting it. His guess was right. Everyone had tried to deal with his speed. The batter looked like a complete fool as he swung at the ball before it slowly reached the plate. The game was over. Mica had thrown a no-hitter.

Mica was mobbed by his teammates as they shook the unique youngster's hand. Mica was bombarded with so many questions that he didn't have an opportunity to answer.

"What's your name?"

"Where're you from?"

"How old are you?"

"Where'd you learn to pitch like that?"

As the activity on the field started to let up, a familiar voice grabbed Mica's attention, "Mica! Mica! We gotta go."

It was Gordon, one of his younger brothers.

Mica walked the younger boy off to the side. "Whadda ya mean, we gotta go?"

"Pa sent me," the boy answered. "Molly got real sick. Ma says we gotta head on home."

Pete was at Mica's side. "Our next game is in two hours. Me and the boys are buying you dinner. Anything you want…it's on the house. Can you pitch another nine for us?"

Mica desired to stay in the worst way, but knew his father would never let him remain behind. "I'm sorry, mister, but I cain't…I gotta go."

"But we don't even know who you are," Pete pleaded.

Gordon was pulling on Mica's arm. "C'mon, Mica, Pa said now!"

Mica removed the spikes quickly as he answered, "Name's Mica. I'm from over in Anthracite. Here's yer spikes back an' thanks fer lettin' me throw a few."

On the way back to their truck, Mica made Gordon promise to never tell that he had been playing ball with a team. Mrs. Sands held Molly in her arms all the way home, with the rest of the kids in the back. They were all upset—the day at the fair had been cut short. Not a word was spoken on the trip back. Mica looked at Gordon on a number of occasions as the young boy appeared to be bursting at the seams to divulge what he knew. Mica knew he wouldn't say anything. Gordon was great at keeping secrets.

It was a week later that a two-tone brown station wagon pulled into the Sands' place. Mr. Sands walked out to meet the stranger who stepped out of the car.

"Howdy. What kin we do fer ya?"

The driver of the car was a fairly young fellow in his early thirties with a crew cut, and an athletic-looking body framed in a pair of jeans and a baggy sweatshirt. The strange thing about the man was that he was carrying a folded newspaper and a ball glove. The man clasped Mr. Sands' hand as he quickly introduced himself. "Frank Denton. I'm the high school baseball coach at Fullerton."

Mr. Sands remained quiet, not sure what the man wanted.

"The reason I came by," explained Denton, "is to speak with your son. I believe you have a boy named Mica."

"He in some kinda trouble?"

"No, quite the opposite. I'd like to talk with Mica about his future. He'll be coming to Fullerton in two years and I'd like him to play ball for me."

Mr. Sands was more confused than he could ever imagine. "My boy don't ever play ball. Practices like crazy, but he's nev'r played anywheres."

"Not according to this article," Denton said.

He unfolded the paper, removed the sports section offering it to Mr. Sands.

Mr. Sands held up his hands in defense. "Don't read all that well,"

Denton tossed the paper back in the open window and went on, "You were over at the state fair a couple of weeks back?"

"Yep, we wuz there, but what's that got ta do with my son?"

"The article says that a twelve-year-old boy by the name of Mica from Anthracite pitched a no-hitter at one of the county ballgames at the fair. It's just a short article—actually I ran across it by accident."

Mr. Sands motioned for Denton to stop talking. "I think we best talk ta Mica `bout this. He's out back o' the barn. C'mon."

Denton smiled when they rounded the corner of the barn. The tall, slender lad stood erect on the treeroot, went though the routine of checking the make-believe runners on first and second, then went into his windup and high kick, followed by a blazing fastball that passed through the center of the tire. Before Denton could utter a word, Mr. Sands yelled, "Mica…git over here! Got somethin' ta ask ya."

Mica quickly ran toward his father and the stranger, removed his battered Reds' hat, and wiped his brow. "What's up, Pa?"

"This man here says ya pitched some ball over at the fair. That true?"

Mica lowered his eyes to the ground. "It's true."

"Why didn't ya say somethin' `bout it?"

"Thought I'd git in trouble."

Mr. Sands reached out, lifting the boy's chin. "This fellah here says ya did okay."

Mica seemed to ease up as he answered, "I sure did! We won an' I hurled a no-hitter. They wanted me ta pitch `nother game but I tol' `em I couldn't."

"Know all `bout it. This fellah's from the high school. Name's Denton. Wants ta speak with ya `bout playin' ball when ya go ta Fullerton. I got work ta do. I'll be leavin' ya ta visit by yerselves. `Member what I said before that chores and schoolin' come first. Nice ta meet ya, Mr. Denton."

An hour later, Denton entered the barn and approached Mica's father. "Excuse me, Mr. Sands. Can we talk for a few minutes?"

Mr. Sands got up from his knees as he responded, "I reckon we kin. How'd ya make out with the boy?"

"Well, I had Mica throw me quite a few pitches. He's got the best fastball—a great curve. Heck, he's the best I've ever seen for his age.

He tells me there isn't anything he can't do on a ballfield. You may not realize it, Mr. Sands, but what your boy did over at the state fair is nothing short of a miracle. He threw a no-hitter against grown men. Struck out twenty-seven batters in a row. Your boy wants to be a ballplayer—I'm talking major leagues here. He has the talent. More than I've ever seen. I told him what a wonderful opportunity he's got, how much money he could earn, how he could change his life. You've got an amazing son, Mr. Sands. He said he really didn't care about all the money, at least for himself. He did say that it would be nice to help his family have a better life. He has a genuine love for the game, and believe me, in today's world, that's rare."

Mr. Sands laid down the wrench he was holding as he took a swig of water from a Mason jar. "So…what're ya sayin?"

Denton smiled. "I'd like to work with Mica. With some finesse, in two years he could be the best fourteen-year-old to ever stand on a ball field. Won't cost you a cent. I'll take care of all that. He needs a pair of spikes and a new glove. I'll supply everything he needs."

"Mr. Denton, I cain't imagine yer're doin' this out o' the kindness o' yer heart. Ev'rybody's got an angle. What's in this fer you?"

"It's like this, Mr. Sands. I grew up over in Hazard, Kentucky. My folks were poor. I had dreams of becoming a big time ballplayer—just like your son. I was good, about the best to ever come out of that part of the state. In high school, I managed to turn a few heads and wound up getting a college scholarship. I even had some pro teams scout me, but they said I needed a couple more years before I was ready for the big leagues. College ball turned out to be a lot different than high school. The players were better hitters and there was more pressure. Turned out, I wasn't good enough for the majors. The thing is…baseball is the reason I received a college education. I studied hard and finally graduated with a degree in teaching sports. Landed me a coaching job here in Fullerton. I've been at it now for four years."

Mr. Sands cleared his throat, then sipped more water. "Ya still ain't answered my question. What'll you git outta trainin' Mica?"

"I love this game, Mr. Sands. Once I realized that I'd never get to play in the big leagues, I decided to spend my time helping other kids to better themselves through the sport. Your son Mica has the combination of two things to go all the way. He's got more raw talent than any boy I've ever seen, and, he has a deep love for the game. I'll tell you what's in it for me: the satisfaction of helping your son realize his dream. Now, what do you say? Do we have a deal? Can I work with him?"

Mica stepped on the smooth, white rubber out on the mound. The infield grass had been recently cut and held the smell of spring. He was fourteen now, in his freshman year at Fullerton. This was the first game of the season and Coach Denton was about to unleash his young pitcher on the league, the likes of which they had never seen.

The youngster from Anthracite was no longer a hillbilly teenager throwing old balls through a tire. He made an imposing appearance out on the elevated mound. He stood straight as an arrow at six-foot-three, weighing in at 182 pounds of hard muscle. His uniform was neat as a pin, not a wrinkle. His spikes had been shined to a high luster and would have made any Marine drill sergeant proud.

Denton's two-year, pre-high school training had honed Mica into what looked like anything but a schoolboy pitcher. He gave the impression of a mature man. He had weathered extensive weight training and stretching exercises. He ran daily and ate balanced meals. He was a baseball machine.

The first batter stepped up to the plate. Three fastballs later, he was the first victim. An hour and a half passed, the final score 6-0. Mica chalked up the second no-hitter if his life. There had only been two players who had even hit the ball. Both had been lazy grounders, which the second baseman fielded without any difficulty. Mica went three for four and stole one base.

Fullerton went undefeated that year. Mica had an unblemished record of six wins and no losses. Four of the games were no-hitters. In the final game of the year, a batter connected with one of Mica's fastballs and knocked it over the center field fence. It was the only one of two hits he had given up all year.

His sophomore year was a sequel of the previous season, leaving the team once again undefeated. Mica was 6-0 again, but only managed to hurl three no-hitters. He was also the home-run champion of the year. Denton counseled Mica and geared him toward concentrating on his schoolwork, as well as his future ball career. He advised him about how to invest the vast amount of money that he would make in the majors, explaining that major league careers could end in just a few short years. There was a long parade of baseball stars who hadn't invested their money only to discover when their careers were over that they had no means to support themselves. Denton, being a Christian man, taught Mica about the virtue of humbleness. A young man with talent, good grades, and a great attitude would get farther and last longer than someone who just had talent.

His third year in high school lifted him to a new level. He was pitching better than the first two seasons, with Fullerton as usual going undefeated. Mica had a flawless record, producing seven no-hitters. There were college and pro scouts at every game. Denton coached Mica well. He interviewed like a mannerly young man, not some starry-eyed kid from the hills. He informed the college scouts that he wasn't going to start looking at any schools until his senior year. As far as the pro scouts were concerned, Mica let Denton do the talking.

His final year at Fullerton was filled with a steady stream of letters and phone calls from colleges and professional teams alike. The team, for the fourth straight year was undefeated, Mica chipping in five no-hitters in twelve games. Life at the Sands' place was anything but boring, with the mailbox always crammed with letters from universities and colleges. There didn't seem to be a weekend that went by where there wasn't a representative from some college or pro team pulling up into the driveway to visit with Mica Sands, the talk of the sporting world.

In June of that year, Mr. Sands took ill and was unable to work, cutting the family income to the bone. There were still six kids at home. Following graduation, Mica was faced with an important decision: college or pro ball. His father was recuperating but still unable to return to work. The family was running out of what little money they had. The older sons who had married and moved away tried to help, but they had families of their own to care for.

Mica didn't see any other way out of the situation but to sign with one of the major league teams that had approached him. He knew coach Denton would be unhappy as he was passing up college, but his folks desperately needed money. Besides that, his motive from the very first day he had returned from Uncle Lutey's was to become a professional ballplayer. He had worked hard, now it was paying off. The Chicago White Sox had offered him the best deal. Fifty-thousand dollars to sign, and a four-year contract worth three million.

The day following his call to Chicago, a long, dark blue Lincoln made its way down the dirt road leading to the Sands' house. Two men dressed in expensive three-piece suits got out and met Mica and Frank Denton in the front yard. An hour later, the Chicago representatives drove off, and Mica Sands, a kid from the poorest part of West Virginia was a member of the Chicago White Sox. That afternoon an old fashioned picnic was held at the farm. Mrs. Sands whipped up a batch of her spicy chicken along with potato salad and baked beans, and four kinds of pie. Frank and his wife attended. It was indeed a time for celebration.

As evening rolled around, the festivities came to an end. The Dentons left for home, while the kids helped Ma tidy up the front yard. Mica slipped off with old Zed. It had been a long day and he wanted to be alone for awhile. He sat by the old tire as he removed the brand-new White Sox hat from his head and stared at the embossed emblem. Tears poured down his cheeks as he pulled the check from his shirt pocket. Fifty thousand dollars! Through the tears, he managed a smile. He would now be able to pull his entire family up out of the dregs of poverty. Time to turn in for the night.

The news of a local youngster making it to the big leagues spread around Anthracite like a summer brushfire. Since the mines had closed, the town had literally gone into hibernation, but he had put the tiny community back on the map.

Mica didn't have to report to Chicago for two weeks. During the first week he set about getting a number of matters accomplished. He deposited the entire sign-on cash in the bank, much to the delight of the bank president, made arrangements for his father's mortgage payment to be prepaid for the next year, purchased a new station wagon for his parents, bought a new washer and dryer for his mother, and a gift for each of the kids.

That Friday, he took a bus over to Charleston, purchased a brand-new, bright yellow Corvette convertible and some new clothes, then set out for Virginia Beach. He had never seen the ocean. A week of relaxing on the sandy beaches and eating all the fresh seafood he wanted was a vacation he well deserved.

After lying on the beach for three days, he was starting to feel guilty. This was the first time since he had returned from Cincinnati years ago that he had not followed his disciplined training. Surely, the short reprieve from daily practice wouldn't have an effect on his ability to pitch or play the game. Maybe he'd cut the vacation short by a couple of days and return home for a few days of old-fashioned training.

The next evening following a movie, he passed a carnival that had been set up one block from the beach. Eating a two-scoop vanilla ice cream cone, he strolled by a pitching-and-hitting booth. Ten pitches for a dollar. There was a large selection of panda bears at the back of the booth. If you managed to hit all ten pitches, you won the grand prize—a six-foot panda. If you hit five pitches, you didn't win anything. Various sized pandas were awarded for the amount of pitches you could hit between six and nine.

Mica stepped up to the booth. "How many o' those giant pandas do ya have?"

The man gave him a look of sarcasm. "I only keep four…got two in the back. The big bears are just kinda on display. Nobody can hit all ten pitches, at least I've never seen it done."

Mica turned to a group of children who were walking by. "You kids wanna win some prizes?"

"Sure!" said one of the boys.

The group crowded around Mica as he addressed the clerk.

"Let's start off with ten dollars worth."

The clerk had a look on his face that reaffirmed his belief that there truly was a sucker born every minute.

Mica stepped into the batter's cage and said, "Let `er rip."

He drove all ten pitches, each a line drive into the back of the padded backstop, turned and smiled at the clerk. "Guess I'll take one of the giant pandas."

Mica handed the panda to the boy standing closest to him, then lined the other three children up and proceeded to hit thirty pitches in a row, each child receiving a large panda. The clerk sadly watched the children run off down the street laughing and shouting as he stated, "Well, you have six dollars left."

"Had `nough of battin,'" said Mica. "Pitchin' is what I'm best at. How's the throwin' part work?"

The clerk lowered his head in wonder as he explained, "You estimate how fast you think you can throw the ball. You then proceed to throw at the target. A speed gun registers your actual speed. If your guess is within five miles per hour of the gun, you win. You get two balls for a dollar. That means you have twelve pitches. If you win, you get your choice of any of the major league batting helmets you see displayed."

Mica picked up the first ball. "My guess will be 102 miles per hour."

The man gave a pig-snort laugh, then stated, "If you say so."

Mica went into his pitching stance, then let loose with a blazing fastball, hitting the small red target dead center. The screen over the speed gun lit up: 103 mph. After telling the man that his guess for the next eleven pitches would be 103, he commenced to slap the target dead center with each throw. He selected eleven White Sox helmets. Taking the helmets down from the shelf, the man informed him that he only had seven and asked him if he wanted five others. Mica decided to take the seven White Sox helmets, thanked the man and walked off leaving the clerk standing in awe. Walking down the street, Mica handed the helmets out to the first seven kids that he met.

That evening, standing on a jetty leading out into the ocean, Mica was pleased with his performance at the carnival. He still had it. Maybe he'd stay one more day, then head back home.

The next morning following a hearty breakfast, he threw his old suitcase in the back of the Corvette, stopped to purchase a box of saltwater taffy for the family, then headed for West Virginia. The sky was overcast and the woman on the radio predicted rainstorms throughout the day.

An hour out from the beach, he stopped for gas and a drink. The rain was starting to pick up as he pulled out onto the four-lane highway. The last thing he remembered was tuning in a station on the radio. There was a loud scrapping metal sound followed by the Corvette being plummeted over the side of a steep embankment, the car rolling over and over, glass smashing, metal and fiberglass parts ripping.

He woke up, staring at the gleaming white ceiling above him. A nurse, seeing that he was awake, left and then returned with a doctor. Fifteen minutes later, the doctor left, stating that he would be back to check on him later. The doctor had informed him that he had been forced off the road by the driver of a tractor trailer. The operator had fallen asleep at the wheel. Mica's car had tumbled over the side of an embankment and exploded. Fortunately, he had been thrown from his vehicle. The truck driver had died at the scene.

It was a miracle that Mica had survived. The amount of injuries to his body was extensive: fractured skull, busted collarbone, one broken arm. Both legs were broken in a number of places, and he was covered with numerous cuts and abrasions. The worst injury of all was that his spine had been badly bent. He would most likely be able to walk again, but he would remain a cripple the remainder of his life. He'd be spending at least six months in rehabilitation. There had to be a period of complete rest during the healing process, then an intensive physical-therapy program.

His folks, brothers and sisters came to visit him every Sunday for the first month. Finally, Mica told his father that he cherished the weekly visits, but he knew they couldn't afford the long drive, plus meals and motel bills. He'd be fine.

When Mica was in the presence of his parents, he put on an act as if things were fine and that he would be back to his old self before long. His positive attitude was no more than a façade. Inside, he was bitter.

The medical staff at the hospital had tactfully explained what life after his eventual release from supervision would be like. He would be confined to a wheelchair for three months, then crutches for another six. Walking normally would never be a part of everyday living. He would have a serious and very noticeable limp in his right leg and would have to slightly drag the left. Running was out of the question and to put it bluntly it would be impossible. Just walking was going to be a difficult experience for a long time. His body was going to be partly twisted, he would never be able to straighten his right arm. The miraculous outcome of the accident was that he had retained complete mental faculties—his mind hadn't been damaged in any way.

Mica never argued with the doctors or objected to daily therapy, but he never accepted their diagnosis. Frank, realizing that the boy was avoiding the obvious, had to point out the grave truth. The afternoon Frank sat by his bed and explained that he would never play ball again was something Mica didn't want to hear. Frank tried to explain to Mica that baseball was a business and that the White Sox were just as upset about the accident as anyone. They had signed possibly the most talented young player of all time and now it was not to be. The contract would be rescinded and the balance of the sign-on fee returned.

It was just about a year and a half later that Mica limped toward the bus outside the terminal at the general store. He sat in the back of the bus and watched Anthracite disappear as they made their way around the first bend in the road. He looked at the ticket clutched in his hand: Oakland, California. It was about as far away as a person could get from West Virginia without stepping into the ocean. He was running away from the way his life had turned out.

Following his release from the hospital, he had retuned home. He felt useless and uncomfortable. He couldn't help his father with his work and he couldn't practice baseball. He couldn't endure to look at the tire hanging in the tree or his old ball field out back in the field. He was back to being poor again, but now it seemed worse. He had been so close to grabbing his dream—blessed by God is the way Frank always put it. Now, God had taken his ability to play ball away.

He felt guilty, as if he had let everyone down. The money he had set aside to pay his father's mortgage had been returned to the White Sox, along with the remaining balance of the fifty-thousand. Mr. Sands had to take a job in Fullerton in order to make ends meet. Between the new job and his repair business, combined with his inferior health, he could hardly stand at the end of the day. Mica, sitting in his wheelchair, followed by months of hobbling around on crutches, was helpless to do any work. He felt guilty about eating his parents' food, even staying under their roof.

Sitting in the backseat and thinking about how he had been cheated out of his future made him feel desolate. Leaving West Virginia, his family and the memories of baseball behind seemed like his only means of escape from his mental torture. In a way, he felt like a criminal. He hadn't told his parents he was leaving. He hadn't mentioned anything to Frank. He just left. He didn't care anymore.

Weeks, months, years drifted by with Mica's life an endless chain of mediocre jobs, his injuries limiting the work he was able to do. Manual labor was too painful and he couldn't keep up with the other workers. He tried his hand at selling clothing in a men's outlet, but eventually was let go. The owner said he was sorry, but Mica just didn't represent the image customers were looking for. About the only type of work he could get was janitorial or dishwashing. After years of trying his best to hold onto low-paying jobs, he could sense himself starting to give up.

He started missing work or quitting jobs after just a few weeks. He was constantly running out of money and he was tired of being a cripple. The bitterness of being robbed of a professional baseball career gripped his mind. It ate at him every day, slowly reducing him to the point where he had to stay at flophouses and eat in soup lines. He had no desire to earn a living. He had no ambition. There didn't seem to be much sense in going on. He thought about returning home. He knew he would be welcomed at the farm, but he was too prideful to return. He was a failure.

He focused on the murky brown water far below. It was strange that after eight years of wandering back and forth across the country that he was going to end his agony in Chicago. At one time, the Windy City was going to be the beginning of everything for him. Now, it was the end. He hadn't eaten in a week—he was frail. He'd been wearing the same clothes for months. He had sunk about as low as he thought a human could get. Four hundred feet below, an oil tanker slowly drifted by. From high up on the bridge, it appeared as a toy. The sun was just starting to sink in the west as he climbed onto the rusted iron railing.

In the distance, he saw the stadium where the Sox played. He had never had the courage to go there. He wouldn't have been able to deal with the pain of wondering how things would have turned out. The Chicago fans were never going to get to see the young man from Anthracite who had struck out twenty-seven grown men at the age of twelve. They'd never get to see him hurl a no-hitter. He had come so close to his dream, and now, no one knew who he was, or even cared. He leaned out further away from the bridge, his right hand the only means of preventing him from dropping to his watery death in the dark river. No one was going to miss some poor backwoods crippled kid from West Virginia.

"Hey, mister, get back from the edge!" The voice startled Mica.

Three young boys on their way home from a day of playing ball at some local park were making their way across the bridge. They were a rough-looking threesome: holes in their jeans, worn-out gloves, a bat that had been broken many times, duct taped and nailed together. All three youngsters wore White Sox hats. One of the boys, tossing a frayed ball up and down in his grubby hand asked, "See ya wear a Sox hat. You a fan, too?"

Mica stepped back down onto the walkway and removed the worn hat from his head, "Yeah, guess I am."

He watched the three boys walk across the bridge, then disappear down into the depths of the vast city. Their timely interruption had stopped his attempt at ending his life. He placed the hat back on his head and started across the bridge. It was getting dark and he needed to find a spot to sleep.

Hours later, he stood warming his hands by a flaming burner barrel at the edge of an alley next to a warehouse. Three other homeless men surrounded the barrel as they passed a bottle. Mica declined the whiskey. The one thing he had never allowed himself was to drink his sorrow away. His grandfather had suffered a hideous death at the hands of alcohol when Mica had been just a small boy. Alcohol had never touched his lips. He had always considered it pathetic that Gramps had drunk himself to death. He gazed into the fire as he thought it wasn't any more ridiculous than trying to jump off some bridge.

Three well-dressed men passed the alley, giving the shabby souls collected around the barrel a quick look, but walked on. One of the men stopped and walked back as he stared at Mica.

"Mica, Mica Sands?"

Mica gave the strange man a confused look wondering who on earth in Chicago knew him. The man smiled as he stuck out his hand. "I see you 're still wearing that White Sox hat."

It took a second, but the face became familiar—a face from the past: Frank Denton.

Mica's head sank in shame. He couldn't face his old mentor. Not this way, not the way he looked. Frank addressed his two friends telling them to go on. He'd be along later. Frank still possessed that tactful way of putting things. He had a knack for putting people at ease, especially in awkward situations. He stepped up to the barrel, stuck his hands over the warming flames, and started talking to

Mica's partners. "Do you gentlemen have any remote idea who you're sharing this barrel with? This is Mica Sands, the greatest pitcher of all time. I oughta know. I was blessed as his coach for four outstanding years when he was in high school. He had one the finest fastballs. Well, let me tell it this way: When he was just twelve ...mind you now, just twelve, he struck out twenty-seven men at the state fair."

One of the men gulped a drink from the bottle, mumbled something and stumbled away, the others following. Frank turned his attention back to Mica. "I guess I could ask you what happened over the years. You know, everybody back home was concerned. You just plain dropped off the face of the earth."

Mica backed away from the barrel, held up his crippled hand, and limped in an awkward circle. "Take a good look, Frank. Does this look like the greatest pitcher o' all time? I'll tell ya what happened ta me. When I went over that embankment it wuz like life itself hit me in the stomach an' drove the wind right outta me. I been tryin' ta catch my breath ev'r since. My father hit the nail right on the head when he tol' me life wuzn't fair."

Frank placed his hands deep into his pockets as he leaned against the brick wall of the warehouse. "Remember back at Fullerton when we talked about making choices? Things like going to college and getting a good education or just going directly into the pros, or how about having a great attitude rather than being a hot dog because you were better than everyone else. You always listened to what I said. You are the finest young man I've ever had the opportunity and the priviledge to coach. Now, you can spend the rest of your life, however long that may be, walking around with a chip on your shoulder or you can start to put things back together. It's your choice. If you'd like some help, drop by the stadium tomorrow morning. Just ask for me. You'll be directed to my offive."

Mica didn't comprehend the meaning of Frank's statement. “"Whadda ya mean…the stadium …yer office?"

Frank pointed at Mica as he answered, "I owe you big time. More than you'll ever realize. When I was in high school, I was well on my way to the major leagues. I didn't have what it takes to get there. You did. You got signed. Maybe you never got to play, but you got further than I did. Leading Fullerton to four consecutive undefeated seasons landed me a college coaching job. Two years later, I found myself coaching Triple-A ball…and finally, two years back, I took over the White Sox."

A Cadillac pulled up, the driver honking the horn, then yelling, "C'mon, Frank!"

Frank smiled. "Please come and see me. I'm not going to give you anything. You'll have to earn it. If you want help, I'm here. See you tomorrow."

Two days later, Mica opened Frank's office door and stood framed in the doorway. He had tried his best to clean himself up but knew he still looked like death warmed over. Frank got up from his swivel chair and offered Mica a seat.

Mica was embarrassed as he looked down at the floor. "I only come by Frank `cause I always respected ya."

"Alright, here's the deal," Frank said. "I'm offering you a job. It's with the grounds crew. You'll be right down there on the field, cutting and watering the infield grass, marking the field and raking the base paths. We'll pay you a fair wage, just like the other men. I've got a spare room behind my office here. It's got a bed and a shower. You can stay there until you get back on your feet. I'm gonna pick you up some clothes and we're going out for dinner tonight…just you and me. I'm going to give you an advance of a few hundred on your wages. Like I said, I'm not giving you anything. You'll have to pay me back for the clothes and the advance. Fair?"

"I ain't got much choice, Frank. I'm standin' on the bottom rung o' the ladder. If I don't start climbin' back…I'm `fraid I'll die." Frank got up and closed the door as Mica broke down in tears.

Three months later, Mica had a small efficiency apartment of his own. It was only a few blocks from the ballpark. Getting back and forth to work was easy. He thought about buying a car, but the only car he had ever owned had almost ended his life. He decided on a bicycle. It was sufficient for getting him the few places he had to go. Besides that, there weren't any fuel or insurance costs.

Surprisingly, Mica's bitterness of never being able to play ball seemed to dwindle away as he went about manicuring the playing field. He was accepted by the other staff members and well liked. He worked five days a week, occasionally four. He wasn't as fast as the other men, but nonetheless, got the job done. Sometimes he would go to the park before any of the others and stand out on the pitcher's mound. He would look down at the batter's box and picture that old used tire hanging in the tree. The Lord sure worked in mysterious ways. The game that seemed as if it had been yanked away from him was back. He was part of baseball again. He got to see all of the games for free and actually got to know all of the players. They had a level of respect for him based on the fact that he at one time had been signed for three million.

In his third season in Chicago, something happened that opened yet another door for Mica. The team mascot, a young man who had held the position for six years got in trouble with the law and carted off to the county jail. It had been totally unexpected. Management was at a loss as to what should be done. There was a scheduled game that afternoon and they had no one to fill in.

Frank had an idea. He called Mica up to the front office and asked him if he was interested. The pay was better and he'd be traveling with the team. He'd still be down there on the field, and besides that he knew the routine.

That afternoon Mica Sands made his debut as the new team mascot. He limped around the infield and in the stands wearing the Sox' outfit, clowning with the fans and the players. He was truly back in baseball. He now had a personal locker right in with the players, his own seat on the bus or plane and got to perform at every field in the league. Eventually, he developed his own cachet of antics and became the most popular mascot in the league. The fans loved him: the children thought he was the greatest.

Mica was especially helpful with the young upcoming players. He knew more about baseball than anyone. He was always ready with tips on their hitting or fielding skills. There was no doubt he was a valuable asset to the entire team.

The game had been called due to rain. The field was covered and the fans who had been looking forward to a Saturday night at the park had long since left for home. Mica flipped up the kickstand of his bike and began to climb on but then noticed a small puppy, sopping wet, shivering and looking like it was half-starved curled up beneath a parked car. He bent down and scooped the little dog up as he checked for any I.D. or license. There wasn't any. "Well," said Mica. "Ya best come home with me."

He dried the pup off and fed him. He was just a mongrel with shaggy long hair and friendly eyes. He couldn't have weighed more than seven or eight pounds. Mica looked down at the now-content pup sleeping soundly at his feet. "Well," said Mica. "Yer'r lucky I found ya. Lucky, yeah Lucky...think that's what I'll name ya."

Lucky became a fixture in the locker room as Mica always brought him to the games. One of the players commented that now they had two mascots. Lucky always remained behind lying next to Mica's locker while he was out on the field going through his routine. The game always got underway as Mica limped to the pitcher's mound where he would pick up the ball and refuse to give it to the pitcher, insisting that he was going to pitch. He'd position himself in an awkward stance and throw the ball toward the plate. It would only travel a few yards, then roll on the ground. Every time he'd throw the ball, the fans roared with approval.

One evening the door hadn't been completely shut, allowing Lucky to get out of the locker room. Walking out onto the field, the small dog spotted Mica out on the mound. Lucky, now ten pounds, raced across the field and began to chase the pitcher who was giving his master a rough time. The umps and players who tried to interfere were equally chased. The fans pointed and laughed at the entertaining spectacle.

The incident had been anything but planned, but the front office enjoyed the way the fans reacted. Lucky became part of Mica's act. They were a team. The player in the clubhouse had been right. Now, they had two mascots.

In the off-season, the grounds crew kept themselves busy preparing the stadium for the next year. There was always painting that needed to be done, screening that needed to be patched, and a ton of other assorted tasks. During Mica's second season as the mascot, the Sox won their division, but lost in the league playoffs. The next season turned out to be special. The All-Star game was to be held in Chicago and Mica was to represent the American League as mascot. Every seat in the house was spoken for. Mica and Lucky were up to their old tricks, causing chaos between innings, much to the delight of the fans.

Every Thanksgiving, Mica and Lucky would catch a bus and head for Anthracite. All the kids were grown now, married and had families of their own. Uncle Mica, as he was referred to was always the center of attention with the children. He was surrounded by the kids and their endless questions.

"Were you really signed years ago with Chicago?"

"Is it true that you had the best fastball they ever saw?"

"Do you really get to travel with the team?"

Life at the Sands' place had become much easier for his parents. The ongoing burden of raising eight children had come to a close. Now, they were being supported by the kids themselves. Mr. Sands still tinkered with cars out in the barn and the Mrs. still canned vegetables and did some sewing.

Halfway through his fourth season, Mica could feel himself slowing down. He couldn't understand why he was getting so tired. He was only in his mid-thirties. He didn't drink or smoke. He thought about going to the team doctor or saying something to Frank, but never seemed to get around to it.

During the sixth inning of the second game of a double-header, Mica fell to the ground as he chased the opposing team's first baseman out toward the outfield, Lucky right behind him. Everyone was laughing. Lucky sat at his master's side waiting for him to get back up. It seemed as if he was staying down too long. Lucky obviously sensed that something was wrong as he licked at Mica's face. The stands were silent as Mica was taken from the field on a stretcher.

It wasn't until two weeks passed that Mica was finally released from the hospital. Denton and his wife had looked after Lucky. The players were concerned and the fans were worried. Mica's hospital room had been so crowded with flowers that it looked like a botanical garden.

It was the perfect night for baseball. Chicago was one game ahead of Baltimore and the four-game homestand would prove to be very crucial. It had been announced that Mica, and of course, Lucky, would be returning as the team mascots.

Something out of the ordinary was going to take place just prior to the game. A man walked to the pitcher's mound, set up a microphone and then returned to the dugout. After a short moment, Mica appeared at the edge of the dugout, then walked toward the mound, Lucky at his side. Mica received a long-standing ovation in honor of his return to the team.

When the clapping finally gave way to complete silence, Mica bent, picked up Lucky and stepped up to the microphone. Taking a deep breath he began. "First o' all, I'd like ta tell ya how happy I am ta be back with the team. As most o' ya know, I had me a mild heart attack a few weeks back. Thanks ta the good doctors here in Chicago I'm still around."

Mica pushed some of the dirt on the mound around with his foot as if he were at a loss for words. A fan from somewhere up in the stands yelled, "We love ya, Mica!"

"I had me a goal," said Mica, "o' one day bein 'able ta pitch in the big leagues. An accident years ago made that dream impossible. But, as ya can see, I still managed ta git here. I love this game. I love ev'ry thin' `bout it. I love the smell o' the popcorn an' the hot dogs. I love the way our nation's flag floats in the wind out there in center field. I love ev'ry pitch, hit, stolen base, home run and out...."

Mica hesitated. It was obvious that he was getting choked up. "Thing I love most `bout the game is you…the fans. If it weren't fer you, well, there wouldn't be no baseball. Tonight 'ill be my las'game. Doctor tells me I cain't keep up the pace. Jus' wanted ta take a few moments an' thank ev'ryone who had a hand in helpin' me when I wuz in need. After tonight, me an' `ol Lucky here, `ill be headin' back home ta West Virginia. We jus' wanted ta say goodbye proper an' let ya'll know that we`ll miss ya'll." Finished, he limped toward the dugout, the standing ovation lasting twenty minutes.

As the large crowd started to settle in for a night of ball, the Sox took the field to the approval of the fans. The pitcher took his warm-up throws, while the first baseman threw ground balls to the infielders. Just as the first batter for the opposing team was walking up to the plate, an announcement came over the P.A. system: *"We are sorry to announce that we have just been notified that Mica Sands collapsed in the clubhouse and has passed away. Following a moment of silence, the game will continue. That's the way Mica would have wanted it. Frank Denton, manager of the Sox, reports that Mica's final words were that he was sorry and that he wanted us to play the game."*

You could have heard a pin drop in the stadium. Then, something unusual happened. In all of the confusion, Lucky had been overlooked. He ran out onto the field just like he was supposed to. He stopped at the mound and looked up at the pitcher, then started to search for Mica. The pitcher's head sank as tears rolled down his cheeks. The little dog didn't understand. Suddenly, it was as if Lucky could sense that something was wrong. He continued to turn in a slow circle looking for his master. Finally, he lay down on the mound and placed his head between his paws, his normally wagging tail perfectly still.

Frank made the long walk to the mound during the silence. He bent down, stroked the dog's head and said softly, "Mica's not here, Lucky. He's gone now."

Denton stood, the mascot held in his arms as he started the walk back to the dugout. He gazed into the dog's eyes, then smiled. "Don't worry, boy. He'll be all right. He really is in the big leagues now. He's pitching for the Lord."

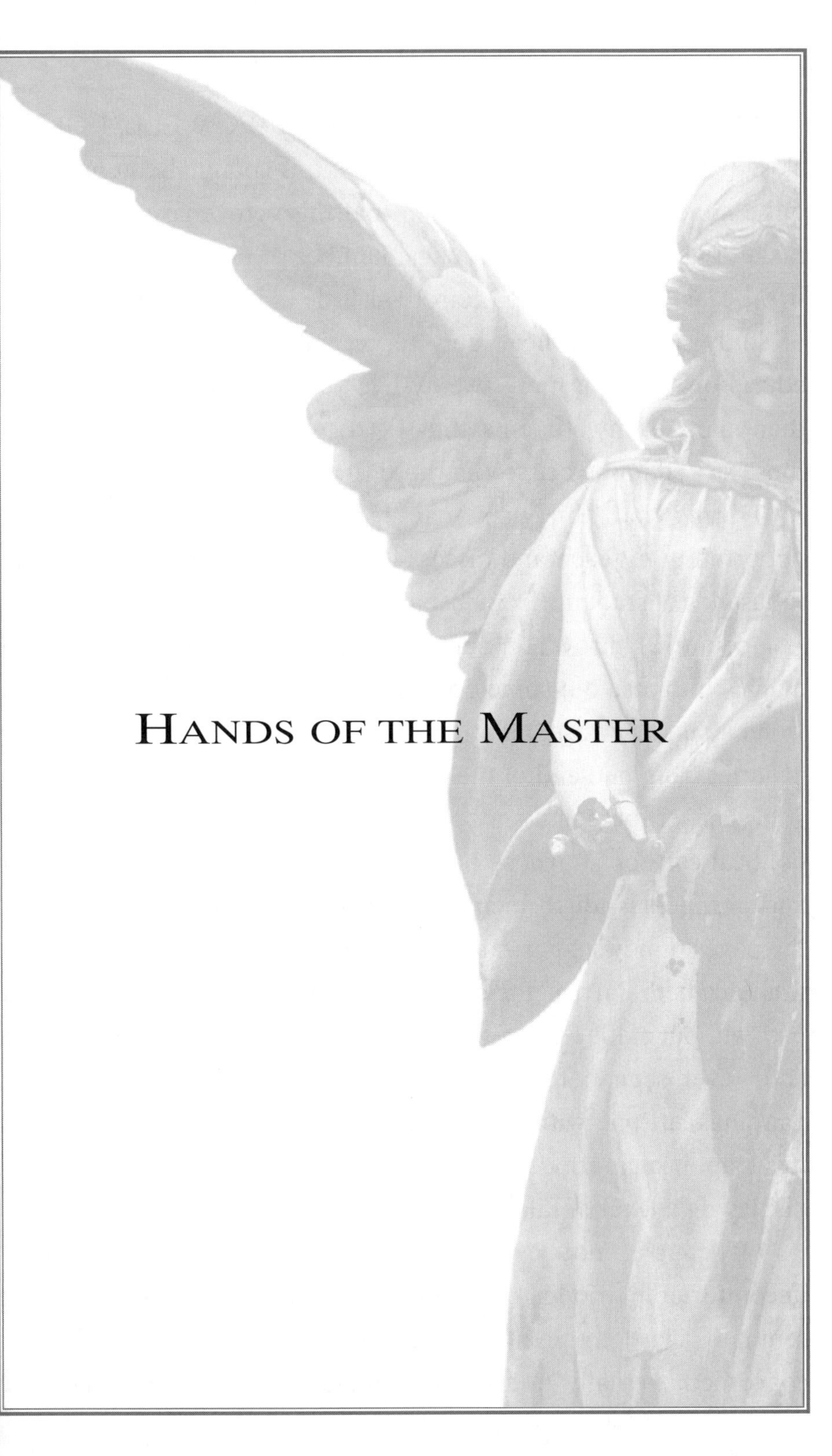

HANDS OF THE MASTER

ANGELS' FOOTPRINTS

I'M RETIRED NOW. HAVE BEEN FOR, WELL, I GUESS close to twenty years. I'll be eighty-one this coming September and quite honestly am of the opinion that this octogenarian just might make it all the way to that magic number of one hundred. When I first began teaching art back in 1940, little did I realize that my time of study spent in college only represented the very debut of my education. Being a mere twenty-five years old, I was barely older than many of my students, thus I struggled to yield the respect of those seated in my classroom those first few years.

During my thirty-six-year tenure, I had the wonderful opportunity to teach and discuss the grand world of art to literally thousands of students from just about every state in the union and a few countries thrown in for good measure. Over the years I've managed to turn out some downright expert artists, young men and women alike, whose paintings and creativity can be viewed in galleries from one end of the country to the other.

I'll never forget students like Robert Diecker, the world-renown political cartoonist, whose hand-drawn caricatures of congressmen and presidents, not to mention assorted world leaders, has graced the pages of newspapers and magazines the world over. Then there was Elizabeth Parrish, the daughter of a Minnesota ironworker. She had, without a doubt, brought nature's wildlife to the canvas as folks had never seen before. David Anthony's Civil War murals and paintings left one with the feeling of actually being present during this important period of history, the detail of his intricate work displaying a level of talent and patience that was hard to fathom.

Of course, not everyone who sat in one of the hard, uncomfortable wooden chairs in my class turned out to be anything remotely close to great, at least as far as the world of art is concerned. Actually, a large percentage of my students graduated from the university with a degree in art under their belt, but never utilized their talent as a means of support in their future lives.

One such student was Reese McCoy, an Indiana farm boy who didn't quite fit into the mold of most art students. I'll never forget that first day he walked into my class: a tall, slender youth, his facial features wearing a weathered mask of long, hot days in the summer heat and bitter winter winds. Despite his gaunt frame, his arms were well-developed, almost appearing out of proportion, years of tossing bales of hay and eighty-pound sacks of grain toning his forearms and biceps into rippling muscle.

His hands were stubby and calloused, the rough skin a dull brown giving the impression of dirt that could not be washed away. He didn't dress like any of the other students, his clothing normally a pair of old denim jeans, an unbuttoned flannel shirt over a white t-shirt and work boots that had seen better days. It was the opinion of his fellow students that he was a common farmer who had simply taken a stab of getting dressed up, since their idea of clothing centered on the latest fashions or acceptable fad.

Reese possessed a jerky gait about his walk and it was perceived by most that he would keel over on his very next step. He had an odd-shaped nose that had obviously been broken at one time, according to Reese by a neighbor's bull, empathic eyes and a neatly trimmed crew cut that any military barber would have surely admired.

Reese took a seat in the middle of the front row, completely unaware of the whispers and comments about his weird appearance. Looking back now, I'm not so sure that he was ignorant of the underlying slurs and detrimental conversation that went on behind his back. It just wasn't an issue to him. He was there to learn, and learn he would.

The reasons why students choose art are as mixed as the students themselves. Sure, there were those who had always displayed a talent for drawing since they had been in elementary school, or those whose abstract painting left most of us wondering what went on inside their minds, the description of their mixture of odd shapes and colors usually leaving many of us in a state of amazement. Some students, like myself, had designs on teaching art or even gaining employment with a prosperous newspaper or ad agency as a member of their art department.

Reese McCoy's reason was that of hunger—a desire to enlarge his knowledge of those who had down through the centuries blessed us with their God-given artistic abilities. He wanted to learn everything about artists like Vincent van Gogh, Pierre Auguste Renoir or America's own Norman Rockwell.

As it turned out, Reese, the inferior-dressed farmer's son, was a walking encyclopedia when it came to individuals of fame. It made no difference if the person was Babe Ruth, General Ulysses S. Grant, Adolf Hitler or just about anybody else of reasonable prominence that could be mentioned. Reese could tell you when and where they were born, the names of their parents, where they attended school, who they married, the ins and outs of their varied careers, including details most people had never heard of, the date of their death, provided they were dead and, finally, where they were buried. The only area of fame that he had never really studied was that of art, thus a totally new world of talented individuals, both alive and deceased would be opened, and no doubt added to his already unbelievable knowledge of biographies.

Just three weeks after Reese walked onto the campus, his uncanny ability to relate what seemed like an endless flow of eloquence left those who listened dumfounded. Somehow, h discussed dates, facts and statistics, which normally had a tendency to lull listeners to sleep, with splashy animation, his rendition of someone's life seemingly unfolding in the form of a well-told story. At noon, or even in between classes, students and teachers alike would convene beneath one of the large Scarlet Oak trees next to the library, munching on brown bag lunches and sipping drinks as Reese presented the life history of some famous person, the information coming forth always direct and delivered with sincere emotion.

On more than one occasion, I joined the ever-increasing crowd as Reese went on about people like Marilyn Monroe—born 1926, Norma Jean Mortenson, later changed to Norma Jean Baker, died 1962—or the famed Mexican revolutionary, Francisco Villa who was born in 1877, as Doroteo Arango, known as Pancho Villa, died 1923….

Toward the end of the year, as usual, the traditional term paper would be due. When I had attended school, I hated the thought and even more the actual preparation of putting together an acceptable subject that would render me a passing grade. That particular year, the year that I met Reese McCoy, I came up with a new slant for the year-end assignment. Each student was to create a term paper of no less than one thousand words and not to exceed three thousand on who they thought the world's greatest artist was—and why.

Aside from the length of their work, there were also a few simplistic ground rules that had to be adhered to: the name of the artist could not be mentioned as well as what I referred to as "major clues," such as where they were born or denoting the identity of any of their creations. Each term paper would be read in front of the entire class by its writer. It would then rest with the students to decide who it was that the paper was about. Each student would write down who he thought the writer was referring to, sign his slip and pass it to the front for review. The author of the paper would then submit the real identity of his or her selected artist in a sealed envelope that would be opened and the name written on the chalkboard. The more students who guessed correctly, the higher grade the writer of the paper received. From the time the rules for the yearly term papers were announced, the students were given six weeks to complete the assignment.

Term paper week was finally at hand and during the course of the week, each student would stand before the class and deliver the clues to their choice of the greatest artist of all time. It was to be conducted in alphabetical order, Reese, unfortunately the last. This in itself presented somewhat of a letdown to the other students as they expected his paper to equal one of his mesmerizing biographical speeches about a famous life. It was Tuesday and Reese wasn't scheduled to speak until Friday afternoon.

Each day, class starting at exactly 1:35 p.m., five students per day would present their paper. As the days passed by, one by one, the students recited their papers and for the most part, honored the rules keeping clues to a minimum, revealing just enough to receive a passing or at least acceptable grade.

I can recall Reese McCoy's paper as if I had just heard it. Actually, his is the only paper that I saved over the years. I must have read it, well…a thousand times. To be truthful, it got to the point after a few years where I practically had the paper memorized.

For some reason, on the day that Reese was to give the class his term paper, he was wearing a brand-new pair of work boots and I remember staring at the glossy finish of the leather as he started. "We have been requested to write about who we feel the greatest artist of all time is…and of course…why. During the week, I have thoroughly relished sitting in the first row hearing about all of your choices, talented individuals like the Frenchman Pablo Picasso, Italy's Leonardo da Vinci and Michelangelo Buonarroti. We have heard of Dutch painters, such as Rembrandt Harmensz van Rijn and Jan Steen. And of course, we mustn't forget James Abbott Moneill Whistler and a host of others who have been your choices as the greatest artist of all time.

"I suppose that no one enjoys being last to present a matter, but perhaps it is a fortunate thing that I bring up the rear as I have no doubt that my choice as the greatest artist of all time is not just my sole opinion but based on fact. For the sake of keeping things interesting, I'm not going to state that any of the individuals already discussed this week are not my choice. As our instructor has indicated, it is up to the class to define the identity of the artist.

"I'm not even going to disclose whether my artist is male or female, however I will ascribe to my selection as he for the benefit of referring to the artist. Now, I realize that some of the ladies in the class might be getting a little upset at this moment feeling that I'm bordering on being chauvinistic, but think about this: the fantastic sailing vessels of history have always been dubbed as she regardless of their given moniker. How many times have we watched on television or heard on the news about the launching of a new vessel, the reporter's rhetoric always including something in regard to her maiden voyage. For this reason, I feel dubbing my artist with he or his, even though I am not hinting that I am not referring to a male is totally acceptable If I have confused anyone at this point, I certainly apologize.

"My initial glimpse at the work of my artist occurred when I was an infant. I'm sure that I enjoyed the colors, but had absolutely no understanding as to what I was looking at. Growing older, I began to understand what the artist had created, but still was a long way from appreciating his work.

"Over my life, I've viewed his trade in a great number of places. It had always been made available to view with ease, the poor being able to enjoy it as much as the rich, the young as well as the old. I think it's safe to say that if you were to make an effort to purchase a painting created by any artist that's been mentioned during the past week, most of us wouldn't even be able to afford its frame. These creations are valued at hundreds of thousands of dollars, maybe millions, depending on the particular painting. The work that my artist had displayed is priceless, but yet available for all to see.

"I'm only going to offer you two examples of his work as I think this should be adequate. I once viewed one of his creations where he had painted the evening sunset along the coast of the Atlantic Ocean. The black gloomy depths had been magically touched by the splendor of the reddish-orange ball located hundred of thousands of miles in the distance. This self-luminous, gaseous central star of the solar system, commonly referred to as the sun, possesses a mass 332,000 times that of the earth, its heat fifteen to twenty million degrees surface temperature. The Atlantic, a vast body of water not only touching the American continents to the west, but Europe and Africa to the east, at its deepest point is estimated at nearly 28,000 feet and covers an expanse of 31,800,000 square miles.

"The greatest artist in the world was able to present to all who saw his work the simplicity of the gentle warmth touching the rolling waves despite the enormity of these two spacious entities. One couldn't help but feel a sense of calmness about themselves.

"My second example of the greatest artist is his painting of the trees. There has been many an artist who has painted these miraculous wonders of nature, but none can attain the change of the seasons as my artist. His paintings of the spring spark of new life, his portraits of redbuds, pink and white dogwoods, flowering peach, the impressive southern magnolia and the shower of cherry blossom petals are truly a welcome sight following the seemingly prolonged months of winter.

"His summer paintings fill our eyesight with the lushness of the mountainside or the meadow, the evergreens: Blue Spruce, Loblolly and White Pines, along with Canadian Hemlock composing a patchwork of color ranging from a gentle lime to a deep radiant green as they stand with prominence in the forest. I once had the pleasure of viewing a group of Crepe Myrtles that he had painted, the frail blooms of white, pink and lavender activating my sense of smell to fill with the essence of the summer fragrance.

"His realistic representation of the bundle of color in the fall is a veritable tapestry of bi-colored combinations adding to the grandeur of the surrounding countryside. His display of the blazing autumn season supplies us with the muted yellow of the Chinese Elm, along with the golden bronze of the American Beech and the Sugar Maple's downpour of brilliant yellow and gold. The Pin Oak displays its foliage bordering between russet and orange, while the Red Maple's leaves offer a shroud of striking crimson.

"His paintings of the winter season leave the trees stripped of their spring and summer coverings, and yet, the exact shape of a tree can only be revealed during this frigid time of the year, its actual frame like an immutable fingerprint outlined by the glistening ice or pure white snow, almost appearing as a winter signature.

"When my artist paints the trees, one can only realize that every tree is indeed different, each leaf suspended high above the ground, a life in itself. The color and texture of his work is without a doubt a sculptural silhouette, leaving us with a clear-cut message that the miracle of trees is not only passed down through generations, but is a bequest of shade, shelter and, most of all,...bliss. Many an artist has tried to duplicate the work of my favorite artist, but to date, no one has been able to catch the realism his brush strokes can create, for he has the hands of the master."

Reese's recital complete, he smiled, his usual ignoble character touching us all as he placed the report and the sealed envelope on my desk, then quietly walked to his chair and was seated. Not only I, but everyone in the class realized that he had delivered what could only be described as a powerful and lavishly detailed paper on his version of the greatest artist of all time.

It seemed to me that there was a very definite flavor of mystery among the students as they glanced at each other as they sat at their desks, tapping their pencils or staring at the wall or ceiling trying to make their individual decisions as to who Reese's choice had been. Their reaction was almost the opposite of how the week had progressed. Following the presentations during the week, in almost every case students had written down who they thought the artist was before the writer had a chance to take their seat. I too, had managed to define most of the artists discussed, but now, like most of the students, I found myself silently reviewing the clues that Reese had given.

As the slips of paper were passed up to the front and laid on my desk, I was still confused, the feeling that Reese's grade might turn out to be rather low as the look on the faces of the students gave an immediate impression that they had done nothing more than take a wild guess at Reese's choice. Opening the papers, one by one, I announced the choice and the name of the student, all the while Reese sitting there, no indication of emotion on his face giving away any signal as to whether anyone had guessed correctly. The guesses were numerous and before long I realized that a passing grade was not in the cards even before Reese's choice was revealed. The class was filled with a sense of repose as I slid back my chair, sliced open the envelope, stared at the one-name artist written on the paper, looked at Reese, who at the moment looked rather peaceful, then stood and chalked the name on the board: GOD.

The students remained quiet for a moment, then as if some sort of signal had been given, an argument began. There wasn't a single person in the room who wasn't talking…well, except for Reese and myself.

"He's right…God is the greatest artist."

"I disagree. How do we know God even exists?"

"God does exist, but I don't think he qualifies according to the rules set forth."

"We have been deceived. God can't be considered."

Reese just sat there, the look of peace that had previously graced his face had disappeared and was now replaced with a genuine facet of concern for having upset the class in its entirety. The class finally settled once I was addressed with a direct question from a girl in the back row: "What do you think? Is God a valid contender for the greatest artist of all time?"

The room was once again back to a state of normalcy as I took my seat and laid the paper back down on my desk. Thinking back, I recall that solitary moment as one where I struggled for the appropriate answer. As a teacher, I had never left a question unanswered. In most cases, I had the wherewithal to deliver an adequate response, and if I wasn't quite sure, then I could always state that I didn't know, but I'd find the answer. This was one of those unique situations where I wasn't quite sure, and claiming that I didn't know wasn't going to be backed up with getting an answer because I didn't know who to consult or what to read. God had always been somewhat of a controversial subject in my life. There were many individuals who believe in God that I could approach, as well as varied religion-related articles or books, including the Bible that would lean strongly in the direction of siding with the fact that God is the greatest artist.

On the flipside of the coin, there were those who were not believers who would state that God is not a valid contender as the greatest artist of all time because He does not exist in the first place. I had always been sort of a fence sitter when it came to God. It really didn't seem to make much difference to me whether there was a creator or not. I really couldn't see where my life would be any different either way.

I answered the girl's question, stating that each student had to make his own choice in the matter. As the instructor, I didn't think that it was my place to inform any of the students that their opinion of the greatest artist was not rational. I also pointed out that the rules had been set up in a fashion to give everyone an equal opportunity to express his opinion and that each grade would be determined by the amount of those who guessed the name written in the sealed envelope. This ignited another conflict between many of the students, some demanding that it didn't seem right for Reese to receive a below par grade as the report itself had been so well written, while others felt that the rules shouldn't be altered in any way. The arguments continued until class finally came to an end. Reese stood up like the others and didn't seem to be the least bit upset about the possibility of receiving a low grade as he walked out of the room.

It was later that evening upon answering my front door, there stood Reese holding a brown bag, which according to him was filled with some of his mother's homemade fudge from back home. Stepping inside, he said that if I could spare a glass of cold milk, we could share the fudge as he had something he wanted to discuss.

An hour later, I found myself sitting alone in my recliner staring at two empty glasses and a collapsed bag now holding only a few small pieces of the delicious sweets from Indiana. Reese had apologized for upsetting the class and told me not to be overly concerned about giving him a low grade. He knew right from the start that choosing God as the world's greatest artist would tilt the apple cart. But in reality, he had chosen God a long time back and what man thought wasn't what was going to matter in the end anyway.

Reese didn't return to my class, but transferred to a university in Indiana where he eventually earned a degree in teaching history, a topic that he was certainly qualified for. The last thing he had said to me before leaving was never to forget what he was really trying to say in his paper. As the years passed, students came and went, but I never could seem to forget Reese McCoy and what was to be the premier term paper of my teaching career.

The first spring following my retirement, I packed up the little wife, our Irish Setter, all of our earthly belongings and moved the family to the West Coast, our new home now a snug, but comfortable cottage no more than fifty yards from the Pacific Ocean. Living along the Oregon coastline had always been a dream of ours that had finally come to be. Long walks on the beach, a small garden out behind the house and shopping in the quaint seaside village just a mile down the road seemed like stepping back in time, the hustle and bustle of city life now nothing more than a memory of a time long ago.

The summer of my fourteenth year of retirement was the year that my eyesight finally gave out on me, the doctors explaining that there was nothing they could do to save my sight. That first year as a member of the community of the blind, I was nothing short of nasty, feeling as if somehow I had been swindled, something that I had possessed all my life now suddenly taken away. During that horrible stretch of time, I had a decision to make: live the last decade or so of my life in resentment or accept my handicap and go on. My wife, during this trying time had a level of patience that can't even be described.

I'll never forget the Sunday evening as we both sat on the porch sipping iced tea. It was a warm summer night and she had commented on how brilliant the stars seemed to be and how she enjoyed watching the ocean waves form, the white caps riding the apex of the rolling water, then finally collapsing in a powerful but peaceful crash as they enveloped the gritty beach with a blanket of wetness that magically disappeared for a moment but then returned with the very next wave.

In those early days of my blindness, her descriptions of the way things looked tended to bring out the worst in me and that particular night was no exception as I blurted out sarcastically that the beauty of the world was for those who possessed sight and talking about what she could see was only making things worse. She calmly ignored my beratement, got up and said that she would be right back—she had something she wanted to read to me.

Moments later, she retuned and read those words to me that I had read many times over in the past. Since the loss of my sight, I hadn't thought too much about reading. It had always been something I had enjoyed and had even taken for granted. The words of Reese McCoy's term paper seemed to stream across the porch that evening as my wife softly read each and every sentence. When she was finished, she placed the paper in my hand and said that she was going in.

That evening, at that precise moment was the night that I was no longer a fencesitter. As the tears fell onto my hands and the paper they held, I knew that God indeed existed. Reese McCoy had been right all along and even though I had read his paper more times than I could recall, I finally understood what he meant when he said never to forget what he was really trying to say.

Today, even though I remain sightless, it's as if I'm seeing more than ever. God is the greatest artist of all time, the proof being that His creations are imbedded in our memory forever, cataloged and filed away for us to bring to life whenever we desire. Now when my wife describes the stars, I can envision them just the way God intended and when I hear the ocean waves, it's as vivid and genuine as I can remember. Reese McCoy, who received the lowest grade in my class surely deserves the highest grade in Heaven for his paper on The Hands of the Master.

Day at the Mall

Angels' Footprints

IT HAD BEEN WELL OVER THREE YEARS SINCE THE two-thousand acre stretch of land in Bristol Valley had been crop-producing. It was said that prior to the acquisition of the tract by Mid-America Development, the fertile land had been farmed as far back as two hundred years.

Residing on the pine-covered side of Hibbs Mountain had for decades given residents a sprawling view of the lush farmland far below, the adjacent fields of corn, beans and tobacco creating a patchwork of green and brown. Jimmy Mueller had been there on the screened-in front porch staring through Harry's binoculars from the very first day the surveyors arrived. It wasn't long after that when the army of men wearing orange hard hats came, driving a long convoy of filthy, yellow heavy equipment.

In just four weeks, the endless fields had been transformed into a vast desert of dirt and rock. A bleary brown cloud of dust hovered over the dozers, earth movers, and mammoth trucks as they pushed, slid and hauled massive piles of dirt from one section to another.

Summer drifted by slowly that first season, and with the intense heat of August came a new group of workers. Flatbed trucks crossed the dusty valley on a daily basis, bringing in tons of lumber, concrete, cinder block, pipe, and wire. Cranes and forklifts heaved pallets and skids of building supplies to specific areas where carpenters, bricklayers, pipefitters, and electricians went about the business of constructing the enormous building.

Jimmy knew more about what was going on down in the valley than anyone in the county. From early morning until mid-afternoon when the workers called it a day, Jimmy peered through the binoculars. He had the work routine of the tradesmen practically memorized. Aside from their hard hats, they wore heavy-duty bib-overalls and jeans, sweatshirts, and steel-toed work boots. They smoked cigars and cigarettes and drank endless cups of coffee in the morning. In the heat of the afternoon, they drank cups of water from five-gallon containers.

The second phase of construction passed as the massive structure took shape, and eventually the surrounding parking lot was paved and striped. The complex had been completed for three months now, except for three large outlets on the outskirts of the mall. The Tri-County Mall drew thousands of shoppers from not only the surrounding counties but from across the state line.

It was eleven o'clock Saturday morning. The sprawling parking lot was already starting to fill up with hundreds of cars. Jimmy swallowed his final swig of orange juice as he placed the binoculars on the lounge chair. It was time.

What he was about to attempt could only result in trouble. He'd thought about it, but what other choice did he have? He'd asked them to take him on three different occasions. They had promised that they would, but so far, it was just that—nothing more than a promise. He had suggested that he go by himself. They had laughed and said that that was impossible. The only way he could go was if he was accompanied by an adult.

Asking them again was out of the question. They were already mad at him for spilling his cereal and juice on the kitchen floor earlier in the morning. Looking over his shoulder, he picked up his worn ball and bat, then opened the screen door leading down to the backyard.

He took three slow steps across the sparse grass, and then stopped. So far, everything was going as planned. He heard Henry on the riding mower out in front of the house. Gwen would be out in the greenhouse tending to her roses. He smiled. He wasn't as stupid as they thought he was. He threw the ball up into the air, trying his best to hit it during its descent, but missed. It always took him three or four attempts to bat the ball. Finally, he connected, the frayed ball traveling just five feet. He walked to the ball, picked it up,and repeated the process until he was two feet from the chain-link fence.

Tossing the ball into the air, he thought, *One more time!* On the fifth try, he was successful, the ball just barely clearing the top of the fence, landing two feet on the other side, and then rolling a little farther. Dropping his bat, he turned and looked back at the house. No one in sight. Up and over the three-foot fence he climbed. He walked to the ball, grabbed it, and threw it back into the yard. Even though he was not supposed to leave the yard, he figured that he was still safe. If he got caught, he could always say that he had to get his ball.

Four cautious steps and he was standing on the dirt road. There was no turning back now. If they saw him, he would have to listen to Gwen go on and on about staying in the yard. Henry never really had too much to say. He seemed to be more understanding. But Gwen, well, you'd think it was the end of the world if you left the yard. If he got caught, it meant being confined to his room for days, but it was worth the risk.

He started down the road, constantly keeping his eyes focused on the house until he was shielded from view by the tall pines. Now, it was a matter of time. He had at least an hour before they would realize he was missing. Once Henry climbed on the mower he kept right on going until the one-acre front yard was mowed. Gwen usually stayed in the greenhouse until around noon on Saturdays.

He rounded the first bend in the road, then stopped to watch two frisky chipmunks dart in and out of an old rotted tree stump. A small flock of wrens had gathered in the top of a tall maple. Jimmy clapped his hands, and the birds quickly fluttered off and disappeared in the blue sky. Farther down the road, a small animal vanished in the thick underbrush. Jimmy smiled. His adventure had just started and he was already enjoying himself.

Better get moving, he thought. He wasn't sure how far it was to the base of the mountain. He'd never walked on the road before. He'd sat in the back of Henry's car on many a trip down the mountain and watched the trees and rocks pass by. Walking on the road was different. There was so much to see: a small furry caterpillar slowly making its way across the road, a gray hawk circling high above, and the long vines hanging in the forest. It would have been great to spend the afternoon exploring the woods, but that wasn't part of the plan.

The morning sunshine stabbed through the dense greenery of pines here and there, reminding Jimmy of massive flashlight beams. The early morning fog surrounding the road had burnt off, but farther back in the trees, a light wisp of lingering condensation hovered gently just above the wildflowers and ferns.

After an hour, he was starting to wonder if he would ever get down to the stone bridge at the foot of the mountain. He was glad that he had decided to wear his brand-new sneakers. His old pair was ripped out and walking down the rough, pitted road would have been difficult. He heard a plane fly over somewhere above. He followed the muffled sound of the twin-engine Cessna as he searched through the intricate branches of the towering trees. The sounds of the aircraft finally faded as he walked around the last bend in the road. The bridge came into sight where the mountain road intersected with a secondary road that led to the freeway overpass.

The stone-arch bridge had a single lane and looked out of place shadowed by the freeway, just yards away. He stopped halfway across the small bridge and watched the speeding traffic. A charter bus sped by, the passengers inside nothing more than opaque figures as they read magazines or watched the passing countryside. Four semis flashed by, their tires making that familiar whining sound that he had heard from the porch many times.

He looked down into the clear, gurgling stream and watched a tiny school of sunfish quickly swim from the edge of the bank out into the middle, then toward some rocks on the other side. He could see clear to the bottom as he looked at the shapes of the moss-covered rocks. He wondered how deep the water was.

A fisherman wearing army-green hip boots waded out into the middle of the water and cast his line downstream, the heavy sinker plunking into the water and slowly sinking to the bottom. Jimmy waved at the man. The lone angler returned his greeting before reeling his line back in.

Jimmy started his excursion up the long, elevated road leading to the overpass. His goal was only ten minutes away and now he was more serious about getting there. There was a better-than-average chance that by now Henry and Gwen had found out that he was no longer on the porch, in the yard, or for that matter, anywhere near the property. He looked back over his shoulder every couple of steps half expecting to see Henry's station wagon emerging from the forest road trailed by a cloud of dust. To get caught now would be so stupid. He would have walked all the way down the mountain only to be nabbed just short of the mall parking lot.

Two cars passed, and one honked. He thought about waving, but decided not to. What if someone, maybe one of the neighbors, saw him. Most of the people who knew Henry and Gwen were aware that he wasn't supposed to leave the yard.

Walking over the concrete overpass caused his stomach to tighten up. He watched the cars and trucks just twenty feet below blasting by, the wind whipping at his face, and blowing his hair in every direction.

On the other side of the overpass, he cut across a well-manicured grassy patch, then stepped onto the hot, black pavement of the parking lot. The mall sat silently in the distance like some sort of shrine, with people parking their cars, then walking toward the enormous structure from every direction. Jimmy almost got hit by a lady driving a long, white car. She gave him a disgusted look before driving off and disappearing in the sea of parked automobiles.

Jimmy moved in between a long row of cars. He wouldn't be quite as easy to be seen there, and he wouldn't have to be worried over getting run down by some lunatic shopper. He looked up at the mountain. His house was up there somewhere. The first thing that he'd do would be to walk over to the area where the last three buildings were still under construction.

It took nearly five minutes to walk the distance, but he finally arrived at the site toward the very edge of the mall. He made himself comfortable on a pile of stacked, chipped cinder blocks, then smiled, realizing that he was in the midst of the workers he had watched from the porch.

Dark, black diesel fumes poured out of a rusted exhaust pipe of a huge crane while it hoisted a skid of blocks from the back of a truck as if it were nothing more than a bundle of feathers. The large, round cylinder of a cement truck slowly turned as the wet cargo slid down a steel runway like lava. Men were carrying blocks, and pushing wheelbarrows full of cement, and building forms from a pile of lumber. The workers reminded Jimmy of an ant colony. Everyone had a task and everyone knew what had to be done.

He sat for a half hour and watched a two-man team of bricklayers as they slapped block and mortar together using pointed metal trowels and wooden levels. Jimmy was amazed. In what seemed like no time at all, the men had constructed a wall nearly seven feet high and twenty feet long.

A muscular man wearing his hard hat backwards walked in front of Jimmy as he drank water from a tin cup. He had the biggest arms Jimmy had ever seen. The man stopped, smiled at Jimmy, then asked if he was with anyone. Jimmy didn't say a word, but smiled back and nodded yes.

Jimmy grew tired of watching the construction men, and, besides that, it was starting to cloud up. Maybe it would rain. He made his way carefully across the gigantic parking lot toward the South Mall Entrance, stopping at each row of cars, and looking in both directions.

At the concrete curb a bus pulled over and stopped. He stood and watched as first the tour director, then the driver were followed by an endless parade of passengers. Jimmy wasn't very good at figuring out where people were from, but was sure from the shape of their eyes that the shoppers were probably from Japan, maybe China. He had watched a television program about people from Japan. The people getting off the bus looked the same.

They carried cameras, shopping bags, and purses. Some wore suits and some dresses, while others had selected the casual look of jeans, tee-shirts, and sandals. Everyone sounded excited as they talked back and forth, at the same time pointing or raising their hands. Jimmy didn't understand a single word that was said.

The tour director followed the last passenger through the large glass doors, and the bus pulled away, leaving Jimmy engulfed in nauseating diesel fumes. He waved his hand in front of his face, coughed, then followed the foreign shoppers.

He took a step inside the entrance onto the polished tile floor, and then froze. He was overwhelmed. He hadn't expected this many people. He stared at the mob of shoppers, some walking slowly as they browsed in shop windows, while others moved along quickly on their way deeper into the depths of the mall. A woman pushing a stroller accidentally forced him to the side. "Excuse me," she said. A teenage girl almost knocked him over as she talked loudly with a friend. She gave Jimmy a rude look and kept right on talking. Jimmy quickly realized that standing directly in front of the main doors was not a very good idea.

After waiting for an old couple to pass, he walked to a wall next to the cinema complex. He looked at the six colorful posters advertising the films being shown. He couldn't read all that well, so he had to be satisfied with looking at the bright pictures. He walked back and forth as he closely examined each poster. Five minutes later, he decided that the third and fifth posters were his choices. The third had a photo of a boy hugging a large black dog, and the fifth one had two men fighting with long swords. He liked animals and he liked pirates. The men on the poster didn't look like pirates, but they had swords. That was close enough.

A steady stream of customers stopped at the ticket counter before walking into the lobby where they stopped for snacks. Jimmy moved down a little farther and watched a girl with a long ponytail dump popcorn into a big round red-and-yellow container. He raised his nose slightly and drew in a deep shot of air. He loved the smell of popcorn. At home, Gwen always put plenty of salt and melted butter on the fluffy white kernels.

He put his hands deeply into his pockets and moved to the next place of business. He looked at the bright flashing lights above the entrance. LET THE GAMES BEGIN. He had no idea what the sign said but knew from the three rows of pinball machines and video games that this was a place that he had to see. Just a few steps inside the arcade a tall man wearing an apron making change gave him a look, but then walked away.

He watched as two boys played a game of air hockey, the circular plastic puck careening loudly against the sides of the table. A woman placed a small child on a multi-colored horse, then put a quarter into the horse's mouth. The horse slowly moved up and down, and back and forth as the little girl giggled and smiled. The woman took a photograph as she smiled approvingly.

In the far corner of the arcade near a row of bowling machines, Jimmy spotted the shiny quarter lying on the carpeted floor. Before picking the coin up, he looked around to see if anybody else saw the money. Everyone was too busy playing a game or talking to notice him. He picked up the coin and once again looked around. No one said or did anything. He placed the quarter inside his front pocket along with the one dollar bill and the other assorted change he had brought along for his journey. He didn't know how much money he had, but now he had a little more than when he had left the house.

He would have liked to play some of the games, but he wasn't sure if he knew how. Back out in the main corridor, he looked at the next store in line. Once again the sign centered above the entrance was a mystery to him. It looked like a place to eat. People stood in line as they talked with two other people behind a bright yellow counter. Pictures of all kinds of sandwiches lined the wall behind the two employees.

Jimmy stood by the counter and watched one of the girls cut open a long sandwich roll, spread mayonnaise, pickles and tomatoes on the bread, then neat rows of sliced cheese and three kinds of meat on the sandwich. The customer paid at the register, grabbed a bag of chips, then moved to the drink machine. The longer he stood there and witnessed the stacks of fixings turn into sandwiches of all sorts, the hungrier he was getting.

Once again out in the main aisle, he had only taken a few steps when a large group of senior citizens, all wearing identical sweatshirts, unintentionally forced him inside a jewelry store as they strolled briskly, following their daily routine of exercise.

The plush, deep burgundy carpet caused him to look down at his feet. It was like walking on air. A crystal chandelier hung directly over the top of a circular glass display case housing an assortment of watches nestled in mint green felt and decorated with intertwining white silk.

Two male clerks, dressed in black tuxedos, starched white shirts, and black bow ties were talking with different couples who were examining an array of diamond rings in a long stainless steel and glass counter stretching the length of the store.

Jimmy had no desire to spend any time looking at watches, gems or anything else the store had to offer. Turning to leave, he bumped into a tall policeman who had entered the store. At first the officer gave him an unfriendly glance, but then much to Jimmy's delight, he smiled and moved to the side.

As soon as he was clear of the jewelry store, Jimmy quickly mingled with the crowd. Policeman were people whom he considered as friends, but in this case, he didn't want to be noticed. If they got the idea that he was not with an adult, his adventure at the mall would come to an end. He had to be careful. There was still so much to see. He picked out an older couple who appeared to be married and followed close behind. If anyone noticed him, maybe they would think that he was part of the family.

Following a ten-minute hike, which included two left turns and a right, he found himself on the opposite side of the mall. The couple that he had been following was finished shopping for the afternoon. They exited the large glass doors and disappeared in the parking lot as they ran through the rain.

Jimmy enjoyed a long sip from a water fountain, then took in his new surroundings: bookstore, pizza stand, travel agency, music shop, and candy store. He couldn't read any of the signs, but he did understand what he saw. He was drawn to a candy display in the large plate-glass window as if he were trapped in a magnetic force field. His previous flight from the police became lost in his mind as he made a beeline for ALICE'S SWEET SHOP.

Strolling slowly down the middle aisle, he felt as if he had been magically placed in a world that, at least for him, was off limits. At home, he was allowed to have one, maybe two, pieces of candy each day. Gwen always said that it wasn't good to eat too many sweets. Jimmy's eyes moved from the right to the left, then back as he stared in wonder at the tilted barrels of candy: jelly beans, gumdrops, chocolate-covered pretzels, coconut bars, and on and on. Every kind of candy in the world had to be right there in front of him. In total surprise, he watched as customers took plastic bags from a large roll, then filled the sacks with whatever their hearts desired. He watched as two teen-aged boys took handful upon handful of candy from a barrel in the corner of the store and stuffed their pockets. When they noticed that Jimmy had spotted them, one of the boys stuck his tongue out, made an awful face, and then the boys left without paying for the sweets.

Looking at all the sweets was making him hungry. Watching the couple back at the sandwich shop, combined with all of the candy, was just too much. His stomach was growling. He had knocked his breakfast on the floor, and he had missed lunch. It was time to find a place to eat. He knew exactly what he wanted. He had overheard Henry say that down at the mall a fellow could get just about anything he wanted to eat. Jimmy ran from the candy store, determined to find his favorite food.

It took nearly an hour, but after passing up four restaurants, a French fry kiosk, an ice cream parlor, a bakery, and a pizza joint, he stopped and stared at the fabulous hot dogs as they slowly rotated on the steel warming bars under the plastic cover. There was nothing in the world like a good hot dog.

Jimmy was startled when the woman behind the counter asked, "May I help you?" He glanced at the woman, and then back at the hot dogs, before looking back at her, but remained silent. Apparently, Jimmy's hypnotic trance directed at the dogs gave the woman a clue as to what he wanted. "Would you like a dog?" she politely inquired.

Jimmy smiled as he nodded yes. He watched her every move as she removed a golden brown bun from an oven. Next, she flipped open the plastic top of the warmer and, using a pair of tongs, removed a hot dog and placed it carefully in the bread. She wrapped the finished product in a white napkin and laid the dog on the counter. "Would you care for something to drink?" she asked.

Another nod from Jimmy, this time indicating no, caused the lady to smile as she stated, "Then, that'll be seventy-five cents."

Jimmy removed a wrinkled one-dollar bill and all of the change from his pocket and laid it on the glass counter, one of the quarters rolling onto the floor near the woman's feet. Jimmy was embarrassed. "That's okay," she said. It was obvious to her that Jimmy didn't have any idea how much seventy-five cents was. After picking up the quarter, she took the bill, punched the amount into the register and gave him back two quarters along with the other change on the counter. "If you want any ketchup, mustard, onions or relish, they're at the end of the counter." Jimmy stuffed the loose change into his front pocket as he looked at his lunch. The grin on his face was thanks enough as far as the clerk was concerned.

Jimmy completely smothered the dog with mustard before walking to a chain of benches next to an elaborate water fountain at center court. He took a seat at the very edge of one of the benches, took his first bite and watched as water from the center of the flat marble fountain spilled out all four sides and cascaded down into a gigantic pool. A man sat down a few feet from him, laid his shopping bag on the floor, then lit up a pipe.

Jimmy was watching a lady operate a stamp machine when a voice startled him. "Enjoying that hot dog?" He turned and saw the tall policeman from the jewelry store towering above him. Before Jimmy could even think of what to do, the officer went on, "They've got the best dogs in town here." He extracted a cigarette from his uniform pocket, then commented, "Think I saw you earlier at the jewelry store."

Smiling through a mustard mustache, Jimmy stood, walked a few feet and took a seat next to a mother and two young daughters. He smiled at the little girl and looked back at the officer. If the policeman had any doubts if Jimmy was with anyone, it looked like he was satisfied. He lit the cigarette, blew out a long stream of light blue smoke and moved off.

The woman got up, retrieved her shopping bags, and instructed the girls that it was time to go. Jimmy wiped his mouth, then walked to a trash container, disposing of the stained napkin. He walked to the edge of the fountain and stared down into the water. He couldn't believe it. The bottom of the pool was practically covered with coins:

quarters, dimes, nickels and pennies. He looked around. No one else seemed worried about the money. A small boy stopped next to the railing. His father reached into his pocket, removed two pennies and gave them to the boy who, without the slightest hesitation threw the coins into the water. There had to be a million dollars in there, thought Jimmy.

He looked around for the policeman. He was gone. He was going to have to be careful. If he was spotted again and he wasn't with the lady and the two girls, he might get caught. He walked in the direction of the part of the mall he hadn't been in yet, as he watched some painters spray the wall of a business that wasn't quite ready to open.

He stopped at a dress shop and watched a woman put the finishing touches on a blue skirt-and-coat outfit on the mannequin in the display window. Jimmy laughed when she bumped the figurine and the long, dark wig fell to the floor. The woman picked up the hairpiece as she smiled at Jimmy and then placed it back on the head, which was minus any facial features. The faceless mannequin reminded Jimmy of the creatures he had seen on a television show about aliens from outer space.

His next visit was to the cookie store. The hot dog had filled him up, but he always had room for dessert. He removed the coins from his pocket, wondering if he had enough money for a cookie. He watched as a woman handed a one dollar-bill to the clerk, who in turn handed her two sugar cookies and some change.

Jimmy gazed at the trays of baked delights. Besides the cookies, there were brownies, sweet rolls and donuts. Then he noticed the giant cookies displayed on the back wall. They were the biggest cookies he had ever seen. He probably couldn't eat one all by himself, but he'd sure like to try.

Suddenly, he realized that he was the only customer there. "Can I help you?" asked the young girl standing behind the counter. Jimmy didn't quite know what to say. He wanted one of the cookies, but wasn't sure if he had enough money. The girl spoke again as she hoisted a tray of chocolate chip cookies onto the counter. "We have a special on these today…only twenty-five cents."

Jimmy took all of the coins from his pocket and gave them to the girl. She took a quarter and handed him back the rest of the change. "You gave me too much," she said. She put one of the delicious-looking cookies in a small bag and gave it to Jimmy as she thanked him.

A half hour later, the cookie was gone. He had enjoyed the treat as he had visited the music store, sporting goods outlet and clothing center. He didn't stay in the clothing center for very long once he spotted the pet shop across the aisle.

He stood near the display window and watched four calico kittens frolic as they scurried back and forth, rolled over top of each other and climbed up and down the carpeted walls. Three of the playful cats finally curled up in the corner for a nap. Jimmy wondered where their mother was.

A long row of cages ran down the center of the shop. Most of the cages were occupied by rare and exotic birds. Some of the birds were perched on top of the cages. One bird in the middle of the store was very active and talkative as he kept repeating, "What's your name? My name's Jo Jo."

Jimmy only looked at the snakes and lizards for a few brief minutes. He could have spent the remainder of the afternoon watching the tropical fish swimming back and forth in the wall of aquariums, but a small white puppy, who at the moment was nibbling at his left foot, got his instant attention. The puppy had been let loose from his cage so a little red-headed, freckle-faced girl could hold him. An attendant dressed in a white smock scooped up the pup and handed him to the girl. The smile on her face gave her mother the answer she was looking for. "We'll take him," said Mom.

For the next hour, Jimmy gazed at the different puppies behind the glass wall. He felt sad for some of the smaller ones that looked on the ugly side He wondered if they, too, would get to go home with someone like the little girl. If he had enough money, he'd buy one.

Walking back out into the main aisle of the mall, he was starting to get tired. He always took a nap in the afternoon. He wasn't used to staying up all day. If he could just find a place to lie down for a few minutes maybe he would feel better.

A huge pile of teddy bears caught his attention. He loved bears. He stopped in front of the toy store window and tried to count all of the bears, but there were too many. Instead of counting all the bears, maybe he'd try and see how many different kinds he could find. There were two polar bears; he knew they were white and lived up north somewhere in the cold. There was a black bear, and a brown bear, a panda and an orange one. Jimmy thought for a moment. Orange! There's no such thing as an orange bear. He didn't like the orange one.

"Excuse me. Are you Jimmy Mueller?"

Jimmy noticed the reflection of the policeman in the glass window. Maybe if he didn't turn around the man in blue would just go away.

The officer moved around to Jimmy's side and touched him lightly on the arm. "Look, I can't help you unless you tell me who you are," the man said.

Jimmy looked at the man's gentle face, then spoke, "Don't need no help."

The policeman gently led Jimmy to a bench and placed his arm around his shoulder. "There are some people looking for you, Jimmy. They're very concerned. They've been looking for you all day. As a matter of fact, a lot of people have been searching for you. You're not in any trouble. You need to come along with me. Everything will be okay. I promise."

The officer stood. Jimmy knew his adventure was over. He knew who the people were who were searching for him. His day of excitement had reached an end. He walked alongside the policeman, his head lowered in shame. He thought about what was going to happen in the next few minutes. He'd probably get confined to his room for the rest of his life. He passed the hot dog stand and remembered how friendly the woman had been. He thought about the little girl with the white puppy. She was probably on her way home with her new puppy sleeping on her lap in the back of her mother's car. Soon, he would be in the back of Henry's car. He wasn't going to be as joyful as the little girl on the way home. Gwen would be leaning over the backseat scolding him, her face red and wrinkled with anger. Henry would be looking in the rearview mirror shaking his head, saying something like, "I can't believe this…I just can't believe it."

Jimmy followed the officer inside the doorway of the mall's main office. "We've found him…he's okay," said the man.

Jimmy took a seat. If he was going to get yelled at he might as well be sitting down. Henry started to say something, but was cut off as Gwen marched across the office and pointed her lanky finger at his face. "Jimmy! Do you have the slightest idea of the problem you have caused? We've been worried to death. You know you're not supposed to leave the backyard. It's too dangerous to be wandering around on your own. We've discussed this more times than I can recall. You can't go walking off wherever you want. Do you realize the position you placed the mall management in? What do you have to say for yourself?"

Jimmy looked at the officer, then back to Gwen. "You told me you would bring me. You promised."

"Jimmy, Jimmy, Jimmy," Gwen said. "That still doesn't mean that you can just walk away from the house...."

Henry could see that things were starting to get out of hand, and besides that, Jimmy was starting to tear up. "Ah, Gwen...why don't we just get Jimmy home? You can see he's upset. He's probably tired and hungry. Let's not make things any worse that they are...please."

Jimmy's head was lowered to his chest, tears were streaming down both cheeks as he whispered, "I sorry...didn't mean no trouble. Just wanted to see mall." He raised his teary eyes toward to officer. "I sorry, Mr. policeman."

The officer had to turn his face toward the door, Jimmy's honest apology being more than he could deal with. Through a choked voice, he answered, "It's okay...it's okay."

After gaining his composure, the officer walked to the main desk. "Look folks, we'll have to fill out a standard incident report. It'll just take a couple of minutes." Two office girls whispered something to each other before leaving the office.

The officer took a seat at the desk, removed an ink pen from his shirt pocket, and asked, "How old is Jimmy?"

Gwen shook her head in disbelief at the events of the afternoon as she said, "He's eighty-one, but he has the mentality of a six-year-old. He doesn't know his phone number or his address. Without us...well, I don't know how he'd manage. Like my husband said, he's probably tired...probably hungry."

Jimmy spoke with anger as he wiped the tears away from his face. "Not true! I had hot dog and cookie."

Inside the officer was smiling. He was glad that Jimmy had spoken up. He felt the couple, especially Gwen, was being somewhat harsh on the old fellow, but it wasn't his place to say anything. He went on, asking the rest of the questions on the form.

It took five minutes for the form to be completed and filed. Gwen stood, saying, "Come on, Jimmy, it's time for you to go home."

Just as they were about to leave, the two girls returned carrying a large shopping bag. One of the girls addressed Gwen, "We really enjoyed having Jimmy here at the mall today. If it's all right with you, we picked him up a few small things."

The compassion of the office girls seemed to relieve the edge of Gwen's sharp attitude. She smiled. "Sure…why not."

As they handed the bag to Jimmy, Henry turned to the officer and the girls. "Listen," he said. "We'd like to thank you for all of your help." His next statement was aimed directly at Gwen. "Starting next week we're going to bring Jimmy to the mall, and not just next week, but one day every week from here on out."

Jimmy was grinning as he clutched the sack. "Can I come see nice ladies and policeman?"

The officer stood. "We'll be looking forward to the visits."

Both girls and the officer waved goodbye to Jimmy as he followed Henry and Gwen down the corridor.

As Henry's station wagon pulled away from the mall parking lot, Jimmy opened the sack: three cookies, a bag of gumdrops, a gift certificate for free fries and a hot dog, a free pass to the cinemas, and five dollars worth of tokens for the game arcade. Jimmy leaned up between the seats, holding a cookie in each hand. "Want a cookie?" Gwen wanted to remain mad, but Jimmy's display of sharing wore down her impatience. She smiled at Henry as she accepted the treat.

Jimmy sat back and took a large bite out of the remaining cookie as he looked up at the towering mall sign. He couldn't read the lettering, but he smiled at the luminous yellow sign as it glowed in the darkness: THANKS FOR SPENDING A DAY AT THE MALL.

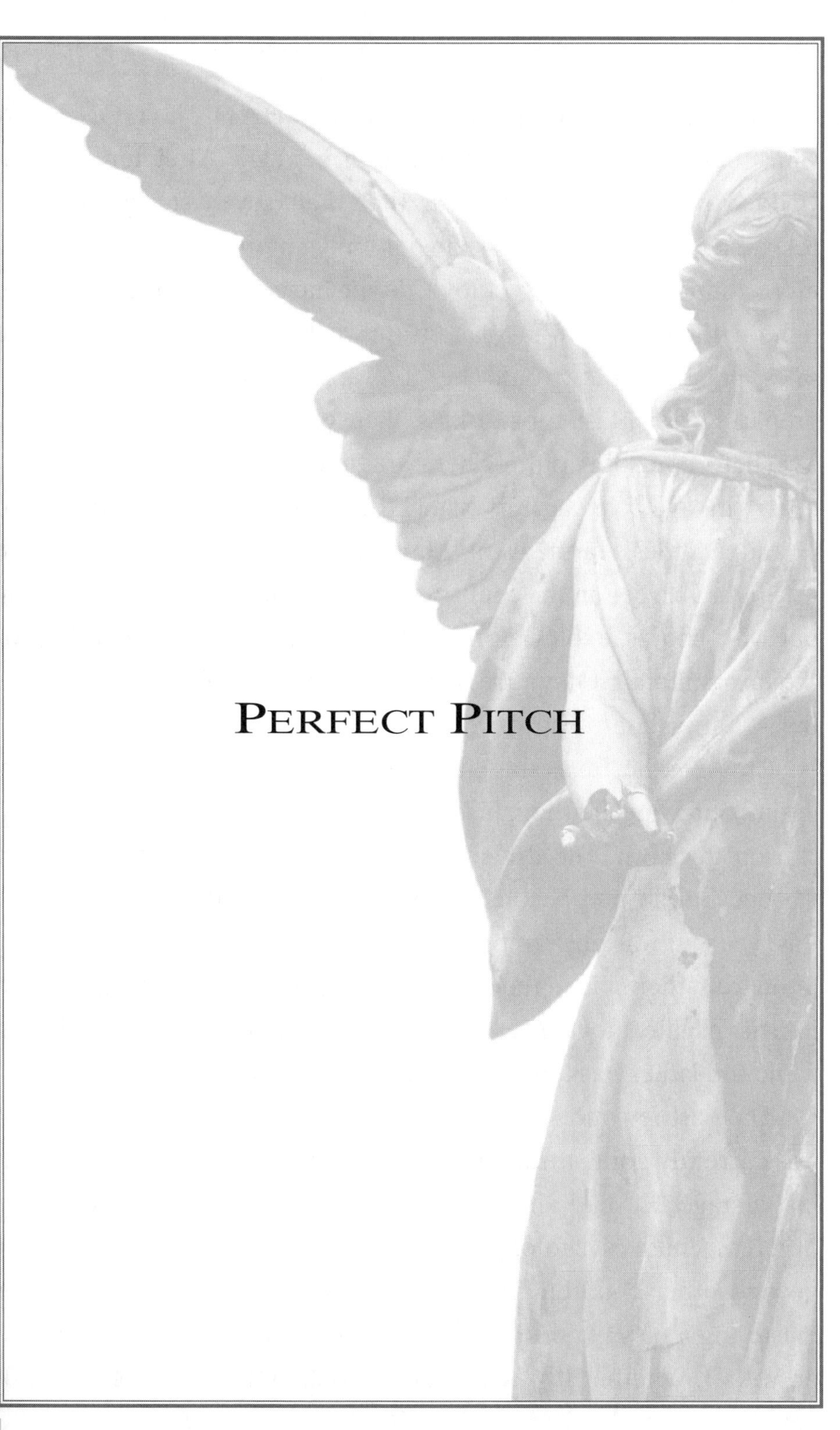

Perfect Pitch

FLOYD AND PATRICA STYLES HADN'T GONE ON what they considered a valid vacation in years. After ten years of wedded bliss, this was the year that their seven straight days of relaxation away from the strains of daily survival were going to be more than just a fantasy. Floyd didn't have to be concerned with fighting the heavy traffic to and from work or with his high-pressure sales position. Pat would be free of the weekend routine of preparing breakfast for the kids, then getting them off to the day care before heading out for her part-time job at the flower shop.

Irwin, age five, and his sister, Renee, four, had been driven to Grandpa Styles's farm, twenty-three miles out into the country from Ft. Smith. A week in the country would be good for the kids, helping out with chores, exploring the surrounding acreage and caring for the farm animals. Of course, the highlight of the weeklong stay was the Arkansas State Fair on Saturday.

Crossing the Texas state line, Pat stuck her head out the window letting out what she thought was an authentic "Rebel yell," as Floyd laid on the horn. The drive from Ft. Smith to her sister's home in Corpus Christi had become an annual summer tradition, although this year it was different. They'd stay the night at Estelle and Leonard's, then pile in the car and head out for a week on the beach in Brownsville. Floyd and Leonard could get in some serious fishing while the ladies basked in the sun and browsed in the local shops.

The past few months had been especially stressful on Pat. Irwin was currently going through what she hoped was nothing more than just a stage. He had already been dubbed as exceptional by three different child psychologists. He had a level of memorization far beyond other children his age. He learned very quickly, and after mastering a new experience tended to destroy anything that had to do with it. Whether it was a coloring book, new toy or some sort of game, it didn't make any difference. Once he figured out how something worked, the process of repeating it over and over was of no interest to him.

It had been a week earlier that a stray kitten had wandered onto their front porch. Irwin had no interest in the small cat until Renee put up a fuss about keeping the animal as a pet. Floyd had never been much of a "pet person," so it was of no concern to him either way.

Pat finally relented, saying that Renee could keep the kitten. Irwin eventually warmed up to their new family pet, but as usual became bored with anything that was new.

"Peachy" disappeared one evening and was accidentally discovered curled up in the back of the refrigerator next to a chocolate cake. The cat appeared alright, but the incident could have been worse. Irwin said that he had placed the cat next to the cake because he thought that she was hungry. Pat was beyond being upset. Destroying a coloring book or a toy was one thing, but this was a living, breathing animal. When they returned from vacation, they were going to have to seek professional help. Maybe Irwin *was* just experiencing a stage, but Pat wanted it to end.

The last day in Brownsville, she finally confided in her sister, filling her in on their problem with Irwin. Estelle said that a woman where she was employed had experienced a similar quandary with one of her boys. He was very advanced, but also, extremely destructive. The physician they talked with suggested a musical instrument, preferably something that would be difficult for the child to destroy. A set of drums turned out to be the key factor in curing the child's desire to destroy everything in sight. He took his frustrations out on the drums and eventually mellowed out to a level of normalcy.

Floyd and Pat didn't have a lot of extra income, so a new set of drums was not in the family budget. They shopped around for a used set, but even that was still out of their range. They looked at a toy set, but from the way that it was constructed they realized that it wouldn't stand up to the beating that Irwin was capable of doling out.

One evening following dinner, the kids tucked away in bed, Pat revealed to Floyd what she hoped would be the solution to their problem. She led Floyd up to the attic where she showed him a toy piano. She felt that it would serve the same purpose as drums. Irwin could bang on the keys to his heart's content. It looked rather sturdy and came with a one-year guarantee. She had paid more for the instrument than they had agreed on, but as responsible parents, they had to make every effort to help their son.

A week later, Irwin turned six. The youngster, like most children, had no patience when it came to the unwrapping of gifts. He tore the ribbon and colorful paper from the box, then ripped the lid open, removed the bright red firetruck, smiled, put the new toy on the floor, and then moved on to the next present. The gun and holster set landed on the floor next to the truck.

The wrappings were gone, and the piano was exposed. The smile on Irwin's face faded and was replaced with a look of confusion. What was this strange-looking object sitting on the floor in front of him? He looked at his parents for the answer. Pat gave Floyd a look of "here goes" as she gently pushed down on one of the keys. A tinny-sounding musical note came from deep inside the toy instrument. Irwin cocked his head to the side as Pat hit a second note.

The new toys lying on the floor and the remaining unwrapped gifts were no longer of any interest to the boy. He moved next to Pat and duplicated her every move, pushing each key. After an hour, she moved away leaving the piano to Irwin's mercy. His intense concentration was such that he skipped ice cream and cake and finally fell asleep on the carpet right next to the piano.

The next morning Pat and Floyd awoke to the sounds of the piano as Irwin sat quietly and pecked away at the black and white keys. He didn't laugh or smile; he just sat there as he experimented with combinations of different notes. The piano came with simplistic instructions for ten nursery rhymes. With Pat's help and Irwin's unusual ability to learn things rapidly, the six-year-old mastered all ten songs in four weeks. This was the turning point. Now that he had conquered all ten songs would he become bored and destructive?

As the weeks passed, Irwin stayed at the piano morning, noon, and night playing the ten tunes over and over. As she watched her son, at times Pat would have sworn that he was trying to make new sounds come from the keyboard. He'd tap a key two or three times, then add a note from an adjacent key. The expression on his face was so serious.

The monthly card party was held at the Styles' house that month. Pat went about preparing finger sandwiches, a veggie tray and dip for the Saturday night get-together of neighboring housewives. Floyd cut the backyard grass, painted the garage, took a nap in the hammock under the maple tree and as evening closed in strolled uptown for a night of football at the neighborhood tavern with his buddies from work.

There was no way he was going to hang around a houseful of gabbing women. In his opinion, the idea of playing cards was just an excuse for the neighbor ladies to get together and gossip. Pat claimed that sitting in a smelly bar, throwing peanut shells on the floor, and drinking beer wasn't any different.

Irwin was somewhat of a dilemma whenever there were guests in the house. Turning your back on the youngster for just a minute resulted in the boy getting into something he shouldn't. All the neighbor ladies wondered what on earth had changed the restless little monster into such a wonderfully behaved child. Irwin positioned himself next to the piano near the front window and played the ten songs for hours as the ladies went about their card game and small talk.

The party finally ending, Irwin curled up on the carpet in front of the piano, his milk and cookies untouched. Once again he had exhausted himself at the tiny keyboard. The woman who lived next door was especially close friends with Pat. As she helped with the dishes, she remarked about how she couldn't get over the change in young Irwin. She asked Pat if she and Floyd had considered giving him piano lessons. Pat said she hadn't thought about the idea. After all, it was just a toy instrument. Just because he enjoyed playing it didn't mean that he had the ability to play a real piano.

That evening in bed, Pat brought up the idea of piano lessons to Floyd. It sounded like a splendid idea since Irwin seemed to enjoy the music from his new toy. The issue of what lessons would cost came up. They were on a tight budget, but Pat said that she could always put in some extra time at the flower shop. It was decided. They would look into lessons.

Pat's employer, Mrs. Temple, had a brother who worked in the administrative office over at the university. Mrs. Temple said that she could ask him if he knew of anyone in town who offered lessons. As it turned out, a retired music professor still gave lessons out of his house. Mrs. Temple supplied Pat with the gentleman's name, address and phone number. She also commented that her brother had said that he was supposed to be excellent, especially with children.

Professor Schuller was most pleasant over the phone. He did indeed still conduct piano lessons. He was currently teaching two students once a week and he had just one opening left at the time. He said that he didn't care to teach more than three students at a time. When Pat told him that Irwin had just recently turned six, Schuller's devotion seemed to subside as he explained that teaching children under eight or nine years of age was difficult to say the least. A six-year-old, in most cases, didn't have the attention span nor the patience to master even the simplest style of playing. Pat informed him that Irwin was gifted. She wanted to at least give it a try. If it didn't work out, she'd understand. But, if there was a chance that her son could play at his age and she and her husband passed the opportunity up, she'd never forgive herself. Schuller told her to bring Irwin by the following Thursday. It wouldn't hurt to take a look at the boy.

The professor and his wife resided on the edge of town on a tree-lined street in a yellow cape cod surrounded by a freshly painted white picket fence. After a short meeting with Schuller and his wife who was also an accomplished pianist, Pat agreed to leave Irwin alone with them for an hour. Irwin wasn't too excited about being left with strangers, but when he saw the two polished pianos in the front room, he smiled. It was almost like he understood why he had been brought to the strange house. Much to the amazement of the three adults present, Irwin walked over to the largest piano, tapped on one of the keys three times, then stated, "Big piano!" Mrs. Schuller said she thought Irwin was going to be just fine. Pat left, saying that she'd be back in an hour.

Pat's prayers were answered that day when she returned. Schuller said that he could teach Irwin how to play. The young boy, according to him, had more raw talent than any other youngster he had ever been associated with. In just one hour, he had mastered the basic musical scales and a simple song. Irwin's ability to learn quickly was uncanny. The lessons would begin the following week.

Professor Schuller updated Pat on Irwin's progress weekly. Three months after the lessons had started, Mr. and Mrs. Styles were invited over to the Schuller's for tea and coffee cake. Of course, Irwin was invited, since he was the reason for the gathering. The young pianist had already conquered fourteen songs, none of which happened to be nursery rhymes. He had quickly graduated to adult music. Floyd and Pat sat in utter amazement as Irwin positioned himself at the Baldwin, then proceeded to gracefully play "Amazing Grace," the movie theme from "The Summer Of 42," finishing up with "The Star Spangled Banner."

"Well, what do you think of your little piano player?" asked the professor.

Pat put down her cup as she answered, "This is so amazing. I…we, can't imagine where this talent comes from. Floyd and I have absolutely no musical ability whatsoever. How could our son be this good? Sitting there playing, he doesn't seem like a child. I mean…sure, he's only four-feet tall and barely weighs sixty pounds, but if you didn't know that it was just a six-year-old that was playing, you would think it was someone much older."

Professor Schuller stood and walked to the piano. "The mystery of where this talent comes from shouldn't be of any concern. The boy has a level of playing that's…well, hard to explain. Usually talent is like gold. One must dig long and hard to find it. In Irwin's case…his talent is like a tall tree standing in the middle of a vast open field. It's so easy to see. Let me put it this way. Your son has what we refer to as perfect pitch. Basically, what the term means is that he has an unusual ear for musical notes. He can actually determine notes simply by their sound. He doesn't have to look at the keyboard or read the notes on a music sheet."

"Isn't that something that most musicians should be able to do?" asked Floyd.

"I'm afraid not," the professor responded. "Don't get me wrong. There are a number of people in the musical field that can identify musical notes, but not at the level of Irwin. Perhaps the best method to explain this elegant talent would be to show you just how perfect pitch works."

Schuller placed Irwin on a chair, turning his back away from the piano. "Patricia," he said. "Please come over here."

Pat walked to the piano and took a seat on a stool as she looked back at Floyd. "I hope you don't expect me to play anything?"

"Quite the contrary," Schuller chuckled. "What I would like you to do at your own discretion is pick a note. Press any key you like."

"Any key?"

"It won't make any difference to Irwin. Any key will suffice."

Pat placed her index finger on a black key and gently pressed.

"B flat," said Irwin.

Schuller nodded his approval at the accurate answer, and then said, "Now, if you will…two different keys at the same time."

Pat pressed a black key and a white key.

"C sharp…E," came Irwin's answer.

The professor smiled, then continued, "Push three keys, please."

After she made her selections, the exact answer came from Irwin: "A sharp…D flat…F."

Four notes with Floyd's assistance followed: "C sharp… D…F…G flat."

"Let's try five notes," the professor stated.

Pat selected three notes, Floyd two.

Irwin thought for a second, then spewed out his answer: A flat…C…B flat…F sharp…G, no *wait*, the fourth note was F."

"End of demonstration," Schuller said. "We haven't gone further than five notes. There's really no reason to. At the piano, the boy is a genius." Reaching over, he ruffled Irwin's shaggy, blond hair. "What we need to do next is not only continue the lessons, but also get little ol` Irwin here exposed to the public. Playing in front of an audience is quite different than in the privacy of someone's living room. With your permission, folks, I'd like to enter your son in a contest. It's in two weeks down at the Knights of Columbus Hall downtown. It's just for children who can play musical instruments. Most of the kids will be older than Irwin, but I think he can hold his own."

Thus, started the career of Irwin Styles. He topped the contest hands down as he banged out a combination of three movie themes. Two weeks later, he swept the audience and judges utterly away at a second event over in the next county. By the time he turned seven, he had a collection of thirty-seven songs and fourteen first-place honors from local contests.

It was the largest crowd he had ever played in front of. Dressed impeccably in a white tux, he marched calmly out onto the massive stage and took a seat at the polished Baby Grand after gently bowing to the hundreds of spectators in the state fair audience. He drew in a deep breath to calm himself, then without further delay played "The Flight Of The Bumblebee," followed by a three-minute version of "The William Tell Overture." When he was finished, he stood erectly, smiled and bowed, then turned and walked from the stage.

Those who had witnessed the performance of the seven-year-old seemed to be stunned. Their applause was delayed, but once it started, it didn't stop. The crowd was on their feet, clapping, talking to one another and cheering. Backstage, Professor Schuller bent on one knee, placed his arm around Irwin and looked directly into the young boy's blue eyes. "Okay, this is it. They want an encore. All you have to do is walk back out there and play the song we talked about."

Pat, Floyd and Renee watched from the second row as Irwin slowly walked back out, took his seat, and then mesmerized the crowd with a flawless rendition of "How Great Thou Art." Finished, he stood, smiled and bowed just like he had done before, then started for the curtain. Suddenly, he stopped, turned, and waved at the crowd. The boy's innocence caused the throng of people to explode into what seemed like an endless applause. Irwin returned for two more curtain calls before the master of ceremonies finally got the audience to calm down and get ready for the next act.

Two hours later, the last act was over and the judges made their final decisions. The crowd was overjoyed as Irwin walked out onto the stage three different times to accept Best Children's Song, Best Child Musician, and Best Overall Performance. Professor Schuller was also pleased, but not surprised. Young Irwin was on the very edge of greatness.

It was the following day that Pat received a phone call from Schuller. He had also received a call—an unusual call from a woman who had been present during Irwin's performance at the state fair. The woman, after introducing herself, had explained that she was an investor. In short, the uniqueness of Irwin's talent combined with his young age equaled an opportunity for a profitable venture. On occasion, in the past, she had invested in upcoming artists. Her idea was to have Irwin cut an album. She would front all of the expenses, and her end would be ten percent of record sales. The earnings that Irwin could derive from the album could not only gain him national exposure, but also ample money for a future college education. After talking with the woman for nearly an hour, Schuller told her that he would contact the family with her proposal.

Pat and Floyd met with the professor and his wife to discuss the possibility of the woman's idea. Schuller had already taken the liberty of checking out Frances M. Marshall. She had excellent credit, no police record, was married to a man who was president of a bank, and had three children in college. Her references checked out. She had indeed sponsored a number of artists, was well-respected, and considered very honest.

Pat was attracted to the image of Irwin attending college in the distant future. Schuller made the point that Irwin, provided he continued to play the piano, would more than likely be attending college regardless of whether Marshall helped him cut a record deal. Irwin's above average talent would ensure that many institutions of higher learning would offer him a music scholarship. He did agree that Marshall was correct about the national exposure that Irwin would gain. There was a lot of money to be made. If there was an opportunity for Irwin to grasp financial independence at his young age...well, what was wrong with that? Another favorable side to the concept was all the folks who would get to hear what could be the greatest seven-year-old to ever play the piano. The Styles talked the idea over with Irwin and it was decided. They would meet with Marshall and, if everything was agreeable, go ahead with the album.

Mrs. Marshall procured a flight ticket to Ft. Smith and met with Irwin, his parents, and Professor Schuller. A month later, Irwin found himself seated in front of an enormous Steinway in a recording studio in New York. Pat and the professor had accompanied him, Floyd unable to go because of his responsibilities at work.

Irwin was a natural as he sat and played for a solid hour with a set of earphones attached to his head. The recording staff said that he didn't seem like a child. When he first walked in, he was without a doubt a seven-year-old. When he positioned himself in front of the piano, he was transformed into a miniature adult, his attention totally focused on his music.

Four months later, the album was released. At first, sales were slow, but then one of Irwin's songs was promoted by a local deejay in New York. One of the takes from the movie theme of "The Sting" had been heard many times by the listening audience, but when it was mentioned that the pianist was only seven years old, the calls started to flood in requesting the song to be played again. Soon, Irwin had the fourth best selling record on the charts.

From that point on, it was straight to the top. Two more of his songs were played by stations all across the country. Irwin was invited to a talk show and positively stunned the audience, not only with his astounding musical talent, but his witty style of answering the host's numerous questions. Little Irwin Styles was making more money than his parents knew what to do with. Professor Schuller suggested a financial advisor. Irwin was going to have enough money to attend any college in the country, for that matter, the world.

Just after Irwin turned eight, he cut his second album. This time he had taken a crack at country music. The album was a hit, following a single from the twelve-song collection. Irwin's rendition of "The Orange Blossom Special" took the Country and Western crowd by storm. It got as far as number two, but never quite made it to the top spot on the charts. At nine years of age, Irwin was invited to play at the Grand Old Opry. The show was televised and once again Irwin was an immediate hit.

The following year he added a Christmas album to his list of accomplishments. He was invited to play on a Christmas TV special. Neighbors and friends gathered at the Styles' house to watch the "boy wonder" of the music world. The seventy-eight piece orchestra sat in silence as they waited for the young pianist to begin. Irwin played flawlessly, as usual.

The next seven years passed as Irwin continued to electrify both young and old alike. The critics said that he could play anything. It was as if the keys were an extension of his inner feelings. During the summer months, he traveled the country giving concerts, often donating a huge percentage of the profits to national charities. People loved to see Irwin Styles play in person. As his fingers floated across the keys during a slow melody, those listening seemed to sense the emotion in his heart. When banging out an upbeat tune, his enthusiasm generated the audience to respond by clapping or singing along. He had the most direct influence on people when he played religious music. He'd raise his face to Heaven and smile as if he were playing just for the Lord.

During his junior year in high school, Irwin flew to Los Angeles over Easter to give a concert to assist the homeless. After the three-hour outdoor concert came to an end, Irwin packed away his music. He sat quietly and watched members of the orchestra gently place saxophones and trumpets inside polished cases and sound technicians roll up endless trails of wiring.

"Excuse me, Mr. Styles." The polite female voice took Irwin by surprise. He hadn't noticed the well-dressed lady walk up onto the stage and then to the piano. The woman repeated herself, "Mr. Styles."

Looking up, Irwin said, "Yes."

The woman continued, "I'm sorry to bother you, but I have to let you know what you have done for me…and my daughter."

Irwin was puzzled and not sure what he was supposed to say. The woman's eyes started to well up in tears as she removed a white hanky from her purse.

"Did I say something wrong?" Irwin asked.

"No, you haven't said anything wrong. Actually, you've done everything right. You saved my daughter's life."

"I'm afraid I'm a wee bit confused," Irwin responded. "You see, I've never saved anyone's life. Perhaps you have me mixed up with someone else."

"Oh no," she said. "You're Irwin Styles, the greatest young pianist of all time. I couldn't possibly have confused you with anyone else. The reason being that no one, I mean *no one*, can perform with the emotional power that you possess."

The woman dabbed her teary eyes as she went on, "My daughter was a hopeless drug addict. My husband and I tried everything we could think of to help her kick the habit, but it was beyond ours means. She was really hooked. She left home, remained addicted to drugs, and even started prostituting herself to support her daily demand for heroin. We spent all of the money that we had in order to help her. She refused any type of medical help or advice from those who could assist. Finally, we were told that until she made the decision to change her life…she was lost. If she waited too long, it might be too late."

Moving closer to the piano, she calmed herself, then continued, "The only thing that we had left was prayer. My husband and I got down on our knees each and every night for three years and asked the Good Lord to send somebody into her life that would shake her from the very depths of Hell." The woman smiled, then reached out and gently touched Irwin's hand. "The Lord sent you."

Irwin was moved by the outpouring of the woman's genuine thankfulness, but was still puzzled. As he opened his mouth to speak, she held up a finger, seeing that he was still confused. "It's your music," she said. "My daughter came to visit us just two weeks ago. She's clean, completely drug-free and off the street. She has a great job as a secretary and is engaged to a promising young lawyer. She claims that she attended one of your concerts and your music just reached out and touched her. My daughter says that she can't explain any of it, but it really doesn't make any difference. Your music saved her." With that, the woman embraced Irwin, then spoke her final words before leaving. "God bless you, Irwin Styles…you surely have the hands of an angel."

The woman's brief visit and tender words lingered inside Irwin's mind. It was difficult for him to understand how his music could save anyone. The more he thought about what she had said, the more he realized how fortunate he was to be blessed with such God-given talent.

Ever since he had entered high school, he had been undecided about what to do with his future. He had already earned more money than he would need for the rest of his life. He certainly didn't want to give up playing the piano. He had mulled over the idea of attending a university that offered a powerful music program, but was hesitant. It might turn out to be a waste of time. He was already being touted as the best pianist ever.

That year at Christmas he announced to his parents that he would attend college. His decision was based on the fact that if his music could reach out and save someone's life, then maybe that's what he was supposed to do. He would take music classes, but would major in working with the handicapped. Graduating from high school, he spent his summer vacation at home working on a new album. He then enrolled in college, and at Thanksgiving, he flew to England to play for the Queen—an honor few artists in the world ever get to experience.

He dove into his schooling with a passion, but still managed to give at least one concert each year, normally geared toward some type of charity. Aside from his school studies, he played at some of the local pubs on Friday nights. Wherever he was playing, the house was packed. He'd sit for hours and play one request after another. He had grown into a handsome young man, standing just above six foot, and weighing in at a slender one hundred and seventy pounds. His blond hair, now fashioned to hang at shoulder length, intent blue eyes, and magnetic smile gave him a stage presence that seemed to captivate those who watched him play.

Sunday night on campus was his favorite time. He'd go to the auditorium at nine in the evening. The large room would always be dark and vacant. He'd sit at the large piano and play all of his favorite songs until midnight. He always placed two candles just above the keyboard. In between songs, he sipped at a bottle of wine and nibbled on cheese and mixed nuts. It wasn't a form of practice, but a chance to get away from everything, an opportunity to sit in the shadows and let the music take him into a state of total relaxation.

At Christmas time in his third year at school, most of the other students had gone home for vacation. Monday morning, he was also pulling out to head home for the holiday. He finished his final song at 12:05, sat back and stretched. It had been a good evening at the piano. As he reached for his glass of wine, he was startled by a frail clapping toward the back of the auditorium. He peered at the darkness, searching for the location of the simple applause. It had an unusual sound to it, almost as if the hands were cupped.

At the very back corner of the auditorium, he could barely make out the shadow of what appeared to be someone sitting in a wheelchair just beneath one of the red exit lights. As the clapping continued, Irwin politely stood and addressed the stranger. "Thank you....thank you very much."

The lone spectator didn't say a word, but stopped clapping, and then steered a wheelchair down the center aisle. For a short stretch of time, the darkness swallowed the wheelchair from view, before it appeared again at the bottom of the stage. His admirer was a girl, a crippled girl, from what he was able to see. She was slightly bent at the waist, a small quilt covering her legs. Her arms were kept close to her sides, both her hands dangling downwards.

Irwin's thoughts were distracted as he gazed at the girl's face: long red hair, hazel green eyes, and a smile that indeed said "Hello." The girl held up one of her hands as she said, "My name's Emily. Most folks just call me Em."

Irwin walked to the edge of the wooden stage, bent downward and offered his hand as he responded, "Pleased to make your acquaintance. My name is Irwin."

As the girl grasped his hand awkwardly, she cut him off. "There's no need to introduce yourself, Mr. Styles. I know who you are. Been a big fan of yours for quite a few years now. I've attended a number of your concerts, and I have all of your albums. You, my friend, are without a doubt the greatest pianist there is."

Irwin struggled for the correct response to the girl's admiration. "You'll have to forgive me," he said. "You seem to have caught me a little off guard. When you play for an audience, provided that you perform well, there's always an applause when it's over. I had no idea that anyone was watching me this evening. Your splendid comments leave me at a loss for words." Irwin glanced at the glass in his hand. "How rude of me. Would you care for a glass of wine? I'm afraid I can only offer a paper cup."

Emily smiled as she accepted. "Wine sounds nice."

For the next two hours, they sat in the pale light of the candles as Emily and Irwin passed the early morning away. In between sips of wine and bites of cheese, Irwin was experiencing one of the most gratifying conversations he could ever remember having with anyone. Emily, as it turned out, had quite a bit in common with him. She was a college student at a private school on the other side of town. It was so ironic. She was also majoring in social work and shared an intent interest in the piano. She had two years of study left before she would graduate.

Emily went on to explain that when she had been eight years of age she had already been playing the piano for four years. Everyone had said that she was quite talented for her age. She held up her hands as she displayed them, telling Irwin that she had been involved in a terrible automobile accident when she was nine. That was the end of her dream of playing the piano. Now, she still played, but only in her mind.

It was at that moment that Irwin was overcome by a strong feeling of compassion. He reached forward, gently taking Emily's crippled hands in his own, then smiled as he looked directly into her tender eyes. "If you really want to play the piano," he said, "it doesn't have all that much to do with your hands. The ability to play comes deep from the heart. I'll teach you to play again."

It took almost a year, but just prior to Irwin's graduation, Emily could play surprisingly well despite her handicap. During that time, they had become very attached without even realizing it, until one evening when Irwin carried her from the stage. As he placed her into her wheelchair, she gently kissed him and thanked him for his patience. A month later, they were engaged, and the next year, married, just a few months after she graduated.

They purchased a beautiful home on the Maine coastline, situated at the edge of a rugged stone cliff overlooking the Atlantic. A huge glassed-in music room housing two pianos faced the ocean and made for the perfect setting for Irwin's goal of teaching the handicapped to play. Business was slow at first, but after a few months, he found himself booked for the next two years. In between students, he continued to give two to three concerts per year, while Emily following her major at college, was deeply involved in social work at a local university.

On rare occasions, Emily would attend concerts and accompany Irwin, who by now was at the top of his field—the greatest pianist of all time. Emily was no slouch herself, leaving people amazed at how well she could perform despite her bent fingers and hands.

The years passed and during the year of their twentieth wedding Anniversary, they were invited to attend and play a duet at the president's birthday. It was a splendid affair with dignitaries, politicians, and movie stars galore in attendance. Following a nonstop two-hour piano marathon, Irwin stood and bowed as he held Em's hand. The president stood and led a five-minute standing ovation.

The following evening, Irwin and Emily sat quietly on the deck at the back of their home, the sinking sun casting a red glow across the ocean below. Sipping at iced tea, they relaxed as they talked about the last twenty years that they had been together. They had indeed been blessed by God. They had gotten over the fact a long time ago that they would never have any children. They had looked into adoption when they discovered that Emily could not conceive children. The system, for some reason, just didn't work for them. They pursued every legal possible solution but the cards just didn't fall in their direction. They finally accepted the fact that having a family was not to be a part of their life. They had decided a long time in the past that they had each other and that was good enough.

Irwin was still offering piano lessons for the handicapped, while Emily had long since retired and busied herself with playing the piano at retirement homes throughout the state. Irwin, at times, went along. It was such a rewarding feeling to sit and watch the smiling faces of the elderly as they listened to Em's music. Irwin still gave an occasional concert and was in the process of creating an album of his most famous songs.

It was an especially cold and rainy Wednesday morning in Maine as the airliner lifted off, slowly disappearing into the dense fog. Irwin was on his way to a weeklong tour in Canada. Em hadn't been feeling too well and had elected to remain at home.

Following concerts in four cities, the plane glided over northern Canada. Irwin sat toward the rear as he wrote a short note on a postcard to Emily. As he reached for his coffee, the aircraft experienced an unexpected dip, causing the hot liquid to spill. Irwin smiled at the man sitting across from him as he commented about the spilled drink, saying that it was one of the hazards of flying. Before the man could even respond, one of the engines on the right side exploded. The plane jerked violently, then banked sharply to the left, the passengers being thrown about like helpless puppets.

Irwin woke up in the freezing rain. He was lying in three feet of snow. There was a huge ball of fire up ahead surrounded by a group of smaller fires. He could hear people screaming, and someone yelling for help. He stood slowly and noticed that he couldn't control the shaking in his hands and arms. It was probably because of the extreme cold, he thought. He stood in the knee-deep snow, his shaking arms folded around his body.

During the crash, he hadn't been wearing a coat, and the short-sleeved cotton shirt and casual slacks he was wearing offered little protection from the ten-degree temperature. He tried to concentrate on controlling the jerky movements of his arms, but the ability to put a stop to the erratic shivering would not occur. Standing in the deep snow, the sense of freezing was replaced with another feeling, one he had never experienced before.

It was a strange, yet, very real semblance of confusion. Why was he here? Who was screaming? What was burning? He staggered toward the largest of the fires around him. In complete shock, he made his way past the blazing fire, the foul odor of burned flesh, rubber, plastic, and scorched metal creating a nauseating stench. He walked past the main section of what remained of the aircraft, and then by mutilated and charred bodies, a number of passengers begging for help. Looking straight ahead, he slowly walked into the dense pines, large white snowflakes, now mixing with the freezing rain.

It took nearly four weeks for the Canadian Air Rescue and a vast amount of volunteers to sift through the horrid carnage. Not one soul had survived. Most of the bodies could only be identified through means of dental records. Of the one-hundred and twenty-three on board, there were thirty-seven that could not be accounted for. It became a ghastly chore as the exhausted volunteers tried to piece together the remaining body parts. Irwin's body was one of those that was never discovered. It was presumed that he was among the scattered remains.

The news of the fatal crash saddened both people in the U.S. and Canada. Many loved ones had been lost. The music world was stunned. The greatest pianist of all time, the little boy who had thrilled onlookers at the state fair was gone. The young high school student who had the hands of an angel had perished. The man who had the patience to teach the handicapped would no longer be able to reach out. Emily went into a six-month mourning period, then finally sold the house in Maine and moved back to North Carolina where she had been raised. Her life was now one of a recluse, living in a cabin in the mountains and keeping to herself.

Irwin's eyes slowly widened as he focused on the V-shaped log ceiling directly above him. He could hear the soft crackling of a fire. He was sweating profusely, his hands still shaking. He didn't understand why. He was no longer cold. A feeling of insecurity flooded his mind. Suddenly, he didn't know who he was or where he was from. Everything seemed to be a blank.

A loud bark caused him to sit up, the warm wool blanket falling to his waist. Near the bottom of the bed lay two large Saint Bernards. A man, well over six-foot, stood over him. He had the appearance of a model who had stepped right out of a hunting and fishing catalogue: handsome, chiseled face nestled in a closely trimmed beard, black-and-white checked flannel shirt supported by wide, red suspenders hooked into heavy-duty camouflage pants. The man spoke with a deep voice that certainly matched his size. "Name's Norm…Norm Smithon. You've been out for almost twenty-four hours. Thought you'd never wake up. Got some of my homemade beef stew here. It'd be best if you get something in your stomach."

Irwin remained quiet, first looking at his trembling hands, then at the two canines at his feet, and finally back to the tall stranger.

"Look," Norm said. "If you don't want to speak, that's fine with me. Actually, I like quiet. That's why I moved up here. On the other side of the coin, if you refuse my world-famous stew, well, I might just get offended."

Irwin glanced at his hands again, then spoke: "Who are you? Where am I and how did I get here?"

Norm placed the bowl of hot stew on a small, wooden nightstand as he replied, "Like I said before my name is Norm. You happen to be in my cabin, which is located in the middle of nowhere. I'm not responsible for you being here. James and John found you."

"James and John?"

"Yeah. Those two overgrown pups at your feet. I named `em after two of Christ's followers. They found you lying down near the creek and drug you up to the front porch." Norm displayed a wide grin, then continued, "They like you."

He got up and started for the front door. "Need to get some wood in for the night. Gonna be a cold one."

Irwin's emotions took over as he started to weep, then through a choked voice stopped Norm from leaving. "I'm hungry."

Norm turned, a look of misunderstanding on his face. "I must've missed something here. That stew really is quite good. My mother used to make it for me when I was young. It always filled me up. All you need to do is reach over there and help yourself. You finish that…you can even have seconds."

Irwin held up his shaking hands. "Look at these. I couldn't hold that bowl if my life depended on it. I don't know why I'm quivering, who I am, my name, where I'm from…nothing."

It took a great deal of patience and persistence, but by the end of the week Irwin was capable of feeding himself. He couldn't explain why he was shaking. As far as he knew, maybe he had always been that way. He had no recollection of his past life, his marriage to Emily, the plane crash or his ability to play the piano. Norm said that something out of the ordinary must have happened. There was no conceivable way that a person from the nearest civilization could have wandered to his remote cabin. He wasn't dressed for traveling in the wilderness and he had no identification. Since they didn't have the luxury of a radio, television, or local newspaper, the business of the outside world was not available.

One evening in front of a warming fire, Norm laid out his idea of living and his reason for his secluded cabin. He had been a high-paid insurance agent back in Boston, but had grown tired of the politics and games of the industry. His wife had left him years earlier and he had never remarried. In short, he just finally got to the point where he wanted to get away from it all.

The nearest town was a six-day hike and that was in good weather conditions. He usually made the journey for supplies during the early spring, mid-summer and late October. During the winter months, he refrained from venturing more than a few miles from the cabin. He liked the lifestyle of being somewhat of a hermit. He didn't have any bills to pay, especially taxes, which just tickled the pink out of him. He did some hunting, fishing, and occasional woodworking. He said that at times he started to miss people, but once he went to town and spent a couple of days, he was always eager to get back to the solitude of the deep Canadian wilderness.

The long winter passed slowly. In early April, Irwin was starting to think that the snow was never going to melt. Later that month, the heavy spring rainfall and the warming sunshine began to diminish the deep, white covering. On April 19, he, Norm, James and John set out on the six-day trip down to Buckhorn. The remaining patches of white were now nothing more than a memory of the past winter.

The first day was mild, but the remaining five days it rained on and off. Following a hearty breakfast each morning, they packed up their tent and gear and hiked through the mountain range until early evening when they stopped to camp for the night. Irwin still had the shakes and had accepted the fact that he was suffering from amnesia. The fact that he knew nothing of his past was puzzling, but for the moment that's the way things were. He had to survive and go on.

Buckhorn turned out to be no more than a few scattered buildings with a rutted dirt road running through the center of the small remote community. Most of the wooden structures were local businesses that serviced the three surrounding logging firms. Besides the post office and combination general store, which seemed to be the center of attraction in town, there was a saloon, rundown garage, doctor's office, and a few residential dwellings, the largest at the edge of a small group of structures belonging to the local sheriff.

Norm, when first arriving in Buckhorn years past, had spent seven months as a logger before retiring to the untamed wilderness. He had remained friends with the owner of one of the mills in the county, and after a short conversation in the saloon over ribeyes, beans and spiked coffee, Irwin had himself a job as a dozer operator if he was interested. Irwin accepted. After all, what was he going to do? He didn't know anyone besides Norm.

Irwin spent the next two years at the logging camp. At first, operating the dozer was awkward, but eventually with practice, he could drive the piece of equipment like a pro. He was well-liked by the other loggers, but for the most part stuck to himself. He saved most of the money that he was paid every two weeks. As long as he worked at the mill, his lodging and meals were part of his employment benefits.

During his two-year stint as a logger, he had quite a bit of time to think. He tried to apply logic in determining his past: where he might have come from or what he had done for a living. He was confident that he was from the United States. His lack of the local rhetoric was a clue that he was not from Canada. He didn't possess a southern drawl of the heavy emphasis on certain words like people from New England. He was positive that he was from either the Midwest or possibly the Pacific coast, maybe even the East Coast: places like Delaware or northern Virginia. The physical work of a logger took its toll. At the end of the long days in the forest, he'd collapse in bed, totally exhausted. He was convinced that whatever type of work he had done prior to the amnesia, it hadn't been one of a hardworking man.

His last day in Canada was a rainy afternoon as he sat with Norm at the saloon over lunch. Norm had come down once again to load up on supplies. Irwin thanked the ex-insurance man for all he had done for him. He'd never forget him and the two Saint Bernards who had dragged him to the cabin. Parting ways at a short paved runway in a large field out behind the garage, Irwin said goodbye and that he would write, keeping Norm informed about his effort to regain his past. The small single-engine aircraft lifted off with Irwin finally on the first leg of his journey to the States.

From Montreal, he took a flight to New York City, then flew down to Roanoke, Virginia. There wasn't any work for someone who had logging experience in and around the city, but he did manage to get a job as a dozer operator with a local construction company. At first, the owner questioned his ability to operate heavy equipment, but following a short demonstration of his driving abilities, his obvious shaking was not a matter of concern. He rented a three-room apartment on the outskirts of town and on weekends drove through the countryside to see if he could recognize anything. He realized that what he was doing was foolish. What were the chances that he was really from Virginia? The more he drove around, the more he started to think that he just needed to accept the way things were.

After spending two years in Roanoke, he decided to move on. For some strange reason, he felt that in the past he had lived near the ocean. He drove down to Jacksonville, North Carolina, secured a position with a builder-contractor and set up housekeeping in a beachside condominium in Moorehead Beach. In the evenings and on days off, he took long walks on the endless beaches. Searching for his past seemed like an impossibility.

He contacted a physician to see if he could get an answer to his constant shaking. After being examined, he was informed that at some point he must have suffered an injury to his spinal cord. The effect on his nervous system could very well be the reason that caused the shaking. The doctor suggested that as long as he wasn't in severe pain and could function there wasn't any reason to operate. Besides that, he couldn't guarantee that his affliction was reversible.

Four more years passed. Irwin had finally given up on his campaign of discovering his past life. He wasn't sure of his age, but the doctor had estimated it to be somewhere in his late fifties. He was still working, and aside from the shaking seemed to be in good health. Maybe it was due to the fact that he was getting old, but sitting around the beach condo at night or walking on the beach was becoming commonplace. He felt like he was rotting away.

Perfect Pitch

One Saturday evening, sitting in a beachside pizza shop, he couldn't help but overhear an intense disagreement between the manager and one of his employees. The young delivery driver had just been yelled at for the second time that evening by an irate customer and stated that he was quitting on the spot. As the boy was walking out the door, the manager, throwing his hands into the air, turned to his cashier and stated that this turn of events really put them in a bind. They were already short two people that had called in sick. Without the delivery driver, they wouldn't be able to make deliveries. They already had seven deliveries ready to go and the phone was ringing off the wall for more deliveries.

Irwin, who at the moment was in the process of paying his check, offered his assistance. "I can deliver your pizzas for you."

The manager was taken off guard as he responded, "Excuse me?"

"Look," said Irwin, "it's simple. You are in need of a delivery man and I'm looking for a part-time job. I have my own car and I'm familiar with the surrounding area. Tell you what we'll do. If you don't trust me, I'll leave my wallet with you. My ID is in there and over two hundred dollars. Stealing four or five pizzas wouldn't be a very good trade off."

The manager hesitated, but then finally commented, "Okay, it's a deal. Pull your car up out back. We'll get you loaded up and see how it goes."

From that moment on, Irwin's boring evenings came to an end. It was almost a year later when Irwin, now a seasoned delivery driver, pulled into a home for the aged. The front desk staff had ordered two large pepperonis. Irwin parked at the circular driveway and entered through the glass double-doors, the hot delivery balanced precariously in his shaking hands. He had never dropped a pizza yet.

Folding the heavy plastic pizza-delivery carrier under his right arm, he turned and started for the main door, but then stopped. Music from down the hall, piano music—grabbed his attention. It was the strangest feeling. The melody not only sounded familiar, but without any effort at all, his mind was defining each and every note. He shook his head, but the musical information continued to flow.

He turned away from the door and walked past the front desk and slowly down the hall, all the while the music getting louder. He stopped at a wooden door that was slightly ajar. The piano music was coming from inside the room. He gently pushed the door open. It was a small chapel lined with three rows of wooden pews. Centered beneath a large stained-glass window there was an old piano. Sitting in front of the Steinway was an older woman in a wheelchair playing the piano.

Irwin stood in silence. Somewhere deep in his memory the realization surfaced that at one time he had played the piano. He quietly walked up the narrow carpeted aisle, but then hesitated when the woman stopped playing. She turned, almost as if she could sense that someone had entered the chapel. When Em's eyes locked on Irwin's, the years that had been erased in the recesses of his brain became clear: *This was his wife. He had been married. He had played the piano. It was all coming back...He had been in a plane crash.*

Emily's eyes filled with tears as her mouth fell open in wonder. Irwin ran to her as he fell to his knees, the pizza carton falling to the floor. "I can't believe this," he sobbed. "I was lost…all those years. I'm so sorry…the plane crashed…I walked off, I just couldn't remember anything. The pain you must have had to go through." He held up his shaking hands. "I'm so sorry, Em…I can't explain any of this."

Emily closed her eyes as she smiled through the tears. "It's all right, Irwin. I thought I had lost you." She looked him over from head to toe. "Do you still play?" she asked.

Irwin displayed his shaking hands as he responded, "They tell me the reason I shake is because of some sort of accident. It wasn't until just a few moments ago that I realized that I had been in that horrible crash. That must be the accident that caused my shaking. It wasn't until I entered this room and saw you that I recalled that I had played the piano before." He looked at the erratic motion of his hands and fingers, and then into Em's eyes. "I couldn't play…look at my condition."

Emily smiled as she reached out, grasping her husband's hands in her crippled palms. "If you really want to play the piano," she emphasized, "it doesn't have that much to do with your hands. The ability to play comes from the heart. I'll teach you to play again."

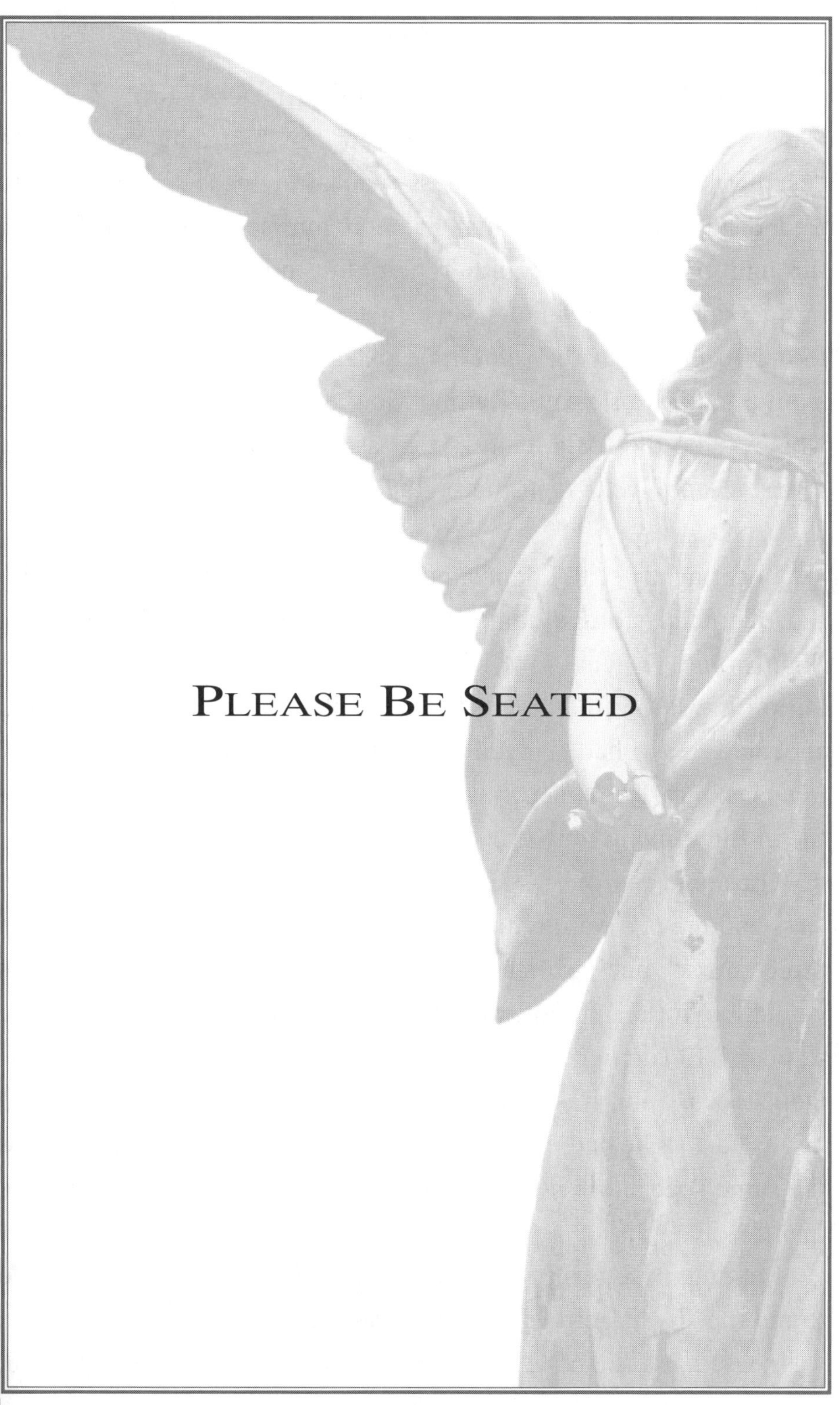

Please Be Seated

STEPPING FROM THE ENCLOSED WALKWAY INTO the interior of the plane, I handed my boarding pass to an exceptionally friendly stewardess who after inspecting my ticket, smiled and informed me that my seat number was D-14. Passing through first class, I couldn't help but notice the well-dressed businessman seated in the very first seat. Rotating his neck, he loosened his tie, at the same time extracting a Wall Street Journal from a leather briefcase. The man looked tired from a long day of whatever he did for a living. As I passed, I gave him one of those sarcastic *enjoy-your-flight* stares, then moved on to my assigned seat in coach.

Locating my seat, I deposited my single piece of luggage up into the overhead storage compartment, then settled in for the long flight home. Fastening my safety belt, my stomach gave me a jab letting me know that I was in need of food, the candy bar and chocolate milk I had enjoyed inside the terminal failing to satisfy my hunger pangs. Looking up at a passing stewardess, I wondered what the in-flight menu for the evening would offer.

For some reason, I started thinking about the man up in first class and how he was no doubt going to be enjoying some succulent three-course meal with unlimited beverages while my tastebuds would be forcing their way though the airline's version of the standard TV dinner. Even though I had no earthly idea what the man's occupation was, I couldn't help but think that I had worked just as hard as he had during the day—was just as tired and deserved the same special attention that he was going to receive during the flight.

Making myself as comfortable as possible, it suddenly occurred to me that I was getting upset just because of where someone else was seated and the benefits of that seat versus where I was located

Please Be Seated

I hadn't thought too much about it up until that moment, but where we sit at different times during our life was a lot more important than I had ever realized.

To say that tradition was a way of life in my family as I was growing up was indeed an understatement. The year always came out of the starting blocks on New Year's Day as we made the three-and-a-half-hour trip up into Ohio, my father sitting rigidly behind the steering wheel of the family van, the braided bead back support wedged in between his back and the vinyl seat. Mother's assignment during the journey was to occupy the time of her three young children with the license plate game, I see something red or the cows versus the horses in the fields contest. As we grew older, and more intelligent, according to Mom, we graduated to more sophisticated challenges like twenty questions or name the state capitals.

After what seemed like an endless drive to us kids, we finally would arrive at the turnoff on Route 62 just across from the big, red barn advertising Mail Pouch Tobacco. Once this old building came into sight, we realized that we had survived the trip once again. The same old tractor was parked next to the large wooden double doors of the barn and I always wondered if it was ever really used or just placed there by the farmer as some sort of a monument indicating to those who drove by that he was indeed a farmer.

The next half mile was a rutted dirt road that intersected with yet another road in equal need of repair, then two miles later, a right turn onto a tree-lined lane leading to Grandma's farm. She and Gramps had retired from farming, the only animals on the seventeen-acre spread a few laying hens, numerous barn cats and Henry, a seventy-pound mongrel who had wandered up the lane at one time in the past and after sampling some table scraps due to the generous nature of Grandma, decided to stay on and had been around ever since.

In the summer, they tended a monstrous garden, Grandma spending hour after hour down in the basement of their house putting up vegetables for the winter, the shelves lined with Mason jars of nutritional goodies as she referred to them. Grandpa balanced his time between fishing down at the nearby creek and woodcarving. There was always a small pile of wood shavings on the screened-in porch directly in front of his rocker.

By the time we pulled up in front of the old farm house, most of the others invited, or I should say, expected to be in attendance, had already arrived, the various vehicles parked at right angles along the barbed wire fence bordering a weed-infested field. We were usually one of the last to arrive, which meant that we had to park all the way down by the chicken coop. The number of cars present was usually around nine or ten and the guests totaling somewhere between thirty-five to forty, depending on rare cancellations.

When I say rare, what I'm really trying to say is that a cancellation was not frequently encountered. Grandma, believe it or not, had an actual sign-in table located just past the spacious walk-in closet. After hanging up their coats, each family had to fill out the register pad listing those attending, the ages of their children and any new additions.

This stipulation of the holiday gathering always seemed out of place to me as if I were attending a funeral or wedding, Grandma said that it was simply used for recordkeeping. It remained a mystery to me over the years why more of the family didn't complain. After all, it was supposed to be a day of great food, pleasant conversation, and a time to kick back and unwind. I had promised myself early on that when I had a family of my own that I was going to rebel and not sign in.

Please Be Seated

The meal itself was always the highlight of the day, the main course being sauerkraut, pork and mashed potatoes. Gram was from back east and claimed that eating this particular combination of food would surely bring good luck for the year, and that partaking of lobster on New Year's Day would equal bad luck. Aunt Doris always had to add that down south consuming black-eyed peas was the secret to starting the year off on a good note.

Easter and Thanksgiving were repeat performances of the New Year's celebration at the farm, except the menu would change from the good luck food to the standard Easter ham or Thanksgiving turkey. My dad's two brothers, their wives and kids, along with my mother's sister's family, were always there, not to mention a number of aunts, uncles, nieces, nephews and cousins.

The seating arrangements at the farm were so organized—almost militaristic. When I was a toddler, I was always seated out on the back porch with others in my age group at a small picnic table right across from the desserts on top of the freezer. From where we were seated, you couldn't even see the big table in the living room.

Once in elementary school, you were positioned in the large pantry off the kitchen—still out of sight of the main table. Junior and senior school high children received the privilege of sitting at a card table in an adjacent room next to the dining area and, depending on which seat you occupied, it was possible to actually see the giant oak table, which seated up to twenty adults.

Graduating from high school in our family not only meant that you had completed the standard twelve years of education required by the state, but now you joined the ranks of relatives that were allowed to sit at the main table at the farm. Just when you were of the opinion that you had finally made it, there was one more level that had to be obtained. There were two seatings during dinner—the first for adults who were married, meaning parents, the second seating for young adults who were single or married but had no children.

When I think back now, it seems to me that where I was seated went far beyond Grandma's farm. Growing up in our conservative four-bedroom brick ranch outside the city limits of Greater Cincinnati, my brother, sister and I at some point had been assigned our own seat at the kitchen or dining room table. There had been times when we had all tried to sit in someone else's spot, which quickly erupted into an argument as to who sat where. Dad sat at the head of the table, Mom on the opposite end, my brother and I flanking good old dad and sis on the right of Mom.

It must have been pretty important as to where we all sat and we never really gave it much thought until during one of our seating arguments at the table, my brother went out on the proverbial limb and questioned my father as to who on earth had decided on where we sat. That night, the limb, so to speak broke, my brother spending the rest of the evening up in his room, my sister and I receiving a long-winded dissertation about discipline and how someday we would have kids of our own and all the stuff that seemed unfair or uncalled for would finally make sense.

This seating business was not only restricted to eating family meals, but just about everything we were involved in. At church, our family sat in the same exact pew for as long as I can remember. There were four elderly ladies who always sat directly in front of us, Doctor Sears, his wife and daughter to our left, the Dougertys and the retired truck driver, Mr. Heig, behind us.

I still remember the Sunday that some visitors had accidentally taken our seats. My mother, who was normally regarded as "very Christian," after glaring at these seat invaders, guided us up and down the aisles taking great pains not to steal someone else's designated seat. We wound up sitting on the far left back in the corner. It was the strangest feeling. The wooden pew beneath my backside just didn't seem as comfortable as my regular seat, the people around us not as friendly and the pastor's sermon not making much sense—more than likely the result of my lack of attention, my mind focused on my old familiar seat toward the front. After that, Mom always got us out the door and on the way to church fifteen minutes earlier than usual. She didn't want to experience the loss of our family pew ever again.

Then there was the seating assignments in the family vehicle. Dad always drove, Mom in the passenger seat, we three kids in the back, my brother and myself each taking a window, sis in the middle. This had come about as Jared and I for some reason once seated in the back of the van became possessed and couldn't travel for more than a mile before we had to start beating on each other, thus my sister, who always remained neutral during these frequent battles sat between us like a protective force field.

The real nightmare set in when Mom took us somewhere and Dad remained at home, which left the much-desired passenger seat *empty!* My brother and I would race to the garage, all the while pushing, shoving, tripping or whatever means was needed to get to that front seat. My sister never displayed any interest in acquiring this special seat. She didn't have to. My mother always solved the argument by allowing her to sit up front, while we stewed in the back.

There was another mode of transportation in my life where seating had been quite important. Who could forget all those early mornings standing at the corner until the long, yellow school bus appeared just up the street? As the bus came to a stop, the doors slowly opened, there sat our driver, Mr. White, a retired Army tank commander. I could never figure it out. I mean, it was hard to picture Mr. White speeding across some foreign terrain in search of enemy tanks now that he had been reduced to babysitting thirty-eight screaming kids.

After returning a "good morning" to Mr. White, I'd always make my way down the narrow aisle, my eyes not quite fully open yet, to my seat toward the middle on the left next to my best friend, Luther Talbert, more commonly known as Luke. I often think about the rainy morning that Ronald Koebler, a 132-pound fifth-grade bully decided that he was going to occupy my seat. Ronald, whom we referred to as the "Cyclops," weighed twice the weight of the normal fifth-grader and towered no less than two feet above the tallest of our class.

The Cyclops pretty much had his own way; stealing lunches, destroying homework, pulling people's hair and somehow never suffering the consequences of his wild unruly behavior. There Ronald sat, *in my seat*, the seat I had been sitting in for close to five years. No one, I mean no one, had ever invaded my space on the bus. There was no reason to. Everyone had his own seat.

Luke had a pleading look on his face as if to make it every clear that I should not do anything stupid as the Cyclops was sitting just inches away from him. Ronald's head always reminded me of the Rottweiler who lived over on the next block. His head seemed out of proportion with the rest of his body, a permanent snarl plastered across his face, his two front teeth missing.

Looking around in a somewhat cocky fashion to make sure those seated nearby received the message that he was in total control, Ronald made his demand, "Gimme yer lunch if ya want yer seat back!"

Please Be Seated

I don't know what came over me that morning, but the fact that the Cyclops was in my seat was more than I could bear. The only thing that I can figure out now when I look back on that moment was that I must have experienced a brief period of total insanity. My response of, "Here's my lunch," was followed by mustering up as much strength as I possibly could in my 78-pound frame and slamming my Davy Crockett lunch box squarely in Ronald's face.

As the Cyclops jumped up from the seat to tear my throat out, old Davy Crockett attacked again with another telling blow, this time Ronald's nose exploding in blood, Luke jumping over the seat as he yelled, "My God—the Cyclops is going to kill us all!"

Ronald just stared at me in disbelief, then staggered back to his seat at the very back of the bus, leaving a trail of blood in the aisle while the other kids were cheering and giving each other high fives.

I never made it to school that day—at least my classroom. After some minor handiwork by the school nurse, Ronald was driven home, while I was delivered to the principal's office to wait for my mother who had been notified about the commotion on the bus.

On the way home, I was surrounded by confusion. There I was sitting in the much-desired passenger seat where I always wanted to be while the van was in motion, but at the moment I certainly wasn't enjoying the ride. I had tried my best to defend my actions by explaining that it wasn't any different than the seating arrangements at the dinner table at home. The Cyclops had taken my seat and seeing that no one was willing to help me—I decided to clobber him in the face with my lunch box. My mother's response to my explanation was that what I had done was not acceptable and the incident would be discussed further when Dad got home later in the evening.

Evening came rather quickly and I found myself seated in the most uncomfortable chair in the entire house.—a stiff, wooden high-back antique that Mom had picked up at a yard sale sometime in the past. This was *the chair* that we as kids were always positioned in during consultations with the parents in regard to questionable behavior on our part. Dad sat quietly across from me in his favorite chair, Mom standing behind him, her arms folded as if she were in total agreement with whatever he was about to say.

An hour later, it was over, my father's final question: "Well, what have we learned from all this?" as he held out my lunch box, patiently waiting for the appropriate answer. My father was usually pretty clear when it came to reprimanding his children and we, as a rule, always got his intended meaning followed by a response that satisfied both he and Mom that we understood. Taking the lunch box from my father, I carefully inspected the metal box then gave my answer, "Yeah, next time I won't use this thing—I mean look at Davy's face—it's all dented in and twisted from Ronald's nose."

This turned out to be one of those extremely rare occasions where my affability was effective, my mother and father staring at each other in silence for a few seconds, not believing what they had just heard, then both bursting forth with laughter. I considered laughing myself, but refrained from doing so. Why push one's luck?

During my junior high years, I experienced a number of times when where one sat was of the utmost importance. My first day at Thaddeus Stevens Junior High was going quite smoothly until lunch time when I entered the school cafeteria. Holding my tray, my eyes scanned the sea of unfamiliar faces in search of just one person that I might know. I just couldn't fathom the idea of flopping down next to a total stranger and being able to enjoy my chicken noodle soup, ham sandwich, chips and banana pudding.

One of the teachers who had been assigned the task of

monitoring the cafeteria must have noticed my hesitation and, obviously aware of my predicament, gently led me to a nearby table and politely asked if those seated there had any objections to my joining the group. Not wishing to display rudeness to the teacher or the students at the table, I pulled out the chair, scooted myself in, took the first bite out of my sandwich and looked across the table. I couldn't believe it. I was sitting directly across from Ronald Koebler. The Cyclops now had a following: a group of comrades that resembled a seventh-grade version of a big-city street gang and no doubt headed for a life of crime that would surely net them a sentence on death row in the coming years.

Just as Ronald was about to open his mouth and honor me with some degrading remark, I felt a friendly hand on my shoulder, accompanied by a voice I knew all too well, "Hey, dude—saved a seat for ya two rows over—com'n." Luke had saved the day and now I would be able to eat without fearing for my very life.

That particular summer, I decided that I wanted to play the trumpet. Why, I'll never know. My mother said that I didn't have a musical bone in my body. The fact that I was displaying an interest in something that had some refinement to it, rather than championship wrestling on television that I had become obsessed with, compelled her to purchase the instrument for me.

Sitting on my bed, dedicated to my one hour of daily practice, some of the most indescribable ear-offending sounds floated down the hall, stairs and, eventually, the first floor, filling the entire house with what my father said sounded like authentic life-ending moans from an actual elephant graveyard. Sometimes, I would position myself next to my bedroom window on warm summer afternoons and entertain the neighborhood with my questionable music abilities, dogs from as far away as two blocks over howling their objections to the strange sounds drifting up and down the streets.

That fall, I joined the school band along with Luther who had been playing the clarinet for a number of years. The band director was more than pleased to have Luke as a new member, but after hearing my feeble attempt at playing asked me if I was really sure this is what I wanted to do. That was the only time during my childhood that Luke and I didn't share a common interest.

Where you sat in the band was a direct reflection on how well you played. We had a total of three clarinet players, the best musician receiving the first seat, the second best, the second seat and so on. This pecking order of young musicians held true to every instrument including the trumpet. We had six trumpet players—I held the honor of sitting in the sixth seat and, to tell you the truth, didn't add much to the listening enjoyment of parents or students during school concerts.

Luke was determined to get the first clarinet seat and the long hours of regimented practice began to cut into our social life. It seemed like all of the band members were motivated to get to the next seat level and once there—keep it. The next summer the trumpet was sold along with numerous other items at our annual July yard sale.

"Excuse me, Mr. Gatewood…could I please see your ticket." My daydreaming of the past seating situations in my life was interrupted by the very stewardess who I had first met when boarding.

Extracting my boarding pass from my inside coat pocket, I asked, "Is there a problem?"

It was at that moment that I noticed another individual standing in the aisle next to the stewardess. The man seemed impatient as he looked up and down the aisle, all the while tapping his boarding pass on the lapel of his sport coat.

Inspecting my ticket, the stewardess confirmed that my seat number was D-14. She informed me with an air of professionalism, no doubt from extensive training in regard to airline scheduling blunders that the flight had been overbooked and my seat had been sold twice. Turning to the nervous man in the aisle, she explained, "This is Mr. Tyler who is also holding a ticket for D-14. His ticket was purchased prior to yours—meaning that he is actually entitled to first seating." Handing my boarding pass back to me, she went on, "I'm sorry for the inconvenience, Mr. Gatewood, but we're going to have to bump you…."

Before she could finish, I politely interrupted, the words flowing from my mouth more than appropriate in my estimation considering how unorganized they seemed to be. "So what you're telling me is that I have to get off the plane?"

Growing up, one of the things my father had tried to instill in his children was to make sure that you had all of the facts about a situation before you opened your mouth. Making comments without all the pertinent information could result in making a fool of yourself.

I should have paid more attention to Dad's wisdom as the stewardess gave me a verbal right hook followed by a sincere jab to the stomach. "We wouldn't think of asking you to leave the flight. You're being bumped up to first class where you'll be receiving all first-class benefits at no additional cost and you're next flight will be covered by the airlines."

"Oh…I see," I stammered. "Well, just let me get my bag then."

Mr. Tyler, who had seconds earlier displayed a look of concern on his face of *You're in my seat* now seemed to become very gracious. "If Mr. Gatewood would rather remain where he is seated…I'll accept the first-class offer."

"That won't be necessary," I said as I unbuckled myself, stood and retrieved my bag. Stepping out into the aisle, I motioned to my previous seat as I smiled at Tyler, then addressed the stewardess, "After you."

Entering first class, the stewardess ushered me to the only seat left on the plane, took my coat and hung it neatly on a wooden hanger, placed it in a small closet, then deposited my bag overhead. After I was in a seat that reminded me more of an expensive recliner rather than just some ordinary airline seat, she asked me if I cared for a magazine, then went on to hand me a beverage list followed by a rundown of the evening meal: veal cutlet, baked potato, honey-glazed carrots, hot rolls and hot fudge sundaes for dessert.

As the 747 was beginning its taxi procedures, I happened to look over at the passenger seated next to me. It was the very same man that I had noticed in first class when I had boarded. *How strange*, I thought. The man's appearance had triggered my brain into a review of seating arrangements during my past life and now I wind up sitting right next to him.

I must have been too obvious as he stuck out his hand. "Hello, there…do I know you from somewhere…I mean the way you were looking at me."

Grasping the man's hand, I answered, " Ah…no, we don't know each other. My name is Roger Gatewood. To be completely honest with you…I think I owe you an apology."

The stranger released his firm grip as he smiled. "First of all…my name is Robert McGuire…Reverend Bob McGuire from Souix City, Iowa. Secondly, I can't imagine why you owe me an apology."

"Well, it's kind of a strange story. You see, when I first boarded I saw you sitting up here in first class and I guess I was jealous because I had to sit back in coach. The more I thought about our seating arrangements the more I started to think about where we sit throughout our lives. My apology stems from the fact that I had no right to think any less of you just because of where you were seated."

The reverend laughed as he placed his hand on my shoulder. "This, believe it or not, is the first time I have ever flown first class. I'm on a rather tight budget these days. The only reason I purchased a first class ticket was because that's all they had available and I need to be home tomorrow for my daughter's wedding."

After explaining that I only wound up in first class due to an airline's overbooking, I gave the reverend the short version of what I had been thinking about seating in my past life. We hadn't even been airborne for more than fifteen minutes when our veal cutlet with all the trimmings was served along with iced tea and imported Columbian coffee.

During our meal at 29,000 feet, Reverend Bob shared quite a few stories of seating arrangements that had occurred in his life, the most amusing being his love affair with the recliner in his finished basement. It was equipped with three pillows, an afghan, footstool, beverage tray, two remotes and fingertip message controls for both his back and legs. The only person in the household who was allowed to occupy the recliner aside from him wasn't an individual at all, but the family dog. This was acceptable to him because the furry pet was simply content to curl up and sleep on the chair, not the slightest bit interested in changing the position of the recliner or rearranging the placement of the pillows. His wife and children always seemed to misplace one of the remotes and throw the afghan on the floor. It was his space—an escape from the gauntlet of problems out there in the world.

Finishing up our fudge sundaes, the reverend removed an envelope from his shirt pocket and handed it to me. "This is the sermon that I have been working on for this coming Sunday," he said. "I've spent the better part of the week putting it together for my congregation, but now that we have met, I feel that the Good Lord had me write this knowing all too well that we would cross paths. You don't have to read it now. We'll be landing in a few minutes. I think that the words in that envelope…especially the last part will give you a pretty good idea how to handle the seating business of life."

I won't keep you in suspense any longer. Later that evening at home, the wife out in the kitchen finishing up the dishes and the kids in bed, I settled down in my own recliner as I read Reverend Bob's sermon. He was right. The ending was the most important part.

During biblical times, there had been a wedding that had been announced—many people had been invited to the celebration. One of the men who had received an invite considered himself as very important, but the fact remained that he was not a very important person. Being of the high opinion of himself as he was, he selected to take a seat near the front of the table where the important wedding guests were to sit. When the wedding party entered and upon seeing the man seated incorrectly, they asked him to step down to a lower seat.

Another man who had been invited was indeed an important man, but did not view himself as such. He decided on a lower seat, whereas, others could sit closer to the front. The wedding party noticing his humbleness invited him to a higher seat. The lesson: Those who exalt themselves will be humbled and those who humble themselves will be exalted.

Just as I was finishing reading the reverend's sermon, my wife entered the den, two cups of steaming coffee balanced in her hands. Sitting across from me offering me one of the beverages, she asked, "What's that you're reading there?"

"Oh…just something a man on the flight in gave me to read. Listen…next week when we head up for Thanksgiving at the farm, how's about if we sit out in the pantry and let the kids sit at the big table?"

My wife, gently sipping at her hot drink asked, "What on earth are you talking about?"

Standing, I took her by the hand. "Have I ever told you the story of Ronald Koebler and the dented Davy Crockett lunch box? Come on, I think I still have that old thing up in the attic. It all started one rainy morning in fifth grade when I was waiting for the bus…."

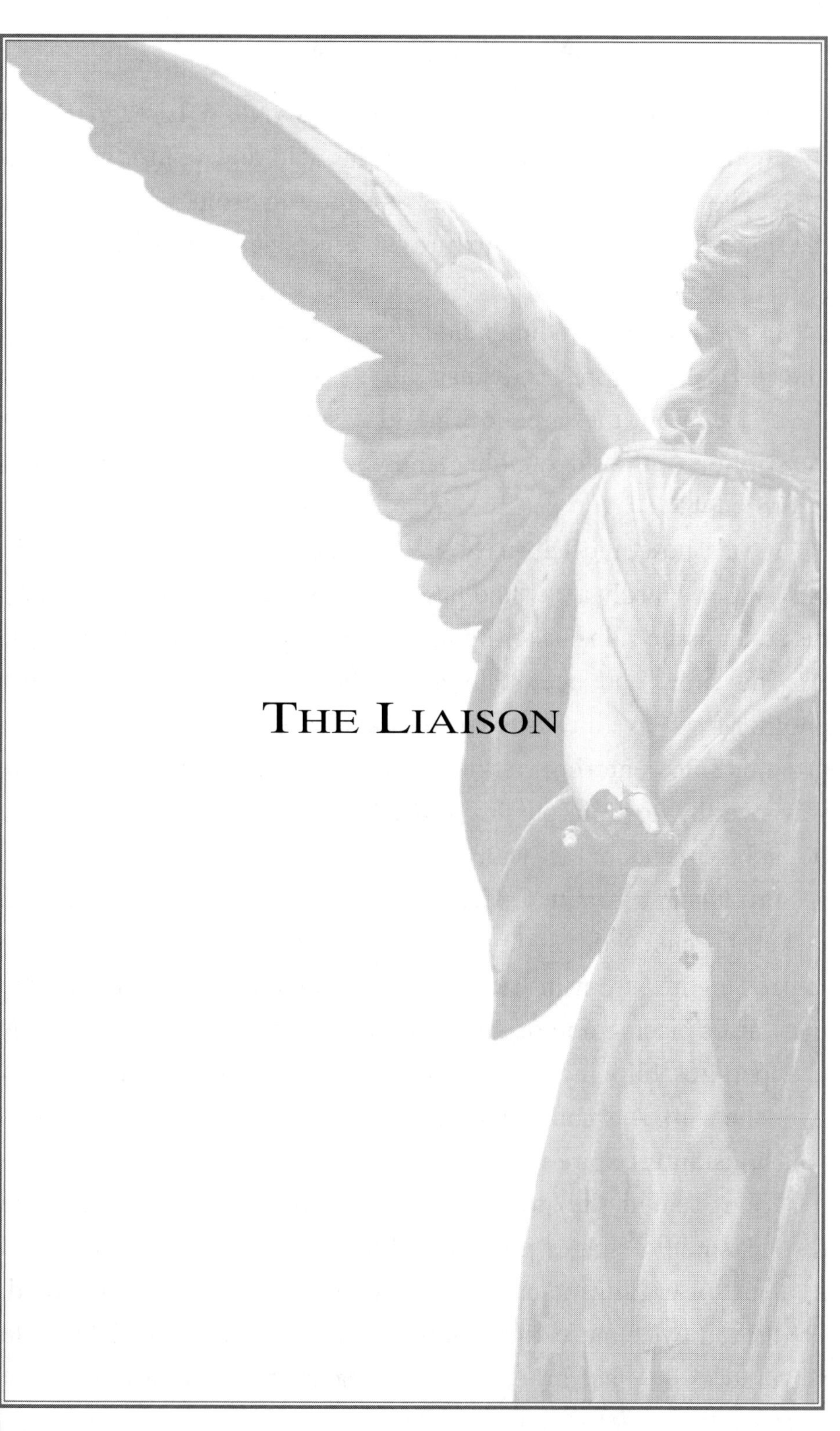

The Liaison

Angels' Footprints

HIS SCUFFED COMBAT BOOT SANK DEEPLY INTO the reddish mud as he stepped from the field down onto the rutted road. The one-lane dirt road was swallowed from sight in either direction from the wintry mixture of snow, sleet and rain creating a swirling white void,

In the spring, the countryside was a patchwork of lush farmland and deep-green forests. At least, that's what the locals said. He'd never been in the area during the spring so the picturesque description of the surrounding landscape simply remained a mental photograph.

It was now mid-February. He had been in France since early November. Hardly a day had passed when it hadn't snowed. Pulling his Army-issue rain slicker up around his neck, he started north.

The snow had been falling for the past three hours, adding another fresh five inches to the foot and a half already covering the ground. Since entering southern France, the division had made its way steadily north in pursuit of the German army. Sooner or later, he had to make contact with American troops.

Producing a rumpled pack of cigarettes from inside his soaked jacket, he checked his supply. Four smokes left. He removed the marred lighter from in between the wrinkled cellophane and the pack after placing one of the addictive white cylinders between his chapped lips. Flipping open the metal top, he flicked the tiny wheel over the flint. A small spark was quickly followed by a low flame, which instantly expired.

He repeated the process. Again; a spark, but no flame. The distinct smell of lighter fluid drifted past his nose, then disappeared as a gust of frigid wind carried the familiar aroma off into the field. He flicked twice more, the results the same. He was out of fluid. He shivered as he placed the lighter and cigarettes back inside his wet jacket.

In most cases, running out of fluid was of no great concern. It was just a matter of turning to one of your comrades and asking for a light. It seemed like everyone in the Army smoked. Maybe it was due to the fact that there was little else to do aside from marching along in the bitter cold one dreary mile after another.

Up ahead, the road was engulfed by a grove of tall pines. A welcome sight, as he had been out in the open on an endless hike into a barren white emptiness. A few yards into the small forest, he stopped. It was still bone-chilling, but at least the cutting wind would be diminished considerably.

The sound of the wind sweeping through the pines reminded him of the hunting lodge back home. He and Uncle Nate had shared some good times there. At the moment, Wisconsin seemed a world away. What would his old pals say if they could see him now; covered with mud, freezing his tail off on some deserted road in the middle of France?

He had been the first one in the neighborhood to join up. A few months later, according to a letter from his mother, Freddy, his best friend had joined the Navy. Months later, a follow-up letter from Mom contained the tragic news that Fred had been lost at sea, the destroyer he had been assigned to falling victim to a well-placed torpedo from a German U-boat. As far as he knew, his other two best friends, Willy and Martin, were still employed at the sawmill back home. One of the first things he needed to do when he arrived at some sort of civilization was to write a letter home updating his family on how the war was progressing.

He stomped his cold feet as he looked back up the lonely road. A set of dim headlights pierced the snow as a jeep slowly lumbered into view. He moved back further into the protection of the trees. If they were Germans, he would remain concealed. He was too tired to fight; too tired to run.

Noting the small American flag flapping wildly on the hood, he stepped back onto the road, raising his hand in a friendly wave. The driver brought the jeep to a stop, the vehicle sliding sideways in the mud.

The driver stared up the road at the lone soldier: four-day beard, uniform caked with mud, an M-16 balanced across his left forearm. The driver stepped down into the mud, scooped up a handful of fresh snow, tossing it onto the mud-streaked windshield, the wipers slowly pushing the wet snow back and forth, the glass eventually clearing. He waved, then signaled the soldier up the road toward the idling jeep. "Looks like you could use a lift. Hop in."

Climbing into the jeep, the young private examined the driver: a tall, lanky man, clean-shaven, friendly eyes, genuine smile, uniform surprisingly spotless. The driver pushed the gearshift into first as the jeep spun out in the mud. Shifting into second gear, he looked across the seat. "You out here alone?"

"Sure am," came the answer.

"What's your name?"

"Charley Brooks…most folks just call me Chuck."

"Well…it's nice to make your acquaintance, Chuck." The driver extended his hand. "Joseph Goodman."

The handshake complete, Chuck cupped his hands together, blowing warm breath over his cold fingers. "God…it's cold." Reaching for his cigarettes, he went on, "Don't suppose ya got a light on ya?"

"No, sure don't," responded Goodman. "Don't smoke myself. Thought I saw some matches over there in the glove compartment."

Chuck fiddled with the stubborn latch, his numb fingers

objecting to the task, the metal lid finally flipping open. After searching through countless candy bar wrappers, tattered road maps, assorted flares and a flashlight, he located the matches.

Seconds later, a cigarette hung from his lips, a long stream of blueish smoke escaping the side of his mouth. "So…tell me, Joe. What is it that you do in this man's army?"

Goodman patted a Bible on the seat between them. "I'm a minister. Had a church of my own before I joined the Army. That was well…about two years back. I was Lutheran then. I'm sort of what you call nondenominational now. I've talked with…and prayed over fellahs from just about every faith there is. How about you? What's your chosen faith?"

"Well," said Chuck, "I don't have any particular beliefs when it comes to this God business."

"How's that?"

Chuck removed the cigarette from his mouth, flicking the ashes to the floorboard. "It's really pretty basic. I don't believe in God, Heaven, Hell, being saved, none of that holier than thou crap."

Goodman downshifted as they came into a long curve, then stepped on the gas as he jammed the gears back up into third. "I wouldn't be doing my job, Mr. Charlie Brooks, if I didn't try to convince you you're wrong."

"Won't do no good," smiled Chuck. "I've heard all that religious babble before. My old man was a preacher. Least that's what my mother told me. He left me and Ma when I was just about two. He didn't leave us with much to live on. Run off with some woman from over at the town diner, took all the church money and spilt. After that, Ma said she didn't have much use for the Lord. It's just the way I was raised."

The cigarette was back in his mouth as he continued, "The next words out of your mouth are probably going to be something like it's not too late for me to change. The thing is…Mr. Goodman, I'm not interested in changing. I just don't believe any of it." He reached over, picking up the Bible. "You people of faith base your beliefs on this one book. Personally, I think this whole religious deal is the greatest rip off of all time. When we die…that's it. We get buried six feet under, then slowly rot. We don't go to Heaven or Hell or anywhere for that matter. We just cease to exist."

Joe held up his hand. "Hold on there, son. There's no need to get so riled up. You see…I've heard it all before, too. I've had men from all walks of life give me an endless list of reasons why they don't believe…"

"If it's all the same," Chuck interrupted, "I'd just as soon not discuss it."

Joe reached across the seat, giving Chuck a soft punch on the shoulder. "That's fine. Actually we won't be together much longer. There's a small village just up the road about a mile. We'll most likely be parting ways there. How'd you get stuck out here anyway?"

Chuck was more at ease since it looked like the topic of religion had come to a close. "Two days back my company got overrun by a large force of Germans. We didn't have a chance. The Krauts were taking prisoners left and right. I managed to escape and got separated from everyone, Germans and Americans alike. Since then, I've been making my way north hoping to catch up with the division." He sucked on the last drag of his smoke, then flicked the butt out into the wind as the town came into sight, a church steeple poking its way up through the falling snow.

Joe brought the jeep to a complete stop. "Looks like this is where we part ways. I'm heading on to the next village. There's a command post over there in that barn. You'd best report there. They can get you reassigned."

Chuck shook Goodman's hand, then stepped down into the street. "Thanks for the ride. I hope you're not too disappointed. I mean…let's face it. Ya can't save everyone."

"Do me a favor," Joe said. He removed a chain suspended medal from around his neck. "Take this with you. You don't have to wear it. You can just stuff it in your pocket if you like. It's a Saint Christopher medal. He's the patron saint of travelers. He's got me through some pretty tight spots. If you're going to survive over here, you're going to need a lot more than just plain old good luck."

Chuck thought for a moment, but then accepted the gift.

Joe smiled. "God bless you Charlie Brooks. I wouldn't worry all that much about not believing in the Good Lord. Fact is, if you stay in this war long enough…you will believe." Following a sloppy salute, he sped up the street.

Chuck glanced down at the medal, then stuffed it inside his jacket as he started toward the barn. Taking in his new surroundings, he noticed that the town had seen plenty of action. Two buildings on the opposite side of the street were charred and gutted, the results of previous bombings. Another structure at the very edge of the town was still smoldering from a recent fire. There were no civilians in sight, only the Army.

The street was a sea of mud as jeeps, halftracks and tanks passed by. The entire operation seemed to be in total confusion. Men were running in every direction, carrying supplies or messages, while others were yelling or giving orders. Everything looked so disorganized. Nothing unusual. That seemed to be standard operating procedure wherever he went.

Wading through the six-inch mud, he stopped as a passing truck threw up a deluge of mud, splattering his already filthy clothing. A soldier standing next to him made an obscene gesture as he spewed out a number of choice metaphors leveled at the driver who could have cared less.

The two-story barn stood at the edge of town, its siding a faded gray from years of exposure to the elements. To the left of the huge wooden double doors, stacks of electronic equipment were rapidly being loaded into a covered truck.

Stopping just inside the doors, Chuck addressed a passing sergeant, "Excuse me, sir. Where might I get reassigned?"

The gruff-looking sergeant gave Chuck an impatient stare, then responded bluntly, "At the moment, private…it don't make a dif. A division o' Panzers is comin' up the road. We've only got 'bout two hundred boys here. We're pullin' out. Make yerself useful. Git out back an' help load up those trucks."

Chuck saluted. "Yes, sir!"

He hadn't even turned when the first enemy shell slammed into the right side of the barn, driving him up and over a desk. Getting slowly to his feet, he saw the sergeant to his left, eyes open wide, blood spewing from his mouth, his right arm completely missing. Men were running, yelling, screaming.

Two more shells exploded just up the street, then a fourth hit in front of the barn. The next shell took out the rest of the building as Chuck was lifted off his feet and catapulted out the front.

Spread-eagled in the middle of the street, he felt dazed, not quite sure of what had happened. He searched for his rifle. It was gone. So was his helmet. A troop transporter was on its side, men scrambling from the back as the motor burst into flames. He stood as he looked up the street. German tanks flanked by infantry were entering town. He watched in horror as a group of American soldiers were machine-gunned to the ground.

A halftrack was coming up the street, some of the men in the back firing at the enemy, but most just crouching in fear, hoping to make good their escape. Chuck jumped up onto the side and threw himself to the floor as a man fell next to him, a crimson red hole appearing on his left cheek.

A shell tore a large divot in the street just to the left of the front tire, mud and dirt exploding into the smoke-filled air as the halftrack was lifted straight up, then tipping to the right as it landed with a jolting thud. Chuck was jammed against the sideboards as the soldiers were thrown to one side, four flying completely out of the vehicle.

Somehow, the driver managed to hang onto the wheel, stomping the gas and dodging a disabled jeep as the halftrack righted itself. Maneuvering up the street between abandoned vehicles and dead bodies, he was finally on the opposite end of the village. He floored the gas. It was clear sailing now.

The soldiers in the back were now seated around the sides or inspecting those who had been wounded. Chuck's right arm and hand were covered with blood. Had he been hit? He quickly examined himself, finally coming to the conclusion that it was someone else's blood.

A mile up the road, the halftrack suddenly lurched to the right, running down into a ditch, coming to an abrupt stop. The German machine guns hidden in the dense trees had opened up spraying a wide, deadly swath of shells into the windshield, killing the driver instantly.

Chuck and two others were thrown over the side landing in the deep snow next to the road. Chuck instinctively rolled back under the truck as the other two started to run for the shelter of the nearby trees. Their bodies were riddled by machine gun fire as they crumbled to the ground like empty potato sacks.

Lying in the deep mud, Chuck stared back at the two soldiers as the halftrack was suddenly surrounded by Germans. He could see their muddy boots as they walked back and forth, some climbing up into the vehicle.

One of the soldiers lying in the snow was still alive. His eyes locked on Chuck's. It was a strange stare, a look of disbelief, a look of fear and shock. Then, suddenly, two sets of boots appeared next to the soldier. Following German dialogue, which Chuck could not understand, there was a laugh, then the sound of a machine gun as the soldier's body was pumped with bullets. The dead soldier was still staring at Chuck, his eyes still open, but now they were filled with death. There were screams from the other side of the road mixed with more gunfire. The Germans had no intentions of taking any prisoners.

One of the enemy soldiers crouched down to inspect the dead Americans lying in the snow. He searched each and every pocket looking for souvenirs. Chuck knew that if the German looked under the halftrack, he would then be spotted, no doubt, and seconds later shot to death. He noticed the Saint Christopher medal lying in the mud. Somehow, it had fallen from his jacket.

The smell of gasoline and the warmth of the fumes flooded over his body as the halftrack was started. A quick count indicated that there were seven Germans standing around the vehicle. He thought about what Goodman had said about needing more than just luck if he expected to survive. He picked up the medal as he realized that once the halftrack was moved he would be in full view of the enemy.

The vehicle was slowly backed up onto the road, then pulled forward. Chuck closed his eyes, lying perfectly still as if he were dead. He could hear boots slopping through the mud in his direction. The warm metal barrel of a machine gun touched the side of his face as his head was pushed to the side. He could feel the warmth of the soldier's breath as he knelt down pulling open his jacket. Chuck gently squeezed the medal in his hand as he thought: *Don't move, don't blink!*

Just then, another voice, a gruff voice, interrupted the German's inspection of his personal belongings. The soldier stood, then was gone. Chuck held his breath for as long as he could, then slowly let out a long, easy flow of air, the tightness in his lungs easing. He opened his eyes, half expecting to see the Germans standing over him. Thick white flakes of snow landed on his face, then melted.

Turning his head to the side he saw the Germans walking toward the town. He remained still until minutes after the last tank disappeared from sight. He sat up, looked in every direction, then quickly rose and ran into the dense trees.

It was twenty minutes later that he stopped, leaning against some large boulders at the edge of the forest. The shelling of the village had all but ceased, the only remaining evidence of battle a few sporadic pops of gunfire.

Catching his breath, he was now faced with the dilemma of what direction he would travel. He stepped back onto the road, deciding the opposite direction of the village would be the safest. Sloshing through the mud, he thought how strange things seemed to be going. It had been less than an hour earlier that he had passed this very spot in Goodman's jeep. He wondered if anyone, anywhere in the entire Army missed his presence. He doubted it.

Rounding a bend in the road, he saw three Germans sprawled in the snow; more casualties of war. Two were dead, the third moaning as he stared up at Chuck, his eyes filled with tears. He clutched at the bright red wound on his upper right chest, a blood-stained photograph in his other hand.

Bending down, Chuck slowly removed the wrinkled picture from the German's hand. Centered in the photo was a proud looking woman flanked by two handsome boys. The German struggled feebly for the picture as he mumbled something that Chuck could not understand. He gently replaced the photograph back in the soldier's hand as he got a good look at his face: a flat nose that looked like it had been broken at one time; thick lips, tired eyes, a scabbed-over scar on his left cheek. He appeared to be in his forties. A number of medals and war decorations hung from his uniform. The German was obviously a grizzled veteran.

He looked at the photo again, wondering if those pictured were his mother and brothers or possibly a wife and sons. He thought about his own mother and about the fact that the man lying on the ground before him wasn't that much different. A different color uniform, a different viewpoint on the war, but nonetheless, a soldier. The general talk among American troops that he had met was that the Germans were nothing but a hoard of savage animals. The enemy on the ground probably missed his home and family just as much as he did.

His thoughts were interrupted by a demanding voice, "What ya got there, G.I.?"

Looking up, Chuck saw the six-foot American lieutenant leading a rag-tag platoon up the road in his direction. The tall officer turned to the two soldiers in the lead and ordered, "Make sure these Jerries are dead."

The two privates responded like mindless robots as they aimed their rifles at two of the Germans, shooting them directly in the head. The officer looked down at the wounded German, asking "What about this one…looks like he's still kicking." Signalling to the soldier standing next to him, he gave his order without the slightest hint of remorse, "Take `im out."

Chuck reacted quickly, "No…let me take care of it. They wiped out my whole company. Just a quick one in the back of the head and I'll be joining up with you fellahs."

Reaching down, he removed the German's revolver from its holster, then rolled the man over onto his stomach, pulling his field jacket up over the back of his head. Chuck knelt, shielding his hand from view, placed the handgun just slightly to the left of the collar and pulled the trigger. He tucked the souvenir revolver into his cammies as he stood. "That's one less Kraut."

Chuck filed in at the end of the platoon as they started up the road. He waited five minutes, then ran up to the lieutenant, explaining that he had forgotten his canteen. He'd run back, get it and be back in no time. The officer gave his permission with a casual wave of his hand.

The German was still on his stomach. Chuck rolled him over gently as he smiled down at the man. "I thought you guys were bad. I guess when it comes right down to it…we're no better." The German couldn't understand a single word, but knew the young American had spared his life.

"It'll be dark soon," Chuck said. "We gotta get ya off this road." Dragging the man by his jacket, he managed to pull him through the deep snow ten yards back into the trees. The snow had stopped and was now replaced by a chilling downpour. The German was shaking uncontrollably from the cold.

"Be right back," Chuck commented.

Moments later, he returned with both jackets from the two dead soldiers back on the road. He considered making a fire. He had matches. He could use branches and leaves for fuel, but the possibility of being seen in the night and the incessant rain dictated a night without warmth.

He shared what rations and water he had left along with his last three smokes with the German. Through the cold, damp pitch black in between rubbing circulation into the man's arms and legs, he rambled on about back home, his old friends, what he was planning on doing when he got out and on and on, all the while the German not comprehending anything that was being said.

The rain had slowed to a misty drizzle as Chuck was awakened by the sound of approaching vehicles. Running to the edge of the trees he saw the German convoy slowly making its way up the road. He ran quickly back to his new friend. "Come on…got to get ya back out there so your comrades can pick you up."

The convoy was still too far off to notice the activity just up ahead. After pulling the German back to the side of the road, he placed the revolver back in its holster, patted the man on his shoulder and smiled. "You'll be alright now." He stood and turned to disappear back into the trees, but then hesitated. He removed the Saint Christopher medal from his pocket and dangled it in front of the German's face. "They tell me this is supposed to be some sort of luck. Well, maybe it's not luck at all. Maybe it's faith. At the moment, I think you need ol' Christopher more than I do." He placed the medal in the man's hand. "Good luck, buddy."

As he stood, the German reached out grabbing his hand with what little strength he had left as he spoke. The German dialect was strange to Chuck, but both men understood the bond the night had brought. Chuck ran back into the tree line and watched as the first vehicle in the convoy halted, seconds later the German was loaded in the back of a covered truck. Minutes later, the last truck gone from sight, Chuck was back on the muddy road, but this time walking south.

Chuck screwed the lid back onto his canteen, then lit his third cigarette in a row. The reported estimation that they were in for an all-day trip hadn't been too far off the mark. They had pulled out just after five in the morning, had stopped to fuel up around noon and were scheduled to continue on until nightfall. The small black hands behind the cracked glass face of his watch displayed the time: 4:09 in the afternoon.

Looking out the rear of the canvas-covered transporter, he could see dark storm clouds starting to form in the distance. He looked at the group of tired soldiers sitting across from him as he thought about the previous winter in France. At times, he had thought he was never going to get warm again. The spring thaw was followed by what seemed like a brief summer, then an unseasonably cold fall.

Back home in Wisconsin, the neighborhood kids would be preparing themselves for Halloween, Ma would be making her famous caramel apples. He unfolded the letter from home once again as he thought about his mother's cooking. In just a few short weeks, Thanksgiving would be rolling around. This would be the second year in a row that he was going to miss her pumpkin pie, spiced apple rings and mouth-watering turkey and dressing.

Compared to his chicken scrawling, she had handwriting that was nothing short of art work. Every letter was slanted at the same angle, the same identical size. The sentences seemed to flow off each page. He read over each line carefully: Willy and Martin had finally joined the Army. His mother had no idea where they were stationed. A memorial service had been held for Freddy, his body never recovered from the sea. Fred's mom said that she had some personal things that she wanted to give him when he got back home. Fred would have wanted him to have them.

The old Rose Street Bridge had been washed away during flash flooding earlier in the summer. The bridge was being replaced by a new modern-looking structure that no one in town seemed to care for. The football team went to the state finals, but lost the game in the last few seconds due to a field goal.

The back end of the transporter bounced up into the air as they passed over a huge pothole. He placed the letter back inside his pocket as he stood, walked to the back, took a final drag on the cigarette and flicked it out into the breeze. To the left of the road, he noticed a small stone barn surrounded by a broken down wooden fence. Two white cows watched peacefully as the small three-truck convoy passed by. He had been told that the winters in this part of the country were brutal. After surviving the winter months in France, he was more than confident that he could endure whatever Poland had to offer.

He sat back down, looking down at his worn boots. It seemed that some of the rules that the military had been so downright picky about in basic training meant absolutely nothing out in the field. He'd spent hours back then shining his boots. Now, they looked like something the homeless would no doubt discard.

Talk was that the Germans were on the run. Some of the boys said that old Hitler was losing control. He had bitten off more than he could chew. Still, the German war machine had plenty of fight left.

A short burst of automatic gunfire ripped his drifting thoughts from daydreaming back to reality as the truck came to an abrupt halt. Four German soldiers suddenly appeared at the rear of the truck, their machine guns leveled directly at the passengers inside. Three more enemy soldiers joined the group as one of the men ordered the American troops to step down as he motioned with his weapon.

A jeep trailed by a German troop truck pulled up, at least twenty more soldiers pouring out onto the road. Stepping down from the transporter, Chuck was shoved roughly into line with the men from all three vehicles.

One of the American soldiers near the end of the line started to scream, "They're going to kill us all!"

The sergeant who had been riding in the lead truck turned and sternly ordered the private, "Shut up…nobody's going to die!"

The young private suddenly broke from the line and ran for the woods. He hadn't even gotten three strides when he crumbled to the road, instantly dead from the piercing bullets that punctured his back. The Germans who hadn't fired stiffened as they aimed their guns at the remaining soldiers in line.

Chuck felt helpless, his hands raised high in the air, his life at the moment in the hands of the enemy. It was a situation he had discussed on many occasions. The rules of warfare were not always strictly adhered to. Sometimes prisoners were taken, while at other times men were just simply gunned down where they stood. He recalled that moment on the muddy road in France where his fellow soldiers had no reservations about killing enemy soldiers rather than taking them prisoner. Was he in the wrong place at the wrong time? He remembered what had been drilled into their brains in basic training: You must make every effort to escape if possible.

More orders in German were given, the line of Americans now being pushed toward the troop truck. Climbing into the back of the truck, Chuck noticed at least fifty German infantry standing in the vicinity. As they pulled out, he glanced at the two German soldiers standing at the front of the truck, their machine guns pointed at the seated prisoners. He was now on his way to a prison-of-war camp. A thought he didn't relish.

He looked across at his fellow soldiers sitting on the opposite side of the truck. Moments earlier, even though the men had been tired from their lengthy ride, they had been laughing and joking, some sleeping, others smoking or talking with each other. Most of the men were strangers, soldiers from all over the states.

It had only been the previous night that he had been assigned to the small convoy. He had only talked with two of the men now sitting next to him in the truck—Billy Flowers, the son of a tobacco farmer from Central Kentucky and Stanley Goldstein from New York. Billy, who was always on the affable side, now sat, a look of disbelief and hopelessness plastered across his normally smiling face. Stanley, a Jewish boy from the city was a wiry little guy who didn't seem to take any guff from anyone. He sat quietly, his eyes constantly moving from one German guard to the other.

As the miles slowly clicked by, the two guards seemed to become less suspect of any escape attempts, their weapons still pointed in the direction of their prisoners, but with a lesser degree of authority. One of the two, momentarily dropped his gun to his side as he groped for his cigarettes, The truck suddenly dipped down into a large rut in the road, the back end sending everyone out of their seats, both guards thrown off balance.

Chuck reacted with the agility of a circus cat as he sprang from the floorboards, catapulting himself over the rear wooden tailgate. He hit the road, rolled to the side on his shoulder, stood and dashed to the trees only yards away. Before the guards inside the truck and the men in the trailing jeep could react, he was fifteen yards into the forest.

He slipped on some wet leaves as he started up a steep incline, losing valuable time as he slid back a few feet. Turning, he saw six Germans advancing into the trees. Grabbing tree limbs, rocks and handfuls of dirt, he struggled up the hill, determined to lose his pursuers.

The incline leveled off, but was followed by yet another hill of equal difficulty. The Germans were now opening up on their target, machine gun shells licking at the dirt at his feet, stripping bark from the surrounding trees and whizzing past his head. There was no sense in looking back. It was a matter of survival. He would not be spared if captured.

At the top of the second hill, he felt a sharp jab of pain as a bullet imbedded itself in his right hand as he grabbed a tree trunk. Withdrawing his hand instantly, another shot of searing pain ripped at his lower right leg. Another bullet nearly found its mark as it nicked his left upper forearm.

He turned again, looking back down through the maze of trees. He spotted three of the enemy, who had stopped advancing, taking a more careful aim, now confident that their prey would soon drop to the ground. Two bullets buried themselves in the dirt at his feet, another ricocheted off a rock to his left. Spinning to reach a gravel road just a few yards away, he slipped, his helmet falling to the ground, rolling down the hill, bouncing off a tree, then stopping.

A barrage of shells blasted over his head as he rolled, then crawled painfully to the edge of the road. Standing awkwardly, he found himself in the middle of a small village. The shooting had stopped. He could hear the enemy soldiers crashing through the trees, someone yelling orders in German.

Limping across the dirt road, he ascended the three steps to a stone church, then turned looking back at the trees as he opened the wooden door. The Germans were just at the very edge of the woods.

The heavy door slammed shut behind with a resounding thud that reverberated through the entire one-room church. Nearly every available seat in the pews was occupied as the Polish villagers turned their eyes to their sudden visitor.

Chuck took three steps up the aisle, then stopped as he pleaded, "Please help me. I'm an American soldier. The Germans are coming up the street. If they find me…they'll kill me! Please…hide me. I have nowhere else to go. Please."

Those who understood English reacted quickly, most who didn't getting the idea as numerous hands guided him to the middle of a pew toward the front, a shaw placed over his head, another around his shoulders. The trail of blood leading up the aisle was wiped clean with coats.

Chuck was no sooner squeezed in between a man and his wife when the Germans busted through the door, once again the heavy entrance banging loudly. The officer in the lead directed two of the men to stand guard at the door while the remaining three followed him to the altar. A man was stationed at either side at the front while the officer and the last soldier took the center aisle.

The officer placed his revolver back into his holster, holding out his hands in friendship. In German, he inquired if anyone in the church understood his language. No one responded. He turned to the soldier across the aisle and gave him a stern order, seconds later the chandelier above the altar crashing to the floor, following a short burst of machine-gun fire. The parishioners winced, those in the first pew shielding their eyes from the shards of flying glass. An older man in the third row slowly stood, explaining that he understood German.

The officer signaled him to the altar, then explained his message which he ordered be interpreted to the congregation. After listening, the man faced his friends and neighbors as he stated in Polish, "We know the American came into your church. He must be taken as a prisoner of war. We will attend to his wounds. We mean no harm to your homes or your families. It is your duty to turn him over to our authority."

The message complete, the old man turned back to the officer. No one in the church made any effort to comply to the demands of the German officer. The officer asked the man to repeat the request, which equaled the same results.

The officer's patience was wearing thin as he ordered the two guards at the end aisles to select two men from the front pew and bring them up to the altar. Guns were then placed at each man's head as the officer told the old man to make it very clear that if the American was not brought forward, the two men would be shot and the process repeated over and over until the demand was met.

Chuck stared down at the faces of two little girls standing next to their parents. Even though he couldn't understand anything that was being said, he understood exactly what was about to happen. As much as he wanted to survive, he just couldn't bring himself to allow helpless people to die in his place. He dropped the shaw from his shoulders and took the second wrap from his head as he held up his bloody hands. "Over here!"

The German officer ordered the two men at the altar released as he smiled. Withdrawing his revolver, he made his way to the end of the row where Chuck was standing as he motioned the six parishioners blocking his way to move out into the aisle.

The officer stepped into the row, took two steps toward Chuck, looking him up and down. The American was nothing but a boy, but nonetheless the enemy, capable of killing Germans. He looked at the muddy worn boots, the small puddle of blood on the floor slowly growing larger. His eyes ran up the filthy uniform, stopping at the dirty face.

The smile on the officer's face was transformed from having the upper hand to one of genuineness as he stared in disbelief. The twenty-year-old American private who stood before him jogged his memory back to that back road in France nearly a year in the past.

He now stood face to face with the young man who had saved his life that cold winter night. The officer stepped closer to Chuck as he holstered his revolver, then removed the Saint Christopher medal from his neck. He held it out to Chuck as he said something in German. He reached out taking Chuck's hand in which he not only placed the medal, but a pack of cigarettes. He ruffled Chuck's blond hair. Following a wide smile, he turned to the congregation, addressed them, then ordered his men to leave. The last German to leave was the officer who hesitated at the door, turned and saluted Chuck.

Chuck couldn't believe what had just happened as he looked down at the medal. The old man who had interpreted the officer's demands approached him. "I don't understand what went on here. He told us to take care of your wounds…to feed you…to get you something to drink. Then he ordered his men to leave saying that they had no business here today."

ANIMAL CRACKERS

THERE WASN'T ANYTHING LITTLE CHARLEY Striker didn't like about the circus. Whether he was gazing through a glass-protected reptile cage at an enormous Anaconda, or watching the playful monkeys frolic in their small replicated version of their native homeland, he smothered his parents with endless questions.

Charley enjoyed attending all of the shows, sitting almost motionless as he watched in amazement as tightrope professionals performed their daring stunts high above the audience, lion tamers fending off fierce jungle cats with nothing more than a whip and a chair. He was always excited about going down on the midway, riding all the rides, eating cotton candy and hot dogs and watching with great anticipation as his father tried to win stuffed animals at the game booths.

The first time he attended the circus had been just after he had turned two years old. He couldn't remember too much about that particular year, but during the next few years his parents continued to take him to the traveling extravaganza when it came to town. Driving home following an evening under the big top, his father had asked him what he liked most about the circus. Five-year-old Charley was quick to respond, saying that the clowns were his favorite. His mother's question of "Why?" led to a simple explanation that clowns made people laugh. People could go to the circus feeling sad, but after watching the clowns, go home feeling happy. Charley added that sometimes the clowns made him laugh so hard his stomach hurt.

The summer of his seventh birthday, the circus was scheduled to arrive in town a month earlier than in past years; the weeklong engagement falling on the same week as his birthday. When his mother suggested that he and four or five of his friends could celebrate his birthday at the circus, his animated excitement caused his rapidly moving right hand to accidentally tumble his orange juice onto the kitchen floor. In the past, knocking food or drink off the table had always led to a stern reprimand about paying more attention to what he was doing. Charley looked at his mother, already quite aware of the look of disappointment that always came across her face following one of his moments of awkwardness. For some reason, much to his bewilderment, she hesitated, her spoonful of cereal halfway to her mouth, then she burst into laughter, saying, "It's okay…get a paper towel."

During the next two days, Charley's mother sat by the phone in the den as she set everything in motion. Five of Charley's close neighborhood pals were invited to the "circus birthday," two of the other mothers volunteering to tag along as helpers.

The night before his birthday, the six boys would spend the night out in the backyard sleeping in Mr. Stryker's old army tent. The next morning, the boys and the three moms would pile into two station wagons and drive over to the local pancake house for a birthday pancake-eating contest. Then, it was off to the fairgrounds and the circus where a lunchtime picnic complete with one of the circus clowns in attendance was planned. The remainder of the day would be spent down on the midway and later that evening at the main show.

Days and weeks passed, the topic of the upcoming day at the circus was discussed daily by the six lads. Finally, "circus week" arrived and with it a sense of festiveness settled over the town. There were billboards advertising the event, television and radio ads, all geared toward enticing the locals to come out to the fairgrounds.

The long convoy of colorful trucks and assorted vehicles arrived in town on Friday morning and the work crews began the process of setting up. Even though the main gates would not open until Monday evening, the chain-link fence surrounding the grounds was packed with children standing shoulder to shoulder as they watched the dirt and grass-covered acreage slowly transformed into a world of wonder.

The Ferris wheel was particularly intriguing as three truckloads of metal parts were somehow miraculously constructed like a giant erector set into the "most popular ride" on the midway. Teams of men unloaded endless rolls of canvas and stacks of poles and rope. Hours later, the gigantic tent, which would house the focal point of the entire circus, stood majestically, a flag flapping at its top: GALLAGHER & BOYLES INTERNATIONAL CIRCUS.

This year the circus had two new animal acts: three black bears and their tumbling female trainer from Russia and a baby elephant by the name of Goldy. Goldy was said to already weigh in at over seven hundred pounds, despite her age of only three months. Her mother, a six-thousand pounder named Tess had been with the circus for years. Goldy's father, Buddha, had been shipped back to the San Diego Zoo from which he had been on loan. The baby pachyderm was expected to be one of the main attractions for the week.

Charley's birthday fell on Thursday so the boys had to wait patiently for three days before they could walk through the main gates at the fairgrounds. On Tuesday, it rained from the moment Charley got up until late that evening. He and the other boys spent the day in the vast field behind Green Street, climbing the trees next to Brushwood Creek and trying their best to blockade the rushing water with logs and rocks from the surrounding banks. Two hours later, deciding that their battle against the creek waters was futile, they ran across the field to the very edge of the forest to the old Buckner Farm.

The three-story stone house, huge barn and assorted sheds had stood abandoned for years. Nobody ever knew what happened to Mr. and Mrs. Buckner. According to Mr. Stryker, they had simply disappeared, never to be heard from again. The Buckners, so his Dad said, had been somewhere in their fifties and had pretty much kept to themselves farming some crops and raising some sheep and hogs. The day that it had been discovered by the local mailman that the family had disappeared, everything on the farm was in order. Nothing as far as the police could tell had been removed from the house. The furniture was clean as a whistle, the old clock above the fireplace ticked away and the icebox was filled with food.

Efforts had been made by viewing the county records to locate the next of kin as the weeks went by, but it seemed that the Buckners had no living relatives that could be notified. Finally, the county took over the property, boarded everything up and sold off all of the livestock, equipment and furnishings at an auction, placing the money from the sale in the bank just in case the Buckners returned. They never did. Eventually, the proceeds were turned over to the city and wound up being donated to three different charities. There was all kinds of speculation as to what had happened to the couple. Some folks said that it was rather obvious that they had just up and left in their old Buick, leaving everything behind. Others said that they had been kidnapped, some going as far as to state that the place was haunted. It was said that the Buckners didn't believe in banks, thus a fortune was hidden somewhere on the property. The most popular version of the disappearance of the Buckners was that they had been murdered and then buried somewhere on the farm, the would-be thieves unable to locate the much-talked about fortune.

As the years passed, even though the local authorities had posted the property against trespassing, adventurous locals had torn the place to pieces in search of the lost money. Anything of apparent value in the house and barn had been carried off, the house now a cold empty shell, any memories of the past family who had lived there completely vanished.

The farm was now a vast playground for Charley and his friends, the police having little concern for those who chose to go there anymore. Whether sitting on the old rusted tractor that sat in the field or jumping from the loft down into the old hay below, the boys always enjoyed themselves. On days when it rained, they spent most of their time inside the house sitting around talking about the supposed hidden treasure and wondering if it really existed.

When Charley arrived home Tuesday evening just prior to supper he had a cough that could only be described as nonstop. Sitting at the dinner table, his mother took one look at her son, who at the moment looked anything but healthy. In between the constant hacking, he tried to force down the fried chicken and mashed potatoes, but it was just too difficult.

Following a hot bath and a dose of cough medicine, Charley was positioned on the living room couch, his pajamas already soaked with perspiration. Shivering, he pulled the wool blanket closer to his neck as his mother placed her cool hand on his forehead. Removing the thermometer from his lips, she looked at the digits, then commented, "We need to get you into see Dr. Holvey."

That evening, on the way home from visiting the family doctor, Charley sat in the back seat of the station wagon as he gazed out the side window at a passing advertisement for the circus. The graphic billboards around town that had hinted at a day of excitement were now just depressing memories that kept reminding him of what the doctor had said: "There's no doubt about it. Charley has a graduated case of bronchitis. I would strongly suggest that he get at least three days rest—bed rest. If he doesn't show some signs of improvement by tomorrow evening, we might have to admit him to the hospital. It's not what I would refer to as severe at this point, but if the symtoms don't start to turn around, we could be looking at pneumonia."

So far, neither one of his parents had said anything about canceling the planned circus trip, but thinking that they would simply ignore the doctor's orders was too much to hope for. Tomorrow was Wednesday—just one day away from his birthday. Some quick addition revealed the fact that three days' bed rest, provided that he was back to his old self, meant that Saturday would be his last chance of going to the circus.

Making his way down the hall to the bathroom he overheard his mother speaking on the phone. It didn't require any great feat of detective work to understand that she was talking with one of the other mothers who was to go along to the circus. Sitting at the top of the carpeted stairs, Charley's last bastion of hope in regards to attending the circus on Saturday vanished as his mother spoke into the phone: "We just didn't have the heart to tell him that the circus for this year is off. He looks so forward to going each year…and this year was going to be special. I guess Herb is going to tell him tomorrow. I'm sorry that we had to cancel. Maybe we can all go next year."

Wednesday morning arrived, Charley's coughing about the same, but his temperature had dropped. He ate some oatmeal and a slice of toast and was pleased to hear that after his mother reported his minor improvement to Dr. Holvey, he wasn't going to be spending any time over at the hospital. Sitting at the breakfast table, he looked out the kitchen window at the pouring rain. He felt about as dreary as the weather. The long-awaited bad news was finally sprung on him as his mother wiped off the stove. "I guess we'll have to forget about the circus this year. I've already called the other mothers...."

Charley didn't let her finish, jumping up from the table and running into the living room and up the stairs to his room as he objected through teary eyes, "It's not fair...it's just not fair!"

Mrs. Stryker entered her young son's room moments later only to find him curled up under the covers as he quietly read one of his favorite books. She tried her best to console the boy, but he protested defiantly saying that he didn't want to talk about it.

He remained in his room the rest of the day, his mother checking in on him every half hour. He dozed off from time to time, refused lunch and wasn't the least bit interested in hearing about how they were going to have cake and ice cream on Thursday even though he was sick.

Charley didn't want to be in attendance at dinner that night, but his father, who didn't put up with any sort of rebellion, told him to get downstairs—pronto! Mr. Stryker stabbed a slab of meat loaf as he looked across the table at his wife, then began the explanation that Charley knew was coming. "Son...sometimes things just don't work out the way we plan. It's a part of life we are all faced with. I suppose at times it even seems unfair. We cannot change what is to be...we can only deal with it. I know how much you were looking forward to going to the circus, but we can't take the chance of allowing you to get pneumonia. Your health is more important than a day at the circus. Your mother and I will try to make this up to you…we promise….”

The following moment was a repeat performance of breakfast, Charley bolting from the table, crying and yelling at the same time, “I don’t care…I hate you, Mom, the doctor…leave me alone!”

Mrs. Stryker rose to follow, but Dad suggested that they leave the boy alone for a bit. An hour later, they both entered their son’s room finding him sleeping soundly. The bedroom door was no sooner closed when Charley opened his eyes, his rendition of being fast asleep had been convincing. He knew what he had to do.

It was 3:30 in the morning, his parents had long since turned in, the thin crack of light at the bottom of their bedroom door finally disappearing. They had checked on him two more times before retiring for the night, each time Charley closing his eyes and remaining perfectly still as they entered his room.

Wrapping himself in the warmest clothes he could find in his dresser, he packed a few small items into his scout knapsack, strapped it on, raised the window, made his way carefully across the shingled roof and finally down the lattice next to the living room wall. Standing by the large maple in the front yard, he took one last look at the house. He had closed the window and turned the light off. Starting slowly up the dark street, he began his journey.

The morning sun was just starting to rise in the east just a few minutes before he arrived at the fence surrounding the fairgrounds. The main gate was wide open as a delivery truck drove through, Charley followed unnoticed. Walking along the inside of the fence, he stopped near some bales of straw after crossing the sprawling dirt parking lot. The rain had stopped sometime during the night, but his shoes were now covered in mud.

He was exhausted, the three-mile walk taking its toll on his already weak body. He sat on a bale of straw as he pulled the collar of his jacket up around his neck, his coughing growing worse. If he could just find out where the clowns lived, then everything would be all right. They'd understand how he felt. After telling them how unfair his parents were, he was sure that they would let him join up.

Suddenly, his attention was drawn to a tent on his left as the large canvas flap was opened. An older man and a younger woman led two adult elephants, followed by a small elephant, a baby he thought. The large elephants were chained to two stakes in the ground while the baby was free to wander, although it didn't seem to stray more than a few feet from its mom.

Charley watched with great interest as the large animals were bathed, the woman operating the water hose, the man gently moving a long-handled scrub brush over the thick gray wrinkled skin. The man didn't pay any attention to Charley, but the woman looked over and smiled.

Of all the animals he knew, the large creatures standing just on the other side of the road were his favorite. He knew all about elephants. There were elephants from Africa and India. One kind had bigger ears than the other, but at the moment he couldn't remember which. If he were back home in his room, he could look it up in one of the three books that he had on elephants. The baby standing next to the mother had to be Goldy. Goldy reminded him of a giant gray puppy as she ran back and forth flipping an old used tire up into the air.

The sun was rising higher in the sky, the warmth taking the edge off his chill. Removing the knapsack from his back, he reached inside and withdrew a small bag of animal crackers. Skipping breakfast, lunch and dinner had resulted in his stomach sending a very clear message to his brain that he was getting hungry. Munching on the crackers, he continued to watch the elephants for the next half hour.

A man walked past, momentarily blocking Charley's view, then stopped. Something about the youngster just didn't seem right. Charley stared back at the man, his appearance causing instant confusion. The man was on the short side, just a shade over five feet. He was wearing one of those wide-brimmed hats that Charley had seen detectives on T.V. wear, loose-fitting blue jeans supported by a pair of black suspenders, no shirt and cowboy boots. The confusion stemmed from the fact that the man's face was that of a clown: bright red, complete with assorted black dots, yellow nose, dazzling eyes and a wide smile.

The man slowly approached Charley realizing that the boy didn't belong to anyone at the circus. Bending over, he placed his hands on his knees, then asked, "Are you by yourself?"

"Yes," answered Charley.

The men ventured his next question: "Where are your parents?"

The answer was simple: "At home."

"And where is home? Do you live here in town?"

"Green Street…I live on Green Street, but not no more."

"So you lived on Green Street but you moved?"

"No, my parents still live there. I ran away today to join the circus. I want to be a clown."

The man smiled as he took a seat on an adjacent bale of straw. "That's pretty serious, I mean running away from home. Why would you do something like that?"

Charley looked down at the mud at his feet as he explained, "Today is my birthday and me and my friends were going to come to the circus, but I got sick and my mom and dad said I couldn't come." Before the man could say anything, Charley looked into his smiling face and pointed as he said, "You're a clown!"

The man laughed as he responded, "Yeah, I am…guess you could tell from my face, huh?" Sticking out his hand, he introduced himself, "My name's Ray."

Charley continued to stare into the man's eyes, then spoke, "Where are your clown clothes?"

"Ah…now I see," said the man. "We don't wear clown clothes all the time…just when we're performing for the audience." He touched his face, slowly smearing his cheek. "This isn't my real face…it's just makeup. Every morning I put on my clown face, then head down to the chow wagon for breakfast. I don't have to get dressed until late in the afternoon."

Charley continued to stare at the man as if he were trying to understand what he had just heard. The man looked at the open bag in Charley's hand, then asked, "I don't suppose those are animal crackers…are they?"

An affirmative nod from Charley, rather than a vocal answer, indicated that they were as the man had guessed. "Seeing as how I haven't had my breakfast yet, maybe you could share some with me?"

Charley held out the bag as he smiled.

The man reached inside the cellophane bag and removed a cracker, then examined it as he went on, "Ya know, when I was about your age I used to eat these things by the box. I haven't had any of these in…I bet thirty years."

Just as he was about to pop the morsel into his mouth, Charley reached out, stopping him: "What's your favorite?"

"Excuse me," said the man.

Charley repeated, but in a more forceful tone, "What's your

favorite animal?"

The man thought for a moment, then replied, "The giraffes…giraffes are my favorite."

"You picked a hippopotamus," said Charley. "You have to pick your favorite first." Searching the contents of the bag, Ray finally withdrew his hand, an animal cracker shaped in the form of a giraffe held between his index finger and thumb.

Ray traded the hippo for the giraffe, then threw the cracker into his mouth. "Tastes just the way I remember," he said. "What's your name?"

"My name is Charley. Why are giraffes your favorite?"

The man held out his hands as if displaying himself. "As you can see, I'm kind of a short fellah, always have been. I've always wanted to be tall. Giraffes are the tallest critters there are…so that's why they're my favorite. How about you? What's your favorite animal?"

Charley pointed at the three elephants as he explained, "The elephants are my favorite." He didn't give Ray the opportunity to ask why but went right ahead and told him why. "My dad says the lion is the king of the jungle, but I think the elephant is king. He's the biggest…and he's the strongest, too."

Ray reached into the bag, extracting yet another cracker. "Ya know, you and I are kind of alike…I mean we have a lot in common."

Charley gave Ray a look of confusion.

"What I mean is that you want to be a clown and I am a clown. I ran away from home when I was a youngster just like you did. Course, I was a little bit older than you are, but just the same I ran off. Things never really seemed to work out for me. When I look back now, I can see that I made a mistake." Ray placed his hand on Charley's thin shoulder as he went on, "I think that you're making a mistake, too. Besides that, why do you want to be a clown? Most kids your age want to be a policeman or an astronaut."

"Clowns make people laugh," said Charley. "I want to make people laugh."

"Well, you're not getting off to a very good start. When your parents discover that you have run off, they're not going to be laughing…even smiling. Eventually, they'll call the police to report you missing. The police won't be laughing either. I'm afraid you've gone and made some people pretty darn sad."

"What should I do?" asked Charley.

"I think you should go home…maybe wait until you're all the way through high school before you decide to join up with the circus."

"But if I go home now…my mom and dad still won't be laughing. I'll just be in more trouble."

Ray leaned in closer. "Tell ya what, if I can promise you that your parents won't be mad at you, will you let me take you back home?" Ray then stood and posed in a funny clown position. "Hey, you said clowns can make people laugh. Who better to take you home? How could they possibly be mad with me there?"

Charley thought for moment, then finally agreed. "Okay, but only if you come."

Ray snapped his suspenders followed by a big smile. "Then, it's a deal, but first, seeing as how it's you're birthday we're gonna do a couple of things before we take you home." He offered his right hand as he motioned with the left. "First, let's go over there and meet Goldy."

It was close to noon when Ray pulled his car to a stop in front of Charley's house. Getting out and walking to the front door, Ray assured Charley that everything was going to be okay. The door was opened shortly after Ray rang the bell, Charley's mother and father flanked by two policemen. Following a ten-minute explanation of what had happened at the fairgrounds, the police left saying they were glad everything had worked out. Minutes later, Ray excused himself once again reminding the Strykers that Charley had only agreed to come home if they would smile. He winked at Mrs. Stryker who smiled as she understood the message and that it had been mentioned for her son's benefit. At the door, Ray turned and waved goodbye to Charley, his last words, "See ya next year at the circus pal. If it's okay with your folks, you can spend the whole week with me. Oh yeah…the next time we meet up, I'll buy the animal crackers."

Getting Charley to quiet down after everyone was gone was no easy task. "Mom…Dad, I can't believe it! I got to meet Goldy and his mother and then we went down to the chow wagon and had a big breakfast where I met three other clowns, the bearded lady, the man who operates the Ferris wheel and a bunch of other people." Running to the large mirror over the hutch, he looked at his image then turned back to his parents as he went on, "Ray took me to his trailer and made me up to look like a real clown. My birthday turned out okay!"

The next morning the front doorbell rang just after ten o'clock. The two detectives standing on the steps introduced themselves and asked if they could step inside for a few moments. Charley was still in bed and his mother had run down to the supermarket for some needed items. Mr. Stryker invited the men in, not understanding what they could possibly want.

Detective Pasco started off the conversation after the three were seated in the living room, "Mr. Stryker, I'm not sure if our visit is really necessary, but we have to ask you some questions."

Mr. Stryker was baffled. "Questions…about what?"

"About your son," Pasco answered.

"My son!"

"Yes…let me get right to the point. Did Charley say anything else after he got home about the time he spent with the clown?"

"Well, yeah, he had quite a bit to say, but it was just a review of what Ray had told all of us. Is there something wrong?"

Pasco shifted in his chair as he loosened his necktie. "What I am about to tell you may come as somewhat of a shock. Ray Stanley, the clown who brought your son home, turned himself in late last night."

Mr. Stryker looked from one detective to the other. "I'm not quite sure what you're driving at."

Detective Waite jumped in on the conversation, offering an explanation: "Ray Stanley is a known child molester. Up until two years ago, he was only labeled as a suspected child molester. About a year and a half back, he was arrested and brought up on charges of molestation of a young boy up in Michigan. He was convicted and sentenced to prison, but during an appeal got off on a technicality—the case was thrown out of court and he was released. As a general rule, individuals who are suspected of child molestation are people that the authorities tend to keep close tabs on, but our Mr. Stanley managed to disappear and hasn't surfaced until last night when he walked into the station downtown. The point of all this is that we just want to make sure that your son wasn't harmed in any way."

"I don't know what to say," said Mr. Stryker. "Ray seemed like such a nice man when he brought Charley home. I'm sure if anything happened that Charley would have said something. I mean…I guess we can ask him."

"That may not be necessary," said Pasco. "We just wanted to make sure. When Stanley turned himself in he assured us that he didn't harm Charley. Actually, your son is the reason that Ray decided to turn himself in. He said that your boy reminded him of himself when he ran away from home years ago. He said that he found it hard to live with himself over the years considering what he had done. He had always taken advantage of the innocence of children, but yet, for some reason, the innocence of Charley had a strange effect on him. He just couldn't live with himself any longer."

Detective Waite stood and said, "I don't think we have anything to worry about. I think the short relationship between Ray Stanley and your son is nothing short of a miracle. There's no dark side to this incident." Pulling an envelope from his coat pocket, he handed it to Mr. Stryker. "Ray didn't have much money on him, only about thirty dollars. He wanted Charley to have it so that next year when the circus comes to town...well, I suppose it's just his way of trying to make up for all the wrong he had done."

Mr. Stryker took the envelope as he walked the detectives to the door. Just before leaving, Pasco snapped his fingers as if remembering something. "I almost forgot." Reaching inside his trench coat he removed a box of animal crackers, handing them to Mr. Stryker. "Ray asked us if we'd stop by the store on the way over here and buy these for Charley. He said the last thing he had said to your son was that the next time they got together, he'd buy the animal crackers. He's going to be spending quite a few years in prison and I guess he just didn't want to disappoint Charley."

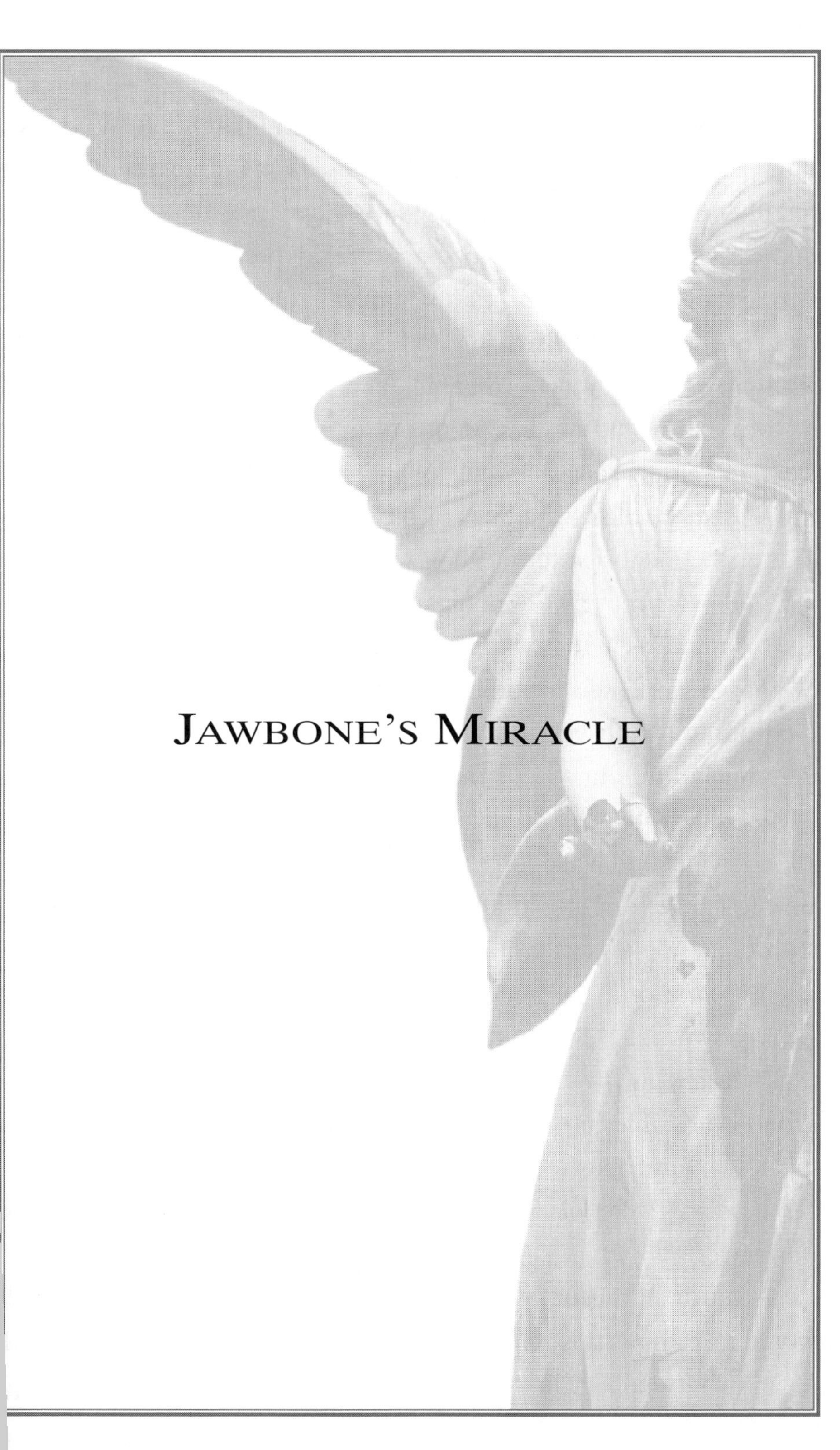

Jawbone's Miracle

ANGELS' FOOTPRINTS

I CAN'T EVEN BEGIN TO INFORM YOU OF HOW MANY times my parents sat around the Sunday dining table and discussed the phenomenon of miracles, my father claiming that "modern-day miracles" in reality were no longer being performed. My mother strongly disagreed, saying that we are surrounded by miracles on a daily basis; things like waking up to yet another day and having the ability to breathe, newborn babies, and the changing of the seasons.

My dad would always point out that even though these things were indeed miraculous, they were not what he meant. He was thinking more along the lines of biblical-type miracles—the parting of the Red Sea or water gushing from a rock.

Mom said there were no grounds for the Lord to perform these kind of miracles in today's society. During biblical times, populations of people witnessed a number of miraculous feats at the hands of God but still refused to change their ways. Society today can't be that much different. "Let's face it," she'd say. "If the Almighty were to bless me with the wherewithal to march down to the local river, split it in half and walk across on dry land in front of the whole town, very few people, if any at all, would avow that it had anything to do with God. Most folks would say that it had occurred due to some scientific reason."

My two sisters, my older brother Robert and I never had too much to say in the midst of these passionate debates. We just sat around the table in silence while we ate roast beef, pork chops, or meat loaf and mashed potatoes along with whatever vegetables Mom decided to cook. Sunday dinner was sort of a tradition around our place.

After dinner, usually out on the front porch, the four of us kids would talk about this miracle business. My sisters always sided with Mom, while Robert leaned toward Dad's philosophy. My siblings were always upset with me because I couldn't make up my mind. They claimed I had to be on *somebody's side*.

In a way, I agreed with Mom. Breathing, babies and the changing of the seasons were indeed miraculous, but I could grasp what Dad was trying to say, too. Breathing seemed so normal. I never thought much about it. I guess it's one of those things we just take for granted. As far as newborn bundles of joy are concerned, babies are born each and every minute of the day. The changing of the seasons happens each year whether we want it to or not.

Dad's comments about biblical-type miracles made sense. I think he was trying to say that there were no more miracles that made folks awestruck. He was probably talking about those "turn from sin, see the light" type of miracles.

I suppose our family is about as Catholic as Catholic could be. My mother was the mainstay of religious activities in our house, making sure that none of us ever missed a Sunday at church. We had to attend every holy day, give up something important during Lent, and as far as I know, follow every single celebration, rule, and regulation regarding Catholicism.

To say that my mother was a devout Christian believer would have been an understatement. On Sundays at church, there wasn't any doubt that she was present during the service. When it came to singing, she raised her voice to an echelon that always caused parishioners in the surrounding pews to turn and stare. I always got embarrassed. Dad always shot me a stern look, indicating for me to "cool it."

My Dad always looked as if he were singing. He always opened his mouth, but I'm not really sure if he ever made a sound. I strained my ears on a number of occasions, listening intently for his deep voice, but Mom drowned him completely out. I tried to pull the same trick of just mouthing the words, but Mom would always give me an elbow. There was no fooling her.

My Mom's brother, Frank, was a priest at the church we attended. I could never figure out if we were supposed to address him as Uncle Frank or Father Frank. Mom said that it was more appropriate to refer to him as Father. It was an official title in the Catholic church. It wasn't any different than the way we referred to the family doctor. We never spoke of him as Harold James, but Doctor James.

Father Frank, to me, was an unusual priest. Maybe it was because he was a younger man. Mom said that he was in his mid-forties. Most of the priests I had met had been much older, in their sixties or seventies. They really didn't do that much aside from performing daily Mass or showing up at the yearly church picnic and bake sale.

Father Frank was involved in just about everything. If he wasn't at the hospital or at someone's home paying a visit to an ill parishioner, he was helping the high school students with a car wash. He was active with the Cub Scouts and the Jaycees. He owned a 1962 Thunderbird that he kept in mint condition., so he was always at all of the local car shows. His list of interests and activities seemed endless, to say the least. He played racquetball, rode his ten-speed twelve miles a day, and was considered in great shape.

It came as a great shock, when we were notified that he had passed away from a heart attack. Not only our family, but everyone who knew the energy-filled man of the cloth, was dazed. The doctor said that Frank woke up in the middle of the night with chest pains. Shortly after he arrived at the parsonage, Frank passed away peacefully.

At the time of his death, I had been an altar boy for just about two years. The day that Father Frank was to be put to rest was a day that I'll never forget. I arrived at the church an hour and a half before the service was to begin. I remember walking through the large front door and standing at the back of the church. The sixteen-foot bronze-plated crucifix on the stone wall always caused me to hesitate. I had served at quite a few services for weddings and funerals, but I never saw so many flowers in all my life. The altar was crammed with floral arrangements of roses, lilies, tulips and daisies.

Father Shehan said that the church was going to be packed to the walls. Everyone who was a member of the parish would be in attendance. Four choirs from neighboring churches would be joining our own choir. Priests from all over the state were expected. Even the bishop and a cardinal were coming. The mayor would be there, members of local businesses, and nuns from the mission downtown. Father Frank had many friends.

Being ten years old and the eldest altar boy, it was my responsibility to get to the church early enough to help get things underway for the service. I had to make sure that all of the vestments were laid out, all of the candles in working order, and designate the first four rows of pews on either side of the aisle for family members and dignitaries.

I was looking around in the old tool shed out behind the church when I heard the first raindrops peck at the metal roof. Father Shehan, in need of a screwdriver and small wrench, had sent me on a seek-and-find mission. The three chairs that had been placed at the side of the altar had to be tightened up. Mrs. Kirkland was supposed to give one of the readings. She weighed close to three hundred pounds. Father Shehan said they weren't taking any chances.

Stepping out of the shed, I closed the rickety door as I noticed a dark brown van pull across the gravel parking lot, the driver guiding the vehicle around to the back and stopping two feet from where I was standing. The bold black lettering on the front of the van caused me to stop in my tracks: LAKEVIEW STATE PENITENTIARY.

The driver and passenger got out. At the same time,the side door of the van opened and three more men exited. All five were dressed in conservative business suits. One of the men was helped out of the van by two others. As he stepped down onto the ground, I noticed the handcuffs and foot shackles. It didn't take any great feat of wisdom on my part to figure out that what I was witnessing was the delivery of some sort of prisoner by four guards to the rear of the church.

The handcuffed man raised his face, permitting the falling rain to caress his skin. He moved as slowly as he possibly could as he gazed out across the fields behind the church. The prisoner and one of the guards smiled at me, but the others remained sober-faced. The guard who smiled at me indicated that I should walk around to the front entrance of the church as they entered the back door.

I located Father Shehan as he was discussing the songs that were to be sung during the ceremony with the choir director. As I handed him the tools he had requested, I mentioned that a man wearing handcuffs had been taken in the back door. He led me gracefully off to the side and told me that the man was expected. He was a prisoner over at the penitentiary, and at Father Frank's last request, the man was to give the eulogy. It was being kept as quiet as possible. Following his brief explanation, he gave me a look of "Do you understand what I'm saying?" He didn't have to utter another word. I was to get on with my duties and remain absolutely quiet about the man in the back of the church.

It wasn't too long after our conversation that people started to file in quietly and take their seats. Father Frank's casket had been placed just to the right of the altar. Many people that I recognized from church and some that I had never seen before walked up to the casket. Some lowered their heads in prayer, while others knelt and wept. Some just walked by, touched the casket, and returned to their seats.

At exactly ten o'clock, the service began. The church was packed just like Father Shehan had predicted. People were standing by the walls all the way to the front pews. The joined voices of the choir members and the organ reverberated through the church as we started up the aisle. Aside from Father Shehan, Robert, and me, there were three other priests and the two people who were to participate in the readings.

As we passed by, Mom gave us her usual nod of approval. She never said anything about it, but I would have bet the farm that she wanted Robert and me to become priests.

The service seemed to drag on endlessly. There was more singing than usual and special readings. Then the moment I had been waiting for occurred. The four guards escorted their prisoner, who had been freed from his bindings, to the main podium. Two guards occupied seats that had been left empty in the first row, and the other two positioned themselves by the entrance doors on the left and right. I was starting to get the drift of the circumstances. The reason for the suits rather than standard prison uniforms was to conform to the situation.

The prisoner stood at the podium and looked out over the crowded church. It was such a strange sight. Everyone in the church remained silent, waiting for him to begin. For the moment, this prisoner, this man from the local penitentiary, was in complete control of people who for the most part probably wouldn't give him the time of day.

He cleared his throat, before beginning, "My name is Benjamin

Sullivan. Many of you know who I am, but for those of you who are not familiar with me, just let me say that I have been seated on death row for the last nineteen years. It's important that you know about me because my life is the exact opposite of Father Frank's."

He looked over at the casket and then raised his hands in an attempt to display humbleness. "Please try and be as patient as you can with me. I have never been known as a public speaker and for the past several years I really haven't had much of an opportunity to talk with a lot of people. I am here today for one reason. To tell you about my good friend Frank.

"Frank and I were both raised right here in town, over on Stiver Avenue. We lived just three houses apart. Our parents were good neighbors. As small boys, we did all the things boys do. We rode bikes, went swimming down at the river, climbed trees, and collected baseball cards. We went to summer camp together, attended the same school, and slept over at each other's house more times than I can recall. We were very close. I never understood just how close a friend Frank was until we turned seven."

Ben took a heavy breath, then continued, "That was the year that my parents were killed in an automobile accident. Frank's parents, actually quite a few folks, were concerned about my future. You see, I had no brothers or sisters. The only living relative in my family was my mother's sister who lived out in California somewhere. She had already had a few run-ins with the law and couldn't seem to hang on to a regular job, so the state wasn't real excited about sending me to the West Coast to live with her. I was virtually alone. No one displayed greater concern for me than Frank. I remember him telling me at my parents' funeral that he didn't know what he was going to do if they decided to send me away.

"The day that they put my folks to rest, a man I had never seen came to the ceremony. He gave the eulogy for my father, saying that he and my dad had been best of friends. He talked about how they had gone to school together and had served in the Navy side by side. I felt good about this strange man who had come to say so many splendid things about my father.

"Later on that day, there was a gathering at Frank's house. People brought hams and cakes and shared their sorrow at the tragic loss of my parents. Frank and I sat out on the back porch. I just didn't feel like eating or being around anybody. Even back then as a young boy, Frank knew how to reach out and touch people. He put his arm around me that afternoon and told me that as long as he lived he'd be there for me.

"I remember crying as I told Frank that he was my best friend. I asked him to do me a favor that day. I asked him if he would come to my funeral and give my eulogy, just like the stranger had done for my father. Frank agreed, but said that there was a bit of a problem. What if he died first? I hadn't even considered Frank dying before me. Before I could answer, he came up with the solution. Frank always had a simple answer for everything. He said that if he died first, I was to give his eulogy. If it turned out the opposite way, then he'd do the honors."

Ben was starting to tear up as he hesitated slightly, turned his head away, composed himself, and picked up where he left off. "That's why I'm here today. I'm here to complete our agreement. The list of terrific things about my friend that can be mentioned seems endless. Most of you folks know what I'm talking about. There probably aren't very many of us here today that Father Frank hasn't reached out and touched in some fashion.

"A few days after they buried my parents, my stay at Frank's house came to an end. Two officials from the state came and took me out to Piney Meadows. That was a long time ago. A lot of you folks probably remember ol' Piney. It's all boarded up now, but at that time it was the largest home for children in the state.

"The day they drove me away, I stared out the back window of the car and watched Frank and his family shrink in the distance. The last thing Frank said to me was not to worry—he'd never abandon me. He kept his word. Every single day for two straight months, rain or shine, Frank would pedal his bike the six miles out to the home, spend the day with me, and then pedal back to his house. He'd always bring my favorite candy bar, which he paid for out of his allowance. The staff at Piney said that I was lucky to have such a great friend.

"Summer came to an end and Frank could no longer visit me every day due to school. His parents had started adoption procedures, but there was a problem. My aunt out in California was interested in taking me in. The state still wasn't willing to give her custody. As things go, the red tape, which seems to be in just about everything we're involved in these days brought everything to a standstill.

"I was to remain at Piney Meadows until the best possible solution to the predicament was reached. I stayed there for another three months. Twice a month, I was permitted to spend the weekend at Frank's. Frank was positive that it was just a question of time until I would be his official brother.

"Eventually, I was adopted, but it wasn't Frank's parents. Don't get me wrong, the folks who took me in couldn't have been kinder. Fortunately, they lived out in Sheldon, so Frank and I could still get to see each other. Sheldon, being seven miles to the north, meant that I wouldn't be attending the same school as Frank. During weekends, we would take turns staying at each other's house. The summers were the best times for us. There was an old oak tree just about halfway between town and Sheldon. We'd always ride our bikes out in the morning and meet at the tree to plan our day.

"Staying at Piney Meadows had changed me. I bumped heads with a few kids who had some temper problems. I wound up developing a temper of my own and my patience was, well, let's just say, on the short side. Looking back, it's easy to see that this was the point in our lives where we started to drift apart. When I say drift apart, I only mean the way that we handled things. Frank continued to deal with situations through reasoning, while I had a tendency to lean toward violence. He always wanted to talk matters over. I always wanted to punch somebody in the mouth.

"By the time high school rolled around, I had become what's more commonly known as a `hood.' Frank and I attended the same high school. I was more interested in driving fast cars, drinking, and running with the wrong crowd. I was involved in everything that was bad, while Frank was in everything that was good. He was president of the student council, a member of the debate team, and a reporter on the school paper. Despite our differences, we still remained the best of friends. Our interests were different, but our friendship held together.

"My senior year turned out to be a total disaster. Besides flunking every single subject I was taking, I got into a fracas with one of the teachers, which netted me getting temporarily expelled. That fall, Frank and I joined the Army on the buddy system. Being the total mess that I was, everyone said that the Army would do me a world of good.

"We weren't even in Vietnam for three months when the night that changed Frank's life occurred. The day before the attack came,

I found Frank, as usual, sitting in his tent in the morning reading his Bible. Over coffee, he told me that he had been reading about a man by the name of Samson, who, believe it or not, had killed three hundred men in combat with nothing more than the jawbone of a donkey. Little did I, or Frank, for that matter, realize how that particular Bible story would affect our lives the following night.

"Our platoon was out on patrol when the unexpected assault came. The enemy was all over us before we knew it. Within seconds, everyone in the entire platoon was killed except for Frank and me. I suffered a machine-gun blast across my legs, then another shell in my right arm. I went down and was rendered helpless. Two enemy soldiers stood over me, their bayonets poised to put an end to my life.

"But then it happened. Those two soldiers fell to the ground, thanks to two well-aimed bullets fired by Frank. He stood over me and ordered me not to worry—no one was going to kill me. I can't even begin to guess how many of the enemy he killed that day. He just stood there, spinning in a circle, a machine gun in each hand. When the guns were empty, he picked up two more from dead soldiers and continued to mow down the oncoming enemy. Near the end he was like a man possessed. A copter landed about twenty yards away and yelled for Frank to get in. He looked down at me and smiled. He wasn't going anywhere without me. The enemy was firing at the copter, the pilot couldn't wait any longer, and he was forced to leave. It was hand-to-hand combat now and Frank was swinging one of the empty machine guns around taking out one soldier after another. He was knocked to the ground, but got back up and threw one of the enemy soldiers into three others. We survived that day, thanks to the air support that drove off the rest of the enemy.

"We were picked up and flown to a local field hospital. We were both too shot up to be of any further service in combat. Frank had been shot seven times, and stabbed twice. I had so much lead in my legs, the doctors joked, saying that I weighed an additional fifty pounds.

"That next morning when I woke up in the hospital, Frank somehow managed to crawl out of his bed and onto the floor. Kneeling next to his bed, his face clutched in his bandaged hands, he cried. I tried to get out of my own bed, but wound up falling on my face. Frank picked me up, his face full of tears as he told me through a choked voice that he had killed so many men. He was afraid that he was going to go to Hell for what he had done.

"Growing up together, Frank always had more emotional strength. But that day, that morning, he was feeling pretty low, and as far as I was concerned, had no reason to be. I told Frank that he had done nothing more than what he had promised me as a kid. I reminded him of what he had said years in the past, that he'd always be there for me. Frank had saved my life.

"Most of you probably don't know this, but Frank had a nickname. I branded him with it that day that we both laid there on that floor. When the nurses came in and got us back into our beds, I just laid there staring up at the ceiling. I kept picturing Frank standing firmly in that muddy field defeating one enemy soldier after another. He had been just like Samson. From that day on, my best friend Frank, had a new name: Jawbone.

"A few weeks later, we were shipped back home. Frank had already decided to start his work for the Lord. Eventually, he went off to study for the priesthood; I returned to my former rotten habits of recklessness and irresponsibility. We stayed in touch and visited when he was home. As time passed, I went through three divorces, more jobs than I could count, and a number of short stays in the county prison.

"When Frank was assigned to the very church he had been raised in, people in town were excited. It was going to be wonderful to have a hometown boy as one of the town's religious leaders. Frank and I returned to our boyhood routine of meeting on Wednesdays. By that time, I was what most folks considered pretty far gone. I was in and out of jail, couldn't hold a job for more than a month, and, in general, one of the local citizens, if you wanted to call me that, whom most people could do without.

"Frank was well aware of my lifestyle of rotten habits. He never really preached to me, but just kept reminding me that he'd always be there. Looking back now, we must have seemed a peculiar-looking pair. Frank usually dressed in a fashion that tipped folks to the fact that he was a priest, while I had a talent of looking like something the cat dragged in. The fact that most people viewed me as a lowlife never entered into Frank's friendship with me. I was about the furthest thing from being a man of faith, but I never allowed the fact that Frank was a priest to interfere with the closeness that we had.

"A little over nineteen years ago, I made the biggest mistake of my life. I needed some cash, so I decided to steal some money from a corner market over in the next county. Me and two of my so-called friends drove over there. I was to hold a gun on the owner while the others went about heisting the place. Things didn't work out the way we had planned. I wound up shooting and eventually killing a girl that worked there. I was convicted and sent to prison. They gave me the death penalty."

Ben stopped as if he were in deep thought, then started again. "Today is the day that the sentence that was passed down years ago will be carried out."

The tears were starting to stream down his cheeks. "Ya know, all that time…nineteen years, the only person who came to visit me on a regular basis was Father Frank. He showed up every Wednesday, never missing a day in all that time. He came on my birthday, at Christmas, and at Thanksgiving. He lived up to what he had promised me: the promise of always being there.

"These last three weeks, he came to see me every day. He told me that he had never been too pushy with me about getting right with the Lord, but time was running out. He reminded me about what he had said when we were kids, about how he didn't know what he'd do if the state shipped me off somewhere. He said that Heaven was the only place to spend eternity and he wanted to make sure that I made it….and that all the praying in the world wouldn't amount to a hill of beans unless I came to terms with the Almighty myself.

"According to the warden, about three hours from now, I'll be taking my last breath when they throw the switch. The clock is ticking and I still haven't asked God to forgive me for the things I've done. I don't want you to think that Father Frank wasn't strong enough to convince me to move toward the Lord. I was just too weak. I could just never imagine God being able to forgive me for taking that girl's life.

"It was just a few days ago that I reminded Frank that he had to perform my eulogy. He said that he would be right there with me, right up to the last moment. I remember laughing, saying that he was going to be hard pressed to find anything good to say about his old friend. Frank just smiled back and said that there was plenty of good things about me he could say.

"When Frank passed on, Father Shehan came to the prison with the sad news. He told me that the last thing that Father Frank said was that I had to give his eulogy, and that I had to ask the Lord for forgiveness. I'll never forget what Frank told me about coming to the Lord. He always said that if a person really accepted Jesus into his heart, there would be a sign.

"Coming here today…to this church wasn't easy. It wasn't something I had planned on. I was supposed to receive my just punishment, and Frank would give my eulogy. I'd like to thank the governor for postponing my execution until this afternoon so I could come here and fulfill my obligation to Frank. Father Frank did a lot of good over at the prison, so I guess the governor figured he owed Frank. The last thing I'd like to say, or I guess, actually do, is to complete Frank's final request. I guess it's true what they say…The Lord works in mysterious ways. It took Frank's untimely death for me to realize that I need to reach out for forgiveness."

Ben backed away from the lectern, then stepped slowly across the altar, knelt down on his knees, and placed his hands on the casket as he closed his eyes. He remained silent for nearly a minute, then finally began, "Dear Lord, I know that this precious man is now with you. I ask forgiveness for the things I have done wrong in my life. I choose to be with you. I know that I am not worthy, but I humbly ask for your blessing."

Ben stood, and gently touched the edge of the casket, as he commented, "Well, Jawbone, I've done what you've asked me to." He turned to one of the guards and went on, "I'm ready now."

Ben and the four guards exited through the side door, leaving the congregation in stunned silence. Then, just as the men disappeared through the doorway, the church tower bell started to ring. Father Shehan gave me a strange look; a look that meant *go and see why that bell is ringing!*

I got up casually, walked through the side door, then ran around to the tower passage. The bell rope was straight as an arrow, but the bell continued to ring as the rope moved up and down. This was an impossibility. The bell was not on any type of automatic timer. The rope had to be manually tugged on in order for the bell to ring.

I ran up the circular stairs, all the while the bell ringing, on and on. When I got to the top of the tower, I saw the prison van pulling away from the church lot. Moments later, the bell no longer ringing, Father Shehan was at my side. Out of breath, he asked, "Who…was…ringing the…bell?"

That moment, I knew who was ringing the ball. I never did answer Father that day. I just smiled and walked back down the stairs. The next time my parents start having one of their miracle debates, well, let's just say, I'll be able to hop right in with some first-hand experience of my own.

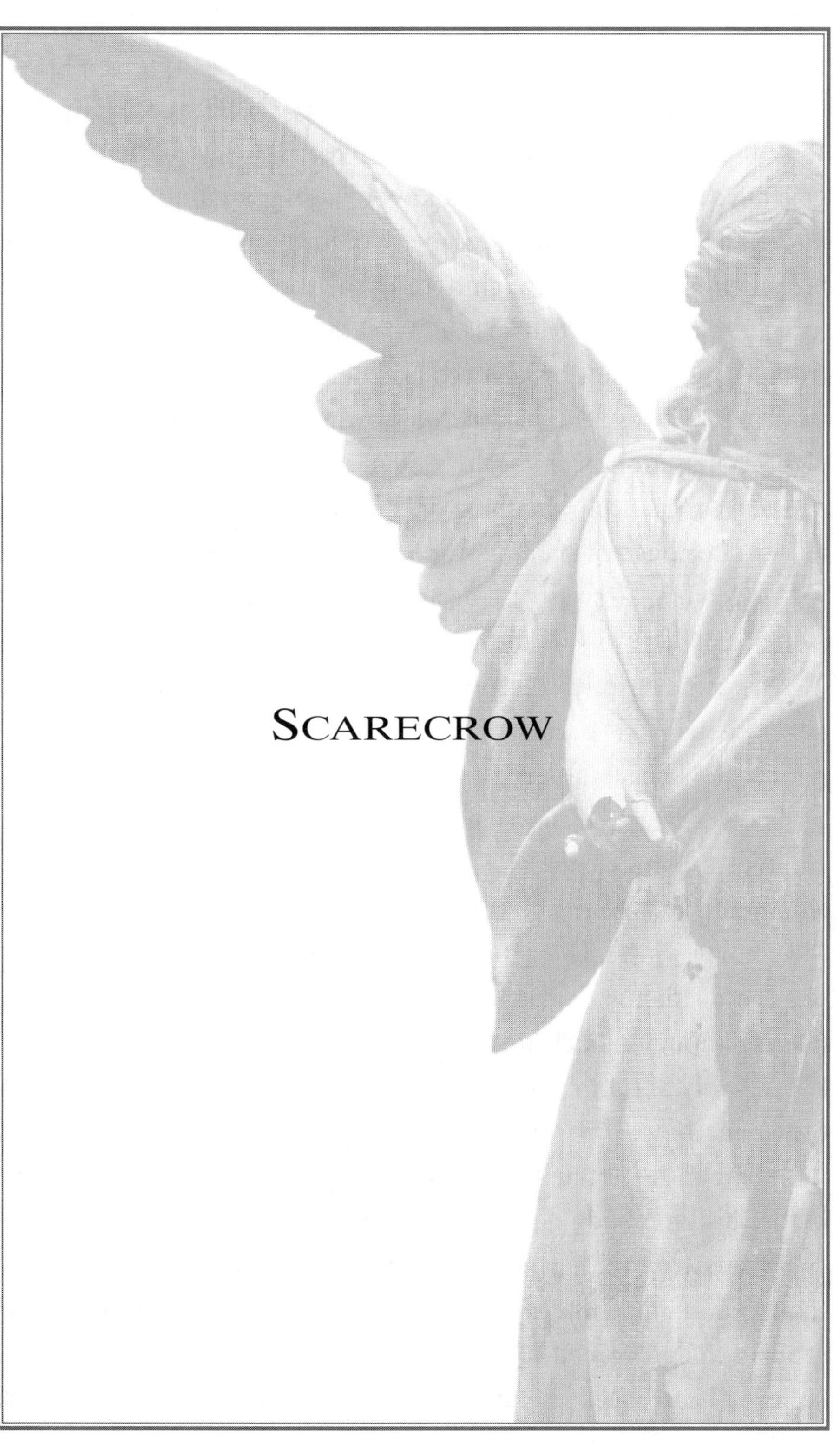

SCARECROW

THE MOSS-COVERED BOULDER OBSTRUCTING HIS chosen route of escape caused him to veer sharply to the right, the twisting sensation in his left ankle delivering a painful message to his leg, his foot stubbing into an exposed tree root. The side of his face slammed into the rough floor of the forest, his hands extended forward plowing pine needles and dirt into small piles. Spitting mud from his mouth, he slowly got to his knees, then winced as the top of a tall maple just six yards away was severed from its thick trunk. The eight-foot section of timber exploded into a mass of splinters, bark and leaves, then fell, snapping off limbs on its journey to the earth below. The constant shelling from cannons belonging to both armies was spreading a swath of destruction over the countryside that would remain for years to come.

His mind briefly transported him to a time in the past. He'd never been in this particular forest before, yet, he couldn't help but ponder how peaceful it must have been here at one time. Birds had probably nested in the safety of the trees, their daily rhapsody creating a calming melody in the branches above. Squirrels and chipmunks had gone about their everyday routine of preparing for the coming winter. Deer foraged in the underbrush for wild berries.

The distinctive and telling sound of a shotgun blast jerked his drifting thoughts back to the situation at hand as he witnessed a fellow soldier crumble to the ground. The wound had not been fatal, the young boy attempting to stand, but the second discharge from the weapon sent the youth sprawling backward, his life ending before his limp body made contact with the moist soil.

"Move...move! he thought. He wasn't even on his feet for more than what seemed like a second when he was hammered back to the ground, the air forced from his lungs. The enemy rider reigned his lathered horse back around for a second attack as the large black

stallion reared up on his back legs. The bearded Confederate horseman skillfully aimed his pistol, pulled the trigger, but then cursed as the hammer clicked. It was empty. Drawing his saber, he spurred the horse forward as he let out a chilling yell, the sharp metal edge of the sword glinting in a ray of sunlight that had filtered down through the trees. The steed stumbled, thudding to the ground, the rider's left leg jammed between horseflesh and dirt.

The rider tried desperately to reload, but the thrashing animal was tossing him back and forth mercilessly. The Union soldier sprang at the chance to cheat death, the throbbing in his ankle now of no concern. Four quick limping strides were immediately followed by yet another collision with the ground as he tripped over a jutting rock. He chanced a short glance back at the flailing horse and its rider. The man had discontinued his attempt to kill any more of the enemy, now his total concern focused on trying to disengage his leg before the panic-stricken animal snapped it like a dry twig.

The blue-clad soldier once again rose, but now was more attentive to where he was stepping. The pain in his ankle had returned and seemed to increase as he weaved in and out between boulders and trees hoping to make himself less of an easy target. Little did he realize that at the moment he was now unnoticed, the remaining gray calvary concentrating their efforts on destroying the rest of the Federal soldiers fleeing deeper into the forest.

As close as he could figure, he must have run for twenty minutes or so. He had fallen two more times, the last failure to remain on his feet had been particularly painful as his right knee was split open by a jagged rock. Suddenly, he found himself confronted by a small stream only five feet in width at its widest point, no more than a few inches deep. It could be forded with little effort.

The idea of proceeding any further was rapidly erased from his thought process. Bending over, his hands resting on his knees, his mouth wide open as he gasped for air, the intense cramp on his left side preventing him from standing erect. Turning slowly and looking back in the direction he had just come from, he peered into the trees in search of the gray riders. No one came into view.

Stepping behind a dense mass of scrub brush, he once again faced the shallow creek, thinking that possibly he may have lost his pursuers. Holding up his sweat and dirt-covered hands, he stared thoughtfully out into the trees on the opposite bank of the water. He had always considered himself an individual who was of a rational nature; a person who was capable of sizing up most situations, dissecting all of the components, then making an intelligent decision on action required.

At the present time, he had so many different raw feelings of emotion tugging at his brain that he wasn't sure what course of action was required to alleviate his pressing problems. He was hungry, thirsty, dead tired, filthy and worst of all, experiencing a sense of fear that prior to this day he couldn't have even imagined.

Two days before their arrival in Sharpsburg, Maryland, his Indiana regiment had covered over sixty miles during the forty-eight hour period. During the forced march, he and the others had been lucky to squeeze in no more than six hours of sleep. They had stumbled into camp a little after four in the morning and had been ordered to try and grab a few hours' rest as the battle would probably begin to form just after dawn.

There had been no time during the exhaustive march for the preparation of warm meals. The only nourishment he had forced into his empty stomach had been a few strips of raw bacon and some green corn they had gleaned from a field they had passed. Just before falling to sleep he had gazed out across the vast fields, the fires of the enemy in plain sight. He wondered if they were as tired as he was.

Morning came quickly and with it the booming of the Confederate cannons. It was the first time in his life that he had ever been awakened by the very ground shaking beneath him. He thought back to his life on the farm and how he had hated his grandmother banging that darn ladle on one of her skillets, which was her way of announcing that breakfast was on. He longed to be back home in Indiana—to hear the peaceful sounds of farm life—even Grandma's skillet in the early morning.

The sleep barely out of their eyes, his regiment was ordered to form up and march to an adjacent rise overlooking the coming battle. Upon arriving, he and three other younger fellows were pulled from line and ordered to an artillery battery about a hundred yards away where they were to unload cassions of ammunition for the cannons. After stacking their rifles, the process of unloading began and continued through the morning.

Hours later, his uniform was completely soaked with sweat, his canteen had long since been emptied. He felt like his arms were going to fall from their sockets as he continued unloading one cassion after another. At times, the smoke from the cannon fire was so thick he could hardly breathe, let alone see.

Finally, about eleven-thirty in the morning, there had been a break in the action as they waited for more ammunition to be brought forward. A light breeze had started to clear away the smoke and he could see the vast cornfield that the Federal cannons were trained on. Picking up a pair of field binoculars that had been dropped by an officer who had been mortally shot, he scanned the thirty acres of corn. It was nothing less than horrid down there in that field. Most of the corn had been shredded to pieces, many of the stalks that were still standing streaked with the blood of the Rebel soldiers who had fallen in the field. He couldn't believe that they just kept advancing—arms, legs, feet and rifles being thrown in every direction. And still they came on. How could man be so brutal toward another man, he had thought.

Just as a group of three cassions pulled up, suddenly from the woods on the left, a band of Southern calvary broke from the trees, guns blazing, the Union soldiers manning the artillery battery being cut to pieces. He had glanced at where his rifle was stacked, but it had been knocked to the ground by one of the riders. The only option that he and those who were left standing had was to run to safety in the trees to the right.

Looking back into the trees again, he realized that he was one of very few that had managed to escape the wrath of the Confederate riders. He had run so hard that he felt as if he couldn't muster up another step. It would be nice just to climb under some of the surrounding brush and try to sleep—but that was too risky. He had heard too many stories about men who had been caught by the enemy while sleeping and taken as prisoners of war. No, he would keep moving away from the sound of the ongoing battle.

For the moment, there was nothing that he could do about his hunger or need for rest, but he could at least get a cool drink and clean himself up in the shallow stream. Checking in every direction once again, he carefully approached the creek and when he was convinced that he was alone, went down on his knees and began to satisfy his thirst. The cool water felt soothing as it rolled across his throat.

Then he heard a distinctive snap. He knew what the sound was before he even looked across the creek into the woods. Someone had stepped on a branch. The Confederate soldier stood on the opposite bank, seemingly not that surprised at seeing an enemy drinking from the stream. The Union soldier jumped to his feet as he grabbed a nearby sizable rock and raised it in defense. Backing up two steps he ordered, "You cross that creek and I'll bash your head in!"

The Confederate, an older man, slightly grinned, then responded, "Fore ya bash my head in, could I at least git my fill first?" With that he knelt down and drank from the stream, not paying any more attention to the young Union soldier. Finished drinking, he sat on a log and placed his dirty bare feet into the water. Reaching inside his shirt pocket he withdrew two strips of jerky. Ripping a bite off one of the strips, he tossed the other across the stream. It landed near the boy's feet. "Gone on," he said, "Looks like ya could use a bite. Don't fret o'er me none. I ain't gonna shoot ya. Ain't ev'n got a gun."

Checking the woods behind the Confederate, he searched for any more of the enemy. "Ain't nobody else with me iffin that's what yer worried o'er," said the man. " Sit down an' work on that jerky."

Bending down, he picked up the jerky, never taking his eyes off the man on the other side of the creek. Sitting down, he placed the rock at his side in case he needed it later. Taking the first bite out of the coarse strip of meat, he looked the Confederate over from head to foot: no shoes or socks, filthy, raggedy-edged pants, a section of hemp for a belt, no shirt, an old gray coat and a wrinkled fishing hat atop the bearded face. A smile came to the young boy's face as he chewed slowly.

"Somethin' wrong?" asked the man.

"Well, I've never been this close to a Reb before," said the boy.

"I haven't been in the Army for more than a few months, but during many a conversation around a campfire, I've heard some of the men say that you Rebs look like scarecrows. Now, that I'm face to face with one—I have to agree. You do look kind of like the scarecrow in my Grannie's garden back in Indiana."

Looking down over himself, the southern soldier responded, "I can assure ya that underneath all these here rags and dirt there's a man…just like you…older, but just an ordinary man." Taking another bite of jerky, he went on as he asked. "So yer'r from Indiana. I've heard it said that they call you fellahs from up there Hoosiers. If I could ask—what's a Hoosier?"

"I'm not really sure, but most folks claim that it stands for something big."

"Big! Ya'll don't look that big ta me. Why, ya couldn't tip the scales at more than, what—maybe 135 pounds."

Taking offense, the boy picked up the rock. "I'm big enough to bash your head in!"

"Take it easy, son, didn't mean nothin' by it." Tipping his hat, the Reb introduced himself, "Name's Amos Dunn. From the hill country down in Texas. Pleasure ta meet ya."

Calming down, the boy put the rock down as he spoke, "I'm Edward Miller from Terre Haute…just this side of the Wabash."

Amos picked up a small rock and tossed it across the stream into the trees as he asked, "What made ya join up?"

Edward seemed more relaxed as he answered, "Seemed like the right thing to do. We talked about slavery in school. Even back then, I didn't think it was right…for one man to actually own another man. That kind of thing would never happen in the north."

"Couldn't agree with ya more. Don't hold with this idea of slavery myself."

Edward stopped chewing for a moment as he stared in wonder. "How can you be against slavery and still fight for the Confederacy?"

"Ya see," answered Amos, "That's where a lot of you folks from up north are a tad confused. The average soldier in the southern Army don't own no slaves. The men who own slaves are the wealthy of the South…politicians, business folk…many of the generals in the Army. My farm's too small fer slaves, but iffin I did have one I'd pay `em a fair wage, an' iffin they was of a mind ta up an leave…so be it. The reason I'm fightin' in this horrible war has nothin' ta do with slavery. I just don't think it's right for Lincoln to intrude into the southern way of life." Rubbing his hand over his rough face, he asked, "That why yer'r fightin'…ta save the slaves?"

"Well, I guess…I mean this war seems to be so complex. The northern section of this country has more manufacturing abilities, more man power and money to support the war, but yet from what I've heard you fellahs have won most of the major battles to date. If we…the north, win the war, slavery will come to an end, but if the South wins, the whole idea of slavery will continue and eventually things will go back to the way they were before this war started."

Amos made no comment about Edward's description of how the war was progressing, but questioned him further about his personal life. "Yer folks…how do they feel `bout ya joinin' up?"

Edward rolled his eyes as he took another bite of the spicy jerky. "They didn't approve at all. My father, who happens to be a preacher doesn't believe in fighting…no matter what the cause may be, and my mother didn't want me to go because I'm her only son. Can't say as I blame her for the way she feels, but I'm old enough to make my own decisions."

"I've had `nough o' this war," said Amos. "This time tomorrow

I'll be well on my way back home to Texas."

"That's real kind of the Army to let you go home."

"Ain't nobody allowin' me ta do nothin'. Leavin' on my own."

Edward looked surprised. "But isn't that desertion?"

"The Army might call it that, but the way I see things it's a matter or gettin' yer priorities in line. I've had and seen `nough killin'. I was at Manassas, Bull Run, White Oak Swamp and a passel of other battles I'd just as soon's fergit. Before I joined the Army, I never come even close ta killin' a man, but these past couple years I've ended many a man's life...and escaped death myself on a number o' occassions. Nah...that's it fer me. Sides that, I got me a letter from my wife a few weeks back. Seems some of yer boys marched through Texas down by where my farm is. They killed everything and burned the place out. My wife and three boys hid in a cellar down under the barn. She said they only had food for maybe a month or so. I gotta get home and see ta my family."

Shaking his head as if in agreement, Edward asked, "What do you miss most about your place down in Texas?"

"The most. I'd say sittin' out behind the barn with my ol' hound Silas, or mebbe one o' my wife's apple pies. Now that's good eatin. An' you...whadda ya miss from up there in Hoosier country?"

Edward didn't even hesitate as he responded, "My Bible....read it through six times over the years. I brought it along with me...read it every night, but somewhere about a week back I lost it. I sure do miss reading about the Lord some each day."

Amos slipped his feet out of the water as he yawned, then asked his next question. "Ya said that yer father was a preacher. What faith do ya practice?"

"We're Southern Baptist."

Amos slapped his hand on his pant leg sending up a small cloud of dust as he laughed. "Southern Baptist! I'm Southern Baptist. Iffin that don't beat all." Looking directly at Edward, he inquired, "How on earth did Southern Baptist get up in Indiana?"

"We're not originally from Indiana. My pa moved the family up there back about seven years ago. My grandma and grandpa owned a pretty big farm in Terre Haute and when Gramps died, Grandma couldn't run the place herself so she wrote my father and said that she'd give him the place if he moved up there and took care of the farm until she passed on. There was a small Methodist church in town, but the preacher ran off with some girl from down at the feed mill…not to mention that he took all the church's money with him. My pa started to hold service at the church and soon just about everybody for miles around had fallen into the fold of Southern Baptist."

Looking upstream, Amos took the last bit of his jerky, then inspected a small streak of blood on his right arm. "Thought I got nipped by a shot earlier today, but it might just be from crashing through the brush."

"Have you ever seen Robert E. Lee?" Edward asked.

Amos smiled. "Sure I've seen him…I guess three or four times. They say he's a short man. Every time I saw him he was seated on his horse so it was kinda hard ta tell just how tall he is. He's here somewhere in all this mess today."

"They say that the men beneath him will do whatever he commands…even if it means giving up their lives."

"He is highly respected…almost looked upon with awe. Myself, I don't pay ol' Bobby Lee much attention. Like most generals, they thrive on a diff'rent level than the normal soldier. I guess they've got their job to do just like the men out on the field."

The sounds of the battle had started to die off, gun shots and the roar of cannons was now merely sporadic. A gunshot that sounded close by in the trees caused Amos and Edward to jump to their feet. "I best be gettin' on," said Amos. "I ain't gettin' any closer to Texas sittin' here. If I was you, I'd be clearin' out. The next Reb that comes `long might not be as friendly as me."

Turning to walk into the woods, he hesitated, then turned back and walked across the stream as he removed something from inside his coat pocket. Holding a well-used Bible in his hand, he offered it to Edward. "Here…want ya ta take this. It might not be yer own Bible, but it reads the same."

Edward objected, "No…I couldn't take another man's Bible. That's not right. I just can't do that."

Reaching out, Amos placed the small Bible in Edward's hand as he explained, "Most folks would say that our meetin' up across from one `nother at this stream is nothin' more than a coincidence. Us Southern Baptists know that that ain't true. The Good Lord amidst all this killin' `round here arranged this meetin `tween us. Seems ta me that yer the kind of fellah that might make it all the way through this war. That ol' Bible has got me through some tough moments…and if ya read just a little each day, ya might just survive all this. Don't fret ov'r me none, son. I got me plenty of verses memorized that `ill get me back home ta Texas."

"I'll accept your Bible," said Edward, "but there's a condition." Sitting down, he started to unlace his shoes. "We've got plenty of shoes back at camp. You'll never make it down to Texas without shoes. Take these…there're a little big for me anyways. I have to stuff leaves in them to make them fit. They look about your size. I won't take no for an answer. It'll be a trade—the Bible for the shoes."

Amos smiled, then spoke, "Sounds fair, Hoosier…I'll take yer shoes."

After placing the shoes on his dirty feet, Amos turned to walk back across the stream, but stopped as he noticed the clear water slowly start to turn a faded red from upstream. Edward looked down at the blood-filled water as he remarked. "Wonder if it's Union or Confederate blood?"

"Don't make a diff'rence," grimaced Amos. "The men from the north wear a diff'rent color uniform than those from down south…but, we all bleed red." He tipped his hat and walked toward the trees, "See ya `round, Hoosier…be careful now."

Edward added his own goodbye as he yelled after the southern veteran, "God go with you, scarecrow."

September 17, 1867. The war had been over for just a little over two years. Edward stood next to his wife Inez at the top of Nicodemus Hill where he had watched the horror during that day in the past at Antietam in Miller's Cornfield. He stood gazing out across the cornfield that had been replanted and now appeared as a vast peaceful sea of cornstalks that swayed in the gentle breeze. It wasn't nearly as hot as it had been when he had been here before. A tear came to his eye as he placed the picnic basket he was carrying on the ground. Inez, holding their 18-month old baby girl, Elizabeth, reached out touching her husband's arm as she reassured him, "It'll be alright, Edward."

This was Edward's first trip back to Antietam. He had told Inez about that bloody day more times than she could remember, but this was the first time he had ever shed a tear.

Smiling through his tear-streaked face, Edward took a deep breath as he tried to gain control of his emotions. "Never really thought I'd come back to this place. Even though the war has been over now for almost three years, they'll be other men who come here today and for years to come to revisit where so many of their friends and the enemy died. Men who survived this battle, who now spend their time in saloons or on their front porch still talk of that day, the single most bloodiest day during the war. Twenty-three thousand casualties." Turning to his wife, he went on, "The name of that cornfield down there back then was Miller's Cornfield. Almost makes me ashamed to have the same last name. I remember sitting around a campfire that night and hearing officers talk about how you couldn't even walk across the field without stepping on a dead body." Pulling his timepiece from his pocket, he picked up the basket as he started down the hill, "Come on, we need to get moving if we're going to be there on time."

Stopping, he noticed the top of the tree that had exploded that day long ago. It was now a rotted shell of a log, no doubt home to countless insects. "This is the spot where I almost met the Good Lord. Guess it just wasn't my time." Edward motioned toward a huge boulder. "That's the way…right through those trees there. It'll probably take about a half hour to get to the stream. If we want to get there on time, we need to keep moving."

It wasn't quite as easy as Edward thought it would have been to retrace his route through the forest two years in the past. He kept stopping, commenting that he had been running for his life, not really paying attention to where he had been going. Finally, they came to the stream, but nothing looked familiar. Four years couldn't have changed the surrounding forest that much. "Well, Inez, this is the stream I came to. I think we're too far downstream though Come on."

Breaking into a small clearing, Edward smiled as he pointe

upstream. “There he is…with his family just like he said he’d be in the letter.” Amos Dunn stood as he waved. Spread out on a blanket sat his wife and three young sons. Edward whispered to Inez, “He brought his whole family…I can’t believe it.”

By the time Edward and Inez got to the edge of the stream, Amos had already crossed as he held a box in his hands. Edward was the first to speak. “Inez, I would like you to meet Mr. Amos Dunn…Amos, this is my wife Inez and our daughter Elizabeth.”

Amos tipped his hat. “My pleasure ma`am. That’s my family ov’r there. Why doncha go on o’er and join ‘em. Me and Edward got some business ta attend ta first. Inez waded across and as she knelt down placing Elizabeth on the blanket looked back as she watched the two enemy soldiers that had bonded in the woods that day in the past.

Edward looked down at the clear water. “There’s no more blood in the stream, Amos. I guess everything has healed itself.”

“Did ya bring yer part o’ the trade with ya,” asked Amos.

Edward reached into his pocket removing the small tattered Bible as Amos lifted the lid from the box, exposing the old shoes. Handing the Bible to Amos, Edward took the box. The trade was complete: an old Confederate Bible for a worn out pair of Union shoes.

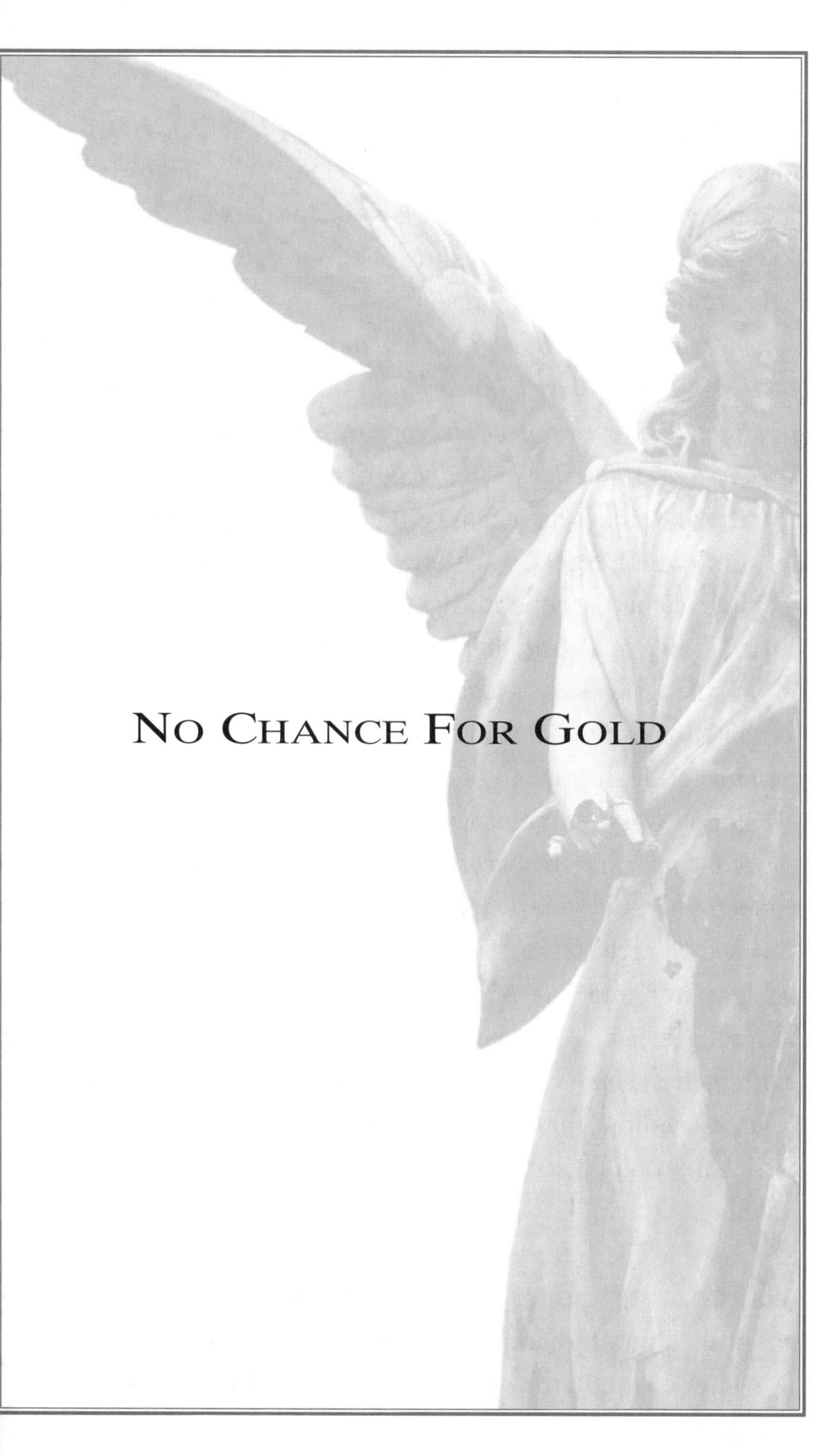

No Chance For Gold

Angels' Footprints

LOCKING THE DOOR OF HIS SECOND-FLOOR apartment, Lyle Campbell tucked his lunch box beneath his arm, then made his way down the dark wooden stairwell, the fourth step down creaking just like it had for the past sixteen years. Each time he heard that all too familiar sound he always had the same thought: *Why not move into a house? He had more than enough money saved up. He could even have a house built—maybe up at Crestwood Valley or in that new development everyone was talking about. He could ask Nora to marry him. He knew she'd say yes.*

After checking his mailbox, he opened the front door leading down to Water Street. Lighting his first cigarette of the day, he cupped his hand around his lighter as the November wind blowing through town made the simple process somewhat difficult. Looking up at the gray sky, which at the moment was filled with a combination of rain, sleet and snow, he started the half mile walk to the mine at the north end of town.

Stopping at the first of two intersections that he had to cross, he noticed that directly across the street three different couples climbed the stone steps leading into the Our Lady of Lourdes Catholic Church. It was Sunday and practically everyone in town would be attending one of the three different churches that the town offered. He had never been big on church. His folks had been anything but what you could call religious. He had always managed to get by without the church, or God, for that matter. As the years passed, he couldn't see why starting to attend church would change anything.

Crossing the intersection, he passed the Nelson County Bank and Trust. A stiff gust of wind almost knocked him off his feet as he was pushed into the brick wall of the building. Pulling the collar of his winter coat up around his neck, he looked in the bank window.

There was Nora's desk, her filing cabinets, her collection of ceramic panda bears and the framed picture of President Nixon on the wall.

Bracing himself against the cold wind, he started up the street once again, passing Ginter's Hardware Store, Bard's Print Shop and the local gin mill more commonly referred to as Mike's Bar and Grill. Every business in town was closed on Sundays, except for the three churches who went about the business of worshiping God. At the last intersection in town, he stopped as a car with a man and a woman in the front and two small children in the back passed by. The woman, obviously, a wife, gave him a subtle, but nonetheless, a degrading glance as she realized that the way he was dressed he was going to work at the mine rather than attending church. He smiled back at the lady as he tossed his finished cigarette into the gutter, the water swishing the butt along for a few yards until it finally disappeared down the street drain.

One block down the street just on the other side of RT. 61, the towering lights of Luken's Coal Company loomed up into the gray sky as if the company were a city itself. Making his way down the final block, he passed a group of boarded up buildings, as if the edge of town had been infected by some sort of cancer that was slowly making its way up the street.

Looking across the street, the view wasn't any more pleasant than the old rotted structures he was walking by. Old Town, or what most people referred to as Patch Town, appeared as if a bomb had been dropped on the area. It wasn't that long ago—maybe two decades in the past, that Patch Town had been the center of most of the miners' lives. Now it was nothing more than a fence-surrounded, dilapidated and dangerous place to enter.

At the very front of Patch Town stood the old mansion where the past mine owner had lived in luxury. The home now resembled a run-down shell of a building, the only hint of past luxury being the massive pillars and the size of the house. At the beginning of the four streets there were four identical dwellings of fair size that had housed the mine bosses, flanked by rows of 14'x 16' shacks that had housed the miners and their families. His grandfather and his father had been raised in Patch Town. He remembered as a young boy listening to his grandfather tell him about struggling to survive in one of the patch houses.

The eight-foot fence was topped with barbed wire and signed every 12 feet with a sign that read, KEEP OUT BY ORDER OF THE GRANITE HILL POLICE. If he remembered correctly, it had been back around the late 1950s that the coal beneath Patch Town had ignited and despite every effort to extinguish the fires, it continued to burn, causing sections of streets and entire houses to sink toward the burning hell down below. The police never really enforced the fact that Patch Town was now off-limits. There was no reason to. No one, even adventurous children, ventured there. It was just understood. It was a place were you might not return from. Lyle thought about how six years ago three youngsters had climbed over the fence for a day of adventure in Patch Town. One of the boys had fallen into a pit and, even after two weeks of extensive searching, was never found. It was as if the bowels of Hell had swallowed him up.

He stopped at the corner of Water Street and Route 61 as two coal trucks and a station wagon passed by. Looking back up Water Street, he noticed the small rectangular sign that read: WELCOME TO GRANITE HILL. Granite Hill, despite its coal and dust-covered buildings was the only town in Nelson County or for that matter, the surrounding counties that had survived the end of the coal era. It was kind of ironic that when the coal boom started to slide downhill, that Patch Town started to sink and was eventually evacuated for the safety of the remaining families.

Old man Lukens had passed on at the age of eighty-three at his desk at the mine. His son, Ralph, assumed responsibilities as the new owner. It was in the mid-fifties that the demand for coal was being replaced by heating oil and other cost-saving commodities other than coal. Ralph utilized the long-lasting relationships that his father had established over the years, convincing many of the huge companies that had purchased coal from his father that the cost of revamping their factories and plants over to oil would be costly and that coal was still a viable means of energy. Young Lukens, a shrewd businessman, cut the tonnage price of his coal, thus retaining many of his father's loyal customers. Lukens Mine survived the downward popularity of coal and so did Granite Hill. Many a mine operation in the northeastern section of Pennsylvania went belly-up, which caused many a town to dissolve right along with the mines. The mine was the heart of the economy of the mining towns. The demand for coal hit an all-time low in the fifties, but many of the companies who still utilized coal purchased it from Lukens, thus, there was work in Granite Hill for men who made their living in the coal fields.

Crossing Route 61, he passed beneath the huge entrance sign that read: SAFETY FIRST. Stepping from the macadam, Lyle slopped his way through the black mud that was rutted with numerous tire treads. Directly in front of him, stood the three-story brick mine office with its discolored shingled roof and dented guttering, the downsprouts at the moment working overtime to dispense the rainwater from the roof. To the right of the main office, there was the boiler room and machine shop, the widows so filthy that they appeared to be painted with a black soot. On the left, there was the long wooden shed that housed bulldozers, scrapers, trucks and other assorted mine equipment.

In the distance, up on the hill, a grimy-black diesel engine slowly pulled a string of loaded coal cars past number 3 coal tipple. Just beyond the three sets of railroad tracks centered in the scarred coal fields sat the old abandoned coal breaker, its windows almost completely broken out from rock throwing youngsters who on occasion wandered amongst the smouldering culm piles that had been burning for years and would continue to do so for as long as they were there. During the night or on a cloud-covered day, the abandoned section of Lukens Mine looked like a small version of what most folks thought Hell probably looked like.

Approaching the carriage that transported the miners down the shaft nearly a half mile below the surface, Lyle waved at the five others who were also working on Sunday. Frank Helms was there along with Asa Martin and the Peterman brothers. The Russian, as he was known, Nicholai Petrovich rounded out the small group. They were all dressed in similar clothing: heavy-duty bib overalls, thick waterproof work socks inside metal-toed boots, flannel shirts, gloves tucked inside belts. They all carried the same equipment: lunch box, canteen or thermos, waterproof flashlight, extra batteries and hard hats equipped with a head lantern. All five men waved or commented as he approached.

Normally, the mine was closed on Sundays, but Mr. Lukens was paying double time and a half for six men who were willing to work on the Sabbath. The state mine inspectors were scheduled to pay the mine one of their quarterly visits in just two weeks. During their last visit, they had pointed out a number of minor infractions, that, if not corrected could be eventually categorized as serious mine violations. Lyle and the other five were the first to volunteer for Sunday work. Lyle had nothing else to do on Sundays, except sit around and watch football on television, so why not pick up some extra cash.

Following a number of greetings and comments between the six miners, they waited as Nicholai knelt and raised his face toward Heaven as he prayed a short prayer for their safety. The Russian had a stronger walk with the Lord than any other man Lyle had ever met. It had become a daily routine for the men to wait for Nicholai to finish his prayer before their descent down into the mine. Finished, Nicholai stood, with that broad smile that he always carried as he spoke with broken English, "Now, ve kin go down."

The six miners filed into the carriage that would lower them down to the main shaft below. As Asa pushed the blue button that activated the carriage, he asked the group if they had seen the high school football game on Saturday. There were numerous remarks not only about the game, but about how things had changed since they were in school and how kids had it easier than they did growing up. Lyle didn't have anything to say during the descent as he watched the square of light above them growing ever smaller. He double-checked his head lantern just as the carriage reached the base of the main shaft.

Stepping out of the carriage, the men walked past the huge ventilator system that kept the mine air circulating. Despite the modern ventilation set-up, the mine still held the constant odor of the creosote and zinc-coated yellow pine timbers that supported the mine shafts. No more than ten yards into the shaft, the group came to the head of the mine car track where the small, heavy-duty battery-operated engine sat, six mine cars strung out behind. The men referred to the mine train as the 6-D train, each car labeled in faded white paint with one of the six D's of mining: Dusty, Deep, Dark, Damp, Dirty and Dangerous.

Chester Flynn, who had worked in the mine for years, started up the engine as the men climbed into the cars, Lyle sitting in the last one as he was the first scheduled to get out. As the small train rounded the first curve in the main shaft, Lyle thought about how vast the track system in the mine was, an intricate maze of tracks that weaved its way through gangways, air shafts and cross headways. The scenery on either side of the main shaft was nothing more than the cold, dripping wet mine walls supported by evenly spaced timbers. Every twelve feet, there was a greasy, coal-stained, wire-protected light and at the head of every cross headway a two-by-two sign emphasizing mine rules and regulations.

The train came to a sudden halt at the Number 9 Headway, where Lyle stepped out, then watched the red light on the end car finally disappear from sight. Placing his lunch box and lantern into a hand-operated cart, he stepped up onto the wooden cart and pulled down on the worn wooden handle that would begin the process of taking him a quarter of a mile up the track into Number 9.

He was alone now. The others had gone deeper into the mine. He enjoyed the time alone. It always gave him time to think about whatever came to his mind. When he had first become a miner years in the past, he had experienced a type of claustrophobia. He had been fortunate to work with Nicholai that first week. The Russian, a grizzled mine veteran, had told him to relax and that he'd get used to being deep in the earth. It didn't take long for Lyle to become accustomed to the ways of mining. It always did and still amazed him how humans could acclimate themselves to almost any condition. When he had been in high school if anyone would have told him that he would spend the next twenty-some years extracting coal from deep down in the mine, he would have said that they were crazy, but yet here he was, going on his twenty-eighth year as a miner.

Today for some reason, his thoughts, at least for the moment, were centered on Nora. He had known her ever since high school. He had been on the football team, and she had been a cheerleader. They started to date, but never became what people referred to as an "item." It was a strange relationship. He never dated anyone else, nor did she. They went to the prom together and eventually graduated the same year.

That summer practically everyone in their graduating class up and left town, many going away to college. Those who chose to step out into the working world were not about to hang around Granite Hill. As far as the young male graduates were concerned, there wasn't that much incentive in claiming a career as a coal miner. It paid well, but the future of most miners always hinged on their survival in the mine. There was the ever-present danger of mine cave-ins or the inevitable probability of acquiring black lung, which usually wound up being fatal and cutting many a miner's life short. Times were changing. Females were no longer interested in waiting for their husband to drag himself home, covered in coal dust following a grueling day down in the mine or raising a family in a rundown coal town.

Nora had been one of those that chose college, while Lyle chose to work in the mine. It was in his blood. His father and his grandfather had worked in the mine. They had both made a good living, but had paid the price. Grandpa died in a horrible mine cave-in back in the forties, and his father passed away at the dreaded hands of black lung. He just couldn't see any reason to go to college. He had no plans of being a doctor or a lawyer—so why not make some money?

Four years later, Nora returned to Granite Hill. She had written to him on a monthly basis while she was away at school. Lyle always had the feeling that she wanted to marry him, despite the fact that he was a miner. Upon returning to town, she got a job at the bank and had worked there ever since. They continued to see each other, going out once a week for dinner or to a movie. It was just three years ago that she had said that if he ever wanted to get married, all he had to do was say the word. He smiled to himself. If he ever did decide to tie the knot, Nora would surely be his choice. He could move out of the old dusty apartment that he had lived in for sixteen years—maybe purchase a house. He had just turned forty-six. He wasn't too old to get married—but starting a family? Maybe he was too old for that?

He had been in Number 9 more times than he could remember. Taking his hand from the wooden handle, the cart came to a stop. He looked at the particularly smooth section of the wall. He knew exactly where he was—about halfway to where he was to start working his way back. Sitting on the edge of the cart, he took a long swallow from his canteen. It was so quiet down in the mine—water dripping from the roof and walls, an occasional creak or movement in the earth surrounding him.

He thought about what his grandfather had said about sounds in the mine. You just sort of got used to the familiar sounds—you really didn't pay them much attention just like when you were on the surface. Up on the top, you could hear the birds and the wind, but seldom gave them a thought. If Gramps had lived, he'd be seventy-one years old, probably retired and spending his days working out in the garden.

Gramps had lived a tough life, working in the mine at eight years of age as a breaker boy, straddled across a colliery chute sorting coal from rock for ten to twelve hours a day, his fingers raw, cracked and bleeding from the sulphur. Years later as a teenager, he was given a job tending the mules, which held much more responsibility and a higher rate of pay. A few years later, he then actually became a bona fide coal miner, but then during a coal strike got involved in bootleg mining, which was illegal. The mine owners back in those days were ruthless toward the miners, especially when there was a strike. Men were shipped in from Pittsburgh to enforce the mine rules and to back the owners. Two of Gramps' close friends had been killed during the strike. Somehow he had managed to avoid prosecution for bootlegging and everything went back to normal when the strike ended.

It was 1943 when fifteen miners had been trapped in the western section of the mine. Gramps had been one of those men. The mine accident had been no one's fault—in the end it was simply unexplainable. It took crews of men and equipment almost five days to dig toward the area of the cave-in. They were too late—all fifteen men had lost their lives. The coroner said that from what he could tell, it hadn't been a matter of lack of food or water, but one of air. He said that it must have been a horrible death for each man. Not everyone had died at the same time. One by one over a period of an hour or so, the miners had watched each other eventually run out of air, taking their last breath, realizing that within a short period of time, their final breath would come.

Lyle drew in a long, deep breath and as he exhaled, he thought about how his grandfather must have felt at the moment of his death. Time to get moving. Climbing back up into the cart, he moved farther back down the track into Number 9.

Minutes later, he stopped the cart at the designated starting point. He laid his canteen and lunch box off to the side as he adjusted his head lantern. Before he got started, he decided on a quick bite. He had skipped breakfast and was starting to get hungry. Opening his lunch box, he removed one of the two hardboiled eggs he had packed earlier that morning. Cracking the egg on the shaft wall, he threw the peelings into the cellophane wrapper, then salted the egg, which he downed in four quick bites. He washed down the egg with a swig of water. Looking at his watch, he noticed the time at 7:15. He'd eat the remaining egg and his two sandwiches around 11:30 or so. Time to get to work.

His task for the day was simple and repetitious. The previous day he and another miner had gone though Number 9 marking all of the spikes in the track that had to be replaced with a fluorescent orange spray paint. He was to remove the marked spikes and replace them with new ones that were piled in a metal compartment at the rear of the cart. Taking the sledge and crowbar from the side of the cart, he twisted and stretched before he started the process.

He placed the notched end of the crowbar around the head of the first spike and, using the rail as a brace, pushed down on the tool. The spike at first didn't budge, but then on the second try, following a rusty scraping sound, the spike popped from the wooden tie. He pitched the old spike into a metal box near the front of the cart, the spike making a heavy metal thudding sound that reverberated up and down the shaft. Next, he removed a new spike and positioned it in the old hole. Then, using the eight-pound sledge, drove it home with four muscular swings.

It didn't take long for his mind to start wandering off on som subject that had absolutely nothing to do with what he was doing a the moment. For some reason, his mind drifted back to the previou summer and how hot it had been. He remembered how pleasant had been to work in the damp, cool mine. He recalled how in the evenings when he had arrived home, he had flipped on the air conditioner and the TV. It was just too hot to go anywhere. His air conditioner was in great working order and, within a few minutes, a cool breeze was blowing through his apartment. Now, the television was completely another matter.

The console model was quite old, and when he turned it on, it took a few seconds of silence as if the set were broken. But then following a crackling sound, the screen started to finally display a pinkish hue of a picture, which over the next minute finally cleared up. He always turned on the TV as soon as he entered the apartment even if he had no plans of watching the set. The noise from the set was almost like someone else being in the place. He remembered one particular hot summer night when he had arrived home, flipped on the air conditioner and TV, then went about preparing his supper and taking a refreshing shower as his leftover chicken and waffles were heating up in the microwave.

Flopping down on the couch with his dinner, he noticed that he was watching a segment of the summer Olympics. A group of four young athletic girls were just taking their place on an elevated stage where they were about to receive gold medals in some sort of swimming event. The girls stood next to each other as a gold medal was hung around their necks followed by the playing of the national anthem. The camera closed in on the faces of the young women, their eyes filled with tears of joy at what they had accomplished.

It was at that moment that Lyle realized that the look on their faces had to do with more than the gold hanging from their necks. It was more like a golden moment, a moment when these girls cashed in on years of rigorous and grueling training to get to the point where they were the best at the event they had won. They were on the top of the heap, numero uno, the best in the world!

Suddenly, the camera switched to another arena where another team, a male team of Gymnasts, were going through the final moments of their event. The commentator said that the male gymnastic team had no chance for gold. As a matter of fact, they were going to return home empty handed—no medals whatsoever. They had been a team that was expected to win the gold, but they had failed to win anything. As Lyle watched the gymnasts go through their final routines, he couldn't spot a single flaw in their performance. Despite the fact that they had no chance to win the gold or any medal at all, they were still giving their very best.

After they finished, the camera moved in for a close up of the team sitting on the bench. There were tears. Not tears of joy like the female swim team had displayed, but tears of frustration and failure. Lyle could just imagine the news the following day in the sports page as the swimmers would be praised as the best in the world while the gymnasts would be looked upon as failures. It didn't seem right. Even though the boys hadn't won any medals, they were still the best that their country had to offer. Just like the girls, they had practiced long and hard to get to the Olympics. Lyle couldn't even comprehend getting to participate in the Olympics let alone win a medal. The gymnasts were not losers. The experience at the Olympics was a moment of gold for them, too. They just didn't realize it at the time. Years down the road, they, too, would be able to tell their children and grandchildren how they had gone to the Olympics.

That evening he had gone to bed, the reactions of the female swimmers and the male gymnasts in regard to winning and losing still fresh on his mind. Lying in bed, he recalled the tears of joy of the women from winning the gold medal and the tears and frowns of the men, who had won nothing. Reviewing his own life, he tried to think of moments in his past life where he had been the best at something—top of the heap—number one. An hour later, he realized that he had never been the best at anything he had ever done. The longer he laid there thinking about how he had never been at the top, the more he began to become depressed.

His mind began to automatically review all of the moments in the past where he had lost. Within fifteen minutes, it was like the roof of his apartment had been ripped open and a cargo plane of failures dumped into his bedroom filling it to the walls and then some. It seemed that every event in his life had been a losing proposition. He had played little league as a youngster, but had never hit a homerun. He had played football in junior high, yet, had never scored a touchdown, intercepted a pass or made a dramatic tackle. He had managed to slide through high school with barely passing grades, received no honors during graduation and stayed behind in Granite Hill to work in the Mine, while it seemed that everyone else had left and moved on to more illustrious careers. He was forty-six years old, living in a rundown second-floor apartment, had never married, had no family—not even a pet. When it came to golden moments in life, they seemed to have passed him by. Just like the commentator on TV had said, "No chance for gold!"

His depression was so strong that he was unable to sleep that night. The next day he worked through the morning down in the mine with neary a word being said to anyone. Nicholai had noticed his unusual behavior as Lyle was always a man who had plenty to say. Nicholai, not one to pry, finally during lunch had asked Lyle if anything was wrong. Lyle opened up and told the Russian about the two different Olympic teams and how they had reacted and about how he had discovered that he had never been the best in the world at anything—that he had never experienced the golden moment.

Sitting in the cold mine shaft that day, the Russian explained that he was not alone and that many people in the world, including himself, had never been the best at anything. This was not something that an individual should be all that concerned over. These were just things of the world, which in the end wouldn't count for anything when it came to the final judgement. The Lord accepts each and everyone of us just the way we are and when we except the fact that his son died on the cross for us so that we can be forgiven and gain Heaven, we are saved. The truth is that we don't have to be number one or the best at something for the Lord to accept us. He accepts us just the way we are, so therefore, we are number one in his book—the book of life. There is gold in life and the true golden moment is when we accept Jesus Christ as our personal Savior... The loud cracking sound from around the corner of Number 9 was instantly followed by a rumbling that traveled down the shaft walls right past him. Lyle had grown accustomed to sounds in the mines and, for the most part, didn't even give them a thought. But this sound was different, out of the ordinary—a death knell. As he turned looking toward the dimly lit headway up ahead, the smell of carbon monoxide and methane filled his nostrils with a nauseating odor as a dark, rushing cloud of dirt and coal dust sped toward him...

His eyes opened slowly, and the first noticeable thing they centered on was a bright ray of light that illuminated a solid wall of loose rock and dirt four feet directly in front of where he was lying. Following the beam of light back to its source, he quickly discovered that it was coming from his head lantern, which was no longer centered on his head but lying at an angle against a fallen timber just to his left. The headlamp gave off enough light that he could see he was buried up to his chest in loose dirt and gravel, his right arm completely covered, except for his right hand that stuck up out of the debris like some kind of monster movie where the dead was trying to rise from the grave. His left arm was completely buried and felt as if it were at a right angle to the rest of his body. It was strange. His entire body seemed smothered, except for the left hand that sensed a cool breeze floating across it.

He moved his head from side to side taking in the small cavity that he had been trapped in, the roof of the tiny area just two feet above him. He tried to move, and with a little effort, released his right arm as he noticed the time on his wristwatch: 10:05. Just a few minutes before the cave-in, he remembered that he had looked at his watch. He recalled that moment as 9:47. That meant that he had been out for approximately fifteen minutes. He tried to move his left arm but the weight of the rubble covering his body was too much. Then he noticed the ragged edge of a timber sticking up from the dirt and he realized that the huge wooden support was lying across his legs. The only part of his body on the left side that he could move was his left hand.

He felt a warm wetness trickle into the side of his left eye. Instinctively, he reached up wiping his eye clear. Looking at his hand, he saw the fresh blood that was coming from somewhere on his head. Running his hand over his matted hair, he couldn't tell if his head was covered in sweat or blood. Bringing his hand back down, he noticed a smear of blood across his palm. There was nothing he could do to stop the bleeding. He had nothing to apply to whatever type of wound he had received.

He thought back to just moments before the walls and roof had collapsed in on him. He had been thinking about what Nicholai had said about the moment of gold and about accepting Jesus as your personal Savior. In his mind, there wasn't any time to think about God now—it was time to figure out what he was going to do—how he was going to survive. Relax, he thought, just relax.

Looking again at his watch, the time was now at 10:48. He must have drifted off for nearly forty-five minutes. He surveyed the small six-by-eight dirt-and-rock enclosed area where he lay trapped. He had been trained many times for just this type of a situation. For the past twenty-eight years, every six months he and the other miners had to attend a required four-hour session on mine survival when involved in a cave-in. Currently, he had been present at fifty-six of these informative meetings. When he had been a novice miner, he had paid close attention to everything that was said or pointed out. As time went by, he eventually became bored with the repetitious methods of survival, the last meeting he had been to was just two months past.

It was all coming back to him. Now, it wasn't just what had to be done if you were in a cave-in. He was faced with a life-and-death dilemma. He was in a cave-in! The first thing he had been trained in was to remain calm—don't panic. An attitude of panic would always bring on a sense of hopelessness, causing an individual to become irrational. Take in your surroundings—evaluate the situation—examine yourself for any noticeable injuries. His surroundings were nothing more than a small closed-in cavity that could get smaller at any moment, or, on the other hand, could remain stable for some time. The situation, as he saw it, looked rather glum. His headlamp was out of reach, and since he couldn't move from the weight of the timber across his legs not to mention a couple of tons of rock and dirt, he wouldn't be able to conserve the light that he now had. Eventually, the lamp would burn out and he would be thrown into total darkness. The only injury that was obvious to him was from the wound around his head area. He noticed that the blood had stopped running down the side of his face. He assumed that the wound or cut must have been minor. He had food in his lunch box, but looking around, it was nowhere in sight. Probably buried. Then he noticed his canteen lying next to the wall of dirt in front of him, just out of reach. There was no way that he could get to the water. Suddenly, he remembered what the coroner had said about his grandfather and the men he had died with years in the past. They had food and water, but the eventual lack of air had been their demise. He drew in a long breath of air. For the moment, he had what seemed like plenty of oxygen.

He considered yelling out for help, but there couldn't possibly be anyone near him. The other five miners had been taken to headways much farther back in the mine. The section that they were in might not even have been affected by the cave-in. Yelling out, at least for now would be a waste of time. He had been on the second floor of the mine office many times and he had been shown an example of how the huge electronic board that displayed the entire underground layout of the mine could pinpoint any area where there was a disturbance in normal mine operations. He was confident that immediately following the cave-in that the board lit up Number 9 as the trouble spot and that the shrill mine warning whistle would be sounded reverberating through the streets of Granite Hill signalling all the miners in town that there was an emergency. It was a code amongst the miners. If that whistle sounded, no matter what you were doing, it was your obligation to report to the mine to assist in any way. He himself had answered that whistle three times over the years. Fortunately, not a man had been lost in any one of those past occasions. He hadn't really thought much about the fact that he could die right there where he was lying, but the possibility was beginning to press in on his brain. Was he to become a fatality despite all the men who would show up to help?

His eyes started to close. He was so tired for some reason. He had to stay awake—decide what he was going to do. What could he do besides just lie there and hope for the best? The mine safety trainers always said that if you were involved in a mining accident that you should make every effort to escape—if possible. Escape was out of the question in this circumstance. The only parts of his body that he could move were his right arm and hand, his left hand and his head. They had said that if escape was not possible, then just remain calm and wait. A rescue team would soon arrive. It was getting increasingly difficult to keep his eyes open. Maybe he'd just shut his eyes for a few minutes' rest.

He was first awakened by the deep rumbling sound coming from somewhere above him. Nearly a quarter of a mile of solid rock, coal, and dirt separated him from the freedom on top. The disturbing sound finally came to a sudden stop, then slowly followed by the collapse of the wall on his right as pebbles and dirt broke loose, the small avalanche covering his right hand and arm and sliding into the side of his face. It was happening so subtlely, so quickly—he was going to suffocate. But then it stopped, the debris stopping just short of his chin. He spit dirt from inside his mouth as he coughed twice then took a deep breath of air. He was okay—for now. He realized that the relief that he was feeling might only be temporary. Another rock movement like that and he'd be buried alive.

His eyes were growing tired again, but now he was becoming too afraid to sleep. This was categorized as stupid in his mind as being buried alive would probably be better if he were asleep than wide awake at that moment. He thought about how thirsty he had become over the last few hours. He looked at his canteen that was lying just to the left of the beam of light coming from his headlamp. It was mentally difficult to lie there unable to reach out to the canteen that was filled with water. He almost wished that the canteen had been buried, so that he could not see the container just feet away from him. Looking at his watch, he noticed the time was 9:07. He had been drifting in and out of sleep for the past eleven hours. It would be night up on top. He could just picture the giant floodlights illuminating the entrance to the mine, men running here and there carrying all sorts of equipment, a taped-off area probably guarded by the local police keeping town folk back from interferring with the rescue operation. He wondered if they had notified Nora or if she had heard about the cave-in.

Suddenly, the headlamp dimmed to a faint light, brightened, then went out casting the chamber into a level of darkness that he had never known. The light had been his last hope of survival. It had been like a friend—that now was gone. He was truly alone now. There was nothing he could do but lie there in the dark and wait for the end. He felt so cut off from the rest of the world.

He thought again about all of the men who were probably digging their way through the blockade of dirt and rock separating him from safety. He wondered if Nicholai would be with them. Nicholai would be one of the first to volunteer. Just like always, he had probably knelt in front of all those present and said a prayer before going down into the mine. Nicholai had such great faith—more than he could ever imagine having. He would never be able to display the kind of faith that Nicholai had. Maybe it was time—time to start praying. What else could he do? No one would see his feeble attempt at prayer deep in the mine. He didn't even know how to start. He felt foolish. He had to try. What if what Nicholai said was true about accepting Jesus Christ as your Savior? He was close to the end. Maybe he should try to contact God in some way. The only thing that was left was prayer. There was nothing else that he could do.

He felt inadequate as he started, "God—it's Lyle Campbell. I guess you know who I am…I just haven't had a need to call on you before today. I've got myself in quite a fix down here. Doesn't look like there's much of a way out of this. I wouldn't blame you if you just blew this prayer off as I haven't been what you would call a Christian man. My friend, Nicholai, who prays to you every day told me at some point in the past that if I had faith in You that in the end everything would work out. Well…it looks like the end might just be around the corner. What I'm trying to say, is that if you decide to allow me to survive this mess, even as horrible as things seem for me, I can't guarantee that I'll change…but I'll try. It's all up to you. Well, I guess that's it then."

The prayer was finished. It had been so short. He pictured the Lord looking down on his dire situation and thinking how he had never made an effort to speak with him beforehand and now that he was facing a terrible death, Lyle could only spare him…what, maybe a minute or even less.

There was a sliding sound that came from his right. He couldn't move his head for fear of the gravel already piled up on the side of his face getting into his mouth, eyes and nose. He could feel the loose dirt slowly building up and moving around to the front of his face, but just as quickly as it had started it stopped. His thoughts of the moving gravel and dirt were replaced by a cool feeling going across his left hand. It was almost as if cool water was being poured over his hand, then wiped away. He concentrated on the strange feeling. It seemed real enough. Then he thought that maybe someone was on the other side of the wall. He called out, "Is there anyone out there…please…help me…help!" No answer came from beyond the dirt. He repeated the shout two more times, but there was no response. No one was there…the feeling was just his imagination, probably from his left hand becoming numb.

He closed his eyes trying to make the feeling in his hand go away, but it remained. Then he had a sudden horrifying thought. Rats—mine rats! They could be out there nibbling away at his flesh. Maybe that's what the feeling was? He remembered what his grandfather had told him as a young boy about the rats that were in the mine. They were huge and there had been many an occasion when these bold creatures attacked the mules and sometimes even the miners when they took short naps during their lunchtime. He tried to jerk his hand back but the weight on his arm was too much. He screamed toward the wall. "Git…get away from me, Get out of here!" Whatever was out there, the feeling would not go away. "God, no…don't let me go out like this."

Taking a deep breath, he realized that he was panicking—exactly what the mine safety trainers had told him not to do. Remain calm—that's what they had said. Then he remembered something else his grandfather had said about the mine rats. Over the years the rats had been completely eliminated from the mines. Maybe so, but what if the cave-in had unearthed a group of mutant rats that had been released into the main part of the mine. Relax, he thought, relax. There are no rats out there. It's just your imagination playing tricks on you.

He had no idea how much time had passed since his panic attack. He could no longer see his watch. He drifted in and out of moments of sleep and each time he was awake, he was aware of the cool feeling on his left hand. It was a constant sensation, cool, firm and solid. He knew that it had to be some sort of numbness. The circulation had probably been cut off from his left arm and hand causing the strange feeling.

He was jerked back to total awareness as something heavy thudded down on top of the dirt covering his body. He had nothing left. Just get it over with, he thought. Why does it have to take so long? At that moment if the wall just fell on him and flattened him to pieces it would be a blessing.

The feeling in his left hand got stronger—probably from just tensing up, he thought. Down near where his feet were located, he heard rocks and dirt moving, then he thought he heard a voice. His mind was really toying with his emotions. He ignored the sounds, but the movement of the rocks became louder. Then suddenly there was a light shining directly at him, eventually finding his eyes. Then he heard the familiar voice of Nicholai, "Lyle…the Lord sent us ta get ya. Ve will hav' ya out of here in a jif." He heard men from behind the Russian cheer.

It took about a half hour to dig him out. He was placed on a stretcher as Nicholai lowered a canteen of cool water to his lips. He could have drunk the entire container, but Nicholai pulled the canteen away saying that he needed to take it easy at first. He could have all the water he wanted, but just not all at once. There was a brief moment when Nicholai left him alone as he walked a few paces away to ask someone a question. Lyle looking to his right noticed something odd—something that was out of place. A white cloth stained with a dirty handprint. Just before they came to carry him off to the mine train, he reached out and grabbed the cloth.

Minutes later he was put in the carriage that would take him up out of the mine. The Russian's face appeared above the stretcher as he smiled and then said, "Lyle…In His hands are the deep places of the earth."

He was no sooner out of the carriage when he felt the driving rain on his face as the dirt and dust were washed away. Looking up into the dark sky he could see that it was a miserable night as far as the weather was concerned. The dark, gray, rain swept sky was the most beautiful sight he had ever seen. He heard someone shout, "Bring that ambulance over here. We gotta get him to the hospital." As he was lifted toward the back of the ambulance, suddenly Nora's face appeared just above him. Her eyes were filled with tears. "Lyle..my dear Lyle…I thought that I had lost you tonight. Thank God you're alive and all right."

Lyle ordered the paramedics, "Wait…wait just a minute." He then reached up caressing Nora's face. "Nora...I'm so sorry that I've been such a…such an uncaring man all these years. As soon as I get out of the hospital, I'm getting you that ring if you'll still have me." The smile on her face gave him the answer. As he was placed in the back of the ambulance, he overheard a television announcer as he spoke into his microphone, "Lyle Campbell has been saved!" The back door was closed and the vehicle pulled away as Lyle held the dirt-stained cloth in his hand. The announcer had been right. He had been saved,but not the way that he meant. Down in the bowels of the earth, he truly had experienced the Golden Moment. God had been right there with him, holding his hand.

BENCHMARK SERIES

MICROSOFT® 365

WORD

LEVELS 1 & 2

AUDREY ROGGENKAMP
Pierce College Puyallup
Puyallup, Washington

IAN RUTKOSKY
Pierce College Puyallup
Puyallup, Washington

A DIVISION OF KENDALL HUNT

Dubuque

Care has been taken to verify the accuracy of information presented in this book. However, the authors, editors, and publisher cannot accept responsibility for web, email, newsgroup, or chat room subject matter or content or for consequences from the application of the information in this book, and make no warranty, expressed or implied, with respect to its content.

Paradigm Education Solutions is independent from Microsoft Corporation and not affiliated with Microsoft in any manner. While this publication may be used in assisting individuals to prepare for a Microsoft Office Specialist certification exam, Microsoft, its designated program administrator, and Paradigm Education Solutions do not warrant that use of this publication will ensure passing a Microsoft Office Specialist certification exam.

Cover Photo Credit: © antishock/Shutterstock.com
Interior Photo Credits: Follow the Indexes.

ISBN 978-1-7924-6949-7

4050 Westmark Drive
Dubuque, IA 52004-1840
Email: ordernow@kendallhunt.com
Website: ParadigmEducation.com

Published in the United States of America

BRIEF CONTENTS

CONTENTS

Word Level 2

PREFACE

Benchmark Series, *Microsoft 365: Word,* Levels 1 & 2, prepares students to work with this popular word processing software for business or personal use. Incorporating an accelerated, step-by-step, project-based approach, this courseware helps students build competency in effectively preparing and formatting as well as enhancing and customizing documents using Word.

A Solution Designed for Student Success

The **Benchmark Series** is powered by Paradigm's Cirrus™ 2.0 platform, which provides a complete solution for learning how to use Microsoft 365 applications. This courseware develops students' skills and knowledge through a learning pathway that includes a series of training, practice, and assessment activities.

With the **Benchmark Series** and Cirrus, students can

- access course content anytime, anywhere through a live internet connection
- use a PC, Mac, or Chromebook
- complete all course activities in a single, seamless environment
- work live in the application without having to install anything
- view Watch and Learn Lessons that demonstrate exactly how to perform chapter activities
- receive immediate, personalized feedback to identify and self-correct errors
- complete Guide and Practice Tutorials to gain training and measured practice that is skill-specific, guided, and interactive
- and more!

ACHIEVING PROFICIENCY

Benchmark Series, *Microsoft 365: Word,* Levels 1 & 2, is designed for students who want to create professional-looking documents for school, work, and personal communication needs. No previous experience with word processing software is required. After successfully completing this course, students will be able to demonstrate the following performance objectives.

- Plan, research, write, revise, and publish documents to meet specific needs.
- Given a workplace scenario requiring a written solution, assess the communication purpose and then prepare the materials that achieve the goal efficiently and effectively.
- Create and edit letters, flyers, announcements, and reports that include headers, footers, references, tables of contents and figures, and hyperlinks.
- Use advanced formatting and editing features as well as building blocks and fields to create and edit a range of document types.
- Add and customize images, text boxes, charts, icons, 3D models, and other elements and objects to enhance written communication.
- Merge documents using a data source file and a main document.
- Manage shared documents that include comments and track changes, check and edit documents for accessibility, and apply document protection features.

Well-designed pedagogy is important, but students learn technology skills through practice and problem solving. Technology provides opportunities for interactive learning as well as excellent ways to quickly and accurately assess student performance. To this end, this course is supported with Cirrus™ 2.0, Paradigm's cloud-based training and assessment platform. Details about Cirrus as well as its integrated student courseware and instructor resources can be found on pages xv–xvii.

PROVEN INSTRUCTIONAL DESIGN

The **Benchmark Series** has long served as a standard of excellence in software instruction. Elements of the series function individually and collectively to create an inviting, comprehensive learning environment that leads to full proficiency in computer applications. The following visual tour highlights the structure and features that comprise the highly popular **Benchmark** model.

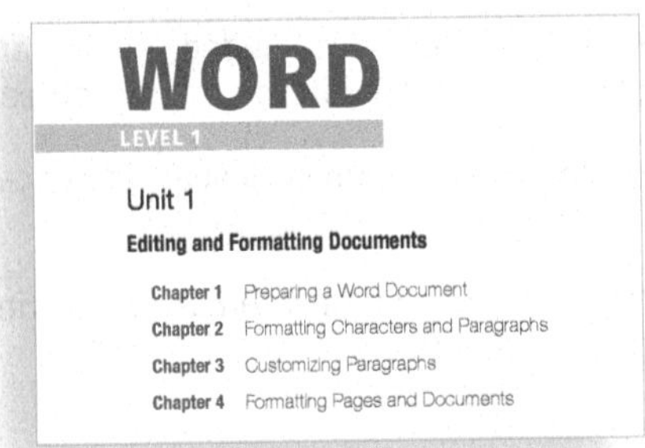

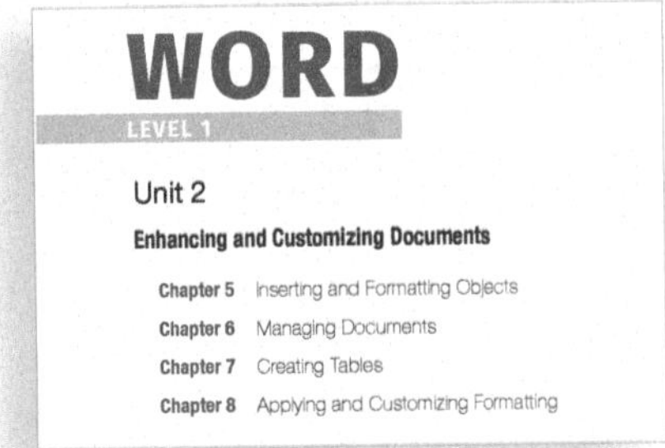

Unit openers display the unit's four chapter titles.

Chapter Openers Present Performance Objectives

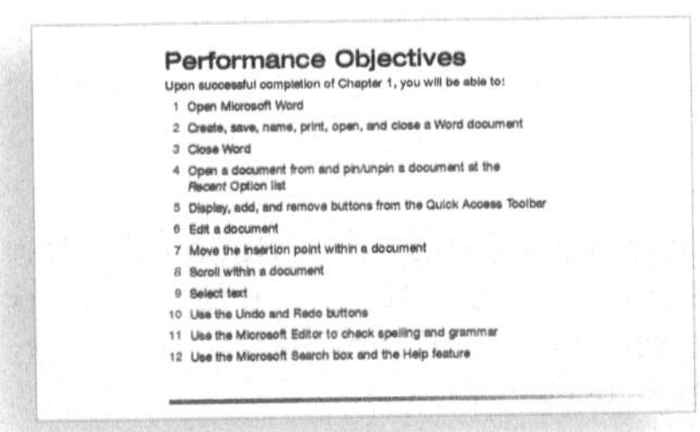

Chapter openers present the performance objectives and an overview of the skills taught.

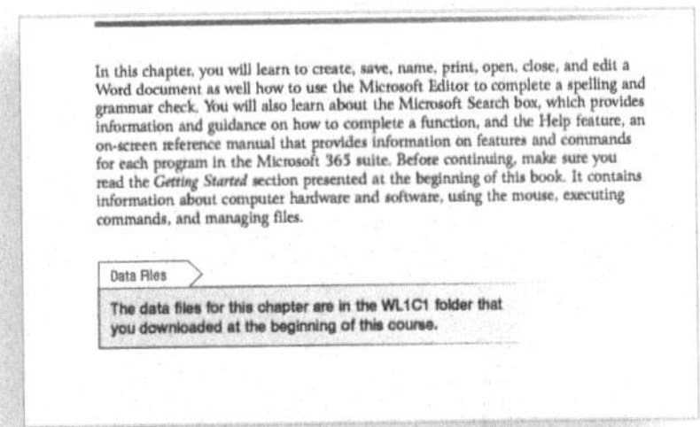

Data files are provided for each chapter. A prominent note reminds students to copy the appropriate chapter data folder and make it active.

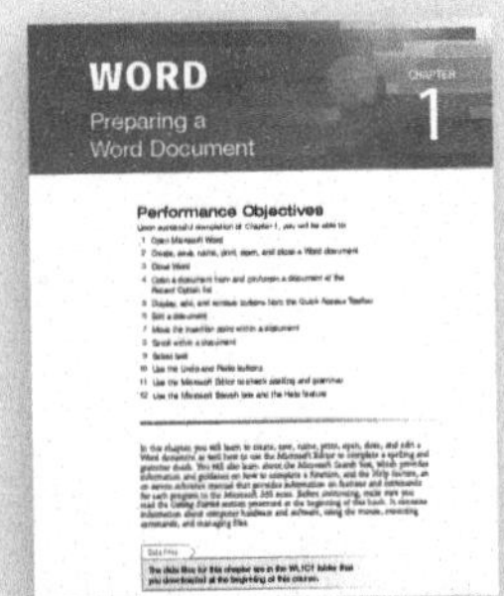

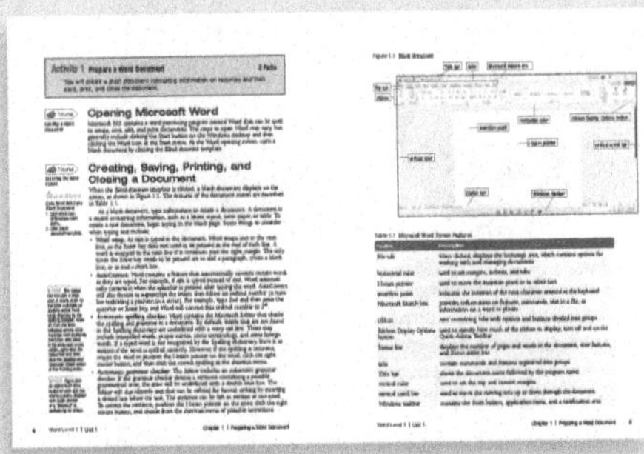

Activities Build Skill Mastery within Realistic Context

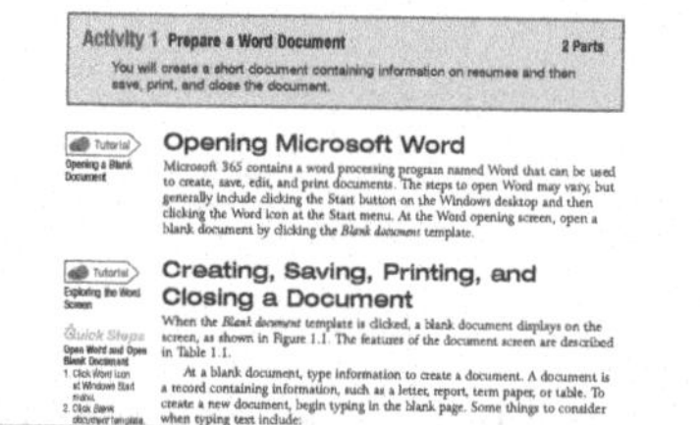

Activity 1 Prepare a Word Document 2 Parts

You will create a short document containing information on resumes and then save, print, and close the document.

Tutorial
Opening a Blank Document

Opening Microsoft Word

Microsoft 365 contains a word processing program named Word that can be used to create, save, edit, and print documents. The steps to open Word may vary, but generally include clicking the Start button on the Windows desktop and then clicking the Word icon at the Start menu. At the Word opening screen, open a blank document by clicking the *Blank document* template.

Tutorial
Exploring the Word Screen

Quick Steps
Open Word and Open Blank Document
1. Click Word icon at Windows Start menu.
2. Click *Blank document* template.

Creating, Saving, Printing, and Closing a Document

When the *Blank document* template is clicked, a blank document displays on the screen, as shown in Figure 1.1. The features of the document screen are described in Table 1.1.

At a blank document, type information to create a document. A document is a record containing information, such as a letter, report, term paper, or table. To create a new document, begin typing in the blank page. Some things to consider when typing text include:

Multipart activities provide a framework for instruction and practice on software features. An activity overview identifies tasks to accomplish and key features to use in completing the work.

Typically, a file remains open throughout all parts of the activity. Students save their work incrementally. At the end of the activity, students save, preview, and then close the file.

Between activity parts, the text presents instruction on the features and skills necessary to accomplish the next portion of the activity.

Tutorial
Moving the Insertion Point Using the Go To Feature

Find

Hint Press Ctrl + G to display the Find and Replace dialog box with the Go To tab selected.

Moving the Insertion Point to a Specific Line or

Word includes a Go To feature that moves the insertion point to a sp location in a document, such as a line or page. To use the feature, cli button arrow in the Editing group on the Home tab and then click G drop-down list. At the Find and Replace dialog box with the Go To ta move the insertion point to a specific page by typing the page numbe *page number* text box and then pressing the Enter key. Move to a spec clicking the *Line* option in the *Go to what* list box, typing the line nun *Enter line number* text box, and then pressing the Enter key. Click the to close the dialog box.

Tutorial
Moving the Insertion Point and Inserting and Deleting Text

Moving the Insertion Point with the Keyboard

To move the insertion point with the keyboard, use the arrow keys to the regular keyboard or use the arrow keys on the numeric keypad. W the arrow keys on the numeric keypad, make sure Num Lock is off. U keys together with other keys to move the insertion point to various the document, as shown in Table 1.2.

Tutorials provide interactive, guided training and measured practice and are accessed in the online course.

Button images provide a quick, visual reference to the buttons introduced in the chapter.

Hints offer useful tips on how to use application features efficiently and effectively.

Quick Steps
Create Columns at Columns Dialog Box
1. Click Layout tab.
2. Click Columns button.
3. Click *More Columns.*
4. Specify column options.
5. Click OK.

Creating Columns with the Columns Dialog Bo

Use the Columns dialog box to create newspaper columns that are unequal in width. To display the Columns dialog box, shown in Fi the Columns button in the Page Setup group on the Layout tab a *More Columns* at the drop-down list.

With options at the Columns dialog box, specify the style and columns, enter specific column measurements, create unequal colu a line between columns. By default, column formatting is applied document. This can be changed to *This point forward* at the *Apply* at the bottom of the Columns dialog box. With the *This point forw* a section break is inserted and the column formatting is applied t the location of the insertion point to the end of the document or column format is encountered. The *Preview* section of the dialog b example of how the columns will appear in the document.

Figure 4.5 Columns Dialog Box

Quick Steps in the margins allow fast reference and review.

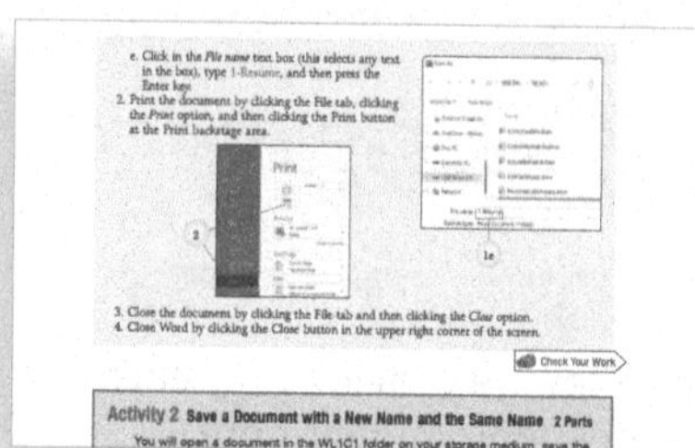

e. Click in the *File name* text box (this selects any text in the box), type 1-Resume, and then press the Enter key.

2. Print the document by clicking the File tab, clicking the *Print* option, and then clicking the Print button at the Print backstage area.

3. Close the document by clicking the File tab and then clicking the *Close* option.
4. Close Word by clicking the Close button in the upper right corner of the screen.

Check Your Work

Activity 2 Save a Document with a New Name and the Same Name 2 Parts

You will open a document in the WL1C1 folder on your storage medium, save the

Step-by-step instructions guide students to the desired outcome for each activity part. Screen captures illustrate what the screen should look like at key points. Magenta identifies text to type.

Check Your Work images and demonstration videos are available in the online course.

Chapter Review and Assessment Reinforces Learning

Chapter Summary

- By default, a Word document contains 1-inch top, bottom, left, and right margins. Change margins with preset margin settings at the Margins button drop-down list or with options at the Page Setup dialog box with the Margins tab selected.
- The default page layout is portrait orientation. It can be changed to landscape orientation with the Orientation button in the Page Setup group on the Layout tab.
- The default paper size is 8.5 inches wide by 11 inches tall. It can be changed with options at the Size button drop-down list or options at the Page Setup dialog box with the Paper tab selected.
- A page break that Word inserts automatically is a *soft page break*. A page break inserted manually is a *hard page break*. Insert a hard page break using the Page Break button in the Pages group on the Insert tab or by pressing Ctrl + Enter.
- Insert a predesigned and formatted cover page by clicking the Cover Page button in the Pages group on the Insert tab and then clicking an option at the drop-down list.
- Insert predesigned and formatted page numbers by clicking the Page Number button in the Header & Footer group on the Insert tab, specifying the location of the page number, and then clicking a page numbering option.
- Insert predesigned headers and footers in a document with the Header button and the Footer button in the Header & Footer group on the Insert tab.
- A watermark is a lightened image that displays behind the text in a document. Use the Watermark button in the Page Background group on the Design tab to

A **Chapter Summary** reviews the purpose and execution of key software features.

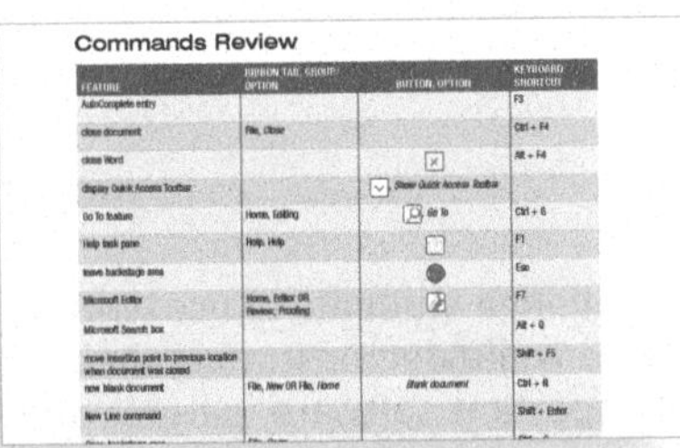

Commands Review

FEATURE	RIBBON TAB, GROUP/ OPTION	BUTTON, OPTION	KEYBOARD SHORTCUT
AutoComplete entry			F3
close document	File, Close		Ctrl + F4
close Word			Alt + F4
display Quick Access Toolbar		*Show Quick Access Toolbar*	
Go To feature	Home, Editing	Go To	Ctrl + G
Help task pane	Help, Help		F1
leave backstage area			Esc
Microsoft Editor	Home, Editor OR Review, Proofing		F7
Microsoft Search box			Alt + Q
move insertion point to previous location when document was closed			Shift + F5
new blank document	File, *New* OR File, *Home*	*Blank document*	Ctrl + N
New Line command			Shift + Enter

Commands Review tables list features taught in the chapter along with ribbon location, button names, and keyboard shortcuts.

Skills Assessment

Assessment 1

Edit a Document on Resume Writing

1. Open Word and then open **WriteResume.docx**.
2. Save the document with the name **1-WriteResume**.
3. Move the insertion point to the end of the document and then type the text shown in Figure 1.9. When typing the text, use the New Line command, Shift + Enter, to end the lines after *Created by Marie Solberg* and *Monday, October 7, 2024*.
4. Make the following changes to the document:
   a. Delete the first occurrence of the word *currently* in the first sentence of the first paragraph.
   b. Select the word *important* in the first sentence in the first paragraph and then type essential.
   c. Type and hard-hitting between the words *concise* and *written* in the second sentence of the second paragraph.
   d. Delete the words *over and over,* (including the comma and the space after the comma) in the third sentence in the second paragraph.
   e. Select and then delete the second sentence of the third paragraph (the sentence that begins *So do not take*).
   f. Move the insertion point to the beginning of the third paragraph and then press the backspace key to join the third paragraph with the second paragraph.

Skills Assessment exercises evaluate the ability to apply chapter skills and concepts in solving realistic problems.

Visual Benchmark

Create a Report about Active Listening Skills

1. Open **ActiveListen.docx** and then save it with the name **2-ActiveListen**.
2. Apply the following formatting to the document so it appears as shown in Figure 2.11:
   a. Select the document and then change the font to 12-point Cambria and the font color to standard dark blue.
   b. Set the title in 16-point Candara bold and center the title.
   c. Set the headings in 14-point Candara bold.
   d. Change the paragraph spacing after the title and headings to 6 points.
   e. Underline the text as shown in the figure.
   f. Create a hanging indent for the paragraphs as shown in the figure. (Do not create the hanging paragraphs using the Tab key.)
3. Save, preview, and then close **2-ActiveListen.docx**.

Figure 2.11 Visual Benchmark

ACTIVE LISTENING SKILLS

Become an Active Listener

Visual Benchmark activities are culminating assessments designed to demonstrate mastery of application features and problem-solving abilities.

Case Study

Part 1

You are the administrative assistant at a mid-sized service-oriented business. Employees frequently use Microsoft Word to create contracts to use with customers. Your boss, Mr. Brewster, wants these saved to a folder named *Contracts* in the Documents folder on your company's shared drive. Mr. Brewster has asked you to create a document for employees with step-by-step instructions for naming and saving contracts. Save your completed document with the name **1-Saving**. Preview and then close the document.

Part 2

Mr. Brewster would like to have a document describing basic Word commands and keyboard shortcuts to help employees work more efficiently in Microsoft Word. He has asked you to prepare a document containing the following information:

- A brief explanation of how to use the Go To feature to move the insertion point to a specific page
- Keyboard shortcuts to move the insertion point to the beginning and end of a line and the beginning and end of a document
- Keyboard commands to delete text from the insertion point to the beginning of a word and from the insertion point to the end of a word
- Steps to select a word and a paragraph using the mouse
- A keyboard shortcut to select the entire document

Save the completed document with the name **1-WordCommands**. Preview and then close the document.

Case Study activities require analyzing a workplace scenario and then planning and executing multipart project. Students may use the search and Help features to locate additional information required to complete the Case Study.

Unit Performance Assessments

Performance assessments for each four-chapter unit provide cross-disciplinary, comprehensive practice.

Data Files

The data files for this unit work are in the WL1U2 folder that you downloaded at the beginning of this course.

Assessing Proficiency

In this unit, you have learned to format and customize objects to enhance the appearance of documents; manage documents; print envelopes and labels; create documents using templates; create and edit tables; visually represent data in SmartArt graphics and charts; create custom numbering and bullet formatting; and customize a document using AutoCorrect options and custom themes.

Assessment 1

Format a Bioinformatics Document

1. Open **Bioinformatics.docx** and then save it with the name **U2-Bioinformatics**.
2. Move the insertion point to the end of the document and then insert the file named **GenomeMapping.docx**.
3. Press Ctrl + Home to move the insertion point to the beginning of the document and then insert the Motion Quote text box with the following

Assessing Proficiency activities check mastery of application functions and features.

Writing Activities

The following activities give you the opportunity to practice your writing skills and demonstrate your understanding of some of the important Word features you have mastered in this unit. Use correct grammar, appropriate word choices, and clear sentence construction.

Activity 1

Create a Letterhead and Compose a Letter

You are the executive assistant to the owner of Clearline Manufacturing, who has asked you to create a letterhead for the company. Use information of your choosing for the letterhead that includes the company name, address, email address, web address, and telephone number. Include an image in the letterhead. Five possible choices are available in your WL1U2 folder, and each image file name begins with *Manufacture*. Save the completed letterhead document as a template in your WL1U2 folder and name the template **CMLtrhdTemplate**. Close the template document.

Use File Explorer to open a document based on the **CMLtrhdTemplate.dotx** template. Write a letter to the president of the board of directors, Mrs. Nancy Logan (you determine her address), that includes the following:

- Explain that the director of the Human Resources Department has created a new employee handbook and that it will be made available to all new employees. Also mention that the attorney for Clearline Manufacturing has

Writing Activities challenge students to use written communication skills while demonstrating their understanding of important software features and functions.

- Apply title and/or heading styles to the title and headings in the document.
- Add a cover page of your choosing to the document and insert the appropriate information in the cover page placeholders.
- Any additional formatting that improves the appearance of the document.

Save, preview, and then close **U2-CMHandbook.docx**.

Internet Research

Create a Flyer on an Incentive Program

The owner of Blue Earth Adventures is offering an incentive to motivate adventure consultants to increase adventure bookings. The incentive is a sales contest with the grand prize of a one-week paid vacation to Cancun, Mexico. The owner has asked you to create a flyer that will be posted on the office bulletin board and that includes information about the incentive program and Cancun. Create this flyer using information about Cancun that you find on the internet. Consider using one (or more) of the images (**Cancun01.jpg**, **Cancun02.jpg**, **Cancun03.jpg**, and **Cancun04.jpg**) in your WL1U2 folder. Include any other information or objects to add visual interest to the flyer. Save the completed flyer with the name **U2-CancunFlyer**. Preview and then close **U2-CancunFlyer.docx**.

Internet Research assignments reinforce the importance of research and information processing skills along with proficiency in the Word environment.

Include any other information or objects to add visual interest to the flyer. Save the completed flyer with the name **U2-CancunFlyer**. Preview and then close **U2-CancunFlyer.docx**.

Job Study

Develop Recycling Program Communications

The chief operating officer of Harrington Engineering has just approved your draft of the company's new recycling policy, the file named **RecyclingPolicy.docx**. Open the file, edit the draft, and prepare a final copy of the policy, along with a memo to all employees describing the new guidelines. To support the company's energy resources conservation effort, you will send hard copies of the new policy to the president of the Somerset Recycling Program and to the directors of the Somerset Chamber of Commerce.

Using the concepts and techniques you learned in this unit, prepare the following documents:

- Format the recycling policy manual, including a cover page, appropriate headers and footers, and page numbers. Add at least one graphic where appropriate. Format the document using styles and a style set. Save the manual with the name **U2-RecyclingManual**. Preview the manual.
- Download a memo template at the New backstage area and then create a memo from Susan Gerhardt, Chief Operating Officer of Harrington Engineering, to all employees that introduces the new recycling program.

A **Job Study** activity included in the Unit 2 assessments presents a capstone activity requiring critical thinking and problem solving.

DRIVE STUDENT SUCCESS WITH CIRRUS

The **Benchmark Series**, powered by Paradigm's Cirrus platform, integrates seamlessly with Blackboard, Canvas, D2L, and Moodle. Students and educators can access all course material anytime, anywhere through a live internet connection. Cirrus delivers students the same learning experience whether they are using a PC, Mac, or Chromebook.

Course content is digitally delivered in a series of scheduled assignments that report to a grade book, thus tracking student progress and achievement through Cirrus's complete solution.

Dynamic Training, Practice, and Assessment

Cirrus course content for the **Benchmark Series** includes interactive assignments to guide student learning and engaging practice and assessment activities to reinforce and assess skills mastery.

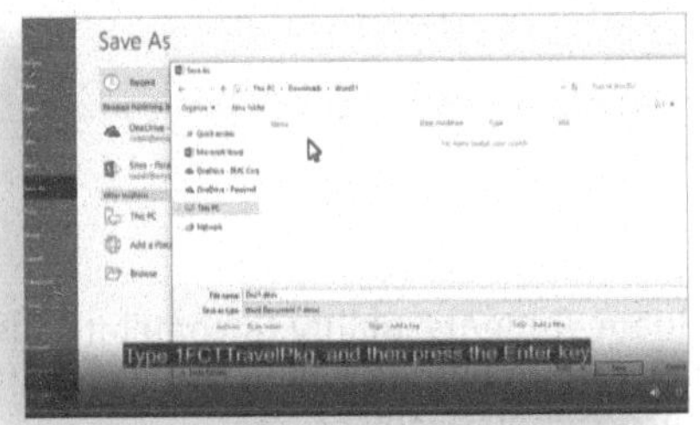

Watch and Learn Lessons explain how to perform each chapter activity part, including short demonstration videos for students to view and content for them to read. Performance objectives, chapter summaries, and Commands Review tables are also included with each lesson.

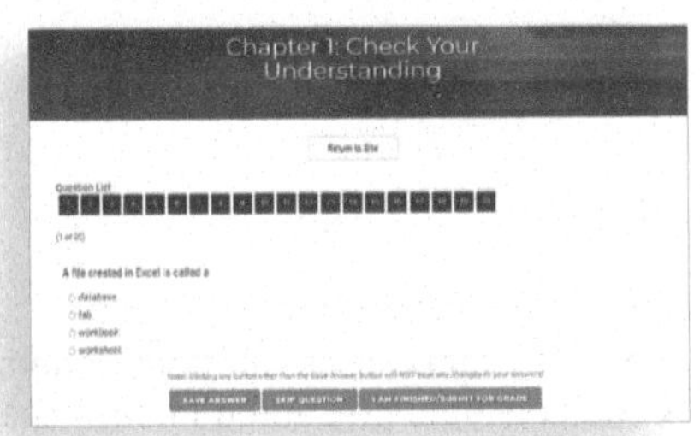

Check Your Understanding Quizzes allow students to check their understanding of the chapter concepts.

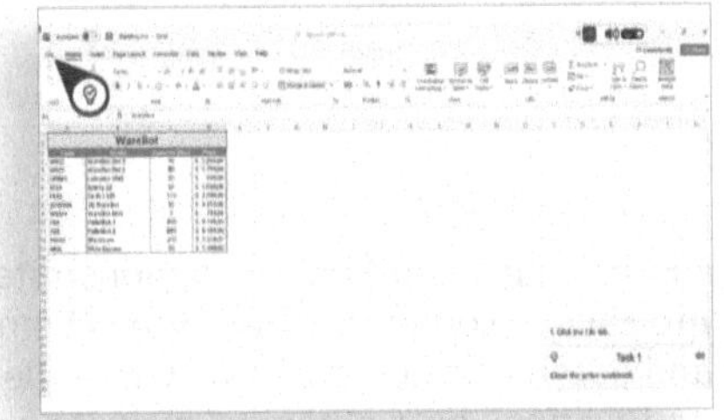

Guide and Practice Tutorials provide interactive, guided training and measured practice.

Chapter Practice and Assessment

Practice and assessment activities for each chapter reinforce and assess student learning.

Hands On Activities provide students the opportunity to practice their skills by completing chapter and end-of-chapter activities on the virtual desktop. Students upload their answers through Cirrus for instructor evaluation.

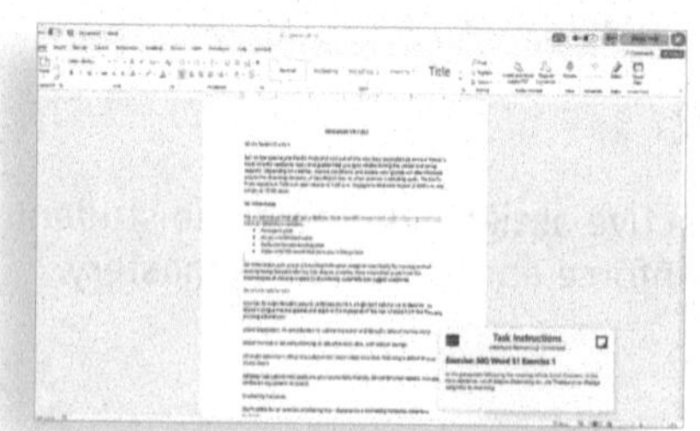

Exercises and Projects provide opportunities to practice and demonstrate skills learned in each chapter. Each is completed live in the Microsoft 365 application and is automatically scored by Cirrus. Detailed feedback and how-to videos help students evaluate and improve their performance.

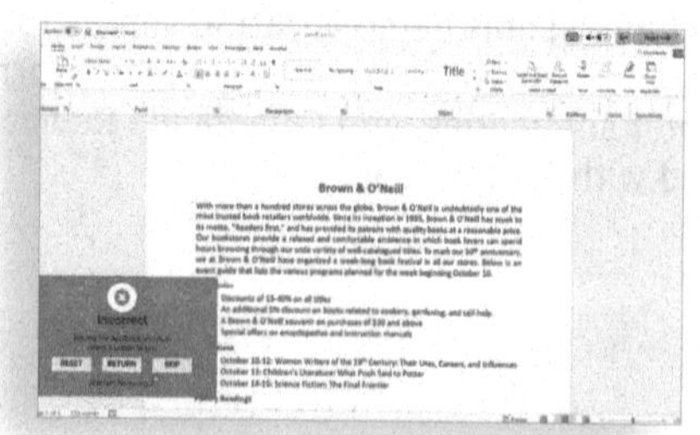

Skills Exams evaluate students' ability to complete specific tasks. Skills Exams are completed live in the Microsoft 365 application and are automatically scored.

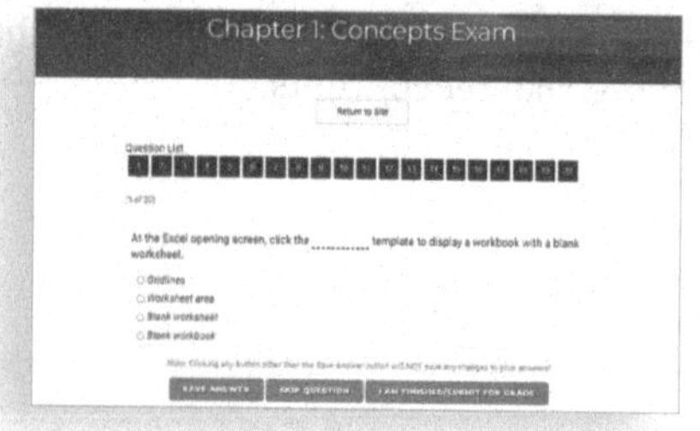

Multiple-choice **Concepts Exams** assess student understanding of key commands and concepts presented in each chapter.

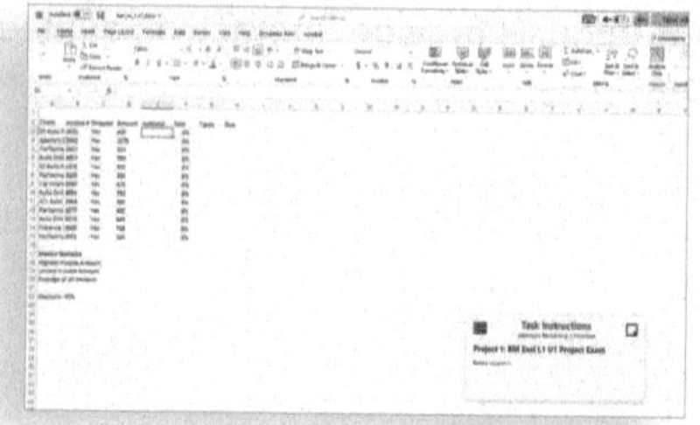

Unit-Level Project Exams allow students to demonstrate skills learned in the unit. Each is completed live in the Microsoft 365 application and automatically scored by Cirrus. Detailed feedback and how-to videos help students evaluate and improve their performance.

SUPPORT EVERY STEP OF THE WAY

Instructor Resources

Cirrus tracks students' step-by-step interactions as they move through each activity, giving instructors visibility into their progress. The Instructor Resources for the **Benchmark Series** include the following support:

- Planning resources, such as syllabus suggestions, course performance objectives, chapter-based performance objectives, and student completion time estimates
- Delivery resources, such as teaching tips, suggestions for using Cirrus demonstration elements in the classroom, and discussion questions
- Assessment resources, including live and annotated PDF model answers for chapter work and review and assessment activities, rubrics for evaluating student work, Knowledge Check completion exercises, chapter-based concept exam item banks, and new capstone projects that allow students to demonstrate their creativity and skills mastery

Faculty Preparation and Technical Assistance

Paradigm is committed to providing educators and students with unparalleled service and support. To prepare everyone for the first day of class and to deliver a smooth and successful experience throughout the course, Paradigm provides the following:

- training for educators teaching with the **Benchmark Series** and Cirrus course customization
- technical support based in the United States
- live chat for questions and assistance
- integration with an institution's learning management system

Visit **pescirrus.com** to access support from Paradigm.

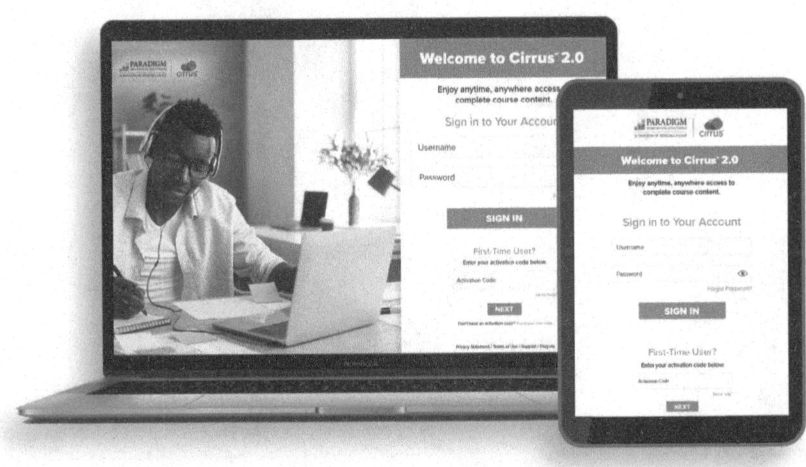

ABOUT THE AUTHORS

Nita Rutkosky began her career teaching business education at Pierce College in Puyallup, Washington, in 1978 and holds a master's degree in occupational education. In her years as an instructor, she taught many courses in software applications to students in postsecondary information technology certificate and degree programs. Since 1987, Nita has been a leading author of courseware for computer applications training and instruction. Her current titles include Paradigm's popular Benchmark Series and Marquee Series. She is a contributor to the Cirrus online content for Microsoft 365 application courses and has also written textbooks for keyboarding, desktop publishing, computing in the medical office, and essential skills for digital literacy.

Audrey Roggenkamp holds a master's degree in adult education and curriculum and has been an adjunct instructor in the Business Information Technology department at Pierce College in Puyallup, Washington, since 2005. Audrey has also been a content provider for Paradigm Education Solutions since 2005. In addition to contributing to the Cirrus online content for Microsoft 365 application courses, Audrey co-authors Paradigm's Benchmark Series, Marquee Series, and Signature Series. Her other available titles include *Keyboarding & Applications I and II* and *Using Computers in the Medical Office: Word, PowerPoint, and Excel.*

Ian Rutkosky has a master's degree in business administration and has been an adjunct instructor in the Business Information Technology department at Pierce College in Puyallup, Washington, since 2010. In addition to joining the author team for the Benchmark Series and Marquee Series, he has co-authored titles on medical office computing and digital literacy and has served as a co-author and consultant for Paradigm's Cirrus training and assessment platform.

ACKNOWLEDGMENTS

The authors and publisher would like to thank the following individuals for their valuable feedback and recommendations.

Julia Basham
Southern State Community College

DeAnne (Dee) Bowersock
Ohio Business College—Sandusky Campus

Heidi Drake
Miller-Motte College of Charleston, SC

Joyce King
Bay College

Marlene Lucas
Westmoreland County Community College

Thomas Mays
Miami University

Mary Kim McDaniel
Wallace Community College—Dothan Campus

Lori McLaughlin
Richmond Community College

Kevin A. Parrett
Elizabethtown Community and Technical College

Crystal Pounds
Colby Community College

Lois Robinson
Reid State Technical College

Kyle Saunders
Bridgerland Technical College

Jane Scott
Spokane, WA

Dennis Sigur
Dillard University

Larrhea Sims
Gadsden State Community College

Melinda Shirey
Fresno City College

Angie Tatro
Pratt Community College

Jennifer Younger
North Central Kansas Technical College

Cirrus Survey Participants

Penny Aldridge
Wallace State Community College

Mary Anderson
Morris Brown College

Terry Ayers
Wallace State Community College

Julia Basham
Southern State Community College

Lani Bogoevska
Interactive College of Technology

DeAnne Bowersock
Ohio Business College—Sandusky Campus

Jeff Brabant
Miles Community College

Robin Bracisiewicz
Miller-Motte College

Tamra Brown
Western Technical College

Hanna Chapman
Chatfield College

Tondrika Dilligard
Miller-Motte College

Heidi Drake
Miller-Motte College

Chuck Durante
Lake-Sumter State College

Laura Fish
Coastal Pines Technical College

Omekia Harrison
Trenholm State Community College

Dr. Regina Henry
Strayer University

Edward Hunter
Skagit Valley College

Mark Kelly
Wallace Community College—Dothan Campus

Joyce King
Bay College

Marlene Lucas
Westmoreland County Community College

Tiffanie Maule
Pierce College

Tom Mays
Miami University

Kim McDaniel
Wallace Community College—Dothan Campus

Lori McLaughlin
Richmond Community College

Kevin Parrett
Elizabethtown Community and Technical College

Raymond Pierce
Wallace State Community College

Crystal Pounds
Colby Community College

Michael Quintieri
Miller-Motte Technical College

Bobbie Rathjens
North Central Michigan College

Lois Robinson
Reid State Technical College

Chris Sargent
Lake-Sumter State College

Kyle Saunders
Bridgerland Technical College

Melinda Shirey
Fresno City College

Dennis Sigur
Dillard University

Larrhea Sims
Gadsden State Community College

David Strickland
Miller-Motte College

Angie Tatro
Pratt Community College

Erica Teague
Gwinnett Technical College

Kershena Thomas
Miller-Motte College

Jonathan Weiss
Ocean County College

Veronica West-Williams
Miller-Motte College

Shawnette L. Williams
Manhattan Area Technical College

Jennifer Younger
North Central Kansas Technical College

GETTING STARTED

Microsoft 365 is a suite of applications for personal computers and other devices. Four applications within the suite include Word, a word processor; Excel, an electronic spreadsheet; Access, a database management system; and PowerPoint, a presentation application used to design and present slide shows. Microsoft 365 is a subscription service that delivers continually updated versions of the applications within the suite. Specific features and functionality of Microsoft 365 vary depending on the user's account, computer setup, and other factors. The Benchmark courseware was developed using features available in Microsoft 365. You may find that with your computer and version of Microsoft 365, the appearance of the application and the steps needed to complete an activity vary slightly from what is presented in the courseware.

Identifying Computer Hardware

The Microsoft 365 suite can run on several types of computer equipment, referred to as *hardware*. You will need access to a laptop or a desktop computer system that includes a PC/tower, monitor, keyboard, printer, drives, and mouse. If you are not sure what equipment you will be operating, check with your instructor. The computer system shown in Figure G.1 consists of six components. Each component is discussed separately in the material that follows.

Figure G.1 Computer System

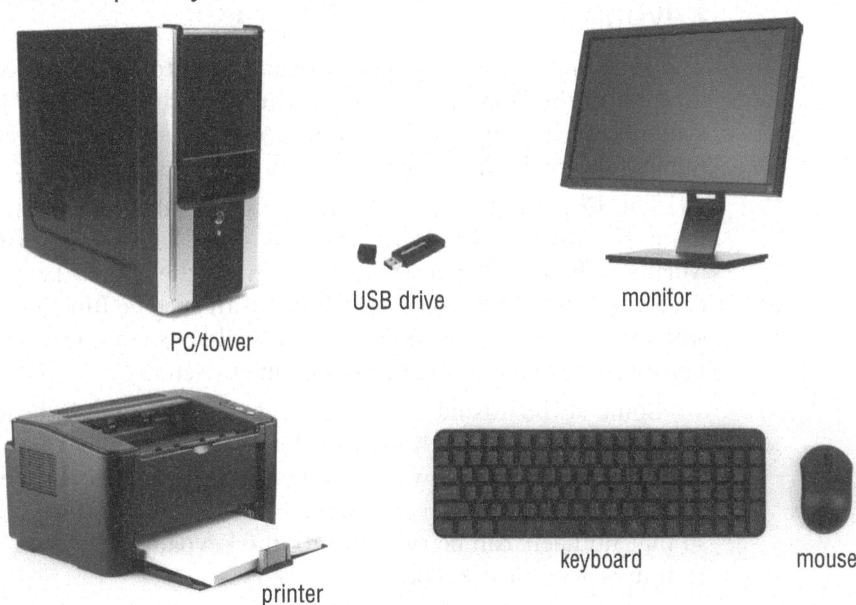

Figure G.2 System Unit Ports

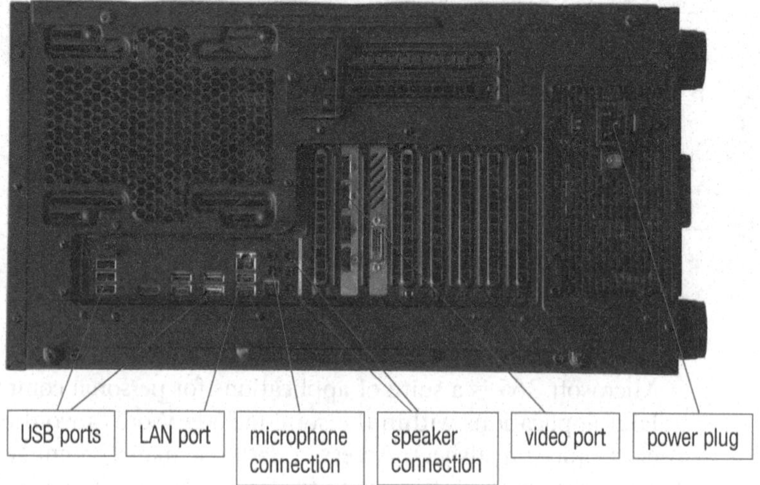

System Unit (PC/Tower)

Traditional desktop computing systems include a system unit known as the *PC (personal computer)* or *tower*. This is the brain of the computer, where all processing occurs. It contains a Central Processing Unit (CPU), hard drives, and video cards plugged into a motherboard. Input and output ports are used for attaching peripheral equipment such as a keyboard, monitor, printer, and so on, as shown in Figure G.2. When a user provides input, the PC computes it and outputs the results.

Monitor

Hint Monitor size is measured diagonally and is generally the distance from the bottom left corner to the top right corner of the monitor.

A computer monitor looks like a television screen. It displays the visual information output by the computer. Monitor size can vary, and the quality of display for monitors varies depending on the type of monitor and the level of resolution.

Keyboard

The keyboard is used to input information into the computer. The number and location of the keys on a keyboard can vary. In addition to letters, numbers, and symbols, most computer keyboards contain function keys, arrow keys, and a numeric keypad. Figure G.3 shows a typical keyboard.

The 12 keys at the top of the keyboard, labeled with the letter *F* followed by a number, are called *function keys*. Use these keys to perform functions within the Microsoft 365 applications. To the right of the regular keys is a group of special or dedicated keys. These keys are labeled with specific functions that will be performed when you press the key. Below the special keys are arrow keys. Use these keys to move the insertion point in the document screen.

Some keyboards include mode indicator lights to indicate that a particular mode, such as Caps Lock or Num Lock, has been turned on. Pressing the Caps Lock key disables the lowercase alphabet so that text is typed in all caps, while pressing the Num Lock key disables the special functions on the numeric keypad so that numbers can be typed using the keypad. When you select these modes, a light appears on the keyboard.

Figure G.3 Keyboard

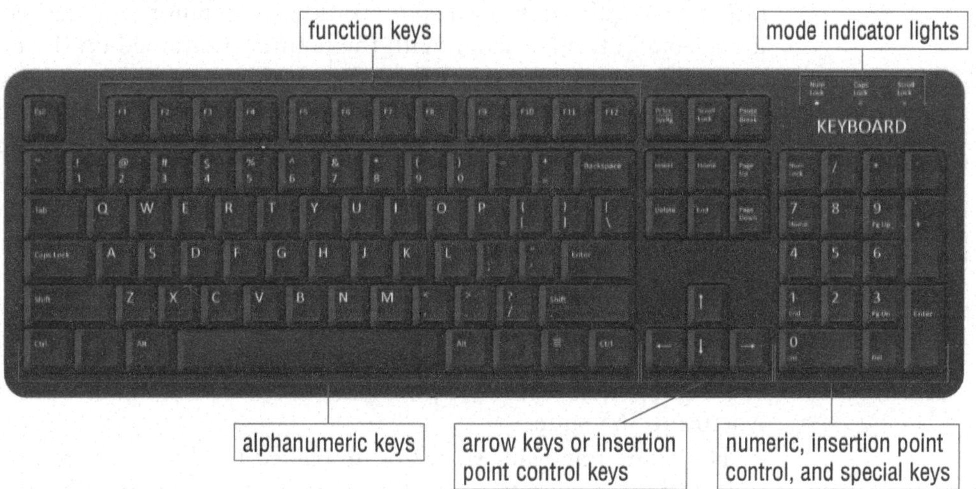

Drives and Ports

An internal hard drive is a disk drive that is located inside the PC and that stores data. External hard drives may be connected via USB ports for additional storage. Ports are the "plugs" on the PC, and are used to connect devices to the computer, such as the keyboard and mouse, the monitor, speakers, USB flash drives and so on. Most PCs will have a few USB ports, at least one display port, audio ports, and possibly an ethernet port (used to physically connect to the internet or a network).

Printer

An electronic version of a file is known as a *soft copy*. If you want to create a hard copy of a file, you need to print it. To print documents, you will need to access a printer, which will probably be either a laser printer or an ink-jet printer. A laser printer uses a laser beam combined with heat and pressure to print documents, while an ink-jet printer prints a document by spraying a fine mist of ink on the page.

Mouse

Most functions and commands in the Microsoft 365 suite are designed to be performed using a mouse or a similar pointing device. A mouse is an input device that sits on a flat surface next to the computer. You can operate a mouse with your left or right hand. Moving the mouse on the flat surface causes a corresponding pointer to move on the screen, and clicking the left or right mouse buttons allows you to select various objects and commands.

Using the Mouse The applications in the Microsoft 365 suite can be operated with the keyboard and a mouse. The mouse generally has two buttons on top, which you press to execute specific functions and commands. A mouse may also contain a wheel, which can be used to scroll in a window or as a third button. To use the mouse, rest it on a flat surface or a mouse pad. Put your hand over it with your palm resting on top of the mouse and your index finger resting on the left mouse button. As you move your hand, and thus the mouse, a corresponding pointer moves on the screen.

When using the mouse, you should understand four terms—*point*, *click*, *double-click*, and *drag*. To *point* means to position the pointer on a desired item, such as an option, button, or icon. With the pointer positioned on the item, *click* the left mouse button once to select the item. (In some cases you may *right-click*, which means to click the right mouse button, but generally, *click* refers to the left button.) To complete two steps at one time, such as choosing and then executing a function, *double-click* the left mouse button by tapping it twice in quick succession. The term *drag* means to click and hold down the left mouse button, move the pointer to a specific location, and then release the button. Clicking and dragging is used, for instance, when moving a file from one location to another.

Hint Instructions in this course use the verb *click* to refer to tapping the left mouse button and the verb *press* to refer to pressing a key on the keyboard.

Using the Pointer The pointer will look different depending on where you have positioned it and what function you are performing. The following are some of the ways the pointer can appear when you are working in an application in the Microsoft 365 suite:

- The pointer appears as an I-beam (called the *I-beam pointer*) when you are inserting text in a file. The I-beam pointer can be used to move the insertion point or to select text.

- The pointer appears as an arrow pointing up and to the left when it is moved to the Title bar, ribbon, Status bar or an option in a dialog box, among other locations.

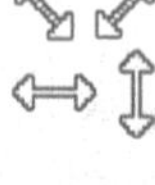

- The pointer becomes a double-headed arrow (either pointing left and right, pointing up and down, or pointing diagonally) when you perform certain functions such as changing the size of an object.

- In certain situations, such as when you move an object or image, the pointer displays with a four-headed arrow attached. The four-headed arrow means that you can move the object left, right, up, or down.

- When a request is being processed or when an application is being loaded, the pointer may appear as a moving circle. The moving circle means "please wait." When the process is completed, the circle is replaced with a normal pointer.

- When the pointer displays as a hand with a pointing index finger, it indicates that more information is available about an item. The pointer also displays as a hand with a pointing index finger when you hover over a hyperlink.

Touchpad

If you are working on a laptop computer, you may be using a touchpad instead of a mouse. A *touchpad* allows you to move the pointer by moving your finger across a surface at the base of the keyboard (as shown in Figure G.4). You click and right-click by using your thumb to press the buttons located at the bottom of the touchpad. Some touchpads have special features such as scrolling or clicking something by tapping the surface of the touchpad instead of pressing a button with a thumb.

Figure G.4 Touchpad

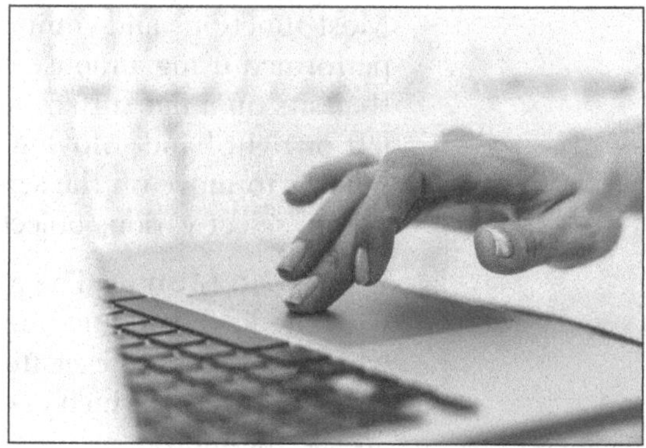

Touchscreen

Smartphones, tablets, and touch monitors all use touchscreen technology (as shown in Figure G.5), which allows users to directly interact with the objects on the screen by touching them with fingers, thumbs, or a stylus. Multiple fingers or both thumbs can be used on most touchscreens, giving users the ability to zoom, rotate, and manipulate items on the screen. While many activities in this textbook can be completed using a device with a touchscreen, a mouse or touchpad might be required to complete a few activities.

Figure G.5 Touchscreen

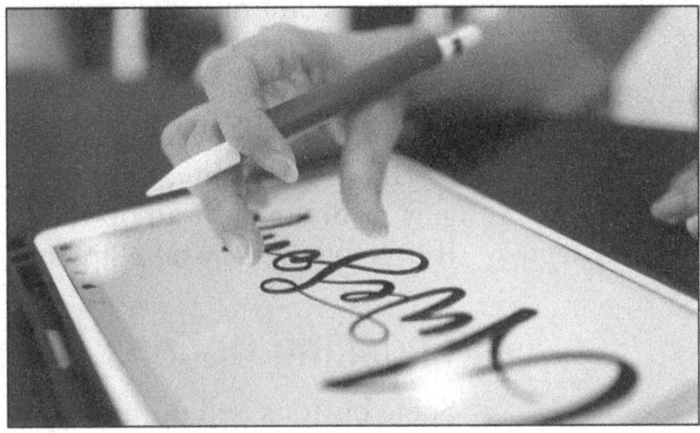

Choosing Commands

A *command* is an instruction that tells an application to complete a certain task. When an application such as Word or PowerPoint is open, the *ribbon* at the top of the window displays buttons and options for commands. To select a command with the mouse, point to it and then click the left mouse button.

Notice that the ribbon is organized into tabs, including File, Home, Insert, and so on. When the File tab is clicked, a *backstage area* opens with options such as opening or saving a file. Clicking any of the other tabs will display a variety of commands and options on the ribbon.

Using Keyboard Shortcuts and Accelerator Keys

As an alternative to using the mouse, keyboard shortcuts can be used for many commands. Shortcuts generally require two or more keys. For instance, in Word, press and hold down the Ctrl key while pressing P to display the Print backstage area, or press Ctrl + O to display the Open backstage area. A complete list of keyboard shortcuts can be found by searching the Help files in a Microsoft 365 application.

Microsoft 365 also provides shortcuts known as *accelerator keys* for every command or action on the ribbon. These accelerator keys are especially helpful for users with motor or visual disabilities or for power users who find it faster to use the keyboard than click with the mouse. To identify accelerator keys, press the Alt key on the keyboard. KeyTips display on the ribbon, as shown in Figure G.6. Press the keys indicated to execute the desired command. For example, to display a list of margin options, press the Alt key, press the P key on the keyboard to display the Layout tab, and then press the letter M on the keyboard.

Figure G.6 Word Home Tab KeyTips

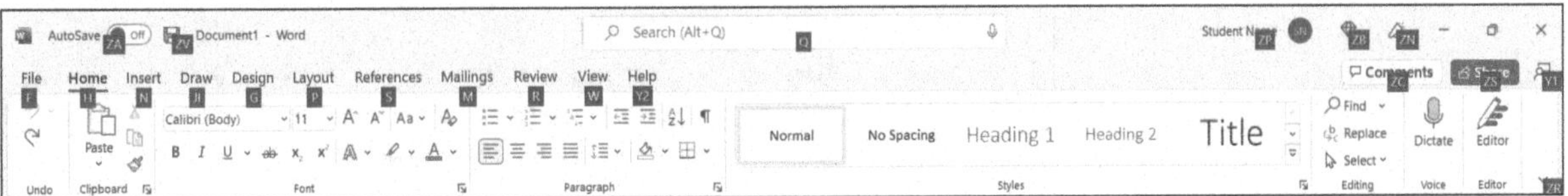

Choosing Commands from a Drop-Down List

Some buttons include arrows that can be clicked to display a drop-down list of options. Point and click with the mouse to choose an option from the list. Some options in a drop-down list may have a letter that is underlined. This indicates that typing the letter will select the option. For instance, to select the option *Insert Table*, type the letter I on the keyboard.

If an option in a drop-down list is not available to be selected, it will appear gray or dimmed. If an option is preceded by a check mark, it is currently active. If it is followed by an ellipsis (...), clicking the option will open a dialog box.

Choosing Options from a Dialog Box or Task Pane

Some buttons and options open a *dialog box* or a task pane containing options for applying formatting or otherwise modifying the data in a file. For example, the Font dialog box shown in Figure G.7 contains options for modifying the font and adding effects. The dialog box contains two tabs—the Font tab and the Advanced tab. The tab that displays in the front is the active tab. Click a tab to make it active or press Ctrl + Tab on the keyboard. Alternately, press the Alt key and then type the letter that is underlined in the tab name.

To choose an option from a dialog box using the mouse, position the arrow pointer on the option and then click the left mouse button. To move forward from option to option using the keyboard, you can press the Tab key. Press Shift + Tab to move back to a previous option. If the option displays with an underlined letter,

Figure G.7 Word Font Dialog Box

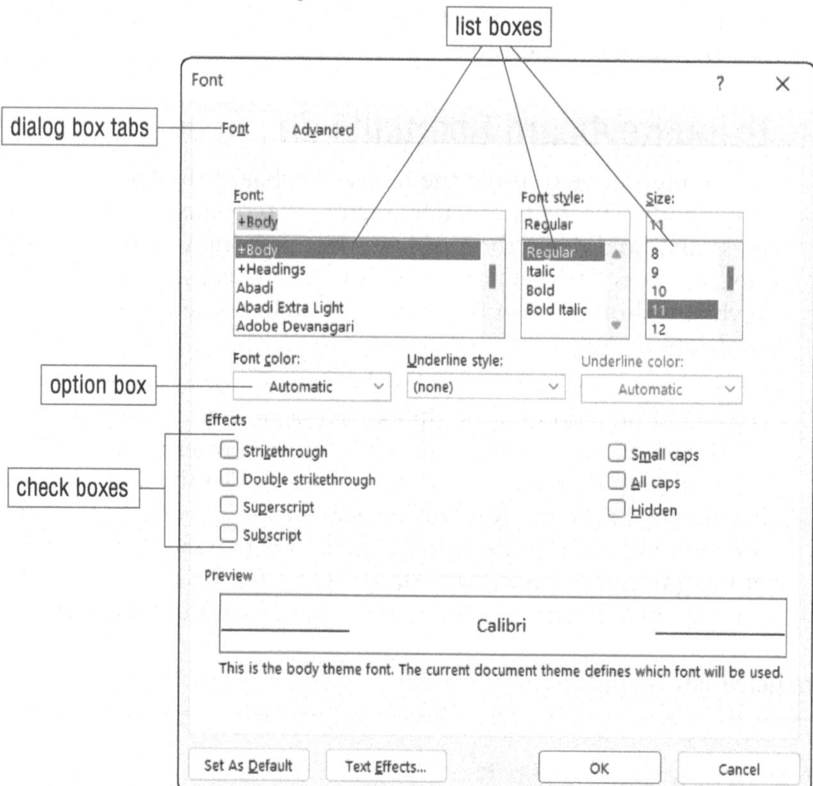

you can choose it by pressing the Alt key and the underlined letter. When an option is selected, it is highlighted in blue or surrounded by a dotted or dashed box called a *marquee*. A dialog box contains one or more of the following elements: list boxes, option boxes, check boxes, text boxes, command buttons, radio buttons, and measurement boxes.

List Boxes and Option Boxes The fonts available at the Font dialog box, shown in Figure G.7 (on the previous page), are contained in a *list box*. Click an option in the list to select it. If the list is long, click the up or down arrows in the *scroll bar* at the right side of the box to scroll through all the options. Alternately, press the up or down arrow keys on the keyboard to move through the list, and press the Enter key when the desired option is selected.

Option boxes contain a drop-down list or gallery of options that opens when the arrow in the box is clicked. An example is the *Font color* option box at the Font dialog box shown in Figure G.7. To display the different color options, click the arrow at the right side of the box. If you are using the keyboard, press Alt + C.

Check Boxes Some options can be selected using a check box, such as the effect options at the dialog box in Figure G.7. If a check mark appears in the box, the option is active (turned on). If the check box does not contain a check mark, the option is inactive (turned off). Click a check box to make the option active or inactive. If you are using the keyboard, press Alt + the underlined letter of the option.

Text Boxes Some options in a dialog box require you to enter text. For example, see the Find and Replace dialog box shown in Figure G.8. In a text box, type or edit text with the keyboard, using the left and right arrow keys to move the insertion point without deleting text and use the Delete key or Backspace key to delete text.

Command Buttons The buttons at the bottom of the dialog box shown in Figure G.8 are called *command buttons*. Use a command button to execute or cancel a command. Some command buttons display with an ellipsis (...), which means another dialog box will open if you click that button. To choose a command button, click with the mouse or press the Tab key until the command button is surrounded by a marquee and then press the Enter key.

Figure G.8 Excel Find and Replace Dialog Box

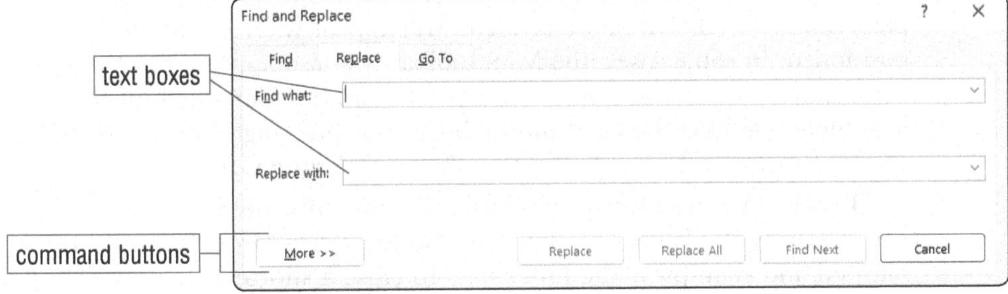

Figure G.9 Word Insert Table Dialog Box

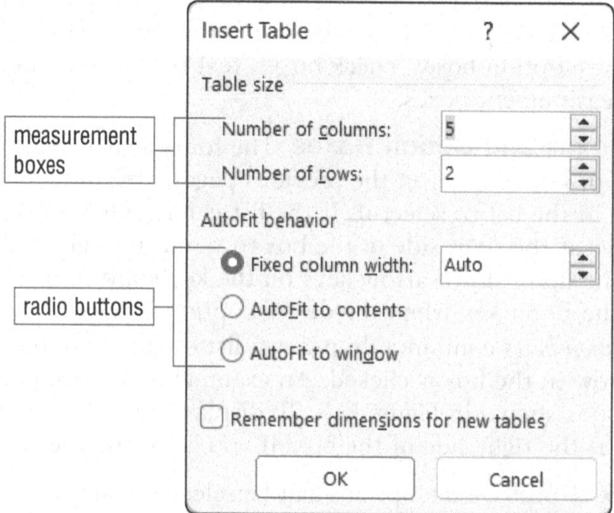

Radio Buttons The Insert Table dialog box shown in Figure G.9 contains an example of *radio buttons* (also referred to as *option buttons*). Only one radio button can be selected at any time. When the button is selected, it is filled with a dark circle. Click a button to select it, or press and hold down the Alt key, press the underlined letter of the option, and then release the Alt key.

Measurement Boxes A *measurement box* contains an amount that can be increased or decreased. An example is shown in Figure G.9. To increase or decrease the number in a measurement box, click the up or down arrow at the right side of the box. Using the keyboard, press and hold down the Alt key and then press the underlined letter for the option, press the Up Arrow key on the keyboard to increase the number or the Down Arrow key to decrease the number, and then release the Alt key.

Choosing Commands with Shortcut Menus

Microsoft 365 applications include shortcut menus that contain commands related to different items. To display a shortcut menu, point to the item for which you want to view more options with the pointer and then click the *right* mouse button, or press Shift + F10. The shortcut menu will appear wherever the insertion point is positioned. In some cases, the Mini toolbar will also appear with the shortcut menu. For example, if the insertion point is positioned in a paragraph of text in a Word document, clicking the right mouse button or pressing Shift + F10 will display the shortcut menu and Mini toolbar, as shown in Figure G.10.

To select an option from a shortcut menu with the mouse, click the option. If you are using the keyboard, press the Up or Down Arrow key until the option is selected and then press the Enter key. To close a shortcut menu without choosing an option, click outside the menu or press the Esc key.

Figure G.10 Shortcut Menu and Mini Toolbar

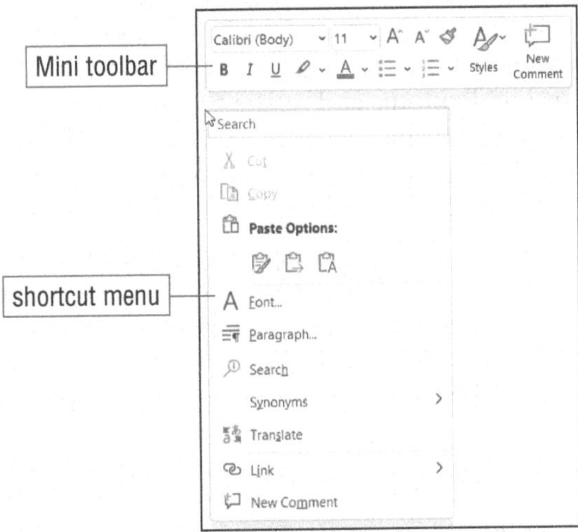

Working with Multiple Applications

As you learn the various applications in the Microsoft 365 suite, you will notice many similarities between them. For example, the steps to save, close, and print are virtually the same whether you are working in Word, Excel, or PowerPoint. This consistency greatly enhances your ability to transfer knowledge learned in one application to another within the suite. Another benefit to using Microsoft 365 is the ability to integrate content from one application with another. For example, you can open Word and create a document, open Excel and create a worksheet, and then copy a worksheet from the workbook into Word.

The Windows taskbar at the bottom of the screen displays buttons representing all the applications that are currently open. For example, Figure G.11 shows the taskbar with Word, Excel, Access, and PowerPoint open. To move from one application to another, click the button on the taskbar representing the desired application.

Maintaining Files and Folders

Windows includes a file management feature named File Explorer that can be used to maintain files and folders. To open File Explorer, click the folder icon on the Windows taskbar. Use File Explorer to complete tasks such as copying, moving, renaming, and deleting files and folders and creating new folders. Some file management tasks can also be completed within Word, Excel, PowerPoint, or Access by clicking File and then *Open* or *Save As* and then clicking the *Browse* option to browse folders and files in a dialog box.

Directions and activities in this course assume that you are managing files and folders stored on a USB flash drive or on your computer's hard drive. If you are using your OneDrive account or another cloud-based storage service, some of the file and folder management tasks may vary.

Figure G.11 Windows Taskbar with Word, Excel, Access, and PowerPoint Open

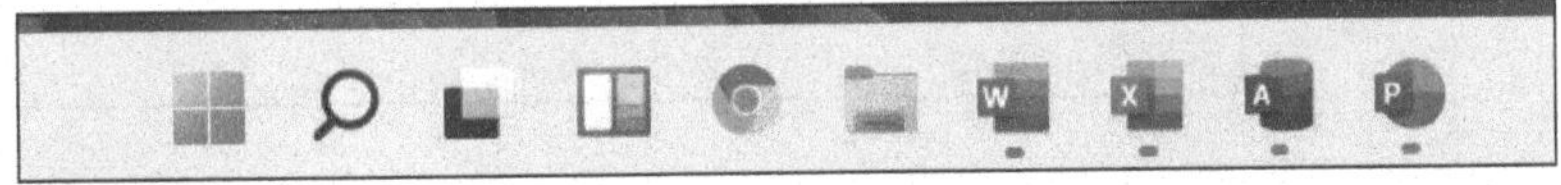

Creating and Naming a Folder

Files (such as Word documents, Excel workbooks, PowerPoint presentations, and Access databases) are easier to find again when they are grouped logically in folders. In File Explorer and at the Open or Save As dialog box, the names of files and folders are displayed in the Content pane. Each file has an icon showing what type of file it is, while folders are identified with the icon of a folder. See Figure G.12 for an example of the File Explorer window.

Create a new folder by clicking the New button at the top of the File Explorer window and then click *Folder* at the drop-down list or click the New folder button in a dialog box. A new folder displays with the name *New folder* highlighted. Type a name for the folder to replace the highlighted text, and then press the Enter key. Folder names can include numbers, spaces, and some symbols.

Selecting and Opening Files and Folders

Select files or folders in a window or dialog box to be managed. To select one file or folder, simply click on it. To select several adjacent files or folders, click the first file or folder, hold down the Shift key, and then click the last file or folder. To select files or folders that are not adjacent, click the first file or folder, hold down the Ctrl key, click any other files or folders, and then release the Ctrl key. To deselect, click anywhere in the window or dialog box.

When a file or folder is selected, the path to the folder displays in the Address bar. If the folder is located on an external storage device, the drive letter and name may display in the path. A right-pointing arrow displays to the right of each folder name in the Address bar. Click the arrow to view a list of subfolders within a folder.

Double-click a file or folder in the Content pane to open it. You can also select one or more files or folders, right-click, and then click the *Open* option at the shortcut menu.

Figure G.12 File Explorer Window

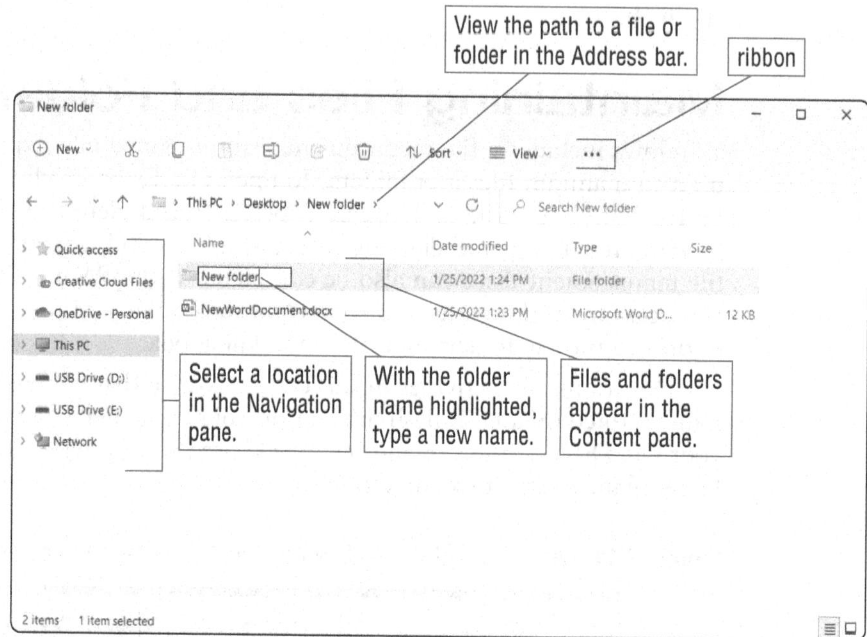

Deleting Files and Folders

Deleting files and folders is part of file maintenance. To delete a file or folder, select it and then press the Delete key. Alternatively, use the Delete button on the ribbon of the File Explorer window, or click the Organize button and then *Delete* at the dialog box. You can also right-click a file or folder and then choose the *Delete* option at the shortcut menu.

Files and folders deleted from the hard drive of the computer are automatically sent to the Recycle Bin, where they can easily be restored if necessary. If a file or folder is stored in another location, such as an external drive or online location, it may be permanently deleted. In this case, a message may appear asking for confirmation. To confirm that the file or folder should be deleted, click Yes.

To view the contents of the Recycle Bin, display the Windows desktop and then double-click the *Recycle Bin* icon. Deleted items in the Recycle Bin can be restored to their original locations, or the Recycle Bin can be emptied to free up space on the hard drive.

Moving and Copying Files and Folders

A file or folder may need to be moved or copied to another location. In File Explorer, select the file or folder and then click the Copy button on the ribbon, use the keyboard shortcut Ctrl + C, or right-click the file and select *Copy* at the shortcut menu. Navigate to the destination folder and then click the Paste button on the ribbon, use the keyboard shortcut Ctrl + V, or right-click and select *Paste*. If a copy is pasted to the same folder as the original, it will appear with the word *Copy* added to its name. To copy files at the Open or Save As dialog box, use the Organize button drop-down list or right-click to access the shortcut menu.

To move a file or folder, follow the same steps, but click the Cut button instead of the Copy button on the ribbon of the File Explorer window, select *Cut* instead of *Copy* or press Ctrl + X instead of Ctrl + C. Files can also be dragged from one location to another. To do this, open two File Explorer windows. Click a file or folder and drag it to the other window while holding down the left mouse button.

Renaming Files and Folders

To rename a file or folder in File Explorer, click its name to highlight it and then type a new name, or right-click the file or folder and then select *Rename* at the shortcut menu. You can also select the file or folder and then click the Rename button on the File Explorer ribbon or click *Rename* from the Organize button drop-down list at the Open or Save As dialog box. Type in a new name and then press the Enter key.

Viewing Files and Folders

Change how files and folders display in the Content pane in File Explorer by clicking the View button on the ribbon and then clicking one of the view options at the drop-down list. View files and folders as extra large, large, medium, or small icons; as tiles; in a list; or with details or information about the file or folder content. At the Open or Save As dialog box, click the Change your view button arrow and a list displays with similar options for viewing folders and files. Click to select an option in the list or click the Change your view button to see different views.

Displaying File Extensions Each file has a file extension that identifies the application and what type of file it is. Excel files have the extension *.xlsx;* Word files end with *.docx,* and so on. By default, file extensions are turned off. To view file extensions, open File Explorer, click the View button on the ribbon, point to *Show* at the drop-down list, and then click *File name extensions* at the side menu. The *File name extensions* option will display with a check mark next to it when file extensions are turned on. Click the option again to stop viewing file extensions.

Displaying All Files The Open or Save As dialog box in a Microsoft 365 application may display only files specific to that application. For example, the Open or Save As dialog box in Word may only display Word documents. Viewing all files at the Open dialog box can be helpful in determining what files are available. Turn on the display of all files at the Open dialog box by clicking the file type button arrow at the right side of the *File Name* text box and then clicking *All Files (*.*)* at the drop-down list.

Managing Files at the Info Backstage Area

The Info backstage area in Word, Excel, and PowerPoint provides buttons for managing files such as uploading and sharing a file, copying a path, and opening File Explorer with the current folder active. To use the buttons at the Info backstage area, open Word, Excel, or PowerPoint and then open a file. Click the File tab and then click the *Info* option. If a file is opened from the computer's hard drive or an external drive, four buttons display near the top of the Info backstage area as shown in Figure G.13.

Figure G.13 Info Backstage Buttons

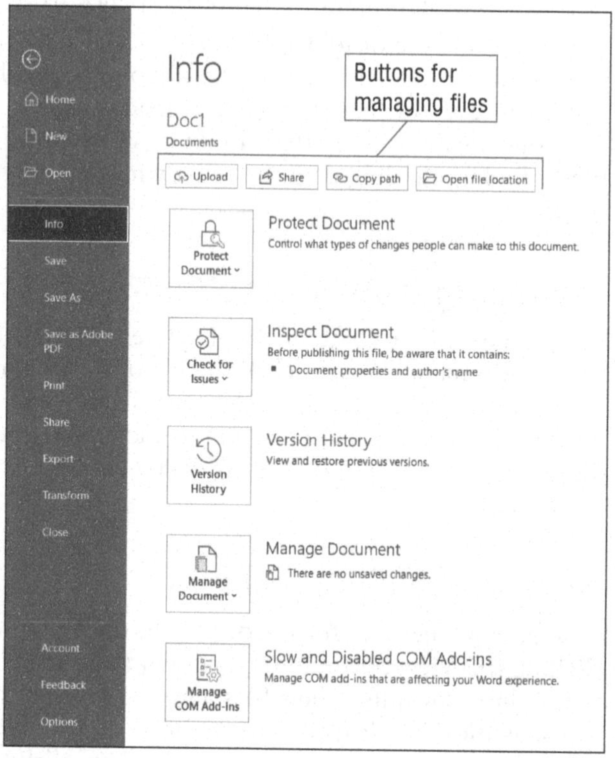

Click the Upload button to upload the open file to a shared location such as a OneDrive account. Click the Share button and a window displays indicating that the file must be saved to OneDrive before it can be shared and provides an option that, when clicked, will save the file to OneDrive. Click the Copy path button and a copy of the path for the current file is saved in a temporary location. This path can be pasted into another file, an email, or any other location where you want to keep track of the file's path. Click the Open file location button and File Explorer opens with the current folder active.

If you open Word, Excel, or PowerPoint and then open a file from OneDrive, three buttons display—Share, Copy path, and Open file location. Click the Share button to display a window with options for sharing the file with others and specifying whether the file can be viewed and edited, or only viewed. Click the Copy path button to save a copy of the path for the current file. Click the Open file location button to open File Explorer with the current folder active.

Customizing Settings

Before beginning computer activities in this textbook, you may need to customize your monitor's settings and change the DPI display setting. Activities in the course assume that the monitor display is set at 1920 × 1080 pixels and the DPI set at 125%. If you are unable to make changes to the monitor's resolution or the DPI settings, the activities can still be completed successfully. Some references in the text might not perfectly match what you see on your screen, so you may not be able to perform certain steps exactly as written. For example, an item in a drop-down gallery might appear in a different column or row than what is indicated in the step instructions.

Before you begin learning applications in the Microsoft 365 suite, take a moment to check the display settings on the computer you are using. Your monitor's display settings are important because the ribbon in the Microsoft 365 suite adjusts to the screen resolution setting of your computer monitor. A computer monitor set at a high resolution will have the ability to show more buttons on the ribbon than will a monitor set to a low resolution. The illustrations in this textbook were created with a screen resolution display set at 1920 × 1080 pixels, as shown in Figure G.14.

Figure G.14 Word Ribbon Set at 1920 x 1080 Screen Resolution

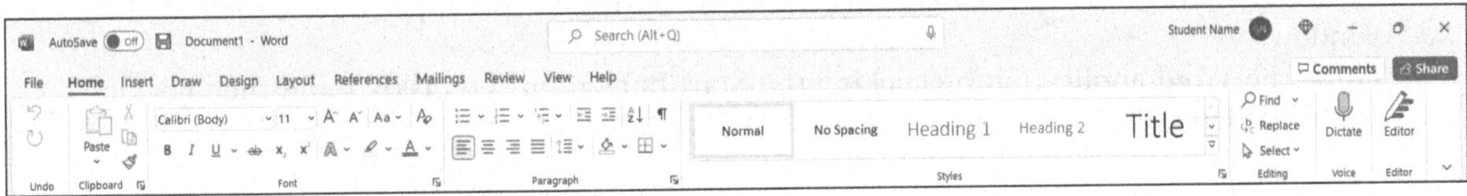

Activity 1 Adjusting Monitor Display and Changing Office Theme

Note: The resolution settings and Office theme may be locked on lab computers. Also, some laptop screens and small monitors may not be able to display in a 1920 × 1080 resolution or change the DPI setting.

1. At the Windows desktop, right-click in a blank area of the screen.
2. At the shortcut menu, click the *Display settings* option.
3. At the Settings window with *System > Display* at the top of the window, scroll down and look at the current setting in the *Display resolution* option box. If your screen is already set to 1920 × 1080, skip ahead to Step 5.
4. Click the *Display resolution* option box and then click the *1920 × 1080* option. ***Note: Depending on the privileges you are given on a school machine, you may not be able to complete Steps 4–5. If necessary, check with your instructor for alternative instructions.***
5. Click the Keep changes button at the message box asking if you want to keep the display settings.
6. At the Settings window, look at the percentage in which the size of text, apps, and other items currently display (also known as the DPI setting) in the *Scale* option box. For example, items on your screen may display at 100%. If the percentage is 125%, skip to Step 8.
7. Click the Scale option box arrow and then click the *125%* option at the drop-down list.

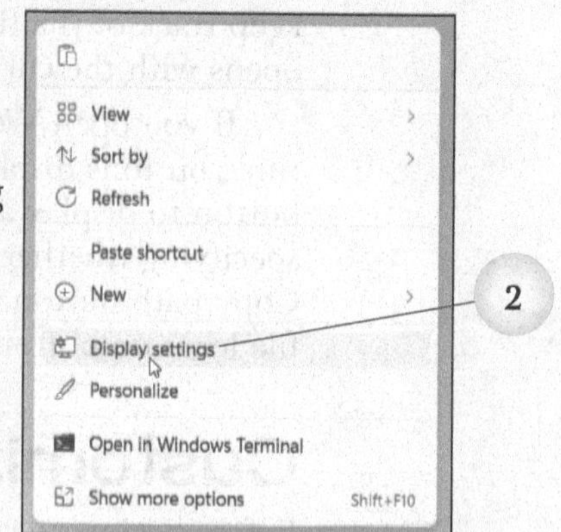

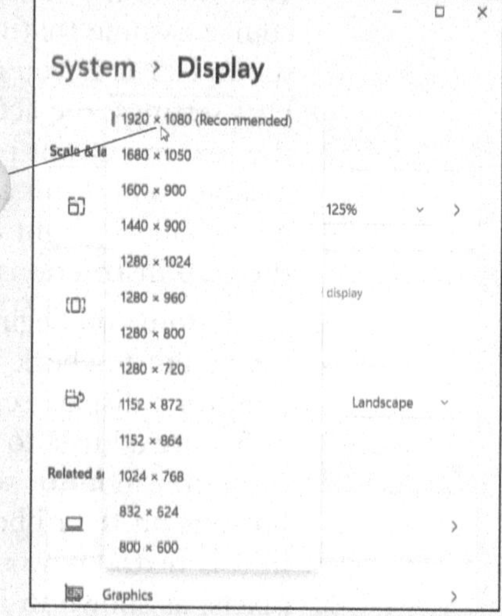

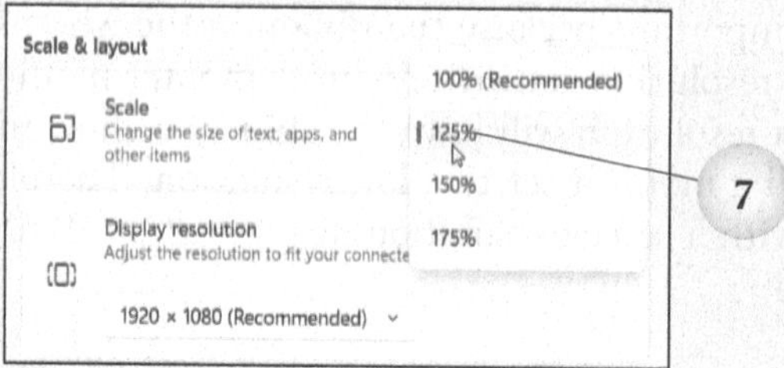

8. Close the Settings window by clicking the Close button in the upper right corner of the window.
9. Open the Word application by clicking the Start button on the taskbar and then clicking the Word icon.

10. At the opening Word screen, click the *Account* option (located near the bottom of the left panel).
11. At the Account backstage area, make sure *Use system setting* displays in the *Office Theme* option box. If it does not, click the *Office Theme* option box arrow and then click *Use system setting* at the drop-down list. If *Use system setting* is not available, click *White* at the drop-down list.
12. Close Word by clicking the Close button in the upper right corner of the screen.

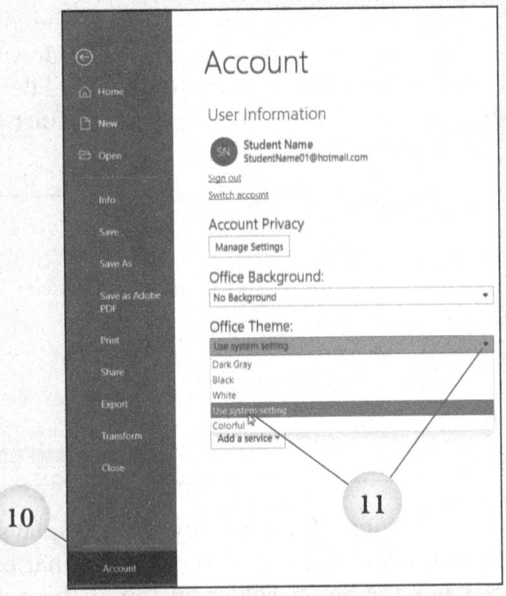

Retrieving and Copying Data Files

While working through the activities in this course, you will often be using data files as starting points. These files are provided through your Cirrus online course, and your instructor may post them in another location such as your school's network drive. You can download all the files at once (described in the activity below), or download only the files needed for a specific chapter.

Activity 2 Downloading Files to a USB Flash Drive

Note: In this activity, you will download data files from your Cirrus online course. Make sure you have an active internet connection before starting this activity. Check with your instructor if you do not have access to your Cirrus online course.

1. Insert your USB flash drive into an available USB port.
2. Navigate to the Course Resources section of your Cirrus online course. ***Note: The steps in this activity assume you are using the Chrome browser. If you are using a different browser, the following steps may vary.***
3. Read the acknowledgment statement about the use of the data files and then click the I Accept hyperlink. A zip file containing the data files will automatically begin downloading from the Cirrus website.

> If you are a PC user running Windows 11 with Microsoft 365/2021 installed on your computer and you wish to access the data files outside of the Cirrus environment, please click I Accept.
>
> 3
>
> **I Accept | Help with the Data Files**

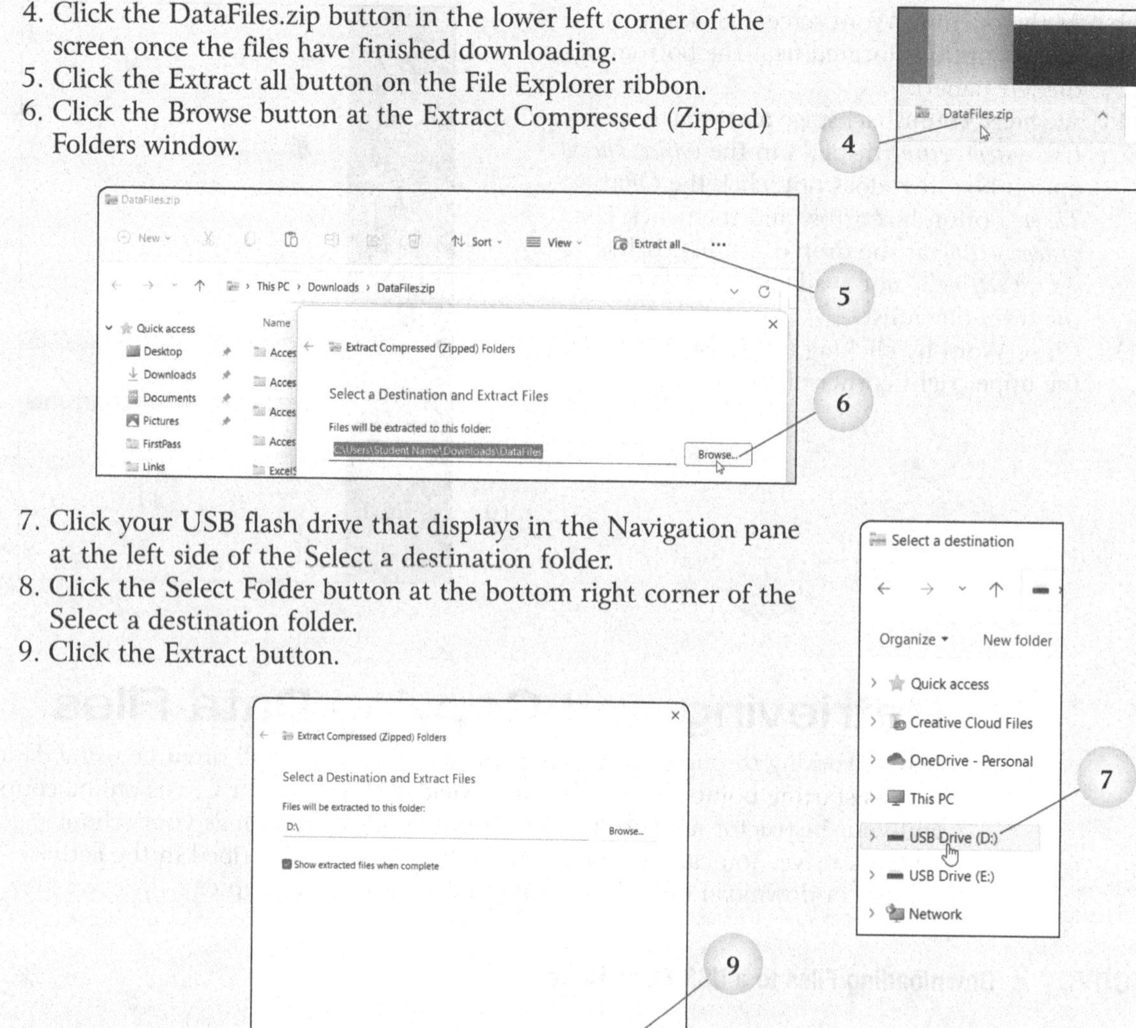

4. Click the DataFiles.zip button in the lower left corner of the screen once the files have finished downloading.
5. Click the Extract all button on the File Explorer ribbon.
6. Click the Browse button at the Extract Compressed (Zipped) Folders window.
7. Click your USB flash drive that displays in the Navigation pane at the left side of the Select a destination folder.
8. Click the Select Folder button at the bottom right corner of the Select a destination folder.
9. Click the Extract button.
10. Close the File Explorer window by clicking the Close button in the upper right corner of the window.

WORD

LEVEL 1

Unit 1

Editing and Formatting Documents

WORD

Preparing a Word Document

CHAPTER 1

Performance Objectives

Upon successful completion of Chapter 1, you will be able to:

1 Open Microsoft Word
2 Create, save, name, print, open, and close a Word document
3 Close Word
4 Open a document from and pin/unpin a document at the *Recent* Option list
5 Display, add, and remove buttons from the Quick Access Toolbar
6 Edit a document
7 Move the insertion point within a document
8 Scroll within a document
9 Select text
10 Use the Undo and Redo buttons
11 Use the Microsoft Editor to check spelling and grammar
12 Use the Microsoft Search box and the Help feature

In this chapter, you will learn to create, save, name, print, open, close, and edit a Word document as well how to use the Microsoft Editor to complete a spelling and grammar check. You will also learn about the Microsoft Search box, which provides information and guidance on how to complete a function, and the Help feature, an on-screen reference manual that provides information on features and commands for each program in the Microsoft 365 suite. Before continuing, make sure you read the *Getting Started* section presented at the beginning of this book. It contains information about computer hardware and software, using the mouse, executing commands, and managing files.

Data Files

The data files for this chapter are in the WL1C1 folder that you downloaded at the beginning of this course.

Activity 1 **Prepare a Word Document** **2 Parts**

You will create a short document containing information on resumes and then save, print, and close the document.

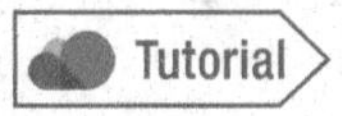

Opening a Blank Document

Opening Microsoft Word

Microsoft 365 contains a word processing program named Word that can be used to create, save, edit, and print documents. The steps to open Word may vary, but generally include clicking the Start button on the Windows desktop and then clicking the Word icon at the Start menu. At the Word opening screen, open a blank document by clicking the *Blank document* template.

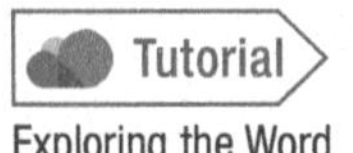

Exploring the Word Screen

Quick Steps

Open Word and Open Blank Document

1. Click Word icon at Windows Start menu.
2. Click *Blank document* template.

Creating, Saving, Printing, and Closing a Document

When the *Blank document* template is clicked, a blank document displays on the screen, as shown in Figure 1.1. The features of the document screen are described in Table 1.1.

At a blank document, type information to create a document. A document is a record containing information, such as a letter, report, term paper, or table. To create a new document, begin typing in the blank page. Some things to consider when typing text include:

- **Word wrap:** As text is typed in the document, Word wraps text to the next line, so the Enter key does not need to be pressed at the end of each line. A word is wrapped to the next line if it continues past the right margin. The only times the Enter key needs to be pressed are to end a paragraph, create a blank line, or to end a short line.
- **AutoCorrect:** Word contains a feature that automatically corrects certain words as they are typed. For example, if *adn* is typed instead of *and*, Word automatically corrects it when the spacebar is pressed after typing the word. AutoCorrect will also format as superscript the letters that follow an ordinal number (a number indicating a position in a series). For example, type *2nd* and then press the spacebar or Enter key, and Word will convert this ordinal number to 2nd.
- **Automatic spelling checker:** Word contains the Microsoft Editor that checks the spelling and grammar in a document. By default, words that are not found in the Spelling dictionary are underlined with a wavy red line. These may include misspelled words, proper names, some terminology, and some foreign words. If a typed word is not recognized by the Spelling dictionary, leave it as written if the word is spelled correctly. However, if the spelling is incorrect, retype the word or position the I-beam pointer on the word, click the right mouse button, and then click the correct spelling at the shortcut menu.
- **Automatic grammar checker:** The Editor includes an automatic grammar checker. If the grammar checker detects a sentence containing a possible grammatical error, the error will be underlined with a double blue line. The Editor will also identify text that can be refined for format writing by inserting a dotted line below the text. The sentence can be left as written or corrected. To correct the sentence, position the I-beam pointer on the error, click the right mouse button, and choose from the shortcut menu of possible corrections.

Hint The Status bar includes a book icon. A check mark on the book indicates no spelling errors have been detected by the spelling checker, while an X on the book indicates errors. Click the book icon to display the Editor task pane. If the book icon is not visible, right-click the Status bar and then click the *Spelling and Grammar Check* option at the shortcut menu.

Hint Right-click an object such as a button or icon and the shortcut menu displays with quick access or a "shortcut" to performing an action.

Figure 1.1 Blank Document

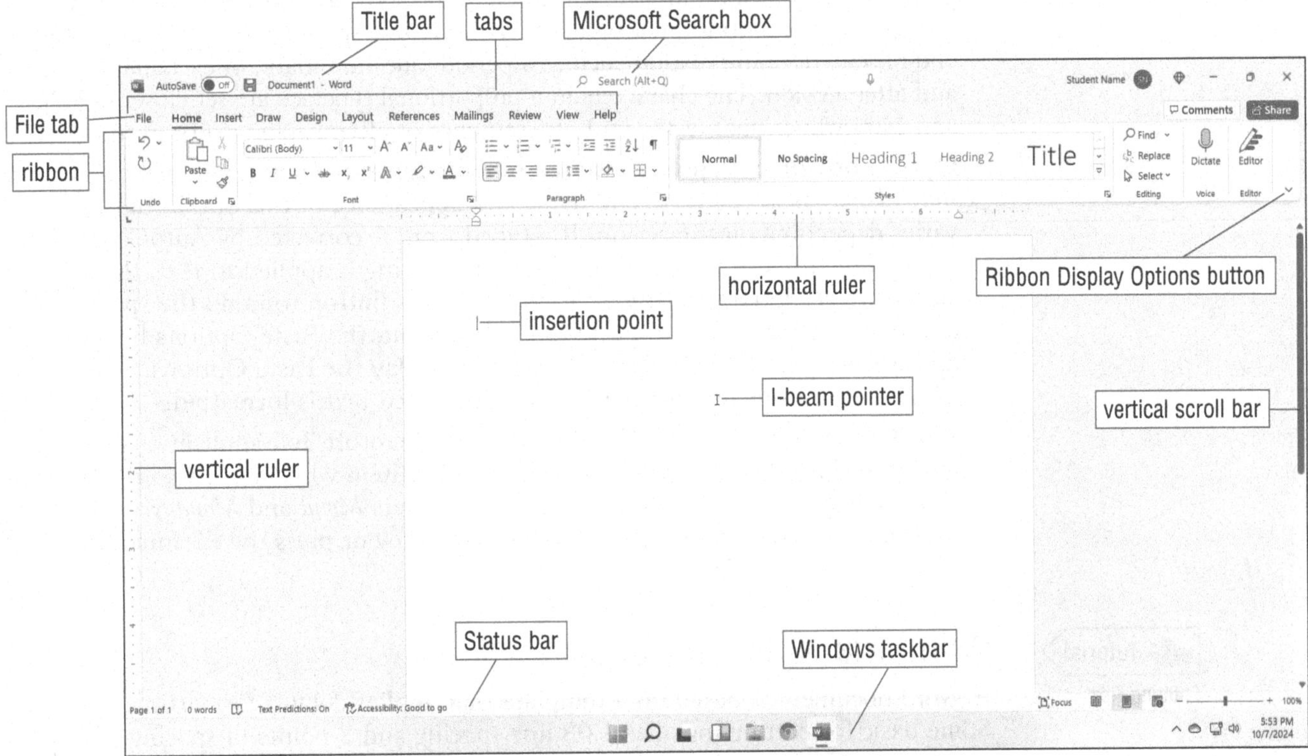

Table 1.1 Microsoft Word Screen Features

Feature	Description
File tab	when clicked, displays the backstage area, which contains options for working with and managing documents
horizontal ruler	used to set margins, indents, and tabs
I-beam pointer	used to move the insertion point or to select text
insertion point	indicates the location of the next character entered at the keyboard
Microsoft Search box	provides information on features, commands, text in a file, or information on a word or phrase
ribbon	area containing tabs with options and buttons divided into groups
Ribbon Display Options button	used to specify how much of the ribbon to display; turn off and on the Quick Access Toolbar
Status bar	displays the number of pages and words in the document, view buttons, and Zoom slider bar
tabs	contain commands and features organized into groups
Title bar	shows the document name followed by the program name
vertical ruler	used to set the top and bottom margins
vertical scroll bar	used to move the viewing area up or down through the document
Windows taskbar	contains the Start button, application icons, and a notification area

- **Spacing punctuation:** The default typeface in Word is Calibri, which is a proportional typeface. (You will learn more about typefaces in Chapter 2.) When typing text in a proportional typeface, use only one space (rather than two) after end-of-sentence punctuation such as a period, question mark, or exclamation point and after a colon. The characters in a proportional typeface are set closer together, and extra white space at the end of a sentence or after a colon is not needed.
- **Option buttons:** As text is inserted or edited in a document, an option button may display near the text. The name and appearance of this option button varies depending on the action. If a typed word is corrected by AutoCorrect, if an automatic list is created, or if autoformatting is applied to text, the AutoCorrect Options button appears. Click this button to undo the specific automatic action. If text is pasted in a document, the Paste Options button appears near the text. Click this button to display the Paste Options gallery, which has buttons for controlling how the pasted text is formatted.
- **AutoComplete:** Microsoft Word and other Microsoft 365 applications include an AutoComplete feature that inserts an entire item when a few identifying characters are typed. For example, type the letters *Mond* and *Monday* displays in a ScreenTip above the letters. Press the Enter key or press the F3 function key and Word inserts *Monday* in the document.

Entering Text

Using the New Line Command

A Word document is based on a template that applies default formatting. Some basic formatting includes 1.08 line spacing and 8 points of spacing after a paragraph. Each time the Enter key is pressed, a new paragraph begins and 8 points of spacing is inserted after the paragraph. To move the insertion point down to the next line without including the additional 8 points of spacing, use the New Line command, Shift + Enter.

Activity 1a Creating a Document

Part 1 of 2

1. Open Word by clicking the Word icon at the Windows Start menu.
2. At the Word opening screen, click the *Blank document* template. (These steps may vary. Check with your instructor for specific instructions.)
3. At a blank document, type the information shown in Figure 1.2 with the following specifications:
   a. Correct any spelling or grammatical errors identified by the Editor as they occur.
   b. Press the spacebar once after end-of-sentence punctuation.
   c. After typing *Created:* press Shift + Enter to move the insertion point to the next line without adding 8 points of additional spacing.
   d. To insert the word *Thursday* at the end of the document, type Thur and then press the F3 function key. (This is an example of the AutoComplete feature. Depending on your system, the AutoComplete feature may not function as indicated.)
   e. To insert the word *December*, type Dece and then press the Enter key. (This is another example of the AutoComplete feature.)
   f. Press Shift + Enter after typing *December 9, 2024*.
   g. When typing the last line (the line containing the ordinal numbers), type the ordinal number text and AutoCorrect will automatically convert the letters in the ordinal number to a superscript.
4. When you are finished typing the text, press the Enter key. (Keep the document open for the next activity.)

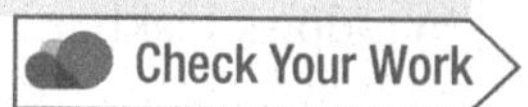

Figure 1.2 Activity 1a

> The traditional chronological resume lists your work experience in reverse-chronological order (starting with your current or most recent position). The functional style deemphasizes the "where" and "when" of your career and instead groups similar experiences, talents, and qualifications regardless of when they occurred.
>
> Like the chronological resume, the hybrid resume includes specifics about where you worked, when you worked there, and what your job titles were. Like a functional resume, a hybrid resume emphasizes your most relevant qualifications in an expanded summary section, in several "career highlights" bullet points at the top of your resume, or in activity summaries.
>
> Created:
> Thursday, December 9, 2024
> Note: The two paragraphs will become the 2nd and 3rd paragraphs in the 5th section.

Saving with a New Name

Save

Quick Steps

Save Document

1. Click File tab.
2. Click *Save As* option.
3. Click *Browse* option.
4. Type document name in *File name* text box.
5. Press Enter key.

Hint Save a document approximately every 15 minutes or when interrupted.

Saving a Document

If a document will be used in the future, it must be saved. To save a new document, click the File tab and then click the *Save* or the *Save As* option. The Save As backstage area displays, as shown in Figure 1.3. Click the *Browse* option to open the Save As dialog box, shown in Figure 1.4. (Pressing the F12 function key will also open this dialog box.) At the dialog box, navigate to the location where the file is to be saved, type a file name, and then press the Enter key or click the Save button. Continue saving periodically whenever edits are made by clicking the Save button on the Title bar or with the keyboard shortcut Ctrl + S.

To save a new version of a document while keeping the original, click the File tab and then click the *Save As* option to display the Save As backstage area. (Do not click *Save*, or changes will be saved to the existing file.) At the Save As backstage area, click the *Browse* option to display the Save As dialog box. Type a new name for the document, select a location where the document is to be saved, and then press the Enter key or click the Save button.

Figure 1.3 Save As Backstage Area

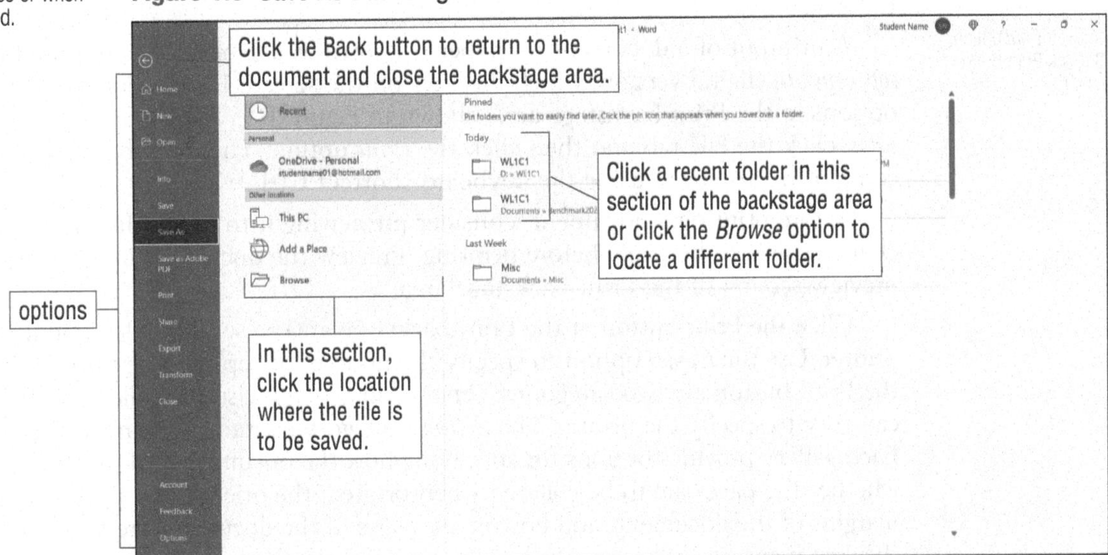

Figure 1.4 Save As Dialog Box

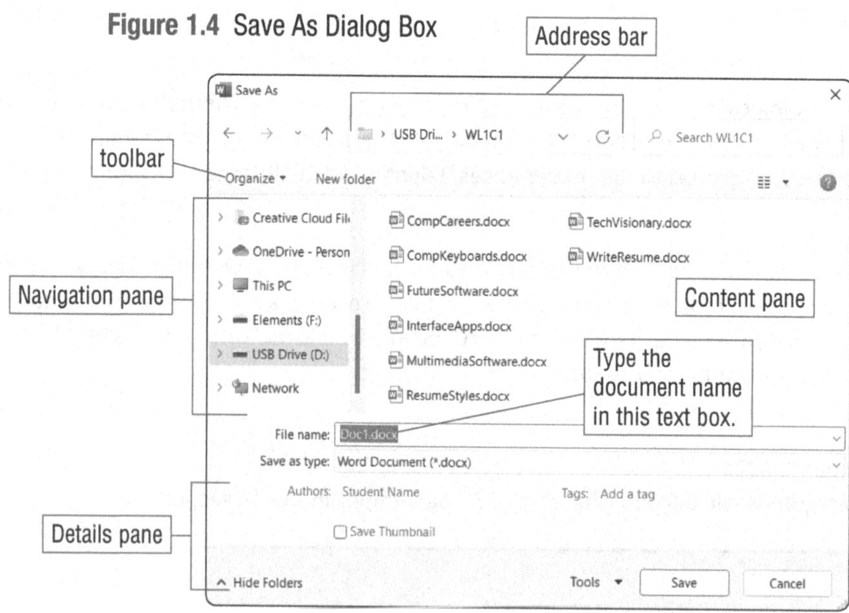

Naming a Document

Hint Word will not allow you to save two documents with the same name in the same folder. This is true even if you make one name uppercase and one lowercase.

Document names created in Word and other applications in the Microsoft 365 suite can be up to 255 characters in length, including the drive letter and any folder names, and they may include spaces. File names cannot include any of the following characters:

forward slash (/)	less-than symbol (<)	quotation marks (" ")
backslash (\)	asterisk (*)	colon (:)
greater-than symbol (>)	question mark (?)	pipe symbol (|)

Tutorial

Printing a Document

Quick Steps

Print Document

1. Click File tab.
2. Click *Print* option.
3. Click Print button.

Printing a Document

Click the File tab and the backstage area displays. The buttons and options at the backstage area change depending on the option selected at the left side of the backstage area. To leave the backstage area without completing an action, click the Back button in the upper left corner of the backstage area, or press the Esc key on the keyboard.

A printout of a document on paper is known as a *hard copy*, as opposed to the *soft copy*, or digital version, which displays on the screen. Print a document with options at the Print backstage area, shown in Figure 1.5. To display this backstage area, click the File tab and then click the *Print* option. The Print backstage area can also be displayed using the keyboard shortcut Ctrl + P.

Before printing a document, consider previewing it to determine if any changes need to be made before printing. Preview the document in the print preview section of the Print backstage area.

Click the Print button at the Print backstage area to send the document to the printer. Use the *Copies* option to specify the number of copies to be printed. Below the Print button are two categories: *Printer* and *Settings*. Use the gallery in the *Printer* category to specify the printer. The *Settings* category contains a number of galleries. Each gallery provides options for specifying how the document will print, including whether the pages are to be collated when printed; the orientation, page size, and margins of the document; and how many pages of the document are to print on a sheet of paper.

Figure 1.5 Print Backstage Area

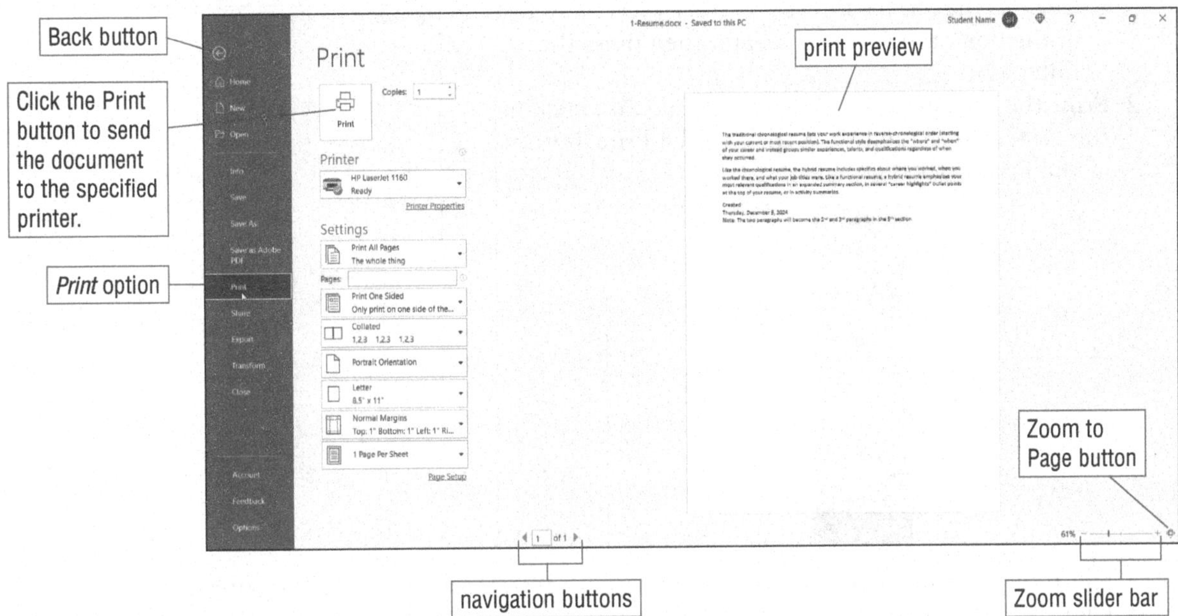

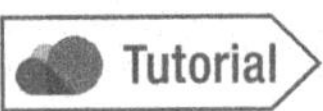

Closing a Document and Closing Word

Quick Steps

Close Document
1. Click File tab.
2. Click *Close* option.

Close Word
Click the Close button.

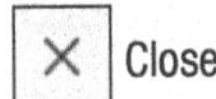

Closing a Document and Closing Word

When a document is saved, it is saved to the specified location and also remains on the screen. To remove the document from the screen, click the File tab and then click the *Close* option or use the keyboard shortcut Ctrl + F4. When a document is closed, it is removed and a blank screen displays. At this screen, open a previously saved document, create a new document, or close Word. To close Word, click the Close button in the upper right corner of the screen. The keyboard shortcut Alt + F4 also closes Word.

Activity 1b Saving, Printing, and Closing a Document and Closing Word — Part 2 of 2

1. Save the document you created for Activity 1a and name it **1-Resume** (*1-* for Chapter 1 and *Resume* because the document is about resumes) by completing the following steps:
   a. Click the File tab.

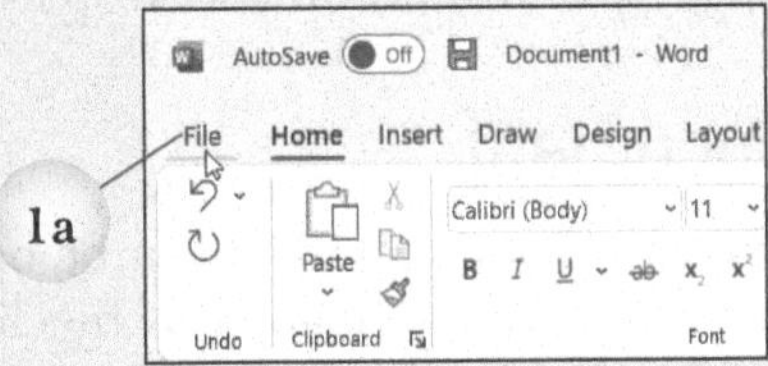

   b. Click the *Save As* option.
   c. At the Save As backstage area, click the *Browse* option.
   d. At the Save As dialog box, if necessary, navigate to the WL1C1 folder on your storage medium.

e. Click in the *File name* text box (this selects any text in the box), type 1-Resume, and then press the Enter key.

2. Print the document by clicking the File tab, clicking the *Print* option, and then clicking the Print button at the Print backstage area.

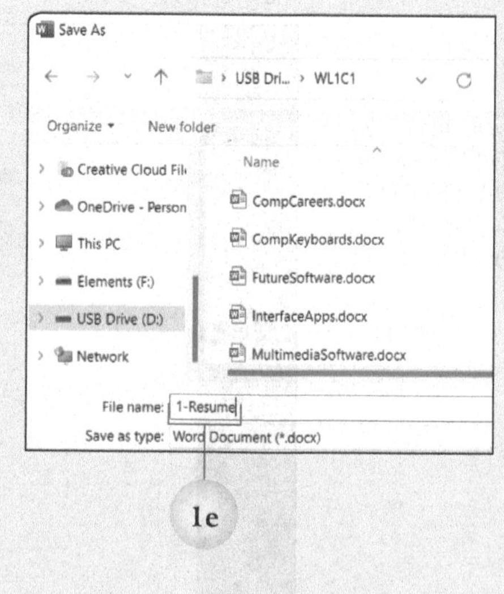

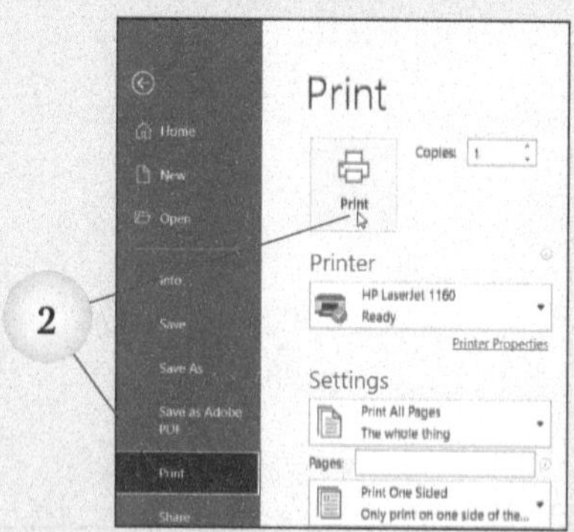

3. Close the document by clicking the File tab and then clicking the *Close* option.
4. Close Word by clicking the Close button in the upper right corner of the screen.

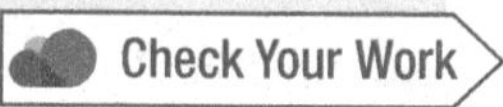

Activity 2 Save a Document with a New Name and the Same Name 2 Parts

You will open a document in the WL1C1 folder on your storage medium, save the document with a new name, add text, and then save the document with the same name. You will also display and add buttons to the Quick Access Toolbar, and then print and close the document.

Creating a New Document

Quick Steps

Create New Document
1. Click File tab.
2. Click *Blank document* template.

When a document is closed, a blank screen displays. To create a new document, click the File tab, click the *New* option, and then click the *Blank document* template. A new document can also be opened with the keyboard shortcut Ctrl + N. Additional templates can be found by clicking the File tab and then clicking the *Home* or *New* option. Double-click the *Single spaced (blank)* template to open a new document with single spacing and no added space after paragraphs.

Opening a Document

Opening a Document at the Open Dialog Box

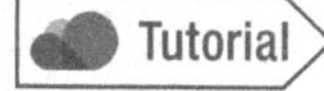

Opening a Document from a Removable Disk

After a document is saved and closed, it can be opened at the Open dialog box, shown in Figure 1.6. Display the dialog box by clicking the File tab, clicking the *Open* option, and then clicking the *Browse* option at the backstage area. Other methods for displaying the Open backstage area include using the keyboard shortcut Ctrl + O and clicking the More documents hyperlink in the lower right corner of the Word opening screen and the Home backstage area.

Figure 1.6 Open Dialog Box

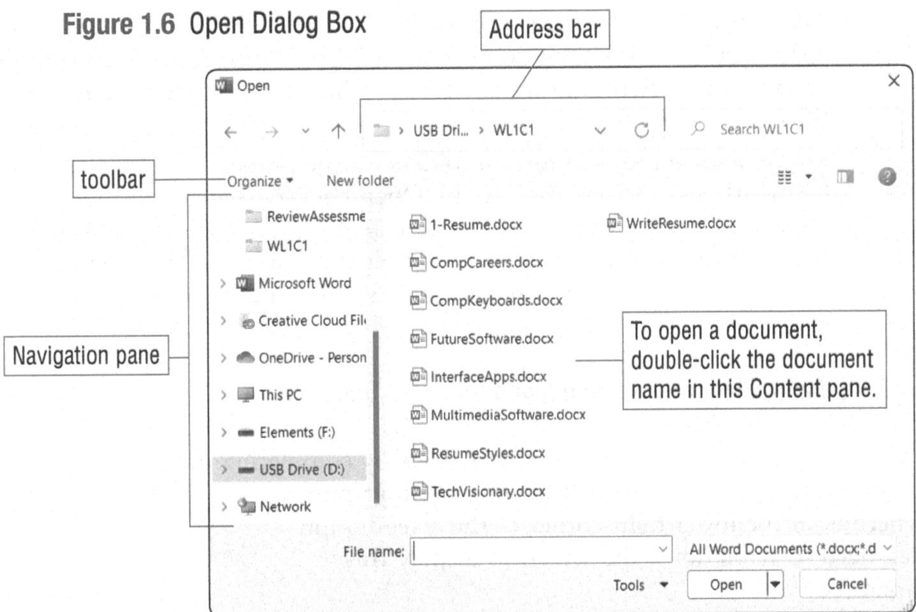

Quick Steps

Open Document

1. Click File tab.
2. Click *Open* option.
3. Click *Browse* option.
4. Double-click document name.

At the Open backstage area, click the *Browse* option and the Open dialog box displays. Go directly to the Open dialog box without displaying the Open backstage area by pressing Ctrl + F12. At the Open dialog box, navigate to the desired location (such as the drive containing your storage medium), open the folder containing the document, and then double-click the document name in the Content pane.

Opening a Document from the *Recent* Option List

Opening a Document from the *Recent* Option List

At the Open backstage area with the *Recent* option selected, the names of the most recently opened documents are listed. By default, Word lists the names of the 50 most recently opened documents and groups them into categories such as *Today*, *Yesterday*, and perhaps another category such as *This Week*. To open a document from the *Recent* option list, scroll down the list and then click the document name. The Word opening screen and the Home backstage area also provide a list of the names of the most recently opened documents. Click a document name in the Recent list to open the document.

Pinning and Unpinning a Document at the *Recent* Option List

Pinning and Unpinning Documents and Folders

If a document is opened on a regular basis, consider pinning it so it can be found more easily. At the Open backstage area, hover the pointer over the document name in the *Recent* option list and then click the pin icon that appears. The document will now appear at the top of the list in the *Pinned* category. A document can also be pinned at the Home backstage area. Click the pin icon next to a document name, and the document will display in the *Pinned* tab. More than one document can be pinned to a list.

To unpin a document from the *Recent* option list at the Open backstage area or the Pinned list at the Home backstage area, click the pin icon to the right of the document name (the pin displays with a circle containing a slash).

Another method for pinning and unpinning documents is to use the shortcut menu. Right-click a document name and then click the *Pin to list* or *Unpin from list* option. The shortcut menu also includes the *Remove from list* option, which removes a document from the *Recent* option list and the Recent list. Right-click a pinned document in the *Recent* option list at the Open backstage area and the shortcut menu includes the option *Clear unpinned items*, which removes all unpinned documents from the *Recent* option list.

In addition to documents, folders can be pinned for easier access. To pin a frequently used folder, display the Open backstage area and then click the *Folders* option. Recently opened folders are listed and grouped into categories such as *Today*, *Yesterday*, and *Last Week* to reflect the time they were last accessed. Click the pin icon to the right of a folder and it will be pinned to the top of the list.

Activity 2a Opening, Pinning, Unpinning, and Saving a Document

Part 1 of 2

1. Open Word and then open **CompCareers.docx** by completing the following steps:
   a. At the Word opening screen, click the More documents hyperlink in the lower right corner of the screen. (You may need to scroll down the screen to display this hyperlink.)
   b. At the Open backstage area, click the *Browse* option.
   c. At the Open dialog box, navigate to the external drive containing your storage medium.
   d. Double-click the ***WL1C1*** folder in the Content pane.
   e. Double-click ***CompCareers.docx*** in the Content pane.
2. Close **CompCareers.docx**.
3. Press Ctrl + F12 to display the Open dialog box and then double-click ***FutureSoftware.docx*** in the Content pane to open the document.
4. Close **FutureSoftware.docx**.
5. Pin **CompCareers.docx** to the *Recent* option list by completing the following steps:
   a. Click the File tab and then click the *Open* option.
   b. At the Open backstage area, hover the pointer over **CompCareers.docx** in the *Recent* option list and then click the pin icon to the right of the document. (The **CompCareers.docx** file will now appear in the *Pinned* category at the top of the list.)

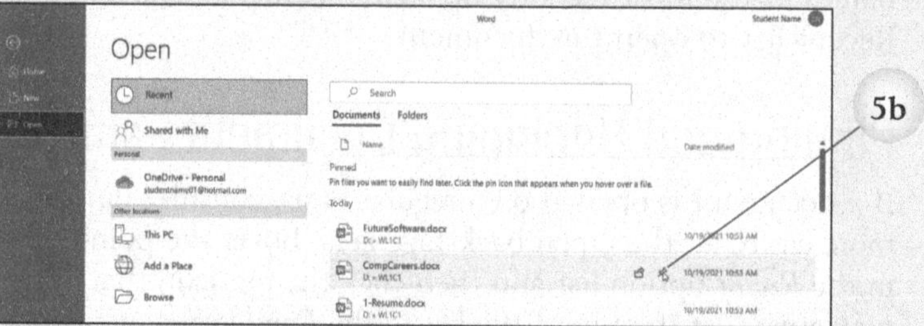

6. Click **CompCareers.docx** in the *Pinned* category at the top of the *Recent* option list to open the document.
7. Unpin **CompCareers.docx** from the *Recent* option list by completing the following steps:
   a. Click the File tab and then click the *Open* option.
   b. At the Open backstage area, hover the pointer over the **CompCareers.docx** document in the *Pinned* category in the *Recent* option list and then click the pin (displays with a circle containing a slash). (This removes the file from the *Pinned* category.)
   c. Click the Back button to return to the document.

8. With **CompCareers.docx** open, save the document with a new name by completing the following steps:
   a. Click the File tab and then click the *Save As* option.
   b. At the Save As backstage area, click the *Browse* option.
   c. At the Save As dialog box, if necessary, navigate to the WL1C1 folder on your storage medium.
   d. Press the Home key on your keyboard to move the insertion point to the beginning of the file name and then type 1-.
   e. Press the Enter key.

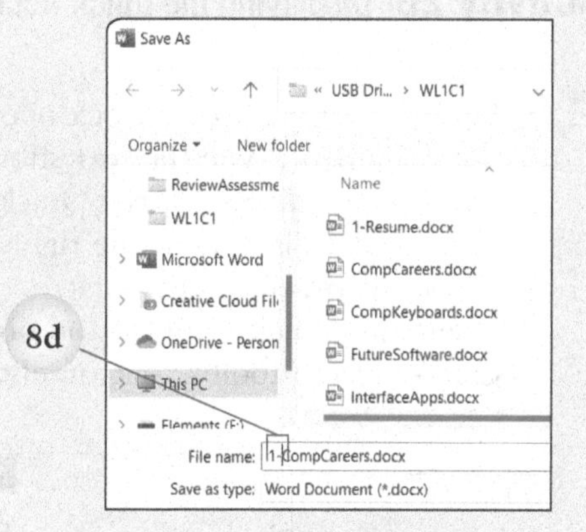

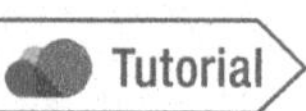

Saving with the Same Name

Quick Steps

Save Document with Same Name

Click Save button on Title bar.

OR

1. Click File tab.
2. Click *Save* option.

OR

Press Ctrl + S.

Saving Changes to a Document

After making changes to a document, save the changes before closing the file. Consider saving on a periodic basis to ensure that no changes are lost if the application crashes or freezes or if power is interrupted. Unless keeping an older version of the document is important, changes can be saved using the same file name. Save a document with the same name using the Save button on the Title bar, the *Save* option at the backstage area, or with the keyboard shortcut Ctrl + S.

Note: If a document is stored in a cloud location such as Microsoft OneDrive or SharePoint Online, any changes to it will be saved automatically with the AutoSave feature. AutoSave can be turned on or off by clicking the toggle switch in the upper left corner of the Word screen.

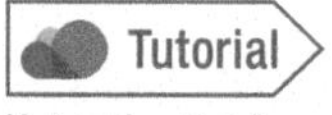

Using the Quick Access Toolbar

Quick Steps

Displaying the Quick Access Toolbar

1. Click Ribbon Display Options button.
2. Click *Show Quick Access Toolbar*.

Using the Quick Access Toolbar

The Quick Access Toolbar is a customizable toolbar that provides easy access to common functions such as opening, saving, and printing a document. Turn on the display of the Quick Access Toolbar by clicking the Ribbon Display Options button at the right side of the ribbon (displays with a down-pointing arrow) and then clicking *Show Quick Access Toolbar* at the drop-down list.

To insert a button on the Quick Access Toolbar, click the Customize Quick Access Toolbar button at the right side of the toolbar and then click the specific button name at the drop-down list. A button can also be inserted on the Quick Access Toolbar by right-clicking the button and then clicking *Add to Quick Access Toolbar* at the shortcut menu that displays. (Right-clicking a button displays the shortcut menu with options for performing an action.) To remove a button from the toolbar, right-click the button and then click *Remove from Quick Access Toolbar* at the shortcut menu.

Specify whether the toolbar displays above or below the ribbon with options at the Customize Quick Access Toolbar button drop-down list. Turn off the display of the Quick Access Toolbar by clicking the Ribbon Display Options button and then clicking *Hide Quick Access Toolbar* at the drop-down list.

Activity 2b Displaying the Quick Access Toolbar; Saving a Document with Same Name Part 2 of 2

1. With **1-CompCareers.docx** open and the insertion point positioned at the beginning of the document, type the text shown in Figure 1.7.
2. Turn on the display of the Quick Access Toolbar by clicking the Ribbon Display Options button that displays at the right side of the ribbon and then clicking *Show Quick Access Toolbar* at the drop-down list.
3. Insert the Quick Print button on the Quick Access Toolbar by clicking the Customize Quick Access Toolbar button and then clicking *Quick Print* at the drop-down list.

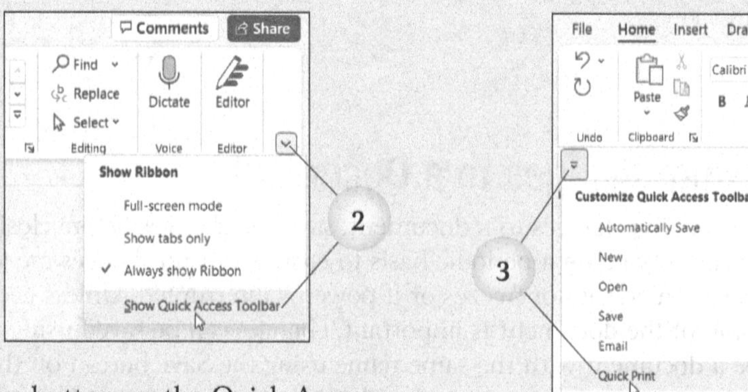

4. Insert the Save button on the Quick Access Toolbar by clicking the Customize Quick Access Toolbar button and then clicking *Save* at the drop-down list.
5. Save the changes you made in Step 1 by clicking the Save button on the Quick Access Toolbar.

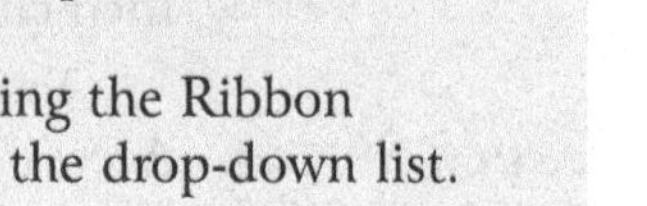

6. Print the document by clicking the Quick Print button on the Quick Access Toolbar.
7. Move the Quick Access Toolbar above the ribbon by clicking the Customize Quick Access Toolbar button and then clicking *Show Above the Ribbon* at the drop-down list.
8. Move the Quick Access Toolbar back below the ribbon by clicking the Customize Quick Access Toolbar button and then clicking *Show Below the Ribbon* at the drop-down list.
9. Close the document by pressing Ctrl + F4.
10. If necessary, turn off the display of the Quick Access Toolbar by clicking the Ribbon Display Options button and then clicking *Hide Quick Access Toolbar* at the drop-down list.

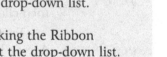

Check Your Work

Figure 1.7 Activity 2b

> The majority of new jobs being created in the United States today involve daily work with computers. Computer-related careers include technical support jobs, sales and training, programming and applications development, network and database administration, and computer engineering.

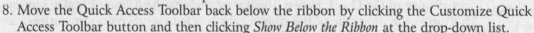

Activity 3 Scroll and Browse in a Document — 2 Parts

You will open a previously created document, save it with a new name, and then use scrolling and browsing techniques to move the insertion point to specific locations in the document.

Scrolling

Editing a Document

When a document is being edited, text may need to be inserted or deleted. To edit a document, use the mouse, the keyboard, or a combination of the two to move the insertion point to specific locations in the document. To move the insertion point using the mouse, position the I-beam pointer where the insertion point is to be positioned and then click the left mouse button.

Scrolling in a document changes the text display, but does not move the insertion point. Use the mouse with the vertical scroll bar, at the right side of the screen, to scroll through text in a document. Click the up scroll arrow at the top of the vertical scroll bar to scroll up through the document, and click the down scroll arrow to scroll down through the document.

The scroll bar contains a scroll box that indicates the location of the text in the document screen in relation to the remainder of the document. To scroll up one screen at a time, position the pointer above the scroll box (but below the up scroll arrow) and then click the left mouse button. Position the pointer below the scroll box and click the left button to scroll down a screen. Click and hold down the left mouse button and the action becomes continuous.

Another method for scrolling is to position the pointer on the scroll box, click and hold down the left mouse button, and then drag the scroll box along the scroll bar to reposition text in the document screen. As the scroll box is dragged along the vertical scroll bar in a longer document, page numbers are shown in a box at the right side of the document screen.

Activity 3a Scrolling in a Document — Part 1 of 2

1. Open **InterfaceApps.docx** (from the WL1C1 folder you copied to your storage medium).
2. Save the document with the new name **1-InterfaceApps** to your WL1C1 folder.
3. Position the I-beam pointer at the beginning of the first paragraph and then click the left mouse button.
4. Click the down scroll arrow on the vertical scroll bar several times. (This scrolls down lines of text in the document.) With the pointer on the down scroll arrow, click and hold down the left mouse button and keep it down until you reach the end of the document.
5. Position the pointer on the up scroll arrow and then click and hold down the left mouse button until you reach the beginning of the document.
6. Position the pointer below the scroll box and then click the left mouse button. Continue clicking the mouse button (with the pointer positioned below the scroll box) until you reach the end of the document.
7. Position the pointer on the scroll box in the vertical scroll bar. Click and hold down the left mouse button, drag the scroll box to the top of the vertical scroll bar, and then release the mouse button. (Notice that the document page numbers are shown in a box at the right side of the document screen.)
8. Click in the title at the beginning of the document. (This moves the insertion point to the location of the pointer.)

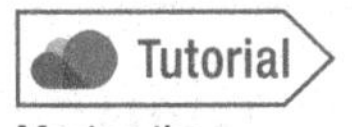

Moving the Insertion Point Using the Go To Feature

Hint Press Ctrl + G to display the Find and Replace dialog box with the Go To tab selected.

Moving the Insertion Point to a Specific Line or Page

Word includes a Go To feature that moves the insertion point to a specific location in a document, such as a line or page. To use the feature, click the Find button arrow in the Editing group on the Home tab and then click *Go To* at the drop-down list. At the Find and Replace dialog box with the Go To tab selected, move the insertion point to a specific page by typing the page number in the *Enter page number* text box and then pressing the Enter key. Move to a specific line by clicking the *Line* option in the *Go to what* list box, typing the line number in the *Enter line number* text box, and then pressing the Enter key. Click the Close button to close the dialog box.

Moving the Insertion Point and Inserting and Deleting Text

Moving the Insertion Point with the Keyboard

To move the insertion point with the keyboard, use the arrow keys to the right of the regular keyboard or use the arrow keys on the numeric keypad. When using the arrow keys on the numeric keypad, make sure Num Lock is off. Use the arrow keys together with other keys to move the insertion point to various locations in the document, as shown in Table 1.2.

When moving the insertion point, Word considers a word to be any series of characters between spaces. A paragraph is any text that is followed by a single press of the Enter key. A page is text that is separated by a soft or hard page break.

Table 1.2 Insertion Point Movement Commands

To move insertion point	Press
one character left	Left Arrow
one character right	Right Arrow
one line up	Up Arrow
one line down	Down Arrow
one word left	Ctrl + Left Arrow
one word right	Ctrl + Right Arrow
to beginning of line	Home
to end of line	End
to beginning of current paragraph	Ctrl + Up Arrow
to beginning of next paragraph	Ctrl + Down Arrow
up one screen	Page Up
down one screen	Page Down
to top of previous page	Ctrl + Page Up
to top of next page	Ctrl + Page Down
to beginning of document	Ctrl + Home
to end of document	Ctrl + End

Resuming Reading or Editing in a Document

If a previously saved document is opened, pressing Shift + F5 will move the insertion point to the position it was last located when the document was closed.

When a multiple-page document is reopened, Word remembers the page where the insertion point was last positioned. A "Welcome back!" message appears at the right side of the screen near the vertical scroll bar, identifying the page where the insertion point was last located. Click the message and the insertion point is positioned at the top of that page.

Activity 3b Moving the Insertion Point in a Document — Part 2 of 2

1. With **1-InterfaceApps.docx** open, move the insertion point to line 15 and then to page 3 by completing the following steps:
   a. Click the Find button arrow in the Editing group on the Home tab and then click *Go To* at the drop-down list.
   b. At the Find and Replace dialog box with the Go To tab selected, click *Line* in the *Go to what* list box.
   c. Click in the *Enter line number* text box, type 15, and then press the Enter key.
   d. Click *Page* in the *Go to what* list box.
   e. Click in the *Enter page number* text box, type 3, and then press the Enter key.
   f. Click the Close button to close the Find and Replace dialog box.

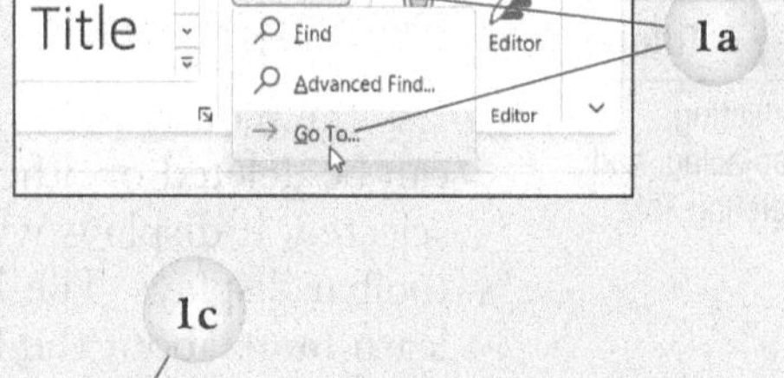

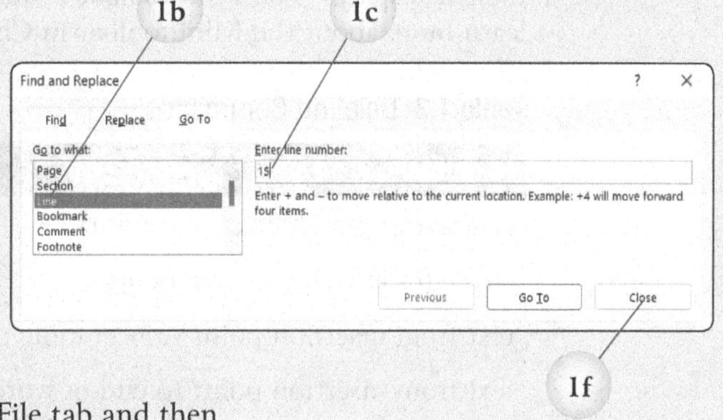

2. Close the document.
3. Open the document by clicking the File tab and then clicking the document name ***1-InterfaceApps.docx*** in the Recent list.
4. Move the pointer to the right side of the screen to display the "Welcome back!" message. Hover the pointer over the message and then click the left mouse button. (This positions the insertion point at the top of the third page—the page the insertion point was positioned when you closed the document.)

5. Press Ctrl + Home to move the insertion point to the beginning of the document.
6. Practice using the keyboard commands shown in Table 1.2 to move the insertion point within the document.
7. Preview the document at the Print backstage area by clicking the File tab and then clicking the *Print* option. At the Print backstage area, view the document at the right side of the screen and then click the Back button (displays with a left-pointing arrow) in the upper left corner of the backstage area to return to the document.
8. Close **1-InterfaceApps.docx**.

Activity 4 Insert and Delete Text — 2 Parts

You will open a previously created document, save it with a new name, and then make editing changes to the document. The editing changes include selecting, inserting, and deleting text and undoing and redoing edits.

Inserting and Deleting Text

Editing a document may include inserting and/or deleting text. To insert text in a document, position the insertion point at the location text is to be typed and then type the text. Existing characters move to the right as text is typed. A number of options are available for deleting text. Some deletion commands are shown in Table 1.3.

Selecting, Replacing, and Deleting Text

Selecting Text

Use the mouse and/or keyboard to select a specific amount of text. Selected text can be deleted or other Word functions can be performed on it. When text is selected, it displays with a gray background, as shown in Figure 1.8, and the Mini toolbar displays. The Mini toolbar contains buttons for common tasks. (You will learn more about the Mini toolbar in Chapter 2.)

Table 1.3 Deletion Commands

To delete	Press
character right of insertion point	Delete key
character left of insertion point	Backspace key
text from insertion point to beginning of word	Ctrl + Backspace
text from insertion point to end of word	Ctrl + Delete

Figure 1.8 Selected Text and Mini Toolbar

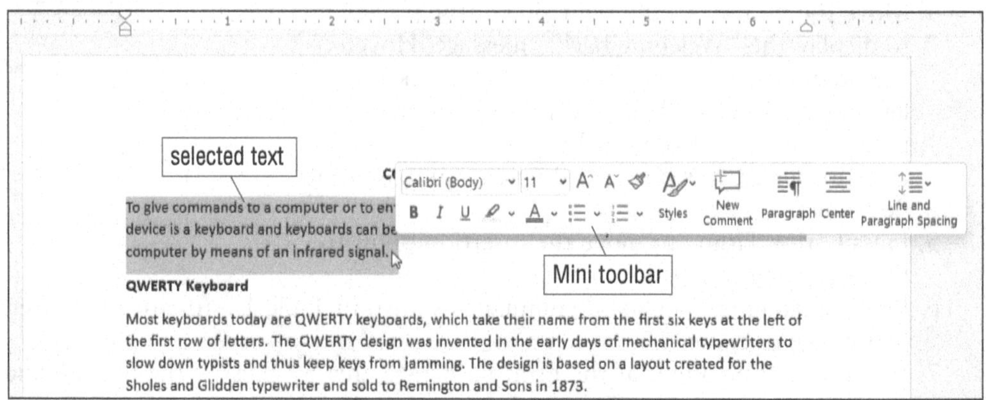

Hint If text is selected, any character you type replaces the selected text.

Selecting Text with the Mouse Use the mouse to select a word, line, sentence, paragraph, or entire document. Table 1.4 indicates the steps to follow to select various amounts of text.

One way to select text is by clicking in the selection bar. The selection bar is the space at the left side of the document screen between the left edge of the page and the text. When the pointer is positioned in the selection bar, the pointer turns into an arrow pointing up and to the right (instead of to the left). Click once to select a line of text, twice to select a paragraph, and three times to select all the text in the document.

Another way to select text is by using the I-beam pointer. Position the pointer on the first character of the text to be selected, click and hold down the left mouse button, drag the I-beam pointer to the last character of the text to be selected, and then release the mouse button. Alternately, position the insertion point where the selection is to begin, press and hold down the Shift key, click the I-beam pointer at the end of the selection, and then release the Shift key. To cancel a selection, simply click in the document screen.

Hint Hold down the Alt key while dragging with the mouse to select text vertically.

Select text vertically in a document by pressing and holding down the Alt key while dragging with the mouse. This is especially useful when selecting a group of text, such as text set in columns.

Selecting Text with the Keyboard To select text using the keyboard, turn on the Selection mode by pressing the F8 function key. With the Selection mode activated, use the arrow keys to select text. To cancel the selection, press the Esc key and then press any arrow key. The Status bar can be customized to indicate that the Selection mode is activated. To do this, right-click on the Status bar and then click *Selection Mode* at the pop-up list. When the F8 function key is pressed to turn on the Selection mode, the words *Extend Selection* display on the Status bar. Text can also be selected with the commands shown in Table 1.5.

Table 1.4 Selecting Text with the Mouse

To select	Complete these steps using the mouse
a word	Double-click the word.
a line of text	Click in the selection bar to the left of the line.
multiple lines of text	Drag in the selection bar to the left of the lines.
a sentence	Press and hold down the Ctrl key and then click in the sentence.
a paragraph	Double-click in the selection bar next to the paragraph, or triple-click in the paragraph.
multiple paragraphs	Drag in the selection bar.
an entire document	Triple-click in the selection bar, or click the Select button in Editing group and then click *Select All*.

Table 1.5 Selecting Text with the Keyboard

To select	Press
one character to right	Shift + Right Arrow
one character to left	Shift + Left Arrow
to end of word	Ctrl + Shift + Right Arrow
to beginning of word	Ctrl + Shift + Left Arrow
to end of line	Shift + End
to beginning of line	Shift + Home
one line up	Shift + Up Arrow
one line down	Shift + Down Arrow
to beginning of paragraph	Ctrl + Shift + Up Arrow
to end of paragraph	Ctrl + Shift + Down Arrow
one screen up	Shift + Page Up
one screen down	Shift + Page Down
to end of document	Ctrl + Shift + End
to beginning of document	Ctrl + Shift + Home
entire document	Ctrl + A

Activity 4a Editing a Document

Part 1 of 2

1. Open **CompKeyboards.docx**. (This document is in the WL1C1 folder you copied to your storage medium.)
2. Save the document with the new name **1-CompKeyboards**.
3. Change the word *give* in the first sentence of the first paragraph to *enter* by double-clicking *give* and then typing enter.
4. Change the second *to* in the first sentence to *into* by double-clicking *to* and then typing into.
5. Select the words *means of* in the last sentence in the first paragraph and then press the Delete key to delete the selected text.

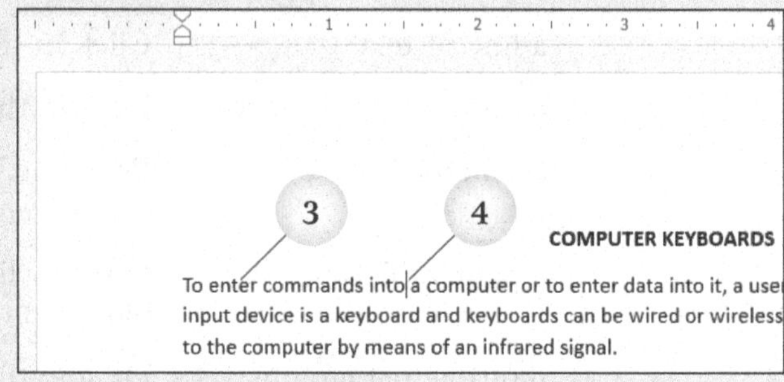

6. Select and then delete the last sentence in the *QWERTY Keyboard* section by completing the following steps:
   a. Position the I-beam pointer anywhere in the last sentence in the *QWERTY Keyboard* section.
   b. Press and hold down the Ctrl key, click the left mouse button, and then release the Ctrl key.
   c. Press the Delete key.

7. Delete the heading *QWERTY Keyboard* using the Selection mode by completing the following steps:
   a. Position the insertion point immediately left of the *Q* in *QWERTY*.
   b. Press the F8 function key to turn on the Selection mode.
   c. Press the Down Arrow key.
   d. Press the Delete key.
8. Complete steps similar to those in Step 7 to delete the heading *DVORAK Keyboard*.
9. Begin a new paragraph with the sentence that reads *Keyboards have different physical appearances* by completing the following steps:
   a. Position the insertion point immediately left of the *K* in *Keyboards* (the first word of the fifth sentence in the last paragraph).
   b. Press the Enter key.
10. Save **1-CompKeyboards.docx**.

7a-
7c

To enter commands into a computer o
input device is a keyboard and keyboar
to the computer by an infrared signal.

QWERTY Keyboard

Most keyboards today are QWERTY ke
the first row of letters. The QWERTY de
slow down typists and thus keep keys f

DVORAK Keyboard

9a-
9b

To enter commands into a computer
input device is a keyboard and keybo
to the computer by an infrared signa

Most keyboards today are QWERTY k
the first row of letters. The QWERTY
slow down typists and thus keep key

The DVORAK keyboard is an alternat
commonly used keys are placed clos
install software on a QWERTY keybo
keyboards is convenient especially w

Keyboards have different physical ap
that of a calculator, containing numb
"broken" into two pieces to reduce s
change the symbol or character ente

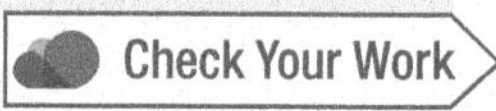

Using the Undo and Redo Buttons

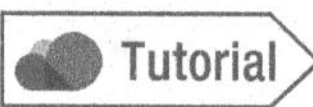

Using Undo and Redo

Undo

Redo

Hint You cannot undo a save.

Hint Use the keyboard shortcut Ctrl + Z to undo an action.

Hint Use the keyboard shortcut Ctrl + Y to redo an action.

Undo typing, formatting, or another action by clicking the Undo button in the Undo group on the Home tab. For example, type text and then click the Undo button and the text is removed. Or apply formatting to text and then click the Undo button and the formatting is removed.

Click the Redo button in the Undo group on the Home tab to reverse the original action. For example, apply formatting such as underlining to text and then click the Undo button and the underlining is removed. Click the Redo button and the underlining formatting is reapplied to the text. Many Word actions can be undone or redone. Some actions, however, such as printing and saving, cannot be undone or redone.

Word maintains actions in temporary memory. To undo an action performed earlier, click the Undo button arrow. This causes a drop-down list to display. To make a selection from this drop-down list, click the desired action; the action, along with any actions listed above it in the drop-down list, is undone.

Activity 4b Undoing and Redoing Deletions

Part 2 of 2

1. With **1-CompKeyboards.docx** open, delete the last sentence in the last paragraph using the mouse by completing the following steps:
   a. Position the I-beam pointer anywhere in the sentence that begins *All keyboards have modifier keys*.
   b. Press and hold down the Ctrl key, click the left mouse button, and then release the Ctrl key.

install software on a QWERTY keyboard that emulates a DVORAK keyboard. The ability to emulate other keyboards is convenient especially when working with foreign languages.

Keyboards have different physical appearances. Many keyboards have a separate numeric keypad, like that of a calculator, containing numbers and mathematical operators. Some keyboards are sloped and "broken" into two pieces to reduce strain. All keyboards have modifier keys that enable the user to change the symbol or character entered when a given key is pressed.

1a-1b

   c. Press the Delete key.
2. Delete the last paragraph by completing the following steps:
   a. Position the I-beam pointer anywhere in the last paragraph (the paragraph that begins *Keyboards have different physical appearances*).
   b. Triple-click the left mouse button.
   c. Press the Delete key.
3. Undo the deletion by clicking the Undo button in the Undo group on the Home tab.

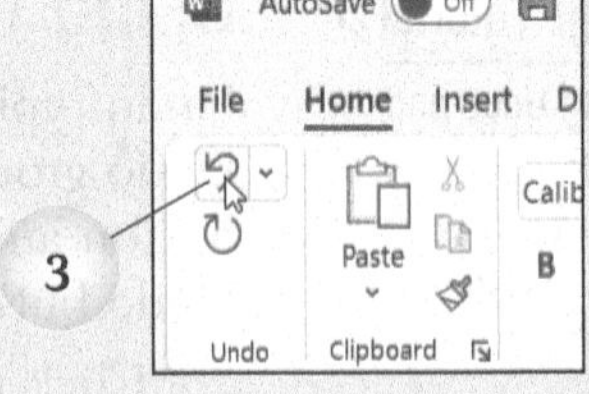

4. Redo the deletion by clicking the Redo button in the Undo group on the Home tab.
5. Select the first sentence in the second paragraph and then delete it.
6. Select the first paragraph in the document and then delete it.
7. Undo the two deletions by completing the following steps:
   a. Click the Undo button arrow.
   b. Click the second *Clear* listed in the drop-down list. (This will redisplay the first paragraph and the first sentence in the second paragraph. The sentence will be selected.)

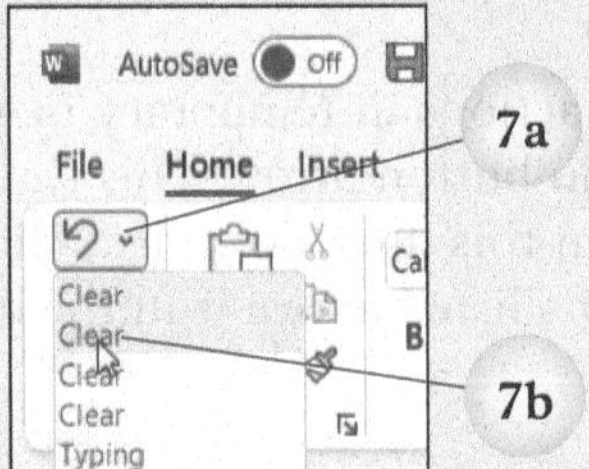

8. Click outside the sentence to deselect it.
9. Save, preview, and then close **1-CompKeyboards.docx**.

Check Your Work

Activity 5 Complete a Spelling and Grammar Check **1 Part**

You will open a previously created document, save it with a new name, and then use the Editor to check the spelling and grammar in the document.

Using the Editor to Check Spelling and Grammar

Quick Steps

Check Spelling and Grammar

1. Click Editor button.
2. Click Editor Score box.
3. Change or ignore errors.
4. Click OK.
5. Click Close button.

Hint Press the F7 function key to display the Editor task pane.

Using the Editor to Check Spelling and Grammar in a Document

Thoughtful and well-written documents are free of errors in spelling and grammar. The Microsoft Editor is a service available in Word that checks a document for spelling and grammar errors and offers suggested corrections. It may also suggest refinements for clarity and conciseness in the writing.

The Editor can find and offer corrections for misspelled words, duplicate words, and irregular capitalizations. To check spelling, it compares the words in the document with the words in its dictionary. If it finds a match, it passes over the word. If the word is not found in its dictionary, it offers possible corrections. Editor will also check a document for grammar issues, such as incorrect use of words, and offer refinement suggestions to improve the writing in the document, such as clarity, conciseness, formality, and punctuation. Editor cannot find all errors so it does not eliminate the need for proofreading.

To complete a spelling and grammar check, click the Editor button in the Editor group on the Home tab, click the Review tab and then click the Editor button in the Proofing group, or press the F7 function key. The Editor task pane opens at the right side of the screen and an Editor Score box displays near the top of the task pane. This box contains a percentage score that represents the number and type of suggestions to be reviewed based on the document length. Below the Editor Score box is an option box with options for specifying the formal level of the document. Click the option box arrow and three options displays. Choose the *Formal* option for an official and highly professional document, choose the *Professional* option for a general business document, or choose *Casual* for a casual or creative document.

The Editor task pane also contains options in the *Corrections* section identifying the number of possible spelling errors and grammar errors and a *Refinements* section identifying the number of areas that may need refining. Click the Editor Score box to search and display spelling and grammar errors as they are encountered. Click the *Spelling* option in the *Corrections* section to review all possible spelling errors and click the *Grammar* option to review all possible grammar errors.

Click the Editor Score box at the Editor task pane and the first spelling or grammar error is selected. The *Suggestions* list box contains one or more possible corrections. Click a suggestion to make the correction in the document. Or, click the arrow to the right of a suggestion for more options, as described in Table 1.6. If none of the suggestions seems right and the word is correct as typed, use the other options in the task pane to ignore the error or add the word to the spelling dictionary. Refer to Table 1.7 for descriptions of the options in the Editor task pane.

Table 1.6 Suggestion Drop-Down List Options

Option	Function
Read Aloud	reads the suggested correction aloud (speaker necessary)
Spell Out	spells the suggested correction aloud (speaker necessary)
Change All	changes all instances of the error to the suggested correction
Add to AutoCorrect	makes a suggested correction automatic by adding it as an option in AutoCorrect

Table 1.7 Editor Task Pane Options

Option	Function
Ignore Once	ignores the selected error
Ignore All	ignores the error and all other occurrences of it in the document
Add to Dictionary	adds the word to the spelling checker dictionary
Delete Repeated Word	deletes one of two repeated words
Stop checking for this	ignores a suspected grammar error and no longer checks for this type of error in the document

If Word detects a grammar error, the text containing the error is selected and possible corrections are provided in the Editor task pane *Suggestions* list box. Depending on the error, some of the options described in Table 1.7 may be available and a grammar rule will be provided near the top of the task pane. Click the down arrow at the right of the grammar rule and information about the rule displays along with suggestions on how to correct the error.

When checking the spelling and grammar in a document, temporarily leave the Editor task pane by clicking in the document. To resume the spelling and grammar check, click the resume button (the name may vary) in the task pane.

Activity 5 Checking the Spelling and Grammar in a Document

Part 1 of 1

1. Open **TechVisionary.docx** and save it with the name **1-TechVisionary**.
2. Click the Editor button in the Editor group on the Home tab (located at the right side of the ribbon).

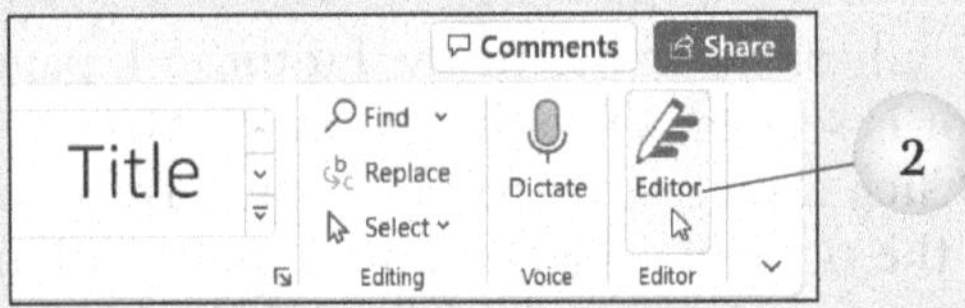

3. The Editor task pane opens and identifies the total number of possible spelling and grammar errors along with information in the *Corrections* section. Change the document's formal level by clicking the *Formal writing* option box and then clicking *Professional* at the drop-down list.
4. Click the Editor Score button near the top of the task pane.

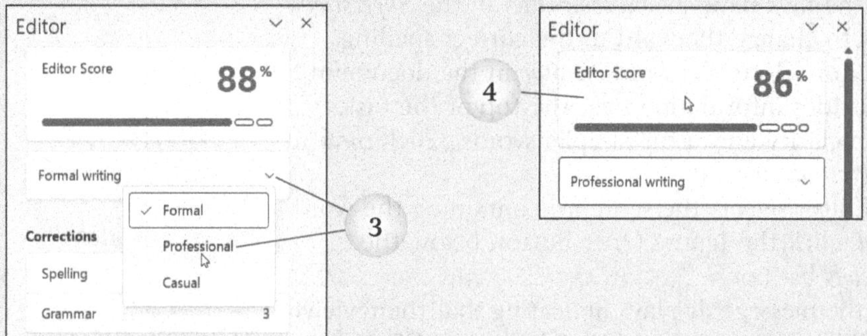

5. The Editor selects the word *chalenged* in the document and provides the correct spelling in the *Suggestions* list box in the task pane. Click *challenged* in the *Suggestions* list box to change the word to the correct spelling.
6. The Editor selects the word *too* in the document and provides the word *to* in the *Suggestions* list box. Click the down arrow to the right of the text *Possible Word Choice Error* near the top of the task pane, read the information provided about a possible word choice error, and then click the up arrow to remove the information.
7. Click *to* in the *Suggestions* list box to correct the grammar error.

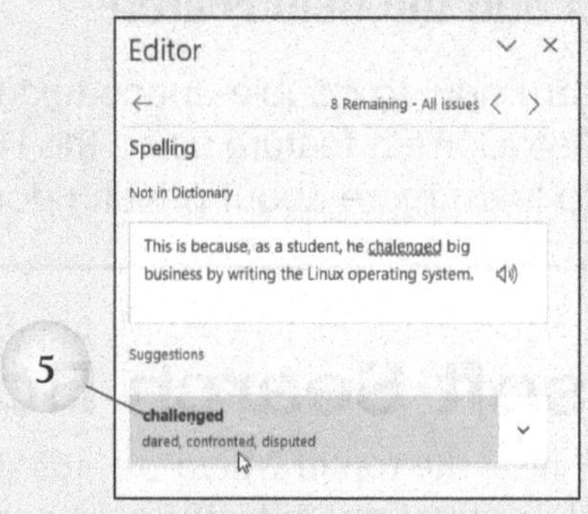

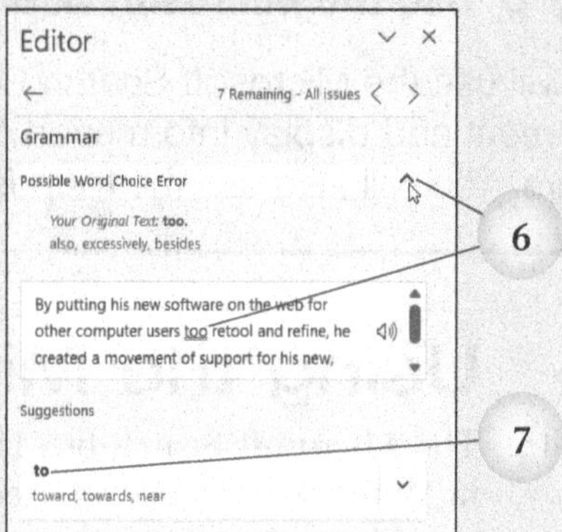

8. If the Editor selects the sentence containing the words *a viable*, click the Ignore Once button below the *Suggestions* list box.
9. The Editor selects the words *operating* and *system*, noting that two spaces appear between the words. The *Suggestions* list box provides an option with the words *operating system* with only one space between the words. Click the option in the *Suggestions* list box to correct the error.

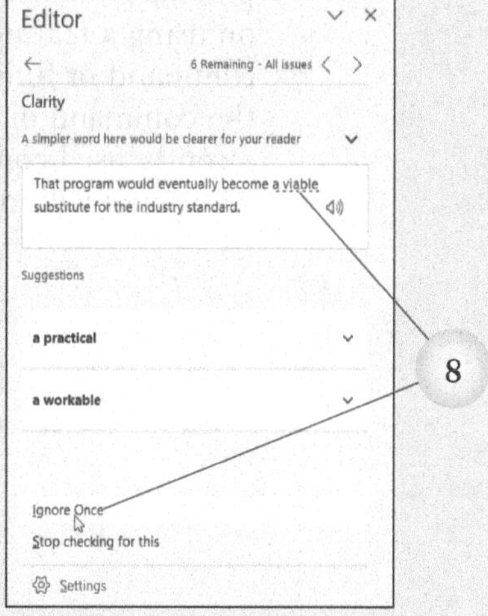

10. The Editor selects the word *the*, which is used two times in a row. Click the *Delete Repeated Word* option in the task pane to delete the second *the*.
11. The Editor selects the word *company's* in the document and provides a grammar suggestion in the *Suggestions* list box in the task pane. Click *companies* in the *Suggestions* list box to change the word to the correct spelling.
12. The Editor selects the word *monitor* in the document and provides information near the top of the task pane on clarity and using simpler words. Click *check* in the *Suggestions* list box.
13. If the Editor selects the sentence containing the word *operated*, click the Ignore Once button below the *Suggestions* list box.
14. When the message displays indicating that the reviewing of the Editor's suggestions is finished, click OK.
15. Close the Editor task pane by clicking the Close button in the upper right corner of the task pane.
16. Save, preview, and then close **1-TechVisionary.docx**.

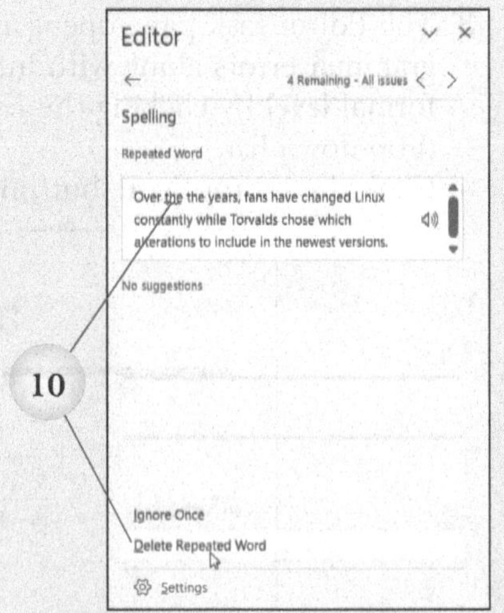

Activity 6 Use the Microsoft Search Box and the Help Feature — 2 Parts

You will use the Microsoft Search Box to learn how to double-space text in a document and display information on the AutoCorrect feature using the Help feature. You will also use the Help feature to learn more about printing documents.

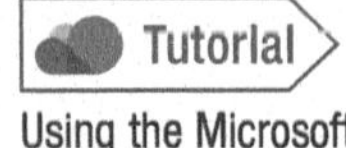

Using the Microsoft Search Box

Using the Microsoft Search Box

The Microsoft Search box is located near the top of Microsoft 365 applications in Windows and can be used to find information on features, commands, text in a file, or information on a word or phrase. The search box can also be used to provide guidance on using a particular feature. To find information or get guidance on using a feature, click in the search box (or press Alt + Q) and then type a command or function. A drop-down list displays with options for completing the command or function. The drop-down list may also contain the most recently used commands, suggested actions based on the current task, how to get additional help on using the command or function, and any recently opened files.

Activity 6a Using the Microsoft Search Box

Part 1 of 2

1. Open **MultimediaSoftware.docx** and then save it with the name **1-MultimediaSoftware**.
2. Press Ctrl + A to select all text in the document.
3. Use the Microsoft Search box to learn how to double-space the text in the document by completing the following steps:
   a. Click in the Microsoft Search box located near the top of the screen.
   b. Type double space.
   c. Click the *2.0 Line and Paragraph Spacing* option in the *Best Action* section. (This double-spaces the selected text in the document.)
   d. Click in the document to deselect the text.

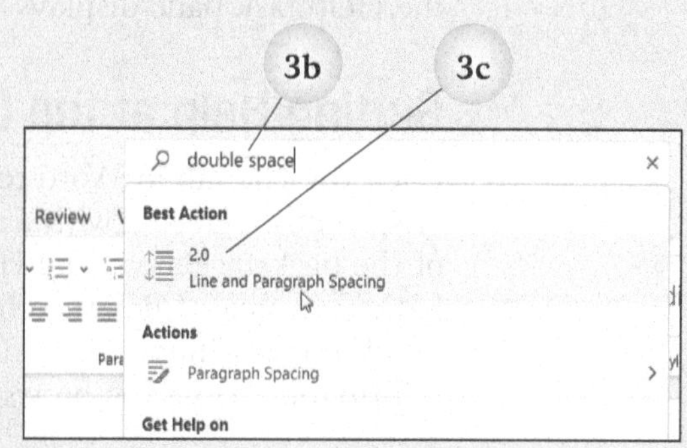

4. Use the Microsoft Search box to display help information on AutoCorrect by completing the following steps:
   a. Click in the Microsoft Search box.
   b. Type autocorrect.
   c. Hover the pointer over the arrow that displays to the right of the *"autocorrect"* option in the *Get Help* section.
   d. At the side menu that displays, click the first option (an article on AutoCorrect). This displays the Help task pane with the article information.
   e. Read the information in the Help task pane and then close the task pane by clicking the the Close button in the upper right corner of the task pane.
5. Save, preview, and then close **1-MultimediaSoftware.docx**.

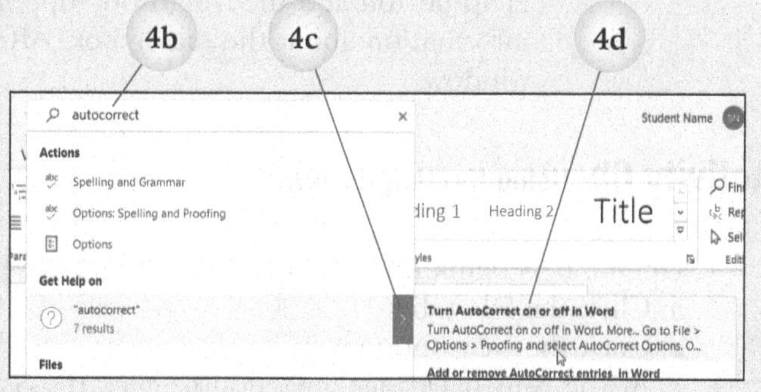

Using the Help Feature

Using the Help Feature

Help

The Help feature is an on-screen reference manual containing information about Word features and commands. The Help feature in Word is similar to the Help features in Excel, PowerPoint, and Access. Get help by using the Microsoft Search box, at the Help task pane, or at the Microsoft support website. Display the Help task pane by pressing the F1 function key or clicking the Help tab and then clicking the Help button.

At the Help task pane, type a topic, feature, or question in the search text box and then press the Enter key. Articles related to the search text are shown in the task pane. Click an article to display the article information in the task pane.

Getting Help from a ScreenTip

Hover the pointer over a certain button, such as the Format Painter button or Font Color button, and the ScreenTip displays with a Help icon and the Tell me more hyperlinked text. Click Tell me more or press the F1 function key and the Help task pane displays with information about the button feature.

Getting Help at the Backstage Area

Click the File tab in Word to display the backstage area. A Microsoft Word Help button, labeled with a question mark (?), appears in the upper right corner of the backstage area. The Help button is also available at many of the other backstage areas. Click the Help button and the Microsoft support website opens in a browser window with information about the backstage area. After reading the information, close the browser window and return to Word.

Getting Help in a Dialog Box

Some dialog boxes contain a Help button. Open a dialog box and then click the Help button and the Microsoft support website opens in a browser window with information about the dialog box. After reading the information, close the browser window.

Activity 6b Using the Help Feature

Part 2 of 2

1. Open a new blank document by completing the following steps:
   a. Click the File tab.
   b. Click the *New* option.
   c. At the New backstage area, double-click the *Single spaced (blank)* template. (You may need to scroll down the screen to display this template.)

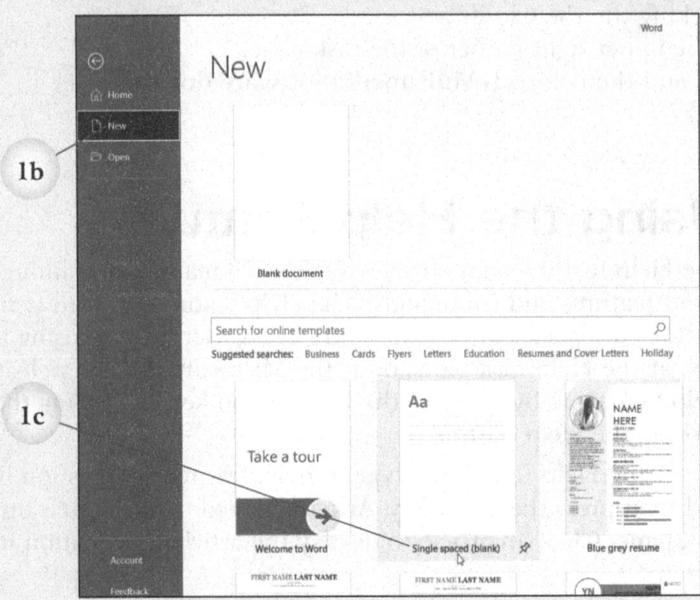

2. Press the F1 function key to display the Help task pane.

3. Type print a document in the task pane search text box and then press the Enter key.
4. When the list of articles displays, click the Print a document in Word hyperlinked article. (You may need to scroll down the task pane to find this article.)
5. Read the information in the task pane about printing a document.
6. Click the Close button to close the Help task pane.
7. Hover the pointer over the Format Painter button in the Clipboard group on the Home tab.
8. Click the Tell me more hyperlinked text at the bottom of the ScreenTip.
9. Read the information in the Help task pane about the Format Painter feature.
10. Click the Help task pane Close button.
11. Click the File tab.
12. Click the Microsoft Word Help button in the upper right corner of the backstage area.

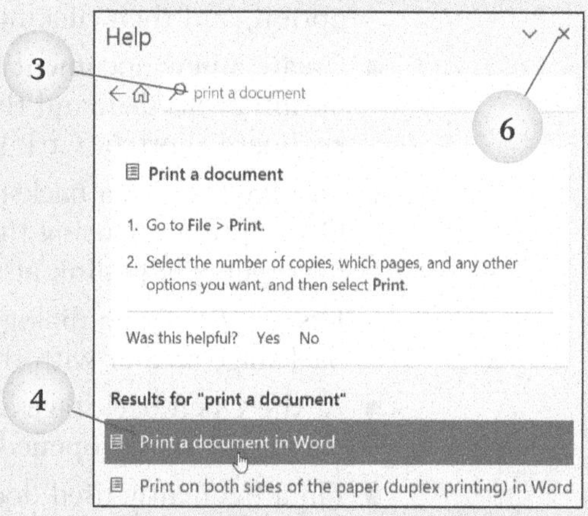

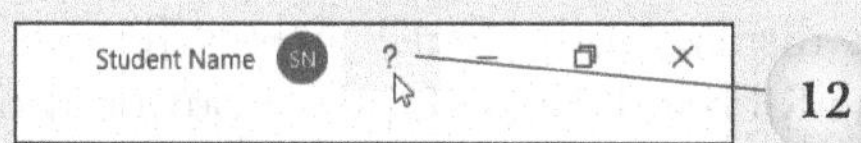

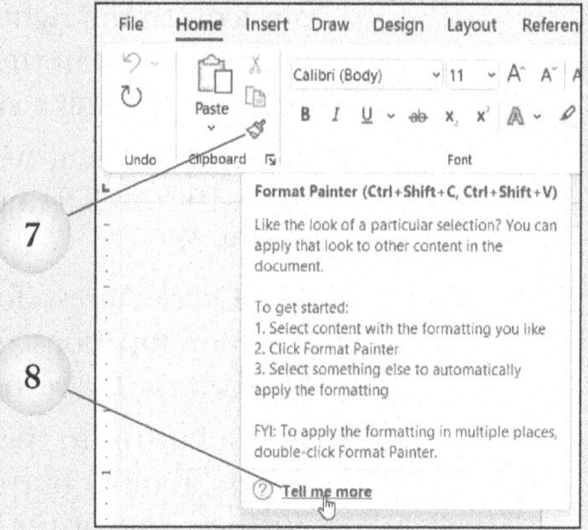

13. Look at the information at the Microsoft support website and then close the browser window.
14. Click the Back button to return to the document.
15. Close the blank document.

Chapter Summary

- Refer to Figure 1.1 and Table 1.1 (on page 5) for an example and a list of key Word screen features respectively.
- Click the File tab and the backstage area displays, containing options for working with and managing documents.
- Document names can contain a maximum of 255 characters, including the drive letter and folder names, and they may include spaces.
- The ribbon contains tabs with options and buttons divided into groups.
- The insertion point displays as a blinking vertical line and indicates the position of the next character to be entered in the document.
- Print a hard copy of a document by clicking the File tab, clicking the *Print* option, and then clicking the Print button.
- Close a document by clicking the File tab and then clicking the *Close* option or with the keyboard shortcut Ctrl + F4.
- Close Word by clicking the Close button in the upper right corner of the screen or with the keyboard shortcut Alt + F4.

- Create a new single-spaced document by clicking the File tab, clicking the *New* option, and then clicking the *Single spaced (blank)* template.
- Create a new document by clicking the File tab, clicking the *Home* or *New* option as needed, and then clicking the *Blank document* template or by using the keyboard shortcut Ctrl + N.
- Display the Open backstage area by clicking the File tab and then clicking the *Open* option; by using the keyboard shortcut Ctrl + O; or by clicking the More documents hyperlink at the Home backstage area or the Word opening screen.
- Display the Open dialog box by clicking the *Browse* option at the Open backstage area or with the keyboard shortcut Ctrl + F12.
- At the Open backstage area with the *Recent* option selected, the names of the 50 most recently opened documents display.
- Pin a frequently used document or folder to the *Recent* option list at the Open backstage area or pin a document at the Home backstage area by clicking the pin icon to the right of the document or folder name. Pinned documents and folders appear in the *Pinned* category. Click the pin icon again (displays with a circle containing a slash) to unpin a document or folder from the list.
- Save a document with the same name by clicking the Save button on the Title bar, with the *Save* option at the backstage area, or with the keyboard shortcut Ctrl + S.
- The Quick Access Toolbar is a customizable toolbar that provides easy access to common functions. Turn on the display of the Quick Access Toolbar with the *Show Quick Access Toolbar* option at the Ribbon Display Options button drop-down list.
- Add a button to the Quick Access Toolbar by clicking the Customize Quick Access Toolbar button at the right side of the toolbar and then clicking the button name at the drop-down list.
- Remove a button from the Quick Access Toolbar by right-clicking the button and then clicking *Remove from Quick Access Toolbar* at the shortcut menu.
- The scroll box on the vertical scroll bar indicates the location of the text in the document screen in relation to the entire of the document.
- The insertion point can be moved throughout the document using the mouse, the keyboard, or a combination of the two.
- The insertion point can be moved by character, word, screen, or page and from the first to the last character in a document. Refer to Table 1.2 (on page 16) for keyboard insertion point movement commands.
- Delete text by character, word, line, several lines, or partial page using specific keys or by selecting text using the mouse or the keyboard. Refer to Table 1.3 (on page 18) for deletion commands.
- A specific amount of text can be selected using the mouse and/or the keyboard. Refer to Table 1.4 (on page 19) for information on selecting with the mouse, and refer to Table 1.5 (on page 20) for information on selecting with the keyboard.
- Use the Undo button on the Home tab to undo an action such as typing, deleting, or formatting text. Use the Redo button to redo something that has been undone with the Undo button.
- Word contains the Microsoft Editor that checks for spelling and grammar errors in the document. Corrections are suggested in the Editor task pane. Refer to Table 1.6 and Table 1.7 (on page 24) for a description of options at the Editor task pane.

- Use the Microsoft Search box, located near the top of the screen, to find information on features, commands, text in a file, or information on a word or phrase.
- Word's Help feature is an on-screen reference manual containing information on Word features and commands. Press the F1 function key to display the Help task pane or click the Help tab and then click the Help button.
- Hover the pointer over a certain button and the ScreenTip displays with a Help icon and the Tell me more hyperlinked text. Click this hyperlinked text to display the Help task pane, which contains information about the button feature.
- Some dialog boxes and the backstage area contain a Help button that links to the Microsoft support website to provide more information about functions and features.

Commands Review

FEATURE	RIBBON TAB, GROUP/ OPTION	BUTTON, OPTION	KEYBOARD SHORTCUT
AutoComplete entry			F3
close document	File, *Close*		Ctrl + F4
close Word			Alt + F4
display Quick Access Toolbar		, *Show Quick Access Toolbar*	
Go To feature	Home, Editing	, *Go To*	Ctrl + G
Help task pane	Help, Help		F1
leave backstage area			Esc
Microsoft Editor	Home, Editor OR Review, Proofing		F7
Microsoft Search box			Alt + Q
move insertion point to previous location when document was closed			Shift + F5
new blank document	File, *New* OR File, *Home*	*Blank document*	Ctrl + N
New Line command			Shift + Enter
Open backstage area	File, *Open*		Ctrl + O
Open dialog box	File, *Open*	*Browse*	Ctrl + F12
Print backstage area	File, *Print*		Ctrl + P
redo action	Undo, Home		Ctrl + Y
save	File, *Save*		Ctrl + S
Save As backstage area	File, *Save As*		
Save As dialog box	File, *Save As*	*Browse*	F12
Selection mode			F8
undo action	Undo, Home		Ctrl + Z

Review and Assessment

CHAPTER 1

Skills Assessment

Assessment 1

Edit a Document on Resume Writing

1. Open Word and then open **WriteResume.docx**.
2. Save the document with the name **1-WriteResume**.
3. Move the insertion point to the end of the document and then type the text shown in Figure 1.9. When typing the text, use the New Line command, Shift + Enter, to end the lines after *Created by Marie Solberg* and *Monday, October 7, 2024*.
4. Make the following changes to the document:
   a. Delete the first occurrence of the word *currently* in the first sentence of the first paragraph.
   b. Select the word *important* in the first sentence in the first paragraph and then type essential.
   c. Type and hard-hitting between the words *concise* and *written* in the second sentence of the second paragraph.
   d. Delete the words *over and over,* (including the comma and the space after the comma) in the third sentence in the second paragraph.
   e. Select and then delete the second sentence of the third paragraph (the sentence that begins *So do not take*).
   f. Move the insertion point to the beginning of the third paragraph and then press the backspace key to join the third paragraph with the second paragraph.
   g. Delete the name *Marie Solberg* and then type your first and last names.
5. Save, preview, and then close **1-WriteResume.docx**.

Figure 1.9 Assessment 1

> Created by Marie Solberg
> Monday, October 7, 2024
> Note: Please insert this information between the 2nd and 3rd sections.

Assessment 2

Check the Spelling and Grammar of a Resume Style Document

1. Open **ResumeStyles.docx**.
2. Save the document with the name **1-ResumeStyles**.
3. Use the Editor to complete a spelling and grammar check on the document and correct the errors.
4. Type the sentence Different approaches work for different people. between the first and second sentences in the first paragraph of text below the title *RESUMES*.
5. Move the insertion point to the end of the document (on the blank line following the last paragraph of text), type your first and last names, press Shift + Enter, and then type the current date.
6. Save, preview, and then close **1-ResumeStyles.docx**.

Assessment 3

Create a Document Describing Keyboard Shortcuts

1. Press the F1 function key to display the Help task pane.
2. Type keyboard shortcuts in the search text box and then press the Enter key.
3. At the Help task pane, click the Keyboard shortcuts in Word hyperlink. (If this article is not available, choose a similar article that describes Word keyboard shortcuts.)
4. Read through the information in the Help task pane.
5. Open a new blank single-spaced document.
6. Create a document with the following specifications:
   a. Type Keyboard Shortcuts as the title.
   b. Describe four keyboard shortcuts by providing a brief description of how each shortcut is used.
   c. Click in the title *Keyboard Shortcuts* and then use the Microsoft Search box to center the title.
7. Save the document with the name **1-KeyboardShortcuts**.
8. Preview and then close **1-KeyboardShortcuts.docx**.

Visual Benchmark

Create a Cover Letter

1. At a new blank document, type the cover letter shown in Figure 1.10, following the directions in red. (A cover letter is a business letter written to accompany a resume. It may be sent electronically or through the mail. When sent through the mail, a cover letter should include the postal address of the writer and the addressee in block paragraph format, as shown in Figure 1.10.)
2. Save the completed letter with the name **1-CoverLtr**.
3. Preview and then close **1-CoverLtr.docx**.

Figure 1.10 Visual Benchmark

(press Enter three times)

4520 South Park Street *(press Shift + Enter)*
Newark, NJ 07122 *(press Shift + Enter)*
Current Date *(press Enter two times)*

Ms. Sylvia Hammond *(press Shift + Enter)*
Sales Director, Eastern Division *(press Shift + Enter)*
Grand Style Products *(press Shift + Enter)*
1205 Sixth Street *(press Shift + Enter)*
Newark, NJ 07102 *(press Enter)*

Dear Ms. Hammond: *(press Enter)*

Thank you for agreeing to meet with me next Wednesday. Based on our initial conversation, I believe that my ability to sell solutions rather than products is a good fit for your needs as you seek to expand your visibility in the region. *(press Enter)*

As noted in the enclosed resume, I have led an underperforming product division to generating 33 percent of total revenue (up from 5 percent) at our location. We now deliver, from a single location, 25 percent of total sales for our 20-site company. Having completed this turnaround over the last 5 years, I'm eager for new challenges that will enable me to use my proven skills in sales, marketing, and program/event planning to contribute to a company's bottom line. *(press Enter)*

I have been thinking about the challenges you described in building your presence at the retail level, and I have some good ideas to share at our meeting. I am excited about the future of Grand Style Products and eager to contribute to the company's growth. *(press Enter)*

Sincerely, *(press Enter two times)*

Student Name *(press Enter)*

Enclosure

Case Study

Part 1

You are the administrative assistant at a mid-sized service-oriented business. Employees frequently use Microsoft Word to create contracts to use with customers. Your boss, Mr. Brewster, wants these saved to a folder named *Contracts* in the Documents folder on your company's shared drive. Mr. Brewster has asked you to create a document for employees with step-by-step instructions for naming and saving contracts. Save your completed document with the name **1-Saving**. Preview and then close the document.

Part 2

Mr. Brewster would like to have a document describing basic Word commands and keyboard shortcuts to help employees work more efficiently in Microsoft Word. He has asked you to prepare a document containing the following information:

- A brief explanation of how to use the Go To feature to move the insertion point to a specific page
- Keyboard shortcuts to move the insertion point to the beginning and end of a line and the beginning and end of a document
- Keyboard commands to delete text from the insertion point to the beginning of a word and from the insertion point to the end of a word
- Steps to select a word and a paragraph using the mouse
- A keyboard shortcut to select the entire document

Save the completed document with the name **1-WordCommands**. Preview and then close the document.

Part 3

According to Mr. Brewster, the company is considering updating its computers to Microsoft 365. He has asked you to go to the Microsoft home page at microsoft.com and then use the Search feature to find information on Microsoft 365 plans for use in business. Determine what applications and services are included and pricing for each plan. When you find the information, type a document that contains information on two different Microsoft 365 plans. Save the document with the name **1-Microsoft365**. Preview and then close the document.

WORD

CHAPTER

2

Formatting Characters and Paragraphs

Performance Objectives

Upon successful completion of Chapter 2, you will be able to:

1 Change the font and font size and choose font effects
2 Format selected text with buttons on the Mini toolbar
3 Apply styles from style sets
4 Apply themes
5 Customize styles and themes
6 Change the alignment of text in paragraphs
7 Indent text in paragraphs
8 Increase and decrease spacing before and after paragraphs
9 Repeat the last action
10 Automate formatting with Format Painter
11 Change line spacing
12 Reveal and compare formatting

The appearance of a document on the screen and when printed is called the *format*. A Word document is based on a template that applies default formatting. Some of the default formats include 11-point Calibri font, line spacing of 1.08, 8 points of spacing after each paragraph, and left-aligned text. In this chapter, you will learn about changing the typeface, type size, and typestyle as well as applying font effects such as bold and italic. You will also learn to format paragraphs by changing text alignment and line spacing, indenting text, and applying formatting with Format Painter.

Data Files

The data files for this chapter are in the WL1C2 folder that you downloaded at the beginning of this course.

Activity 1 Apply Font Formatting to Characters in a Document — 4 Parts

You will open a document containing a glossary of terms and then format the document by changing the font and the font size; adding bold, italics, and underlining; and applying font effects.

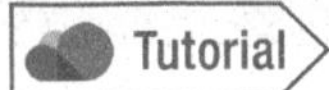

Applying Font Formatting Using the Font Group

Applying Font Formatting

One of the most visible aspects of a document's format is the font. Font formatting can be applied to the individual characters of text, including letters, numbers, and symbols. Applying font formatting can draw the reader's attention to specific parts of a document, make information accessible to the reader by formatting items such as headings, highlight key words, and emphasize important information.

A font consists of three elements: typeface, type size, and typestyle. By default, a Word document is formatted with the Calibri typeface in 11-point size. The typestyle is roman type; that is, regular and not bold or italic. This default may need to be changed to another font for such reasons as altering the mood of the document, enhancing its visual appeal, and increasing its readability.

Hint Change the default font by selecting the font at the Font dialog box and then clicking the Set As Default button.

The Font group on the Home tab, shown in Figure 2.1, contains a number of options and buttons for applying font formatting to characters in a document. The top row contains options for changing the font and font size as well as buttons for increasing and decreasing the size of the font and changing the text case. The bottom row contains buttons for applying typestyles such as bold, italic, and underline and for applying text effects, highlighting, and color. Use the Clear All Formatting button in the top row of the Font group to remove all formatting applied to characters and paragraphs in the text. To remove only character formatting, select text and then use the keyboard shortcut Ctrl + spacebar.

Hint Use a serif typeface for text-intensive documents.

A typeface is a set of characters with a common design and shape and can be decorative or plain and either monospaced or proportional. Word refers to a typeface as a *font*. A monospaced typeface allots the same amount of horizontal space for each character, while a proportional typeface allots varying amounts of space for different characters. Typefaces are divided into two main categories: serif and sans serif. A serif is a small line at the end of a character stroke. Consider using a serif typeface for text-intensive documents because the serifs help move the reader's eyes across the page. Use a sans serif typeface for headings, headlines, and advertisements. Some popular typefaces are shown in Table 2.1.

Figure 2.1 Font Group Option Boxes and Buttons

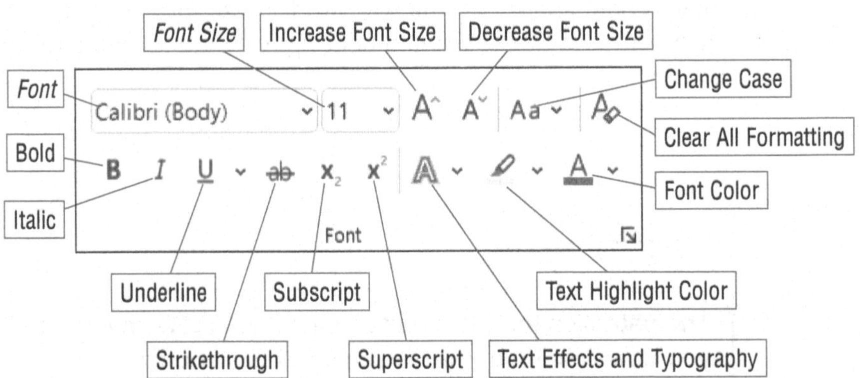

Table 2.1 Categories of Typefaces

Serif Typefaces	Sans Serif Typefaces	Monospaced Typefaces
Cambria	Calibri	Consolas
Constantia	Candara	Courier New
Times New Roman	Corbel	Lucida Console
Bookman Old Style	Arial	MS Gothic

Hint Press Ctrl +] to increase font size by 1 point and press Ctrl + [to decrease font size by 1 point.

Type is generally set in proportional size. The size of proportional type is measured vertically in units called *points*. A point is approximately 1/72 of an inch—the higher the point size, the larger the characters. Within a typeface, characters may have varying styles, including regular, bold, italic, bold italic, and underlined.

Use the *Font* option box in the Font group to change the font. Select the text in the document, click the *Font* option box arrow, and then click a font option at the drop-down gallery. Another method for changing the font is to click the current font name in the *Font* option box to select it and then type the new font name. Change the font size by clicking the *Font Size* option box arrow and then clicking the font size at the drop-down gallery. Or, click the current font size in the *Font Size* option box to select it and then type the new font size number.

To see a live preview of the text in different fonts and sizes before changing the formatting in the document, select the text and then display the *Font* or *Font Size* drop-down gallery. Hover the pointer over different font options to see how the selected text displays in each font or size.

Activity 1a Changing the Font and Font Size — Part 1 of 4

1. Open **CompTerms.docx** and then save it with the name **2-CompTerms**.
2. Change the typeface to Cambria by completing the following steps:
   a. Select all text in the document by clicking the Select button in the Editing group and then clicking *Select All* at the drop-down list. (You can also select the entire document by pressing Ctrl + A.)
   b. Click the *Font* option box arrow, scroll down the drop-down gallery until *Cambria* displays, and then hover the pointer over *Cambria*. This displays a live preview of the text set in Cambria.
   c. Click the *Cambria* option.

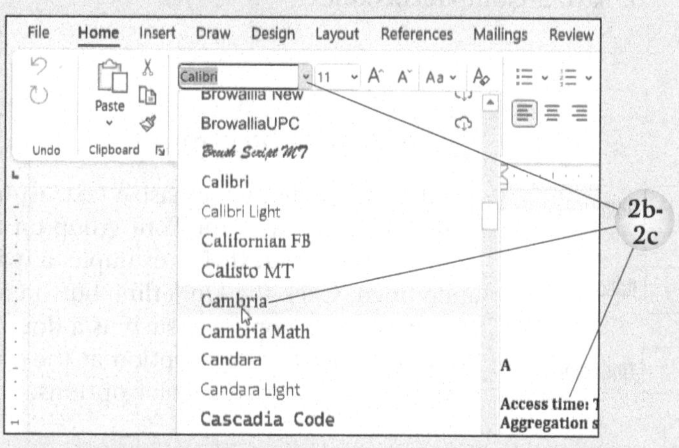

3. Change the type size to 14 points by completing the following steps:
   a. With the text in the document still selected, click the *Font Size* option box arrow.
   b. At the drop-down gallery, hover the pointer over *14* and look at the live preview of the text with 14 points applied.
   c. Click the *14* option.

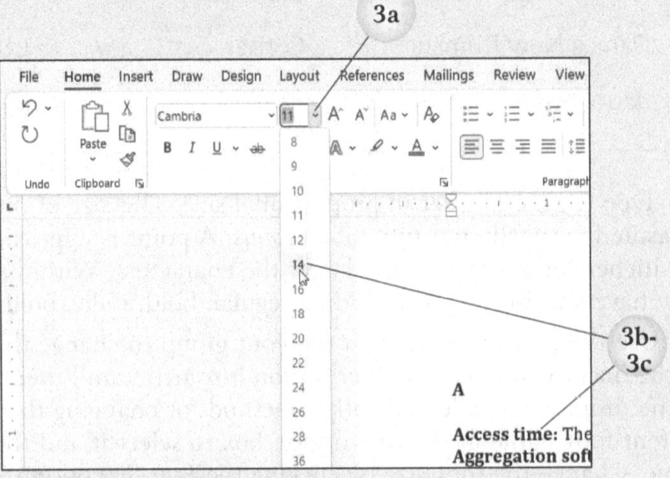

4. Change the type size and typeface by completing the following steps:
   a. Click the Decrease Font Size button in the Font group three times. (This decreases the size to 10 points.)
   b. Click the Increase Font Size button two times. (This increases the size to 12 points.)
   c. Click the *Font* option box arrow, scroll down the drop-down gallery, and then click *Constantia*. (The most recently used fonts are listed at the beginning of the gallery, followed by a listing of all fonts.)

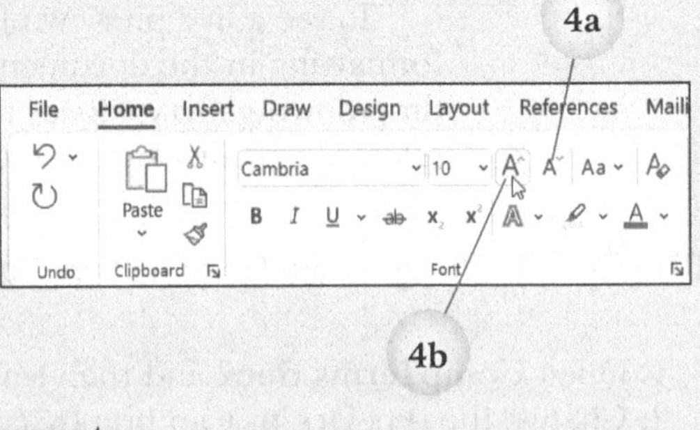

5. Deselect the text by clicking anywhere in the document.
6. Save **2-CompTerms.docx**.

Check Your Work

Choosing a Typestyle

B Bold

I Italic

U Underline

Apply a typestyle to emphasize text using the Bold, Italic, and Underline buttons in the bottom row in the Font group on the Home tab. More than one typestyle can be applied to text. For example, a word may be set as bold italic and also underlined. Click the Underline button arrow and a drop-down gallery displays with underlining options, such as a double line, dashed line, and thicker underline. Click the *Underline Color* option at the Underline button drop-down gallery and a side menu displays with color options.

Activity 1b Applying Font Formatting to Characters as You Type

1. With **2-CompTerms.docx** open, press Ctrl + Home to move the insertion point to the beginning of the document.
2. Type a heading for the document by completing the following steps:
   a. Click the Bold button in the Font group. (This turns on bold formatting.)
   b. Click the Underline button in the Font group. (This turns on underline formatting.)
   c. Type Glossary of Terms.

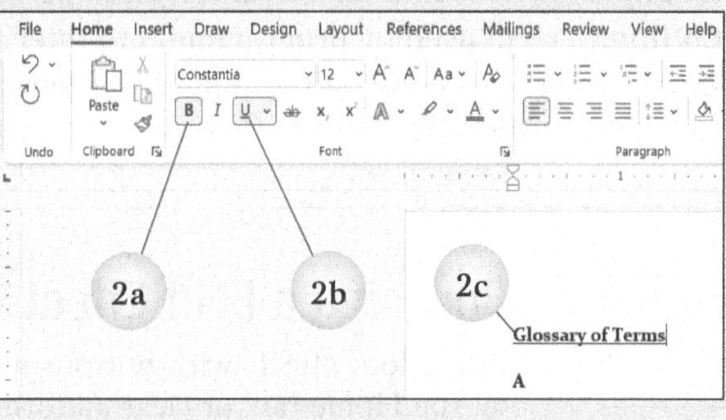

3. Press Ctrl + End to move the insertion point to the end of the document.
4. Type the text shown in Figure 2.2 with the following specifications:
   a. While typing, make the appropriate text bold, as shown in the figure, by completing the following steps:
      1) Click the Bold button. (This turns on bold formatting.)
      2) Type the text.
      3) Click the Bold button. (This turns off bold formatting.)
   b. Press the Enter key two times after typing the C heading.
   c. While typing, italicize the appropriate text, as shown in the figure, by completing the following steps:
      1) Click the Italic button in the Font group.
      2) Type the text.
      3) Click the Italic button.
5. After typing the text, press the Enter key two times and then press Ctrl + Home to move the insertion point to the beginning of the document.
6. Change the underlining below the title by completing the following steps:
   a. Select the title <u>*Glossary of Terms*</u>.
   b. Click the Underline button arrow and then click the third underline option from the top of the drop-down gallery (*Thick underline*).

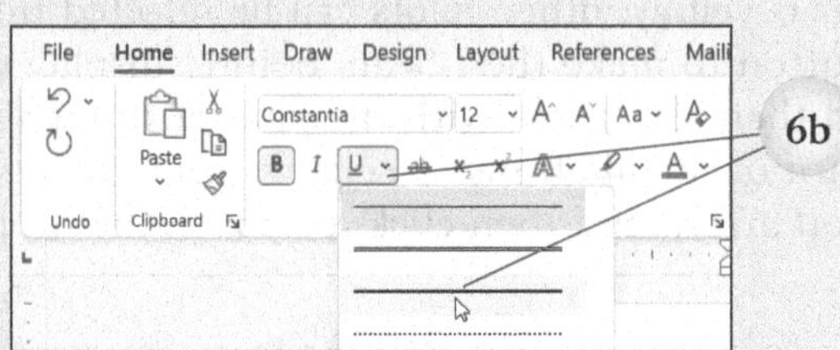

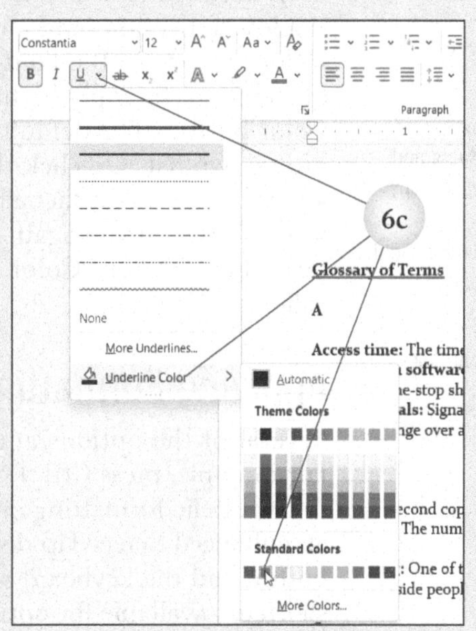

   c. Click the Underline button arrow, point to the *Underline Color* option, and then click the *Red* color (second color option in the *Standard Colors* section).
7. With the title still selected, change the font size to 14 points.
8. Save **2-CompTerms.docx**.

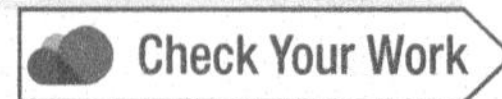
Check Your Work

Figure 2.2 Activity 1b

> **C**
>
> **Chip:** A thin wafer of *silicon* containing electronic circuitry that performs various functions, such as mathematical calculations, storage, and controlling computer devices.
> **Coding:** A term used by programmers to refer to the act of writing source code.
> **Crackers:** A term coined by computer hackers for those who intentionally enter (or hack) computer systems to damage them.

Tutorial — Highlighting Text

Tutorial — Applying Text Effects Using the Ribbon

Choosing a Font Effect

Apply font effects with buttons in the top and bottom rows in the Font group on the Home tab, or clear all formatting from selected text with the Clear All Formatting button. Change the case of text with the Change Case button drop-down list. Click the Change Case button in the top row in the Font group and then click one of the options in the drop-down list: *Sentence case*, *lowercase*, *UPPERCASE*, *Capitalize Each Word*, and *tOGGLE cASE*. The case of selected text can also be changed with the keyboard shortcut Shift + F3. Each time Shift + F3 is pressed, the selected text displays in the next case option in the list.

Clear All Formatting

Change Case

The bottom row in the Font group contains buttons for applying font effects. Use the Strikethrough button to draw a line through selected text. This has a practical application in some legal documents in which deleted text must be retained in the document. Use the Subscript button to create text that is lowered slightly below the line, as in the chemical formula H_2O. Use the Superscript button to create text that is raised slightly above the text line, as in the mathematical equation four to the third power (written as 4^3).

Strikethrough

Subscript

Superscript

Click the Text Effects and Typography button in the bottom row and a drop-down gallery displays with predesigned effect options along with outline, shadow, reflection, and glow text effects. The Text Highlight Color and Font Color buttons in the Font group are used to highlight text or change the color of the font. To apply highlighting, select text and then click the Text Highlight Color button. The default color is yellow; other colors can be selected from the drop-down list. Or, click the button to make the I-beam pointer display with a highlighter pen attached, and then select text with the pointer to highlight it. Click the button again to turn off highlighting. To change font color, select text, click the Font Color button arrow, and then click a color at the drop-down gallery.

Text Effects and Typography

Text Highlight Color

Font Color

Applying Formatting Using Keyboard Shortcuts

Several of the options and buttons in the Font group have keyboard shortcuts. For example, press Ctrl + B to turn bold formatting on or off and press Ctrl + I to turn italic formatting on or off. Position the pointer on an option or button and an enhanced ScreenTip displays with the name and description of the option or button and the keyboard shortcut, if it has one. Table 2.2 identifies the keyboard shortcuts available for options and buttons in the Font group.

Table 2.2 Font Group Option and Button Keyboard Shortcuts

Font Group Option/Button	Keyboard Shortcut
Font	Ctrl + Shift + F
Font Size	Ctrl + Shift + P
Increase Font Size	Ctrl + Shift + > OR Ctrl +]
Decrease Font Size	Ctrl + Shift + < OR Ctrl + [
Bold	Ctrl + B
Italic	Ctrl + I
Underline	Ctrl + U
Subscript	Ctrl + =
Superscript	Ctrl + Shift + +
Change Case	Shift + F3

Applying Font Formatting Using the Mini Toolbar

Formatting with the Mini Toolbar

When text is selected, the Mini toolbar displays above the selected text, as shown in Figure 2.3. Click a button on the Mini toolbar to apply formatting to the selected text. When the pointer is moved away from the Mini toolbar, the toolbar disappears.

Figure 2.3 Mini Toolbar

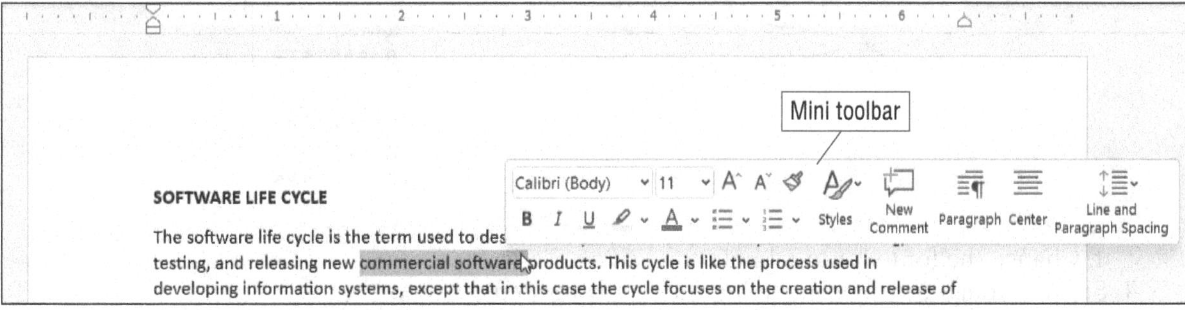

Activity 1c Applying Font Effects

Part 3 of 4

1. With **2-CompTerms.docx** open, move the insertion point to the beginning of the term *Chip*, press the Enter key, and then press the Up Arrow key.
2. Type the text shown in Figure 2.4 on page 45. Create each superscript number by clicking the Superscript button, typing the number, and then clicking the Superscript button.

3. Remove formatting and then change the case and size of the text, and apply text effects to the title by completing the following steps:
   a. Select the title *Glossary of Terms*.
   b. Remove all formatting from the title by clicking the Clear All Formatting button in the Font group.
   c. Click the Change Case button in the Font group and then click *UPPERCASE* at the drop-down list.
   d. Click the Text Effects and Typography button in the Font group and then click the option in the second column, second row (the option with blue gradient fill and reflection).
   e. Apply a dark blue outline text effect to the selected title by clicking the Text Effects and Typography button, pointing to *Outline*, and then clicking the *Dark Blue* color (ninth color option in the *Standard Colors* section).

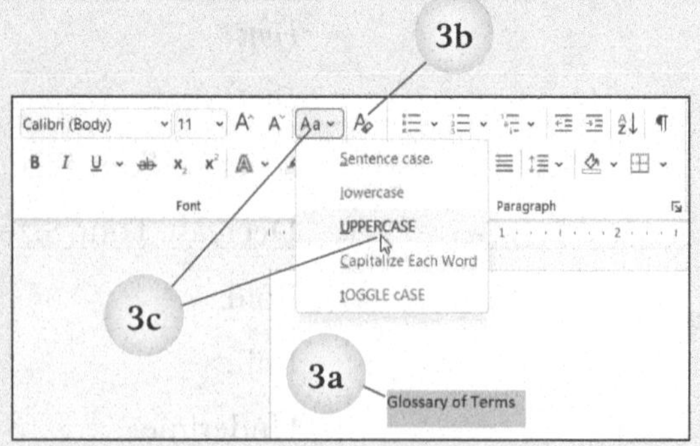

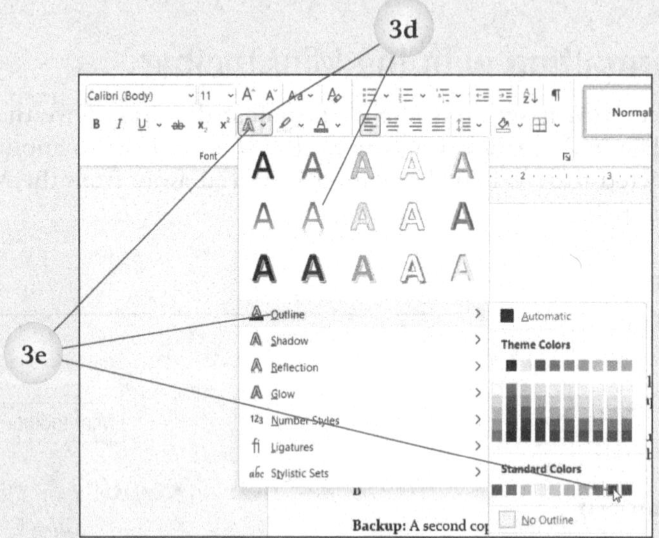

   f. Change the font size to 14 points.
4. Strike through text by completing the following steps:
   a. In the *Crackers* definition, select the phrase *or hack* and the parentheses around it.
   b. Click the Strikethrough button in the Font group.

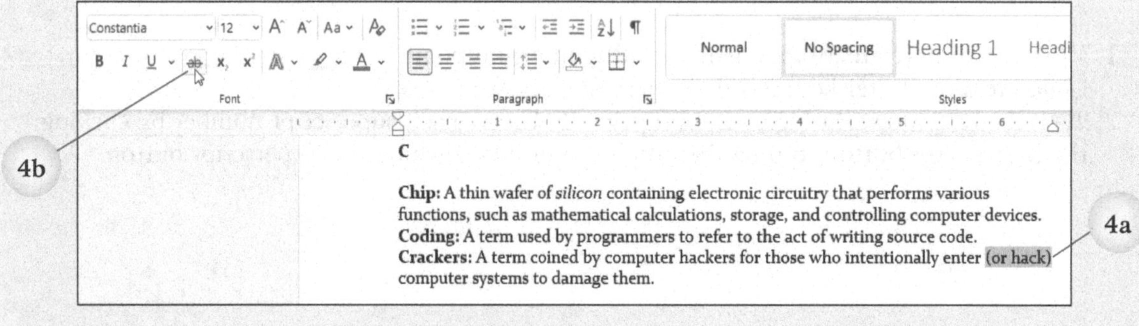

5. Change the font color for the entire document by completing the following steps:
   a. Press Ctrl + A to select the entire document.
   b. Click the Font Color button arrow.
   c. Click the *Dark Red* color (first color option in the *Standard Colors* section) at the drop-down gallery.
   d. Click in the document to deselect text.

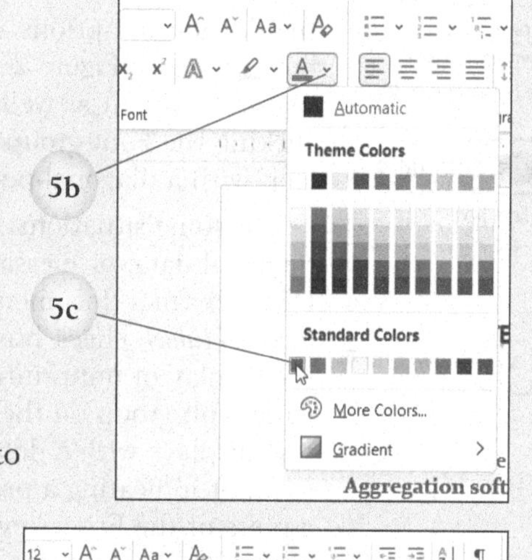

6. Highlight text in the document by completing the following steps:
   a. Select the term *Beta testing* and the definition that follows.
   b. Click the Text Highlight Color button in the Font group. (This applies yellow text highlighting color to the selected text.)
   c. Click the Text Highlight Color button arrow and then click the *Turquoise* color (third column, first row) at the drop-down palette. (This turns on highlighting and the pointer displays as an I-beam pointer with a highlighter pen attached.)
   d. Select the term *Coding* and the definition that follows.
   e. Click the Text Highlight Color button arrow and then click the *Yellow* color (first column, first row) at the drop-down gallery.
   f. Click the Text Highlight Color button to turn off highlighting.

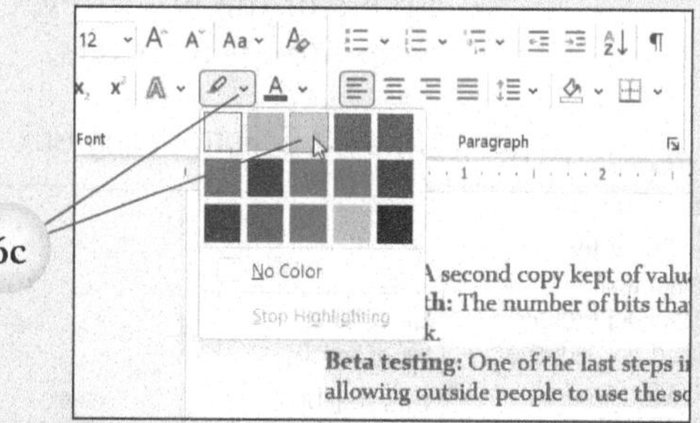

7. Apply italic formatting using the Mini toolbar by completing the following steps:
   a. In the definition for *Aggregation software*, select the phrase *one-stop shopping* (When you select the text, the Mini toolbar displays.)
   b. Click the Italic button on the Mini toolbar.
   c. In the definition for *Bandwidth*, select the word *bits* and then click the Italic button on the Mini toolbar.
8. Save **2-CompTerms.docx**.

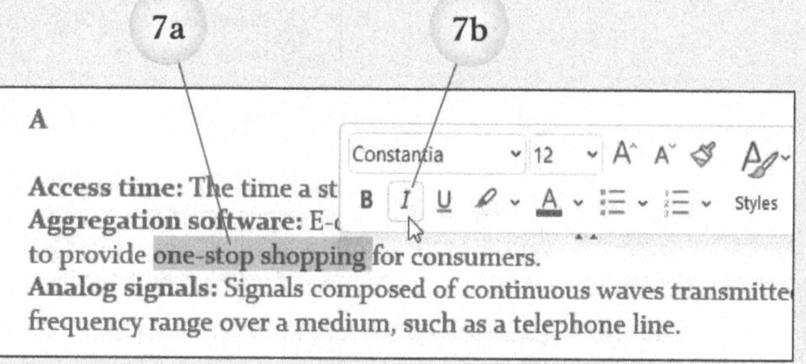

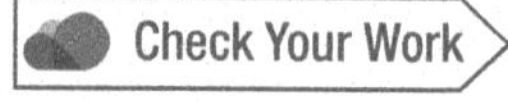

Figure 2.4 Activity 1c

> **Chinese abacus:** Pebbles strung on a rod inside a frame. Pebbles in the upper part of an abacus correspond to 5 x 10^0, or 5, for the first column; 5 x 10^1, or 50, for the second column; 5 x 10^2, or 500, for the third column; and so on.

Applying Font Formatting Using the Font Dialog Box

Hiding Text

Applying Font Formatting Using the Font Dialog Box

In addition to options and buttons in the Font group, options at the Font dialog box, shown in Figure 2.5, can be used to change the typeface, type size, and typestyle of text as well as apply font effects. Display the Font dialog box by clicking the Font group dialog box launcher. The dialog box launcher is a small icon with a diagonal-pointing arrow in the lower right corner of the Font group.

In some situations, sensitive data in a document such as personal information, financial data, or messages to specific people may need to be hidden from view. Hide text in a document by selecting the text and then inserting a check mark in the *Hidden* check box at the Font dialog box. To display hidden data, turn on the display of nonprinting characters by clicking the Show/Hide ¶ button in the Paragraph group on the Home tab. With the Show/Hide ¶ button active, hidden text displays with a dotted underline. Other nonprinting symbols displays such as a dot indicating a press of the spacebar and the paragraph symbol ¶ indicating a press of the Enter key. Click the Show/Hide ¶ to turn off the display of nonprinting characters.

Quick Steps

Change Font at Font Dialog Box

1. Select text.
2. Click Font group dialog box launcher.
3. Choose options at dialog box.
4. Click OK.

Figure 2.5 Font Dialog Box

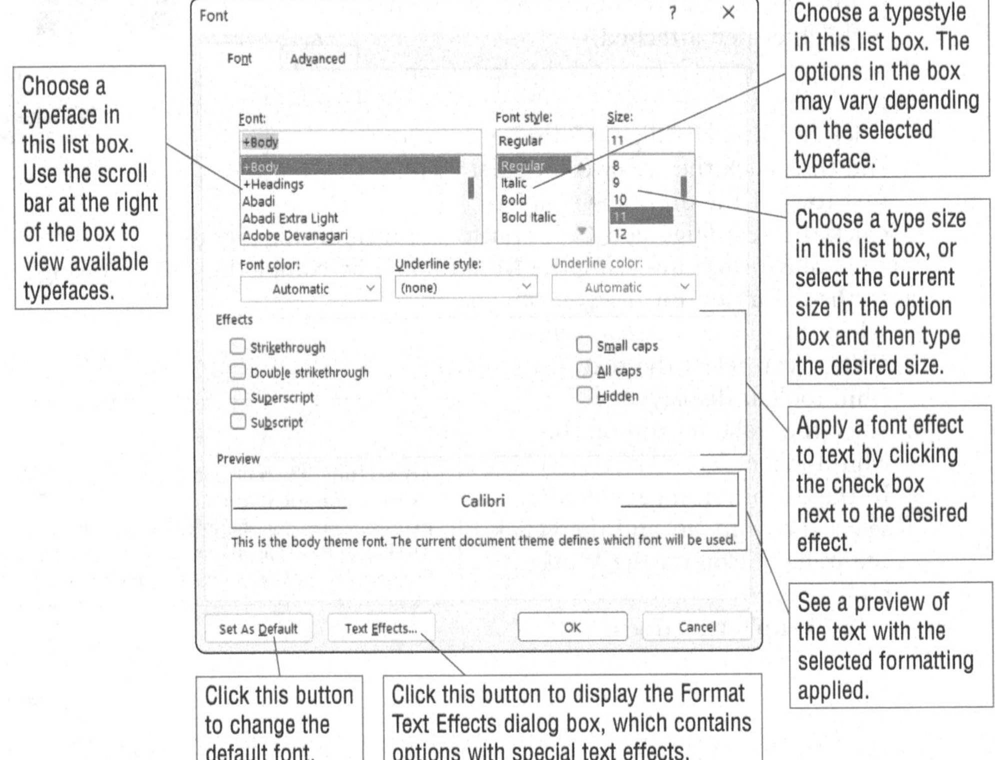
Font
Font
Advanced
Font:
Font style:
Size:
+Body
Regular
11
+Body
+Headings
Abadi
Abadi Extra Light
Adobe Devanagari
Regular
Italic
Bold
Bold Italic
8
9
10
11
12
Font color:
Underline style:
Underline color:
Automatic
(none)
Automatic
Effects
Strikethrough
Double strikethrough
Superscript
Subscript
Small caps
All caps
Hidden
Preview
Calibri
This is the body theme font. The current document theme defines which font will be used.
Set As Default
Text Effects...
OK
Cancel
Choose a typeface in this list box. Use the scroll bar at the right of the box to view available typefaces.
Choose a typestyle in this list box. The options in the box may vary depending on the selected typeface.
Choose a type size in this list box, or select the current size in the option box and then type the desired size.
Apply a font effect to text by clicking the check box next to the desired effect.
See a preview of the text with the selected formatting applied.
Click this button to change the default font.
Click this button to display the Format Text Effects dialog box, which contains options with special text effects.

Activity 1d Changing the Font at the Font Dialog Box

Part 4 of 4

1. With **2-CompTerms.docx** open, press Ctrl + End to move the insertion point to the end of the document (a double space below the last line of text).
2. Type Created by Susan Ashby and then press the Enter key.
3. Type Wednesday, February 21, 2024.

4. Change the font for the entire document to 13-point Candara in standard dark blue color by completing the following steps:
   a. Press Ctrl + A to select the entire document.
   b. Click the Font group dialog box launcher.
   c. At the Font dialog box, type can in the *Font* option box (this displays fonts that begin with *can*) and then click *Candara* in the *Font* list box.
   d. Click in the *Size* option box and then type 13.
   e. Click the *Font color* option box arrow and then click the *Dark Blue* color (ninth color option in the *Standard Colors* section).
   f. Click OK to close the dialog box.
5. Double-underline text by completing the following steps:
   a. Select *Wednesday, February 21, 2024*.
   b. Click the Font group dialog box launcher.
   c. At the Font dialog box, click the *Underline style* option box arrow and then click the double-line option at the drop-down list.
   d. Click OK to close the dialog box.
6. Change text to small caps and hide text by completing the following steps:
   a. Select the text *Created by Susan Ashby* and *Wednesday, February 21, 2024*.
   b. Display the Font dialog box.
   c. Click the *Small caps* check box in the *Effects* section. (This inserts a check mark in the check box.)
   d. Click the *Hidden* check box to insert a check mark.
   e. Click OK to close the dialog box.

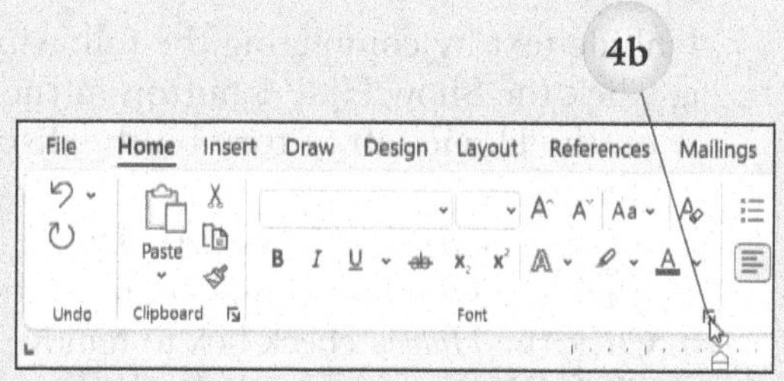

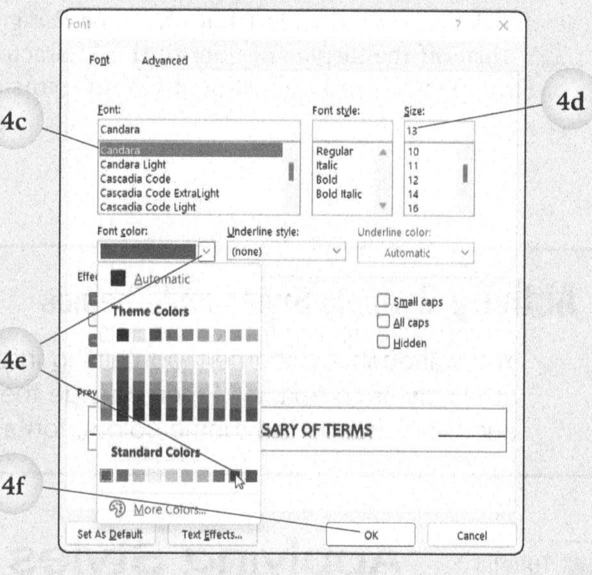

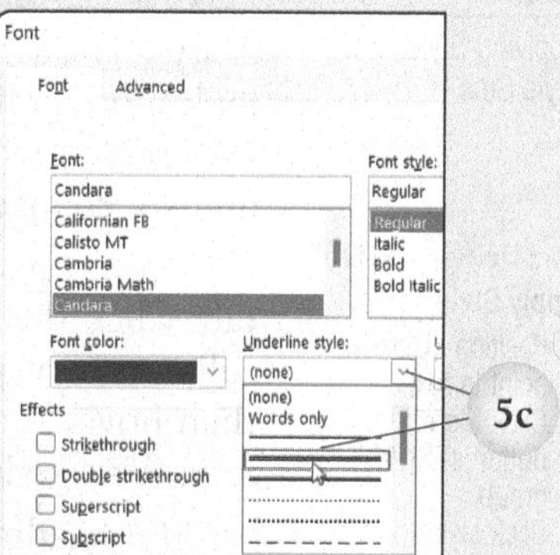

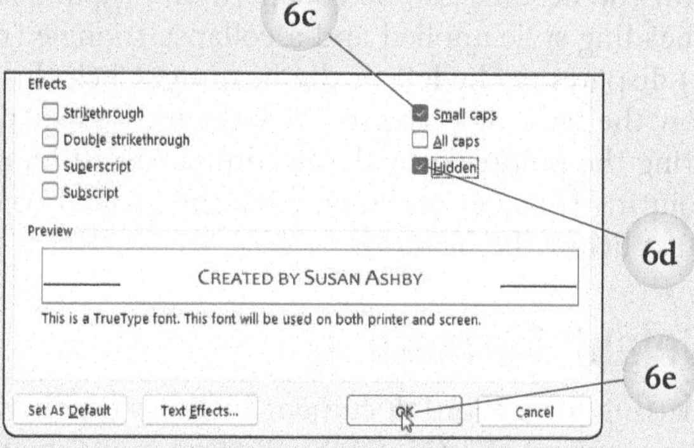

7. Unhide text by completing the following steps:
   a. Click the Show/Hide ¶ button in the Paragraph group on the Home tab to turn on the display of nonprinting characters.
   b. Select *CREATED BY SUSAN ASHBY*.
   c. Click the Font group dialog box launcher.
   d. Click the *Hidden* check box to remove the check mark.
   e. Click OK to close the dialog box.
   f. Click the Show/Hide ¶ button in the Paragraph group to turn off the display of nonprinting characters.
8. Save, preview, and then close **2-CompTerms.docx**.

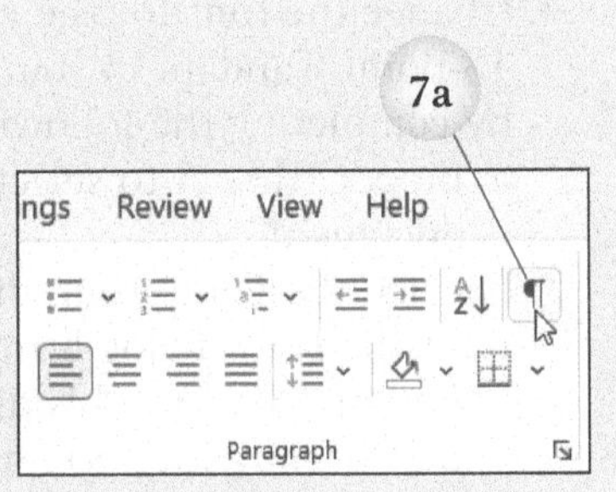

Activity 2 Apply Styles and Themes — 3 Parts

You will open a document containing information on the life cycle of software, apply styles to text, and then change the style set. You will also apply a theme and then change the theme colors, fonts, and paragraph spacing.

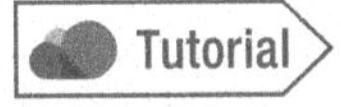

Applying Styles and Style Sets

Quick Steps

Apply Style
1. Position insertion point in text.
2. Click More Styles button in Styles group.
3. Click style.

Applying Styles from a Style Set

A style is a set of predefined formats that can be applied to a document to make it look more polished and professional and provide a structure that can be discerned by a screen reader. When styles are applied, the look of a document can be quickly changed by choosing a different style set.

Word provides a set of predesigned styles in the Styles group on the Home tab. Click the More Styles button (the arrow button at the right side of the gallery) to display all the style options. Position the insertion point in the text and then hover the pointer over the options in the gallery to see how the text will look in various styles and then click a style to apply it.

If a heading style (such as Heading 1, Heading 2, and so on) is applied to text, the text below the heading can be collapsed and expanded. Hover the pointer over text with a heading style applied and a collapse triangle (right- and down-pointing triangle) displays to the left of the heading. Click this collapse triangle and any text below the heading collapses (is hidden). Redisplay the text below a heading by hovering the pointer over the heading text until an expand triangle displays (right-pointing triangle) and then click the expand triangle. This expands (redisplays) the text below the heading.

Removing Default Formatting

The default formatting for a Word document includes 8 points of spacing after paragraphs and line spacing of 1.08. (You will learn more about these formatting options later in this chapter.) This default formatting, as well as any character formatting applied to text in the document, can be removed by applying the No Spacing style to the text. This style is in the styles gallery in the Styles group.

Changing the Style Set

Quick Steps
Change Style Set
1. Click Design tab.
2. Click style set.

To quickly change the look of an entire document, choose a new style set. Style sets can be found in a gallery on the Design tab in the Document Formatting group. Each set contains a different combination of title, heading, and paragraph styles. To apply a new style set, click the Design tab and then click the style set in the style sets gallery in the Document Formatting group.

Activity 2a Applying Styles and Changing the Style Set — Part 1 of 3

1. Open **SoftwareCycle.docx** and then save it with the name **2-SoftwareCycle**.
2. Position the insertion point anywhere in the title *SOFTWARE LIFE CYCLE* and then click the *Heading 1* style in the Styles group.

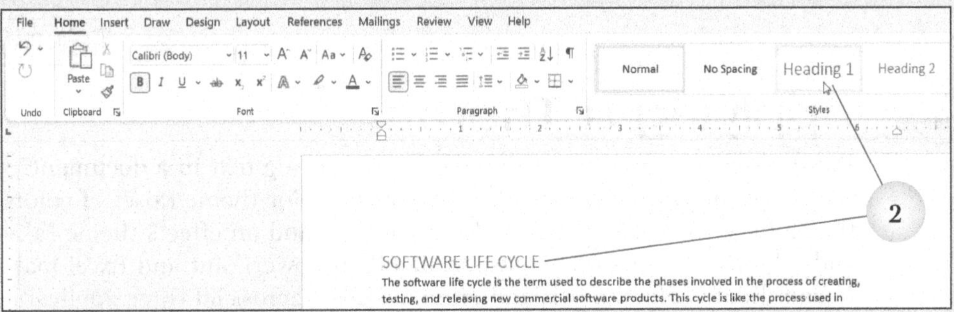

3. Position the insertion point anywhere in the heading *Proposal and Planning* and then click the *Heading 2* style in the styles gallery.

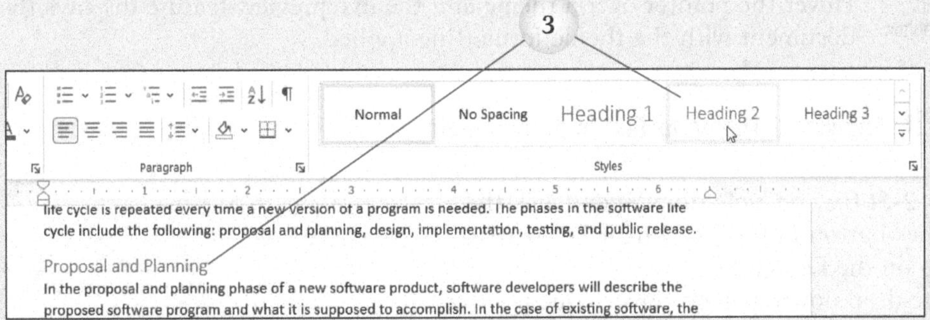

4. Position the insertion point anywhere in the heading *Design* and then click the *Heading 2* style in the styles gallery.
5. Apply the Heading 2 style to the remaining headings (*Implementation*, *Testing*, and *Public Release and Support*).
6. Collapse and expand text below the heading with the Heading 1 style applied by completing the following steps:
   a. Hover the pointer over the heading *SOFTWARE LIFE CYCLE* until a collapse triangle displays at the left of the heading and then click the triangle. (This collapses all the text below the heading.)
   b. Click the expand triangle at the left of the heading *SOFTWARE LIFE CYCLE*. (This redisplays the text in the document.)

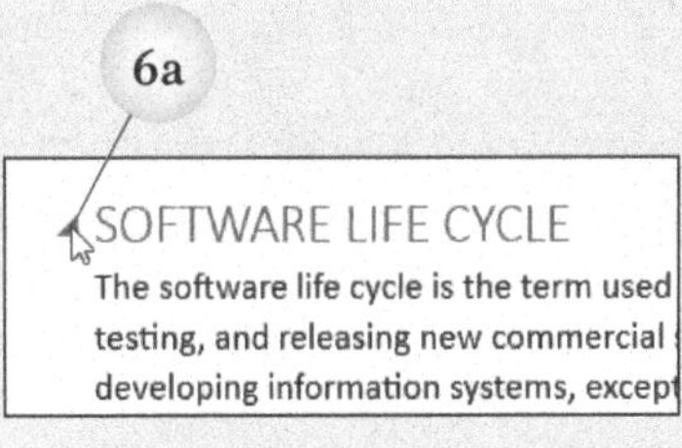

7. Click the Design tab.
8. Click the *Casual* style set in the style sets gallery in the Document Formatting group (the ninth option in the style set; this location may vary). (Notice how the Heading 1 and Heading 2 formatting changes.)

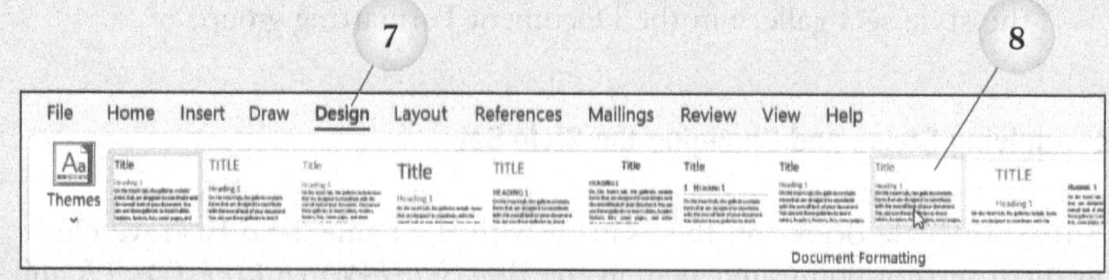

9. Save and then preview **2-SoftwareCycle.docx**.

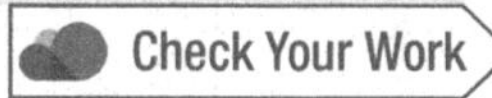

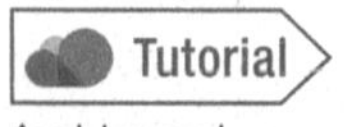

Applying and Modifying a Theme

Applying a Theme

Word provides a number of themes for formatting text in a document. A theme is a set of formatting choices that includes a color theme (a set of colors), a font theme (a set of heading and body text fonts), and an effects theme (a set of line and fill effects). Themes are also available in PowerPoint and Excel making it easy to coordinate colors, fonts, and graphic effects across all three applications and give files a consistent and cohesive appearance.

Quick Steps

Apply Theme

1. Click Design tab.
2. Click Themes button.
3. Click theme.

To apply a theme, click the Design tab, click the Themes button in the Document Formatting group, and then click the theme at the drop-down gallery. Hover the pointer over a theme and the live preview feature displays the document with the theme formatting applied.

Activity 2b Applying a Theme to Text in a Document — Part 2 of 3

1. With **2-SoftwareCycle.docx** open, click the Themes button in the Document Formatting group on the Design tab.
2. At the drop-down gallery, hover your pointer over several different themes and notice how the text formatting changes in your document.
3. Click the *Organic* theme.
4. Save and then preview **2-SoftwareCycle.docx**.

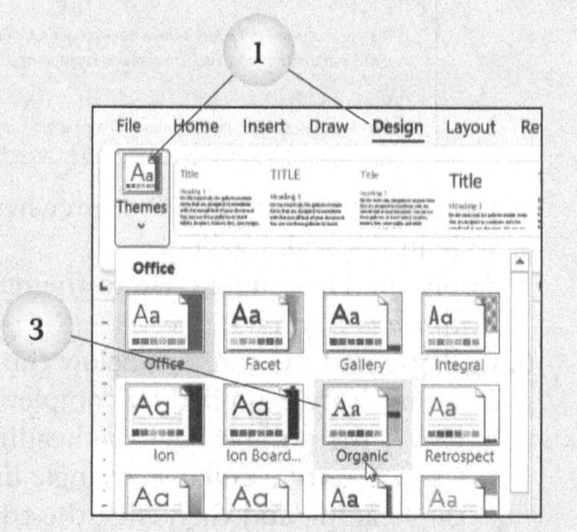

Check Your Work

Modifying a Theme

Quick Steps

Change Theme Color
1. Click Design tab.
2. Click Colors button.
3. Click theme color option.

Change Theme Fonts
1. Click Design tab.
2. Click Fonts button.
3. Click theme font option.

Change Paragraph Spacing
1. Click Design tab.
2. Click Paragraph Spacing button.
3. Click paragraph spacing option.

Theme Colors

Theme Fonts

Theme Effects

Paragraph Spacing

The color and font of a style or theme can be modified using buttons in the Document Formatting group on the Design tab. Click the Colors button and a drop-down gallery displays with various color schemes. Click the Fonts button in this group and a drop-down gallery displays with font choices. Each font group in the drop-down gallery contains two choices. The first choice is the font that is applied to headings, and the second choice is applied to body text in the document. If a document contains graphics with lines and fills, a specific theme effect can be applied with options at the Effects button drop-down gallery.

The buttons in the Document Formatting group provide a visual representation of the current theme. If the theme colors are changed, the small color squares in the Themes button and the larger squares in the Colors button reflect the change. Change the theme fonts and the *A*s on the Themes button and the uppercase *A* on the Fonts button reflect the change. If the theme effects are changed, the circle in the Effects button reflects the change.

The Paragraph Spacing button in the Document Formatting group on the Design tab contains predesigned paragraph spacing options. To change paragraph spacing, click the Paragraph Spacing button and then click an option at the drop-down gallery. Hover the pointer over an option at the drop-down gallery and after a moment a ScreenTip displays with information about the formatting applied by the option. For example, hover the pointer over the *Compact* option at the side menu and a ScreenTip displays indicating that selecting the *Compact* option will change the spacing before paragraphs to 0 points, the spacing after paragraphs to 4 points, and the line spacing to single line spacing.

Activity 2c Modifying a Theme — Part 3 of 3

1. With **2-SoftwareCycle.docx** open, click the Colors button in the Document Formatting group on the Design tab and then click the *Red Orange* option at the drop-down gallery. (Notice how the colors in the title and headings change.)
2. Click the Fonts button and then click the *Corbel* option. (Notice how the document text font changes.)

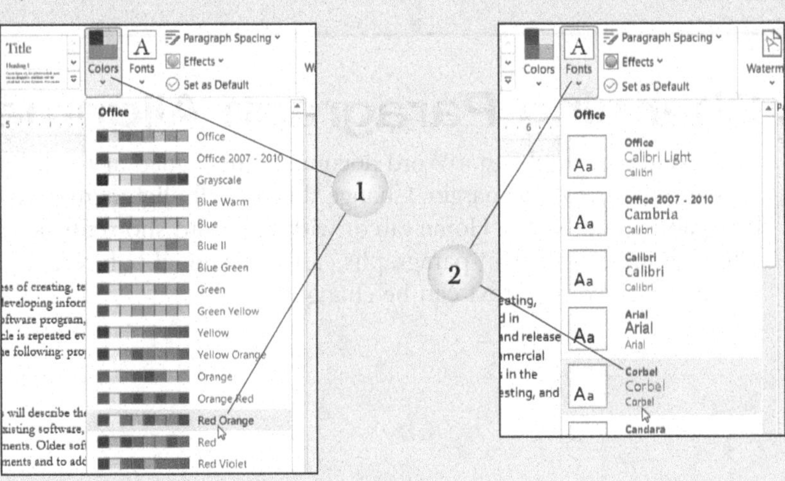

3. Click the Paragraph Spacing button and then, one at a time, hover the pointer over each paragraph spacing option, beginning with *Compact*. For each option, read the ScreenTip that explains the paragraph spacing applied by the option.
4. Click the *Double* option.

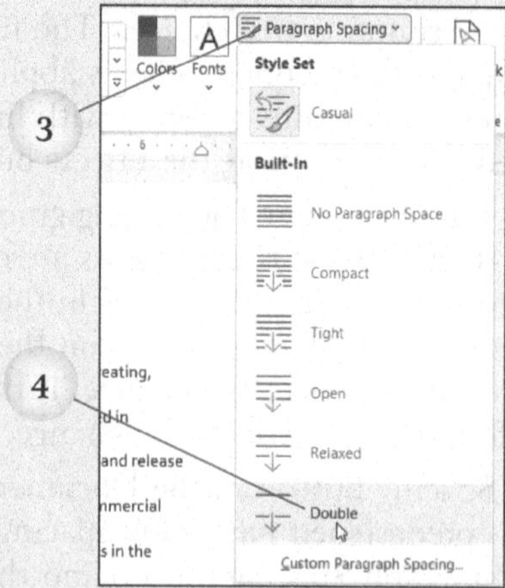

5. Scroll through the document and notice the paragraph spacing.
6. Change the paragraph spacing by clicking the Paragraph Spacing button and then clicking the *Compact* option.
7. Save, preview, and then close **2-SoftwareCycle.docx**.

Activity 3 Apply Paragraph Formatting and Use Format Painter 5 Parts

You will open a report on intellectual property and fair use issues and then format the report by changing the alignment and indent of text in paragraphs, changing spacing before and after paragraphs of text, and repeating the last formatting command. You will also format headings using Format Painter and change the line spacing of text.

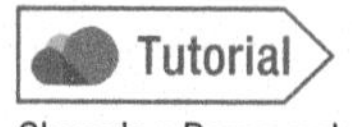

Changing Paragraph Alignment

Changing Paragraph Alignment

By default, paragraphs in a Word document are aligned at the left margin and are ragged at the right margin. Change this default alignment with buttons in the Paragraph group on the Home tab or with keyboard shortcuts, as shown in Table 2.3. The alignment of text in paragraphs can be changed before text is typed, or the alignment of existing text can be changed.

Table 2.3 Paragraph Alignment Buttons and Keyboard Shortcuts

To align text	Paragraph Group Button	Keyboard Shortcut
At the left margin		Ctrl + L
Between margins		Ctrl + E
At the right margin		Ctrl + R
At the left and right margins		Ctrl + J

Changing Paragraph Alignment as Text Is Typed

If the alignment is changed before text is typed, the alignment formatting is inserted in the paragraph mark. Type text and press the Enter key and the paragraph formatting is continued. For example, click the Center button in the Paragraph group on the Home tab, type text for the first paragraph, and then press the Enter key; the center alignment formatting is still active and the insertion point is centered between the left and right margins. To display the paragraph symbols in a document, click the Show/Hide ¶ button in the Paragraph group. With the Show/Hide ¶ button active (displays with a gray background), nonprinting formatting symbols display.

Changing Paragraph Alignment of Existing Text

Hint Align text to help the reader follow the message of a document and to make the layout look appealing.

To change the alignment of existing text in a paragraph, position the insertion point anywhere within the paragraph. The entire paragraph does not need to be selected. To change the alignment of several adjacent paragraphs in a document, select a portion of the first paragraph through a portion of the last paragraph. All the text in the paragraphs does not need to be selected.

To return paragraph alignment to the default (left-aligned), click the Align Left button in the Paragraph group. All paragraph formatting can also be returned to the default with the keyboard shortcut Ctrl + Q. This keyboard shortcut removes paragraph formatting from selected text. To remove all formatting from selected text, including character and paragraph formatting, click the Clear All Formatting button in the Font group.

Changing Alignment at the Paragraph Dialog Box

Quick Steps

Change Paragraph Alignment

Click alignment button in Paragraph group on Home tab.
OR
1. Click Paragraph group dialog box launcher.
2. Click *Alignment* option box arrow.
3. Click alignment option.
4. Click OK.

Along with buttons in the Paragraph group on the Home tab and keyboard shortcuts, options in the *Alignment* option box at the Paragraph dialog box, shown in Figure 2.6, can be used to change paragraph alignment. Display this dialog box by clicking the Paragraph group dialog box launcher. At the Paragraph dialog box, click the *Alignment* option box arrow. At the drop-down list, click the alignment option and then click OK to close the dialog box.

Figure 2.6 Paragraph Dialog Box with the Indents and Spacing Tab Selected

Change paragraph alignment by clicking the *Alignment* option box arrow and then clicking the alignment option at the drop-down list.

Use these options to adjust spacing before and after paragraphs.

Activity 3a Changing Paragraph Alignment

Part 1 of 5

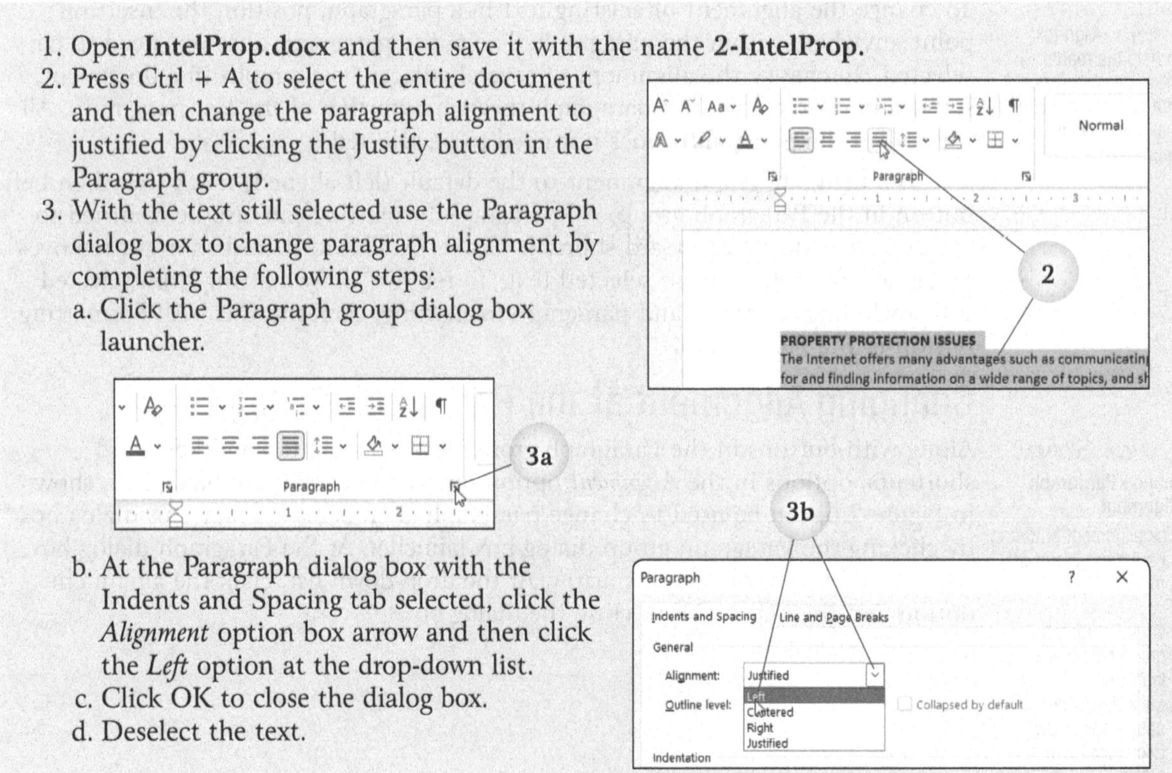

1. Open **IntelProp.docx** and then save it with the name **2-IntelProp**.
2. Press Ctrl + A to select the entire document and then change the paragraph alignment to justified by clicking the Justify button in the Paragraph group.
3. With the text still selected use the Paragraph dialog box to change paragraph alignment by completing the following steps:
   a. Click the Paragraph group dialog box launcher.
   b. At the Paragraph dialog box with the Indents and Spacing tab selected, click the *Alignment* option box arrow and then click the *Left* option at the drop-down list.
   c. Click OK to close the dialog box.
   d. Deselect the text.

4. Change paragraph alignment by completing the following steps:
   a. Press Ctrl + End to move the insertion point to the end of the document and then position the insertion point anywhere in the text *Prepared by Clarissa Markham*.
   b. Click the Paragraph group dialog box launcher.
   c. At the Paragraph dialog box with the Indents and Spacing tab selected, click the *Alignment* option box arrow and then click the *Right* option at the drop-down list.
   d. Click OK to close the dialog box. (The line of text containing the name *Clarissa Markham* and the line of text containing the name *Joshua Streeter* are both aligned at the right because the New Line command, Shift + Enter, was used to separate the lines of text without creating a new paragraph.)
5. Save **2-IntelProp.docx**.

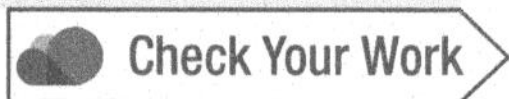

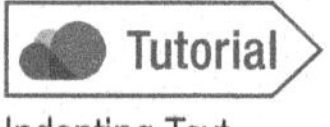

Indenting Text

Quick Steps

Indent Text

Drag indent marker(s) on horizontal ruler.

OR

Press keyboard shortcut keys.

OR

1. Click Paragraph group dialog box launcher.
2. Insert measurement in *Left*, *Right*, and/or *By* measurement box.
3. Click OK.

Indenting Text in Paragraphs

The first line of a paragraph is commonly indented to show paragraph breaks in a document. Paragraphs may also be indented from the left and right margins to set them off from the rest of the text. For instance, a long quotation or a bulleted or numbered list may be indented in this manner.

To indent text from the left margin, the right margin, or both margins, use the indent buttons in the Paragraph group on the Layout tab, keyboard shortcuts, options from the Paragraph dialog box, markers on the horizontal ruler, or the Alignment button above the vertical ruler. Figure 2.7 identifies indent markers on the horizontal ruler as well as the Alignment button. Refer to Table 2.4 for methods for indenting text in a document. If the horizontal ruler is not visible, display the ruler by clicking the View tab and then clicking the *Ruler* check box in the Show group to insert a check mark.

Figure 2.7 Horizontal Ruler and Indent Markers

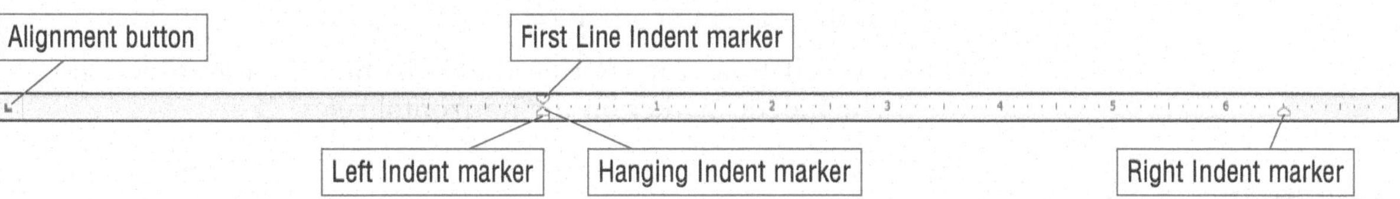

Table 2.4 Methods for Indenting Text

Indent	Methods for Indenting
First line of paragraph	• Press the Tab key. • Display the Paragraph dialog box, click the *Special* option box arrow, click *First line*, and then click OK. • Drag the First Line Indent marker on the horizontal ruler. • Click the Alignment button above the vertical ruler until the First Line Indent symbol displays and then click the horizontal ruler at the desired location.

Continues

Table 2.4 Methods for Indenting Text—*Continued*

Indent	Methods for Indenting
Text from left margin	• Click the Increase Indent button in the Paragraph group on the Home tab to increase the indent or click the Decrease Indent button to decrease the indent. • Insert a measurement in the *Indent Left* measurement box in the Paragraph group on the Layout tab. • Press Ctrl + M to increase the indent or press Ctrl + Shift + M to decrease the indent. • Display the Paragraph dialog box, type the indent measurement in the *Left* measurement box, and then click OK. • Drag the Left Indent marker on the horizontal ruler.
Text from right margin	• Insert a measurement in the *Indent Right* measurement box in the Paragraph group on the Layout tab. • Display the Paragraph dialog box, type the indent measurement in the *Right* measurement box, and then click OK. • Drag the Right Indent marker on the horizontal ruler.
All lines of text except first (called a *hanging indent*)	• Press Ctrl + T. (Press Ctrl + Shift + T to remove a hanging indent.) • Display the Paragraph dialog box, click the *Special* option box arrow, click *Hanging*, and then click OK. • Click the Alignment button, left of the horizontal ruler and above the vertical ruler, until the Hanging Indent symbol displays and then click the horizontal ruler at the desired location. • Drag the Hanging Indent marker on the horizontal ruler.
Text from both left and right margins	• Display the Paragraph dialog box, type the indent measurement in the *Left* measurement box, type the indent measurement in the *Right* measurement box, and then click OK. • Insert measurements in the *Indent Right* and *Indent Left* measurement boxes in the Paragraph group on the Layout tab. • Drag the Left Indent marker on the horizontal ruler and then drag the Right Indent marker on the horizontal ruler.

Activity 3b Indenting Text

Part 2 of 5

1. With **2-IntelProp.docx** open, indent the first line of text in each paragraph by completing the following steps:
   a. Select the text in the document after the title *PROPERTY PROTECTION ISSUES* and before the heading *Intellectual Property*.
   b. Make sure the horizontal ruler is visible. (If it is not, click the View tab and then click the *Ruler* check box in the Show group to insert a check mark.)
   c. Position the pointer on the First Line Indent marker on the horizontal ruler, click and hold down the left mouse button, drag the marker to the 0.5-inch mark, and then release the mouse button.

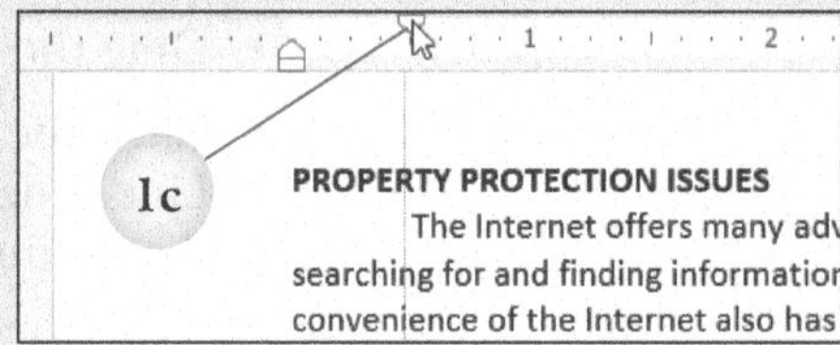

d. Select the text in the *Intellectual Property* section and then drag the First Line Indent marker on the horizontal ruler to the 0.5-inch mark.

e. Select the text in the *Fair Use* section, click the Alignment button above the vertical ruler until the First Line Indent symbol displays, and then click the horizontal ruler at the 0.5-inch mark.

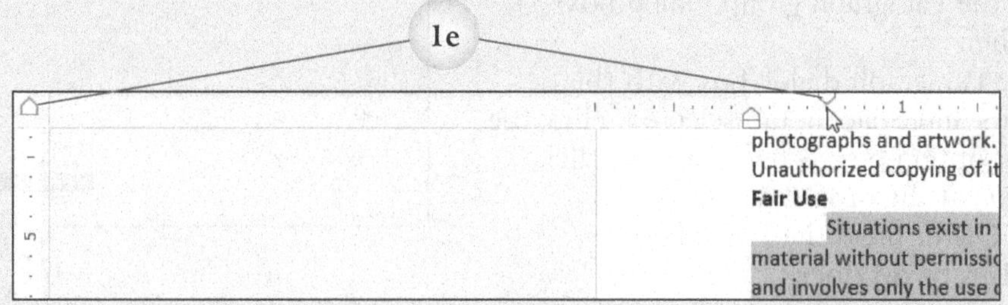

f. Position the insertion point anywhere in the paragraph of text below the heading *Intellectual Property Protection*, make sure the First Line Indent symbol displays on the Alignment button, and then click the 0.5-inch mark on the horizontal ruler.

2. Since the text in the second paragraph in the *Fair Use* section is a quote, indent the text from the left and right margins by completing the following steps:
   a. Position the insertion point anywhere in the second paragraph in the *Fair Use* section (the paragraph that begins *[A] copyrighted work, including such*).
   b. Click the Paragraph group dialog box launcher.
   c. At the Paragraph dialog box with the Indents and Spacing tab selected, select the current measurement in the *Left* measurement box and then type 0.5.
   d. Select the current measurement in the *Right* measurement box and then type 0.5.
   e. Click the *Special* option box arrow and then click *(none)* at the drop-down list.
   f. Click OK.

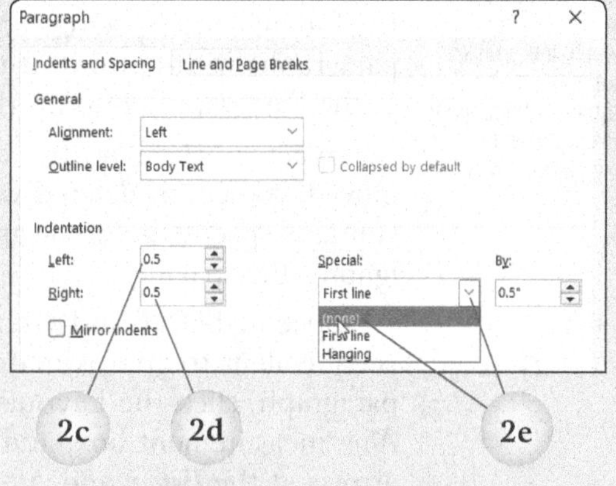

3. Create a hanging indent for the first paragraph in the *REFERENCES* section by positioning the insertion point anywhere in the first paragraph below the heading *REFERENCES* (on the third page) and then pressing Ctrl + T.

4. Create a hanging indent for the second paragraph in the *REFERENCES* section by completing the following steps:
   a. Position the insertion point anywhere in the second paragraph in the *REFERENCES* section.
   b. Click the Alignment button until the Hanging Indent symbol displays.
   c. Click the 0.5-inch mark on the horizontal ruler.

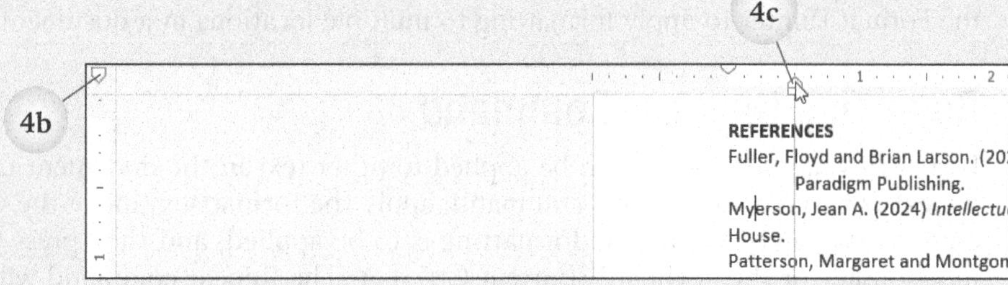

5. Create a hanging indent for the third and fourth paragraphs by completing the following steps:
   a. Select a portion of the third and fourth paragraphs.
   b. Click the Paragraph group dialog box launcher.
   c. At the Paragraph dialog box with the Indents and Spacing tab selected, click the *Special* option box arrow and then click *Hanging* at the drop-down list.
   d. Click OK or press the Enter key.
6. Save **2-IntelProp.docx**.

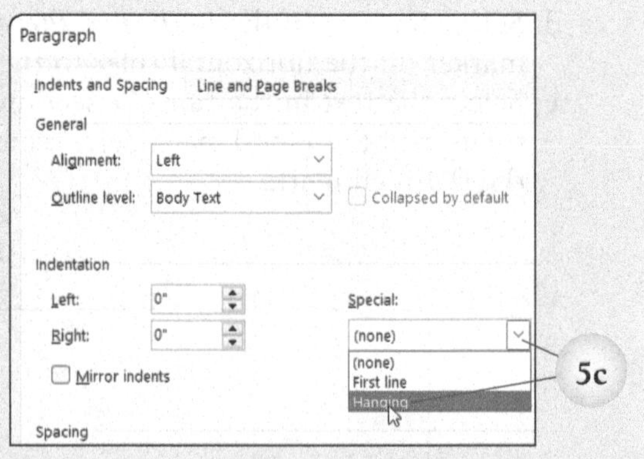

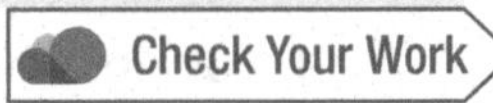

Changing Spacing Before and After Paragraphs

Hint Line spacing determines the amount of vertical space between lines, while paragraph spacing determines the amount of space above or below paragraphs of text.

Spacing Before and After Paragraphs

By default, Word applies 8 points of additional spacing after a paragraph. This spacing can be removed or it can be increased or decreased, and spacing can be inserted above the paragraph. To change spacing before or after a paragraph, use the *Before* and *After* measurement boxes in the Paragraph group on the Layout tab, or use the *Before* and *After* measurement boxes at the Paragraph dialog box with the Indents and Spacing tab selected. Spacing can also be added before and after paragraphs with options at the Line and Paragraph Spacing button drop-down list in the Paragraph group on the Home tab.

Spacing before or after a paragraph is part of the paragraph and will be moved, copied, or deleted with the paragraph. If a paragraph, such as a heading, contains spacing before it and the paragraph falls at the top of a page, Word ignores the spacing.

Spacing before and after paragraphs is added in points. One vertical inch is equivalent to approximately 72 points. To add spacing before or after a paragraph, click the Layout tab, select the current measurement in the *Before* or *After* measurement box, and then type the number of points. The up or down arrows at the *Before* and *After* measurement boxes can also be clicked to increase or decrease the amount of spacing.

Automating Formatting

Applying consistent formatting in a document, especially a multiple-page document, can be time consuming. Word provides options for applying formatting automatically. Use the Repeat command to repeat the last action, such as applying formatting, or the Format Painter to apply formatting to multiple locations in a document.

Repeating the Last Command

Quick Steps

Repeat Last Action

Press F4.
OR
Press Ctrl + Y.

Repeating the Last Command

Formatting applied to text can be applied to other text in the document using the Repeat command. To use this command, apply the formatting, move the insertion point to the next location the formatting is to be applied, and then press the F4 function key or the keyboard shortcut Ctrl + Y. The Repeat command will repeat only the last command executed.

Activity 3c Changing Spacing Before and After Paragraphs and Repeating the Last Command

Part 3 of 5

1. With **2-IntelProp.docx** open, add 6 points of spacing before and after each paragraph in the document by completing the following steps:
   a. Select the entire document.
   b. Click the Layout tab.
   c. Click the *Before* measurement box up arrow in the Paragraph group. (This inserts *6 pt* in the box.)
   d. Click the *After* measurement box up arrow two times. (This inserts *6 pt* in the box.)

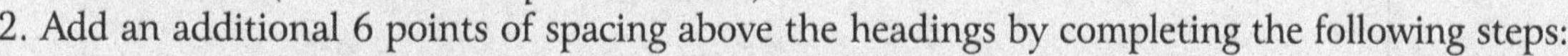

2. Add an additional 6 points of spacing above the headings by completing the following steps:
   a. Position the insertion point anywhere in the heading *Intellectual Property* and then click the *Before* measurement box up arrow. (This changes the measurement to *12 pt.*)

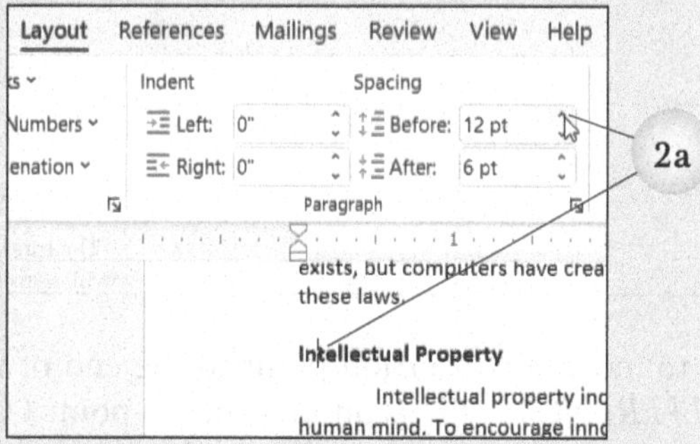

   b. Position the insertion point anywhere in the heading *Fair Use* and then press the F4 function key. (F4 is the Repeat command.)
   c. Position the insertion point anywhere in the heading *Intellectual Property Protection* and then press the F4 function key.
   d. Position the insertion point anywhere in the heading *REFERENCES* and then press Ctrl + Y. (Ctrl + Y is also the Repeat command.) (When a heading displays at the beginning of a page, the spacing above is ignored.)
3. Save **2-IntelProp.docx**.

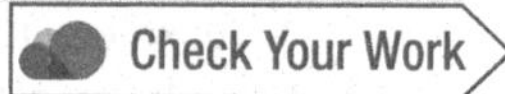

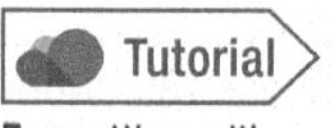

Formatting with Format Painter

Format Painter

Quick Steps

Format with Format Painter

1. Click in formatted text.
2. Click Format Painter button.
3. Select text.

Formatting with Format Painter

The Home tab contains a button for copying formatting, which displays in the Clipboard group with a paintbrush. To use this button, called Format Painter, position the insertion point anywhere in text containing the desired formatting, click the Format Painter button, and then select the text to which the formatting is to be applied. When the Format Painter button is clicked, the I-beam pointer displays with a paintbrush attached. To apply the formatting a single time, click the Format Painter button. To apply the formatting in more than one location in the document, double-click the Format Painter button and then select the text to which the formatting is to be applied. When finished, click the Format Painter button to turn it off. The Format Painter button can also be turned off by pressing the Esc key.

Activity 3d Formatting Headings with Format Painter

1. With **2-IntelProp.docx** open, click the Home tab.
2. Select the entire document and then change the font to 12-point Cambria.
3. Select the title *PROPERTY PROTECTION ISSUES*, click the Center button in the Paragraph group, and then change the font to 16-point Candara.
4. Apply 16-point Candara and center-alignment formatting to the heading *REFERENCES* by completing the following steps:
   a. Click in the title *PROPERTY PROTECTION ISSUES*.
   b. Click the Format Painter button in the Clipboard group.

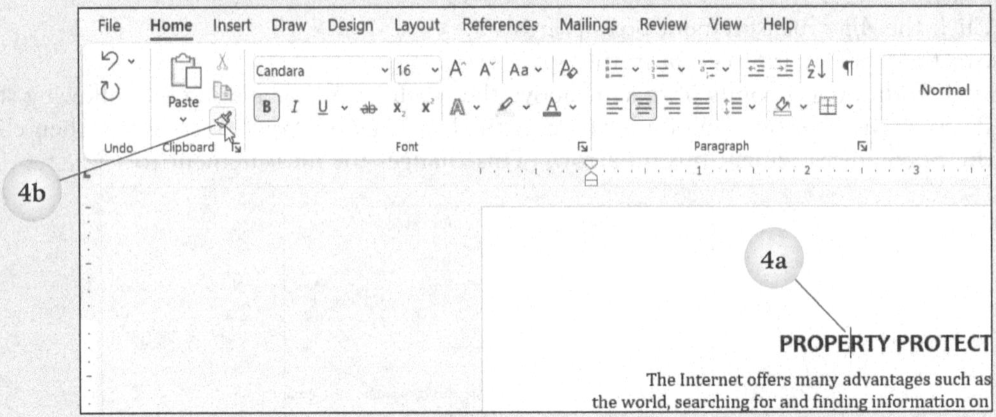

   c. Press Ctrl + End to move the insertion point to the end of the document and then click in the heading *REFERENCES*. (This applies the 16-point Candara formatting and centers the text.)
5. Select the heading *Intellectual Property* and then change the font to 14-point Candara.
6. Use the Format Painter button to apply 14-point Candara formatting to the other headings by completing the following steps:
   a. Position the insertion point anywhere in the heading *Intellectual Property*.
   b. Double-click the Format Painter button in the Clipboard group.
   c. Using the mouse, select the heading *Fair Use*.
   d. Using the mouse, select the heading *Intellectual Property Protection*.
   e. Click the Format Painter button in the Clipboard group. (This turns off the feature and deactivates the button.)
   f. Deselect the heading.
7. Save **2-IntelProp.docx**.

Changing Line Spacing

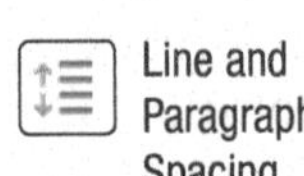

Line and Paragraph Spacing

Changing Line Spacing

The default line spacing for a document is 1.08. (The line spacing for the IntelProp file, which you opened at the beginning of Activity 3, had been changed to single line spacing.) In certain situations, Word automatically adjusts the line spacing. For example, if a large character or object, such as a graphic, is inserted into a line, Word increases the line spacing of that line. The line spacing for a paragraph, section, or an entire document can be changed.

Quick Steps

Change Line Spacing

1. Click Line and Paragraph Spacing button.
2. Click option.

OR

Press keyboard shortcut command.

OR

1. Click Paragraph group dialog box launcher.
2. Click *Line spacing* option box arrow.
3. Click line spacing option.
4. Click OK.

OR

1. Click Paragraph group dialog box launcher.
2. Type line measurement in *At* measurement box.
3. Click OK.

Change line spacing using the Line and Paragraph Spacing button in the Paragraph group on the Home tab, keyboard shortcuts, or options in the Paragraph dialog box. Table 2.5 shows the keyboard shortcuts to change line spacing.

Line spacing can also be changed at the Paragraph dialog box with the *Line spacing* option or the *At* measurement box. Click the *Line spacing* option box arrow and a drop-down list displays with a variety of spacing options, such as *Single*, *1.5 lines*, and *Double*. A specific line spacing measurement can be entered in the *At* measurement box. For example, to change the line spacing to 1.75 lines, type *1.75* in the *At* measurement box.

Table 2.5 Line Spacing Keyboard Shortcuts

Press	To change line spacing to
Ctrl + 1	single line spacing (1.0)
Ctrl + 2	double line spacing (2.0)
Ctrl + 5	1.5 line spacing

Activity 3e Changing Line Spacing

Part 5 of 5

1. With **2-IntelProp.docx** open, change the line spacing for all paragraphs to double spacing by completing the following steps:
   a. Select the entire document.
   b. Click the Line and Paragraph Spacing button in the Paragraph group on the Home tab.
   c. Click *2.0* at the drop-down list.
2. With the entire document still selected, press Ctrl + 5. (This changes the line spacing to 1.5 lines.)
3. Change the line spacing to 1.2 lines at the Paragraph dialog box by completing the following steps:
   a. With the entire document still selected, click the Paragraph group dialog box launcher.
   b. At the Paragraph dialog box, make sure the Indents and Spacing tab is selected, click in the *At* measurement box, and then type 1.2. (This measurement box is to the right of the *Line spacing* option box.)
   c. Click OK or press the Enter key.
   d. Deselect the text.
4. Save, preview, and then close **2-IntelProp.docx**.

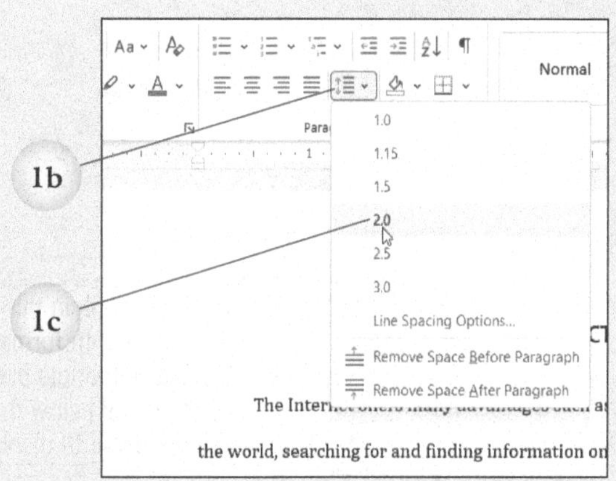

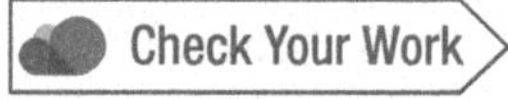

Activity 4 Reveal and Compare Formatting in a Document — 2 Parts

You will open a document containing two computer-related problems to solve, reveal the formatting, compare the formatting, and make formatting changes.

Revealing and Comparing Formatting

Display formatting applied to specific text in a document at the Reveal Formatting task pane, shown in Figure 2.8. The Reveal Formatting task pane displays font, paragraph, and section formatting applied to text where the insertion point is positioned or to selected text. Display the Reveal Formatting task pane with the keyboard shortcut Shift + F1. Generally, a collapse triangle (a solid right-and-down-pointing triangle) precedes *Font* and *Paragraph* and an expand triangle (a hollow right-pointing triangle) precedes *Section* in the *Formatting of selected text* list box in the Reveal Formatting task pane. Click the collapse triangle to hide any items below a heading and click the expand triangle to reveal items. Some of the items below headings in the *Formatting of selected text* list box are hyperlinks. Click a hyperlink and a dialog box displays with the specific option.

Figure 2.8 Reveal Formatting Task Pane

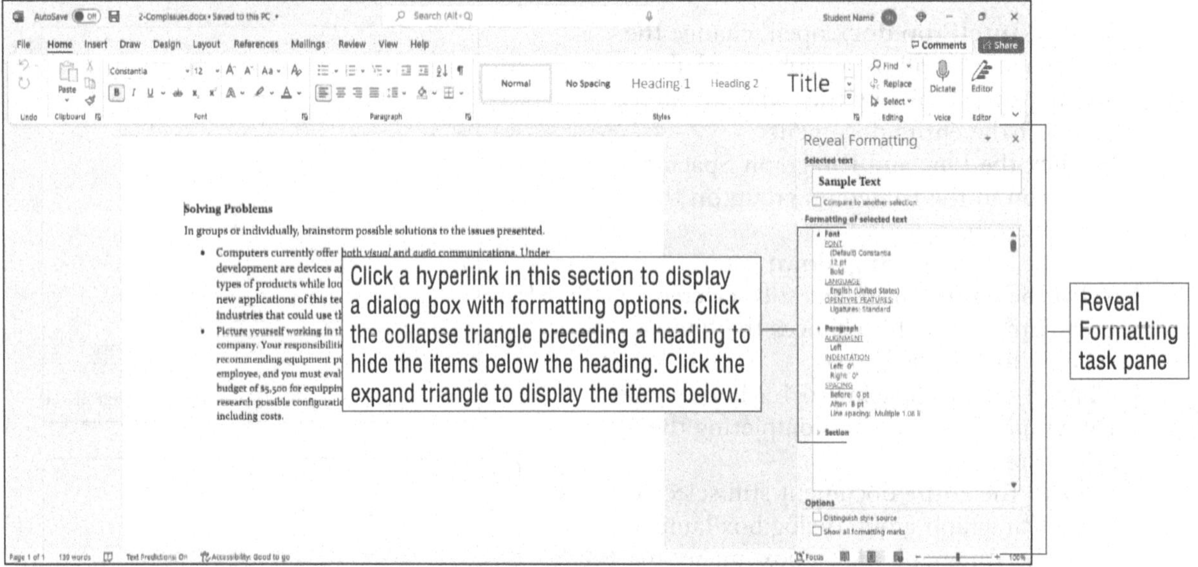

Activity 4a Revealing Formatting — Part 1 of 2

1. Open **CompIssues.docx** and then save it with the name **2-CompIssues**.
2. Press Shift + F1 to display the Reveal Formatting task pane.
3. Click in the heading *Solving Problems* and then notice the formatting information in the Reveal Formatting task pane.
4. Click in the bulleted paragraph and then notice the formatting information in the Reveal Formatting task pane.
5. Leave **2-CompIssues.docx** open for the next activity.

Quick Steps

Compare Formatting

1. Press Shift + F1 to display Reveal Formatting task pane.
2. Click or select text.
3. Click *Compare to another selection* check box.
4. Click or select text.

Along with displaying formatting applied to text, the Reveal Formatting task pane can be used to compare formatting in two text selections to determine what is different. To compare formatting, select the first instance of formatting to be compared, click the *Compare to another selection* check box, and then select the second instance of formatting to be compared. Any differences between the two selections display in the *Formatting differences* list box.

Activity 4b Comparing Formatting

Part 2 of 2

1. With **2-CompIssues.docx** open, make sure the Reveal Formatting task pane is visible. If it is not, turn it on by pressing Shift + F1.
2. Select the first bulleted paragraph (the paragraph that begins *Computers currently offer both*).
3. Click the *Compare to another selection* check box to insert a check mark.
4. Select the second bulleted paragraph (the paragraph that begins *Picture yourself working in the*).
5. Determine the formatting differences by reading the information in the *Formatting differences* list box. (The list box shows *12 pt -> 11 pt* below the FONT hyperlink, indicating that the difference is point size.)
6. Format the second bulleted paragraph so it is set in 12-point size.
7. Click the *Compare to another selection* check box to remove the check mark.
8. Select the word *visual*, which is used in the first sentence in the first bulleted paragraph.
9. Click the *Compare to another selection* check box to insert a check mark.
10. Select the word *audio*, which is used in the first sentence of the first bulleted paragraph.
11. Determine the formatting differences by reading the information in the *Formatting differences* list box.
12. Format the word *audio* so it matches the formatting of the word *visual*.
13. Click the *Compare to another selection* check box to remove the check mark.
14. Close the Reveal Formatting task pane by clicking the Close button in the upper right corner of the task pane.
15. Save, preview, and then close **2-CompIssues.docx**.

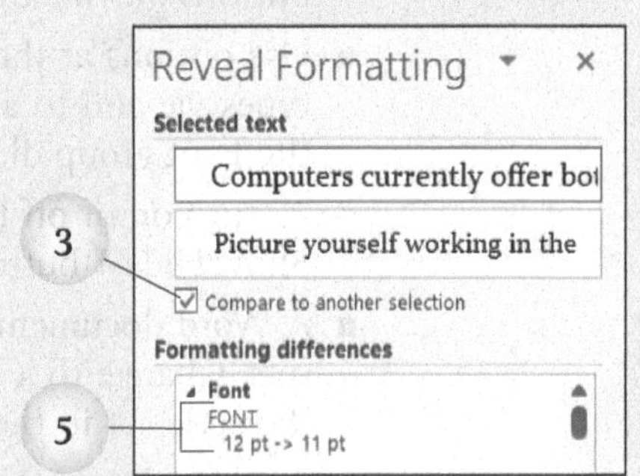

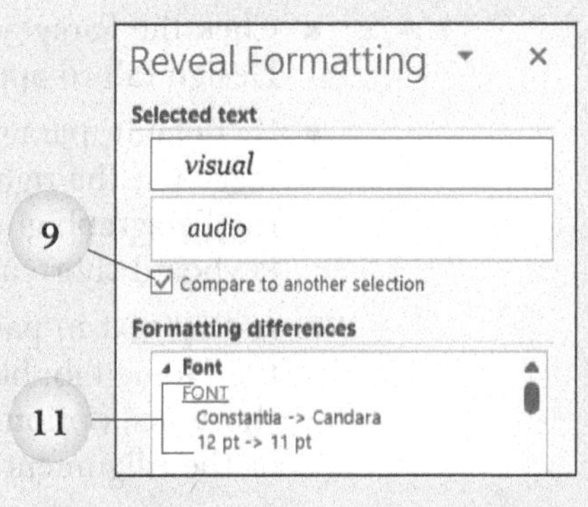

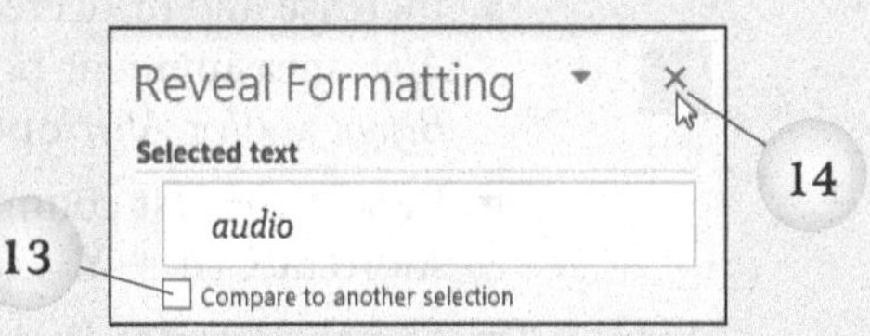

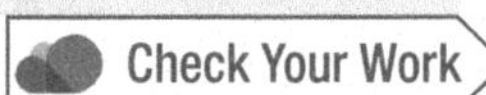

Chapter Summary

- A font consists of three elements: typeface, type size, and typestyle.
- A typeface (font) is a set of characters with a common design and shape. Typefaces are monospaced, allotting the same amount of horizontal space for each character, or proportional, allotting varying amounts of space for different characters. Typefaces are divided into two main categories: serif and sans serif.
- Type size is measured in points; the higher the point size, the larger the characters.
- A typestyle is a variation of style within a certain typeface, such as bold, italic, or underline. Apply typestyles with buttons in the Font group on the Home tab.
- Apply font effects, such as superscript, subscript, and strikethrough formatting, with buttons in the second row in the Font group on the Home tab.
- The Mini toolbar automatically displays above selected text. Use options and buttons on this toolbar to apply formatting to the selected text.
- Use options at the Font dialog box to change the typeface, type size, and typestyle and to apply specific font effects. Display this dialog box by clicking the Font group dialog box launcher in the Font group on the Home tab.
- To turn on or off the display of nonprinting characters and hidden text, click the Show/Hide ¶ button in the Paragraph group on the Home tab.
- A Word document contains a number of predesigned formats grouped into style sets. Change to a different style set by clicking the Design tab and then clicking the style set in the style set gallery in the Document Formatting group.
- Apply a theme and change theme colors, fonts, and effects with buttons in the Document Formatting group on the Design tab.
- Click the Paragraph Spacing button in the Document Formatting group on the Design tab to apply a predesigned paragraph spacing option to text.
- By default, paragraphs in a Word document are aligned at the left margin and ragged at the right margin. Change this default alignment with buttons in the Paragraph group on the Home tab, at the Paragraph dialog box, or with keyboard shortcuts.
- Indent text in paragraphs with indent buttons in the Paragraph group on the Home tab, buttons in the Paragraph group on the Layout tab, keyboard shortcuts, options at the Paragraph dialog box, markers on the horizontal ruler, or the Alignment button above the vertical ruler.
- Increase and/or decrease spacing before and after paragraphs using the *Before* and *After* measurement boxes in the Paragraph group on the Layout tab or using the *Before* and/or *After* options at the Paragraph dialog box.
- Repeat the last command by pressing the F4 function key or the keyboard shortcut Ctrl + Y.
- Use the Format Painter button in the Clipboard group on the Home tab to copy formatting already applied to text to different locations in the document.
- Change line spacing with the Line and Paragraph Spacing button in the Paragraph group on the Home tab, keyboard shortcuts, or options at the Paragraph dialog box.
- Display the Reveal Formatting task pane with the keyboard shortcut Shift + F1. Use the *Compare to another selection* option in the task pane to compare formatting of two text selections to determine what is different.

Commands Review

FEATURE	RIBBON TAB, GROUP	BUTTON	KEYBOARD SHORTCUT
bold text	Home, Font		Ctrl + B
center-align text	Home, Paragraph		Ctrl + E
change case of text	Home, Font		Shift + F3
clear all formatting	Home, Font		
clear character formatting			Ctrl + spacebar
clear paragraph formatting			Ctrl + Q
decrease font size	Home, Font		Ctrl + Shift + < OR Ctrl + [
decrease indent	Home, Paragraph		
display or hide nonprinting characters	Home, Paragraph		Ctrl + Shift + *
font	Home, Font		
font color	Home, Font		
Font dialog box	Home, Font		Ctrl + D
font size	Home, Font		
Format Painter	Home, Clipboard		
highlight text	Home, Font		
increase font size	Home, Font		Ctrl + Shift + > OR Ctrl +]
increase indent	Home, Paragraph		
italicize text	Home, Font		Ctrl + I
justify text	Home, Paragraph		Ctrl + J
left-align text	Home, Paragraph		Ctrl + L
line spacing	Home, Paragraph		Ctrl + 1 (single) Ctrl + 2 (double) Ctrl + 5 (1.5)

Continues

FEATURE	RIBBON TAB, GROUP	BUTTON	KEYBOARD SHORTCUT
Paragraph dialog box	Home, Paragraph		
paragraph spacing	Design, Document Formatting		
repeat last action			F4 or Ctrl + Y
Reveal Formatting task pane			Shift + F1
right-align text	Home, Paragraph		Ctrl + R
spacing after paragraph	Layout, Paragraph		
spacing before paragraph	Layout, Paragraph		
strikethrough text	Home, Font		
subscript text	Home, Font		Ctrl + =
superscript text	Home, Font		Ctrl + Shift + +
text effects and typography	Home, Font		
theme colors	Design, Document Formatting		
theme effects	Design, Document Formatting		
theme fonts	Design, Document Formatting		
themes	Design, Document Formatting		
underline text	Home, Font		Ctrl + U

Review and Assessment

CHAPTER 2

Skills Assessment

Assessment 1

Apply Character Formatting to a Lease Agreement Document

1. Open **LeaseAgrmnt.docx** and then save it with the name **2-LeaseAgrmnt**.
2. Press Ctrl + End to move the insertion point to the end of the document, press the Enter key, and then type the text shown in Figure 2.9. Bold, italicize, and underline text as shown.
3. Select the entire document and then change the font to Candara and the font size to 12 points.
4. Select and then bold *THIS LEASE AGREEMENT* in the first paragraph.
5. Select and then italicize *12 o'clock midnight* in the *Term* section.
6. Select the title *LEASE AGREEMENT* and then change the font to 16-point Corbel and the font color to standard dark blue. (The title should remain bold.)
7. Select the heading *Term*, change the font to 14-point Corbel, and then apply small caps formatting. (The heading should remain bold.)
8. Use Format Painter to change the formatting to small caps in 14-point Corbel bold for the remaining headings (*Rent*, *Damage Deposit*, *Use of Premises*, *Condition of Premises*, *Damage to Premises*, and *Inspection of Premises*).
9. Save, preview, and then close **2-LeaseAgrmnt.docx**.

Figure 2.9 Assessment 1

Inspection of Premises

Lessor shall have the right to exhibit the Premises and to display a *for rent* sign on the Premises at any time within <u>forty-five</u> days before the expiration of this Lease.

Assessment 2 Apply Styles, a Style Set, and a Modified Theme in a Document on New Zealand

1. Open **NewZealand.docx** and then save it with the name **2-NewZealand**.
2. Apply the Heading 1 style to the title *NEW ZEALAND*.
3. Apply the Heading 2 style to the headings in the document (*Culture*, *Nature*, and *Sailing Nation*).
4. Apply the Lines (Stylish) style set.
5. Apply the Banded theme.
6. Apply the Orange theme colors.
7. Apply the Candara theme fonts.
8. Apply the Open paragraph spacing.
9. Highlight in yellow the text *New Zealand has it all!* at the end of the first paragraph of text below the title.
10. Save, preview, and then close **2-NewZealand.docx**.

Assessment 3 Apply Character and Paragraph Formatting to an Employee Privacy Document

1. Open **WorkPrivacy.docx** and then save it with the name **2-WorkPrivacy**.
2. Select the text from the beginning of the first paragraph to the end of the document (including the blank line following the last paragraph) and then make the following changes:
   a. Change the line spacing to 1.5 lines.
   b. Change the spacing after paragraphs to 0 points.
   c. Indent the first line of each paragraph 0.5 inch.
   d. Change the paragraph alignment to justified.
3. Move the insertion point to the end of the document, drag the First Line Indent marker on the horizontal ruler back to 0 inches, and then type the text shown in Figure 2.10. (Create a hanging indent as shown in the figure without using the Tab key.)
4. Select the entire document and then change the font to Constantia.
5. Select the title *WORKPLACE PRIVACY* and then apply the following formatting:
   a. Center the title.
   b. Change the font to 14-point Calibri.
   c. Click the Text Effects and Typography button and then click the option in the second column, first row (blue fill and shadow).
6. Use the Format Painter to apply the same formatting to the title *BIBLIOGRAPHY* that you applied to the title *WORKPLACE PRIVACY*.
7. Save, preview, and then close **2-WorkPrivacy.docx**.

Figure 2.10 Assessment 3

BIBLIOGRAPHY

Nye, H. G. (2024). *Privacy in the workplace*, 2nd edition (pp. 103-112). Denver, CO: Goodwin Publishing Group.

Visual Benchmark

Create a Report about Active Listening Skills

1. Open **ActiveListen.docx** and then save it with the name **2-ActiveListen**.
2. Apply the following formatting to the document so it appears as shown in Figure 2.11:
   a. Select the document and then change the font to 12-point Cambria and the font color to standard dark blue.
   b. Set the title in 16-point Candara bold and center the title.
   c. Set the headings in 14-point Candara bold.
   d. Change the paragraph spacing after the title and headings to 6 points.
   e. Underline the text as shown in the figure.
   f. Create a hanging indent for the paragraphs as shown in the figure. (Do not create the hanging paragraphs using the Tab key.)
3. Save, preview, and then close **2-ActiveListen.docx**.

Figure 2.11 Visual Benchmark

ACTIVE LISTENING SKILLS

Listening is a two-way activity. When the audience pays attention, the speaker gains confidence, knowing that their message is being received and appreciated. At the same time, alert listeners obtain information, hear an amusing or interesting story, and otherwise benefit from the speaker's presentation.

Become an Active Listener

Active listeners pay attention to the speaker and to what is being said. They are respectful of the speaker and eager to be informed or entertained. In contrast, *passive listeners* "tune out" the presentation and may even display rudeness by not paying attention to the speaker. Here are ways in which you can become an active listener:

Listen with a purpose: Stay focused on what the speaker is saying, and you will gain useful information or hear a suspenseful story narrated well. Try to avoid letting your attention wander.

Be courteous: Consider that the speaker spent time preparing for the presentation and thus deserves your respect.

Take brief notes: If the speaker is providing information, take brief notes on the main ideas. Doing so will help you understand and remember what is being said. If you have questions or would like to hear more about a particular point, ask the speaker for clarification after the presentation.

Practice Active Listening Skills in Conversation

Most people have had the experience of being in a one-way conversation, in which one person does all the talking and the others just listen. In fact, this is not a conversation, which is an exchange of information and ideas. In a true conversation, everyone has a chance to be heard. Do not monopolize conversation. Give the other person or persons an opportunity to talk. Pay attention when others are speaking and show your interest in what is being said by making eye contact and asking questions. Avoid interrupting, since this shows your disinterest and suggests that what you have to say is more important.

Case Study

Part 1

You work for the local chamber of commerce and are responsible for assisting the office manager, Teresa Alexander. Ms. Alexander would like to maintain consistency in articles submitted for publication in the monthly chamber newsletter. She wants you to explore various decorative and plain fonts. She would like you to choose two handwriting fonts, two decorative fonts, and two plain fonts and then prepare a document containing an example of each font. Save the document with the name **2-Fonts**. Preview and then close the document.

Part 2

Ms. Alexander has asked you to write a short article for the chamber newsletter. In the article, you are to describe an upcoming event at your school or in your community. Effectively use at least two of the fonts you selected in Case Study Part 1. Save the document with the name **2-Article**. Preview and then close the document.

Part 3

Ms. Alexander will be posting the newsletter to the chamber's website and would like you to explain how to save a Word document as a web page. Display the Save As dialog box and then determine how to save a document as a filtered web page using the *Save as type* option box. Create a Word document with step-by-step instructions. Save the document with the name **2-WebPage**. Close the document. Open **2-Article.docx**, the document you created in Case Study Part 2, and then save the document as a filtered web page.

WORD

CHAPTER 3

Customizing Paragraphs

Performance Objectives

Upon successful completion of Chapter 3, you will be able to:

1 Apply numbered and bulleted formatting to text
2 Apply paragraph borders and shading
3 Sort paragraphs of text
4 Set, clear, and move tabs on the horizontal ruler and at the Tabs dialog box
5 Cut, copy, and paste text in a document
6 Use the Paste Options button to specify how text is pasted in a document
7 Use the Clipboard task pane to copy and paste text within and between documents

As you learned in Chapter 2, Word contains a variety of options for formatting text in paragraphs. In this chapter, you will learn how to apply numbered and bulleted formatting as well as borders and shading. You will also learn how to sort paragraphs of text in alphabetical, numerical, and date order and to set and modify tabs on the horizontal ruler and at the Tabs dialog box. Editing some documents might include selecting and then deleting, moving, or copying text. You can perform these types of editing tasks with buttons in the Clipboard group on the Home tab or with keyboard shortcuts.

Data Files

The data files for this chapter are in the WL1C3 folder that you downloaded at the beginning of this course.

Activity 1 Format a Document on Computer Technology 3 Parts

You will open a document containing information on computer technology, type numbered and bulleted text in the document, and apply numbered and bulleted formatting to paragraphs in the document.

Applying Numbering and Bullets

Numbering

Bullets

When typing a list of items, use numbers to indicate the sequence or importance of the items and use bullets when the order of the items is not important. Word provides buttons for automatically numbering or bulleting text. Use the Numbering button in the Paragraph group on the Home tab to insert numbers before specific paragraphs and use the Bullets button to insert bullets.

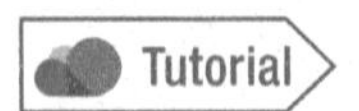

Creating Numbered Lists

Quick Steps

Type Numbered Paragraphs

1. Type 1.
2. Press spacebar.
3. Type text.
4. Press Enter key.

Hint Define a new numbering format by clicking the Numbering button arrow and then clicking *Define New Number Format.*

Creating Numbered Lists

To type a numbered list, type *1.* and then press the spacebar, and Word indents the number 0.25 inch from the left margin. Text typed after the number will be indented 0.5 inch. When the Enter key is pressed to end the first item, the next number, *2.*, is automatically inserted at the beginning of the next paragraph. Continue typing items and Word inserts the next number in the list. To insert a line break without inserting a number, press Shift + Enter.

To turn off numbering, press the Enter key two times or click the Numbering button in the Paragraph group on the Home tab. To turn numbering back on, simply type the next number in the list (and the period) followed by a space. Word will automatically indent the number and the text. (Numbered and bulleted formatting can be removed from a paragraph with the keyboard shortcut Ctrl + Q. Remove all formatting from selected text by clicking the Clear All Formatting button in the Font group on the Home tab.)

When the AutoFormat feature inserts numbering and indents text, the AutoCorrect Options button displays. Click this button and a drop-down list displays with options for undoing and/or stopping the automatic numbering.

Activity 1a Creating a Numbered List — Part 1 of 3

1. Open **TechInfo.docx** and then save it with the name **3-TechInfo**.
2. Press Ctrl + End to move the insertion point to the end of the document and then type the text shown in Figure 3.1. Apply bold formatting and center the title *Technology Career Questions*. When typing the numbered paragraphs, complete the following steps:
   a. Type 1. and then press the spacebar. (The *1.* is indented 0.25 inch from the left margin and typed text is indented 0.5 inch from the left margin. Also, the AutoCorrect Options button displays. Use this button if you want to undo or stop automatic numbering.)
   b. Type the paragraph of text and then press the Enter key. (This moves the insertion point down to the next paragraph and inserts an indented number *2* followed by a period.)
   c. Continue typing the remaining text. (Remember, you do not need to type the paragraph number and period—they are automatically inserted. The last numbered item will wrap differently on your screen than shown in Figure 3.1.)
   d. After typing the last question, press the Enter key two times. (This turns off paragraph numbering.)
3. Save **3-TechInfo.docx**.

Check Your Work

Figure 3.1 Activity 1a

Technology Career Questions

1. What is your ideal technical job?
2. Which job suits your personality?
3. Which is your first-choice certificate?
4. How does the technical job market look in your state right now?

Automatic numbering is turned on by default. Turn off automatic numbering at the AutoCorrect dialog box with the AutoFormat As You Type tab selected, as shown in Figure 3.2. To display this dialog box, click the File tab and then click *Options*. At the Word Options dialog box, click the *Proofing* option in the left panel and then click the AutoCorrect Options button in the *AutoCorrect options* section of the dialog box. At the AutoCorrect dialog box, click the AutoFormat As You Type tab and then click the *Automatic numbered lists* check box to remove the check mark. Click OK to close the AutoCorrect dialog box and then click OK to close the Word Options dialog box.

Quick Steps

Create Numbered List

1. Select text.
2. Click Numbering button.

To create a numbered list, click the Numbering button in the Paragraph group on the Home tab. Type text and it will be formatted as a numbered list. Click the button again to turn off numbering, or select existing text and then click the Numbering button to apply numbered formatting.

Figure 3.2 AutoCorrect Dialog Box with the AutoFormat As You Type Tab Selected

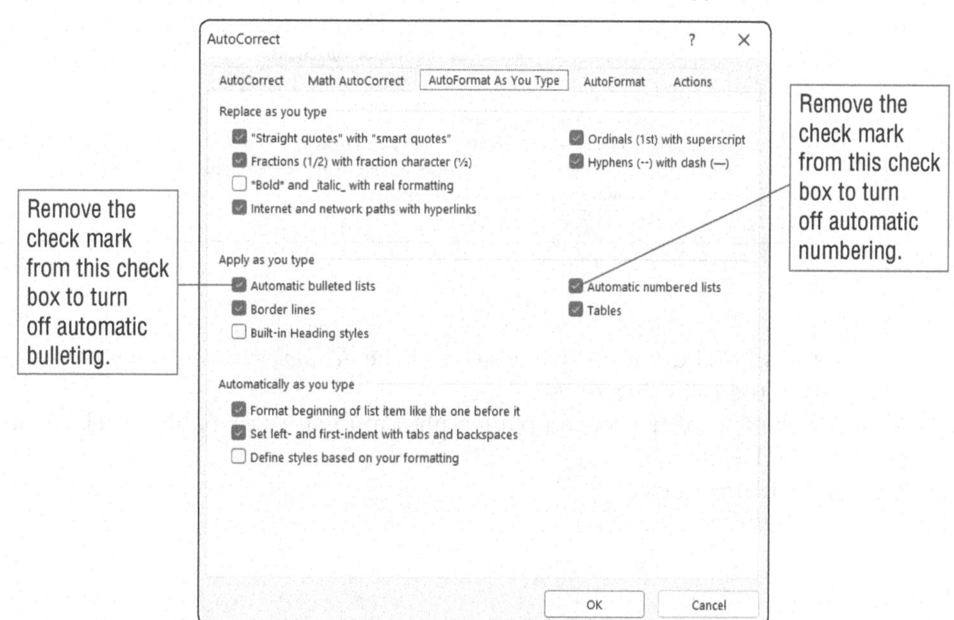

Activity 1b Applying Numbered Formatting

Part 2 of 3

1. With **3-TechInfo.dox** open, apply numbers to paragraphs by completing the following steps:
   a. Select the five paragraphs of text in the *Technology Information Questions* section.
   b. Click the Numbering button in the Paragraph group on the Home tab.

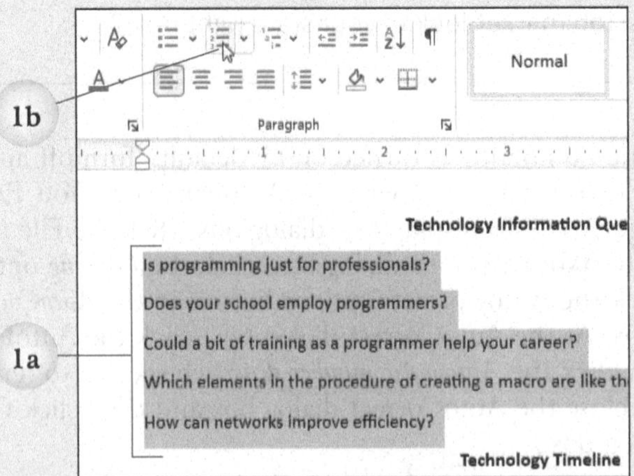

2. Add text between paragraphs 4 and 5 in the *Technology Information Questions* section by completing the following steps:
   a. Position the insertion point immediately right of the question mark at the end of the fourth paragraph.
   b. Press the Enter key.
   c. Type What kinds of networks are used in your area?

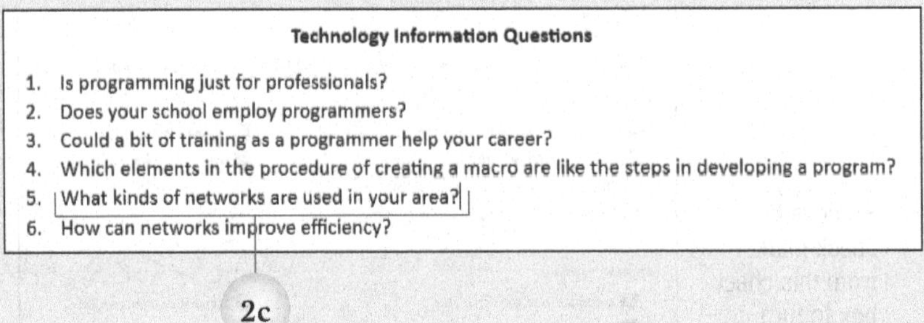

3. Delete the second question (paragraph) in the *Technology Information Questions* section by completing the following steps:
   a. Select the text of the second paragraph. (You will not be able to select the number.)
   b. Press the Delete key.
4. Save **3-TechInfo.docx**.

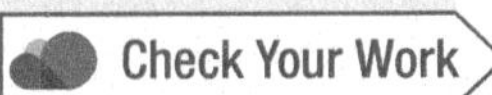

Creating Bulleted Lists

Quick Steps

Type Bulleted List
1. Type *, >, or - symbol.
2. Press spacebar.
3. Type text.
4. Press Enter key.

Create Bulleted List
1. Select text.
2. Click Bullets button.

Creating Bulleted Lists

In addition to automatically numbering paragraphs, Word's AutoFormat feature creates bulleted lists. A bulleted list with a hanging indent is automatically created when a paragraph begins with the symbol *, >, or -. Type one of the symbols and then press the spacebar and the AutoFormat feature inserts a bullet 0.25 inch from the left margin and indents the text following the bullet another 0.25 inch. Change the indent of bulleted text by pressing the Tab key to demote text or pressing Shift + Tab to promote text. Word uses different bullets for demoted text.

Bulleted formatting can be turned on or applied to existing text with the Bullets button in the Paragraph group on the Home tab. Click the Bullets button to turn on bulleting, type text, and then click the button again to turn off bulleting. Or select existing text and then click the Bullets button to apply bulleted formatting. When the AutoFormat feature inserts bullets and indents text, the AutoCorrect Options button displays. This button contains options for undoing and/or stopping the automatic bulleting. The automatic bulleting feature can be turned off at the AutoCorrect dialog box with the AutoFormat As You Type tab selected.

Activity 1c Creating a Bulleted List and Applying Bulleted Formatting — Part 3 of 3

1. With **3-TechInfo.docx** open, press Ctrl + End to move the insertion point to the end of the document.
2. Turn on bold formatting, change to center alignments, and then type Technology Visionaries as shown in Figure 3.3.
3. Press the Enter key, turn off bold formatting, and change to left alignment.
4. Type a greater-than symbol (>), press the spacebar, type the text of the first bulleted item in Figure 3.3, and then press the Enter key.
5. Press the Tab key (which demotes the bullet to a hollow circle) and then type the remaining bulleted text, pressing the Enter key after each entry. After typing the last bulleted item, press the Enter key three times to turn off automatic bulleting.
6. Promote *Robert Noyce* by positioning the insertion point at the beginning of *Robert Noyce* and then pressing Shift + Tab.
7. Format the paragraphs of text in the *Technology Timeline* section as a bulleted list by completing the following steps:
   a. Select the paragraphs of text in the *Technology Timeline* section.
   b. Click the Bullets button in the Paragraph group. (Word will insert the same arrow bullets that you inserted in Step 4. Word keeps the same bullet formatting until you choose a different bullet style.)
8. Save, preview, and then close **3-TechInfo.docx**.

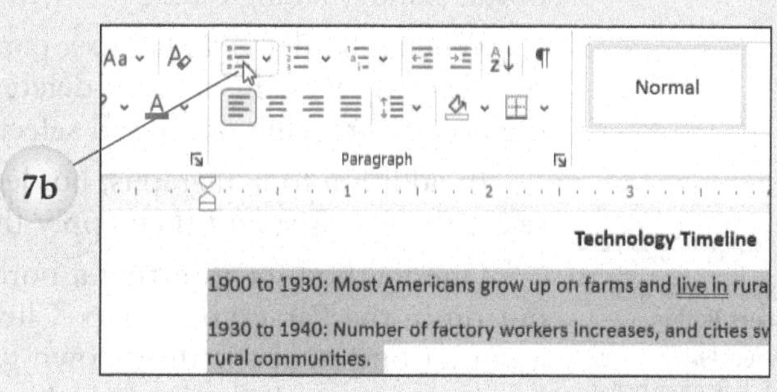

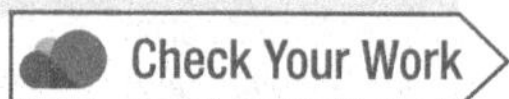

Figure 3.3 Activity 1c

Technology Visionaries

- Jack Kilby
    - Inventor of the handheld calculator
    - Credited with designing the first integrated circuit
    - Robert Noyce
    - Co-founder of Intel
    - Developed an integrated circuit using silicon

Activity 2 Customize a Document on Chapter Questions — 3 Parts

You will open a document containing chapter questions and then apply border and shading formatting to text.

Adding Emphasis to Paragraphs

To call attention to or to highlight specific text in a document, consider adding emphasis to the text by applying paragraph borders and/or shading. Apply borders with the Borders button in the Paragraph group on the Home tab and shading with the Shading button. Additional border and shading options are available at the Borders and Shading dialog box.

Applying Borders

Borders

Applying Paragraph Borders

Every paragraph in a Word document contains an invisible frame, and a border can be applied to the frame around the paragraph. Apply a border to specific sides of the paragraph frame or to all sides. Add borders to paragraphs using the Borders button in the Paragraph group on the Home tab or using options at the Borders and Shading dialog box with the Border tab selected.

When a border is added to a paragraph of text, the border expands and contracts as text is inserted or deleted from the paragraph. Insert a border around the active paragraph or around selected paragraphs.

In addition to paragraphs, borders can be applied to specific text. To do this, select the text first and then apply the border(s).

Quick Steps

Apply Borders with Borders Button

1. Select text.
2. Click Borders button arrow.
3. Click border option at drop-down gallery.

One method for inserting a border is to use options from the Borders button in the Paragraph group. Click the Borders button arrow and then choose a border option at the drop-down gallery. For example, to insert a border at the bottom of the paragraph, click the *Bottom Border* option. Clicking an option will add the border to the paragraph where the insertion point is located. To add a border to more than one paragraph, select the paragraphs first and then click the option.

Activity 2a Applying Borders to Paragraphs of Text

Part 1 of 3

1. Open **Questions.docx** and then save it with the name **3-Questions**.
2. Insert an outside border to specific text by completing the following steps:
   a. Select text from the heading *Chapter 1 Questions* through the four bulleted paragraphs.
   b. Click the Borders button arrow in the Paragraph group on the Home tab.
   c. Click the *Outside Borders* option at the drop-down gallery.
3. Select text from the heading *Chapter 2 Questions* through the five bulleted paragraphs and then click the Borders button (The button will apply the border option that was previously selected.)
4. Save **3-Questions.docx**.

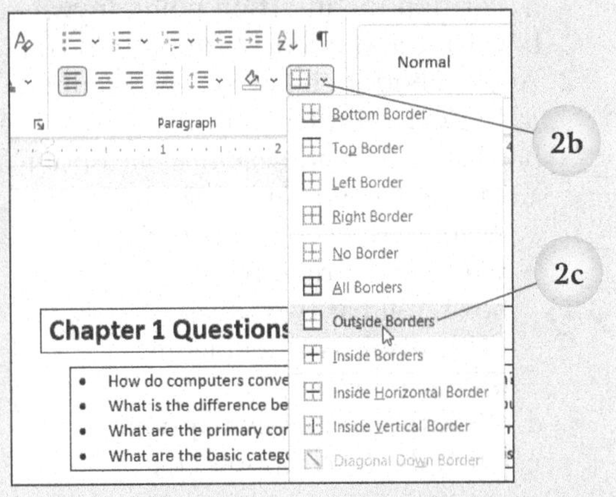

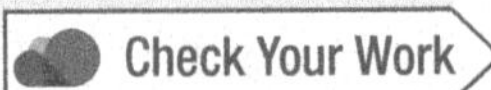

Quick Steps

Apply Borders at Borders and Shading Dialog Box

1. Select text.
2. Click Borders button arrow.
3. Click *Borders and Shading* option.
4. Choose options in dialog box.
5. Click OK.

To further customize paragraph borders, use options at the Borders and Shading dialog box with the Borders tab selected, as shown in Figure 3.4. Display this dialog box by clicking the Borders button arrow and then clicking *Borders and Shading* at the drop-down list. At the Borders and Shading dialog box, specify the border setting, style, color, and width.

Figure 3.4 Borders and Shading Dialog Box with the Borders Tab Selected

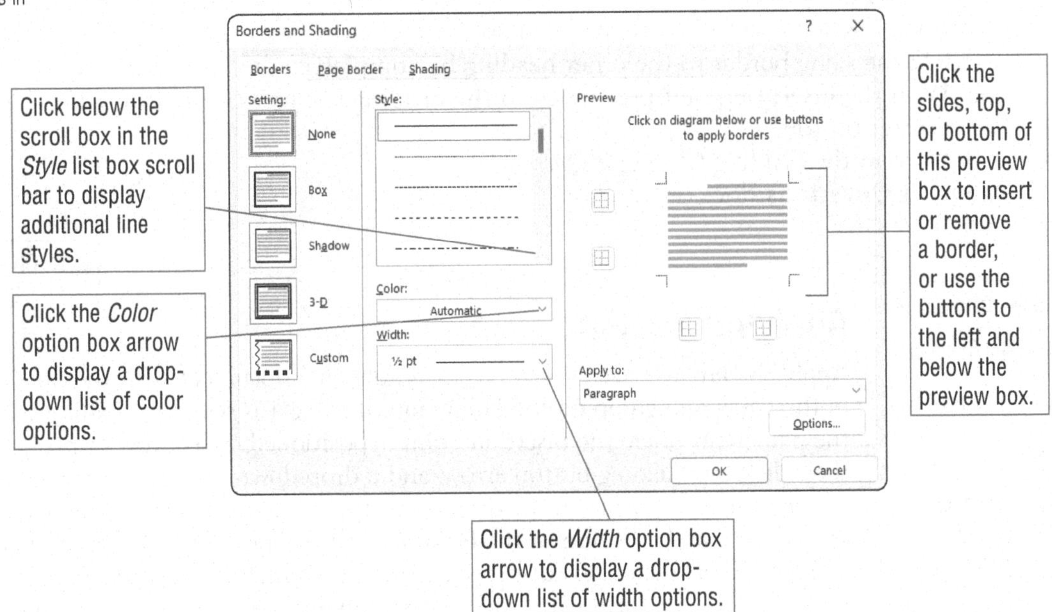

Activity 2b Applying Borders at the Borders and Shading Dialog Box — Part 2 of 3

1. With **3-Questions.docx** open, remove the borders around the heading *Chapter 1 Questions* by completing the following steps:
   a. Position the insertion point anywhere in the heading *Chapter 1 Questions*.
   b. Click the Borders button arrow and then click *No Border* at the drop-down gallery.
2. Apply a bottom border to the heading *Chapter 1 Questions* by completing the following steps:
   a. Click the Borders button arrow.
   b. Click the *Borders and Shading* option.
   c. At the Borders and Shading dialog box, click below the scroll box in the *Style* list box scroll bar two times. (This displays a double-line option.)
   d. Click the double-line option.
   e. Click the *Color* option box arrow.
   f. Click the *Blue* color (eighth color option in the *Standard Colors* section).
   g. Click the *Width* option box arrow.
   h. Click the *3/4 pt* option at the drop-down list.
   i. Click the *None* option in the *Setting* section.
   j. Click the bottom border of the box in the *Preview* section.
   k. Click OK to close the dialog box and apply the border.

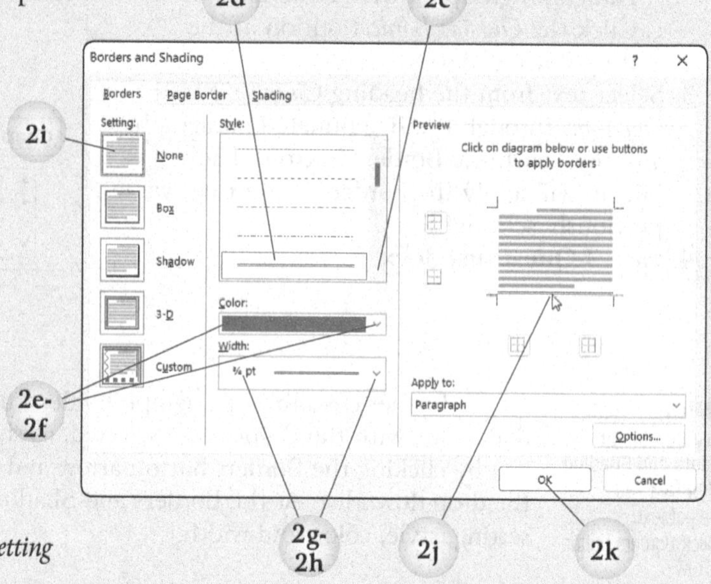

3. Apply the same border to the other heading by completing the following steps:
   a. With the insertion point positioned in the heading *Chapter 1 Questions*, click the Format Painter button.
   b. Click in the heading *Chapter 2 Questions*.
4. Save **3-Questions.docx**.

Check Your Work

Tutorial

Applying Shading

Shading

Quick Steps

Apply Shading
1. Select text.
2. Click Shading button.

OR

1. Click Borders button arrow.
2. Click *Borders and Shading* option.
3. Click Shading tab.
4. Choose options in dialog box.
5. Click OK.

Applying Shading

Apply shading to selected text or paragraphs in a document with the Shading button in the Paragraph group on the Home tab. If no text is selected, shading is applied to the paragraph where the insertion point is positioned. Select text or paragraphs and then click the Shading button arrow, and a drop-down gallery displays. Shading colors are presented in themes in the drop-down gallery. Use one of the theme colors or click one of the standard colors at the bottom of the gallery. Click the *More Colors* option and the Colors dialog box displays. At the Colors dialog box with the Standard tab selected, click a color or click the Custom tab and then specify a custom color.

Shading can also be applied using options at the Borders and Shading dialog box. Display this dialog box by clicking the Borders button arrow and then clicking the *Borders and Shading* option. At the Borders and Shading dialog box, click the Shading tab. Use options in the dialog box to specify a fill color, choose a pattern style, and specify a color for the dots that make up the pattern.

Activity 2c Applying Paragraph Shading

1. With **3-Questions.docx** open, apply shading to the paragraph containing the heading *Chapter 1 Questions* by completing the following steps:
   a. Click in the heading *Chapter 1 Questions*.
   b. Click the Shading button arrow.
   c. Click the *Blue, Accent 5, Lighter 80%* option (ninth column, second row in the *Theme Colors* section).

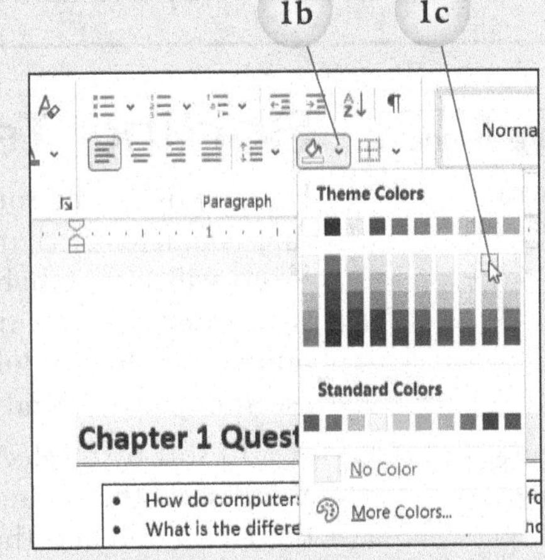

2. Apply the same blue shading to the other heading by completing the following steps:
   a. With the insertion point positioned in the heading *Chapter 1 Questions*, click the Format Painter button.
   b. Click in the heading *Chapter 2 Questions*.
3. Apply shading to selected paragraphs with options at the Borders and Shading dialog box by completing the following steps:
   a. Select the four bulleted paragraphs below the heading *Chapter 1 Questions*.
   b. Click the Borders button arrow.
   c. Click the *Borders and Shading* option.
   d. At the Borders and Shading dialog box, click the Shading tab.
   e. Click the *Fill* option box arrow.
   f. Click the *Gold, Accent 4, Lighter 80%* option (eighth column, second row in the *Theme Colors* section).
   g. Click the *Style* option box arrow.
   h. Click the *5%* option.
   i. Click the *Color* option box arrow.
   j. Click the *Blue, Accent 5, Lighter 60%* option (ninth column, third row in the *Theme Colors* section).
   k. Click OK to close the dialog box.

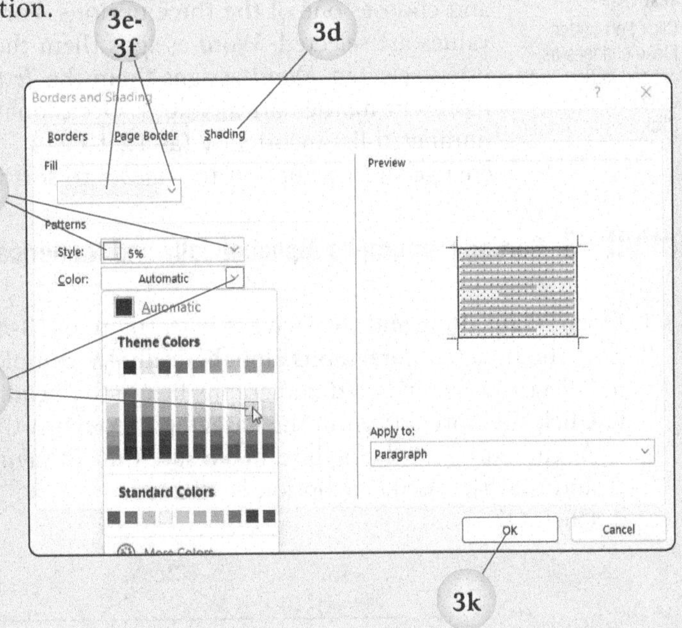

4. Apply the same shading to the bulleted paragraphs below the heading *Chapter 2 Questions* by completing the following steps:
   a. Click in the bulleted paragraphs below the heading *Chapter 1 Questions*.
   b. Click the Format Painter button.
   c. Select the five bulleted paragraphs below the heading *Chapter 2 Questions*.
5. Save, preview, and then close **3-Questions.docx**.

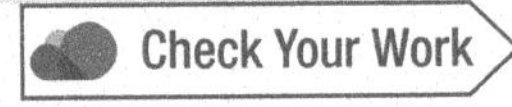

Activity 3 Sort Text in a Document on Maui — 1 Part

You will open a document on Maui and then sort several different paragraphs of text alphabetically and numerically.

Sorting Text in Paragraphs

Sorting Text in Paragraphs

Paragraphs can be sorted alphabetically, numerically, or by date, based on the first character or characters in each paragraph. If the first character is a letter, Word will sort alphabetically from A to Z or from Z to A. This can be useful for such things as a list of names or a glossary of terms. Paragraphs that begin with a number, such as a dollar amount or measurement, can be arranged numerically in ascending or descending order.

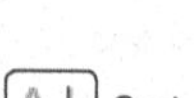

To sort text, select the specific paragraphs to be sorted. (If text is not selected, Word sorts the entire document.) Click the Sort button in the Paragraph group on the Home tab and the Sort Text dialog box displays. At this dialog box, click OK.

Quick Steps

Sort Paragraphs of Text

1. Click Sort button.
2. Make changes as needed at Sort Text dialog box.
3. Click OK.

The *Type* option at the Sort Text dialog box provides the options *Text, Number,* or *Date* depending on the text selected. Word attempts to determine the data type and chooses one of the three options. For example, if numbers with mathematical values are selected, Word assigns them the *Number* type. However, if a numbered list is selected, Word assigns them the *Text* type since the numbers do not represent mathematical values. Occasionally this will result in Word reorganizing a numbered list incorrectly (as 1., 10., 11., 12., 2., for example). If this occurs, change the *Type* option to *Number* to sort in correct numerical order.

Activity 3 Sorting Paragraphs Alphabetically and Numerically — Part 1 of 1

1. Open **Maui.docx** and then save it with the name **3-Maui**.
2. Sort the bulleted paragraphs alphabetically by completing the following steps:
   a. Select the five bulleted paragraphs below the heading *Maui Activities*.
   b. Click the Sort button in the Paragraph group on the Home tab.
   c. At the Sort Text dialog box, make sure that *Paragraphs* displays in the *Sort by* option box and that the *Ascending* option is selected.
   d. Click OK.

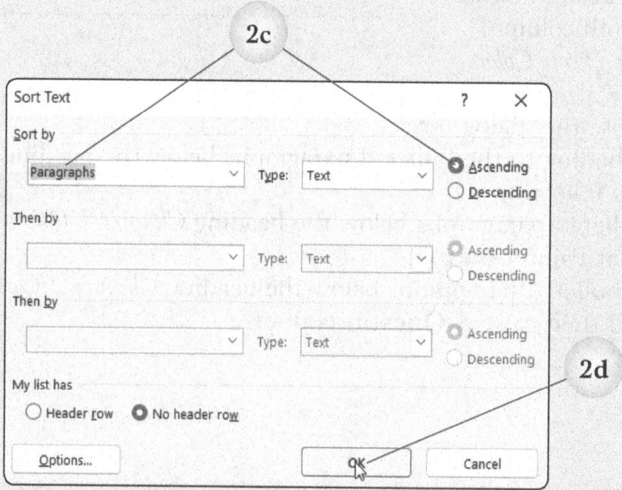

3. Sort the numbered paragraphs by completing the following steps:
   a. Select the ten numbered paragraphs below the heading *Maui Sites*.
   b. Click the Sort button in the Paragraph group.
   c. At the Sort Text dialog box, click the *Type* option box arrow and then click *Number* at the drop-down list.
   d. Click OK.
4. Sort the prices below the heading *Adventure Deals* in descending numerical order by completing the following steps:
   a. Select the paragraphs below the heading *Adventure Deals*.
   b. Click the Sort button in the Paragraph group.
   c. Click the *Type* option box arrow and then click *Number* at the drop-down list.
   d. Click the *Descending* option.
   e. Click OK.
5. Save, preview, and then close **3-Maui.docx**.

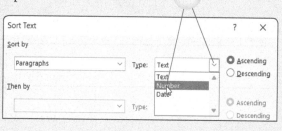

Activity 4 Prepare a Document on Workshops and Training Dates 4 Parts

You will set and move tabs on the horizontal ruler and at the Tabs dialog box and type tabbed text about workshops, training dates, and a table of contents.

Setting and Modifying Tabs

Blocks of text can be organized by setting tabs to separate the text and to give the text a more uniform appearance. Tabs allow text to be aligned at different points in the document. When typing blocks of text, only press the Tab key one time between the blocks. The default setting for tabs in Word is a left tab set every 0.5 inch. When the Tab key is pressed, the insertion point moves to the right 0.5 inch. In some situations, these default tabs are appropriate; in others, custom tabs may be needed. Tabs can be set on the horizontal ruler or at the Tabs dialog box.

Setting and Modifying Tabs on the Horizontal Ruler

Quick Steps

Set Tabs on Horizontal Ruler

1. Click Alignment button above vertical ruler.
2. Click tab locations on horizontal ruler.

Setting and Modifying Tabs on the Horizontal Ruler

Use the horizontal ruler to set, move, and delete tabs. If the ruler is not visible, click the View tab and then click the *Ruler* check box in the Show group to insert a check mark. By default, tabs are set every 0.5 inch on the horizontal ruler. To set a new tab, first click the Alignment button to the left of the ruler and above the vertical ruler to specify how text will be aligned on the tab. The types of tabs that can be set on the ruler are left, center, right, decimal, and bar. These tab types are represented with the symbols shown in Table 3.1. Text is aligned at the left edge of a left tab, in the middle of a center tab, at the right edge of a right tab, and at the decimal point with a decimal tab. Setting a bar tab causes a vertical bar (line) to be inserted in the document at the point where the tab is set. Refer to Figure 3.7 on page 86 to see an example of a document with a bar tab.

Table 3.1 Alignment Button Tab Symbols

Alignment Button Symbol	Type of Tab
∟	left
⊥	center
┘	right
⊥.	decimal
|	bar

Hint When setting tabs on the horizontal ruler, a dotted guideline displays to help align them.

Hint Position the insertion point in any paragraph of text, and tabs for the paragraph appear on the horizontal ruler.

When the Alignment button displays the correct tab symbol, position the pointer on the ruler where the tab should be set, and then click the left button to set the tab. When a new tab is set, any default tabs to the left of it are automatically deleted by Word. If the tab symbol on the Alignment button is changed, the symbol remains in place until it is changed again or Word is closed. If Word is closed and then reopened, the Alignment button displays with the left tab symbol.

To set a tab at a specific measurement on the horizontal ruler, press and hold down the Alt key, position the pointer at the desired position, and then click and hold down the left mouse button. This displays two measurements in the white portion of the horizontal ruler. The first measurement is the location of the pointer on the ruler in relation to the left margin. The second measurement is the distance from the pointer to the right margin. With the left mouse button held down, position the tab symbol at the desired location and then release the mouse button followed by the Alt key.

Tabs can be used to type text in columns. Type text and then press the Tab key to create a new column. At the end of a line, press the Enter key or press Shift + Enter. If the Enter key is used to end each line, all lines of text in columns will need to be selected to make paragraph formatting changes. To make changes to columns of text with line breaks inserted using Shift + Enter, the insertion point needs to be positioned in only one location in the columns of text.

Activity 4a Setting Left, Center, and Right Tabs on the Horizontal Ruler

Part 1 of 4

1. Press Ctrl + N to open a new blank document.
2. Type WORKSHOPS and apply bold formatting and center alignment, as shown in Figure 3.5.
3. Press the Enter key and then change the paragraph alignment back to left and turn off bold formatting.
4. Set a left tab at the 0.5-inch mark, a center tab at the 3.25-inch mark, and a right tab at the 6-inch mark by completing the following steps:
   a. Click the Show/Hide ¶ button in the Paragraph group on the Home tab to turn on the display of nonprinting characters.
   b. Make sure the horizontal ruler is visible. (If it is not, click the View tab and then click the *Ruler* check box in the Show group to insert a check mark.)

c. Make sure the left tab symbol displays in the Alignment button above the vertical ruler.
d. Position the pointer on the 0.5-inch mark on the horizontal ruler and then click the left mouse button.

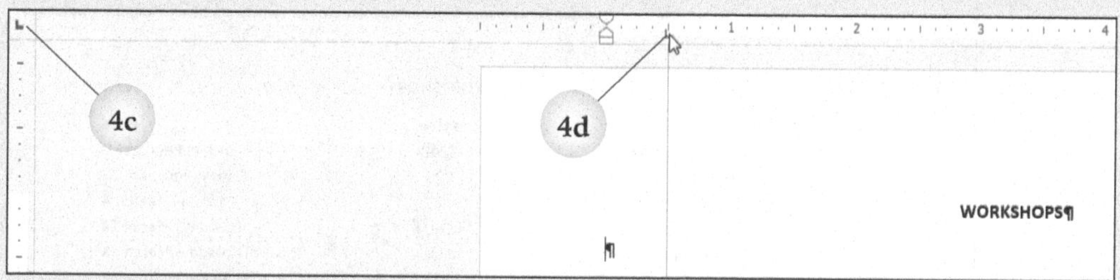

e. Position the pointer on the Alignment button and then click the left mouse button until the center tab symbol displays (see Table 3.1).
f. Position the pointer on the 3.25-inch mark on the horizontal ruler. Press and hold down the Alt key and then click and hold down the left mouse button. Make sure the first measurement on the horizontal ruler displays as approximately *3.25"* and then release the mouse button followed by the Alt key. (If *3.25"* does not display, consider increasing the zoom.)

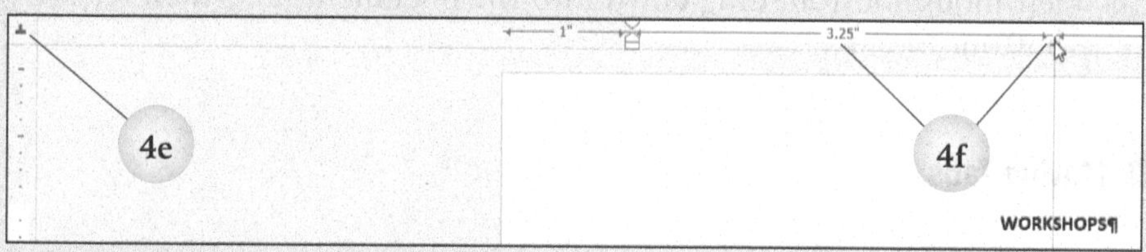

g. Position the pointer on the Alignment button and then click the left mouse button until the right tab symbol displays (see Table 3.1).
h. Position the pointer below the 6-inch mark on the horizontal ruler. Press and hold down the Alt key and then click and hold down the left mouse button. Make sure the first measurement on the horizontal ruler displays as approximately *6"* and then release the mouse button followed by the Alt key.

5. Type the text in columns, as shown in Figure 3.5 on page 84. Press the Tab key before typing each column entry and press Shift + Enter after typing each entry in the third column. Apply bold formatting to column headings, as shown in the figure.
6. After typing the final entry in the last column entry, press the Enter key two times.
7. Press Ctrl + Q to remove paragraph formatting (tab settings) below the columns from the current paragraph.
8. Click the Show/Hide ¶ button to turn off the display of nonprinting characters.
9. Save the document with the name **3-Tabs**.

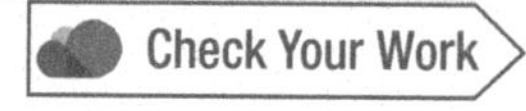

Figure 3.5 Activity 4a

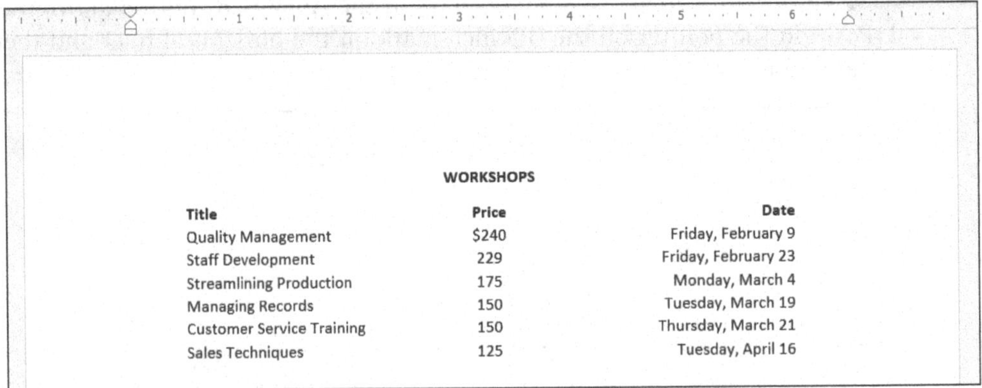

WORKSHOPS

Title	Price	Date
Quality Management	$240	Friday, February 9
Staff Development	229	Friday, February 23
Streamlining Production	175	Monday, March 4
Managing Records	150	Tuesday, March 19
Customer Service Training	150	Thursday, March 21
Sales Techniques	125	Tuesday, April 16

After a tab has been set on the horizontal ruler, it can be moved to a new location. To move a tab, position the pointer on the tab symbol on the ruler, click and hold down the left mouse button, drag the symbol to the new location on the ruler, and then release the mouse button. To delete a tab from the ruler, position the pointer on the tab symbol to be deleted, click and hold down the left mouse button, drag down into the document, and then release the mouse button.

Activity 4b Moving Tabs

Part 2 of 4

1. With **3-Tabs.docx** open, position the insertion point anywhere in the first entry in the tabbed text.
2. Position the pointer on the left tab symbol at the 0.5-inch mark on the horizontal ruler, click and hold down the left mouse button, drag the left tab symbol to the 1-inch mark on the ruler, and then release the mouse button. ***Hint: Use the Alt key to help you position the tab symbol precisely.***

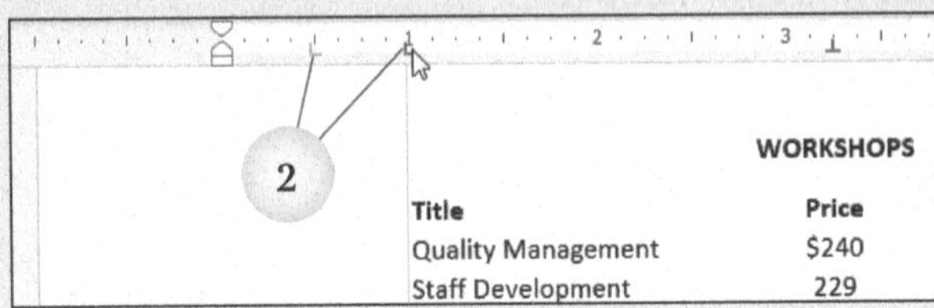

3. Position the pointer on the right tab symbol at the 6-inch mark on the horizontal ruler, click and hold down the left mouse button, drag the right tab symbol to the 5.5-inch mark on the ruler, and then release the mouse button. ***Hint: Use the Alt key to help you position the tab symbol precisely.***
4. Save **3-Tabs.docx**.

Check Your Work

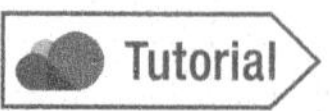

Setting and Clearing Tabs at the Tabs Dialog Box

Quick Steps

Set Tabs at Tabs Dialog Box

1. Click Paragraph group dialog box launcher.
2. Click Tabs button.
3. Specify tab positions, alignments, and leader options.
4. Click OK.

Setting and Modifying Tabs at the Tabs Dialog Box

Use the Tabs dialog box, shown in Figure 3.6, to set tabs at specific measurements and clear one tab or all tabs. To display the Tabs dialog box, click the Paragraph group dialog box launcher. At the Paragraph dialog box, click the Tabs button in the lower left corner of the dialog box.

A left, right, center, decimal, or bar tab can be set at the Tabs dialog box. (For an example of a bar tab, refer to Figure 3.7 on page 86.) To set a tab, click the type of tab in the *Alignment* section of the dialog box, type the tab measurement in the *Tab stop position* text box, and then click the Set button. To clear an individual tab at the Tabs dialog box, select or enter the tab position and then click the Clear button. To clear all tabs, click the Clear All button.

Figure 3.6 Tabs Dialog Box

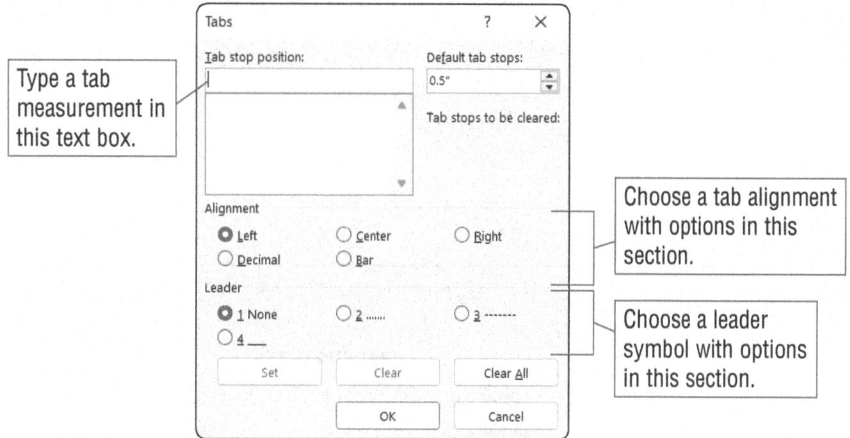

Activity 4c Setting Left Tabs and a Bar Tab at the Tabs Dialog Box

Part 3 of 4

1. With **3-Tabs.docx** open, press Ctrl + End to move the insertion point to the end of the document.
2. Type the title TRAINING DATES and apply bold formatting and center alignment, as shown in Figure 3.7. Press the Enter key, return the paragraph alignment to left, and then turn off bold formatting.
3. Display the Tabs dialog box and then set left tabs and a bar tab by completing the following steps:
   a. Click the Paragraph group dialog box launcher.
   b. At the Paragraph dialog box, click the Tabs button in the lower left corner of the dialog box.
   c. Make sure *Left* is selected in the *Alignment* section of the dialog box.
   d. Type 1.75 in the *Tab stop position* text box.
   e. Click the Set button.
   f. Type 4 in the *Tab stop position* text box and then click the Set button.
   g. Type 3.25 in the *Tab stop position* text box, click *Bar* in the *Alignment* section, and then click the Set button.
   h. Click OK to close the Tabs dialog box.

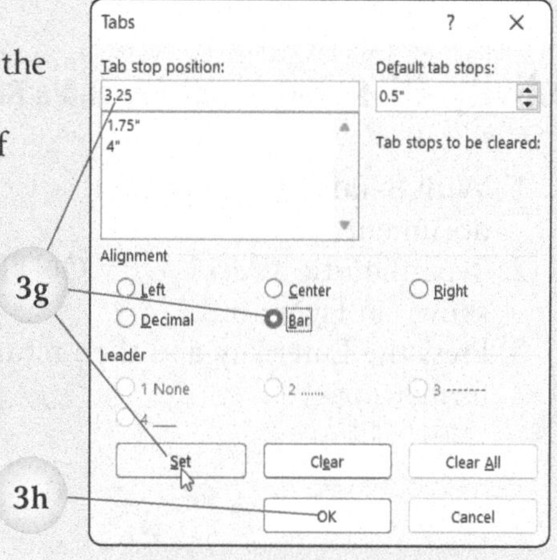

4. Type the text in columns, as shown in Figure 3.7. Press the Tab key before typing each column entry and press Shift + Enter to end each line. After typing *February 26*, press the Enter key.
5. Clear tabs below the columns from the current paragraph by completing the following steps:
   a. Click the Paragraph group dialog box launcher.
   b. At the Paragraph dialog box, click the Tabs button.
   c. At the Tabs dialog box, click the Clear All button.
   d. Click OK.
6. Press the Enter key.
7. Remove the 8 points of spacing after the last entry in the text by completing the following steps:
   a. Position the insertion point anywhere in the *January 29* entry.
   b. Click the Line and Paragraph Spacing button in the Paragraph group on the Home tab.
   c. Click the *Remove Space After Paragraph* option.
8. Save **3-Tabs.docx**.

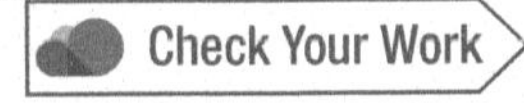

Figure 3.7 Activity 4c

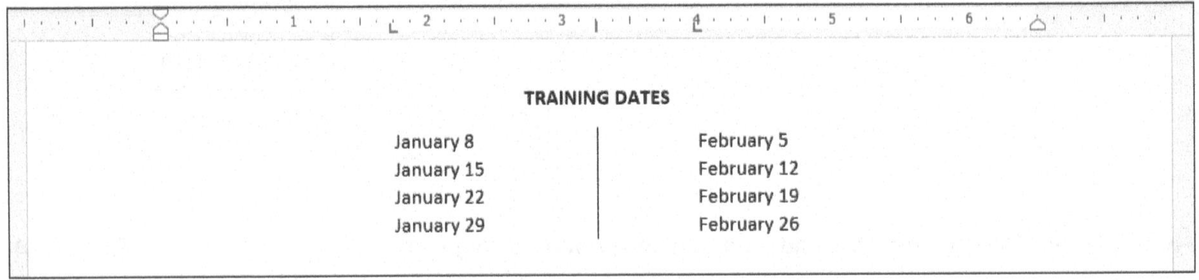

Four types of tabs (left, right, center, and decimal) can be set with leaders at the Tabs dialog box. Leaders are useful in a table of contents or other material where the reader's eyes should be directed across the page. Figure 3.8 shows an example of leaders. Leaders can be periods (.), hyphens (-), or underlines (_). To add leaders to a tab, click the type of leader in the *Leader* section of the Tabs dialog box.

Activity 4d Setting a Left Tab and a Right Tab with Period Leaders

Part 4 of 4

1. With **3-Tabs.docx** open, press Ctrl + End to move the insertion point to the end of the document.
2. Type the title TABLE OF CONTENTS and apply bold formatting and center alignment, as shown in Figure 3.8.
3. Press the Enter key and then return the paragraph alignment to left and turn off bold formatting.

4. Set a left tab and then a right tab with period leaders by completing the following steps:
   a. Click the Paragraph group dialog box launcher.
   b. Click the Tabs button.
   c. At the Tabs dialog box, make sure *Left* is selected in the *Alignment* section of the dialog box.
   d. With the insertion point positioned in the *Tab stop position* text box, type 1 and then click the Set button.
   e. Type 5.5 in the *Tab stop position* text box.
   f. Click *Right* in the *Alignment* section.
   g. Click *2 ......* in the *Leader* section and then click the Set button.
   h. Click OK to close the dialog box.

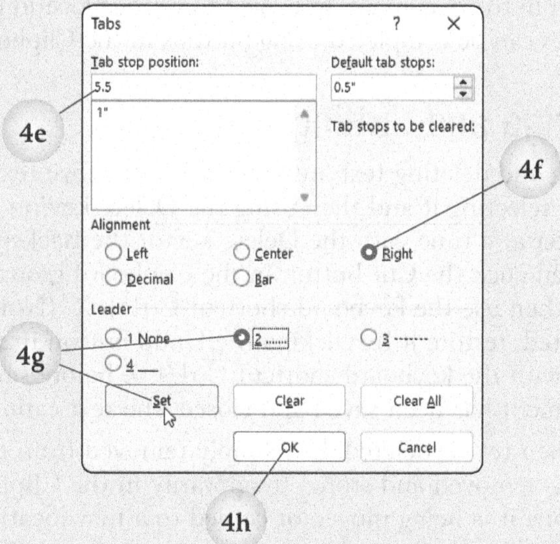

5. Type the text in columns, as shown in Figure 3.8. Press the Tab key before typing each column entry and press Shift + Enter to end each line.
6. Save, preview, and then close **3-Tabs.docx**.

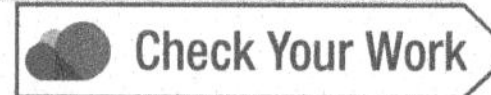

Figure 3.8 Activity 4d

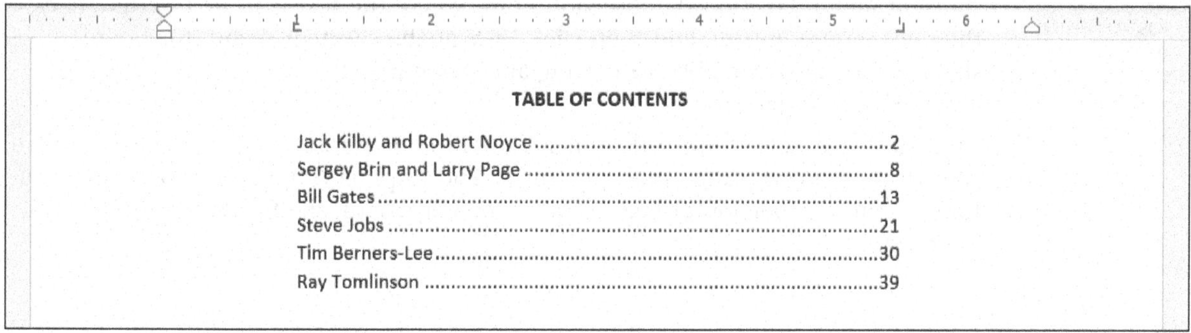

TABLE OF CONTENTS

Jack Kilby and Robert Noyce 2
Sergey Brin and Larry Page 8
Bill Gates 13
Steve Jobs 21
Tim Berners-Lee 30
Ray Tomlinson 39

Activity 5 Move and Copy Text in a Document on Volcanoes — 2 Parts

You will open a document containing information on volcanoes and then cut, copy, and paste text in the document.

Cutting, Copying, and Pasting Text

Cutting, Copying, and Pasting Text

When editing a document, specific text may need to be deleted, moved to a different location in the document, or copied to various locations in the document. These activities can be completed using buttons in the Clipboard group on the Home tab.

Deleting and Cutting Text

Cut

Cutting and deleting text are two ways to remove text from a document. Delete text by selecting it and then using the Delete key on the keyboard, or delete one character at a time with the Delete key or the Backspace key. To cut text, select it and then click the Cut button in the Clipboard group on the Home tab, or select it and then use the keyboard shortcut Ctrl + X. (Note: If text is accidentally cut or deleted, restore it by clicking the Undo button in the Undo group on the Home tab or with the keyboard shortcut Ctrl + Z before saving or closing the file. After a document has been saved and closed, the text cannot be restored.)

Hint The Clipboard content is deleted when the computer is turned off. Text you want to save permanently should be saved as a separate document.

When text is deleted, it is simply removed from the document. When text is cut, it is removed and stored temporarily in the Clipboard. The Clipboard holds text while it is being moved or copied to a new location in the document or to a different document.

Cutting and Pasting Text

Paste

Quick Steps

Move Selected Text

1. Select text.
2. Click Cut button or use Ctrl + X.
3. Position insertion point.
4. Click Paste button or use Ctrl + V.

To move text to a different location in the document, select the text, click the Cut button, position the insertion point at the location the text is to be inserted, and then click the Paste button in the Clipboard group.

Selected text can also be moved using the shortcut menu. To do this, select the text and then position the insertion point inside the selected text until it turns into an arrow pointer. Click the right mouse button and then click *Cut* at the shortcut menu. Position the insertion point where the text is to be inserted, click the right mouse button, and then click *Paste* at the shortcut menu. Keyboard shortcuts are also available for cutting and pasting text. Use Ctrl + X to cut text and Ctrl + V to paste text.

When text is cut from a document, it will remain in the Clipboard while Word is open and can be pasted multiple times. The Clipboard holds only one item at a time. If another portion of text is cut to the Clipboard, the first selection will be removed.

Quick Steps

Move Text with Mouse

1. Select text.
2. Position pointer in selected text.
3. Click and hold down left mouse button and drag to new location.
4. Release left mouse button.

Moving Text by Dragging with the Mouse

The mouse can be used to move text. To do this, select text to be moved and then click and drag the selection with the pointer. As the text is being dragged, the pointer will display as an arrow with a small gray box attached. Move to the location the selected text is to be inserted, and then release the button. If the selected text is inserted in the wrong location, click the Undo button immediately.

Activity 5a Cutting and Dragging Selected Text

Part 1 of 2

1. Open **Volcanoes.docx** and then save it with the name **3-Volcanoes.**
2. Move a paragraph by completing the following steps:
   a. Select the paragraph that begins with *Eruption Stage.*
   b. Click the Cut button in the Clipboard group on the Home tab.
   c. Position the insertion point at the beginning of the paragraph that begins with *Cooling Stage.*
   d. Click the Paste button (make sure you click the Paste button and not the Paste button arrow) in the Clipboard group on the Home tab.

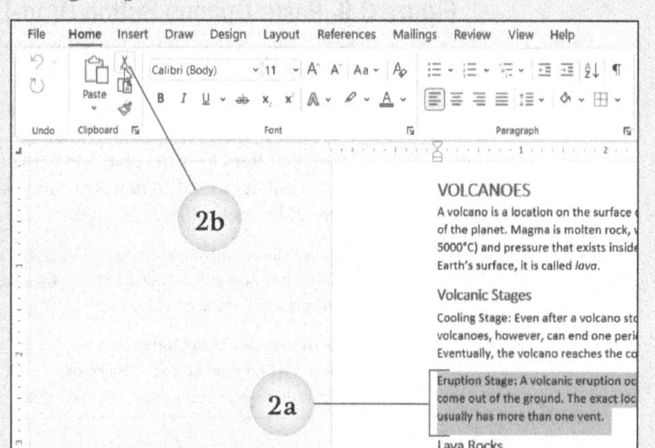

3. Following steps similar to those in Step 2, move the paragraph that begins with *Basalt* before the paragraph that begins with *Andesite.*
4. Move a paragraph using the mouse by completing the following steps:
   a. Use the mouse to select the paragraph that begins with *Shield Volcanoes.*
   b. Move the I-beam pointer inside the selected text until it displays as an arrow pointer.
   c. Click and hold down the left mouse button, drag the arrow pointer (which displays with a small gray box attached) so that the insertion point (which displays as a black vertical bar) is positioned at the beginning of the paragraph that begins with *Composite Volcanoes* and then release the mouse button.

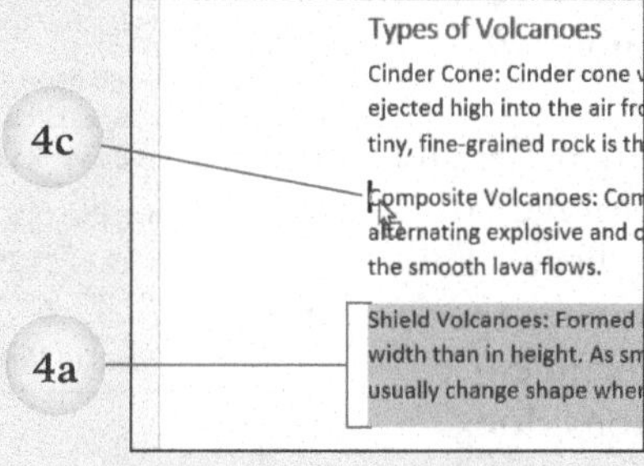

5. Deselect the text.
6. Save **3-Volcanoes.docx.**

Copying and Pasting Text and Formatting

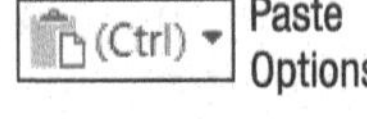

Paste Options

Using the Paste Options Button

When text is pasted in a document, the Paste Options button displays in the lower right corner of the text. Click this button (or press the Ctrl key on the keyboard) and the Paste Options gallery displays, as shown in Figure 3.9. The gallery can also be displayed by clicking the Paste button arrow in the Clipboard group.

The Paste Options gallery contains buttons for specifying the formatting of pasted text.(The number of buttons may vary depending on what is cut or copied.) The first button, Keep Source Formatting, is the default and pastes the text with the original formatting. Click the second button, Merge Formatting, and pasted text will take on the formatting of the text where it is pasted. Click the third button, Keep Text Only, to paste only the text and not the text formatting. Hover the pointer over a button in the gallery and the live preview displays the text in the document as it will appear when pasted.

Figure 3.9 Paste Options Button Drop-Down Gallery

Lava Rocks
Obsidian: Sometimes called volcanic glass, obsidian (pronounced ub-SID-ee-en) is semi-translucent glass that contains a large amount of silicon. Obsidian is usually black or dark gray in color, and occasionally red or brown. Obsidian that is green is rare but does exist. When lava cools so quickly that it does not have time to crystallize, obsidian is formed.
Basalt: Basalt (pronounced buh-SAL... composed of mostly feldspar and pyroxene. Dark in color, basalt is a fine-grained rock. ... basalt, and some contain iron, magnesium, silica, or aluminum.
(Ctrl)
Paste Options:
Set Default Paste...
Andesite: Like basalt, andesite (pro... mposed of feldspar and pyroxene and is a fine-grained rock. Unlike ba... t to medium gray in color.
Andesite is one of the most common volcanic rocks and can contain olivine, a green mineral.
Click the button that specifies the formatting for the pasted text.

Activity 5b Using the Paste Options Button — Part 2 of 2

1. With **3-Volcanoes.docx** open, open **LavaRocks.docx**.
2. In the **LavaRocks.docx** document, select the paragraph of text that begins with *Obsidian* and then click the Cut button in the Clipboard group on the Home tab.
3. Close the **LavaRocks.docx** document without saving it.
4. Position the insertion point at the beginning of the paragraph that begins with *Basalt*.
5. Click the Paste button.
6. Click the Paste Options button at the end of the paragraph and then click the Merge Formatting button in the Paste Options gallery. (This changes the font so that it matches the font of the other paragraphs in the document.)
7. Save and then close **3-Volcanoes.docx**.

Lava Rocks
Obsidian: Sometimes called volcanic glass, obsidian (pronounce...
translucent glass that contains a large amount of silicon. Obsidi...
color, and occasionally red or brown. Obsidian that is green is r...
cools so quickly that it does not have time to crystallize, obsidia...
Basalt: Basalt (pronounced buh-SALT) is rock composed of most...
color, basalt is a fine-grained rock. There are many varieties of b...
magnesium, silica, or aluminum.
Paste Options:
Andesite: Like basalt, andesite (pro...
and is a fine-grained rock. Unlike ba...
Andesite is one of the most commo...
Set Default Paste...
Types of Volcanoes
6

Check Your Work

Activity 6 Copy Text in a Staff Meeting Announcement — 1 Part

You will copy and paste text in a document announcing a staff meeting for the Technical Support Team.

Copying and Pasting Text

Copy

Quick Steps

Copy Selected Text

1. Select text.
2. Click Copy button or use Ctrl + C.
3. Position insertion point.
4. Click Paste button or use Ctrl + V.

Use copy and paste to copy text from one document and paste it into another. Or, paste copied text into one document multiple times to insert duplicate portions of text without needing to retype it. Copy selected text and then paste it in a different location using the Copy and Paste buttons in the Clipboard group on the Home tab or the keyboard shortcuts Ctrl + C and Ctrl + V.

Text can also be copied and pasted using the mouse. To do this, select the text and then click inside the selected text. Hold down the left mouse button and also press and hold down the Ctrl key while dragging the selected text with the mouse. While text is being dragged, the pointer displays with a small gray box and a box containing a plus [+] symbol and a black vertical bar moves with the pointer. Position the black bar in the desired location, release the mouse button, and then release the Ctrl key to paste the text.

Activity 6 Copying Text — Part 1 of 1

1. Open **StaffMtg.docx** and then save it with the name **3-StaffMtg**.
2. Copy the text in the document to the end of the document by completing the following steps:
   a. Select all the text in the document and include one blank line below the text. ***Hint: Click the Show/Hide ¶ button to turn on the display of nonprinting characters. When you select the text, select one of the paragraph markers below the text.***
   b. Click the Copy button in the Clipboard group on the Home tab.
   c. Press Ctrl + End to move the insertion point to the end of the document.
   d. Click the Paste button.
3. Paste the text again at the end of the document. To do this, click the Paste button. (This inserts a copy of the text from the Clipboard.)
4. Select all the text in the document using the mouse and include one blank line below the text.
5. Move the I-beam pointer inside the selected text until it becomes an arrow pointer.
6. Click and hold down the Ctrl key and then the left mouse button. Drag the arrow pointer (which displays with a box containing a plus symbol) so the vertical black bar is positioned at the end of the document, release the mouse button, and then release the Ctrl key.
7. Deselect the text.
8. Make sure all the text fits on one page. If not, consider deleting any extra blank lines.
9. Save, preview, and then close **3-StaffMtg.docx**.

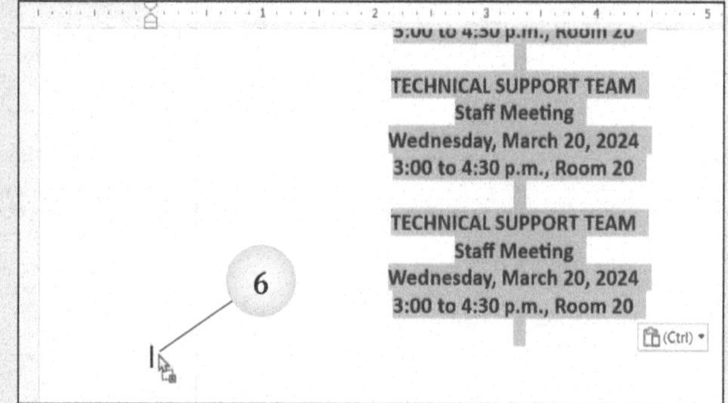

Activity 7 Create a Contract Negotiations Document — 1 Part

You will use the Clipboard task pane to copy and paste paragraphs to and from separate documents to create a contract negotiations document.

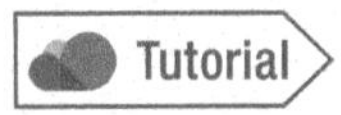

Using the Clipboard Task Pane

Quick Steps

Use the Clipboard

1. Click Clipboard group task pane launcher.
2. Select and copy or cut text.
3. Position insertion point.
4. Click option in Clipboard task pane.

Hint You can copy or cut items to the Clipboard from various Microsoft 365 applications and then paste them into any Microsoft 365 file.

Using the Clipboard Task Pane

Use the Clipboard task pane to collect up to 24 different items, such as text, images, and objects, and then paste the items multiple times and in multiple locations in Word as well as other applications, such as Excel, PowerPoint, and Access. The Clipboard allows cutting and copying multiple items without limiting pasting to only the last item cut or copied.

To display the Clipboard task pane, click the Clipboard group task pane launcher in the lower right corner of the Clipboard group on the Home tab. The Clipboard task pane displays at the left side of the screen in a manner similar to what is shown in Figure 3.10.

Select the item to be copied and then click the Copy button or Cut button in the Clipboard group. Continue selecting items and clicking the Copy or Cut button. To insert an item from the Clipboard task pane into the document, position the insertion point in the desired location and then click the option in the Clipboard task pane representing the item. Click the Paste All button to paste all the items in the Clipboard task pane into the document. If the copied or cut item is text, the first 50 characters display in the list box on the Clipboard task pane. When all the items are inserted, click the Clear All button to clear all items from the task pane.

Figure 3.10 Clipboard Task Pane

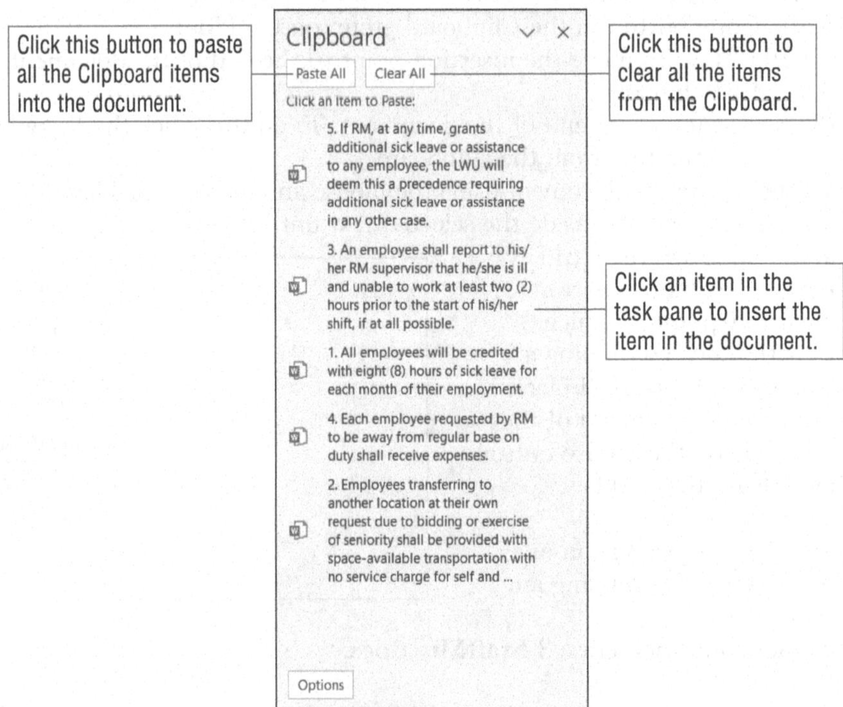

Activity 7 Collecting and Pasting Paragraphs of Text

1. Open **ContractItems.docx**.
2. Display the Clipboard task pane by clicking the Clipboard group task pane launcher in the bottom right corner of the Clipboard group on the Home tab. (If the Clipboard task pane list box contains any items, click the Clear All button at the top of the Clipboard task pane.)

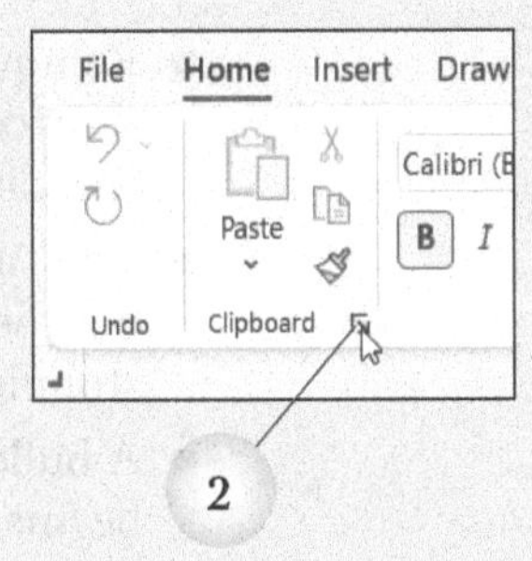

3. Select paragraph 1 in the document (the *1.* is not selected) and then click the Copy button.
4. Select paragraph 3 in the document (the *3.* is not selected) and then click the Copy button.
5. Close **ContractItems.docx**.
6. Paste the paragraphs by completing the following steps:
   a. Press Ctrl + N to open a new blank document. (If the Clipboard task pane does not display, click the Clipboard group task pane launcher.)
   b. Type CONTRACT NEGOTIATION ITEMS and apply bold formatting and center alignment.
   c. Press the Enter key, turn off bold formatting, and return the paragraph alignment to left.
   d. Click the Paste All button in the Clipboard task pane to paste both paragraphs in the document.
   e. Click the Clear All button in the Clipboard task pane.

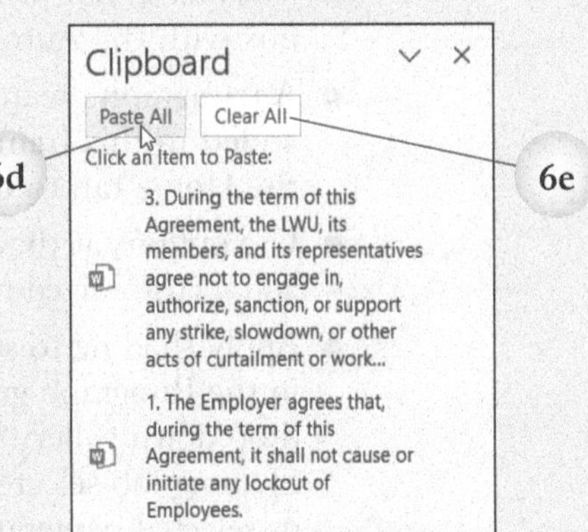

7. Open **UnionContract.docx**.
8. Select and then copy each of the following paragraphs:
   a. Paragraph 2 in the *Transfers and Moving Expenses* section.
   b. Paragraph 4 in the *Transfers and Moving Expenses* section.
   c. Paragraph 1 in the *Sick Leave* section.
   d. Paragraph 3 in the *Sick Leave* section.
   e. Paragraph 5 in the *Sick Leave* section.
9. Close **UnionContract.docx**.
10. Make sure the insertion point is positioned at the end of the document on a new line and then paste the paragraphs by completing the following steps:
    a. Click the button in the Clipboard task pane representing paragraph 2. (When the paragraph is inserted in the document, the paragraph number changes to *3.*)
    b. Click the button in the Clipboard task pane representing paragraph 4.
    c. Click the button in the Clipboard task pane representing paragraph 3.
    d. Click the button in the Clipboard task pane representing paragraph 5.

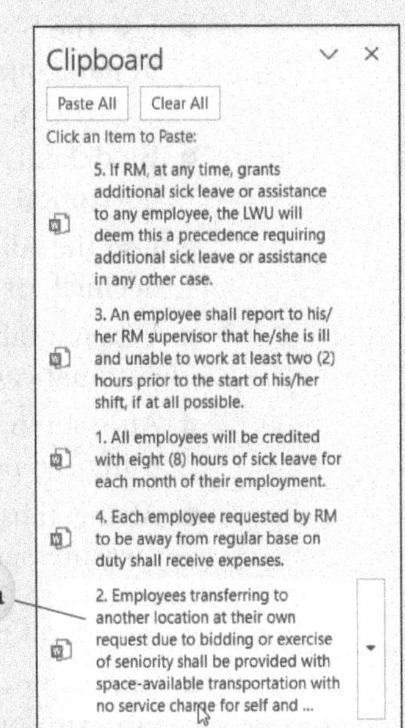

11. Click the Clear All button.
12. Close the Clipboard task pane.
13. Save the document with the name **3-NegotiateItems**.
14. Preview and then close **3-NegotiateItems.docx**.

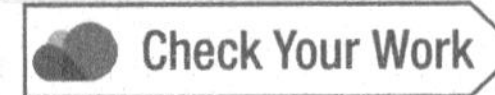

Chapter Summary

- Number paragraphs using the Numbering button in the Paragraph group on the Home tab and insert bullets before paragraphs using the Bullets button.
- Remove all paragraph formatting from a paragraph by using the keyboard shortcut Ctrl + Q. Remove all character and paragraph formatting by clicking the Clear All Formatting button in the Font group.
- The AutoCorrect Options button displays when the AutoFormat feature inserts numbers or bullets. Click this button to display options for undoing and/or stopping automatic numbering or bulleting.
- A bulleted list with a hanging indent is automatically created when a paragraph begins with *, >, or -. The type of bullet inserted depends on the type of character entered.
- Automatic numbering and bulleting can be turned off at the AutoCorrect dialog box with the AutoFormat As You Type tab selected.
- A paragraph created in Word contains an invisible frame and a border can be added to this frame. Click the Borders button arrow in the Paragraph group on the Home tab to display a drop-down gallery of border options.
- Use options at the Borders and Shading dialog box with the Borders tab selected to add a customized border to a paragraph, selected paragraphs, or selected text.
- Apply shading to selected text or paragraphs by clicking the Shading button arrow in the Paragraph group on the Home tab and then clicking a color option at the drop-down gallery. Use options at the Borders and Shading dialog box with the Shading tab selected to add shading and/or a pattern to selected text, a paragraph, or selected paragraphs.
- Use the Sort button in the Paragraph group on the Home tab to sort text in paragraphs alphabetically or numerically by the first character of each paragraph, which can be a number, symbol, or letter.
- By default, tabs are set every 0.5 inch. Tab settings can be changed on the horizontal ruler or at the Tabs dialog box.
- Use the Alignment button above the vertical ruler to select a left, right, center, decimal, or bar tab.
- When a tab is set on the horizontal ruler, any default tabs to the left are automatically deleted.
- After a tab has been set on the horizontal ruler, it can be moved or deleted using the pointer.
- At the Tabs dialog box, any of the five types of tabs can be set at a specific measurement. Four types of tabs (left, right, center, and decimal) can be set with preceding leaders, which can be periods, hyphens, or underlines. Individual tabs or all tabs can be cleared at the Tabs dialog box.
- Cut, copy, and paste text using buttons in the Clipboard group on the Home tab, with options at the shortcut menu, or with keyboard shortcuts.
- When selected text is pasted, the Paste Options button displays in the lower right corner of the text. Click the button and the Paste Options gallery displays with buttons for specifying how text and formatting is pasted in the document.
- With the Clipboard task pane, up to 24 items can be cut or copied and then pasted in various locations in a document or other document.
- Display the Clipboard task pane by clicking the Clipboard group task pane launcher in the Clipboard group on the Home tab.

Commands Review

FEATURE	RIBBON TAB, GROUP	BUTTON, OPTION	KEYBOARD SHORTCUT
borders	Home, Paragraph		
Borders and Shading dialog box	Home, Paragraph	, *Borders and Shading*	
bullets	Home, Paragraph		
clear all formatting	Home, Font		
clear paragraph formatting			Ctrl + Q
Clipboard task pane	Home, Clipboard		
copy text	Home, Clipboard		Ctrl + C
cut text	Home, Clipboard		Ctrl + X
numbering	Home, Paragraph		
Paragraph dialog box	Home, Paragraph		
paste text	Home, Clipboard		Ctrl + V
shading	Home, Paragraph		
Sort Text dialog box	Home, Paragraph		
Tabs dialog box	Home, Paragraph	, Tabs	

Review and Assessment

CHAPTER 3

Skills Assessment

Assessment 1

Format and Sort an Adventure Tours Document

1. Open **Tours.docx** and then save it with the name **3-Tours**.
2. Move the insertion point to the end of the document and then type the text shown in Figure 3.11. (Type the > symbol and press the spacebar for the first item and the symbol will be formatted as an arrow bullet, and the bullet for each remaining item will be inserted automatically as you type.)
3. Select the four paragraphs below the heading *Tour Specials* and then apply numbered formatting.
4. Type the following paragraph of text between paragraphs 3 and 4 below the heading *Tour Specials*: 7-day tours beginning at $1,779 per person. ***Note: The new paragraph will be the fourth item in the numbered list.***
5. Select the nine paragraphs below the heading *European Tours* and then apply bulleted formatting. (Arrow bullets will be applied to the paragraphs.)
6. With the nine paragraphs still selected, sort the paragraphs in ascending order.
7. Move the insertion point to the beginning of the document and then apply the Shaded style set. (Click the Design tab to display style sets; you will need click the more style sets button to display this style set.)
8. Apply the Slice theme. (Click the Design tab to display the Theme button.)
9. Select the nine paragraphs below the heading *European Tours* and then apply Dark Green, Accent 4, Lighter 80% paragraph shading (eighth column, second row in the *Theme Colors* section) to the selected paragraphs.
10. Apply the same Dark Green, Accent 4, Lighter 80% paragraph shading to the five numbered paragraphs below the heading *TOUR SPECIALS* and the three bulleted paragraphs below the heading *TOP TOURS*.
11. Save, preview, and then close **3-Tours.docx**.

Figure 3.11 Assessment 1

➢ Taste of Italy
➢ Hallmarks of Europe
➢ Best of England

Assessment 2 Type Tabbed Text and Apply Formatting to a Computer Software Document

1. Open **ProdSoftware.docx** and then save it with the name **3-ProdSoftware**.
2. Move the insertion point to the end of the document and then set left tabs at the 0.75-inch, 2.75-inch, and 4.5-inch marks on the horizontal ruler. Type the text in Figure 3.12 at the tabs you set. Use the New Line command, Shift + Enter, after typing each line of text in columns (except the last line).
3. Apply the Retrospect theme.
4. Select the productivity software categories in the *Productivity Software* section (from *Word processing* through *Computer-aided design*) and then sort the text alphabetically.
5. With the text still selected, apply bulleted formatting. (Solid circle bullets will be applied to the text.)
6. Select the personal-use software categories in the *Personal-Use Software* section (from *Personal finance software* through *Games and entertainment software*) and then sort the text alphabetically in ascending order.
7. With the text still selected, apply bulleted formatting.
8. Apply to the heading *Productivity Software* a single-line top border and Olive Green, Text 2, Lighter 80% paragraph shading (fourth column, second row in the *Theme Colors* section).
9. Apply the same single-line top border and olive green shading to the other two headings (*Personal-Use Software* and *Software Training Schedule*).
10. Position the insertion point in the first line of tabbed text and then move the tab symbols on the horizontal ruler as follows:
    a. Move the tab at the 0.75-inch mark to the 1-inch mark.
    b. Move the tab at the 4.5-inch mark to the 4-inch mark.
11. Save, preview, and then close **3-ProdSoftware.docx**.

Figure 3.12 Assessment 2

Word	April 16	8:30 to 11:30 a.m.
PowerPoint	April 18	1:00 to 3:30 p.m.
Excel	May 14	8:30 to 11:30 a.m.
Access	May 16	1:00 to 3:30 p.m.

Assessment 3 Type and Format a Table of Contents Document

1. At a new blank document, type the document shown in Figure 3.13 with the following specifications:
    a. Change the font to 11-point Cambria.
    b. Apply bold formatting and center alignment to the title as shown.
    c. Before typing the tabbed text, display the Tabs dialog box. Set a left tab at the 1-inch mark and the 1.5-inch mark and a right tab with period leaders at the 5.5-inch mark.
    d. When typing the text, press the Enter key to end each line of text.
2. Save the document with the name **3-TofC**.
3. Preview **3-TofC.docx**.
4. Select the tabbed text and then make changes as follows. (Because you pressed the Enter key instead of Shift + Enter at the end of each line of text, you need to select all the tabbed text before moving the tabs.)

a. Delete the left tab symbol at the 1.5-inch mark.
b. Set a new left tab at the 0.5-inch mark.
c. Move the right tab at the 5.5-inch mark to the 6-inch mark.

5. Insert single-line borders above and below the title *TABLE OF CONTENTS*.
6. Apply Orange, Accent 2, Lighter 80% paragraph shading (sixth column, second row in the *Theme Colors* section) to the title *TABLE OF CONTENTS*.
7. Save, preview, and then close **3-TofC.docx**.

Figure 3.13 Assessment 3

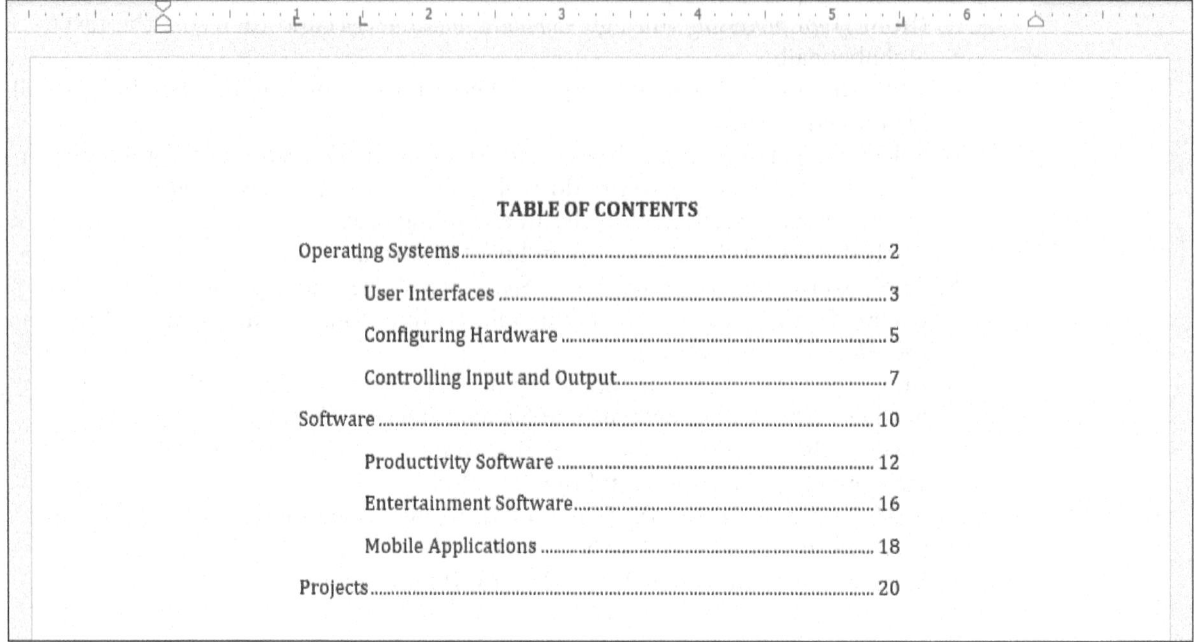

TABLE OF CONTENTS

Operating Systems.......... 2
    User Interfaces.......... 3
    Configuring Hardware.......... 5
    Controlling Input and Output.......... 7
Software.......... 10
    Productivity Software.......... 12
    Entertainment Software.......... 16
    Mobile Applications.......... 18
Projects.......... 20

Assessment 4 Format a Building Construction Agreement Document

1. Open **ConstructAgrmnt.docx** and then save it with the name **3-ConstructAgrmnt**.
2. Select and then delete the paragraph that begins *SUPERVISION OF WORK*.
3. Move the paragraph that begins *FINANCE AGREEMENT* before the paragraph that begins *START OF CONSTRUCTION*.
4. Open **AgrmntItems.docx**.
5. Display the Clipboard task pane and then clear all the contents, if necessary.
6. Select and then copy the first paragraph.
7. Select and then copy the second paragraph.
8. Select and then copy the third paragraph.
9. Close **AgrmntItems.docx**.
10. With **3-ConstructAgrmnt.docx** open, display the Clipboard task pane.
11. Position the insertion point at the beginning of the *CHANGES AND ALTERATIONS* paragraph and then paste the *SUPERVISION* paragraph and merge the formatting.
12. Position the insertion point at the beginning of the *POSSESSION OF RESIDENCE* paragraph and then paste the *PAY REVIEW* paragraph and merge the formatting.
13. Clear all items from the Clipboard and then close the Clipboard task pane.
14. Save, preview, and then close **3-ConstructAgrmnt.docx**.

Assessment 5

Hyphenate Words in a Report

1. In some Word documents, especially documents with left and right margins wider than 1 inch, the right margin may appear quite ragged. If the paragraph alignment is changed to justified alignment, the right margin will appear even, but extra space will be added between words throughout the line. In these situations, hyphenating long words that fall at the ends of text lines provides the document with a more balanced look. Click the Layout tab and then explore the options available in the Hyphenation button drop-down list in the Page Setup group. Figure out how to automatically hyphenate words in a document and how to limit the number of consecutive hyphens using an option at the Hyphenation dialog box.
2. Open **Costumes.docx** and then save it with the name **3-Costumes**.
3. Automatically hyphenate words in the document, limiting the number of consecutive hyphens to two. ***Hint: Display the Hyphenation dialog box by clicking the Hyphenation button in the Page Setup group on the Layout tab and then clicking* Hyphenation Options.**
4. Save, preview, and then close **3-Costumes.docx**.

Visual Benchmark

Create a Resume

1. Open **Resume.docx** and then save it with the name **3-Resume**.
2. Apply character and paragraph formatting to the resume so it appears as shown in Figure 3.14.
3. Save, preview, and then close **3-Resume.docx**.

Figure 3.14 Visual Benchmark

DEVON CHAMBERS

344 North Anderson Road * Oklahoma City, OK 73177 * (404) 555-3228

PROFILE

Business manager with successful track record at entrepreneurial start-up and strong project management skills. Keen ability to motivate and supervise employees, a strong hands-on experience with customer service, marketing, and operations. Highly organized and motivated professional looking to leverage strengths in leadership and organizational skills in a project coordinator role.

PROFESSIONAL EXPERIENCE

Midwest Deli, Oklahoma City, OK .... 07/21 to present
Assistant Manager

- Coordinated the opening of a new business, which included budgeting start-up costs, establishing relationships with vendors, ordering supplies, purchasing and installing equipment, and marketing the business to the community
- Manage business personnel, which includes recruitment, interviewing, hiring, training, motivating staff, and resolving conflicts
- Manage daily business operations through customer satisfaction, quality control, employee scheduling, process improvement, and product inventory maintenance

Marin Associates, Shawnee, OK............ 06/19 to 06/21
Projects Coordinator

- Developed and maintained a secure office network and installed and repaired computers
- Provided support for hardware and software issues
- Directed agency projects such as equipment purchases, office reorganization, and building maintenance and repair

Moore Insurance Agency, Shawnee, OK............ 04/17 to 05/19
Administrative Assistant

- Prepared documents and forms for staff and clients
- Organized and maintained paper and electronic files and scheduled meetings and appointments
- Disseminated information using the telephone, mail services, websites, and email

EDUCATION

Associate of Arts, Business 2021
Oklahoma City Community College

TECHNOLOGY SKILLS

- Proficient in Microsoft Word, Excel, and PowerPoint
- Knowledgeable in current and previous versions of the Windows operating system
- Experience with networking, firewalls, and security systems

REFERENCES

Professional and personal references available upon request.

Case Study

Part 1

You are the assistant to Gina Coletti, manager of La Dolce Vita, an Italian restaurant. She has been working on updating and formatting the lunch menu. She has asked you to complete the menu by opening **Menu.docx**, determining how the appetizer section is formatted, and then applying the same formatting to the sections *Soups and Salads*; *Sandwiches, Calzones, and Burgers*; and *Individual Pizzas*. Save the document with the name **3-Menu**. Preview and then close the document.

Part 2

Ms. Coletti has reviewed the completed menu and is pleased with it, but she wants to add a border around the entire page to increase visual interest. Open **3-Menu.docx** and then save it with the name **3-MenuPgBorder**. Display the Borders and Shading dialog box with the Page Border tab selected and then experiment with the options available. Apply an appropriate page border to the menu. (Consider applying an art image border.) Save, preview, and then close **3-MenuPgBorder.docx**.

Part 3

Each week, the restaurant offers daily specials. Ms. Coletti has asked you to create a new menu for specials using the text in **MenuSpecials.docx**. She has asked you to format the specials menu in a similar manner as the main menu, but to change some elements to make it unique. Make the formatting changes, and then apply the same page border to the specials menu document that you applied to the main menu document. Save the document with the name **3-MenuSpecials**. Preview and then close the document.

Part 4

You have been asked by the head chef to research a new recipe for an Italian dish. Using the internet, find a recipe that interests you and then prepare a Word document containing the recipe steps and ingredients. Bullet the items in the list of ingredients and number the steps in the recipe preparation. Save the document with the name **3-Recipe**. Preview and then close the document.

WORD

Formatting Pages and Documents

CHAPTER 4

Performance Objectives

Upon successful completion of Chapter 4, you will be able to:

1. Change margins, page orientation, and paper size
2. Format pages at the Page Setup dialog box
3. Insert a page break, blank page, and cover page
4. Insert and remove page numbers
5. Insert and edit predesigned headers and footers
6. Insert a watermark, page background color, and page border
7. Insert section breaks
8. Create and format text in columns
9. Hyphenate words automatically and manually
10. Create a drop cap
11. Use the Click and Type feature
12. Vertically align text
13. Find and replace text

Word provides a number of options for changing the layout of a document, such as adjusting page margins, orientation, and paper size. Word also includes features that can be inserted in a document, such as a page break, blank page, cover page, and watermark, as well as page numbers, headers, footers, page color, and page borders. You will learn about these features in this chapter along with other page and document formatting options, such as inserting section breaks, formatting text into columns, hyphenating words, creating a drop cap, and vertically aligning text. You will also learn how to find and replace text in a document.

Data Files

The data files for this chapter are in the WL1C4 folder that you downloaded at the beginning of this course.

Activity 1 Format a Document on Photography 2 Parts

You will open a document containing information on photography and then change the margins, page orientation, and paper size.

Changing Page Setup

The Page Setup group on the Layout tab contains a number of options for changing the layout of pages in a document. Use options in the Page Setup group to perform such actions as changing margins, orientation, and paper size and inserting page breaks. The Pages group on the Insert tab contains three buttons for inserting a cover page, blank page, or page break.

Changing Margins

Changing Margins

A page in a Word document, by default, has a one-inch top, bottom, left, and right margin. Situations may occur where these margins may need to be increased to allow space for binding a document, room in the margins for making notes or inserting objects, or decreased to allow for more text on the page.

Margins

Change page margins with options at the Margins button drop-down list, as shown in Figure 4.1. To display this drop-down list, click the Layout tab and then click the Margins button in the Page Setup group. To change the margins, click one of the preset margins in the drop-down list. Be aware that most printers require a minimum margin (between ¼ and ⅜ inch) because they cannot print to the edge of the page.

Quick Steps

Change Margins
1. Click Layout tab.
2. Click Margins button.
3. Click margin option.

Change Page Orientation
1. Click Layout tab.
2. Click Orientation button.
3. Click *Portrait* or *Landscape*.

Change Paper Size
1. Click Layout tab.
2. Click Size button.
3. Click paper size.

Figure 4.1 Margins Button Drop-Down List

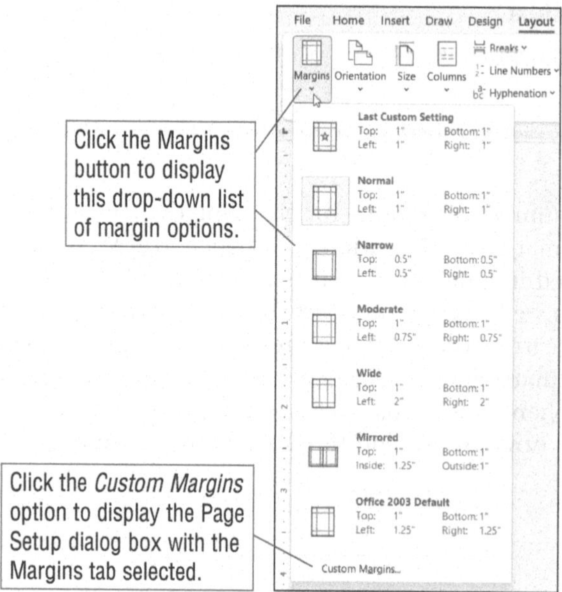

Changing Page Orientation

Orientation

Changing Page Orientation

Click the Orientation button in the Page Setup group on the Layout tab and two options display: *Portrait* and *Landscape*. At the portrait orientation, which is the default, the page is 8.5 inches wide and 11 inches tall. At the landscape orientation, the page is 11 inches wide and 8.5 inches tall. Change the page orientation and the page margins automatically shift: The left and right margin measurements become the top and bottom margin measurements.

Changing Paper Size

Size

Changing Paper Size

By default, Word formats documents for printing on standard letter-sized paper that is 8.5 inches wide and 11 inches tall. Change this default setting with options at the Size button drop-down list. Display this drop-down list by clicking the Size button in the Page Setup group on the Layout tab.

Activity 1a Changing Margins, Page Orientation, and Paper Size

Part 1 of 2

1. Open **Photography.docx** and then save it with the name **4-Photography**.
2. Click the Layout tab.
3. Click the Margins button in the Page Setup group and then click the *Narrow* option.

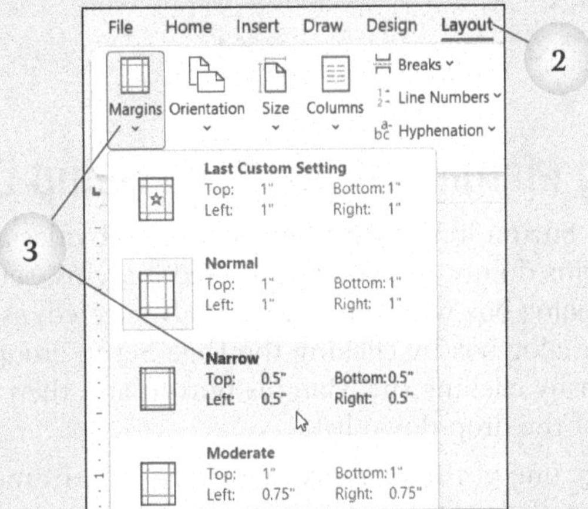

4. Click the Orientation button in the Page Setup group and then click *Landscape* at the drop-down list.

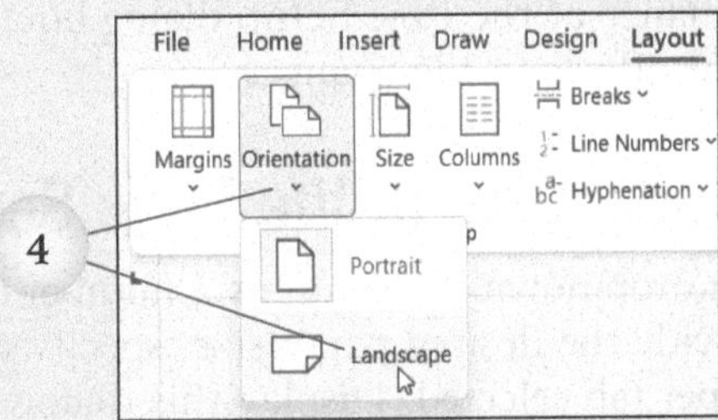

5. Scroll through the document and notice how the text displays on the page in landscape orientation.
6. Click the Orientation button in the Page Setup group and then click *Portrait* at the drop-down list. (This changes the orientation back to the default.)

7. Click the Size button in the Page Setup group and then click the *Executive* option (*7.25" × 10.5"*). Paper size options may vary. If this option is not available, choose an option with a similar paper size.

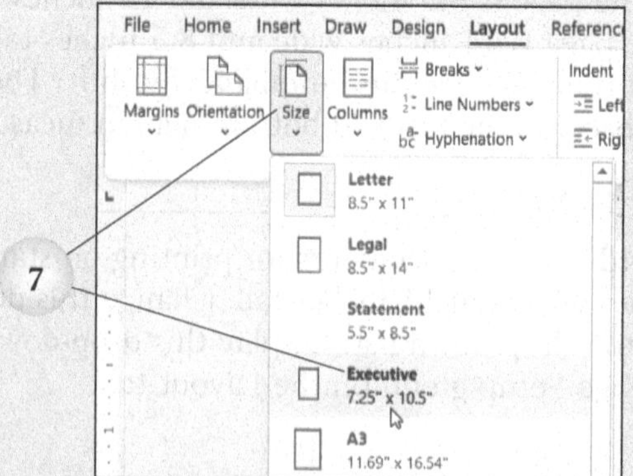

8. Scroll through the document and notice how the text displays on the page.
9. Click the Size button and then click *Legal* (*8.5" × 14"*).
10. Scroll through the document and notice how the text displays on the page.
11. Click the Size button and then click *Letter* (*8.5" × 11"*). (This returns the size back to the default.)
12. Save **4-Photography.docx**.

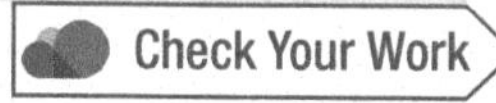

Changing Margins at the Page Setup Dialog Box

Quick Steps

Change Margins at Page Setup Dialog Box

1. Click Layout tab.
2. Click Page Setup group dialog box launcher.

OR

1. Click Layout tab.
2. Click Margins button.
3. Click *Custom Margins*.
4. Specify margins.
5. Click OK.

Change Paper Size at Page Setup Dialog Box

1. Click Layout tab.
2. Click Size button.
3. Click *More Paper Sizes*.
4. Specify size.
5. Click OK.

The Margins button in the Page Setup group provides a number of preset margins. If these margins do not provide the desired margins, set specific margins at the Page Setup dialog box with the Margins tab selected, as shown in Figure 4.2. Display this dialog box by clicking the Page Setup group dialog box launcher on the Layout tab or by clicking the Margins button and then clicking *Custom Margins* at the bottom of the drop-down list.

To change one of the margins, select the current measurement in the *Top*, *Bottom*, *Left*, or *Right* measurement box and then type the new measurement, or click the measurement box up arrow to increase the measurement or the measurement box down arrow to decrease the measurement. As the margin measurements change at the Page Setup dialog box, the sample page in the *Preview* section shows the effects of the changes.

Changing Paper Size at the Page Setup Dialog Box

The Size button drop-down list contains a number of preset paper sizes. If these sizes do not provide the desired paper size, specify a size at the Page Setup dialog box with the Paper tab selected. Display this dialog box by clicking the Size button in the Page Setup group and then clicking *More Paper Sizes* at the bottom of the drop-down list.

Figure 4.2 Page Setup Dialog Box with the Margins Tab Selected

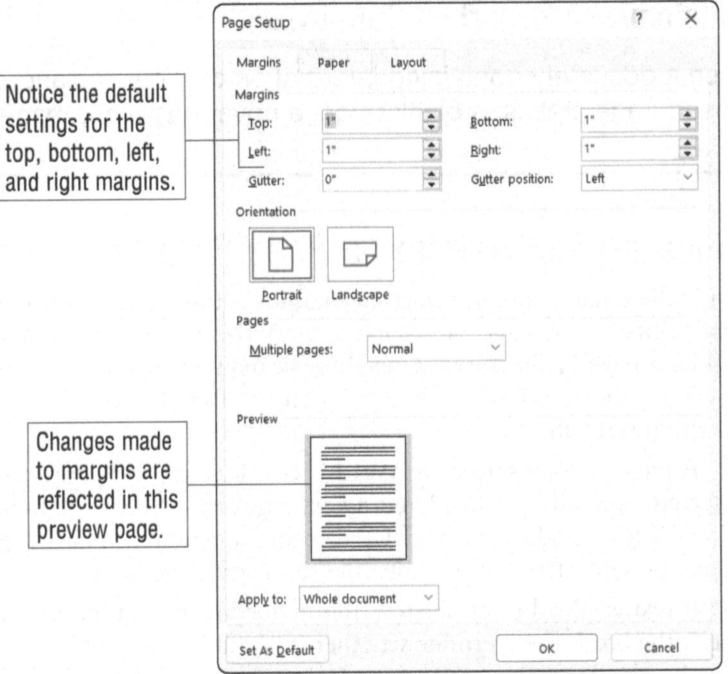

Activity 1b Changing Margins and Paper Size at the Page Setup Dialog Box

Part 2 of 2

1. With **4-Photography.docx** open, make sure the Layout tab is selected.
2. Click the Page Setup group dialog box launcher.
3. At the Page Setup dialog box with the Margins tab selected, click the *Top* measurement box up arrow until *0.7"* displays.
4. Click the *Bottom* measurement box up arrow until *0.7"* displays.
5. Select the current measurement in the *Left* measurement box and then type 0.75.
6. Select the current measurement in the *Right* measurement box and then type 0.75.
7. Click OK to close the dialog box.
8. Click the Size button in the Page Setup group and then click *More Paper Sizes* at the drop-down list.
9. At the Page Setup dialog box with the Paper tab selected, click the *Paper size* option box arrow and then click *Legal* at the drop-down list.
10. Click OK to close the dialog box.
11. Scroll through the document and notice how the text displays on the page.
12. Click the Size button in the Page Setup group and then click *Letter* at the drop-down list.
13. Save, preview, and then close **4-Photography.docx**.

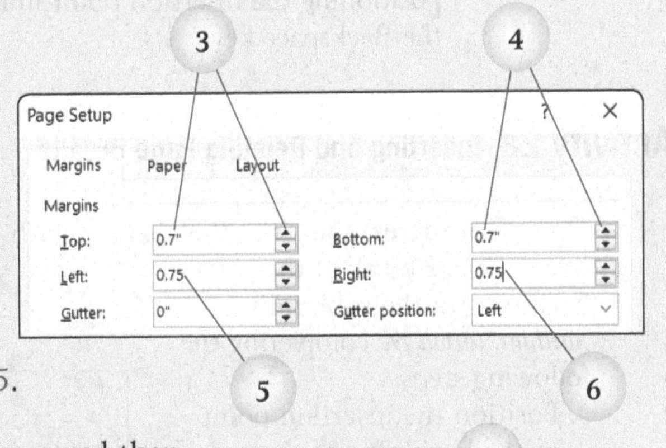

Check Your Work

Activity 2 Customize a Report on Countries — 3 Parts

You will open a document containing information on New Zealand and Australia and then insert page breaks, a blank page, a cover page, and page numbers.

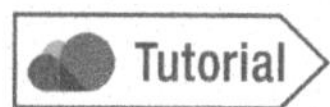

Inserting and Deleting a Page Break

Inserting and Deleting a Page Break

With the default top and bottom margins set at 1 inch, approximately 9 inches of text prints on the page. At approximately the 10-inch mark, Word automatically inserts a page break. Insert a page break manually in a document with the keyboard shortcut Ctrl + Enter or with the Page Break button in the Pages group on the Insert tab.

A page break inserted by Word is considered a *soft page break* and a page break inserted manually is considered a *hard page break*. Soft page breaks automatically adjust if text is added to or deleted from a document. Hard page breaks do not adjust and are therefore less flexible than soft page breaks.

Quick Steps

Insert Page Break

1. Click Insert tab.
2. Click Page Break button.

OR

Press Ctrl + Enter.

If text is added to or deleted from a document containing a hard page break, check the break to determine whether it is still in a desirable location. Display a hard page break, along with other nonprinting characters, by clicking the Show/Hide ¶ button in the Paragraph group on the Home tab. A hard page break displays as a row of dots with the words *Page Break* in the center. To delete a hard page break, position the insertion point at the beginning of the page break and then press the Delete key or double-click the words *Page Break* and then press the Delete key. If the display of nonprinting characters is turned off, delete a hard page break by positioning the insertion point immediately below the page break and then pressing the Backspace key.

Activity 2a Inserting and Deleting Page Breaks — Part 1 of 3

1. Open **Countries.docx** and then save it with the name **4-Countries**.
2. Insert a page break at the beginning of the subheading *Sailing Nation* by completing the following steps:
   a. Position the insertion point at the beginning of the subheading *Sailing Nation* (near the bottom of page 1).
   b. Click the Insert tab and then click the Page Break button in the Pages group.
3. Move the insertion point to the beginning of the heading *AUSTRALIA* (on the second page) and then insert a page break by pressing Ctrl + Enter.

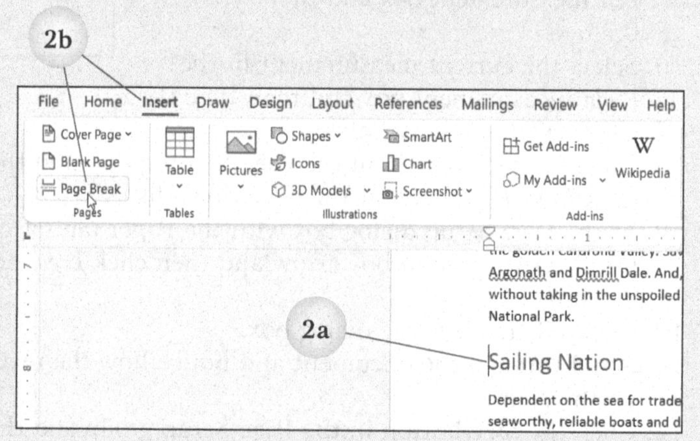

4. Delete a page break by completing the following steps:
   a. Move the insertion point to the end of the second paragraph in the *Nature* section (at the end of page 1).
   b. Click the Home tab.
   c. Turn on the display of nonprinting characters by clicking the Show/Hide ¶ button in the Paragraph group.
   d. Position the insertion point at the beginning of the page break.
   e. Press the Delete key two times.
   f. Click the Show/Hide ¶ button to turn off the display of nonprinting characters.
5. Save **4-Countries.docx**.

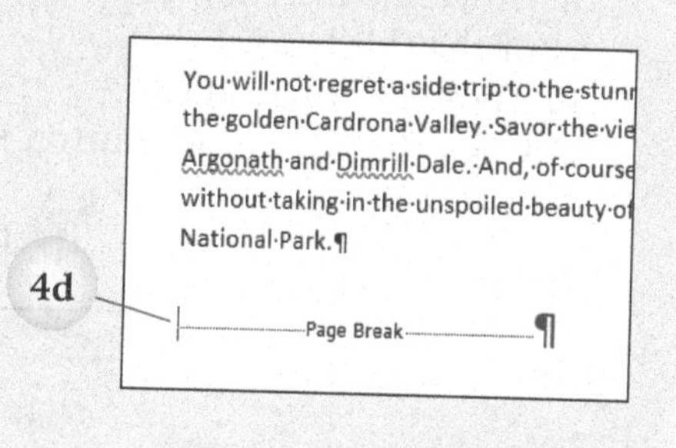

Inserting and Removing a Blank Page

Inserting and Removing a Blank Page

Click the Blank Page button in the Pages group on the Insert tab to insert a blank page at the position of the insertion point. This might be useful in a document where a blank page is needed for an illustration, graphic, or figure. When a blank page is inserted, Word inserts a page break and then inserts another page break to create the blank page. To remove a blank page, turn on the display of nonprinting characters and then delete the page breaks.

Inserting and Removing a Cover Page

Quick Steps

Insert Blank Page
1. Click Insert tab.
2. Click Blank Page button.

Insert Cover Page
1. Click Insert tab.
2. Click Cover Page button.
3. Click cover page option.

Hint Adding a cover page gives a document a polished and professional look.

Inserting and Removing a Cover Page

An educational paper, such as a report, thesis, or dissertation or a scientific or professional paper, may include a cover page that introduces the document by including a title, subtitle, image, abstract, or other elements. Word provides several predesigned cover pages. Click the Cover Page button in the Pages group on the Insert tab and a drop-down list displays with visual representations of the cover pages. Scroll through the list and then click a cover page option.

A predesigned cover page contains location placeholders, in which specific text is entered. For example, a cover page might contain the placeholder *[Document title]*. Click the placeholder to select it and then type the title of the document. Delete a placeholder by clicking to select it, clicking the placeholder tab, and then pressing the Delete key. Remove a cover page by clicking the Cover Page button and then clicking *Remove Current Cover Page* at the drop-down list.

Activity 2b Inserting and Removing a Blank Page and Inserting a Cover Page

1. With **4-Countries.docx** open, create a blank page by completing the following steps:
   a. Move the insertion point to the beginning of the heading *AUSTRALIA* at the beginning of the third page.
   b. Click the Insert tab.
   c. Click the Blank Page button in the Pages group.

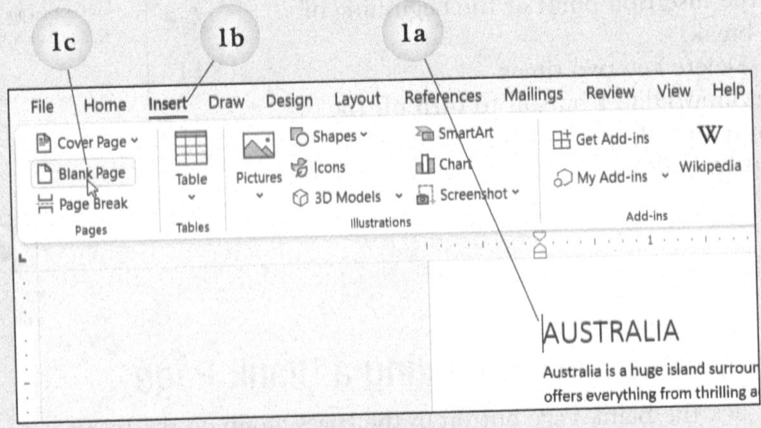

2. Insert a cover page by completing the following steps:
   a. Press Ctrl + Home to move the insertion point to the beginning of the document.
   b. Click the Cover Page button in the Pages group.
   c. Scroll down the drop-down list and then click the *Banded* option.

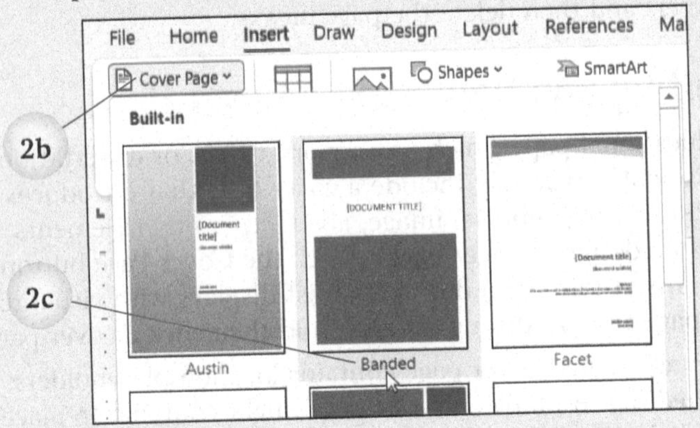

   d. Click the *[DOCUMENT TITLE]* placeholder and then type south pacific countries. (The text you type will display in uppercase letters.)

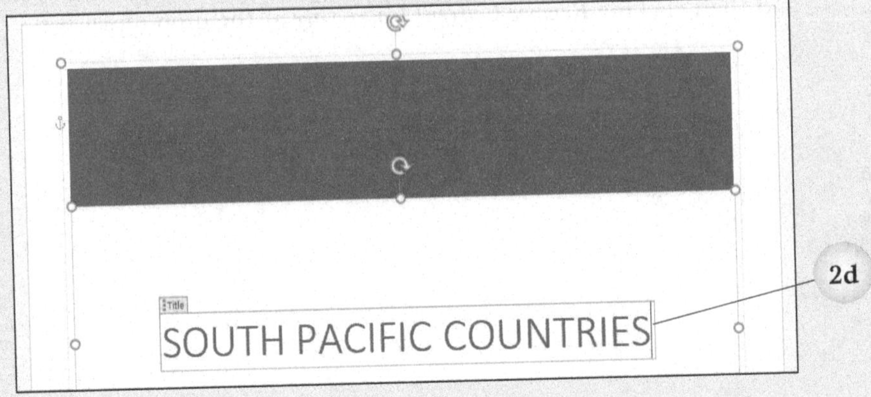

e. Click the *[COMPANY NAME]* placeholder and then type premier college. (The text you type will display in uppercase letters.) (If a name appears in the placeholder, select the name and then type premier college.)
f. Select the name above the company name and then type your first and last names. If instead of a name, the *[Author name]* placeholder displays above the company name, click the placeholder and then type your first and last names.

3. Delete the [Company address] placeholder by completing the following steps:
   a. Click the *[Company address]* placeholder.
   b. Click the *Address* placeholder tab.
   c. Press the Delete key.

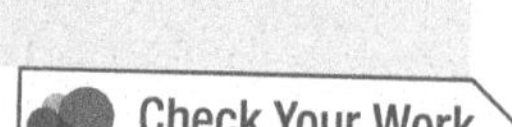

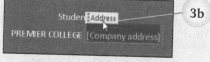

4. Remove the blank page you inserted in Step 1 by completing the following steps:
   a. Move the insertion point immediately right of the period that ends the last sentence in the paragraph of text below the subheading *Transport Options* (on page 3).
   b. Press the Delete key on the keyboard approximately five times until the heading *AUSTRALIA* displays on page 3.
5. Save **4-Countries.docx.**

Check Your Work

Inserting and Removing Page Numbers

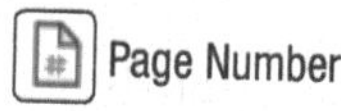

Quick Steps
Insert Page Numbers
1. Click Insert tab.
2. Click Page Number button.
3. Click number option.

Inserting and Removing Page Numbers

Word by default does not include page numbers on pages. Consider inserting page numbers in a document to help readers find specific parts of a document, know the size of the complete text by checking the last page number, and to allow for citations of particular pages.

To insert page numbers in a document, click the Page Number button in the Header & Footer group on the Insert tab. A drop-down list displays with options for placing page numbers in the top margin of the page (in the Header pane), in the bottom margin of the page (in the Footer pane), in a page margin (either in a Header or Footer pane), or at the location of the insertion point. Click or point to an option and a drop-down list will appear showing several predesigned page number formats. Scroll through the list and then click an option.

Choose a page number option other than *Current Position*, and the Header and Footer panes open. Changes can be made to the page numbering format in the Header pane or Footer pane. To do this, select the page number and then apply formatting, such as a different font size, style, or color. A page number inserted in a document with the *Current Position* option is positioned in the document, not in the Header or Footer pane. Format the page number like any other text in the document.

After formatting page numbers inserted in the Header or Footer pane, click the Close Header and Footer button, or simply double-click anywhere in the document outside the Header or Footer pane. Remove page numbers from the document by clicking the Page Number button in the Header & Footer group and then clicking *Remove Page Numbers* at the drop-down list.

Activity 2c Inserting and Removing Predesigned Page Numbers

1. With **4-Countries.docx** open, insert page numbers by completing the following steps:
   a. Move the insertion point so it is positioned anywhere in the heading *NEW ZEALAND*.
   b. If necessary, click the Insert tab.
   c. Click the Page Number button in the Header & Footer group and then point to *Top of Page*.
   d. Scroll through the drop-down list and then click the *Brackets 2* option.

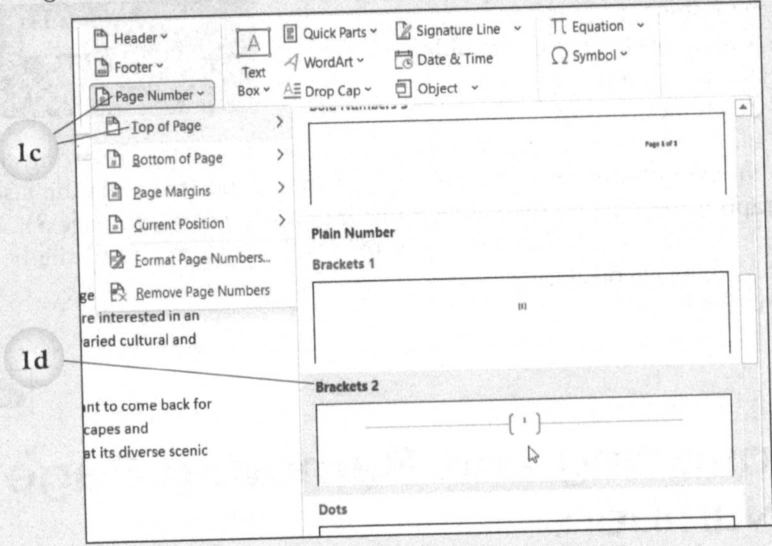

   e. Click the Close Header and Footer button in the Close group on the Header & Footer tab.
2. Scroll through the document and notice the page numbers at the top of each page except the cover page. (The cover page and text are divided by a page break. Word does not include the cover page when numbering pages.)
3. Remove the page numbering by clicking the Insert tab, clicking the Page Number button, and then clicking *Remove Page Numbers* at the drop-down list.
4. Click the Page Number button, point to *Bottom of Page*, scroll down the drop-down list, and then click the *Accent Bar 2* option.

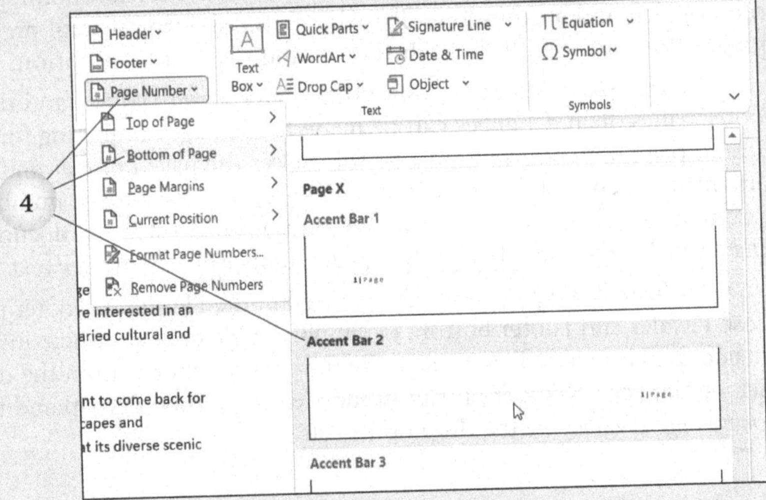

5. Click the Close Header and Footer button.
6. Save, preview, and then close **4-Countries.docx**.

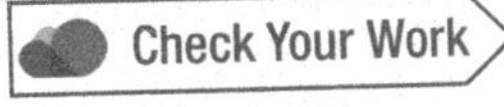

Activity 3 Add Elements to a Report on the Writing Process 3 Parts

You will open a document containing information on the process of writing effectively, insert a predesigned header and footer, remove a header, and format and delete header and footer elements.

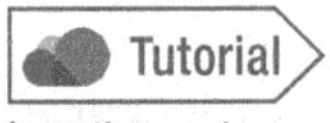

Tutorial

Inserting and Removing a Predesigned Header and Footer

Inserting Predesigned Headers and Footers

As mentioned in the last section, text that appears in the top margin of a page is called a *header* and text that appears in the bottom margin of a page is referred to as a *footer*. Headers and footers are common in manuscripts, textbooks, reports, and other publications. They typically include page numbers and other information, such as the author's name, the title of the publication, and/or the chapter title.

Header

Quick Steps

Insert Predesigned Header or Footer

1. Click Insert tab.
2. Click Header button or Footer button.
3. Click header or footer option.
4. Type text in specific placeholders in header or footer.
5. Click Close Header and Footer button.

Insert a predesigned header in a document by clicking the Insert tab and then clicking the Header button in the Header & Footer group. This displays the Header button drop-down list. At this drop-down list, click a predesigned header option and the header is inserted in the document.

A predesigned header or footer may contain location placeholders, such as [Document title] or [Type here]. Click in the placeholder text to select it and type the title of the document or other personalized text. Delete a placeholder by clicking to select it and then pressing the Delete key. If the placeholder contains a tab, delete the placeholder by clicking the placeholder tab and then pressing the Delete key.

To return to the document after inserting a header or footer, double-click in the document outside the Header or Footer pane or click the Close Header and Footer button.

Activity 3a Inserting a Predesigned Header Part 1 of 3

1. Open **WritingProcess.docx** and then save it with the name **4-WritingProcess**.
2. With the insertion point positioned at the beginning of the document, insert a header by completing the following steps:
   a. If necessary, click the Insert tab.
   b. Click the Header button in the Header & Footer group.
   c. Scroll to the bottom of the drop-down list and then click the *Sideline* option.

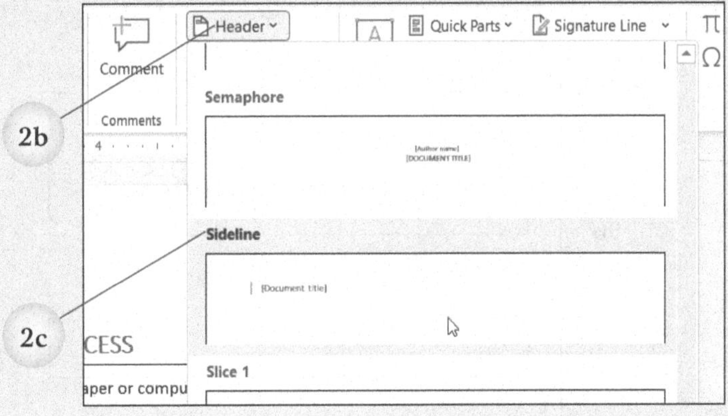

d. Click the *[Document title]* placeholder and then type The Writing Process.
e. Double-click in the document text. (This makes the document text active and dims the header.)

5. Scroll through the document to see how the header will print.
6. Save and then preview **4-WritingProcess.docx**.

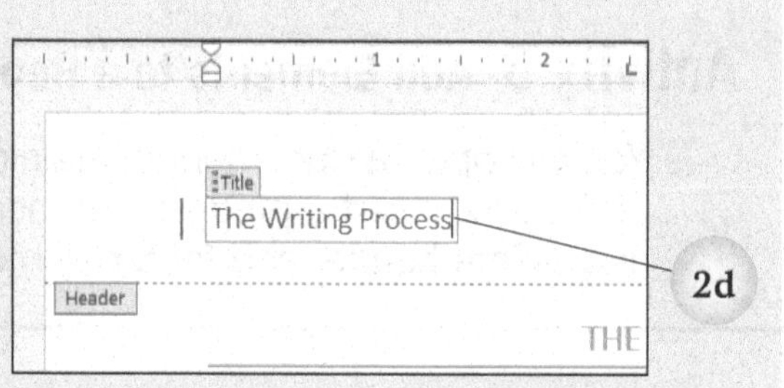

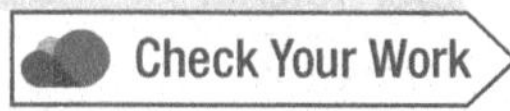

Insert a predesigned footer in the same manner as a header. Click the Footer button in the Header & Footer group on the Insert tab and a drop-down list displays that is similar to the Header button drop-down list. Click a footer and the predesigned footer is inserted in the document.

Removing a Header or Footer

Remove a header from a document by clicking the Insert tab and then clicking the Header button in the Header & Footer group. At the drop-down list, click the *Remove Header* option. Complete similar steps to remove a footer.

Activity 3b Removing a Header and Inserting a Predesigned Footer

Part 2 of 3

1. With **4-WritingProcess.docx** open, press Ctrl + Home to move the insertion point to the beginning of the document.
2. Remove the header by clicking the Insert tab, clicking the Header button in the Header & Footer group, and then clicking the *Remove Header* option at the drop-down list.
3. Insert a footer in the document by completing the following steps:
   a. Click the Footer button in the Header & Footer group.
   b. Scroll down the drop-down list and then click *Ion (Light)*.

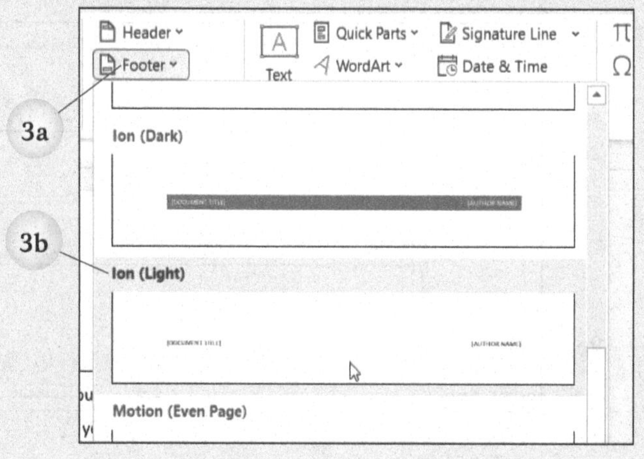

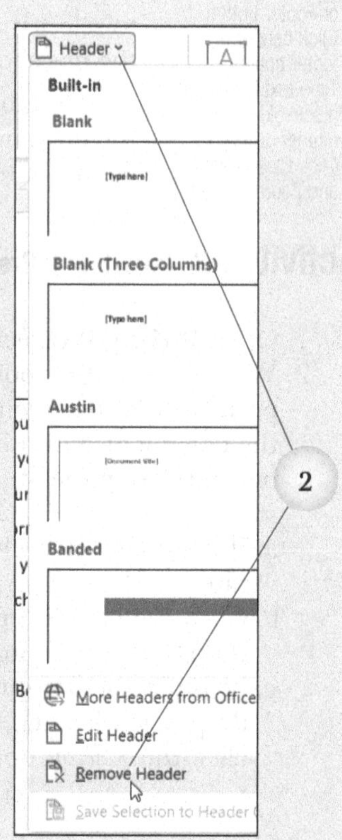

c. Notice that Word inserted the document title at the left side of the footer. (Word remembered the document title you entered in the header.) Word also inserted your name at the right side of the footer. If the document title does not appear, click the *[DOCUMENT TITLE]* placeholder and then type THE WRITING PROCESS. If your name does not appear, click the *[AUTHOR NAME]* placeholder and then type your first and last names.

d. Click the Close Header and Footer button to close the Footer pane and return to the document.

4. Scroll through the document to see how the footer will print.
5. Save and then preview **4-WritingProcess.docx**.

Editing a Predesigned Header or Footer

Predesigned headers and footers contain elements such as page numbers, a title, and an author's name. The formatting of an element can be changed by clicking the element and then applying formatting. Delete an element from a header or footer by selecting the element and then pressing the Delete key.

Activity 3c Formatting and Deleting Header and Footer Elements — Part 3 of 3

1. With **4-WritingProcess.docx** open, remove the footer by clicking the Insert tab, clicking the Footer button, and then clicking *Remove Footer* at the drop-down list.
2. Insert and then format a header by completing the following steps:
   a. Click the Header button in the Header & Footer group on the Insert tab, scroll down the drop-down list, and then click *Grid*. (This header inserts the document title and a date placeholder.)
   b. Delete the date placeholder by clicking the *[Date]* placeholder, clicking the placeholder tab, and then pressing the Delete key.
   c. Click the Close Header and Footer button.

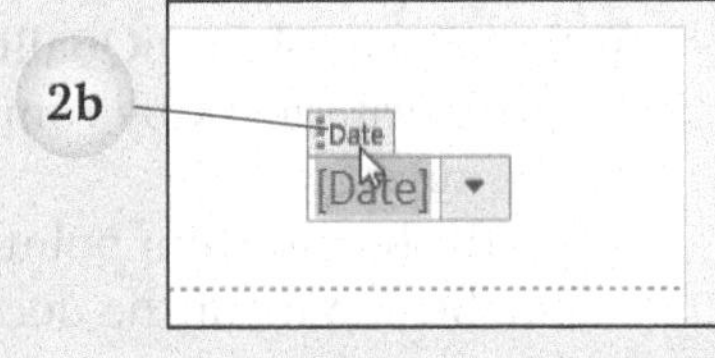

3. Insert and then format a footer by completing the following steps:
   a. Click the Insert tab.
   b. Click the Footer button, scroll down the drop-down list, and then click *Retrospect*.
   c. Select the name in the author placeholder at the left side of the footer and then type your first and last names.
   d. Select your name and the page number, apply bold formatting, and then change the font size to 10 points.
   e. Double-click in the document text.
4. Scroll through the document to see how the header and footer will print.
5. Save, preview, and then close **4-WritingProcess.docx**.

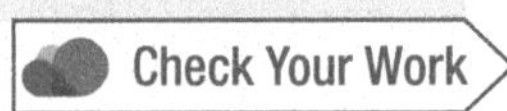

Activity 4 Format a Report on Desirable Employee Qualities — 2 Parts

You will open a document containing information on desirable employee qualities and then insert a watermark, change the page background color, and insert a page border.

Quick Steps

Insert Watermark

1. Click Design tab.
2. Click Watermark button.
3. Click watermark option.

Apply Page Background Color

1. Click Design tab.
2. Click Page Color button.
3. Click color option.

Formatting the Page Background

The Page Background group on the Design tab contains three buttons for customizing the page background. Click the Watermark button and choose a predesigned watermark from options at the drop-down list. If a document will be shared electronically or published online, consider adding a page background color with the Page Color button. Use the Page Borders button to apply a border to the background of a page. Customize the style of the page border by using options in the Borders and Shading dialog box.

Inserting and Removing a Watermark

Inserting a Watermark

A watermark is a lightened image that displays behind the text in a document. Use a watermark to add visual appeal or to identify a document as a draft, sample, or confidential document. Word provides a number of predesigned watermarks. View watermark options by clicking the Watermark button in the Page Background group on the Design tab. Scroll through the list and then click an option.

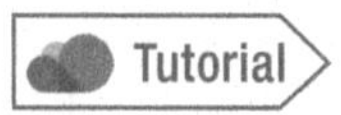

Applying a Page Background Color

Applying a Page Background Color

Use the Page Color button in the Page Background group on the Design tab to apply a background color to a document. This background color is intended for documents that will be viewed on-screen or online, as color is visible on the screen but does not print. Insert a page color by clicking the Page Color button and then clicking a color at the drop-down color palette.

Activity 4a Inserting and Removing a Watermark and Applying a Page Background Color — Part 1 of 2

1. Open **EmpQualities.docx** and then save it with the name **4-EmpQualities**.
2. Insert a watermark by completing the following steps:
   a. With the insertion point positioned at the beginning of the document, click the Design tab.
   b. Click the Watermark button in the Page Background group.
   c. At the drop-down list, click the *CONFIDENTIAL 1* option.
3. Scroll through the document and notice how the watermark displays behind the text.

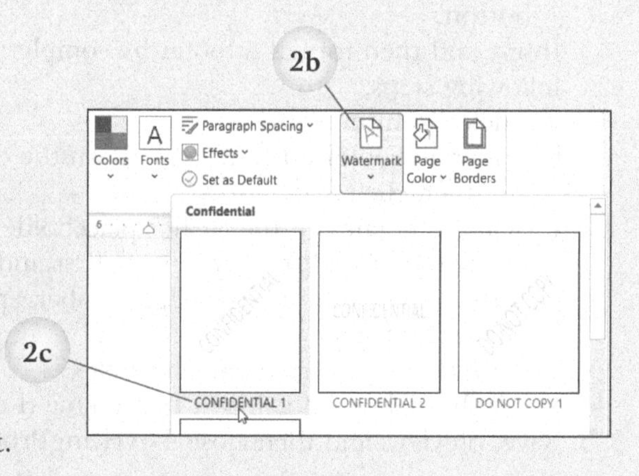

4. Remove the watermark and insert a different one by completing the following steps:
   a. Click the Watermark button and then click *Remove Watermark* at the drop-down list.
   b. Click the Watermark button and then click the *DO NOT COPY 1* option at the drop-down list.
5. Scroll through the document and notice how the watermark displays.
6. Move the insertion point to the beginning of the document.
7. Click the Page Color button in the Page Background group and then click the *Gray, Accent 3, Lighter 80%* option (seventh column, second row in the *Theme Colors* section).
8. Save **4-EmpQualities.docx**.

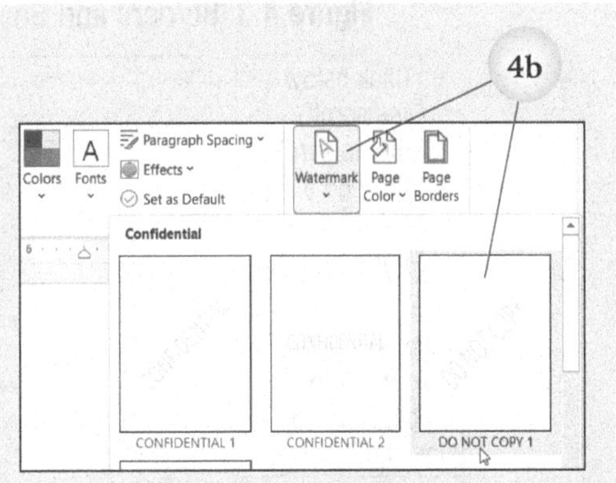

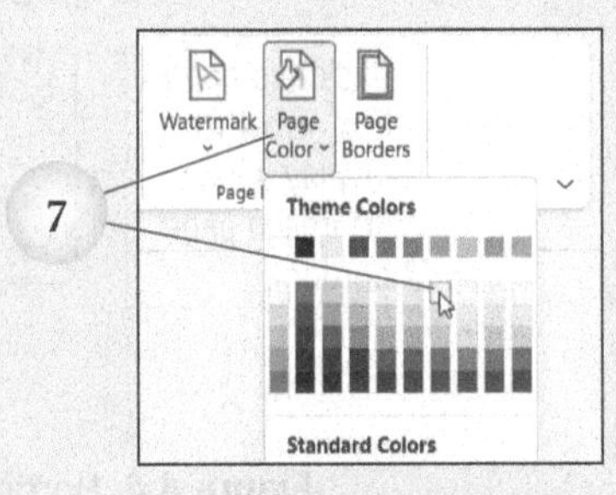

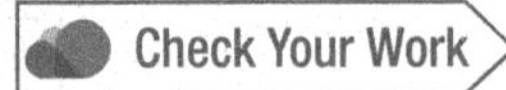

Inserting a Page Border

Quick Steps

Insert Page Border
1. Click Design tab.
2. Click Page Borders button.
3. Specify options at dialog box.
4. Click OK.

Inserting a Page Border

To improve the visual interest of a document, make the text stand out, or to make a document look finished, consider inserting a page border. When a page border is inserted in a multiple-page document, it prints on each page. To insert a page border, click the Page Borders button in the Page Background group on the Design tab. This displays the Borders and Shading dialog box with the Page Border tab selected, as shown in Figure 4.3 on the next page. At this dialog box, specify the border style, color, and width.

The dialog box contains an option for inserting a page border containing an art image. To display the images available, click the *Art* option box arrow and then scroll through the drop-down list. Click an image to insert the art image page border in the document.

Changing Page Border Options

By default, a page border appears and prints 24 points from the top, left, right, and bottom edges of the page. Some printers, particularly inkjet printers, have a nonprinting area around the outside edges of the page that can interfere with the printing of a border. Before printing a document with a page border, click the File tab and then click the *Print* option. Look at the preview of the page at the right side of the Print backstage area and determine whether the entire border is visible. If a portion of the border is not visible in the preview page (generally at the bottom and right sides of the page), consider changing measurements at the Border and Shading Options dialog box, shown in Figure 4.4 on the next page.

Figure 4.3 Borders and Shading Dialog Box with the Page Border Tab Selected

Click below the scroll box to scroll through a list of page border styles.

Click this option box arrow to display a list of line width options.

Click this option box arrow to display a list of art image page borders.

Preview the page border in this section.

Click this option box arrow to display a palette of page border colors.

Click this button to display the Border and Shading Options dialog box.

Borders and Shading

Borders | Page Border | Shading

Setting: None, Box, Shadow, 3-D, Custom

Style:

Color: Automatic

Width: ½ pt

Art: (none)

Preview

Click on diagram below or use buttons to apply borders

Apply to: Whole document

Options...

Cancel

Figure 4.4 Border and Shading Options Dialog Box

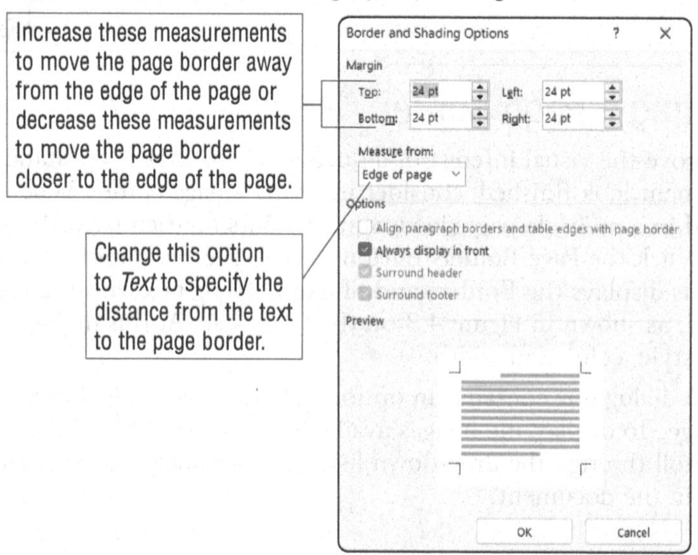

Display the Border and Shading Options dialog box by clicking the Design tab and then clicking the Page Borders button. At the Borders and Shading dialog box with the Page Border tab selected, click the Options button in the lower right corner of the dialog box. The options at the Border and Shading Options dialog box change depending on whether the Borders tab or the Page Border tab is selected when the Options button is clicked.

If a printer contains a nonprinting area and the entire page border will not print, consider increasing the spacing from the page border to the edge of the page. Do this with the *Top*, *Left*, *Bottom*, and/or *Right* measurement boxes. The *Measure from* option box has a default setting of *Edge of page*. To fit the border more closely around the text of the document, choose the *Text* option in the option box. This option sets the top and bottom margins at *1 pt* and the side margins at *4 pt*. These measurements can be increased or decreased by clicking the arrows in the measurement boxes.

Change the *Measure from* option to *Text* and the *Surround header* and *Surround footer* options become available and the check boxes contain check marks. With check marks in the check boxes, header and footer text is positioned inside the page border. To specify that header and footer text should be positioned outside the page border, remove the check marks from the check boxes.

Activity 4b Inserting a Page Border

Part 2 of 2

1. With **4-EmpQualities.docx** open, remove the page color by clicking the Page Color button in the Page Background group on the Design tab and then clicking the *No Color* option.
2. Insert a page border by completing the following steps:
   a. Click the Page Borders button in the Page Background group on the Design tab.
   b. At the Borders and Shading dialog box with the Page Border tab selected, click the *Box* option in the *Setting* section.
   c. Scroll down the list of line styles in the *Style* list box to the last line style and then click the third line from the end.
   d. Click the *Color* option box arrow and then click the *Orange, Accent 2* option (sixth column, first row in the *Theme Colors* section).
   e. Click OK to close the dialog box.

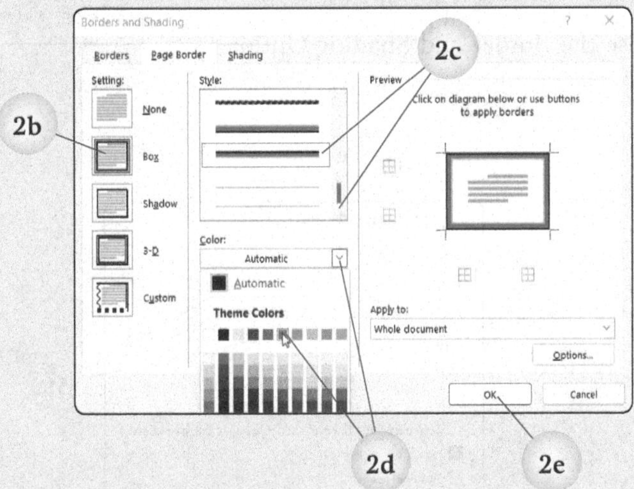

3. Increase the spacing from the page border to the edges of the page by completing the following steps:
   a. Click the Page Borders button.
   b. At the Borders and Shading dialog box with the Page Border tab selected, click the Options button in the lower right corner.
   c. At the Border and Shading Options dialog box, click the *Top* measurement box up arrow until *31 pt* displays. (This is the maximum measurement allowed.)
   d. Increase the measurements in the *Left, Bottom,* and *Right* measurement boxes to *31 pt*.
   e. Click OK to close the Border and Shading Options dialog box.
   f. Click OK to close the Borders and Shading dialog box.

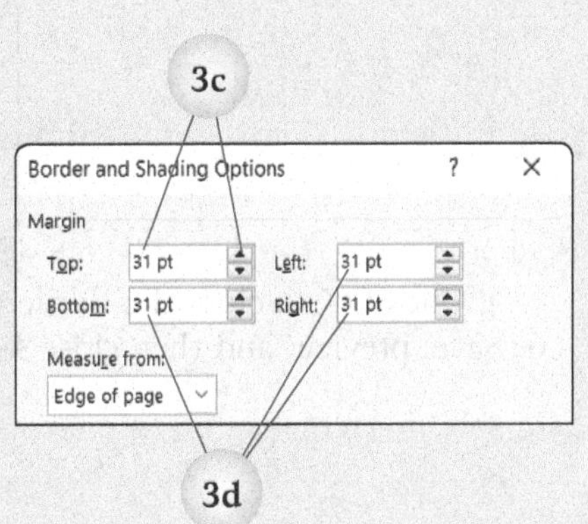

4. Save and then preview **4-EmpQualities.docx**.
5. Insert an art image page border and change the page border spacing options by completing the following steps:
   a. Click the Page Borders button.
   b. Click the *Art* option box arrow and then click the border image shown at the right (approximately one-third of the way down the drop-down list).
   c. Click the Options button in the lower right corner of the Borders and Shading dialog box.
   d. At the Border and Shading Options dialog box, click the *Measure from* option box arrow and then click *Text* at the drop-down list.
   e. Click the *Top* measurement box up arrow until *4 pt* displays.
   f. Increase the measurement in the *Bottom* measurement box to *4 pt* and the measurements in the *Left* and *Right* measurement boxes to *10 pt*.
   g. Click the *Surround header* check box to remove the check mark.
   h. Click the *Surround footer* check box to remove the check mark.
   i. Click OK to close the Border and Shading Options dialog box.

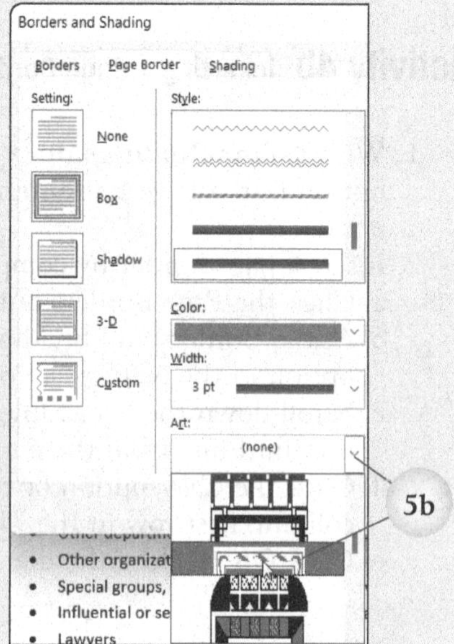

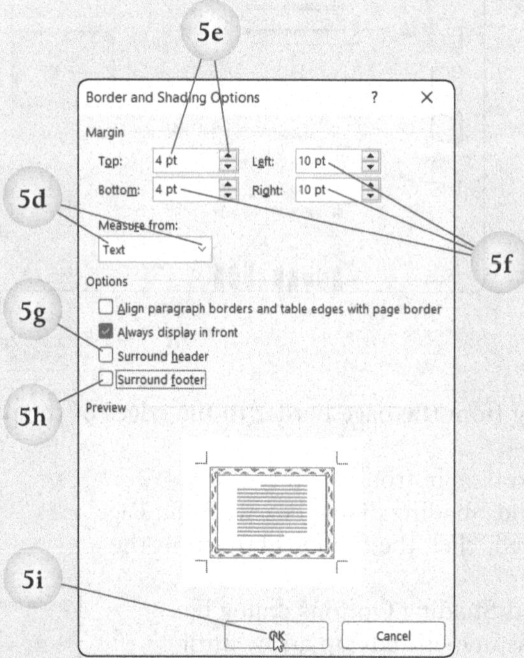

   j. Click OK to close the Borders and Shading dialog box.
6. Save, preview, and then close **4-EmpQualities.docx**.

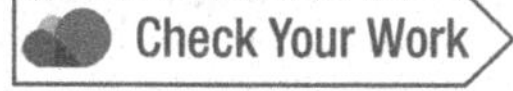

Activity 5 Format a Document on Singapore — 6 Parts

In a document on Singapore, you will format text into columns, improve the readability by hyphenating long words, and improve the visual interest by inserting a drop cap.

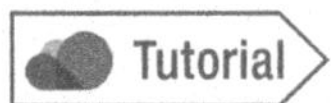

Inserting and Deleting a Section Break

Breaks

Quick Steps

Insert Section Break

1. Click Layout tab.
2. Click Breaks button.
3. Click section break option.

Hint When you delete a section break, the text that follows takes on the formatting of the text preceding the break.

Inserting a Section Break

Some documents may have several sections of text that need to be formatted in different ways. To help make formatting easier, insert section breaks. Formatting changes that are made to one section—such as narrower margins, a paragraph border, colored text, and so on—will only apply to that section and not to the rest of the document.

Insert a section break in a document by clicking the Breaks button in the Page Setup group on the Layout tab. Choose from four types of section breaks in the drop-down list: *Next Page*, *Continuous*, *Even Page*, and *Odd Page*. Click *New Page* to insert a section break and start a new section on the next page. Click *Continuous* to insert a section break and start a new section on the same page. Click *Even Page* or *Odd Page* to insert a section break and then start a new section on either the next even or the next odd page.

To see the locations of section breaks in a document, click the Show/Hide ¶ button on the Home tab to turn on the display of nonprinting characters. A section break is shown in the document as a double row of dots with the words *Section Break* in the middle. Word will identify the type of section break. For example, if a continuous section break is inserted, the words *Section Break (Continuous)* display in the middle of the row of dots. To delete a section break, click the Show/Hide ¶ button to turn on the display of nonprinting characters, click on the section break, and then press the Delete key.

Activity 5a Inserting a Continuous Section Break — Part 1 of 6

1. Open **Singapore.docx** and then save it with the name **4-Singapore**.
2. Insert a continuous section break by completing the following steps:
   a. Move the insertion point to the beginning of the heading *Climate*.
   b. Click the Layout tab.
   c. Click the Breaks button in the Page Setup group and then click *Continuous* in the *Section Breaks* section of the drop-down list.
3. Click the Home tab, click the Show/Hide ¶ button in the Paragraph group, and then notice the section break at the end of the first paragraph of text.
4. Click the Show/Hide ¶ button to turn off the display of nonprinting characters.

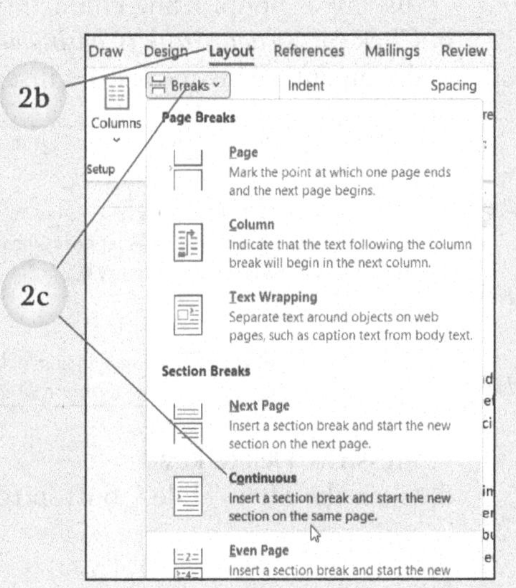

5. With the insertion point positioned at the beginning of the heading *Climate*, change the left and right margins to 1.5 inches. (The margin changes affect only the text after the continuous section break.)
6. Save and then preview **4-Singapore.docx**.

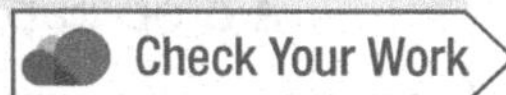

Formatting Text into Columns

Formatting Text into Columns

When preparing a document containing text, an important point to consider is its readability. *Readability* refers to the ease with which a person can read and understand groups of words. The line length of text in a document can enhance or detract from its readability. If the line length is too long, the reader may lose his or her place and have a difficult time moving to the next line below.

To improve the readability of a document, consider formatting the text in columns. One common type is the newspaper column, which is typically used for text in newspapers, newsletters, and magazines.

Format text in one, two, or three columns with the Columns button in the Page Setup group on the Layout tab. To customize the column width and spacing, click the *More Columns* option to display the Columns dialog box. Adjust the measurement to create columns of varying widths. A document can include as many columns as will fit on the page. Word determines how many columns can be included based on the page width, the margin widths, and the size and spacing of the columns. Columns should be at least 0.5 inch in width.

Quick Steps

Create Columns

1. Click Layout tab.
2. Click Columns button.
3. Click number of columns.

Activity 5b Formatting Text into Columns — Part 2 of 6

1. With **4-Singapore.docx** open, make sure the insertion point is positioned below the section break and then change the left and right margins back to 1 inch.
2. Delete the section break by completing the following steps:
   a. Click the Show/Hide ¶ button in the Paragraph group on the Home tab to turn on the display of nonprinting characters.
   b. Click on *Section Break (Continuous)* at the end of the first paragraph below the title in the document. (This moves the insertion point to the beginning of the section break.)

SINGAPORE¶

Steeped·in·tradition,·Singapore·is·the·ideal·destination·for·travelers·in·pursuit·of·that·elusive·and·eclectic·culture·mix.·Before·you·experience·Singapore's·unique·lifestyle·op-tions,·look·at·some·of·the·basic·facts·about·this·fascinating·country.¶ Section Break (Continuous)

Climate¶

Singapore's·climate·is·warm·and·humid,·ideal·for·sunbathing,·swimming,·sailing,·surfing,·and·other·water·sports.·But·there·is·respite·for·those·who·need·a·break·from·the·tropical·climate:·almost·all·shops,·

2b

   c. Press the Delete key.
   d. Click the Show/Hide ¶ button to turn off the display of nonprinting characters.

3. Move the insertion point to the beginning of the first paragraph of text below the title and then insert a continuous section break.
4. Format the text into columns by completing the following steps:
   a. Make sure the insertion point is positioned below the section break.
   b. If necessary, click the Layout tab.
   c. Click the Columns button in the Page Setup group.
   d. Click *Two* at the drop-down list.
5. Save **4-Singapore.docx**.

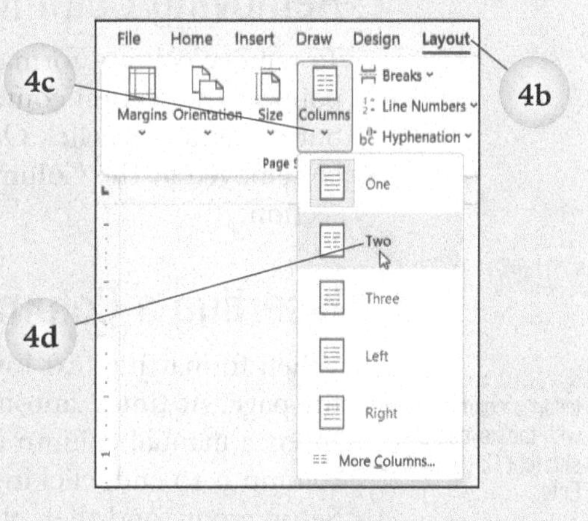

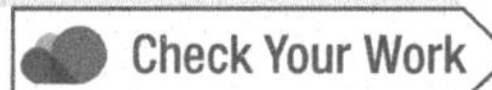

Creating Columns with the Columns Dialog Box

Quick Steps

Create Columns at Columns Dialog Box
1. Click Layout tab.
2. Click Columns button.
3. Click *More Columns*.
4. Specify column options.
5. Click OK.

Use the Columns dialog box to create newspaper columns that are equal or unequal in width. To display the Columns dialog box, shown in Figure 4.5, click the Columns button in the Page Setup group on the Layout tab and then click *More Columns* at the drop-down list.

With options at the Columns dialog box, specify the style and number of columns, enter specific column measurements, create unequal columns, and insert a line between columns. By default, column formatting is applied to the whole document. This can be changed to *This point forward* at the *Apply to* option box at the bottom of the Columns dialog box. With the *This point forward* option, a section break is inserted and the column formatting is applied to text from the location of the insertion point to the end of the document or until another column format is encountered. The *Preview* section of the dialog box shows an example of how the columns will appear in the document.

Figure 4.5 Columns Dialog Box

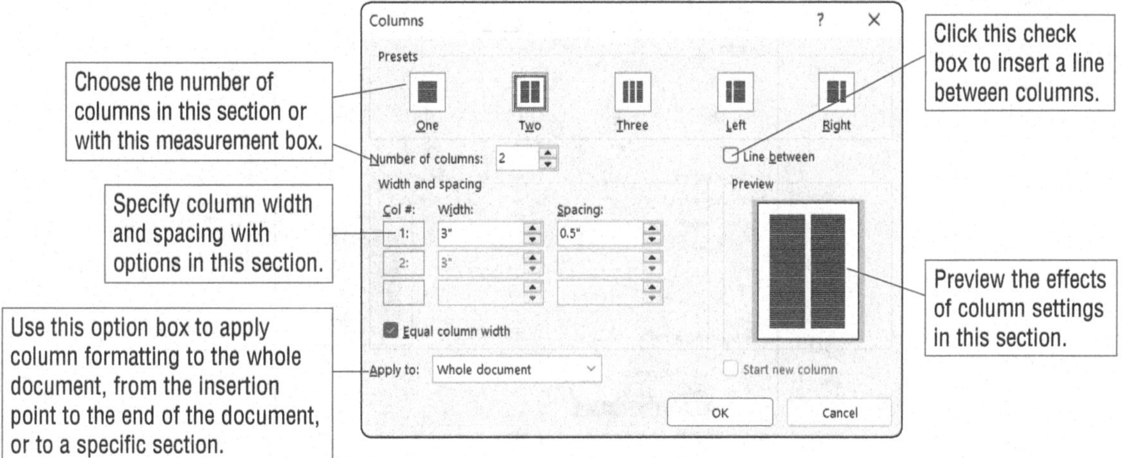

Removing Column Formatting

To remove column formatting using the Columns button, position the insertion point in the section containing columns, click the Layout tab, click the Columns button, and then click *One* at the drop-down list. Column formatting can also be removed at the Columns dialog box by selecting the *One* option in the *Presets* section.

Inserting a Column Break

Hint You can also insert a column break with the keyboard shortcut Ctrl + Shift + Enter.

When formatting text into columns, Word automatically breaks the columns to fit the page. At times, automatic column breaks may appear in undesirable locations. Insert a manual column break by positioning the insertion point where the column is to end, clicking the Layout tab, clicking the Breaks button in the Page Setup group, and then clicking *Column* at the drop-down list.

Activity 5c Formatting Text into Columns at the Columns Dialog Box — Part 3 of 6

1. With **4-Singapore.docx** open, delete the section break by completing the following steps:
   a. If necessary, click the Home tab.
   b. Click the Show/Hide ¶ button in the Paragraph group to turn on the display of nonprinting characters.
   c. Click on *Section Break (Continuous)* and then press the Delete key.
   d. Click the Show/Hide ¶ button to turn off the display of nonprinting characters.
2. Remove column formatting by clicking the Layout tab, clicking the Columns button, and then clicking *One* at the drop-down list.
3. Format the text into columns by completing the following steps:
   a. If necessary, position the insertion point at the beginning of the first paragraph of text below the title.
   b. Click the Columns button and then click *More Columns* at the drop-down list.
   c. At the Columns dialog box, click *Two* in the *Presets* section.
   d. Click the *Spacing* measurement box down arrow until *0.3"* displays.
   e. Click the *Line between* check box to insert a check mark.
   f. Click the *Apply to* option box arrow and then click *This point forward* at the drop-down list.
   g. Click OK to close the dialog box.

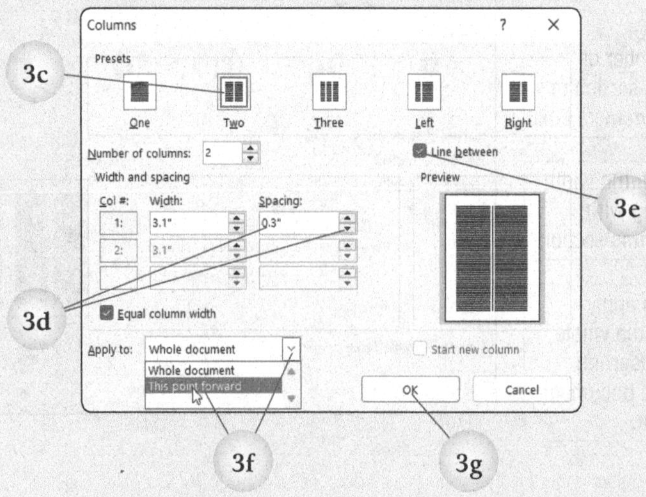

4. Insert a column break by completing the following steps:
   a. Position the insertion point at the beginning of the heading *Entertainment* (at the bottom of the first column).
   b. Click the Breaks button in the Page Setup group and then click *Column* at the drop-down list.
5. Save and then preview **4-Singapore.docx**.

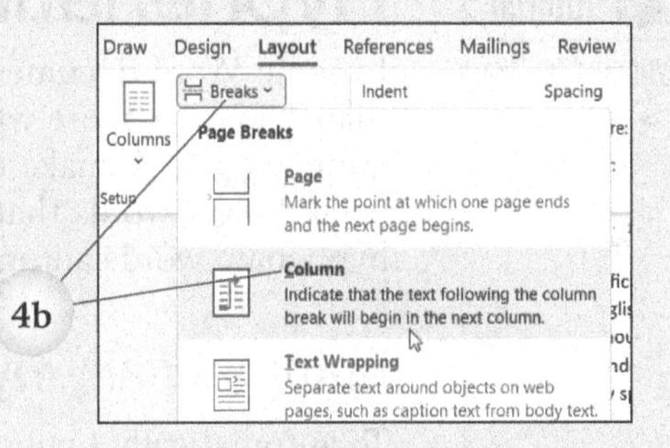

Balancing Columns on a Page

In a document containing text formatted into columns, Word automatically lines up (balances) the last lines of text at the bottoms of the columns, except on the last page. Text in the last column of the last page may end far short of the bottom of the page, and the page will look unbalanced. Balance columns by inserting a continuous section break at the end of the text.

Activity 5d Formatting and Balancing Columns of Text

Part 4 of 6

1. With **4-Singapore.docx** open, delete the column break by positioning the insertion point at the beginning of the heading *Entertainment*, if necessary, and then pressing the Backspace key.
2. Select the entire document and then change the font to 12-point Constantia.
3. Move the insertion point to the end of the document and then balance the columns by clicking the Layout tab, clicking the Breaks button in the Page Setup group, and then clicking *Continuous* at the drop-down list.

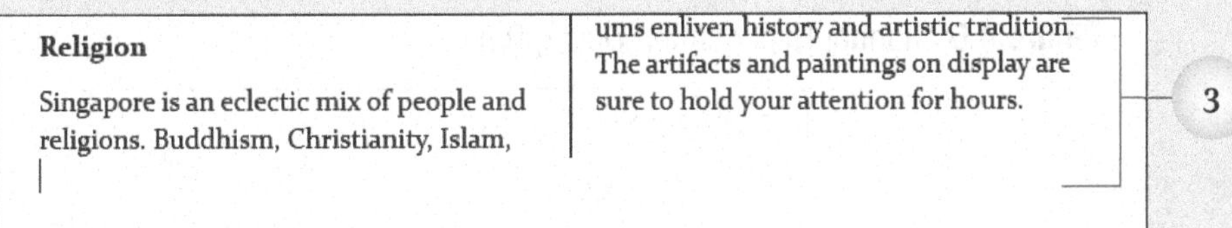

Religion
Singapore is an eclectic mix of people and religions. Buddhism, Christianity, Islam,
ums enliven history and artistic tradition. The artifacts and paintings on display are sure to hold your attention for hours.
3

4. Apply the Green, Accent 6, Lighter 60% paragraph shading (last column, third row) to the title *SINGAPORE*.
5. Apply the Green, Accent 6, Lighter 80% paragraph shading (last column, second row) to each heading in the document.
6. Insert page numbers that print at the bottom center of each page using the *Plain Number 2* option.
7. Double-click in the document to make it active.
8. Save **4-Singapore.docx**.

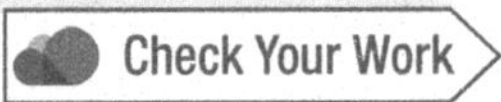

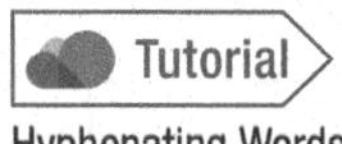

Hyphenating Words

Hyphenating Words

In some Word documents, especially those with left and right margins wider than 1 inch or those with text set in columns, the right margin may appear quite ragged. To make the margin neater and more uniform, use hyphens to break longer words that fall at the ends of lines. Use the hyphenation feature to hyphenate words automatically or manually.

Automatically Hyphenating Words

Hyphenation

Hint Avoid dividing words at the ends of more than two consecutive lines.

To automatically hyphenate words in a document, click the Layout tab, click the Hyphenation button in the Page Setup group, and then click *Automatic* at the drop-down list. Scroll through the document and check to see whether hyphens were added in appropriate locations within the words. To undo hyphenation, immediately click the Undo button in the Undo group on the Home tab.

Manually Hyphenating Words

Quick Steps

Automatically Hyphenate Document

1. Click Layout tab.
2. Click Hyphenation button.
3. Click *Automatic*.

Manually Hyphenate Document

1. Click Layout tab.
2. Click Hyphenation button.
3. Click *Manual*.
4. Click Yes or No to hyphenate indicated words.
5. When complete, click OK.

To control where hyphens appear in words during hyphenation, choose manual hyphenation. To do this, click the Layout tab, click the Hyphenation button in the Page Setup group, and then click *Manual* at the drop-down list. This displays the Manual Hyphenation dialog box, as shown in Figure 4.6. (The word in the *Hyphenate at* text box will vary.)

At this dialog box, click Yes to hyphenate the word as indicated in the *Hyphenate at* text box, click No if the word should not be hyphenated, or click Cancel to cancel hyphenation. The hyphen can be repositioned in the word in the *Hyphenate at* text box. Word shows the word with syllable breaks indicated by hyphens and a blinking black bar indicates the location where the manual hyphen will be inserted. To hyphenate a word at a different place, click and drag the blinking black bar to the position desired and then click Yes. Continue clicking Yes or No at the Manual Hyphenation dialog box.

Figure 4.6 Manual Hyphenation Dialog Box

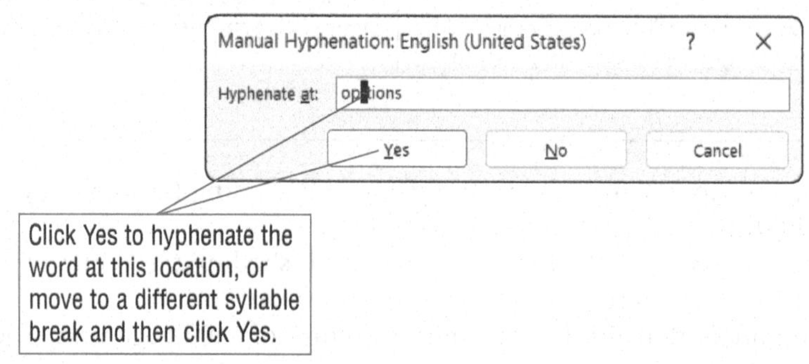
Manual Hyphenation: English (United States)
Hyphenate at:
options
Yes
No
Cancel
Click Yes to hyphenate the word at this location, or move to a different syllable break and then click Yes.

Activity 5e Automatically and Manually Hyphenating Words

Part 5 of 6

1. With **4-Singapore.docx** open, hyphenate words automatically by completing the following steps:
   a. Press Ctrl + Home.
   b. Click the Layout tab.
   c. Click the Hyphenation button in the Page Setup group and then click *Automatic* at the drop-down list.

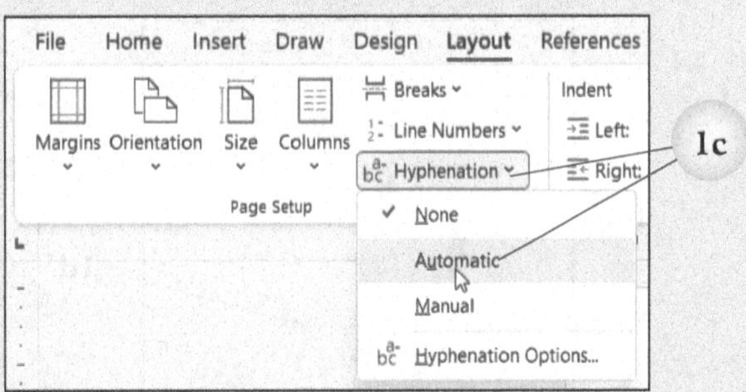

2. Scroll through the document and notice the hyphenation.
3. Click the Home tab and then click the Undo button to remove the hyphens.
4. Manually hyphenate words by completing the following steps:
   a. Click the Layout tab, click the Hyphenation button in the Page Setup group, and then click *Manual* at the drop-down list.
   b. At the Manual Hyphenation dialog box, make one of the following choices (proper names and capitalized text should not be hyphenated):
      - Click Yes to hyphenate the word as indicated in the *Hyphenate at* text box.
      - Click and drag the hyphen in the word to break the word on a different syllable and then click Yes.
      - Click No if the word should not be hyphenated.
   c. Continue clicking Yes or No at the Manual Hyphenation dialog box.
   d. At the message indicating that hyphenation is complete, click OK.
5. Save **4-Singapore.docx**.

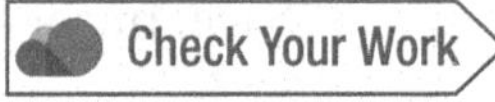

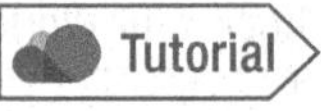

Creating and Removing a Drop Cap

Quick Steps

Create Drop Cap

1. Click Insert tab.
2. Click Drop Cap button.
3. Click drop cap option.

Creating a Drop Cap

Use a drop cap to enhance the appearance of text. A drop cap is the first letter of the first word of a paragraph that is set into the paragraph with formatting that differentiates it from the rest of the paragraph. Drop caps can be used to identify the beginnings of major sections or parts of a document.

Create a drop cap with the Drop Cap button in the Text group on the Insert tab. The drop cap can be set in the paragraph or in the margin. At the Drop Cap dialog box, specify a font, the number of lines the letter should drop, and the distance the letter should be positioned from the text of the paragraph. Add a drop cap to the entire first word of a paragraph by selecting the word and then clicking the Drop Cap button.

Activity 5f Inserting a Drop Cap

1. With **4-Singapore.docx** open, create a drop cap by completing the following steps:
   a. Position the insertion point in the first word of the first paragraph below the title (the word *Steeped*).
   b. Click the Insert tab.
   c. Click the Drop Cap button in the Text group.
   d. Click *In margin* at the drop-down gallery.

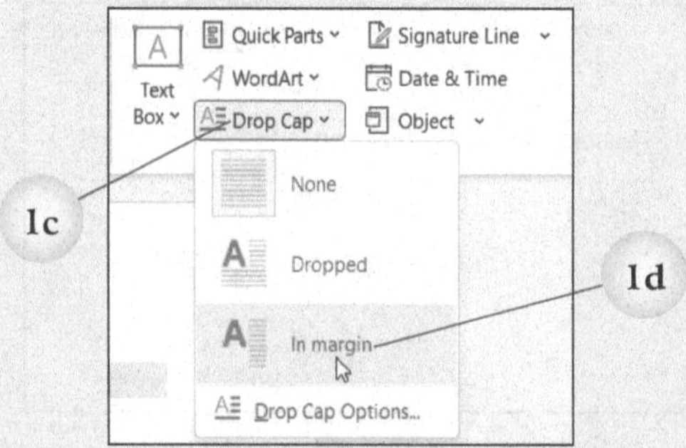

2. Looking at the drop cap, you decide that you do not like it positioned in the margin and want it to be a little smaller. To change the drop cap, complete the following steps:
   a. With the *S* in the word *Steeped* selected, click the Drop Cap button and then click *None* at the drop-down gallery.
   b. Click the Drop Cap button and then click *Drop Cap Options* at the drop-down gallery.
   c. At the Drop Cap dialog box, click *Dropped* in the *Position* section.
   d. Click the *Font* option box arrow, scroll up the drop-down list, and then click *Cambria*.
   e. Click the *Lines to drop* measurement box down arrow to change the number to *2*.
   f. Click OK to close the dialog box.
   g. Click outside the drop cap to deselect it.
3. Save, preview, and then close **4-Singapore.docx**.

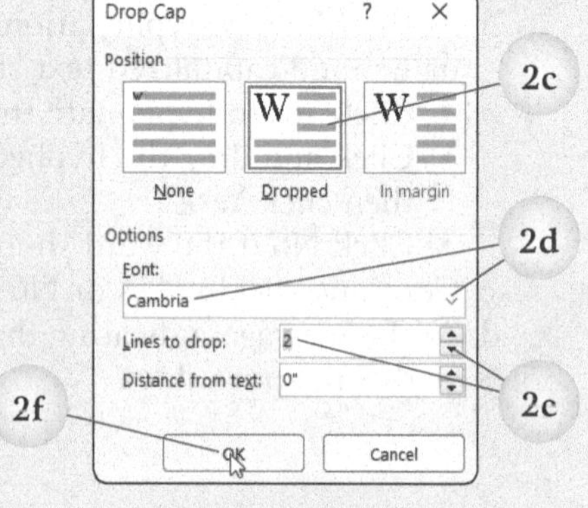

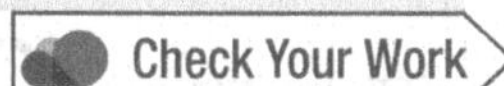

Activity 6 Create an Announcement about Supervisor Training

2 Parts

You will create an announcement about upcoming supervisor training and use the Click and Type feature to center and right-align text. You also will vertically center the text on the page.

Using Click and Type

Using the Click and Type Feature

Word contains a Click and Type feature that allows text to be aligned left, right, or center beginning at a specific point in the document. This feature can be used to position text as it is being typed rather than typing the text and then selecting and formatting the text, which requires multiple steps.

Quick Steps

Use Click and Type

1. Hover mouse at left margin, between left and right margins, or at right margin.
2. When horizontal lines display next to pointer, double-click left mouse button.

To use the Click and Type feature, open a new blank document and move the pointer slowly over the page, going from left to right. The pointer will appear as an I-beam with horizontal lines representing the text alignment. Near the left margin, the horizontal lines are left-aligned. In the center of the page, the lines are centered. At the right margin, the horizontal lines are right-aligned. Double-click in the document and begin typing. Text should automatically align to match the horizontal lines indicated on the I-beam pointer. (Note: Make sure the horizontal lines display near the pointer before double-clicking the mouse button. Double-clicking when the alignment lines are not shown will insert a tab instead of changing the text alignment.)

Activity 6a Using Click and Type

Part 1 of 2

1. Press Ctrl + N to open a blank document and then create the centered text shown in Figure 4.7 by completing the following steps:
   a. Position the I-beam pointer between the left and right margins at about the 3.25-inch mark on the horizontal ruler and at the top of the vertical ruler.
   b. When the center-alignment lines display below the I-beam pointer, double-click the left mouse button.

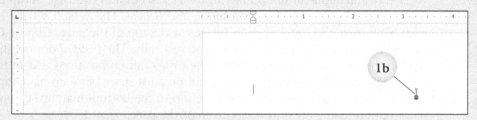

   c. Type the centered text shown in Figure 4.7. Press Shift + Enter to end each line except the last line.
2. Change to right alignment by completing the following steps:
   a. Position the I-beam pointer near the right margin at approximately the 1.25-inch mark on the vertical ruler until the right-alignment lines display at the left of the I-beam pointer.

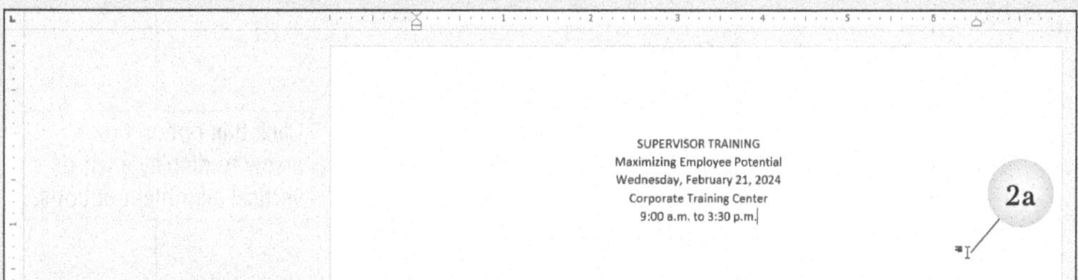

   b. Double-click the left mouse button.
   c. Type the right-aligned text shown in Figure 4.7. Press Shift + Enter to end the first line.
3. Select the centered text and then change the font to 14-point Candara bold and the line spacing to double spacing.
4. Select the right-aligned text, change the font to 10-point Candara bold, and then deselect the text.
5. Save the document with the name **4-Training**.

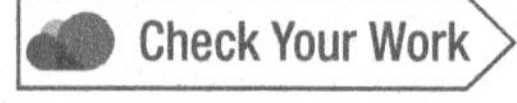

Figure 4.7 Activity 6a

SUPERVISOR TRAINING
Maximizing Employee Potential
Wednesday, February 21, 2024
Corporate Training Center
9:00 a.m. to 3:30 p.m.

Sponsored by
Cell Systems

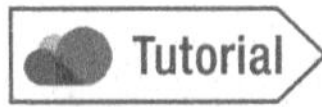

Changing Vertical Alignment

Changing Vertical Alignment

Text or items in a Word document are aligned at the top of the page by default. Change this alignment with the *Vertical alignment* option box at the Page Setup dialog box with the Layout tab selected, as shown in Figure 4.8. Display this dialog box by clicking the Layout tab, clicking the Page Setup group dialog box launcher, and then clicking the Layout tab at the Page Setup dialog box.

Quick Steps

Vertically Align Text

1. Click Layout tab.
2. Click Page Setup group dialog box launcher.
3. Click Layout tab.
4. Click *Vertical alignment* option box.
5. Click alignment.
6. Click OK.

The *Vertical alignment* option box in the *Page* section of the Page Setup dialog box contains four choices: *Top*, *Center*, *Justified*, and *Bottom*. The default setting is *Top*, which aligns text and items such as images at the top of the page. Choose *Center* to position the text in the middle of the page vertically. The *Justified* option aligns text between the top and bottom margins. The *Center* option positions text in the middle of the page vertically, while the *Justified* option adds space between paragraphs of text (not within) to fill the page from the top to the bottom margins. Choose the *Bottom* option to align text at the bottom of the page.

Figure 4.8 Page Setup Dialog Box with the Layout Tab Selected

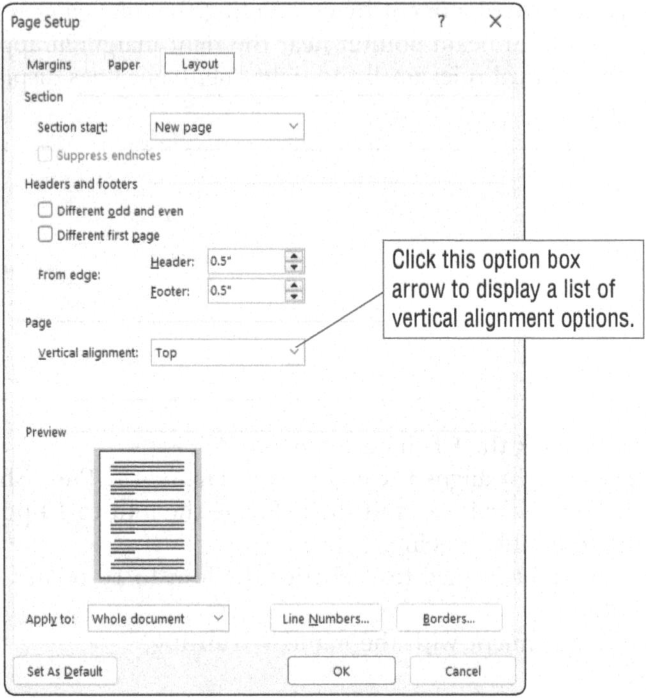

Activity 6b Vertically Centering Text

Part 2 of 2

1. With **4-Training.docx** open, click the Layout tab and then click the Page Setup group dialog box launcher.
2. At the Page Setup dialog box, click the Layout tab.
3. Click the *Vertical alignment* option box arrow in the *Page* section and then click *Center* at the drop-down list.
4. Click OK to close the dialog box.
5. Save, preview, and then close **4-Training.docx**.

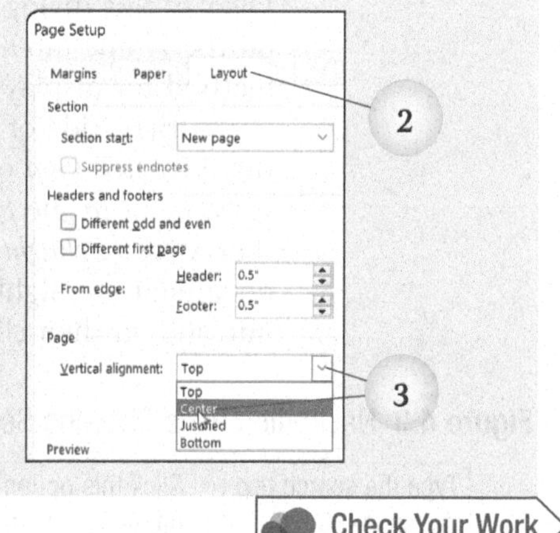

Check Your Work

Activity 7 Format a Lease Agreement

3 Parts

You will open a lease agreement, search for specific text, and then search for specific text and replace it with other text.

Editing Text with Find and Replace

Find

Replace

The Editing group on the Home tab contains the Find button and the Replace button. Use the Find button to search for specific text in a document and use the Replace button to search for and then replace specific text.

Finding Text

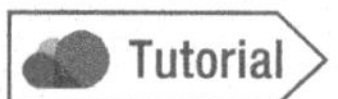

Finding Text Using the Navigation Pane

Finding Text Using the Find and Replace Dialog Box

Quick Steps

Find Text

1. Click Find button.
2. Type search text.
3. Click Next button.

Click the Find button in the Editing group on the Home tab (or press the keyboard shortcut Ctrl + F) and the Navigation pane displays at the left side of the screen with the Results tab selected. With this tab selected, type *search text* in the search text box and any occurrence of the text in the document is highlighted. A fragment of the text surrounding the search text is shown in a thumbnail in the Navigation pane. For example, when searching for *Lessee* in **4-LeaseAgrmnt.docx** in Activity 7a (on page 133), the screen displays as shown in Figure 4.9. Any occurrence of *Lessee* displays highlighted in yellow in the document and the Navigation pane shows thumbnails of the text surrounding the occurrences of *Lessee*.

Click a text thumbnail in the Navigation pane and the occurrence of the search text is selected in the document. Hover the pointer over a text thumbnail in the Navigation pane and the page number location displays in a small box near the pointer. Move to the next occurrence of the search text by clicking the Next button (contains a down arrow) below and to the right of the search text box. Click the Previous button (contains an up arrow) to move to the previous occurrence of the search text.

Click the down arrow at the right side of the search text box and a drop-down list displays. It shows options for displaying dialog boxes, such as the Find Options dialog box and the Find and Replace dialog box. It also shows options for specifying what should be found in the document, such as figures, tables, and equations.

The search text in a document can be highlighted with options at the Find and Replace dialog box with the Find tab selected as shown in Figure 4.10. Display this dialog box by clicking the Find button arrow in the Editing group on the Home tab and then clicking *Advanced Find* at the drop-down list. Another method for displaying the Find and Replace dialog box is to click the down arrow at the right side of the search text box in the Navigation pane and then click the *Advanced Find* option at the drop-down list. To highlight found text, type the search text in the *Find what* text box, click the Reading Highlight button, and then click *Highlight All* at the drop-down list. All occurrences of the text in the document are highlighted. To remove highlighting, click the Reading Highlight button and then click *Clear Highlighting* at the drop-down list.

Figure 4.9 Navigation Pane Showing Search Results

Type the search text in this text box.

Click this option box arrow to display options for finding and replacing text.

Click this button to move to the next occurrence of the search text.

Click this button to move to the previous occurrence of the search text.

Occurrences of the search text are highlighted in the document.

Text thumbnails show instances of the search text along with the sentence or phrase it is found in.

Figure 4.10 Find and Replace Dialog Box with Find Tab Selected

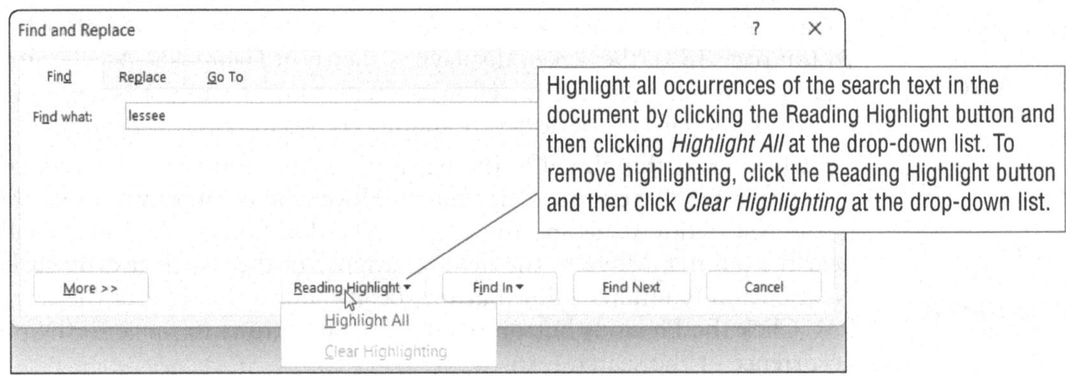
Find and Replace
Find
Replace
Go To
Find what:
lessee
Highlight all occurrences of the search text in the document by clicking the Reading Highlight button and then clicking *Highlight All* at the drop-down list. To remove highlighting, click the Reading Highlight button and then click *Clear Highlighting* at the drop-down list.
More >>
Reading Highlight
Find In
Find Next
Cancel
Highlight All
Clear Highlighting

Activity 7a Finding and Highlighting Text

Part 1 of 3

1. Open **LeaseAgrmnt.docx** and then save it with the name **4-LeaseAgrmnt**.
2. Find all occurrences of *lessee* by completing the following steps:
   a. Click the Find button in the Editing group on the Home tab.
   b. If necessary, click the Results tab in the Navigation pane.
   c. Type lessee in the search text box in the Navigation pane.
   d. After a moment, all occurrences of *lessee* in the document are highlighted and text thumbnails display in the Navigation pane. Click a couple of the text thumbnails in the Navigation pane to select the text in the document.
   e. Click the Previous button (contains an up arrow) to select the previous occurrence of *lessee* in the document.

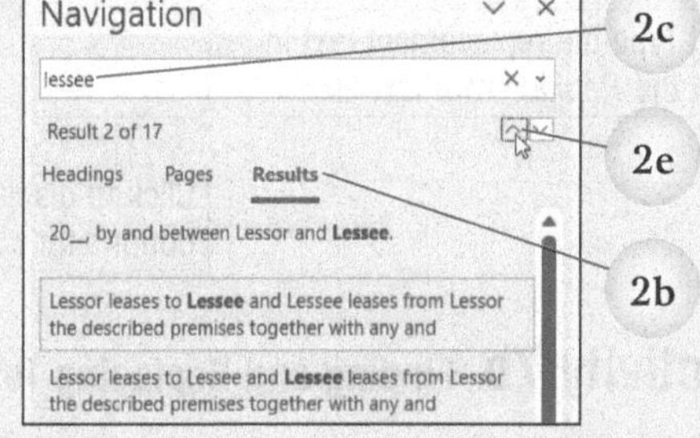

3. Use the Find and Replace dialog box with the Find tab selected to highlight all occurrences of *Premises* in the document by completing the following steps:
   a. Click in the document and press Ctrl + Home to move the insertion point to the beginning of the document.
   b. Click the search option box arrow in the Navigation pane and then click *Advanced Find* at the drop-down list.
   c. At the Find and Replace dialog box with the Find tab selected (and *lessee* selected in the *Find what* text box), type Premises.
   d. Click the Reading Highlight button and then click *Highlight All* at the drop-down list.
   e. Click in the document to make it active and then scroll through the document and notice the occurrences of highlighted text.
   f. Click in the dialog box to make it active.
   g. Click the Reading Highlight button and then click *Clear Highlighting* at the drop-down list.
   h. Click the Close button to close the Find and Replace dialog box.
4. Close the Navigation pane by clicking the Close button in the upper right corner of the pane.

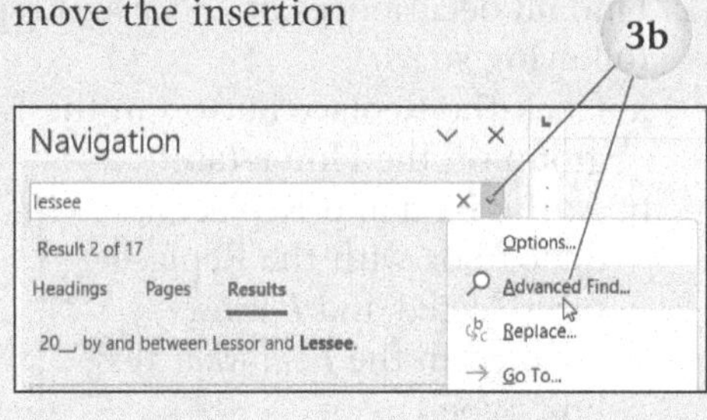

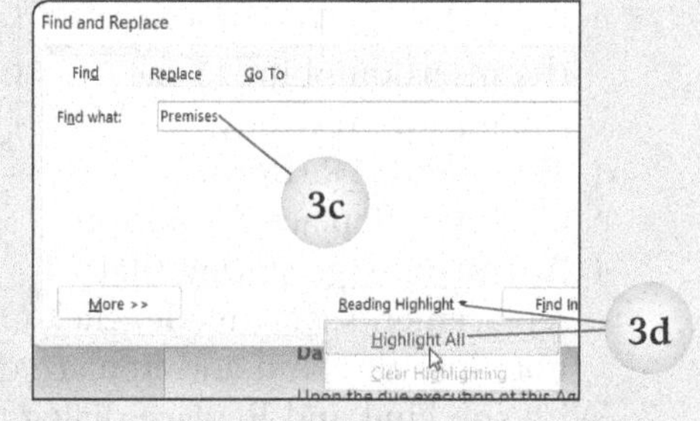

Finding and Replacing Text

Quick Steps

Find and Replace Text

1. Click Replace button.
2. Type search text.
3. Press Tab key.
4. Type replacement text.
5. Click Replace or Replace All button.

Finding and Replacing Text

To find and replace text, click the Replace button in the Editing group on the Home tab or use the keyboard shortcut Ctrl + H. This displays the Find and Replace dialog box with the Replace tab selected, as shown in Figure 4.11. Type the search text in the *Find what* text box, press the Tab key, and then type the replacement text in the *Replace with* text box.

The Find and Replace dialog box contains several command buttons. Click the Find Next button to tell Word to find the next occurrence of the text. Click the Replace button to replace the text and find the next occurrence. If all occurrences of the text in the *Find what* text box are to be replaced with the text in the *Replace with* text box, click the Replace All button.

Hint If the Find and Replace dialog box is in the way of specific text, drag it to a different location.

Figure 4.11 Find and Replace Dialog Box with the Replace Tab Selected

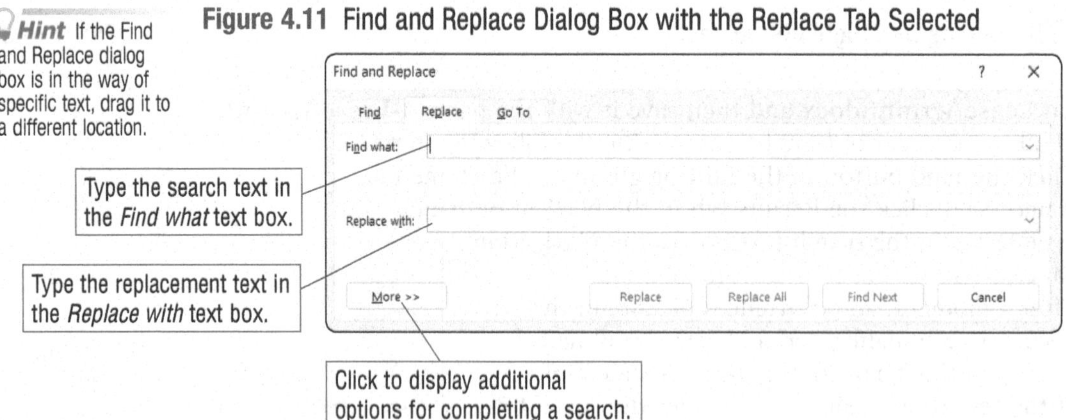

Activity 7b Finding and Replacing Text

Part 2 of 3

1. With **4-LeaseAgrmnt.docx** open, make sure the insertion point is positioned at the beginning of the document.
2. Find all occurrences of *Lessor* and replace them with *Tracy Hartford* by completing the following steps:
   a. Click the Replace button in the Editing group on the Home tab.
   b. At the Find and Replace dialog box with the Replace tab selected and *Premises* selected in the *Find what* text box, type Lessor.
   c. Press the Tab key to move the insertion point to the *Replace with* text box.
   d. Type Tracy Hartford.
   e. Click the Replace All button.
   f. At the message stating that 11 replacements were made, click OK. (Do not close the Find and Replace dialog box.)

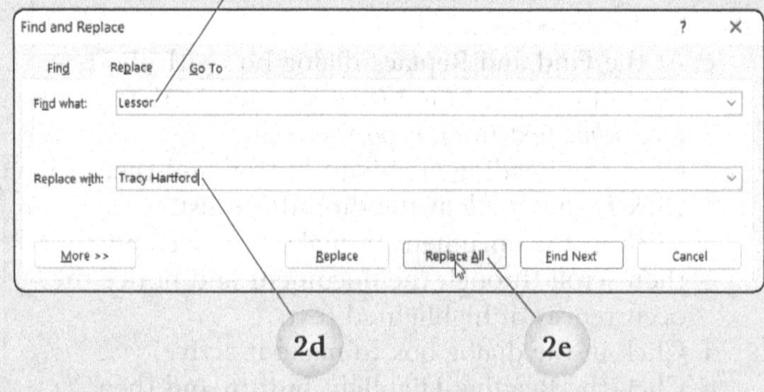

3. With the Find and Replace dialog box still open, complete steps similar to those in Step 2 to find all occurrences of *Lessee* and replace them with *Michael Iwami*.
4. Click the Close button to close the Find and Replace dialog box.
5. Save **4-LeaseAgrmnt.docx**.

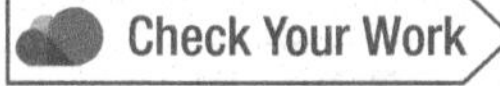

Specifying Search Options

The Find and Replace dialog box provides more options for completing a search. To display these options, click the More button in the lower left corner of the dialog box. This causes the Find and Replace dialog box to expand, as shown in Figure 4.12. Search Options in the dialog box are described in Table 4.1. Click check boxes to select options for customizing the search, and then click the Less button (previously the More button) to hide the options and shrink the dialog box again. If a mistake was made when replacing text, close the Find and Replace dialog box and then click the Undo button in the Undo group on the Home tab.

Figure 4.12 Expanded Find and Replace Dialog Box

Click this button to remove the display of search options.

Specify search options using the check boxes in this section.

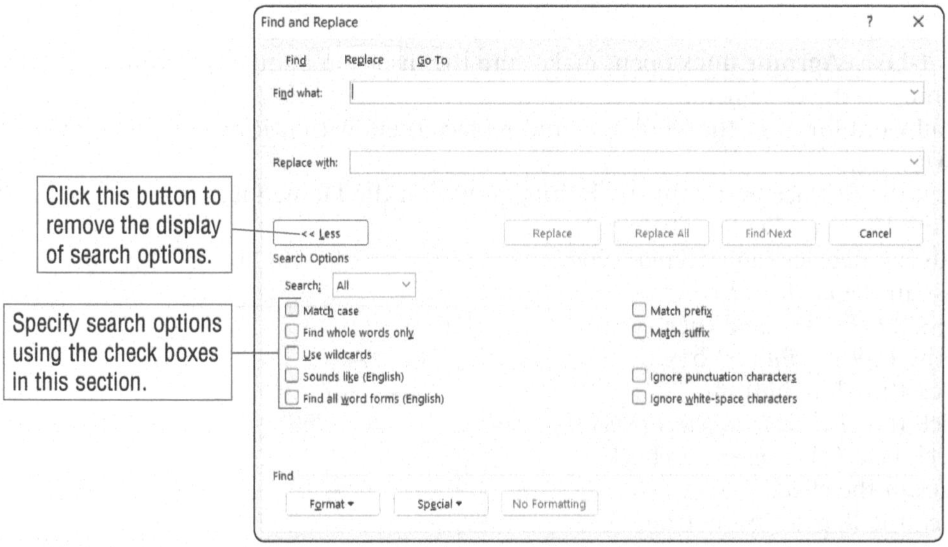

Table 4.1 Options at the Expanded Find and Replace Dialog Box

Choose this option	To
Match case	Exactly match the case of the search text. For example, search for *Book* and select the *Match case* option and Word will stop at *Book* but not *book* or *BOOK*.
Find whole words only	Find a whole word, not a part of a word. For example, search for *her* without selecting *Find whole words only* and Word will stop at *there*, *here*, *hers*, and so on.
Use wildcards	Use special characters as wildcards to search for specific text.
Sounds like (English)	Match words that sound alike but are spelled differently, such as *know* and *no*.
Find all word forms (English)	Find all forms of the word entered in the *Find what* text box. For example, enter *hold* and Word will stop at *held* and *holding*.
Match prefix	Find only those words that begin with the letters in the *Find what* text box. For example, enter *per* and Word will stop at words such as *perform* and *perfect* but skip words such as *super* and *hyperlink*.
Match suffix	Find only those words that end with the letters in the *Find what* text box. For example, enter *ly* and Word will stop at words such as *accurately* and *quietly* but skip words such as *catalyst* and *lyre*.
Ignore punctuation characters	Ignore punctuation within characters. For example, enter *US* in the *Find what* text box and Word will stop at *U.S.*
Ignore white-space characters	Ignore spaces between letters. For example, enter *F B I* in the *Find what* text box and Word will stop at *FBI*.

Activity 7c Finding and Replacing Word Forms and Suffixes

Part 3 of 3

1. With **4-LeaseAgrmnt.docx** open, make sure the insertion point is positioned at the beginning of the document.
2. Find all word forms of the word *lease* and replace them with *rent* by completing the following steps:
   a. Click the Replace button in the Editing group on the Home tab.
   b. At the Find and Replace dialog box with the Replace tab selected, type lease in the *Find what* text box.
   c. Press the Tab key and then type rent in the *Replace with* text box.
   d. Click the More button.
   e. Click the *Find all word forms (English)* check box. (This inserts a check mark in the check box.)
   f. Click the Replace All button.
   g. At the message stating that the Replace All button is not recommended when the *Find all word forms* check box is selected, click OK.
   h. At the message stating that six replacements were made, click OK.
   i. Click the *Find all word forms* check box to remove the check mark.

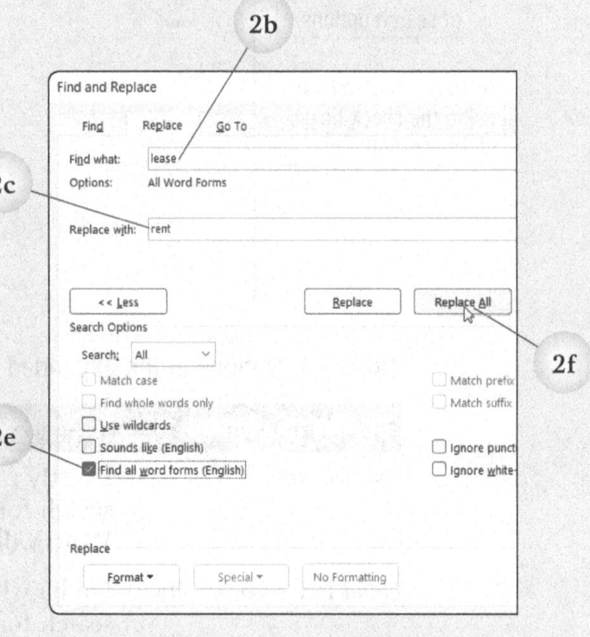

3. Find the word *less* and replace it with the word *minus* and specify that you want Word to find only those words that end in *less* by completing the following steps:
   a. At the expanded Find and Replace dialog box, select the text in the *Find what* text box and then type less.
   b. Select the text in the *Replace with* text box and then type minus.
   c. Click the *Match suffix* check box to insert a check mark (telling Word to find only words that end in *less*).
   d. Click the Replace All button.
   e. Click OK at the message stating that two replacements were made.
   f. Click the *Match suffix* check box to remove the check mark.
   g. Click the Less button.
   h. Close the Find and Replace dialog box.

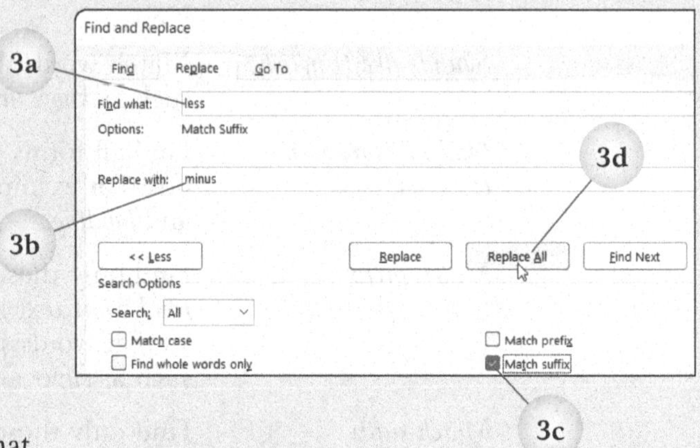

4. Save, preview, and then close **4-LeaseAgrmnt.docx**.

Check Your Work

Chapter Summary

- By default, a Word document contains 1-inch top, bottom, left, and right margins. Change margins with preset margin settings at the Margins button drop-down list or with options at the Page Setup dialog box with the Margins tab selected.
- The default page layout is portrait orientation. It can be changed to landscape orientation with the Orientation button in the Page Setup group on the Layout tab.
- The default paper size is 8.5 inches wide by 11 inches tall. It can be changed with options at the Size button drop-down list or options at the Page Setup dialog box with the Paper tab selected.
- A page break that Word inserts automatically is a *soft page break*. A page break inserted manually is a *hard page break*. Insert a hard page break using the Page Break button in the Pages group on the Insert tab or by pressing Ctrl + Enter.
- Insert a predesigned and formatted cover page by clicking the Cover Page button in the Pages group on the Insert tab and then clicking an option at the drop-down list.
- Insert predesigned and formatted page numbers by clicking the Page Number button in the Header & Footer group on the Insert tab, specifying the location of the page number, and then clicking a page numbering option.
- Insert predesigned headers and footers in a document with the Header button and the Footer button in the Header & Footer group on the Insert tab.
- A watermark is a lightened image that displays behind the text in a document. Use the Watermark button in the Page Background group on the Design tab to insert a watermark.
- Insert a page background color in a document with the Page Color button in the Page Background group on the Design tab. The page background color is designed for viewing a document onscreen and does not print.
- Click the Page Borders button in the Page Background group on the Design tab and the Borders and Shading dialog box with the Page Border tab selected displays. Use options at this dialog box to insert a page border or an art image page border in a document.
- Apply formatting to a portion of a document by inserting a continuous section break or a section break that begins a new page. Turn on the display of nonprinting characters to display section breaks.
- Set text in columns to improve the readability of documents, such as newsletters and reports. Format text in columns using the Columns button in the Page Setup group on the Layout tab or with options at the Columns dialog box.
- Remove column formatting with the Columns button in the Page Setup group on the Layout tab or at the Columns dialog box.
- Insert a column break by clicking the Layout tab, clicking the Breaks button, and then clicking the *Column* option. Balance column text on the last page of a document by inserting a continuous section break at the end of the text.
- Improve the appearance of text by hyphenating long words that fall at the ends of lines. Use the hyphenation feature to hyphenate words automatically or manually. Click the Hyphenation button in the Page Setup group on the Layout tab to display a drop-down list with hyphenation options.
- To enhance the appearance of text, use drop caps to identify the beginnings of major sections or paragraphs. Create drop caps with the Drop Cap button in the Text group on the Insert tab.

- Use the Click and Type feature to center, right-align, and left-align text.
- Vertically align text in a document with the *Vertical alignment* option box at the Page Setup dialog box with the Layout tab selected.
- Use the Find button in the Editing group on the Home tab to search for specific text. Use the Replace button to search for specific text and replace it with other text.
- At the Find and Replace dialog box, click the Find Next button to find the next occurrence of the text. Click the Replace button to replace the text and find the next occurrence or click the Replace All button to replace all occurrences of the text.
- Click the More button at the Find and Replace dialog box to display additional search options.

Commands Review

FEATURE	RIBBON TAB, GROUP	BUTTON, OPTION	KEYBOARD SHORTCUT
blank page	Insert, Pages		
Border and Shading Options dialog box	Design, Page Background	, Options	
Borders and Shading dialog box with Page Border tab selected	Design, Page Background		
column break	Layout, Page Setup	, *Column*	Ctrl + Shift + Enter
columns	Layout, Page Setup		
Columns dialog box	Layout, Page Setup	, *More Column*	
continuous section break	Layout, Page Setup	, *Continuous*	
cover page	Insert, Pages		
drop cap	Insert, Text		
Find and Replace dialog box with Find tab selected	Home, Editing	, *Advanced Find*	
Find and Replace dialog box with Replace tab selected	Home, Editing		Ctrl + H
footer	Insert, Header & Footer		
header	Insert, Header & Footer		
hyphenate words automatically	Layout, Page Setup	, *Automatic*	
Manual Hyphenation dialog box	Layout, Page Setup	, *Manual*	
margins	Layout, Page Setup		
Navigation pane	Home, Editing		Ctrl + F
orientation	Layout, Page Setup		
page background color	Design, Page Background		
page break	Insert, Pages		Ctrl + Enter
page numbers	Insert, Header & Footer		
Page Setup dialog box with Margins tab selected	Layout, Page Setup	, *Custom Margins* OR	
Page Setup dialog box with Paper tab selected	Layout, Page Setup	, *More Paper Sizes*	
paper size	Layout, Page Setup		
watermark	Design, Page Background		

Review and Assessment

CHAPTER 4

Skills Assessment

Assessment 1

Format a Cover Letter Document and Insert a Cover Page

1. Open **CoverLetter.docx** and then save it with the name **4-CoverLetter**.
2. Change the left and right margins to 1.25 inches.
3. Move the insertion point to the beginning of the heading *Writing Cover Letters to People You Know* and then insert a blank page.
4. Insert a page break at the beginning of the heading *Writing Cover Letters to People You Do Not Know*.
5. Move the insertion point to the beginning of the document, insert the Filigree cover page, and then insert the following text in the specified fields:
   a. Type job search strategies in the *[DOCUMENT TITLE]* placeholder.
   b. Type Writing a Cover Letter in the *[Document subtitle]* placeholder.
   c. Type the current date in the *[DATE]* placeholder.
   d. Type career finders in the *[COMPANY NAME]* placeholder.
   e. Delete the *[Company address]* placeholder.
6. Move the insertion point to anywhere in the subtitle *WRITING A COVER LETTER* (on the page after the cover page) and then insert the Brackets 1 page numbering at the bottom of the page. (The page numbering will not appear on the cover page.)
7. Make the document active and turn on the display of nonprinting characters.
8. Move the insertion point to the blank line below the first paragraph of text (and above the page break) and then press the Delete key six times. (This deletes the page break on the first page and the page break creating a blank page 2, as well as extra blank lines.) Turn off the display of nonprinting characters.
9. Save, preview, and then close **4-CoverLetter.docx**.

Assessment 2

Format a Photography Report into Columns

1. Open **PhotoReport.docx** and then save it with the name **4-PhotoReport**.
2. Format the text from the first paragraph of text below the title to the end of the document into two columns with a line between and with 0.4 inch between columns.
3. Create a drop cap with the first letter of the first paragraph below the title. Specify that the drop cap is in the paragraph rather than the margin and is dropped two lines.
4. Move the insertion point to the end of the document and then insert a continuous section break to balance the columns on the second page.
5. Manually hyphenate the document. (Do not hyphenate headings and names.)
6. Save, preview, and then close **4-PhotoReport.docx**.

Assessment 3 Format an Intellectual Property Report and Insert Headers and Footers

1. Open **ProtectIssues.docx** and then save it with the name **4-ProtectIssues**.
2. Change the top margin to 1.5 inches.
3 Change the page layout to landscape orientation.
4. With the insertion point positioned at the beginning of the document, insert the Retrospect footer. Select the name at the left side of the footer and then type your first and last names.
5. Save the document and then preview only page 1.
6. Change the page layout back to portrait orientation.
7. Apply the Moderate page margins.
8. Remove the footer.
9. Insert the Ion (Dark) header.
10. Insert the Ion (Dark) footer. Type property protection issues as the title and make sure your first and last names display at the right side of the footer.
11. Select the footer text (document name and your name), apply bold formatting, and then change the font size to 8 points.
12. Insert the DRAFT 1 watermark in the document.
13. Apply the Green, Accent 6, Lighter 80% page color (last column, second row in the *Theme Colors* section).
14. Save and then preview **4-ProtectIssues.docx**.
15. With the document still open, change the paper size to Legal (8.5 inches by 14 inches).
16. Save the document with Save As and name it **4-ProtectIssues-Legal**.
17. Check with your instructor to determine if you can print legal-sized documents. If so, print page 1 of the document.
18. Save, preview, and then close **4-ProtectIssues-Legal.docx**.

Assessment 4 Format a Real Estate Agreement

1. Open **REAgrmnt.docx** and then save it with the name **4-REAgrmnt**.
2. Find all occurrences of *BUYER* (matching the case) and replace them with *James Berman*.
3. Find all occurrences of *SELLER* (matching the case) and replace them with *Mona Trammell*.
4. Find all word forms of the word *buy* and replace them with *purchase*.
5. Insert Plain Number 2 page numbering at the bottom center of the page.
6. Insert a page border with the following specifications:
   - Choose the first double-line border in the *Style* list box.
   - Change the color of the page border to the standard dark red color (first color in the *Standard Colors* section).
   - Change the width of the page border to 1 1/2 points.
7. Display the Border and Shading Options dialog box for the page border and then change the top, left, bottom, and right measurements to 30 points. ***Hint: Display the Border and Shading Options dialog box by clicking the Options button at the Borders and Shading dialog box with the Page Border tab selected.***
8. Save, preview, and then close **4-REAgrmnt.docx**.

Visual Benchmark

Format a Resume Styles Report

1. Open **Resumes.docx** and then save it with the name **4-Resumes**.
2. Format the document so it appears as shown in Figure 4.13 with the following specifications:
   a. Change the top margin to 1.5 inches.
   b. Change the line spacing for the entire document to 1.5 lines.
   c. Apply the Heading 1 style to the title and the Heading 2 style to the headings.
   d. Apply the Lines (Simple) style set.
   e. Apply the Savon theme.
   f. Apply the Blue Green theme colors.
   g. Change the paragraph spacing after the title to 9 points. Apply 6 points of paragraph spacing after the three headings.
   h. Insert the Austin cover page. Insert text in the placeholders and delete the Abstract placeholder as shown in the figure. (If a name appears in the author placeholder, delete it and then type your first and last names.)
   i. Insert the Ion (Dark) header and the Ion (Dark) footer.
3. Save, preview, and then close **4-Resumes.docx**.

Figure 4.13 Visual Benchmark

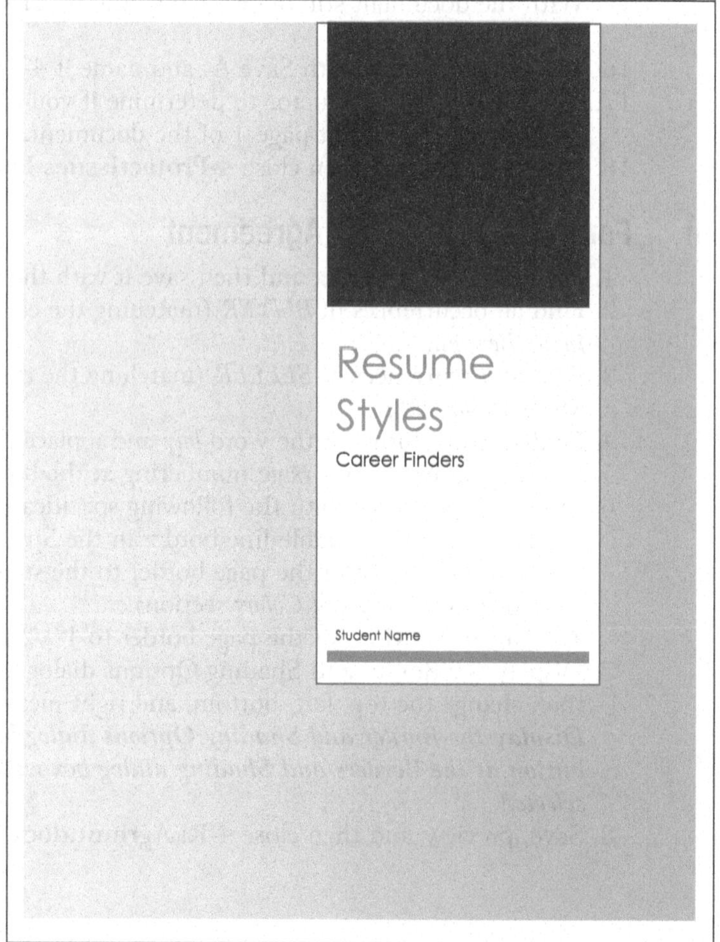

Continues

Figure 4.13 Visual Benchmark—*Continued*

1

RESUME STYLES

You can write a resume several different ways. The three most popular resume styles include: chronological resumes, functional resumes, and hybrid resumes. To these three we will add the structured interview resume. Although not used often, this resume format enables people to set out the benefits that they offer an employer in a conversational style. It's inviting to read and enables you to convey a lot of targeted information. It is particularly useful if you are able to anticipate the types of questions that will be asked at an interview. By presenting your resume in this way, you provide the employer with an expectation of how you might perform in an interview, giving the employer a reason to consider your application further.

The Chronological Resume

This resume style is the one most commonly used. It lists the individual's training and jobs by the date he or she started each of them. Typically, people list their most recent training or jobs first and proceed backward to the things they did in the past. This is called "reverse chronological" order. The components of this resume include:

- Personal contact information
- Employment history, including names of employers, dates of employment, positions held, and achievements
- Educational qualifications
- Professional development

The Functional Resume

This is the style that emphasizes an individual's skills and achie[illegible] the applicant does not have a degree or has educational qu[illegible] that are not relevant to the job being sought. This style might [illegible] had many different jobs with no clear pattern or progression, [illegible] several gaps.

RESUME STYLES

2

The Hybrid Resume

This is an increasingly popular approach that combines the best of both the chronological resume and the functional resume. A hybrid resume retains much of the fixed order of the chronological resume, but it includes more emphasis on skills and achievements—sometimes in a separate section. The hybrid approach is the one that we recommend to most people. It provides more opportunity for job seekers to explain how they stand out from the crowd. Now that many resumes are uploaded electronically without a cover letter attached, a hybrid resume that emphasizes your skills and achievements may be the best choice for marketing yourself to prospective employers.

RESUME STYLES STUDENT NAME

Case Study

Part 1

You work for Citizens for Consumer Safety, a nonprofit organization that provides information on household safety. Your supervisor, Melinda Johansson, has asked you to format a document on smoke detectors. She will use the document as an informational handout during a presentation on smoke detectors. Open **SmokeDetectors.docx** and then save it with the name **4-SmokeDetectors-1**. Apply a style set, apply appropriate styles to the title and headings, and then apply a theme and theme colors to the document. Ms. Johansson has asked you to change the page layout to landscape orientation and to change the left and right margins to 1.5 inches. She wants to allow extra space at the left and right margins so audience members can write notes in these areas. Use the Help feature or experiment with the options on the Header & Footer tab and figure out how to put page numbers on every page but the first page. Insert page numbers in the document that print at the top right of every page except the first page. Save, preview, and then close **4-SmokeDetectors-1.docx**.

Part 2

After reviewing the formatted document on smoke detectors, Ms. Johansson has decided that she would like it to print in the default orientation (portrait) and that she would like to see different theme and style choices. She has also decided that the term *smoke alarm* should be replaced with *smoke detector*. She has asked you to open and then make changes to the original document. Open **SmokeDetectors.docx** and then save it with the name **4-SmokeDetectors-2**. Apply styles to the title and headings and apply a theme and theme colors to the document (other than the one you chose for Part 1). Search for all occurrences of *Smoke Alarm* and replace them with *Smoke Detector* matching the case. Search for all occurrences of *smoke alarm* and replace them with *smoke detector* without matching the case. Insert a cover page of your choosing and then insert the appropriate information on the page. Use the current date and your name as the author and delete all unused placeholders. Make any other formatting changes to improve the appearance and layout of the document. Save, preview, and then close **4-SmokeDetectors-2.docx**.

Part 3

Ms. Johansson has asked you to prepare a document on infant car seats and infant car seat safety to be available for distribution at a local community center. Find websites that provide information on child and infant car seats and car seat safety. Using the information you find, write a report that covers at least the following topics:

- Description of types of infant car seats (such as rear-facing, convertible, forward-facing, built-in, and booster)
- Safety rules and guidelines for safe installation
- Websites that sell infant car seats, along with price ranges for specific models
- Websites that provide safety information

Format the report using styles and a theme and include a cover page and headers and/or footers. Save the completed document with the name **4-CarSeats**. Preview and then close the document.

WORD LEVEL 1

Unit 1 Performance Assessment

Data Files

The data files for this unit work are in the WL1U1 folder that you downloaded at the beginning of this course.

Assessing Proficiency

In this unit, you have learned to create, edit, save, and print Word documents. You have also learned to format characters, paragraphs, pages, and documents.

Assessment 1

Format a Document on Website Design

1. Open **Website.docx** and then save it with the name **U1-Website**.
2. Use the Editor to complete a spelling and grammar check on the document.
3. Select the text from the paragraph that begins *Make your home page work for you.* through the end of the document and then apply bulleted formatting.
4. Select and then apply bold formatting to the first sentence of each bulleted paragraph.
5. Apply a single-line bottom border to the document title and apply Gold, Accent 4, Lighter 80% paragraph shading (eighth column, second row in the *Theme Colors* section) to the title.
6. Save and then preview **U1-Website.docx**.
7. Change the top, left, and right margins to 1.5 inches.
8. Select the bulleted paragraphs, change the paragraph alignment to justified, and then apply numbered formatting.
9. Select the entire document and then change the font to 12-point Cambria.
10. Insert the text shown in Figure U1.1 after paragraph number 2. (The number *3.* should automatically be inserted preceding the text you type.)
11. Save, preview, and then close **U1-Website.docx**.

Figure U1.1 Assessment 1

Avoid a cluttered look. In design, less is more. Strive for a clean look to your pages, using ample margins and white space.

Assessment 2 Format an Accumulated Returns Document

1. Open **TotalReturns.docx** and then save it with the name **U1-TotalReturns**.
2. Select the entire document and then make the following changes:
   a. Apply the No Spacing style.
   b. Change the line spacing to 1.5 lines.
   c. Change the font to 12-point Cambria.
   d. Apply 6 points of spacing after paragraphs.
3. Select the title *TOTAL RETURN CHARTS*, change the font to 14-point Corbel bold, change the alignment to centered, and apply Blue-Gray, Text 2, Lighter 80% paragraph shading (fourth column, second row in the *Theme Colors* section).
4. Apply bold formatting to the following text that appears at the beginnings of the second through the fifth paragraphs:
   Average annual total return:
   Annual total return:
   Accumulation units:
   Accumulative rates:
5. Select the paragraphs of text in the body of the document (all paragraphs except the title) and then change the paragraph alignment to justified.
6. Select the paragraphs that begin with the bolded words, sort the paragraphs in ascending order, and then indent the text 0.5 inch from the left margin.
7. Insert a watermark that prints *DRAFT* diagonally across the page.
8. Save, preview, and then close **U1-TotalReturns.docx**.

Assessment 3 Format a Technology Visionaries Report

1. Open **TechVisionaries.docx** and then save it with the name **U1-TechVisionaries**.
2. Apply the Heading 1 style to the titles *TECHNOLOGY VISIONARIES* and *REFERENCES*.
3. Apply the Heading 2 style to the headings in the document (*Konrad Zuse*, *William Hewlett and David Packard*, *Gordon E. Moore*, and *Jack S. Kilby*).
4. Apply the Centered style set.
5. Apply the Tight paragraph spacing.
6. Apply the Frame theme and then change the theme fonts to Candara.
7. Change the paragraph spacing after each heading from 2 points to 6 points.
8. Create a hanging indent for the paragraphs of text below the title *REFERENCES*.
9. Insert page numbers that print at the bottom center of each page.
10. Save, preview, and then close **U1-TechVisionaries.docx**.

Assessment 4 Set Tabs and Type Income by Division Text in Columns

1. At a new blank document, type the text shown in Figure U1.2 with the following specifications:
   a. Apply bold formatting to and center the title as shown.
   b. You determine the tab settings for the text in columns.
   c. Select the entire document and then change the font to 12-point Arial.
2. Save the document with the name **U1-Income**.
3. Preview and then close **U1-Income.docx**.

Figure U1.2 Assessment 4

INCOME BY DIVISION			
	2022	**2023**	**2024**
Public Relations	$14,375	$16,340	$16,200
Database Services	9,205	15,055	13,725
Graphic Design	18,400	21,790	19,600
Technical Support	5,780	7,325	9,600

Assessment 5

Set Tabs and Type Table of Contents Text

1. At a blank document, type the text shown in Figure U1.3 with the following specifications:
   a. Apply bold formatting to and center the title as shown.
   b. You determine the tab settings for the text in columns.
   c. Select the entire document, change the font to 12-point Cambria, and then change the line spacing to 1.5 lines.
2. Save the document with the name **U1-TofC**.
3. Preview and then close **U1-TofC.docx**.

Figure U1.3 Assessment 5

TABLE OF CONTENTS

Ancient Astronomy.. 3
Laws of Nature 7
Modern Astronomy.. 12
Our Solar System 23
Laws of Planetary Motion 31
Earth and Sky.. 45

Assessment

Format a Union Agreement Contract

1. Open **LaborContract.docx** and then save it with the name **U1-LaborContract**.
2. Find *AERO MANUFACTURING* and replace all occurrences with *KEIL CORPORATION*.
3. Find *AM* (matching the case) and replace all occurrences with *KC*.
4. Find *LABOR WORKERS' UNION* and replace all occurrences with *SERVICE EMPLOYEES' UNION*.
5. Find *LWU* and replace all occurrences with *SEU*.
6. Select the entire document and then change to 1.15 line spacing.
7. Select the numbered paragraphs in the section *Transfers and Moving Expenses* and change them to bulleted paragraphs.

8. Select the numbered paragraphs in the section *Sick Leave* and change them to bulleted paragraphs.
9. Change to landscape orientation and change the top margin to 1.5 inches.
10. Save and then preview **U1-LaborContract.docx**.
11. Change the top margin back to 1 inch and then change back to portrait orientation.
12. Insert the Whisp cover page and then insert the current date in the date placeholder, the title *Union Agreement* as the document title, and *Keil Corporation* as the document subtitle. Select the author placeholder (or the name) at the bottom of the cover page and then type your first and last names. Delete the company name placeholder.
13. Move the insertion point to the page after the cover page, insert the Ion (Dark) footer, and then make sure *UNION AGREEMENT* displays in the title placeholder and your name displays in the author placeholder. If not, type UNION AGREEMENT in the title placeholder and your first and last names in the author placeholder.
14. Save, preview, and then close **U1-LaborContract.docx**.

Assessment 7 Copy and Paste Text in a Health Plan Document

1. Open **KeyLifePlan.docx** and then save it with the name **U1-KeyLifePlan**.
2. Open **PlanOptions.docx** and then display the Clipboard task pane. Make sure the Clipboard is empty.
3. Select the heading *Plan Highlights* and the six paragraphs of text below it and then copy the selected text to the Clipboard.
4. Select the heading *Plan Options* and the two paragraphs of text below it and then copy the selected text to the Clipboard.
5. Select the heading *Quality Assessment* and the six paragraphs of text below it (located at the end of the document) and then copy the selected text to the Clipboard.
6. Close **PlanOptions.docx**.
7. With **U1-KeyLifePlan.docx** open, display the Clipboard task pane.
8. Move the insertion point to the beginning of the heading *Provider Network*, paste the *Plan Options* item from the Clipboard, and merge the formatting.
9. With the insertion point positioned at the beginning of the heading *Provider Network*, paste the *Plan Highlights* item from the Clipboard and merge the formatting.
10. Move the insertion point to the beginning of the heading *Plan Options*, paste the *Quality Assessment* item from the Clipboard, and merge the formatting.
11. Clear the Clipboard and then close it.
12. Apply the Heading 1 style to the title *KEY LIFE HEALTH PLAN*.
13. Apply the Heading 2 style to the four headings in the document.
14. Change the top margin to 1.5 inches.
15. Apply the Lines (Simple) style set.
16. Apply the Compact paragraph spacing.
17. Apply the Red Orange theme colors.
18. Insert a double-line page border in the standard dark red color.
19. Insert the Slice 1 header.
20. Insert the Slice footer and type your first and last names in the author placeholder.
21. Insert a page break at the beginning of the heading *Plan Highlights*.
22. Save, preview, and then close **U1-KeyLifePlan.docx**.

Assessment 8

Format a Bioinformatics Document

1. Open **Bioinformatics.docx** and then save it with the name **U1-Bioinformatics**.
2. Change the line spacing for the entire document to 1.5 spacing.
3. Insert a continuous section break at the beginning of the first paragraph of text (the paragraph that begins *Bioinformatics is the mixed application*).
4. Format the text below the section break into two columns.
5. Balance the columns on the second page.
6. Create a drop cap with the first letter of the first word *Bioinformatics* that begins the first paragraph of text. Specify that the drop cap is in the paragraph and not the margin and make the drop cap two lines in height.
7. Manually hyphenate the words in the document.
8. Insert page numbers at the bottoms of the pages using the Thin Line page numbering option. (The Thin Line page number option is located in the *Plain Number* section of the Page Number button side menu.)
9. Save, preview, and then close **U1-Bioinformatics.docx**.

Assessment 9

Create and Format a Resume

1. Open **Resume.docx** and then save it with the name **U1-Resume**.
2. Apply the following formatting so your document appears as shown in Figure U1.4:
   a. Change the font for the entire document to Candara.
   b. Change the top margin measurement to 1.25 inches.
   c. Apply character and paragraph formatting as shown (including bold formatting, paragraph alignment, bulleted formatting, borders and shading formatting, and adding leaders to the right tab in the *PROFESSIONAL EXPERIENCE* section, as shown in the figure).
3. Save, preview, and then close **U1-Resume.docx**.

Figure U1.4 Assessment 9

KIERNAN O'MALLEY

1533 Baylor Street East, Auburn, WA 98020 (253) 555-3912

NETWORK ADMINISTRATION PROFESSIONAL
Pursuing **CCNA Cloud certification** and **Network+** credentials
Proficient in Microsoft Office applications in Windows environment

EDUCATION

Information Systems (IS), Western Washington University, Bellingham, WA......................2024
Medical Specialist, Seattle University, Seattle, WA .... 2020 to 2023
Medical Terminology, Green River Community College, Auburn, WA..................................2019

APPLIED RESEARCH PROJECTS

Completed **Applied Research Projects (ARPs)**, in conjunction with IS degree requirements, covering all aspects of design and management of organizational technical resources, as follows:

- **Organizational Culture and Leadership** (2024): Evaluated the organizational culture of Bellevue Surgery Center's endoscopy unit and operating room (OR) to ensure that the mission and vision statements were being appropriately applied at the staff level.
- **Human Resources (HR) Management** (2024): Established a comprehensive orientation package for the Bellevue Surgery Center's clinical staff.
- **Strategic Management and Planning** (2023): Conducted internal/external environmental assessments in order to identify an approach for Bellevue Surgery Center to expand its OR facilities.
- **Financial Accounting** (2023): Created a quarterly operating budget for the Bellevue Surgery Center and implemented an expenditure tracking system.
- **Database Management Systems** (2022): Created an inventory-control system that optimizes inventory maintenance in a cost-effective manner.
- **Statistics and Research Analysis** (2022): Generated graphics to illustrate the Valley Hospital's assisted-reproduction success rate.
- **Management Support System** (2021): Identified solutions to resolve inventory-control vulnerabilities at minimal cost for Valley Hospital.

PROFESSIONAL EXPERIENCE

CERTIFIED SURGICAL TECHNOLOGIST

Bellevue Surgery Center, Bellevue, WA...2022 to present
Valley Hospital, Renton, WA ....2020 to 2021
Kenmore Ambulatory Surgery Center, Kenmore, WA ....2018 to 2020
South Sound Medical Center, Auburn, WA.. 2017 to 2018

Writing Activities

The following activities give you the opportunity to practice your writing skills and to demonstrate your understanding of some of the important Word features you have mastered in this unit. Use correct grammar, appropriate word choices, and clear sentence construction. Follow the steps in Figure U1.5 to improve your writing skills.

Activity 1

Write Paragraph on Button Functions

Explore the three buttons in the Editing group on the Home tab. Learn what functions are performed by each button. At a blank document, write a paragraph describing the functions performed by each button. After writing the paragraph, add steps on how to find text using the Navigation pane. Save the completed document with the name **U1-EditingGroupButtons**. Preview and then close **U1-EditingGroupButtons.docx**.

Activity 2

Write Information on Advanced Word Options

Use Word's Help feature and the search text *word options advanced* to learn how to customize display options at the Word Options dialog box with the *Advanced* option selected. After learning about the display options, create a document that describes the steps to change the display of the *Show this number of Recent Documents* option to *10*. Assume that the steps begin at a blank document. Describe the steps to turn on the *Quickly access this number of Recent Documents* option and change the number to *6*. Again, assume that the steps begin at a blank document. Add any additional information, such as a title, heading, and/or explanatory text, that helps the reader understand the contents of the document. Save the completed document with the name **U1-DisplayOptions**. Preview and then close **U1-DisplayOptions.docx**.

Internet Research

Research Business Desktop Computer Systems

You hold a part-time job at the local chamber of commerce, where you assist the office manager, Rianna Woods. Ms. Woods will be purchasing new desktop computers for the office staff. She has asked you to research using the internet and identify at least three PCs that can be purchased, and she wants you to put your research and recommendations in writing. Ms. Woods is looking for solid, reliable, economical, and powerful desktop computers with good warranties and service plans. She has given you a budget of $900 per unit.

Search the internet for three desktop PC systems from three different manufacturers. Consider price, specifications (processor speed, amount of RAM, hard drive space, and monitor type and size), performance, warranties, and service plans when choosing the systems. Include your research findings with your report.

Using Word, write a brief report in which you summarize the capabilities and qualities of each of the three computer systems you recommend. Include a final paragraph detailing which system you suggest for purchase and why. If possible, incorporate user opinions and/or reviews about the system to support your decision. Format your report using the concepts and techniques you learned in Unit 1. Save the report with the name **U1-InternetResearch**. Preview and then close the document.

Figure U1.5 The Writing Process

The Writing Process

Plan Gather ideas, select which information to include, and choose the order in which to present the information.

Checkpoints
- What is the purpose?
- What information does the reader need to reach your intended conclusion?

Write Following the information plan and keeping the reader in mind, draft the document using clear, direct sentences that say what you mean.

Checkpoints
- What subpoints support each main thought?
- How can you connect paragraphs so the reader moves smoothly from one idea to the next?

Revise Improve what is written by changing, deleting, rearranging, or adding words, sentences, and paragraphs.

Checkpoints
- Is the meaning clear?
- Do the ideas follow a logical order?
- Have you included any unnecessary information?
- Have you built your sentences around strong nouns and verbs?

Edit Check spelling, sentence construction, word use, punctuation, and capitalization.

Checkpoints
- Can you spot any redundancies or clichés?
- Can you reduce any phrases to effective words (for example, change *the fact that* to *because*)?
- Have you used commas only where there is a strong reason for doing so?
- Did you proofread the document for errors that your spelling checker cannot identify?

Publish Prepare a final copy that can be reproduced and shared with others.

Checkpoints
- Which design elements, such as bold formatting and different fonts, will help highlight important ideas or sections?
- Will charts or other graphics help clarify meaning?

WORD

LEVEL 1

Unit 2

Enhancing and Customizing Documents

WORD

Inserting and Formatting Objects

CHAPTER 5

Performance Objectives

Upon successful completion of Chapter 5, you will be able to:

1 Insert symbols, special characters, and the date and time

2 Insert, format, and customize images, text boxes, shapes, and WordArt

3 Insert and customize a screenshot

4 Insert, format, and modify a SmartArt graphic

Documents in Word may include special characters and symbols as well as the current date and time. The visual interest of a document can be enhanced by graphics, such as images, text boxes, shapes, WordArt, and screenshots. Word's SmartArt feature can be used to insert a graphic, such as a diagram or organizational chart. This chapter covers how to insert and customize these elements using buttons in the Illustrations group, the Text group, and the Symbols group on the Insert tab.

Data Files

The data files for this chapter are in the WL1C5 folder that you downloaded at the beginning of this course.

Activity 1 Format a Document on Computer Input Devices 2 Parts

In a document on computer input devices, you will insert a special character, symbols, and the date and time.

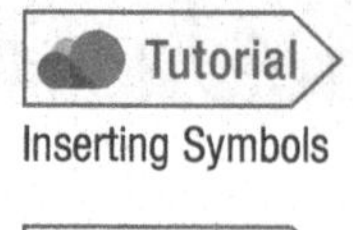

Inserting Symbols

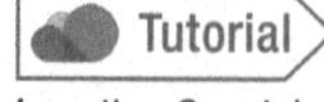

Inserting Special Characters

Symbol

Quick Steps

Insert Symbol

1. Click Insert tab.
2. Click Symbol button.
3. Click symbol.

OR

1. Click Insert tab.
2. Click Symbol button.
3. Click *More Symbols*.
4. Double-click symbol.
5. Click Close.

Quick Steps

Insert Special Character

1. Click Insert tab.
2. Click Symbol button.
3. Click *More Symbols*.
4. Click Special Characters tab.
5. Double-click special character.
6. Click Close.

Inserting Symbols and Special Characters

Use the Symbol button on the Insert tab to insert special symbols in a document. Click the button and a drop-down list displays the most recently inserted symbols. Click one of the symbols in the list to insert it in the document or click the *More Symbols* option to display the Symbol dialog box, as shown in Figure 5.1. Double-click a symbol to insert it, or click it once and then click the Insert button. Click Close to exit the dialog box. Another method for selecting a symbol at the Symbol dialog box is to type the symbol code in the *Character code* text box. Click a symbol in the dialog box and the character code displays in the *Character code* text box. If a symbol is used on a regular basis, remembering the character code can be useful for inserting the symbol in a document.

At the Symbol dialog box with the Symbols tab selected, the font can be changed with the *Font* option box. When the font is changed, different symbols display in the dialog box. Click the Special Characters tab at the Symbol dialog box and a list of special characters displays along with keyboard shortcuts for creating them.

Figure 5.1 Symbol Dialog Box with the Symbols Tab Selected

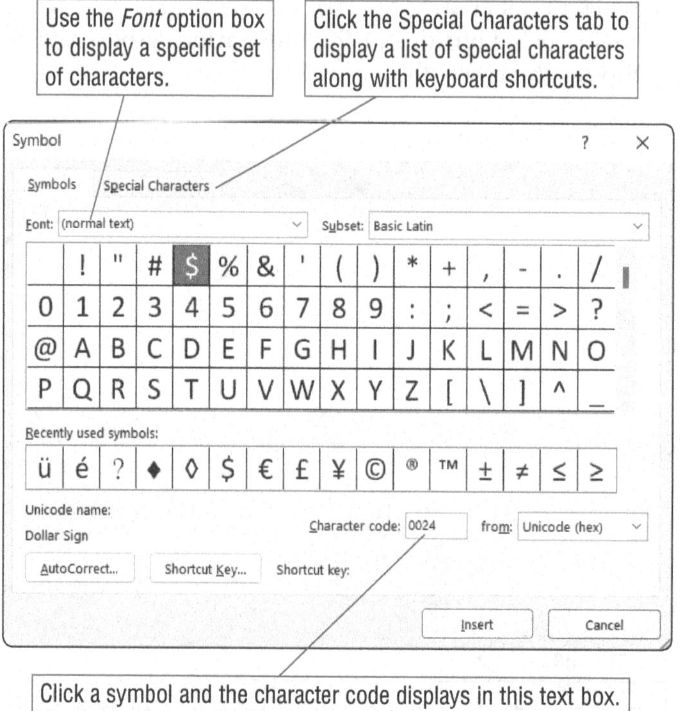

Activity 1a Inserting Symbols and Special Characters

1. Open **InputDevices.docx** and then save it with the name **5-InputDevices**.
2. Press Ctrl + End to move the insertion point to the end of the document.
3. Type Prepared by: and then press the spacebar.
4. Type the first name Matthew and then press the spacebar.
5. Insert the last name *Viña* by completing the following steps:
   a. Type Vi.
   b. Click the Insert tab.
   c. Click the Symbol button in the Symbols group.
   d. Click *More Symbols* at the drop-down list.
   e. At the Symbol dialog box, make sure *(normal text)* appears in the *Font* option box and then double-click the *ñ* symbol (located in approximately the twelfth row).
   f. Click the Close button.
   g. Type a.
6. Press Shift + Enter.
7. Insert the keyboard symbol (🖮) by completing the following steps:
   a. Click the Symbol button and then click *More Symbols*.
   b. At the Symbol dialog box, click the *Font* option box arrow and then click *Wingdings* at the drop-down list. (You will need to scroll down the list to see this option.)
   c. Select the current number in the *Character code* text box and then type 55.
   d. Click the Insert button and then click the Close button.
8. Type SoftCell Technologies.
9. Insert the registered trademark symbol (®) by completing the following steps:
   a. Click the Symbol button and then click *More Symbols*.
   b. At the Symbol dialog box, click the Special Characters tab.
   c. Double-click the ® symbol (tenth option from the top).
   d. Click the Close button.
   e. Press Shift + Enter.
10. Select the keyboard symbol (🖮) and then change the font size to 18 points.
11. Save and then preview **5-InputDevices.docx**.

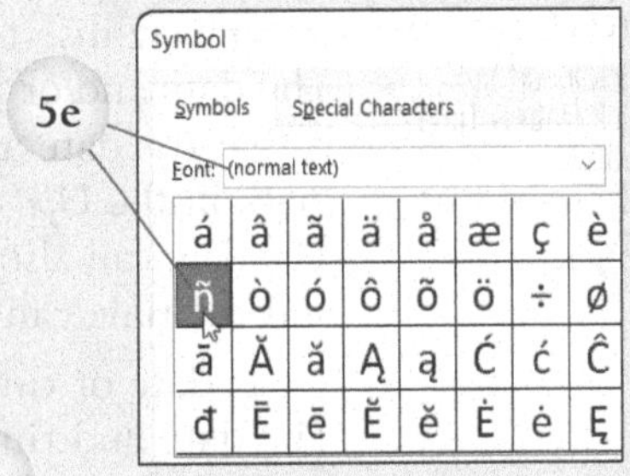

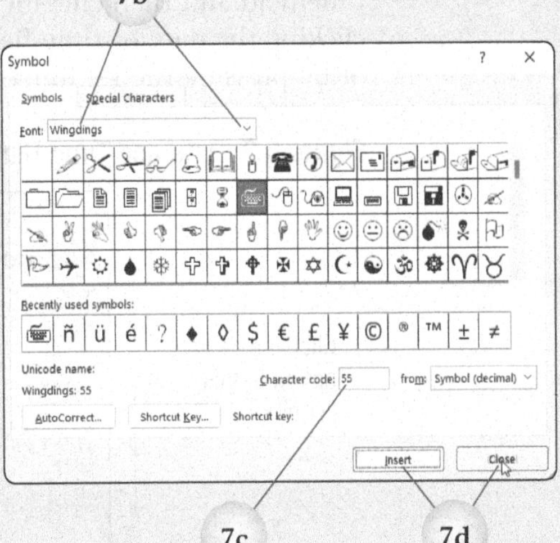

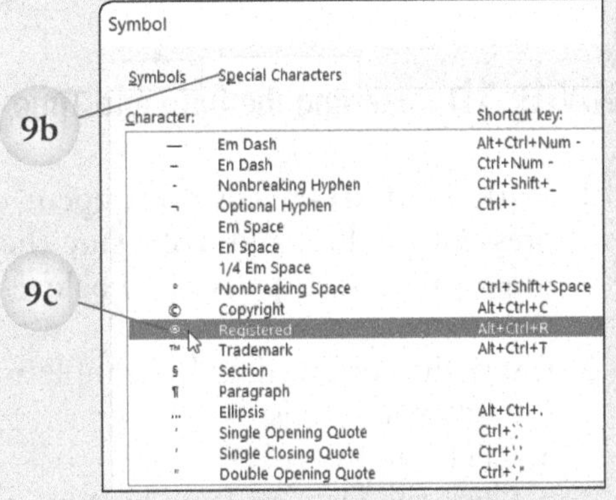

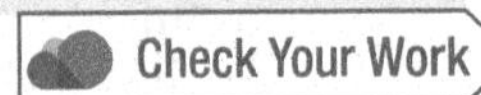

Inserting the Date and Time

Quick Steps

Insert Date and Time

1. Click Insert tab.
2. Click Date & Time button.
3. Click option in list box.
4. Click OK.

Inserting the Date and Time

Use the Date & Time button in the Text group on the Insert tab to insert the current date and time in a document. Click this button and the Date and Time dialog box displays, as shown in Figure 5.2. (Your date will vary from what you see in the figure.) At the Date and Time dialog box, click the desired date and/or time format in the *Available formats* list box.

If the *Update automatically* check box does not contain a check mark, the date and/or time are inserted in the document as text that can be edited in the normal manner. The date and/or time can also be inserted as a field. The advantage to using a field is that the date and time are updated when a document is reopened. Insert a check mark in the *Update automatically* check box to insert the date and/or time as a field. The date can also be inserted as a field using the keyboard shortcut Alt + Shift + D, and the time can be inserted as a field with the keyboard shortcut Alt + Shift + T.

A date or time field will automatically update when a document is reopened. The date and time can also be updated in the document by clicking the date or time field and then clicking the Update tab that appears above the field, by right-clicking the date or time field and then clicking *Update Field* at the shortcut menu, or by pressing the F9 function key.

Figure 5.2 Date and Time Dialog Box

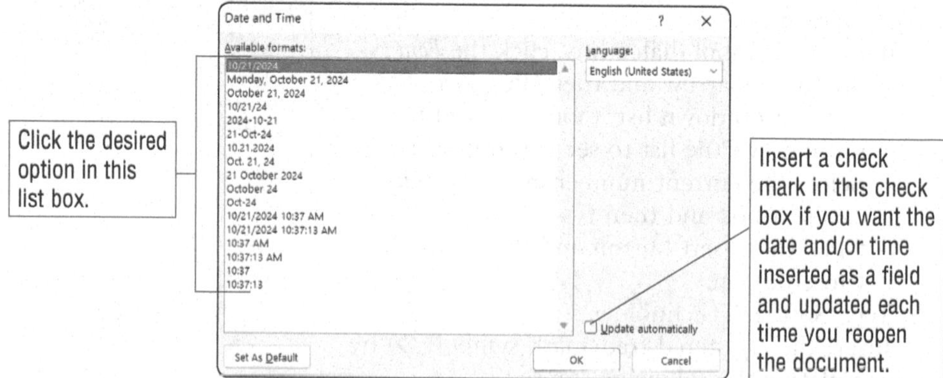

Activity 1b Inserting the Date and Time

Part 2 of 2

1. With **5-InputDevices.docx** open, press Ctrl + End and make sure the insertion point is positioned below the company name.
2. Insert the current date by completing the following steps:
   a. Click the Insert tab.
   b. Click the Date & Time button in the Text group.
   c. At the Date and Time dialog box, click the third option from the top in the *Available formats* list box. (Your date and time will vary from what you see in the image at the right.)
   d. If necessary, click in the *Update automatically* check box to insert a check mark.
   e. Click OK to close the dialog box.

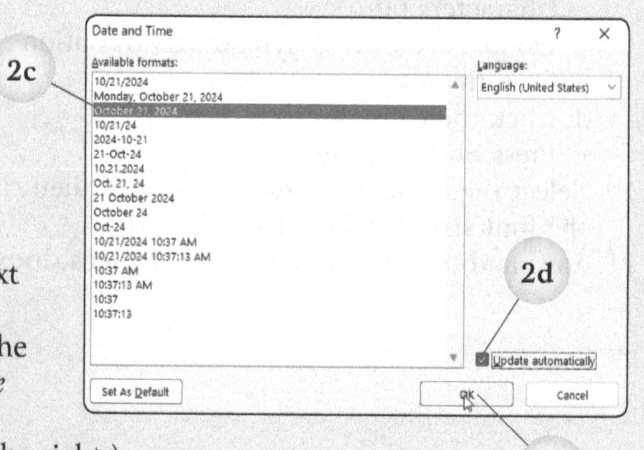

3. Press Shift + Enter.
4. Insert the current time by pressing Alt + Shift + T.
5. Save **5-InputDevices.docx**.
6. Update the time by clicking the time and then pressing the F9 function key.
7. Save, preview, and then close **5-InputDevices.docx**.

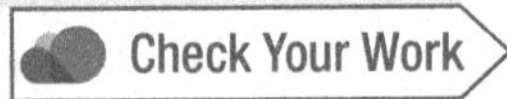

Activity 2 **Insert Images in a Tour Document** **2 Parts**

You will open a document with information on an Australian tour and add visual interest to the document by inserting and formatting images.

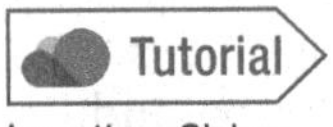

Inserting, Sizing, and Positioning an Image

Inserting and Formatting an Image

Insert an image, such as a photo or clip art, in a Word document with buttons in the Illustrations group on the Insert tab. Use the Pictures button in the Illustrations group to insert an image from a folder on the computer's hard drive or removable drive or an online source. Insert an image in a document to illustrate important information and to add visual interest.

Inserting an Image

Click the Pictures button in the Illustrations group on the Insert tab and a drop-down list displays with options for searching for images on the computer's hard drive or external storage medium, displaying a window with stock images (images available from Microsoft), or opening the Online Pictures window containing categories of images.

Click the *This Device* option at the Pictures button drop-down list and the Insert Picture dialog box displays. At this dialog box, navigate to the folder containing the desired image and then double-click the image to insert it in the document. Click the *Stock Images* option at the drop-down list and a window opens with royalty-free images that can be used in Microsoft 365 applications. To insert a stock image, click a category, and then double-click an image. Or, type key words in the search text box and then press the Enter key to find a specific type of image.

Click the *Online Pictures* option at the Pictures button drop-down list and the Online Pictures window displays. At this window, type the search term or topic in the search text box and then press the Enter key. Images that match the search text are shown in the window. Insert the image by clicking the image and then clicking the Insert button or by double-clicking the image. Be aware that many of the images available online are copyrighted. Before using an image in a document that will be shared publicly, make sure the image is either in the public domain (and thus not copyrighted) or determine how to get permission to use the image.

Sizing and Cropping an Image

When an image is inserted in a document, the Picture Format tab is active. The Size group on the Picture Format tab contains buttons for changing the size of an image and cropping an image. Change the size of an image by typing a measurement in the *Shape Height* and/or *Shape Width* measurement boxes or by clicking the up or down arrows in the measurement box.

Images in Word can also be sized using the mouse. Click an image to select it and circular sizing handles display around the image. Position the pointer on a sizing handle until the pointer turns into a double-headed arrow and then click and hold down the left mouse button. Drag the sizing handle in or out to decrease or increase the size of the image and then release the mouse button. Use the middle sizing handles at the left and right sides of the image to make the image wider or thinner. Use the middle sizing handles at the top and bottom of the image to make the image taller or shorter. Use the sizing handles at the corners of the image to change both the width and height at the same time.

Crop

Use the Crop button in the Size group to remove any unnecessary parts of an image. Click the Crop button and crop handles display around the image. Position the pointer on a crop handle and the pointer displays as a crop tool. Drag a crop handle to remove parts of the image.

Arranging an Image

The Arrange group on the Picture Format tab contains buttons for positioning, aligning, and rotating images. The group also contains buttons for wrapping text around an image and specifying if an image should appear in front of or behind text or other items.

Wrap Text

Layout Options

Use the Wrap Text button in the Arrange group to specify how text or other objects in the document should wrap around a selected image. The Wrap Text button drop-down list contains options for specifying square or tight wrapping, wrapping text above or below the image, and positioning the image behind or in front of text. The Layout Options button can also be used to specify text wrapping. When an image is selected, the Layout Options button displays outside the upper right corner of the image. Click the Layout Options button and then click a wrapping option at the drop-down list. Another method for specifying text wrapping is to right-click an image, point to *Wrap Text* at the shortcut menu, and click a text wrapping option at the side menu.

Position

Move an image to a specific location on the page with options at the Position button drop-down gallery in the Arrange group. Choose an option from this gallery and the image is moved to the specified location and square text wrapping is applied to it.

Rotate Objects

Rotate an image by positioning the pointer on the rotation handle, a circular arrow that appears above a selected image. The pointer will display with a black circular arrow attached. Click and hold down the left mouse button, drag in the desired direction, and then release the mouse button. An image can also be rotated or flipped with options at the Rotate Objects button drop-down gallery in the Arrange group.

Moving an Image

In addition to the Position button in the Arrange group on the Picture Format tab, an image can be moved using the mouse. Before moving an image with the mouse, specify how text should wrap around the image. After specifying text wrapping, position the pointer on the image until the pointer displays with a four-headed arrow attached. Click and hold down the left mouse button, drag the image to the new location, and then release the mouse button.

As an image is moved to the top, left, right, or bottom margin or to the center of the document, green alignment guides display. Use these guides to help

position the image on the page. If alignment guides do not display, turn them on by clicking the Align button in the Arrange group and then clicking *Use Alignment Guides* at the drop-down list. In addition to alignment guides, gridlines can be turned on to help position an image precisely. Turn on the display of gridlines by clicking the Align button and then clicking *View Gridlines*.

Activity 2a Inserting and Customizing an Image

Part 1 of 2

1. Open **Tour.docx** and then save it with the name **5-Tour**.
2. Insert an image by completing the following steps:
   a. Click the Insert tab, click the Pictures button in the Illustrations group, and then click the *This Device* option at the drop-down list.
   b. At the Insert Picture dialog box, navigate to your WL1C5 folder.
   c. Double-click the ***Uluru.jpg*** image file in the Content pane.

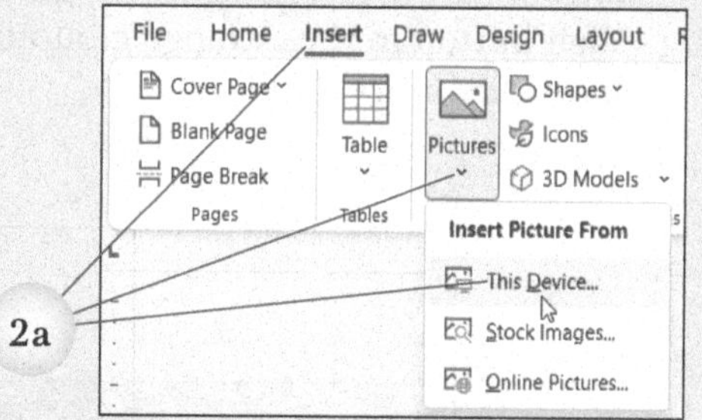

3. Crop the image by completing the following steps:
   a. Click the Crop button in the Size group on the Picture Format tab.
   b. Position the pointer on the bottom middle crop handle (which appears as a short black line) until the pointer turns into the crop tool (which appears as a small black T).
   c. Click and hold down the left mouse button, drag up to just below the rock (as shown at the right), and then release the mouse button.
   d. Click the Crop button in the Size group to turn the feature off.

4. Change the size of the image by clicking in the *Shape Height* measurement box in the Size group, typing 3, and then pressing the Enter key.
5. Specify text wrapping by clicking the Wrap Text button in the Arrange group and then clicking *Tight* at the drop-down list.

6. Change to a different text wrapping by completing the following steps:
   a. Click the Layout Options button outside the upper right corner of the image.
   b. Click the *Behind Text* option at the side menu (second column, second row in the *With Text Wrapping* section).
   c. Close the side menu by clicking the Close button in the upper right corner of the side menu.

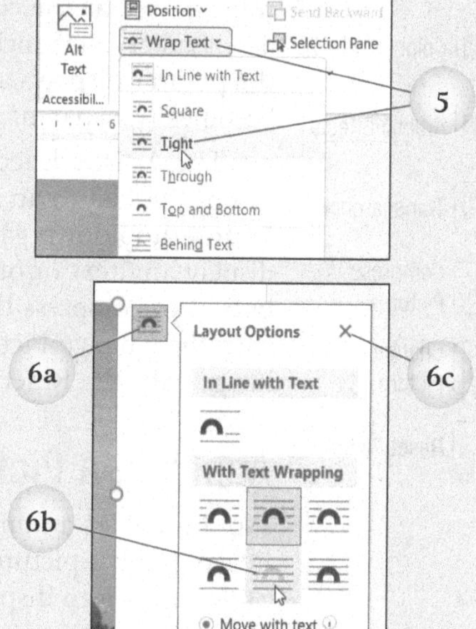

7. Rotate the image by clicking the Rotate Objects button in the Arrange group and then clicking *Flip Horizontal* at the drop-down gallery.
8. Position the pointer on the border of the selected image until the pointer displays with a four-headed arrow attached. Click and hold down the left mouse button, drag the image up and slightly to the right until you see green alignment guides at the top margin and the center of the page, and then release the mouse button. (If the green alignment guides do not display, turn on the guides by clicking the Align button in the Arrange group on the Picture Format tab and then clicking the *Use Alignment Guides* option.)

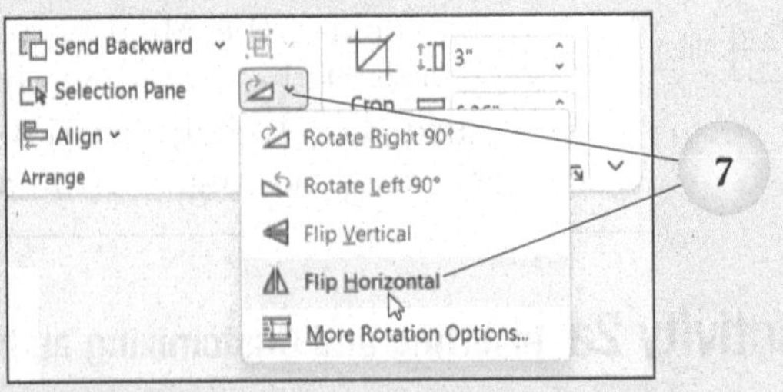

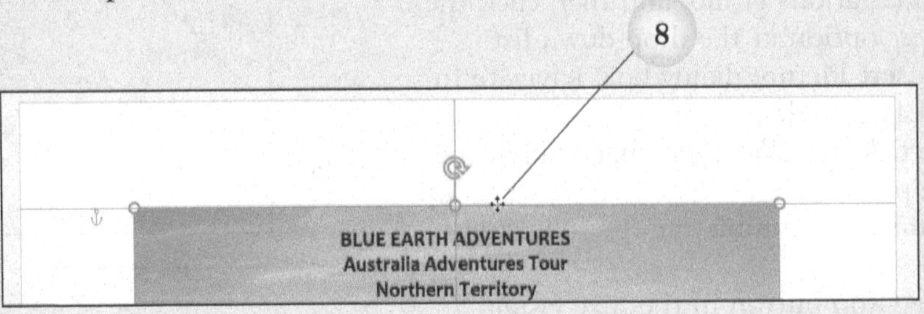

9. Save and then preview **5-Tour.docx**.

Formatting an Image

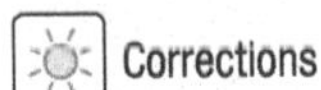

Adjusting an Image

The Adjust group on the Picture Format tab contains buttons for adjusting the background, color, brightness, and contrast of an image. Click the Remove Background button to display the Background Removal tab with buttons for removing unwanted portions of an image. Soft or sharpen an image or change the brightness and/or contrast with options at the Corrections button drop-down gallery. Use options at the Color button drop-down gallery to change the image color as well as the color saturation and color tone. The Color button drop-down gallery also includes the *Set Transparent Color* option. Click this option and the pointer displays as a dropper tool. Click a color in the image and that color becomes transparent.

The Artistic Effects button drop-down gallery offers a variety of effects that can be applied to an image. Lighten an image with options at the Transparency button drop-down gallery. For example, make an image more transparent to display any text or other objects behind the image. Use the Compress Pictures button to compress the size of images in a document. Remove or replace an image with the Change Picture button and discard all formatting changes and reset an image with the Reset Picture button.

Applying a Picture Style

Word provides a number of predesigned picture styles that can be applied to an image. Click a picture style in the Picture Styles group or click the More Picture Styles button to display a drop-down gallery of picture styles.

Creating Alternative Text for an Image

When an image is inserted in a document, consider adding *alternative text*. Alternative text, also known as alt text, is a brief description of an image or object that can be read by a screen reader and helps a person with a visual impairment understand what the image or object represents. Create alternative text at the Alt Text task pane. Display this task pane by clicking the Alt Text button in the Accessibility group on the Picture Format tab or by right-clicking the image and then clicking *Edit Alt Text* at the shortcut menu. At the Alt Text task pane, type a description of the image. If the image is only decorative and not important for understanding the content of the document, insert a check mark in the *Mark as decorative* check box. An image marked as decorative will not include any description for screen readers.

Activity 2b **Formatting and Adjusting Images** — Part 2 of 2

1. With **5-Tour.docx** open and the image selected, apply an artistic effect by clicking the Artistic Effects button in the Adjust group and then clicking the *Watercolor Sponge* option (second column, third row).
2. Lighten the image by clicking the Transparency button in the Adjust group and then clicking the *Transparency: 30%* option (third option in the drop-down gallery).
3. After looking at the artistic effect and transparency, remove the artistic effect and transparency by clicking the Reset Picture button in the Adjust group.

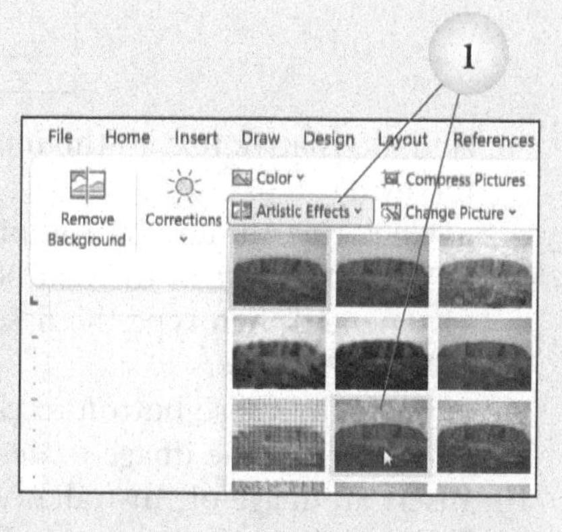

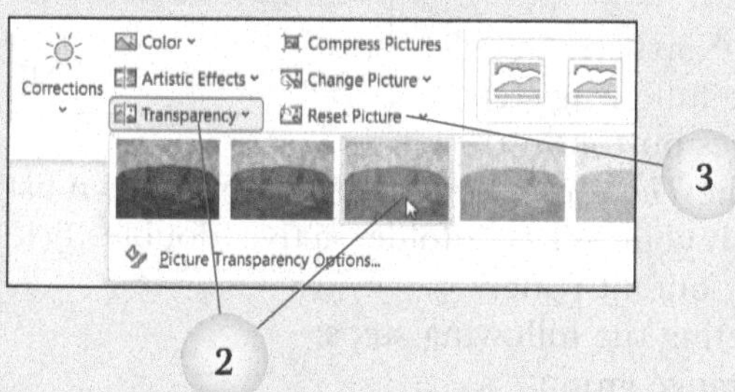

4. Sharpen the image by clicking the Corrections button in the Adjust group and then clicking the *Sharpen: 25%* option (fourth option in the *Sharpen/Soften* section).
5. Change the contrast of the image by clicking the Corrections button in the Adjust group and then clicking the *Brightness: 0% (Normal) Contrast: +40%* option (third column, bottom row in the *Brightness/Contrast* section).

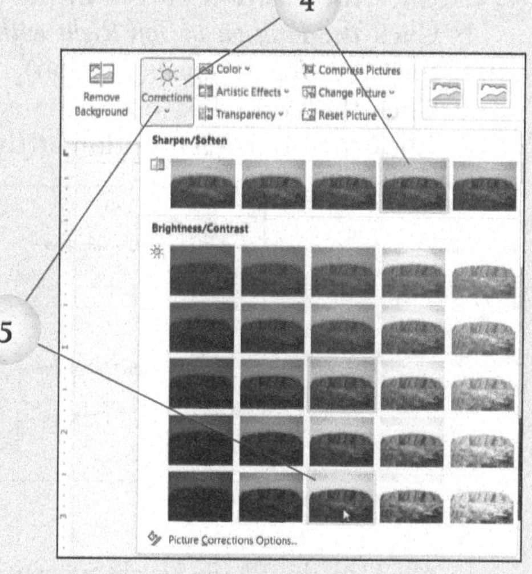

6. Compress the image by completing the following steps:
   a. Click the Compress Pictures button in the Adjust group.
   b. At the Compress Pictures dialog box, make sure check marks appear in the check boxes for both options in the *Compression options* section and then click OK.

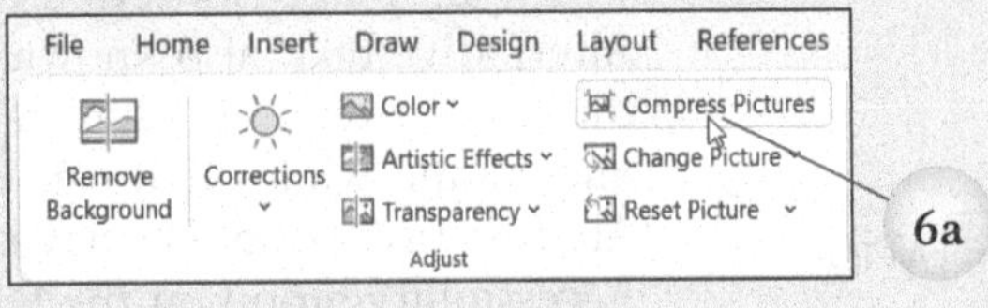

7. Apply a picture style by clicking the More Pictures Styles button in the Picture Styles group and then clicking the *Simple Frame, Black* option (second column, second row at the drop-down gallery).

8. Add alternative text to the image by completing the following steps:
   a. Click the Alt Text button in the Accessibility group.
   b. Select the text in the text box in the Alt Text task pane and then type the description Uluru (also known as Ayers Rock).
   c. Click the Close button to close the task pane.

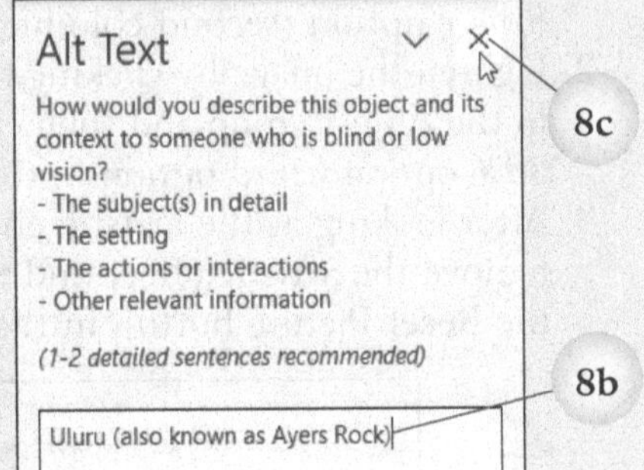

9. Click outside the image to deselect it.
10. Insert an image of Australia (with the Northern Territory identified) by completing the following steps:
    a. Click the Insert tab, click the Pictures button in the Illustrations group, and then click the *This Device* option at the drop-down list.
    b. At the Insert Picture dialog box, with your WL1C5 folder active, double-click the ***NT-Australia.png*** image file in the Content pane.
11. Position and size the image by completing the following steps:
    a. Click the Position button in the Arrange group.
    b. Click the *Position in Top Right with Square Text Wrapping* option (third column, first row in the *With Text Wrapping* section).
    c. Click the Wrap Text button.
    d. Click the *Behind Text* option at the drop-down gallery.

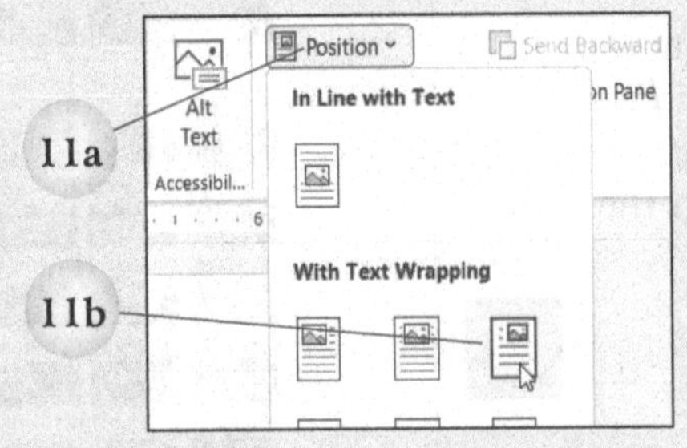

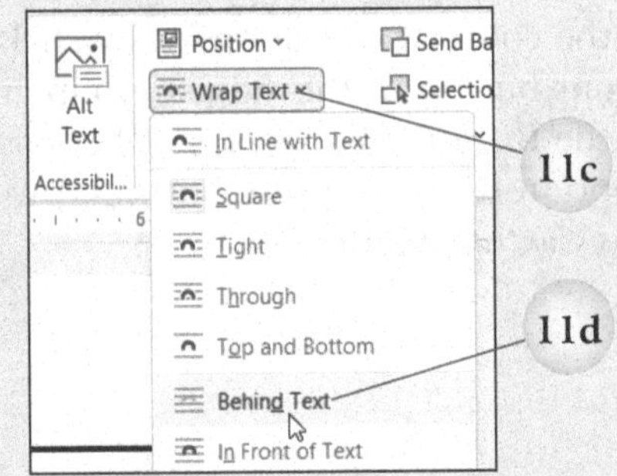

    e. Click in the *Shape Height* measurement box in the Size group, type 1, and then press the Enter key.

12. Make the white background of the image transparent by completing the following steps:
    a. Click the Color button in the Adjust group.
    b. Click the *Set Transparent Color* option at the bottom of the drop-down list. (The pointer turns into a dropper tool.)
    c. Position the dropper tool on any white portion of the image and then click the left mouse button.
13. Click the Color button and then click the *Orange, Accent color 2 Dark* option (third column, second row in the *Recolor* section).
14. Insert an airplane image by clicking the Insert tab, clicking the Pictures button, clicking the *This Device* option, and then double-clicking the ***Airplane.jpg*** image file in your WL1C5 folder.
15. With the airplane image selected, remove the background by completing the following steps:
    a. Click the Remove Background button in the Adjust group on the Picture Format tab.
    b. Click the Mark Areas to Remove button. (The pointer changes to a pen.)
    c. Position the pointer (pen) in the white area above the wing at the left side of the airplane, press and hold down the left mouse button, drag around the white area above the airplane to below the wing at the right side of the airplane (do not drag through any portion of the airplane), and then release the mouse button. (The white background the pointer passes through should be removed.)
    d. Use the pointer to drag in the remaining white background just above the wing and below the body of the airplane (Do not drag through any portion of the airplane.)
    e. If you are not satisfied with the background removal, click the Discard All Changes button and start again. If you are satisfied with the background removal, click the Keep Changes button.

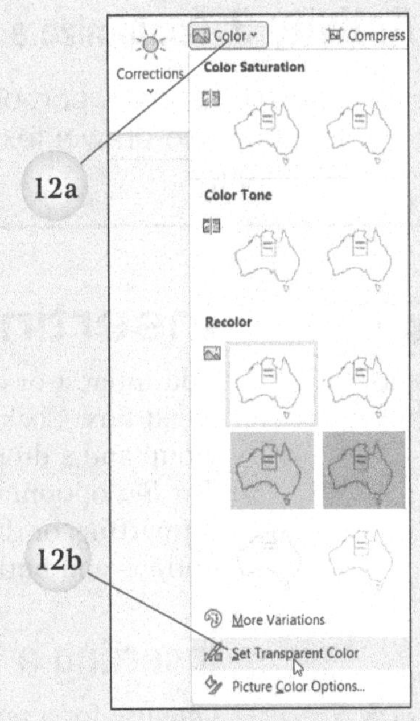

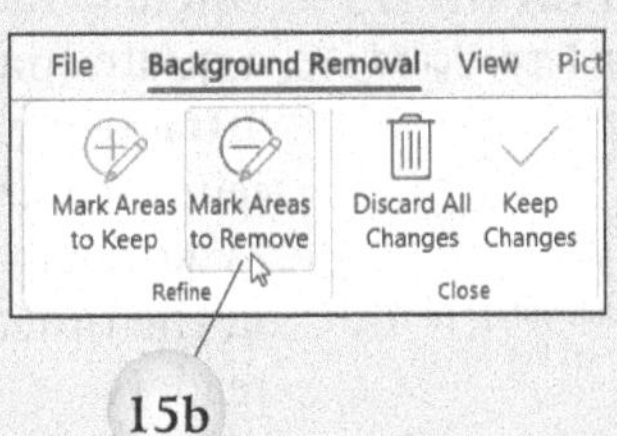

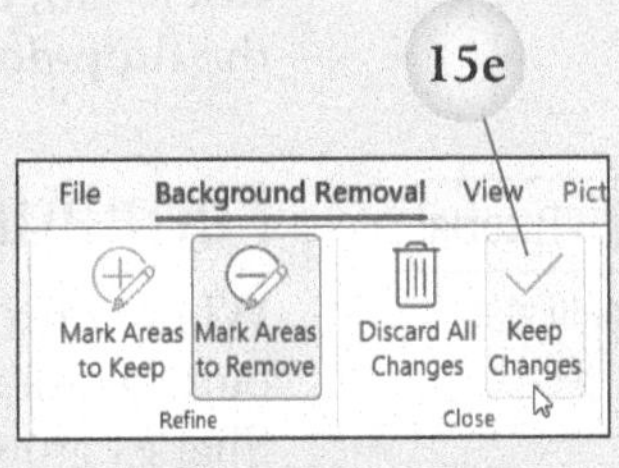

16. Position the airplane by clicking the Position button and then clicking the *Position in Top Left with Square Text Wrapping* option (first column, top row in the *With Text Wrapping* section).
17. Specify text wrapping by clicking the Wrap Text button and then clicking the *Behind Text* option.
18. Change the image width by clicking in the *Shape Width* measurement box, typing 2.1, and then pressing the Enter key.
19. Save, preview, and then close **5-Tour.docx**.

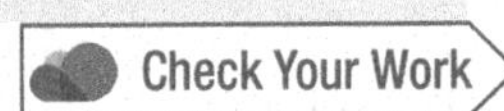

Activity 3 Customize a Report on Robots **2 Parts**

You will open a report on robots and then add a pull quote using a predesigned text box and draw a text box and type information about an upcoming conference.

Inserting a Text Box

Inserting and Formatting a Text Box

Add interest or create a location in a document for text by inserting or drawing a text box. Click the Insert tab and then click the Text Box button in the Text group and a drop-down list displays with predesigned text boxes and the *Draw Text Box* option. Choose one of the predesigned text boxes, which already contain formatting, or draw a text box and then customize or apply formatting to it with options and buttons on the Shape Format tab.

Inserting a Predesigned Text Box

Quick Steps

Insert Predesigned Text Box

1. Click Insert tab.
2. Click Text Box button.
3. Click option at drop-down list.

One use for a text box in a document is to insert a pull quote. A pull quote is a quote from the text that is "pulled out" and enlarged and positioned in an attractive location on the page. Some advantages of using pull quotes are that they reinforce important concepts, summarize the message, and break up text blocks to make them easier to read. If a document contains multiple pull quotes, keep them in the order in which they appear in the text to ensure clear comprehension by readers.

A text box for a pull quote can be drawn in a document or a predesigned text box can be inserted in the document. To insert a predesigned text box, click the Insert tab, click the Text Box button, and then click the predesigned text box at the drop-down list.

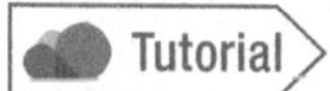

Formatting a Text Box

Formatting a Text Box

When a text box is selected, the Shape Format tab is active. This tab contains buttons for formatting and customizing the text box. Use options in the Insert Shapes group to insert a shape in the text box or in another location in the document. Apply predesigned styles to a text box and change the shape fill, outline, and effects with options in the Shape Styles group. Change the formatting of the text in the text box with options in the WordArt Styles group. Click the More WordArt Styles button in the WordArt Styles group and then click a style at the drop-down gallery. Further customize the formatting of text in the text box with the Text Fill, Text Outline, and Text Effects buttons in the Text group. Use options in the Arrange group to position the text box on the page, specify text wrapping in relation to the text box, align the text box with other objects in the document, and rotate the text box. Specify the text box size with the *Shape Height* and *Shape Width* measurement boxes in the Size group.

Activity 3a Inserting and Formatting a Predesigned Text Box

Part 1 of 2

1. Open **Robots.docx** and then save it with the name **5-Robots.**
2. Insert a predesigned text box by completing the following steps:
   a. Click the Insert tab.
   b. Click the Text Box button in the Text group.
   c. Scroll down the drop-down list and then click the *Ion Quote (Dark)* option.
3. Type the following text in the text box:
   "The task of creating a humanlike body has proven incredibly difficult."
4. Delete the line and the source placeholder in the text box by pressing the F8 function key (which turns on the Selection mode), pressing Ctrl + End (which selects text from the location of the insertion point to the end of the text box), and then pressing the Delete key.
5. With the Shape Format tab active, click the More Shape Styles button in the Shape Styles group and then click the *Subtle Effect - Blue, Accent 5* option (sixth column, fourth row in the *Theme Styles* section).
6. Click the Shape Effects button in the Shape Styles group, point to *Shadow*, and then click the *Offset: Bottom Right* option (first column, first row in the *Outer* section).

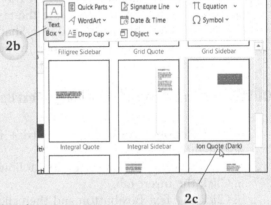

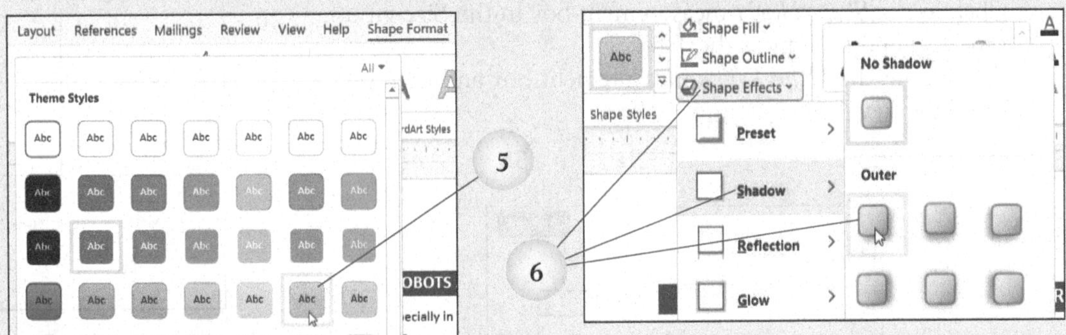

7. Position the pointer on the border of the selected text box until the pointer turns into a four-headed arrow and then drag the text box so it is positioned as shown below.

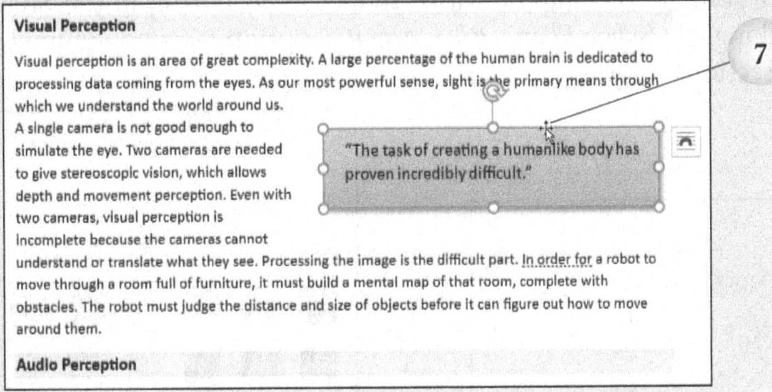

Visual Perception

Visual perception is an area of great complexity. A large percentage of the human brain is dedicated to processing data coming from the eyes. As our most powerful sense, sight is the primary means through which we understand the world around us.

A single camera is not good enough to simulate the eye. Two cameras are needed to give stereoscopic vision, which allows depth and movement perception. Even with two cameras, visual perception is incomplete because the cameras cannot understand or translate what they see. Processing the image is the difficult part. In order for a robot to move through a room full of furniture, it must build a mental map of that room, complete with obstacles. The robot must judge the distance and size of objects before it can figure out how to move around them.

"The task of creating a humanlike body has proven incredibly difficult."

Audio Perception

8. Click outside the text box to deselect it.
9. Save **5-Robots.docx.**

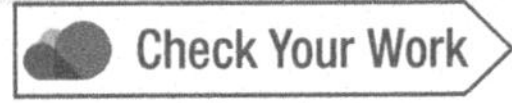

Drawing a Text Box

Quick Steps

Draw Text Box

1. Click Insert tab.
2. Click Text Box button.
3. Click *Draw Text Box*.
4. Click or drag in document to create box.

To draw a text box rather than inserting a predesigned one, click the Insert tab, click the Text Box button in the Text group, and then click *Draw Text Box* at the drop-down list. With the pointer displaying as crosshairs (a plus [+] symbol), click in the document to insert the text box or position the crosshairs in the document and then drag to create the text box with the desired size and dimensions. When a text box is selected, the Shape Format tab is active. Use buttons on this tab to format a drawn text box in the same manner as a built-in text box.

Activity 3b Inserting and Formatting a Text Box

Part 2 of 2

1. With **5-Robots.docx** open, press Ctrl + End to move the insertion point to the end of the document.
2. Insert a text box by completing the following steps:
   a. Click the Insert tab.
   b. Click the Text Box button and then click the *Draw Text Box* option.
   c. Position the pointer (displays as crosshairs) on the insertion point and then click the left mouse button. (This inserts the text box in the document.)
3. Change the text box height and width by completing the following steps:
   a. Click in the *Shape Height* measurement box in the Size group, type 1.2, and then press the Tab key.
   b. Type 4.5 in the *Shape Width* measurement box and then press the Enter key.

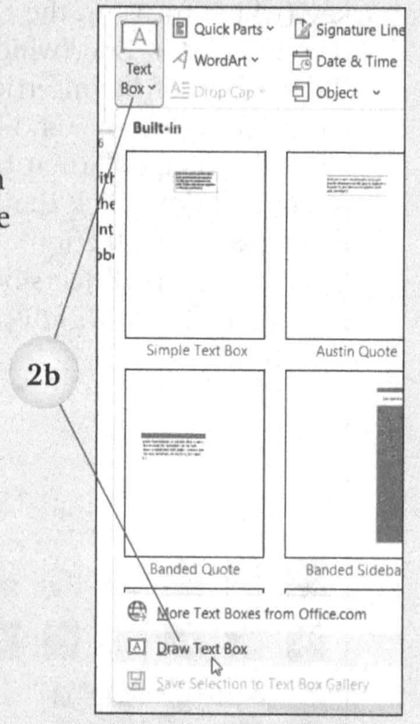

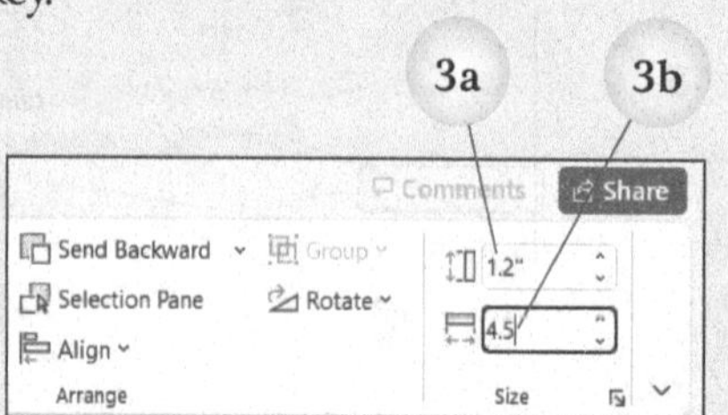

4. Center the text box by clicking the Align button in the Arrange group and then clicking *Align Center* at the drop-down list.
5. Apply a shape style by clicking the More Shape Styles button in the Shape Styles group and then clicking the *Subtle Effect - Blue, Accent 1* option (second column, fourth row in the *Theme Styles* section).

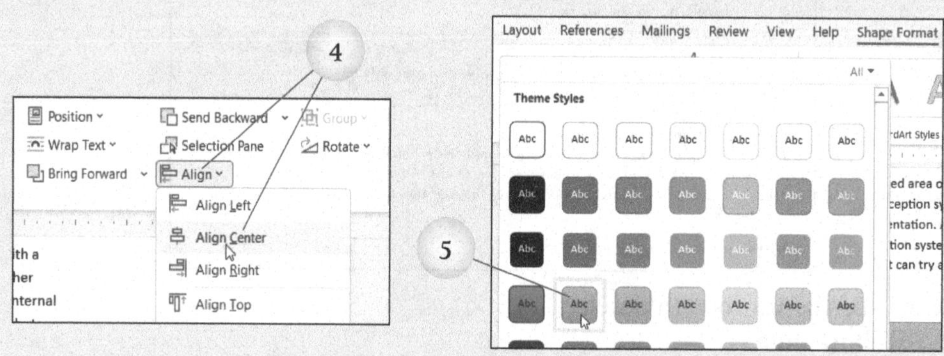

6. Apply a bevel shape effect by clicking the Shape Effects button, pointing to the *Bevel* option, and then clicking the *Soft Round* option at the side menu (second column, second row in the *Bevel* section).
7. Apply a 3-D shape effect by clicking the Shape Effects button, pointing to *3-D Rotation*, and then clicking the *Perspective: Above* option (first column, second row in the *Perspective* section).

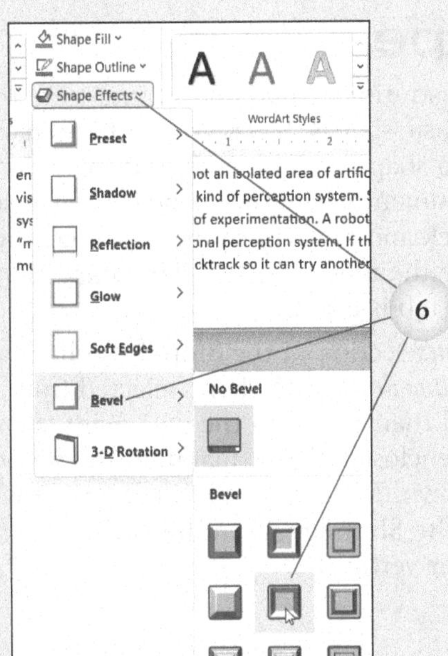

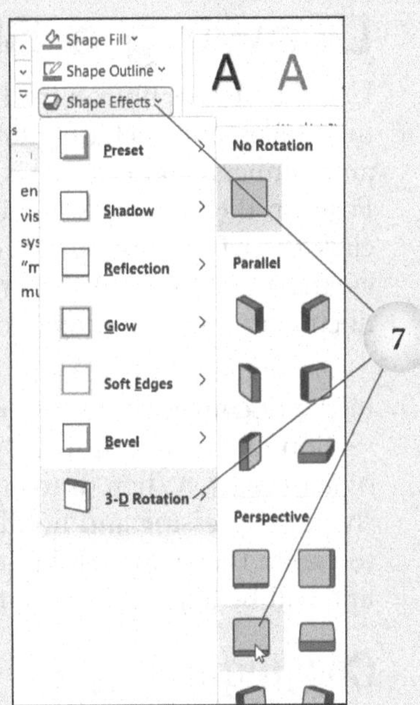

8. Insert and format text in the text box by completing the following steps:
   a. Press the Enter key two times. (The insertion point should be positioned in the text box.)
   b. Click the Home tab.
   c. Change the font size to 14 points, apply bold formatting, and change the font color to Dark Blue (ninth color option in the *Standard Colors* section).
   d. Click the Center button in the Paragraph group.
   e. Type International Conference on Artificial Intelligence Summer 2025.
   f. Click outside the text box to deselect it. (Your text box should appear as shown below.)

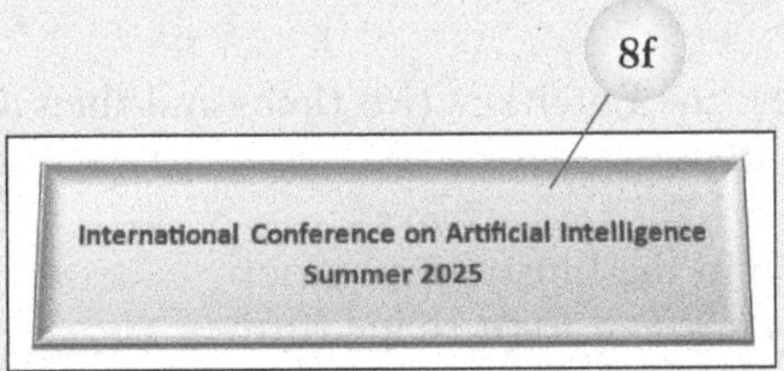

9. Save, preview, and then close **5-Robots.docx**.

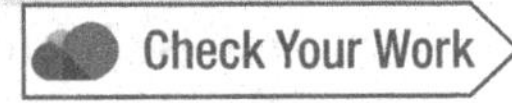

Activity 4 Prepare a Company Flyer

2 Parts

You will create a company flyer document and increase the visual interest in the document by inserting and customizing shapes and WordArt.

Inserting, Sizing, and Positioning a Shape and Line

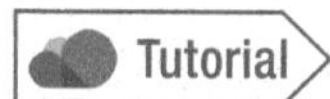

Formatting a Shape and Line

Shapes

Quick Steps

Draw Shape

1. Click Insert tab.
2. Click Shapes button.
3. Click shape.
4. Click or drag in document to create shape.

Hint To draw a square, choose the Rectangle shape and then press and hold down the Shift key while drawing.

Drawing a Shape

Use the Shapes button in the Illustrations group on the Insert tab to draw shapes in a document, including lines, basic shapes, block arrows, flow chart shapes, stars and banners, and callouts. Click a shape and the pointer displays as crosshairs. Position the crosshairs in the document where the shape is to be inserted and then click the left mouse button or click and hold down the left mouse button, drag to create the shape, and then release the mouse button. The shape is inserted in the document and the Shape Format tab is active.

A shape selected from the *Lines* section of the drop-down list and then drawn in the document is considered a *line drawing*. A shape selected from another section of the drop-down list and then drawn in the document is considered an *enclosed object*. When drawing an enclosed object, maintain the proportions of the shape by pressing and holding down the Shift key while dragging with the mouse to create the shape. Hold down the Shift key when drawing a straight line and the line will be aligned horizontally or vertically.

Copying a Shape

To copy a shape, select the shape and then click the Copy button in the Clipboard group on the Home tab. Position the insertion point at the location the copied shape is to be inserted and then click the Paste button. A selected shape can also be copied by right-clicking the shape and then clicking *Copy* at the shortcut menu. Position the insertion point where the shape is to be copied, right-click, and then click *Paste* at the shortcut menu. Another method for copying shapes is to press and hold down the Ctrl key while dragging a copy of the shape to the new location.

Activity 4a Drawing and Copying Arrow Shapes

Part 1 of 2

1. At a blank document, press the Enter key two times and then draw an arrow shape by completing the following steps:
   a. Click the Insert tab.
   b. Click the Shapes button in the Illustrations group and then click the *Arrow: Striped Right* shape (fifth column, second row in the *Block Arrows* section).
   c. Position the pointer (which displays as crosshairs) on the insertion point and then click the left mouse button. (This inserts the arrow shape in the document and makes the Shape Format tab active.)
2. Format the arrow by completing the following steps:
   a. Click in the *Shape Height* measurement box in the Size group, type 2.4, and then press the Tab key.
   b. Type 4.5 in the *Shape Width* measurement box and then press the Enter key.

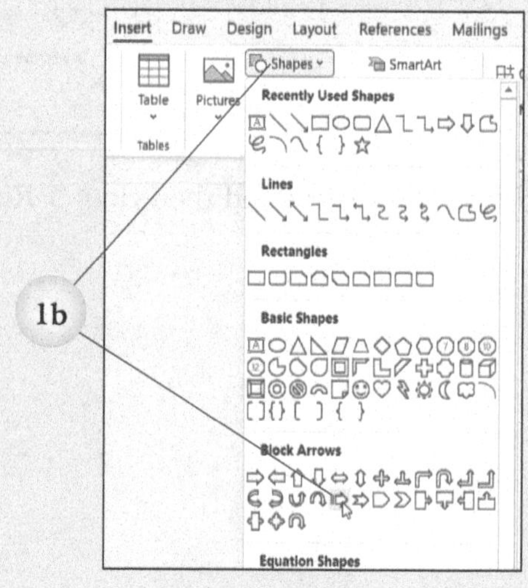

c. Horizontally align the arrow by clicking the Align button in the Arrange group and then clicking *Distribute Horizontally* at the drop-down list.

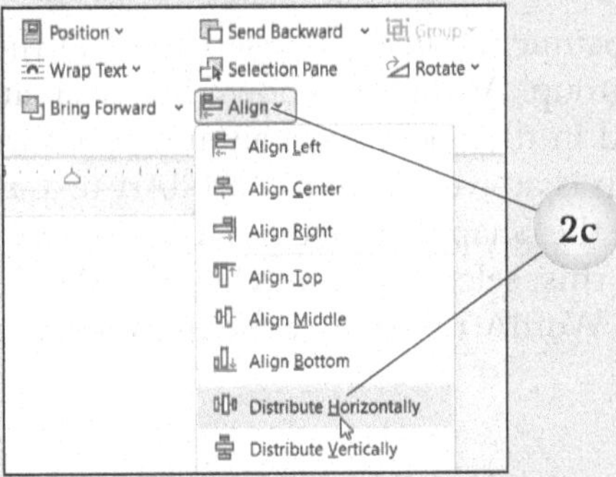

d. Click the More Shape Styles button in the Shape Styles group and then click the *Intense Effect - Green, Accent 6* option (last option in the *Theme Styles* section at the drop-down gallery).

e. Click the Shape Effects button in the Shape Styles group, point to *Bevel*, and then click the *Angle* option (first column, second row in the *Bevel* section).

f. Click the Shape Outline button arrow in the Shape Styles group and then click the *Dark Blue* color (ninth color option in the *Standard Colors* section).

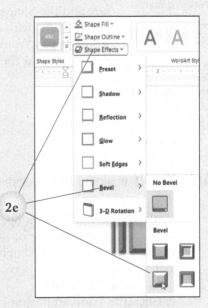

3. Copy the arrow by completing the following steps:
   a. With the pointer positioned in the arrow (pointer displays with a four-headed arrow attached), press and hold down the Ctrl key and click and hold down the left mouse button. Drag down until the copied arrow appears just below the top arrow, release the mouse button, and then release the Ctrl key.
   b. Copy the selected arrow by pressing and holding down the Ctrl key and clicking and holding down the left mouse button, dragging the copied arrow just below the second arrow, and then releasing the Ctrl key and the mouse button.
4. Flip the middle arrow by completing the following steps:
   a. Click the middle arrow to select it.
   b. Click the Rotate button in the Arrange group on the Shape Format tab and then click the *Flip Horizontal* option at the drop-down gallery.

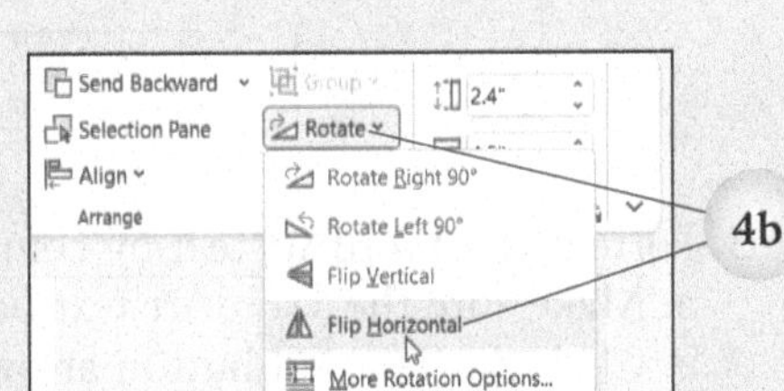

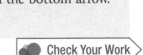

5. Insert the text *Financial* in the top arrow by completing the following steps:
   a. Click the top arrow to select it.
   b. Type Financial.
   c. Select *Financial*.
   d. Click the Home tab.
   e. Change the font size to 16 points, apply bold formatting, and change the font color to Dark Blue (ninth color option in the *Standard Colors* section).
6. Complete steps similar to those in Step 5 to insert the word *Direction* in the middle arrow.
7. Complete steps similar to those in Step 5 to insert the word *Retirement* in the bottom arrow.
8. Save the document with the name **5-FinConsult**.

Inserting, Sizing, and Positioning WordArt

Formatting WordArt

Quick Steps

Create WordArt Text

1. Click Insert tab.
2. Click WordArt button.
3. Click option.
4. Type WordArt text.

Creating and Formatting WordArt

Use the WordArt feature to distort or modify text to conform to a variety of shapes. This is useful for creating company logos, letterheads, flyer titles, and headings.

To insert WordArt in a document, click the Insert tab and then click the WordArt button in the Text group. At the drop-down list, click an option and a WordArt text box is inserted in the document containing the words *Your text here* and the Shape Format tab is active. Type the WordArt text and then format the WordArt with options on the Shape Format tab. Existing text can also be formatted as WordArt. To do this, select the text, click the WordArt button on the Insert tab, and then click the WordArt option at the drop-down list.

Activity 4b Inserting and Modifying WordArt

Part 2 of 2

1. With **5-FinConsult.docx** open, press Ctrl + Home to move the insertion point to the beginning of the document.
2. Insert WordArt text by completing the following steps:
   a. Type Miller Financial Services and then select *Miller Financial Services*.
   b. Click the Insert tab.
   c. Click the WordArt button in the Text group and then click the option in the third column, first row (orange fill and outline).

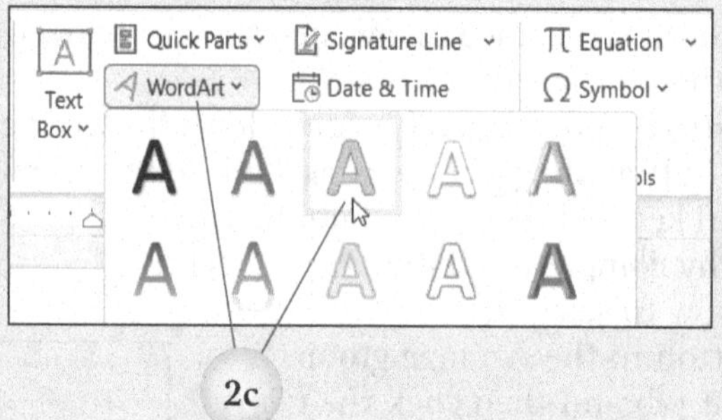

3. Format the WordArt text by completing the following steps:
   a. Make sure the WordArt text border displays as a solid line.
   b. Click the Text Fill button arrow in the WordArt Styles group on the Shape Format tab and then click the *Light Green* color (fifth color option in the *Standard Colors* section).
   c. Click the Text Outline button arrow in the WordArt Styles group and then click the *Green, Accent 6, Darker 50%* option (last option in the *Theme Colors* section).

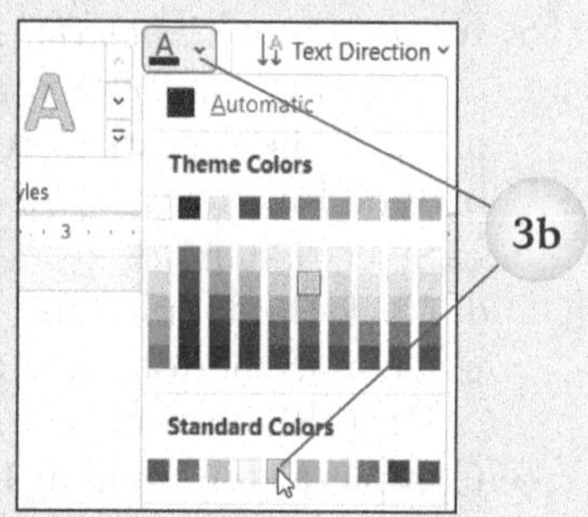

d. Click the Text Effects button in the WordArt Styles group, point to *Glow*, and then click the *Glow: 5 point; Blue, Accent color 1* option (first column, first row in the *Glow Variations* section).

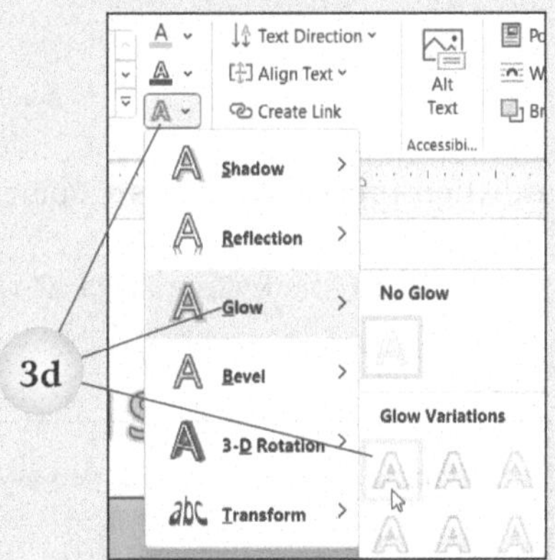

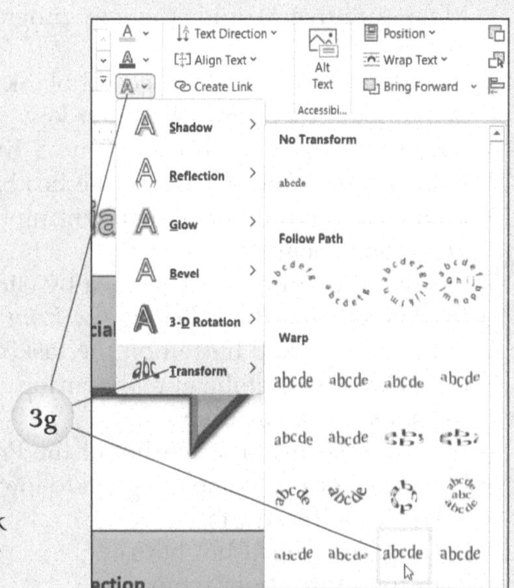

e. Click in the *Shape Height* measurement box in the Size group, type 1, and then press the Tab key.

f. Type 6 in the *Shape Width* measurement box in the Size group and then press the Enter key.

g. Click the Text Effects button in the WordArt Styles group, point to *Transform*, and then click the *Warp Up* option (third column, fourth row in the *Warp* section).

h. Click the Position button in the Arrange group and then click the *Position in Top Center with Square Text Wrapping* option (second column, first row in the *With Text Wrapping* section).

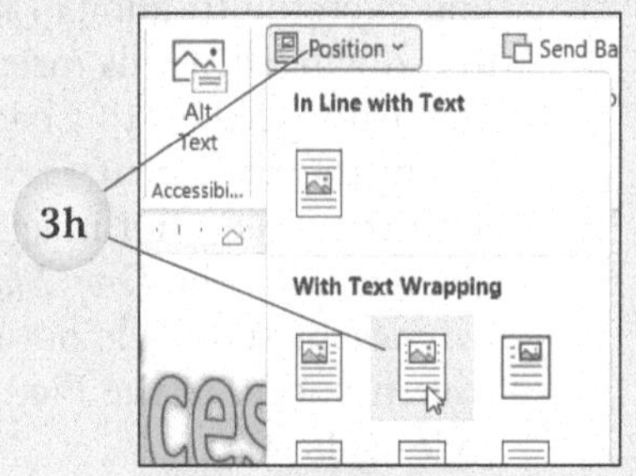

4. Click outside the WordArt to deselect it.
5. Move the arrows as needed to ensure they do not overlap the WordArt or each other and that they all fit on one page.
6. Save, preview, and then close **5-FinConsult.docx**.

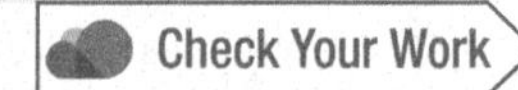

Activity 5 Insert and Format Screenshots — 2 Parts

You will create a document with screenshots of the Print and Info backstage areas and create another document with screen clippings of sample cover pages.

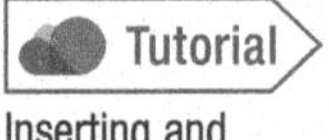

Inserting and Formatting Screenshot and Screen Clipping Images

Inserting a Screenshot

The Illustrations group on the Insert tab contains a Screenshot button, which captures a screen or part of a screen as an image. To capture the entire screen, open a new document, click the Insert tab, click the Screenshot button in the Illustrations group, and then click the screen thumbnail at the drop-down list. (The currently active document does not appear as a thumbnail at the drop-down list—only other documents or files that are open.) Click the specific thumbnail at the drop-down list and a screenshot is inserted as an image in the open document. Once the screenshot is inserted in the document, the Picture Format tab is active. Use buttons on this tab to customize the screenshot image.

Activity 5a Inserting and Formatting Screenshots

Part 1 of 2

1. Make sure that Word is the only program open and then press Ctrl + N to open a blank document.
2. Press Ctrl + N to open a second blank document, type Print Backstage Area at the left margin, and then press the Enter key.
3. Save the document with the name **5-BackstageAreas.**
4. Point to the Word button on the taskbar and then click the thumbnail representing the blank document.
5. Display the Print backstage area by clicking the File tab and then clicking the *Print* option.
6. Point to the Word button on the taskbar and then click the thumbnail representing **5-BackstageAreas.docx.**
7. Insert and format a screenshot of the Print backstage area by completing the following steps:
    a. Click the Insert tab.
    b. Click the Screenshot button in the Illustrations group and then click the thumbnail in the drop-down list. (This inserts a screenshot of the Print backstage area in the document.)
    c. With the screenshot image selected, click the *Drop Shadow Rectangle* picture style option (fourth option in the Picture Styles gallery).
    d. Select the measurement in the *Shape Width* measurement box, type 5.5, and then press the Enter key.

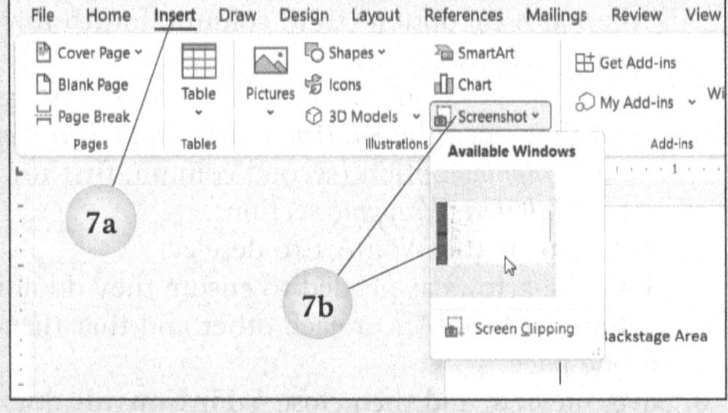

8. Press Ctrl + End and then press the Enter key. (The insertion point should be positioned below the screenshot image and at the left margin. You may need to press the Enter key again so that the insertion point is positioned at the left margin.)
9. Type Info Backstage Area at the left margin and then press the Enter key.
10. Point to the Word button on the taskbar and then click the thumbnail representing the blank document (with the Print backstage area displayed).
11. At the backstage area, click the *Info* option. (This displays the Info backstage area.)
12. Point to the Word button on the taskbar and then click the thumbnail representing **5-BackstageAreas.docx.**
13. Insert and format a screenshot of the Info backstage area by completing steps similar to those in Step 7.
14. Press Ctrl + Home to move the insertion point to the beginning of the document.
15. Save, preview, and then close **5-BackstageAreas.docx.**
16. At the Info backstage area, press the Esc key to redisplay the blank document.
17. Close the blank document.

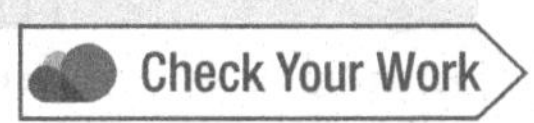

To create a screenshot of only part of the image on the screen, use the *Screen Clipping* option at the Screenshot button drop-down list. Click this option and the other open document, file, or Windows Start screen or desktop displays in a dimmed manner and the pointer displays as crosshairs. Using the mouse, draw a border around the specific area of the screen to be captured. The area identified is inserted in the other document as an image, the image is selected, and the Picture Format tab is active.

Activity 5b Inserting and Formatting a Screen Clipping

Part 2 of 2

1. Open **NSSLtrhd.docx** and then save it with the name **5-NSSCoverPages.**
2. Type the text Sample Cover Pages and then press the Enter key two times.
3. Select the text you just typed, change the font to 18-point Copperplate Gothic Bold, and then center the text.
4. Press Ctrl + End to move the insertion point below the text.
5. Open **NSSCoverPg01.docx** and then change the zoom to 50% by clicking approximately five times on the Zoom Out button at the left of the Zoom slider bar on the Status bar.
6. Point to the Word button on the taskbar and then click the thumbnail representing **5-NSSCoverPages.docx.**
7. Insert and format a screen clipping image by completing the following steps:
   a. Click the Insert tab.
   b. Click the Screenshot button and then click the *Screen Clipping* option.
   c. When **NSSCoverPg01.docx** displays in a dimmed manner, position the mouse crosshairs in the upper left corner of the cover page, click and hold down the left mouse button, drag down to the lower right corner of the cover page, and then release the mouse button. (See the image below and to the right.)
   d. With the cover page screen clipping image inserted in **5-NSSCoverPages.docx**, make sure the image is selected. (The sizing handles should appear around the cover page image.)
   e. Click the Wrap Text button in the Arrange group on the Picture Format tab and then click *Square* at the drop-down gallery.
   f. Select the current measurement in the *Shape Width* measurement box, type 3, and then press the Enter key.
   g. Click the Picture Border button arrow and then click the *Black, Text 1* option (second column, first row in the *Theme Colors* section).
8. Point to the Word button on the Taskbar and then click the thumbnail representing **NSSCoverPg01.docx.**

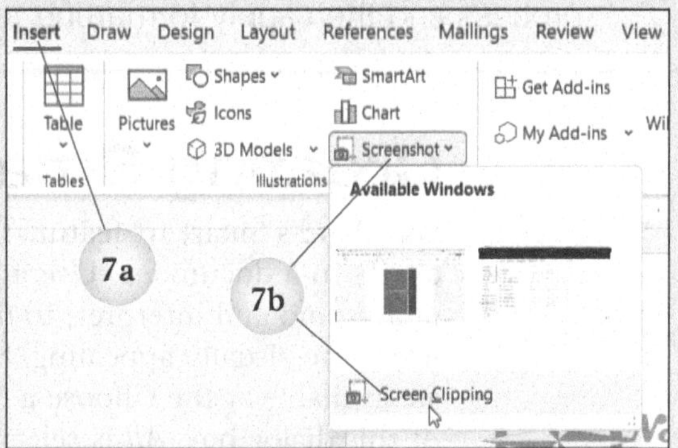

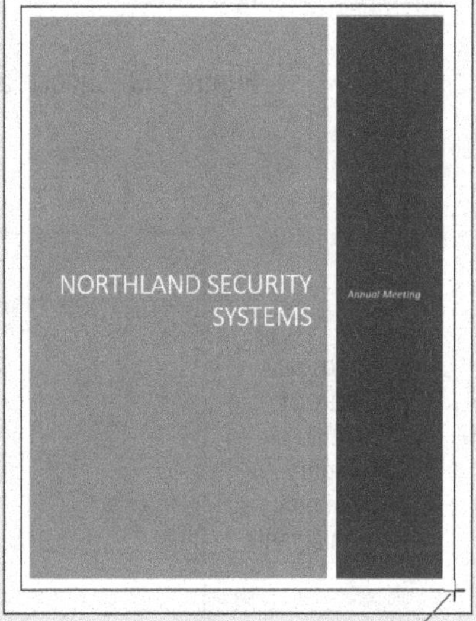

9. Close **NSSCoverPg01.docx**.
10. Open **NSSCoverPg02.docx** and then, if necessary, change the zoom to 50%.
11. Point to the Word button on the Taskbar and then click the thumbnail representing **5-NSSCoverPages.docx**.
12. Insert and format a screen clipping image of the cover page by completing steps similar to those in Step 7.
13. Using the mouse, position the two cover page screenshot images side by side in the document.
14. Save, preview, and then close **5-NSSCoverPages.docx**.
15. With **NSSCoverPg02.docx** the active document, change the zoom to 100% and then close the document.

Activity 6 Prepare and Format a SmartArt Graphic — 2 Parts

You will prepare SmartArt process graphics that identify steps in the production process and then apply formatting to enhance the graphics.

Creating SmartArt

Hint Use SmartArt to communicate your message and ideas in a visual manner.

Use Word's SmartArt feature to insert graphics, such as diagrams and organizational charts in a document. Use a SmartArt graphic to make information easier to understand and interpret, to draw attention to important information, or to make text more visually appealing. SmartArt offers a variety of predesigned graphics that are available at the Choose a SmartArt Graphic dialog box, as shown in Figure 5.3. At this dialog box, *All* is selected by default in the left panel and all the available predesigned SmartArt graphics are shown in the middle panel.

Figure 5.3 Choose a SmartArt Graphic Dialog Box

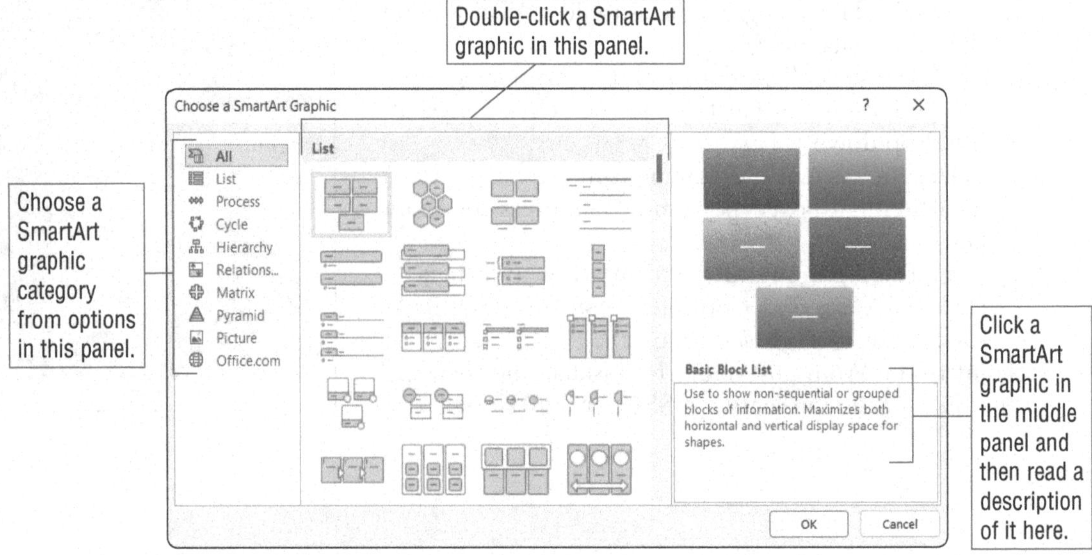

Inserting, Sizing, and Positioning SmartArt

Quick Steps

Insert SmartArt Graphic

1. Click Insert tab.
2. Click SmartArt button.
3. Double-click graphic.

Inserting a SmartArt Graphic

To insert a SmartArt graphic, click the Insert tab and then click the SmartArt button in the Illustrations group to open the Choose a SmartArt Graphic dialog box (see Figure 5.3). Predesigned SmartArt graphics are shown in the middle panel of the dialog box. Use the scroll bar at the right side of the middle panel to scroll down the list of choices. Click a graphic in the middle panel and its name displays in the right panel along with a description. SmartArt includes graphics for presenting a list of data; showing processes, cycles, and relationships; and presenting data in a matrix or pyramid. Double-click a graphic in the middle panel of the dialog box (or click the graphic and then click OK) and the graphic is inserted in the document.

When a SmartArt graphic is inserted in a document, a Text pane may appear at the left of the graphic. Type text in the Text pane or type directly in the graphic.

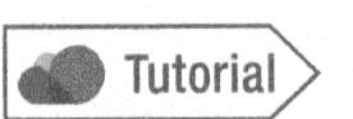

Formatting a SmartArt Graphic

Hint Limit the number of shapes and amount of text in your SmartArt graphic.

Formatting a SmartArt Graphic

Apply formatting to a SmartArt graphic with options at the SmartArt Design tab. This tab becomes active when the graphic is inserted in the document. Use options and buttons on this tab to add objects, change the graphic layout, apply a style to the graphic, and reset the graphic to the original formatting.

Formatting can also be applied to a SmartArt graphic with options on the SmartArt Format tab. Use options and buttons on this tab to change the sizes and shapes of objects in the graphic; apply shape styles and WordArt styles; change the shape fill, outline, and effects; and arrange and size the graphic.

Activity 6a Inserting and Formatting SmartArt Graphics — Part 1 of 2

1. At a blank document, insert the SmartArt graphic shown in Figure 5.4 by completing the following steps:
   a. Click the Insert tab.
   b. Click the SmartArt button in the Illustrations group.
   c. At the Choose a SmartArt Graphic dialog box, click *Process* in the left panel and then double-click the *Alternating Flow* graphic (second column, second row).
   d. If the Text pane does not display at the left of the graphic, click the Text Pane button in the Create Graphic group on the SmartArt Design tab to display it.
   e. With the insertion point positioned after the top bullet in the Text pane, type Design.
   f. Click the *[Text]* placeholder below *Design* and then type Mock-up.
   g. Continue clicking occurrences of the *[Text]* placeholder and typing text so the Text pane displays as shown at the right.
   h. Close the Text pane by clicking the Close button in the upper right corner of the pane. (You can also click the Text Pane button in the Create Graphic group.)

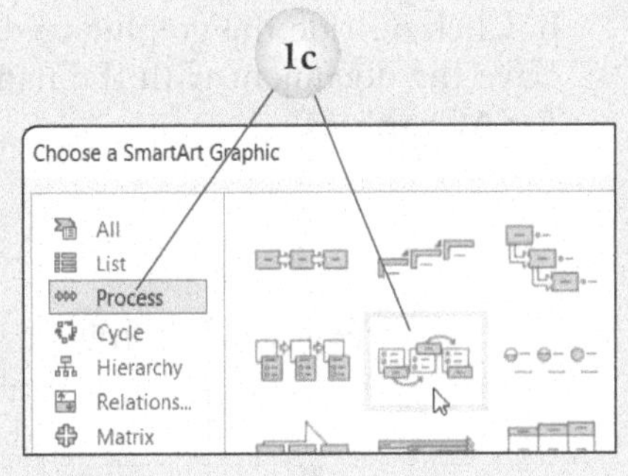

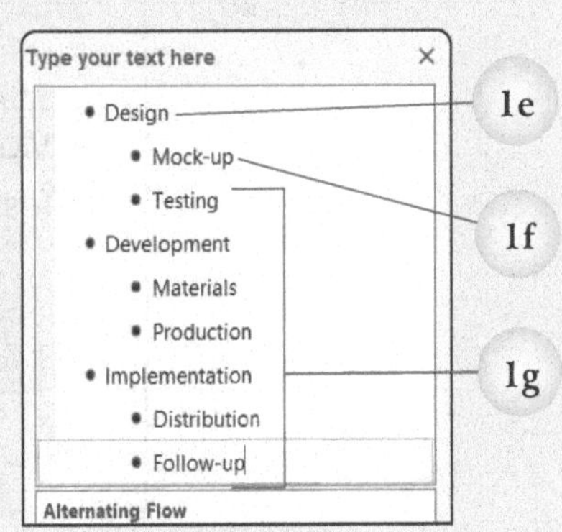

2. Change the graphic colors by clicking the Change Colors button in the SmartArt Styles group and then clicking the *Colorful Range - Accent Colors 5 to 6* option (last option in the *Colorful* section).
3. Apply a style by clicking the More SmartArt Styles button in the SmartArt Styles group and then clicking the *Inset* option (second option in the *3-D* section).

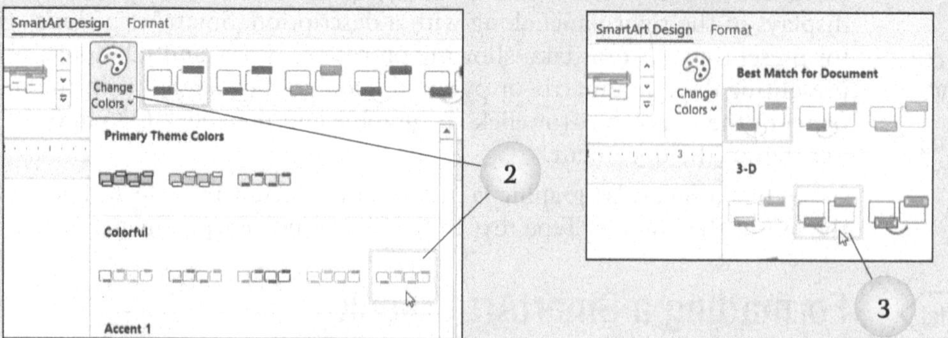

4. Copy the graphic and then change the layout by completing the following steps:
   a. Click inside the SmartArt graphic border but outside any shapes.
   b. Click the Home tab and then click the Copy button in the Clipboard group.
   c. Press Ctrl + End, press the Enter key, and then press Ctrl + Enter to insert a page break.
   d. Click the Paste button in the Clipboard group.
   e. Click inside the copied SmartArt graphic border but outside any shapes.
   f. Click the SmartArt Design tab.
   g. Click the More Layouts button in the Layouts group and then click the *Continuous Block Process* layout (second column, second row).
   h. Click outside the graphic to deselect it.
5. Save the document with the name **5-SAGraphics**.

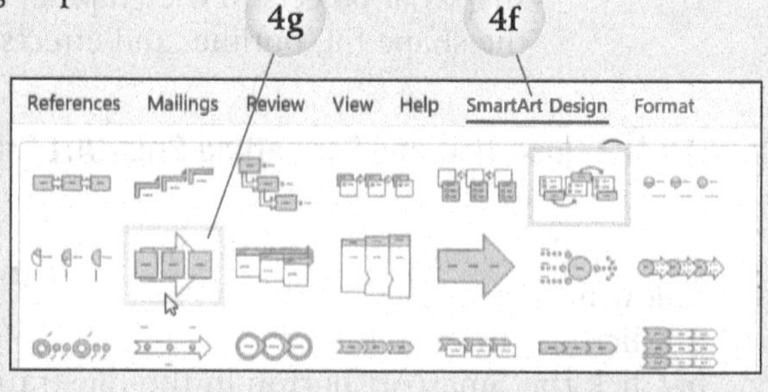

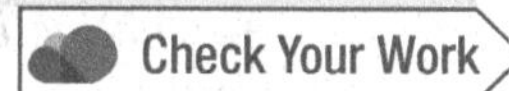

Figure 5.4 Activity 6a

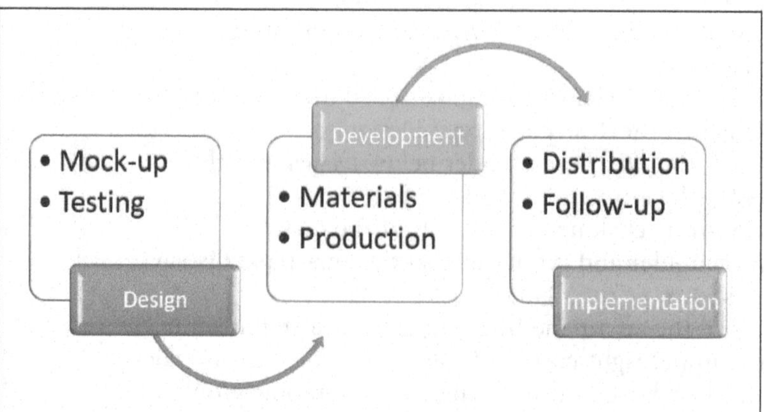

Arranging and Moving a SmartArt Graphic

Position

Wrap Text

Position a SmartArt graphic by clicking the Position button in the Arrange group on the SmartArt Format tab. Apply text wrapping to a SmartArt graphic using options in the Arrange group, with the Layout Options button, or by right-clicking the graphic and clicking *Wrap Text* at the shortcut menu.

Move a SmartArt graphic by positioning the pointer on the graphic until the pointer displays with a four-headed arrow attached, clicking and holding down the left mouse button, and then dragging the graphic to the new location. The SmartArt graphic or shapes within it can also be moved using the up, down, left, and right arrow keys on the keyboard.

Activity 6b Formatting SmartArt Graphics

Part 2 of 2

1. With **5-SAGraphics.docx** open, format shapes by completing the following steps:
   a. Click the SmartArt graphic on the first page to select it (a border surrounds the graphic).
   b. Click the SmartArt Format tab.
   c. In the SmartArt graphic, click the rectangle shape containing the word *Design*.
   d. Press and hold down the Shift key and then click the shape containing the word *Development*.
   e. With the Shift key still held down, click the shape containing the word *Implementation* and then release the Shift key. (All three shapes should now be selected.)
   f. Click the Change Shape button in the Shapes group.
   g. Click the *Arrow: Pentagon* arrow shape (seventh column, second row in the *Block Arrows* section).
   h. With the shapes still selected, click the Larger button in the Shapes group.
   i. With the shapes still selected, click the Shape Outline button arrow in the Shape Styles group and then click the *Dark Blue* color (ninth color option in the *Standard Colors* section).

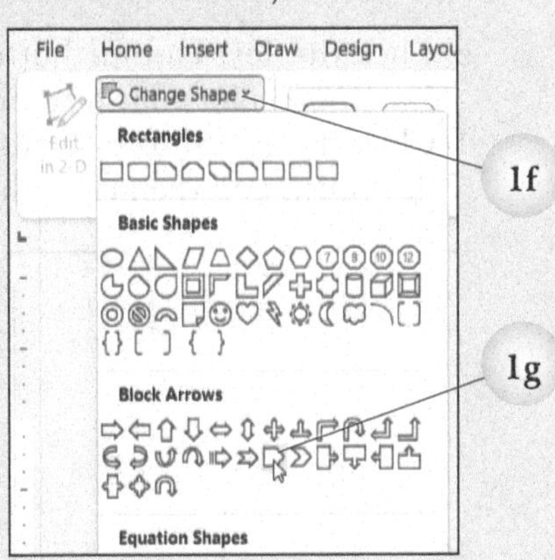

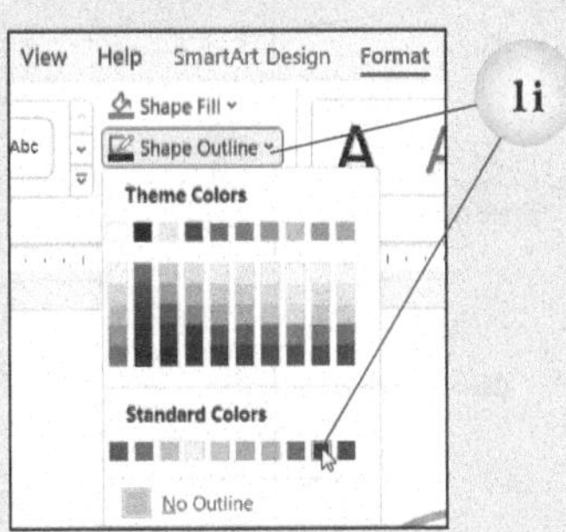

   j. Click inside the SmartArt graphic border but outside any shapes. (This deselects the shapes, but keeps the graphic selected.)
2. Click the Size button, click in the *Height* measurement box in, type 4, and then press the Enter key.

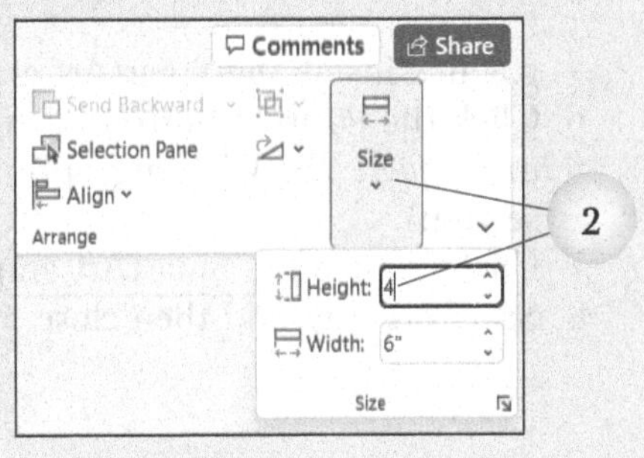

3. Click the Position button and then click the *Position in Middle Center with Square Text Wrapping* option (second column, second row in the *With Text Wrapping* section).
4. Click outside the SmartArt graphic to deselect it.
5. Format the bottom SmartArt graphic by completing the following steps:
   a. Press Ctrl + End to move to the end of the document and then click in the bottom SmartArt graphic to select it.
   b. Press and hold down the Shift key and then click each of the three shapes.
   c. Click the More WordArt Styles button in the WordArt Styles group on the SmartArt Format tab.
   d. Click the option in the first column, first row (black fill, shadow).

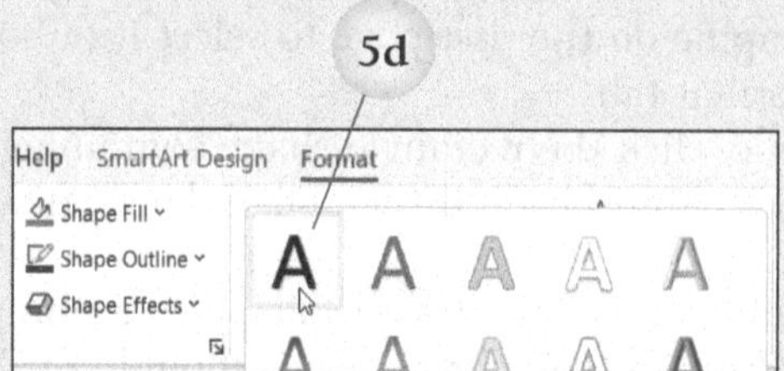

   e. Click the Text Outline button arrow in the WordArt Styles group and then click the *Dark Blue* color (ninth color option in the *Standard Colors* section).
   f. Click the Text Effects button in the WordArt Styles group, point to *Glow* at the drop-down list, and then click the *Glow: 5 point; Orange, Accent color 2* option (second column, first row).

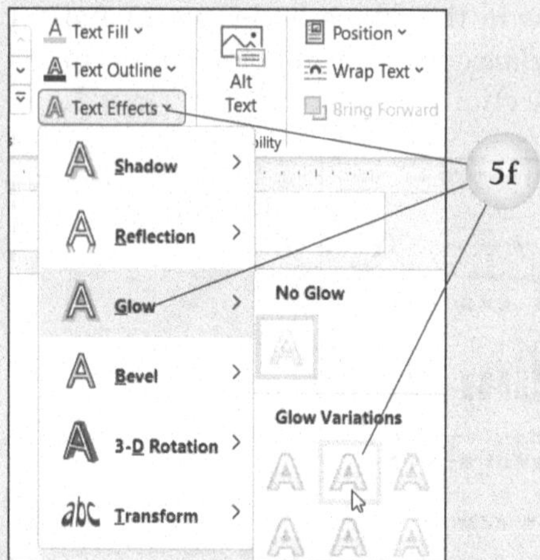

   g. Click inside the SmartArt graphic border but outside any shapes.
6. Click the Position button in the Arrange group and then click the *Position in Middle Center with Square Text Wrapping* option (second column, second row in the *With Text Wrapping* section).
7. Click outside the SmartArt graphic to deselect it.
8. Save, preview, and then close **5-SAGraphics.docx**.

Activity 7 Prepare and Format a Company Organizational Chart 1 Part

You will prepare an organizational chart for a company and then apply formatting to enhance the appearance of the chart.

Creating an Organizational Chart with SmartArt

Quick Steps

Insert Organizational Chart

1. Click Insert tab.
2. Click SmartArt button.
3. Click *Hierarchy*.
4. Double-click organizational chart.

To visually illustrate hierarchical data, consider using a SmartArt option to create an organizational chart. To display organizational chart SmartArt options, click the Insert tab and then click the SmartArt button in the Illustrations group. At the Choose a SmartArt Graphic dialog box, click *Hierarchy* in the left panel. Organizational chart options display in the middle panel of the dialog box. Double-click an organizational chart and the chart is inserted in the document. Type text in a SmartArt graphic by selecting the shape and then typing text in it or type text in the Text pane at the left of the graphic. Format a SmartArt organizational chart with options and buttons on the SmartArt Design tab and the SmartArt Format tab, and with the Layout Options button.

Activity 7 Creating and Formatting a SmartArt Organizational Chart Part 1 of 1

1. At a blank document, create the SmartArt organizational chart shown in Figure 5.5. To begin, click the Insert tab.
2. Click the SmartArt button in the Illustrations group.
3. At the Choose a SmartArt Graphic dialog box, click *Hierarchy* in the left panel of the dialog box and then double-click the *Organization Chart* option (first option in the middle panel).

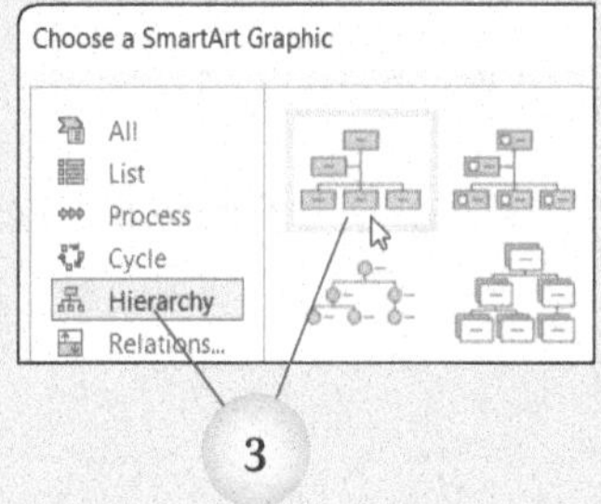

4. If the Text pane displays at the left of the organizational chart, close it by clicking the Text Pane button in the Create Graphic group.
5. Delete one of the boxes in the organizational chart by clicking the border of the box in the lower right corner to select it and then pressing the Delete key. (Make sure that the selection border surrounding the box is a solid line and not a dashed line. If a dashed line appears, click the box border again. This should change the border to a solid line.)
6. With the bottom right box selected, click the Add Shape button arrow in the Create Graphic group and then click the *Add Shape Below* option.

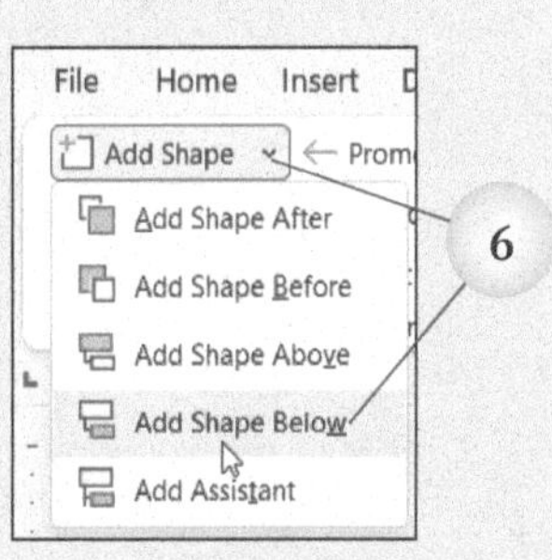

7. Click the *[Text]* placeholder in the top box, type Blaine Willis, press Shift + Enter, and then type President. Click in each of the remaining boxes and type the text as shown in Figure 5.5. (Press Shift + Enter after typing each name.)
8. Click the More SmartArt Styles button in the SmartArt Styles group and then click the *Inset* style (second option in the *3-D* section).
9. Click the Change Colors button and then click the *Colorful Range - Accent Colors 4 to 5* option (fourth option in the *Colorful* section).

10. Click the SmartArt Format tab.
11. Click the text pane control (displays with a left-pointing arrow) at the left side of the graphic border. (This displays the Text pane.)
12. Using the mouse, select all the text in the Text pane.
13. Click the Change Shape button in the Shapes group and then click the *Rectangle: Top Corners Rounded* option (eighth option in the *Rectangles* section).

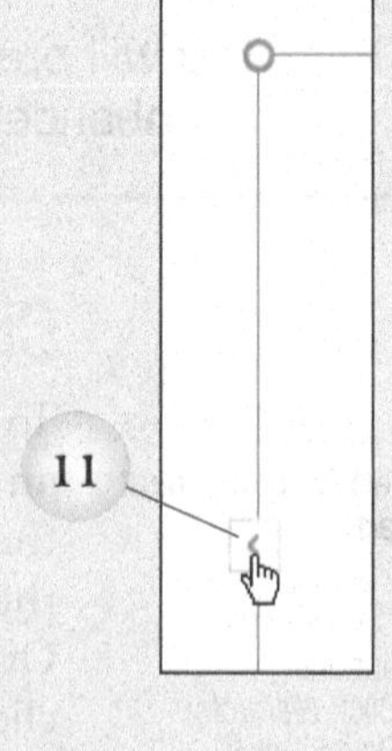

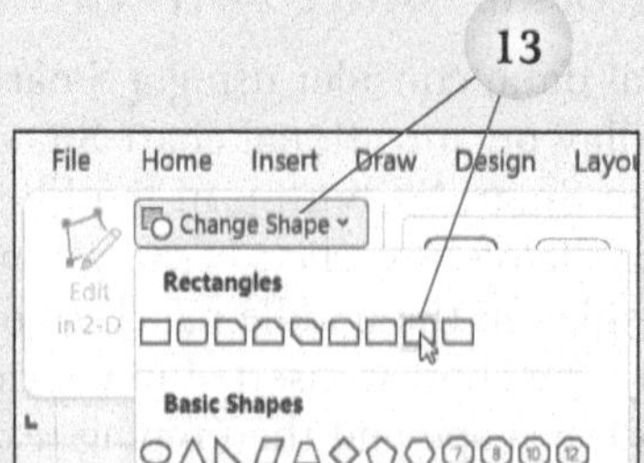

14. Click the Shape Outline button arrow in the Shape Styles group and then click the *Dark Blue* color (ninth color option in the *Standard Colors* section).
15. Close the Text pane.
16. Click inside the organizational chart border but outside any shapes.
17. Click the Size button, click in the *Height* measurement box, and then type 4.
18. Click in the *Width* measurement box, type 6.5, and then press the Enter key.
19. Click outside the organizational chart to deselect it.
20. Save the document with the name **5-OrgChart**.
21. Preview and then close **5-OrgChart.docx**.

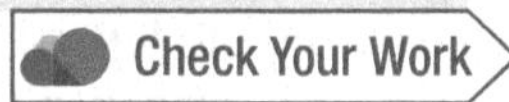

Figure 5.5 Activity 7

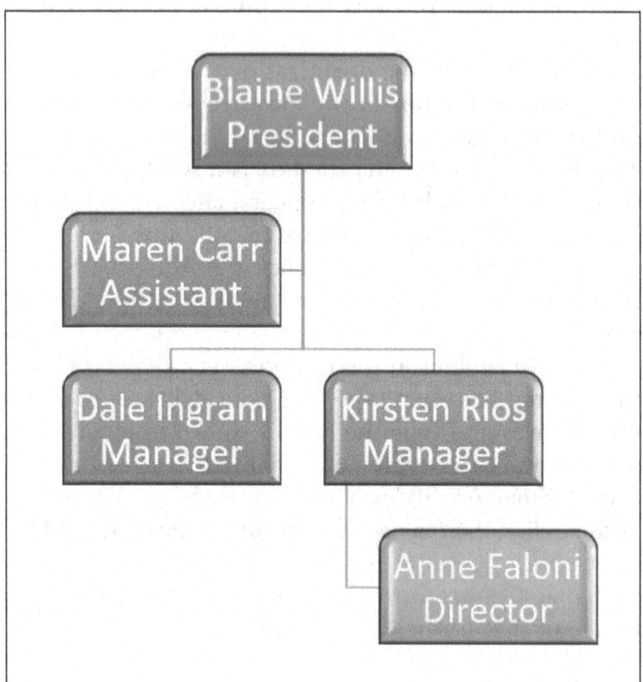

Chapter Summary

- Insert symbols with options at the Symbol dialog box with the Symbols tab selected, and insert special characters with options at the Symbol dialog box with the Special Characters tab selected.
- Click the Date & Time button in the Text group on the Insert tab to display the Date and Time dialog box. Insert the date or time with options at this dialog box or with keyboard shortcuts. If the date or time is inserted as a field, update the field by clicking the Update tab or pressing the F9 function key.
- Insert an image, such as a photo or clip art, with the Pictures button in the Illustrations group on the Insert tab.
- To insert an image from a folder on the computer's hard drive or removable storage medium, click the Insert tab, click the Pictures button in the Illustrations group, and then click the *This Device* option at the drop-down list. At the Insert Picture dialog box, navigate to the specific folder and then double-click the image file.
- To insert a stock image available from Microsoft 365, click the Insert tab, click the Pictures button, and then click *Stock Images* at the drop-down list. At the window that displays, chose an image, click a category and then chose an image, or search for a specific image and then click the image. Click the Insert button and then close the Close button to close the window. You can also double-click an image and then click the Close button to close the stock images window.
- To insert an online image, click the Insert tab, click the Pictures button, and then click *Online Pictures* at the drop-down list. At the Online Pictures window, type the search text or topic and then press the Enter key. Click an image to select it and then click the Insert button.
- Use the *Shape Height* and *Shape Width* measurement boxes in the Size group on the Picture Format tab to change the size of an image. The size of an image can also be changed with the sizing handles around a selected image.
- Use the Crop button in the Size group to remove unnecessary parts of an image. To crop an image, click the Crop button and then use the crop handles to specify what part of the image should be cropped.
- The Arrange group on the Picture Format tab contains buttons for positioning, aligning, and rotating text.
- Use the Wrap Text button in the Arrange group to specify how text or other objects should wrap around a selected image. The Layout Options button that displays outside the upper right corner of a selected image can also be used to specify text wrapping.
- Move an image using options at the Position button drop-down gallery on the Picture Format tab or by choosing a text wrapping style and then moving the image by dragging it with the mouse.
- Rotate a selected image using the pointer on the rotation handle (circular arrow) that appears above the image.
- The Adjust group on the Picture Format tab contains buttons for adjusting the background, color, brightness, and contrast of an image. An artistic effect can be applied to a selected image using the Artistic Effects button in the Adjust group. Use the *Set Transparent Color* option at the Color button drop-down gallery to make a color transparent in the selected image. Adjust the transparency of an image with options at the Transparency button drop-down gallery.

- Apply a predesigned picture style to a selected image with styles in the Picture Styles group on the Picture Format tab.
- Create alternative text to describe images in a document for readers with visual impairments. Type a description of an image at the Alt Text task pane. Display this task pane by clicking the Alt Text button on the Picture Format tab or right-clicking an image and then clicking *Edit Alt Text* at the shortcut menu.
- Click the Text Box button in the Text group on the Insert tab to display a drop-down list of predesigned text boxes (text boxes that already contain formatting) that can be inserted in a document.
- Draw a text box by clicking the Text Box button in the Text group on the Insert tab, clicking the *Draw Text Box* option at the drop-down list, and then clicking or dragging in the document.
- Customize a text box with options on the Shape Format tab.
- Draw shapes in a document by clicking the Shapes button in the Illustrations group on the Insert tab, clicking a shape at the drop-down list, and then clicking or dragging in the document to draw the shape. Customize a shape with options on the Shape Format tab.
- Copy a selected shape by clicking the Copy button in the Clipboard group on the Home tab, positioning the insertion point in the new location, and then clicking the Paste button. Another method for copying a selected shape is to press and hold down the Ctrl key while dragging the selected shape.
- Use WordArt to distort or modify text to conform to a variety of shapes. Customize WordArt with options on the Shape Format tab.
- Use the Screenshot button in the Illustrations group on the Insert tab to capture part or all of a window visible on the screen. Use buttons on the Picture Format tab to customize a screenshot image.
- Use the SmartArt feature to insert predesigned graphics and organizational charts in a document. Click the SmartArt button in the Illustrations group on the Insert tab to display the Choose a SmartArt Graphic dialog box containing a variety of graphics.
- Format a SmartArt graphic with options and buttons on the SmartArt Design tab and the SmartArt Format tab.
- Position a SmartArt graphic by clicking the Position button in the Arrange group on the SmartArt Format tab and then clicking a position option at the drop-down gallery.
- Specify how text or other objects should wrap around a SmartArt graphic with options at the Wrap Text button drop-down gallery. The Layout Options button that appears outside the upper right corner of the selected SmartArt graphic can also be used to specify text wrapping.
- Move a selected SmartArt graphic by dragging it with the mouse or using the up, down, left, and right arrow keys on the keyboard. Before moving a SmartArt graphic, apply text wrapping.
- Use a SmartArt option to create an organizational chart, which is a visual illustration of hierarchical data.

Commands Review

FEATURE	RIBBON TAB, GROUP	BUTTON, OPTION	KEYBOARD SHORTCUT
Alt Text task pane	Picture Format, Accessibility		
Choose a SmartArt Graphic dialog box	Insert, Illustrations		
Date and Time dialog box	Insert, Text		
insert date as field			Alt + Shift + D
Insert Picture dialog box	Insert, Illustrations	, *This Device*	
insert time as field			Alt + Shift + T
predesigned text box	Insert, Text		
screenshot	Insert, Illustrations		
shapes	Insert, Illustrations		
Symbol dialog box	Insert, Symbols	, *More Symbols*	
text box	Insert, Text		
update field			F9
WordArt	Insert, Text		

Review and Assessment

CHAPTER 5

Skills Assessment

Assessment 1 Add Visual Interest to a Report on Intellectual Property

1. Open **ProtectIssues.docx** and then save it with the name **5-ProtectIssues**.
2. Insert the **Hackers.png** image file from your WL1C5 folder. (Do this at the Insert Picture dialog box. Display this dialog box by clicking the Insert tab, clicking the Pictures button, and then clicking the *This Device* option at the drop-down list.)
3. Format the image with the following specifications:
   a. Change the height to 1 inch.
   b. Change the color of the image to Blue, Accent color 1 Light (second column, third row in the *Recolor* section).
   c. Correct the contrast to Brightness: 0% (Normal) Contrast: +20% (third column, fourth row in the *Brightness/Contrast* section).
   d. Change the position of the image to Position in Middle Left with Square Text Wrapping (first column, second row in the *With Text Wrapping* section).
   e. Use the Rotate Objects button in the Arrange group to flip the image horizontally.
4. Move the insertion point to the beginning of the paragraph immediately below the heading *Intellectual Property Protection* (on the second page). Insert the Austin Quote text box and then make the following customizations:
   a. Type the following text in the text box: "Plagiarism may be punished by law, and in many educational institutions it can result in suspension or even expulsion."
   b. Select the text and then change the font size to 11 points.
   c. Change the width of the text box to 2.8 inches.
   d. Change the position of the text box to Position in Top Center with Square Text Wrapping (second column, first row in the *With Text Wrapping* section).
5. Move the insertion point to the end of the document, insert the Plaque shape (tenth column, second row in the *Basic Shapes* section) at the location of the insertion point, and then make the following customizations:
   a. Change the shape height to 1.4 inches and the shape width to 3.9 inches.
   b. Use the Align button in the Arrange group to distribute the shape horizontally.
   c. Apply the Subtle Effect - Blue, Accent 1 shape style (second column, fourth row).
   d. Type the text Felicité Compagnie inside the shape. Insert the *é* symbol at the Symbol dialog box with the *(normal text)* font selected.
   e. Use options at the Date and Time dialog box to insert the current date below *Felicité Compagnie* and the current time below the date. Make sure the date and time will not update automatically.
   f. Select the text in the shape, change the font size to 14 points, and then apply bold formatting.
6. Save, preview, and then close **5-ProtectIssues.docx**.

Assessment 2

Create a Sales Meeting Announcement

1. At a blank document, press the Enter key two times and then create WordArt with the following specifications:
   a. Insert WordArt with the option in the first column, third row of the WordArt button drop-down list (black fill, white outline, blue hard shadow) and then type Inlet Corporation in the WordArt text box.
   b. Change the width of the WordArt text box to 6.5 inches.
   c. Use the *Transform* option from the Text Effects button in the WordArt Styles group to apply the Chevron: Up text effect (first column, second row in the *Warp* section) to the WordArt text.
2. Press Ctrl + End and then press the Enter key three times. Change the font to 18-point Candara, apply bold formatting, change to center alignment, and then type the following text, pressing the Enter key after each line of text except the fourth line:

   National Sales Meeting
   Pacific Division
   Ocean View Resort
   May 13 through May 15, 2024
3. Insert the **Ocean.jpg** image file from your WL1C5 folder and then make the following changes to the image:
   a. Crop approximately 1 inch off the bottom of the image.
   b. Apply the Brightness: 0% (Normal) Contrast: +20% correction (third column, fourth row in the *Brightness/Contrast* section).
   c. Apply the Compound Frame, Black picture style (fourth column, second row in the Picture Styles gallery).
   d. Change the position of the image to Position in Top Center with Square Text Wrapping (second column, first row in the *With Text Wrapping* section).
   e. Change text wrapping to Behind Text.
4. Save the announcement document with the name **5-SalesMtg**.
5. Preview and then close **5-SalesMtg.docx**.

Assessment 3

Create an Announcement

1. Open **FirstAidCourse.docx** and then save it with the name **5-FirstAidCourse**.
2. Format the announcement as shown in Figure 5.6. Insert the **FirstAid.png** image file from your WL1C5 folder with the following specifications:
   a. Change the text wrapping to Tight.
   b. Change the image color to Blue, Accent color 5 Light (sixth column, third row in the *Recolor* section).
   c. Correct the brightness and contrast to Brightness: 0% (Normal) Contrast: +40% (third column, bottom row in the *Brightness/Contrast* section).
   d. Size and move the image as shown in the figure.
3. Apply paragraph shading, insert the page border, and add period leaders to the right tab, as shown in Figure 5.6.
4. Save, preview, and then close **5-FirstAidCourse.docx**. (If printing the document and some of the page border does not print, consider increasing the measurements at the Border and Shading Options dialog box.)

Figure 5.6 Assessment 3

First Aid at Work

The Safety Committee is offering a two-day first aid course for employees. The objective of the course is to equip employees with the essential knowledge and practical experience to enable them to carry out first aid in the workplace. Course content includes health and safety administration, handling an incident and developing an action plan, recognizing and treating injuries and illnesses, and cardio-pulmonary resuscitation (CPR).

Dates .... March 4 and 5

Times.. 9:00 a.m. to 4:30 p.m.

Location .... Administration Building

Room.. Conference Room 200

Registration is available from February 12 until the course begins on March 4. Before registering, please check with your immediate supervisor to ensure that you can be excused from your normal duties for the two days.

For more information, contact Maxwell Singh at extension 3505.

Assessment 4 Insert Screen Clippings in a Memo

1. Open **FirstAidMemo.docx** and then save it with the name **5-FirstAidMemo**.
2. Insert and format screen clippings so that your document appears as shown in Figure 5.7. Use the document **FirstAidAnnounce.docx** to create the first screen clipping, and use the document **5-FirstAidCourse.docx** you created in Assessment 3 for the second screen clipping. ***Hint: Decrease the display percentage of the document so the entire document is visible on the screen.***
3. Move the insertion point below the screen clipping images and then insert the text as shown in the figure. Insert your initials in place of the *XX*.
4. Save, preview, and then close **5-FirstAidMemo.docx**.

Figure 5.7 Assessment 4

DATE:	January 10, 2024
TO:	Carmen Singleton
FROM:	Maxwell Singh
SUBJECT:	FIRST AID COURSE ANNOUNCEMENTS

As you requested, I have created two announcements for the first aid course in March. Please review the two announcements shown below and let me know which one you prefer.

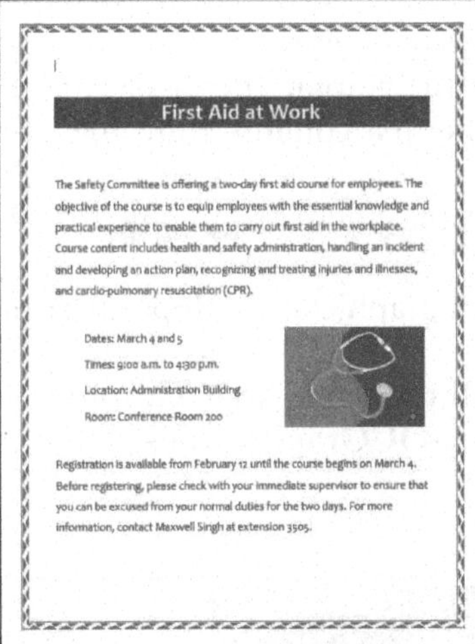

First Aid at Work

The Safety Committee is offering a two-day first aid course for employees. The objective of the course is to equip employees with the essential knowledge and practical experience to enable them to carry out first aid in the workplace. Course content includes health and safety administration, handling an incident and developing an action plan, recognizing and treating injuries and illnesses, and cardio-pulmonary resuscitation (CPR).

Dates: March 4 and 5

Times: 9:00 a.m. to 4:30 p.m.

Location: Administration Building

Room: Conference Room 200

Registration is available from February 12 until the course begins on March 4. Before registering, please check with your immediate supervisor to ensure that you can be excused from your normal duties for the two days. For more information, contact Maxwell Singh at extension 3505.

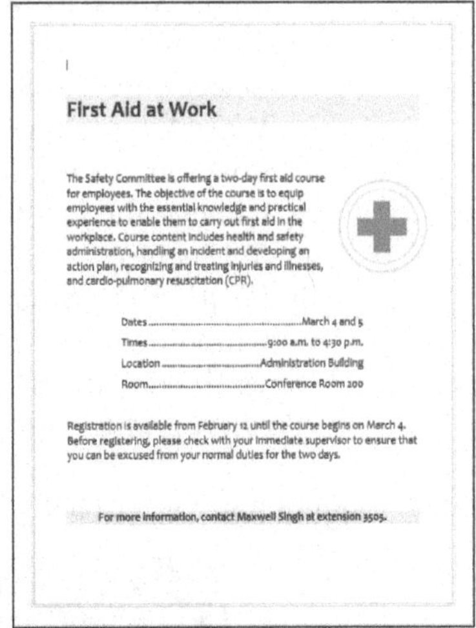

First Aid at Work

The Safety Committee is offering a two-day first aid course for employees. The objective of the course is to equip employees with the essential knowledge and practical experience to enable them to carry out first aid in the workplace. Course content includes health and safety administration, handling an incident and developing an action plan, recognizing and treating injuries and illnesses, and cardio-pulmonary resuscitation (CPR).

Dates .... March 4 and 5
Times .... 9:00 a.m. to 4:30 p.m.
Location .... Administration Building
Room .... Conference Room 200

Registration is available from February 12 until the course begins on March 4. Before registering, please check with your immediate supervisor to ensure that you can be excused from your normal duties for the two days.

For more information, contact Maxwell Singh at extension 3505.

XX
5-FirstAidMemo.docx

Assessment 5 Create and Format a Company SmartArt Graphic

1. At a blank document, create the SmartArt graphic shown in Figure 5.8 with the following specifications:
   a. Use the Titled Matrix SmartArt graphic (second option in the *Matrix* group).
   b. Apply the Colorful - Accent Colors SmartArt style (first option in the *Colorful* section).
   c. Apply the Polished SmartArt style (first option in the *3-D* section).
   d. With the middle shape selected, apply the Intense Effect - Green, Accent 6 shape style. (Click the SmartArt Format tab, click the More Shape Styles button in the Shape Styles group, and then click the last option in the *Theme Styles* section.)
   e. Type all the text shown in Figure 5.8.
   f. Select only the SmartArt graphic (not a specific shape) and then apply the WordArt option in the first column, third row of the WordArt button drop-down list to the text.
   g. Change the height of the SmartArt graphic to 3.2 inches and the width to 5.3 inches.
   h. Position the SmartArt graphic at the top center of the page with square text wrapping.
2. Save the document with the name **5-OCGraphic**.
3. Preview and then close **5-OCGraphic.docx**.

Figure 5.8 Assessment 5

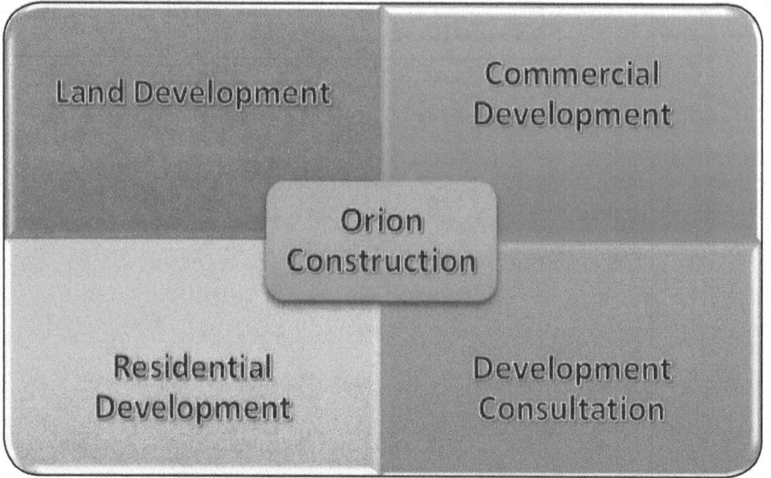

Assessment 6

Create and Format a Company Organizational Chart

1. At a blank document, create the organizational chart shown in Figure 5.9 with the following specifications:
   a. Use the Hierarchy SmartArt graphic (second column, second row with *Hierarchy* selected in the left panel).
   b. With the top text box selected, add a shape above it.
   c. Select the text box at the right in the third row and then add a shape below it.
   d. Type the text shown in the organizational chart in Figure 5.4.
   e. Apply the Colorful Range - Accent Colors 3 to 4 SmartArt style (third option in the *Colorful* section).
   f. Increase the height to 4.5 inches and the width to 6.5 inches.
   g. Position the organizational chart in the middle of the page with square text wrapping.
2. Save the document with the name **5-CoOrgChart**.
3. Preview and then close **5-CoOrgChart.docx**.

Figure 5.9 Assessment 6

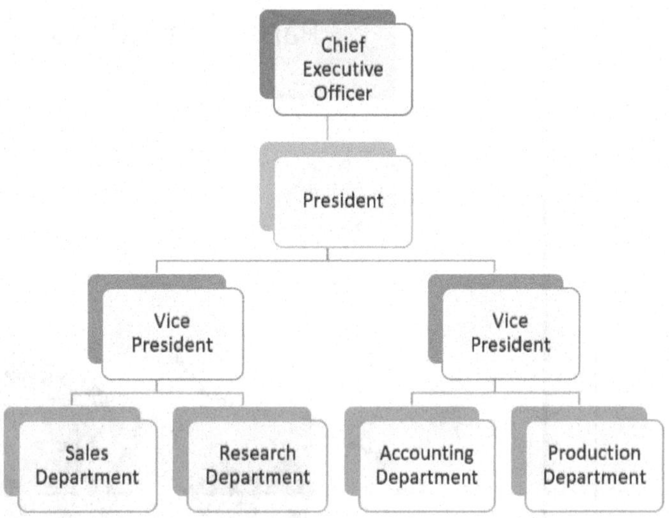

Visual Benchmark

Activity 1

Create a Flyer

1. Create the flyer shown in Figure 5.10 with the following specifications:
   - Create the title *Pugs on Parade!* as WordArt using the option in the first column, first row in the WordArt button drop-down list. Change the width to 6.5 inches, apply the Warp Up transform effect (third column, fourth row in the *Warp* section), and then change the text fill color to standard dark red.
   - Create the shape containing the text *Admission is free!* using the Explosion: 8 Points shape (first column, first row in the *Stars and Banners* section of the Shapes button drop-down list).
   - Insert the **Pug.jpg** image file from your WL1C5 folder. Change the text wrapping for the image to Behind Text and then size and position the image as shown in the figure.

- Create the line above the last line of text as a top border. Change the color to standard dark red and the width to 3 points.
- Make any other changes so your document appears similar to Figure 5.10.

2. Save the document with the name **5-PugFlyer**.
3. Preview and then close **5-PugFlyer.docx**.

Figure 5.10 Visual Benchmark 1

Pugs on Parade!

Come join us for the sixth annual "Pugs on Parade" party, Saturday, July 27, at Mercer Way Park from 1:00 to 3:30 p.m.

Prizes awarded for the best costumes.

Activity 2

Format a Report

1. Open **Resume.docx** and then save it with the name **5-Resume**.
2. Format the report so it appears as shown in Figure 5.11 with the following specifications:
   a. Insert the WordArt text *Résumé Writing* with the following specifications:
      - Use the option in the first column, third row of the WordArt button drop-down list.
      - Type the text Résumé Writing and insert the *é* symbol using the Symbol dialog box.
      - Change the position to Position in Top Center with Square Text Wrapping.
      - Change the width of the WordArt to 5.5 inches.
      - Apply the Warp Up transform text effect (third column, fourth row in the *Warp* section).

   b. Insert the pull quote with the following specifications:
      - Use the Motion Quote text box.
      - Type the text shown in the pull quote text box in Figure 5.11. (Use the Symbol dialog box to insert the two *é* symbols in the word *résumé*.)
      - Select the text box and then change the font size of the text to 11 points.
      - Change the width of the text box to 2.3 inches.
      - Position the text box in the middle center with square text wrapping.

   c. Insert the cake image with the following specifications:
      - Insert the **Cake.png** image file from your WL1C5 folder.
      - Change the width to 1.2 inches.
      - Change the text wrapping to Tight.
      - Position the cake image as shown in Figure 5.11.
3. Save, preview, and then close **5-Resume.docx**.

Activity 3

Create and Format a SmartArt Graphic

1. At a blank document, create the document shown in Figure 5.12 (on page 195). Create and format the SmartArt graphic as shown in the figure. ***Hint: Use the* Step Up Process *graphic*.** Change the width of the SmartArt graphic to 6.5 inches. (Bold the white text with the dark blue paragraph shading. When formatting the SmartArt, you will need to change the colors of each shape separately.)
2. Save the completed document with the name **5-SalesGraphic**.
3. Preview and then close **5-SalesGraphic.docx**.

Figure 5.11 Visual Benchmark 2

Résumé Writing

To produce the best "fitting" résumé, you need to know about yourself, and you need to know about the job you are applying for. Before you do anything else, ask yourself why you are preparing a résumé. The answer to this question is going to vary from one person to the next, and here are our top ten reasons for writing a résumé:

1. You have seen a job that appeals to you advertised in the paper.
2. You want to market yourself to win a contract or a proposal or be elected to a committee or organization.
3. You have seen a job that appeals to you on an internet job site.
4. Your friends or family told you of a job opening at a local company.
5. You want to work for the local company and thought that sending a résumé to them might get their attention.
6. You have seen a job advertised internally at work.
7. You are going for a promotion.
8. You are feeling fed up and writing down all your achievements will cheer you up and might motivate you to look for a better job.
9. You are thinking "Oh, so that's a résumé! I suppose I ought to try to remember what I've been doing with my life."
10. Your company is about to be downsized and you want to update your résumé to be ready for any good opportunities.

All these certainly are good reasons to write a résumé, but the résumé serves many different purposes. One way of seeing the different purposes is to ask yourself who is going to read the résumé in each case.

Résumés 1 through 5 will be read by potential employers who probably do not know you. Résumés 6 and 7 are likely to be read by your boss or other people who know you. Résumés 8 through 10 are really for your own benefit and should not be considered as suitable for sending out to employers.

The Right Mix

Think about the list of reasons again. How else can you divide up these reasons? An important difference is that, in some cases, you will have a good idea of what the employer is looking for because you have a job advertisement in front of you and can tailor your résumé accordingly. For others, you have no idea what the reader might want to see.

"Updating your résumé from time to time is a good idea so you do not forget important details..."

Updating your résumé from time to time is a good idea so you do not forget important details but remember that the result of such a process will not be a winning résumé. It will be a useful list of tasks and achievements.

Writing a résumé is like baking a cake. You need all the right ingredients: flour, butter, eggs, and so on. It is what you do with the ingredients that makes the difference between a great résumé (or cake) and failure.

Keeping your résumé up-to-date is like keeping a stock of ingredients in the pantry—it is potentially very useful, but do not imagine that is the end of it!

Figure 5.12 Visual Benchmark 3

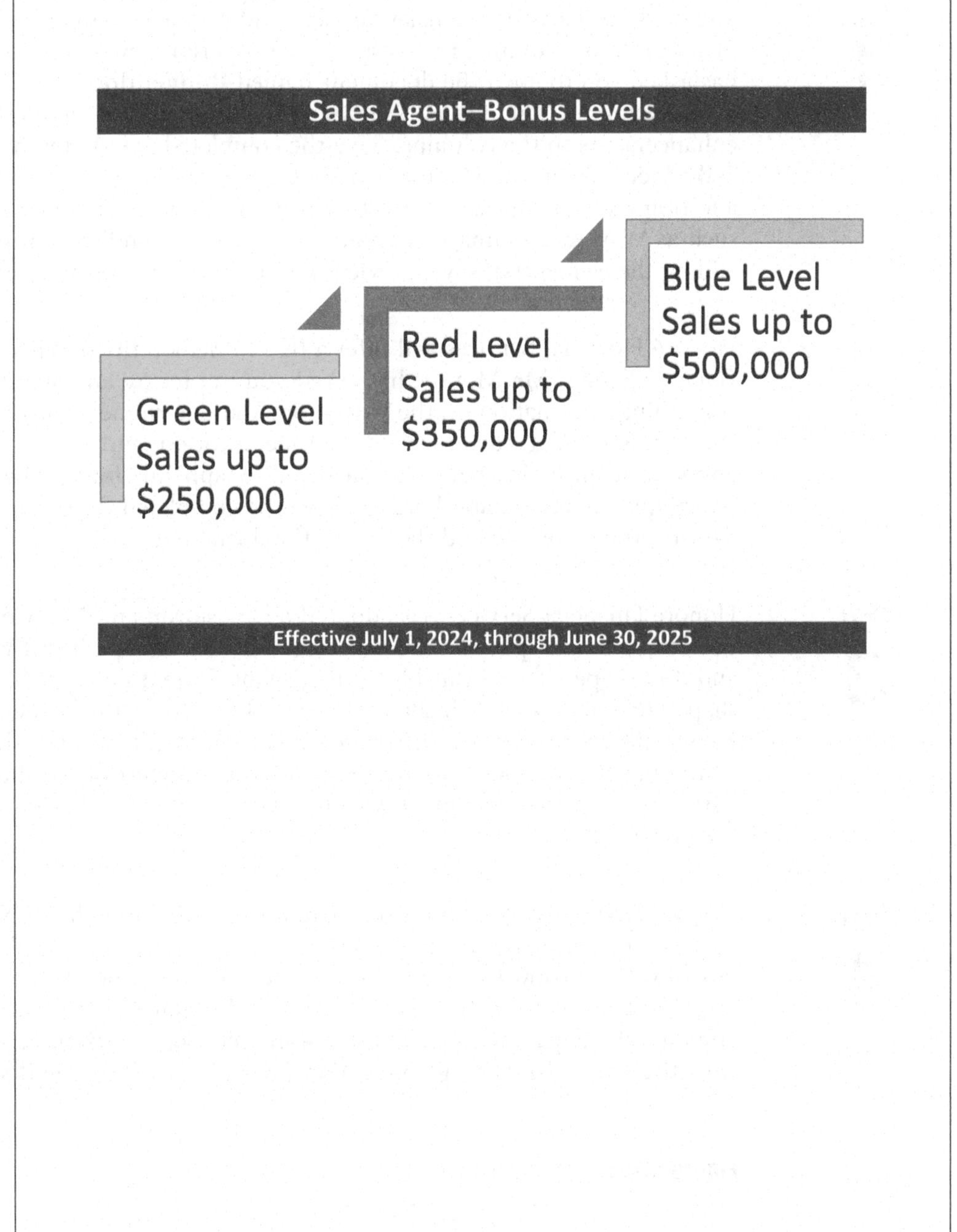

Case Study

Part 1

You work for Honoré Financial Services and have been asked by the office manager, Jason Monroe, to prepare an information newsletter. Mr. Monroe has asked you to open the document named **Budget.docx** and then format it into columns. You are to decide the number of columns and any additional enhancements to the columns. Save the completed newsletter, naming it **5-Budget**. When Mr. Monroe reviews the newsletter, he decides that it needs additional visual appeal. He wants you to insert visual elements in the newsletter, such as WordArt, an image, a predesigned text box, and/or a drop cap. After adding the element(s), save, preview, and then close **5-Budget.docx**.

Part 2

Honoré Financial Services will offer a free workshop titled *Planning for Financial Success*. Mr. Monroe has asked you to prepare an announcement containing information on the workshop. You determine what to include in the announcement, such as the date, time, location, and so forth. Enhance the announcement by inserting an image and by applying formatting such as font, paragraph alignment, and borders. Save the completed document with the name **5-Announce**. Preview and then close the document.

Part 3

Honoré Financial Services has adopted a new slogan and Mr. Monroe has asked you to create a shape with the new slogan inside it. Experiment with the shadow and 3-D shape effects available on the Shape Format tab and then create a shape and enhance it with shadow and/or 3-D effects. Insert the new Honoré Financial Services slogan, *Retirement Planning Made Easy*, in the shape. Include any additional enhancements to improve the visual interest of the shape and slogan. Save the completed document with the name **5-Slogan**. Preview and then close the document.

Part 4

Mr. Monroe has asked you to prepare an organization chart that will become part of the company profile. Create a SmartArt organizational chart using the position titles shown in Figure 5.13. Use the order and structure in Figure 5.13 to guide the layout of the SmartArt chart. Format the organizational chart to enhance the appearance. Save the completed organizational chart document with the name **5-HFSOrgChart**. Preview and then close the document.

Figure 5.13 Case Study, Part 4

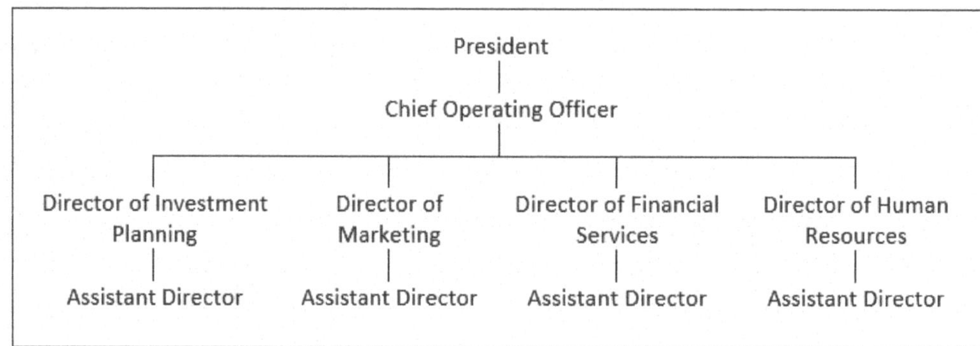

Part 5

Mr. Monroe has asked you to prepare a document containing information on teaching children how to budget. Use the internet to find websites and articles that provide information on this topic. Write a synopsis of the information and include at least four suggestions for teaching children to manage their money. Format the text into newspaper columns. Add additional enhancements to improve the appearance of the document. Save the completed document with the name **5-ChildBudget**. Preview and then close the document.

WORD

CHAPTER 6

Managing Documents

Performance Objectives

Upon successful completion of Chapter 6, you will be able to:

1. Change the view of a document
2. Use learning tools to aid reading fluency and comprehension
3. Change page movement, display percentage, and ribbon display options
4. Hide and show white space
5. Split a window, view documents side by side, and open a new window
6. Insert a file into an open document
7. Preview and print specific text and pages in a document
8. Prepare and print envelopes and labels
9. Create a document using a template
10. Save documents in different file formats
11. Save a template and open a template using File Explorer

Word provides a number of options for managing documents, including customizing the document view, using learning tools, changing the display and display percentage, and changing ribbon display options. Managing documents can also include working with windows and performing such actions as arranging windows, splitting windows, viewing documents side by side, and opening a new window. In this chapter, you will learn these techniques, as well as saving documents in different file formats and saving and opening a template. You will also learn how to create and print envelopes and labels.

Data Files

The data files for this chapter are in the WL1C6 folder that you downloaded at the beginning of this course.

Activity 1 Change Views and Display and Use Immersive Options in a Report on Navigating and Searching the Web — 3 Parts

You will open a document on navigating and searching the web, change the document view, use immersive reader options, change page movement to side to side, change display percentages, and hide and show white space at the tops and bottoms of pages.

Changing Document Views

Changing the Document View

By default, a Word document displays in Print Layout view. This view displays the document on the screen as it will appear when printed. Other views are available, such as Draft and Read Mode. Change views with buttons in the view area on the Status bar (see Figure 6.1) or with options on the View tab.

Displaying a Document in Draft View

Draft

Change to Draft view and the document displays in a format for efficient editing and formatting. In this view, margins and other features such as headers and footers do not appear on the screen. Change to Draft view by clicking the View tab and then clicking the Draft button in the Views group.

Displaying a Document in Web Layout View

To see what a document would look like as a web page, click the Web Layout button on the View tab or click the Web Layout button on the Status bar. In Web Layout view, the document margins are wider; this can be useful for viewing objects such as tables and graphics.

Displaying a Document in Read Mode View

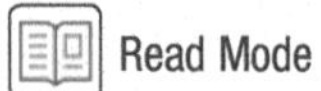

Read Mode view displays a document in a format for easy viewing and reading. Change to Read Mode view by clicking the Read Mode button in the view area on the Status bar or by clicking the View tab and then clicking the Read Mode button in the Views group. Navigate in Read Mode view using the keys on the keyboard, as shown in Table 6.1. Another way to navigate in Read Mode is to click the Next and Previous arrow buttons at the right and left sides of the screen to page forward and backward through the document.

The File, Tools, and View tabs appear in the upper left corner of the screen in Read Mode view. Click the File tab to display the backstage area. Click the Tools tab and a drop-down list displays with options for finding specific text in the document, searching for information on the internet, and translating text in the document.

Figure 6.1 View Buttons and the Zoom Slider Bar

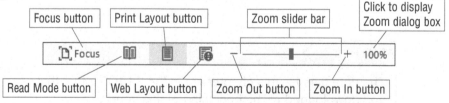

Focus button
Print Layout button
Zoom slider bar
Click to display Zoom dialog box
Focus
100%
Read Mode button
Web Layout button
Zoom Out button
Zoom In button

Table 6.1 Keyboard Commands in Read Mode View

Press this key	To complete this action
Page Down key, Right Arrow key, or spacebar	display next two pages
Page Up key, Left Arrow key, or Backspace key	display previous two pages
Home	display first page in document
End	display last page in document
Esc	return to previous view

Click the View tab to customize Read Mode view. Use View tab options to switch to Focus Mode, display the Navigation pane to navigate to specific locations in the document, or to show comments inserted in the document. The View tab also includes options for making text more readable by changing column width, page color, and page layout; showing syllable breaks; increasing spacing between characters, words, and lines; and hearing text read aloud. These options are also available on the Immersive Reader tab, described on the next page.

If a document contains an object such as a table, SmartArt graphic, image, or shape, zoom in on the object in Read Mode view by double-clicking it. The display size of the object increases and a button containing a magnifying glass with a plus symbol inside (🔍) appears just outside the upper right corner of the object. Click the magnifying glass to zoom in and out. Click outside the object to exit the zoom view. To close Read Mode view and return to the previous view, press the Esc key or click the View tab and then click *Edit Document* at the drop-down list.

Activity 1a Changing Views

Part 1 of 3

1. Open **WebReport.docx** and then save it with the name **6-WebReport**.
2. Display the document in Draft view by clicking the View tab and then clicking the Draft button in the Views group.

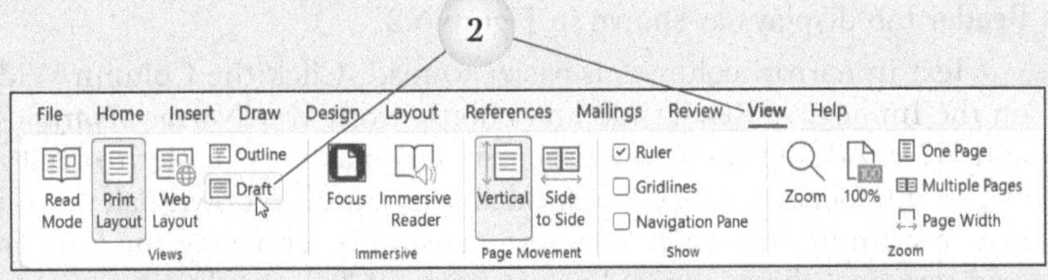

3. Click the Web Layout button in the Views group to display the document as it would appear if published as a web page.
4. Display the document in Read Mode view by clicking the Read Mode button in the view area on the Status bar.

5. If a speaker is connected to your computer, have the text read out loud by clicking the View tab and then clicking the *Read Aloud* option at the drop-down list. After listening for a short period of time, turn off the reading by clicking the View tab and then clicking the *Read Aloud* option.
6. Increase the display size of the table at the right side of the screen by double-clicking the table. (If the table is not visible, click the Next button at the right side of the screen to view the next page.)
7. Click the button containing a magnifying glass with a plus symbol that displays outside the upper right corner of the table. (This increases the zoom.)

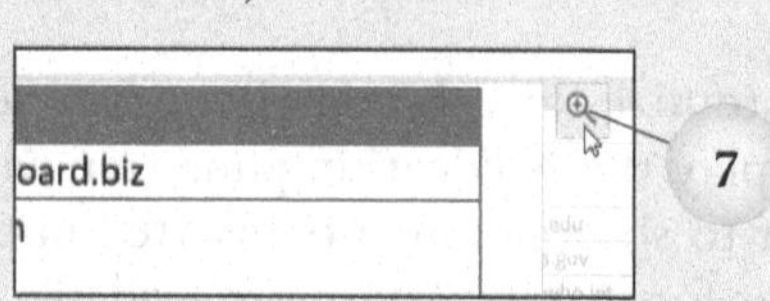

8. Click outside the table to return it to the original display size.
9. Practice navigating in Read Mode view using the actions shown in Table 6.1 (except the last action).
10. Press the Esc key to return to the Print Layout view.

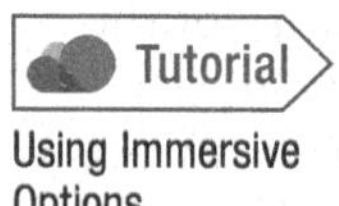

Using Immersive Options

Using Immersive Options

Focus

Immersive Reader

The Immersive group on the View tab contains a Focus button and an Immersive Reader button. Click the Focus button to switch to Focus Mode and only the document displays without the distraction of other screen features. Edit a document in Focus Mode in the normal manner. Move the insertion point to the top of the screen and the ribbon displays. To close Focus Mode, press the Esc key or move the insertion point to the top of the screen and then click the Focus button on the View tab. Another option for switching to Focus Mode is to click the Focus button on the Status bar.

The same learning tools available in Read Mode view can also be found on the Immersive Reader tab, along with additional options. Click the View tab and then click the Immersive Reader button in the Immersive group and the Immersive Reader tab displays as shown in Figure 6.2.

Column Width

Page Color

Line Focus

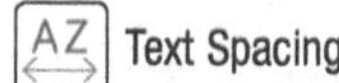
Text Spacing

Syllables

Read Aloud

Text in narrow columns is easier to read. Click the Column Width button on the Immersive Reader tab and choose from *Very Narrow, Narrow, Moderate,* and *Wide*. Adding color to a page can also make text easier to read and reduce eye strain. Click the Page Color button and a drop-down palette of color choices displays. Improve focus and comprehension by choosing the Line Focus button to read text one, three, or five lines at a time. Click the Text Spacing button to make text easier to read by increasing space between words, characters, and lines. Click the Syllables button to display syllable breaks in words, making words easier to recognize and pronounce.

If audio output is available, click the Read Aloud button to hear the text read. Each word is highlighted as it is being read. A playback toolbar displays with buttons for controlling the narration, as shown in Figure 6.3. Turn off reading by clicking the Stop button on the playback toolbar or by clicking the Read Aloud button again. The Read Aloud button is also available in the Speech group on the Review tab.

Figure 6.2 Immersive Reader Tab

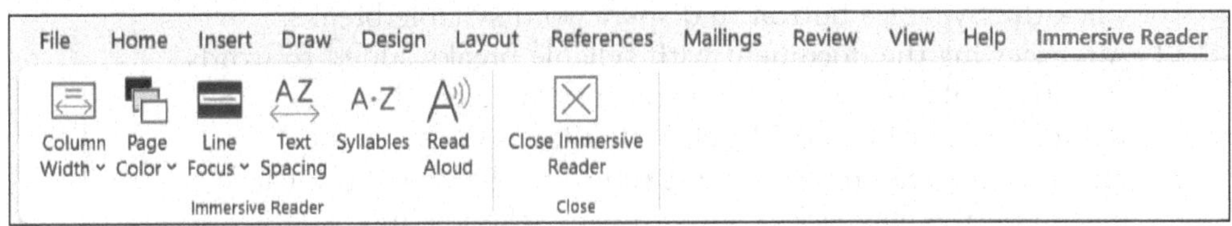

Figure 6.3 Playback Toolbar

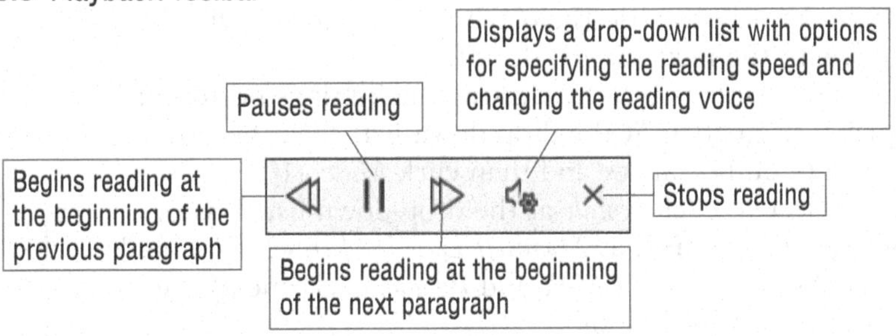

Activity 1b Using Immersive Reader Option

Part 2 of 3

1. With **6-WebReport.docx** open, display the document in Focus Mode by clicking the View tab and then clicking the Focus button in the Immersive group. Return to the Print Layout view by moving the pointer to the top of the screen and then clicking the Focus button.
2. Display the Immersive Reader tab by clicking the View tab, if necessary, and then clicking the Immersive Reader button in the Immersive group.
3. Change column width by clicking the Column Width button on the Immersive Reader tab and then clicking *Moderate* at the drop-down list.
4. Change page background color by clicking the Page Color button and then clicking the *Light Gray* option (last column, first row in the color palette).
5. Focus on only a few lines in the document by clicking the Line Focus button and then clicking *Five Lines* at the drop-down list.

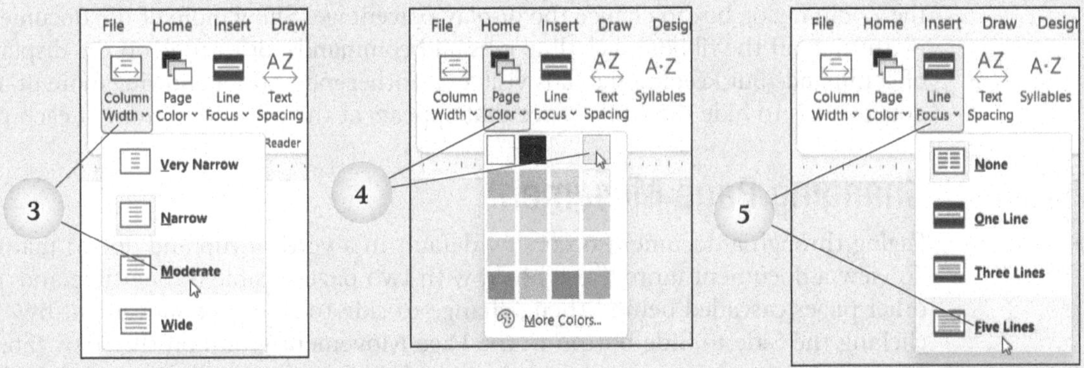

6. Click the down arrow at the right side of the screen to scroll down five lines in the document.
7. Remove the line focus by clicking the Line Focus button and then clicking *None* at the drop-down list.
8. If the Text Spacing button is active (displays with a gray background), click the button to remove spacing between characters.
9. After viewing the document with extra spacing, click the Text Spacing button to turn off text spacing.

10. Click the Syllables button to display word syllable breaks.
11. After viewing the document with syllable breaks added to words, click the Syllables button to turn off syllable breaks.
12. If audio output is available, click the Read Aloud button.
13. Listen to the reading for a short time and then click the Pause button on the playback toolbar to pause the reading.
14. Click the Play button (previously the Pause button) to resume the reading.
15. Click the Next button on the playback toolbar to begin the reading with the next paragraph of text.
16. Change the reading voice by clicking the Settings button on the playback toolbar. At the drop-down list, click the *Voice Selection* option box arrow and then click *Male*. (If *Male* is already selected, click *Female* at the drop-down list. If your choices are names such as *Microsoft David*, *Microsoft Zira*, and *Microsoft Mark* instead of *Male* and *Female*, click one of the names at the drop-down list.)
17. After listening to the reading by a male voice, return to the female voice by clicking the Settings button, clicking the *Voice Selection* option box arrow, and then clicking *Female*.
18. Click the Stop button on the playback toolbar to turn off reading.
19. Remove the page color by clicking the Page Color button and then clicking the *None* option (first column, first row) at the color palette.
20. Close the Immersive Reader tab by clicking the Close Immersive Reader button on the Immersive Reader tab.

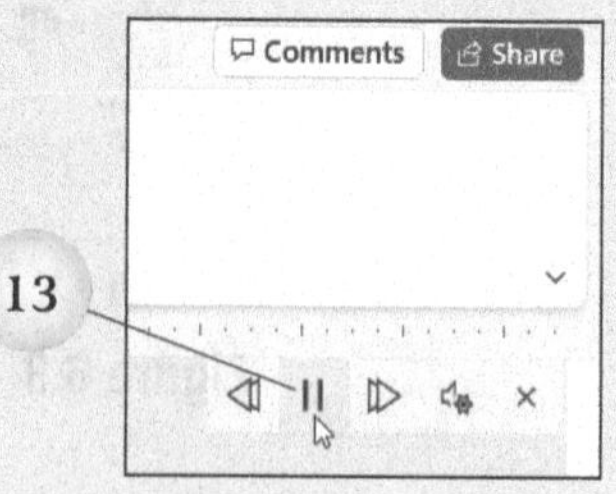

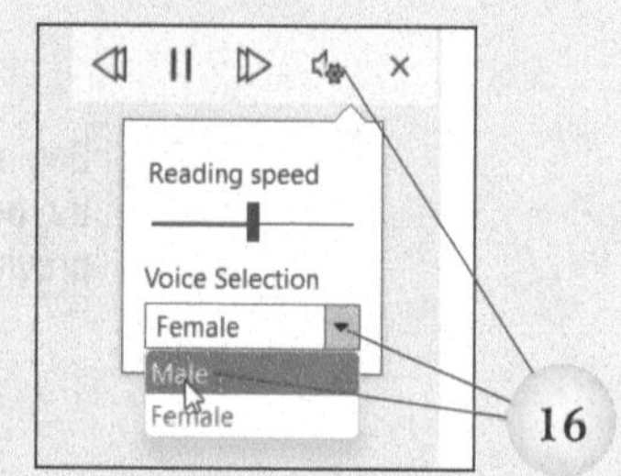

Changing the Document Display

Word includes a number of options for changing the way a document displays on the screen. Show pages in a document like pages in a book with the Side to Side button in the Page Movement group on the View tab. Use options on the Zoom slider bar or the Zoom dialog box to change the display percentage. Show more of the document by turning off the ribbon, including tabs and commands, or turning off the display of commands but keeping the tabs visible. Another method for showing more of a document is to hide the white space that appears at the top and bottom of each page.

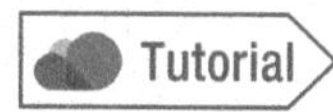

Changing Page Movement

Changing Page Movement

Paging through a document occurs by default in a vertical (up and down) manner. To view a document more like a book, with two pages visible at one time and other pages cascaded behind them, change to side-to-side page movement by clicking the Side to Side button in the Page Movement group on the View tab. Figure 6.4 shows how pages appear in the 6-WebReport.docx document with the Side to Side button active.

Scroll through pages on a touch screen using a finger to flip through pages. If the computer screen is not a touch screen, use the horizontal scroll bar or the mouse wheel to scroll through pages. To use the horizontal scroll bar, click the Next button (right-pointing triangle) at the right side of the scroll bar to display the next page or click the Previous button (left-pointing triangle) at the left side of the scroll bar to display the previous page; drag the scroll box on the scroll bar; or click to the left or right of the scroll box. The mouse wheel can also be used to scroll through pages.

Figure 6.4 Side-to-Side Page Movement

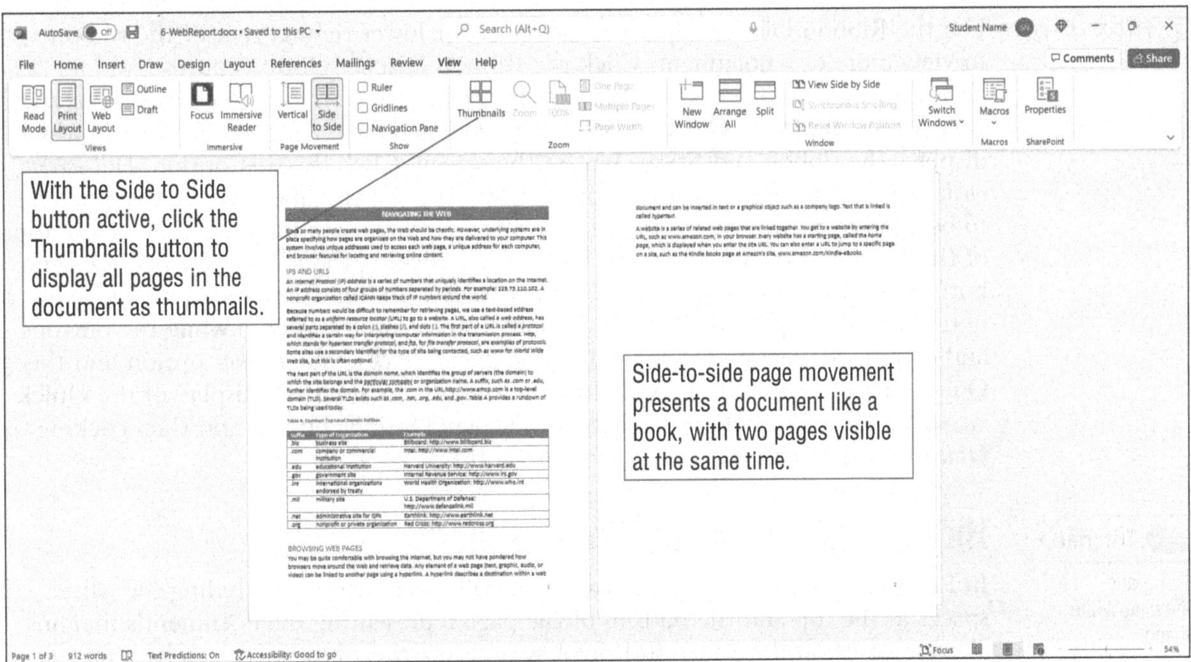

With the Side to Side button active, click the Thumbnails button to display all pages in the document as thumbnails.
Side-to-side page movement presents a document like a book, with two pages visible at the same time.

Thumbnails

When the Side to Side button is active, the Thumbnails button appears in the Zoom group on the View tab and other options in the Zoom group are unavailable. Click the Thumbnails button and all pages in the document display as thumbnails. Click a thumbnail to move the insertion point to the beginning of the page represented by the thumbnail and that page along with the next or previous page displays side to side. Another method for displaying page thumbnails is to hold down the Ctrl key while moving the mouse wheel. Return to the default vertical page movement by clicking the Vertical button in the Page Movement group on the View tab.

Vertical

Tutorial

Changing the Display Percentage

Changing the Display Percentage

By default, a document displays at 100%. This display percentage can be changed with the Zoom slider bar at the right side of the Status bar and with options in the Zoom group on the View tab. To change the display percentage with the Zoom slider bar, drag the button on the bar to increase or decrease the percentage. Click the Zoom Out button at the left of the slider bar to decrease the display percentage or click the Zoom In button to increase the display percentage.

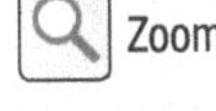
Zoom

100%

One Page

Multiple Pages

Page Width

Click the Zoom button in the Zoom group on the View tab to display the Zoom dialog box, which contains options for changing the display percentage. If the display percentage has been changed, return to the default by clicking the 100% button in the Zoom group on the View tab. Click the One Page button to display the entire page on the screen and click the Multiple Pages button to display multiple pages on the screen. Click the Page Width button and the document expands across the screen.

Hint Click the percentage at the right of the Zoom slider bar to display the Zoom dialog box.

Changing Ribbon Display Options

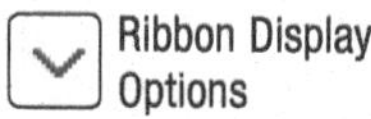

Use the Ribbon Display Options button in the lower right corner of the ribbon to view more of a document. Click the Ribbon Display Options button and a drop-down list displays with four options: *Full-screen mode*, *Show tabs only*, *Always show Ribbon* and *Show Quick Access Toolbar*. The default is *Always show Ribbon*, which displays the ribbon and Status bar on the screen. Click the first option, *Full-screen mode*, and the ribbon and Status bar are hidden, allowing more of the document to be visible on the screen. To temporarily redisplay these features, click at the top of the screen. Turn these features back on by clicking the Ribbon Display Options button and then clicking the *Always show Ribbon* option. Click the *Show tabs only* option at the drop-down list and the tabs display on the ribbon while the buttons and commands remain hidden. Click the *Show Quick Access Toolbar* option and the Quick Access Toolbar displays below the ribbon. Turn off the display of the Quick Access Toolbar by clicking the Ribbon Display Options button and then clicking *Hide Quick Access Toolbar* at the drop-down list.

Hiding and Showing White Space

Hiding and Showing White Space

In Print Layout view, a page appears as it will when printed, including the white spaces at the top and the bottom of the page representing the document's margins. To save space on the screen in Print Layout view, the white space can be removed from view by positioning the pointer at the top edge or bottom edge of a page or between pages until the pointer displays as the Hide White Space icon and then double-clicking the left mouse button. To redisplay the white space, position the pointer on the thin gray line separating pages until the pointer turns into the Show White Space icon and then double-click the left mouse button.

Activity 1c Changing Views, Changing Display, and Hiding/Showing White Space — Part 3 of 3

1. With **6-WebReport.docx** open, press Ctrl + Home to move the insertion point to the beginning of the document.
2. Change to side-to-side page movement by clicking the View tab and then clicking the Side to Side button in the Page Movement group. (This displays pages 1 and 2 side by side.)
3. Click the Next button at the right side of the horizontal scroll bar to display pages 2 and 3.
4. Display page thumbnails by clicking the Thumbnails button in the Zoom group.
5. Click the page 1 thumbnail.

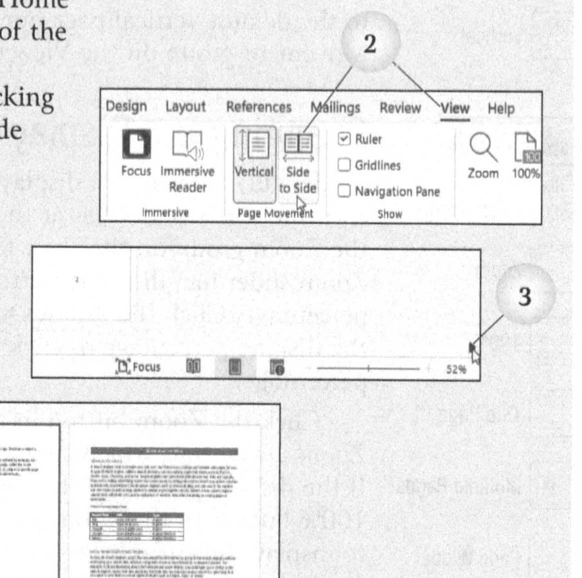

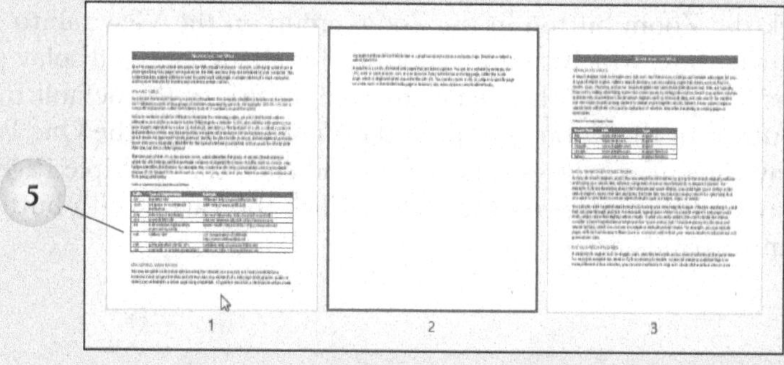

6. Return to the default page movement by clicking the Vertical button in the Page Movement group.
7. Click the Zoom button in the Zoom group on the View tab.
8. At the Zoom dialog box, click the *75%* option and then click OK.
9. Return the display percentage to the default by clicking the 100% button in the Zoom group.
10. Click the Ribbon Display Options button in the lower right corner of the ribbon and then click *Full-screen mode* at the drop-down list.
11. Press the Page Down key until the end of the document displays.
12. Click at the top of the screen to temporarily redisplay the ribbon and Status bar.
13. Click the Ribbon Display Options button and then click *Show tabs only* at the drop-down list.
14. Double-click the Home tab to redisplay the ribbon.
15. Press Ctrl + Home to move the insertion point to the beginning of the document.
16. Hide the white spaces at the tops and bottoms of pages by positioning the pointer at the top edge of the page until the pointer turns into the Hide White Space icon and then double-clicking the left mouse button.
17. Scroll through the document and notice the appearance of pages.
18. Redisplay the white spaces at the tops and bottoms of pages by positioning the pointer on any thin gray line separating pages until the pointer turns into the Show White Space icon and then double-clicking the left mouse button.
19. Close **6-WebReport.docx**.

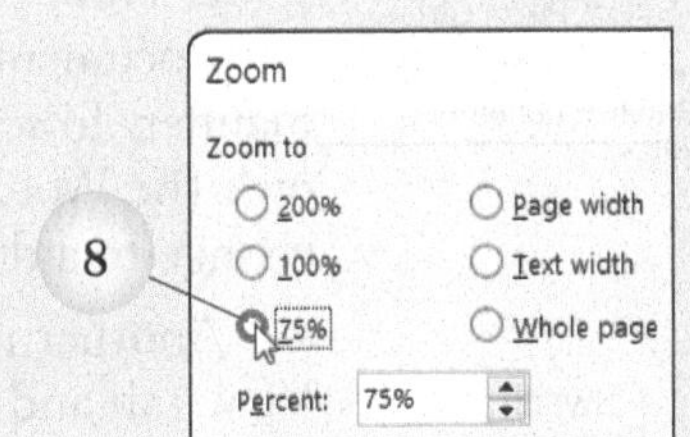

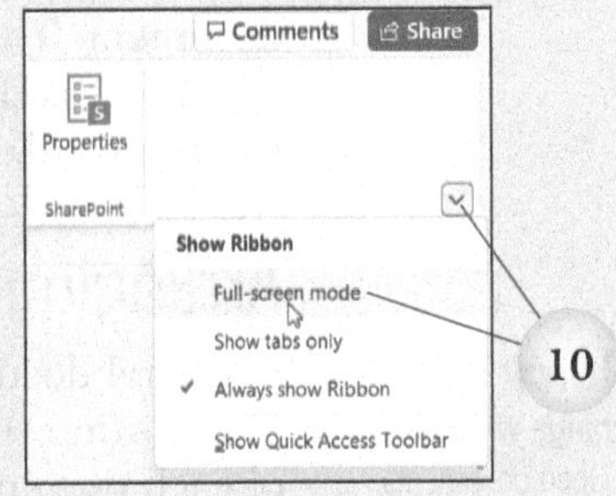

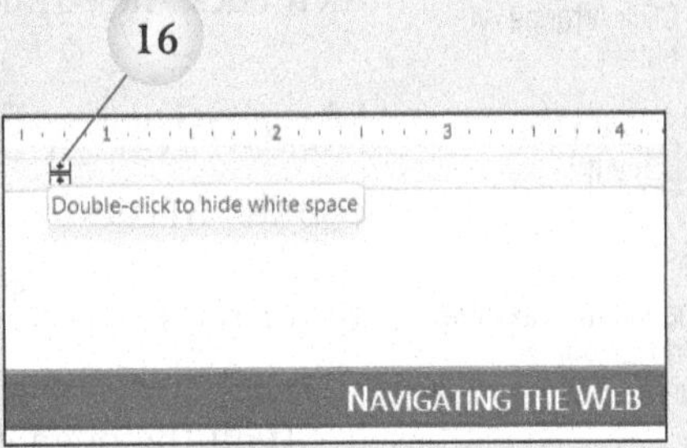

browsers move around the Web and retrieve d video) can be linked to another page using a hy document an Double-click to show white space ap called *hypertext*.

18

Activity 2 Manage Multiple Documents — 7 Parts

You will open multiple documents and then arrange, maximize, restore, and minimize windows; move selected text between split windows; compare formatting of documents side by side; and print specific text, pages, and multiple copies.

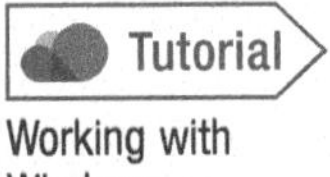

Working with Windows

Hint Press Ctrl + F6 to switch between open documents.

Working with Windows

Multiple documents can be opened in Word, the insertion point can be moved between documents, and information can be moved or copied from one document and pasted into another. When a new document is opened, it displays on top of any previously opened document. With multiple documents open, the window containing each document can be resized to see all or a portion of it on the screen.

Hint Press Ctrl + W or Ctrl + F4 to close the active document window.

A Word button appears on the taskbar when a document is open. If more than one document is open, another button will appear behind the first in a cascading manner. To see all documents that are currently open in Word, hover the pointer over the Word button. A thumbnail of each document will appear. To make a change to a document, click the thumbnail that represents the document.

Switch Windows

Another method for determining what documents are open is to click the View tab and then click the Switch Windows button in the Window group. The document name in the list with the check mark in front of it is the active document. The active document contains the insertion point. To make a different document active, click the document name. To switch to another document using the keyboard, type the number shown in front of the document.

Arranging Windows

Quick Steps

Arrange Windows

1. Open documents.
2. Click View tab.
3. Click Arrange All button.

If several documents are open, they can be arranged so a portion of each appears. The portion that appears includes the title (if present) and the opening paragraph of each document. To arrange a group of open documents, click the View tab and then click the Arrange All button in the Window group.

Arrange All

Maximizing, Restoring, and Minimizing Documents

Hint The keyboard shortcut to maximize a document is Ctrl + F10.

Use the Maximize and Minimize buttons in the upper right corner of the active document to change the size of a document window. The two buttons are at the left of the Close button. (The Close button is in the upper right corner of the screen and contains an X.)

Maximize

Minimize

Restore

If all the open documents are arranged on the screen, clicking the Maximize button in the active document causes that document to expand to fill the screen. Any other open windows will be hidden behind it. In addition, the Maximize button changes to the Restore button. To return the active document back to its original size, click the Restore button. Click the Minimize button in the active document and the document is reduced to a button on the taskbar. To maximize a document that has been minimized, hover the pointer over the taskbar button and click the thumbnail of the document.

Activity 2a Arranging, Maximizing, Restoring, and Minimizing Windows

Part 1 of 7

Note: If you are using Word on a network system that contains a virus checker, you may not be able to open multiple documents at once. Continue by opening each document individually.

1. Open the following documents: **AptLease.docx**, **IntelProp.docx**, **NSS.docx**, and **Visionaries.docx**. (To open all the documents at one time, display the Open dialog box, hold down the Ctrl key, click each document name, release the Ctrl key, and then click the Open button.)
2. Arrange the windows by clicking the View tab and then clicking the Arrange All button in the Window group.
3. Make **AptLease.docx** the active document by clicking the Switch Windows button in the Window group on the View tab of the document at the top of your screen and then clicking ***AptLease.docx*** at the drop-down list.
4. Close **AptLease.docx**.
5. Make **IntelProp.docx** active and then close it.

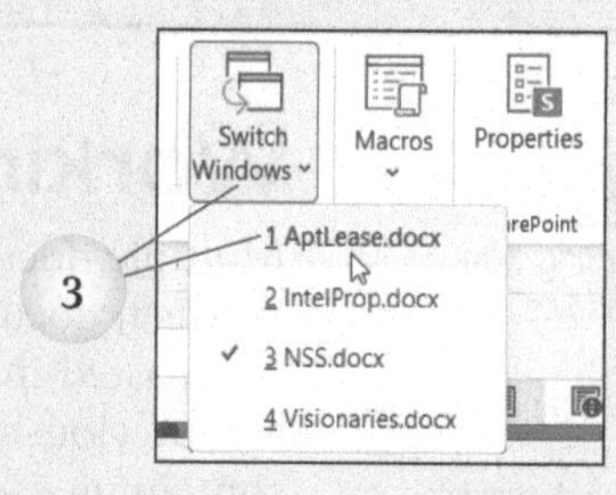

6. Make **Visionaries.docx** active and minimize it by clicking the Minimize button in the upper right corner of the active window.
7. Maximize **NSS.docx** by clicking the Maximize button immediately left of the Close button.
8. Close **NSS.docx**.
9. Restore **Visionaries.docx** by clicking the button on the taskbar that represents the document.
10. Maximize **Visionaries.docx**.

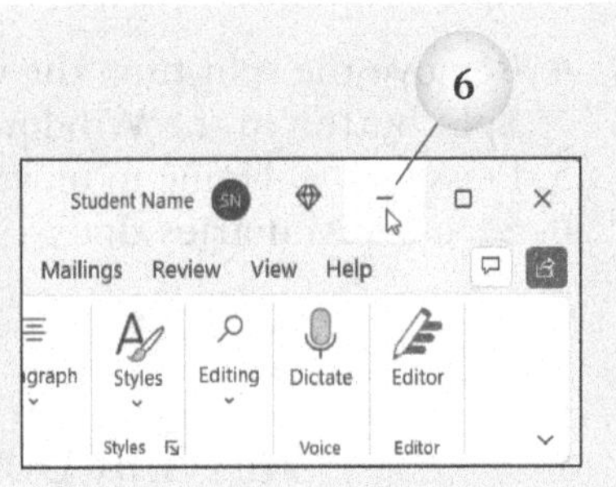

Splitting a Window

Quick Steps
Split Window
1. Open document.
2. Click View tab.
3. Click Split button.

Split

Hint The keyboard shortcut to split a window is Alt + Ctrl + S.

Remove Split

A window can be split into two panes so that two different parts of a document can be seen at once. For example, show an outline for a report in one pane and the part of the report to be edited in the other pane. The original window is split into two panes that extend horizontally across the screen.

Split a window by clicking the View tab and then clicking the Split button in the Window group. This splits the window in two with a split bar and another horizontal ruler. The location of the split bar can be changed by positioning the pointer on the split bar until the pointer displays as an up-and-down-pointing arrow with two small lines in the middle, holding down the left mouse button, dragging to the new location, and then releasing the mouse button.

When a window is split, the insertion point is positioned in the bottom pane. To move the insertion point to the other pane with the mouse, position the I-beam pointer in the other pane and then click the left mouse button. To remove the split bar from the document, click the View tab and then click the Remove Split button in the Window group. The split bar can also be double-clicked or dragged to the top or bottom of the screen.

Activity 2b Moving Selected Text between Split Windows

Part 2 of 7

1. With **Visionaries.docx** open, save the document with the name **6-Visionaries.**
2. Click the View tab and then click the Split button in the Window group.
3. Move the *William Hewlett and David Packard* section just above the *Gordon E. Moore* section by completing the following steps:
   a. Click in the top pane and then click the Home tab.
   b. Select the heading *William Hewlett and David Packard* and the three paragraphs below the heading.
   c. Click the Cut button in the Clipboard group on the Home tab.
   d. Click in the bottom pane, scroll down the document, and then position the insertion point at the beginning of the heading *Gordon E. Moore*.
   e. Click the Paste button in the Clipboard group on the Home tab.

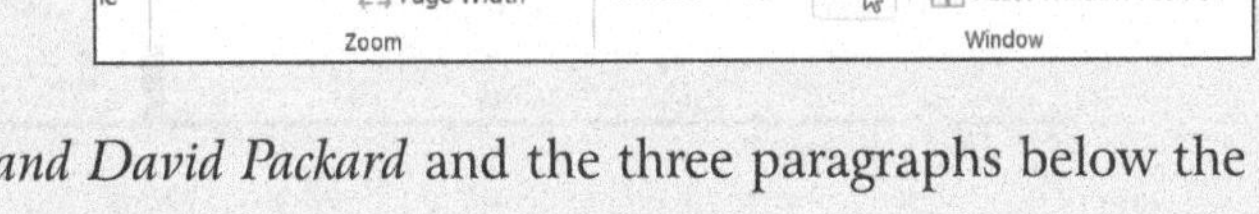

4. Remove the split from the window by clicking the View tab and then clicking the Remove Split button in the Window group.
5. Press Ctrl + Home to move the insertion point to the beginning of the document.
6. Save **6-Visionaries.docx**.

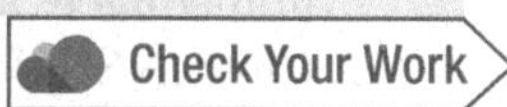
Check Your Work

Viewing Documents Side by Side

View Side by Side

Synchronous Scrolling

Quick Steps

View Documents Side by Side
1. Open two documents.
2. Click View tab.
3. Click View Side by Side button.

The contents of two documents can be compared on screen by opening both documents, clicking the View tab, and then clicking the View Side by Side button in the Window group. The documents are arranged on the screen side by side, as shown in Figure 6.5. By default, synchronous scrolling is active. With this feature active, scrolling in one document causes the same scrolling in the other document. This feature is useful for comparing the text, formatting, or other features between documents. To scroll in one document and not the other, click the Synchronous Scrolling button in the Window group to turn it off.

Figure 6.5 Viewing Documents Side by Side

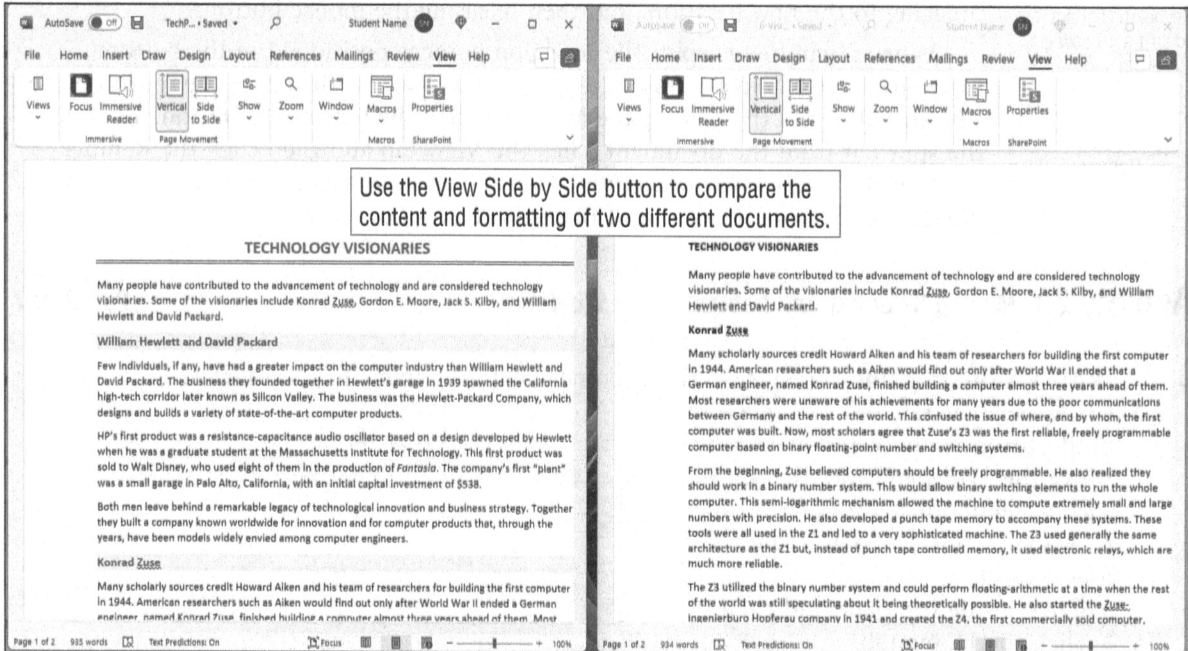
Use the View Side by Side button to compare the content and formatting of two different documents.
TECHNOLOGY VISIONARIES
TECHNOLOGY VISIONARIES

Activity 2c Viewing Documents Side by Side

Part 3 of 7

1. With **6-Visionaries.docx** open, open **TechPioneers.docx**.
2. Click the View tab and then click the View Side by Side button in the Window group.

3. Scroll through both documents simultaneously. Notice the difference between the two documents. (The titles and headings are set in different alignment, font color and size, and/or shading.) Format the title and headings in **6-Visionaries.docx** so that they match the formatting in **TechPioneers.docx**. ***Hint: Use the Format Painter button to copy the formatting.***
4. Turn off synchronous scrolling by clicking the View tab in the active document, clicking the Window button, and then clicking the Synchronous Scrolling button at the drop-down list.

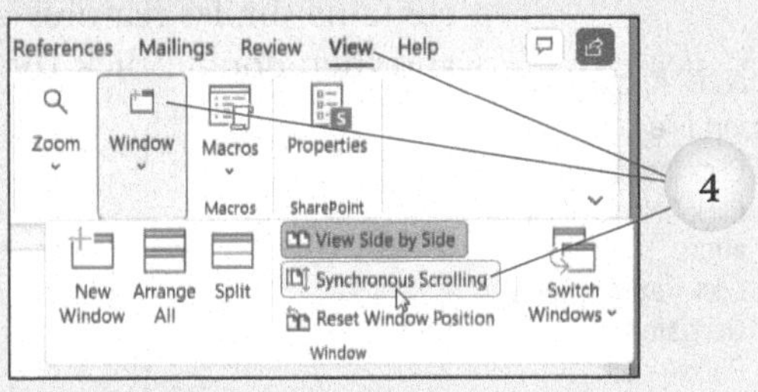

5. Click in the document and then scroll through the document and notice that no scrolling occurs in the other document.
6. Make **TechPioneers.docx** the active document and then close it.
7. Save **6-Visionaries.docx**.

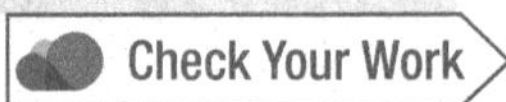

Opening a New Window

Quick Steps

Open New Window

1. Open document.
2. Click View tab.
3. Click New Window button.

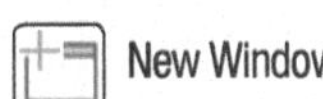

A second copy of a document can be opened in a new window so that two copies of the same document may be viewed side by side. To do this, first open a document and then click the New Window button in the Window group on the View tab. When a new window is opened, the document name in the Title bar is followed by *- 2*. The document name in the original window is followed by *- 1*. Any change made to the document in one window is reflected in the document in the other window, as both windows display the exact same file.

Activity 2d Opening a New Window

Part 4 of 7

1. With **6-Visionaries.docx** open, open a second copy of the document in a new window by clicking the New Window button in the Window group on the View tab. (Notice that the document name in the Title bar displays followed by *- 2*.)
2. Click the View tab and then click the View Side by Side button in the Window group.
3. Click the Window button on the View tab and then click the Synchronous Scrolling button to turn off synchronous scrolling.
4. Click in the **6-Visionaries.docx - 2** window to make the document active. Look at the first paragraph of text and notice the order in which the names are listed in the last sentence of the paragraph (Konrad Zuse, Gordon E. Moore, Jack S. Kilby, and William Hewlett and David Packard).
5. Click in the **6-Visionaries.docx - 1** window and then cut and paste the headings and text so that each name and text following the name appears in the order listed in the first paragraph.
6. Click the Save button on the Title bar.
7. Close the second copy of the document by clicking the Word button on the taskbar and then clicking the Close button in the upper right corner of the **6-Visionaries.docx - 2** thumbnail (above the Word button on the taskbar).
8. With **6-Visionaries.docx** active, scroll to the bottom of the first page and make sure the title *Jack S. Kilby* displays on the same page as the paragraph of text that follows.
9. Save **6-Visionaries.docx**.

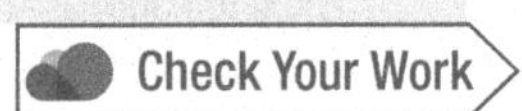

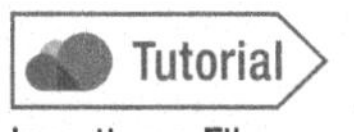
Inserting a File

Object

Quick Steps

Insert File
1. Click Insert tab.
2. Click Object button arrow.
3. Click *Text from File*.
4. Navigate to folder.
5. Double-click document.

Inserting a File into a Document

The contents of one document can be inserted into another using the Object button in the Text group on the Insert tab. Click the Object button arrow and then click *Text from File* and the Insert File dialog box displays. This dialog box contains similar features as the Open dialog box. Navigate to the specific folder and then double-click the document to be inserted in the open document.

Activity 2e Inserting a File — Part 5 of 7

1. With **6-Visionaries.docx** open, move the insertion point to the blank line above the title *REFERENCES*.
2. Insert a file into the open document by completing the following steps:
   a. Click the Insert tab.
   b. Click the Object button arrow in the Text group and then click *Text from File* at the drop-down list.
   c. At the Insert File dialog box, navigate to your WL1C6 folder and then double-click ***Torvalds.docx***.
3. Save **6-Visionaries.docx**.

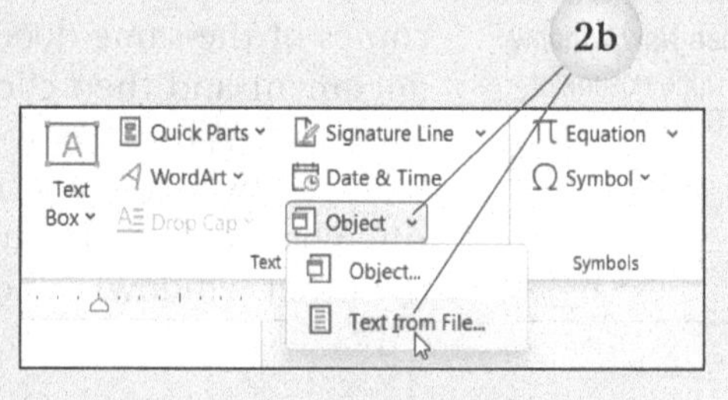

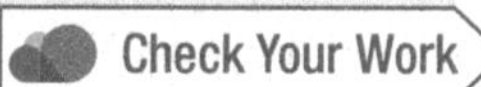
Check Your Work

Previewing and Printing

Hint The Print backstage area can also be displayed with the keyboard shortcut Ctrl + P.

Previewing and Printing

Use options at the Print backstage area, shown in Figure 6.6, to specify what is to be printed and to preview pages before printing them. To display the Print backstage area, click the File tab and then click the *Print* option. If the Quick Access Toolbar displays, the Print Preview and Print button can be added to the toolbar so that, when clicked, the Print backstage area displays. Display the Quick Access Toolbar by clicking the Ribbon Display Options button at the right side of the ribbon and then clicking *Show Quick Access Toolbar*. Insert the button on the Quick Access Toolbar by clicking the Customize Quick Access Toolbar button at the right side of the toolbar and then clicking *Print Preview and Print* at the drop-down list.

Previewing Pages

Zoom to Page

At the Print backstage area, a preview of the current page is shown (see Figure 6.6). Click the Next Page button to view the next page in the document preview, and click the Previous Page button to display the previous page. Use the Zoom slider bar to increase or decrease the size of the page and click the Zoom to Page button to fit the entire page in the viewing area.

Figure 6.6 Print Backstage Area

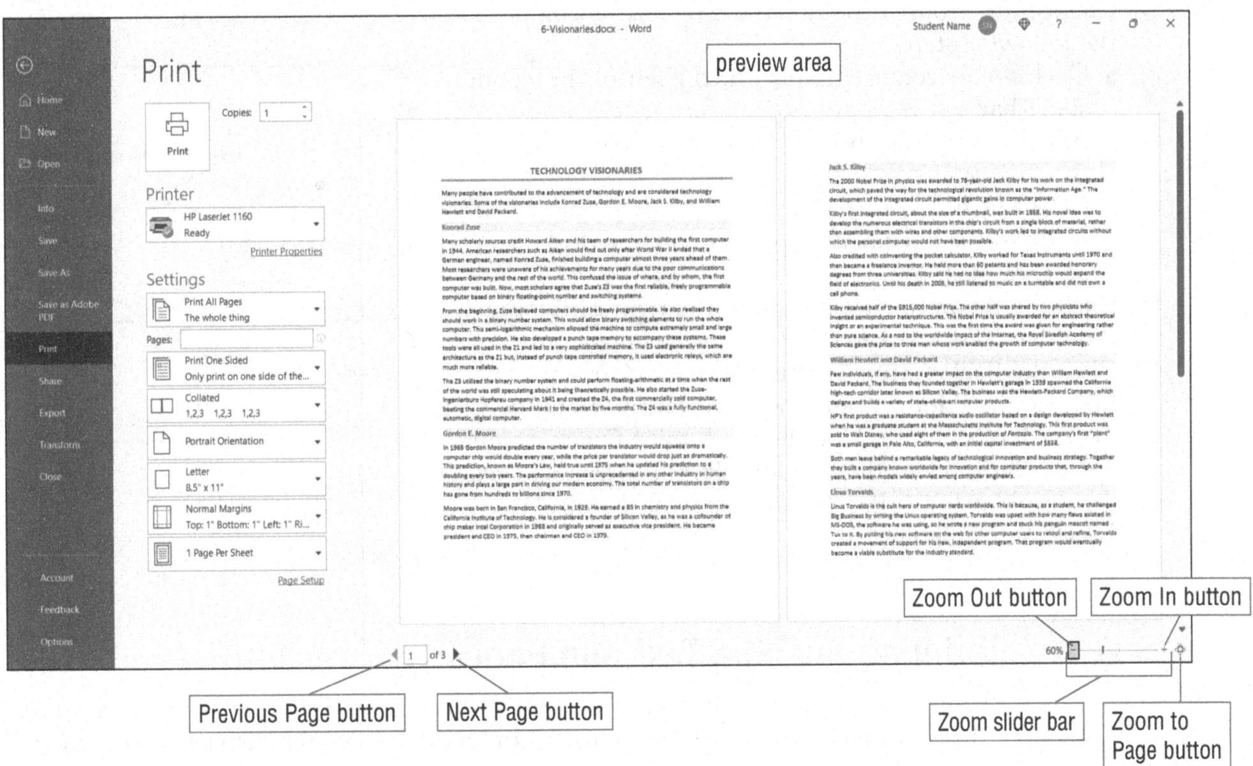

Activity 2f Previewing Pages

Part 6 of 7

1. With **6-Visionaries.docx** open, press Ctrl + Home to move the insertion point to the beginning of the document.
2. If necessary, turn on the display of the Quick Access Toolbar by clicking the Ribbon Display Options button and then clicking *Show Quick Access Toolbar* at the drop-down list.
3. Insert the Print Preview and Print button on the Quick Access Toolbar by clicking the Customize Quick Access Toolbar button and then clicking *Print Preview and Print* at the drop-down list.

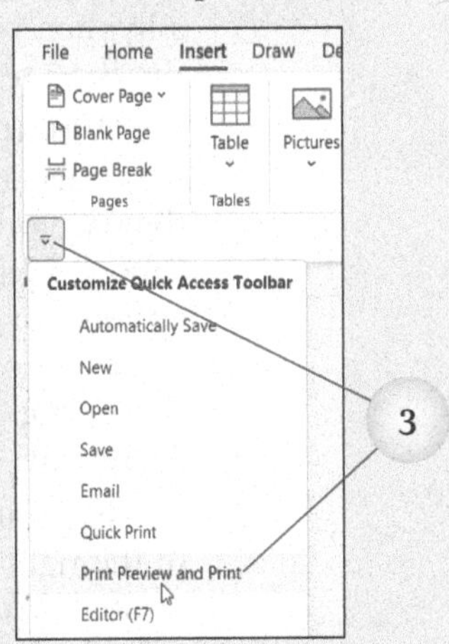

4. Preview the document by clicking the Print Preview and Print button on the Quick Access Toolbar.
5. Click the Zoom In button (plus [+] symbol) at the right of the Zoom slider bar two times. (This increases the size of the preview page.)
6. At the Print backstage area, click the Next Page button below and to the left of the preview page. (This displays page 2 in the preview area.)

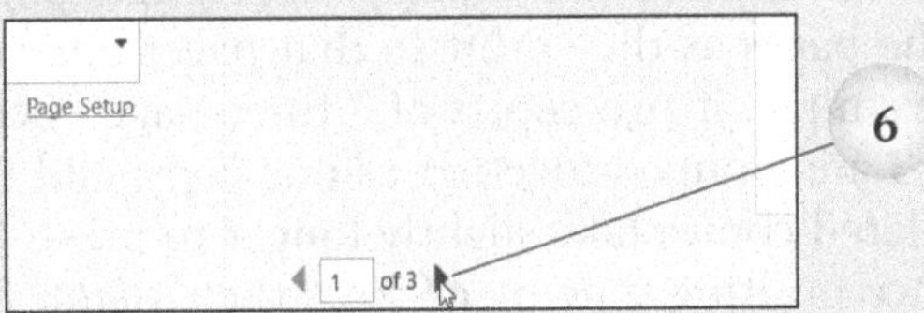

7. Click the Zoom Out button (minus [–] symbol) at the left of the Zoom slider bar until two pages of the document display in the preview area.

8. Change the zoom at the Zoom dialog box by completing the following steps:
   a. Click the percentage number at the left of the Zoom slider bar.
   b. At the Zoom dialog box, click the *Many pages* option in the *Zoom to* section.
   c. Click OK to close the dialog box. (Notice that all the pages in the document appear as thumbnails in the preview area.)
9. Click the Zoom to Page button at the right of the Zoom slider bar. (This returns the page to the default size.)
10. Click the Back button to return to the document.
11. Remove the Print Preview and Print button from the Quick Access Toolbar by clicking the Customize Quick Access Toolbar button and then clicking *Print Preview and Print* at the drop-down list. If necessary, turn off the display of the Quick Access Toolbar.

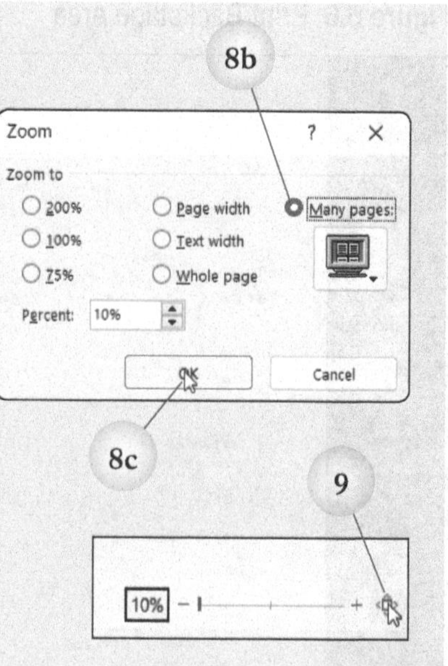

Printing Specific Text and Pages

Hint Save a document before printing it.

Control what prints in a document with options at the Print backstage area. Click the first gallery in the *Settings* category and a drop-down list displays with options for printing. All pages in the document may be printed; or, print only selected text, the current page, or a custom range of pages.

Print a portion of a document by selecting the text and then choosing the *Print Selection* option at the Print backstage area. With this option, only the selected text prints. (If no text is selected, this option is dimmed.) Click the *Print Current Page* option to print only the page on which the insertion point is located. Use the *Custom Print* option to identify a specific page, multiple pages, or a range of pages to print. To print specific pages, use a comma (,) to indicate *and* and use a hyphen (-) to indicate *through*. For example, to print pages 2 and 5, type 2,5 in the *Pages* text box and to print pages 6 through 10, type 6-10.

With the other galleries available in the *Settings* category of the Print backstage area, specify whether to print on one or both sides of the page, change the page orientation (portrait or landscape), specify how the pages are collated, choose a paper size, and specify document margins. The last gallery contains options for printing 1, 2, 4, 6, 8, or 16 pages of a multiple-page document on one sheet of paper. This gallery also contains the *Scale to Paper Size* option. Click this option and then use the side menu to choose the paper size to scale the document.

To print more than one copy of a document, use the *Copies* measurement box to the right of the Print button. If several copies of a multiple-page document are printed, Word collates the pages as they print so that pages appear in sequential order in each copy. For example, if two copies of a three-page document are printed, pages 1, 2, and 3 are grouped together as one copy, and then the pages print a second time. Collated copies take slightly longer to print. If copies do not need to be collated, reduce printing time by clicking the *Collated* gallery in the Print backstage area and then clicking the *Uncollated* option.

To send a document directly to the printer without displaying the Print backstage area, consider adding the Quick Print button to the Quick Access Toolbar. To do this, display the Quick Access Toolbar, click the Customize Quick Access Toolbar button and then click *Quick Print* at the drop-down gallery. Click the Quick Print button and all the pages of the active document will print.

Activity 2g Printing Specific Text and Pages

Part 7 of 7

1. With **6-Visionaries.docx** open, print selected text by completing the following steps:
   a. Select the heading *Konrad Zuse* and the three paragraphs of text that follows it.
   b. Click the File tab and then click the *Print* option.
   c. At the Print backstage area, click the first gallery in the *Settings* category (displays with *Print All Pages*) and then click *Print Selection* at the drop-down list.
   d. Click the Print button.
2. Change the margins and page orientation and then print only the first page by completing the following steps:
   a. Press Ctrl + Home to move the insertion point to the beginning of the document.
   b. Click the File tab and then click the *Print* option.
   c. At the Print backstage area, click the fourth gallery (displays with *Portrait Orientation)* in the *Settings* category and then click *Landscape Orientation* at the drop-down list.
   d. Click the sixth gallery (displays with *Normal Margins*) in the *Settings* category and then click *Narrow* at the drop-down list.
   e. Click the first gallery (displays with *Print All Pages*) in the *Settings* category and then click *Print Current Page* at the drop-down list.
   f. Click the Print button. (The first page of the document prints in landscape orientation with 0.5-inch margins.)

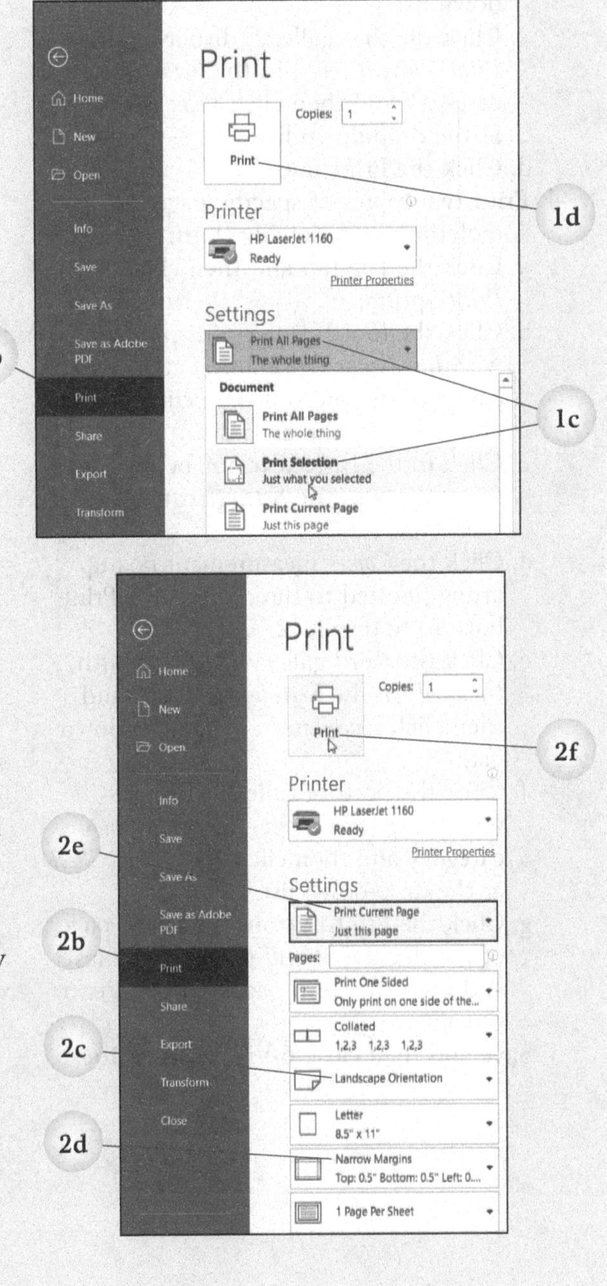

3. Print all the pages as thumbnails on one page by completing the following steps:
   a. Click the File tab and then click the *Print* option.
   b. At the Print backstage area, click the bottom gallery (displays with *1 Page Per Sheet*) in the *Settings* category and then click *4 Pages Per Sheet* at the drop-down list.
   c. Click the first gallery (displays with *Print Current Page*) in the *Settings* category and then click *Print All Pages* at the drop-down list.
   d. Click the Print button.
4. Print two copies of specific pages by completing the following steps:
   a. Click the File tab and then click the *Print* option.
   b. Click the fourth gallery (displays with *Landscape Orientation*) at the *Settings* category and then click *Portrait Orientation* in the drop-down list.
   c. Click in the *Pages* text box below the first gallery in the *Settings* category and then type 1,3.
   d. Click the *Copies* measurement box up arrow (located to the right of the Print button) to display *2*.
   e. Click the third gallery (displays with *Collated*) in the *Settings* category and then click *Uncollated* at the drop-down list.
   f. Click the bottom gallery (displays with *4 Pages Per Sheet*) in the *Settings* category and then click *1 Page Per Sheet* at the drop-down list.
   g. Click the Print button. (The first page of the document will print two times and then the third page will print two times.)
5. Save and then close **6-Visionaries.docx**.

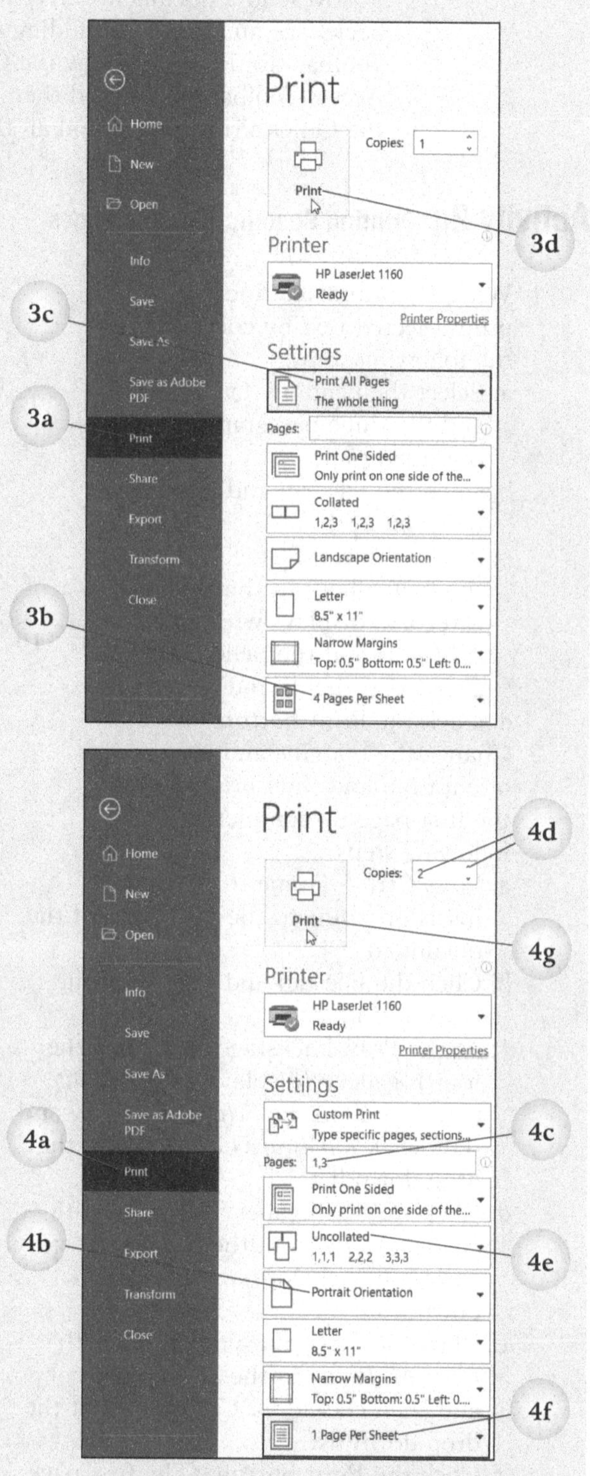

Check Your Work

Activity 3 Prepare Envelopes — 2 Parts

You will create an envelope document and type the return address and delivery address using envelope addressing guidelines issued by the United States Postal Service. You will also open a letter document and then prepare an envelope using the inside address on the business letter.

Preparing an Envelope

Envelopes

Preparing Envelopes

Word automates the creation of envelopes with options at the Envelopes and Labels dialog box with the Envelopes tab selected, as shown in Figure 6.7. Display this dialog box by clicking the Mailings tab and then clicking the Envelopes button in the Create group. At the dialog box, type the delivery address in the *Delivery address* text box and the return address in the *Return address* text box. Print the envelope immediately by clicking the Print button, or prepare the envelope to be printed along with a letter or other document by clicking the Add to document button.

Quick Steps

Prepare Envelope

1. Click Mailings tab.
2. Click Envelopes button.
3. Type delivery address.
4. Click in *Return address* text box.
5. Type return address.
6. Click Add to Document button or Print button.

When a return address is entered in the dialog box, Word will display the question *Do you want to save the new return address as the default return address?* At this question, click Yes to save the current return address for future envelopes or click No if the return address should not be used as the default. To omit a return address, insert a check mark in the *Omit* check box.

The Envelopes and Labels dialog box contains a *Preview* sample box and a *Feed* sample box. The *Preview* sample box shows how the envelope will appear when printed and the *Feed* sample box shows how the envelope should be fed into the printer.

Figure 6.7 Envelopes and Labels Dialog Box with the Envelopes Tab Selected

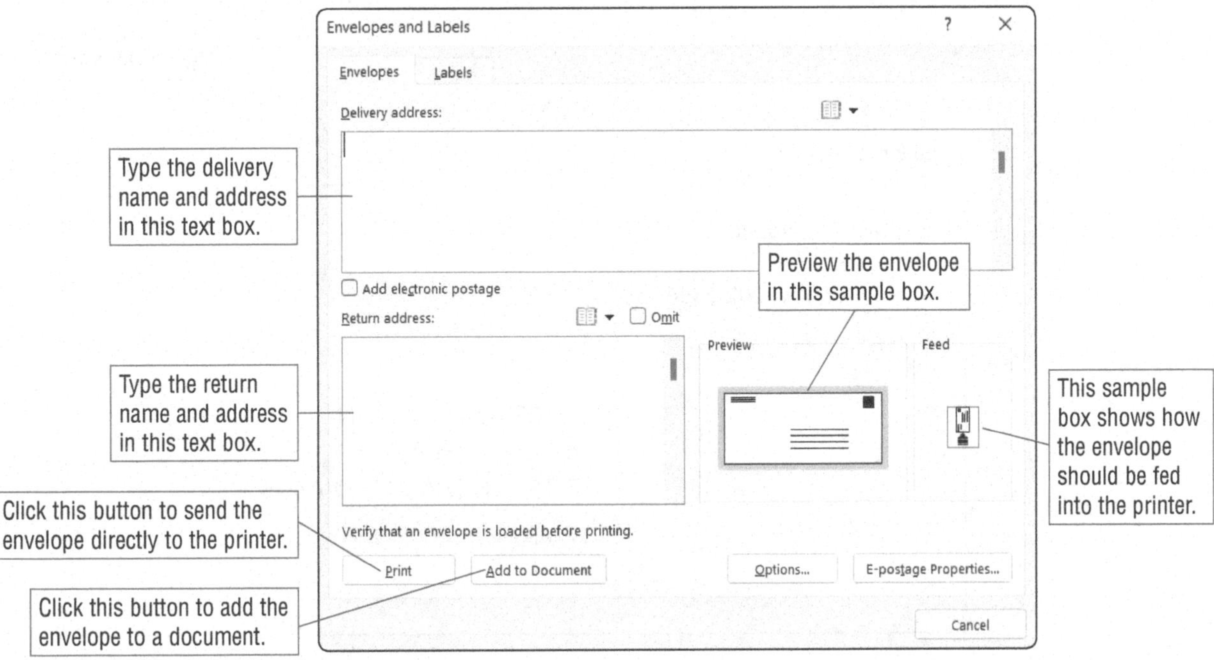
Envelopes and Labels
Envelopes
Labels
Delivery address:
Type the delivery name and address in this text box.
Add electronic postage
Return address:
Omit
Preview the envelope in this sample box.
Preview
Feed
Type the return name and address in this text box.
This sample box shows how the envelope should be fed into the printer.
Click this button to send the envelope directly to the printer.
Verify that an envelope is loaded before printing.
Print
Add to Document
Options...
E-postage Properties...
Click this button to add the envelope to a document.
Cancel

When addressing envelopes, consider following general guidelines issued by the United States Postal Service (USPS). The USPS guidelines suggest using all capital letters with no commas or periods for return and delivery addresses. Figure 6.8 shows envelope addresses that follow the USPS guidelines. Use abbreviations for street suffixes (such as *ST* for *Street* and *AVE* for *Avenue*). For a complete list of address abbreviations, visit the USPS.com website and then search for *Official USPS Abbreviations.*

Activity 3a Preparing an Envelope

Part 1 of 2

1. At a blank document, create an envelope document with the delivery address and return address shown in Figure 6.8. Begin by clicking the Mailings tab.
2. Click the Envelopes button in the Create group.
3. At the Envelopes and Labels dialog box with the Envelopes tab selected, type the delivery address shown in Figure 6.8 (the one containing the name *GREGORY LINCOLN*). (Press the Enter key to end each line in the name and address.)
4. Click in the *Return address* text box. (If any text displays in the *Return address* text box, select and then delete it.)
5. Type the return address shown in Figure 6.8 (the one containing the name *WENDY STEINBERG*). (Press the Enter key to end each line in the name and address.)
6. Click the Add to Document button.
7. At the message *Do you want to save the new return address as the default return address?*, click No.
8. Save the document with the name **6-Env**.
9. Preview and then close **6-Env.docx**.

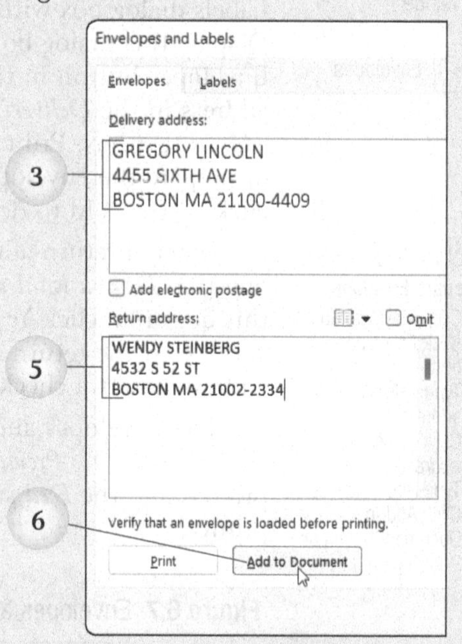

Check Your Work

Figure 6.8 Activity 3a

WENDY STEINBERG
4532 S 52 ST
BOSTON MA 21002-2334

GREGORY LINCOLN
4455 SIXTH AVE
BOSTON MA 21100-4409

After typing a letter in Word, prepare an envelope to mail the letter by clicking the Envelopes button. Word automatically inserts the first address in the document in the *Delivery address* text box. (Note: Each line of the address must end with a press of the Enter key, and not Shift + Enter, for Word to recognize it.)

Alternately, select the delivery address in the letter document and then click the Envelopes button. When using this method, the address will be formatted exactly as it appears in the letter and may not conform to the USPS guidelines; however, these guidelines are only suggestions, not requirements.

Activity 3b Creating an Envelope in an Existing Document — Part 2 of 2

1. Open **LAProgram.docx**.
2. Click the Mailings tab.
3. Click the Envelopes button in the Create group.
4. At the Envelopes and Labels dialog box (with the Envelopes tab selected), make sure the delivery address appears properly in the *Delivery address* text box.
5. If any text appears in the *Return address* text box, insert a check mark in the *Omit* check box (located to the right of the *Return address* option). (This tells Word not to print the return address on the envelope.)
6. Click the Print button.
7. Close **LAProgram.docx** without saving the changes.

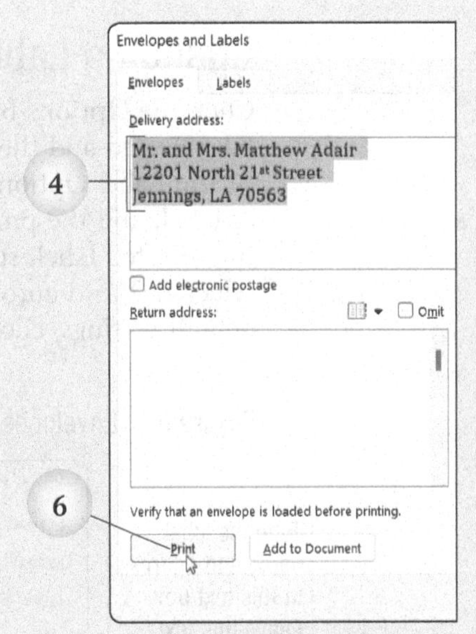

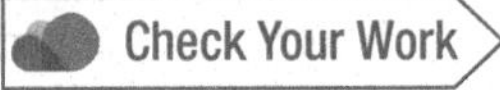

Activity 4 Prepare Labels — 2 Parts

You will create mailing labels containing different names and addresses, labels with the same name and address, and labels with an image.

Preparing Labels

Use Word's Labels feature to print text on mailing labels, file folder labels, and other types of labels. Word formats text for a variety of brands and sizes of labels that can be purchased at most office supply stores. Use the Labels feature to create a sheet of mailing labels with a different name and address on each label or with the same name and address or image on each label.

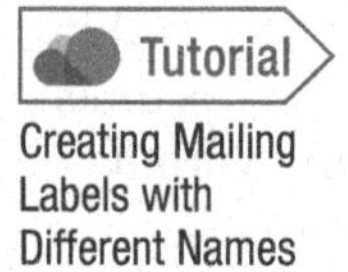

Creating Mailing Labels with Different Names and Addresses

Labels

Creating Mailing Labels with Different Names and Addresses

To create a sheet of mailing labels with a different name and address on each label, click the Labels button in the Create group on the Mailings tab. At the Envelopes and Labels dialog box with the Labels tab selected, as shown in Figure 6.9, leave the *Address* text box empty and then click the New Document button to insert the labels in a new document. The insertion point is positioned in the first label. Type the name and address in the label and then press the Tab key one or two times (depending on the label) to move the insertion point to the next label. Pressing Shift + Tab will move the insertion point to the preceding label.

Changing Label Options

Click the Options button at the Envelopes and Labels dialog box with the Labels tab selected and the Label Options dialog box displays, as shown in Figure 6.10. At the Label Options dialog box, choose the type of printer, the type and brand of label, and the product number. This dialog box also provides information about the selected label, such as type, height, width, and paper size. When a label is selected, Word automatically determines the label margins. To customize these default settings, click the Details button at the Label Options dialog box.

Figure 6.9 Envelopes and Labels Dialog Box with the Labels Tab Selected

Figure 6.10 Label Options Dialog Box

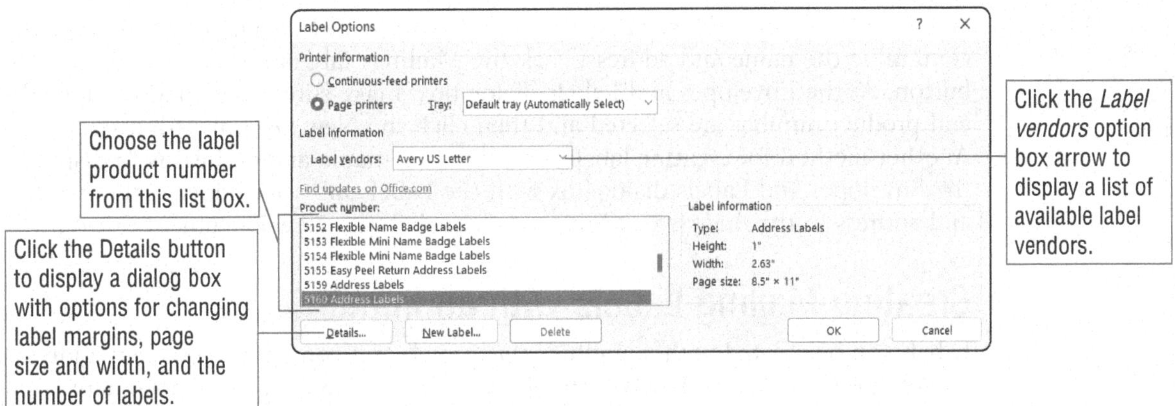

Activity 4a Creating Mailing Labels with Different Names and Addresses

Part 1 of 2

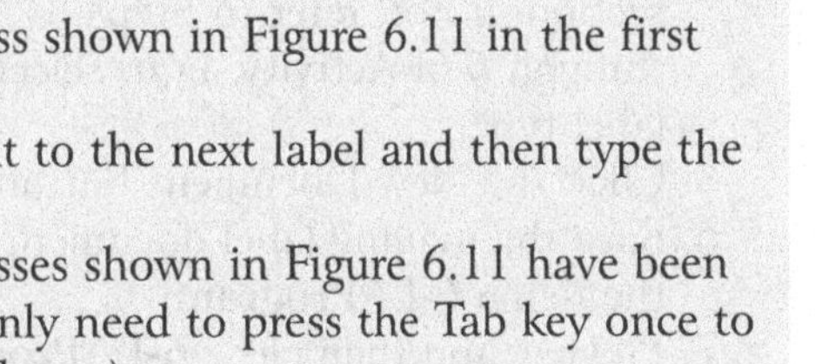

1. At a blank document, click the Mailings tab.
2. Click the Labels button in the Create group.
3. At the Envelopes and Labels dialog box with the Labels tab selected, click the Options button.
4. At the Label Options dialog box, click the *Label vendors* option box arrow and then click *Avery US Letter* at the drop-down list. (You may need to scroll down the list to see this option.)
5. Scroll down the *Product number* list box and then click *5160 Address Labels*.
6. Click OK or press the Enter key.
7. At the Envelopes and Labels dialog box, click the New Document button.
8. At the document screen, type the first name and address shown in Figure 6.11 in the first label.
9. Press the Tab key two times to move the insertion point to the next label and then type the second name and address shown in Figure 6.11.
10. Continue in this manner until all the names and addresses shown in Figure 6.11 have been typed. (After typing the third name and address, you only need to press the Tab key once to move the insertion point to the first label in the second row.)
11. Save the document with the name **6-Labels**.
12. Preview and then close **6-Labels.docx**.
13. Close the blank document without saving changes.

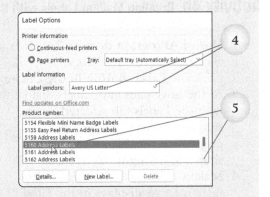

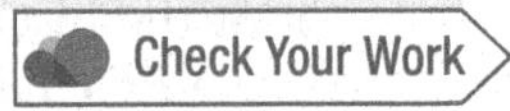

Figure 6.11 Activity 4a

DAVID LOWRY 12033 S 152 ST HOUSTON TX 77340	MARCELLA SANTOS 394 APPLE BLOSSOM DR FRIENDSWOOD TX 77533	KEVIN DORSEY 26302 PRAIRIE DR HOUSTON TX 77316
AL AND DONNA SASAKI 1392 PIONEER DR BAYTOWN TX 77903	JACKIE RHYNER 29039 107 AVE E HOUSTON TX 77302	MARK AND TINA ELLIS 607 FORD AVE HOUSTON TX 77307

Creating Mailing Labels with the Same Name and Address and an Image

Creating Mailing Labels with the Same Name and Address

To create labels with the same name and address on each label, open a document containing the name and address, click the Mailings tab, and then click the Labels button. At the Envelopes and Labels dialog box, make sure the desired label vendor and product number are selected and then click the New Document button. Another method for creating labels with the same name and address is to display the Envelopes and Labels dialog box with the Labels tab selected, type the name and address in the *Address* text box, and then click the New Document button.

Creating Mailing Labels with an Image

Labels can be created with a graphic image, such as a company's logo and address and/or slogan. To create labels with an image, insert the image in a document, select the image, click the Mailings tab, and then click the Labels button. At the Envelopes and Labels dialog box, make sure the correct vendor and product number are selected and then click the New Document button.

Activity 4b Creating Mailing Labels with the Same Name and Address and an Image Part 2 of 2

1. Open **LAProgram.docx** and create mailing labels with the delivery address. Begin by clicking the Mailings tab.
2. Click the Labels button in the Create group.
3. At the Envelopes and Labels dialog box with the Labels tab selected, make sure the delivery address displays properly in the *Address* text box, as shown at the right.
4. Make sure *Avery US Letter, 5160 Address Labels* displays in the *Label* section; if not, refer to Steps 3 through 6 of Activity 4a to select the label type.
5. Click the New Document button.
6. Save the mailing label document with the name **6-LAProgram.**
7. Preview and then close **6-LAProgram.docx.**

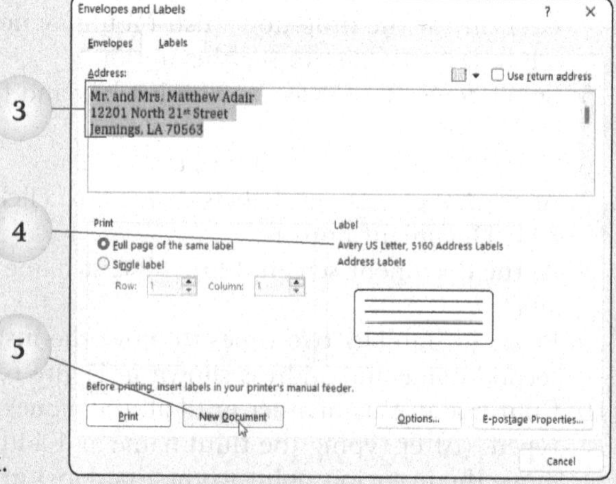

8. Close **LAProgram.docx.**
9. At a blank document, insert an image by completing the following steps:
   a. Click the Insert tab, click the Pictures button in the Illustrations group, and then click the *This Device* option at the drop-down list.
   b. At the Insert Picture dialog box, navigate to your WL1C6 folder and then double-click the ***BGCLabels.png*** image file.
10. With the image selected in the document, click the Mailings tab and then click the Labels button.
11. At the Envelopes and Labels dialog box, make sure *Avery US Letter, 5160 Address Labels* displays in the *Label* section and then click the New Document button.
12. Save the document with the name **6-BGCLabels.**
13. Preview and then close **6-BGCLabels.docx.**
14. Close the document containing the image without saving changes.

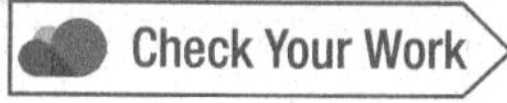

Activity 5 Create a Business Letter Using a Template **1 Part**

You will use a letter template provided by Word to create a business letter.

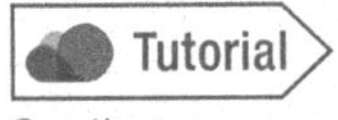

Creating a Document Using a Template

Quick Steps

Create Document Using Template

1. Click File tab.
2. Click *New* option.
3. Click or double-click template.

OR

1. Click File tab.
2. Click *New* option.
3. Click in search text box.
4. Type search text.
5. Press Enter.
6. Double-click template.

Creating a Document Using a Template

Word includes a number of document templates that are formatted for specific uses. Each Word document is based on a template document and the Normal template is the default. Choose from other available Word templates to create a variety of documents with special formatting, such as letters, calendars, and certificates.

View available templates by clicking the File tab and then clicking the *New* option. Thumbnails of various templates display in the New backstage area, as shown in Figure 6.12. Open one of the templates by double-clicking it. This opens a new document based on the template.

In addition to the templates that are shown at the New backstage area, templates can be downloaded from the internet. To do this, click in the search text box, type the search text or category, and then press the Enter key. Templates that match the search text or category display in the New backstage area. Click the template and then click the Create button or double-click the template. This downloads the template and opens a document based on it. Placeholders or content controls may appear in the document as suggested locations for personalized text. Click the placeholder or content control and then type text to personalize the document.

If a template is used on a regular basis, consider pinning it to the New backstage area. To do this, search for the template, hover the pointer over it, and then click the pin (Pin to list) to the right of the template name. To unpin a template, click the pin (Unpin from list).

Figure 6.12 New Backstage Area

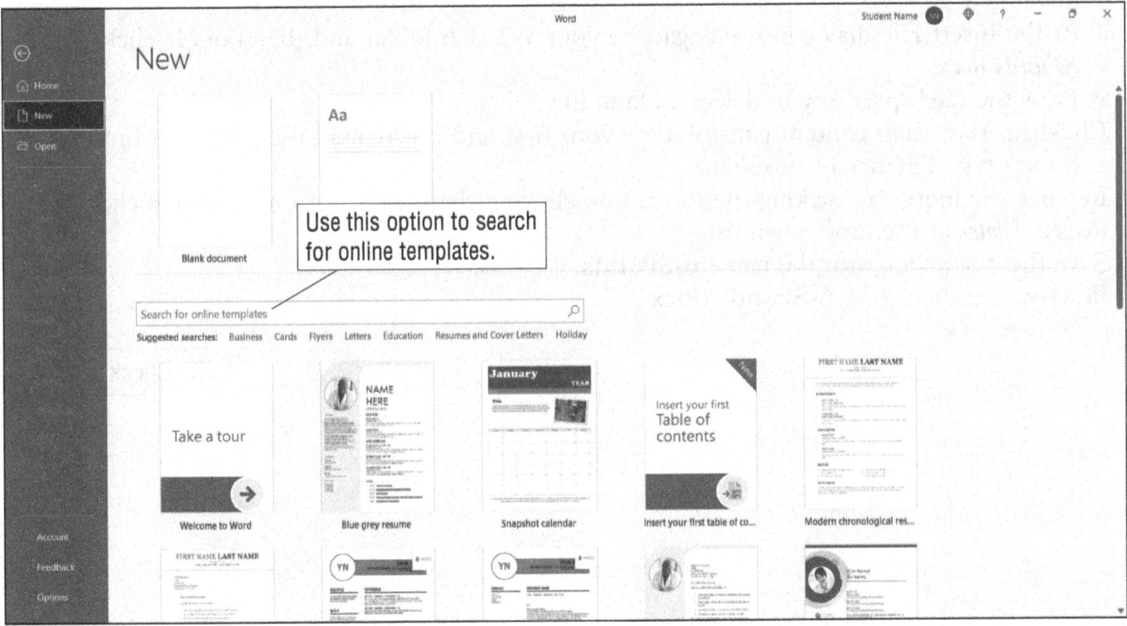

Activity 5 Creating a Business Letter Using a Template

Part 1 of 1

1. Click the File tab and then click the *New* option.
2. At the New backstage area, click in the search text box, type business letter simple design and then press the Enter key.
3. Double-click the *Business letter (simple design)* template. (If this template is not available, open **BusinessLetter.docx** from your WL1C6 folder.)

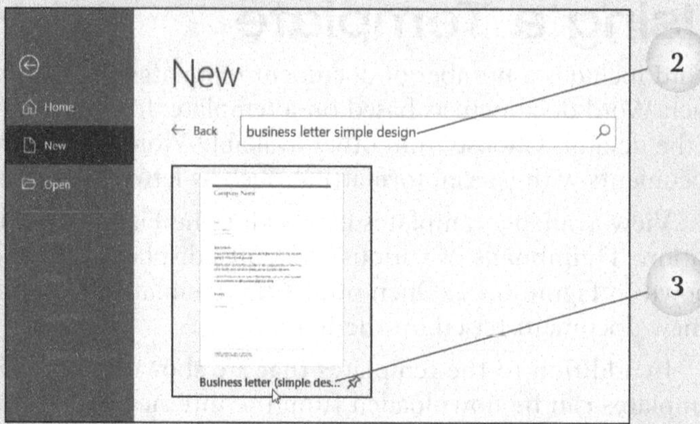

4. When the business letter document displays on the screen, click the *Company Name* content control and then type Sorenson Funds. (Clicking anywhere in the *Company Name* content control selects the entire control.)
5. Click the *Date* content control and then type the current date.
6. Click the *Street Address City, ST ZIP Code* content control. Type Ms. Jennifer Gonzalez, press the Enter key, type 12990 Boyd Street, press the Enter key, and then type Baltimore, MD 20375.
7. Click the *Recipient* content control and then type Ms. Gonzalez.
8. Insert a file in the document by completing the following steps:
    a. Click in the three paragraphs of text in the body of the letter and then press the Delete key.
    b. Click the Insert tab.
    c. Click the Object button arrow in the Text group and then click *Text from File* at the drop-down list.
    d. At the Insert File dialog box, navigate to your WL1C6 folder and then double-click ***SFunds.docx***.
    e. Press the Backspace key to delete a blank line.
9. Click the *Your Name* content control, type your first and last names, press Shift + Enter, and then type Financial Consultant.
10. Remove the footer by clicking the Insert tab, clicking the Footer button, and then clicking *Remove Footer* at the drop-down list.
11. Save the document with the name **6-SFunds**.
12. Preview and then close **6-SFunds.docx**.

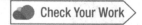

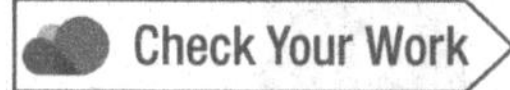

Activity 6 Save Documents in Different File Formats — 2 Parts

You will save an apartment lease agreement document in different file formats, including Word 97-2003 and plain text. You will also save a company document as a PDF file and then edit the file in Word.

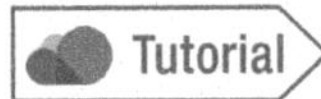

Saving in a Different Format

Quick Steps

Save in Different Format at Save As Dialog Box

1. Press F12 to display Save As dialog box.
2. Type document name.
3. Click *Save as type* option box.
4. Click format.
5. Click Save button.

Saving in a Different Format

When a document is saved, it is saved as a Word document with the file extension *.docx*. If the document is to be shared with someone who is using a different word processing program or a different version of Word, consider saving the document in another format. Save a document in a different file format by clicking the File tab and then clicking the *Export* option. At the Export backstage area, click the *Change File Type* option. Available file types display as shown in Figure 6.13. Save the Word document with the default file format, in a previous version of Word, in the OpenDocument Text format, or as a template. The OpenDocument Text format is an XML-based file format free from licensing and restrictions. It was designed to make word processing, spreadsheet, and presentation files easier to share across applications.

If a document is being sent to a user who does not have access to Microsoft Word, consider saving the document in plain text or rich text file format. Use the *Plain Text (*.txt)* option to save the document with all the formatting stripped, which is good for universal file exchange. Use the *Rich Text Format (*.rtf)* option to save the document and preserve most of the formatting, including bold, italic, underline, bullets, and fonts. With the *Single File Web Page (*.mht, *.mhtml)* option, a document can be saved as a single-page web document. Double-click the *Save as Another File Type* option and the Save As dialog box opens. Use the *Save as type* option box to specify the file format.

In addition to displaying the Save As dialog box through the Export backstage area, the dialog box can be displayed by clicking the File tab, clicking the *Save As* option, and then clicking the *Browse* option. (Pressing the F12 function key will also display the Save As dialog box.) Click the *Save as type* option box at the Save As dialog box and a drop-down list displays containing all the available file formats for saving a document. Click the specific format and then click the Save button.

Figure 6.13 Export Backstage Area with the *Change File Type* Option Selected

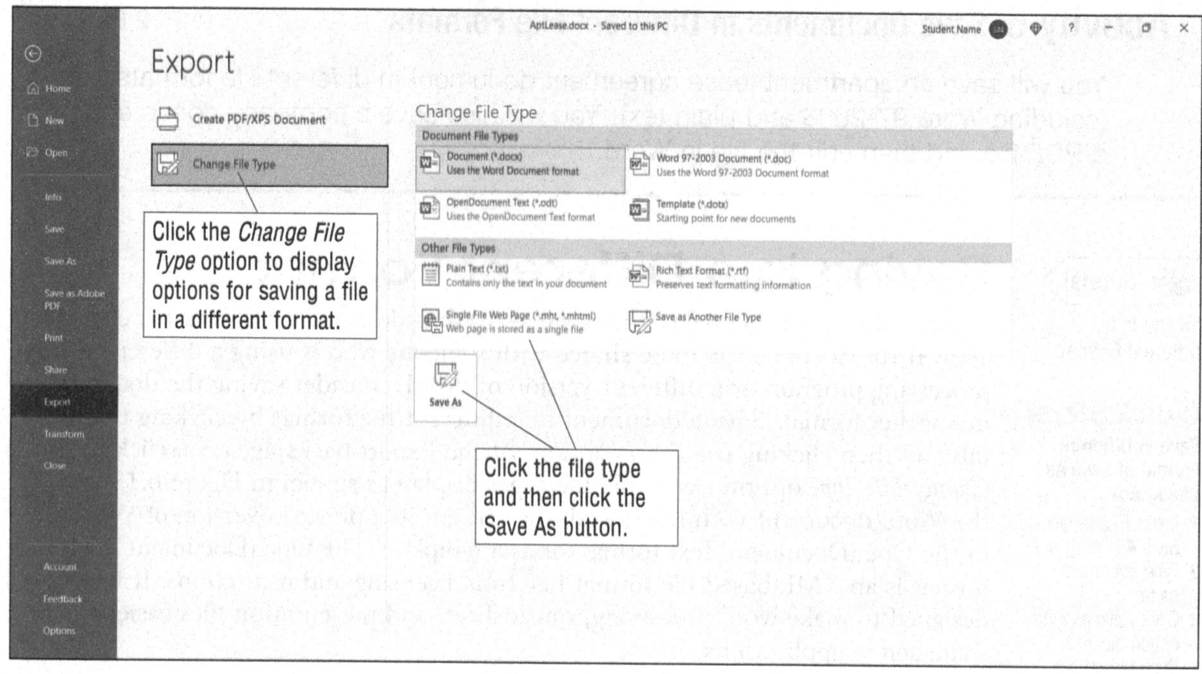

Activity 6a **Saving in Different File Formats**

Part 1 of 2

1. Open **AptLease.docx** and then save it in Word 97-2003 format by completing the following steps:
   a. Click the File tab and then click the *Export* option.
   b. At the Export backstage area, click the *Change File Type* option.
   c. Click the *Word 97-2003 Document (*.doc)* option in the *Document File Types* section.
   d. Click the Save As button.

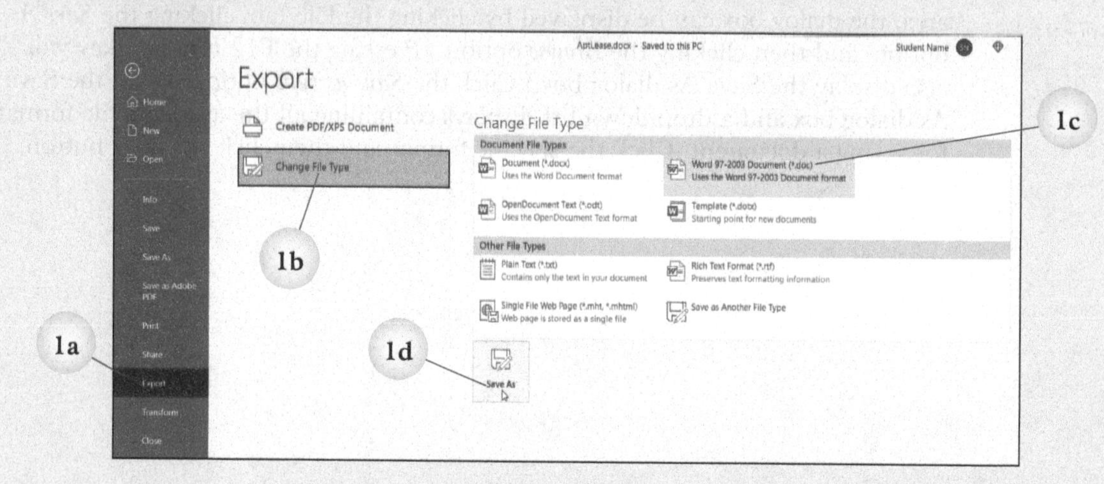

e. At the Save As dialog box with the *Save as type* option changed to *Word 97-2003 Document (*.doc)*, type 6-AptLease-Word97-2003 in the *File name* text box and then press the Enter key.

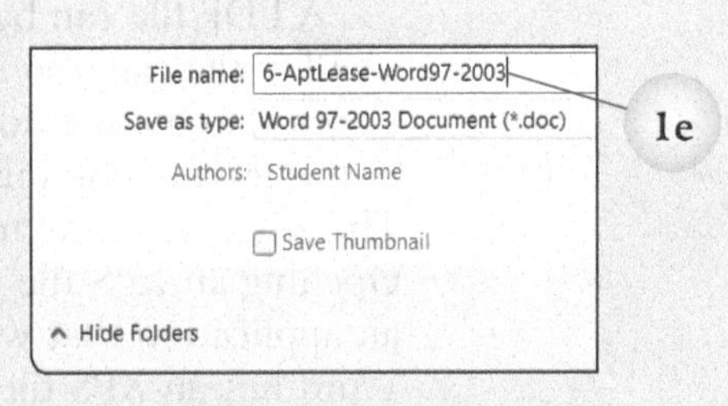

2. At the document, notice *Compatibility Mode* after the document name.
3. Click the Design tab and notice that the Themes, Colors, and Fonts buttons are dimmed. (This is because the themes features were not available in Word 97 through 2003.)
4. Close **6-AptLease-Word97-2003.doc**.
5. Open **AptLease.docx**.
6. Save the document in OpenDocument Text format at the Save As dialog box by completing the following steps:
   a. Press the F12 function key to display the Save As dialog box.
   b. At the Save As dialog box, type 6-AptLease-OpenDocTxt in the *File name* text box.
   c. Click the *Save as type* option box.
   d. Click *OpenDocument Text (*.odt)* at the drop-down list.
   e. Click the Save button.
   f. At the message that displays, click the Yes button.

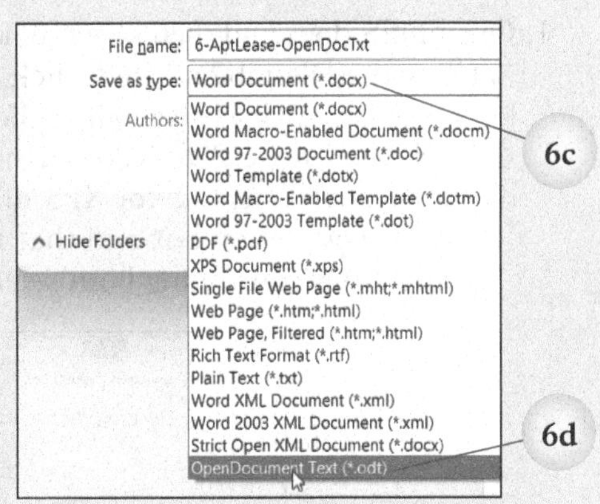

7. Close **6-AptLease-OpenDocTxt.odt**.
8. Display the Open dialog box and, if necessary, display all the files. To do this, click the file type button at the right of the *File name* text box and then click *All Files (*.*)* at the drop-down list.

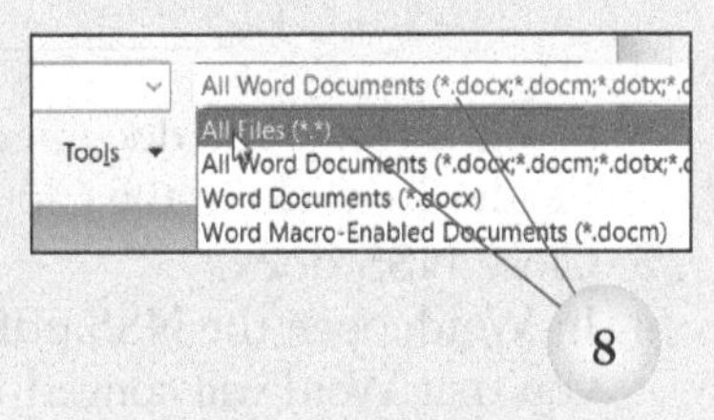

9. Double-click ***6-AptLease-OpenDocTxt.odt***. (Notice that the document has retained the formatting.)
10. Close **6-AptLease-OpenDocTxt.odt**.

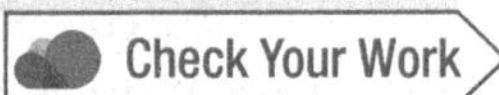

Saving and Opening a Document as a PDF File

Quick Steps

Save a PDF File or in XPS Format
1. Click File tab.
2. Click *Export* option.
3. Click Create PDF/XPS button.
4. At Publish as PDF or XPS dialog box, specify PDF or XPS format.
5. Click Publish button.

A Word document can be saved as a PDF file or in the XPS file format. PDF stands for *portable document format* and is a file format that preserves fonts, formatting, and images in a printer-friendly version that looks the same on most computers. A person who receives a Word file saved as a PDF file does not need to have the Word application on their computer to open, read, and print the file. Exchanging PDF files is a popular method for collaborating, since this file type has cross-platform compatibility, allowing users to open PDF files on both Macintosh and Windows-based computers, as well as different brands of tablets and smartphones. The XML paper specification (XPS) format, which was developed by Microsoft, is a fixed-layout format with all the formatting preserved (similar to PDF).

To save a document as a PDF file or in XPS format, click the File tab, click the *Export* option, and then click the Create PDF/XPS button. This displays the Publish as PDF or XPS dialog box with the *PDF (*.pdf)* option selected in the *Save as type* option box. To save the document in XPS format, click the *Save as type* option box and then click *XPS Document (*.xps)* at the drop-down list. At the Save As dialog box, type a name in the *File name* text box and then click the Publish button.

A PDF file can be opened in Adobe Acrobat Reader, Microsoft Edge, or Word. (A PDF file can also be opened in other available web browsers, such as Google Chrome.) One method for opening a PDF file is to open File Explorer, navigate to the folder containing the file, right-click the file, and then point to *Open with*. This displays a side menu with the programs that can be used to open the file. Opening an XPS file may require opening the Microsoft Store and searching for an application that will open the file. A PDF file can be opened and edited in Word but an XPS file cannot.

Activity 6b Saving as a PDF File and Editing a PDF File in Word

Part 2 of 2

1. Open **NSS.docx** and then save the document as a PDF file by completing the following steps:
   a. Click the File tab and then click the *Export* option.
   b. At the Export backstage area, click the *Create PDF/XPS Document* option.
   c. Click the Create PDF/XPS button.
   d. At the Publish as PDF or XPS dialog box, make sure that *PDF (*.pdf)* is selected in the *Save as type* option box and that the *Open file after publishing* check box contains a check mark. After confirming both selections, click the Publish button.

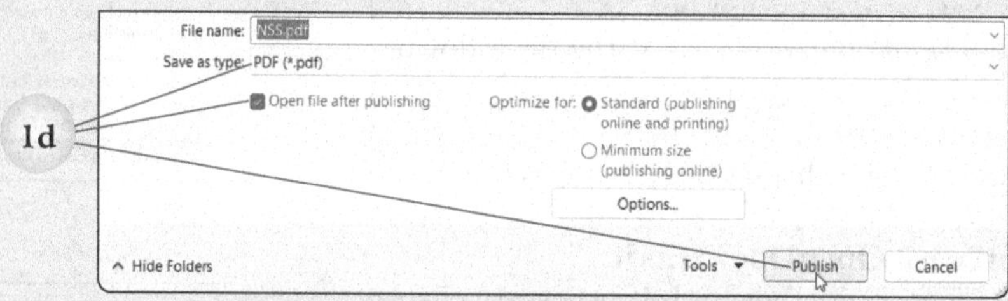

2. Scroll through the document in Adobe Acrobat Reader and then close Adobe Acrobat Reader by clicking the Close button in the upper right corner of the window.
3. Close **NSS.docx**.
4. In Word, open the **NSS.pdf** PDF file you saved to your WL1C6 folder. At the message telling you that Word will convert the file to an editable Word document, click OK.
5. Notice that the formatting of the text is slightly different from the original formatting. Edit the file by completing the following steps:
   a. Click the Design tab and then click the *Lines (Distinctive)* style set.
   b. Delete the text *We are* in the text below the first heading and replace it with Northland Security Systems is.
6. Save the file with Save As with the name **6-NSS**. (The file will be saved as a Word file.)
7. Preview and then close **6-NSS.docx**.
8. Make a screen capture of the Open dialog box and then paste it in a Word document and print the document by completing the following steps:
   a. Display the Open dialog box.
   b. Press and hold down the Alt key, press the Print Screen button on your keyboard, and then release the Alt key.
   c. Close the Open dialog box and close the Open backstage area.
   d. Press Ctrl + N to open a blank document.
   e. Click the Paste button.
9. Save the document with the name **6-ScreenCapture**.
10. Preview and then close **6-ScreenCapture.docx**.

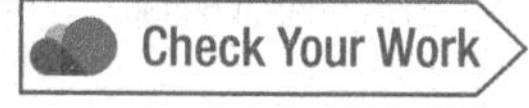

Activity 7 Save and Open a Document Based on a Template 2 Parts

You will open a summons document, save it as a template, use it to create a summons, and then find and replace text within the document. You will also save the summons document as a template in your WL1C6 folder and then use File Explorer to locate the template and open a new document based on it.

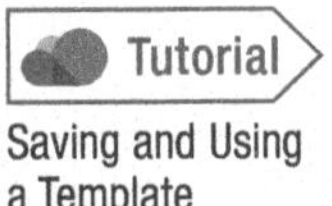

Saving and Using a Template

Saving a Template

Using a template to create a document has several advantages. A template provides consistency and uniformity in documents, reduces document preparation time, offers increased flexibility, and templates are easy to update. Save a template by changing the *Save as type* option at the Save As dialog box to *Word Template (*.dotx)*.

Saving a Template in the Custom Office Templates Folder

When the *Save as type* option is changed to *Word Template (*.dotx)*, Word will save the document as a template in the Custom Office Templates folder. To use the template, click the File tab and then click the *New* option. At the New backstage area, click the *Personal* option. This displays custom templates in the New backstage area. Double-click a template to open a new document based on that template.

Activity 7a Saving and Opening a Document Based on a Template Part 1 of 2

1. Open **Summons.docx** and then save it as a template in the Custom Office Templates folder by completing the following steps:
   a. Press the F12 function key to display the Save As dialog box.
   b. At the Save As dialog box, click the *Save as type* option box and then click *Word Template (*.dotx)* at the drop-down list. (When the *Save as type* option is changed to *Word Template (*.dotx)*, Word automatically makes Custom Office Templates the active folder.)
   c. Select the name in the *File name* text box, type your last name followed by Summons, and then press the Enter key.

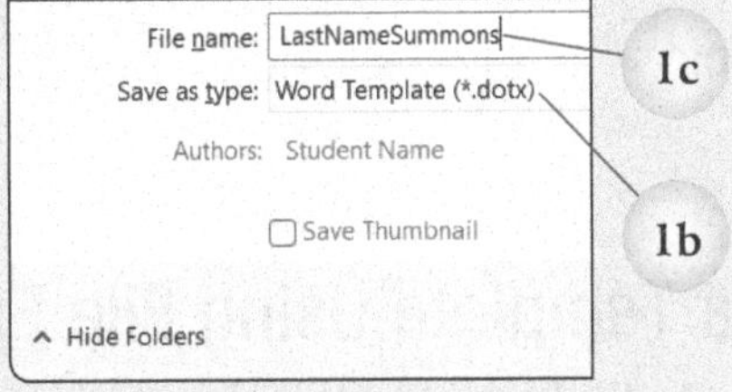

2. Close the summons template.

3. Open a document based on the summons template by completing the following steps:
   a. Click the File tab and then click the *New* option.
   b. At the New backstage area, click the *Personal* option.
   c. Click the summons template that is preceded by your last name.
4. With the summons document open, find and replace text as follows:
   a. Find *NAME1* and replace all occurrences with *AMY GARCIA*.
   b. Find *NAME2* and replace all occurrences with *NEIL CARLIN*.
   c. Find *NUMBER* and replace with *C-98002*.
5. Save the document in your WL1C6 folder with the name **6-SummonsGarcia**.
6. Preview and then close **6-SummonsGarcia.docx**.
7. Delete the summons template from the hard drive by completing the following steps:
   a. Press Ctrl + F12 to display the Open dialog box.
   b. At the Open dialog box, click the *Documents* folder in the Navigation pane.
   c. Double-click the *Custom Office Templates* folder in the Content pane.
   d. Click the summons template that begins with your last name.
   e. Click the Organize button and then click *Delete* at the drop-down list.

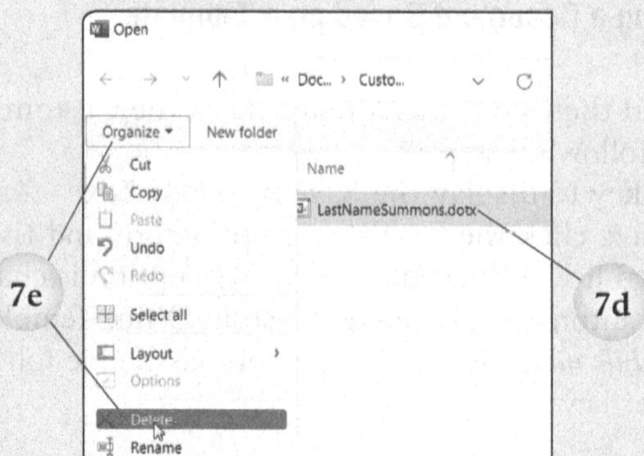

8. Close the Open dialog box.

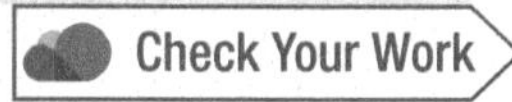

Opening a Template Using File Explorer

In Word, opening a document based on a template is accomplished through the New backstage area with the *Personal* option selected. If a template is saved in a location other than the Custom Office Templates folder, File Explorer can be used to open a document based on the template. To do this, click the File Explorer button on the taskbar, navigate to the folder containing the template, and then double-click the template. This will open a new document based on the template.

Activity 7b Using File Explorer to Open a Document Based on a Template

1. Open **Summons.docx** and then save it as a template in your WL1C6 folder by completing the following steps:
   a. Click the File tab and then click the *Export* option.
   b. At the Export backstage area, click the *Change File Type* option.
   c. Click the *Template (*.dotx)* option in the *Document File Types* section.
   d. Click the Save As button.

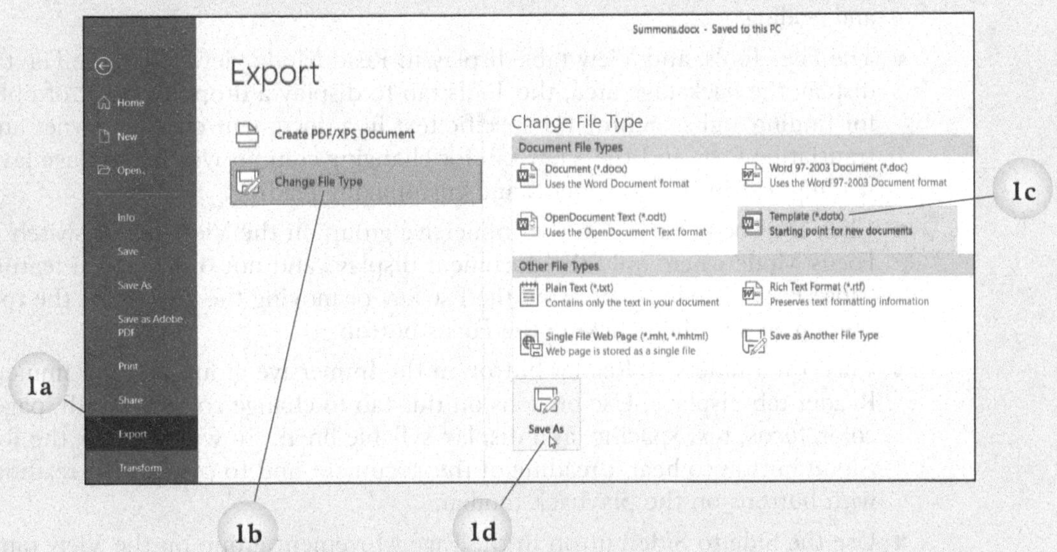

   e. At the Save As dialog box with *Word Template (*.dotx)* in the *Save as type* option box, type 6-SummonsTemplate in the *File name* text box.
   f. Navigate to your WL1C6 folder and then click the Save button.
2. Close the summons template.
3. Open a document based on the summons template using File Explorer by completing the following steps:
   a. Click the File Explorer button on the taskbar. (The taskbar displays along the bottom of the screen.)
   b. Navigate to your WL1C6 folder and then double-click ***6-SummonsTemplate.dotx***.
4. With the summons document open, find and replace text as follows:
   a. Find *NAME1* and replace all occurrences with *CASEY NYE*.
   b. Find *NAME2* and replace all occurrences with *SANDRA IVERS*.
   c. Find *NUMBER* and replace with *C-99743*.
5. Save the document in your WL1C6 folder with the name **6-SummonsNye**.
6. Preview and then close **6-SummonsNye.docx**.

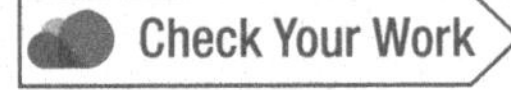

Chapter Summary

- Change the document view with buttons in the view area on the Status bar or with options in the Views group on the View tab.
- Print Layout is the default view but this can be changed to other views, such as Draft view, Web Layout view and Read Mode view.
- Draft view displays the document in a format for efficient editing and formatting. Change to Web Layout view to display a document as it would appear online. Read Mode view displays a document in a format for easy viewing and reading.
- The File, Tools, and View tabs display in Read Mode view. Click the File tab to display the backstage area, the Tools tab to display a drop-down list of options for finding and searching for specific text in a document or the internet and translating text, and the View tab for changing column width and page layout, reading text in the document, and customizing reading.
- Click the Focus button in the Immersive group on the View tab to switch to Focus Mode where only the document displays and not other screen features. Close Focus Mode by pressing the Esc key or moving the pointer to the top of the screen and then clicking the Focus button.
- Click the Immersive Reader button in the Immersive group and the Immersive Reader tab displays. Use buttons on this tab to change column width, page color, focus, text spacing, and display syllable breaks in words. Click the Read Aloud button to hear a reading of the document and to control the reading with buttons on the playback toolbar.
- Use the Side to Side button in the Page Movement group on the View tab to change page movement in a document from the default of vertical to side to side, where two pages are shown at one time. On a screen without touch screen capabilities, scroll through the side to side pages using the horizontal scroll bar or the mouse wheel. Click the Vertical button on the View tab to return to the default page movement.
- Use the Zoom slider bar or buttons in the Zoom group on the View tab to change the display percentage.
- Use options at the Ribbon Display Options button drop-down list to specify if the Quick Access Toolbar, ribbon, and Status bar should be visible or hidden.
- Save space on the screen by hiding white space at the top and bottom of pages. Hide white space using the Hide White Space icon, which appears when the pointer is positioned at the top or bottom edge of a page. Redisplay white space using the Show White Space icon, which appears when the pointer is positioned on the thin gray line separating pages.
- Move among open documents by hovering the pointer over the Word button on the taskbar and then clicking the thumbnail of the document or by clicking the View tab, clicking the Switch Windows button in the Window group, and then clicking the document name.
- View portions of all open documents by clicking the View tab and then clicking the Arrange All button in the Window group.
- Use the Minimize, Restore, and Maximize buttons in the upper right corner of the active window to reduce or increase the size of the window.
- Divide a window into two panes by clicking the View tab and then clicking the Split button in the Window group.

- View the contents of two open documents side by side by clicking the View tab and then clicking the View Side by Side button in the Window group.
- Open a new window containing the same document by clicking the View tab and then clicking the New Window button in the Window group.
- Insert a document into the open document by clicking the Insert tab, clicking the Object button arrow, and then clicking *Text from File* at the drop-down list. At the Insert File dialog box, double-click the document.
- Preview a document at the Print backstage area. Scroll through the pages in the document with the Next Page and the Previous Page buttons, which are below the preview page. Use the Zoom slider bar to increase or decrease the display size of the preview page.
- Use options at the Print backstage area to customize a print job by changing the page orientation, size, and margins; specify how many pages to print on one page; indicate the number of copies and whether to collate the pages; and specify the printer.
- Prepare and print an envelope at the Envelopes and Labels dialog box with the Envelopes tab selected.
- If the Envelopes and Labels dialog box is opened in a document containing a name and address (with each line ending with a press of the Enter key), that information is automatically inserted in the *Delivery address* text box in the dialog box.
- Use Word's labels feature to print text on mailing labels, file labels, and other types of labels. Create labels at the Envelopes and Labels dialog box with the Labels tab selected.
- Available templates are shown in the New backstage area. Double-click a template to open a document based on it. Search for templates online by typing the search text or category in the search text box and then pressing the Enter key.
- Click the *Change File Type* option at the Export backstage area and options display for saving the document in a different file format. Documents can also be saved in different file formats with the *Save as type* option box at the Save As dialog box.
- Save a document as a PDF file or in XPS format at the Publish as PDF or XPS dialog box. Display this dialog box by clicking the *Create PDF/XPS Document* option at the Export backstage area and then clicking the Create PDF/XPS button. A PDF file can be opened and edited in Word.
- Change the *Save as type* option at the Save As dialog box to *Word Template (*.dotx)* and the Custom Office Templates folder becomes the active folder. A template saved in this folder is available at the New backstage area with the *Personal* option selected. Open a document based on a template at the New backstage area with the *Personal* option selected.
- If a template is saved in a location other than the Custom Office Templates folder, File Explorer can be used to open a document based on the template.

Commands Review

FEATURE	RIBBON TAB, GROUP/OPTION	BUTTON, OPTION	KEYBOARD SHORTCUT
arrange documents	View, Window		
Draft view	View, Views		
Envelopes and Labels dialog box with Envelopes tab selected	Mailings, Create		
Envelopes and Labels dialog box with Labels tab selected	Mailings, Create		
Export backstage area	File, *Export*		
Focus mode	View, Immersive		
Immersive Reader	View, Immersive		
Insert File dialog box	Insert, Text	, *Text from File*	
maximize document			Ctrl + F10
minimize document			
New backstage area	File, *New*		
new window	View, Window		
Print backstage area	File, *Print*		Ctrl + P
Read Mode view	View, Views		
restore document to previous size			
side to side page movement	View, Page Movement		
split window	View, Window		Alt + Ctrl + S
switch windows	View, Window		
synchronous scrolling	View, Window		
vertical page movement	View, Page Movement		
view documents side by side	View, Window		
Web Layout view	View, Views		

Review and Assessment

CHAPTER 6

Skills Assessment

Assessment 1

Manage Documents

1. Open **OMSHandbook.docx**.
2. Change to Draft view.
3. Change to Read Mode view and then return to the document. ***Hint: To return to the document, click the View tab and then click the* Edit Document *option.***
4. Display the Immersive Reader tab and then make the following changes:
   a. Change the column width to Wide.
   b. Change the page color to Sepia (third column, first row).
   c. If a speaker is connected to your computer, start the reading of the document.
   d. Use buttons on the playback toolbar to skip to the next paragraph, skip to the previous paragraph, change the reading voice to the male voice, and then change back to female voice.
   e. Close Immersive Reader.
5. Change the page movement to side to side, display page thumbnails, remove the display of thumbnails, and then change page movement back to vertical.
6. Close **OMSHandbook.docx**.
7. Open **StaffMtg.docx**, **Agreement.docx**, and **Robots.docx**.
8. Make **Agreement.docx** the active document.
9. Make **StaffMtg.docx** the active document.
10. Arrange all the windows.
11. Make **Robots.docx** the active document and then minimize it.
12. Minimize the remaining documents.
13. Restore **StaffMtg.docx**.
14. Restore **Agreement.docx**.
15. Restore **Robots.docx**.
16. Maximize and then close **StaffMtg.docx** and then maximize and close **Robots.docx**.
17. Maximize **Agreement.docx** and then save the document with the name **6-Agreement**.
18. Open **AptLease.docx**.
19. View **6-Agreement.docx** and **AptLease.docx** side by side.
20. Scroll through both documents simultaneously and notice the formatting differences between the titles, headings, and fonts in the two documents. Change the font and apply shading to only the title and headings in **6-Agreement.docx** to match the font and shading of the title and headings in **AptLease.docx**.
21. Make **AptLease.docx** active and then close it.
22. Save **6-Agreement.docx**.
23. Move the insertion point to the end of the document and then insert the document **Terms.docx**.

24. Apply formatting to the inserted text so it matches the formatting of the previous text in **6-Agreement.docx**.
25. Move the insertion point to the end of the document and then insert the document **Signature.docx**.
26. Save, preview, and then close **6-Agreement.docx**.

Assessment 2

Prepare an Envelope

1. At a blank document, prepare an envelope with the text shown in Figure 6.14.
2. Save the envelope document with the name **6-EnvMiller**.
3. Preview and then close **6-EnvMiller.docx**.

Figure 6.14 Assessment 2

DR ROSEANNE HOLT
21330 CEDAR DR
LOGAN UT 84598

GENE MILLER
4559 CORRIN AVE
SMITHFIELD UT 84521

Assessment 3

Prepare Mailing Labels

1. Prepare mailing labels with the names and addresses shown in Figure 6.15. Use a label option of your choosing. (You may need to check with your instructor before choosing an option.) When entering a street number such as *147TH*, Word will convert the *th* to superscript letters when you press the spacebar after typing *147TH*. To remove the superscript formatting, immediately click the Undo button in the Undo group on the Home tab.
2. Save the document with the name **6-LabelsOhio**.
3. Preview and then close **6-LabelsOhio.docx**.
4. At the blank document screen, close the document without saving changes.

Figure 6.15 Assessment 3

SUSAN LUTOVSKY 1402 MELLINGER DR FAIRHOPE OH 43209	JIM AND PAT KEIL 413 JACKSON ST AVONDALE OH 43887	IRENE HAGEN 12930 147TH AVE E CANTON OH 43296
VINCE KILEY 14005 288TH ST CANTON OH 43287	LEONARD KRUEGER 13290 N 120TH ST CANTON OH 43291	HELGA GUNDSTROM PO BOX 3112 AVONDALE OH 43887

Assessment 4

Prepare an Award Certificate

1. Display the New backstage area, search for *formal award certificate*, and then download the *Formal award certificate* template. (If the template is not available at the New backstage area, open the **Certificate.docx** document from your WL1C6 folder.) Insert the following information in the specified fields:

Recipient Name	Curtis Sayers
Program / Project Name	Community Outreach / Micro Loans
Month, Day, Year	(insert current month, day, year)
SIGNED, Signature Name, Title	Emerson Day, President
Company Logo	(insert the image file **GoldStar.png**)

2. Save the document with the name **6-Certificate**.
3. Preview and then close **6-Certificate.docx**.

Assessment 5

Save a Document as a Web Page

1. Experiment with the *Save as type* option box at the Save As dialog box and figure out how to save a document as a single-file web page.
2. Open **NSS.docx**, display the Save As dialog box, and then change the *Save as type* option to *Single File Web Page (*.mht;*.mhtml)*. Click the Change Title button in the Save As dialog box. At the Enter Text dialog box, type Northland Security Systems in the *Page title* text box and then click OK to close the dialog box. Click the Save button in the Save As dialog box.
3. Close the **NSS.mht** web page file.
4. **Optional:** If possible, open your web browser and then open the **NSS.mht** web page file. You may need to check with your instructor to determine the specific steps on opening the web browser and opening the file.
5. Close your web browser.

Assessment

Prepare Personal Mailing Labels

1. At a blank document, type your name and address and then apply formatting to enhance the appearance of the text. (You determine the font, font size, and font color.)
2. Create labels with your name and address. (You determine the label vendor and product number.)
3. Save the label document with the name **6-PersonalLabels**.
4. Preview and then close **6-PersonalLabels.docx**.
5. Close the document containing your name and address without saving the changes.

Assessment 7

Save a Template; Open a Document Based on the Template

1. Open **Labels.docx** and then save it in the *Word Template* (**.dotx*) format in your WL1C6 folder and name the template **6-LabelsTemplate**.
2. Close **6-LabelsTemplate.dotx**.
3. Open File Explorer and then open a document based on the **6-LabelsTemplate.dotx** template document.
4. Click in the *Name* content control and then type Jack Stiles. (When you click in the Street Address content control in the next step, Word will automatically update the name on all labels.)
5. Click in the *Street Address* content control and then type 4493 Second Street. (When you click in the City, ST ZIP Code content control in the next step, Word will automatically update the street address on all labels.)
6. Click in the *City, ST ZIP Code* content control and then type Stowe, VT 05661.
7. Click anywhere in the label document and Word will automatically update the city, state, and zip code in all labels.
8. Save the completed document with the name **6-StilesLabels**.
9. Preview and then close **6-StilesLabels.docx**.

Assessment 8

Download and Complete an Award Certificate

1. Display the New backstage area and then search for and download an award template of your choosing. (Type award in the search text box and then download an award template that interests you.)
2. Insert the appropriate information in the award placeholders or content controls.
3. Save the completed award and name the document **6-Award**.
4. Preview and then close **6-Award.docx**.

Visual Benchmark

Activity 1

Prepare Custom Labels

1. You can create a sheet of labels with the same information in each label by typing the information in the *Address* text box at the Envelopes and Labels dialog box. Or you can type the information, select it, and then create the label. Using this technique, create the sheet of labels shown in Figure 6.16 with the following specifications:
   - Open **NSSLabels.docx**.
   - Set the text in 12-point Magneto.
   - Select the entire document and then create the labels using the Avery US Letter label vendor and the 5161 product number.
2. Save the labels document with the name **6-NSSLabels**.
3. Preview and then close **6-NSSLabels.docx**.
4. Close **NSSLabels.docx** without saving it.

Figure 6.16 Visual Benchmark 1

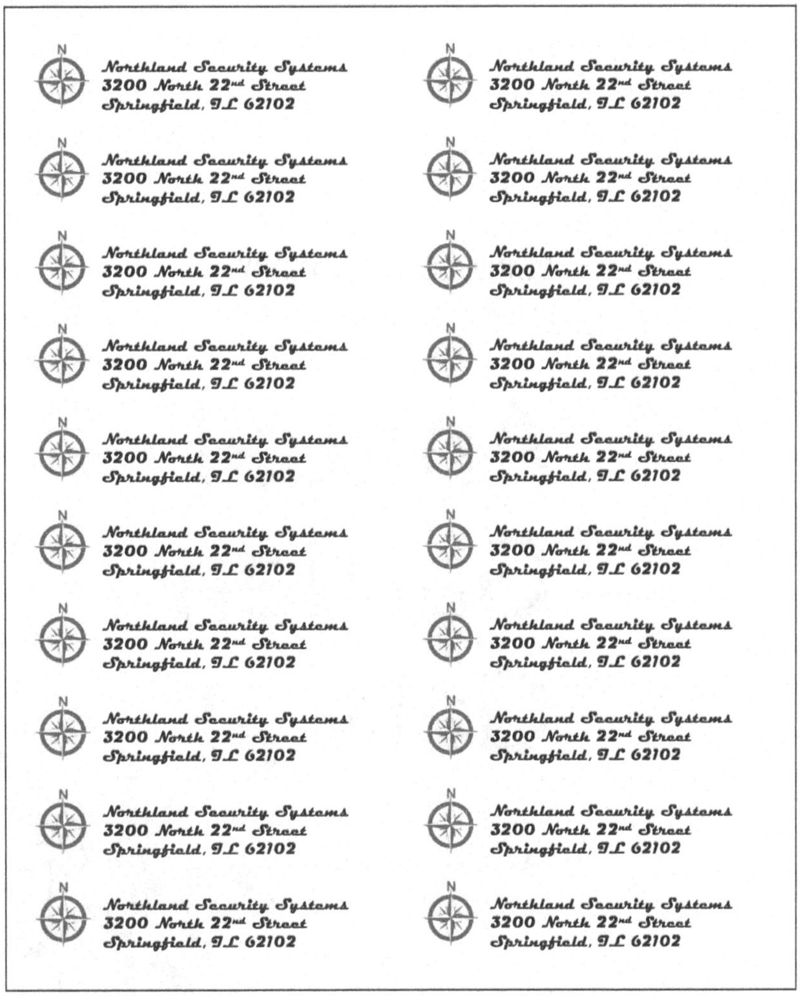

Northland Security Systems 3200 North 22nd Street Springfield, IL 62102	Northland Security Systems 3200 North 22nd Street Springfield, IL 62102
Northland Security Systems 3200 North 22nd Street Springfield, IL 62102	Northland Security Systems 3200 North 22nd Street Springfield, IL 62102
Northland Security Systems 3200 North 22nd Street Springfield, IL 62102	Northland Security Systems 3200 North 22nd Street Springfield, IL 62102
Northland Security Systems 3200 North 22nd Street Springfield, IL 62102	Northland Security Systems 3200 North 22nd Street Springfield, IL 62102
Northland Security Systems 3200 North 22nd Street Springfield, IL 62102	Northland Security Systems 3200 North 22nd Street Springfield, IL 62102
Northland Security Systems 3200 North 22nd Street Springfield, IL 62102	Northland Security Systems 3200 North 22nd Street Springfield, IL 62102
Northland Security Systems 3200 North 22nd Street Springfield, IL 62102	Northland Security Systems 3200 North 22nd Street Springfield, IL 62102
Northland Security Systems 3200 North 22nd Street Springfield, IL 62102	Northland Security Systems 3200 North 22nd Street Springfield, IL 62102
Northland Security Systems 3200 North 22nd Street Springfield, IL 62102	Northland Security Systems 3200 North 22nd Street Springfield, IL 62102
Northland Security Systems 3200 North 22nd Street Springfield, IL 62102	Northland Security Systems 3200 North 22nd Street Springfield, IL 62102

Activity 2

Create an Invitation

1. Open File Explorer and then open a document based on the template **GalaTemplate.dotx** located in your WL1C6 folder.
2. Type the text in the appropriate content controls as shown in Figure 6.17.
3. Change the color of the text *Annual Garden Gala* to Blue (eighth color in the *Standard Colors* section).
4. Change the color of the date and time text to Green, Accent 6, Darker 25% (last column, fifth row in the *Theme Colors* section).
5. Insert the **Flowers.png** image file from your WL1C6 folder with the following specifications:
   - Change the text wrapping to behind the text.
   - Set the light background as transparent. ***Hint: Use the* Set Transparent Color *option from the Color button on the Picture Format tab.***
   - Size and position the image so it appears as shown in Figure 6.17.
6. Save the invitation with the name **6-Gala**.
7. Save the invitation document as a PDF file with the same name.
8. Open the **6-Gala.pdf** file in Adobe Acrobat Reader, review the file, and then close Adobe Acrobat Reader.
9. Save, preview, and then close **6-Gala.docx**.

Figure 6.17 Visual Benchmark 2

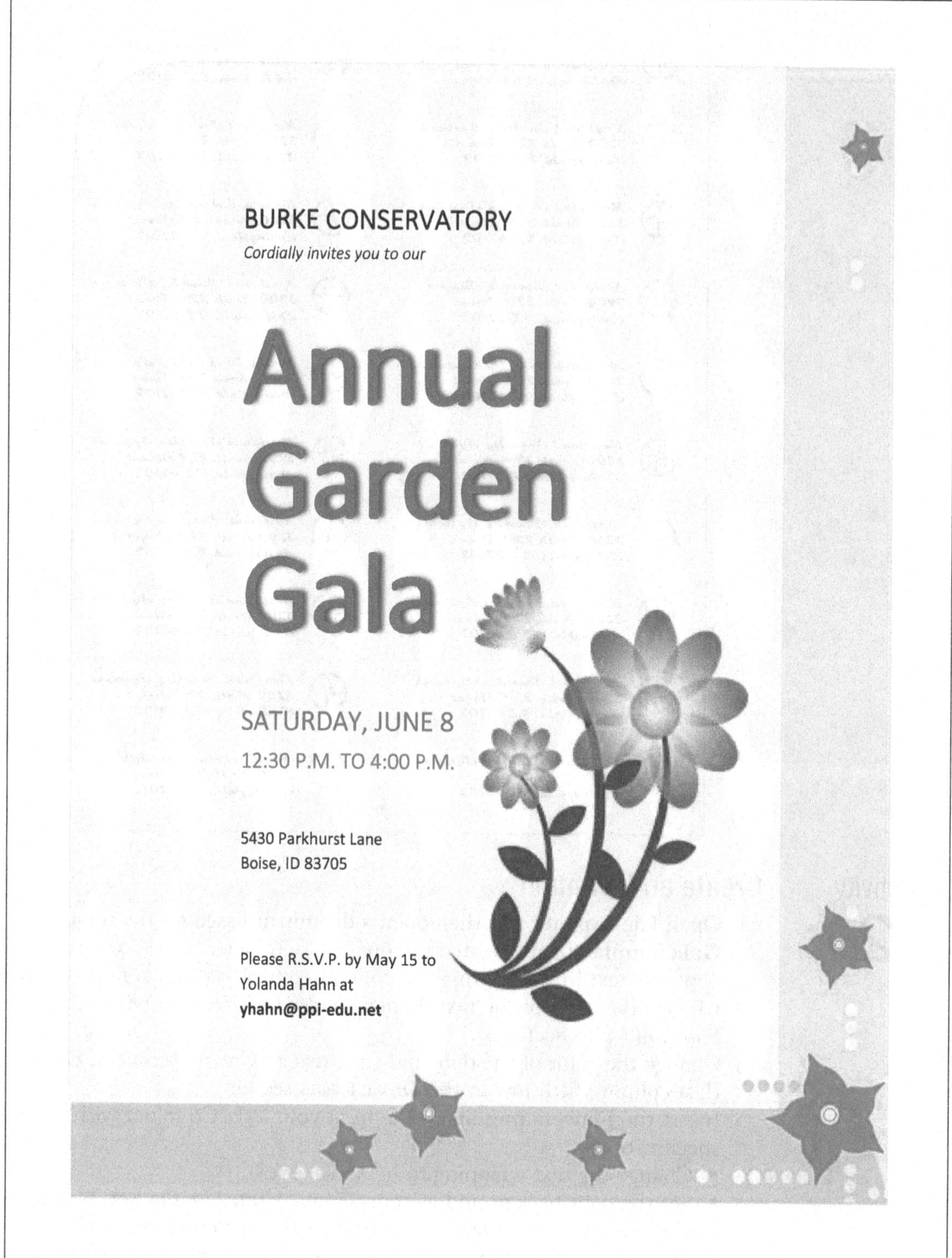

Case Study

Part 1

You are the office manager for a real estate company, Macadam Realty, and have been asked by the senior sales associate, Lucy Hendricks, to prepare mailing labels for the company. Include on the labels the company name, Macadam Realty, and the address, 100 Third Street, Suite 210, Denver, CO 80803. Use a decorative font for the name and address and make the *M* in *Macadam* and the *R* in *Realty* larger and more pronounced than the surrounding text. Save the completed document with the name **6-RELabels**. Preview and then close **6-RELabels.docx**.

Part 2

One of your responsibilities at Macadam Realty is to format contract forms. Open **REConAgrmnt.docx** and then save it with the name **6-REConAgrmnt**. Ms. Hendricks has asked you to insert signature information at the end of the document using the file named **RESig.docx**. With **6-REConAgrmnt.docx** still open, open **REBuildAgrmnt.docx**. Format **6-REConAgrmnt.docx** so it is formatted in a manner similar to **REBuildAgrmnt.docx**. Consider the following when specifying formatting: fonts, font sizes, font formatting, and paragraph shading. Save and then close **6-REConAgrmnt.docx**. Close **REBuildAgrmnt.docx**.

Part 3

Ms. Hendricks has asked you to insert document properties in **REBuildAgrmnt.docx** and **6-REConAgrmnt.docx**. Use the Help feature to learn how to insert document properties. With the information you learn from the Help feature, open each document separately, display the Info backstage area, click the Show All Properties hyperlink (you may need to scroll down the backstage area to locate this hyperlink), and then insert document properties in the following fields (you determine the information to type): *Title*, *Subject*, *Company*, and *Category*. Print the document properties for each document. (Change the first gallery in the *Settings* category in the Print backstage area to *Document Info*.) Save each document with the original name and then close the documents.

Part 4

A client of the real estate company, Anna Hurley, is considering purchasing several rental properties and has asked for information on how to locate real estate rental forms. Using the internet, locate at least three websites that offer real estate rental forms. Write a letter to Anna Hurley at 2300 South Poplar Street, Denver, CO 80205. In the letter, list the websites you found and include information on which site you thought offered the most resources. Also include in the letter that Macadam Realty is very interested in helping her locate and purchase rental properties. Save the document with the name **6-RELtr**. Create an envelope for the letter and add it to the letter document. Save, preview, and then close **6-RELtr.docx**. (If printing, you may need to manually feed the envelope into the printer.)

WORD

CHAPTER

7

Creating Tables

Performance Objectives

Upon successful completion of Chapter 7, you will be able to:

1 Create a table
2 Change the table design
3 Select cells in a table
4 Change the table layout
5 Convert text to a table and a table to text
6 Draw a table
7 Insert a Quick Table
8 Perform calculations on data in a table
9 Insert an Excel spreadsheet

Use the Tables feature in Word to organize data in tables with any number of columns and rows. The data can consist of text, values, and/or mathematical formulas. Presenting information in a table can show patterns and relationships and help with data comprehension.

This chapter will introduce the steps for creating a table in Word using the Table button drop-down grid and options at the Insert Table dialog box. You will also learn to draw a table in a document and apply formatting to tables using buttons and options on the Table Design and Table Layout tabs. Finally, you will learn to perform calculations in a table and practice inserting an Excel spreadsheet into a Word document to display text and numerical data.

Data Files

The data files for this chapter are in the WL1C7 folder that you downloaded at the beginning of this course.

Activity 1 Create and Format Tables with Company Information — 8 Parts

You will create a table containing contact information and another containing information on employee benefit plans offered by a company. You will then change the design and layout of each table.

Creating a Table

Creating a Table

Create a table in a document to organize and provide a visual grouping of data and make the data easier to read and interpret. Tables are grids containing boxes of information called *cells*. Each cell is the intersection between a row and a column. A cell can contain text, characters, numbers, data, graphics, or formulas.

Table

Quick Steps

Create Table

1. Click Insert tab.
2. Click Table button.
3. Point to create number of columns and rows.
4. Click mouse button.

OR

1. Click Insert tab.
2. Click Table button.
3. Click *Insert Table*.
4. Specify number of columns and rows.
5. Click OK.

Hint You can create a table within a table, creating a *nested* table.

Insert a table in a document by clicking the Insert tab and then clicking the Table button in the Tables group. Move the pointer down and to the right in the drop-down grid to select the number of rows and columns to include in the table. A table can also be created with options at the Insert Table dialog box. Display this dialog box by clicking the Table button in the Tables group on the Insert tab and then clicking *Insert Table* at the drop-down list.

Figure 7.1 shows an example of a table with four columns and four rows. Various parts of the table are identified in the figure. These include the gridlines, move table column markers, table move handle, and resize handle. In a table, nonprinting characters identify the ends of cells and the ends of rows. To view these characters, click the Show/Hide ¶ button in the Paragraph group on the Home tab. The end-of-cell marker appears inside each cell and the end-of-row marker appears at the end of each row of cells. These markers are identified in Figure 7.1.

Columns in a table are generally referred to using the letters A–Z, while rows are numbered. When a table is inserted in a document, the insertion point is positioned in the first cell in the upper left corner of the table. This is referred to as cell A1, as it is located in column A, row 1. Cell B1 is to the right of A1, and cell A2 is directly below it.

When the insertion point is positioned in a cell in the table, move table column markers display on the horizontal ruler. These markers represent the ends of columns and can be moved to change the widths of columns. Figure 7.1 identifies move table column markers.

Figure 7.1 Table with Nonprinting Characters Displayed

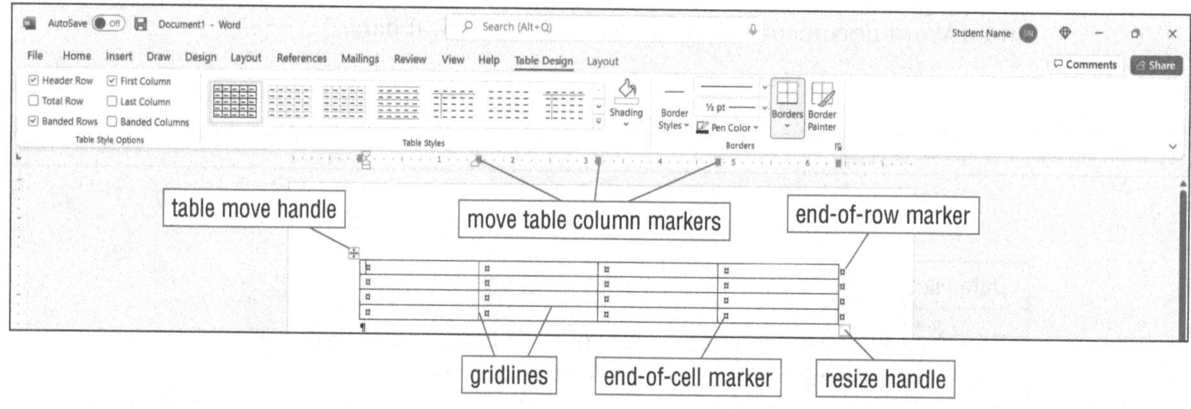

Entering Text in Cells

Hint Pressing the Tab key in a table moves the insertion point to the next cell. Pressing Ctrl + Tab moves the insertion point to the next tab within a cell.

With the insertion point positioned in a cell, type or edit text. Point and click with the mouse to move the insertion point from cell to cell, or press the Tab key to move to the next cell and Shift + Tab to move to the preceding cell.

Text typed in a cell automatically wraps to the next line to fit the width of the column. The Enter key can also be pressed to move to the next line within a cell. The cell expands vertically to accommodate the text, and all cells in that row also expand. Pressing the Tab key in a table causes the insertion point to move to the next cell in the table. To move the insertion point to a tab within a cell, press Ctrl + Tab. If the insertion point is in the last cell of the table, pressing the Tab key adds another row to the table. Insert a page break within a table by pressing Ctrl + Enter. The page break is inserted between rows, not within a row.

Moving the Insertion Point within a Table

To use the mouse to move the insertion point to a different cell within the table, click in the specific cell. To use the keyboard to move the insertion point to a different cell within the table, refer to the information shown in Table 7.1.

Table 7.1 Insertion Point Movement within a Table Using the Keyboard

To move the insertion point	Press
to next cell	Tab
to preceding cell	Shift + Tab
forward one character	Right Arrow key
backward one character	Left Arrow key
to previous row	Up Arrow key
to next row	Down Arrow key
to first cell in row	Alt + Home
to last cell in row	Alt + End
to top cell in column	Alt + Page Up
to bottom cell in column	Alt + Page Down

Activity 1a Creating a Table

1. At a blank document, turn on bold formatting and then type the title CONTACT INFORMATION, as shown in Figure 7.2.
2. Turn off bold formatting and then press the Enter key.
3. Create the table shown in Figure 7.2 by completing the following steps:
   a. Click the Insert tab.
   b. Click the Table button in the Tables group.
   c. Move the pointer down and to the right in the drop-down grid until the label above the grid displays as *3x5 Table* and then click the left mouse button.

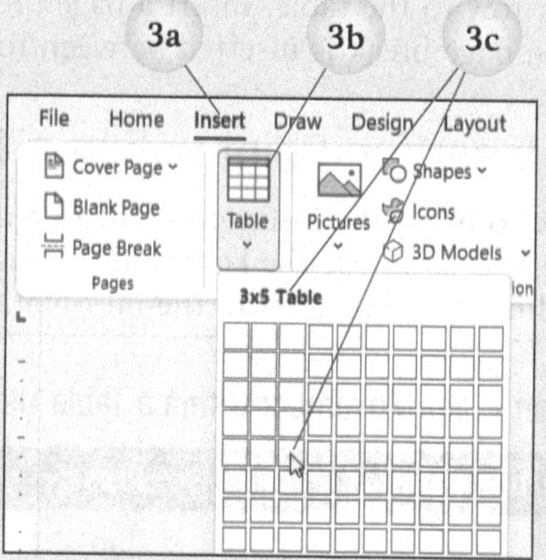

4. Type the text in the cells as indicated in Figure 7.2. Press the Tab key to move to the next cell and press Shift + Tab to move to the preceding cell. (If you accidentally press the Enter key within a cell, immediately press the Backspace key. Do not press the Tab key after typing the text in the last cell. If you do, another row is inserted in the table. If this happens, immediately click the Undo button in the Undo group on the Home tab or press Ctrl + Z.)
5. Save the table document with the name **7-Tables**.

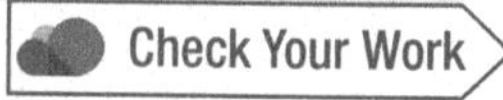

Figure 7.2 Activity 1a

CONTACT INFORMATION

Maggie Rivera	First Trust Bank	(203) 555-3440
Les Cromwell	Madison Trust	(602) 555-4900
Cecilia Nordyke	American Financial	(509) 555-3995
Regina Stahl	United Fidelity	(301) 555-1201
Justin White	Key One Savings	(360) 555-8963

Using the Insert Table Dialog Box

A table can also be created with options at the Insert Table dialog box, shown in Figure 7.3. To display this dialog box, click the Insert tab, click the Table button in the Tables group, and then click *Insert Table*. At the Insert Table dialog box, enter the number of columns and the number of rows and then click OK.

Figure 7.3 Insert Table Dialog Box

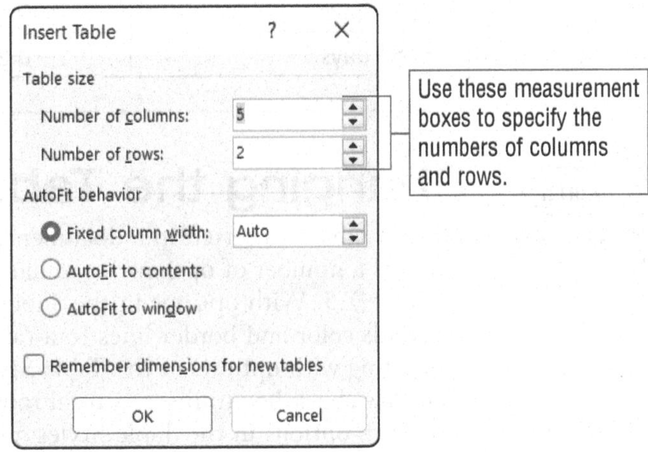

Activity 1b Creating a Table with the Insert Table Dialog Box

Part 2 of 8

1. With **7-Tables.docx** open, press Ctrl + End to move the insertion point below the table.
2. Press the Enter key two times.
3. Turn on bold formatting and then type the title OPTIONAL PLAN PREMIUM RATES, as shown in Figure 7.4.
4. Turn off bold formatting and then press the Enter key.
5. Click the Insert tab, click the Table button in the Tables group, and then click *Insert Table* at the drop-down list.
6. At the Insert Table dialog box, type 3 in the *Number of columns* measurement box. (The insertion point is automatically positioned in this measurement box.)
7. Press the Tab key (this moves the insertion point to the *Number of rows* measurement box) and then type 5.
8. Click OK.
9. Type the text in the cells as indicated in Figure 7.4. Press the Tab key to move to the next cell and press Shift + Tab to move to the preceding cell. To indent the text in cells B2 through B5 and cells C2 through C5, press Ctrl + Tab to move the insertion point to a tab within a cell and then type the text.
10. Save **7-Tables.docx**.

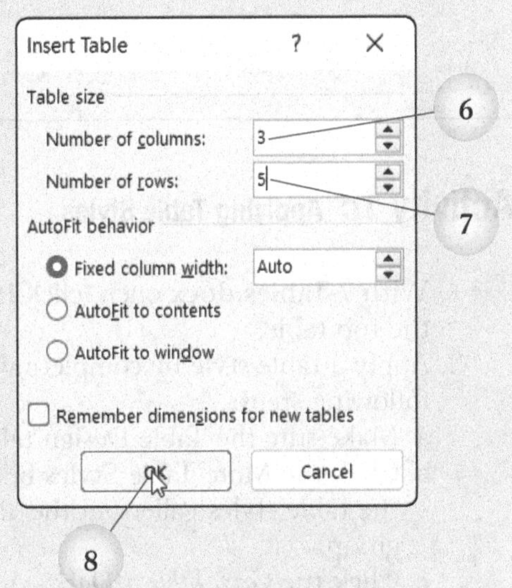

Check Your Work

Figure 7.4 Activity 1b

OPTIONAL PLAN PREMIUM RATES

Waiting Period	Basic Plan Employees	Plan Gold Employees
60 days	0.67%	0.79%
90 days	0.49%	0.59%
120 days	0.30%	0.35%
180 days	0.23%	0.26%

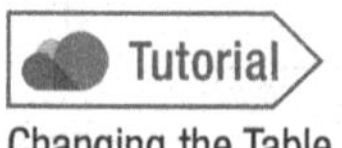

Changing the Table Design

Changing the Table Design

When a table is inserted in a document, the Table Design tab is active. This tab contains a number of options for enhancing the appearance of the table, as shown in Figure 7.5. With options in the Table Styles group, apply a predesigned style that adds color and border lines to a table and shading to cells. Customize the formatting with options in the Table Style Options group. For example, click the *Total Row* check box to insert a total row in the table. Apply a predesigned table style with options in the Table Styles group.

Border Styles

Border Painter

Use options in the Borders group to change the look of cell borders in a table. Click the Border Styles button to display a drop-down list of available styles. Use other buttons in the Borders group to change the line style, width, and color and to add or remove borders. Apply the same border style to other cells with the Border Painter button.

Figure 7.5 Table Design Tab

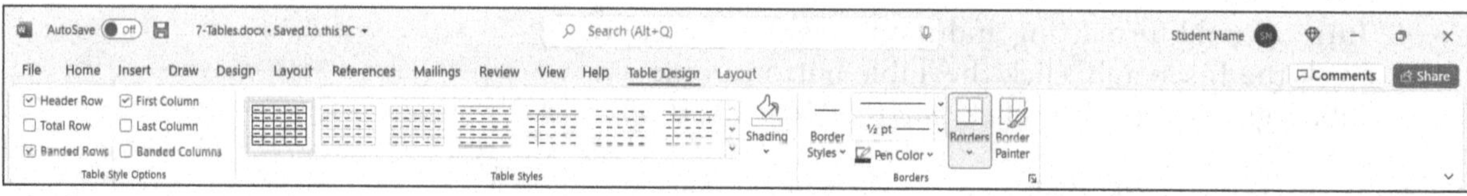

Activity 1c Applying Table Styles

Part 3 of 8

1. With **7-Tables.docx** open, click in any cell in the top table.
2. Apply a table style by completing the following steps:
   a. Make sure the Table Design tab is active.
   b. Click the More Table Styles button in the table styles gallery in the Table Styles group.
   c. Click the *Grid Table 5 Dark - Accent 5* table style (sixth column, fifth row in the *Grid Tables* section).

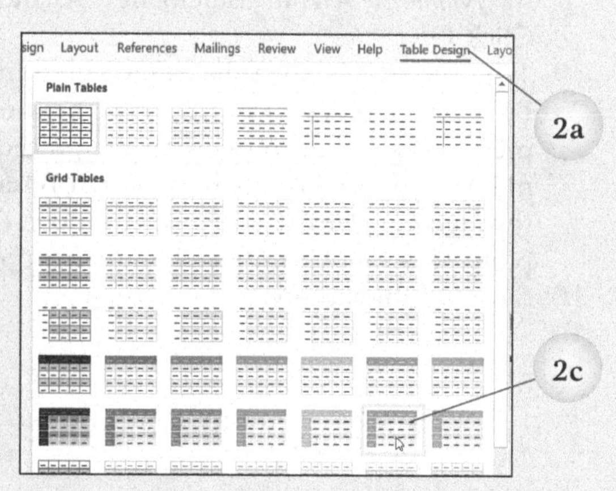

3. After looking at the table, you realize that the first row is not a header row and the first column should not be formatted differently from the other columns. To format the first row and the first column in the same manner as the other rows and columns, click the *Header Row* check box and the *First Column* check box in the Table Style Options group to remove the check marks.

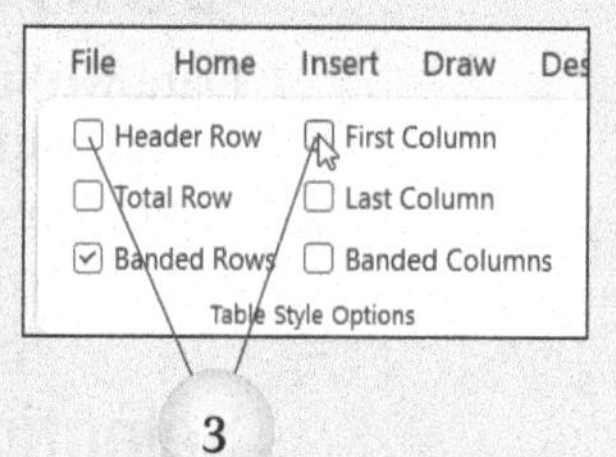

4. Click in any cell in the bottom table and then apply the List Table 6 Colorful - Accent 5 table style (sixth column, sixth row in the *List Tables* section).
5. Add color borders to the top table by completing the following steps:
   a. Click in any cell in the top table.
   b. Click the Pen Color button arrow in the Borders group on the Table Design tab and then click the *Orange, Accent 2, Darker 50%* color option (sixth column, last row in the *Theme Colors* section).
   c. Click the *Line Weight* option box arrow in the Borders group and then click *1 ½ pt* in the drop-down list. (When you choose a line weight, the Border Painter button is automatically activated.)

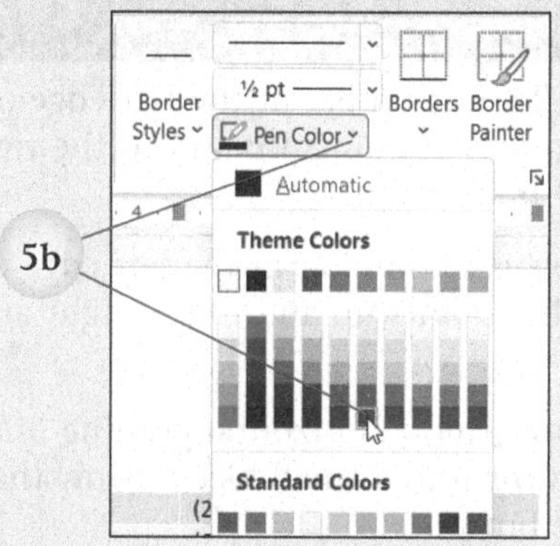

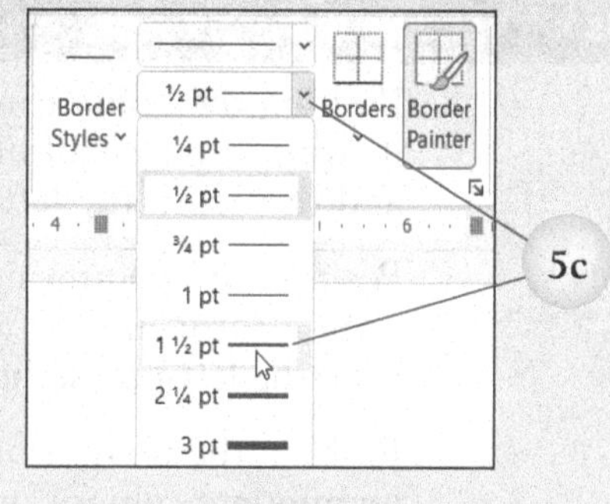

   d. Using the mouse (the pointer appears as a pen), drag along all four sides of the table. (As you drag with the mouse, a thick brown line is inserted. If you make a mistake or the line does not appear as you intended, click the Undo button and then continue drawing along each side of the table.)
6. Click the Border Styles button arrow and then click the *Double solid lines, 1/2 pt, Accent 2* option (third column, third row in the *Theme Borders* section).
7. Drag along all four sides of the bottom table.
8. Click the Border Painter button to turn off the feature.
9. Save **7-Tables.docx**.

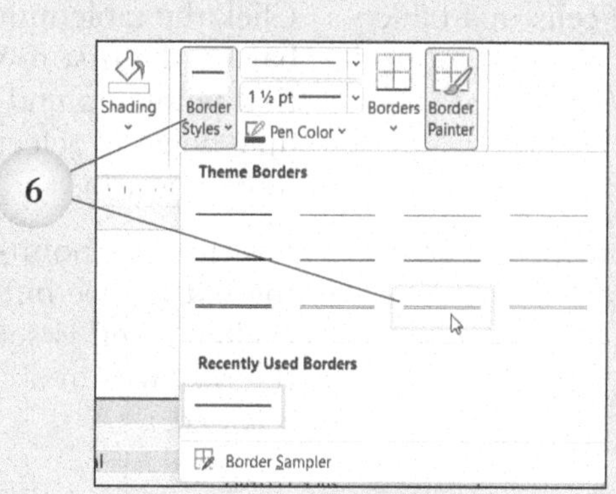

Check Your Work

Selecting Cells

Data within a table can be formatted in several ways. For example, the alignment of text within cells or rows can be changed, rows or columns can be moved or copied, and character formatting, such as bold, italic, and underlining, can be applied to text. To make changes to a cell, row, or column, first select the cells.

Selecting in a Table with the Mouse

Use the pointer to select a cell, row, or column or to select an entire table. Table 7.2 describes methods for selecting in a table with the mouse. To select a cell, position the pointer in the *cell selection bar*, an invisible strip just inside the left edge of a cell. The pointer turns into a small black arrow pointing up and to the right. Click to select the cell. Each row in a table contains a *row selection bar*, which is the space just outside the left edge of the table. Position the pointer in the row selection bar and the pointer turns into a white arrow that points up and to the right. Click to select the row.

Table 7.2 Selecting in a Table with the Mouse

To select this	Do this
cell	Position the pointer in the cell selection bar at the left edge of the cell until it turns into a small black arrow that points up and to the right and then click the left mouse button.
row	Position the pointer in the row selection bar at the left edge of the table until it turns into an arrow that points up and to the right and then click the left mouse button.
column	Position the pointer on the uppermost horizontal gridline of the table in the appropriate column until it turns into a small black arrow that points down and then click the left mouse button.
adjacent cells	Position the pointer in the first cell to be selected, click and hold down the left mouse button, drag the pointer to the last cell to be selected, and then release the mouse button.
all cells in a table	Click the table move handle or position the pointer in the row selection bar for the first row at the left edge of the table until it turns into an arrow that points up and to the right, click and hold down the left mouse button, drag down to select all the rows in the table, and then release the left mouse button.
text within a cell	Position the pointer at the beginning of the text, click and hold down the left mouse button, and then drag the mouse across the text. (When a cell is selected, its background color changes to gray. When the text within a cell is selected, only those lines containing text are selected.)

Selecting in a Table with the Keyboard

In addition to the mouse, the keyboard can be used to select specific cells within a table. Table 7.3 shows the commands for selecting specific elements of a table.

To select only the text within a cell, rather than the entire cell, position the insertion point in front of text in a cell and then press the F8 function key to turn on the Extend mode. Move the insertion point with an arrow key to select one character at a time, being careful not to select the entire cell. When a cell is selected, its background color changes to gray. When the text within a cell is selected, only those lines containing text are selected.

Table 7.3 Selecting in a Table with the Keyboard

To select	Press
next cell's contents	Tab
preceding cell's contents	Shift + Tab
entire table	Alt + 5 (on numeric keypad with Num Lock off)
adjacent cells	Press and hold down the Shift key and then press an arrow key repeatedly.
column	Position the insertion point in the top cell of the column, press and hold down the Shift key, and then press and hold down the Down Arrow key until the column is selected.

Activity 1d Selecting, Moving, and Formatting Cells in a Table

Part 4 of 8

1. With **7-Tables.docx** open, move two rows in the top table by completing the following steps:
   a. Position the pointer in the row selection bar at the left edge of the row containing the name *Cecilia Nordyke* until the pointer turns into an arrow that points up and to the right, click and hold down the left mouse button, and then drag down to select two rows (the *Cecilia Nordyke* row and the *Regina Stahl* row).

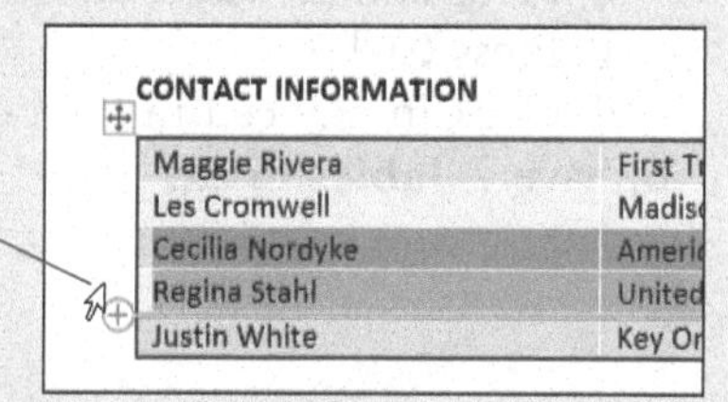

   b. Click the Home tab and then click the Cut button in the Clipboard group.
   c. Position the insertion point at the beginning of the name *Les Cromwell* and then click the Paste button in the Clipboard group.
2. Move the third column in the bottom table by completing the following steps:
   a. Position the pointer on the top border of the third column in the bottom table until the pointer turns into a short black arrow that points down and then click the left mouse button. (This selects the entire column.)
   b. Click the Cut button.
   c. With the insertion point positioned at the beginning of the text *Basic Plan Employees*, click the Paste button. (Moving the column removed the right border.)
   d. Insert the right border by clicking the Table Design tab, clicking the Border Styles button arrow, and then clicking the *Double solid lines, 1/2 pt, Accent 2* option at the drop-down list (third column, third row in the *Theme Borders* section).

e. Drag along the right border of the bottom table.
f. Click the Border Painter button to turn off the feature.

3. Apply shading to a row by completing the following steps:
   a. Position the pointer in the row selection bar at the left edge of the first row in the bottom table until the pointer turns into an arrow that points up and to the right and then click the left mouse button. (This selects the entire first row of the bottom table.)
   b. Click the Shading button arrow in the Table Styles group on the Table Design tab and then click the *Orange, Accent 2, Lighter 80%* color option (sixth column, second row in the *Theme Colors* section).

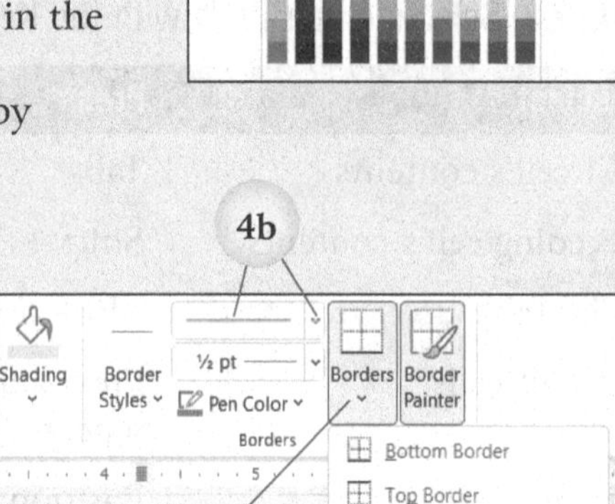

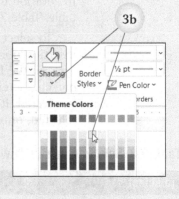

4. Apply a border line to the right sides of two columns by completing the following steps:
   a. Position the pointer on the top border of the first column in the bottom table until the pointer turns into a short black arrow that points down and then click the left mouse button.
   b. Click the *Line Style* option box arrow and then click the top line option (a single line).
   c. Click the Borders button arrow and then click *Right Border* at the drop-down list.
   d. Select the second column in the bottom table.
   e. Click the Borders button arrow and then click *Right Border* at the drop-down list.

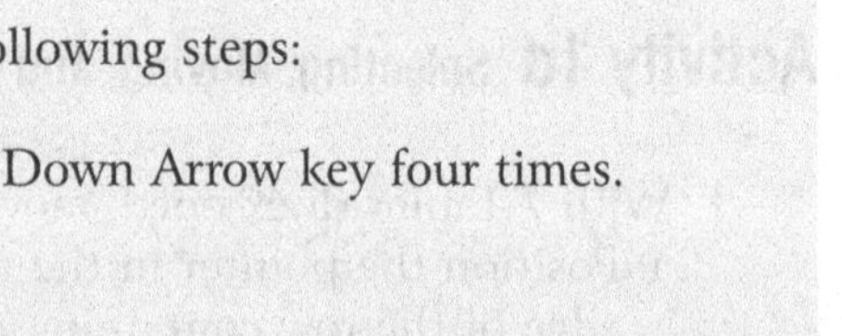

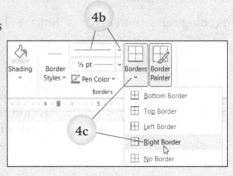

5. Apply italic formatting to a column by completing the following steps:
   a. Click in the first cell of the first row in the top table.
   b. Press and hold down the Shift key and then press the Down Arrow key four times. (This should select all the cells in the first column.)
   c. Press Ctrl + I.
   d. Click in any cell in the table to deselect the column.
6. Save **7-Tables.docx**.

Check Your Work

Changing the Table Layout

Changing the Table Layout

To further customize a table, consider changing the layout by inserting or deleting columns and rows and specifying how text should align in cells. Change the table layout with options on the Table Layout tab, shown in Figure 7.6. Use options and buttons on the tab to select specific cells, delete and insert rows and columns, merge and split cells, specify cell height and width, sort data in cells, and insert formulas.

Figure 7.6 Table Layout Tab

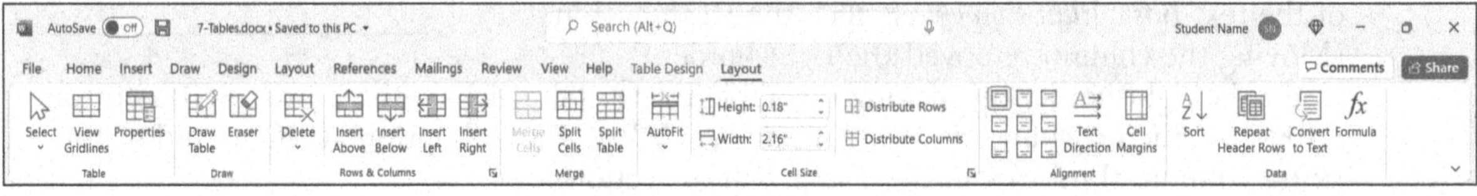

Selecting with the Select Button

Along with selecting cells with the keyboard and mouse, specific cells can be selected with the Select button in the Table group on the Table Layout tab. Position the insertion point in the specific cell, column, or row and then click the Select button. At the drop-down list, specify what is to be selected: the entire table or a column, row, or cell.

Viewing Gridlines

Hint Some table layout options are available at a shortcut menu that can be viewed by right-clicking in a table.

By default, the cells in a table are bordered by a grid of thin black horizontal and vertical lines. These borders can be modified or removed using options on the Table Design tab, as shown on page 248. If the design of a table is changed so that the table does not contain visible borders, seeing the boundaries of each cell when entering data can be difficult. In this case, turn on the display of nonprinting gridlines to be used as a reference when working with the table. These gridlines appear as dashed lines on the screen, but they will not print. Turn on or off the display of nonprinting dashed gridlines with the View Gridlines button in the Table group on the Table Layout tab.

Inserting and Deleting Rows and Columns

Insert or delete a row or a column with buttons in the Rows & Columns group on the Table Layout tab. Click a button in the group to insert the row or column above, below, to the left, or to the right. To delete a cell, a row, a column, or the entire table, click the Delete button and then click the option identifying what is to be deleted. The shortcut menu can also be used to insert or delete a row or column. To use the shortcut menu to insert a row or column, right-click in a cell, point to the *Insert* option, and then click an insert option at the side menu. To delete a row or column, right-click in a cell and then click the *Delete Cells* option. This displays the Delete Cells dialog box with options for deleting cells, a row, or a column.

In addition to using options on the Table Layout tab, rows or columns can be inserted using an Insert Control. Display the Insert Control for a row by positioning the pointer just outside the left border of the table at the left edge of the row border. When the Insert Control displays (a plus symbol in a circle and a border line), click the control and a row is inserted below the Insert Control border line. To insert a column, position the pointer above the column border line until the Insert Control displays and then click the control. This inserts a new column immediately left of the Insert Control border line.

Activity 1e Selecting, Inserting, and Deleting Columns and Rows — Part 5 of 8

1. Make sure **7-Tables.docx** is open.
2. The table style applied to the bottom table removed row border gridlines. If you do not see dashed row border gridlines in the bottom table, turn on the display of nonprinting gridlines by positioning your insertion point in the table, clicking the Table Layout tab, and then clicking the View Gridlines button in the Table group. (The button should appear with a gray background, indicating it is active. Skip this step if the button is already active.)
3. Select a column and apply formatting by completing the following steps:
   a. Click in any cell in the first column in the top table.

b. Make sure the Table Layout tab is active, click the Select button in the Table group, and then click *Select Column* at the drop-down list.

c. With the first column selected, press Ctrl + I to remove italic formatting and then press Ctrl + B to apply bold formatting.

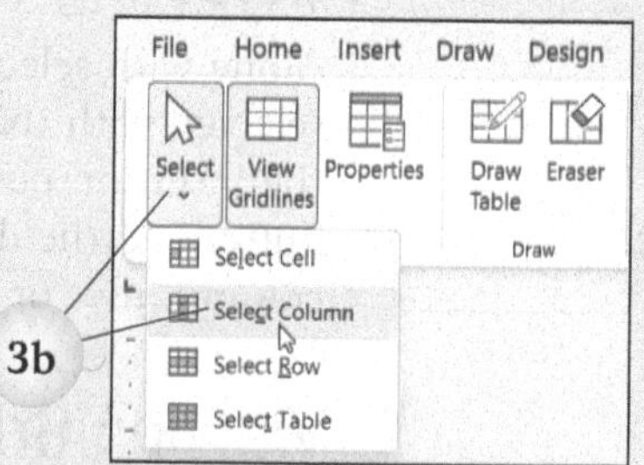

4. Select a row and apply formatting by completing the following steps:

a. Click in any cell in the first row in the bottom table.

b. Click the Select button in the Table group and then click *Select Row* at the drop-down list.

c. With the first row selected in the bottom table, press Ctrl + I to apply italic formatting.

5. Insert a new row in the bottom table and type text in the new cells by completing the following steps:

a. Click in the cell containing the text *60 days*.

b. Click the Insert Above button in the Rows & Columns group.

c. Type 30 days in the first cell of the new row. Press the Tab key, press Ctrl + Tab, and then type 0.85% in the second cell of the new row. Press the Tab key, press Ctrl + Tab, and then type 0.81% in the third cell of the new row.

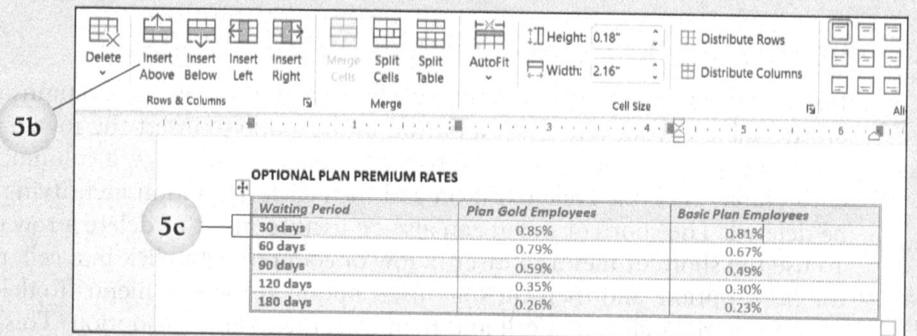

OPTIONAL PLAN PREMIUM RATES

Waiting Period	*Plan Gold Employees*	*Basic Plan Employees*
30 days	0.85%	0.81%
60 days	0.79%	0.67%
90 days	0.59%	0.49%
120 days	0.35%	0.30%
180 days	0.26%	0.23%

6. Insert two new rows in the top table by completing the following steps:

a. Select the two rows of cells that begin with the names *Cecilia Nordyke* and *Regina Stahl*.

b. Click the Insert Below button in the Rows & Columns group.

c. Click in any cell of the top table to deselect the new rows.

7. Insert a new row in the top table by positioning the pointer at the left edge of the table next to the border line below *Regina Stahl* until the Insert Control displays and then clicking the Insert Control.

CONTACT INFORMATION

Maggie Rivera	
Cecilia Nordyke	
Regina Stahl	
Les Cromwell	
Justin White	

8. Type the following text in the new cells:

Teresa Getty	Meridian Bank	(503) 555-9800
Michael Vazquez	New Horizon Bank	(702) 555-2435
Samantha Roth	Cascade Mutual	(206) 555-6788

Maggie Rivera	First Trust Bank	(203) 555-3440
Cecilia Nordyke	American Financial	(509) 555-3995
Regina Stahl	United Fidelity	(301) 555-1201
Teresa Getty	Meridian Bank	(503) 555-9800
Michael Vazquez	New Horizon Bank	(702) 555-2435
Samantha Roth	Cascade Mutual	(206) 555-6788
Les Cromwell	Madison Trust	(602) 555-4900
Justin White	Key One Savings	(360) 555-8963

9. Delete a row by completing the following steps:
   a. Click in the cell containing the name *Les Cromwell*.
   b. Click the Delete button in the Rows & Columns group and then click *Delete Rows* at the drop-down list.

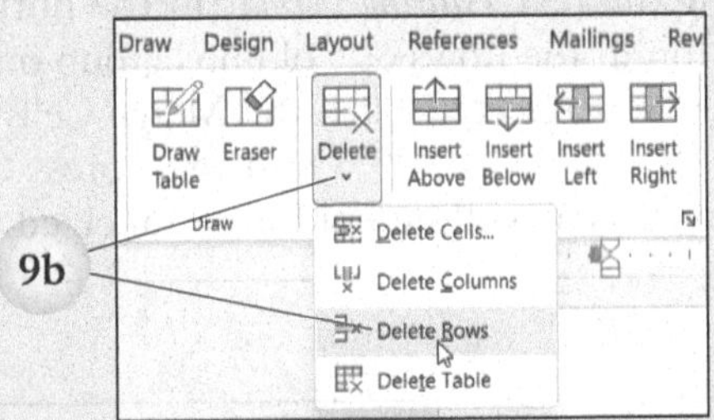

10. Insert a new column in the top table by positioning the pointer immediately above the border line between the first and second columns until the Insert Control displays and then clicking the Insert Control.

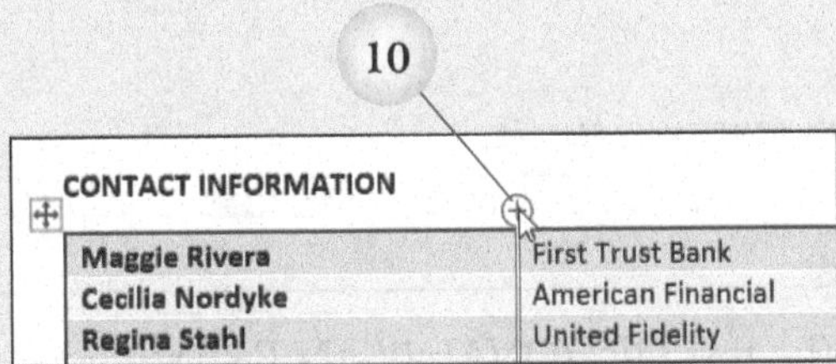

11. Type the following text in the new cells:
    B1 = Vice President
    B2 = Loan Officer
    B3 = Account Manager
    B4 = Branch Manager
    B5 = President
    B6 = Vice President
    B7 = Regional Manager
12. Save **7-Tables.docx**.

CONTACT INFORMATION

Maggie Rivera	Vice President	First Tru
Cecilia Nordyke	Loan Officer	America
Regina Stahl	Account Manager	United F
Teresa Getty	Branch Manager	Meridia
Michael Vazquez	President	New Ho
Samantha Roth	Vice President	Cascade
Justin White	Regional Manager	Key One

11

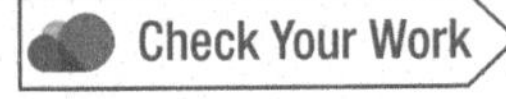

Merging and Splitting Cells and Tables

Merge Cells

Split Cells

Split Table

Click the Merge Cells button in the Merge group on the Table Layout tab to merge selected cells and click the Split Cells button to split the currently active cell. Click the Split Cells button and the Split Cells dialog box displays with options for specifying the number of columns or rows into which the active cell should be split. To split one table into two tables, position the insertion point in a cell in the row that will be the first row in the new table and then click the Split Table button.

Activity 1f Merging and Splitting Cells and Splitting a Table

1. With **7-Tables.docx** open, insert a new row and merge cells in the row by completing the following steps:
   a. Click in the cell containing the text *Waiting Period* (in the bottom table).
   b. Click the Insert Above button in the Rows & Columns group on the Table Layout tab.
   c. With all the cells in the new row selected, click the Merge Cells button in the Merge group.
   d. Type OPTIONAL PLAN PREMIUM RATES and then press Ctrl + E to center-align the text in the cell. (The text you type will be bold and italicized.)

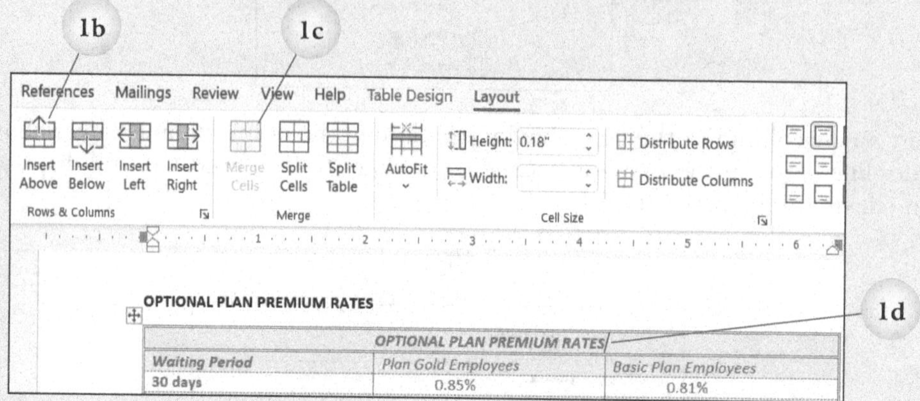

2. Select and then delete the text *OPTIONAL PLAN PREMIUM RATES* above the bottom table.
3. Insert rows and text in the top table and merge cells by completing the following steps:
   a. Click in the cell containing the text *Maggie Rivera*.
   b. Click the Table Layout tab.
   c. Click the Insert Above button two times. (This inserts two rows at the top of the table.)
   d. With the cells in the top row selected, click the Merge Cells button.
   e. Type CONTACT INFORMATION, NORTH and then press Ctrl + E to center-align the text in the cell.
   f. Type the following text in the four cells in the new second row.

      Name Title Company Telephone

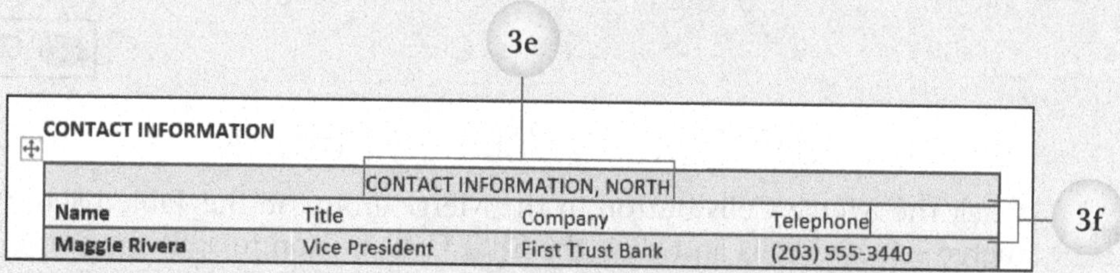

4. Apply heading formatting to the new top row by completing the following steps:
   a. Click the Table Design tab.
   b. Click the *Header Row* check box in the Table Style Options group to insert a check mark.
5. Select and then delete the text *CONTACT INFORMATION* above the top table.
6. Split a cell by completing the following steps:
   a. Click in the cell containing the telephone number *(301) 555-1201*.
   b. Click the Table Layout tab.
   c. Click the Split Cells button in the Merge group.
   d. At the Split Cells dialog box, click OK. (The telephone number will wrap to a new line. You will change this in the next activity.)
   e. Click in the new cell.

f. Type x453 in the new cell. If AutoCorrect automatically capitalizes the *x*, hover the pointer over the *X* until the AutoCorrect Options button displays. Click the AutoCorrect Options button and then click *Undo Automatic Capitalization* or click *Stop Auto-capitalizing First Letter of Table Cells*.

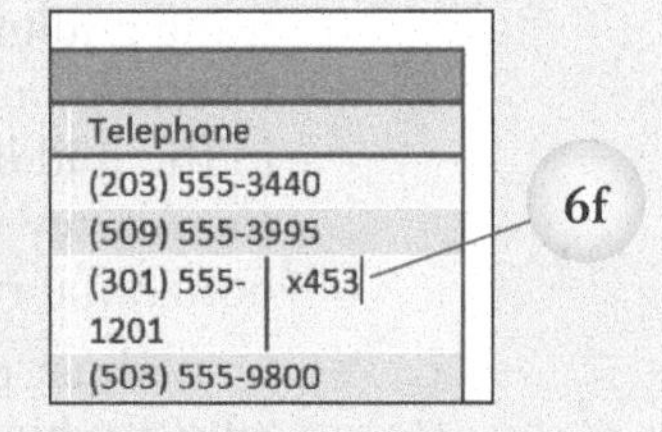

7. Split the cell containing the telephone number *(206) 555-6788* and then type x2310 in the new cell. (If necessary, make the *x* lowercase.)
8. Split the top table into two tables by completing the following steps:
   a. Click in the cell containing the name *Teresa Getty*.
   b. Click the Split Table button in the Merge group.
   c. Click in the cell containing the name *Teresa Getty* (in the first row of the new table).
   d. Click the Insert Above button in the Rows & Columns group on the Table Layout tab.
   e. With the new row selected, click the Merge Cells button.
   f. Type CONTACT INFORMATION, SOUTH in the new row and then press Ctrl + E to center-align the text.
9. Save and then preview **7-Tables.docx**.
10. Delete the middle table by completing the following steps:
    a. Click in any cell in the middle table.
    b. Click the Table Layout tab.
    c. Click the Delete button in the Rows & Columns group and then click *Delete Table* at the drop-down list.
11. Draw a dark-orange border at the bottom of the top table by completing the following steps:
    a. Click in any cell in the top table and then click the Table Design tab.
    b. Click the *Line Weight* option box arrow in the Borders group and then click *1½ pt* at the drop-down list. (This activates the Border Painter button.)
    c. Click the Pen Color button and then click the *Orange, Accent 2, Darker, 50%* color option (sixth column, bottom row in the *Theme Colors* section).
    d. Using the mouse, drag along the bottom border of the top table.
    e. Click the Border Painter button to turn off the feature.
12. Save **7-Tables.docx**.

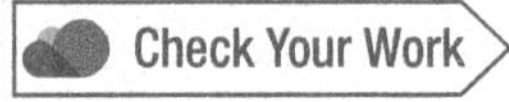

Customizing Cell Size

Customizing Cells in a Table

Distribute Rows

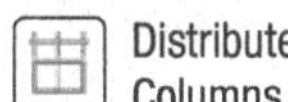

Distribute Columns

When a table is created, the column widths are equal and the row heights are equal. Both can be customized with buttons in the Cell Size group on the Table Layout tab. Use the *Table Row Height* measurement box to increase or decrease the heights of rows and use the *Table Column Width* measurement box to increase or decrease the widths of columns. The Distribute Rows button will make all the selected rows the same height and the Distribute Columns button will make all the selected columns the same width.

Column width can also be changed using the move table column markers on the horizontal ruler or using the table gridlines. To change column width using the horizontal ruler, position the pointer on a move table column marker until it turns into a left-and-right-pointing arrow and then drag the marker on the horizontal ruler to the specific position. Press and hold down the Shift key while dragging a table column marker and the horizontal ruler remains stationary while the table column marker moves. Press and hold down the Alt key while dragging a table column marker and measurements display on the horizontal ruler. To change column width using gridlines, position the pointer on the gridline separating columns until the insertion point turns into a left-and-right-pointing arrow with a vertical double-line in the middle and then drag the gridline to the new position. Press and hold down the Alt key while dragging the gridline and column measurements display on the horizontal ruler.

Adjust row height in a manner similar to adjusting column width. Drag the adjust table row marker on the vertical ruler or drag the gridline separating rows. Press and hold down the Alt key while dragging the adjust table row marker or the row gridline and measurements display on the vertical ruler.

AutoFit

Use the AutoFit button in the Cell Size group to make the column widths in a table automatically fit the contents. To do this, position the insertion point in any cell in the table, click the AutoFit button in the Cell Size group, and then click *AutoFit Contents* at the drop-down list.

Activity 1g Changing Column Width and Row Height

Part 7 of 8

1. With **7-Tables.docx** open, change the width of the first column in the top table by completing the following steps:
   a. Click in the cell containing the name *Maggie Rivera*.
   b. Position the pointer on the Move Table Column marker just right of the 1.5-inch mark on the horizontal ruler until the pointer turns into a left-and-right-pointing arrow.
   c. Press and hold down the Shift key and then click and hold down the left mouse button.
   d. Drag the marker to the 1.25-inch mark, release the mouse button, and then release the Shift key.

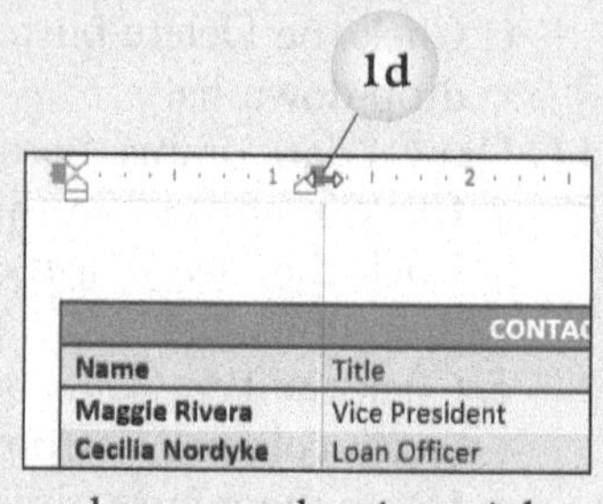

2. Complete steps similar to those in Step 1 to drag the move table column marker just right of the 3-inch mark on the horizontal ruler to the 2.75-inch mark. (Make sure the text *Account Manager* in the second column does not wrap to the next line. If it does, slightly increase the width of the column.)
3. Change the width of the third column in the top table by completing the following steps:
   a. Position the pointer on the gridline separating the third and fourth columns until the pointer turns into a left-and-right-pointing arrow with a vertical double-line in the middle.
   b. Press and hold down the Alt key, click and hold down the left mouse button, drag the gridline to the left until the measurement for the third column on the horizontal ruler displays as *1.31"*, and then release the mouse button followed by the Alt key.

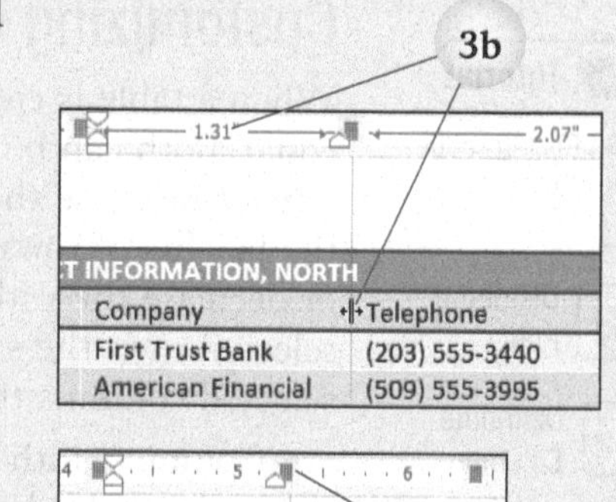

4. Position the pointer on the gridline that separates the telephone number *(301) 555-1201* from the extension *x453* and then drag the gridline to the 5.25-inch mark on the horizontal ruler. (Make sure the phone number does not wrap down to the next line.)
5. Drag the right border of the top table to the 5.75-inch mark on the horizontal ruler.

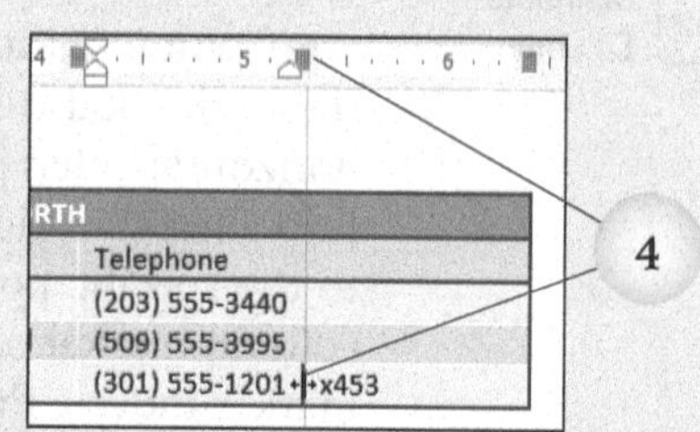

6. Automatically fit the columns in the bottom table by completing the following steps:
   a. Click in any cell in the bottom table.
   b. Click the AutoFit button in the Cell Size group on the Table Layout tab and then click *AutoFit Contents* at the drop-down list.
7. Increase the height of the first row in the bottom table by completing the following steps:
   a. Make sure the insertion point is positioned in one of the cells in the bottom table.
   b. Position the pointer on the top adjust table row marker on the vertical ruler.
   c. Press and hold down the Alt key and then click and hold down the left mouse button.
   d. Drag the Adjust Table Row marker down until the first row measurement on the vertical ruler displays as *0.39"*, release the mouse button, and then release the Alt key.

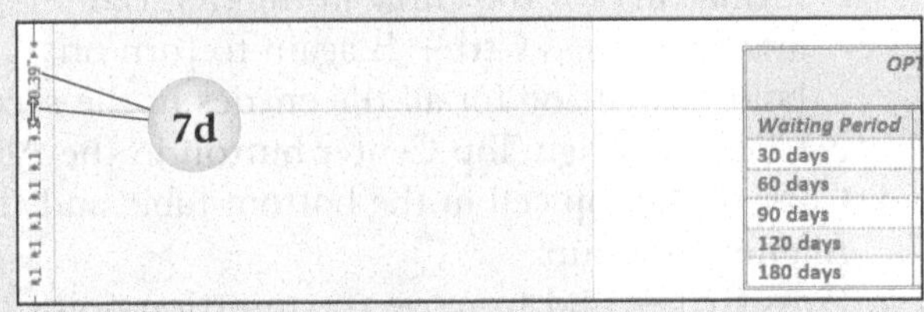

8. Increase the height of the first row in the top table by completing the following steps:
   a. Click in any cell in the top table.
   b. Position the pointer on the gridline at the bottom of the top row until the pointer turns into an up-and-down-pointing arrow with a vertical double-line in the middle.
   c. Click and hold down the left mouse button and then press and hold down the Alt key.
   d. Drag the gridline down until the first row measurement on the vertical ruler displays as *0.39"*, release the mouse button, and then release the Alt key.

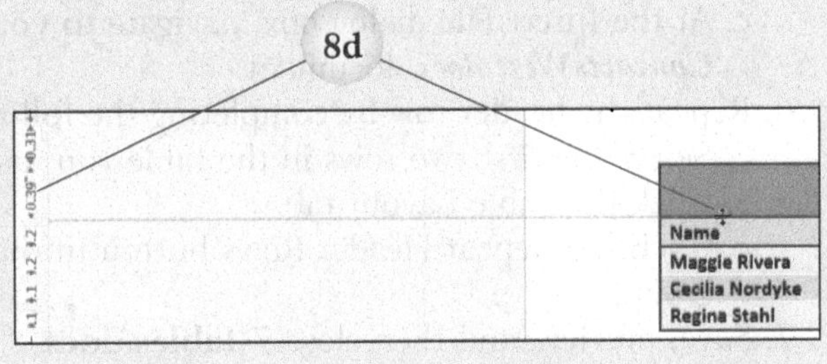

9. Save **7-Tables.docx**.

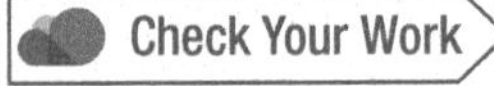

Changing Cell Alignment

The Alignment group on the Table Layout tab contains a number of buttons for specifying the horizontal and vertical alignment of text in cells. Each button contains a visual representation of the alignment. Hover the pointer over a button to display a ScreenTip with the button name and description.

Repeating a Header Row

Quick Steps

Repeat Header Row
1. Click in header row or select rows.
2. Click Table Layout tab.
3. Click Repeat Header Rows button.

Repeat Header Rows

If a table continues over two or more pages, consider adding the header row at the beginning of each page for easier reference while reading. To repeat a header row, click in the first row (header row) and then click the Repeat Header Rows button in the Data group on the Table Layout tab. To repeat more than one header row, select the rows and then click the Repeat Header Rows button.

Activity 1h Aligning Text in Cells and Repeating Header Rows — Part 8 of 8

1. With **7-Tables.docx** open, click in the top cell in the top table (the cell containing the title *CONTACT INFORMATION, NORTH*).
2. Click the Align Center button in the Alignment group on the Table Layout tab.
3. Format and align the text in the second row in the top table by completing the following steps:
   a. Select the second row.
   b. Press Ctrl + B to turn off bold formatting for the entry in the first cell and then press Ctrl + B again to turn on bold formatting for all the entries in the second row.
   c. Click the Align Top Center button in the Alignment group.
4. Click in the top cell in the bottom table and then click the Align Center button in the Alignment group.
5. Press Ctrl + End to move the insertion point to the end of the document, press the Enter key four times, and then insert a table into the current document by completing the following steps:
   a. Click the Insert tab.
   b. Click the Object button arrow in the Text group and then click *Text from File* at the drop-down list.
   c. At the Insert File dialog box, navigate to your WL1C7 folder and then double-click the ***ContactsWest.docx*** document.
6. Repeat the header row by completing the following steps:
   a. Select the first two rows in the table you just inserted.
   b. Click the Table Layout tab.
   c. Click the Repeat Header Rows button in the Data group.
7. Save, preview, and then close **7-Tables.docx**.

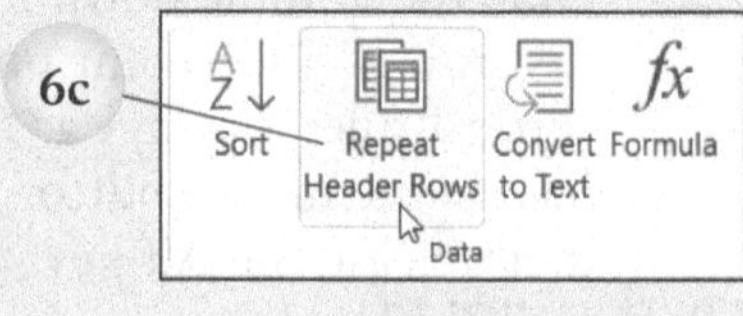

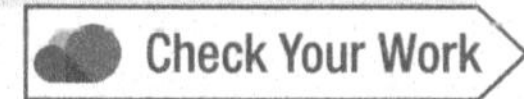

Activity 2 Create and Format Tables with Employee Information — 6 Parts

You will create and format a table containing information on the names and departments of employees of Tri-State Products, two tables containing additional information on employees, and a calendar quick table.

Changing Cell Margin Measurements

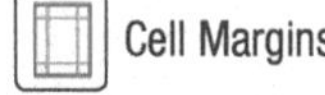
Cell Margins

By default, the cells in a table contain specific margin measurements. The top and bottom margins in a cell have a default measurement of 0 inch and the left and right margins have a default measurement of 0.08 inch. Change these default measurements with options at the Table Options dialog box, shown in Figure 7.7. Display this dialog box by clicking the Cell Margins button in the Alignment group on the Table Layout tab. Use the measurement boxes in the *Default cell margins* section to change the top, bottom, left, and/or right cell margin measurements.

Figure 7.7 Table Options Dialog Box

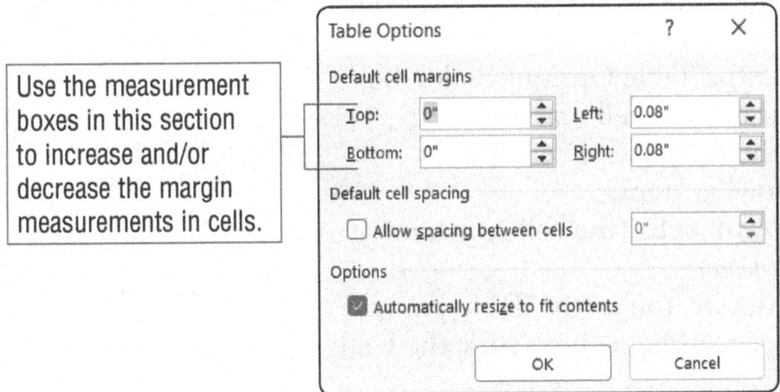

Changes to cell margins will affect all the cells in a table. To change the cell margin measurements for one cell or selected cells, position the insertion point in the cell or select the cells and then click the Properties button in the Table group on the Table Layout tab (or click the Cell Size group dialog box launcher). At the Table Properties dialog box, click the Cell tab and then the Options button in the lower right corner of the dialog box. This displays the Cell Options dialog box, shown in Figure 7.8.

Before setting the new cell margin measurements, remove the check mark from the *Same as the whole table* check box. With the check mark removed, the cell margin options become available. Specify the new cell margin measurements and then click OK to close the dialog box.

Figure 7.8 Cell Options Dialog Box

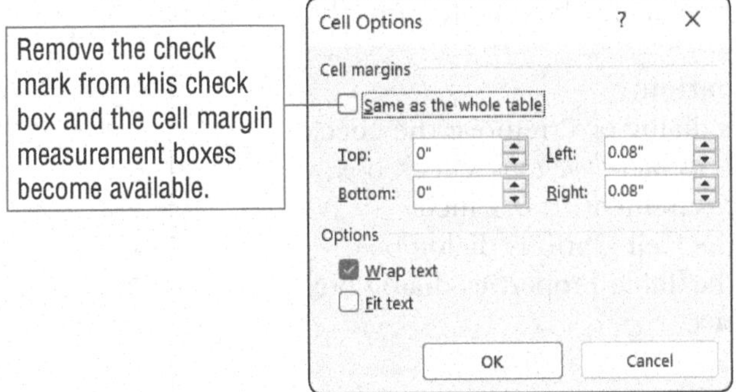

Activity 2a Changing Cell Margin Measurements

Part 1 of 6

1. Open **TSPTables.docx** and then save it with the name **7-TSPTables**.
2. Change the top and bottom cell margin measurements for all the cells in the table by completing the following steps:
   a. Position the insertion point in any cell in the table and then click the Table Layout tab.
   b. Click the Cell Margins button in the Alignment group.

c. At the Table Options dialog box, change the *Top* and *Bottom* measurements to 0.05 inch.
d. Click OK to close the Table Options dialog box.

3. Change the top and bottom cell margin measurements for the first row of cells by completing the following steps:
   a. Select the first row of cells (the cells containing *Name* and *Department*).
   b. Click the Properties button in the Table group.
   c. At the Table Properties dialog box, click the Cell tab.
   d. Click the Options button in the lower right corner of the dialog box.
   e. At the Cell Options dialog box, click the *Same as the whole table* check box to remove the check mark.
   f. Change the *Top* and *Bottom* measurements to 0.1 inch.
   g. Click OK to close the Cell Options dialog box.
   h. Click OK to close the Table Properties dialog box.
4. Change the left cell margin measurement for specific cells by completing the following steps:
   a. Select all the rows in the table *except* the top row.
   b. Click the Cell Size group dialog box launcher.
   c. At the Table Properties dialog box, make sure the Cell tab is active.
   d. Click the Options button.
   e. At the Cell Options dialog box, remove the check mark from the *Same as the whole table* check box.
   f. Change the *Left* measurement to 0.3 inch.
   g. Click OK to close the Cell Options dialog box.
   h. Click OK to close the Table Properties dialog box.
5. Save **7-TSPTables.docx**.

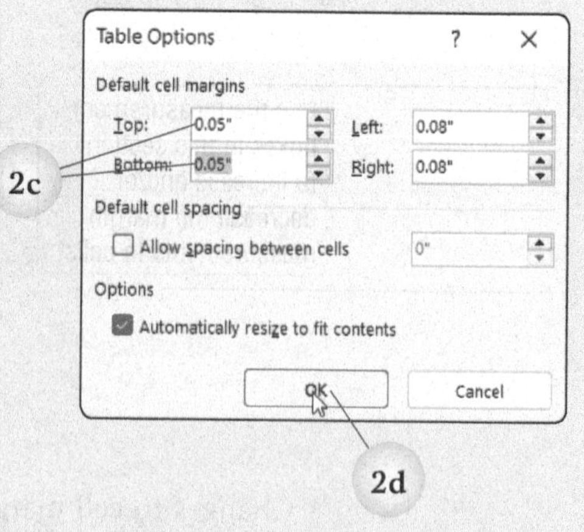

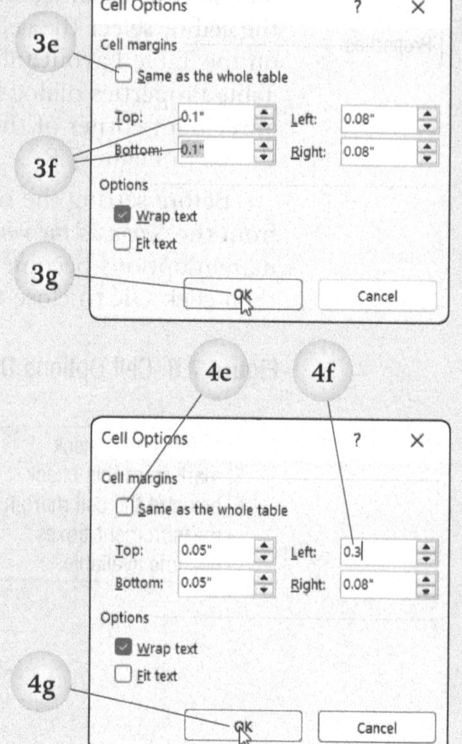

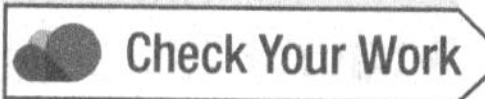

Changing Text Direction in a Cell

Text Direction

Change the direction of text in a cell using the Text Direction button in the Alignment group on the Table Layout tab. Each time the Text Direction button is clicked, the text in the cell rotates 90 degrees.

Changing Table Alignment and Dimensions

By default, a table aligns at the left margin. Change this alignment with options at the Table Properties dialog box with the Table tab selected, as shown in Figure 7.9. To change the alignment, click the specific alignment option in the *Alignment* section of the dialog box. Change table dimensions by clicking the

Preferred width check box to insert a check mark. This makes active both the width measurement box and the *Measure in* option box. Type a width measurement in the measurement box and specify whether the measurement type is inches or a percentage with the *Measurement in* option box.

Figure 7.9 Table Properties Dialog Box with the Table Tab Selected

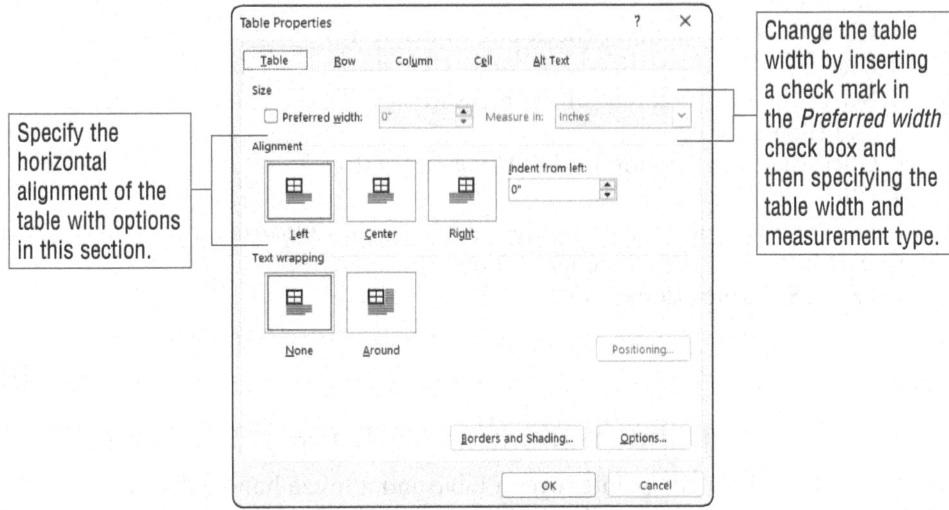

Activity 2b Changing Size and Cell Alignment and Text Direction

Part 2 of 6

1. With **7-TSPTables.docx** open, insert a new column and change text direction by completing the following steps:
   a. Click in any cell in the first column.
   b. Click the Insert Left button in the Rows & Columns group on the Table Layout tab.
   c. With the cells in the new column selected, click the Merge Cells button in the Merge group.
   d. Type Tri-State Products.
   e. Click the Align Center button in the Alignment group.
   f. Click two times on the Text Direction button in the Alignment group.

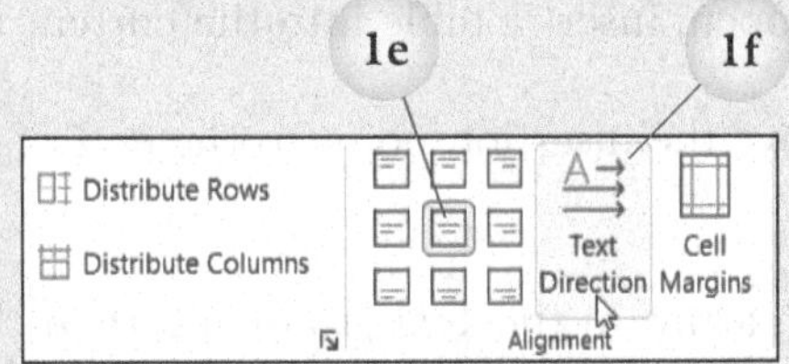

   g. With *Tri-State Products* selected, click the Home tab and then increase the font size to 16 points.
2. Automatically fit the contents by completing the following steps:
   a. Click in any cell in the table.
   b. Click the Table Layout tab.
   c. Click the AutoFit button in the Cell Size group and then click *AutoFit Contents* at the drop-down list.

3. Change the table width and alignment by completing the following steps:
   a. Click the Properties button in the Table group on the Table Layout tab.
   b. At the Table Properties dialog box, click the Table tab.
   c. Click the *Preferred width* check box to insert a check mark.
   d. Select the measurement in the measurement box and then type 4.5.
   e. Click the *Center* option in the *Alignment* section.
   f. Click OK.

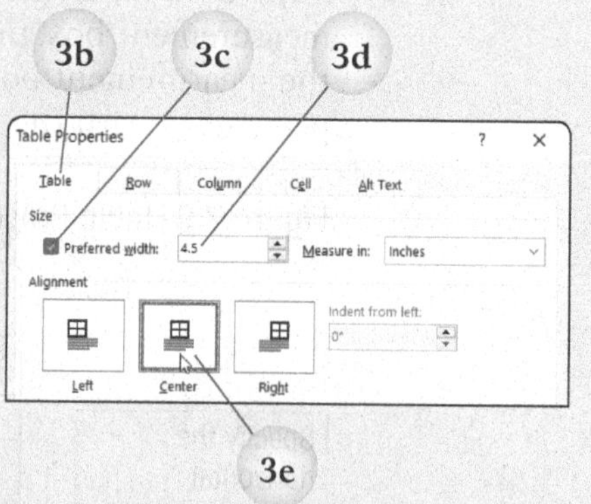

4. Select the two cells containing the text *Name* and *Department* and then click the Align Center button in the Alignment group.
5. Save **7-TSPTables.docx**.

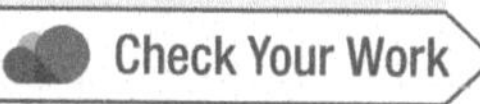

Changing Table Size with the Resize Handle

Hover the pointer over a table and a resize handle displays in the lower right corner. The resize handle displays as a small white square. Drag this resize handle to increase and/or decrease the size and proportion of the table.

Quick Steps

Move Table
1. Position pointer on table move handle until pointer displays with four-headed arrow attached.
2. Click and hold down left mouse button.
3. Drag table to new location.
4. Release mouse button.

Moving a Table

Position the pointer in a table and a table move handle displays in the upper left corner. Use this handle to move the table within the document. To move a table, position the pointer on the table move handle until the pointer displays with a four-headed arrow attached, click and hold down the left mouse button, drag the table to the new location, and then release the mouse button.

Activity 2c Resizing and Moving Tables — Part 3 of 6

1. With **7-TSPTables.docx** open, insert a table into the current document by completing the following steps:
   a. Press Ctrl + End to move the insertion point to the end of the document and then press the Enter key.
   b. Click the Insert tab.
   c. Click the Object button arrow in the Text group and then click *Text from File* at the drop-down list.
   d. At the Insert File dialog box, navigate to your WL1C7 folder and then double-click the ***TSPEmps.docx*** document.
2. Automatically fit the bottom table by completing the following steps:
   a. Click in any cell in the bottom table.
   b. Click the Table Layout tab.
   c. Click the AutoFit button in the Cell Size group and then click *AutoFit Contents* at the drop-down list.

3. Format the bottom table by completing the following steps:
   a. Click the Table Design tab.
   b. Click the More Table Styles button in the table styles gallery, scroll down the gallery, and then click the *List Table 4 - Accent 6* table style (last column, fourth row in the *List Tables* section).
   c. Click the *First Column* check box in the Table Style Options group to remove the check mark.
   d. Select the first and second rows, click the Table Layout tab, and then click the Align Center button in the Alignment group.
   e. Select the second row and then press Ctrl + B to apply bold formatting.

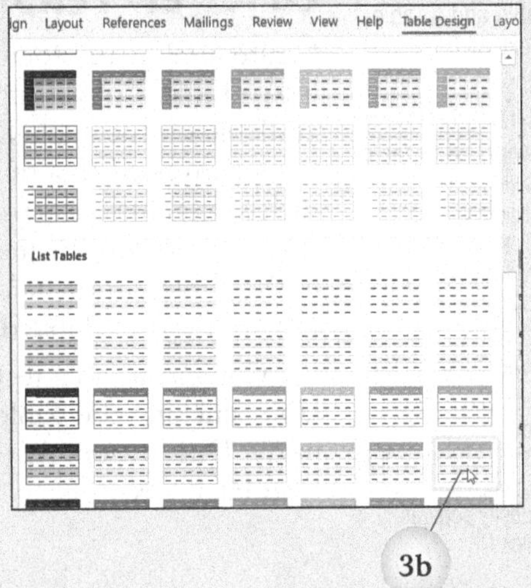

4. Size the bottom table by completing the following steps:
   a. Position the pointer on the resize handle in the lower right corner of the bottom table.
   b. Click and hold down the left mouse button, drag down and to the right until the width and height of the table increase approximately 1 inch, and then release the mouse button.

TRI-STATE PRODUCTS		
Name	**Employee #**	**Department**
Whitaker, Christine	1432-323-09	Financial Services
Higgins, Dennis	1230-933-21	Public Relations
Coffey, Richard	1321-843-22	Research and Development
Lee, Yong	1411-322-76	Human Resources
Fleishmann, Jim	1246-432-90	Public Relations
Schaffer, Mitchell	1388-340-44	Purchasing
Porter, Robbie	1122-361-38	Public Relations
Buchanan, Lillian	1432-857-87	Research and Development
Kensington, Jacob	1112-473-31	Human Resources

4a-4b

5. Move the bottom table by completing the following steps:
   a. Move the pointer over the bottom table and then position the pointer on the table move handle that appears just outside the upper left corner of the table until the pointer displays with a four-headed arrow attached.
   b. Click and hold down the left mouse button, drag the table so it is positioned equally between the left and right margins, and then release the mouse button.

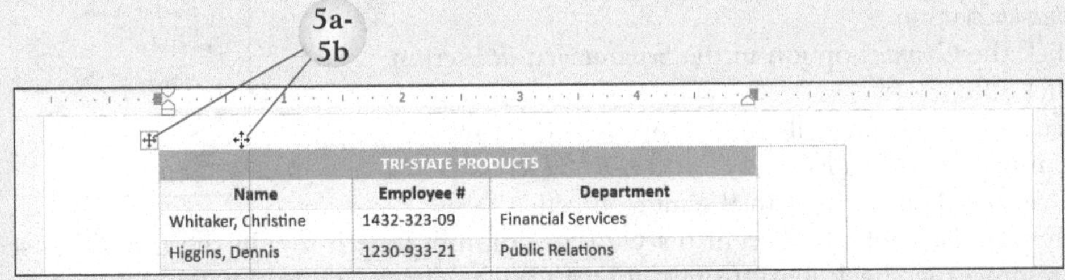

6. Select the cells in the column below the heading *Employee #* and then click the Align Top Center button in the Alignment group.
7. Save **7-TSPTables.docx**.

Converting Text to a Table and a Table to Text

Converting Text to a Table and a Table to Text

Create a table and then enter text in the cells or create the text and then convert it to a table. Converting text to a table provides formatting and layout options available on the Table Design tab and the Table Layout tab. When typing the text to be converted to a table, separate units of information using separator characters, such as commas or tabs. These characters identify where the text is divided into columns. To convert text, select the text, click the Insert tab, click the Table button in the Tables group, and then click *Convert Text to Table* at the drop-down list. At the Convert Text to Table dialog box, specify the separator and then click OK.

Convert a table to text by positioning the insertion point in any cell of the table, clicking the Table Layout tab, and then clicking the Convert to Text button in the Data group. At the Convert Table To dialog box, specify the separator and then click OK.

Quick Steps

Convert Text to Table

1. Select text.
2. Click Insert tab.
3. Click Table button.
4. Click *Convert Text to Table.*
5. Click OK.

Convert Table to Text

1. Click Table Layout tab.
2. Click Convert to Text button.
3. Specify separator.
4. Click OK.

Convert to Text

Activity 2d Converting Text to a Table

Part 4 of 6

1. With **7-TSPTables.docx** open, press Ctrl + End to move the insertion point to the end of the document. (If the insertion point does not display below the second table, press the Enter key until the insertion point displays below the table.)
2. Insert the document named **TSPExecs.docx** into the current document.
3. Convert the text to a table by completing the following steps:
   a. Select the text you just inserted.
   b. Make sure the Insert tab is active.
   c. Click the Table button in the Tables group and then click *Convert Text to Table* at the drop-down list.
   d. At the Convert Text to Table dialog box, type 2 in the *Number of columns* measurement box.
   e. Click the *AutoFit to contents* option in the *AutoFit behavior* section.
   f. Click the *Commas* option in the *Separate text at* section.
   g. Click OK.

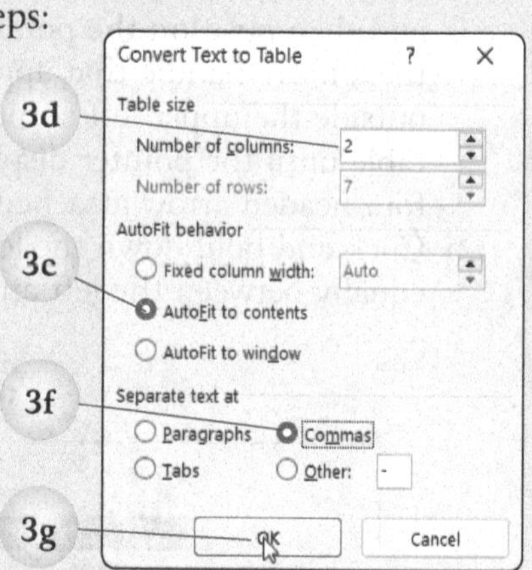

4. Select and merge the cells in the top row (the row containing the title *TRI-STATE PRODUCTS*) and then center-align the text in the merged cell.
5. Apply the List Table 4 - Accent 6 style (last column, fourth row in the *List Tables* section) and remove the check mark from the *First Column* check box in the Table Style Options group on the Table Design tab.
6. Drag the table so it is centered below the table above it.
7. Apply the List Table 4 - Accent 6 style to the top table. Increase the widths of the columns so the text *Tri-State Products* is visible and the text in the second and third columns displays on one line.
8. Drag the table so it is centered above the middle table. Make sure the three tables fit on one page.

9. Click in the middle table and then convert the table to text by completing the following steps:
   a. Click the Table Layout tab and then click the Convert to Text button in the Data group.
   b. At the Convert Table To dialog box, make sure *Tabs* is selected and then click OK.
10. Preview **7-TSPTables.docx**.
11. Click the Undo button to return the text to a table.
12. Save **7-TSPTables.docx**.

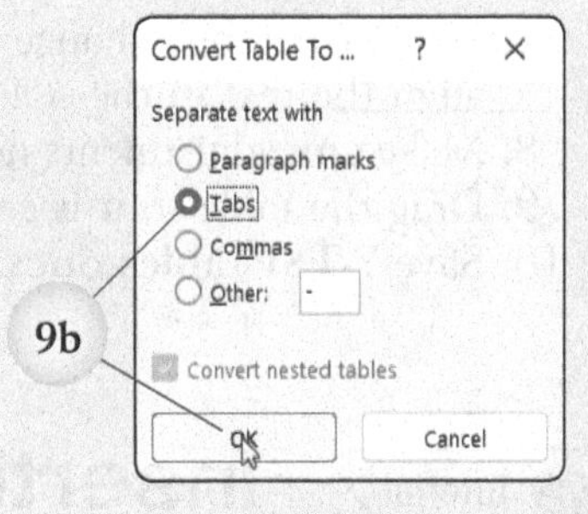

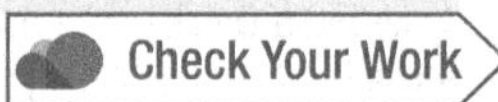

Drawing a Table

In Activity 1, options in the Borders group on the Table Design tab were used to draw borders around an existing table. These options can also be used to draw an entire table. To draw a table, click the Insert tab, click the Table button in the Tables group, and then click *Draw Table* at the drop-down list. Or click the Draw Table button in the Draw group on the Table Layout tab; this turns the pointer into a pen. Drag the pen pointer in the document to create the table. To correct an error when drawing a table, click the Eraser button in the Draw group on the Table Layout tab (which changes the pointer to an eraser) and then drag over any border lines to be erased. Clicking the Undo button will also undo the most recent action. To turn off the draw feature, click the Draw Table button in the Draw group or press the Esc key on the keyboard.

Activity 2e Drawing and Formatting a Table — Part 5 of 6

1. With **7-TSPTables.docx** open, select and then delete three rows in the middle table from the row that begins with the name *Lee, Yong* through the row that begins with the name *Schaffer, Mitchell*.
2. Move the insertion point to the end of the document (outside any table) and then press the Enter key. (Make sure the insertion point is positioned below the third table.)
3. Click the Insert tab, click the Table button, and then click the *Draw Table* option at the drop-down list. (This turns the insertion point into a pen.)
4. Using the mouse, drag in the document (below the bottom table) to create the table shown at the right, drawing the outside border first. If you make a mistake, click the Undo button. You can also click the Eraser button in the Draw group on the Table Layout tab and drag over a border line to erase it. Click the Draw Table button in the Draw group to turn off the draw feature.

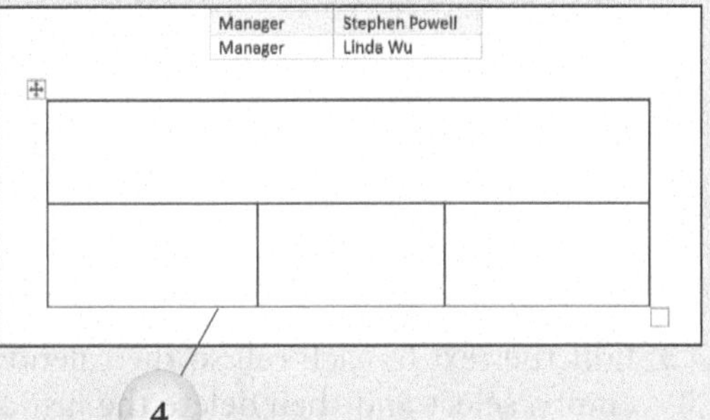

5. After drawing the table, type Tri-State Products in the top cell, Washington Division in the cell at the left, Oregon Division in the middle bottom cell, and California Division in the cell at the right.
6. Apply the Grid Table 4 - Accent 6 table style (last column, fourth row in the *Grid Tables* section).

7. Select the table, change the font size to 12 points, apply bold formatting, and then center-align the text in the cells using the Align Center button in the Alignment group.
8. Make any adjustments needed to the border lines so the text in each cell is on one line.
9. Drag the table so it is centered and positioned below the bottom table.
10. Save **7-TSPTables.docx**.

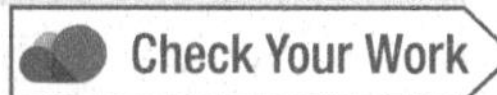

Inserting a Quick Table

Inserting a Quick Table

Word includes a Quick Tables feature for inserting predesigned tables in a document. To insert a quick table, click the Insert tab, click the Table button in the Tables group, point to *Quick Tables*, and then click a table at the side menu. Additional formatting can be applied to a quick table with options on the Table Design tab and the Table Layout tab.

Activity 2f Inserting a Quick Table — Part 6 of 6

1. With **7-TSPTables.docx** open, press Ctrl + End to move the insertion point to the end of the document and then press Ctrl + Enter to insert a page break.
2. Insert a quick table by clicking the Insert tab, clicking the Table button, pointing to *Quick Tables*, and then clicking the *Calendar 3* option at the side menu.

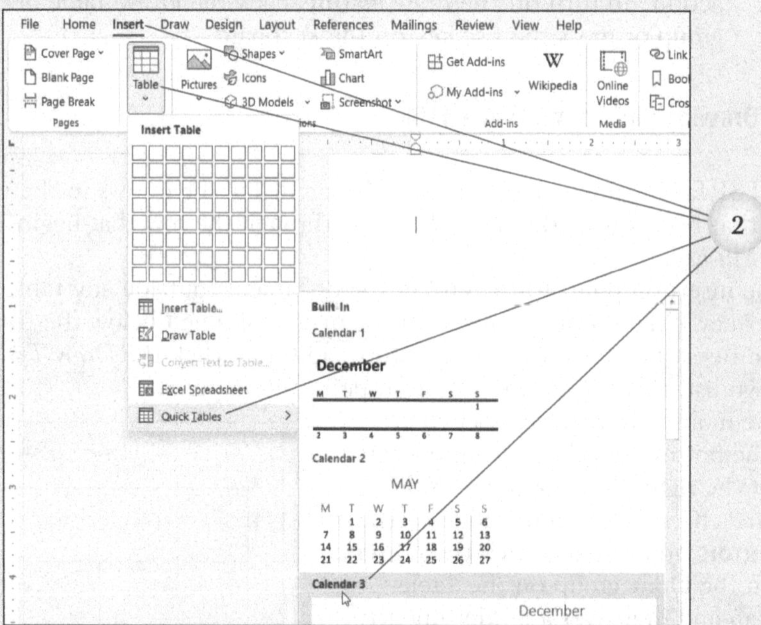

3. Edit the text in each cell so the calendar reflects the current month. (If the bottom row is empty, select and then delete the last and second to last rows.)
4. Select the entire table by clicking the Table Layout tab, clicking the Select button in the Table group, and then clicking the *Select Table* option. With the table selected, change the font to Copperplate Gothic Light.
5. Drag the table so it is centered between the left and right margins.
6. Save, preview, and then close **7-TSPTables.docx**.

Activity 3 Calculate Sales Data — 1 Part

You will insert formulas in a Tri-State Products sales table to calculate total sales, average sales, and top sales.

Performing Calculations in a Table

Performing Calculations in a Table

Use the Formula button in the Data group on the Table Layout tab to insert formulas that perform calculations on data in a table. The numbers in cells can be added, subtracted, multiplied, and divided. Other calculations can be performed, such as determining averages, counting items, and identifying minimum and maximum values. For more complex calculations, consider using an Excel worksheet.

Formula

Quick Steps

Insert Formula in Table

1. Click in cell.
2. Click Table Layout tab.
3. Click Formula button.
4. Type formula in Formula dialog box.
5. Click OK.

To perform a calculation on the data in a table, position the insertion point in the cell where the result of the calculation is to be inserted and then click the Formula button in the Data group on the Table Layout tab. This displays the Formula dialog box, as shown in Figure 7.10. At this dialog box, accept the default formula in the *Formula* text box or type a calculation and then click OK.

Four basic operators are available for writing a formula, including the plus symbol (+) for addition, the minus symbol (–) for subtraction, the asterisk (*) for multiplication, and the forward slash (/) for division. If a calculation contains two or more operators, Word performs the operations from left to right. To change the order of operations, put parentheses around the part of the calculation to be performed first.

In the default formula, the SUM part of the formula is called a *function*. Word also provides other functions for inserting formulas. These functions are available in the *Paste function* option box in the Formula dialog box. For example, use the AVERAGE function to average numbers in cells.

Specify the numbering format with the *Number format* option box in the Formula dialog box. For example, when calculating amounts of money, specify the number of digits that should follow the decimal point.

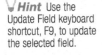

Hint Use the Update Field keyboard shortcut, F9, to update the selected field.

If changes are made to a formula, the result of the formula needs to be updated. To do this, right-click the formula result and then click *Update Field* at the shortcut menu. Another method is to click the formula result and then press the F9 function key, which is the Update Field keyboard shortcut. To update the results of all the formulas in a table, select the entire table and then press the F9 function key.

Figure 7.10 Formula Dialog Box

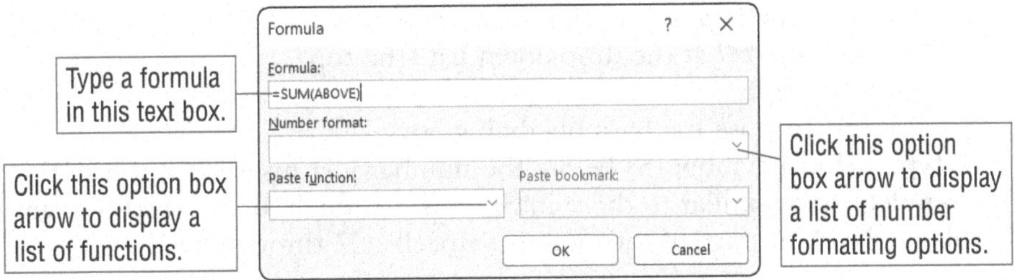
Formula
?
Formula:
=SUM(ABOVE)
Number format:
Paste function:
Paste bookmark:
OK
Cancel
Type a formula in this text box.
Click this option box arrow to display a list of functions.
Click this option box arrow to display a list of number formatting options.

Activity 3 Inserting and Recalculating Formulas

Part 1 of 1

1. Open **TSPSalesTable.docx** and then save it with the name **7-TSPSalesTable**.
2. Insert a formula in the table by completing the following steps:
   a. Click in cell B9. (Cell B9 is the empty cell immediately below the cell containing the amount *$375,630*.)
   b. Click the Table Layout tab.
   c. Click the Formula button in the Data group.
   d. At the Formula dialog box, make sure *=SUM(ABOVE)* appears in the *Formula* text box.
   e. Click the *Number format* option box arrow and then click *#,##0* at the drop-down list (the top option in the list).
   f. Click OK to close the Formula dialog box.

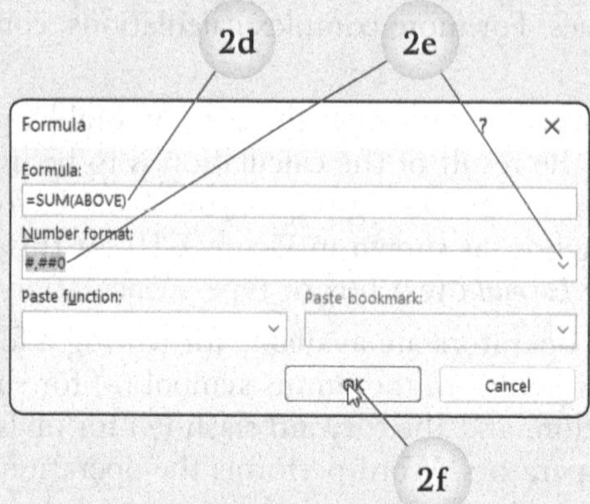

   g. In the table, type a dollar symbol ($) before the number just inserted in cell B9.
3. Complete steps similar to those in Steps 2c through 2g to insert a formula in cell C9. (Cell C9 is the empty cell immediately below the cell containing the amount *$399,120*.)
4. Insert a formula that calculates the average of amounts by completing the following steps:
   a. Click in cell B10. (Cell B10 is the empty cell immediately right of the cell containing the word *Average*.)
   b. Click the Formula button in the Data group.
   c. At the Formula dialog box, delete the formula in the *Formula* text box *except* for the equals (=) sign.
   d. With the insertion point positioned immediately right of the equals sign, click the *Paste function* option box arrow and then click *AVERAGE* at the drop-down list.
   e. With the insertion point positioned between the left and right parentheses, type B2:B8. (When typing cell designations in a formula, you can type either uppercase or lowercase letters.)
   f. Click the *Number format* option box arrow and then click *#,##0* at the drop-down list (the top option in the list).

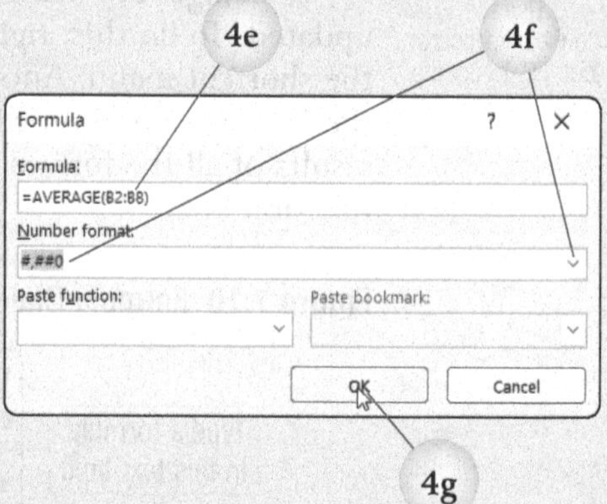

   g. Click OK to close the Formula dialog box.
   h. Type a dollar symbol ($) before the number just inserted in cell B10.
5. Complete steps similar to those in Steps 4b through 4h to insert a formula in cell C10 that calculates the average of the amounts in cells C2 through C8.

6. Insert a formula that calculates the maximum number by completing the following steps:
   a. Click in cell B11. (Cell B11 is the empty cell immediately right of the cell containing the words *Top Sales*.)
   b. Click the Formula button in the Data group.
   c. At the Formula dialog box, delete the formula in the *Formula* text box *except* for the equals sign.
   d. With the insertion point positioned immediately right of the equals sign, click the *Paste function* option box arrow and then click *MAX* at the drop-down list. (You will need to scroll down the list to locate the *MAX* option.)
   e. With the insertion point positioned between the left and right parentheses, type B2:B8.
   f. Click the *Number format* option box arrow and then click *#,##0* at the drop-down list.
   g. Click OK to close the Formula dialog box.
   h. Type a dollar symbol ($) before the number just inserted in cell B11.
7. Complete steps similar to those in Steps 6b through 6h to insert the maximum number in cell C11.
8. Save and then preview **7-TSPSalesTable.docx**.
9. Change the amount in cell B2 from *$543,241* to *$765,700*.
10. Recalculate all the formulas in the table by completing the following steps:
    a. Make sure the Table Layout tab is active and then click the Select button in the Table group.
    b. Click the *Select Table* option.
    c. Press the F9 function key.
11. Save, preview, and then close **7-TSPSalesTable.docx**.

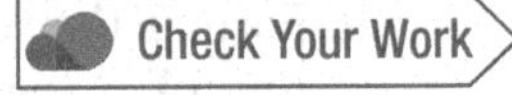

Activity 4 Insert an Excel Worksheet — 1 Part

You will insert an Excel worksheet in a blank document, decrease the number of rows and columns in the worksheet, insert data from a Word document, and calculate data in the worksheet.

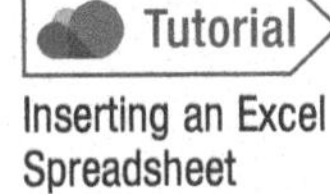

Inserting an Excel Spreadsheet

Inserting an Excel Spreadsheet

An Excel spreadsheet (usually referred to as a *worksheet*) can be inserted into a Word document, which provides some Excel functions for modifying and formatting the data. To insert an Excel worksheet, click the Insert tab, click the Table button in the Tables group, and then click the *Excel Spreadsheet* option at the drop-down list. This inserts a worksheet in the document with seven columns and ten rows visible. Increase or decrease the number of visible cells by dragging the sizing handles around the worksheet. Use buttons on the Excel ribbon tabs to format the worksheet. Click outside the worksheet and the Excel ribbon tabs are removed. Double-click the table to redisplay the Excel ribbon tabs.

Activity 4 Inserting and Formatting an Excel Worksheet

1. Open **SalesIncrease.docx.**
2. Press Ctrl + N to open a blank document.
3. Insert an Excel spreadsheet into the blank document by clicking the Insert tab, clicking the Table button in the Tables group, and then clicking *Excel Spreadsheet* at the drop-down list.

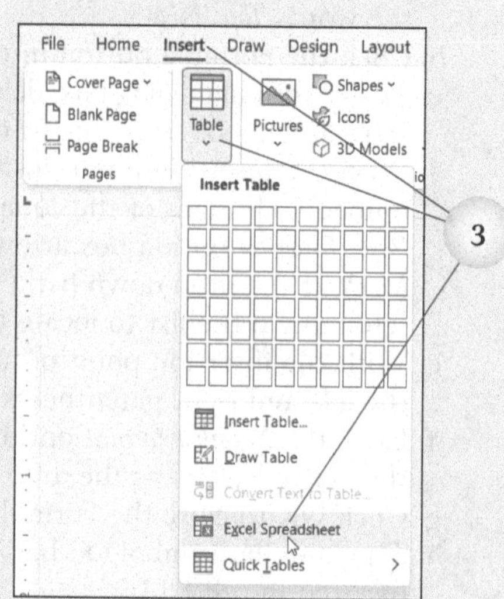

4. Decrease the size of the worksheet by completing the following steps:
   a. Position the pointer on the sizing handle (small black square) in the lower right corner of the worksheet until the pointer displays as a black, diagonal, two-headed arrow.
   b. Click and hold down the left mouse button, drag up and to the left, and then release the mouse button. Continue dragging the sizing handles until only columns A, B, and C and rows 1 through 7 are visible.
5. Copy a table into the Excel worksheet by completing the following steps:
   a. Position the pointer on the Word button on the taskbar and then click the *SalesIncrease.docx* thumbnail.
   b. Position the pointer over the table and then click the table move handle (small square containing a four-headed arrow) in the upper left corner of the table. (This selects all the cells in the table.)
   c. Click the Copy button in the Clipboard group on the Home tab.
   d. Close **SalesIncrease.docx.**
   e. With the first cell in the worksheet active, click the Paste button in the Clipboard group.
6. Format the worksheet and insert a formula by completing the following steps:
   a. Increase the width of the second column by positioning the pointer on the column boundary between columns B and C and double-clicking the left mouse button.
   b. Click in cell C3, type the formula =B3*1.02, and then press the Enter key.

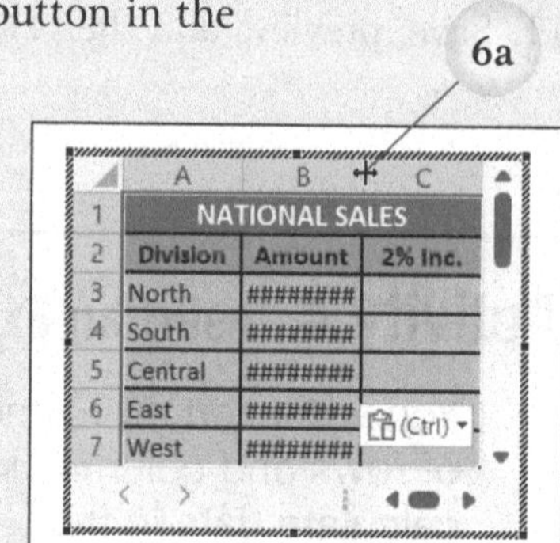

7. Copy the formula in cell C3 to the range C4:C7 by completing the following steps:
   a. Position the pointer (white plus symbol) in cell C3, click and hold down the left mouse button, drag into cell C7, and then release the mouse button.
   b. Click the Fill button in the Editing group on the Home tab and then click *Down* at the drop-down list.

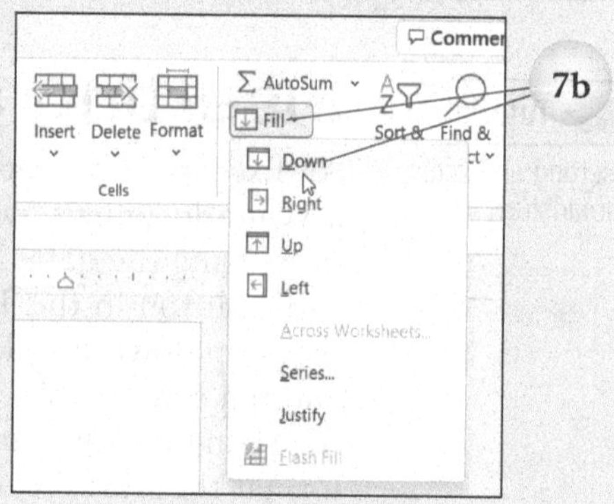

8. Click outside the worksheet to remove the Excel ribbon tabs.
9. Save the document with the name **7-Worksheet.**
10. Preview and then close **7-Worksheet.docx.**

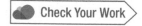

Check Your Work

Chapter Summary

- Create a table in a document to organize and provide a visual grouping of data and make the data easier to read and interpret.
- Use the Tables feature to create a table with columns and rows of information. Create a table with the Table button in the Tables group on the Insert tab or with options at the Insert Table dialog box.
- A cell is the intersection between a row and a column. The lines that form the cells of the table are called *gridlines*.
- Press the Tab key to move the insertion point to the next cell or press Shift + Tab to move the insertion point to the preceding cell.
- Press Ctrl + Tab to move the insertion point to a tab within a cell.
- Move the insertion point to cells in a table using the mouse by clicking in a cell or using the keyboard commands shown in Table 7.1.
- Change the table design with options and buttons on the Table Design tab.
- Refer to Table 7.2 for a list of mouse commands for selecting specific cells in a table and Table 7.3 for a list of keyboard commands for selecting specific cells in a table.
- Change the layout of a table with options and buttons on the Table Layout tab.
- Select a table, column, row, or cell using the Select button in the Table group on the Table Layout tab.
- Turn on and off the display of gridlines by clicking the View Gridlines button in the Table group on the Table Layout tab.
- Insert and delete columns and rows with buttons in the Rows & Columns group on the Table Layout tab.
- Merge selected cells with the Merge Cells button and split cells with the Split Cells button, both in the Merge group on the Table Layout tab.
- Change the column width and row height using the height and width measurement boxes in the Cell Size group on the Table Layout tab; by dragging move table column markers on the horizontal ruler, adjust table row markers on the vertical ruler, or gridlines in the table; or using the AutoFit button in the Cell Size group.
- Change the alignment of text in cells with buttons in the Alignment group on the Table Layout tab.
- If a table spans two pages or more, a header row can be inserted at the beginning of each page. To do this, click in the header row or select the header rows and then click the Repeat Header Rows button in the Data group on the Table Layout tab.
- Change cell margins with options in the Table Options dialog box.
- Change text direction in a cell with the Text Direction button in the Alignment group on the Table Layout tab.
- Change the table dimensions and alignment with options at the Table Properties dialog box with the Table tab selected.
- Use the resize handle to change the size of the table and the table move handle to move the table.
- Convert text to a table with the *Convert Text to Table* option at the Table button drop-down list. Convert a table to text with the Convert to Text button in the Data group on the Table Layout tab.

- Draw a table in a document by clicking the Insert tab, clicking the Table button in the Tables group, and then clicking *Draw Table* at the drop-down list. Using the mouse, drag in the document to create the table.
- Quick tables are predesigned tables that can be inserted in a document by clicking the Insert tab, clicking the Table button in the Tables group, pointing to *Quick Tables*, and then clicking a table at the side menu.
- Perform calculations on data in a table by clicking the Formula button in the Data group on the Table Layout tab and then specifying the formula and number format at the Formula dialog box.
- Insert an Excel spreadsheet (worksheet) into a Word document to provide Excel functions by clicking the Insert tab, clicking the Table button in the Tables group, and then clicking *Excel Spreadsheet* at the drop-down list.

Commands Review

FEATURE	RIBBON TAB, GROUP	BUTTON, OPTION
AutoFit table contents	Table Layout, Cell Size	, *AutoFit Contents*
cell alignment	Table Layout, Alignment	
convert table to text	Table Layout, Data	
convert text to table	Insert, Tables	, *Convert Text to Table*
delete column	Table Layout, Rows & Columns	, *Delete Columns*
delete row	Table Layout, Rows & Columns	, *Delete Rows*
distribute columns	Table Layout, Cell Size	
distribute rows	Table Layout, Cell Size	
draw table	Insert, Tables	, *Draw Table*
Formula dialog box	Table Layout, Data	*fx*
insert column left	Table Layout, Rows & Columns	
insert column right	Table Layout, Rows & Columns	
Insert Excel spreadsheet	Insert, Tables	, *Excel Spreadsheet*
insert row above	Table Layout, Rows & Columns	
insert row below	Table Layout, Rows & Columns	
Insert Table dialog box	Insert, Tables	, *Insert Table*
merge cells	Table Layout, Merge	
Quick Table	Insert, Tables	, *Quick Tables*
repeat header row	Table Layout, Data	
Split Cells dialog box	Table Layout, Merge	
table	Insert, Tables	
Table Options dialog box	Table Layout, Alignment	
text direction	Table Layout, Alignment	
view gridlines	Table Layout, Table	

CHAPTER 7

Review and Assessment

Skills Assessment

Assessment 1

Create, Format, and Modify a Training Schedule Table

1. At a blank document, create a table with four columns and five rows.
2. Type text in the cells as shown in Figure 7.11.
3. Insert a new column at the right side of the table and then type the following text in the new cells:

   Trainer
   Marsden
   Trujillo
   Yong
   Stein
4. Change the widths of the columns to the following measurements:

   First column = 0.8 inch
   Second column = 1.2 inches
   Third column = 0.7 inch
   Fourth column = 1.3 inches
   Fifth column = 0.9 inch
5. Insert a new row above the first row and then, with the new row selected, merge the cells. Type APPLICATION TRAINING SCHEDULE in the cell and then center-align the text.
6. Select the second row (contains the text *Section*, *Training*, *Days*, and so on) and then apply bold formatting to and center-align the text.
7. Make the Table Design tab active, apply the Grid Table 4 table style (first column, fourth row in the *Grid Tables* section), and then remove the check mark from the *First Column* check box.
8. Horizontally center the table on the page. ***Hint: Do this at the Table Properties dialog box with the Table tab selected.***
9. Save the document with the name **7-SchTable**.
10. Preview and then close **7-SchTable.docx**.

Figure 7.11 Assessment 1

Section	Training	Days	Time
WD100	Word Level 1	MWF	9:00 to 10:00 a.m.
WD110	Word Level 2	TTh	1:30 to 3:00 p.m.
EX100	Excel Level 1	MTW	3:00 to 4:00 p.m.
EX110	Excel Level 2	TTh	2:00 to 3:30 p.m.

Assessment 2 Create, Format, and Modify a Property Replacement Costs Table

1. At a blank document, create a table with two columns and six rows.
2. Type the text in the cells in the table as shown in Figure 7.12. (Press the Enter key after typing the word *PROPERTY* in the first cell.)
3. Merge the cells in the top row and then change the alignment to align top center.
4. Change the alignment to align top right for the text in the cells containing money amounts and the blank cell below the last amount (cells B2 through B6).
5. Click in the *Accounts receivable* cell and then insert a row below it. Type Equipment in the new cell at the left and type $83,560 in the new cell at the right.
6. Insert a formula in cell B7 that sums the amounts in cells B2 through B6 and then change the number format to *#,##0*. Type a dollar symbol ($) before the amount in cell B7.
7. Automatically fit the contents of the cells.
8. Apply the Grid Table 4 - Accent 1 table style (second column, fourth row in the *Grid Tables* section) and remove the check mark from the *First Column* check box.
9. Click the Border Styles button arrow, click the *Double solid lines, 1/2 pt* option (first column, third row in the *Theme Borders* section), and then draw a border around all four sides of the table.
10. Save the document with the name **7-CostsTable**.
11. Preview and then close **7-CostsTable.docx**.

Figure 7.12 Assessment 2

PROPERTY REPLACEMENT COSTS	
Accounts receivable	$95,460
Business personal property	$1,367,340
Legal liability	$75,415
Earnings and expenses	$945,235
Total	

Assessment 3 Format a Table on Transportation Services

1. Open **ServicesTable.docx** and then save it with the name **7-ServicesTable**.
2. Insert a new column at the left of the table and then merge the cells. Type Metro Area in the merged cell, press the Enter key, and then type Transportation Services.
3. Select the text in the first column, change the font size to 16 points, and then click the Text Direction button two times to rotate the text. ***Hint: The Text Direction button is in the Alignment group on the Table Layout tab.***
4. Center-align (using the Align Center button) the text in the first column.
5. Change the width of the first column to 0.9 inch and the width of the third column to 1.1 inches.
6. Apply the Grid Table 5 Dark - Accent 5 table style (sixth column, fifth row in the *Grid Tables* section).

7. Horizontally center the table on the page.
8. Indent the text in the three cells below the cell containing the text *Valley Railroad*, as shown in Figure 7.13. ***Hint: Use Ctrl + Tab to create the indent in each cell.***
9. Apply italic and bold formatting to the four headings in the second column (*Langley City Transit*, *Valley Railroad*, *Mainline Bus*, and *Village Travel Card*).
10. Save, preview, and then close **7-ServicesTable.docx**.

Figure 7.13 Assessment 3

Metro Area Transportation Services	Service	Telephone
	Langley City Transit	
	Subway and bus information	(507) 555-3049
	Service status hotline	(507) 555-4123
	Travel information	(507) 555-4993
	Valley Railroad	
	Railway information	(202) 555-2300
	Status hotline	(202) 555-2343
	Travel information	(202) 555-2132
	Mainline Bus	
	Bus routes	(507) 555-6530
	Emergency hotline	(507) 555-6798
	Travel information	(507) 555-7542
	Village Travel Card	
	Village office	(507) 555-1232
	Card inquiries	(507) 555-1930

Assessment 4

Insert Formulas in a Table

1. In this chapter, you learned how to insert formulas in a table. Experiment with writing formulas (consider using the Help feature or another reference) and then open **FinAnalysis.docx**. Save the document with the name **7-FinAnalysis**.
2. Apply the Grid Table 4 - Accent 6 table style (last column, fourth row in the *Grid Tables* section) to the table and then apply other formatting so your table appears similar to the one in Figure 7.14.
3. Insert a formula in cell B13 that sums the amounts in cells B6 through B12. Apply the #,##0 format. Type a dollar symbol ($) before the amount. Complete similar steps to insert formulas and dollar symbols in cells C13, D13, and E13.
4. Insert a formula in cell B14 that subtracts the amount in B13 from the amount in B4. Apply the #,##0 format. ***Hint: The formula should look like this:* =(B4-B13)**. Type a dollar symbol before the amount. Complete similar steps to insert formulas and dollar symbols in cells C14, D14, and E14.
5. Save, preview, and then close **7-FinAnalysis.docx**.

Figure 7.14 Assessment 4

TRI-STATE PRODUCTS				
Financial Analysis				
	First Qtr.	**Second Qtr.**	**Third Qtr.**	**Fourth Qtr.**
Revenue	$1,450,348	$1,538,239	$1,634,235	$1,523,455
Expenses				
Facilities	$250,220	$323,780	$312,485	$322,655
Materials	$93,235	$102,390	$87,340	$115,320
Payroll	$354,390	$374,280	$380,120	$365,120
Benefits	$32,340	$35,039	$37,345	$36,545
Marketing	$29,575	$28,350	$30,310	$31,800
Transportation	$4,492	$5,489	$5,129	$6,349
Miscellaneous	$4,075	$3,976	$4,788	$5,120
Total				
Net Revenue				

Visual Benchmark

Activity 1

Create a Cover Letter Containing a Table

1. Click the File tab, click the *New* option, and then double-click the *Single spaced (blank)* template.
2. At the single-spaced blank document, type the letter shown in Figure 7.15. Create and format the table in the letter as shown in the figure. ***Hint: Apply the Grid Table 4 - Accent 1 table style*** (second column, fourth row in the *Grid Tables* section).
3. Save the completed document with the name **7-CoverLtr**.
4. Preview and then close **7-CoverLtr.docx**.

Activity 2

Insert and Format a Quick Table

1. At a blank document, insert the Calendar 1 quick table and then format the calendar so that it appears as shown in Figure 7.16. (You may want to turn on gridlines to see the cells in the calendar.) Consider the following when formatting the calendar:
   a. Increase the size of the calendar so that it is approximately 6.5 inches wide and 8 inches tall.
   b. Change *December* to *October 2024* and then change the font size as shown in the figure for all cells.
   c. Type the dates (1 2, 3, and so on) and the information in cells.
   d. Position the days of the week (M, T, W, and so on) in the cells as shown.
   e. Apply bold formatting and change the font color to Orange, Accent 2, Darker 50% (sixth column, bottom row in the *Theme Colors* section) for all text in the document.
   f. Insert the **FallLeaves.png** image file from your WL1C7 folder. Change the wrapping to behind text and then size and position the image as shown.
   g. Change the color of the black border lines below each week to Orange, Accent 2, Darker 50% (sixth column, bottom row in the *Theme Colors* section).
   h. Make any other formatting changes so your document looks similar to the document in Figure 7.16.
2. Save the completed document with the name **7-OctCalendar**.
3. Preview and then close **7-OctCalendar.docx**.

Figure 7.15 Visual Benchmark 1

10234 Larkspur Drive *(press Enter)*
Cheyenne, WY 82002 *(press Enter)*
July 15, 2024 *(press Enter five times)*

Dr. Theresa Sullivan *(press Enter)*
Rocky Mountain News *(press Enter)*
100 Second Avenue *(press Enter)*
Cheyenne, WY 82001 *(press Enter two times)*

Dear Dr. Sullivan: *(press Enter two times)*

Your advertised opening for a corporate communications staff writer describes interesting challenges. As you can see from the table below, my skills and experience are excellent matches for the position. *(press Enter two times)*

QUALIFICATIONS AND SKILLS	
Your Requirement	**My Experience, Skills, and Value Offered**
Two years of business writing experience	Four years of experience creating diverse business messages, from corporate communications to feature articles and radio broadcast material.
Ability to complete projects on deadline	Proven project coordination skills and tight deadline focus. My current role as producer of a daily three-hour talk-radio program requires planning, coordination, and execution of many detailed tasks, always in the face of inflexible deadlines.
Oral presentation skills	Unusually broad experience, including high-profile roles as an on-air radio presence and "the voice" for an on-hold telephone message company.
Relevant education (BA or BS)	BA in Mass Communications; one year post-graduate study in Multimedia Communications.

As you will note from the enclosed résumé, my experience encompasses corporate, print media, and multimedia environments. I offer a diverse and proven skill set that can help your company create and deliver its message to various audiences to build image, market presence, and revenue. I look forward to meeting with you to discuss the value I can offer your company. *(press Enter two times)*

Sincerely, *(press Enter four times)*

Marcus Tolliver *(press Enter two times)*

Enclosure: Résumé

Figure 7.16 Visual Benchmark 2

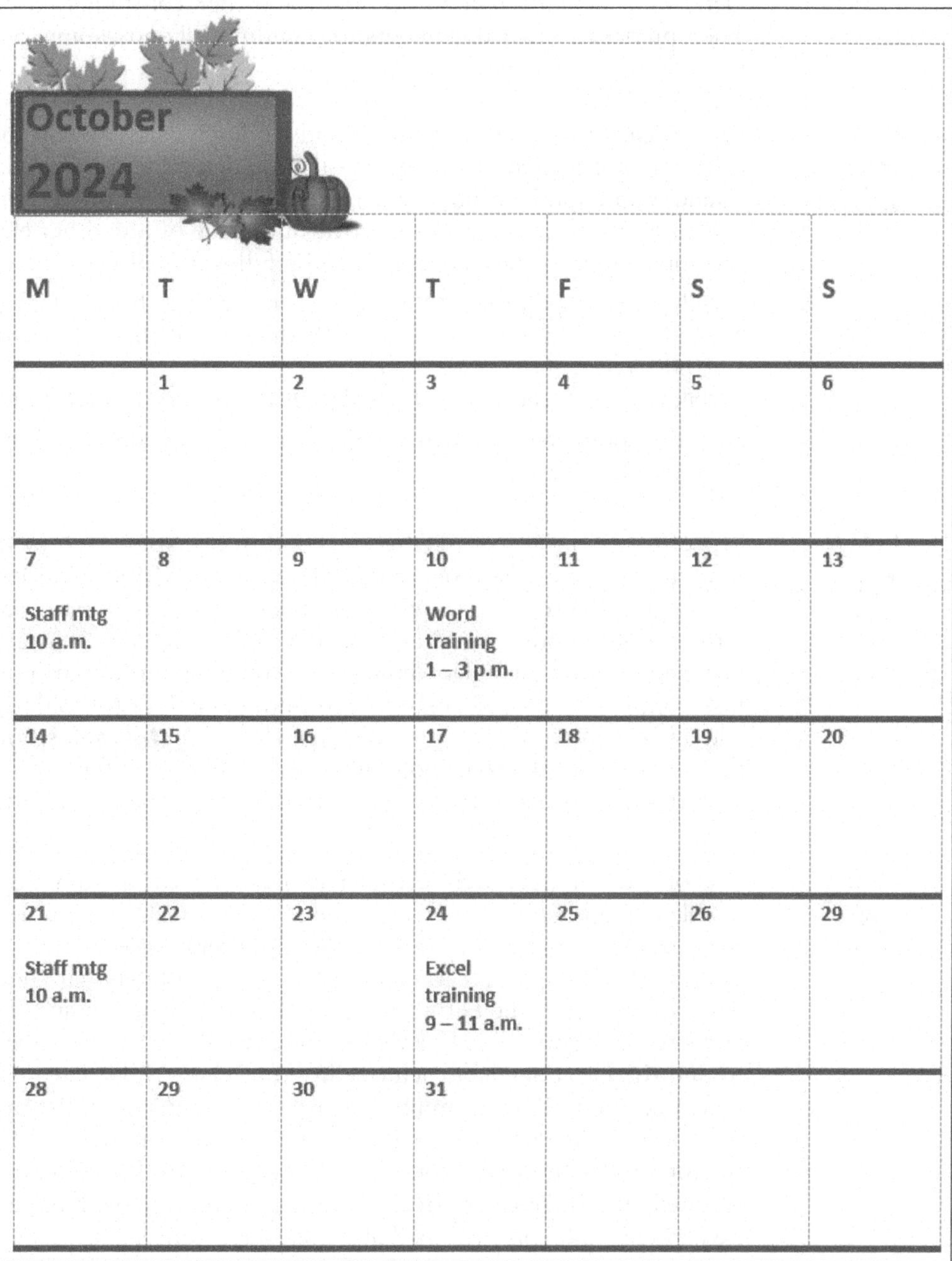

October 2024

M	T	W	T	F	S	S
	1	2	3	4	5	6
7 Staff mtg 10 a.m.	8	9	10 Word training 1 – 3 p.m.	11	12	13
14	15	16	17	18	19	20
21 Staff mtg 10 a.m.	22	23	24 Excel training 9 – 11 a.m.	25	26	29
28	29	30	31			

Case Study

Part 1

You have recently been hired as an office clerk for a landscaping business, Landmark Landscaping, which has two small offices in your city. The person who held the position before you kept track of monthly sales using Word, and the office manager would prefer that you continue using that application. Open the document **LLMoSales.docx** and then save it with the name **7-LLMoSales**. After reviewing the information, you decide that a table would be a better format for maintaining and presenting the data. Convert the data to a table and modify its appearance so that it is easy to read and understand. Insert a total row at the bottom of the table and then insert formulas to sum the totals in the columns that contain amounts. Apply formatting to the table to enhance its appearance. Determine a color theme for the table and then continue to use that color theme when preparing other documents for Landmark Landscaping. Save, preview, and then close the document.

Part 2

The office manager of Landmark Landscaping would like you to create a monthly calendar (use the current month) using a quick table. Insert the dates in the calendar and apply formatting using the color theme you determined for the company in Part 1. Consider inserting an image or any other element to enhance the appearance of the calendar. Add the following information to the calendar:

- Sales meeting on the first Tuesday of the month from 10:00 to 11:30 a.m.
- Product presentation the second Wednesday of the month from 9:00 to 10:00 a.m.
- Sales training the fourth Thursday of the month from 2:00 to 4:30 p.m.

Save the completed calendar with the name **7-LLCalendar**. Preview and then close the document.

Part 3

The office manager has asked you to find information on how to add alt text to a table to make the table accessible to people with disabilities. Use the Help feature and the search text *table properties* or the search text *table alt text* to find information on how to add alt text to a table. If a video is available in the Help task pane, watch the video along with reading any information provided in the task pane. With the information you find, open **7-LLMOSales.docx** and then add alt text to the table. Save and then close **7-LLMOSales.docx**. At a blank document, write the steps you followed to add the alt text. Save the document with the name **7-AltText**. Preview and then close the document.

Part 4

One of the landscape architects at Landmark Landscaping has asked you to prepare a table containing information on the trees that need to be ordered next month. She would also like you to include the Latin names for the trees because this information is important when ordering. Create a table that contains the common name of each tree, the Latin name, the quantity required, and the price per tree, as shown in Figure 7.17. Use the internet (or any other resource available to you) to find the Latin name of each tree listed in Figure 7.17. Create a column in the table that multiplies the number of trees to be ordered by the price and include this formula for each tree. Create a row at the bottom of the table that calculates the total order (note that totals are not required for the columns with the quantity required and the price per tree). Format and enhance the table so it is attractive and easy to read and apply colors that match the color scheme you chose in Part 1. Save the document with the name **7-LLTrees**. Preview and then close the document.

Figure 7.17 Case Study, Part 4

Douglas Fir, 15 required, $2.99 per tree
Elm, 10 required, $4.49 per tree
Western Hemlock, 10 required, $3.89 per tree
Red Maple, 8 required, $8.99 per tree
Ponderosa Pine, 5 required, $4.69 per tree

WORD

Applying and Customizing Formatting

CHAPTER 8

Performance Objectives

Upon successful completion of Chapter 8, you will be able to:

1 Create and insert custom numbers and bullets
2 Create and insert multilevel list formatting
3 Specify AutoCorrect exceptions
4 Add and delete AutoCorrect text
5 Use the AutoCorrect Options button
6 Customize AutoFormatting
7 Create custom theme colors and theme fonts
8 Save, apply, edit, and delete a custom theme
9 Reset the template theme

Word offers a number of features to apply and customize formatting and to help streamline the formatting of a document. In this chapter, you will learn how to define and insert custom numbers and bullets and to format text in a multilevel list. You will use Word's AutoCorrect and Autoformatting features and customize them for your convenience when creating documents. The Microsoft 365 suite offers design themes that provide consistent formatting and help create documents with a professional and polished look. This chapter provides instruction on how to customize a theme by modifying the color and fonts and applying theme effects.

Data Files

The data files for this chapter are in the WL1C8 folder that you downloaded at the beginning of this course.

Activity 1 **Apply Number Formatting to an Agenda** **2 Parts**

You will open an agenda document, apply formatting that includes number formatting, and then define and apply custom numbering.

Inserting and Creating Custom Numbers and Bullets

Number paragraphs or insert bullets before paragraphs using buttons in the Paragraph group on the Home tab. Use the Numbering button to insert numbers before specific paragraphs and use the Bullets button to insert bullets. To insert custom numbering or bullets, click the button arrow and then choose from the drop-down gallery that displays.

Inserting Custom Numbers

Insert numbers as text is typed or select text and then apply a numbering format. Type *1.* and then press the spacebar and Word indents the number approximately 0.25 inch. Type text after the number and then press the Enter key and Word indents all the lines in the paragraph 0.5 inch from the left margin (called a *hanging indent*). At the beginning of the next paragraph, Word inserts the number *2* followed by a period 0.25 inch from the left margin. Continue typing items and Word numbers successive paragraphs in the list. To number existing paragraphs of text, select the paragraphs and then click the Numbering button in the Paragraph group on the Home tab.

Hint If the automatic numbering or bulleting feature is on, press Shift + Enter to insert a line break without inserting a number or bullet.

Click the Numbering button in the Paragraph group and arabic numbers (1., 2., 3., etc.) are inserted in the document. This default numbering can be changed by clicking the Numbering button arrow and then clicking an option at the drop-down gallery.

To change list levels, click the Numbering button arrow, point to the *Change List Level* option at the bottom of the drop-down gallery, and then click a list level at the side menu. Set the numbering value with options at the Set Numbering Value dialog box, shown in Figure 8.1. Display this dialog box by clicking the Numbering button arrow and then clicking the *Set Numbering Value* option at the bottom of the drop-down gallery.

Figure 8.1 Set Numbering Value Dialog Box

Activity 1a Inserting Custom Numbers

Part 1 of 2

1. Open **FDAgenda.docx** and then save it with the name **8-FDAgenda.**
2. Restart the list numbering at 1 by completing the following steps:
   a. Select the numbered paragraphs.
   b. Click the Numbering button arrow in the Paragraph group on the Home tab and then click *Set Numbering Value* at the drop-down gallery.
   c. At the Set Numbering Value dialog box, select the number in the *Set value to* measurement box, type 1, and then press the Enter key.

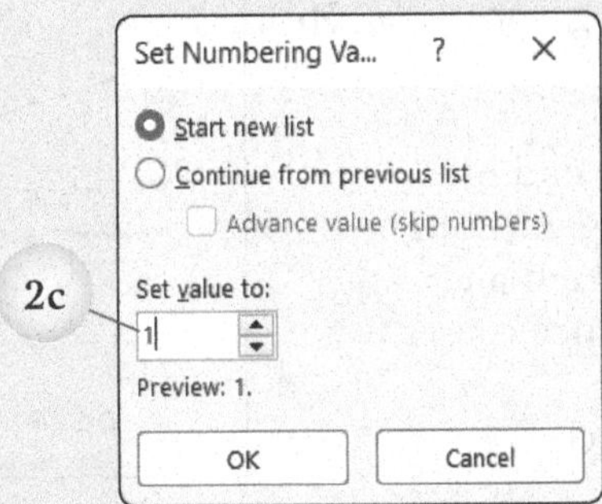

3. Change the paragraph numbers to letters by completing the following steps:
   a. With the numbered paragraphs selected, click the Numbering button arrow.
   b. At the Numbering button drop-down gallery, click the option that uses capital letters followed by a period (second column, second row in the *Numbering Library* section [this location may vary]).

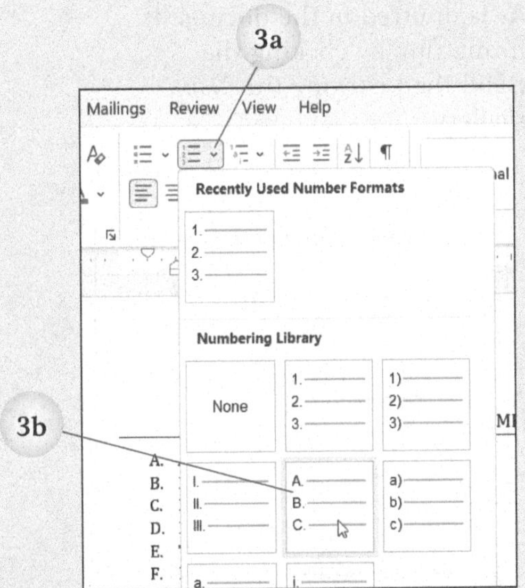

4. Add text by positioning the insertion point immediately right of the text *Introductions*, pressing the Enter key, and then typing Organizational Overview.

5. Demote the lettered list by completing the following steps:
   a. Select the lettered paragraphs.
   b. Click the Numbering button arrow, point to the *Change List Level* option, and then click the *a.* option at the side menu (*Level 2*).
6. With the paragraphs still selected, promote the list by clicking the Decrease Indent button in the Paragraph group on the Home tab. (The lowercase letters change back to capital letters.)
7. Move the insertion point to the end of the document and then type The meeting will stop for lunch, which is catered and will be held in the main conference center from 12:15 to 1:30 p.m.
8. Press the Enter key and then click the Numbering button.
9. Click the AutoCorrect Options button next to the *A.* inserted in the document and then click *Continue Numbering* at the drop-down list. (This changes the letter from *A.* to *H.*)
10. Type Future Goals, press the Enter key, type Proposals, press the Enter key, and then type Adjournment.
11. Press the Enter key and *K.* is inserted in the document. Turn off the numbering formatting by clicking the Numbering button arrow and then clicking the *None* option at the drop-down gallery.

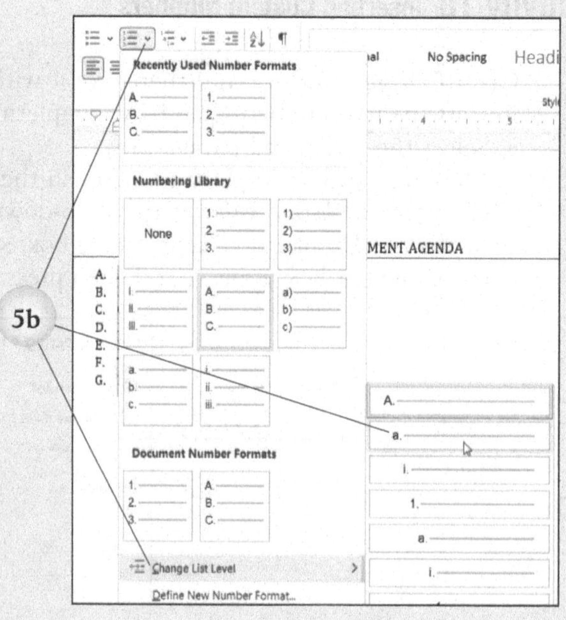

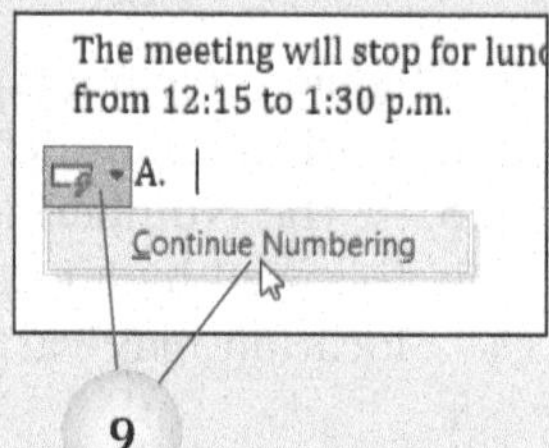

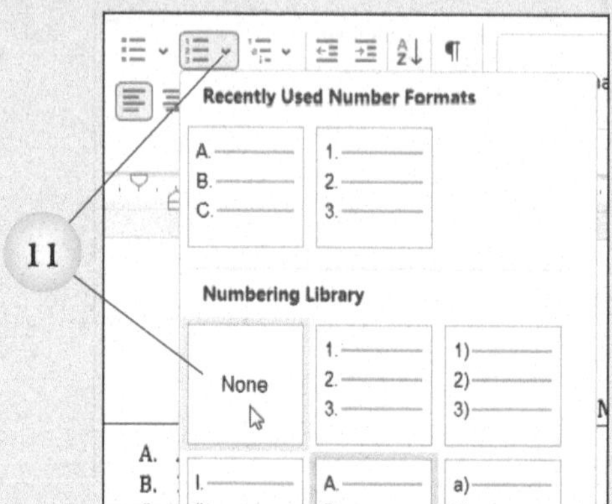

12. Decrease the paragraph indent by clicking the Decrease Indent button in the Paragraph group on the Home tab.
13. Save and then preview **8-FDAgenda.docx**.
14. Select and then delete the paragraph of text in the middle of the list (the paragraph that begins *The meeting will stop*). (All the lettered items should be listed consecutively and the same amount of space should appear between them.)
15. Save **8-FDAgenda.docx**.

Creating Custom Numbering Formats

Quick Steps

Define New Number Format

1. Click Numbering button arrow.
2. Click *Define New Number Format.*
3. Specify format.
4. Click OK.

Creating Custom Numbering Formats

Along with default and custom numbers, custom numbering formats can be created with options at the Define New Number Format dialog box, shown in Figure 8.2. Display this dialog box by clicking the Numbering button arrow and then clicking *Define New Number Format* at the drop-down gallery. Use options at the dialog box to specify the number style, font, and alignment. Preview the formatting in the *Preview* section.

Any number format created at the Define New Number Format dialog box is automatically included in the *Numbering Library* section of the Numbering button drop-down gallery. Remove a number format from the drop-down gallery by right-clicking the format and then clicking *Remove* at the shortcut menu.

Figure 8.2 Define New Number Format Dialog Box

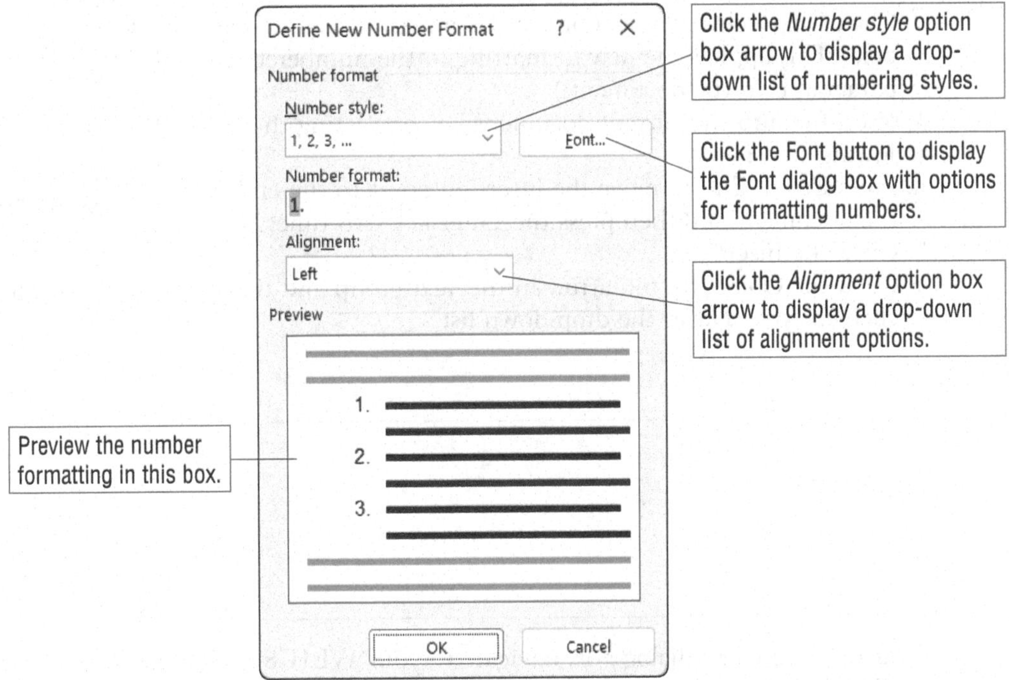

Activity 1b Creating a Numbering Format

Part 2 of 2

1. With **8-FDAgenda.docx** open, define a new numbering format by completing the following steps:
   a. With the insertion point positioned anywhere in the numbered paragraphs, click the Numbering button arrow in the Paragraph group on the Home tab.
   b. Click *Define New Number Format* at the drop-down gallery.
   c. At the Define New Number Format dialog box, click the *Number style* option box arrow and then click the *I, II, III, …* option.
   d. Click the Font button at the right of the *Number style* list box.

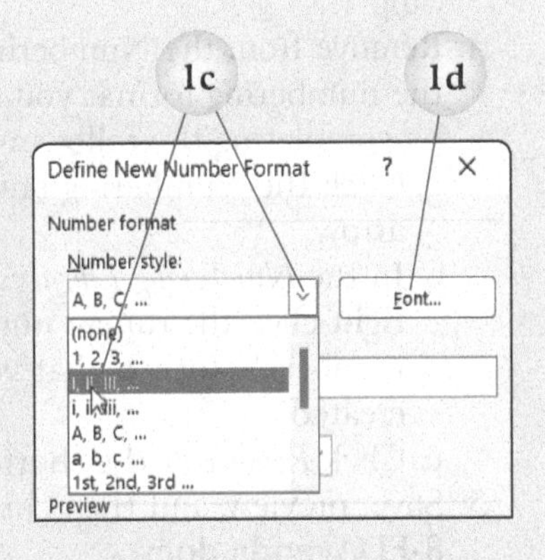

e. At the Font dialog box, scroll down the *Font* list box and then click *Calibri*.
f. Click *Bold* in the *Font style* list box.

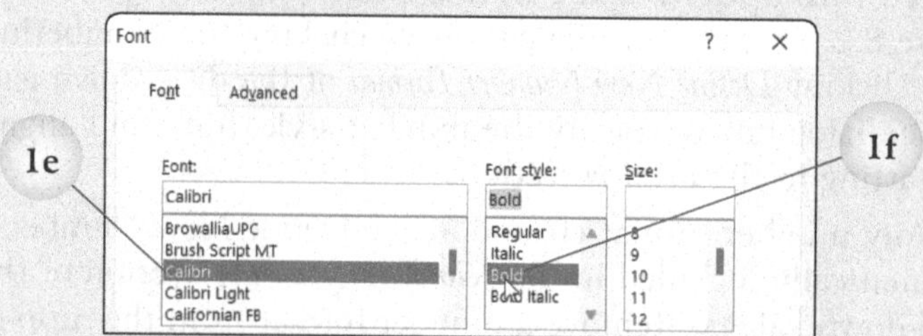

g. Click OK to close the Font dialog box.
h. Click the *Alignment* option box arrow and then click *Right* at the drop-down list.
i. Click OK to close the Define New Number Format dialog box. (This applies the new formatting to the numbered paragraphs in the document.)

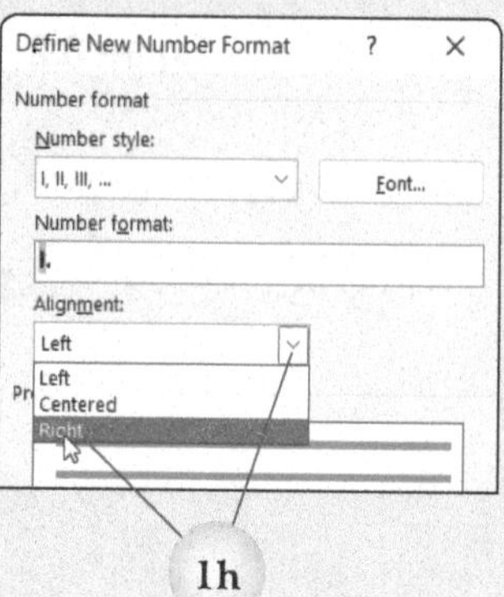

2. Insert a file into the current document by completing the following steps:
   a. Press Ctrl + End to move the insertion point to the end of the document and then press the Enter key two times.
   b. Click the Insert tab.
   c. Click the Object button arrow in the Text group and then click *Text from File* at the drop-down list.

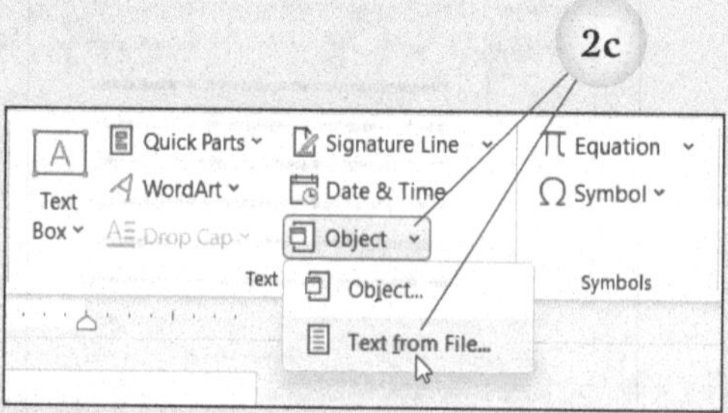

   d. At the Insert File dialog box, navigate to your WL1C8 folder and then double-click the ***PDAgenda.docx*** document.
3. Select the text below the title *PRODUCTION DEPARTMENT AGENDA*, click the Home tab, click the Numbering button arrow, and then click the roman numeral style created in Step 1.
4. Remove from the Numbering Library the numbering format you created by completing the following steps:
   a. Click the Numbering button arrow.
   b. In the *Numbering Library* section, right-click the roman numeral numbering format that you created.
   c. Click *Remove* at the shortcut menu.
5. Save, preview, and then close **8-FDAgenda.docx**.

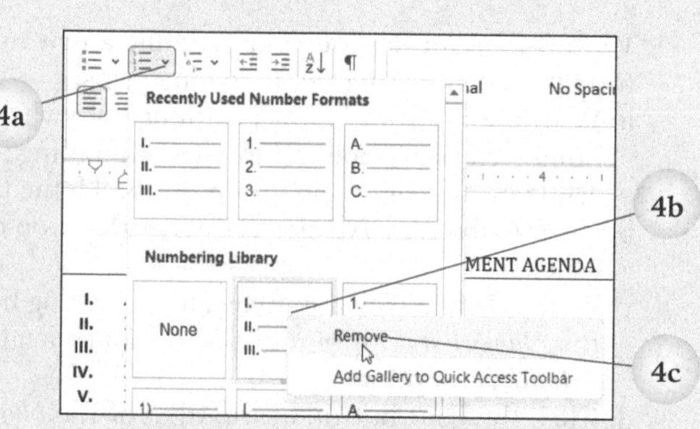

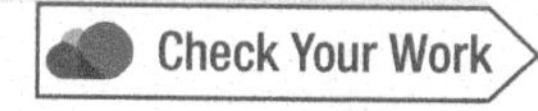

Activity 2 Apply Custom Bullets to an Adventure Document 1 Part

You will open an adventure document and then define and insert custom picture and symbol bullets.

Creating Custom Bullets

Quick Steps

Define Custom Bullet

1. Click Bullets button arrow.
2. Click *Define New Bullet* at drop-down gallery.
3. Click Symbol button or Picture button.
4. Click symbol or picture.
5. Click OK.
6. Click OK.

Hint Create a picture bullet to add visual interest to a document.

Creating Custom Bullets

Click the Bullets button in the Paragraph group and a round bullet is inserted in the document. Insert custom bullets by clicking the Bullets button arrow and then clicking a bullet type at the drop-down gallery. This drop-down gallery displays the most recently used bullets along with an option for defining a new bullet.

Click the *Define New Bullet* option and the Define New Bullet dialog box displays, as shown in Figure 8.3. Use options at the dialog box to choose a symbol or picture bullet, change the font size of the bullet, and specify the alignment of the bullet. When creating a custom bullet, consider matching the theme or mood of the document to maintain a consistent look or create a picture bullet to add visual interest.

A custom bullet created at the Define New Bullet dialog box is automatically included in the *Bullet Library* section of the Bullets button drop-down gallery. Remove a custom bullet from the drop-down gallery by right-clicking the bullet and then clicking *Remove* at the shortcut menu.

As with the level of a numbered list, the level of a bulleted list can be changed. To do this, click the item or select the items to be changed, click the Bullets button arrow, and then point to *Change List Level*. At the side menu of bullet options that displays, click a bullet. To insert a line break in the list while the automatic bullets feature is on without inserting a bullet, press Shift + Enter. (A line break can also be inserted in a numbered list without inserting a number by pressing Shift + Enter.)

Figure 8.3 Define New Bullet Dialog Box

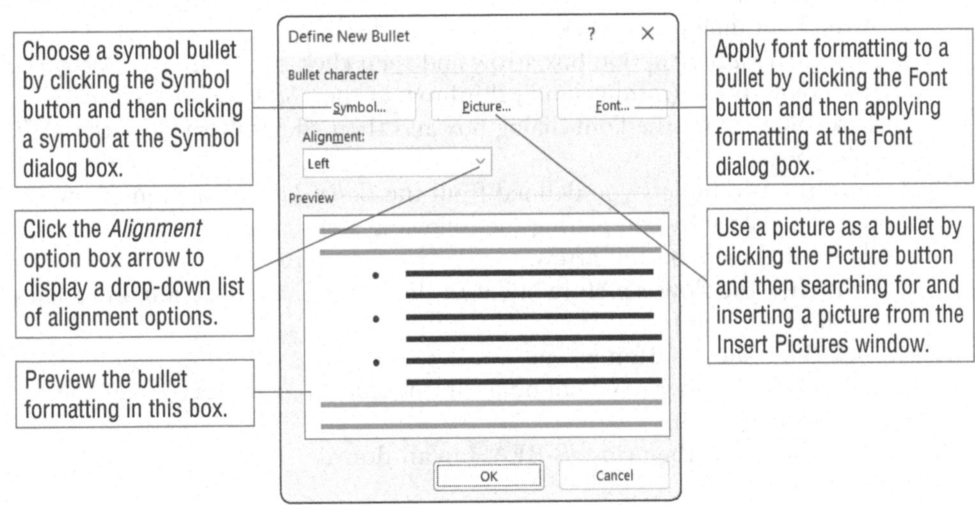
Choose a symbol bullet by clicking the Symbol button and then clicking a symbol at the Symbol dialog box.
Click the *Alignment* option box arrow to display a drop-down list of alignment options.
Preview the bullet formatting in this box.
Define New Bullet
Bullet character
Symbol...
Picture...
Font...
Alignment:
Left
Preview
OK
Cancel
Apply font formatting to a bullet by clicking the Font button and then applying formatting at the Font dialog box.
Use a picture as a bullet by clicking the Picture button and then searching for and inserting a picture from the Insert Pictures window.

Activity 2 Creating Custom Bullets

Part 1 of 1

1. Open **BEAHawaii.docx** and then save it with the name **8-BEAHawaii.**
2. Define and insert a picture bullet by completing the following steps:
   a. Select the four paragraphs of text below the heading *Rainy Day Activities*.
   b. Click the Bullets button arrow in the Paragraph group on the Home tab and then click *Define New Bullet* at the drop-down gallery.
   c. At the Define New Bullet dialog box, click the Picture button.
   d. At the Insert Pictures window, click the *Browse* option at the right of the *From a file* option, navigate to your WL1C8 folder, and then double-click the ***Flower.png*** image file.
   e. Click OK to close the Define New Bullet dialog box. (The new bullet is applied to the selected paragraphs.)

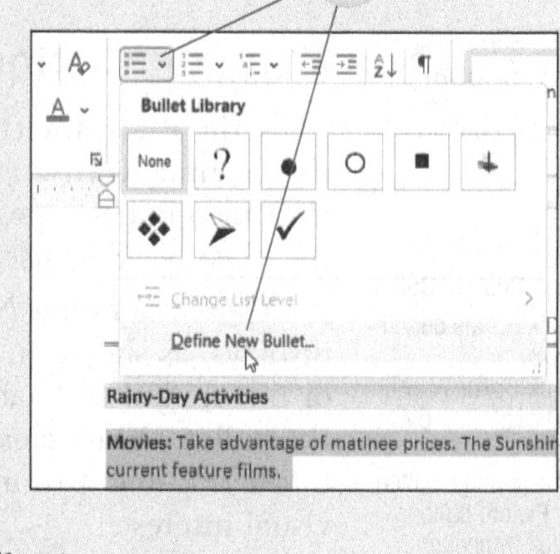

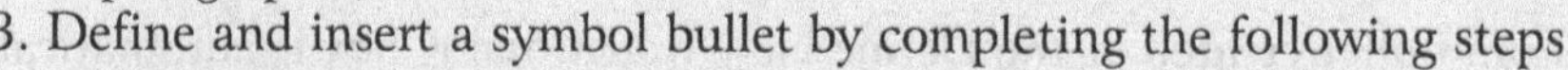

3. Define and insert a symbol bullet by completing the following steps:
   a. Select the six paragraphs below the heading *Kauai Sights*.
   b. Click the Bullets button arrow and then click *Define New Bullet* at the drop-down gallery.
   c. At the Define New Bullet dialog box, click the Symbol button.
   d. At the Symbol dialog box, click the *Font* option box arrow, scroll down the drop-down list, and then click *Wingdings*.
   e. Click the flower symbol shown at the right (character code 124).
   f. Click OK to close the Symbol dialog box.
   g. At the Define New Bullet dialog box, click the Font button.
   h. At the Font dialog box, click *11* in the *Size* list box.
   i. Click the *Font color* option box arrow and then click the *Light Blue, Background 2, Darker 25%* color option (third column, third row in the *Theme Colors* section).
   j. Click OK to close the Font dialog box and then click OK to close the Define New Bullet dialog box.
4. Remove the two bullets you defined from the *Bullet Library* section of the Bullets button drop-down gallery by completing the following steps:
   a. Click the Bullets button arrow.
   b. Right-click the flower picture bullet in the *Bullet Library* section and then click *Remove* at the shortcut menu.
   c. Click the Bullets button arrow.
   d. Right-click the flower symbol bullet in the *Bullet Library* section and then click *Remove* at the shortcut menu.
5. Save, preview, and then close **8-BEAHawaii.docx.**

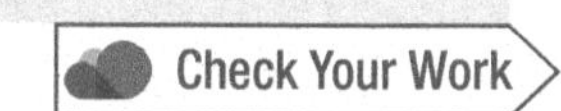

Activity 3 Apply Multilevel List Numbering to a Job Search Document

2 Parts

You will open a document containing a list of job search terms, apply multilevel list numbering to the text, and then define and apply a new multilevel list numbering style.

Applying Multilevel List Formatting

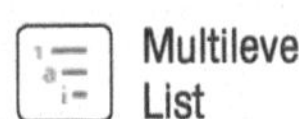

Multilevel List

Quick Steps

Insert Multilevel List Formatting

1. Click Multilevel List button.
2. Click style at drop-down gallery.

Applying Multilevel List Formatting

Use the Multilevel List button in the Paragraph group on the Home tab to specify the type of list formatting for paragraphs of text at the left margin, first tab, second tab, and so on. To apply predesigned multilevel list formatting to text in a document, click the Multilevel List button and then click a list style at the drop-down list.

Some options at the Multilevel List button drop-down list have labels such as *Heading 1*, *Heading 2*, and so on after the numbers. Click one of these options and Word inserts the numbering and applies the heading styles to the text.

Activity 3a Inserting Multilevel List Formatting

Part 1 of 2

1. Open **JSList.docx** and then save it with the name **8-JSList(3a)**.
2. Select the paragraphs of text below the title and then apply multilevel list formatting by completing the following steps:
   a. Click the Multilevel List button in the Paragraph group on the Home tab.
   b. At the drop-down list, click the middle option in the top row of the *List Library* section.

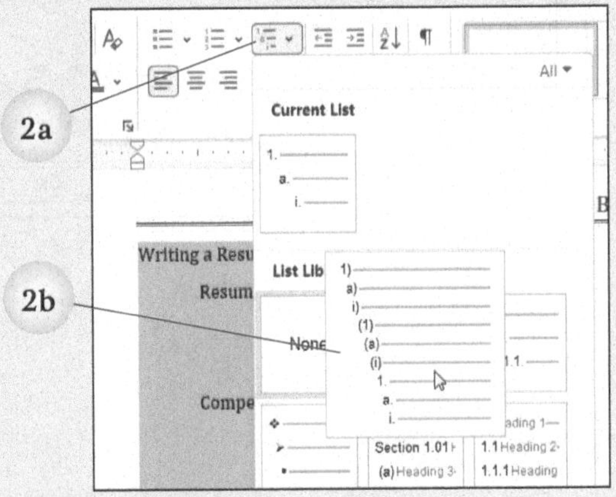

   c. Deselect the text.
3. Save, preview, and then close **8-JSList(3a).docx**.

Check Your Work

Creating a Custom Multilevel List Option

Quick Steps

Define Multilevel List

1. Click Multilevel List button.
2. Click *Define New Multilevel List.*
3. Choose level, list format, and/or position.
4. Click OK.

Hint When defining a multilevel list, you can mix numbers and bullets in the same list.

Creating a Custom Multilevel List

The Multilevel List button drop-down list contains predesigned level formatting options. If the drop-down list does not contain the type of list formatting required, create custom list formatting. To do this, click the Multilevel List button and then click the *Define New Multilevel List* option. This displays the Define new Multilevel list dialog box, shown in Figure 8.4. At this dialog box, click a level in the *Click level to modify* list box and then specify the level format, style, position, and alignment.

Typing a Multilevel List

Select text and then apply a multilevel list or apply the list and then type the text. When typing the text, press the Tab key to move to the next level or press Shift + Tab to move to the previous level.

Figure 8.4 Define New Multilevel List Dialog Box

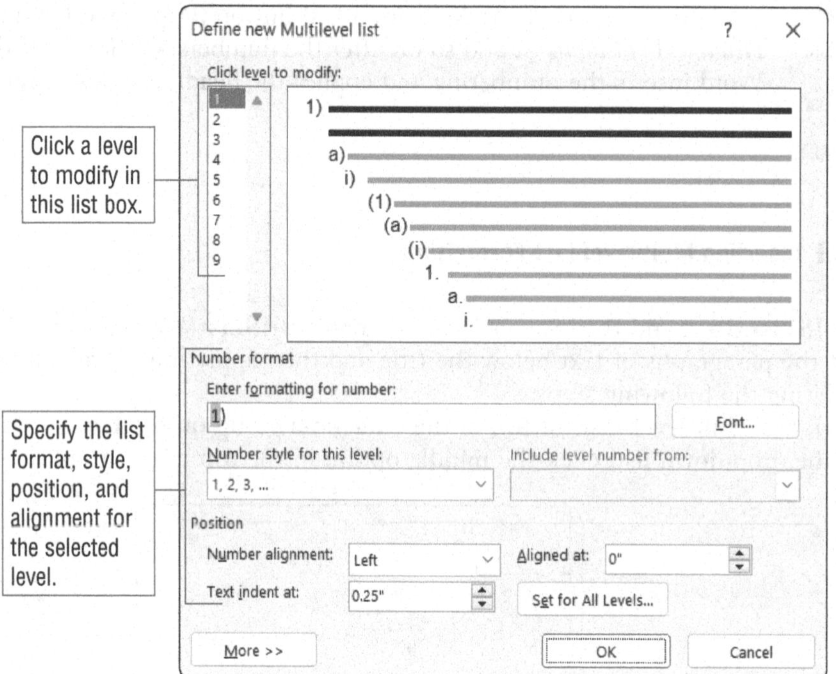

Activity 3b Creating and Applying a New Multilevel List

1. Open **JSList.docx** and then save it with the name **8-JSList(3b)**.
2. Select the paragraphs of text below the title.
3. Click the Multilevel List button in the Paragraph group on the Home tab.
4. Click the *Define New Multilevel List* option at the drop-down list.
5. At the Define new Multilevel list dialog box, make sure *1* is selected in the *Click level to modify* list box.
6. Click the *Number style for this level* option box arrow and then click *A, B, C, …* at the drop-down list.
7. Click in the *Enter formatting for number* text box, delete any text after *A*, and then type a period. (See image at the right.)
8. Click the *Aligned at* measurement box up arrow until *0.3"* displays in the measurement box.
9. Click the *Text indent at* measurement box up arrow until *0.6"* displays in the measurement box.

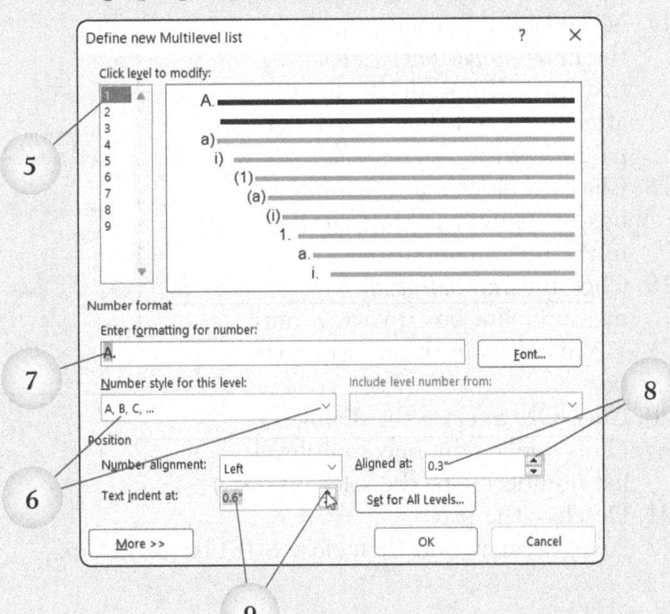

10. Click *2* in the *Click level to modify* list box.
11. Click the *Number style for this level* option box arrow and then click *1, 2, 3, …* at the drop-down list.
12. Click in the *Enter formatting for number* text box, delete any text after the *1*, and then type a period.
13. Click the *Aligned at* measurement box up arrow until *0.6"* displays in the measurement box.
14. Click the *Text indent at* measurement box up arrow until *0.9"* displays in the measurement box.

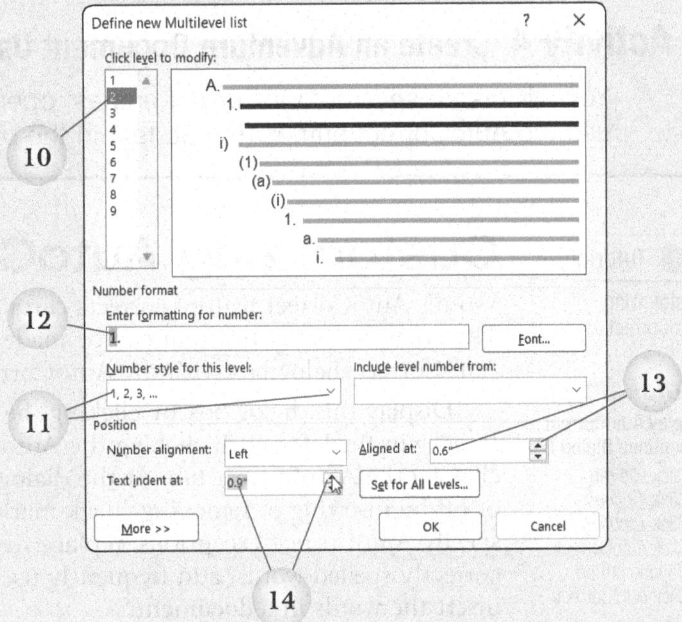

15. Click *3* in the *Click level to modify* list box.
16. Click the *Number style for this level* option box arrow and then click *a, b, c, ...* at the drop-down list.
17. Make sure that *a)* appears in the *Enter formatting for number* text box. (If not, delete any text after the *a* and then type a right parenthesis.)
18. Click the *Aligned at* measurement box up arrow until *0.9"* displays in the measurement box.
19. Click the *Text indent at* measurement box up arrow until *1.2"* displays in the measurement box.
20. Click OK to close the dialog box. (This applies the new multilevel list numbering to the selected text.)
21. Deselect the text.
22. Save, preview, and then close **8-JSList(3b).docx**.

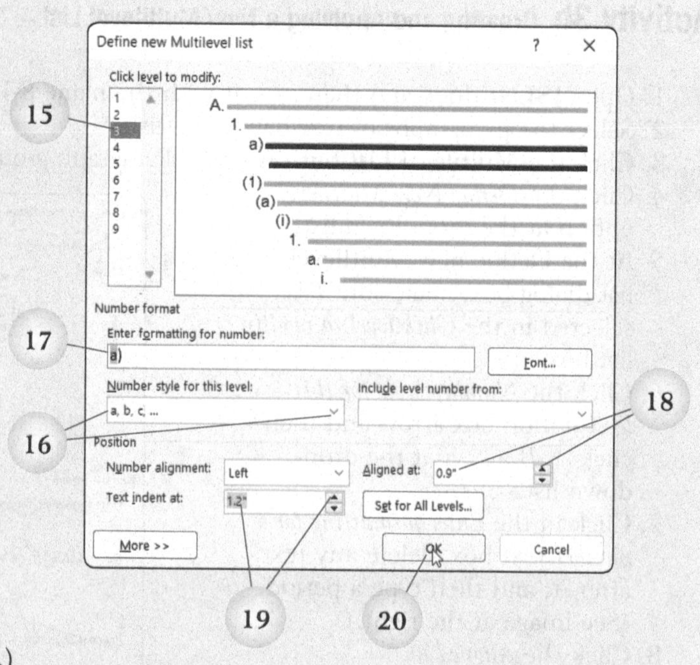

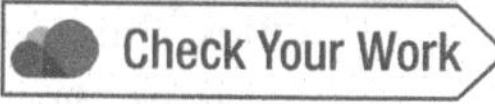

Activity 4 Create an Adventure Document Using AutoCorrect — 4 Parts

You will create several AutoCorrect entries, open a letterhead document, and then use the AutoCorrect entries to type text in the document.

Customizing AutoCorrect

Quick Steps

Display AutoCorrect Exceptions Dialog Box

1. Click File tab.
2. Click *Options.*
3. Click *Proofing.*
4. Click AutoCorrect Options button.
5. Click AutoCorrect tab.
6. Click Exceptions button.

Customizing AutoCorrect

Word's AutoCorrect feature corrects certain text automatically as it is typed. The types of corrections that can be made are specified with options at the AutoCorrect dialog box with the AutoCorrect tab selected, as shown in Figure 8.5.

Display this dialog box by clicking the File tab, clicking *Options*, clicking *Proofing* in the left panel, clicking the AutoCorrect Options button, and then clicking the AutoCorrect tab. At the dialog box, turn AutoCorrect features on or off by inserting or removing check marks from the check boxes. In addition, specify AutoCorrect exceptions, replace frequently misspelled words with the correctly spelled words, add frequently used words, and specify keys to quickly insert the words in a document.

Figure 8.5 AutoCorrect Dialog Box with the AutoCorrect Tab Selected

AutoCorrect: English (United States)
AutoCorrect | Math AutoCorrect | AutoFormat As You Type | AutoFormat | Actions
Show AutoCorrect Options buttons
Correct TWo INitial CApitals
Capitalize first letter of sentences
Capitalize first letter of table cells
Capitalize names of days
Correct accidental usage of cAPS LOCK key
Exceptions...
Replace text as you type
Replace: With: Plain text Formatted text
(c) ©
(e) €
(r) ®
(tm) ™
... …
:(☹
:-(☹
Add Delete
Automatically use suggestions from the spelling checker
OK Cancel

Remove the check marks from the check boxes identifying corrections that should not be made by AutoCorrect.

Click this button to display the AutoCorrect Exceptions dialog box.

Type the text shown in the first column of this list box in a document and then press the spacebar or press the Enter key and the text is replaced by the symbol or text shown in the second column.

Specifying AutoCorrect Exceptions

The check box options at the AutoCorrect dialog box with the AutoCorrect tab selected identify the types of corrections made by AutoCorrect. Specify which corrections should not be made with options at the AutoCorrect Exceptions dialog box, shown in Figure 8.6. Display this dialog box by clicking the Exceptions button at the AutoCorrect dialog box with the AutoCorrect tab selected.

AutoCorrect usually capitalizes a word that comes after a period, since a period usually ends a sentence. This automatic capitalization may be incorrect in some cases, as when the period is used in an abbreviation. Exceptions to this general practice are shown in the AutoCorrect Exceptions dialog box with the First Letter tab selected. Many exceptions already display in the dialog box but additional exceptions can be added by typing each exception in the *Don't capitalize after* text box and then clicking the Add button.

Figure 8.6 AutoCorrect Exceptions Dialog Box

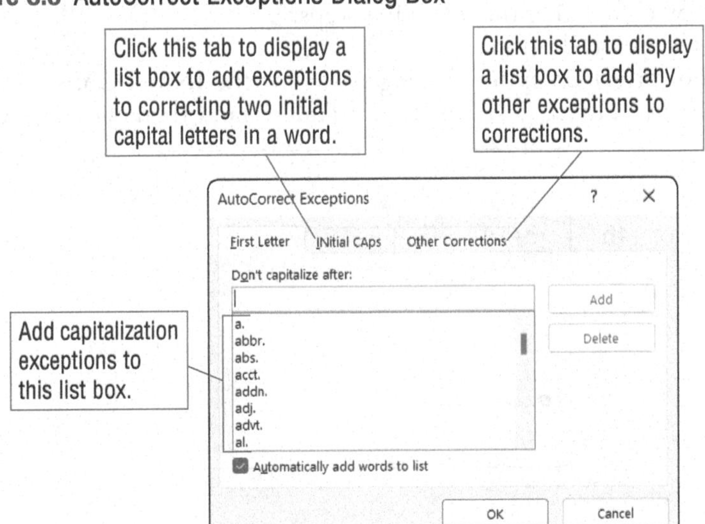
Click this tab to display a list box to add exceptions to correcting two initial capital letters in a word.
Click this tab to display a list box to add any other exceptions to corrections.
AutoCorrect Exceptions
First Letter
INitial CAps
Other Corrections
Don't capitalize after:
Add
Delete
a.
abbr.
abs.
acct.
addn.
adj.
advt.
al.
Automatically add words to list
OK
Cancel
Add capitalization exceptions to this list box.

By default, AutoCorrect corrects the use of two initial capital letters in a word. If AutoCorrect should not correct these instances, display the AutoCorrect Exceptions dialog box with the INitial CAps tab selected and then type the exception text in the *Don't correct* text box. At the AutoCorrect Exceptions dialog box with the Other Corrections tab selected, type the text that should not be corrected in the *Don't correct* text box. Delete an exception from the dialog box with any of the tabs selected by clicking the text in the list box and then clicking the Delete button.

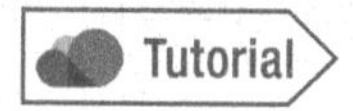

Adding and Deleting an AutoCorrect Entry

Adding and Deleting an AutoCorrect Entry

Commonly misspelled words and/or typographical errors can be added to AutoCorrect. For example, if a user consistently types *relavent* instead of *relevant*, *relavent* can be added to the AutoCorrect dialog box with the AutoCorrect tab selected with the direction to correct it to *relevant*. The AutoCorrect dialog box also contains a few symbols that can be inserted in a document. For example, type *(c)* and AutoCorrect changes the text to © (copyright symbol). Type *(r)* and AutoCorrect changes the text to ® (registered trademark symbol). The symbols display at the beginning of the AutoCorrect dialog box list box.

Quick Steps

Add Word to AutoCorrect

1. Click File tab.
2. Click *Options*.
3. Click *Proofing*.
4. Click AutoCorrect Options button.
5. Click AutoCorrect tab.
6. Type misspelled or abbreviated word.
7. Press Tab.
8. Type correctly spelled or complete word.
9. Click Add button.
10. Click OK.

An abbreviation can be added to AutoCorrect that will insert the entire word (or words) in the document when it is typed. For example, in Activity 4a, the abbreviation *fav* will be added to AutoCorrect and *Family Adventure Vacations* will be inserted when *fav* is typed followed by a press of the spacebar or Enter key. The capitalization of the abbreviation can also be controlled. For example, in Activity 4a, the abbreviation *Na* will be added to AutoCorrect and *Namibia* will be inserted when *Na* is typed and *NAMIBIA* will be inserted when *NA* is typed.

AutoCorrect text can be deleted from the AutoCorrect dialog box. To do this, display the AutoCorrect dialog box with the AutoCorrect tab selected, click the word or words in the list box, and then click the Delete button.

Activity 4a Adding Text and Specifying Exceptions to AutoCorrect — Part 1 of 4

1. At a blank screen, click the File tab and then click *Options*.
2. At the Word Options dialog box, click *Proofing* in the left panel.
3. Click the AutoCorrect Options button in the *AutoCorrect options* section.
4. At the AutoCorrect dialog box with the AutoCorrect tab selected, add an exception to AutoCorrect by completing the following steps:
   a. Click the Exceptions button.
   b. At the AutoCorrect Exceptions dialog box, click the INitial CAps tab.
   c. Click in the *Don't correct* text box, type STudent, and then click the Add button.

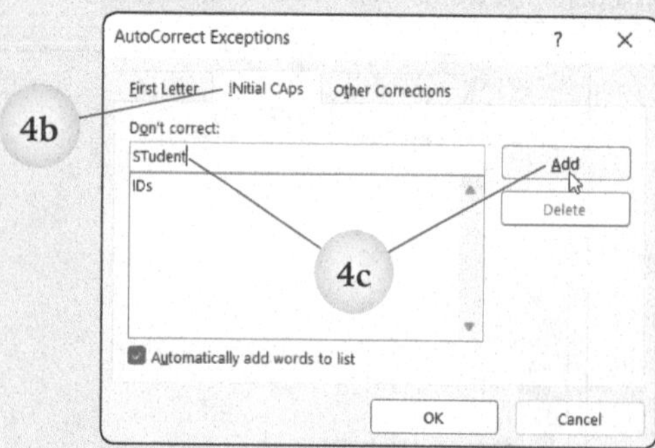

d. Click in the *Don't correct* text box, type STyle, and then click the Add button.
e. Click OK.
5. At the AutoCorrect dialog box with the AutoCorrect tab selected, click in the *Replace* text box and then type fav.
6. Press the Tab key (which moves the insertion point to the *With* text box) and then type Family Adventure Vacations.
7. Click the Add button. (This adds *fav* and *Family Adventure Vacations* to AutoCorrect and also selects *fav* in the *Replace* text box.)

8. Type Na in the *Replace* text box. (The text *fav* is automatically removed when you begin typing *Na*.)
9. Press the Tab key and then type Namibia.
10. Click the Add button.
11. With the insertion point positioned in the *Replace* text box, type vf.
12. Press the Tab key and then type Victoria Falls.
13. Click the Add button.
14. With the insertion point positioned in the *Replace* text box, type bea.
15. Press the Tab key and then type Blue Earth Adventures.
16. Click the Add button.
17. Click OK to close the AutoCorrect dialog box and then click OK to close the Word Options dialog box.
18. Open **BEALtrhd.docx** and then save it with the name **8-BEAAfrica**.
19. Type the text shown in Figure 8.7. Type the text exactly as shown (including applying bold formatting and centering *fav* at the beginning of the document). AutoCorrect will correct the words as they are typed.
20. Save **8-BEAAfrica.docx**.

Figure 8.7 Activity 4a

> **fav**
>
> Na and vf Adventure
>
> bea is partnering with fav to provide adventurous and thrilling family vacations. Our first joint adventure is a holiday trip to Na. Na is one of the most fascinating holiday destinations in Africa and offers comfortable facilities, great food, cultural interaction, abundant wildlife, and a wide variety of activities to interest people of all ages. During the 12-day trip, you and your family will travel across Na through national parks, enjoying the beautiful and exotic scenery and watching wildlife in natural habitats.
>
> If you or your family member is a college student, contact one of our college travel adventure consultants to learn more about the newest Student Travel package titled "STudent STyle" that offers a variety of student discounts, rebates, and free travel accessories for qualifying participants.
>
> bea and fav are offering a 15 percent discount if you sign up for this once-in-a-lifetime trip to Na. This exciting adventure is limited to 20 people, so don't wait to sign up.

Undoing an AutoCorrect Correction

Using the AutoCorrect Options Button

After AutoCorrect corrects a portion of text, hover the pointer near the text and a small blue box displays below it. Move the pointer to this blue box and the AutoCorrect Options button displays. Click this button to display a drop-down list with the options to change the text back to the original version, stop automatically correcting the specific text, and display the AutoCorrect dialog box.

AutoCorrect Options

If the AutoCorrect Options button does not display, turn on the feature. To do this, display the AutoCorrect dialog box with the AutoCorrect tab selected, click the *Show AutoCorrect Options buttons* check box to insert a check mark, and then click OK to close the dialog box.

Activity 4b Using the AutoCorrect Options Button

Part 2 of 4

1. With **8-BEAAfrica.docx** open, select and then delete the last paragraph.
2. With the insertion point positioned on the blank line below the last paragraph of text (you may need to press the Enter key), type the following text. (AutoCorrect will automatically change *Ameria* to *America*, which you will change in the next step.) Through the sponsorship of Ameria Resorts, we are able to offer you a 15 percent discount for groups of 12 or more people.
3. Change the spelling of *America* back to *Ameria* by completing the following steps:
   a. Position the pointer over *America* until a blue box displays below it.
   b. Position the pointer on the blue box until the AutoCorrect Options button displays.

c. Click the AutoCorrect Options button and then click the *Change back to "Ameria"* option.

4. Save and then preview **8-BEAAfrica.docx**.

3c

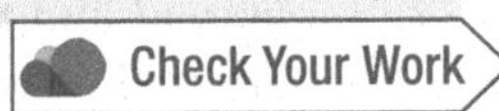

Inserting Symbols Automatically

AutoCorrect recognizes and replaces symbols as well as text. Several symbols included in AutoCorrect are shown in the AutoCorrect dialog box and are listed first in the *Replace* text box. Table 8.1 lists these symbols along with the characters to insert them.

In addition to the symbols provided by Word, other symbols can be inserted in the AutoCorrect dialog box with the AutoCorrect button in the Symbol dialog box. To insert a symbol in the AutoCorrect dialog box, click the Insert tab, click the Symbol button in the Symbols group, and then click *More Symbols* at the drop-down list. At the Symbol dialog box, click the specific symbol and then click the AutoCorrect button in the lower left corner of the dialog box. This displays the AutoCorrect dialog box with the symbol inserted in the *With* text box and the insertion point positioned in the *Replace* text box. Type the text that will insert the symbol, click the Add button, and then click OK to close the AutoCorrect dialog box. Click the Close button to close the Symbol dialog box.

Table 8.1 AutoCorrect Symbols Available at the AutoCorrect Dialog Box

Type	To insert
(c)	©
(r)	®
(tm)	™
...	…
:) or :-)	☺
:| or :-|	😐
:(or :-(	☹
-->	→
<--	←
==>	➔
<==	🡐
<=>	⇔

Activity 4c Inserting Symbols Using AutoCorrect

Part 3 of 4

1. With **8-BEAAfrica.docx** open, click immediately right of the last *s* in *Resorts* (located in the last paragraph) and then type (r). (This inserts the registered trademark symbol.)
2. Click immediately left of the *1* in *15* and then type ==>. (This inserts the ➔ symbol.)
3. Move the insertion point immediately right of the *t* in *discount* and then type <==. (This inserts the 🡐 symbol.)
4. Insert the pound (£) currency unit symbol in AutoCorrect by completing the following steps:
   a. Click the Insert tab.
   b. Click the Symbol button and then click *More Symbols* at the drop-down list.
   c. At the Symbol dialog box, make sure that *(normal text)* displays in the *Font* option box. If it does not, click the *Font* option box arrow and then click *(normal text)* at the drop-down list (first option in the list).
   d. Scroll through the list of symbols and then click the pound (£) currency unit symbol (located in approximately the sixth or seventh row; character code *00A3*).
   e. Click the AutoCorrect button in the lower left corner of the dialog box.
   f. At the AutoCorrect dialog box, type pcu in the *Replace* text box and then click the Add button.
   g. Click OK to close the AutoCorrect dialog box.

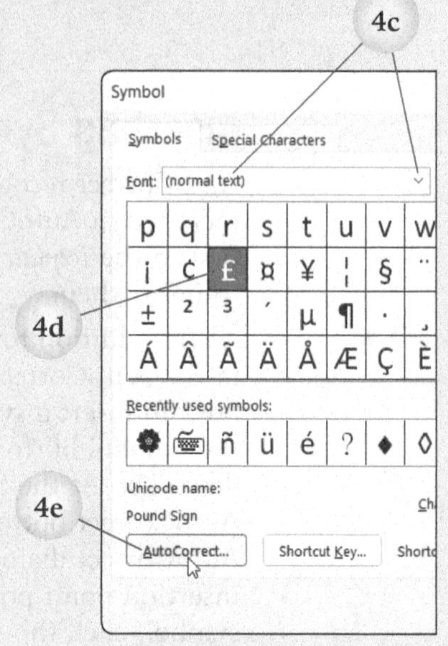

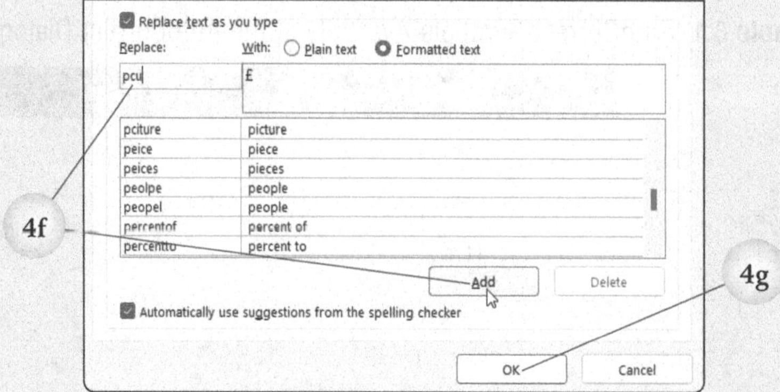

   h. Click the Close button to close the Symbol dialog box.
5. Press Ctrl + End to move the insertion point to the end of the document and then press the Enter key.
6. Type the text shown in Figure 8.8. (Press Shift + Enter or the Enter key as indicated in the figure.) Create the pound currency unit symbol by typing pcu and then pressing the spacebar. Press the Backspace key once and then type 2,999. (Complete similar steps when typing *£2,549 (UK)*.)
7. Save **8-BEAAfrica.docx**.

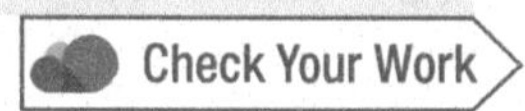

Figure 8.8 Activity 4c

> **Individual price:** *(press Shift+ Enter)*
> $3,999 (US) *(press Shift+ Enter)*
> £2,999 (UK) *(press Enter)*
>
> **Individual price for groups of 12 or more:** *(press Shift+ Enter)*
> $3,399 (US) *(press Shift+ Enter)*
> £2,549 (UK)

Customizing AutoFormatting

Customizing AutoFormatting

When typing text, Word provides options to automatically apply some formatting, such as changing a fraction to a fraction character (1/2 to ½), changing numbers to ordinals (1st to 1st), changing an internet or network path to a hyperlink (https://ppi-edu.net to https://ppi-edu.net), and applying bullets or numbers to text. The autoformatting options display in the AutoCorrect dialog box with the AutoFormat As You Type tab selected, as shown in Figure 8.9.

Display this dialog box by clicking the File tab and then clicking *Options*. At the Word Options dialog box, click *Proofing* in the left panel and then click the AutoCorrect Options button. At the AutoCorrect dialog box, click the AutoFormat As You Type tab. At the dialog box, remove the check marks from those options to be turned off and insert check marks for those options to be formatted automatically.

Figure 8.9 AutoCorrect Dialog Box with the AutoFormat As You Type Tab Selected

AutoCorrect ? ×

AutoCorrect | Math AutoCorrect | AutoFormat As You Type | AutoFormat | Actions

Replace as you type
- [x] "Straight quotes" with "smart quotes"
- [x] Ordinals (1st) with superscript
- [x] Fractions (1/2) with fraction character (½)
- [x] Hyphens (--) with dash (—)
- [ ] *Bold* and _italic_ with real formatting
- [x] Internet and network paths with hyperlinks

Apply as you type
- [x] Automatic bulleted lists
- [x] Automatic numbered lists
- [x] Border lines
- [x] Tables
- [ ] Built-in Heading styles

Automatically as you type
- [x] Format beginning of list item like the one before it
- [x] Set left- and first-indent with tabs and backspaces
- [ ] Define styles based on your formatting

OK | Cancel

Insert check marks in the check boxes for formatting options that Word should apply automatically.

Click this tab to display options for formats that Word should apply automatically as text is being typed.

Activity 4d Changing AutoFormatting and Deleting AutoCorrect Text

1. Make sure **8-BEAAfrica.docx** is open.
2. Suppose that you need to add a couple of web addresses to a document and do not want the addresses automatically formatted as hyperlinks (since you are sending the document as hard copy rather than electronically). Turn off the autoformatting of web addresses by completing the following steps:
   a. Click the File tab and then click *Options*.
   b. At the Word Options dialog box, click *Proofing* in the left panel.
   c. Click the AutoCorrect Options button.
   d. At the AutoCorrect dialog box, click the AutoFormat As You Type tab.
   e. Click the *Internet and network paths with hyperlinks* check box to remove the check mark.

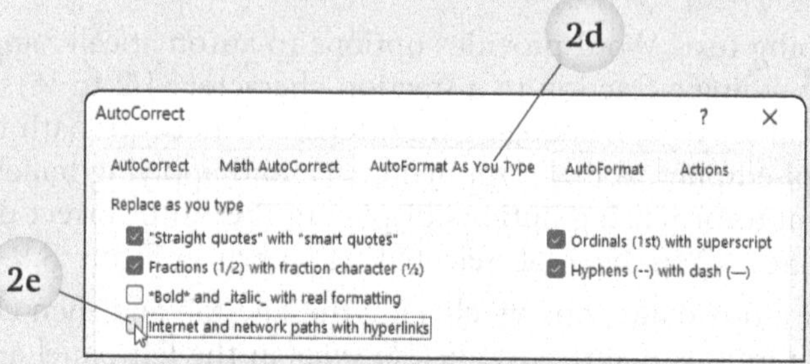

   f. Click OK to close the AutoCorrect dialog box.
   g. Click OK to close the Word Options dialog box.
3. Press Ctrl + End to move the insertion point to the end of the document, press the Enter key, and then type the text shown in Figure 8.10.
4. Turn on the autoformatting of web addresses that was turned off in Step 2 by completing Steps 2a through 2g (except in Step 2e, insert the check mark rather than remove it).
5. Delete *fav* from AutoCorrect by completing the following steps:
   a. Click the File tab and then click *Options*.
   b. At the Word Options dialog box, click *Proofing* in the left panel.
   c. Click the AutoCorrect Options button.
   d. At the AutoCorrect dialog box, click the AutoCorrect tab.
   e. Click in the *Replace* text box and then type fav. (This selects the entry in the list box.)
   f. Click the Delete button.
6. Complete steps similar to those in Steps 5e and 5f to delete the *Na*, *vf*, and *bea* AutoCorrect entries.

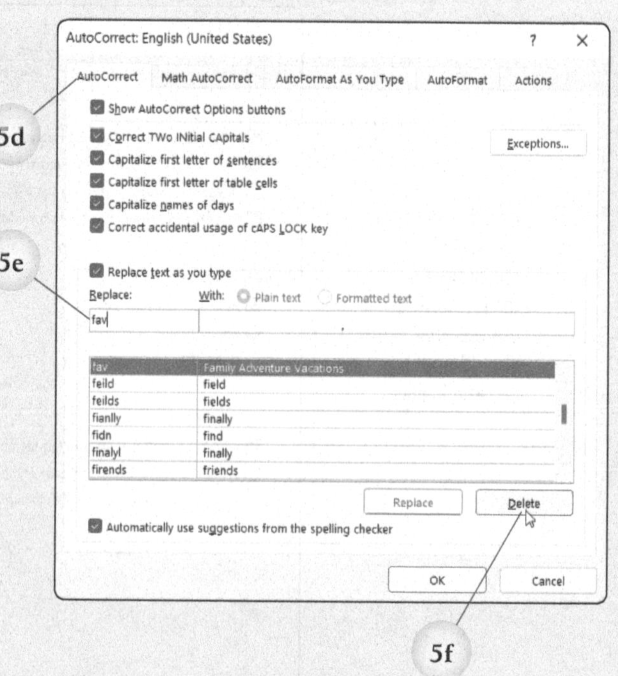

7. Delete the exceptions added to the AutoCorrect Exceptions dialog box by completing the following steps:
   a. At the AutoCorrect dialog box with the AutoCorrect tab selected, click the Exceptions button.
   b. At the AutoCorrect Exceptions dialog box, if necessary, click the INitial CAps tab.
   c. Click *STudent* in the list box and then click the Delete button.
   d. Click *STyle* in the list box and then click the Delete button.
   e. Click OK to close the AutoCorrect Exceptions dialog box.
8. Click OK to close the AutoCorrect dialog box.
9. Click OK to close the Word Options dialog box.
10. Save, preview, and then close **3-BEAAfrica.docx**.

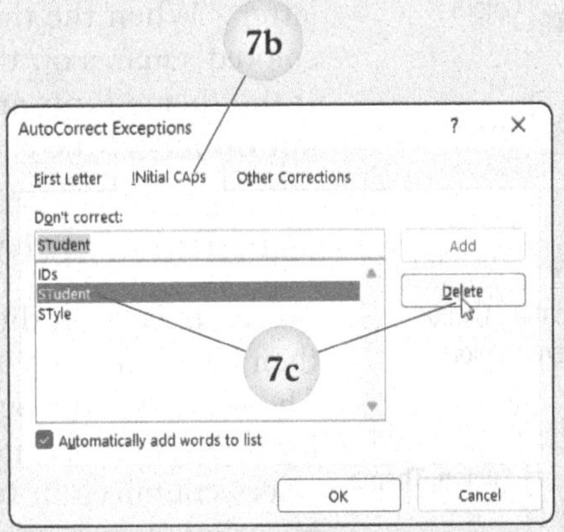

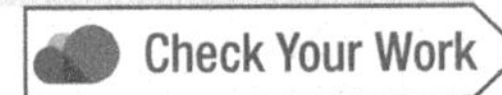

Figure 8.10 Activity 4d

For additional information on the Na adventure, as well as other exciting vacation specials, please visit our website at https://ppi-edu.net/BlueEarth or visit https://ppi-edu.net/FamAdvs.

Activity 5 Apply Custom Themes to Company Documents — 5 Parts

You will create custom theme colors and theme fonts and then apply theme effects. You will save the changes as a custom theme, apply the custom theme to a company services document and a company security document, and then delete the theme.

Customizing Themes

A document created in Word is based on the Normal template. This template provides a document with default layout, formatting, styles, and themes. The Normal template provides a number of built-in or predesigned themes. Some of these built-in themes have been used in previous chapters to apply colors, fonts, and effects to content in documents. The same built-in themes are available in Microsoft Word, Excel, Access, PowerPoint, and Outlook. Because the same themes are available across these applications, business files—such as documents, workbooks, databases, and presentations—can be branded with a consistent and professional appearance.

Hint Every document created in Word has a theme applied to it.

A theme is a combination of theme colors, theme fonts, and theme effects. Within a theme, any of these three elements can be changed with the additional buttons in the Document Formatting group on the Design tab. Apply one of the built-in themes or create a custom theme. A custom theme will display in the *Custom* section of the Themes button drop-down gallery. To create a custom theme, change the theme colors, theme fonts, and/or theme effects.

The Themes, Colors, and Fonts buttons in the Document Formatting group on the Design tab provide representations of the current theme. For example, the Themes button shows uppercase and lowercase *Aa* with colored squares below the letters. When the theme colors are changed, the changes are reflected in the small colored squares on the Themes button and the four squares on the Colors button. If the theme fonts are changed, the letters on the Themes button and the Fonts button reflect the change.

Tutorial

Creating Custom Theme Colors

Quick Steps

Create Custom Theme Colors

1. Click Design tab.
2. Click Colors button.
3. Click *Customize Colors*.
4. Type name for custom theme colors.
5. Change background, accent, and hyperlink colors.
6. Click Save button.

Creating Custom Theme Colors

To create custom theme colors, click the Design tab, click the Colors button, and then click *Customize Colors* at the drop-down gallery. This displays the Create New Theme Colors dialog box, similar to the one shown in Figure 8.11. Type a name for the custom theme colors in the *Name* text box and then change colors. Theme colors contain four text and background colors, six accent colors, and two hyperlink colors, as shown in the *Theme colors* section of the dialog box. Change a color in the list box by clicking the color button at the right of the color option and then clicking a color at the color palette.

After making all the changes to the colors, click the Save button. This saves the custom theme colors and also applies the color changes to the active document. Display the custom theme colors by clicking the Colors button. The custom theme colors will display at the top of the drop-down gallery in the *Custom* section.

Resetting Custom Theme Colors

If changes have been made to colors at the Create New Theme Colors dialog box, the colors can be reset by clicking the Reset button in the lower left corner of the dialog box. Clicking this button restores the colors to the default Office theme colors.

Figure 8.11 Create New Theme Colors Dialog Box

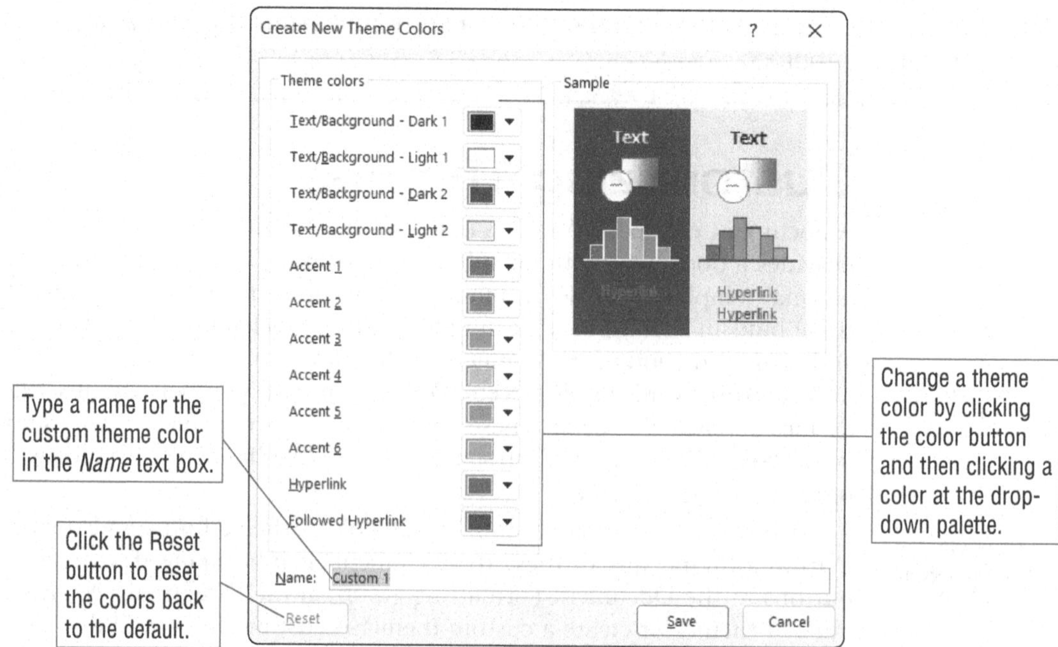

Activity 5a Creating Custom Theme Colors

Note: If you are running Word on a computer connected to a network in a public environment, such as a school, you may need to complete all five parts of Activity 5 during the same session. Network system software may delete your custom themes when you exit Word. Check with your instructor.

1. At a blank document, click the Design tab.
2. Click the Colors button in the Document Formatting group and then click *Customize Colors* at the drop-down gallery.
3. At the Create New Theme Colors dialog box, type your first and last names in the *Name* text box.
4. Click the color button to the right of the *Text/Background - Light 1* option and then click the *Dark Red* color (first color option in the *Standard Colors* section).

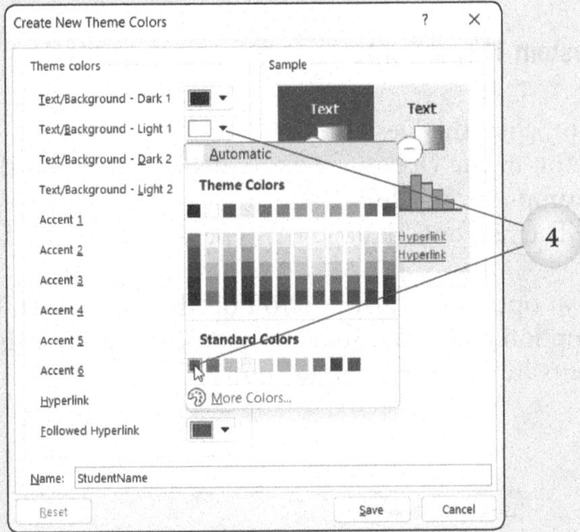

5. Click the color button to the right of the *Accent 1* option and then click the *Yellow* color (fourth color option in the *Standard Colors* section).
6. You decide that you do not like the colors you have chosen and want to start over. To do this, click the Reset button in the lower left corner of the dialog box.
7. Click the color button to the right of the *Text/Background - Dark 2* option and then click the *Blue* color (eighth color option in the *Standard Colors* section).
8. Change the color for the *Accent 1* option by completing the following steps:
   a. Click the color button to the right of the *Accent 1* option.
   b. Click the *More Colors* option below the color palette.
   c. At the Colors dialog box, click the Standard tab.
   d. Click the dark green color, as shown at the right.
   e. Click OK to close the dialog box.
9. Save the custom theme colors by clicking the Save button.
10. Close the document without saving it.

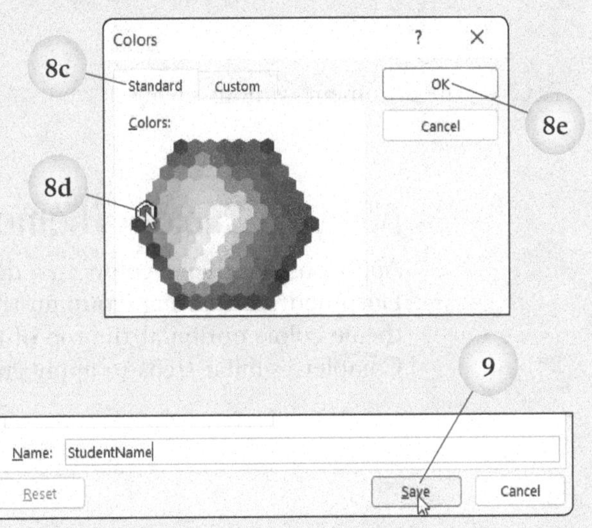

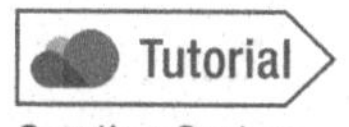

Creating Custom Theme Fonts

Creating Custom Theme Fonts

To create a custom theme font, click the Design tab, click the Fonts button, and then click *Customize Fonts* at the drop-down gallery. This displays the Create New Theme Fonts dialog box. At this dialog box, type a name for the custom font in the *Name* text box. Choose a font for headings and a font for body text and then click the Save button.

Quick Steps

Create Custom Theme Fonts

1. Click Design tab.
2. Click Fonts button.
3. Click *Customize Fonts*.
4. Choose fonts.
5. Type name for custom theme fonts.
6. Click Save button.

Activity 5b Creating Custom Theme Fonts

Part 2 of 5

1. At a blank document, click the Design tab.
2. Click the Fonts button in the Document Formatting group and then click the *Customize Fonts* option at the drop-down gallery.
3. At the Create New Theme Fonts dialog box, type your first and last names in the *Name* text box.
4. Click the *Heading font* option box arrow, scroll up the drop-down list, and then click *Arial*.
5. Click the *Body font* option box arrow, scroll down the drop-down list, and then click *Cambria*.
6. Save the custom fonts by clicking the Save button.

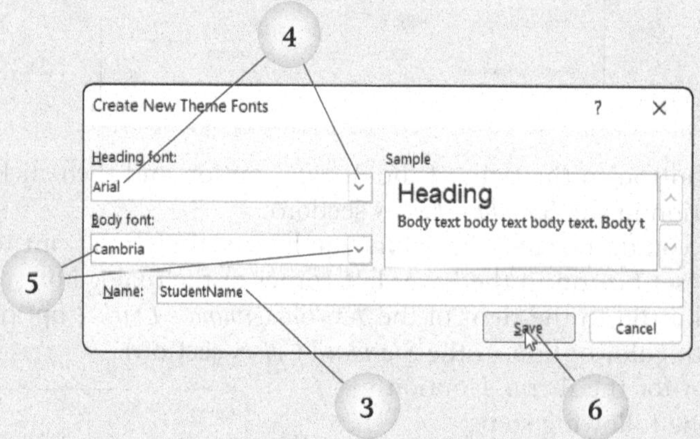

7. Close the document without saving it.

Applying Custom Theme Colors and Fonts

Apply custom theme colors to a document by clicking the Colors button in the Document Formatting group on the Design tab and then clicking the custom theme colors option at the top of the drop-down gallery in the *Custom* section. Complete similar steps to apply custom theme fonts.

Applying Theme Effects

The options in the Theme Effects button drop-down gallery apply sets of line and fill effects to the graphics in a document. Custom theme effects cannot be created, but a theme effect can be applied to a document and the formatting can then be saved in a custom theme.

Saving a Custom Document Theme

Quick Steps

Save Custom Document Theme

1. Click Design tab.
2. Click Themes button.
3. Click *Save Current Theme*.
4. Type name for theme.
5. Click Save button.

Saving a Custom Document Theme

A custom document theme containing custom theme colors, fonts, and effects can be saved. To do this, create and apply custom theme colors, fonts, and theme effects to a document, click the Themes button on the Design tab, and then click *Save Current Theme* at the drop-down gallery. This displays the Save Current Theme dialog box, which has many of the same options as the Save As dialog box. Type a name for the custom document theme in the *File name* text box and then click the Save button.

Activity 5c Applying Theme Effects and Saving a Custom Document Theme — Part 3 of 5

1. Open **NSSServices.docx** and then save it with the name **8-NSSServices.**
2. Make the following changes to the document:
   a. Apply the Title style to the company name *Northland Security Systems.*
   b. Apply the Heading 1 style to the heading *Northland Security Systems Mission.*
   c. Apply the Heading 2 style to the remaining headings, *Security Services* and *Security Software.*
   d. Apply the Word 2010 style set (the last option in the expanded style set gallery on the Design tab).
3. Apply the custom theme colors you saved by completing the following steps:
   a. Click the Colors button in the Document Formatting group on the Design tab.
   b. Click the theme colors option with your name at the top of the drop-down gallery in the *Custom* group.

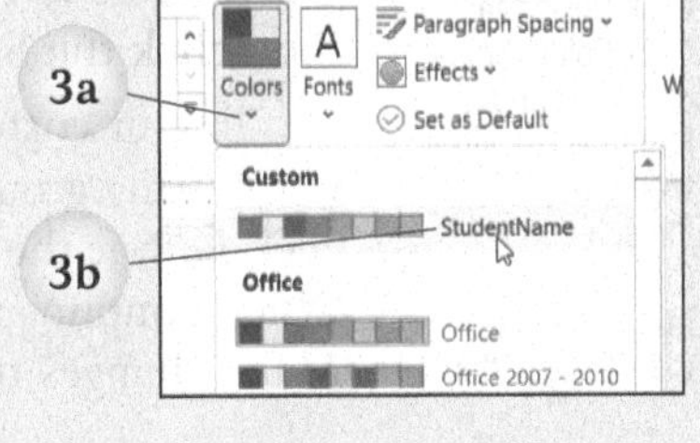

4. Apply the custom theme fonts you saved by clicking the Fonts button in the Document Formatting group and then clicking the custom theme fonts with your name.
5. Apply a theme effect by clicking the Effects button in the Document Formatting group and then clicking *Glossy* at the drop-down gallery (last option).
6. Make the following changes to the SmartArt graphic:
   a. Click the graphic to select it. (When the graphic is selected, a border displays around it.)
   b. Click the SmartArt Design tab.
   c. Click the Change Colors button and then click *Colorful Range - Accent Colors 5 to 6* (last option in the *Colorful* section).

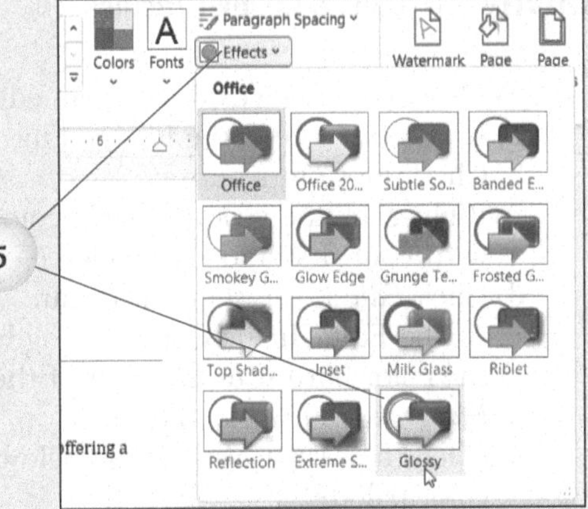

d. Click the More SmartArt Styles button in the SmartArt Styles group and then click *Cartoon* (third option in the *3-D* section).
e. Click outside the SmartArt graphic to deselect it.

7. Save the custom theme colors and fonts, as well as the Glossy theme effect, as a custom document theme by completing the following steps:
   a. Click the Design tab.
   b. Click the Themes button in the Document Formatting group.
   c. Click the *Save Current Theme* option at the bottom of the drop-down gallery.
   d. At the Save Current Theme dialog box, type your first and last names (without a space between) in the *File name* text box and then click the Save button.

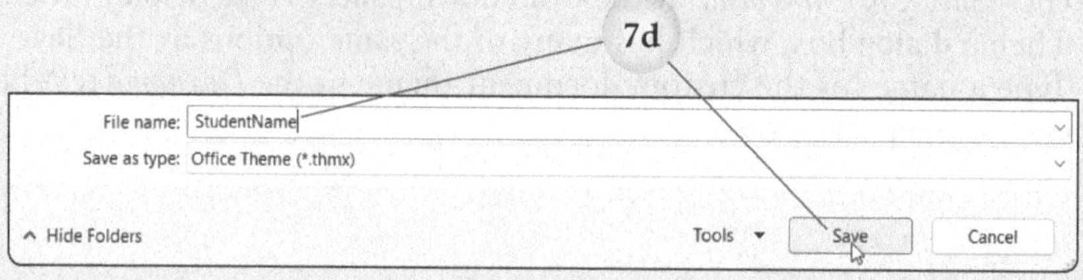

8. Save and then preview **8-NSSServices.docx**.

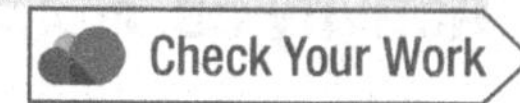

Editing a Custom Theme

Editing Custom Themes

Custom theme colors and theme fonts can be edited. To edit custom theme colors, click the Design tab and then click the Colors button in the Document Formatting group. At the drop-down gallery of custom and built-in theme colors, right-click the custom theme colors and then click *Edit* at the shortcut menu. This displays the Edit Theme Colors dialog box, which contains the same options as the Create New Theme Colors dialog box. Make changes to the theme colors and then click the Save button.

To edit custom theme fonts, click the Fonts button in the Document Formatting group on the Design tab, right-click the custom theme fonts, and then click *Edit* at the shortcut menu. This displays the Edit Theme Fonts dialog box, which contains the same options as the Create New Theme Fonts dialog box. Make changes to the theme fonts and then click the Save button.

Quick Steps

Edit Custom Theme Colors or Fonts

1. Click Design tab.
2. Click Colors button or Fonts button.
3. Right-click custom theme colors or fonts.
4. Click *Edit*.
5. Make changes.
6. Click Save button.

Activity 5d Editing Custom Themes

Part 4 of 5

1. With **8-NSSServices.docx** open, edit the theme colors by completing the following steps:
   a. If necessary, click the Design tab.
   b. Click the Colors button.
   c. Right-click the custom theme colors named with your first and last names.
   d. Click *Edit* at the shortcut menu.
   e. At the Edit Theme Colors dialog box, click the color button to the right of the *Text/ Background - Dark 2* option.
   f. Click the *More Colors* option below the color palette.

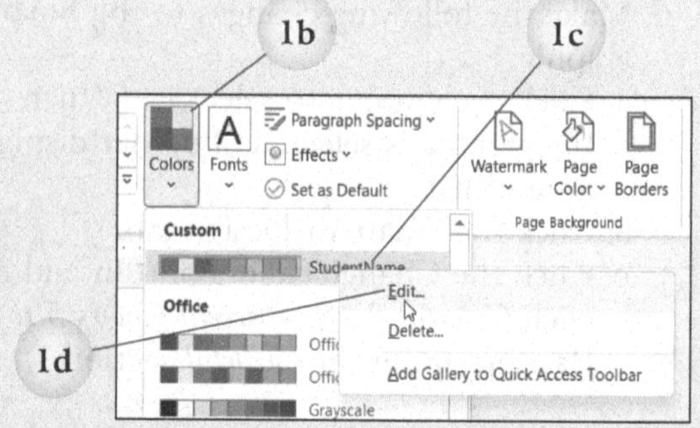

g. At the Colors dialog box, click the Standard tab.
h. Click the dark green color. (This is the same color you chose for *Accent 1* in Activity 5a.)
i. Click OK to close the dialog box.
j. Click the Save button.

2. Edit the theme fonts by completing the following steps:
   a. Click the Fonts button in the Document Formatting group.
   b. Right-click the custom theme fonts named with your first and last names and then click *Edit* at the shortcut menu.
   c. At the Edit Theme Fonts dialog box, click the *Body font* option box arrow, scroll down the drop-down list, and then click *Constantia*.
   d. Click the Save button.
3. Apply a different theme effect by clicking the Effects button and then clicking *Extreme Shadow* at the drop-down gallery (second column, last row). (This applies a shadow behind each shape.)
4. Save the changes to the custom theme by completing the following steps:
   a. Click the Themes button and then click *Save Current Theme* at the drop-down gallery.
   b. At the Save Current Theme dialog box, click the theme named with your first and last names in the content pane.
   c. Click the Save button.
   d. At the message stating that the theme already exists and asking if you want to replace it, click Yes.
5. Save, preview, and then close **8-NSSServices.docx**.

Resetting a Template Theme

Quick Steps

Resetting Template Theme
1. Click Design tab.
2. Click Themes button.
3. Click *Reset to Theme from Template*.

If a built-in theme other than the Office default theme or a custom theme is applied to a document, the theme can be reset to the default by clicking the Themes button and then clicking *Reset to Theme from Template* at the drop-down gallery. If the document is based on the default template provided by Word, clicking this option resets the theme to the Office default theme.

Deleting Custom Themes

Tutorial

Deleting a Custom Theme

Quick Steps

Delete Custom Theme Colors or Fonts
1. Click Design tab.
2. Click Colors or Fonts button.
3. Right-click custom theme.
4. Click *Delete*.
5. Click Yes.

Delete a Custom Theme
1. Click Design tab.
2. Click Themes button.
3. Right-click custom theme.
4. Click *Delete*.
5. Click Yes.

Delete custom theme colors from the Colors button drop-down gallery, delete custom theme fonts from the Fonts drop-down gallery, and delete custom themes at the Themes button drop-down gallery or the Save Current Theme dialog box.

To delete custom theme colors, click the Colors button, right-click the theme to be deleted, and then click *Delete* at the shortcut menu. At the confirmation message, click Yes. To delete custom theme fonts, click the Fonts button, right-click the theme to be deleted, and then click *Delete* at the shortcut menu. At the confirmation message, click Yes.

Delete a custom theme (including custom colors, fonts, and effects) at the Themes button drop-down gallery or the Save Current Theme dialog box. To delete a custom theme from the drop-down gallery, click the Themes button, right-click the custom theme, click *Delete* at the shortcut menu, and then click Yes at the confirmation message. To delete a custom theme from the Save Current Theme dialog box, click the Themes button and then click *Save Current Theme* at the drop-down gallery. At the dialog box, click the custom theme document name, click the Organize button on the dialog box toolbar, and then click *Delete* at the drop-down list. If a confirmation message displays, click Yes.

Changing Default Settings

If formatting is applied to a document—such as a specific style set, theme, and paragraph spacing—it can be saved as the default formatting. To do this, click the Set as Default button in the Document Formatting group on the Design tab. At the message asking if the current style set and theme should be set as the default and indicating that the settings will be applied to new documents, click Yes.

Activity 5e Applying and Deleting Custom Themes — Part 5 of 5

1. Open **NSSSecurity.docx** and then save it with the name **8-NSSSecurity**.
2. Apply the Title style to the company name, apply the Heading 1 style to the two headings in the document, and then apply the Word 2010 style set.
3. Apply your custom theme by completing the following steps:
   a. If necessary, click the Design tab.
   b. Click the Themes button.
   c. Click the custom theme named with your first and last names at the top of the drop-down gallery in the *Custom* section.

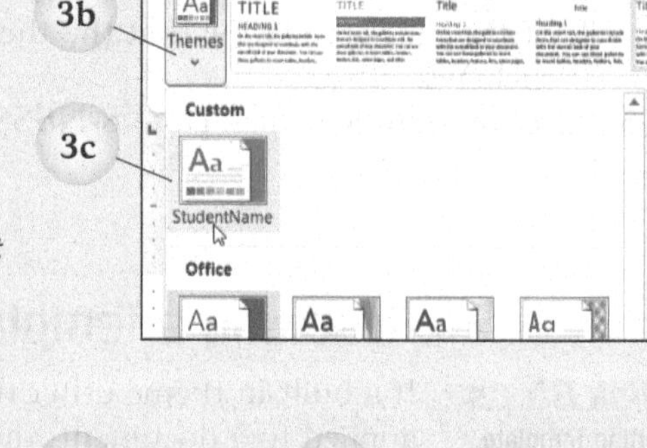

4. Save and then preview **8-NSSSecurity.docx**.
5. Reset the theme to the Office default theme by clicking the Themes button and then clicking *Reset to Theme from Template* at the drop-down gallery.
6. Save and then close **8-NSSSecurity.docx**.
7. Press Ctrl + N to display a new blank document.
8. Delete the custom theme colors by completing the following steps:
   a. Click the Design tab.
   b. Click the Colors button in the Document Formatting group.
   c. Right-click the custom theme colors named with your first and last names.
   d. Click *Delete* at the shortcut menu.
   e. At the message that displays asking if you want to delete the theme colors, click Yes.

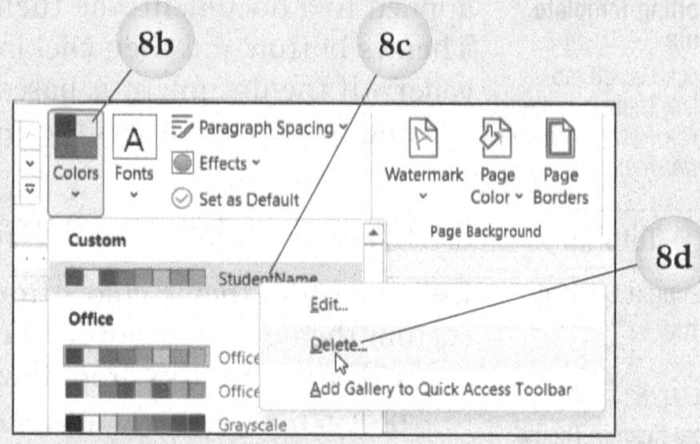

9. Complete steps similar to those in Step 8 to delete the custom theme fonts named with your first and last names.
10. Delete the custom theme by completing the following steps:
    a. Click the Themes button.
    b. Right-click the custom theme named with your first and last names.
    c. Click *Delete* at the shortcut menu.
    d. At the message asking if you want to delete the theme, click Yes.
11. Close the document without saving it.

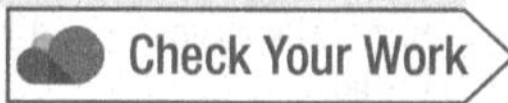

Chapter Summary

- Use the Bullets button to insert bullets before specific paragraphs of text and use the Numbering button to insert numbers.
- Insert custom numbers by clicking the Numbering button arrow and then clicking an option at the drop-down gallery.
- Set the numbering value at the Set Numbering Value dialog box. Display this dialog box by clicking the Numbering button arrow and then clicking the *Set Numbering Value* option.
- Define custom numbering formatting at the Define New Number Format dialog box. Display this dialog box by clicking the Numbering button arrow and then clicking the *Define New Number Format* option.
- Insert custom bullets by clicking the Bullets button arrow and then clicking an option at the drop-down gallery. Define new custom bullets at the Define New Bullet dialog box. Display this dialog box by clicking the Bullets button arrow and then clicking the *Define New Bullet* option.
- Apply list formatting to multilevel paragraphs of text by clicking the Multilevel List button in the Paragraph group on the Home tab. Define new custom multilevel list formatting at the Define new Multilevel list dialog box. Display this dialog box by clicking the Multilevel List button and then clicking the *Define New Multilevel List* option.
- When typing a multilevel list, press the Tab key to move to the next level and press Shift + Tab to move to the previous level.
- Words can be added to AutoCorrect at the AutoCorrect dialog box. Display this dialog box by clicking the File tab, clicking *Options*, clicking *Proofing*, clicking the AutoCorrect Options button, and then clicking the AutoCorrect tab.
- Specify exceptions to AutoCorrect at the AutoCorrect Exceptions dialog box. Display this dialog box by clicking the Exceptions button at the AutoCorrect dialog box with the AutoCorrect tab selected.
- Use the AutoCorrect Options button, which displays when the pointer is hovered over corrected text, to change corrected text back to the original spelling, stop automatically correcting specific text, or display the AutoCorrect dialog box.
- The AutoCorrect dialog box contains several symbols that can be inserted in a document by typing specific text or characters. To add more symbols, display the Symbol dialog box, click the specific symbol, and then click the AutoCorrect button.
- When typing text, control what Word formats automatically with options at the AutoCorrect dialog box with the AutoFormat As You Type tab selected.
- A Word document is based on the Normal template that provides a document with default layout, formatting, styles, and themes. The Normal template provides a number of predesigned themes that are available in the Document Formatting group on the Design tab.
- A theme is a combination of theme colors, theme fonts, and theme effects. A custom theme can be created that includes custom theme colors, theme fonts, and/or theme effects.
- Create custom theme colors with options at the Create New Theme Colors dialog box. Display this dialog box by clicking the Colors button on the Design tab and then clicking *Customize Colors* at the drop-down gallery. Click the Reset button in the dialog box to return to the default Office theme colors.

- Create custom theme fonts with options at the Create New Theme Fonts dialog box. Display this dialog box by clicking the Fonts button on the Design tab and then clicking *Customize Fonts* at the drop-down gallery.
- A theme effect is a set of lines and fill effects that can be applied to a document. Custom theme effects cannot be created, but a theme effect can be applied to a document and then saved in a custom theme.
- Save a custom theme at the Save Current Theme dialog box. Display this dialog box by clicking the Themes button on the Design tab and then clicking *Save Current Theme* at the drop-down gallery.
- Apply custom theme colors by clicking the Colors button in the Document Formatting group on the Design tab and then clicking the custom theme colors option at the top of the drop-down gallery. Complete similar steps to apply custom theme fonts.
- Edit custom theme colors by clicking the Design tab and then clicking the Colors button in the Document Formatting group. At the drop-down gallery, right-click the custom theme colors and then click *Edit* at the shortcut menu. This displays the Edit Theme Colors dialog box where changes can be made to the theme colors. Edit custom theme fonts in a similar manner.
- Click the *Reset to Theme from Template* option at the Themes button drop-down gallery to reset to the Office default theme.
- Delete a custom theme at the Themes button drop-down gallery or at the Save Current Theme dialog box.
- Formatting applied to a document can be saved as the default formatting by clicking the Set as Default button in the Document Formatting group on the Design tab.

Commands Review

FEATURE	RIBBON TAB, GROUP/OPTION	BUTTON, OPTION
AutoCorrect dialog box	File, *Options, Proofing*	AutoCorrect Options
bullets	Home, Paragraph	
Create New Theme Colors dialog box	Design, Document Formatting	, *Customize Colors*
Create New Theme Fonts dialog box	Design, Document Formatting	A, *Customize Fonts*
Define New Bullet dialog box	Home, Paragraph	, *Define New Bullet*
Define new Multilevel list dialog box	Home, Paragraph	, *Define New Multilevel List*
Define New Number Format dialog box	Home, Paragraph	, *Define New Number Format*
numbering	Home, Paragraph	
Save Current Theme dialog box	Design, Document Formatting	Aa, *Save Current Theme*

Review and Assessment

CHAPTER 8

Skills Assessment

Assessment 1

Define and Apply Custom Bullets and Multilevel Lists to a Document

1. Open **TechTimeline.docx** and then save it with the name **8-TechTimeline**.
2. Select the questions below the heading *Early Computer Technology Questions* and then insert check mark (✓) bullets.
3. Define a computer symbol bullet in 14-point font size and then apply the symbol bullet to the 12 paragraphs of text below the heading *Technology Timeline: 1800 - 1970*. (To find the computer symbol, select the Wingdings font at the Symbol dialog box and then type 58 in the *Character code* text box.)
4. Select the paragraphs of text below the heading *Information Systems and Commerce* (on page 2), click the Multilevel List button, and then click the middle option in the top row of the *List Library* section.
5. Select the paragraphs of text below the heading *Internet* (on page 3) and then apply the same multilevel list formatting.
6. Save and then preview page 3 of **8-TechTimeline.docx**.
7. Select the paragraphs of text below the heading *Information Systems and Commerce* and then define a new multilevel list with the following specifications:
   a. Level 1 inserts arabic numbers (1, 2, 3), each followed by a period. The numbers are aligned at the left margin (at 0 inch) and the text indent is 0.25 inch.
   b. Level 2 inserts capital letters (A, B, C), each followed by a period. The letters are aligned 0.25 inch from the left margin and the text indent is 0.5 inch.
   c. Level 3 inserts arabic numbers (1, 2, 3), each followed by a right parenthesis. The numbers are aligned 0.5 inch from the left margin and the text indent is 0.75 inch.
   d. Make sure the new multilevel list formatting is applied to the selected paragraphs.
8. Select the paragraphs of text below the heading *Internet* and then apply the new multilevel list formatting.
9. Save, preview, and then close **8-TechTimeline.docx**.

Assessment 2

Format a Health Plan Document with AutoCorrect

1. Open **KLHPlan.docx** and then save it with the name **8-KLHPlan**.
2. Add the following text to AutoCorrect:
   a. Type kl in the *Replace* text box and type Key Life Health Plan in the *With* text box.
   b. Type m in the *Replace* text box and type medical in the *With* text box.
3. With the insertion point positioned at the beginning of the document, type the text shown in Figure 8.12.
4. Move the insertion point to the blank line below the first paragraph of text below the heading *Quality Assessment*. Insert a bullet symbol by typing > and then pressing the Tab key. Type Member rights, press the Enter key, and then type the following lines of text (each should be preceded by the bullet symbol):

   Preventative health care
   Provider quality standards
   Clinical care review

5. If necessary, turn off autoformatting of web addresses. ***Hint: Do this at the AutoCorrect dialog box with the AutoFormat As You Type tab selected.***
6. Move the insertion point to the end of the document and then type the text shown in Figure 8.13. ***Hint: Type** (tm) **to insert the trademark symbol.***
7. Make the following changes to the document:
   a. Apply the Heading 1 style to the title *Key Life Health Plan*.
   b. Apply the Heading 2 style to the heading *How the Plan Works*.
   c. Apply the Frame theme.
8. Save and then preview **8-KLHPlan.docx**.
9. Delete the two entries you made at the AutoCorrect dialog box.
10. Turn on the autoformatting of web addresses.
11. Close 8-**KLHPlan.docx**.

Figure 8.12 Assessment 2

kl

How the Plan Works

When you enroll in the kl, you and each eligible family member select a plan option. A kl option includes a main m clinic, any affiliated satellite clinics, and designated hospitals. kl provides coverage for emergency m services outside the service area. If the m emergency is not life threatening, call your primary care physician to arrange for care before going to an emergency facility. If you have a life-threatening emergency, go directly to the nearest appropriate facility.

Figure 8.13 Assessment 2

Key Life Health Plan™

https://ppi-edu.net/KeyLife

Assessment 3 Create and Apply Custom Themes to a Company Document

1. At a blank document, create custom theme colors named with your initials that make the following color changes:
   a. Change the Text/Background - Dark 2 color to Orange, Accent 2, Darker 50% (sixth column, last row in the *Theme Colors* section).
   b. Change the Accent 1 color to Green, Accent 6, Darker 50% (tenth column, last row in the *Theme Colors* section).
   c. Change the Accent 4 color to Orange, Accent 2, Darker 50%.
   d. Change the Accent 6 color to Green, Accent 6, Darker 25% (tenth column, fifth row in the *Theme Colors* section).
2. Create custom theme fonts named with your initials that change the heading font to Copperplate Gothic Bold and the body font to Constantia.
3. Apply the *Riblet* effect (last column, third row in the Effects button drop-down list).
4. Save the custom document theme with the name *WL1C8* followed by your initials. ***Hint: Do this with the* Save Current Theme *option at the Themes button drop-down gallery.***
5. Close the document without saving the changes.
6. Open **DIRevenues.docx** and then save it with the name **8-DIRevenues**.
7. Move the insertion point to the end of the document and then insert the document named **DIGraphic.docx**. ***Hint: Do this with the Object button arrow on the Insert tab.***
8. Apply the WL1C8 (followed by your initials) custom document theme to the document.
9. Save, preview, and then close **8-DIRevenues.docx**.
10. Open a blank document.
11. Make a screen capture of the Colors button drop-down gallery by completing the following steps:
    a. Click the Design tab and then click the Colors button. (Make sure your custom theme colors display.)
    b. Press the Print Screen button on your keyboard.
    c. Click in the document, click the Home tab, and then click the Paste button in the Clipboard group. (This inserts the screen capture in your document.)
12. Press Ctrl + End, press the Enter key two times, and then complete steps similar to those in Step 11 to insert a screen capture of the Fonts button drop-down gallery. (Make sure your custom theme fonts display.)
13. Press Ctrl + End, press the Enter key two times, and then complete steps similar to those in Step 11 to insert a screen capture of the Themes button drop-down gallery. (Make sure your custom theme displays.)
14. If necessary, size the three images so that they fit on one page.
15. Save the document with the name **8-ScreenImages**.
16. Preview and then close **8-ScreenImages.docx**.
17. Open a blank document; delete the custom theme colors, custom theme fonts, and custom document theme you created; and then close the blank document.

Assessment 4

Customize AutoCorrect and Edit an Adventure Document

1. Open **BEAAdventures.docx** and then save it with the name **8-BEAAdventures.**
2. In this chapter, you learned how to customize AutoCorrect. Continue exploring AutoCorrect and determine how to turn off automatic bulleted lists, automatic numbered lists, and the formatting of ordinals as superscripts. Turn off these three features.
3. Position the insertion point at the beginning of the adventure *European Grand Tour*, type >, and then press the spacebar. (With the bulleted list feature turned off, the text you type should not be converted to an arrow bullet.) Type > and press the spacebar before each of the three remaining adventures.
4. Position the insertion point at the beginning of *Antarctic Exploration*, type 1., and then press the spacebar. (With the numbered list feature turned off, the text you type should not be indented.) Sequentially number the remaining three Antarctic adventures (2., 3., and 4.).
5. Move the insertion point to the end of the document and then type For more information on Antarctic adventures, please visit us at our San Diego office at 9880 43rd Street East or call 619-555-9090. (With the formatting of ordinals as superscripts turned off, the text *rd* in *43rd* will not be formatted as a superscript.)
6. Save, preview, and then close **8-BEAAdventures.docx.**
7. At the blank screen, turn on the three features you turned off in Step 2 (automatic bulleted lists, automatic numbered lists, and the formatting of ordinals as superscripts).

Visual Benchmark

Create and Format an International Correspondence Document

1. Open **IntlCorres.docx** and then save it with the name **8-IntlCorres.**
2. Apply the following formatting so your document appears similar to the document shown in Figure 8.14:
   - Change the top margin to 1.5 inches and the left and right margins to 1.25 inches.
   - Apply the Heading 1 style to the title and the Heading 2 style to the three headings.
   - Apply the Shaded style set. (You will need to click the More Style Sets button in the Document Formatting group on the Design tab to display this style set.)
   - Change the theme colors to Green.
   - Apply check mark bullets as shown in the figure.
   - Apply symbol bullets as shown in the figure. (The globe bullet is available in the Webdings font, character code 254, at the Symbol dialog box.)
   - Apply automatic numbering as shown in the figure and start numbering with 11 after the heading *CANADIAN CODES AND TERRITORIES.*
   - Apply any other formatting required to make your document similar to the document shown in Figure 8.14.
3. Save, preview, and then close **8-IntlCorres.docx.**

Figure 8.14 Visual Benchmark

INTERNATIONAL CORRESPONDENCE

With the increased number of firms conducting business worldwide, international written communication has assumed new importance. Follow these guidelines when corresponding internationally, especially with people for whom English is not the primary language:

- ✓ Use a direct writing style and clear, precise words.
- ✓ Avoid slang, jargon, and idioms.
- ✓ Develop an awareness of cultural differences that may interfere with the communication process.

INTERNATIONAL ADDRESSES

Use the company's letterhead or a business card as a guide for spelling and other information. Include the following when addressing international correspondence:

- Line 1: Addressee's Name, Title
- Line 2: Company Name
- Line 3: Street Address
- Line 4: City and Codes
- Line 5: COUNTRY NAME (capitalized)

CANADIAN CODES AND PROVINCES

1. ON – Ontario
2. QC – Quebec
3. NS – Nova Scotia
4. NB – New Brunswick
5. MB – Manitoba
6. BC – British Columbia
7. PE – Prince Edward Island
8. SK – Saskatchewan
9. AB – Alberta
10. NL – Newfoundland and Labrador

CANADIAN CODES AND TERRITORIES

11. NT – Northwest Territories
12. YT – Yukon
13. NU – Nunavut

Case Study

Part 1

You work in the Human Resources Department of Oceanside Medical Services and your supervisor has asked you to create a custom document theme. Open **OMSOrgChart.docx** and then save it with the name **8-OMSOrgChart**. Open **OMSLtrhd.docx** and look at the colors in the letterhead. Make **8-OMSOrgChart.docx** the active document, and then create and save custom theme colors that match the letterhead. Create and save custom theme fonts that apply the Arial font to the headings and the Constantia font to the body text. Apply the Glossy effect. Save the custom document theme in the Save Current Theme dialog box and then name it with your initials followed by *OMS*. Save, preview, and then close **8-OMSOrgChart.docx**. Close **OMSLtrhd.docx**.

Part 2

Open **OMSHandbook.docx** and then save it with the name **8-OMSHandbook**. Apply the custom document theme you created and saved in Part 1 (named with your initials followed by *OMS*). Apply or insert the following in the document:

- Create an AutoCorrect entry that will replace *OMS* with *Oceanside Medical Services*. Position the insertion point on the blank line below the heading *NEW EMPLOYEE ORIENTATION* (located near the bottom of the first page) and then type the text shown in Figure 8.15.
- Define a new symbol bullet (you determine the symbol) and then apply it to all the currently bulleted paragraphs in the handbook document.
- Select the lines of text on the first page beginning with *Section 1: General Information* through *Compensation Procedures* and then define and apply a new multilevel list number format that applies capital letters followed by periods to the first level and arabic numbers (1, 2, 3) followed by periods to the second level. You determine the indents.
- Insert a cover page of your choosing and insert the appropriate information in the placeholders.

Save, preview, and then close **8-OMSHandbook.docx**.

Figure 8.15 Case Study, Part 2

> The OMS New Employee Orientation Program is designed to welcome new employees into the spirit and culture of OMS, to clearly establish health care performance expectations, and to set the stage for success. New personnel are encouraged to begin their jobs with the monthly orientation in order to be introduced to the overall operations of OMS.

Part 3

At a blank document, make a screen capture (use the Print Screen button) of the Colors button drop-down gallery (in the Document Formatting group on the Design tab) and paste it in the document. (Refer to Assessment 3, Step 11.) Make a screen capture of the Fonts button drop-down gallery (in the Document Formatting group on the Design tab) and paste it in the document. Make a screen capture of the Themes button drop-down gallery and paste it in the document. Make sure all the screen capture images are visible and fit on one page. Save the document with the name **8-OMSScreenImages**. Preview and then close **8-OMSScreenImages.docx**. Open a blank document and then delete your custom theme colors, custom theme fonts, and custom document theme. Delete the *OMS* AutoCorrect entry and then close the document.

WORD LEVEL 1

Unit 2 Performance Assessment

Data Files

The data files for this unit work are in the WL1U2 folder that you downloaded at the beginning of this course.

Assessing Proficiency

In this unit, you have learned to format and customize objects to enhance the appearance of documents; manage documents; print envelopes and labels; create documents using templates; create and edit tables; visually represent data in SmartArt graphics and charts; create custom numbering and bullet formatting; and customize a document using AutoCorrect options and custom themes.

Assessment 1 Format a Bioinformatics Document

1. Open **Bioinformatics.docx** and then save it with the name **U2-Bioinformatics**.
2. Move the insertion point to the end of the document and then insert the file named **GenomeMapping.docx**.
3. Press Ctrl + Home to move the insertion point to the beginning of the document and then insert the Motion Quote text box with the following specifications:
   a. Type "Understanding our DNA is similar to understanding a number that is billions of digits long." in the text box.
   b. Select the text in the text box and then change the font size to 12 points.
   c. Change the width of the text box to 2.6 inches.
   d. Position the text box in the middle of the page with square text wrapping.
4. Insert page numbering at the bottom of the page using the Thin Line page numbering option.
5. Save, preview, and then close **U2-Bioinformatics.docx**.

Assessment 2 Create a Workshop Flyer

1. Create the flyer shown in Figure U2.1 with the following specifications:
   a. Create the WordArt with the following specifications:
      - Use the option in the fourth column, first row in the WordArt button drop-down gallery (white fill, blue outline, shadow).
      - Increase the width to 6.5 inches and the height to 1 inch.
      - Apply the Deflate text effect transform shape (second column, sixth row in the *Warp* section).
      - Position the WordArt in the top center of the page with square text wrapping.
      - Change the text fill color to Green, Accent 6, Lighter 40% (last column, fourth row in the *Theme Colors* section).

   b. Type the text shown in the figure. Change the font to 22-point Calibri, apply bold formatting, and center-align the text.
   c. Insert the **WorldGlobe.png** image file from your WL1U2 folder. Change the wrapping style to Square and size and position the image as shown in Figure U2.1.
2. Save the document with the name **U2-BEAFlyer**.
3. Preview and then close **U2-BEAFlyer.docx**.

Figure U2.1 Assessment 2

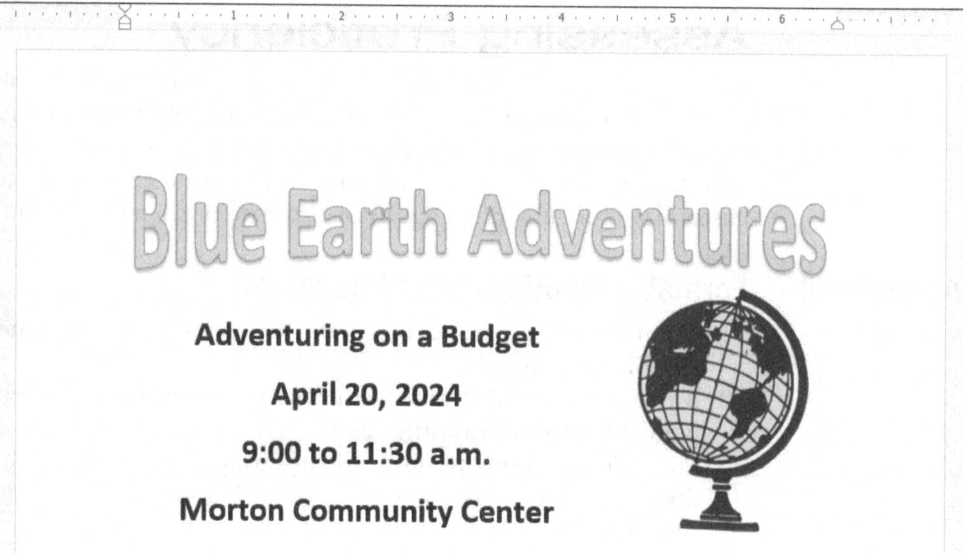

Assessment 3 Create a Staff Meeting Announcement

1. Click the File tab, click the *New* option, and then double-click the *Single spaced (blank)* template.
2. Create the announcement shown in Figure U2.2 with the following specifications:
   a. Use the Hexagon shape in the *Basic Shapes* section of the Shapes button drop-down list (ninth column, first row) to create the shape. (You determine the size of the shape.)
   b. Apply the Subtle Effect - Blue, Accent 1 shape style (second column, fourth row in the *Theme Styles* section).
   c. Apply the Divot bevel shape effect (first column, third row in the *Bevel* section).

d. Type the text in the shape as shown in Figure U2.2. Insert the *ñ* as a symbol (in the normal text font, character code 00F1) and insert the clock as a symbol (in the Wingdings font, character code 185). Set the text and clock symbol in larger font sizes.

3. Save the completed document with the name **U2-MeetNotice**.
4. Preview and then close **U2-MeetNotice.docx**.

Figure U2.2 Assessment 3

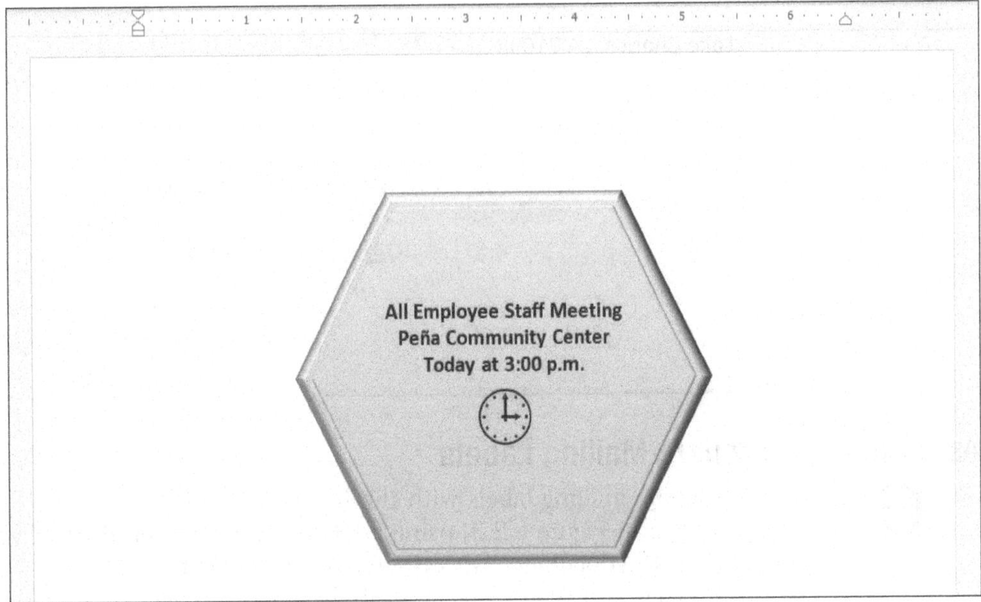

Assessment 4

Create a Snorkeling Flyer

1. At a blank document, insert the **Snorkeling.jpg** image file from your WL1U2 folder.
2. Crop off some of the bottom of the image.
3. Correct the brightness and contrast to Brightness: 0% (Normal) Contrast: +20% (third column, fourth row in the *Brightness/Contrast* section).
4. Use the Position button to position the image in the top center with square text wrapping and then use the Wrap Text button to wrap the image behind text.
5. Apply the Double Frame, Black picture style to the image.
6. Press the Enter key twice and then change to center alignment. Type the text Snorkeling Adventures on the first line; Blue Island Bay on the second line; and 1-888-555-3322 on the third line. Change the font for the text to 18-point Castellar and apply bold formatting. Make sure the text fits in the water portion of the image.
7. Save the document with the name **U2-SnorkelingFlyer**.
8. Preview and then close **U2-SnorkelingFlyer.docx**.

Assessment 5 Prepare an Envelope

1. At a blank document, prepare an envelope with the text shown in Figure U2.3.
2. Save the envelope document with the name **U2-Env**.
3. Preview and then close **U2-Env.docx**.

Figure U2.3 Assessment 5

Mrs. Eileen Hebert
15205 East 42nd Street
Lake Charles, LA 71098

Mr. Earl Robicheaux
1436 North Sheldon Street
Jennings, LA 70542

Assessment 6 Prepare Mailing Labels

1. Prepare mailing labels with the name and address for Mrs. Eileen Hebert, shown in Figure U2.3, using a label vendor and product of your choosing.
2. Save the document with the name **U2-Labels**.
3. Preview and then close **U2-Labels.docx**.

Assessment 7 Create and Format a Table with Software Training Information

1. At a blank document, create the table shown in Figure U2.4. Format the table and the text (do not apply a table style) in a manner similar to what is shown in Figure U2.4.
2. Insert a formula in cell B8 that totals the numbers in cells B4 through B7.
3. Insert a formula in cell C8 that totals the numbers in cells C4 through C7.
4. Save the document with the name **U2-TechTraining**.
5. Preview and then close **U2-TechTraining.docx**.

Figure U2.4 Assessment 7

TRI-STATE PRODUCTS		
Computer Technology Department Microsoft 365® Training		
Application	**# Enrolled**	**# Completed**
Access 365	20	15
Excel 365	62	56
PowerPoint 365	40	33
Word 365	80	72
Total		

Assessment 8

Edit and Format a Table Containing Training Scores

1. Open **TrainingScores.docx** and then save it with the name **U2-TrainingScores**.
2. Insert formulas that calculate the averages in the appropriate rows and columns. (When writing the formulas, change the *Number format* option to *0*.)
3. Autofit the contents of the table.
4. Apply a table style of your choosing.
5. Apply any other formatting to enhance the appearance of the table.
6. Save, preview, and then close **U2-TrainingScores.docx**.

Assessment

Create an Organizational Chart

1. Use SmartArt to create an organizational chart for the text shown in Figure U2.5 (in the order shown). Change the colors to Colorful Range - Accent Colors 4 to 5 and apply the Metallic Scene SmartArt style.
2. Save the completed document with the name **U2-OrgChart**.
3. Preview and then close **U2-OrgChart.docx**.

Figure U2.5 Assessment 9

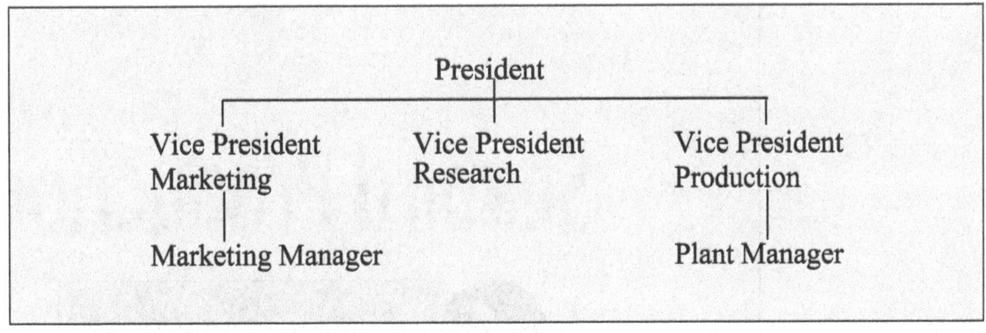

Assessment 10

Create a SmartArt Graphic

1. At a blank document, create the WordArt graphic and SmartArt graphic shown in Figure U2.6 with the following specifications:
   a. Create the WordArt text using the option in the third column, third row of the WordArt button drop-down list. Change the shape height to 1 inch and the shape width to 6 inches and then apply the Square transform text effect (first effect in the *Warp* section). Position the WordArt at the top center of the page with square text wrapping.
   b. Create the SmartArt graphic using the Vertical Picture Accent List graphic. Click the picture icon in the top circle and then insert the **SP-Seagull.png** image file from your WL1U2 folder. Insert the same image file in the other two circles. Type the text in each rectangle shape as shown in Figure U2.6. Change the colors to Colorful Range - Accent Colors 5 to 6 and apply the Cartoon SmartArt style.
2. Save the document with the name **U2-SPGraphic**.
3. Preview and then close **U2-SPGraphic.docx**.

Figure U2.6 Assessment 10

Assessment 11

Format a Stock Awards Document

1. Open **CMStocks.docx** and then save it with the name **U2-CMStocks**.
2. Apply the Title style to the title *Clearline Manufacturing*.
3. Apply the Heading 1 style to the headings *Stock Awards* and *Employee Stock Plan*.
4. Apply the Centered style set.
5. Select the bulleted paragraphs of text and then define and apply a new picture bullet using the **BlueCircle.png** image file in your WL1U2 folder.
6. Select the lines of text below the heading *Employee Stock Plan* and then apply a multilevel list (middle option in the top row of the *List Library* section of the Multilevel List button drop-down list).
7. With the text still selected, define a new multilevel list that inserts capital letters followed by periods (A., B., C.) for level 2 and arabic numbers followed by periods (1., 2., 3.) for level 3. (Make sure the new multilevel list applies to the selected text.)
8. Save, preview, and then close **U2-CMStocks.docx**.

Assessment 12

Format an Equipment Rental Agreement

1. At a blank document, create custom theme colors named with your initials that change the Text/Background - Dark 2 color to Orange, Accent 2, Darker 50% (sixth column, last row in the *Theme Colors* section) and the Accent 1 color to Green, Accent 6, Darker 25% (tenth column, fifth row in the *Theme Colors* section).
2. Create custom theme fonts named with your initials that apply the Verdana font to headings and the Cambria font to body text.
3. Save the custom document theme and name it with your initials. (Do this with the *Save Current Theme* option at the Themes button drop-down gallery).
4. Close the document without saving the changes.
5. Open **MRCForm.docx** and then save it with the name **U2-MRCForm**.
6. Add the following text to AutoCorrect:
   a. Type mrc in the *Replace* text box and type Meridian Rental Company in the *With* text box.
   b. Type erag in the *Replace* text box and type Equipment Rental Agreement in the *With* text box.
7. Move the insertion point to the blank line below the heading *Default* (on the third page) and then type the text shown in Figure U2.7. Use the Numbering feature to number each paragraph with a lowercase letter followed by a right parenthesis. (If the AutoCorrect feature capitalizes the first word after the letter and right parenthesis, use the AutoCorrect options button to return the letter to lowercase.)
8. Apply the Centered style set.
9. Apply your custom document theme to the document.
10. Delete the two entries you made at the AutoCorrect dialog box.
11. Save, preview, and then close **U2-MRCForm.docx**.
12. Open a blank document; delete the custom theme colors, custom theme fonts, and custom document theme named with your initials; and then close the document.

Figure U2.7 Assessment 12

> Upon the occurrence of default, mrc may, without any further notice, exercise any one or more of the following remedies:
>
> a) terminate this erag as to any or all items of Equipment;
>
> b) cause Lessee to return the Equipment to mrc in the condition set forth in this erag;
>
> c) dispose of the Equipment without affecting the obligations of Lessee as provided by this erag;
>
> d) exercise any other rights accruing to mrc upon a default by Lessee of this erag.

Writing Activities

The following activities give you the opportunity to practice your writing skills and demonstrate your understanding of some of the important Word features you have mastered in this unit. Use correct grammar, appropriate word choices, and clear sentence construction.

Activity 1

Create a Letterhead and Compose a Letter

You are the executive assistant to the owner of Clearline Manufacturing, who has asked you to create a letterhead for the company. Use information of your choosing for the letterhead that includes the company name, address, email address, web address, and telephone number. Include an image in the letterhead. Five possible choices are available in your WL1U2 folder, and each image file name begins with *Manufacture*. Save the completed letterhead document as a template in your WL1U2 folder and name the template **CMLtrhdTemplate**. Close the template document.

Use File Explorer to open a document based on the **CMLtrhdTemplate.dotx** template. Write a letter to the president of the board of directors, Mrs. Nancy Logan (you determine her address), that includes the following:

- Explain that the director of the Human Resources Department has created a new employee handbook and that it will be made available to all new employees. Also mention that the attorney for Clearline Manufacturing has reviewed the handbook and approved its content.
- Open **CMHandbook.docx** and then use the headings to summarize the contents of the handbook in a paragraph in the letter. Explain in the letter that a draft of the handbook is enclosed.

Save the completed letter document with the name **U2-CMLetter**. Preview and then close **U2-CMLetter.docx**.

Activity 2

Create a Custom Document Theme

Create a custom document theme for formatting Clearline Manufacturing documents that includes the colors and/or fonts you chose for the company letterhead. Open **CMHandbook.docx** and then save it with the name **U2-CMHandbook**. Apply at least the following to the document:

- Apply the custom document theme you created.
- Apply title and/or heading styles to the title and headings in the document.
- Add a cover page of your choosing to the document and insert the appropriate information in the cover page placeholders.
- Any additional formatting that improves the appearance of the document.

Save, preview, and then close **U2-CMHandbook.docx**.

Internet Research

Create a Flyer on an Incentive Program

The owner of Blue Earth Adventures is offering an incentive to motivate adventure consultants to increase adventure bookings. The incentive is a sales contest with the grand prize of a one-week paid vacation to Cancun, Mexico. The owner has asked you to create a flyer that will be posted on the office bulletin board and that includes information about the incentive program and Cancun. Create this flyer using information about Cancun that you find on the internet. Consider using one (or more) of the images (**Cancun01.jpg**, **Cancun02.jpg**, **Cancun03.jpg**, and **Cancun04.jpg**) in your WL1U2 folder. Include any other information or objects to add visual interest to the flyer. Save the completed flyer with the name **U2-CancunFlyer**. Preview and then close **U2-CancunFlyer.docx**.

Job Study

Develop Recycling Program Communications

The chief operating officer of Harrington Engineering has just approved your draft of the company's new recycling policy, the file named **RecyclingPolicy.docx**. Open the file, edit the draft, and prepare a final copy of the policy, along with a memo to all employees describing the new guidelines. To support the company's energy resources conservation effort, you will send hard copies of the new policy to the president of the Somerset Recycling Program and to the directors of the Somerset Chamber of Commerce.

Using the concepts and techniques you learned in this unit, prepare the following documents:

- Format the recycling policy manual, including a cover page, appropriate headers and footers, and page numbers. Add at least one graphic where appropriate. Format the document using styles and a style set. Save the manual with the name **U2-RecyclingManual**. Preview the manual.
- Download a memo template at the New backstage area and then create a memo from Susan Gerhardt, Chief Operating Officer of Harrington Engineering, to all employees that introduces the new recycling program.

- Copy the *Procedure* section of the recycling policy manual into the memo where appropriate. Include a table listing five employees who will act as recycling coordinators at Harrington Engineering (make up the names). Add columns for the employees' department names and telephone extensions. Save the memo with the name **U2-RecylingMemo**. Preview the memo.
- Write a letter to the president of the Somerset Recycling Program, William Elizondo, indicating that Harrington Engineering has approved a new recycling policy and that a copy of the new policy is enclosed with the letter. Identify some of the new recycling guidelines in the policy. Add a notation indicating that copies with enclosures were sent to all the members of the Somerset Chamber of Commerce. Save the letter with the name **U2-RecyclingLetter**. Preview the letter.
- Create mailing labels (see Figure U2.8). Save the labels with the name **U2-RecyclingLabels**. Preview the labels.

Figure U2.8 Mailing Labels

William Elizondo
Somerset Recycling Program
700 West Brighton Road
Somerset, NJ 55123

Paul Schwartz
Somerset Chamber of Commerce
45 Wallace Road
Somerset, NJ 55123

Ashley Crighton
Somerset Chamber of Commerce
45 Wallace Road
Somerset, NJ 55123

Carol Davis
Somerset Chamber of Commerce
45 Wallace Road
Somerset, NJ 55123

Robert Knight
Somerset Chamber of Commerce
45 Wallace Road
Somerset, NJ 55123

INDEX

D

E

F

G

H

I

K

L

M

N

U

V

W

X

Z

Interior Photo Credits

All screen captures provided by the authors.

Preface

Page x: © LightField Studios/Shutterstock.com; **Page xii:** © Neyman Kseniya/Shutterstock.com; **Page xiv:** © Cameron Prins/Shutterstock.com; **Page xvii:** laptop: © Kite_rin/Shutterstock.com, tablet: © guteksk7/Shutterstock.com; **Page xviii:** © KucherAV/Shutterstock.com; **Page xix:** © Prostock-studio/Shutterstock.com

Getting Started

GS-1: clockwise from top left: © Alexander Selyunin/Shutterstock.com, © Paradigm Education Solutions, © rangizzz/Shutterstock.com, © NetPhotographer/Shutterstock.com, © Bborriss.67/Shutterstock.com; **GS-2:** © Aleksey Mnogosmyslov/Shutterstock.com; **GS-3:** © Paradigm Education Solutions; **GS-4:** © Pixels Hunter/Shutterstock.com; **GS-5:** © AngieYeoh/Shutterstock.com

Chapter 5

Page 161: photo © Kelly Rutkosky; **Page 163:** photos © Kelly Rutkosky; **Page 165:** Australia outlines: publicdomainvectors.org; **Page 188:** first aid icon: publicdomainvectors.org; **Page 189:** stethoscope: publicdomainvectors.org, first aid icon: publicdomainvectors.org; **Page 192:** photo: Audrey Roggenkamp; **Page 194:** cake: publicdomainvectors.org

Chapter 6

Page 239: compass: publicdomainvectors.org; **Page 240:** flowers: publicdomainvectors.org

Chapter 7

Page 281: fall imagery: publicdomainvectors.org

Unit 2 Performance Assessment

Page 320: globe: publicdomainvectors.org; **Page 324:** seagulls: publicdomainvectors.org

WORD

LEVEL 2

Unit 1

Formatting and Customizing Documents

Chapter 1 Applying Advanced Formatting

Chapter 2 Proofing Documents

Chapter 3 Inserting Headers, Footers, and References

Chapter 4 Creating Specialized Tables and Navigating in a Document

WORD

Applying Advanced Formatting

CHAPTER 1

Performance Objectives

Upon successful completion of Chapter 1, you will be able to:

1 Adjust character spacing, use OpenType features, apply text effects, and change the default font
2 Insert intellectual property symbols, hyphens, dashes, and nonbreaking spaces
3 Find and replace font formatting, paragraph formatting, special characters, styles, and body and heading fonts, and use wildcard characters
4 Manage document properties
5 Inspect a document for confidentiality, accessibility, and compatibility issues

Microsoft Word is a powerful word processing program containing many features for making documents look polished, professional, and publication-ready. This chapter will introduce you to some advanced formatting that will bring your skills to the next level. Use options at the Font dialog box with the Advanced tab selected to apply advanced character formatting such as scaling, spacing, and kerning, as well as OpenType features such as ligatures, number styles, and stylistic sets. Insert special symbols such as intellectual property symbols, hyphens, and nonbreaking spaces at the Symbol dialog box or with keyboard shortcuts. To make designing a document faster and easier, use Word's Find and Replace feature to find and replace formatting, special characters, styles, and body and heading fonts. Finally, you'll learn to prepare documents for sharing by managing document properties and inspecting a document for confidentiality, accessibility, and compatibility issues.

Data Files

The data files for this chapter are in the WL2C1 folder that you downloaded at the beginning of this course.

Activity 1 Apply Advanced Character Formatting to a Letter **5 Parts**

You will open a document containing a donor appreciation letter and then apply advanced character formatting to the text, including character scaling, spacing, and kerning; and apply OpenType features such as ligatures, number styles, and stylistic sets. You will also apply text effects and change the default font for all new documents.

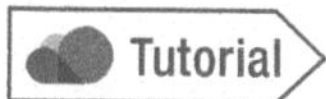

Applying Advanced Character Formatting

Applying Character Formatting

The Font dialog box with the Advanced tab selected contains a number of options for improving the appearance of text in a document, stretching or shrinking text to fit in a specified area, and to create a specific mood in a document. Use options at the dialog box to adjust character spacing, apply OpenType features, and apply text effects to selected text.

Quick Steps

Adjust Character Spacing

1. Click Font group dialog box launcher.
2. Click Advanced tab.
3. Specify scaling, spacing, positioning, and/or kerning.
4. Click OK.

Adjusting Character Spacing

Each typeface is designed with a specific amount of space between characters. This character spacing can be changed with options in the *Character Spacing* section of the Font dialog box with the Advanced tab selected, as shown in Figure 1.1. Display this dialog box by clicking the Font group dialog box launcher on the Home tab and then clicking the Advanced tab at the dialog box.

Choose the *Scale* option to stretch or compress text horizontally as a percentage of the current size from 1% to 600%. Expand or condense the spacing

Figure 1.1 Font Dialog Box with the Advanced Tab Selected

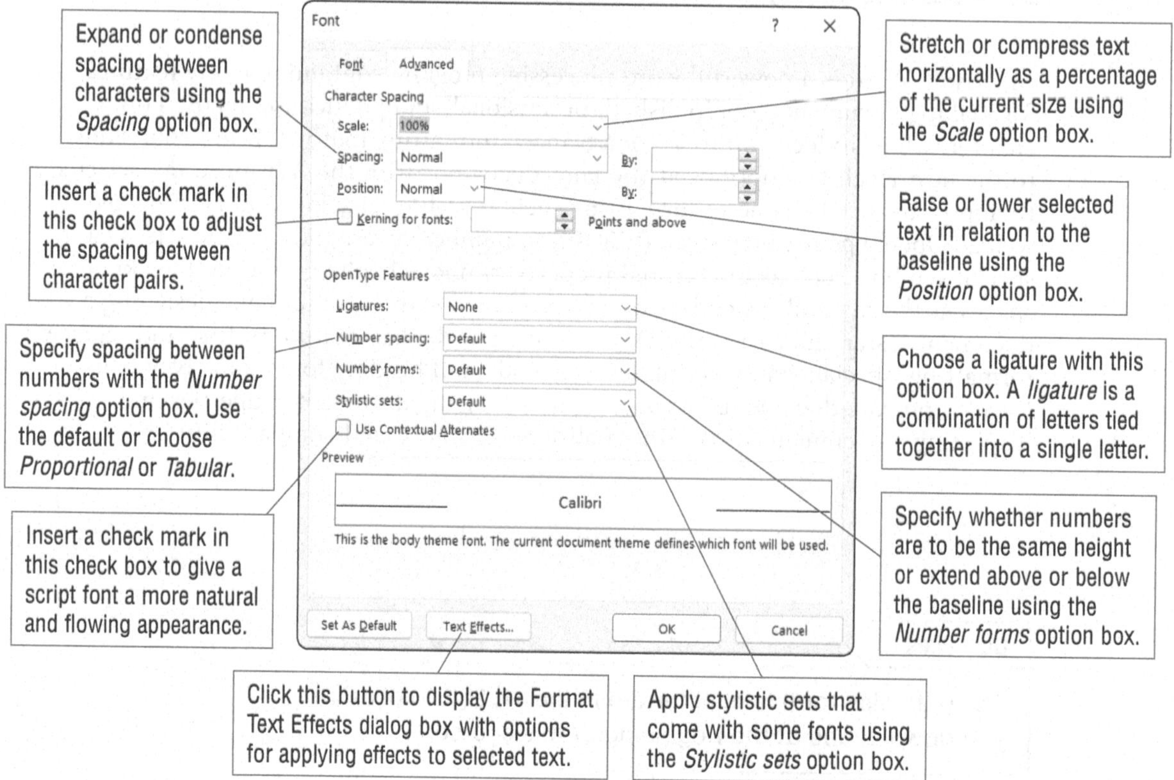
Expand or condense spacing between characters using the Spacing option box.
Insert a check mark in this check box to adjust the spacing between character pairs.
Specify spacing between numbers with the Number spacing option box. Use the default or choose Proportional or Tabular.
Insert a check mark in this check box to give a script font a more natural and flowing appearance.
Font
Font
Advanced
Character Spacing
Scale:
100%
Spacing:
Normal
By:
Position:
Normal
By:
Kerning for fonts:
Points and above
OpenType Features
Ligatures:
None
Number spacing:
Default
Number forms:
Default
Stylistic sets:
Default
Use Contextual Alternates
Preview
Calibri
This is the body theme font. The current document theme defines which font will be used.
Set As Default
Text Effects...
OK
Cancel
Stretch or compress text horizontally as a percentage of the current size using the Scale option box.
Raise or lower selected text in relation to the baseline using the Position option box.
Choose a ligature with this option box. A ligature is a combination of letters tied together into a single letter.
Specify whether numbers are to be the same height or extend above or below the baseline using the Number forms option box.
Click this button to display the Format Text Effects dialog box with options for applying effects to selected text.
Apply stylistic sets that come with some fonts using the Stylistic sets option box.

Hint Subtle adjustments to the scaling and spacing of characters can have a big impact on the visual display of text in a document.

Hint Apply kerning for fonts set 14 points or larger or for italic text.

between characters with the *Spacing* option box. Choose the *Expanded* or *Condensed* option and then enter a specific point size in the *By* text box. Raise or lower selected text in relation to the baseline with the *Position* option box. Choose the *Raised* or *Lowered* option and then enter the point size in the *By* text box.

Insert a check mark in the *Kerning for fonts* check box to apply kerning to selected text in a document. Kerning involves adjusting the spacing between certain character combinations by positioning two characters closer together than normal and uses the shapes and slopes of the characters to improve their appearance. Kerning allows more text to fit in a specific amount of space; kerned characters also look more natural and help the eye move along the text when reading. Consider kerning text set in larger font sizes, such as 14 points and larger, and text set in italics. Figure 1.2 displays text with and without kerning applied. Notice how the letters *Te* and *Va* are closer together in the kerned text compared with the text that is not kerned.

Turn on automatic kerning by displaying the Font dialog box with the Advanced tab selected and then inserting a check mark in the *Kerning for fonts* check box. Specify the beginning point size to be kerned in the *Points and above* measurement box.

Figure 1.2 Text with and without Kerning Applied

Tennison Valley (kerned)
Tennison Valley (not kerned)

Activity 1a Adjusting Character Spacing and Kerning Text

Part 1 of 5

1. Open **PRDonorApp.docx** and then save it with the name **1-PRDonorApp**.
2. Select the title *Donor Appreciation*.
3. With the Home tab active, click the Font group dialog box launcher.
4. At the Font dialog box, click the Advanced tab.
5. Click the *Scale* option box arrow and then click *150%* at the drop-down list.
6. Click the *Spacing* option box arrow and then click *Condensed* at the drop-down list.
7. Click the *Kerning for fonts* check box to insert a check mark.
8. Click OK to close the dialog box.
9. Select the text *Enjoy the "flavor of Tanzania" and an evening of cultural entertainment....*
10. Click the Font group dialog box launcher to display the Font dialog box with the Advanced tab selected.
11. Click the *Kerning for fonts* check box to insert a check mark.
12. Click OK to close the dialog box.
13. Save **1-PRDonorApp.docx**.

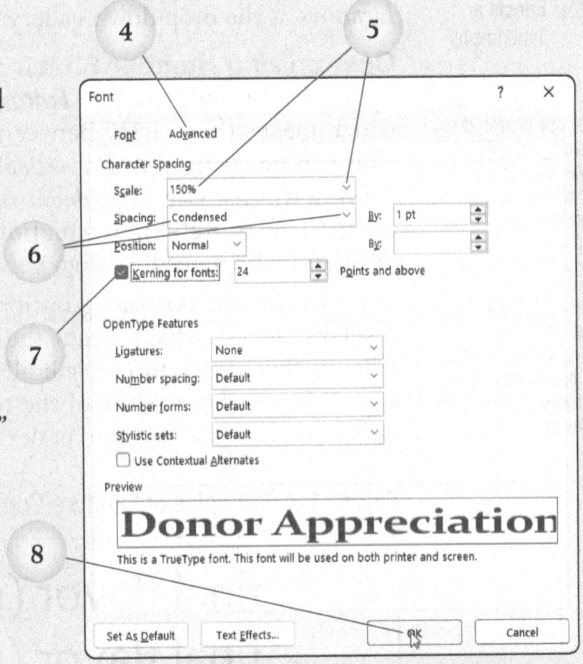

Check Your Work

Applying OpenType Features

Quick Steps

Apply OpenType Features

1. Click Font group dialog box launcher.
2. Click Advanced tab.
3. Specify ligatures, number spacing and forms, and/or stylistic sets.
4. Click OK.

Hint Microsoft and Adobe worked cooperatively to create OpenType fonts, which are scalable fonts based on TrueType fonts.

Applying OpenType Features

The OpenType font file format was developed by Adobe and Microsoft to work on both Macintosh and Windows computers. The benefits of the OpenType format are cross-platform compatibility, which means font files can be moved between Macintosh and Windows computers; the ability to support expanded character sets and layout figures; and the capability for web page designers to create high-quality fonts for online documents. Microsoft Word offers some advanced OpenType features in the Font dialog box with the Advanced tab selected (refer to Figure 1.1 on page 4) that desktop publishers and web and graphic designers can use to enhance the appearance of text.

Using Ligatures to Combine Characters At the Font dialog box with the Advanced tab selected, *Ligatures* is the first option box in the *OpenType Features* section. A ligature is a combination of characters joined into a single letter. The OpenType standard specifies four categories of ligatures: *Standard Only*, *Standard and Contextual*, *Historical and Discretionary*, and *All*. The font designer decides which category to support and in which group to put combinations of characters.

With the *Standard Only* option selected, the standard set of ligatures that most typographers and font designers determine are appropriate for the font are applied to text. Common ligatures include letter combinations with the letter *f*, as shown in Figure 1.3. Notice how the *fi* and *fl* letter pairs are combined when ligatures are applied.

Use the other ligature options to specify *Contextual* ligatures, which are ligatures that the font designer believes are appropriate for use with the font, but are not standard. Choose the option *Historical and Discretionary* to apply ligatures that were once standard, but are no longer commonly used; use them to create a historical or "period" effect. The *All* ligatures option applies all the ligature combinations to selected text. Another method for applying ligatures to selected text is to click the Text Effects and Typography button in the Font group on the Home tab, point to *Ligatures* at the drop-down gallery and then click an option at the side menu.

Text Effects and Typography

Hint Some fonts that use proportional spacing and old style number forms by default include Candara, Constantia, and Corbel.

Hint Some fonts that use tabular spacing and lining number forms include Cambria, Calibri, and Consolas.

Customizing Number Spacing and Number Forms The *Number spacing* option box in the *OpenType Features* section will automatically display *Default*, which means the spacing between numbers is determined by the font designer. This can be changed to *Proportional*, which adjusts the spacing for numbers with varying widths. Use the *Tabular* option to specify that each number is the same width. This is useful in a situation in which the numbers are set in columns and all the numbers need to align vertically.

Like the *Number spacing* option box, the *Number forms* option box automatically displays *Default*, which means the font designer determines the number form. Change this option to *Lining* if all the numbers should be the same height and not extend below the baseline of the text. Generally, lining numbers are used in tables and forms because they are easier to read. With the *Old-style* option, the lines of

Figure 1.3 Examples of Ligature Combinations

ﬁnal ﬂavor (using ligatures)
final flavor (not using ligatures)

the numbers can extend above or below the baseline of the text. For some fonts, changing the *Number forms* option to *Old-style* results in numbers such as *3* and *5* extending below the baseline or being centered higher on the line. See Figure 1.4 for examples of number form and spacing.

The spacing and form of numbers can also be adjusted with the Text Effects and Typography button in the Font group. Click the button arrow and then hover the pointer over the *Number Styles* option in the drop-down gallery to display a side menu of options.

Figure 1.4 Number Form and Spacing

Old-style form and proportional spacing (in Candara):

123456789

Lining form and tabular spacing (in Cambria):

123456789

Activity 1b Applying a Ligature and Number Form

Part 2 of 5

1. With **1-PRDonorApp.docx** open, select the text *Enjoy the "flavor of Tanzania" and an evening of cultural entertainment....*
2. Click the Font group dialog box launcher and, if necessary, click the Advanced tab.
3. At the Font dialog box with the Advanced tab selected, click the *Ligatures* option box arrow and then click *Standard and Contextual* at the drop-down list.
4. Click OK to close the dialog box.
5. Select the text *2025 – 2026* and *$3,500,000.*
6. Click the Text Effects and Typography button in the Font group, point to *Number Styles* at the drop-down gallery, and then click *Tabular Old-style* at the side menu.
7. Save **1-PRDonorApp.docx**.

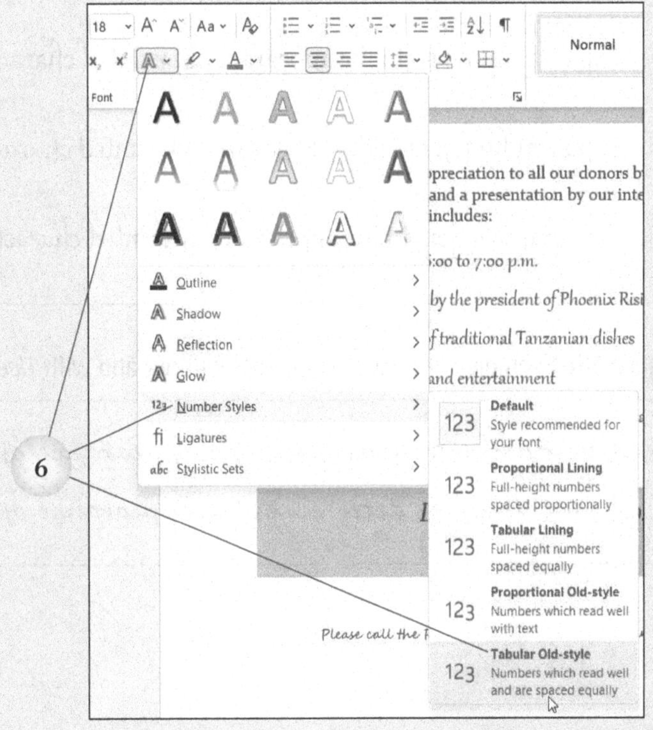

Check Your Work

Applying Stylistic Sets A font designer may include a number of stylistic sets for a specific font. A different stylistic set may apply additional formatting to the characters in a font. For example, the sentences in Figure 1.5 are set in 16-point Gabriola. Notice the slight variations in characters in some of the stylistic sets. Choose a stylistic set and see a visual representation of the characters with the stylistic set applied in the *Preview* section of the dialog box. A stylistic set can also be applied by clicking the Text Effects and Typography button in the Font group, pointing to *Stylistic Sets* at the drop-down gallery, and then clicking the stylistic set at the side menu.

Insert a check mark in the *Use Contextual Alternates* check box in the Font dialog box with the Advanced tab selected to fine-tune letter combinations based on the surrounding characters. Use this feature to give script fonts a more natural and flowing appearance. Figure 1.6 shows text set in 12-point Segoe Script. The first line of text is set with the default setting and the second line of text is set with the *Use Contextual Alternates* option selected. Notice the slight differences in letters such as *t*, *n*, *s*, and *h*.

Not all fonts are developed in the OpenType file format. Experiment with a font using the OpenType features at the Font dialog box with the Advanced tab selected to determine what features are supported by the font.

Figure 1.5 Examples of Gabriola Font Stylistic Sets

Typography refers to the appearance of printed characters on the page. (Default set)

Typography refers to the appearance of printed characters on the page. (Stylistic set 4)

Typography refers to the appearance of printed characters on the page. (Stylistic set 5)

Typography refers to the appearance of printed characters on the page. (Stylistic set 6)

Figure 1.6 Examples of Segoe Script Font without and with *Use Contextual Alternates* Selected

A font designer determines the appearance of each character in a font.

A font designer determines the appearance of each character in a font.

Activity 1c Applying a Stylistic Set and Using Contextual Alternates

Part 3 of 5

1. With **1-PRDonorApp.docx** open, select the bulleted text.
2. Display the Font dialog box with the Advanced tab selected.
3. Click the *Stylistic sets* option box arrow and then click *4* at the drop-down list.
4. Click OK to close the dialog box.
5. Select the text *Please call the Phoenix Rising office to let us know if you will be joining us.*
6. Display the Font dialog box with the Advanced tab selected.
7. Click the *Use Contextual Alternates* check box to insert a check mark.

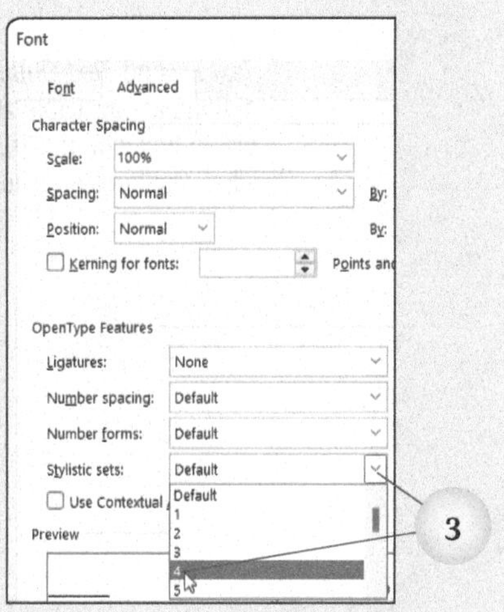

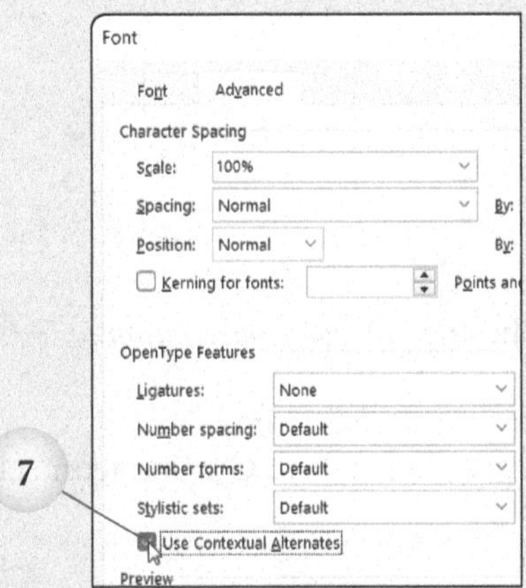

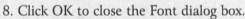

8. Click OK to close the Font dialog box.
9. Save **1-PRDonorApp.docx**.

Check Your Work

Tutorial

Applying Text Effects at the Format Text Effects Dialog Box

Quick Steps

Apply Text Effects

1. Click Font group dialog box launcher.
2. Click Text Effects button.
3. Choose options at Format Text Effects dialog box.
4. Click OK.

Applying Text Effects

Text effects can enhance the look of a document by adding color and interest. Use text effects to create attention-getting flyers and brochures. Or add effects to titles and subtitles to give reports and other documents a more professionally designed look and feel. Click the Text Effects button at the bottom of the Font dialog box with the Advanced tab selected and the Format Text Effects dialog box displays with the Text Fill & Outline icon selected, as shown in Figure 1.7. Click *Text Fill* or *Text Outline* to display the text formatting options. Click the Text Effects icon to display additional effects formatting options. Many of the options available at the dialog box also are available by clicking the Text Effects and Typography button in the Font group on the Home tab.

Figure 1.7 Format Text Effects Dialog Box

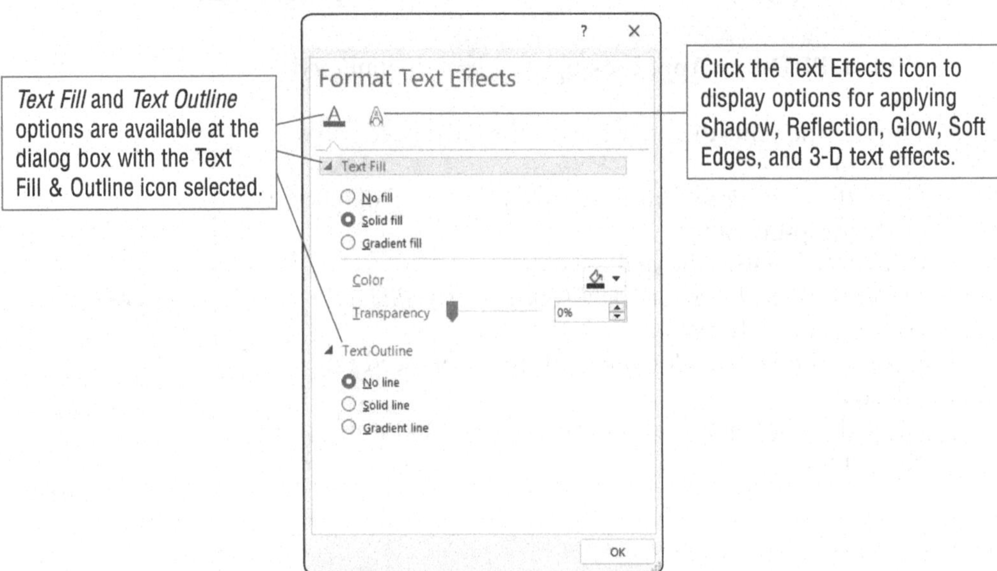

Activity 1d Applying Text Effects

Part 4 of 5

1. With **1-PRDonorApp.docx** open, select the title *Donor Appreciation*.
2. Display the Font dialog box.
3. Click the Text Effects button at the bottom of the dialog box.
4. At the Format Text Effects dialog box with the Text Fill & Outline icon selected, click *Text Fill* to expand the options.
5. Click *Gradient fill* to select the option.
6. Click the Preset gradients button and then click the *Medium Gradient - Accent 6* option (last column, third row).

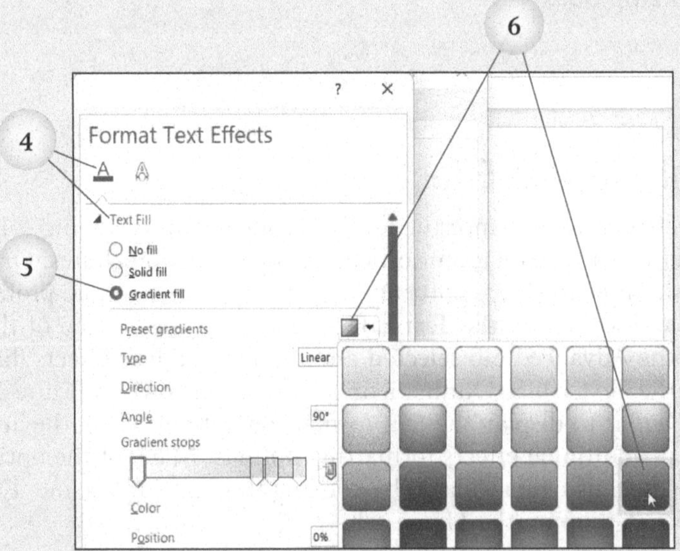

7. Click the Direction button and then click the *Linear Down* option (second column, first row).

8. Scroll down the dialog box and then click *Text Outline* to expand the options.
9. Click *Solid line* to select the option.
10. Click the Color button and then click the *Orange, Accent 6, Darker 50%* option (last column, last row in the *Theme Colors* section).

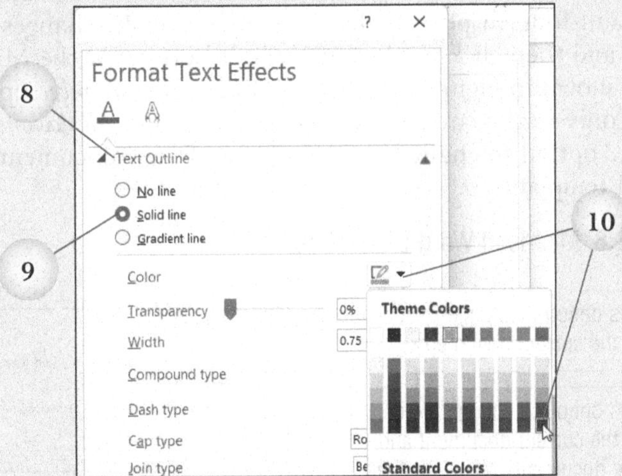

11. Click the Text Effects icon.
12. Click *Shadow* to expand the options.
13. Click the Presets button and then click the *Offset: Left* option (third column, second row in the *Outer* section).

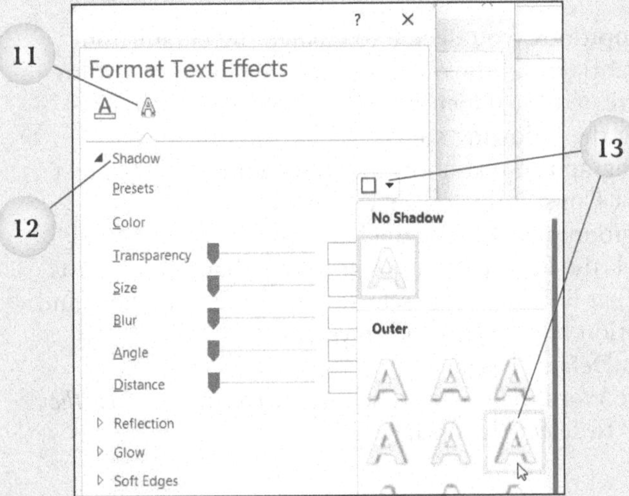

14. Click *Glow* to expand the options.
15. Click the Presets button in the *Glow* section and then click the *Glow: 5 point; Orange, Accent color 6* option (last column, first row in the *Glow Variations* section).
16. Click OK to close the Format Text Effects dialog box.
17. Click OK to close the Font dialog box and then deselect the title.
18. Save **1-PRDonorApp.docx**.

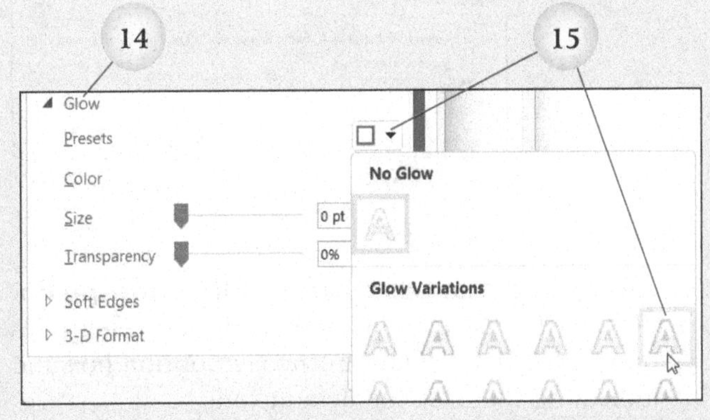

Check Your Work

Changing the Default Font

Quick Steps

Change Default Font

1. Click Font group dialog box launcher.
2. Change font and/or effects.
3. Click Set As Default button.
4. Click *This document only?* or *All documents based on the Normal template?*
5. Click OK.

Changing the Default Font

If documents are generally created with a font other than the default, the default can be changed with the Set As Default button at the Font dialog box. The default font can be changed for the current document or it can be changed in the Normal template, which is the template on which all new documents are based. To change the default font, display the Font dialog box, make changes to the font and/or effects, and then click the Set As Default button. At the Microsoft Word dialog box, as shown in Figure 1.8, click the *This document only?* option to apply the default only to the current document or click the *All documents based on the Normal template?* option to change the default for all new documents based on the default Normal template.

Figure 1.8 Microsoft Word Dialog Box

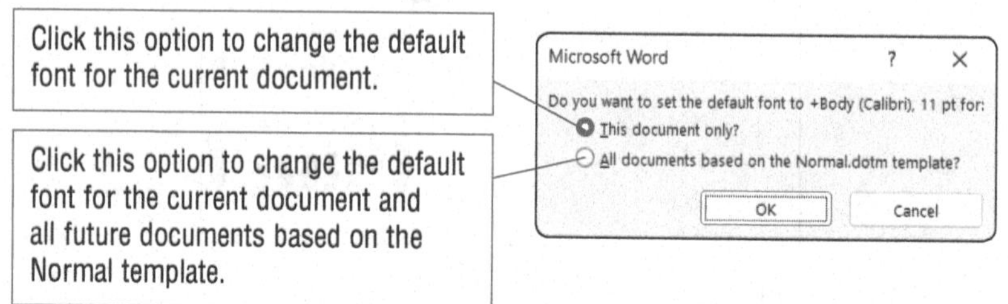

Activity 1e Changing the Default Font

Part 5 of 5

1. For **1-PRDonorApp.docx**, you decide to change the default font to 12-point Constantia in a brown color, since this font is used for most documents created for Phoenix Rising. Change the default font by completing the following steps:
   a. Click in the paragraph of text above the bulleted text. (This text is set in 12-point Constantia and in a brown color.)
   b. Click the Font group dialog box launcher.
   c. If necessary, click the Font tab and then notice that *Constantia* is selected in the *Font* list box, *12* is selected in the *Size* list box, and the *Font color* option box displays a brown color.
   d. Click the Set As Default button.
   e. At the Microsoft Word dialog box, click *All documents based on the Normal template?* to select the option.
   f. Click OK.

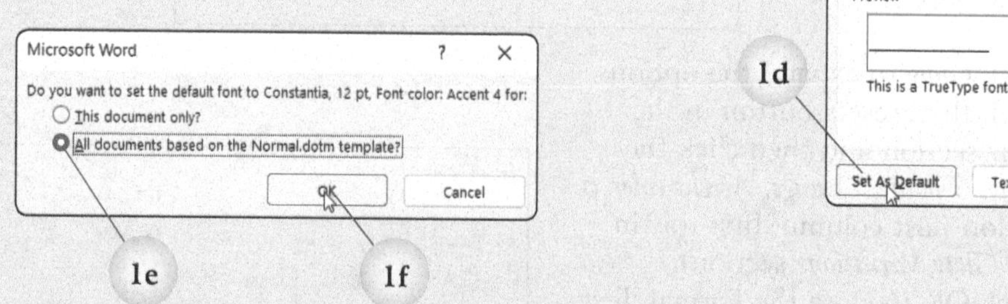

2. Save, preview, and then close **1-PRDonorApp.docx**.
3. Press Ctrl + N to open a new blank document based on the Normal template. Notice that *Constantia* displays in the *Font* option box and *12* displays in the *Font Size* option box, indicating that it is the default font.

4. Change the font back to the original default by completing the following steps:
   a. Click the Font group dialog box launcher.
   b. Scroll up the *Font* list box and then click *+Body*. (This is the original default font, which applies the Calibri font to body text in a document.)
   c. Click *11* in the *Size* list box.
   d. Click the *Font color* option box arrow and then click the *Automatic* option at the top of the drop-down list.
   e. Click the Set As Default button.
   f. At the Microsoft Word dialog box, click the *All documents based on the Normal template?* option.
   g. Click OK.
5. Close the blank document without saving changes.

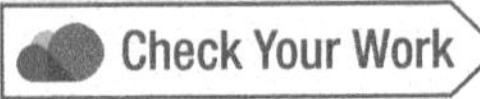

Activity 2 Create a Document with Symbols and Special Characters **3 Parts**

You will create a document that includes intellectual property symbols; nonbreaking, em dash, and en dash hyphens; and nonbreaking spaces.

Inserting Symbols and Special Characters

Symbols and special characters can be inserted in a document with options at the Symbol dialog box with either the Symbols tab or Special Characters tab selected. Display this dialog box by clicking the Insert tab, clicking the Symbol button, and then clicking the *More Symbols* option. Symbols can also be inserted by typing a sequence of characters or by using keyboard shortcuts. Word creates some special characters automatically as text is typed.

Inserting Intellectual Property Symbols

Inserting Intellectual Property Symbols

Among the symbols that can be inserted in a document are three intellectual property protection symbols: ©, ™, and ®. Insert the © symbol to identify copyrighted intellectual property indicating that someone legally owns the rights to make and distribute copies of a particular work; use the ™ symbol to specify a trademark that a company uses for a particular word, phrase, or logo that represents the business; and use the ® symbol to identify a registered trademark that has been granted by the United States Patent and Trademark Office for a word, phrase, or logo for a company's product or service.

Insert these symbols with options at the Symbol dialog box with the Special Characters tab selected, by typing a sequence of characters, or by using a keyboard shortcut. Insert a © symbol by typing (c) or pressing Alt + Ctrl + C, insert a ™ symbol by typing (tm) or pressing Alt + Ctrl + T, and insert a ® symbol by typing (r) or pressing Alt + Ctrl + R.

Activity 2a Inserting Intellectual Property Symbols

Part 1 of 3

1. At a blank document, type the text shown in Figure 1.9. Bold and center the title as shown and insert each intellectual property symbol using the appropriate sequence of characters or keyboard shortcut. To insert the sequence of characters for each symbol rather than the actual symbol, type the sequence of characters and then immediately click the Undo button. This changes the symbol back to the sequence of characters. (The text in your document will wrap differently than what is shown in the figure.)
2. Save the document with the name **1-Symbols**.

Check Your Work

Figure 1.9 Activity 2a

INTELLECTUAL PROPERTY PROTECTION

A copyright protects original works in areas such as publishing, music, literature, and drama. Use the © symbol to identify copyrighted intellectual property. Create this symbol by typing (c), by using the keyboard shortcut Alt + Ctrl + C, or by clicking the symbol at the Symbol dialog box with the Special Characters tab selected.

A trademark identifies a word, symbol, device, or name such as a brand name. Use the ™ symbol to identify a trademarked name or product. Create this symbol by typing (tm), by using the keyboard shortcut Alt + Ctrl + T, or by clicking the symbol at the Symbol dialog box with the Special Characters tab selected.

A registered trademark is a trademark that has been registered with the US Patent and Trademark Office. Use the ® symbol to identify a registered trademark. Create this symbol by typing (r), by using the keyboard shortcut Alt + Ctrl + R, or by clicking the symbol at the Symbol dialog box with the Special Characters tab selected.

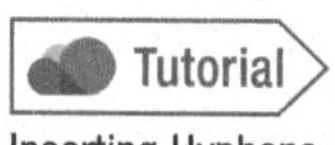

Inserting Hyphens and Nonbreaking Characters

Inserting Hyphens and Dashes

A hyphen (-) is a punctuation mark used to join compound words, such as *fresh-looking* or *sister-in-law*. Use the hyphen key on the keyboard to insert such hyphens. Hyphens can also be used to divide words that fall at the ends of lines. This can create a more even-looking right margin and is especially useful when formatting text in narrow columns.

To hyphenate words that fall at the ends of lines, use the Hyphenation button in the Page Setup group on the Layout tab. This button includes options for automatically or manually hyphenating words that fall at the end of a line. If words are automatically hyphenated, Word inserts an optional hyphen, which displays only when the word is divided across two lines or if the display of nonprinting characters is turned on. If the document is changed so that the word no longer breaks on a line, the hyphen is removed. To control where hyphens appear in words during hyphenation, choose manual rather than automatic hyphenation.

Some text should not be hyphenated and divided across lines. For example, a company name such as *Knowles-Myers Corporation* should not be divided between *Knowles* and *Myers* and set on two lines. To avoid a break like this, insert a nonbreaking hyphen by clicking the *Nonbreaking Hyphen* option at the Symbol dialog box with the Special Characters tab selected or with the keyboard shortcut Ctrl + Shift + -.

An em dash (—) is used to indicate a break in thought or to highlight a term or phrase by separating it from the rest of the sentence. Em dashes are particularly useful in long sentences and sentences with multiple phrases and commas. For example, the sentence "The main focus of this document is on general-purpose, single-user computers—personal computers—that enable users to complete a variety of computing tasks." contains two em dashes: before and after the words *personal computers*.

To create an em dash in a Word document, type a word, type two hyphens, type the next word, and then press the spacebar. When the spacebar is pressed, Word automatically converts the two hyphens to an em dash. If automatic formatting of em dashes is turned off, an em dash can be inserted with the *Em Dash* option at the Symbol dialog box with the Special Characters tab selected or with the keyboard shortcut Alt + Ctrl + - (on the numeric keypad).

Hint An em dash is the width of the capital letter *M* and an en dash is the width of the capital letter *N*.

En dashes (–) are used between inclusive dates, times, and numbers to mean "through." For example, in the text *9:30–11:00 a.m.*, the numbers should be separated by an en dash rather than a regular hyphen. Word does not automatically convert hyphens to en dashes, as it does with em dashes. To create an en dash, click the *En Dash* option at the Symbol dialog box with the Special Characters tab selected or use the keyboard shortcut Ctrl + - (on the numeric keypad).

Activity 2b Inserting Hyphens and Dashes

Part 2 of 3

1. With **1-Symbols.docx** open, press Ctrl + End, press the Enter key, and then type the text shown in Figure 1.10 with the following specifications:
   a. Type an en dash between the times *9:00* and *10:30 a.m.* by pressing Ctrl + - (on the numeric keypad). If you are working on a laptop that does not have a numeric keypad, insert an en dash by clicking the Insert tab, clicking the Symbol button, and then clicking *More Symbols*. At the Symbol dialog box, click the Special Characters tab, click the *En Dash* option, click the Insert button, and then click the Close button.
   b. Create the em dashes before and after the phrase *Excel, PowerPoint, and Access* by typing hyphens (two hyphens for each em dash).
   c. Insert a nonbreaking hyphen within *Tri-State* by pressing Ctrl + Shift + -.
2. Save **1-Symbols.docx**.

Check Your Work

Figure 1.10 Activity 2b

SOFTWARE TRAINING

The Microsoft® 365 Word training is scheduled for Thursday, March 7, 2024, from 9:00–10:30 a.m. Additional training for other applications in the Microsoft suite—Excel, PowerPoint, and Access—will be available during the month of April. Contact the Training Department for additional information. All Tri-State employees are eligible for the training.

Inserting Nonbreaking Spaces

As text is typed in a document, Word makes decisions about where to end lines and automatically wraps text to the beginning of new lines. In some situations, a line may break between two words or phrases that should remain together. To control where text breaks across lines, consider inserting nonbreaking spaces between words that should remain together.

Insert a nonbreaking space with the *Nonbreaking Space* option at the Symbol dialog box with the Special Characters tab selected or with the keyboard shortcut Ctrl + Shift + spacebar. If nonprinting characters are turned on, a normal space displays as a dot and a nonbreaking space displays as a degree symbol.

Activity 2c Inserting Nonbreaking Spaces

Part 3 of 3

1. With **1-Symbols.docx** open, click the Show/Hide ¶ button in the Paragraph group on the Home tab.

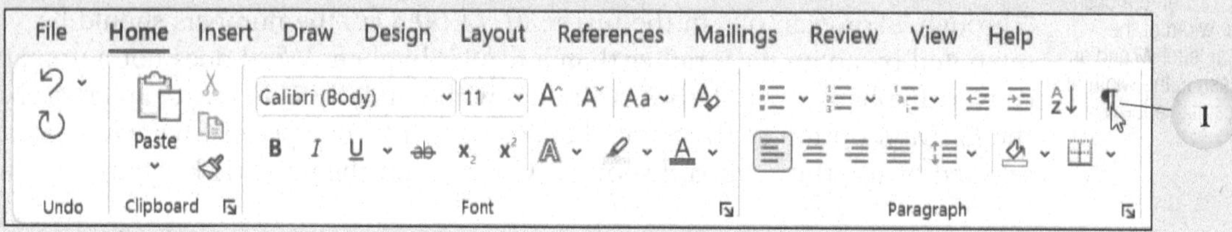

2. Press Ctrl + End, press the Enter key, and then type the text in Figure 1.11. Insert nonbreaking spaces in the keyboard shortcuts by pressing Ctrl + Shift + spacebar before and after each plus (+) symbol.
3. Turn off the display of nonprinting characters.
4. Save, preview, and then close **1-Symbols.docx**.

Figure 1.11 Activity 2c

KEYBOARD SHORTCUTS

Microsoft Word includes a number of keyboard shortcuts you can use to access commands. The ScreenTip for some buttons and options displays the keyboard shortcut for executing the command. Hovering the pointer over the *Font* option box on the Home tab causes the ScreenTip to display Ctrl + Shift + F as the keyboard shortcut. Additional Home tab Font group keyboard shortcuts include Ctrl + B to bold text, Ctrl + I to italicize text, and Ctrl + U to underline text. You can also press Ctrl + Shift + + to turn on superscript and press Ctrl + = to turn on subscript.

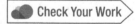

Activity 3 Use Find and Replace Options in a Lease Agreement 5 Parts

You will open a commercial lease agreement; find and replace font formatting, paragraph formatting, special characters, styles, and body and heading fonts; and then find and replace text using a wildcard character.

Using Find and Replace Options

The Find and Replace dialog box can be used to find and replace fonts, special characters, and body and heading fonts. The expanded Find and Replace dialog box contains a *Use wildcards* option. With this option selected, a wildcard character can be used to find specific text or characters in a document. Display the Find and Replace dialog box by clicking the Replace button in the Editing group on the Home tab.

Finding and Replacing Formatting

Finding and Replacing Font Formatting

Use options at the Find and Replace dialog box with the Replace tab selected to search for characters containing specific font formatting and replace them with other characters or font formatting. With the insertion point positioned in the *Find what* text box, specify the font formatting to be found in the document by clicking the More button to expand the dialog box, clicking the Format button in the lower left corner of the dialog box, and then clicking the *Font* option at the drop-down list. At the Find Font dialog box, specify the formatting to be found and then close the dialog box. Click in the *Replace with* text box and then complete similar steps to specify the replacement font formatting.

Finding and Replacing Paragraph Formatting

The Find and Replace dialog box contains options for searching for and replacing specific paragraph formatting. Identify the paragraph formatting to be found in the document by clicking in the *Find what* text box, clicking the Format button in the lower left corner of the dialog box, and then clicking *Paragraph* at the drop-down list. At the Paragraph dialog box, specify the formatting to be found and then close the dialog box. Click in the *Replace with* text box and then complete similar steps to specify the replacement paragraph formatting.

Activity 3a Finding and Replacing Font and Paragraph Formatting Part 1 of 5

1. Open **ComLease.docx** and then save it with the name **1-ComLease**.
2. Find text set in the Corbel font with dark red color and replace it with text set in Constantia with automatic color by completing the following steps:
   a. Click the Replace button in the Editing group on the Home tab.
   b. At the Find and Replace dialog box, click the More button to expand the dialog box.

c. Click in the *Find what* text box, click the Format button in the lower left corner of the dialog box, and then click *Font* at the drop-down list.
d. At the Find Font dialog box, scroll down the *Font* list box and then click *Corbel*.
e. Click the *Font color* option box arrow and then click the *Dark Red* color (first color option in the *Standard Colors* section).
f. Click OK to close the dialog box.
g. Click in the *Replace with* text box.
h. Click the Format button in the lower left corner of the dialog box and then click *Font* at the drop-down list.
i. At the Replace Font dialog box, scroll down the *Font* list box and then click *Constantia*.
j. Click the *Font color* option box arrow and then click the *Automatic* option.
k. Click OK to close the dialog box.
l. At the Find and Replace dialog box, click the Replace All button.
m. At the message indicating 40 replacements were made, click OK.

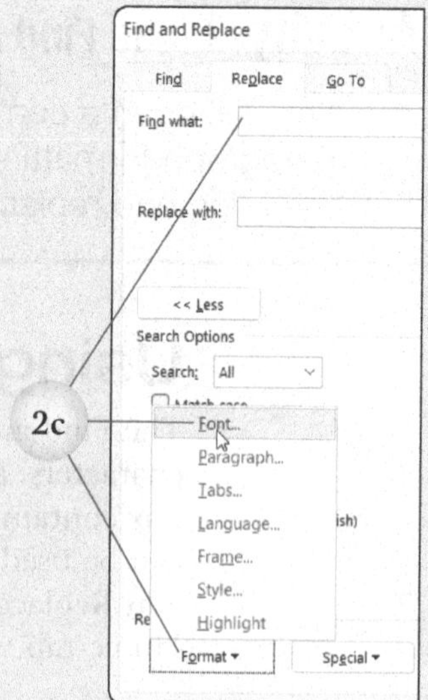

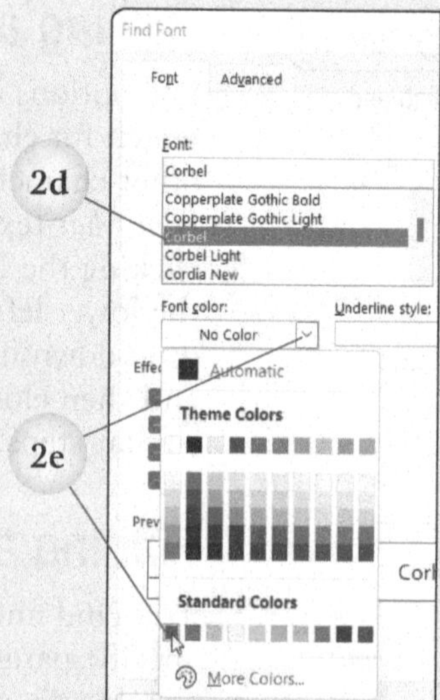

3. With the Find and Replace dialog box open, search for all first-line indents in the document and remove the indents by completing the following steps:
   a. With the insertion point positioned in the *Find what* text box, click the No Formatting button.
   b. Click the Format button and then click *Paragraph* at the drop-down list.
   c. At the Find Paragraph dialog box, click the *Special* option box arrow in the *Indentation* section and then click *First line* at the drop-down list.
   d. Click OK to close the Find Paragraph dialog box.
   e. At the Find and Replace dialog box, click in the *Replace with* text box.
   f. Click the No Formatting button.
   g. Click the Format button and then click *Paragraph* at the drop-down list.
   h. At the Replace Paragraph dialog box, click the *Special* option box arrow in the *Indentation* section and then click *(none)* at the drop-down list.
   i. Click OK to close the Replace Paragraph dialog box.
   j. Click the Replace All button.
   k. At the message indicating 7 replacements were made, click OK.

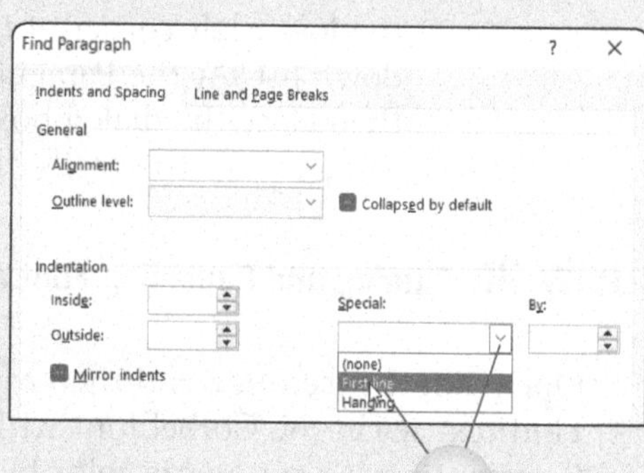

4. Close the Find and Replace dialog box.
5. Save **1-ComLease.docx**.

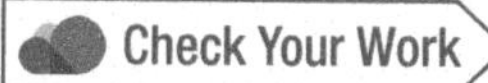

Finding and Replacing Special Characters

Quick Steps

Find and Replace Special Character

1. Click Replace button.
2. Click More button.
3. Click Special button.
4. Click character at drop-down list.
5. Click in *Replace with* text box.
6. Insert replacement character.
7. Click Replace All button.
8. Click OK.

Finding and Replacing Special Characters

Find or find and replace special characters with the Special button at the expanded Find and Replace dialog box. Click the Special button and a drop-down list displays similar to the one shown in Figure 1.12. Click a special character in the drop-down list and a code representing the character is inserted in the text box where the insertion point is positioned. For example, with the insertion point positioned in the *Find what* text box, clicking *Paragraph Mark* at the Special button drop-down list inserts the code ^*p* in the text box. If a character code is known, it can be typed directly in the *Find what* or *Replace with* text box

Figure 1.12 Special Button Drop-Down List

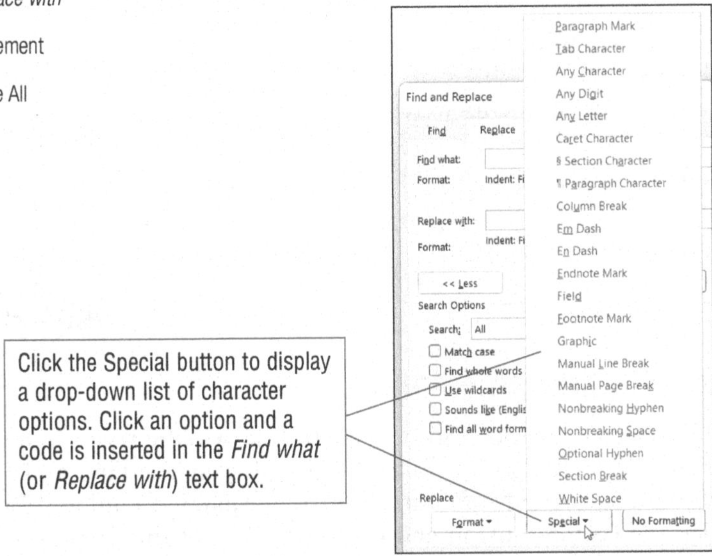

Click the Special button to display a drop-down list of character options. Click an option and a code is inserted in the *Find what* (or *Replace with*) text box.

Activity 3b Finding and Replacing Special Characters

Part 2 of 5

1. With **1-ComLease.docx** open, search for and delete all continuous section breaks by completing the following steps:
   a. Click the Replace button in the Editing group on the Home tab.
   b. If necessary, expand the Find and Replace dialog box.
   c. If formatting information displays below the *Find what* text box, click the No Formatting button.
   d. Click the Special button at the bottom of the dialog box.
   e. Click *Section Break* in the drop-down list. (This inserts ^*b* in the *Find what* text box.)
   f. Click in the *Replace with* text box and make sure the text box is empty. If formatting information displays below the text box, click the No Formatting button.

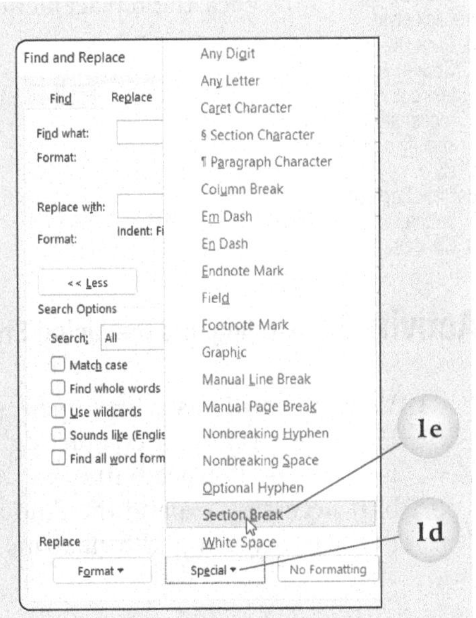

g. Click the Replace All button.
h. At the message indicating 3 replacements were made, click OK.

2. With the expanded Find and Replace dialog box open, find all occurrences of regular hyphens and replace them with nonbreaking hyphens by completing the following steps:
   a. With ^*b* selected in the *Find what* text box, type - (a hyphen).
   b. Press the Tab key to move the insertion point to the *Replace with* text box.
   c. Click the Special button at the bottom of the dialog box.
   d. Click *Nonbreaking Hyphen* at the drop-down list.
   e. Click the Replace All button.
   f. At the message indicating 19 replacements were made, click OK.
   g. Close the Find and Replace dialog box.
3. Save **1-ComLease.docx**.

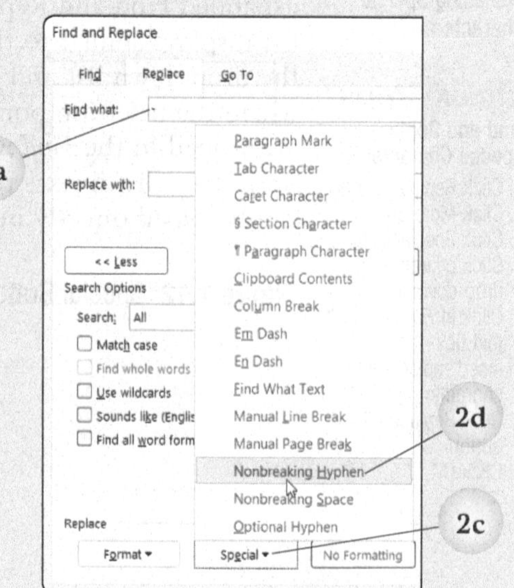

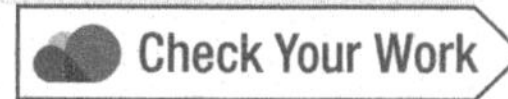

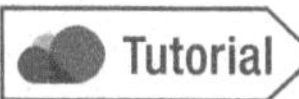

Finding and Replacing Styles

Quick Steps

Find and Replace Style

1. Click Replace button.
2. Click More button.
3. Click Format button.
4. Click *Style*.
5. Click style.
6. Click OK.
7. Click in *Replace with* text box and then repeat steps 3-6 to specify replacement style.
8. Click Replace All button.
9. Click OK.

Finding and Replacing Styles

The Find and Replace dialog box can be used to find specific styles in a document and replace them with other styles. To find styles, display the Find and Replace dialog box and then click the More button. At the expanded Find and Replace dialog box, click the Format button and then click *Style* at the drop-down list. At the Find Style dialog box, click the style in the *Find what style* list box and then click OK. Click in the *Replace with* text box at the Find and Replace dialog box, click the Format button, and then click *Style*. At the Replace Style dialog box, click the replacement style in the *Replace With Style* list box and then click OK.

Activity 3c Finding and Replacing Styles

Part 3 of 5

1. With **1-ComLease.docx** open, search for Heading 3 styles and replace them with Heading 2 styles by completing the following steps:
   a. Click the Replace button in the Editing group on the Home tab.
   b. If necessary, expand the Find and Replace dialog box.
   c. Clear any text and formatting from the *Find what* and *Replace with* text boxes.

d. With the insertion point positioned in the *Find what* text box, click the Format button and then click *Style* at the drop-down list.
e. At the Find Style dialog box, scroll down the *Find what style* list box and then click *Heading 3*.
f. Click OK to close the Find Style dialog box.

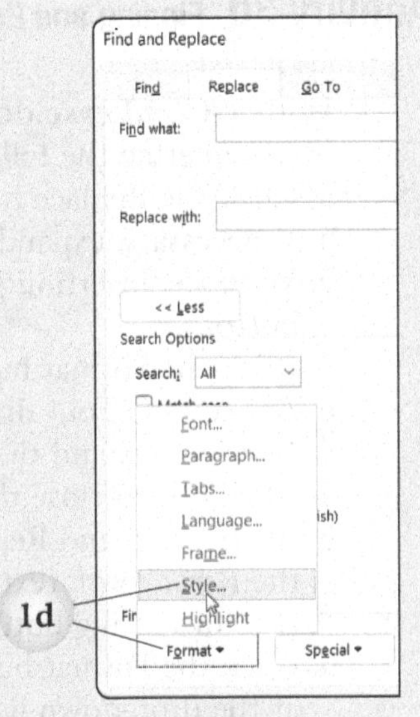

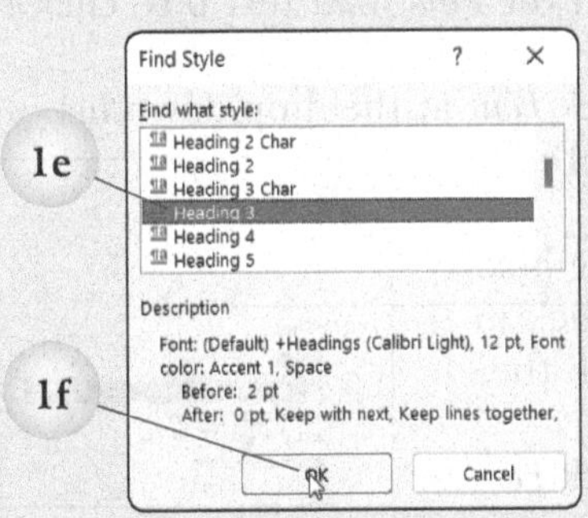

g. At the Find and Replace dialog box, click in the *Replace with* text box.
h. Click the Format button and then click *Style* at the drop-down list.
i. At the Replace Style dialog box, scroll down the *Replace With Style* list box, click *Heading 2*, and then click OK.
j. At the Find and Replace dialog box, click the Replace All button.
k. At the message indicating 6 replacements were made, click OK.
l. Click the Close button to close the Find and Replace dialog box.

2. Save **1-ComLease.docx**.

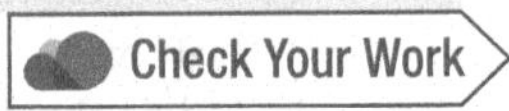

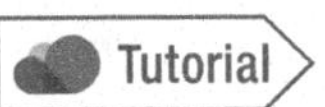

Finding and Replacing Body and Heading Fonts

Quick Steps

Find and Replace Body or Heading Font

1. Click Replace button.
2. Click More button.
3. Click Format button.
4. Click *Font*.
5. Click *+Body* or *+Headings* in *Font* list box.
6. Click OK.
7. Click in *Replace with* text box.
8. Insert replacement font.
9. Click Replace All button.
10. Click OK.

Finding and Replacing Body and Heading Fonts

By default, a Word document has the Office theme applied, which applies the Office set of colors, fonts, and effects. The theme fonts include a body font and heading font. The default settings for theme fonts are *Calibri (Body)* and *Calibri Light (Headings)*. These fonts display at the beginning of the *Font* option box drop-down gallery. If a different theme has been applied, other body and heading fonts will be used; they can be viewed at the *Font* option box drop-down gallery.

A document can be searched for one body or heading font and then replaced with a different font. To do this, display the Find and Replace dialog box with the Replace tab selected. Expand the dialog box, click the Format button, and then click *Font* at the drop-down list. At the Find Font dialog box, scroll up the *Font* list box and then click *+Body* if searching for the body font or click *+Headings* if searching for the heading font. Click in the *Replace with* text box and then complete the steps to insert the replacement font.

Activity 3d Finding and Replacing Body and Heading Fonts

1. With **1-ComLease.docx** open, search for the +Body font and replace it with Constantia by completing the following steps:
   a. Click the Replace button in the Editing group on the Home tab.
   b. If necessary, expand the Find and Replace dialog box.
   c. With the insertion point positioned in the *Find what* text box, click the No Formatting button.
   d. Click the Format button and then click *Font* at the drop-down list.
   e. At the Find Font dialog box, scroll up the *Font* list box and then click *+Body*.
   f. Click OK to close the Find Font dialog box.
   g. At the Find and Replace dialog box, click in the *Replace with* text box and then click the No Formatting button.
   h. Click the Format button and then click *Font* at the drop-down list.
   i. At the Replace Font dialog box, scroll down the *Font* list box and then click *Constantia*.
   j. Click OK to close the Replace Font dialog box.
   k. At the Find and Replace dialog box, click the Replace All button.
   l. At the message indicating 43 replacements were made, click OK.

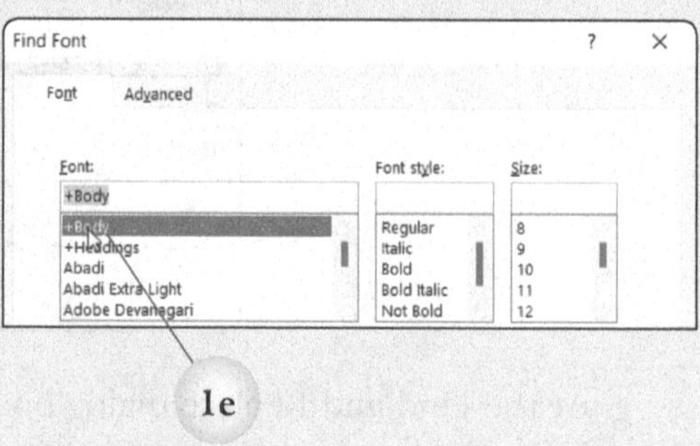

2. With the Find and Replace dialog box open, search for text set in the +Headings font and replace it with text set in 14-point Corbel bold and the standard dark blue color, and then change the paragraph alignment to center alignment by completing the following steps:
   a. With the insertion point positioned in the *Find what* text box, click the No Formatting button.
   b. Click the Format button and then click *Font* at the drop-down list.
   c. At the Find Font dialog box, click *+Headings* in the *Font* list box.
   d. Click OK to close the Find Font dialog box.
   e. At the Find and Replace dialog box, click in the *Replace with* text box.
   f. Click the No Formatting button.
   g. Click the Format button and then click *Font* at the drop-down list.
   h. At the Replace Font dialog box, scroll down and then click *Corbel* in the *Font* list box, click *Bold* in the *Font style* list box, scroll down and then click *14* in the *Size* list box, and click the *Font color* option box arrow and then click the *Dark Blue* option (ninth color option in the *Standard Colors* section).
   i. Click OK to close the Replace Font dialog box.
   j. With the insertion point positioned in the *Replace with* text box at the Find and Replace dialog box, click the Format button and then click *Paragraph* at the drop-down list.

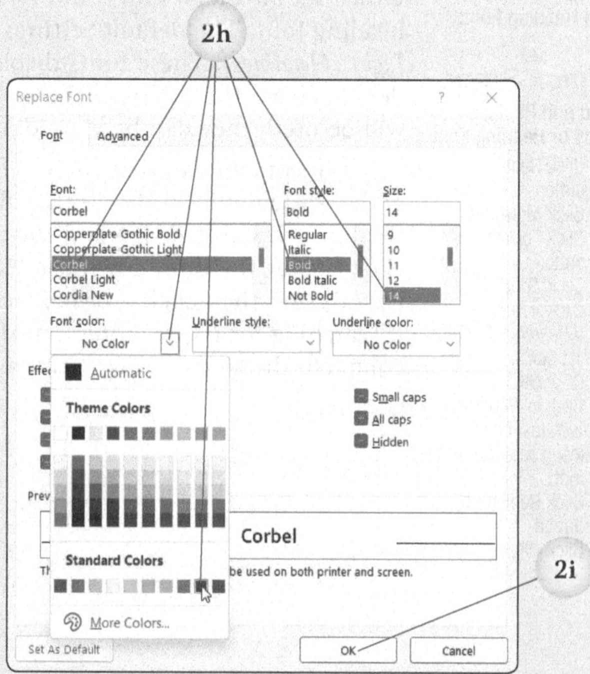

k. At the Replace Paragraph dialog box, click the *Alignment* option box arrow and then click *Centered* at the drop-down list.

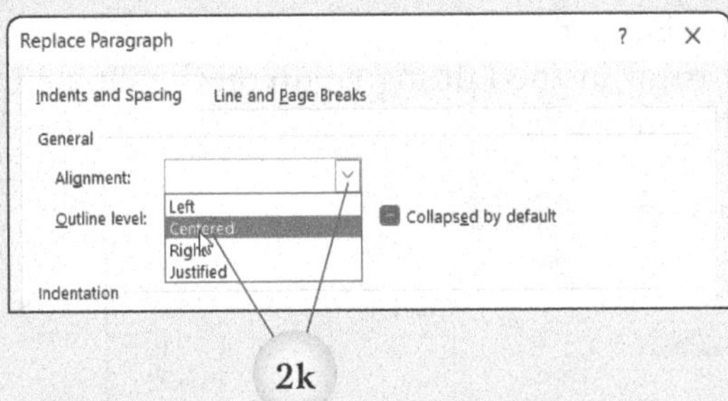

l. Click OK to close the Replace Paragraph dialog box.
m. Click the Replace All button.
n. At the message indicating 7 replacements were made, click OK.

3. Click the Less button and then close the Find and Replace dialog box.
4. Scroll through the document and notice the heading, formatting, and paragraph changes made to the document.
5. Save **1-ComLease.docx**.

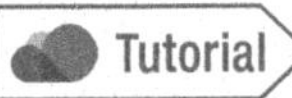

Finding and Replacing Text Using a Wildcard Character

Quick Steps

Find and Replace Text Using Wildcard Character

1. Click Replace button.
2. Click More button.
3. Click *Use wildcards* check box.
4. Click in *Find what* text box.
5. Type find text using wildcard character.
6. Click in *Replace with* text box.
7. Type replacement text.
8. Click Replace All button.
9. Click OK.

Finding and Replacing Using Wildcard Characters

The expanded Find and Replace dialog box contains a *Use wildcards* check box. Insert a check mark in this check box to use wildcard characters in a search to find or find and replace data. For example, suppose the company name *Hansen Products* also mistakenly appears in a document as *Hanson Products*. Both spellings can be found by typing *Hans?n* in the *Find what* text box. Word will find *Hansen* and *Hanson* if the *Use wildcards* check box contains a check mark. If the *Use wildcards* check box does not contain a check mark, Word will try to find the exact spelling *Hans?n* and not find either spelling in the document. Table 1.1 identifies some common wildcard characters along with the functions they perform. For information on additional wildcard characters, use the Help feature.

Table 1.1 Wildcard Characters

Wildcard Character	Function
*	Indicates any characters. For example, type le*s and Word finds *less*, *leases*, and *letters*.
?	Indicates one character. For example, type gr?y and Word finds *gray* and *grey*.
@	Indicates any occurrence of the previous character. For example, type cho@se and Word finds *chose* and *choose*.
<	Indicates the beginning of a word. For example, type <(med) and Word finds *medical*, *medicine*, and *media*.
>	Indicates the ending of a word. For example, type (tion)> and Word finds *election*, *deduction*, and *education*.

Activity 3e Finding and Replacing Using a Wildcard Character

Part 5 of 5

1. With **1-ComLease.docx** open, use a wildcard character to search for words beginning with *leas* by completing the following steps:
   a. Click the Find button arrow in the Editing group on the Home tab and then click *Advanced Find* at the drop-down list.

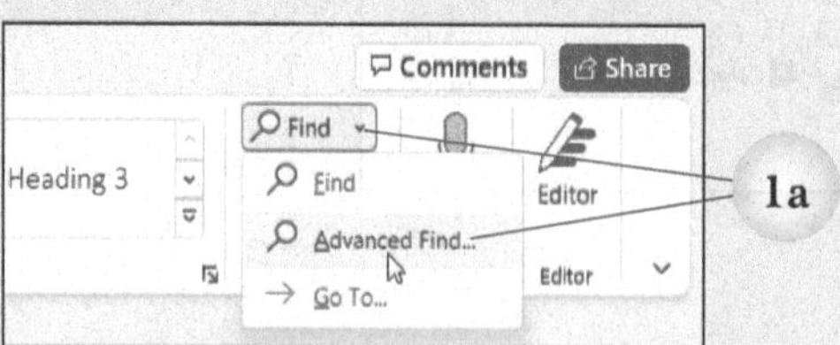

   b. At the Find and Replace dialog box, click the More button.
   c. Click the No Formatting button.
   d. Click the *Use wildcards* check box to insert a check mark.
   e. Click in the *Find what* text box and then type <(leas).
   f. Click the Find Next button to find the first occurrence of a word that begins with *leas*.
   g. Click the Find Next button four more times.
   h. Press the Esc key to end the find and close the Find and Replace dialog box.
2. The name *Arigalason* is spelled a variety of ways in the document. Use a wildcard character to search for all the versions of the name and replace them with the correct spelling by completing the following steps:
   a. Press Ctrl + Home to move the insertion point to the beginning of the document.
   b. Click the Replace button.
   c. At the Find and Replace dialog box, delete the text in the *Find what* text box and then type Ar?galas?n.
   d. Make sure that the dialog box is expanded and that the *Use wildcards* check box contains a check mark.
   e. Press the Tab key.
   f. Click the No Formatting button.
   g. Type Arigalason (the correct spelling) in the *Replace with* text box.
   h. Click the Replace All button.

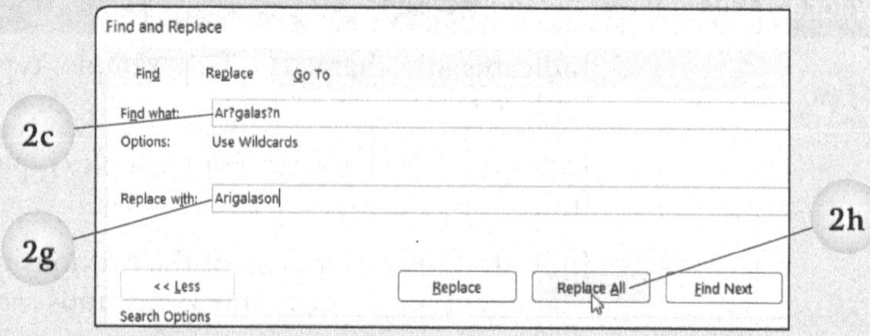

   i. At the message indicating that 23 replacements were made, click OK.
3. Close the Find and Replace dialog box.
4. Save, preview, and then close **1-ComLease.docx**.

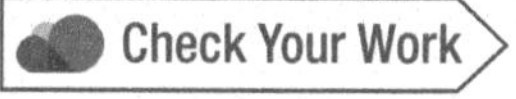

Activity 4 Insert Properties and Inspect a Document — 4 Parts

You will open a document (an advertising flyer), insert document properties, inspect the document and remove specific elements, and then check the compatibility and accessibility of the document.

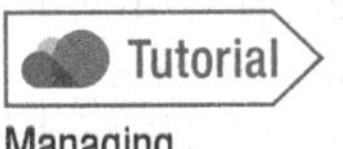

Managing Document Properties

Managing Document Properties

Every document has properties associated with it, such as the type of document, the location in which it has been saved, and when it was created, modified, and accessed. Document properties can be viewed and modified at the Info backstage area. To display information about the open document, click the File tab and then click the *Info* option. Document property information displays at the right side of the Info backstage area, as shown in Figure 1.13.

The document property information at the Info backstage area includes the file size, number of pages and words, total editing time, and any tags or comments that have been added. Some properties, such as the title, tags, or comments, may be edited. Hover over the property and a rectangular text box with a light blue border displays. Click inside the text box to type or edit information. In the *Related Dates* section, dates display for when the document was created and when it was last modified and printed. The *Related People* section includes the name of the author of the document and provides options for adding additional author names. Display additional document properties by clicking the Show All Properties hyperlink.

Figure 1.13 Info Backstage Area

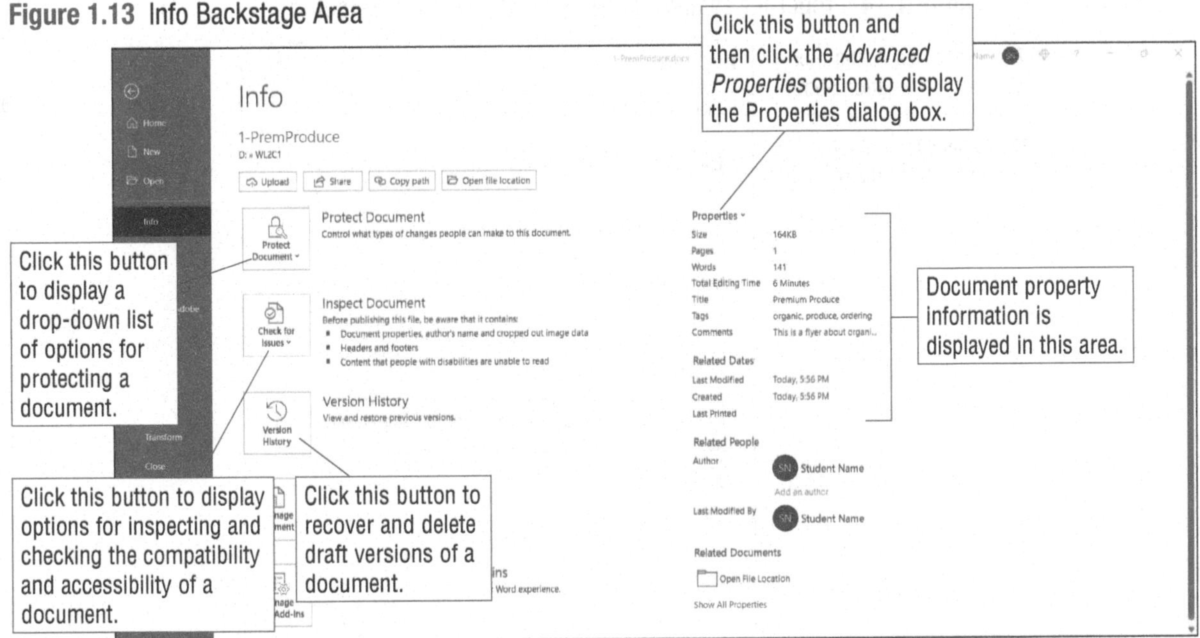

Quick Steps

Display Properties Dialog Box

1. Click File tab.
2. Click *Info* option.
3. Click Properties button.
4. Click *Advanced Properties*.

In addition to adding or updating document property information at the Info backstage area, specific information about a document can be viewed, added, edited, and customized with options at the Properties dialog box, shown in Figure 1.14. Open the dialog box by displaying the Info backstage area, clicking the Properties button, and then clicking *Advanced Properties* at the drop-down list.

The Properties dialog box with the General tab selected displays information about the document type, size, and location. Click the Summary tab to view fields such as *Title*, *Subject*, *Author*, *Company*, *Category*, *Keywords*, and *Comments*. Some fields may contain data and others may be blank. Insert, edit, or delete text in the fields. With the Statistics tab selected, information displays such as the number of pages, paragraphs, lines, words, and characters. With the Contents tab selected, the dialog box displays the document title. Click the Custom tab to add custom properties to the document. For example, a property can be added that displays the date the document was completed, information on the department in which the document was created, and much more.

Another method for displaying document properties is to display the Open dialog box, click the document in the Content pane, click the Organize button, and then click *Properties* at the drop-down list. Or right-click the file name in the Content pane and then click *Properties* at the shortcut menu. The Properties dialog box that displays contains the tabs General, Security, Details, and Previous Versions. Some of the information in this Properties dialog box is the same as the information in the Properties dialog box that is accessed through the Info backstage area, while some of the information is different. Generally, consider using the Properties dialog box accessed through the Info backstage area to add, edit, and create custom properties and use the Properties dialog box accessed through the Open dialog box to view document properties.

Figure 1.14 Properties Dialog Box with the General Tab Selected

The Properties dialog box displays information about the document. Click each tab to display additional document information.

Properties ? ×

General Summary Statistics Contents Custom

1-PremProduce.docx

Type: Microsoft Word Document
Location: D:\WL2C1
Size: 164KB (168,676 bytes)

MS-DOS name: 1-PREM~1.DOC
Created: Monday, December 27, 2021 5:56:39 PM
Modified: Monday, December 27, 2021 5:56:40 PM
Accessed: Monday, December 27, 2021

Attributes: Read only Hidden Archive System

OK Cancel

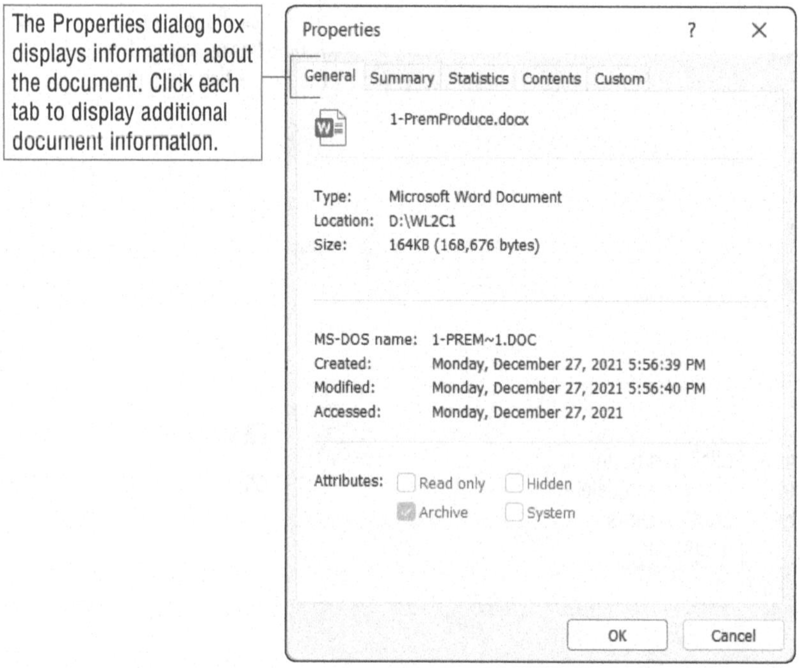

Activity 4a Inserting Document Properties

1. Open **PremProduce.docx** and then save it with the name **1-PremProduce**.
2. Insert document properties by completing the following steps:
   a. Click the File tab and then click the *Info* option.
   b. Hover the pointer over the text *Add a title* at the right of the *Title* document property, click in the text box, and then type Premium Produce.
   c. Display the Properties dialog box by clicking the Properties button and then clicking *Advanced Properties* at the drop-down list.

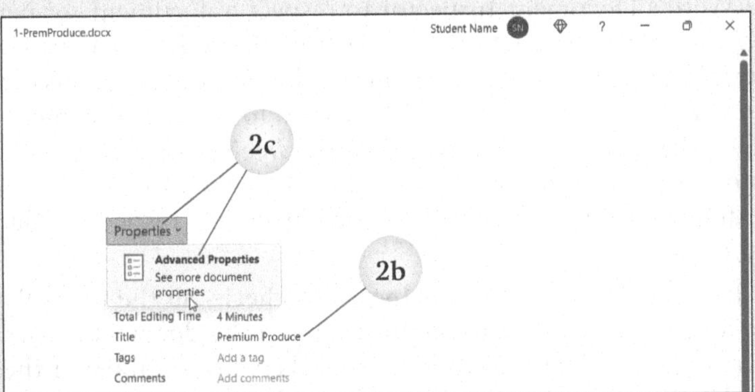

   d. At the Properties dialog box with the Summary tab selected, press the Tab key to make the *Subject* text box active and then type Organic produce.
   e. Click in the *Category* text box and then type Premium Produce flyer.
   f. Press the Tab key and then type the following words, separated by commas, in the *Keywords* text box: organic, produce, ordering.
   g. Press the Tab key and then type the following text in the *Comments* text box: This is a flyer about organic produce and the featured produce of the month.
   h. Click OK to close the dialog box.

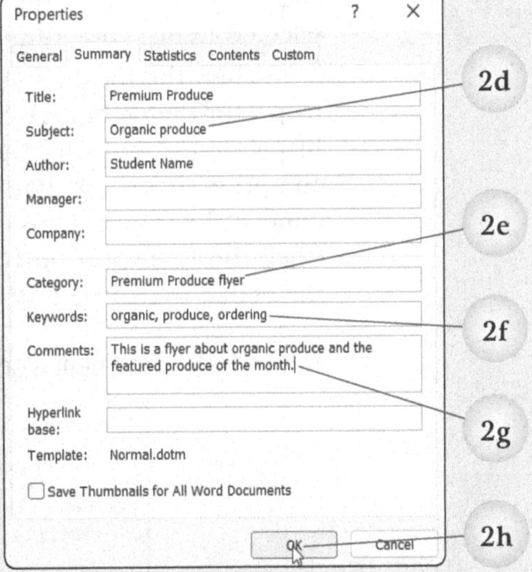

3. Click the Back button to return to the document.
4. Save **1-PremProduce.docx**.
5. Print only the document properties by completing the following steps:
   a. Click the File tab and then click the *Print* option.
   b. At the Print backstage area, click the first gallery in the *Settings* category and then click *Document Info* at the drop-down list.
   c. Click the Print button.
6. Save **1-PremProduce.docx**.

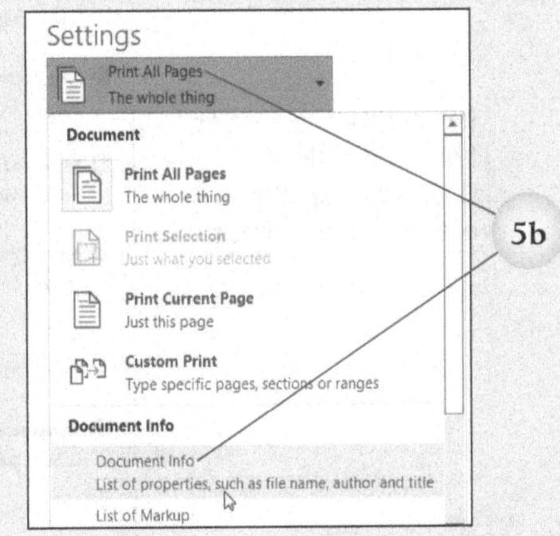

Check Your Work

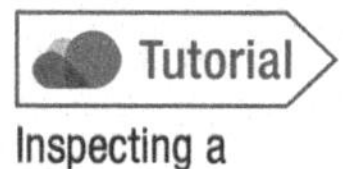

Inspecting a Document

Inspecting Documents

Use options from the Check for Issues button drop-down list at the Info backstage area to inspect a document for personal and hidden data along with compatibility and accessibility issues. Click the Check for Issues button at the Info backstage area and a drop-down list displays with the options *Inspect Document*, *Check Accessibility*, and *Check Compatibility*.

Using the Document Inspector

Check for Issues

Use Word's Document Inspector to inspect a document for personal data, hidden data, and metadata (data that describes other data, such as document properties). In certain situations, some personal or hidden data may need to be removed before a document is shared with others. To check a document for personal and hidden data, click the File tab, click the *Info* option, click the Check for Issues button at the Info backstage area, and then click the *Inspect Document* option at the drop-down list. This displays the Document Inspector dialog box, shown in Figure 1.15.

By default, the Document Inspector checks all the items listed in the dialog box. To control what items are inspected in the document, remove the check marks preceding items that should not be checked. For example, if the headers and footers in a document do not need to be checked, click the *Headers, Footers, and Watermarks* check box to remove the check mark. To scan the document to check for the selected items, click the Inspect button at the bottom of the dialog box.

When the inspection is complete, the results display in the Document Inspector dialog box. A check mark before an option indicates that the Document Inspector did not find the specific items. If an exclamation point displays before an option, it means that the items were found and a list of the items displays. To remove the found items, click the Remove All button at the right of the option. Click the Reinspect button to ensure that the specific items were removed and then click the Close button.

Figure 1.15 Document Inspector Dialog Box

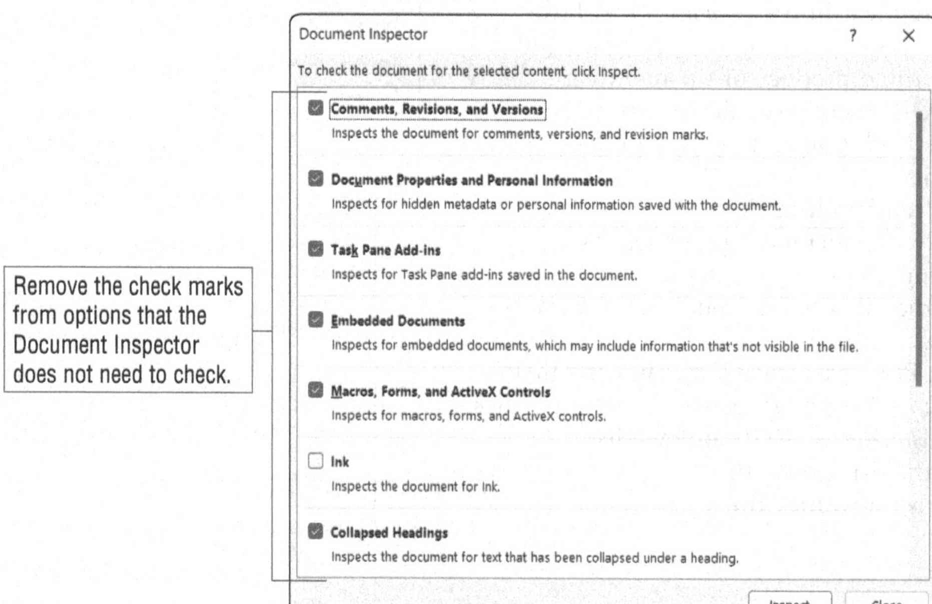

Activity 4b Inspecting a Document

1. With **1-PremProduce.docx** open, type and then hide text by completing the following steps:
   a. Press Ctrl + Home to move the insertion point to the beginning of the document and then type Before distributing the flyer, make sure the Pricing link is active.
   b. Select the text you just typed.
   c. Click the Home tab, if necessary.
   d. Click the Font group dialog box launcher.
   e. At the Font dialog box with the Font tab selected, click the *Hidden* check box in the *Effects* section to insert a check mark.
   f. Click OK to close the dialog box.

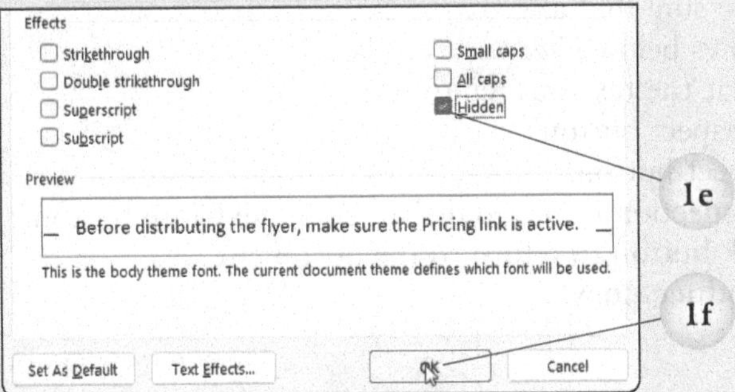

2. Click the Save button on the Title bar.
3. Inspect the document by completing the following steps (this document contains a watermark, a footer, document properties, and hidden text):
   a. Click the File tab and then click the *Info* option.
   b. Click the Check for Issues button at the Info backstage area and then click *Inspect Document* at the drop-down list.
   c. At the Document Inspector dialog box, specify not to check the document for collapsed headings by clicking the *Collapsed Headings* check box to remove the check mark.
   d. Click the Inspect button.

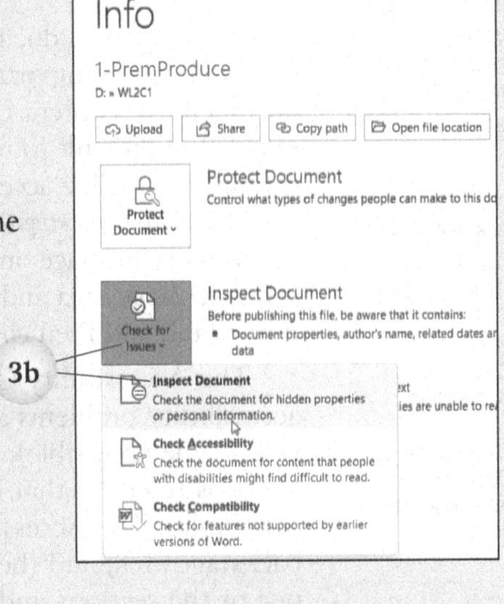

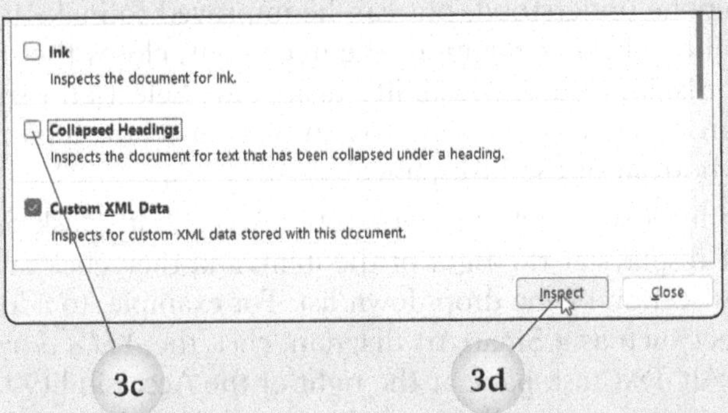

   e. Notice that the results show the document contains document properties and personal information. Scroll down the list box showing the inspection results and notice that the results show that the document also contains a header, a footer, and hidden text.

f. Remove the footer and watermark by clicking the Remove All button at the right of the *Headers, Footers, and Watermarks* section. (Make sure that a message displays below *Headers, Footers, and Watermarks* stating that the text was removed.)
g. Remove the hidden text by clicking the Remove All button at the right of the *Hidden Text* section. (Make sure that a message displays below *Hidden Text* stating that the text was removed.)
h. Click the Reinspect button.
i. Click the Inspect button.
j. Review the inspection results and then click the Close button.
k. Click the Back button to return to the document.

4. Save **1-PremProduce.docx**.

Checking for Accessibility and Compatibility Issues

Quick Steps

Check Accessibility

1. Click File tab.
2. Click *Info* option.
3. Click Check for Issues button.
4. Click *Check Accessibility*.

OR

1. Click Review tab.
2. Click Check Accessibility button.

Checking for Accessibility Issues

When preparing a document, making sure the content is accessible to people of all abilities is important. Word provides the Accessibility Checker to check a document for content that a person with disabilities (such as a visual impairment) might find difficult to read or understand using assistive technology. If a document contains a possible accessibility issue, a message will display on the Status bar such as *Accessibiltiy: Investigate*. Check the accessibility of a document by clicking the accessibility message on the Status bar or clicking the Check for Issues button at the Info backstage area and then clicking *Check Accessibility*. Another option is to click the Review tab and then click the Check Accessibility button in the Accessibility group.

The Accessibility Checker examines the document for the most common accessibility problems and sorts them into three categories: errors (content that will not be accessible); warnings (content that may be difficult to understand); and tips (content that may be understood, but can be improved to make it more accessible). The Accessibility Checker examines the document, closes the Info backstage area, and then displays the Accessibility task pane. Select an issue in one of the sections and an explanation of why it is an issue and how it can be corrected displays at the bottom of the task pane.

To correct an accessibility issue, click the item in the Accessibility task pane, click the down arrow that displays at the right of the item, and then click an option in the *Recommended Actions* section of the drop-down list. For example, to add alternative text to an object such as a SmartArt diagram, click the *Add a description* option. This displays the Alt Text task pane at the right of the Accessibility task pane. Click in the Alt Text task pane text box and then type a description of the object. If a person with a visual impairment uses a screen reader to hear a reading of the document, the screen reader will read the text in the Alt Text text box describing the item. Microsoft includes the Intelligent Services feature that will generate an alternative description for an object such as a picture or clip art. When checking accessibility, verify the generated text or create new alternative text.

Activity 4c Checking for Accessibility Issues

1. With **1-PremProduce.docx** open, conduct an accessibility check by completing the following steps:
   a. Click the File tab and then click the *Info* option.
   b. At the Info backstage area, click the Check for Issues button and then click *Check Accessibility* at the drop-down list.
   c. Notice the Accessibility task pane at the right side of the screen, which contains an *Errors* section.
   d. Click the *Missing alternative text (2)* option to expand it.
   e. Click *Picture 2* in the *Errors* section and then read the information at the bottom of the task pane describing why the error should be fixed and how to fix it.

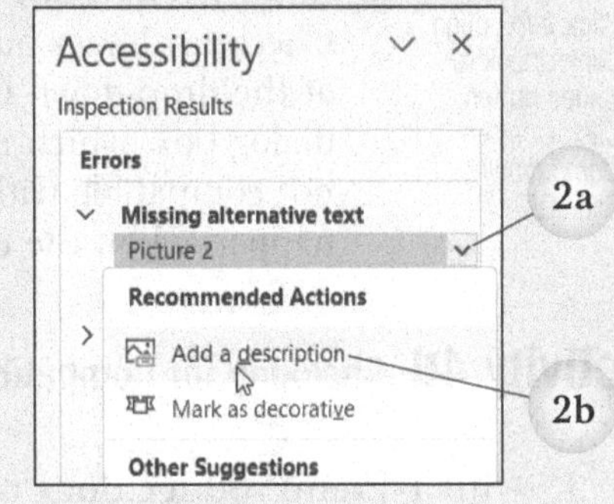

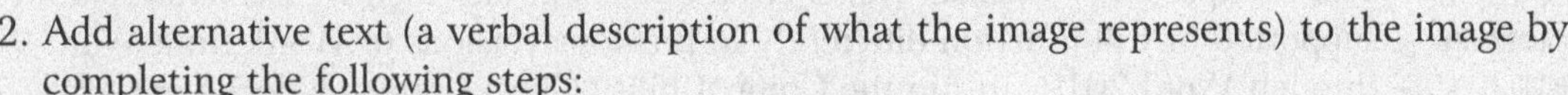

2. Add alternative text (a verbal description of what the image represents) to the image by completing the following steps:
   a. Click the down arrow at the right of *Picture 2*.
   b. Click the *Add a description* option at the drop-down list. (This displays the Alt Text task pane and the Accessibility task pane is reduced to a button at the right side of the Alt Text task pane.)
   c. At the Alt Text task pane, type Image of fruits and vegetables representing Premium Produce. in the text box.
3. Expand the Accessibility task pane by clicking the Accessibility button at the right side of the Alt Text task pane.

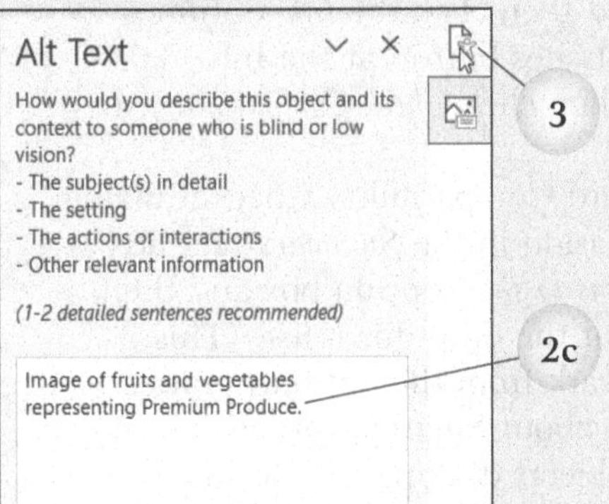

4. Hover the pointer over *Diagram 1* below *Missing alternative text*, click the down arrow at the right of the option, and then click *Add a description* at the drop-down list.
5. Type SmartArt graphic indicating no pesticides, no herbicides, and organically grown produce. in the Alt Text task pane text box.
6. Close the Alt Text task pane.
7. At the Accessibility task pane, click the *Image or object not inline* option to expand it.

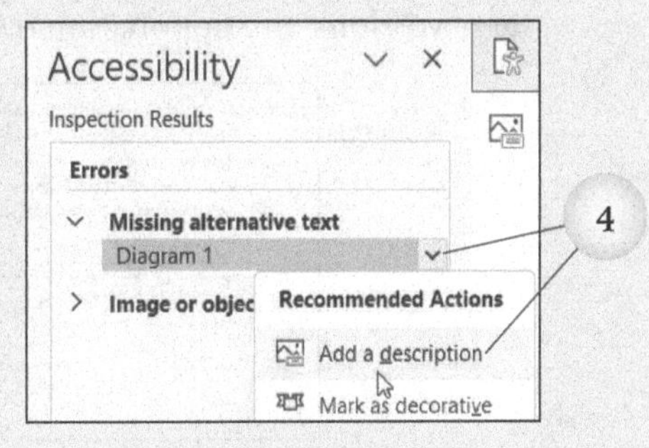

8. Hover the pointer over *Diagram 1* and then click the down arrow.
9. Click *Place this inline* at the drop-down list. (This changes the text wrapping of the SmartArt to *In Line with Text*.)
10. Close the Accessibility task pane.
11. Save **1-PremProduce.docx**.

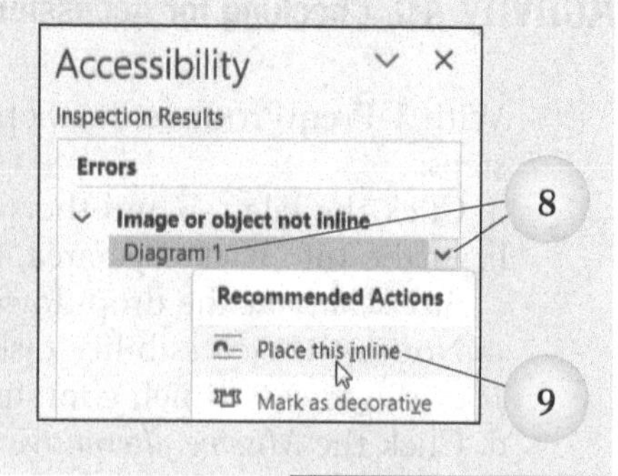

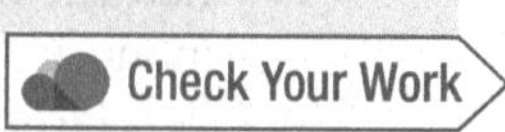

Checking for Compatibility Issues

Quick Steps

Check Compatibility

1. Click File tab.
2. Click *Info* option.
3. Click Check for Issues button.
4. Click *Check Compatibility*.
5. Click OK.

The Compatibility Checker will check a document and identify elements that are not supported or will function differently in previous versions of Word, from Word 97 through Word 2010. To run the Compatibility Checker, open a document, click the Check for Issues button at the Info backstage area, and then click *Check Compatibility* at the drop-down list. This displays the Microsoft Word Compatibility Checker dialog box, which includes a summary of the elements in the document that are not compatible with previous versions of Word. This box also indicates what will happen when the document is saved and then opened in a previous version.

Activity 4d Checking for Compatibility Issues — Part 4 of 4

1. With **1-PremProduce.docx** open, check the compatibility of elements in the document by completing the following steps:
   a. Click the File tab and then click the *Info* option.
   b. Click the Check for Issues button at the Info backstage area and then click *Check Compatibility* at the drop-down list.
   c. At the Microsoft Word Compatibility Checker dialog box, read the information in the *Summary* text box.
   d. Click the *Select versions to show* option box and then click *Word 97-2003* at the drop-down list. (This removes the check mark from the option.) Notice that the information about SmartArt graphics being converted to static objects disappears from the *Summary* text box. This is because Word 2007 and later versions all support SmartArt graphics.

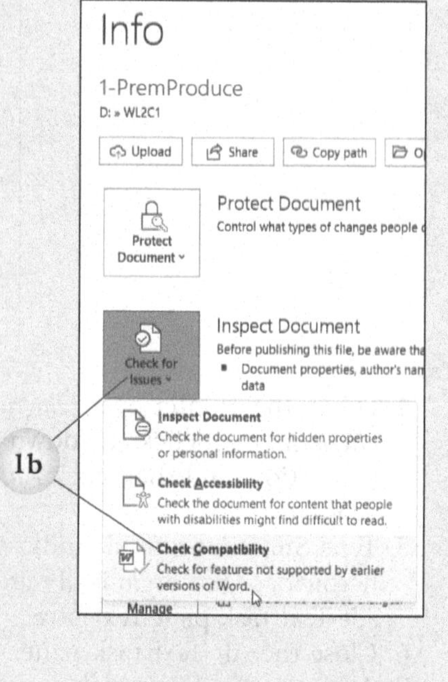

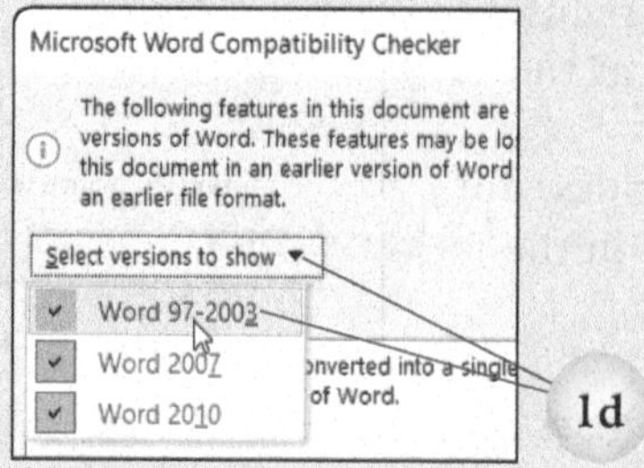

   e. Click OK to close the dialog box.

2. Save the document in Word 2003 format by completing the following steps:
   a. Press the F12 function key to display the Save As dialog box with WL2C1 the active folder.
   b. At the Save As dialog box, click the *Save as type* option box and then click *Word 97-2003 Document (*.doc)* at the drop-down list.
   c. Select the text in the *File name* text box and then type 1-PremProduce-2003format.
   d. Click the Save button.

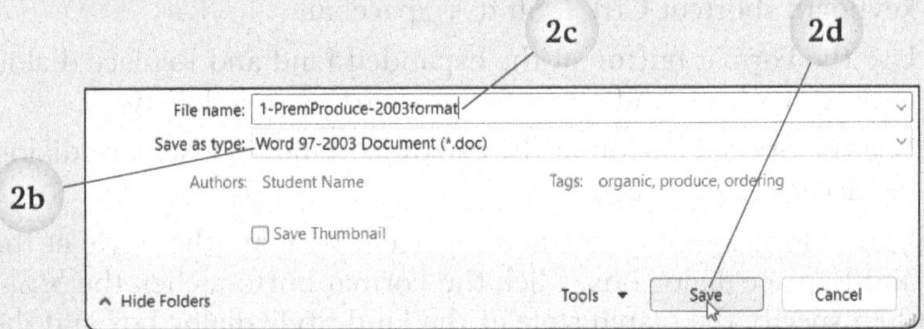

   e. Click the Continue button at the Microsoft Word Compatibility Checker dialog box.
3. Close **1-PremProduce-2003format.doc.**

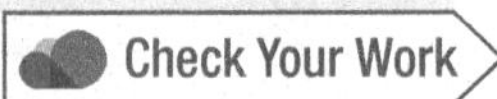

Chapter Summary

- Use options in the *Character Spacing* section of the Font dialog box with the Advanced tab selected to adjust character spacing and turn on kerning.
- The OpenType features available at the Font dialog box with the Advanced tab selected include options for choosing a ligature style, specifying number spacing and form, and applying stylistic sets.
- The Text Effects and Typography button in the Font group on the Home tab contains options for applying text effects such as outline, shadow, reflection, and glow effects as well as typography options such as number styles, ligatures, and stylistic sets.
- Click the Text Effects button at the Font dialog box to display the Format Text Effects dialog box. Use options at this dialog box to apply text fill and text outline effects to selected text.
- Change the default font with the Set As Default button at the Font dialog box. The default font can be changed for the current document or all new documents based on the Normal template.
- Use the © symbol to identify copyrighted intellectual property, use the ™ symbol to identify a trademark, and use the ® symbol to identify a registered trademark.
- Insert a nonbreaking hyphen by clicking the *Nonbreaking Hyphen* option at the Symbol dialog box with the Special Characters tab selected or by using the keyboard shortcut Ctrl + Shift + -.
- Use an em dash to indicate a break in thought or to highlight a term or phrase by separating it from the rest of the sentence. Insert an em dash by typing a word, typing two hyphens, typing the next word, and then pressing the spacebar. An em dash can also be inserted with the keyboard shortcut Alt + Ctrl + - (on the numeric keypad) or at the Symbol dialog box with the Special Characters tab selected.

- Use an en dash to indicate inclusive dates, times, and numbers. To insert an en dash, click the *En Dash* option at the Symbol dialog box with the Special Characters tab selected or use the keyboard short Ctrl + - (on the numeric keypad).
- Insert nonbreaking spaces between words that should not be separated across a line break. Insert a nonbreaking space by clicking the *Nonbreaking Space* option at the Symbol dialog box with the Special Characters tab selected or with the keyboard shortcut Ctrl + Shift + spacebar.
- Use the Format button at the expanded Find and Replace dialog box to find and replace character and paragraph formatting in a document.
- Use the Special button at the expanded Find and Replace dialog box to find and replace special characters.
- Search for a specific style and replace it with another style at the expanded Find and Replace dialog box. Click the Format button, click the *Style* option, and then specify the search style at the Find Style dialog box and the replacement style at the Replace Style dialog box.
- A Word document contains a body font and a heading font. A document can be searched to find a body or heading font and replace it with a different font.
- Wildcard characters can be used to find text in a document. To use a wildcard, display the expanded Find and Replace dialog box and then click the *Use wildcards* check box to insert a check mark.
- Document properties can be viewed and modified at the Info backstage area and at the Properties dialog box. Display the Properties dialog box by clicking the Properties button at the Info backstage area and then clicking *Advanced Properties* at the drop-down list.
- Inspect a document for personal data, hidden data, and metadata with options at the Document Inspector dialog box. Display this dialog box by clicking the Check for Issues button at the Info backstage area and then clicking *Inspect Document* at the drop-down list.
- The Accessibility Checker checks a document for content that a person with disabilities might find difficult to read or understand with the use of assistive technology. Run the Accessibility Checker by clicking the Check for Issues button at the Info backstage area and then clicking *Check Accessibility* at the drop-down list, by clicking the accessibility message on the Status bar, or by clicking the Review tab and then clicking the Check Accessibility button.
- Run the Compatibility Checker to check a document and identify elements that are not supported or that will function differently in previous versions of Word. Run the Compatibility Checker by clicking the Check for Issues button at the Info backstage area and then clicking *Check Compatibility* at the drop-down list.

Commands Review

FEATURE	RIBBON TAB, GROUP/OPTION	BUTTON, OPTION	KEYBOARD SHORTCUT
Accessibility Checker	File, *Info*	, *Check Accessibility*	
Compatibility Checker	File, *Info*	, *Check Compatibility*	
copyright symbol	Insert, Symbols	, *More Symbols*	Alt + Ctrl + C
Document Inspector dialog box	File, *Info*	, *Inspect Document*	
em dash	Insert, Symbols	, *More Symbols*	Alt + Ctrl + - (on numeric keypad)
en dash	Insert, Symbols	, *More Symbols*	Ctrl + - (on numeric keypad)
Find and Replace dialog box	Home, Editing	, *Replace*	Ctrl + H
Font dialog box	Home, Font		Ctrl + D
nonbreaking hyphen	Insert, Symbols	, *More Symbols*	Ctrl + Shift + -
nonbreaking space	Insert, Symbols	, *More Symbols*	Ctrl + Shift + spacebar
Properties dialog box	File, *Info*	Properties, *Advanced Properties*	
registered trademark symbol	Insert, Symbols	, *More Symbols*	Alt + Ctrl + R
Symbol dialog box	Insert, Symbols	, *More Symbols*	
Text Effects and Typography button	Home, Font		
trademark symbol	Insert, Symbols	, *More Symbols*	Alt + Ctrl + T

Review and Assessment

CHAPTER 1

Skills Assessment

Assessment 1
Apply Character Spacing and OpenType Features to a Donations Document

1. Open **PRDonations.docx** and then save it with the name **1-PRDonations**.
2. Select the quote text *"In every community there is work to be done. In every nation there are wounds to heal. In every heart there is the power to do it."* and then apply stylistic set 4. (Do this at the Font dialog box with the Advanced tab selected.)
3. Select the heading *Domestic Donations* and change the scale to 90% and the spacing to Expanded. (Do this at the Font dialog box with the Advanced tab selected.)
4. Apply the same formatting in Step 3 to the heading *International Donations*.
5. Select the numbers in the *Domestic Donations* section. ***Hint: To select only the numbers, position the pointer at the beginning of $450,000, press and hold down the Alt key, use the pointer to drag down and select the four numbers in the second column, and then release the Alt key.***
6. With the numbers selected, change the number spacing to Tabular spacing. (Do this at the Font dialog box with the Advanced tab selected.)
7. Select the numbers in the *International Donations* section and then change the number spacing to Tabular spacing.
8. Select the text *We are dedicated to working toward a more just and peaceful world.* and then insert a check mark in the *Use Contextual Alternates* check box at the Font dialog box with the Advanced tab selected.
9. Save, preview, and then close **1-PRDonations.docx**.

Assessment 2
Find and Replace Formatting and Use a Wildcard Character in an Employee Guide Document

1. Open **EmpGuide.docx** and then save it with the name **1-EmpGuide**.
2. Find text set in the +Headings font and replace the font with Candara.
3. Find text set in the +Body font and replace the font with Constantia.
4. Find text set in 11-point Candara and replace it with 12-point Candara italic.
5. Using a wildcard charcter, find all occurrences of *Ne?land?Davis* and replace them with *Newland-Davis*.
6. Select the title *Newland-Davis Medical* and then change the scale option to 150% and the spacing option to Expanded. (Do this at the Font dialog box with the Advanced tab selected.)
7. Save, preview, and then close **1-EmpGuide.docx**.

Assessment 3

Replace Special Characters, Insert Document Properties, and Inspect and Check the Accessibility of a First Aid Training Flyer

1. Open **FirstAidTraining.docx** and then save it with the name **1-FirstAidTraining**.
2. Move the insertion point immediately right of *Health* in the subtitle *Sponsored by Frontline Health* and then insert a trademark symbol.
3. Search for all occurrences of hyphens and replace them with nonbreaking hyphens.
4. Search for all occurrences of em dashes and replace them with en dashes.
5. Display the Info backstage area and then type First Aid Training in the *Title* document property text box.
6. Display the Properties dialog box and then type the following in each specified document property:
   a. Subject: Training
   b. Company: Tri-State Products
   c. Keywords: first aid, training, CPR
7. Save the document and then inspect the document and remove headers, footers, and watermarks.
8. Complete an accessibility check and then insert alternative text for the picture image by typing Stethoscope image in the text box in the Alt Text task pane. Position the picture image inline with text and then close all open task panes.
9. Print only the document properties.
10. Save, preview, and then close **1-FirstAidTraining.docx**.

Assessment 4

Check an Adventures Document for Accessibility Issues

1. Open **BEAdventures.docx** and then save it with the name **1-BEAdventures**.
2. Using the Help feature, learn more about the rules for the Accessibility Checker.
3. After reading the information, complete an accessibility check on the document. Look at the errors that appear in the Accessibility task pane and then correct each error.
4. Save and then close **1-BEAdventures.docx**.
5. Open a blank document and then type text explaining the errors that were found in **1-BEAdventures.docx** by the Accessibility Checker and what you did to correct the errors.
6. Save the completed document with the name **1-BEAAccessibility**.
7. Preview and then close **1-BEAAccessibility.docx**.

Visual Benchmark

Format an Hawaiian Adventures Document

1. Open **Hawaii.docx** and then save it with the name **1-Hawaii**.
2. Complete the steps formatting so your document appears similar to the document shown in Figure 1.16:
   - Inspect the document and remove the watermark (the watermark is in the footer) and the header.
   - Expand the spacing (by increasing the spacing point size) for the title and apply a stylistic set so your title appears similar to the title in the figure.
   - Expand the spacing (by increasing the spacing point size) and apply a stylistic set to the two headings in the document so the headings appear similar to the headings in the figure.

- Apply a stylistic set to the quote and the author of the quote near the bottom of the page.
- Select the tabbed text and then use the Text Effects and Typography button in the Font group on the Home tab to apply the tabular lining number style.
- Search for all occurrences of em dashes and replace each with a colon followed by a space.
- Search for all occurrences of hyphens and replace each with an en dash.

3. Save, preview, and then close **1-Hawaii.docx**.

Figure 1.16 Visual Benchmark

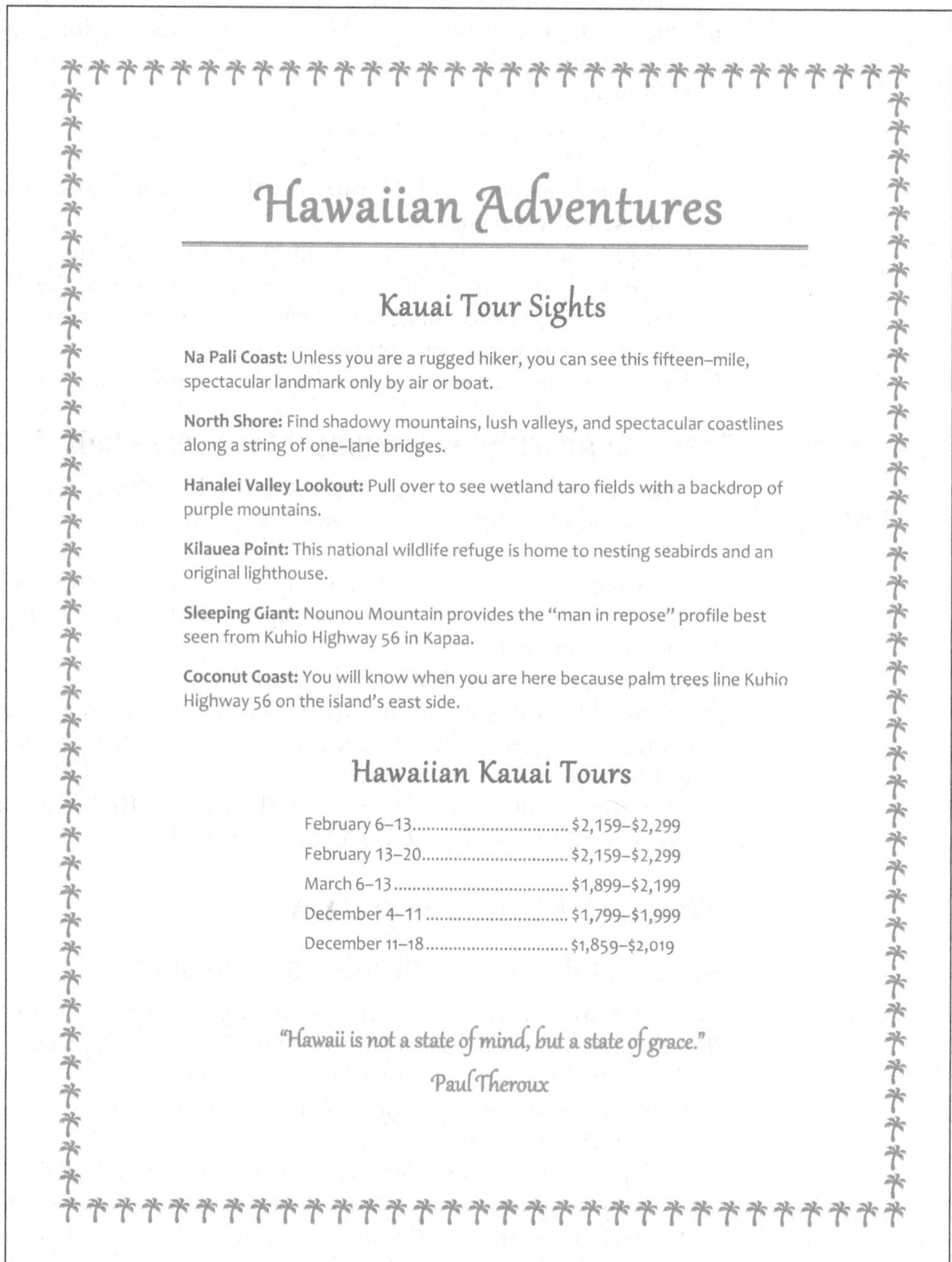

Hawaiian Adventures

Kauai Tour Sights

Na Pali Coast: Unless you are a rugged hiker, you can see this fifteen–mile, spectacular landmark only by air or boat.

North Shore: Find shadowy mountains, lush valleys, and spectacular coastlines along a string of one–lane bridges.

Hanalei Valley Lookout: Pull over to see wetland taro fields with a backdrop of purple mountains.

Kilauea Point: This national wildlife refuge is home to nesting seabirds and an original lighthouse.

Sleeping Giant: Nounou Mountain provides the "man in repose" profile best seen from Kuhio Highway 56 in Kapaa.

Coconut Coast: You will know when you are here because palm trees line Kuhio Highway 56 on the island's east side.

Hawaiian Kauai Tours

February 6–13................................ $2,159–$2,299
February 13–20.............................. $2,159–$2,299
March 6–13.................................... $1,899–$2,199
December 4–11 .... $1,799–$1,999
December 11–18............................. $1,859–$2,019

"Hawaii is not a state of mind, but a state of grace."
Paul Theroux

Case Study

Part 1

You are the assistant to the executive director of Phoenix Rising, a nonprofit organization. Phoenix Rising is sponsoring an affordable housing forum and you need to format a flyer for the event. Open **PRForum.docx** and then save it with the name **1-PRForum**. The information about the forum is provided in the document and your responsibility is to apply attractive and appealing formatting to the information. To provide a frame of reference for formatting, open **1-PRDonations.docx** and **1-PRDonorApp.docx** to see how those documents are formatted and then apply similar formatting to **1-PRForum.docx**. Replace any regular hyphens with en dashes and consider whether you want to have an em dash or other punctuation after *Date*, *Time*, and *Location*. Save, preview, and then close **1-PRForum.docx**. Close all open documents.

Part 2

The executive director of Phoenix Rising needs a new organizational chart. Open **PRLtrhd.docx** and then save it with the name **1-PROrgChart**. Look at the information in Figure 1.17 below and then create a SmartArt organizational chart to display the information. Provide a title for the organizational chart and apply formatting so that the title and organizational chart appear similar to the other documents you prepared in this case study. Save, preview, and then close **1-PROrgChart.docx**.

Figure 1.17 Case Study, Part 2

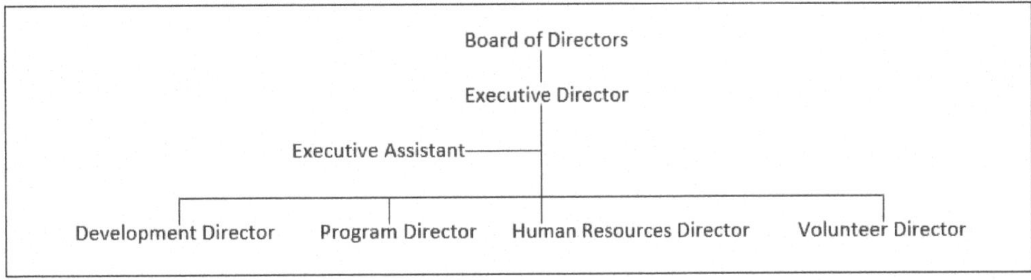

Part 3

The executive director wants to ensure that all documents you prepare for Phoenix Rising are checked for accessibility issues and has asked you to check two documents. Open **1-PRForum.docx**, run an accessibility check on the document, and fix any errors identified by the Accessibility Checker. Save and then close **1-PRForum.docx**. Open **1-PROrgChart.docx**, run an accessibility check, and fix any errors identified by the Accessibility Checker. Save and then close **1-PROrgChart.docx**. Open **PRLtrhd.docx** and then save it with the name **1-PRAccessibility.docx**. Write a letter to the executive director explaining any accessibility issues found in each document by the Accessibility Checker and the steps you took to correct them. Save, preview, and then close **1-PRAccessibility.docx**.

Part 4

To further identify a document and its contents, the executive director has asked you to provide document properties for **1-PROrgChart.docx**. Open **1-PROrgChart.docx** and then insert at least the following document properties:

- Title
- Author (use your name)
- Company
- Keywords

After inserting the document properties, save **1-PROrgChart.docx**, print only the document properties, and then close the document.

WORD

Proofing Documents

CHAPTER 2

Performance Objectives

Upon successful completion of Chapter 2, you will be able to:

1 Use the Editor to complete a spelling check and a grammar check
2 Display readability statistics
3 Create a custom dictionary, change the default dictionary, and remove a dictionary
4 Display document word, paragraph, and character counts
5 Insert line numbers
6 Display synonyms and antonyms for specific words using the thesaurus
7 Use the Search and Researcher task panes to find information on a specific topic
8 Translate text to and from different languages
9 Sort text in paragraphs, columns, and tables

Microsoft Word includes proofing tools to help you create well-written, error-free documents. These tools include the Microsoft Editor that checks spelling and grammar in a document and the thesaurus that displays words with similar or opposite meanings. If documents will be created with specific words, terms, or acronyms not found in the main spelling dictionary, a custom dictionary can be created. When completing a spelling check, the Editor will compare words in a document with the main dictionary as well as a custom dictionary. Word provides a translation feature for translating text into different languages. In Word, text in paragraphs, columns and tables can be sorted alphabetically or numerically in ascending or descending order. In this chapter, you will learn how to use the proofing tools, create a custom dictionary, translate text to and from different languages, and sort text.

Data Files

The data files for this chapter are in the WL2C2 folder that you downloaded at the beginning of this course.

Activity 1 Check Spelling in an Investment Plan Document **1 Part**

You will open an investment plan document and then use the Editor to complete a spelling and grammar check.

Checking Spelling and Grammar

Editor

Word contains the Microsoft Editor that checks the spelling and grammar of a document. To use the Editor, click the Editor button at the right side of the Home tab, click the Review tab and then click the Editor button in the Proofing group, or press the F7 function key. When checking a document, the Editor flags misspelled words, potential grammar errors, and writing clarity issues and offers corrections.

The Editor's spell checking feature can find and correct misspelled words, duplicate words, and irregular capitalizations. To check spelling, it compares the words in the document with the words in its dictionary. If it finds a match, it passes over the word. The Editor will identify misspelled words (any words not found in the Editor's dictionary), typographical errors (such as transposed letters), double occurrences of a word, irregular capitalizations, some proper names and jargon or technical terms.

The Editor's grammar checking feature searches a document for errors in grammar, punctuation, and word usage and will also identify text with writing clarity or conciseness issues. Using the Editor can help create well-written documents, but does not replace the need for proofreading.

Editing during a Spelling and Grammar Check

When checking the spelling and grammar in a document, edits or corrections can be made in the document. Do this by clicking in the document outside the Editor task pane, making the change or edit, and then clicking the Resume checking all results button in the task pane.

Customizing Spelling and Grammar Checking

Customizing Spell Checking

Customize the Editor spelling checker with options at the Word Options dialog box with the *Proofing* option selected, as shown in Figure 2.1. Display this dialog box by clicking the File tab and then clicking *Options*. At the Word Options dialog box, click *Proofing* in the left panel. Use options at this dialog box to specify what the Editor should review or ignore.

Hint Read grammar suggestions carefully. Some may not be valid in a specific context and a problem identified by the grammar checker may not actually be an issue.

Using the Editor Task Pane Reading Feature

The Editor task pane includes a reading feature that will read aloud the text that displays in the Editor task pane. To hear a reading of the text, click the speaker icon to the right of the sentence. The suggested word and definition that display in the *Suggestions* list box can also be read aloud by clicking the word in the list box and then clicking the *Read Aloud* option at the drop-down list. For the reading feature to work, the computer speakers must be turned on.

Figure 2.1 Word Options Dialog Box with the *Proofing* Option Selected

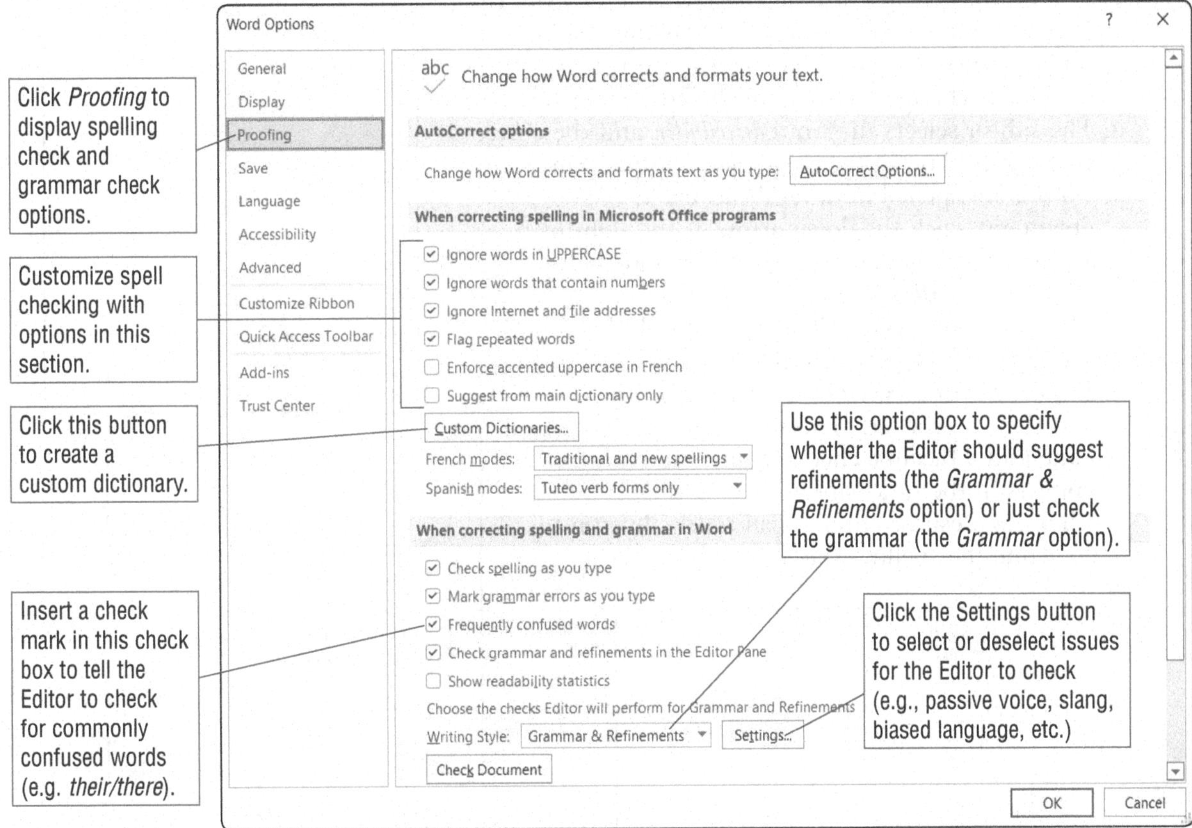

Activity 1 Spell Checking a Document with Uppercase Words

Part 1 of 1

Note: The Microsoft Editor is updated on a continuous basis so some of the steps in this activity may vary. Ignore any suggestions provided by Editor that are not specifically addressed in this activity.

1. Open **PlanDists.docx** and then save it with the name **2-PlanDists**.
2. Change a spell checking option by completing the following steps:
   a. Click the File tab.
   b. Click *Options*.
   c. At the Word Options dialog box, click the *Proofing* option in the left panel.
   d. Click the *Ignore words in UPPERCASE* check box to remove the check mark.
   e. Click OK to close the dialog box.

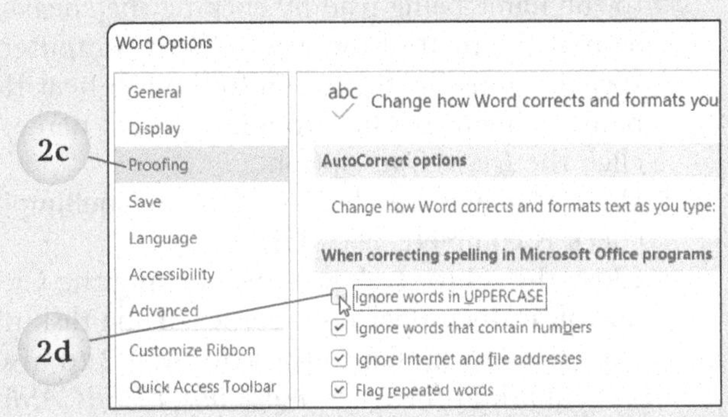

3. Complete a spelling check on the document by completing the following steps:
   a. Click the Editor button in the Editor group on the Home tab.
   b. At the Editor task pane, click the Editor Score box near the top of the task pane.

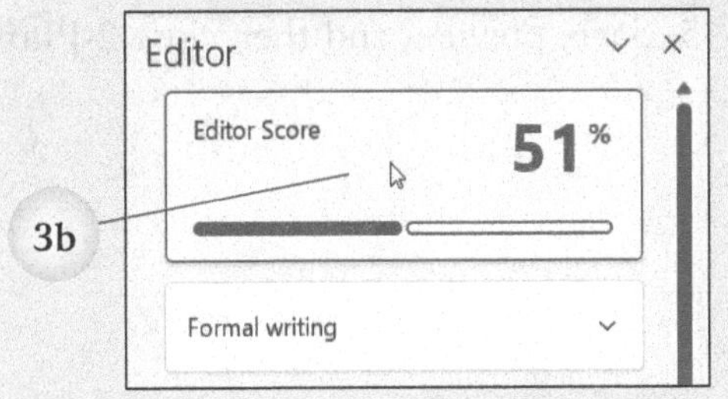

c. The Editor displays *AERLY DISTRIBUTIONS* in the Editor task pane and the correct spelling displays in the *Suggestions* list box. Click *EARLY* in the *Suggestions* list box to change the word to the correct spelling.

d. The Editor selects the word *distributin* and the correct spelling displays in the *Suggestions* list box. Since this word is misspelled in other locations in the document, click the down arrow at the right of *distribution* in the *Suggestions* list box and then click *Change All* at the drop-down list.

e. The Editor selects *eter*. The word should be *after* and the proper spelling is not available in the *Suggestions* list box. Double-click *eter* in the document and then type after. (This dims the Editor task pane and a Resume checking all results button appears in the task pane.)

f. Click the Resume checking all results button to continue the spelling check.

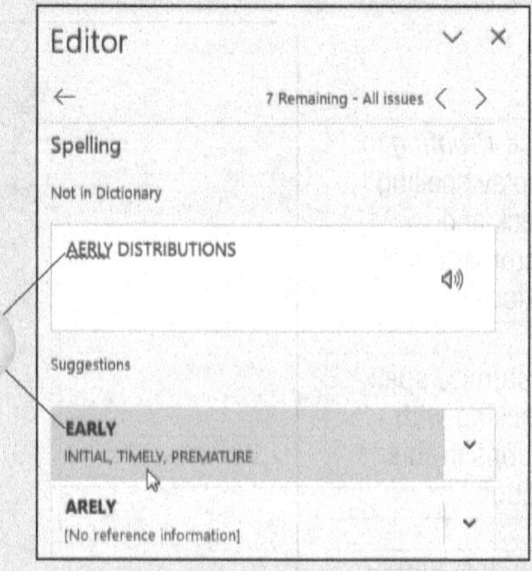

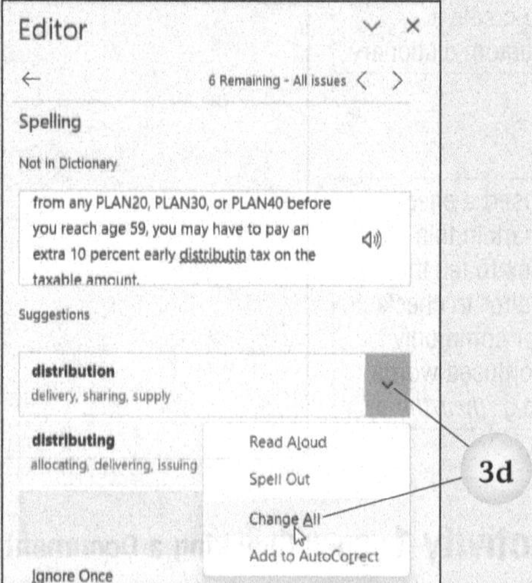

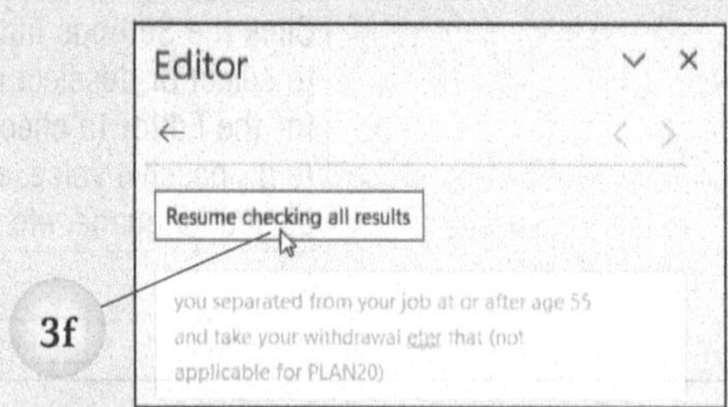

g. The spelling checker selects *to*. (This is a double word occurrence.) Click the *Delete Repeated Word* option to delete the second occurrence of *to*.

h. The spelling checker selects *Ingstrom* and displays *Logan Ingstrom* in the Editor task pane. Listen to the name being read by clicking the speaker icon at the right of the name. (Your computer speakers must be turned on for you to hear the name being read.) Ingstrom is a proper name, so click the *Ignore Once* option.

i. When the message displays that the spelling check is complete, click OK.

j. Close the Editor task pane by clicking the Close button in the upper right corner of the task pane.

4. Complete steps similar to those in Step 2 to insert a check mark in the *Ignore words in UPPERCASE* check box.
5. Save, preview, and then close **2-PlanDists.docx**.

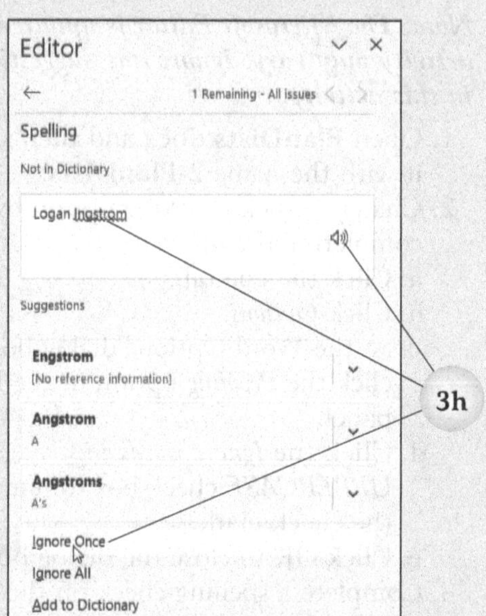

Check Your Work

Activity 2 Change Grammar Options and Check the Grammar in a Company Letter — 2 Parts

You will check the grammar in a company letter, change grammar options, and then check the document for spelling and grammar errors. You will also display readability statistics for the document.

Changing Grammar Checking Options

Quick Steps

Change Grammar Checking Options

1. Click File tab.
2. Click *Options*.
3. Click *Proofing*.
4. Change options in the dialog box.
5. Click OK.

When performing a spelling and grammar check, Word highlights text that may contain grammatical errors and displays the potential errors in the Editor task pane. By default, the grammar checker also looks for ways to refine the writing, such as by eliminating wordiness. To simply check the grammar and not look for refinements, change the option in the Word Options dialog box (see Figure 2.1 on page 43) from *Grammar & Refinements* to *Grammar*.

Click the Settings button at the Word Options dialog box with *Proofing* selected in the left panel and the Grammar Settings dialog box displays with a list of issues the Editor can consider when checking a document (e.g., errors in punctuation, misused words, biased language, and so on). Each option is preceded by a check box. If a check box contains a check mark, the option is active and the Editor will check for the issue. Scroll down the list box to see the issues available for checking in a document. Customize by inserting or removing check marks.

Activity 2a Changing Grammar Options and Checking Grammar — Part 1 of 2

1. Open **MCFLetter.docx** and save it with the name **2-MCFLetter.**
2. Look at the document and notice the dotted line below the text *all of* and *main focus* in the document indicating a possible grammar error.
3. Change the grammar option by completing the following steps:
   a. Click the File tab and then click *Options*.
   b. Click *Proofing* in the left panel.
   c. Click the *Writing Style* option box arrow and then click *Grammar* at the drop-down list.

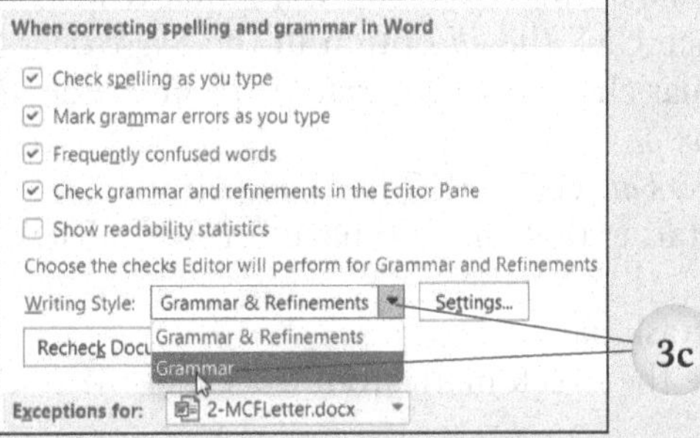

   d. Click OK.
4. At the document, notice that most of the dotted lines have been removed. This is because the *Grammar* option does not check a document for grammar issues such as wordiness and conciseness.

5. Change the grammar option back to the default and specify that the grammar checker is to check for passive voice by completing the following steps:
   a. Click the File tab and then click *Options*.
   b. Click *Proofing* in the left panel.
   c. Click the *Writing Style* option box arrow and then click *Grammar & Refinements* at the drop-down list.
   d. Click the Settings button.
   e. At the Grammar Settings dialog box, scroll down the *Options* list box to the *Clarity* section and then click the *Passive Voice* check box to insert a check mark. (Skip this step if the option already contains a check mark.)
   f. Click OK to close the Grammar Settings dialog box.
   g. Click OK to close the Word Options dialog box.

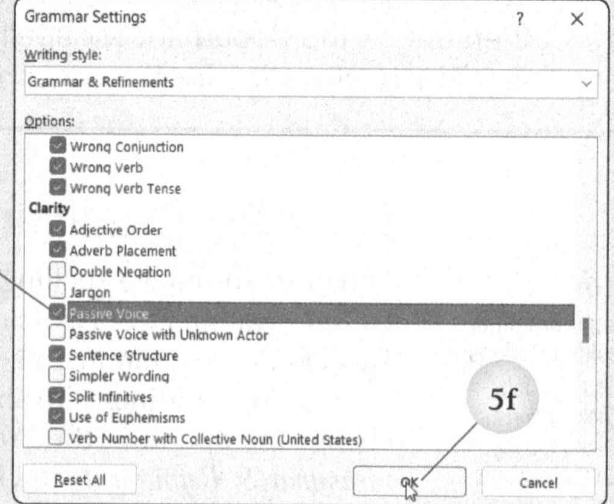

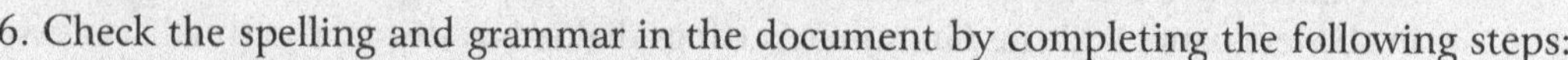

6. Check the spelling and grammar in the document by completing the following steps:
   a. Click the Editor button in the Editor group on the Home tab.
   b. At the Editor task pane, click the Editor Score box.
   c. The grammar checker selects the text *Expense charges are being lowered by McCormack Funds* and does not offer any suggestions in the *Suggestions* list box.
   d. Click the down arrow at the right of the text *Saying who or what did the action would be clearer* in the Editor task pane and then read the information that displays below the text about active voice.
   e. Click in the document and then edit the first sentence in the first paragraph so it reads as *McCormack Funds is lowering expense charges beginning May 1, 2024*.
   f. Click the Resume checking all results button in the Editor task pane.
   g. When the grammar checker selects *all of* in the document, notice the information *More concise language would be clearer for your reader* that displays below *Conciseness* in the Editor task pane and then click the *all* option in the *Suggestions* list box.
   h. When the grammar checker selects *main focus* in the document, click *focus* in the *Suggestions* list box.
   i. If the Editor selects *at*, click the *Ignore Once* option.
   j. At the message stating that the you have finished reviewing Editor's suggestion, click OK.
   k. Close the Editor task pane.
7. If necessary, remove the check mark from the *Passive Voice* check box by completing the following steps:
   a. Click the File tab and then click *Options*.
   b. Click *Proofing* in the left panel.
   c. Click the Settings button.

d. At the Grammar Settings dialog box, scroll down the *Options* list box to the *Clarity* section and then click the *Passive Voice* check box to remove the check mark.
e. Click OK to close the Grammar Settings dialog box.
f. Click OK to close the Word Options dialog box.

8. Save **2-MCFLetter.docx**.

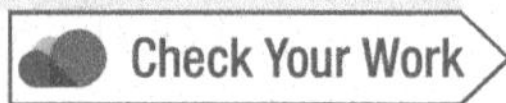

Setting the Proofing Language

Quick Steps

Choose Proofing Language

1. Click Review tab.
2. Click Language button.
3. Click *Set Proofing Language.*
4. Click language in list box.
5. Click OK.

Microsoft provides a number of dictionaries for proofing text in various languages. To change the language used for proofing a document, click the Review tab, click the Language button in the Language group, and then click *Set Proofing Language* at the drop-down list. At the Language dialog box, click a language in the *Mark selected text as* list box. To make the selected language the default, click the Set As Default button in the lower left corner of the dialog box. Click OK to close the Language dialog box.

Displaying Readability Statistics

Quick Steps

Show Readability Statistics

1. Click File tab.
2. Click *Options.*
3. Click *Proofing.*
4. Click *Show readability statistics* check box.
5. Click OK.
6. Complete spelling and grammar check.

Readability statistics about a document can be displayed when completing a spelling and grammar check. Figure 2.2 lists the readability statistics for the document used in Activity 2b. The statistics include word, character, paragraph, and sentence counts; average number of sentences per paragraph, words per sentence, and characters per word; and readability information such as the percentage of passive sentences in the document, the Flesch Reading Ease score, and the Flesch-Kincaid Grade Level score. Control the display of readability statistics with the *Show readability statistics* check box in the Word Options dialog box with *Proofing* selected.

The Flesch Reading Ease score is based on the average number of syllables per word and the average number of words per sentence. The higher the score, the greater the number of people who will be able to understand the text in the document. Standard writing generally scores in the 60 to 70 range.

The Flesch-Kincaid Grade Level score is based on the average number of syllables per word and the average number of words per sentence. The score indicates a grade level. Standard writing is generally scored at the seventh or eighth grade level.

Figure 2.2 Readability Statistics Dialog Box

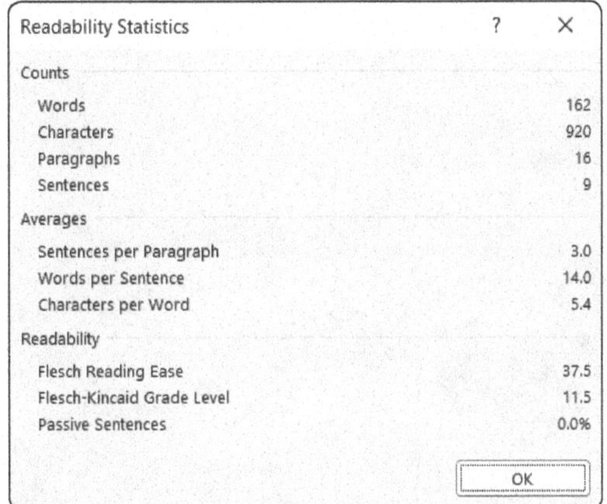

Activity 2b Displaying Readability Statistics

1. With **2-MCFLetter.docx** open, display readability statistics about the document by completing the following steps:
   a. Click the File tab and then click *Options*.
   b. At the Word Options dialog box, click *Proofing* in the left panel.
   c. Click the *Show readability statistics* check box to insert a check mark.

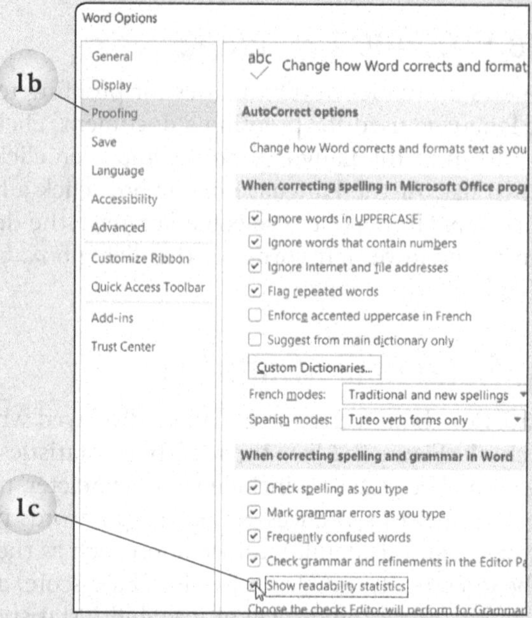

   d. Click OK to close the Word Options dialog box.
   e. At the document, click the Editor button in the Editor group on the Home tab.
   f. Look at the readability statistics that display in the Readability Statistics dialog box and then click OK to close the dialog box.
   g. Click OK at the message indicating that you have finished reviewing Editor's suggestions.
   h. If necessary, close the Editor task pane.
2. Complete steps similar to those in Steps 1a–1d to remove the check mark from the *Show readability statistics* check box.
3. Save, preview, and then close **2-MCFLetter.docx**.

Activity 3 Use Proofing Tools and Search for Information in a Document on Endangered Trees — 4 Parts

You will open an endangered trees document, create a custom dictionary, add specific terms to the custom dictionary, and then complete a spelling check. You will also display the word count, use the Thesaurus feature to replace a word with a synonym, insert line numbers, and find information on specific topics using the Search and Researcher task panes.

Creating and Removing a Custom Dictionary

Quick Steps

Create Custom Dictionary

1. Click File tab.
2. Click *Options*.
3. Click *Proofing*.
4. Click Custom Dictionaries button.
5. Click New button.
6. Type name for dictionary.
7. Press Enter key.

Hint When you change the custom dictionary settings in one Microsoft 365 application, the changes affect all the other applications in the suite.

Creating a Custom Dictionary

When completing a spelling check on a document, the Editor uses the main dictionary, named *RoamingCustom.dic*, to compare words. This main dictionary contains most common words, but may not include specific proper names, medical and technical terms, acronyms, or other text related to a specific field or business. If documents will be created with specific words, terms, or acronyms not found in the main dictionary, consider creating a custom dictionary. When completing a spelling check, the Editor will compare words in a document with the main dictionary as well as a custom dictionary.

To create a custom dictionary, display the Word Options dialog box with *Proofing* selected and then click the Custom Dictionaries button. This displays the Custom Dictionaries dialog box, shown in Figure 2.3. To create a new dictionary, click the New button. At the Create Custom Dictionary dialog box, type a name for the dictionary in the *File name* text box and then press the Enter key. The new dictionary name displays in the *Dictionaries* list box in the Custom Dictionaries dialog box. More than one dictionary can be used when spell checking a document. Insert a check mark in the check box next to each dictionary to be used when spell checking.

Changing the Default Dictionary

At the Custom Dictionaries dialog box, the default dictionary displays in the *Dictionaries* list box followed by *(Default)*. Change this default by clicking the dictionary name in the list box and then clicking the Change Default button.

Figure 2.3 Custom Dictionaries Dialog Box

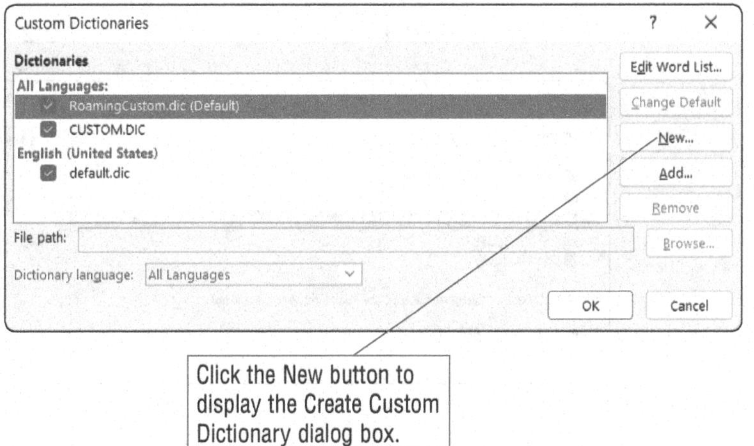

Removing a Dictionary

Quick Steps

Remove Custom Dictionary

1. Click File tab.
2. Click *Options*.
3. Click *Proofing*.
4. Click Custom Dictionaries button.
5. Click custom dictionary name.
6. Click Remove button.
7. Click OK.

Remove a custom dictionary with the Remove button at the Custom Dictionaries dialog box. To do this, display the Custom Dictionaries dialog box, click the dictionary name in the *Dictionaries* list box, and then click the Remove button. No prompt will display confirming the deletion, so make sure the correct dictionary name is selected before clicking the Remove button.

Activity 3a Creating a Custom Dictionary and Changing the Default Dictionary — Part 1 of 4

1. Open **EndangeredTrees.docx**, notice the wavy red lines indicating words not recognized by the Editor (words not in the main dictionary), and then close the document.
2. Create a custom dictionary, add words to the dictionary, and then change the default dictionary by completing the following steps:
   a. Click the File tab and then click *Options*.
   b. At the Word Options dialog box, click *Proofing* in the left panel.
   c. Click the Custom Dictionaries button.
   d. At the Custom Dictionaries, click the New button.
   e. At the Create Custom Dictionary dialog box, type your first and last names (without a space between them) in the *File name* text box and then press the Enter key.
   f. At the Custom Dictionaries dialog box, add a word to your dictionary by completing the following steps:
      1) Click the name of your dictionary in the *Dictionaries* list box.
      2) Click the Edit Word List button.

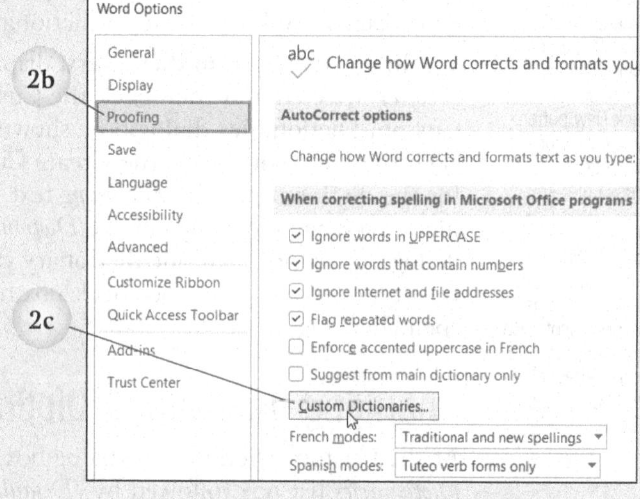

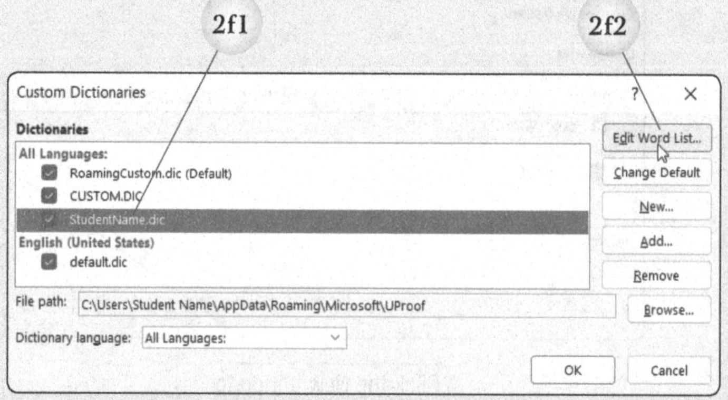

3) At the dialog box for your custom dictionary, type acerifolia in the *Word(s)* text box.
4) Click the Add button.

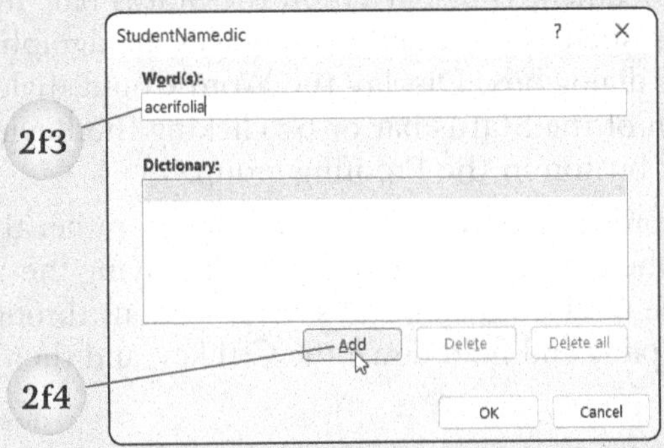

g. Add another word to the dictionary by clicking in the *Word(s)* text box, typing floridana, and then pressing the Enter key.
h. Add another word to the dictionary by clicking in the *Words(s)* text box, typing giganteum, and then pressing the Enter key.
i. Click OK to close the dialog box.
j. At the Custom Dictionaries dialog box, click the name of your dictionary in the list box and then click the Change Default button. (Notice that the word *(Default)* displays after your custom dictionary.)

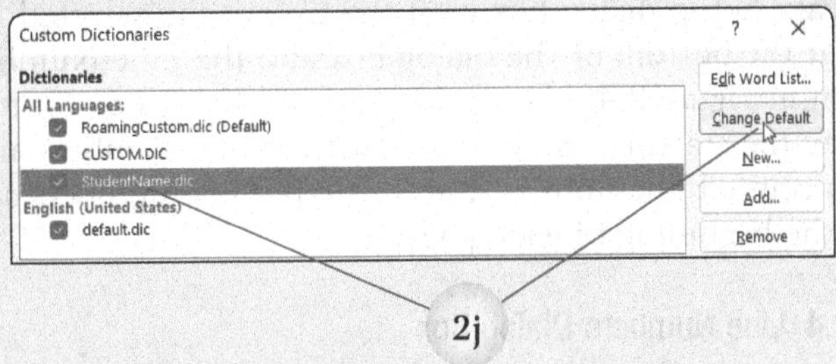

k. Click OK to close the Custom Dictionaries dialog box.
l. Click OK to close the Word Options dialog box.

3. Open **EndangeredTrees.docx** and then save it with the name **2-EndangeredTrees**.
4. Use the Editor to complete a spelling and grammar check on the document and accept all spelling and grammar suggestions. (The Editor will not stop at the words you added to your custom dictionary.)
5. Save **2-EndangeredTrees.docx**.
6. Change the default dictionary and then remove your custom dictionary by completing the following steps:
   a. Click the File tab and then click *Options*.
   b. At the Word Options dialog box, click *Proofing* in the left panel.
   c. Click the Custom Dictionaries button.
   d. At the Custom Dictionaries dialog box, click *RoamingCustom.dic* in the *Dictionaries* list box.
   e. Click the Change Default button. (This changes the default back to the RoamingCustom.dic dictionary.)
   f. Click the name of your dictionary in the *Dictionaries* list box.
   g. Click the Remove button. (If a message displays, click the Yes button.)
   h. Click OK to close the Custom Dictionaries dialog box.
   i. Click OK to close the Word Options dialog box.

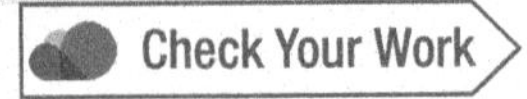

Displaying Word Count

Quick Steps

Display Word Count Dialog Box

Click word count section of Status bar.
OR
1. Click Review tab.
2. Click Word Count button.

 Word Count

Displaying Word Count

Words are counted as they are typed in a document and the total number of words in a document is displayed on the Status bar. To display more information—such as the numbers of pages, paragraphs, and lines—display the Word Count dialog box. Display the Word Count dialog box by clicking the word count section of the Status bar or by clicking the Review tab and then clicking the Word Count button in the Proofing group.

Count words in a portion of the document, rather than the entire document, by selecting the portion of text and then displaying the Word Count dialog box. To determine the total word count of several sections throughout a document, select the first section, press and hold down the Ctrl key, and then select the other sections.

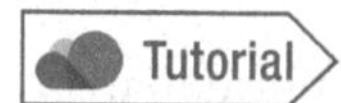

Inserting Line Numbers

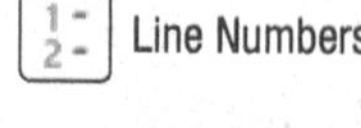

Quick Steps

Insert Line Numbers

1. Click Layout tab.
2. Click Line Numbers button.
3. Click line number option.

Inserting Line Numbers

Use the Line Numbers button in the Page Setup group on the Layout tab to insert line numbers in a document. Numbering lines has practical applications for certain legal papers and reference purposes. To number lines in a document, click the Layout tab, click the Line Numbers button in the Page Setup group, and then click a line number option at the drop-down list.

To have more control over inserting line numbers in a document, click the Line Numbers button and then click *Line Numbering Options* at the drop-down list. At the Page Setup dialog box with the Layout tab selected, click the Line Numbers button at the bottom of the dialog box and the Line Numbers dialog box displays, as shown in Figure 2.4. Use options at this dialog box to insert line numbers and to specify the starting number, the location line numbers are printed, the interval between printed line numbers, and whether line numbers are consecutive or start over at the beginning of each page.

Figure 2.4 Line Numbers Dialog Box

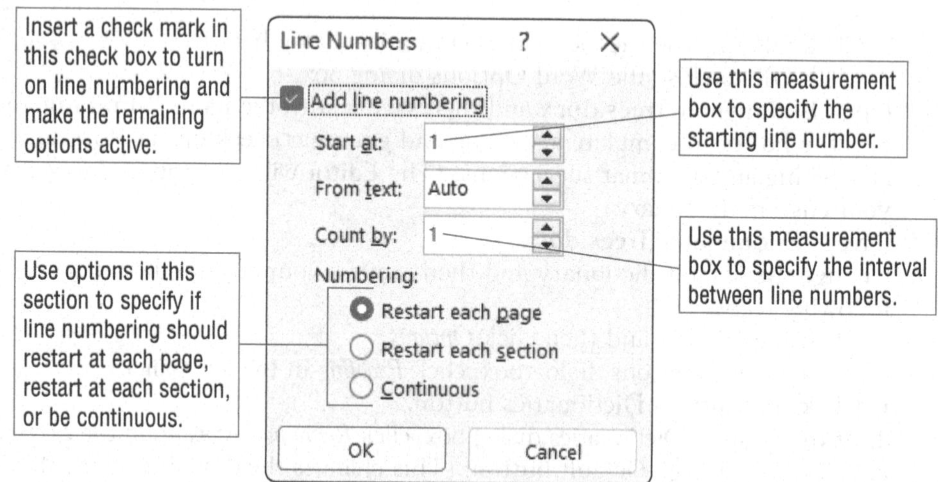

Using the Thesaurus

Quick Steps

Use Thesaurus

1. Click Review tab.
2. Click Thesaurus button.
3. Type word in search text box.
4. Press Enter key.

Using the Thesaurus

Word offers a Thesaurus feature for finding synonyms, antonyms, and related words for a particular word. Synonyms are words that have the same or nearly the same meaning. When the Thesaurus feature is used, antonyms may display for some words, which are words with opposite meanings.

To use the Thesaurus feature, click the Review tab and then click the Thesaurus button in the Proofing group or use the keyboard shortcut Shift + F7. At the Thesaurus task pane, click in the search text box at the top of the task pane, type a word, and then press the Enter key or click the Start searching button (which contains a magnifying glass icon). A list of synonyms and antonyms for the typed word displays in the task pane list box. Another method for finding synonyms and antonyms is to select a word and then display the Thesaurus task pane. Figure 2.5 shows the Thesaurus task pane with synonyms and antonyms for the word *normally.*

Depending on the word typed in the search text box, words in the Thesaurus task pane list box may appear followed by *(n.)* for *noun*, *(adj.)* for *adjective,* or *(adv.)* for *adverb*. Any antonyms at the end of the list of related synonyms will be followed by *(Antonym)*. If a dictionary is installed on the computer, a definition of the selected word will appear below the task pane list box.

The Thesaurus feature provides synonyms for the selected word as well as a list of related synonyms. For example, in the Thesaurus task pane list box shown in Figure 2.5, the main synonym *usually* displays for *normally* and is preceded by a collapse triangle (a right-and-down-pointing triangle). The collapse triangle indicates that the list of related synonyms is displayed. Click the collapse triangle

Figure 2.5 Thesaurus Task Pane

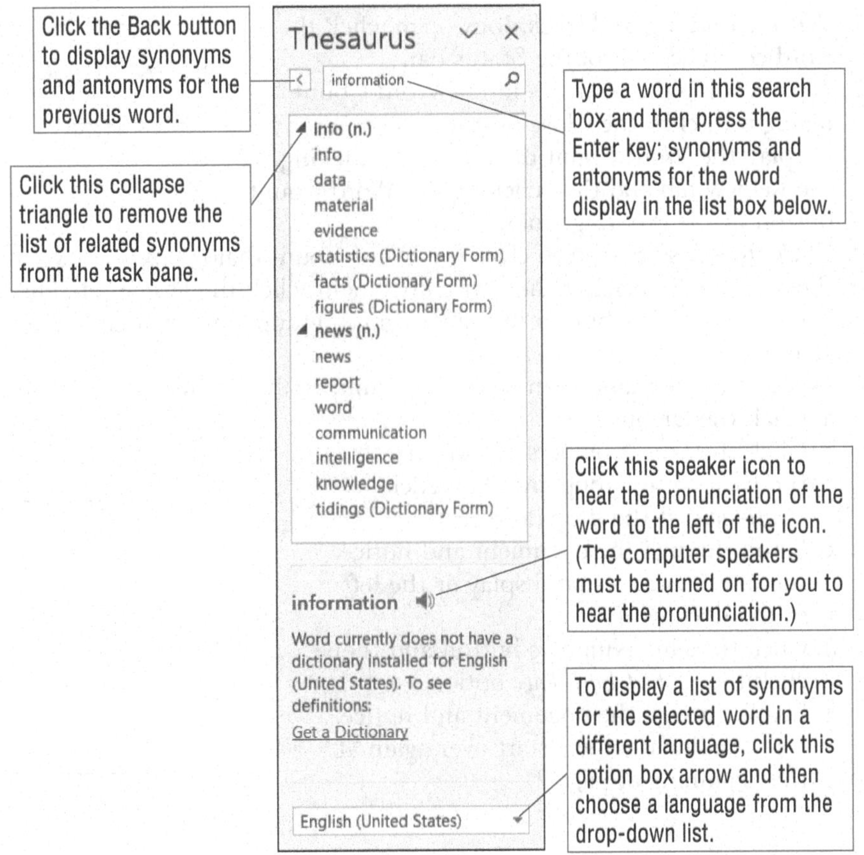

and the list of related synonyms is removed from the task pane list box and the collapse triangle changes to an expand triangle (a right-pointing triangle). Click a word in the Thesaurus task pane list box to see synonyms for it.

When reviewing synonyms and antonyms for words within a document, display the list of synonyms and antonyms for the previous word by clicking the Back button (left-pointing arrow) at the left of the search text box. Click the down-pointing triangle at the left of the Close button in the upper right corner of the task pane and a drop-down list displays with options for moving, sizing, and closing the task pane.

To replace a selected word in the document with a synonym in the Thesaurus task pane, point to the synonym in the task pane list box using the mouse. This displays a down arrow to the right of the word. Click the down arrow and then click the *Insert* option at the drop-down list.

The Thesaurus task pane, like the Editor task pane, includes a reading feature that will speak the word currently selected in the task pane. To hear the word pronounced, click the speaker icon at the right of the word below the task pane list box. (For this feature to work, the computer speakers must be turned on.)

The Thesaurus task pane also includes a language option for displaying synonyms of the selected word in a different language. To use this feature, click the option box arrow at the bottom of the task pane and then click a language at the drop-down list.

Activity 3b Displaying the Word Count, Inserting Line Numbers, and Using the Thesaurus

Part 2 of 4

1. With **2-EndangeredTrees.docx** open, click the word count section of the Status bar.
2. After reading the statistics in the Word Count dialog box, click the Close button.
3. Display the Word Count dialog box by clicking the Review tab and then clicking the Word Count button in the Proofing group.
4. Click the Close button to close the Word Count dialog box.
5. Press Ctrl + A to select the entire document, click the Home tab, click the Line and Paragraph Spacing button in the Paragraph group, and then click *2.0* at the drop-down gallery.
6. Deselect the text and then insert line numbers by completing the following steps:
   a. Click the Layout tab.
   b. Click the Line Numbers button in the Page Setup group and then click *Continuous* at the drop-down list.
   c. Scroll through the document and notice the line numbers that display at the left of the document.
   d. Click the Line Numbers button and then click the *Restart Each Page* option.
   e. Scroll through the document and notice that the line numbers start over again at the beginning of page 2.

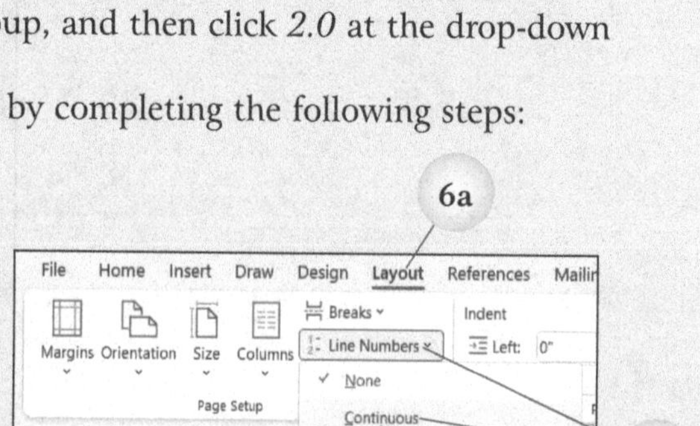

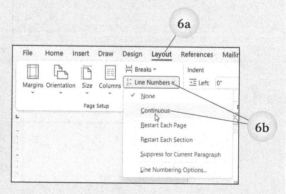

f. Click the Line Numbers button and then click *Line Numbering Options* at the drop-down list.
g. At the Page Setup dialog box, click the Line Numbers button at the bottom of the dialog box.
h. At the Line Numbers dialog box, select the current number in the *Start at* measurement box and then type 30.
i. Click the *Count by* measurement box up arrow. (This displays *2* in the measurement box.)
j. Click the *Continuous* option in the *Numbering* section.
k. Click OK to close the Line Numbers dialog box.

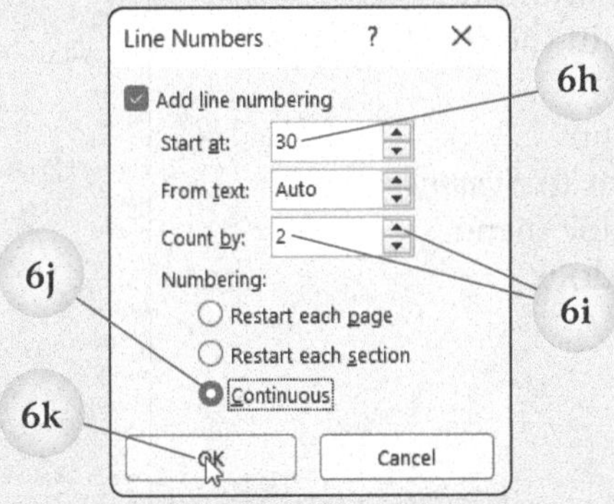

l. Click OK to close the Page Setup dialog box.
m. Scroll through the document and notice the line numbers that display at the left side of the document. The numbers start with *30* and increase by intervals of two.
n. Click the Line Numbers button and then click *None* at the drop-down list.

7. Select the document, click the Home tab, click the Line and Paragraph Spacing button in the Paragraph group, and then click *1.0* at the drop-down gallery.
8. Use the Thesaurus feature to change the word *information* in the first paragraph to *knowledge* by completing the following steps:
   a. Click in the word *information* in the second sentence of the first paragraph.
   b. Click the Review tab.
   c. Click the Thesaurus button in the Proofing group.
   d. At the Thesaurus task pane, point to *knowledge* in the task pane list box, click the down arrow at the right of the word, and then click *Insert* at the drop-down list.
   e. Close the Thesaurus task pane.

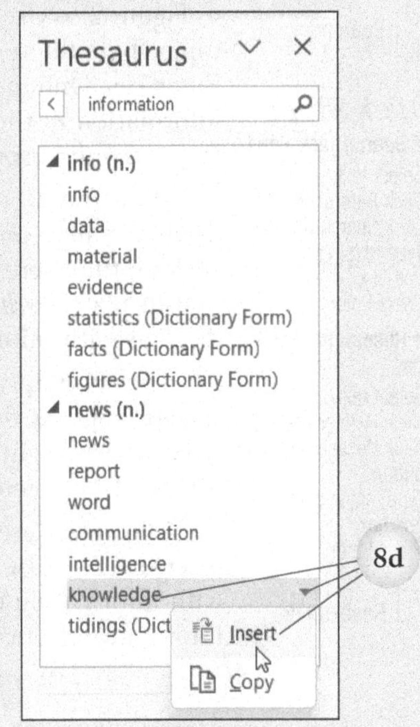

9. Follow steps similar to those in Step 8 to use the Thesaurus to replace *exact* with *precise* (located in the second sentence of the second paragraph).
10. Save **2-EndangeredTrees.docx**.

Check Your Work

Another method for displaying synonyms of a word is to use a shortcut menu. To do this, position the pointer on the word and then click right mouse button. At the shortcut menu, point to *Synonyms* and then click a synonym at the side menu. Click the *Thesaurus* option at the bottom of the side menu to display synonyms and antonyms for the word in the Thesaurus task pane.

Activity 3c Replacing Synonyms Using the Shortcut Menu

Part 3 of 4

1. With **2-EndangeredTrees.docx** open, position the pointer on the word *unique* in the first sentence in the third paragraph.
2. Click the right mouse button.
3. At the shortcut menu, point to *Synonyms* and then click *rare* at the side menu.
4. Save **2-EndangeredTrees.docx**.

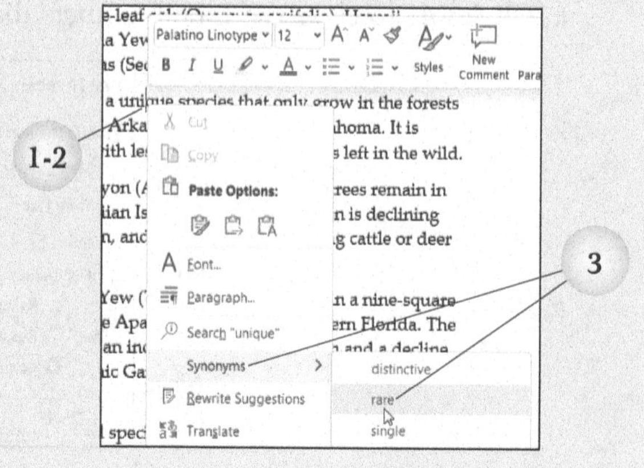

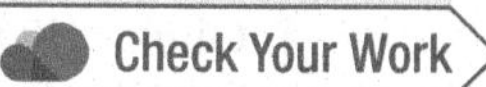

Using Research Tools

Search

Quick Steps

Use Search Task Pane

1. Select text.
2. Click References tab.
3. Click Search button.
4. Type text in search text box.
5. Press Enter.

Use Researcher Task Pane

1. Select text.
2. Click References tab.
3. Click Researcher button.
4. Type text in search text box.
5. Press Enter.

Researcher

Using Research Tools

The Research group on the References tab contains two buttons—Search and Researcher. Click the Search button and the Search task pane displays as shown in Figure 2.6. Use the Search task pane to find information online for a specific topic. Type the text on which to search in the Search text box and then press the Enter key. Online sources containing the topic display in the task pane. Read the information in the task pane or click a hyperlink to display additional information from an online source.

With the *All* option selected in the Search task pane, the task pane will display sources on the web and media resources. Specify what to display by clicking the More button in the task pane and then clicking one of the options that display—*Web*, *Media*, or *Help*. Click the *Help* option and the Help task pane displays with information on the text in the search text box.

The shortcut menu provides another method for displaying information on a specific topic at the Search task pane. To use the shortcut menu, click in a word or select words, right-click the word(s), and then click the *Search* option (followed by the word or selected words) at the shortcut menu.

Click the Researcher button and the Researcher task pane displays as shown in Figure 2.7. Use the Researcher task pane to search for websites and journals with information on a specific topic. Type a topic in the search text box and information from journals and websites displays in the task pane.

Figure 2.6 Search Task Pane

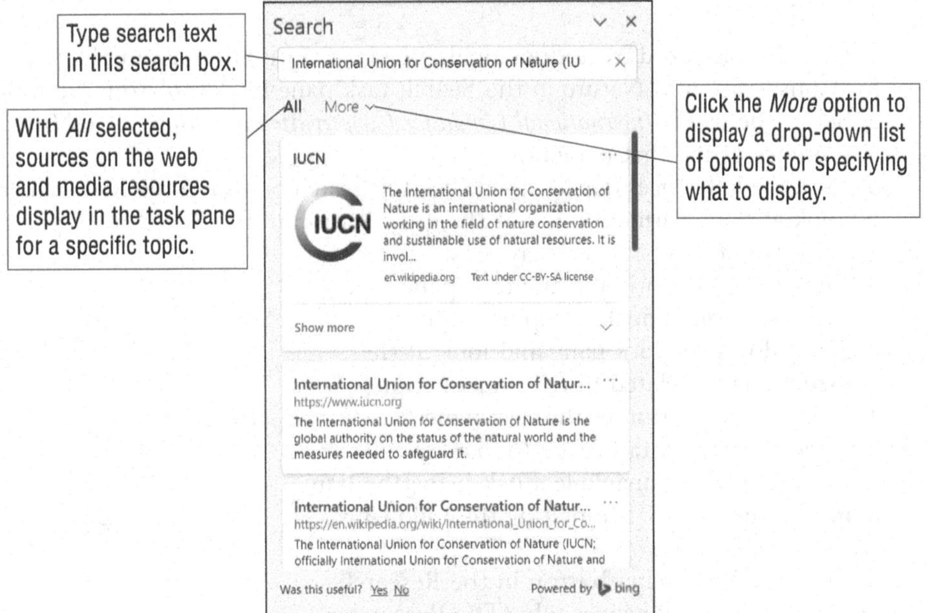

Figure 2.7 Researcher Task Pane

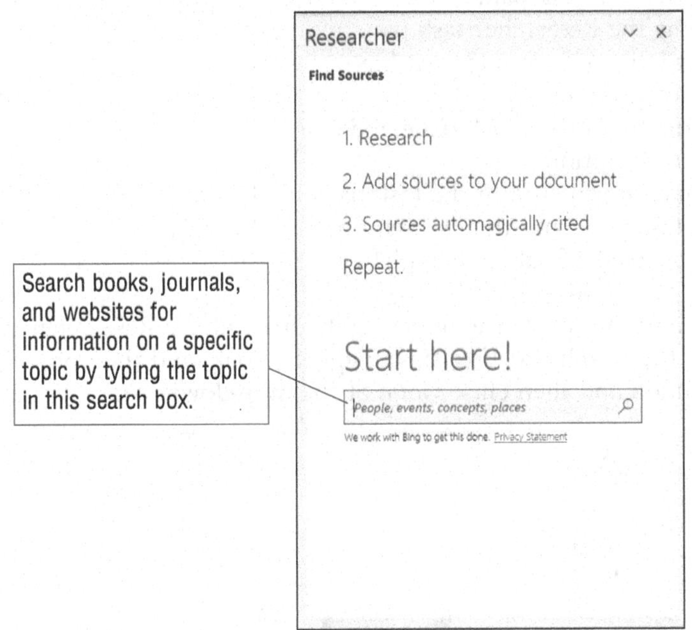

Activity 3d Using the Search and Researcher Task Panes

Part 4 of 4

1. With **2-EndangeredTrees.docx** open, display information about the International Union for Conservation of Nature in the Search task pane by completing the following steps:
   a. Select the words *International Union for Conservation of Nature (IUCN)* in the first sentence of the first paragraph.
   b. Click the References tab and then click the Search button in the Research group.
   c. Look at the information about the organization in the Search task pane. (Note that options in this task pane may vary.)
   d. Click the *More* option in the task pane and then click *Media* at the drop-down list.
   e. Scroll down the task pane and look at the media images related to the organization.
   f. Click the *All* option in the task pane.

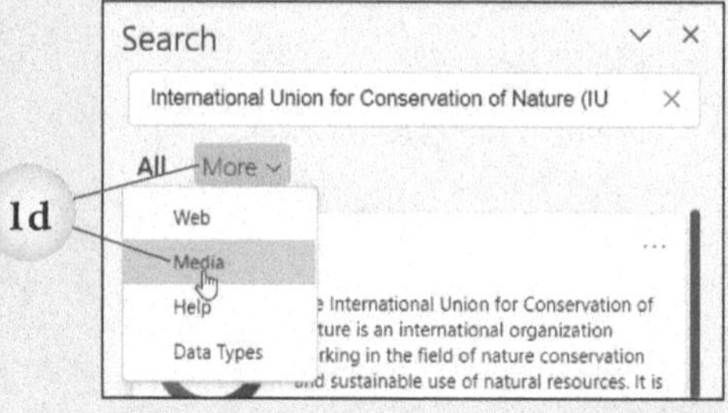

2. Use the Researcher task pane to display information on the maple-leaf oak using the latin name for the tree by completing the following steps:
   a. Click the Researcher button in the Research group on the References tab. (The Researcher task pane opens and the Search task pane is reduced to a button that display outside the upper right corner of the task pane above a button representing the Researcher task pane.)
   b. Type quercus acerifolia in the search text box and then press the Enter key.
   c. Look at the information in the task pane and then click the *Journals* option.
   d. Look at the journal information in the task pane.

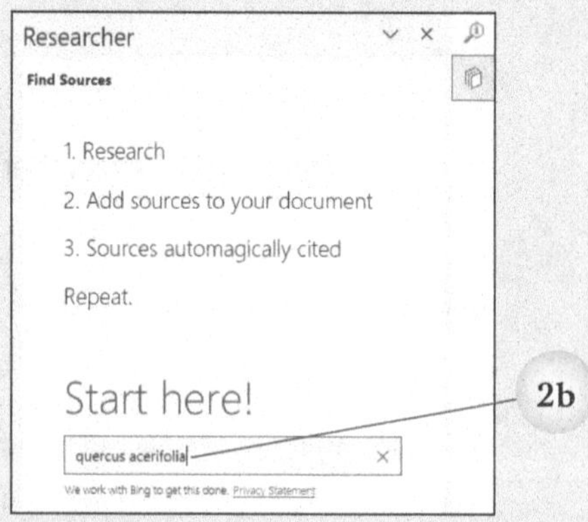

3. Display the Search task pane and then search for information on the maple-leaf oak by completing the following steps:
   a. Click the Search button outside the upper right corner of the Researcher task pane.
   b. Select the text in the search text box, type maple-leaf oak, and then press the Enter key.
   c. Click the *More* option and then click *Media* at the drop-down list.

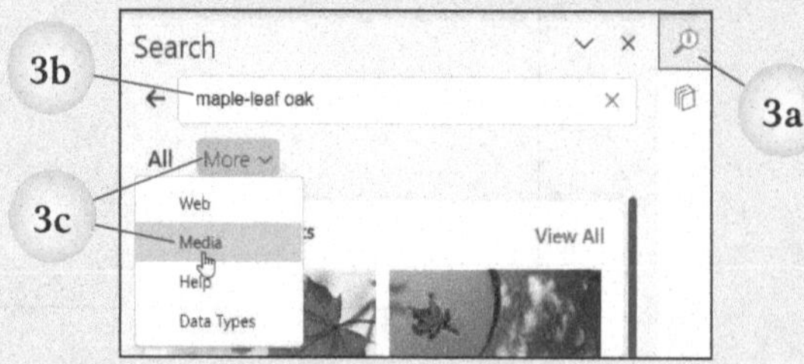

   d. Scroll down the list of images of the maple-leaf oak.
4. Close the Search task pane.
5. Close the Researcher task pane.
6. Save, preview, and then close **2-EndangeredTrees.docx**.

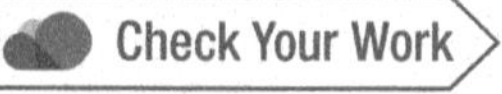

Activity 4 Translate Text in Documents — 2 Parts

You will use the translation feature to translate selected text from English to Spanish and English to French. You will also translate a document from English to Spanish.

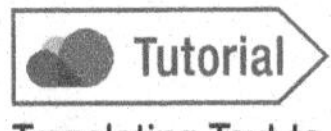

Translating Text to and from Different Languages

Translate

Translating Text to and from Different Languages

Word includes a Translate feature that will translate text to and from different languages. To use the Translate feature, click the Review tab and then click the Translate button in the Language group. At the drop-down list, click the *Translate Selection* option to translate selected text or click the *Translate Document* to translate the contents of the open document.

Translating Selected Text

Quick Steps

Translate Selected Text

1. Click Review tab.
2. Click Translate button.
3. Click *Translate Selection.*

To translate specific text in a document, click the Translate button in the Language group on the Review tab and then click the *Translate Selection* option. This opens the Translator task pane at the right side of the screen with the *Selection* option selected, similar to what is shown in Figure 2.8.

By default, the Translate feature will automatically detect the language in the document and *Auto-detect* will display in the *From* option box. A specific language can be selected by clicking the *From* option box and then clicking the language at the drop-down list. Click the *To* option box and then click the translation language at the drop-down list. Select text in the document and then click the Insert button near the bottom of the task pane. The selected text is replaced by the translated text.

Figure 2.8 Translator Task Pane

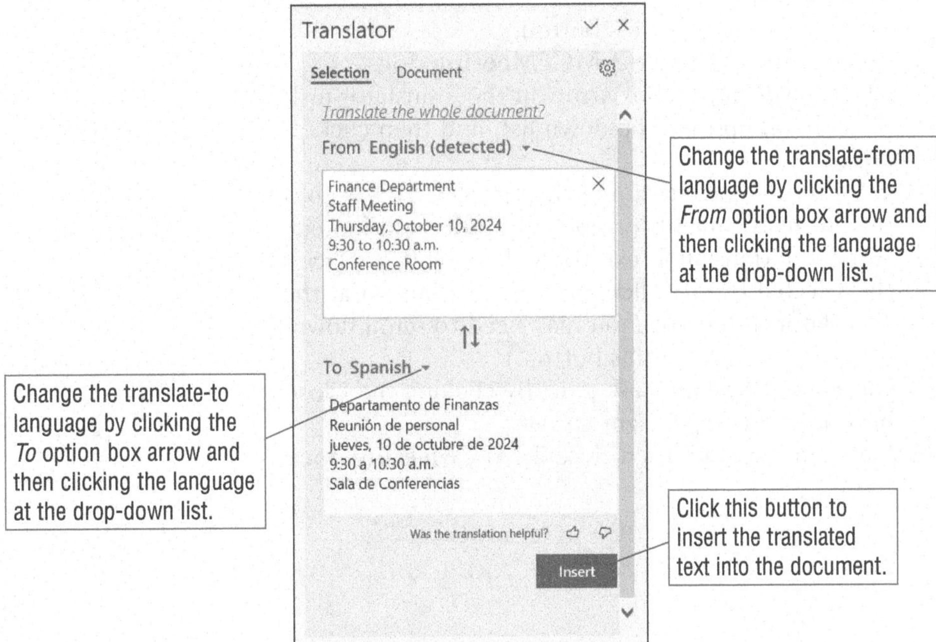

Activity 4a Translating Selected Text

Part 1 of 2

Note: Check with your instructor before completing this activity to make sure you have access to the internet.

1. Open **MCFMeeting.docx** and then save it with the name **2-MCFMeeting.docx**.
2. Display the Translator task pane by clicking the Review tab, clicking the Translate button in the Language group, and then clicking *Translate Selection* at the drop-down list.

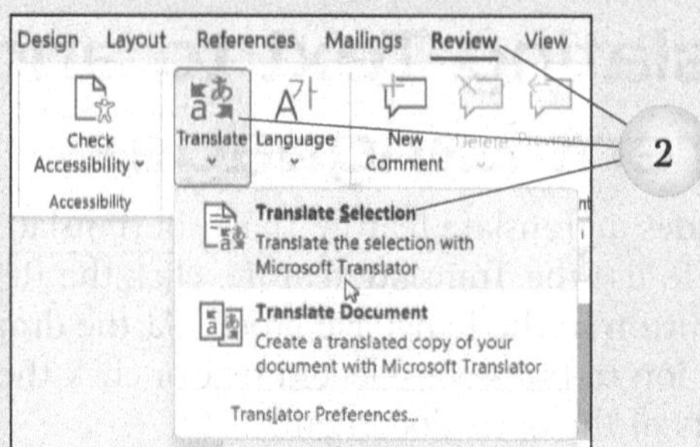

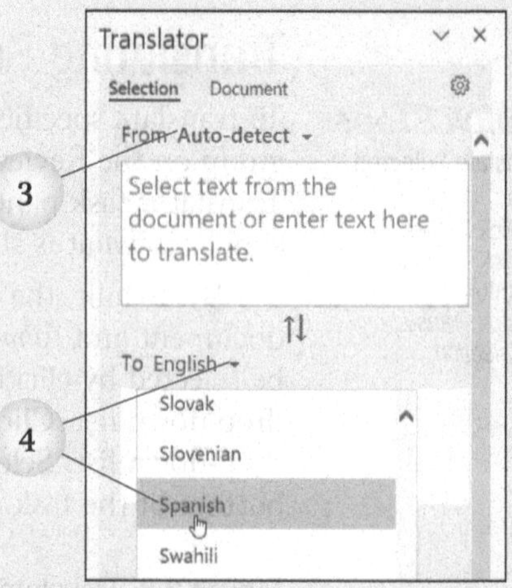

3. At the Translator task pane with the *Selection* option selected, check to make sure the *From* option box displays with *Auto-detect* (or it might also display as *English*).
4. Click the *To* option box arrow, scroll down the drop-down list, and then click *Spanish*. (The language names display in alphabetical order in the drop-down list.)
5. Click in the document and then press Ctrl + A to select the entire document (except the header and footer). Notice that the translation of the selected text displays below the *To* option box in the Translator task pane.
6. Insert the translated text in the document in place of the selected text by clicking the Insert button at the Translator task pane. (You may need to scroll down the task pane to display this button.)
7. Preview and then save **2-MCFMeeting.docx**.
8. Click the *To* option box arrow in the Translator task pane, scroll up the drop-down list, and then click *French*.
9. Click in the document and then press Ctrl + A to select the entire document (except the header and footer).
10. Insert the translated text in the document in place of the selected text by clicking the Insert button at the Translator task pane. (You may need to scroll down the task pane to display this button.)
11. Close the Translator task pane by clicking the Close button in the upper right corner.
12. Save, preview, and then close **2-MFCMeeting.docx**.

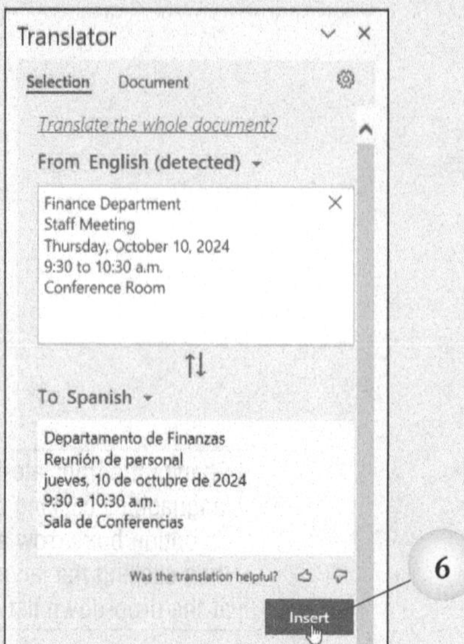

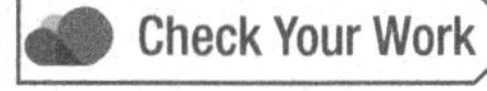

Translating a Document

Quick Steps

Translate Document

1. Click Review tab.
2. Click Translate button.
3. Click *Translate Document*.

To translate an entire document, click the Translate button in the Language group on the Review tab and then choose the *Translate Document* option. The Translator task pane opens with the *Document* option selected. Select the language to translate from and to, and then click the Translate button. A new document opens with the translated text. Click the Translate button and then click the *Translator Preferences* option to narrow the list of languages to be included in the translation list, or click the gear icon in the task pane.

Preparing a Document for Translation

Word's Translate feature is considered a machine translation because a machine, rather than a person, does the translating. While this method is fast and convenient, it is prone to errors. Before sharing a machine-translated document, ask someone familiar with the target language to proofread the text to be sure the information is properly translated. For important or sensitive information to be used in a business context, always rely on a professional translator. To optimize machine translation and reduce errors, follow these guidelines:

- Use standard, formal language. Avoid abbreviations, acronyms, slang, colloquialisms, and idioms, as these may not translate well to a different language.
- Write simple, direct sentences that express only one idea.
- Avoid ambiguities. Use articles (such as *the*) in sentences whenever possible and repeat the noun in a sentence rather than use a pronoun.
- Before translating, run a spelling and grammar check to be sure all words are spelled correctly and that proper punctuation and grammar are used.
- Apply predesigned heading styles to any headings in the document.

Activity 4b Translating a Document — Part 2 of 2

1. Open **Australia.docx** and then save it with the name **2-Australia**.
2. Display the Translator task pane by clicking the Review tab, clicking the Translate button, and then clicking *Translate Document* at the drop-down list. (If a new document opens with translated text, close the document without saving changes.)
3. At the Translator task pane with the *Document* option selected, make sure that *Auto-detect* or *English* displays in the *From* option box.
4. Click the *To* option box arrow, scroll down the drop-down list, and then click *Spanish*.
5. Click the Translate button at the Translator task pane. (This opens a new document with the translated document.)
6. Save the document with the name **2-TranslatedDoc**.
7. Preview and then close **2-TranslatedDoc.docx**.
8. At the **2-Australia.docx** document, close the Translator task pane and then close the document.

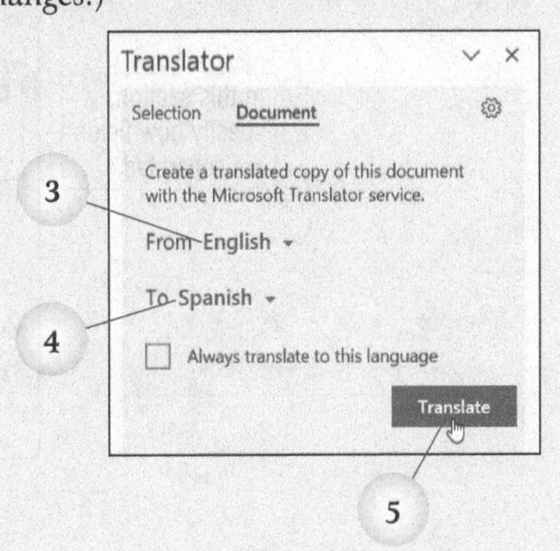

Check Your Work

Activity 5 Sort Company Information **3 Parts**

You will open a document containing information on company employees and then sort data in paragraphs, columns, and tables.

Sorting Text

Text in a document can be sorted alphanumerically, numerically, or chronologically. In an alphanumeric sort, punctuation marks and special symbols are sorted first, followed by numbers and then text. Use options at the Sort Text dialog box to specify what is to be sorted. Text in paragraphs, columns, and tables can be sorted.

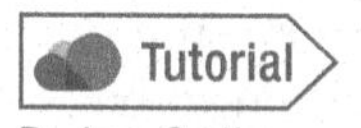

Review: Sorting Text in Paragraphs

Sort

Quick Steps

Sort Paragraphs of Text

1. Click Sort button.
2. Make changes as needed at Sort Text dialog box.
3. Click OK.

Sorting Text in Paragraphs

To sort paragraphs of text, select the text and then click the Sort button in the Paragraph group on the Home tab. This displays the Sort Text dialog box, which contains sorting options.

The *Type* option at the Sort Text dialog box will display *Text*, *Number*, or *Date* depending on the text selected. Word attempts to determine the data type and chooses one of the three options. For example, if numbers with mathematical values are selected, Word assigns them the *Number* type. However, if a numbered list is selected, Word assigns them the *Text* type since the numbers do not represent mathematical values.

By default, paragraphs of text are sorted by the first word of each paragraph. This can be changed with options at the Sort Options dialog box, shown in Figure 2.9. Display this dialog box by clicking the Options button at the Sort Text dialog box. Use the options in the *Separate fields at* section to specify how text is separated in the document. For example, to sort text by the second word of each paragraph, click the *Other* option box (this moves the insertion point into the text box to the right of the *Other* option box) and then press the spacebar.

Figure 2.9 Sort Options Dialog Box

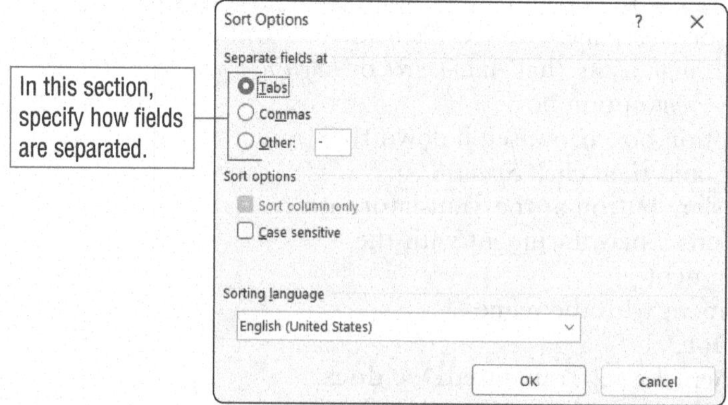

Activity 5a Sorting Text in Paragraphs

Part 1 of 3

1. Open **Sorting.docx** and then save it with the name **2-Sorting**.
2. Sort the text alphabetically by first name by completing the following steps:
   a. Select the seven lines of text at the beginning of the document.
   b. Click the Sort button in the Paragraph group on the Home tab.
   c. At the Sort Text dialog box, click OK.
3. Sort the text by last name by completing the following steps:
   a. With the seven lines of text still selected, click the Sort button.
   b. At the Sort Text dialog box, click the Options button.
   c. At the Sort Options dialog box, click *Other* and then press the spacebar. (This indicates that the first and last names are separated by a space.)

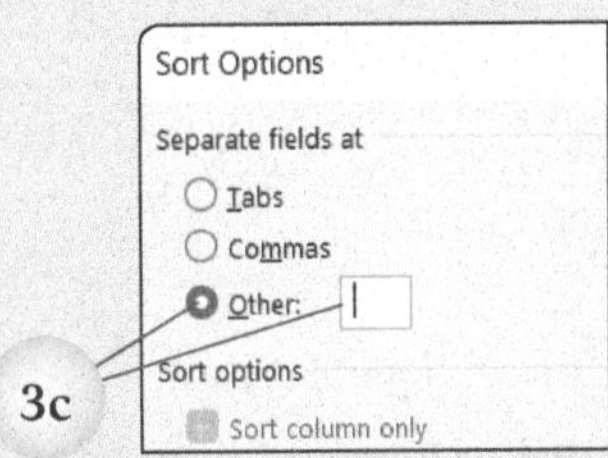

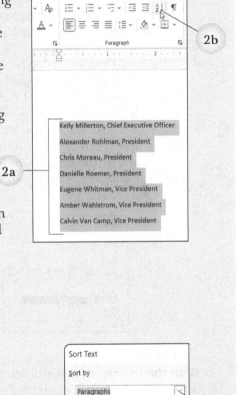

   d. Click OK.
   e. At the Sort Text dialog box, click the *Sort by* option box arrow and then click *Word 2* at the drop-down list.
   f. Click OK.
4. Save **2-Sorting.docx**.

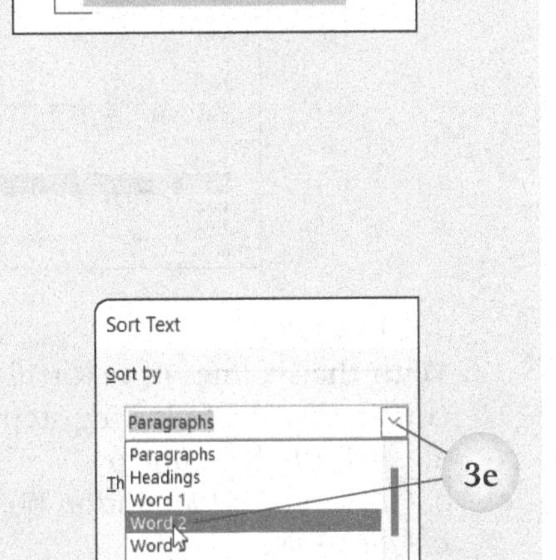

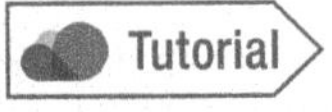

Sorting Text in Columns

Quick Steps

Sort Text in Columns
1. Select specific text.
2. Click Sort button.
3. Click Options button.
4. Specify *Tabs* as separator.
5. Click OK.
6. Make changes at Sort Text dialog box.
7. Click OK.

Sorting Text in Columns

To sort text set in columns, the text must be separated with tabs. When sorting text in columns, Word considers the left margin *Field 1*, text typed at the first tab *Field 2*, and so on. When sorting text in columns, make sure the columns are separated with only one tab because Word recognizes each tab as beginning a separate column. Thus, using more than one tab between columns may result in field numbers that correspond to empty columns.

Sorting on More than One Field

Text can be sorted on more than one field. For example, in Activity 5b, Step 3, the department entries will be sorted alphabetically and then the employee names will be sorted alphabetically within the departments. To do this, specify the *Department* column in the *Sort by* option box and then specify the *Employee* column in the *Then by* option box. If a document contains columns with heading text, click the *Header row* option in the *My list has* section.

Activity 5b **Sorting Text in Columns** Part 2 of 3

1. With **2-Sorting.docx** open, sort text in the first column by last name by completing the following steps:
   a. Select the six lines of text below the column headings *Employee*, *Department*, and *Ext.*
   b. Click the Sort button in the Paragraph group on the Home tab.
   c. At the Sort Text dialog box, click the Options button.
   d. At the Sort Options dialog box, make sure the *Tabs* option is selected in the *Separate fields at* section and then click OK to close the dialog box.
   e. At the Sort Text dialog box, click the *Sort by* option box arrow and then click *Field 2* at the drop-down list. (The left margin is *Field 1* and the first tab is *Field 2*.)

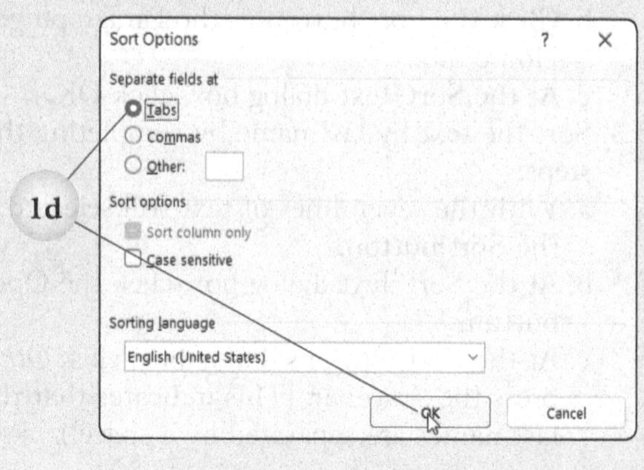

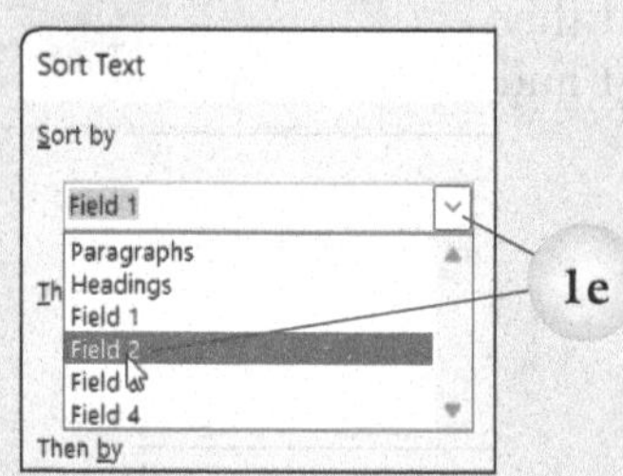

   f. Click OK.
2. With the six lines of text still selected, sort the third column of text numerically by completing the following steps:
   a. Click the Sort button.
   b. Click the *Sort by* option box arrow and then click *Field 4* at the drop-down list.
   c. Click OK.
3. Sort the text in the first two columns by completing the following steps:
   a. Select the seven lines of text set in the columns, including the headings.
   b. Click the Sort button.
   c. At the Sort Text dialog box, click the *Header row* option in the *My list has* section.
   d. If necessary, click the *Sort by* option box arrow and then click *Department*.
   e. Click the *Type* option box arrow in the *Sort by* section and then click *Text*.
   f. Click the *Then by* option box arrow and then click *Employee* at the drop-down list.
   g. Click OK.
4. Save **2-Sorting.docx**.

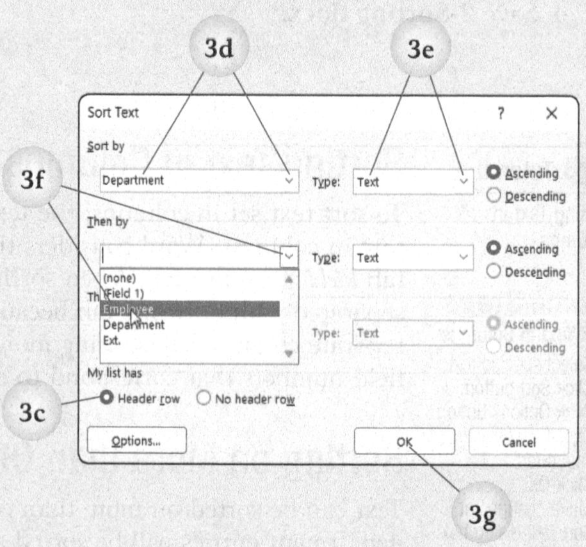

Check Your Work

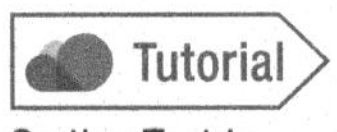

Sorting Text in a Table

Quick Steps

Sort Text in Table

1. Position insertion point in table.
2. Click Sort button.
3. Make changes at Sort dialog box.
4. Click OK.

Sorting Text in a Table

Sorting text in columns within tables is similar to sorting columns of text separated by tabs. When sorting text in a table, the dialog box is named the Sort dialog box rather than the Sort Text dialog box. If a table contains a header, click the *Header row* option in the *My list has* section of the Sort dialog box to tell Word not to include the header row when sorting. To sort only specific cells in a table, select the cells and then complete the sort.

Activity 5c Sorting Text in a Table

Part 3 of 3

1. With **2-Sorting.docx** open, sort the text in the first column of the table by completing the following steps:
   a. Position the insertion point in any cell in the table.
   b. Click the Sort button.
   c. At the Sort dialog box, make sure the *Header row* option is selected in the *My list has* section.
   d. Click the *Sort by* option box arrow and then click *Sales, First Half* at the drop-down list.
   e. Make sure nothing displays in the *Then by* option box. If necessary, click the *Then by* option box arrow and then click *(none)* at the drop-down list.
   f. Click OK.

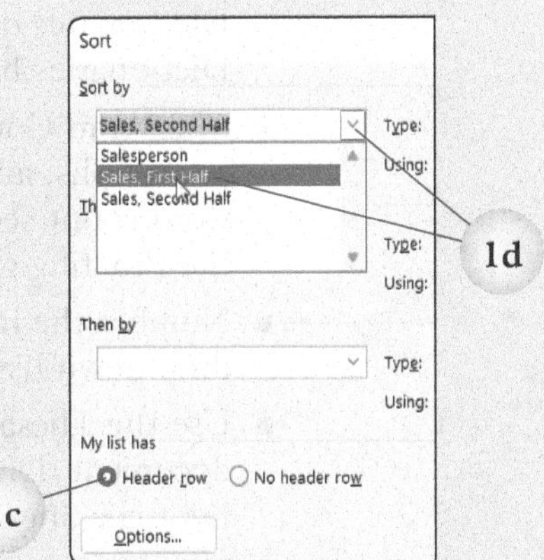

2. Sort the numbers in the third column in descending order by completing the following steps:
   a. Select all the cells in the table except the cells in the first row.
   b. Click the Sort button.
   c. Click the *Sort by* option box arrow and then click *Column 3* at the drop-down list.
   d. Click *Descending*.

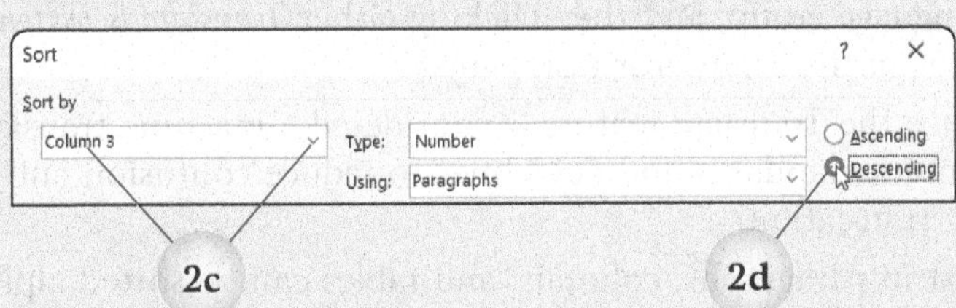

   e. Click OK.
3. Save, preview, and then close **2-Sorting.docx**.

Check Your Work

Chapter Summary

- Word's Editor contains a spelling and grammar checker. The spelling checker checks text against its dictionary and suggests corrections. The grammar checker finds errors in grammar, punctuation, and word usage.
- When checking spelling and grammar, make changes by clicking in the document outside the Editor task pane. Make the changes and then click the Resume checking all results button in the task pane.
- Customize spelling and grammar checking options at the Word Options dialog box with *Proofing* selected in the left panel.
- Change the proofing language at the Language dialog box. Display this dialog box by clicking the Review tab, clicking the Language button in the Language group, and then clicking *Set Proofing Language*.
- To display readability statistics for a document, insert a check mark in the *Show readability statistics* check box in the Word Options dialog box with *Proofing* selected and then complete a spelling and grammar check.
- Word uses the main dictionary when spell checking a document. Change the default dictionary and add or remove a custom dictionary at the Custom Dictionaries dialog box. Display this dialog box by clicking the Custom Dictionaries button at the Word Options dialog box with *Proofing* selected.
- The Word Count dialog box displays the numbers of pages, words, characters, paragraphs, and lines in a document. Display this dialog box by clicking the word count section of the Status bar or by clicking the Word Count button in the Proofing group on the Review tab.
- Number the lines in a document with options at the Line Numbers button drop-down list or the Line Numbers dialog box.
- Use the Thesaurus feature to find synonyms and antonyms for words in a document. Display synonyms and antonyms at the Thesaurus task pane or by right-clicking a word and then pointing to *Synonyms* at the shortcut menu.
- Use the Search button in the Research group on the References tab to find information online for a specific topic and use the Researcher button to search for websites and journals with information on a specific topic.
- Translate text by clicking the Review tab, clicking the Translate button in the Language group, and then clicking either *Translate Selection* or *Translate Document* to open the Translator task pane.
- Since the Translate feature is considered a machine translation, consider content standards and guidelines to reduce confusion and errors and optimize the translation.
- Text in paragraphs, columns, and tables can be sorted alphabetically, numerically, or chronologically. Sort text by clicking the Sort button in the Paragraph group on the Home tab and then using options at the Sort Text dialog box to specify what is to be sorted.
- By default, paragraphs of text are sorted by the first word of each paragraph. This can be changed with options at the Sort Options dialog box. Display the dialog box by clicking the Options button at the Sort Text dialog box. Use the options in the *Separate fields at* section of the dialog box to specify how text is separated in the document.

- When sorting text set in columns, Word considers text typed at the left margin *Field 1*, text typed at the first tab *Field 2*, and so on.
- Sort on more than one field with the *Sort by* and *Then by* options at the Sort dialog box.
- Use the *Header row* option in the *My list has* section in the Sort Text dialog box to sort all the text in rows in a table except the first row.

Commands Review

FEATURE	RIBBON TAB, GROUP	BUTTON, OPTION	KEYBOARD SHORTCUT
line numbers	Layout, Page Setup		
proofing language	Review, Language	, *Set Proofing Language*	
Researcher task pane	References, Research		
Search task pane	References, Research		
Sort Options dialog box	Home, Paragraph	, Options	
Sort Text dialog box	Home, Paragraph		
spelling and grammar checker	Review, Proofing		F7
Thesaurus task pane	Review, Proofing		Shift + F7
Translator task pane	Review, Language	, *Translate Selection* OR *Translate Document*	
Word Count dialog box	Review, Proofing		

Review and Assessment

CHAPTER 2

Skills Assessment

Assessment 1
Check Spelling and Grammar in a Document

1. Open **QuoteMarks.docx** and then save it with the name **2-QuoteMarks**.
2. Complete a spelling and grammar check on the document. (Ignore any quoted text selected by the Editor.)
3. Apply the Heading 1 style to the title of the document and the Heading 2 style to the headings in the document (which currently display with bold formatting).
4. Apply the Parallax theme.
5. Center the document title.
6. Save, preview, and then close **2-QuoteMarks.docx**.

Assessment 2
Check Spelling and Grammar and Proofread a Letter

1. Open **AirMiles.docx** and then save it with the name **2-AirMiles**.
2. Complete a spelling and grammar check on the document.
3. After completing the spelling and grammar check, proofread the letter and correct any errors not identified by the Editor. Replace the *XX* near the end of the document with your initials.
4. Select the entire document and then change the font to 12-point Candara.
5. Save, preview, and then close **2-AirMiles.docx**.

Assessment 3
Check Spelling and Grammar and Display Readability Statistics and Word Count in a Document

1. Open **KonradZuse.docx** and then save it with the name **2-KonradZuse**.
2. Turn on the display of readability statistics and then complete a spelling and grammar check on the document. (All proper names are spelled correctly.)
3. Make a note of the number of words, the Flesch Reading Ease score, and the Flesch-Kincaid Grade Level score. Type that information in the appropriate locations at the end of the document.
4. Turn off the display of readability statistics.
5. Insert continuous line numbering.
6. Save, preview, and then close **2-KonradZuse.docx**.

Assessment 4
Translate Selected Text in a Document

1. Open **PRConference.docx** and then save it with the name **2-PRConference**.
2. Select all the text in the first cell in the table (begins with *Annual Conference*).
3. Display the Translator task pane with the *Selection* option selected.
4. Specify that the text is to be translated into Spanish.
5. Click in the empty row at the bottom of the table and then insert the translated text.
6. Close the Translator task pane.
7. Save, preview, and then close **2-PRConference.docx**.

Assessment 5

Translate an Entire Document

1. Open **Announcement.docx** and then save it with the name **2-Announcement**.
2. Translate the entire document into French.
3. Save the translated document with the name **2-Announce-French**.
4. Preview and then close **2-Announce-French.docx**.
5. Close the Translator task pane and then close **2-Announcement.docx**.

Assessment 6

Sort Text in a Document

1. Open **SFSSorting.docx** and then save it with the name **2-SFSSorting**.
2. Select the nine lines of text below the heading *Executive Team* and then sort the text alphabetically by last name.
3. Sort the three columns of text below the title *New Employees* by date of hire in ascending order.
4. Sort the text in the *First Qtr.* column in the table numerically in descending order.
5. Save, preview, and then close **2-SFSSorting.docx**.

Visual Benchmark

Activity 1

Sort Data in a Document

1. Open **Natura.docx** and then save it with the name **2-Natura**.
2. Complete sorts so that your text appears as shown in Figure 2.10. ***Hint: Sort the text in the table first by the country and then by the customer name.***
3. Save, preview, and then close **2-Natura.docx**.

Activity 2

Translate Text

1. Open **CCDonations.docx** and then save it with the name **2-CCDonations**.
2. Select the paragraph of text below the heading *English:* and then translate the paragraph into Spanish and then into French. Insert the translated text into the document, as shown in Figure 2.11. (Your translations may vary from those shown in the figure.)
3. Use the Curlz MT font with bold formatting to format the heading at the beginning of each paragraph and the quote (without bold formatting) that displays near the end of the letter. Center the quote and apply the Blue font color to the quote and then apply paragraph shading as shown in the figure.
4. Save, preview, and then close **2-CCDonations.docx**.

Figure 2.10 Visual Benchmark 1

Natura Representatives

Denise Beaulieu	206-555-3901
Marcus Brown	347-555-2389
Charles Collins	202-555-9954
Dallas Conway	305-555-3492
Midori Fujita	504-555-7384
Isaac Hill	520-555-4366
Finn McDougal	312-444-0394
Paulina Menzel	346-555-2348
Hamilton Pierce	410-555-2384
Genevieve Salinger	602-555-4392

Natura Customers

Customer	Street Address	City	State/ Province	Postal Code	Country
Flying Queen	478 River Ave.	Winnipeg	MB	V4B 4A9	Canada
Rose	467 Seventh St. E.	Saskatoon	SK	S7H1A3	Canada
Swan	347 Park St.	Halifax	NS	B3H 2W2	Canada
Wave Rider	342 W. Georgia	Vancouver	BC	V6E 3H7	Canada
Beauty	89 Kiefer Creek Rd.	Ballwin	MO	63021	USA
Belle	P.O. Box 359	Belt	MT	59412	USA
Blue Fairy	307 Gold Hill Dr.	Grass Valley	CA	95945	USA
Maiden	345 Polk St.	San Francisco	CA	94109	USA
Melody	P.O. Box 789	Stromsburg	NE	68666	USA
Nautilus	45 Scarborough St.	Hartford	CT	06105	USA
Nina's Gift	784 Arizona Ave.	Santa Monica	CA	90401	USA
Red Coral	67 N. 73rd St.	Omaha	NE	68114	USA
Sailing Beauty	358 Fifth Ave.	Anchorage	AK	99501	USA
Sea Princess	876 N. Roxboro St.	Durham	NC	27701	USA
Suzanna	2331 S. Pioneer St.	Abilene	TX	79605	USA
The Dolphin	478 Dodson Dr.	East Point	GA	30344	USA
The Mermaid	782 West Fairway Pl.	Chandler	AZ	85224	USA
The Picasso	784 Parks St.	Duxbury	MA	02331	USA
Water Spirit	215 Vine St.	Cincinnati	OH	45202	USA
Woodwinds	34 Downey Ave.	Modesto	CA	95354	USA

Figure 2.11 Visual Benchmark 2

Cordova Children's Community Center

Support Your Local Community Center

English:
As you consider your donation contributions for the coming year, we ask that you consider your community by supporting the Cordova Children's Community Center. The center is a nonprofit agency providing educational and recreational activities for children. Please stop by for a visit. Our dedicated staff will be available to discuss with you the services offered by the center, how the center spends your donation dollars, and provide information on current and future activities and services.

Spanish:
Al considerar sus contribuciones de donación para el próximo año, le pedimos que considere su comunidad apoyando al Centro Comunitario infantil de Cordova. El centro es una agencia sin fines de lucro que ofrece actividades educativas y recreativas para los niños. Por favor, pase por aquí para una visita. Nuestro dedicado personal estará disponible para discutir con usted los servicios ofrecidos por el centro, cómo el centro gasta sus dólares de donación, y proporcionar información sobre las actividades y servicios actuales y futuros.

French:
Alors que vous considérez vos contributions de dons pour l'année à venir, nous vous demandons de considérer votre communauté en soutenant le Cordova Children's Community Center. Le centre est une agence à but non lucratif offrant des activités éducatives et récréatives pour les enfants. S'il vous plaît arrêtez-vous pour une visite. Notre personnel dévoué sera disponible pour discuter avec vous des services offerts par le centre, de la façon dont le centre dépense vos dons et fournir des informations sur les activités et services actuels et futurs.

"Children are our most valuable natural resource." ~ Herbert Hoover

770 Sunrise Terrace ◆ Santa Fe, NM 87509 ◆ 505-555-7700

Case Study

Part 1

You work in the executive offices at Nickell Industries and have been asked to develop a writing manual for employees. The company has not used a consistent theme when formatting documents, so you decide to choose a theme and use it when formatting all Nickell documents. Open **NIManual.docx** and then save the document with the name **2-NIManual**. Check the spelling and grammar in the document. (You determine whether to accept or ignore grammar suggestions made by the Editor.)

Make the following changes to the document:

- Insert a next page section break at the beginning of the title *Editing and Proofreading*.
- Apply styles of your choosing to the titles and headings in the document.
- Apply the theme you have chosen for company documents.
- Insert headers and/or footers.
- Create a cover page.
- Save the document.

Part 2

As you review the writing manual document you have created for Nickell Industries, you decide to highlight the points for developing sections of documents. You decide that a vertical block list SmartArt graphic will present the ideas in an easy-to-read format and provide some visual interest to the manual. Insert a page break at the end of the text in **2-NIManual.docx**, type the title *Developing a Document*, and then insert the following in the SmartArt graphic in the appropriate shapes:

Beginning

- Introduce main idea.
- Get reader's attention.
- Establish a positive tone.

Middle

- Provide detail for main idea.
- Lead reader to intended conclusion.

End

- State conclusion.
- State action reader should take.

Apply colors that follow the theme you have chosen for company documents. Save and then close the document.

Part 3

Nickell Industries does business in other countries, including Mexico. One of the executives in the Finance Department has asked you to translate into Spanish some terms that will be used to develop an invoice. Create a document that translates the following terms from English to Spanish and also include in the document the steps for translating text. Your reason for doing this is that if the executives know the steps, they can translate the text at their own computers.

- city
- telephone
- invoice
- product
- description
- total

Format the document with the theme you have chosen for company documents and add any other enhancements to improve the appearance of the document. Save the completed document with the name **2-NITranslations**. Preview and then close **2-NITranslations.docx**.

Part 4

While working on the writing manual for Nickell Industries, you decide to purchase some reference books on grammar and punctuation. Using the internet, search for books that provide information on grammar and punctuation and then choose three books. You know that the books will be purchased soon, so you decide to add the information in the writing manual document, telling readers what reference books are available. Open **2-NIManual.docx** and then include this information on a separate page at the end of the text in the document. Save, preview, and then close the document.

WORD

CHAPTER 3

Inserting Headers, Footers, and References

Performance Objectives

Upon successful completion of Chapter 3, you will be able to:

1 Insert headers and footers in documents
2 Format, edit, and remove headers and footers
3 Insert and print sections
4 Keep text together on a page
5 Insert footnotes and endnotes
6 Insert and edit sources and citations
7 Insert, modify, and format sources lists

Word provides a number of predesigned headers (text that displays and prints at the tops of pages) and footers (text that displays and prints at the bottoms of pages) that can be inserted in documents, or custom headers and footers can be created. A document can be divided into sections and different formatting can be applied to each section, such as different headers, footers, and page numbers. In this chapter, you will learn how to create custom headers and footers, how to format and print sections in a document, and how to control soft page breaks within a document. You will also learn how to reference documents and acknowledge sources using footnotes, endnotes, and source lists.

Data Files

The data files for this chapter are in the WL2C3 folder that you downloaded at the beginning of this course.

Activity 1 **Insert Headers and Footers in a Computer Software Report** **8 Parts**

You will open a report on computer software and then create, customize, and position headers and footers in the document. You will also create headers and footers for different pages in a document, divide a document into sections, and then create footers for specific sections.

Inserting Headers and Footers

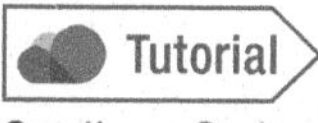

Creating a Custom Header and Footer

Editing a Header and Footer

Hint One method for formatting a header or footer is to select the header or footer text and then use the options on the Mini toolbar.

Text that appears in the top margin of a page is called a *header* and text that appears in the bottom margin of a page is called a *footer*. Headers and footers are commonly used in manuscripts, textbooks, reports, and other publications to display the page numbers and section or chapter titles. For example, see the footer at the bottom of this page.

Insert a predesigned header by clicking the Insert tab and then clicking the Header button in the Header & Footer group. This displays a drop-down list of header choices. Click the predesigned header and the formatted header is inserted in the document. Complete similar steps to insert a predesigned footer.

If the predesigned headers and footers do not meet specific needs, create a custom header or footer. To create a custom header, click the Insert tab, click the Header button in the Header & Footer group, and then click *Edit Header* at the drop-down list. This displays a Header pane in the document along with the Header & Footer tab, as shown in Figure 3.1. Use options on this tab to insert elements such as page numbers, and images; to navigate to other headers and footers in the document; and to position headers and footers on different pages in a document.

Inserting Elements in Headers and Footers

Use buttons in the Insert group on the Header & Footer tab to insert elements into the header or footer, such as the date and time, Quick Parts, and images. Click the Date & Time button in the Insert group and the Date and Time dialog box displays. Choose a date and time option in the *Available formats* list box of the dialog box and then click OK.

Click the Document Info button to display a drop-down list of document information fields that can be inserted into the document. Hover the pointer over the *Document Property* option in the Document Info button drop-down list to display a side menu of document properties, such as *Author*, *Comments*, and *Company*, that can be inserted in the header or footer.

Figure 3.1 Header & Footer Tab

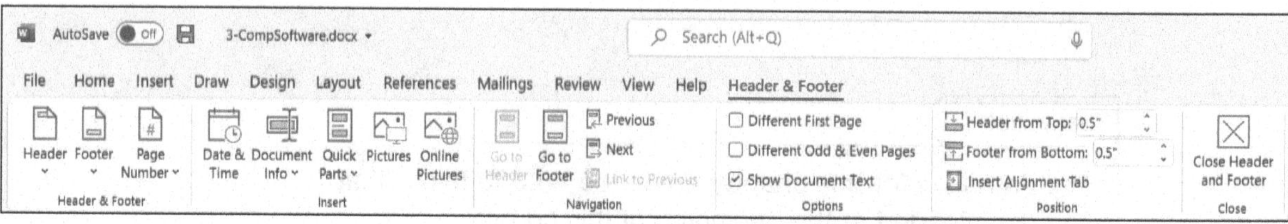

The Quick Parts button in the Insert group on the Header & Footer tab contains options for inserting document properties, fields, and other elements. Click the Pictures button to display the Insert Picture dialog box and insert an image from the computer's hard drive or removable drive. Click the Online Pictures button and the Online Pictures window opens with options for searching for and then downloading an image into the header or footer.

Activity 1a Inserting Elements in a Header and Footer

Part 1 of 8

1. Open **CompSoftware.docx** and then save it with the name **3-CompSoftware**.
2. Insert a header by completing the following steps:
   a. Click the Insert tab.
   b. Click the Header button in the Header & Footer group and then click *Edit Header* at the drop-down list.
   c. With the insertion point positioned in the Header pane, click the Pictures button in the Insert group on the Header & Footer tab.

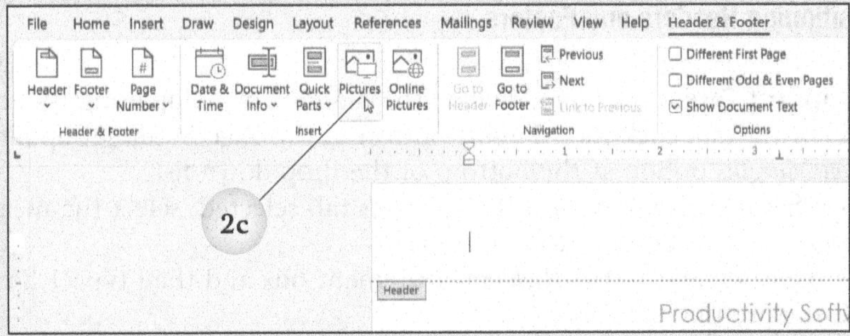

   d. At the Insert Picture dialog box, navigate to your WL2C3 folder and then double-click the ***Worldwide.png*** image file.
   e. With the image selected, click in the *Shape Height* measurement box in the Size group, type 0.5 and then press the Enter key.
   f. Click the Wrap Text button in the Arrange group and then click *Behind Text* at the drop-down list.
   g. Drag the image up approximately one-third of an inch.
   h. Click outside the image to deselect it.
   i. Press the Tab key two times. (Pressing the Tab key moves the insertion point to the right margin.)
   j. Click the Header & Footer tab and then click the Date & Time button in the Insert group.
   k. At the Date and Time dialog box, click the twelfth option from the top (the option that displays the date in numbers and the time) and then click OK to close the dialog box.
   l. Select the date and time text and then use the Mini toolbar to apply bold formatting and change the font size to 9 points.
   m. Double-click in the document to make it active. (The text in the header will display dimmed.)
3. Save **3-CompSoftware.docx**.

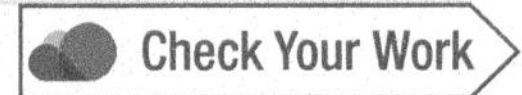

Positioning Headers and Footers

Word inserts a header 0.5 inch from the top of the page and a footer 0.5 inch from the bottom of the page. These default positions can be changed with buttons in the Position group on the Header & Footer tab. Use the *Header from Top* and the *Footer from Bottom* measurement boxes to adjust the position of the header and the footer, respectively, on the page.

By default, headers and footers contain two tab settings. A center tab is set at 3.25 inches and a right tab is set at 6.5 inches. If the document contains default left and right margin settings of 1 inch, the center tab set at 3.25 inches is the center of the document and the right tab set at 6.5 inches is at the right margin. If the default margins are changed, the default center tab may need to be changed before inserting header or footer text at the center tab. Position tabs with the Insert Alignment Tab button in the Position group. Click this button and the Alignment Tab dialog box displays. Use options at this dialog box to change tab alignment and set tabs with leaders.

Activity 1b Positioning Headers and Footers

Part 2 of 8

1. With **3-CompSoftware.docx** open, change the margins by completing the following steps:
   a. Click the Layout tab, click the Margins button in the Page Setup group, and then click the *Custom Margins* option at the bottom of the drop-down list.
   b. At the Page Setup dialog box with the Margins tab selected, select the measurement in the *Left* measurement box and then type 1.25.
   c. Select the measurement in the *Right* measurement box and then type 1.25.
   d. Click OK to close the dialog box.
2. Create a footer by completing the following steps:
   a. Click the Insert tab.
   b. Click the Footer button in the Header & Footer group and then click *Edit Footer* at the drop-down list.
   c. With the insertion point positioned in the Footer pane, type your first and last names at the left margin.
   d. Press the Tab key. (This moves the insertion point to the center tab position.)
   e. Click the Page Number button in the Header & Footer group, point to *Current Position*, and then click *Accent Bar 2* at the drop-down list.

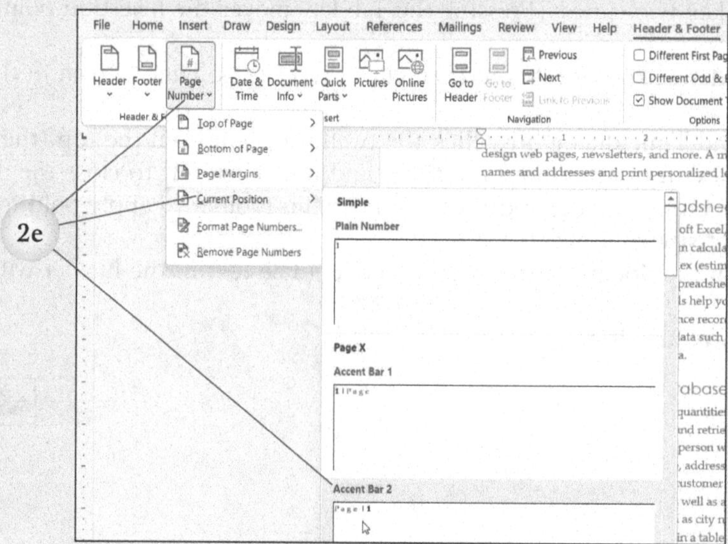

f. Press the Tab key.

g. Click the Document Info button in the Insert group and then click *File Name* at the drop-down list.

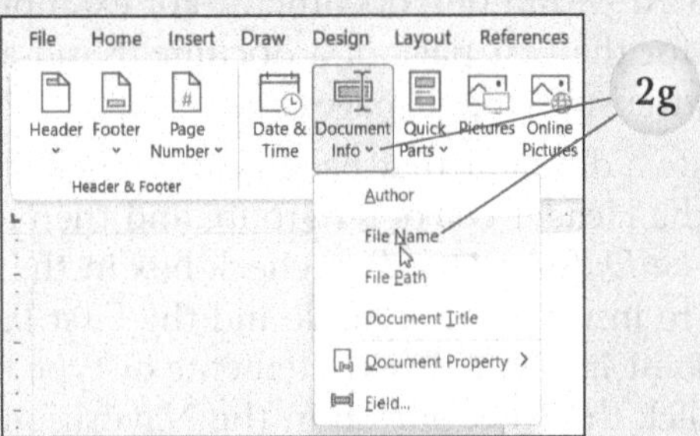

h. You notice that the center tab and right tab are slightly off, because the left and right margins in the document are set at 1.25 inches instead of 1 inch. To align the tabs correctly, drag the center tab marker to the 3-inch mark on the horizontal ruler and drag the right tab marker to the 6-inch mark on the horizontal ruler.

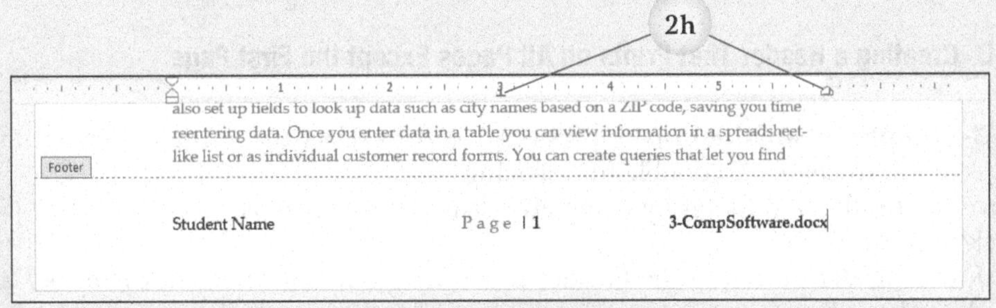

i. Select all the footer text and then apply bold formatting and change the font size to 9 points.

3. Change the position of the header and footer by completing the following steps:
   a. Click the Header & Footer tab.
   b. Click the Go to Header button in the Navigation group.
   c. Click the *Header from Top* measurement box up arrow to display *0.6"*.
   d. Click the Go to Footer button in the Navigation group.
   e. Click in the *Footer from Bottom* measurement box, type 0.6, and then press the Enter key.
   f. Click the Close Header and Footer button.

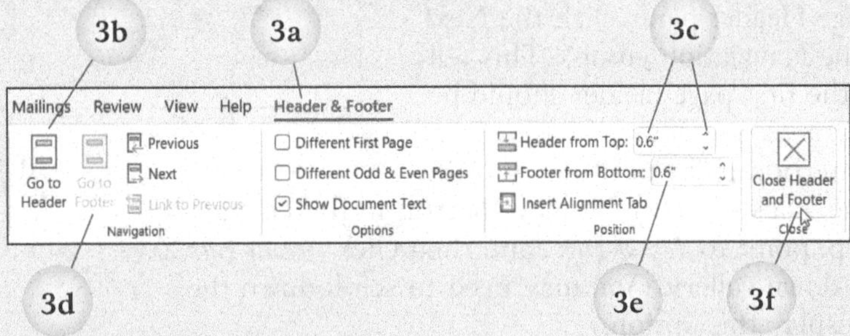

4. Save and then preview **3-CompSoftware.docx**.

Check Your Work

Creating a Different First Page Header and Footer

Quick Steps

Create Different First Page Header or Footer

1. Click Insert tab.
2. Click Header or Footer button.
3. Click *Edit Header* or *Edit Footer* at drop-down list.
4. Click *Different First Page* check box.
5. Insert elements and/or text.
6. Click Next button.
7. Insert elements and/or text.

Creating a Different First Page Header or Footer

A header and/or footer inserted in a document will display and print on every page in the document by default. However, different headers and footers can be created within one document. For example, a unique header or footer can be created for the first page of a document and a different header or footer can be created for the subsequent pages.

To create a different first page header, click the Insert tab, click the Header button in the Header & Footer group, and then click *Edit Header* at the drop-down list. Click the *Different First Page* check box in the Options group on the Header & Footer tab to insert a check mark and the First Page Header pane displays with the insertion point inside it. Insert elements or type text to create the first page header and then click the Next button in the Navigation group. This displays the Header pane with the insertion point positioned inside it. Insert elements and/or type text to create the header. Complete similar steps to create a different first page footer.

In some situations, the first page header or footer should be blank. This is particularly useful if a document contains a title page and the header or footer should not display and print on it.

Activity 1c Creating a Header That Prints on All Pages Except the First Page — Part 3 of 8

1. With **3-CompSoftware.docx** open, press Ctrl + A to select the entire document and then press Ctrl + 2 to change to double-line spacing.
2. Remove the header and footer by completing the following steps:
   a. Click the Insert tab.
   b. Click the Header button in the Header & Footer group and then click *Remove Header* at the drop-down list.
   c. Click the Footer button in the Header & Footer group and then click *Remove Footer* at the drop-down list.
3. Press Ctrl + Home and then create a header that prints on all pages except the first page by completing the following steps:
   a. With the Insert tab active, click the Header button in the Header & Footer group.
   b. Click *Edit Header* at the drop-down list.
   c. Click the *Different First Page* check box in the Options group on the Header & Footer tab to insert a check mark.
   d. With the insertion point positioned in the First Page Header pane, click the Next button in the Navigation group. (This tells Word that the first page header should be blank.)
   e. With the insertion point positioned in the Header pane, click the Page Number button in the Header & Footer group, point to *Top of Page*, and then click *Accent Bar 2* at the drop-down gallery. (You may need to scroll down the gallery to display this option.)
   f. Click the Close Header and Footer button.
4. Scroll through the document and notice that the header appears on the second, third, fourth, and fifth pages.
5. Save and then preview **3-CompSoftware.docx**.

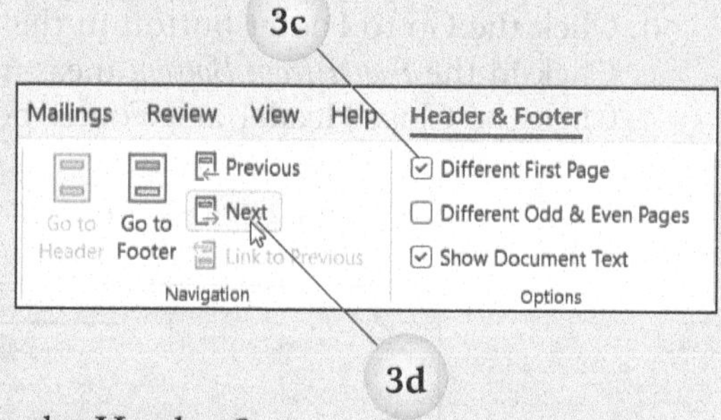

Check Your Work

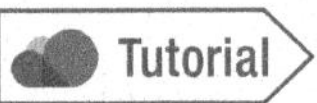

Creating Odd Page and Even Page Headers and Footers

Quick Steps

Create Odd and Even Page Headers or Footers

1. Click Insert tab.
2. Click Header or Footer button.
3. Click *Edit Header* or *Edit Footer*.
4. Click *Different Odd & Even Pages* check box.
5. Insert elements and/or text.

Creating Odd and Even Page Headers or Footers

If a document will be read in book form, consider inserting odd and even page headers or footers. When presenting pages in a document in book form with facing pages, the outside margins are the left side of the left page and the right side of the right page. Also, when a document has facing pages, the right-hand page is generally numbered with an odd number and the left-hand page is generally numbered with an even number.

Create even and odd headers or footers to insert this type of page numbering. Use the *Different Odd & Even Pages* check box in the Options group on the Header & Footer tab to create odd and even headers and/or footers.

Activity 1d Creating Odd and Even Page Footers

Part 4 of 8

1. With **3-CompSoftware.docx** open, remove the header from the document by completing the following steps:
   a. Click the Insert tab.
   b. Click the Header button in the Header & Footer group and then click *Edit Header* at the drop-down list.
   c. Click the *Different First Page* check box in the Options group to remove the check mark.
   d. Click the Header button in the Header & Footer group and then click *Remove Header* at the drop-down list. (This displays the insertion point in an empty Header pane.)
2. Create one footer that prints on odd pages and another that prints on even pages by completing the following steps:
   a. Click the Go to Footer button in the Navigation group.
   b. Click the *Different Odd & Even Pages* check box in the Options group to insert a check mark. (This displays the Odd Page Footer pane with the insertion point inside it.)
   c. Click the Page Number button in the Header & Footer group, point to *Bottom of Page*, and then click *Plain Number 3* at the drop-down list.
   d. Click the Next button in the Navigation group. (This displays the Even Page Footer pane with the insertion point inside it.)

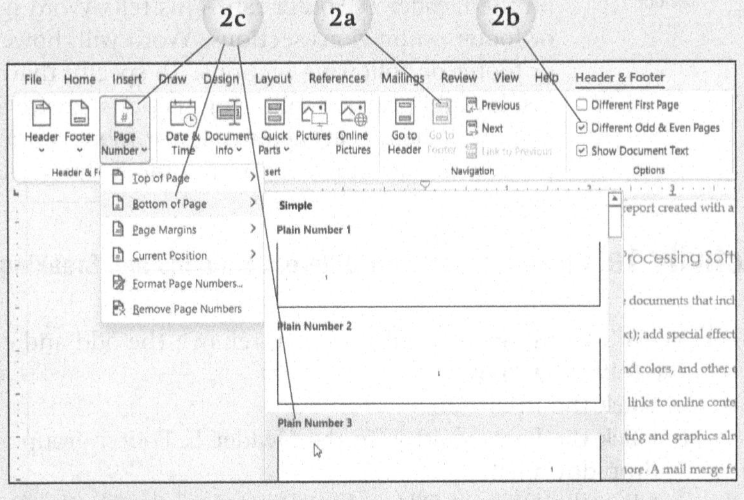

e. Click the Page Number button, point to *Current Position*, and then click *Plain Number* at the drop-down list.
f. Click the Close Header and Footer button.
3. Scroll through the document and notice the page numbers at the right sides of the odd page footers and the left sides of the even page footers.
4. Save and then preview **3-CompSoftware.docx**.

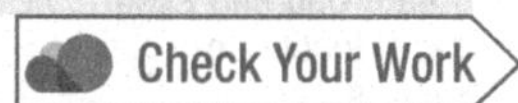

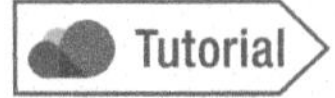

Creating a Header and Footer for Different Sections

Quick Steps

Create Headers or Footers for Different Sections

1. Insert section break.
2. Click Insert tab.
3. Click Header or Footer button.
4. Click *Edit Header* or *Edit Footer*.
5. Click Link to Previous button to deactivate.
6. Insert elements and/or text.
7. Click Next button.
8. Insert elements and/or text.

Creating a Header and Footer for Different Sections

A document can be divided into sections by inserting section breaks and then different formatting can be applied to each section. A section break can be inserted that begins a new page or a section break can be inserted that allows the sections to be formatted differently, but does not begin a new page. A section break can also be inserted that starts a new section on the next even-numbered page or the next odd-numbered page.

To insert different headers and/or footers on pages in a document, divide the document into sections. For example, if a document contains several chapters, each chapter can be a separate section and a different header and footer can be created for each section. When dividing a document into sections by chapter, insert section breaks that also begin new pages.

Breaking a Section Link

When a header or footer is created for a specific section in a document, it can be created for all the previous and following sections or only the following sections. By default, each section in a document is linked to the other sections. To display and print a header or footer only on the pages within a section and not the previous section, deactivate the Link to Previous button in the Navigation group on the Header & Footer tab. This tells Word not to display and print the header or footer on previous sections. Word will, however, display and print the header or footer on following sections. To specify that the header or footer should not display and print on following sections, create a blank header or footer at the next section. When creating a header or footer for a specific section in a document, preview the document to determine if the header or footer appears on the correct pages.

Activity 1e Creating Footers for Different Sections and Breaking a Section Link — Part 5 of 8

1. With **3-CompSoftware.docx** open, remove the odd and even page footers by completing the following steps:
   a. Click the Insert tab.
   b. Click the Footer button in the Header & Footer group and then click *Edit Footer* at the drop-down list.
   c. Click the *Different Odd & Even Pages* check box in the Options group to remove the check mark.
   d. Click the Footer button in the Header & Footer group and then click *Remove Footer* at the drop-down list.
   e. Click the Close Header and Footer button.

2. Remove the page break before the second title in the document by completing the following steps:
   a. Move the insertion point immediately right of the period that ends the paragraph in the section *Presentation Software* (near the middle of page 3).
   b. Press the Delete key two times. (The title *Graphics and Multimedia Software* should now display below the paragraph on the third page.)
3. Insert an odd page section break (a section break that starts a section on the next odd page) by completing the following steps:
   a. Position the insertion point at the beginning of the title *Graphics and Multimedia Software*.
   b. Click the Layout tab, click the Breaks button in the Page Setup group, and then click *Odd Page* at the drop-down list.

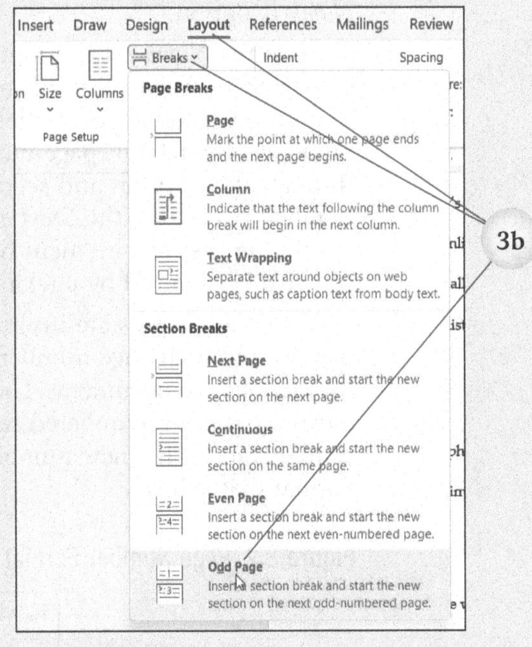

4. Create section titles and footers with page numbers for the two sections by completing the following steps:
   a. Position the insertion point at the beginning of the document.
   b. Click the Insert tab.
   c. Click the Footer button in the Header & Footer group and then click *Edit Footer* at the drop-down list.
   d. At the Footer -Section 1- pane, type Section 1 Productivity Software and then press the Tab key two times. (This moves the insertion point to the right margin.)
   e. Type Page and then press the spacebar.
   f. Click the Page Number button in the Header & Footer group, point to *Current Position*, and then click *Plain Number* at the side menu.
   g. Click the Next button in the Navigation group.
   h. Click the Link to Previous button to deactivate it. (This removes the message *Same as Previous* from the top right side of the footer pane.)
   i. In the footer, change the text *Section 1 Productivity Software* to *Section 2 Graphics and Multimedia Software*.
   j. Click the Close Header and Footer button.

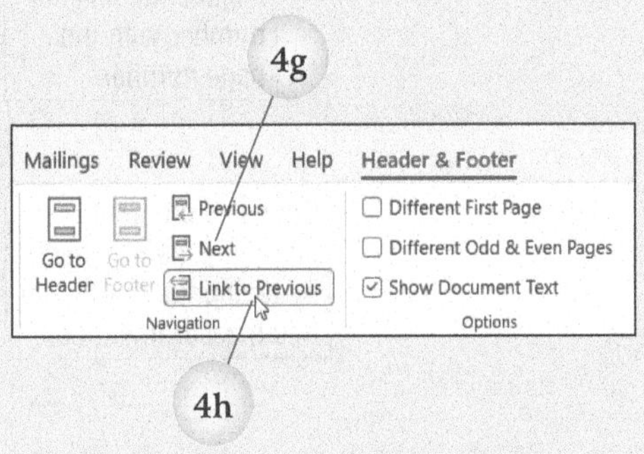

5. Scroll through the document and notice the footers and page numbers in the sections. (Note that due to the section break, there is no page 4 shown in the document. A blank page 4 will display in print preview and, if the document is printed, a blank page 4 will print.)
6. Save **3-CompSoftware.docx**.

Check Your Work

Customizing Page Numbers

Page Number

Customizing Page Numbers

By default, Word inserts arabic numbers (1, 2, 3, and so on) and numbers pages sequentially beginning with 1. These default settings can be customized with options at the Page Number Format dialog box, shown in Figure 3.2. To display this dialog box, click the Insert tab, click the Page Number button in the Header & Footer group, and then click *Format Page Numbers* at the drop-down list. Another method for displaying the dialog box is to click the Page Number button in the Header & Footer group on the Header & Footer tab and then click the *Format Page Numbers* option.

Use the *Number format* option at the Page Number Format dialog box to change from arabic numbers to arabic numbers preceded and followed by hyphens, lowercase letters, uppercase letters, lowercase roman numerals, or uppercase roman numerals. By default, page numbering begins with 1 and continues sequentially through all the pages and sections in a document. Change the beginning page number by clicking the *Start at* option and then typing the beginning page number in the measurement box. The number in the *Start at* measurement box can also be changed by clicking the measurement box up or down arrow.

If section breaks are inserted in a document and then a header and footer are inserted with page numbers for each section, the page numbers are sequential throughout the document. The document used in Activity 1f has a section break, but the pages are numbered sequentially. If the page numbering in a section should start with a new number, use the *Start at* option at the Page Number Format dialog box.

Figure 3.2 Page Number Format Dialog Box

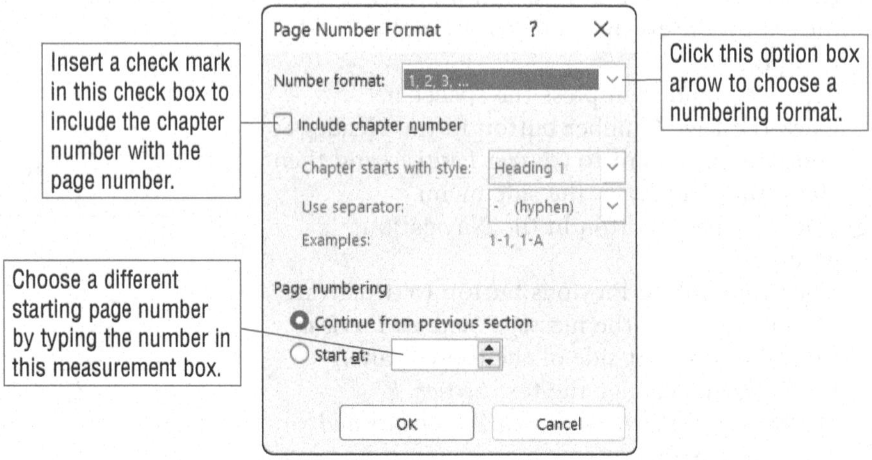

Activity 1f Customizing Page Numbering

Part 6 of 8

1. With **3-CompSoftware.docx** open, change the page numbers to lowercase roman numerals and change the starting page number by completing the following steps:
   a. Press Ctrl + Home.
   b. Click the Insert tab.
   c. Click the Page Number button in the Header & Footer group and then click *Format Page Numbers* at the drop-down list.
   d. At the Page Number Format dialog box, click the *Number format* option box arrow and then click *i, ii, iii, ...* at the drop-down list.
   e. Click the *Start at* option and then type 4.
   f. Click OK to close the dialog box.
2. Scroll through the document and notice the lowercase roman numeral page numbers (beginning with *iv*) that display at the right margins at the bottoms of the pages.
3. Scroll to the bottom of the page containing the title *Graphics and Multimedia Software* and notice that the page numbers did not change. (This is because the sections were unlinked.)
4. Position the insertion point in the first paragraph of text below the title *Graphics and Multmedia Software* and then change the page numbering by completing the following steps:
   a. Click the Page Number button and then click *Format Page Numbers* at the drop-down list.
   b. At the Page Number Format dialog box, click the *Number format* option box arrow and then click *i, ii, iii, ...* at the drop-down list.
   c. Click the *Start at* option and then type 7.
   d. Click OK to close the dialog box.
5. Save and then preview **3-CompSoftware.docx**.

Page Number Format
Number format: i, ii, iii, ...
Include chapter number
Chapter starts with style: Heading 1
Use separator: - (hyphen)
Examples: 1-1, 1-A
Page numbering
Continue from previous section
Start at: 4
OK Cancel
1d 1e 1f

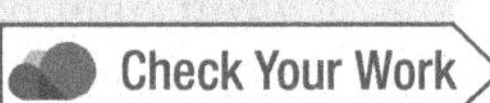

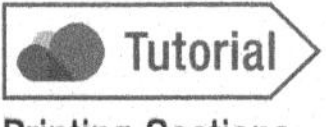

Printing Sections

Printing Sections

Print specific pages in a document by inserting page numbers in the *Pages* text box at the Print backstage area. When entering page numbers in this text box, use a hyphen to indicate a range of consecutive pages or a comma to specify nonconsecutive pages.

Quick Steps

Print Section

1. Click File tab.
2. Click *Print* option.
3. Click in *Pages* text box.
4. Type s followed by section number.
5. Click Print button.

In a document that contains sections, use the *Pages* text box at the Print backstage area to specify the section and pages within the section to be printed. For example, if a document is divided into three sections, print only section 2 by typing *s2* in the *Pages* text box. If a document contains six sections, print sections 3 through 5 by typing *s3-s5* in the *Pages* text box. Specific pages within or between sections can also be identified for printing. For example, to print pages 2 through 5 of section 4, type p2s4-p5s4; to print from page 3 of section 1 through page 5 of section 4, type p3s1-p5s4; to print page 1 of section 3, page 4 of section 5, and page 6 of section 8, type p1s3,p4s5,p6s8.

Activity 1g Changing Section Page Numbering and Printing Section Pages

1. With **3-CompSoftware.docx** open, press Ctrl + Home to move the insertion point to the beginning of the document.
2. Change the number formats and starting page numbers for sections 1 and 2 by completing the following steps:
   a. Click the Insert tab, click the Footer button in the Header & Footer group, and then click *Edit Footer* at the drop-down list.
   b. At the Footer -Section 1- footer pane, click the Page Number button in the Header & Footer group and then click the *Format Page Numbers* option at the drop-down list.
   c. Click the *Number format* option box arrow and then click the *1, 2, 3, ...* option at the drop-down list.
   d. Select the current number in the *Start at* measurement box and then type 1.
   e. Click OK to close the dialog box.
   f. Display the section 2 footer by clicking the Next button in the Navigation group.
   g. At the Footer -Section 2- footer pane, click the Page Number button and then click the *Format Page Numbers* option at the drop-down list.
   h. At the Page Number Format dialog box, click the *Number format* option box arrow and then click the *1, 2, 3, ...* option at the drop-down list.
   i. Select the current number in the *Start at* measurement box and then type 1.
   j. Click OK to close the dialog box.
   k. Click the Close Header and Footer button.

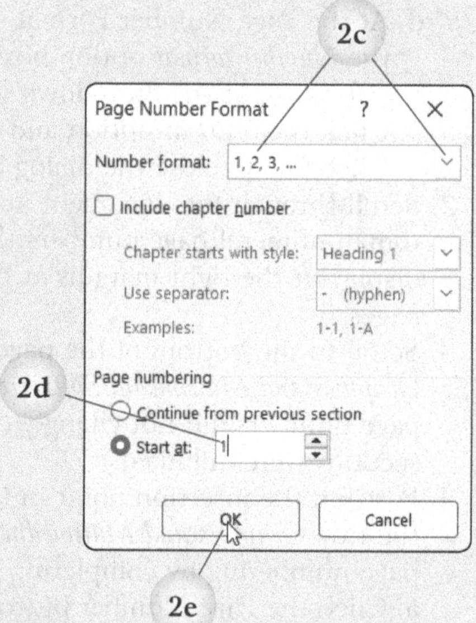

3. Print only page 1 of section 1 and page 1 of section 2 by completing the following steps:
   a. Click the File tab and then click the *Print* option.
   b. At the Print backstage area, click in the *Pages* text box in the *Settings* category and then type p1s1,p1s2.
   c. Click the Print button.
4. Save **3-CompSoftware.docx.**

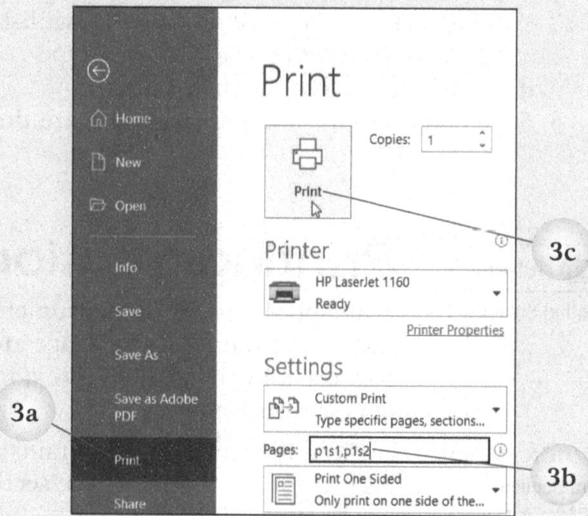

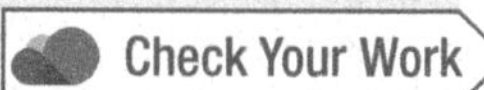

Keeping Text Together

Quick Steps

Keep Text Together

1. Click Paragraph group dialog box launcher.
2. Click Line and Page Breaks tab.
3. Click *Keep with next, Keep lines together,* and/or *Page break before.*
4. Click OK.

Hint Text formatted with the *Keep with next* option applied to it is identified with the nonprinting character ■ in the left margin.

Keeping Text Together

In a multipage document, Word automatically inserts soft page breaks, which are page breaks that adjust when data is added or deleted from the document. However, a soft page break may occur in an undesirable location. For example, a soft page break may cause a heading to display at the bottom of a page while the text related to the heading displays at the top of the next page. A soft page break may also create a widow or orphan. A widow is the last line of text in a paragraph that appears by itself at the top of a page and an orphan is the first line of text in a paragraph that appears by itself at the bottom of a page.

Use options at the Paragraph dialog box with the Line and Page Breaks tab selected, as shown in Figure 3.3, to control widows and orphans and keep a paragraph, group of paragraphs, or group of lines together. Display this dialog box by clicking the Paragraph group dialog box launcher on the Home tab and then clicking the Line and Page Breaks tab at the dialog box.

By default, the *Widow/Orphan control* option is active and Word tries to avoid creating widows and orphans when inserting soft page breaks. The other three options in the *Pagination* section of the dialog box are not active by default. Use the *Keep with next* option to keep a line together with the next line. This is useful for keeping a heading together with the first line of text below it. To keep a group of selected lines together, use the *Keep lines together* option. Use the *Page break before* option to insert a page break before selected text.

Figure 3.3 Paragraph Dialog Box with the Line and Page Breaks Tab Selected

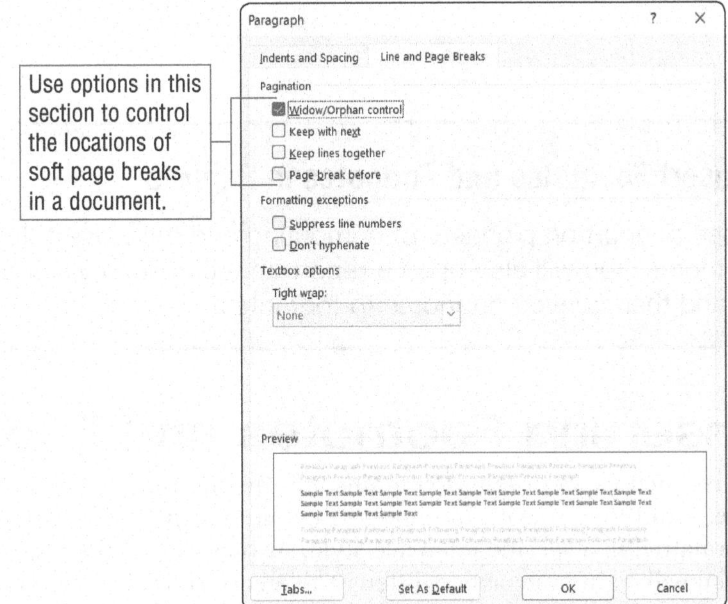

Activity 1h Keeping Text Together Part 8 of 8

1. With **3-CompSoftware.docx** open, scroll through the document and notice that the heading *Spreadsheet Software* displays at the bottom of page 1 and the paragraph that follows the heading displays at the top of page 2. Keep the heading and paragraph together by completing the following steps:
   a. Position the insertion point in the heading *Spreadsheet Software*.
   b. Make sure the Home tab is active and then click the Paragraph group dialog box launcher.
   c. At the Paragraph dialog box, click the Line and Page Breaks tab.
   d. Click the *Keep with next* check box to insert a check mark.
   e. Click OK to close the dialog box.
2. Scroll through the document and notice the heading *Multimedia Software* near the end of the document. Insert a soft page break at the beginning of the heading by completing the following steps:
   a. Move the insertion point to the beginning of the heading *Multimedia Software*.
   b. Click the Paragraph group dialog box launcher.
   c. At the Paragraph dialog box with the Line and Page Breaks tab selected, click the *Page break before* check box to insert a check mark.
   d. Click OK to close the dialog box.
3. Save, preview, and then close **3-CompSoftware.docx**.

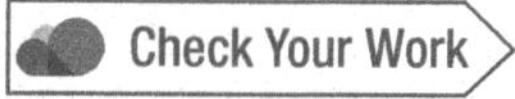

Activity 2 Insert Footnotes and Endnotes in Reports — 3 Parts

You will open a report on pioneers of computing and then insert, format, and modify footnotes. You will also open a report on technology visionaries, insert endnotes, and then convert endnotes to footnotes.

Inserting Footnotes and Endnotes

Hint Ctrl + Alt + F is the keyboard shortcut to insert a footnote and Ctrl + Alt + D is the keyboard shortcut to insert an endnote.

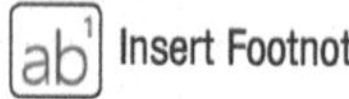
Insert Footnote

Insert Endnote

Inserting Footnotes and Endnotes

A research paper or report contains information from a variety of sources. To give credit to those sources, footnotes or endnotes can be inserted in a document formatted in a specific reference style, such as that of the *Chicago Manual of Style*. (You will learn more about different reference styles in the next activity.) A footnote is an explanatory note or source reference that is printed at the bottom of the page on which the corresponding information appears. An endnote is also an explanatory note or reference, but it is printed at the end of the document.

Two steps are involved in creating a footnote or endnote. First, the note reference number is inserted in the document where the corresponding information appears. Second, the note entry text is typed. Footnotes and endnotes are created in a similar manner.

Quick Steps

Insert Footnote

1. Click References tab.
2. Click Insert Footnote button.
3. Type footnote text.

Insert Endnote

1. Click References tab.
2. Click Insert Endnote button.
3. Type endnote text.

To create a footnote, position the insertion point where the reference number is to appear, click the References tab, and then click the Insert Footnote button in the Footnotes group. This inserts a number in the document along with a separator line at the bottom of the page and a superscript number below it. With the insertion point positioned immediately right of the superscript number, type the note entry text. By default, Word numbers footnotes with superscript arabic numbers and endnotes with superscript lowercase roman numerals.

Activity 2a Creating Footnotes

Part 1 of 3

1. Open **CompPioneers.docx** and then save it with the name **3-CompPioneers.**
2. Create the first footnote shown in Figure 3.4 by completing the following steps:
   a. Position the insertion point at the end of the first paragraph of text below the heading *Konrad Zuse* (immediately following the period).
   b. Click the References tab.
   c. Click the Insert Footnote button in the Footnotes group.
   d. With the insertion point positioned at the bottom of the page immediately following the superscript number, type the first footnote shown in Figure 3.4. (Italicize the text as shown in the figure.)

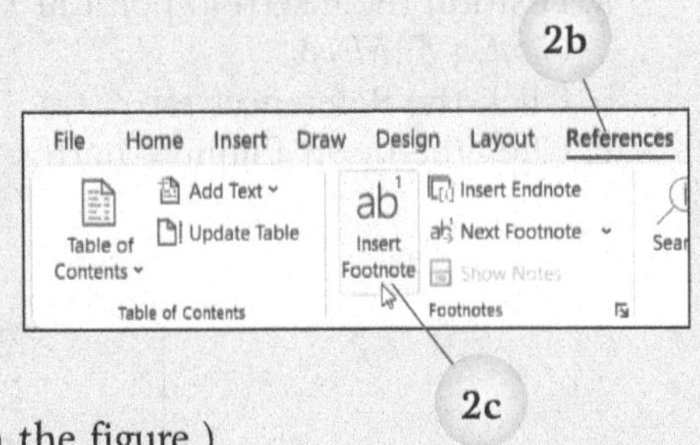

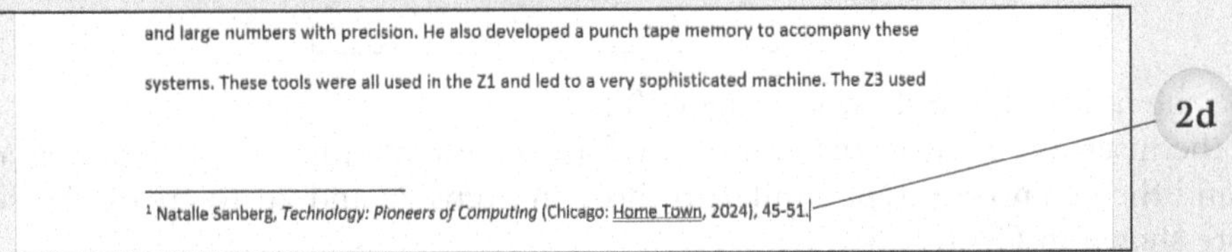

3. Move the insertion point to the end of the third paragraph below the heading *Konrad Zuse*. Using steps similar to those in Steps 2c and 2d, create the second footnote shown in Figure 3.4. (Italicize the text as shown in the figure.)
4. Move the insertion point to the end of the last paragraph below the heading *Konrad Zuse* and then create the third footnote shown in Figure 3.4.
5. Move the insertion point to the end of the third paragraph below the heading *William Hewlett and David Packard* and then create the fourth footnote shown in Figure 3.4.
6. Move the insertion point to the end of the last paragraph in the document and then create the fifth foonote shown in Figure 3.4.
7. Save, preview, and then close **3-CompPioneers.docx.**

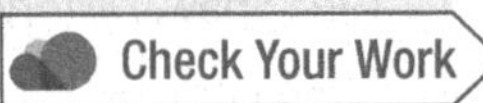

Figure 3.4 Activity 2a

Natalie Sanberg, *Technology: Pioneers of Computing* (Chicago: Home Town, 2024), 45-51.

Miguel Whitworth and Danielle Reyes, "Development of Computing," *Design Technologies* (2024): 24-26.

Sam Wells, *Biographies of Computing Pioneers* (San Francisco: Laurelhurst, 2024), 20-23.

Terrell Montgomery, *History of Computers* (Boston: Langley-Paulsen, 2024), 13-15.

Justin Evans, "Hewlett-Packard's Impact on Computing," *Computing Technologies* (2024): 7-12.

Printing Footnotes and Endnotes

When printing a document that contains footnotes, Word automatically reduces the number of text lines on a page to create space for the number of lines in the footnotes and the separator line. If the page does not contain enough space, the footnote number and entry text are moved to the next page. Word separates the footnotes from the text with a 2-inch separator line that begins at the left margin. When endnotes are created in a document, Word prints all the endnotes at the end of the document, separated from the text by a 2-inch line.

Activity 2b Creating Endnotes

Part 2 of 3

1. Open **TechVisionaries.docx** and then save it with the name **3-TechVisionaries**.
2. Create the first endnote shown in Figure 3.5 by completing the following steps:
   a. Position the insertion point at the end of the second paragraph below the heading *Gordon E. Moore*.
   b. Click the References tab.
   c. Click the Insert Endnote button in the Footnotes group.

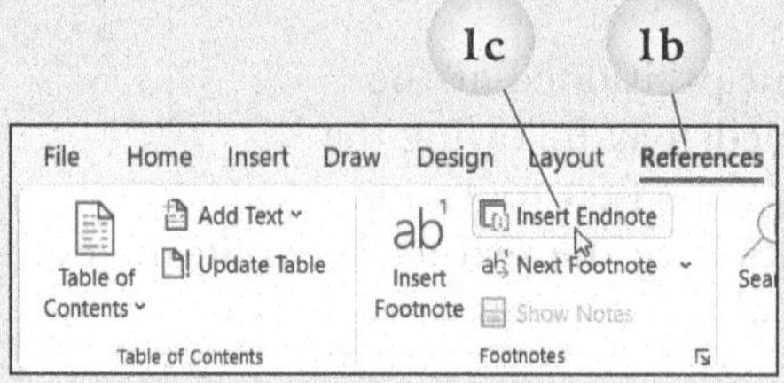

   d. Type the first endnote shown in Figure 3.5.
3. Move the insertion point to the end of the fourth paragraph below the heading *Jack S. Kilby* and then complete steps similar to those in Steps 2c and 2d to create the second endnote shown in Figure 3.5.
4. Move the insertion point to the end of the first paragraph below the heading *Linus Torvalds* and then create the third endnote shown in Figure 3.5.
5. Move the insertion point to the end of the last paragraph in the document and then create the fourth endnote shown in Figure 3.5.
6. Save **3-TechVisionaries.docx**.

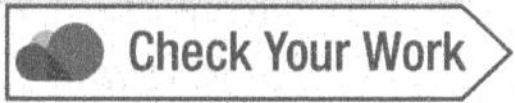

Figure 3.5 Activity 2b

Gina Shaw, *History of Computing Technologies* (Los Angeles: Gleason Rutherford Publishing, 2024): 11-14.

Ellen Littleton, "Jack Kilby: Nobel Prize Winner," *Horizon Computing* (Boston: Robison Publishing House, 2024): 23-51.

Eric Ventrella, "Computer Nerd Hero," *Computing Today* (2024): 5-10.

Joseph Daniels, "Linus Torvalds: Technology Visionary," *Connections* (2024): 13-17.

Viewing and Editing Footnotes and Endnotes

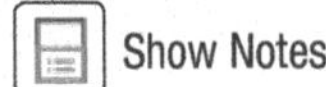

Hint To view the entry text for a footnote or endnote where the note occurs within the document, position the pointer on the note reference number. The footnote or endnote text displays in a box above the number.

Viewing and Editing Footnotes and Endnotes

To view the footnotes in a document, click the Next Footnote button in the Footnotes group on the References tab. This moves the insertion point to the first footnote reference number following the insertion point. To view the endnotes in a document, click the Next Footnote button arrow and then click *Next Endnote* at the drop-down list. Use other options at the Next Footnote button drop-down list to view the previous footnote, next endnote, or previous endnote. Move the insertion point to specific footnote text with the Show Notes button.

If a footnote or endnote reference number is moved, copied, or deleted, all the remaining footnotes or endnotes automatically renumber. To move a footnote or endnote, select the reference number and then click the Cut button in the Clipboard group on the Home tab. Position the insertion point at the new location and then click the Paste button in the Clipboard group. To delete a footnote or endnote, select the reference number and then press the Delete key. This deletes the reference number as well as the footnote or endnote text.

Click the Footnotes group dialog box launcher and the Footnote and Endnote dialog box displays, as shown in Figure 3.6. Use options at this dialog box to convert footnotes to endnotes and endnotes to footnotes; change the locations of footnotes or endnotes; change the number formatting; start footnote or endnote numbering with a specific number, letter, or symbol; or change numbering within sections in a document.

Figure 3.6 Footnote and Endnote Dialog Box

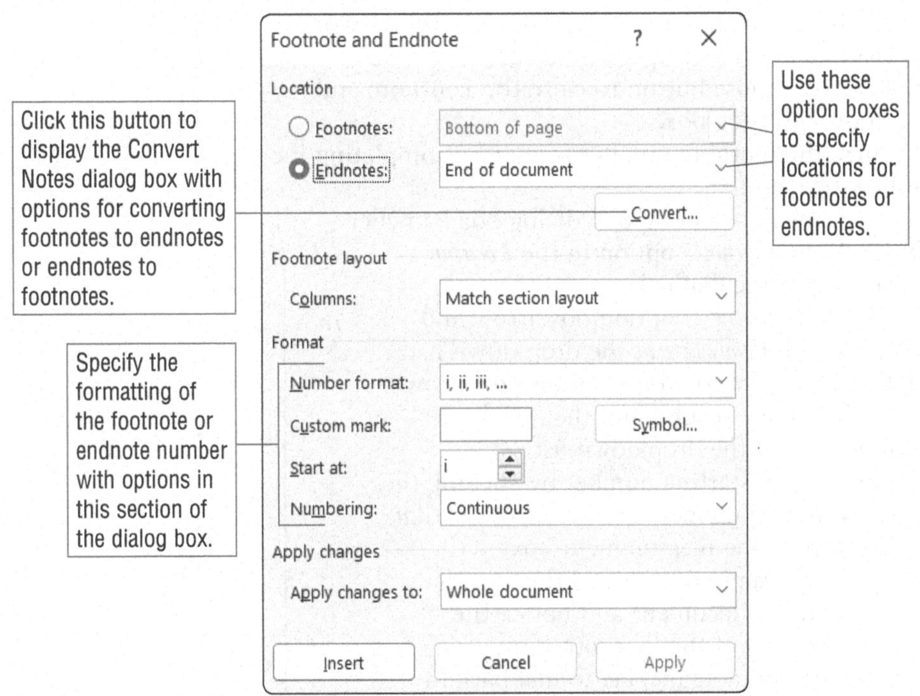

Activity 2c Editing Endnotes, Converting Endnotes to Footnotes, and Editing Footnotes

Part 3 of 3

1. With **3-TechVisionaries.docx** open, press Ctrl + Home to move the insertion point to the beginning of the document and then edit the endnotes by completing the following steps:
   a. If necessary, click the References tab.
   b. Click the Next Footnote button arrow in the Footnotes group and then click *Next Endnote* at the drop-down list.
   c. Click the Show Notes button in the Footnotes group to display the endnote text.
   d. Change the page numbers for the Gina Shaw entry from *11-14* to *6-10*.
   e. Click the Show Notes button again to return to the reference number in the document.

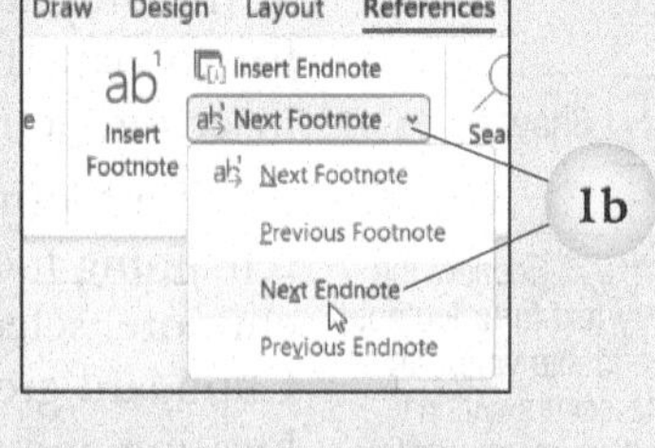

2. Press Ctrl + A to select the document (but not the endnote entry text) and then change the font to Constantia.
3. Change the font for the endnotes by completing the following steps:
   a. Press Ctrl + End to move the insertion point to the end of the document.
   b. Click in any endnote entry and then press Ctrl + A to select all the endnote entries.
   c. Change the font to Constantia.
   d. Press Ctrl + Home.
4. Convert the endnotes to footnotes by completing the following steps:
   a. Click the References tab and then click the Footnotes group dialog box launcher.
   b. At the Footnote and Endnote dialog box, click the Convert button.
   c. At the Convert Notes dialog box with the *Convert all endnotes to footnotes* option selected, click OK.
   d. Click the Close button to close the Footnote and Endnote dialog box.

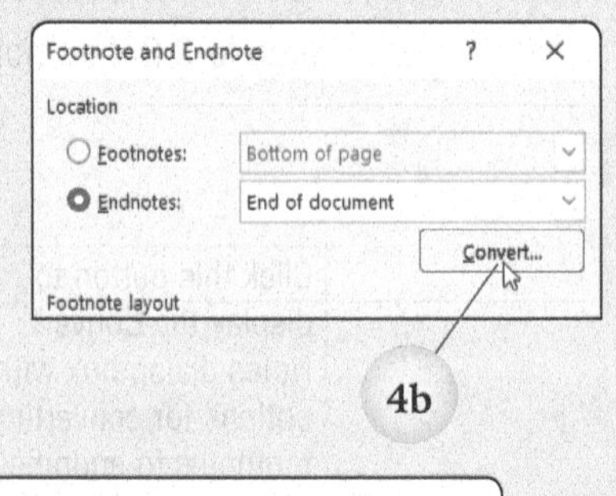

5. Change the footnote number format by completing the following steps:
   a. Click the Footnotes group dialog box launcher.
   b. Click the *Footnotes* option in the *Location* section of the dialog box.
   c. Click the *Footnotes* option box arrow and then click *Below text* at the drop-down list.
   d. Click the *Number format* option box arrow in the *Format* section and then click *a, b, c, …* at the drop-down list.
   e. Change the starting number by clicking the *Start at* measurement box up arrow until *d* displays in the measurement box.
   f. Click the Apply button and then scroll through the document and notice the renumbering of the footnotes.
6. Change the footnote number format back to arabic numbers by completing the following steps:
   a. With the References tab active, click the Footnotes group dialog box launcher.
   b. At the Footnote and Endnote dialog box, click the *Footnotes* option in the *Location* section.

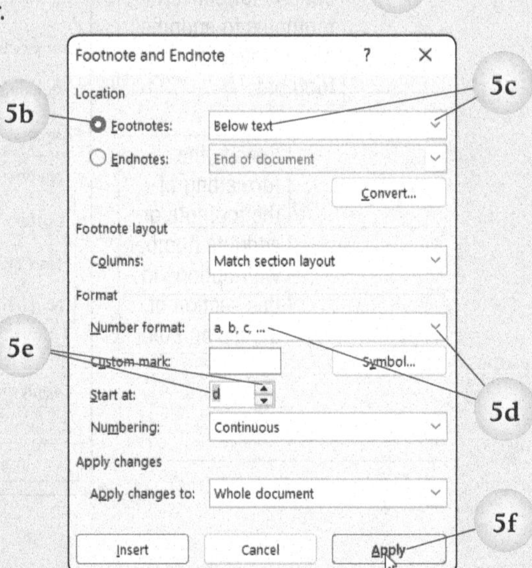

c. Click the *Number format* option box arrow in the *Format* section and then click *1, 2, 3, …* at the drop-down list.
d. Change the starting number back to 1 by clicking the *Start at* measurement box down arrow until *1* displays in the measurement box.
e. Click the Apply button.

7. Delete the third footnote by completing the following steps:
   a. Press Ctrl + Home.
   b. Make sure the References tab is active and then click the Next Footnote button three times.
   c. Select the third footnote reference number (superscript number) and then press the Delete key.
8. Save, preview, and then close **3-TechVisionaries.docx**.

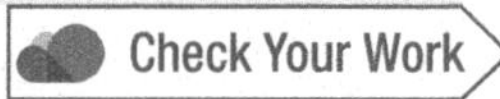
Check Your Work

Activity 3 Cite Sources in a New Zealand Report — 8 Parts

You will open a report on New Zealand, add information and insert source citations and a bibliography, and then modify and customize citation styles.

Citing and Editing Sources

In addition to using footnotes and endnotes to credit sources in a research paper or manuscript, consider inserting in-text citations and a sources list to identify sources of quotations, facts, theories, and other borrowed or summarized material. An in-text citation acknowledges that information is being borrowed from a source. Not acknowledging someone else's words or ideas is called *plagiarizing*.

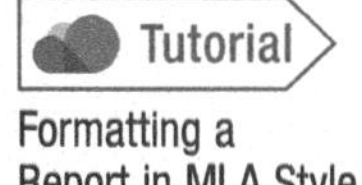
Tutorial
Formatting a Report in MLA Style

Tutorial
Formatting a Report in APA Style

Formatting a Report Using an Editorial Style

Word provides a number of commonly used editorial styles for citing references in research papers and reports, including the American Psychological Association (APA) reference style, which is generally used in the social sciences and research fields; the Modern Language Association (MLA) style, which is generally used in the humanities and English composition; and the *Chicago Manual of Style* (Chicago), which is used both in the humanities and the social sciences and is considered more complex than either APA or MLA style.

To prepare a research paper or report in APA or MLA style, format the document according to the following general guidelines:

- Use standard-sized paper (8.5 × 11 inches)
- Set 1-inch top, bottom, left, and right margins
- Format the text in a 12-point serif typeface (such as Cambria or Times New Roman)
- Double-space text
- Indent the first line of each paragraph 0.5 inch
- Insert page numbers in the header, positioned at the right margin.

When formatting a research paper or report according to MLA or APA style, follow certain guidelines for properly formatting the first page of the document. With MLA style, at the beginning of the first page, at the left margin, insert the author's name (the person writing the report), the instructor's name, the course title, and the current date. Double-space after each of the four lines. After the current date, double-space and then type and center the title of the document. Also double-space between the title and the first line of text. The text should be left-aligned and double-spaced. Finally, insert a header in the upper right corner of the document that includes the author's last name and the page number.

When using APA style, create a title page that is separate from the body of the document. On this page, include the title of the paper, the author's name, and the school's name, all double-spaced, centered, and positioned on the upper half of the page. Also include a header with the text *Running Head:* followed by the title of the paper in uppercase letters at the left margin and the page number at the right margin.

Activity 3a Formatting the First Page of a Research Paper in MLA Style — Part 1 of 8

1. Open **NewZealand.docx** and then save it with the name **3-NewZealand**.
2. Format the document in MLA style by completing the following steps:
   a. Press Ctrl + A to select the entire document.
   b. Display the Font dialog box with the Font tab selected and change the font to Cambria and the font size to 12 points. Click the Set As Default button in the lower left corner of the dialog box and then click OK at the Microsoft Word dialog box. (This changes the default setting to 12-point Cambria for the current document only.)
   c. Press Ctrl + Home to position the insertion point at the beginning of the document.
   d. Type your first and last names and then press the Enter key.
   e. Type your instructor's name and then press the Enter key.
   f. Type your course title and then press the Enter key.
   g. Type the current date.

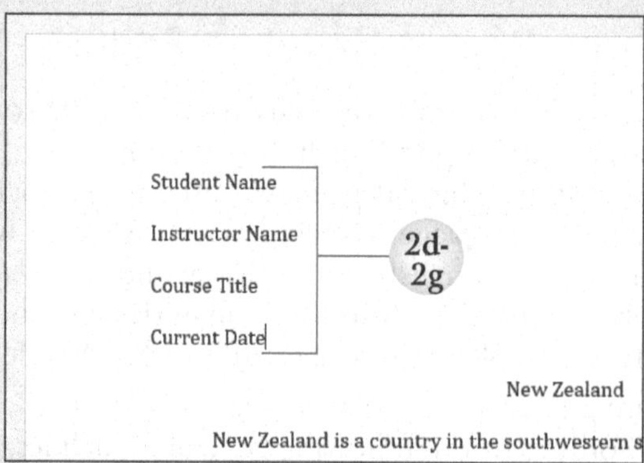

3. Insert a header in the document by completing the following steps:
   a. Click the Insert tab.
   b. Click the Header button in the Header & Footer group and then click *Edit Header* at the drop-down list.
   c. Press the Tab key two times to move the insertion point to the right margin in the Header pane.

d. Type your last name and then press the spacebar.
e. Click the Page Number button in the Header & Footer group on the Header & Footer tab, point to *Current Position*, and then click the *Plain Number* option.

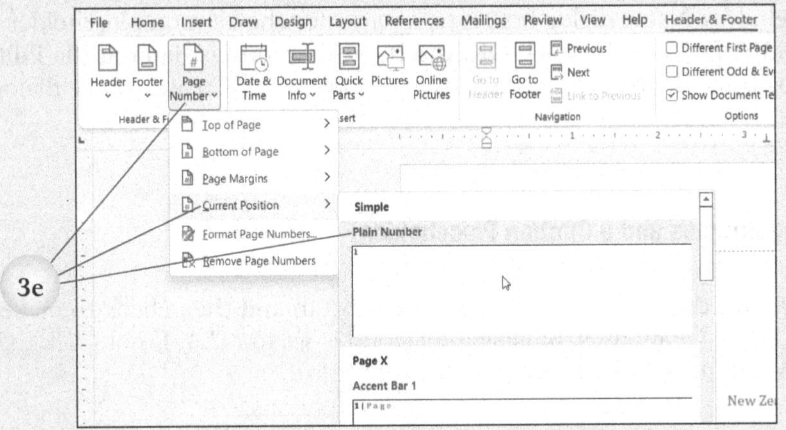

f. Double-click in the body of the document.
4. Save **3-NewZealand.docx**.

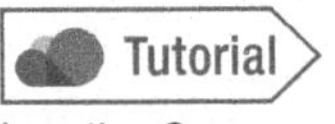

Inserting Sources and Citations

Quick Steps

Insert New Citation

1. Click References tab.
2. Click Insert Citation button.
3. Click *Add New Source*.
4. Type source information.
5. Click OK.

Inserting Source Citations

When creating an in-text source citation, enter the information about the source in fields at the Create Source dialog box. To insert a citation in a document, click the References tab, click the Insert Citation button in the Citations & Bibliography group, and then click *Add New Source* at the drop-down list. At the Create Source dialog box, shown in Figure 3.7, select the type of source to be cited (such as a book, journal article, or report) and then type the bibliographic information in the required fields. To include more information than required in the displayed fields, click the *Show All Bibliography Fields* check box to insert a check mark and then type the additional bibliographic details in the extra fields. After filling in the necessary source information, click OK. The citation is automatically inserted in the document at the location of the insertion point.

Figure 3.7 Create Source Dialog Box

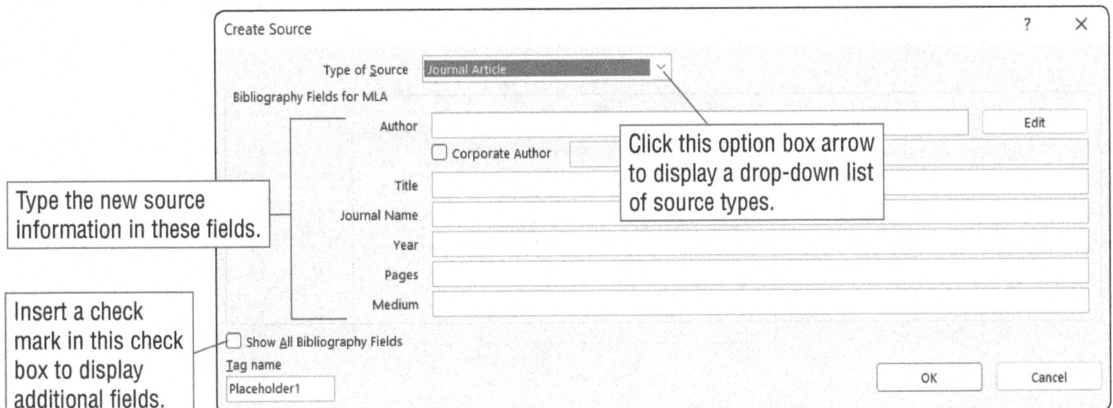

Inserting Citation Placeholders

Quick Steps

Insert Citation Placeholder

1. Click References tab.
2. Click Insert Citation button.
3. Click *Add New Placeholder.*
4. Type citation name.
5. Click OK.

If information for an in-text source citation will be inserted later, insert a citation placeholder. To do this, click the Insert Citation button in the Citations & Bibliography group and then click *Add New Placeholder* at the drop-down list. At the Placeholder Name dialog box, type a name for the citation placeholder and then press the Enter key or click OK. Insert the citation text later at the Edit Source dialog box, which contains the same options as the Create Source dialog box.

Activity 3b **Inserting Sources and a Citation Placeholder** Part 2 of 8

1. With **3-NewZealand.docx** open, click the References tab and then check to make sure the *Style* option box in the Citations & Bibliography group is set to *MLA*. If not, click the *Style* option box arrow and then click *MLA* at the drop-down list.

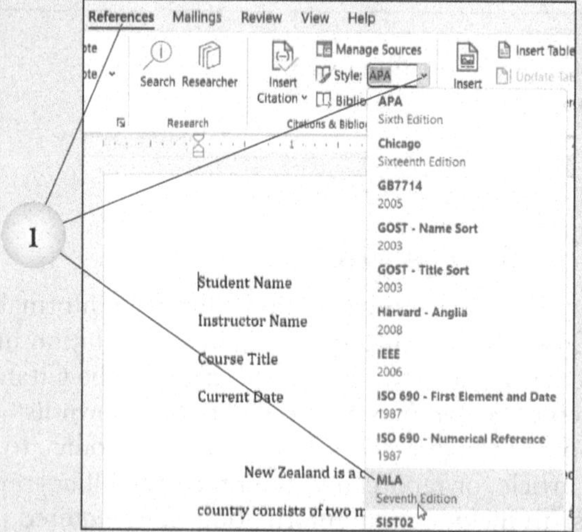

2. Select and then delete the text *(Jefferson)* at the end of the first paragraph of text (before the period that ends the sentence).
3. With the insertion point positioned between the word *city* and the period that ends the last sentence in the first paragraph, press the spacebar and then insert a citation by completing the following steps:
   a. Click the Insert Citation button in the Citations & Bibliography group and then click *Add New Source* at the drop-down list.

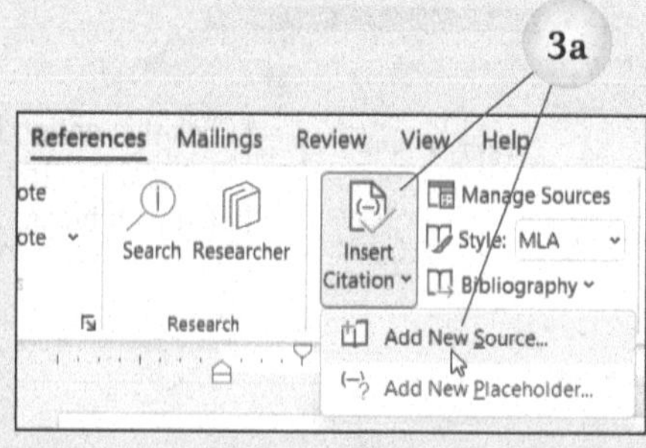

b. At the Create Source dialog box, if necessary, click the *Type of Source* option box arrow and then click *Journal Article* at the drop-down list.
c. In the *Bibliography Fields for MLA* section, click in the *Author* text box, type Gabe Jefferson, and then press the Tab key three times.
d. In the *Title* text box, type Exploring New Zealand and then press the Tab key.
e. In the *Journal Name* text box, type Island Countries and then press the Tab key.
f. In the *Year* text box, type 2024 and then press the Tab key.
g. In the *Pages* text box, type 8-10.
h. Click OK.

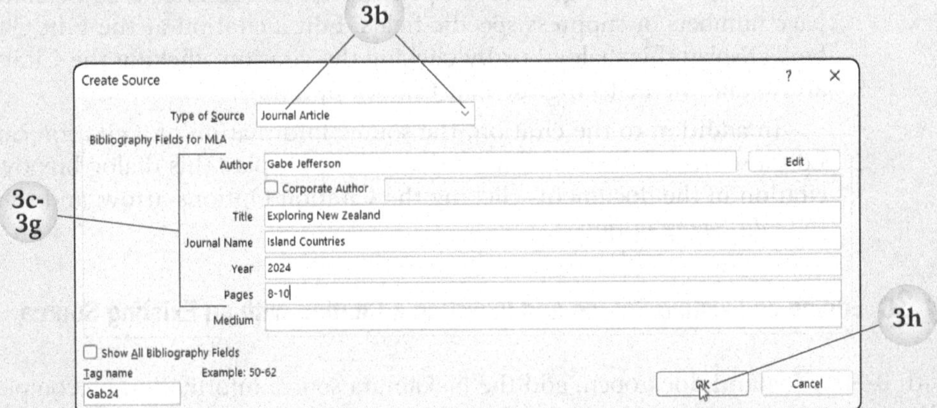

4. Select and then delete the text *(Lopez)* at the end of the third paragraph.
5. With the insertion point positioned between the word *language* and the period that ends the last sentence in the third paragraph, press the spacebar and then insert the following source information for a book. (At the Create Source dialog box, click the *Type of Source* option box arrow and then click *Book* at the drop-down list.)

Author	Rafael Lopez
Title	South Pacific Countries
Year	2024
City	Chicago
Publisher	Great Lakes

6. Select and then delete the text *(Nakamura)* in the last paragraph of text.
7. With the insertion point positioned between the word *constitution* and the period that ends the last sentence in the last paragraph of text, press the spacebar and then insert a citation placeholder by completing the following steps:
   a. Click the Insert Citation button.
   b. Click *Add New Placeholder* at the drop-down list.
   c. At the Placeholder Name dialog box, type Nakamura and then press the Enter key. (You will create the citation and fill in the source information in the next activity.)
8. Save **3-NewZealand.docx**.

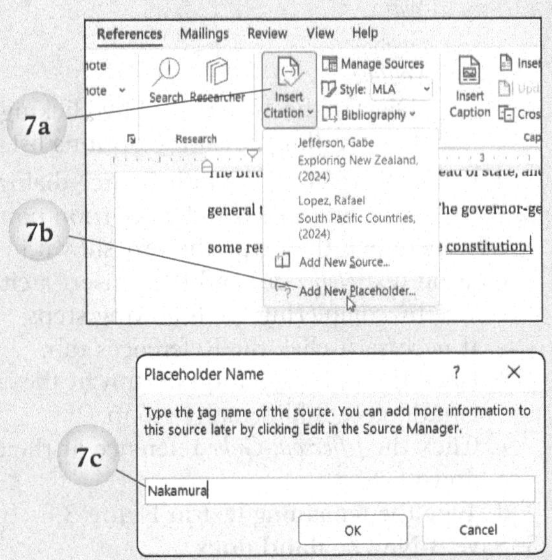

Check Your Work

Quick Steps

Insert Citation with Existing Source

1. Click References tab.
2. Click Insert Citation button.
3. Click source.

Inserting a Citation with an Existing Source

Once source information is inserted at the Create Source dialog box, Word automatically saves it. To insert a citation in a document for source information that has already been saved, click the Insert Citation button in the Citations & Bibliography group and then click the source at the drop-down list.

Editing a Citation and Source

Editing a Citation and Source

After source information is inserted in a document, it may need to be edited to correct errors or change data. Or perhaps the citation needs to be edited to add page numbers or suppress specific fields. Edit a citation at the Edit Citation dialog box. Display this dialog box by clicking the citation, clicking the Citation Options arrow, and then clicking the *Edit Citation* option.

In addition to the citation, the source information of a citation can be edited. Edit a source at the Edit Source dialog box. Display this dialog box by clicking the citation in the document, clicking the Citation Options arrow, and then clicking the *Edit Source* option.

Activity 3c Editing an Existing Source and Inserting a Citation with an Existing Source **Part 3 of 8**

1. With **3-NewZealand.docx** open, add the Nakamura source information by completing the following steps:
   a. Click the *Nakamura* citation in the document.
   b. Click the Citation Options arrow at the right side of the selected citation.
   c. Click *Edit Source* at the drop-down list.
   d. At the Edit Source dialog box, click the *Type of Source* option box arrow and then click *Journal Article*.
   e. Type the following information in the specified text boxes:

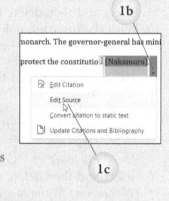

Author	Janet Nakamura
Title	New Zealand Government
Journal Name	International Governmental Organizations
Year	2024
Pages	15-28
Volume	6

   (Display the *Volume* field by clicking the *Show All Bibliography Fields* check box and then scrolling down the options list.)
   f. Click OK to close the Edit Source dialog box.
2. Press Ctrl + End to move the insertion point to the end of the document and then type the text shown in Figure 3.8 up to the citation text *(Jefferson)* and then insert a citation from an existing source by completing the following steps:
   a. If necessary, click the References tab.
   b. Click the Insert Citation button in the Citations & Bibliography group.
   c. Click the *Jefferson, Gabe* reference at the drop-down list.
   d. Type the remaining text in Figure 3.8.
3. Save **3-NewZealand.docx**.

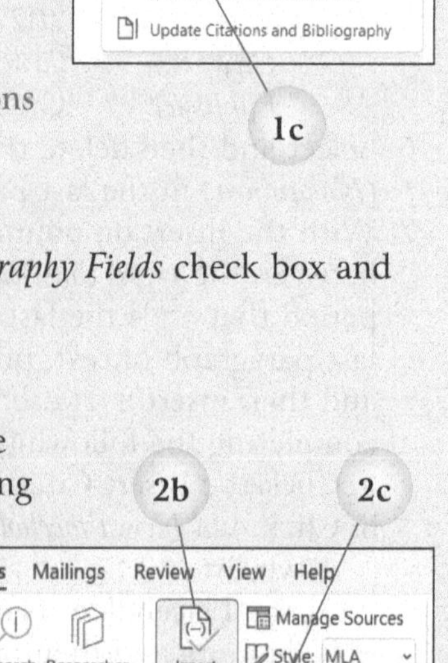

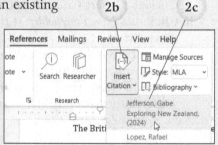

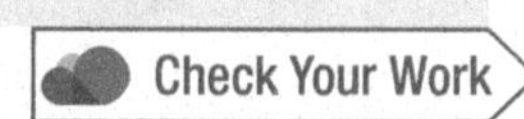
Check Your Work

Figure 3.8 Activity 3c

> An interesting fact about New Zealand is that in 1893 it was the first country to approve the right for women to vote (Jefferson). Other interesting facts are that over thirty percent of the country is a national reserve, the country has more sheep than people, it has the most southerly capital in the world, and it was the last country in the world inhabited by humans.

Quick Steps
Insert Page Number in Citation
1. Click citation to display placeholder.
2. Click Citation Options arrow.
3. Click *Edit Citation*.
4. Type page number(s).
5. Click OK.

Inserting Page Numbers in a Citation

If a direct quote from a source is included in a report, insert quotation marks around the text used from that source and insert in the citation the page number or numbers of the quoted material. To insert specific page numbers in a citation, click the citation to select the citation placeholder. Click the Citation Options arrow and then click *Edit Citation* at the drop-down list. At the Edit Citation dialog box, type the page number or numbers of the source from which the quote was borrowed and then click OK.

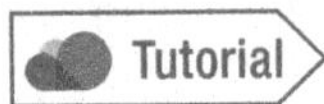

Managing Sources

Manage Sources

Quick Steps
Manage Sources
1. Click References tab.
2. Click Manage Sources button.
3. Edit, add, and/or delete sources.
4. Click Close.

Hint Click the Browse button in the Source Manager dialog box to select another master list.

Managing Sources

All the sources cited in the current document and in previous documents display in the Source Manager dialog box, as shown in Figure 3.9. Display this dialog box by clicking the References tab and then clicking the Manage Sources button in the Citations & Bibliography group. The *Master List* list box in the Source Manager dialog box displays all the sources that have been created in Word. The *Current List* list box displays all the sources used in the currently open document.

Use options at the Source Manager dialog box to copy a source from the master list to the current list, delete a source, edit a source, and create a new source. To copy a source from the master list to the current list, click the source in the *Master List* list box and then click the Copy button between the two list boxes. Click the Delete button to delete a source. Edit a source by clicking the source, clicking the Edit button, and then making changes at the Edit Source dialog box. Click the New button to create a new source at the Create Source dialog box.

If the *Master List* list box contains a large number of sources, search for a specific source by typing keywords in the *Search* text box. As text is typed, the list narrows to sources that match the text. After making all the changes at the Source Manager dialog box, click the Close button.

Figure 3.9 Source Manager Dialog Box

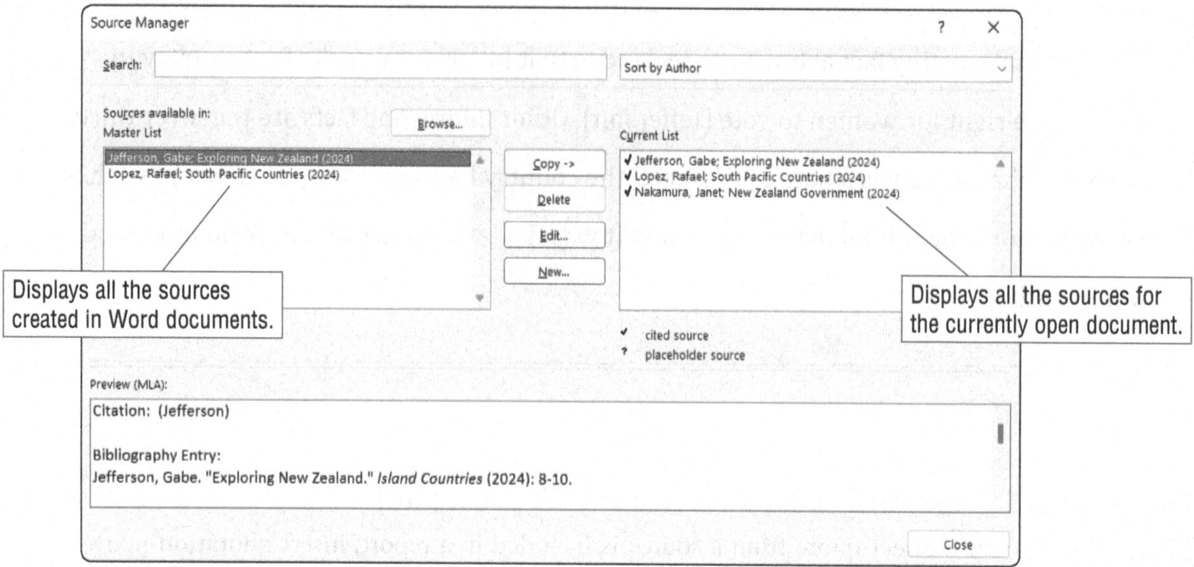

Activity 3d Managing Sources

Part 4 of 8

1. With **3-NewZealand.docx** open, edit a source by completing the following steps:
   a. If necessary, click the References tab.
   b. Click the Manage Sources button in the Citations & Bibliography group.
   c. At the Source Manager dialog box, click the *Jefferson, Gabe* source entry in the *Master List* list box.
   d. Click the Edit button.

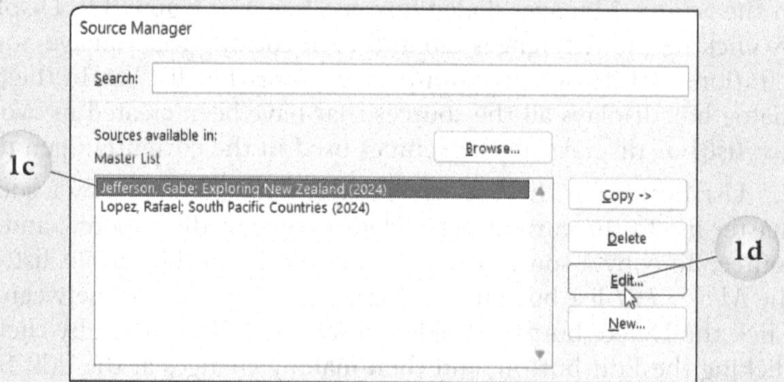

   e. At the Edit Source dialog box, delete the text in the *Author* text box and then type Gabriel Jackson.
   f. Click OK to close the Edit Source dialog box.
   g. At the message asking if you want to update both the master list and current list with the changes, click Yes.
   h. Click the Close button to close the Source Manager dialog box. (Notice that the last name changed in both of the Jefferson citations to reflect the edit.)
2. Delete a source by completing the following steps:
   a. Select and then delete the last sentence in the third paragraph in the document (the sentence beginning Te reo *is another name*), including the citation.
   b. Click the Manage Sources button.

c. At the Source Manager dialog box, click the *Lopez, Rafael* entry in the *Current List* list box. (This entry will not contain a check mark because you deleted the citation from the document.)
d. Click the Delete button.

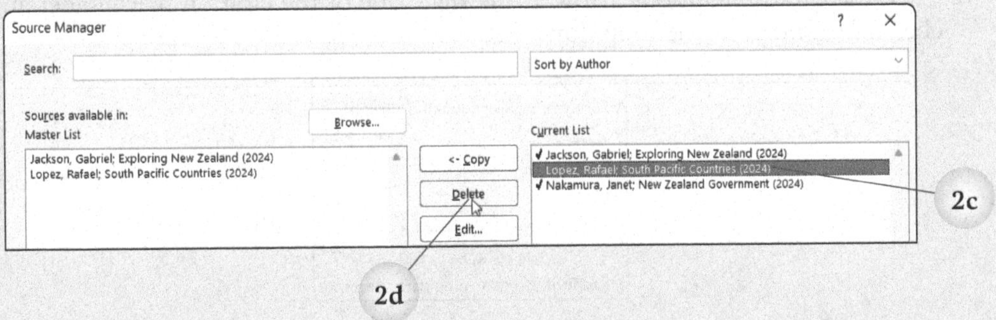

e. Click the Close button to close the Source Manager dialog box.

3. Create and insert a new source in the document by completing the following steps:
   a. Click the Manage Sources button.
   b. Click the New button in the Source Manager dialog box.
   c. Type the following book information in the Create Source dialog box. (Change the *Type of Source* option to *Book*.)

Author	Georgia Miraldi
Title	World Climates
Year	2024
City	Houston
Publisher	Rio Grande

   d. Click OK to close the Create Source dialog box.
   e. Click the Close button to close the Source Manager dialog box.
   f. Position the insertion point between the last word *snowfall* at the end of the fourth paragraph and the period that ends the sentence and then press the spacebar.
   g. Insert a citation for Georgia Miraldi by clicking the Insert Citation button in the Citations & Bibliography group and then clicking *Miraldi, Georgia* at the drop-down list.

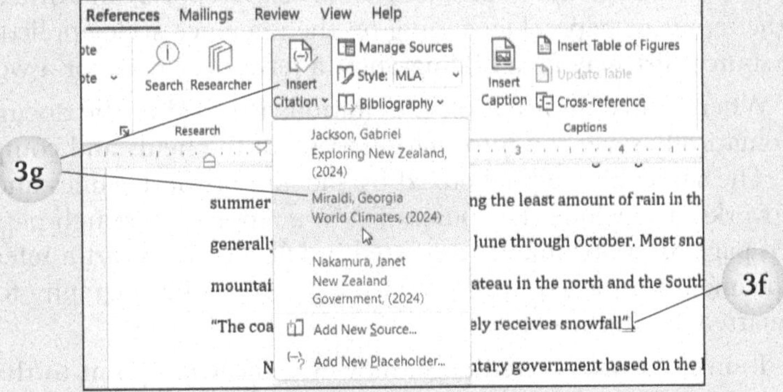

4. To correctly acknowledge the direct quote from Georgia Miraldi, the page on which the quote appears in the book needs to be added. Insert the page number in the citation by completing the following steps:
   a. Click the *Miraldi* citation in the document.
   b. Click the Citation Options arrow at the right side of the citation placeholder and then click *Edit Citation* at the drop-down list.

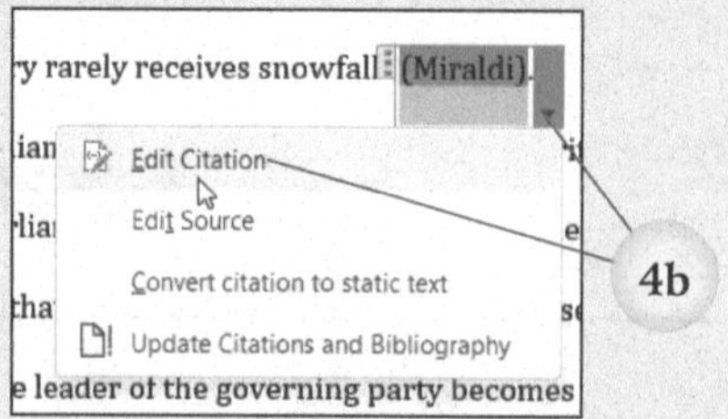

   c. At the Edit Citation dialog box, type 19 in the *Pages* text box.
   d. Click OK.

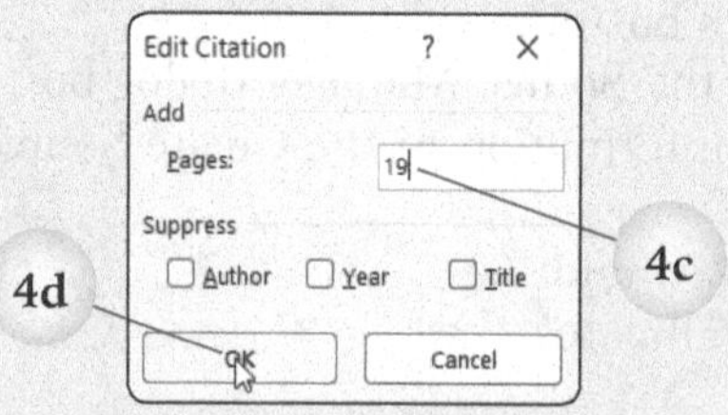

5. Save **3-NewZealand.docx**.

Inserting a Works Cited Page

Quick Steps

Insert Sources List
1. Insert new page at end of document.
2. Click References tab.
3. Click Bibliography button.
4. Click works cited, reference, or bibliography option.

Inserting a Sources List

If citations are included in a report or research paper, a sources list needs to be inserted as a separate page at the end of the document. A sources list is an alphabetical list of the books, journal articles, reports, and other sources referenced in the report or paper. Depending on the reference style applied to the document, the sources list may be a bibliography, a references page, or a works cited page.

When source information for citations is typed in the document, Word automatically saves the information from all the fields and compiles a sources list. The sources are alphabetized by the authors' last names and/or the titles of the works. To include the sources list in a report or research paper, insert a works cited page for a document formatted in MLA style, insert a references page for a document formatted in APA style, and insert a bibliography for a document formatted in Chicago style.

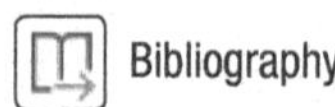

To insert a works cited page, move the insertion point to the end of the document and then insert a new page. Click the References tab and make sure the *Style* option box is set to *MLA*. Click the Bibliography button in the Citations & Bibliography group and then click the *Works Cited* option. For a document formatted in the APA style, click the Bibliography button and then click the *References* option.

Activity 3e Inserting a Works Cited Page

Part 5 of 8

1. With **3-NewZealand.docx** open, insert a works cited page at the end of the document by completing these steps:
   a. Press Ctrl + End to move the insertion point to the end of the document.
   b. Press Ctrl + Enter to insert a page break.
   c. If necessary, click the References tab.
   d. Click the Bibliography button in the Citations & Bibliography group.
   e. Click the *Works Cited* option in the *Built-In* section of the drop-down list.

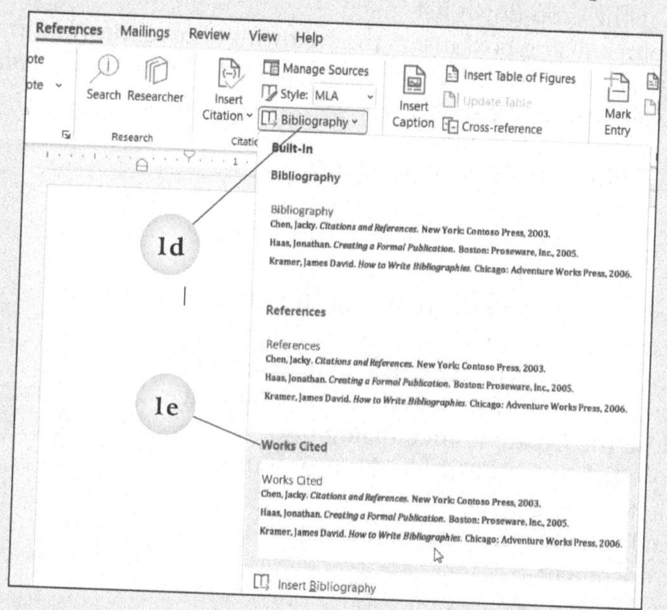

2. Format the works cited page to meet MLA requirements with the following changes:
   a. Select the *Works Cited* heading and all the entries and click the *No Spacing* style in the Styles group on the Home tab.
   b. Change the spacing to 2.0.
   c. Press Ctrl + T to format the works cited entries with a hanging indent.
   d. Center the title *Works Cited*.
3. Save **3-NewZealand.docx**.

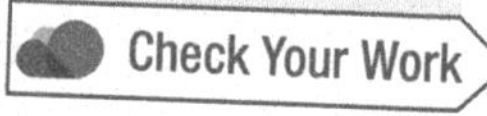

Modifying and Updating a Sources List

Quick Steps

Update Sources List
1. Click in sources list.
2. Click Update Citations and Bibliography tab.

If a new source is inserted at the Source Manager dialog box or an existing source is modified, Word automatically inserts the source information in the sources list. If a new citation requires a new source to be added, Word will not automatically update the sources list. To update the sources list, click in the list and then click the Update Citations and Bibliography tab. The updated sources list reflects any changes made to the citations and source information in the document.

Activity 3f Modifying and Updating a Works Cited Page

Part 6 of 8

1. With **3-NewZealand.docx** open, create a new source and citation by completing the following steps:
   a. Position the insertion point immediately left of the period that ends the last sentence in the third paragraph of the document (after the word *Language*).
   b. Press the spacebar.
   c. If necessary, click the References tab.
   d. Click the Insert Citation button in the Citations & Bibliography group and then click *Add New Source* at the drop-down list.
   e. At the Create Source dialog box, insert the following source information for a website. (Change the *Type of Source* option to *Web site* and click the *Show All Bibliography Fields* check box to display all the fields.)

Author	Chay Suong
Name of Web Page	New Zealand Sign Language
Year	2024
Month	April
Day	21
Year Accessed	(type current year in numbers)
Month Accessed	(type current month in letters)
Day Accessed	(type current day in numbers)
URL	https://ppi-edu.net/signlanguage

   f. Click OK to close the Create Source dialog box.
2. Update the works cited page to include the new source by completing the following steps:
   a. Press Ctrl + End to move the insertion point to the end of the document.
   b. Click in the works cited text.
   c. Click the Update Citations and Bibliography tab above the heading *Works Cited*. (Notice that the updated sources list includes the Suong reference.)
3. Save **3-NewZealand.docx**.

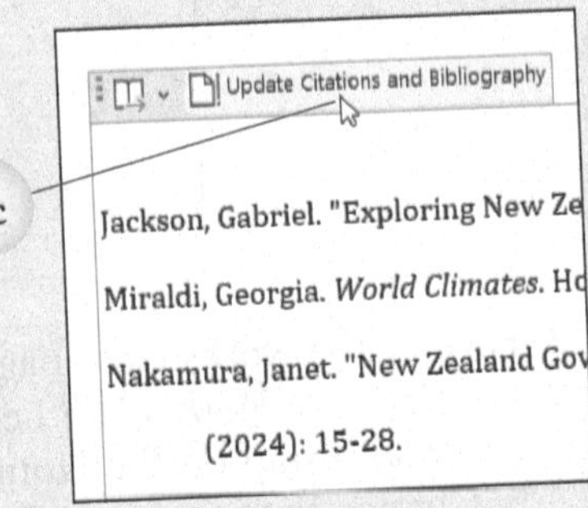

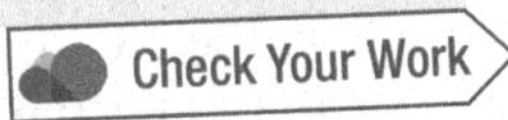

Formatting a Sources List

The formatting applied by Word to the sources list may need to be changed to meet the specific guidelines of MLA, APA, or Chicago style. For example, MLA and APA styles require the following formats for a sources list:

- Begin the sources list on a separate page after the last page of text in the report.
- Include the title *Works Cited*, *References*, or *Bibliography* at the top of the page and center it on the width of the page.
- Use the same font for the sources list as for the main document.
- Double-space between and within entries.
- Begin each entry at the left margin and format subsequent lines in each entry with a hanging indent.
- Alphabetize the entries.

The general formatting requirements for Chicago style are similar except that single spacing is applied within entries and double spacing is applied between entries.

Activity 3g Formatting a Works Cited Page

Part 7 of 8

1. With **3-NewZealand.docx** open, notice that the works cited entries are set in 12-point Cambria and a hanging indent is applied to the entries.
2. Select the four reference entries below the *Works Cited* title, click the Home tab, and then click the *No Spacing* style in the Styles group.
3. With the four entries still selected, press Ctrl + 2 to apply double spacing to the entries and then press Ctrl + T to apply a hanging indent to the entries. (Applying the *No Spacing* style in Step 2 removed the hanging indent.)
4. Save and then preview **3-NewZealand.docx**.

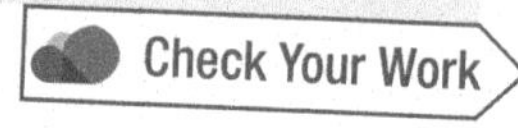

Choosing a Citation Style

Quick Steps

Change Citation Style
1. Click References tab.
2. Click *Style* option box arrow.
3. Click a style.

Different subjects and different instructors or professors may require different formats for citing references. The style for reference citations can be changed before beginning a new document or while working in an existing document. To change the style of citations in an existing document, click the References tab, click the *Style* option box arrow, and then click the style at the drop-down list.

Activity 3h Choosing a Citation Style

Part 8 of 8

1. With **3-NewZealand.docx** open, change the document and works cited page from MLA style to APA style by completing the following steps:
   a. Click the References tab.
   b. Click the *Style* option box arrow in the Citations & Bibliography group and then click *APA* at the drop-down list.

   c. Notice the changes made to the works cited entries.
   d. Scroll up the document and notice the changes to the citations.
   e. Press Ctrl + End to move the insertion point to the end of the document.
   f. Change the title *Works Cited* to *References*.
2. Save, preview, and then close **3-NewZealand.docx**.
3. Display a blank document, click the References tab, change the style to *MLA*, and then close the document without saving it.

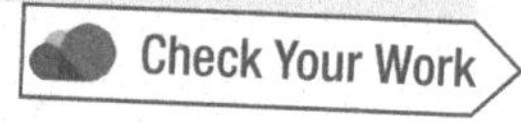

Chapter Summary

- Text that appears in the top margin of a page is called a *header*; text that appears in the bottom margin of a page is called a *footer*. Insert predesigned headers and footers in a document or create custom headers and footers.
- To create a custom header, click the Header button in the Header & Footer group on the Insert tab and then click *Edit Header*. At the Header pane, insert elements or text. Complete similar steps to create a custom footer.
- Use buttons in the Insert group on the Header & Footer tab to insert elements such as the date and time, Quick Parts, and images into a header or footer.
- Word inserts headers and footers 0.5 inch from the edge of the page. Reposition a header or footer with buttons in the Position group on the Header & Footer tab.
- A unique header or footer can be created on the first page; a header or footer can be omitted on the first page; different headers or footers can be created for odd and even pages; or different headers or footers can be created for sections in a document. Use options in the Options group on the Header & Footer tab to specify the type of header or footer to be created.
- Each section in a document is linked to the other sections in the document. To specify that a header or footer prints only on the pages within a section and not the previous sections, click the Link to Previous button in the Navigation group on the Header & Footer tab to deactivate the button.
- Insert page numbers in a document in a header or footer or with options at the Page Number button in the Header & Footer group on the Insert tab.
- Format page numbers with options at the Page Number Format dialog box.
- To print sections or specific pages within a section, use the *Pages* text box at the Print backstage area. When specifying sections and pages, use the letter *s* before a section number and the letter *p* before a page number.
- Word attempts to avoid creating widows and orphans when inserting soft page breaks. Turn on or off the *Widow/Orphan control* option at the Paragraph dialog box with the Line and Page Breaks tab selected. This dialog box also contains options for keeping a paragraph, group of paragraphs, or group of lines together.
- Footnotes and endnotes provide explanatory notes and source citations. Footnotes are inserted and printed at the bottoms of pages and endnotes are inserted and printed at the end of the document.
- By default, footnotes are numbered with arabic numbers and endnotes are numbered with lowercase roman numerals.
- Move, copy, or delete a footnote/endnote reference number in a document and all the other footnotes/endnotes automatically renumber.
- Delete a footnote or endnote by selecting the reference number and then pressing the Delete key.
- Consider using in-text citations to acknowledge sources in a paper. Commonly used citation and reference styles include those of the American Psychological Association (APA), Modern Language Association (MLA), and *Chicago Manual of Style* (Chicago).
- Insert a citation using the Insert Citation button in the Citations & Bibliography group on the References tab. Specify source information at the Create Source dialog box.

- Insert a citation placeholder in a document if the source information will be added at a later time.
- Insert a citation in a document for source information that has already been saved by clicking the Insert Citation button in the Citations & Bibliography group and then clicking the source at the drop-down list.
- Edit a source at the Edit Source dialog box. Display this dialog box by clicking the source citation in the document, clicking the Citation Options arrow, and then clicking *Edit Source* at the drop-down list. Another option is to display the Source Manager dialog box, click the source to be edited, and then click the Edit button.
- Copy, delete, and edit sources and create new sources with options at the Source Manager dialog box. Display this dialog box by clicking the Manage Sources button in the Citations & Bibliography group on the References tab.
- Insert a sources list, such as a works cited page, references page, or bibliography, at the end of the document on a separate page. To do so, use the Bibliography button in the Citations & Bibliography group on the References tab.
- To update a sources list, click in the list and then click the Update Citations and Bibliography tab.
- The MLA and APA styles require specific formatting for a list of sources. Refer to page 104 for a list of formatting requirements.
- Change the reference style with the *Style* option box in the Citations & Bibliography group on the References tab.

Commands Review

FEATURE	RIBBON TAB, GROUP	BUTTON, OPTION	KEYBOARD SHORTCUT
bibliography	References, Citations & Bibliography		
create footer	Insert, Header & Footer	, *Edit Footer*	
create header	Insert, Header & Footer	, *Edit Header*	
citation style	References, Citations & Bibliography		
Create Source dialog box	References, Citations & Bibliography	, *Add New Source*	
endnote	References, Footnotes		Alt + Ctrl + D
footer	Insert, Header & Footer		
footnote	References, Footnotes		Alt + Ctrl + F
header	Insert, Header & Footer		
next footnote	References, Footnotes		
page number	Insert, Header & Footer		
show notes	References, Footnotes		
Source Manager dialog box	References, Citations & Bibliography		

Review and Assessment

CHAPTER 3

Skills Assessment

Assessment 1 — Insert Specialized Footers in a Report

1. Open **Robots.docx** and then save it with the name **3-Robots**.
2. Keep the heading *NAVIGATION* together with the paragraph of text that follows it.
3. Move the insertion point to the beginning of the document and then create an odd page footer that includes the following:
   a. Insert the current date at the left margin. (Choose the date option that displays the month spelled out, such as *January 1, 2024*.)
   b. Using the Pictures button in the Insert group on the Header & Footer tab, insert the **RobotWalking.jpg** image file in the middle of the footer. Change the height of the robot image to 0.5 inch and the text wrapping to Behind Text. If necessary, drag the robot image below the footer pane border.
   c. At the right margin, type Page, press the spacebar, and then insert a plain page number at the current position.
4. Create an even page footer that includes the following:
   a. At the left margin, type Page, press the spacebar, and then insert a plain page number at the current position.
   b. Insert the **RobotWalking.jpg** image file in the middle of the footer and apply the same formatting as you did to the image in the odd page footer.
   c. Insert the current date at the right margin in the same format you chose for the odd page footer.
5. Save, preview, and then close **3-Robots.docx**.

Assessment 2 — Insert a Header and Footer in a Report on All Pages Except the First Page

1. Open **Volcanoes.docx** and then save it with the name **3-Volcanoes**.
2. Create a header for all pages except the first page and type Volcano Report at the right margin of the Header pane. (Make sure the First Page Header pane is blank.)
3. Create a footer for all pages except the first page and insert the Banded predesigned footer in the Footer pane. (Make sure the First Page Footer pane is blank.)
4. Save, preview, and then close **3-Volcanoes.docx**.

Assessment 3 Insert a Section Break and Format and Print Sections

1. Open **CompViruses.docx** and then save it with the name **3-CompViruses**.
2. Insert a section break that begins a new page at the beginning of the title *CHAPTER 2 SECURITY RISKS*.
3. Move the insertion point to the beginning of the document and then create a footer for the first section in the document with *Chapter 1* at the left margin, the page number in the middle, and your first and last names at the right margin.
4. Edit the footer for the second section to Chapter 2 instead of Chapter 1. ***Hint: Make sure you break the link.***
5. Print only the pages in section 2.
6. Save, preview, and then close **3-CompViruses.docx**.

Assessment 4 Insert Footnotes in a Designing Newsletters Document

1. Open **DesignNwsltr.docx** and then save it with the name **3-DesignNwsltr**.
2. Create the first footnote shown in Figure 3.10 at the end of the first paragraph in the *Applying Guidelines* section.
3. Create the second footnote shown in the figure at the end of the last paragraph in the *Applying Guidelines* section.
4. Create the third footnote shown in the figure at the end of the only paragraph in the *Choosing Paper Size and Type* section.
5. Create the fourth footnote shown in the figure at the end of the only paragraph in the *Choosing Paper Weight* section.
6. Save and then preview **3-DesignNwsltr.docx**.
7. Select the entire document and then change the font to Constantia.
8. Select all the footnotes and then change the font to Constantia. ***Note: Pressing Ctrl + A will select all the footnotes in the document.***
9. Delete the second footnote (*Maddock*).
10. Save, preview, and then close **3-DesignNwsltr.docx**.

Figure 3.10 Assessment 4

James Haberman, "Designing a Newsletter," *Desktop Designs* (2024): 23-29.

Arlita Maddock, "Guidelines for a Better Newsletter," *Desktop Publisher* (2023): 32-38.

Monica Alverso, "Paper Styles for Newsletters," *Design Technologies* (2024): 45-51.

Keith Sutton, "Choosing Paper Styles," *Design Techniques* (2024): 8-11.

Assessment 5 Insert Sources and Citations in a Privacy Rights Document

1. Open **PrivRights.docx** and then save it with the name **3-PrivRights-MLA**.
2. Make sure that MLA style is selected in the Citations & Bibliography group on the References tab.
3. With the insertion point positioned at the beginning of the document, type your name, press the Enter key, type your instructor's name, press the Enter key, type the title of your course, press the Enter key, and then type the current date.
4. Set the text in the document to 12-point Cambria and then make this the default font for the document. ***Hint: Do this with the Set As Default button at the Font dialog box.***

5. Insert a header that displays your last name and the page number at the right margin.
6. Select and then delete the text *(Hartley)* that appears in the second paragraph.
7. With the insertion point positioned between the word *policy* and the period that ends the third sentence in the second paragraph, press the spacebar and then insert the source information for a journal article written by Kenneth Hartley using the following information:

Author	Kenneth Hartley
Title	Privacy Laws
Journal Name	Business World
Year	2024
Pages	33-46
Volume	XII

8. Select and then delete the text *(Ferraro)* that appears in the second paragraph.
9. With the insertion point positioned between the word *place* and the period that ends the fourth sentence in the second paragraph, press the spacebar and then insert the following source information for a book:

Author	Ramona Ferraro
Title	Business Employee Rights
Year	2024
City	Tallahassee
Publisher	Everglades Publishing House

10. Select and then delete the text *(Aldrich)* that appears in the last paragraph.
11. With the insertion point positioned between the word *limit"* and the period that ends the second sentence in the last paragraph, press the spacebar and then insert the following information for an article in a periodical:

Author	Kelly Aldrich
Title	What Rights Do Employees Have?
Periodical Title	Great Plains Times
Year	2024
Month	May
Day	6
Pages	18-22

12. Insert page number 20 in the Kelly Aldrich citation using the Edit Citation dialog box.
13. Edit the Kenneth Hartley source title to read *Small Business Privacy Laws* in the *Master List* section of the Source Manager dialog box. (Update both the Master List and the Current List.)
14. Insert a works cited page on a separate page at the end of the document.
15. Create a new source in the document using the Source Manager dialog box and include the following source information for a website:

Author	Harold Davidson
Name of Web Page	Small Business Policies and Procedures
Year	2023
Month	December
Day	12
Year Accessed	2024
Month Accessed	February
Day Accessed	23
URL	https://ppi-edu.net/policies

16. Insert a citation for Harold Davidson at the end of the last sentence in the first paragraph.
17. Update the works cited page.

18. Format the works cited page to meet MLA requirements with the following changes:
    a. Select the *Works Cited* heading and all the entries and then click the *No Spacing* style.
    b. Change the spacing to 2.0.
    c. Format the works cited entries with a hanging indent.
    d. Center the title *Works Cited*.
19. Save and then preview **3-PrivRights-MLA.docx**.
20. Save the document with the name **3-PrivRights-APA**.
21. Change the document and works cited page from MLA style to APA style. Make sure you change the title of the sources list to *References*. Select the references in the list and then change the line spacing to double spacing.
22. Save, preview, and then close **3-PrivRights-APA.docx**.

Visual Benchmark

Format a Report in MLA Style

1. Open **SecurityDefenses.docx** and then save it with the name **3-SecurityDefenses**.
2. Format the document so it displays as shown in Figure 3.11 with the following specifications:
    a. Change the document font to 12-point Cambria and then set 12-point Cambria as the default.
    b. Use the information from the works cited page when inserting citations into the document. The Hollingsworth citation is for a journal article, the Montoya citation is for a book, and the Gillespie citation is for a website.
    c. Format the works cited page to meet MLA requirements.
3. Save, preview, and then close **3-SecurityDefenses.docx**.

Figure 3.11 Visual Benchmark

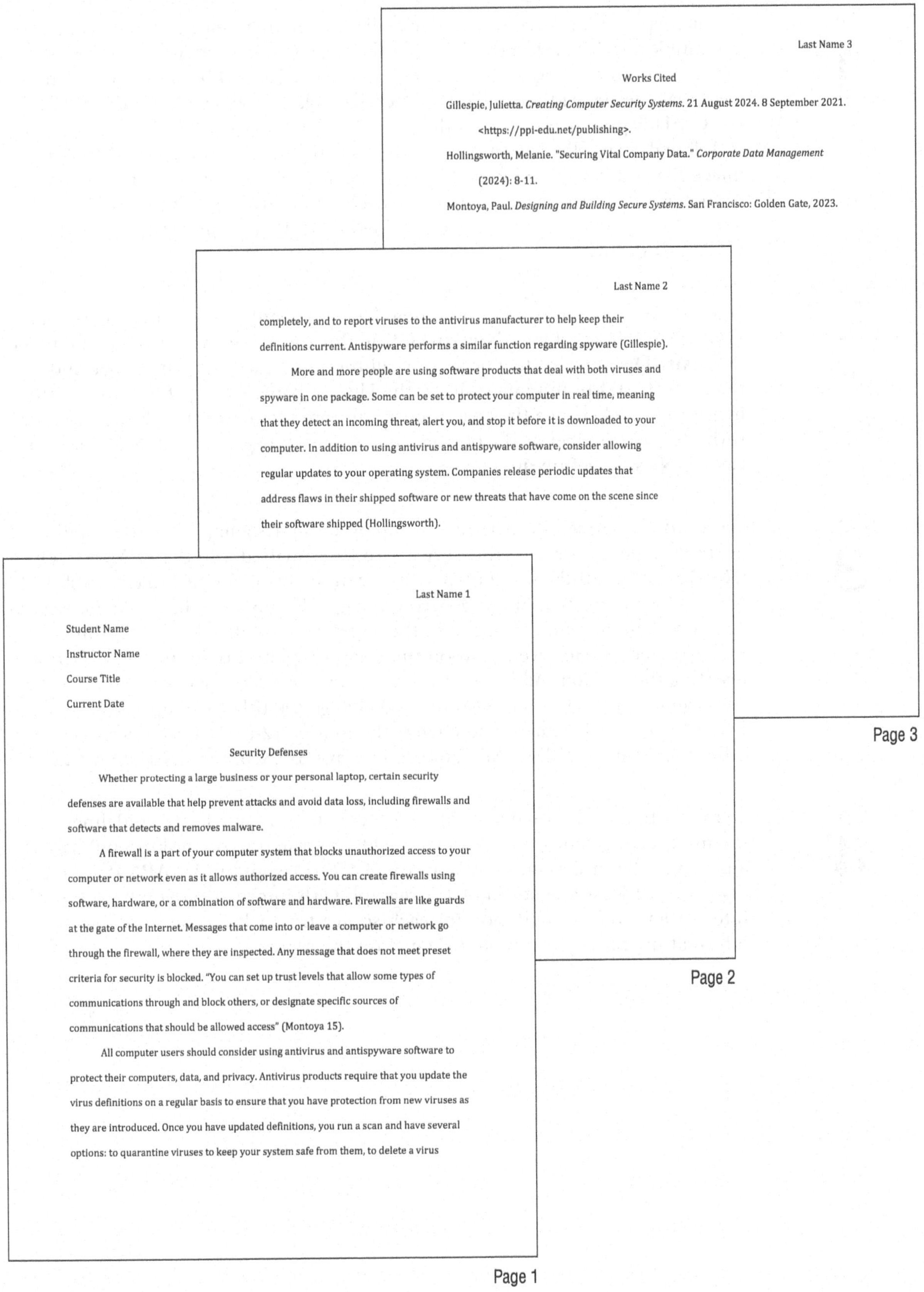

Last Name 3

Works Cited

Gillespie, Julietta. *Creating Computer Security Systems.* 21 August 2024. 8 September 2021. <https://ppi-edu.net/publishing>.

Hollingsworth, Melanie. "Securing Vital Company Data." *Corporate Data Management* (2024): 8-11.

Montoya, Paul. *Designing and Building Secure Systems.* San Francisco: Golden Gate, 2023.

Page 3

Last Name 2

completely, and to report viruses to the antivirus manufacturer to help keep their definitions current. Antispyware performs a similar function regarding spyware (Gillespie).

More and more people are using software products that deal with both viruses and spyware in one package. Some can be set to protect your computer in real time, meaning that they detect an incoming threat, alert you, and stop it before it is downloaded to your computer. In addition to using antivirus and antispyware software, consider allowing regular updates to your operating system. Companies release periodic updates that address flaws in their shipped software or new threats that have come on the scene since their software shipped (Hollingsworth).

Page 2

Last Name 1

Student Name

Instructor Name

Course Title

Current Date

Security Defenses

Whether protecting a large business or your personal laptop, certain security defenses are available that help prevent attacks and avoid data loss, including firewalls and software that detects and removes malware.

A firewall is a part of your computer system that blocks unauthorized access to your computer or network even as it allows authorized access. You can create firewalls using software, hardware, or a combination of software and hardware. Firewalls are like guards at the gate of the Internet. Messages that come into or leave a computer or network go through the firewall, where they are inspected. Any message that does not meet preset criteria for security is blocked. "You can set up trust levels that allow some types of communications through and block others, or designate specific sources of communications that should be allowed access" (Montoya 15).

All computer users should consider using antivirus and antispyware software to protect their computers, data, and privacy. Antivirus products require that you update the virus definitions on a regular basis to ensure that you have protection from new viruses as they are introduced. Once you have updated definitions, you run a scan and have several options: to quarantine viruses to keep your system safe from them, to delete a virus

Page 1

Case Study

Part 1

You just opened a new company, Chrysalis Media, that helps businesses creatively communicate with customers. Some of the media design services you offer are business letterhead, logos, flyers, newsletters, signage, and business cards. Create a company letterhead document by opening a blank document and then inserting the **CMHdr.png** image file as a first page header. Change the height of the image to 1.4" and change the header position from the top to 0.3". Insert the **CMFtr.png** image file as a first page footer. If necessary, make adjustments to the header and/or footer to improve the appearance of each on the page Save the completed letterhead document with the name **3-CMLtrhd**. Preview and then close **3-CMLtrhd.docx**.

Part 2

You have a document on defining newsletter elements that you want to make available to clients. Open **Nwsltr-Define.docx** and then save it with the name **3-Nwsltr-Define**. Create a header for all the pages except the first page and insert the **CMHdr.png** image file in the Header pane. Change the width of the image to 2" and change the header position from the top to 0.3". Insert a footer with the page number at the bottom center of each page. Save, preview, and then close **3-Nwsltr-Define.docx**.

Part 3

You want to provide information for employees on designing newsletters and have a report on newsletter design that needs to be formatted into the APA style. Open **CM-DesignNwsltr.docx** and then save it with the name **3-CM-DesignNwsltr-APA**. Look at the information in Figure 3.10 (on page 110) and then insert the information as in-text journal article citations in the locations indicated in Steps 2 through 5 in Assessment 4. However, position the insertion point inside the period before inserting the citation. Add a reference page on a separate page at the end of the document. Center the title *References* and change the title to all uppercase letters. Select the entire document and change the font to 12-point Cambria. Apply any other formatting to follow APA guidelines. Save **3-CM-DesignNwsltr-APA.docx**.

Part 4

You want to include some additional information on newsletter guidelines. Using the internet, look for websites that provide information on desktop publishing and/or newsletter design. Include in the **3-CM-DesignNwsltr-APA.docx** report document at least one additional paragraph with information you found on the internet and include a citation for each source from which you have borrowed information. Save, preview, and then close the report.

WORD

CHAPTER 4

Creating Specialized Tables and Navigating in a Document

Performance Objectives

Upon successful completion of Chapter 4, you will be able to:

1. Insert a table of contents
2. Number the table of contents page
3. Navigate using a table of contents
4. Customize, update, or remove a table of contents
5. Assign levels to table of content entries
6. Mark table of contents entries as fields
7. Insert, update, or delete a table of figures
8. Create and customize captions for figures
9. Navigate in a document using the Navigation pane, bookmarks, hyperlinks, and cross-references
10. Insert hyperlinks to a location in the same document, a different document, a file in another program, or an email address

---

A book, textbook, report, or manuscript often includes sections such as a table of contents and a table of figures. Creating these sections manually can be tedious. However, using Word's automated features, these sections can be created quickly and easily. In this chapter, you will learn how to mark text for a table of contents and a table of figures and how to insert captions. You will also learn how to insert hyperlinks, bookmarks, and cross-references to allow for more efficient navigation within a document.

Data Files

The data files for this chapter are in the WL2C4 folder that you downloaded at the beginning of this course.

Activity 1 Create a Table of Contents for a Computer Interface Report **2 Parts**

You will open a report on computer interfaces, insert a section break, insert the table of contents in the document, and then number the table of contents page. You will also customize and update the table of contents.

Creating a Table of Contents

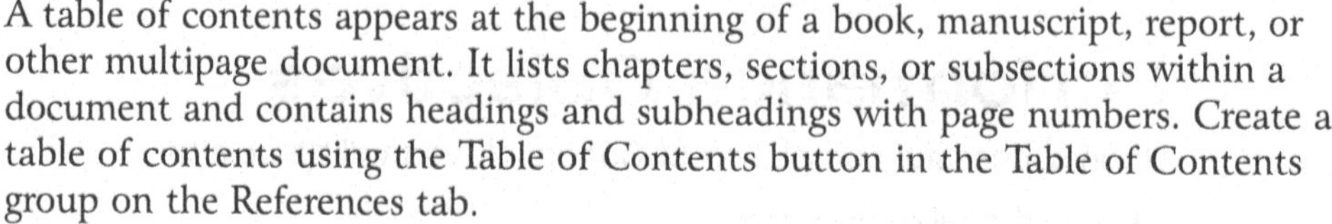

A table of contents appears at the beginning of a book, manuscript, report, or other multipage document. It lists chapters, sections, or subsections within a document and contains headings and subheadings with page numbers. Create a table of contents using the Table of Contents button in the Table of Contents group on the References tab.

Table of Contents

One method for identifying text to be included in a table of contents is to apply built-in heading styles. Apply built-in heading styles with options in the Styles group on the Home tab. Text with the Heading 1 style applied is used for the first level of the table of contents, text with the Heading 2 style applied is used for the second level, and so on.

Inserting a Table of Contents

Quick Steps

Insert Table of Contents

1. Apply heading styles.
2. Click References tab.
3. Click Table of Contents button.
4. Click option at drop-down list.

Inserting a Table of Contents

After applying styles to the headings, insert the table of contents in the document. To do this, position the insertion point at the beginning of the document where the table of contents is to appear, click the References tab, click the Table of Contents button, and then click the specific option at the drop-down list.

Page Number

Quick Steps

Number Table of Contents Page

1. Click Insert tab.
2. Click Page Number button.
3. Click *Format Page Numbers.*
4. Change number format to lowercase roman numerals.
5. Click OK.

Numbering the Table of Contents Page

Generally, the page or pages containing the table of contents are numbered with lowercase roman numerals (*i, ii, iii*). Format the page numbers as lowercase roman numerals at the Page Number Format dialog box, shown in Figure 4.1. Display this dialog box by clicking the Insert tab, clicking the Page Number button in the Header & Footer group, and then clicking *Format Page Numbers* at the drop-down list.

The first page of text in the main document, which usually comes immediately after the table of contents, should begin with arabic number 1. To change from roman to arabic page numbers within the same document, separate the table of contents from the first page of the document with a section break that begins a new page.

Figure 4.1 Page Number Format Dialog Box

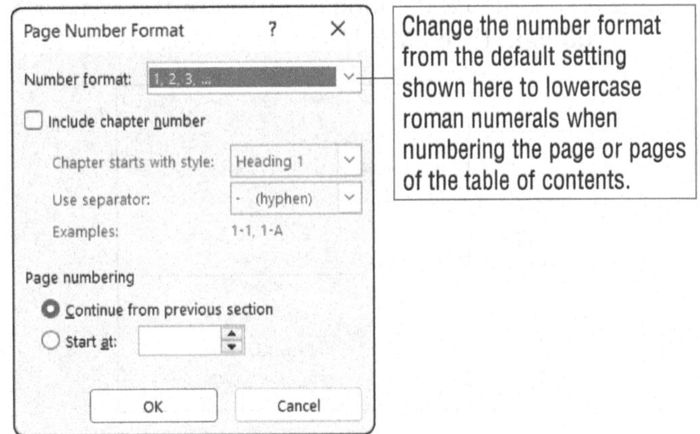

Navigating Using a Table of Contents

Hint You can use a table of contents to navigate quickly in a document and to get an overview of the topics it covers.

When a table of contents is inserted in a document, each entry automatically becomes a hyperlink that can be used to navigate within the document. To navigate in a document using the table of contents, click in the table of contents to select it. Position the pointer over an entry and a ScreenTip displays with the path and file name as well as the text *Ctrl+Click to follow link.* Press and hold down the Ctrl key, click the left mouse button, and then release the Ctrl key to go directly to the page where the content is located.

Activity 1a Inserting a Table of Contents

Part 1 of 2

1. Open **AIReport.docx** and then save it with the name **4-AIReport**. (This document contains headings with heading styles applied.)
2. Position the insertion point immediately left of the first *N* in *NATURAL INTERFACE* and then insert a section break by completing the following steps:
   a. Click the Layout tab.
   b. Click the Breaks button in the Page Setup group.
   c. Click the *Next Page* option in the *Section Breaks* section.
3. With the insertion point positioned immediately left of the *N* (and below the section break), insert page numbers and change the beginning number to *1* by completing the following steps:
   a. Click the Insert tab.
   b. Click the Page Number button in the Header & Footer group, point to *Bottom of Page*, and then click *Plain Number 2*.

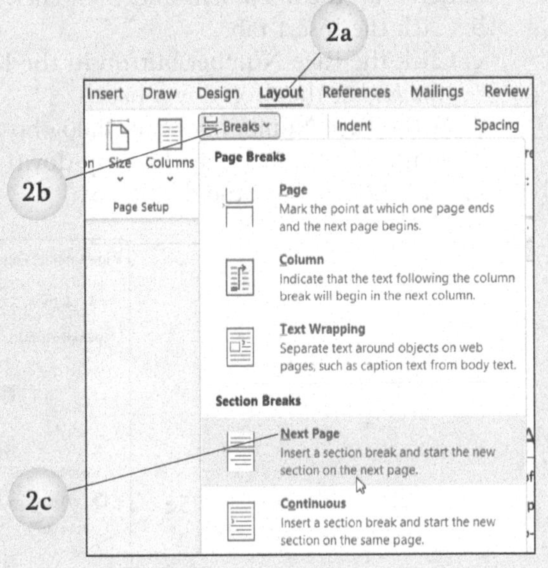

c. Click the Page Number button in the Header & Footer group on the Header & Footer tab and then click *Format Page Numbers* at the drop-down list.

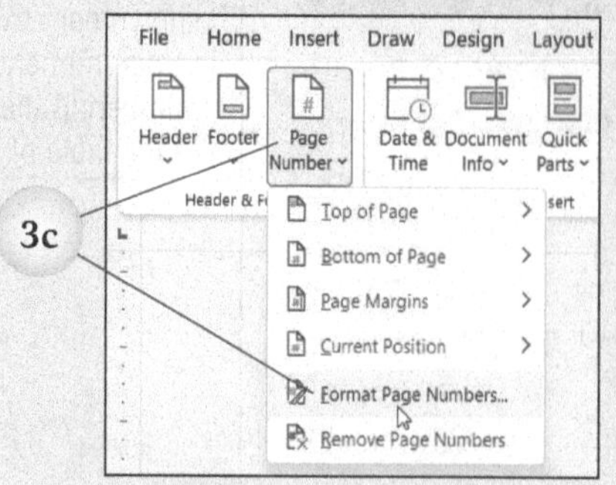

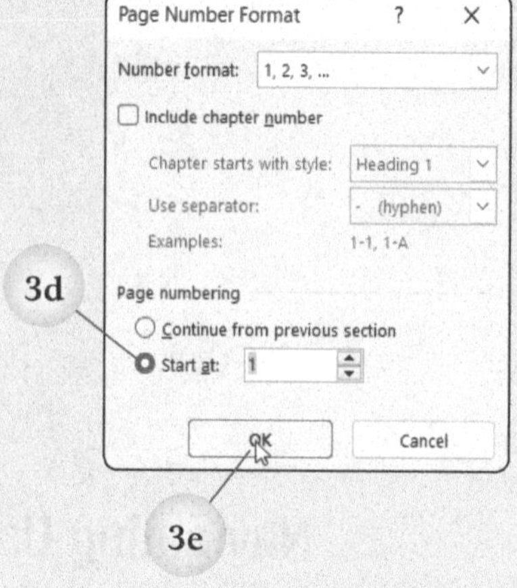

d. At the Page Number Format dialog box, click *Start at* in the *Page numbering* section. (This inserts *1* in the *Start at* measurement box.)

e. Click OK to close the Page Number Format dialog box.

f. Click the Close Header and Footer button.

4. Insert a table of contents at the beginning of the document by completing the following steps:

   a. Press Ctrl + Home to move the insertion point to the beginning of the document.

   b. Click the References tab.

   c. Click the Table of Contents button in the Table of Contents group and then click the *Automatic Table 1* option in the *Built-In* section of the drop-down list.

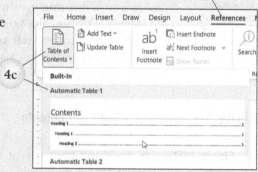

5. Modify the page number on the table of contents page by completing the following steps:

   a. Scroll up the document and then click in the heading *Contents*.

   b. Click the Insert tab.

   c. Click the Page Number button in the Header & Footer group and then click *Format Page Numbers* at the drop-down list.

   d. At the Page Number Format dialog box, click the *Number format* option box arrow and then click *i, ii, iii, …* at the drop-down list.

   e. Click OK to close the dialog box.

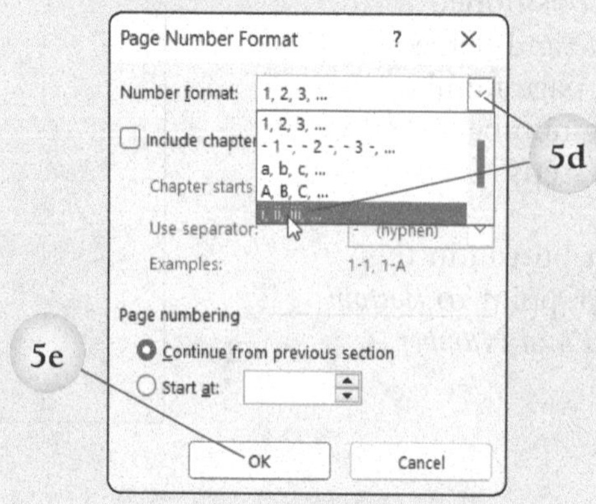

6. Navigate in the document using the table of contents by completing the following steps:
   a. Click in the table of contents.
   b. Position the pointer on the entry *Virtual Reality*, press and hold down the Ctrl key, click the left mouse button, and then release the Ctrl key. (This moves the insertion point to the beginning of the heading *Virtual Reality* in the document.)
   c. Press Ctrl + Home to move the insertion point to the beginning of the document.
7. Save and then preview **4-AIReport.docx**.

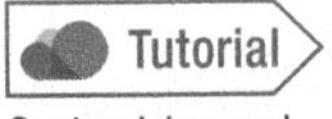

Customizing and Updating a Table of Contents

Customizing a Table of Contents

Customize an existing table of contents in a document with options at the Table of Contents dialog box, shown in Figure 4.2. Display this dialog box by clicking the Table of Contents button on the References tab and then clicking *Custom Table of Contents* at the drop-down list.

At the Table of Contents dialog box, a sample table of contents appears in the *Print Preview* section. Change the table of contents format by clicking the *Formats* option box arrow in the *General* section. At the drop-down list, click a format. When a different format is selected, that format displays in the *Print Preview* section.

Page numbers in a table of contents will display after the text or aligned at the right margin, depending on what option is selected. Page number alignment can also be specified with the *Right align page numbers* option. The possible number of levels in the contents list that appears in a table of contents depends on the number of heading levels in the document. Control the number of levels that display with the *Show levels* measurement box in the *General* section. Tab leaders help guide readers' eyes from the table of contents heading to the page number. The default tab leader is a period or dotted line leader. To choose a different leader, click the *Tab leader* option box arrow and then click to select a dotted line, dashed line, or solid underline at the drop-down list.

Figure 4.2 Table of Contents Dialog Box

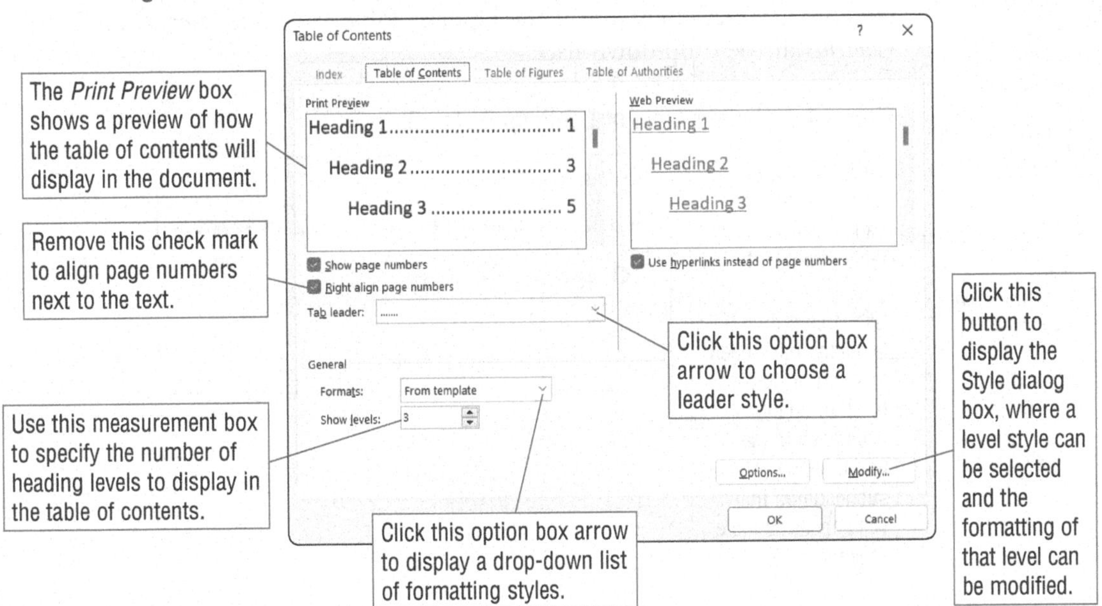

Word automatically formats the entries in a table of contents as hyperlinks and inserts page numbers. Each hyperlink can be used to move to a specific location in the document.

The *Use hyperlinks instead of page numbers* check box in the *Web Preview* section of the Table of Contents dialog box contains a check mark by default. With this option active, if the document is posted to the web, readers will only need to click the hyperlink to view specific content in the document. If the document is viewed in a web browser or the table of contents is used to navigate in the document, page numbers are not necessary and can be removed from the table of contents by removing the check mark from the *Show page numbers* check box at the Table of Contents dialog box.

If changes are made to the options at the Table of Contents dialog box, clicking OK will cause a message to display asking if the selected table of contents should be replaced. At this message, click Yes.

Updating a Table of Contents

Update Table

Quick Steps

Update Table of Contents
1. Click in table of contents.
2. Click References tab.
3. Click Update Table button, click Update Table tab, or press F9.
4. Click *Update page numbers only* or *Update entire table*.
5. Click OK.

Remove Table of Contents
1. Click References tab.
2. Click Table of Contents button.
3. Click *Remove Table of Contents*.

OR
1. Click in table of contents.
2. Click Table of Contents tab.
3. Click *Remove Table of Contents*.

If headings or other text in a document is deleted, moved, or edited after the table of contents is inserted, the table of contents will need to be updated. To do this, click in the current table of contents and then click the Update Table button in the Table of Contents group, click the Update Table tab, or press the F9 function key (the Update Field key). At the Update Table of Contents dialog box, shown in Figure 4.3, click *Update page numbers only* if changes were made that only affect page numbers or click *Update entire table* if changes were made to the headings or subheadings in the document. Click OK or press the Enter key to close the dialog box.

Removing a Table of Contents

Remove a table of contents from a document by clicking the Table of Contents button on the References tab and then clicking *Remove Table of Contents* at the drop-down list. Another way to remove a table of contents is to click in the table of contents, click the Table of Contents tab in the upper left corner of the table of contents (immediately left of the Update Table tab), and then click *Remove Table of Contents* at the drop-down list.

Figure 4.3 Update Table of Contents Dialog Box

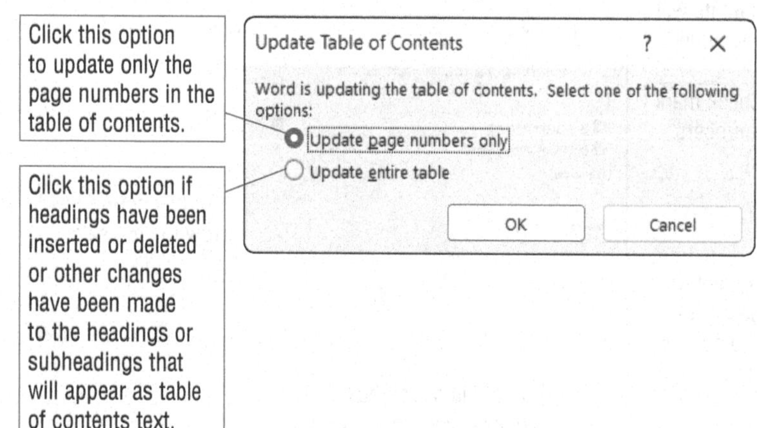
Click this option to update only the page numbers in the table of contents.
Click this option if headings have been inserted or deleted or other changes have been made to the headings or subheadings that will appear as table of contents text.
Update Table of Contents
?
×
Word is updating the table of contents. Select one of the following options:
Update page numbers only
Update entire table
OK
Cancel

Activity 1b Customizing and Updating a Table of Contents

1. With **4-AIReport.docx** open and the insertion point positioned at the beginning of the document, apply a different formatting style to the table of contents by completing the following steps:
   a. Click the References tab, click the Table of Contents button, and then click *Custom Table of Contents* at the drop-down list.
   b. At the Table of Contents dialog box with the Table of Contents tab selected, click the *Formats* option box arrow in the *General* section and then click *Formal* at the drop-down list.
   c. Click the *Tab leader* option box arrow and then click the solid line option (bottom option) at the drop-down list.
   d. Click the *Show levels* measurement box down arrow to change the number to *2*.
   e. Click OK to close the dialog box.
   f. At the message asking if you want to replace the selected table of contents, click the Yes button.

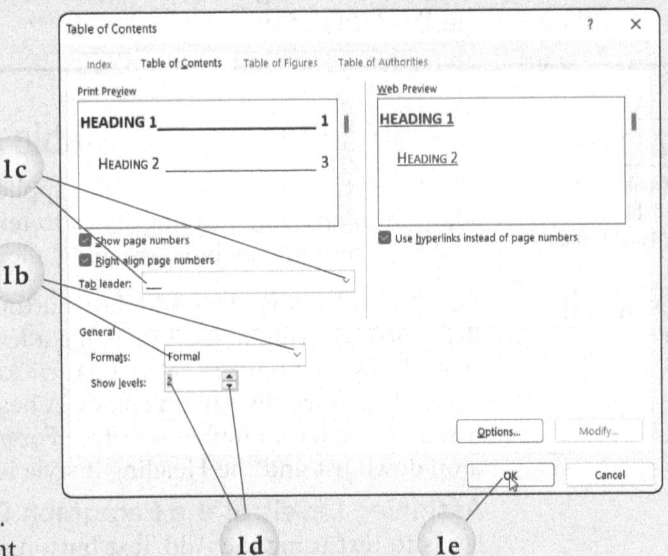

2. Use the table of contents to move the insertion point to the beginning of the heading *Audio Perception*.
3. Press Ctrl + Enter to insert a page break.
4. Update the table of contents by completing the following steps:
   a. Press Ctrl + Home and then click in the table of contents.
   b. Click the Update Table tab.
   c. At the Update Table of Contents dialog box, make sure *Update page numbers only* is selected and then click OK.

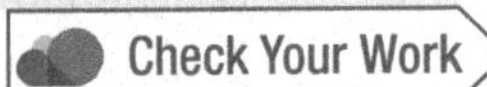

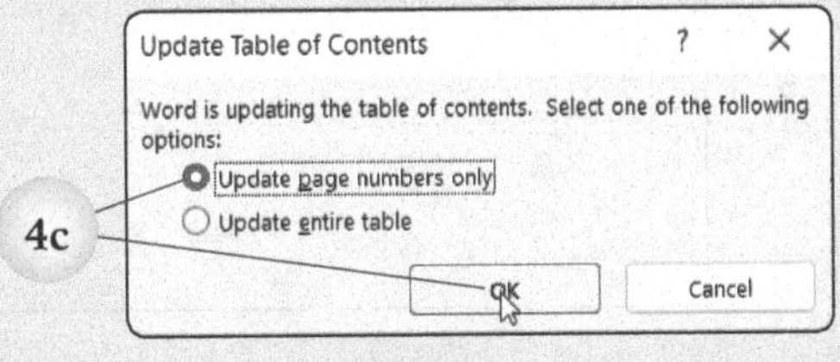

5. Save, preview, and then close **4-AIReport.docx**.

Check Your Work

Activity 2 Assign Levels, Mark Text, and Insert a Table of Contents in Company Documents

3 Parts

You will open documents that contain employee pay and evaluation information, mark text as table of contents fields, and then insert a table of contents. You will also insert a file containing additional information on employee classifications and then update the table of contents.

Assigning Levels for Table of Contents Entries

Assigning Levels for a Table of Contents

Word uses text with heading styles applied to create a table of contents. In addition to applying heading styles to text, other methods for identifying text for a table of contents include assigning a level to text and marking text as a field.

Assigning Levels The Add Text button in the Table of Contents group on the References tab can be used to assign a level to text, which also applies a heading style. To use the button, select text, click the button, and then click a specific level at the drop-down list that displays. A heading style is applied to the selected text based on the level number selected. For example, click the Level 2 option at the drop-down list and the Heading 2 style is applied to the selected text.

Assigning Levels at the Paragraph Dialog Box Applying styles or assigning levels to text using the Add Text button applies specific formatting. The *Outline level* option box at the Paragraph dialog box can be used to assign a level to text for a table of contents that does not apply a style. To use this option, select text, display the Paragraph dialog box, click the *Outline level* option box arrow, and then click the specific level at the drop-down list.

Activity 2a Assigning Levels to Text

Part 1 of 3

1. Open **EmployeeEval.docx** and then save it with the name **4-EmployeeEval.**
2. Select the title *EMPLOYEE MANUAL* at the beginning of the second page.
3. Assign a level to the title by clicking the References tab, clicking the Add Text button in the Table of Contents group, and then clicking *Level 1* at the drop-down list.
4. Select the heading *Evaluation* and then assign a level by completing the following steps:
   a. Click the Home tab.
   b. Click the Paragraph group dialog box launcher.
   c. At the Paragraph dialog box with the Indents and Spacing tab selected, click the *Outline level* option box arrow and then click *Level 2* at the drop-down list.
   d. Click OK.

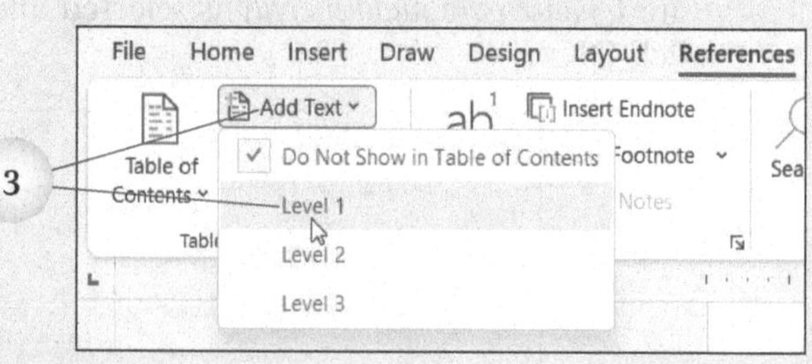

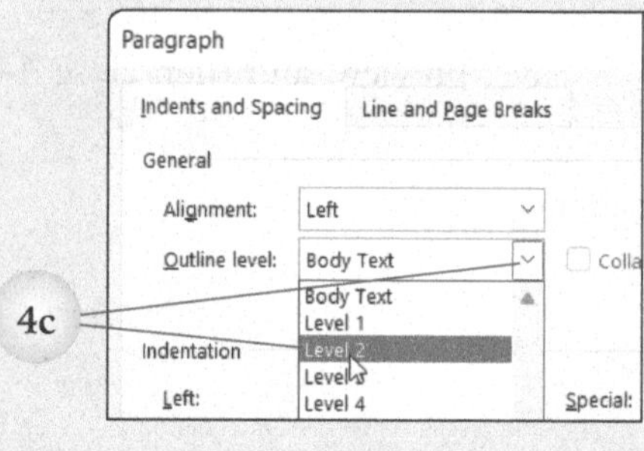

5. Complete steps similar to those in Step 4 to assign Level 3 to the subheadings *Performance Standards*, *Performance Evaluation*, and *Employee Records*.
6. Insert a page break at the beginning of the subheading *Employee Records*. (This heading and the text that follows should display on page 3.)
7. Move the insertion point to the beginning of the document (on the blank page) and then insert insert the Automatic Table 1 table of contents.
8. Save, preview, and then close **4-EmployeeEval.docx**.

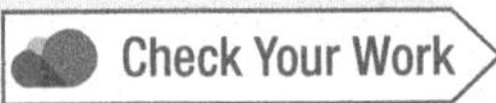

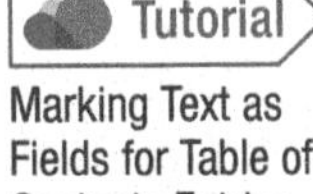

Marking Text as Fields for Table of Contents Entries

Marking Text as Fields Another method for identifying titles and/or headings for a table of contents without applying style formatting is to mark each title or heading as a field entry. To do this, select the text to be included in the table of contents and then press Alt + Shift + O. This displays the Mark Table of Contents Entry dialog box, shown in Figure 4.4. In the dialog box, the selected text displays in the *Entry* text box. Specify the text level using the *Level* measurement box and then click the Mark button. This turns on the display of nonprinting characters in the document and also inserts a field code immediately after the selected text.

For example, when the title is selected in Activity 2a, the following code is inserted immediately after the title *COMPENSATION*: { TC "COMPENSATION" \f C \l "1" }. The Mark Table of Contents Entry dialog box also remains open. To mark the next entry for the table of contents, select the text and then click the Title bar of the Mark Table of Contents Entry dialog box. Specify the level and then click the Mark button. Continue in this manner until all the table of contents entries have been marked.

The *Table identifier* option box at the Mark Table of Contents Entry dialog box has a default setting of *C*. (For a table of figures discussed later in this chapter, the table identifier is *F*.) To create more than one table of contents for a document, mark text with a specific table identifer and then use that identifer when inserting the table of contents.

If the table of contents entries are marked as fields, the *Table entry fields* option will need to be activated when inserting the table of contents. To do this, display the Table of Contents dialog box and then click the Options button. At the Table of Contents Options dialog box, shown in Figure 4.5, click the *Table entry fields* check box to insert a check mark and then click OK.

Figure 4.4 Mark Table of Contents Entry Dialog Box

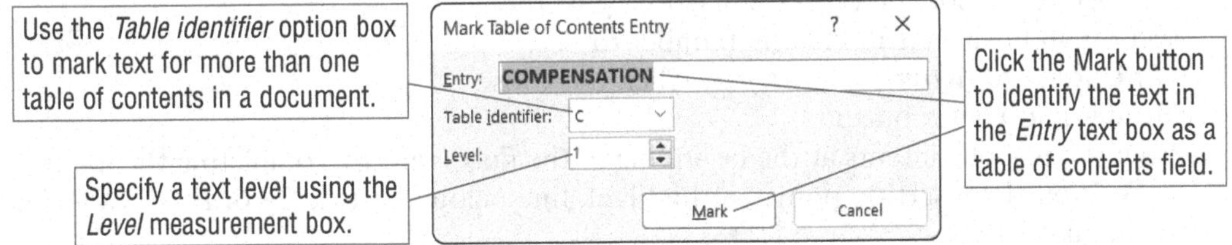

Figure 4.5 Table of Contents Options Dialog Box

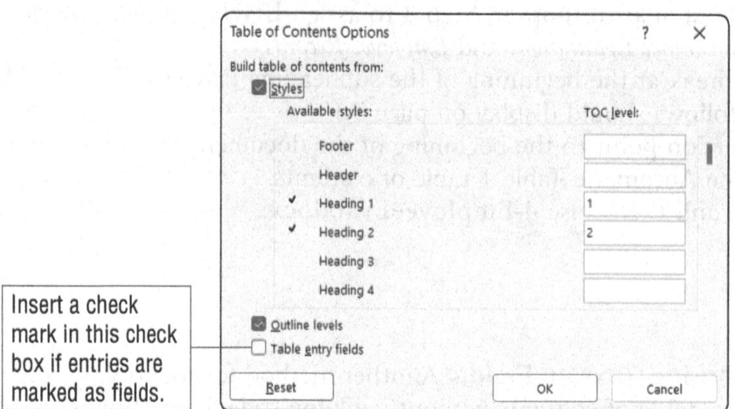

Activity 2b Marking Headings as Fields

Part 2 of 3

1. Open **EmployeeComp.docx** and then save it with the name **4-EmployeeComp**.
2. Mark the titles and headings as fields for insertion in a table of contents by completing the following steps:
   a. Select the title *COMPENSATION* (on the second page).
   b. Press Alt + Shift + O.
   c. At the Mark Table of Contents Entry dialog box, make sure the *Level* measurement box is set at *1* and then click the Mark button. (This turns on the display of nonprinting characters.)
   d. Click in the document and then select the heading *Rate of Pay*.
   e. Click the dialog box Title bar.
   f. Click the *Level* measurement box up arrow in the Mark Table of Contents Entry dialog box to display *2*.
   g. Click the Mark button.
   h. Mark the headings *Direct Deposit Options* and *Pay Progression* as level 2.
   i. Click the Close button to close the Mark Table of Contents Entry dialog box.
3. Position the insertion point at the beginning of the title *COMPENSATION*. Insert a page number at the bottom center of each page of the section and change the starting number to *1*. ***Hint: Refer to Activity 1a, Step 3.*** Click the Close Header and Footer button.
4. Insert a table of contents at the beginning of the document by completing the following steps:
   a. Position the insertion point on the blank line below the title *TABLE OF CONTENTS* on the first page.
   b. Click the References tab.
   c. Click the Table of Contents button and then click *Custom Table of Contents* at the drop-down list.
   d. At the Table of Contents dialog box, click the Options button.

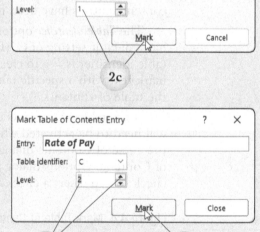

Mark Table of Contents Entry
Entry: COMPENSATION
Table identifier: C
Level: 1
Mark
Cancel
2c

Mark Table of Contents Entry
Entry: Rate of Pay
Table identifier: C
Level: 2
Mark
Close
2f
2g

e. At the Table of Contents Options dialog box, click the *Table entry fields* check box to insert a check mark.
f. Click OK to close the Table of Contents Options dialog box.
g. Click OK to close the Table of Contents dialog box.
5. Insert a lowercase roman numeral page number on the table of contents page. ***Hint: Refer to Activity 1a, Step 5.***
6. Click the Show/Hide ¶ button in the Paragraph group on the Home tab to turn off the display of nonprinting characters.
7. Save and then preview **4-EmployeeComp.docx**.

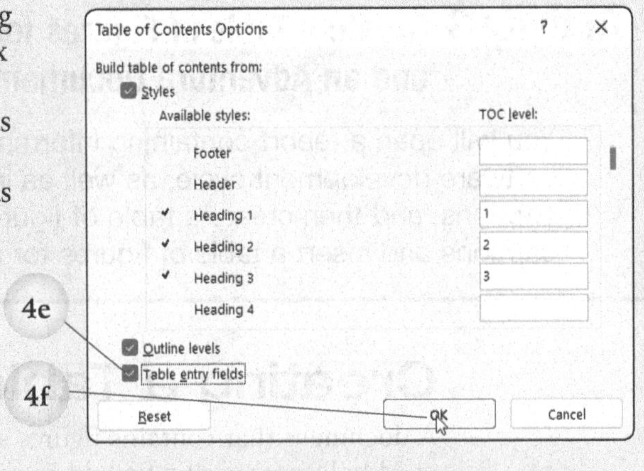

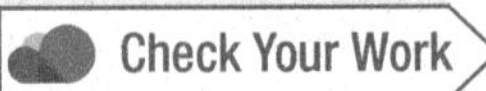

If additional information is inserted in a document with headings marked as fields, the table of contents can be easily updated. To do this, insert the text and then mark the text with options at the Mark Table of Contents Entry dialog box. Click in the table of contents and then click the Update Table tab. At the Update Table of Contents dialog box, click the *Update entire table* option and then click OK.

Activity 2c Updating an Entire Table of Contents

Part 3 of 3

1. With **4-EmployeeComp.docx** open, move the insertion point to the end of the document and then insert a file in the document by completing the following steps:
   a. Click the Insert tab.
   b. Click the Object button arrow in the Text group and then click *Text from File* at the drop-down list.
   c. At the Insert File dialog box, navigate to your WL2C4 folder and then double-click ***PosClass.docx***. (This document contains a title that has already been marked as a level 1 field.)

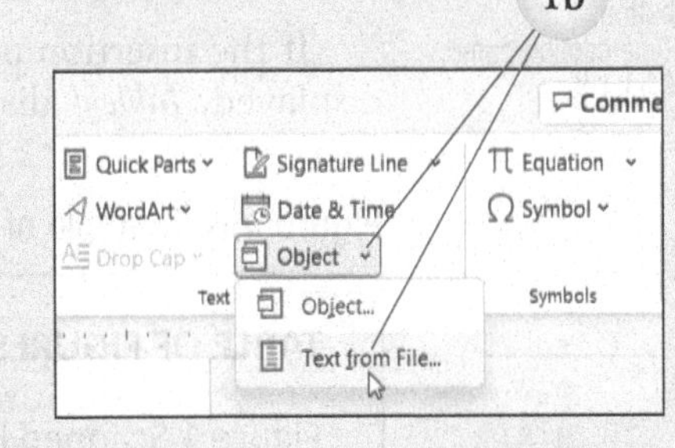

2. Update the table of contents by completing the following steps:
   a. Select the entire table of contents (excluding the title).
   b. Click the References tab.
   c. Click the Update Table button in the Table of Contents group.
   d. At the Update Table of Contents dialog box, click the *Update entire table* option.
   e. Click OK.
3. Save, preview, and then close **4-EmployeeComp.docx**.

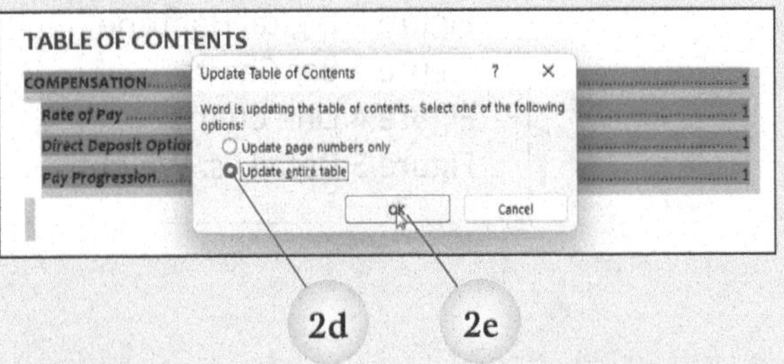

Check Your Work

Activity 3 Create a Table of Figures for a Technology Report and an Adventure Document — 3 Parts

You will open a report containing information on software, output devices, and the software development cycle, as well as images and a SmartArt diagram; insert captions; and then create a table of figures. You will also create and customize captions and insert a table of figures for an adventure document.

Creating a Table of Figures

Insert Table of Figures

A document that contains figures should include a table of figures so readers can quickly locate specific figures, images, tables, equations, and charts. Figure 4.6 shows an example of a table of figures. Create a table of figures by marking text or images with captions and then using the caption names to create the table. The Captions group on the References tab includes the Insert Caption button for creating captions and the Insert Table of Figures button for inserting a table of figures in a document.

Creating and Customizing Captions

Quick Steps

Create Caption

1. Select text or image.
2. Click References tab.
3. Click Insert Caption button.
4. Type caption name.
5. Click OK.

Creating a Caption

A caption is text that describes an item such as a figure, image, table, equation, or chart. The caption generally displays below the item. Create a caption by selecting the figure text or image, clicking the References tab, and then clicking the Insert Caption button in the Captions group. This displays the Caption dialog box, shown in Figure 4.7. At the dialog box, *Figure 1* displays in the *Caption* text box and the insertion point is positioned after *Figure 1*. Type a name for the figure and then press the Enter key. Word inserts *Figure 1* followed by the typed caption below the selected text or image.

If the insertion point is positioned in a table when the Caption dialog box is displayed, *Table 1* displays in the *Caption* text box instead of *Figure 1*.

Figure 4.6 Example of Table of Figures

TABLE OF FIGURES

Figure 4.7 Caption Dialog Box

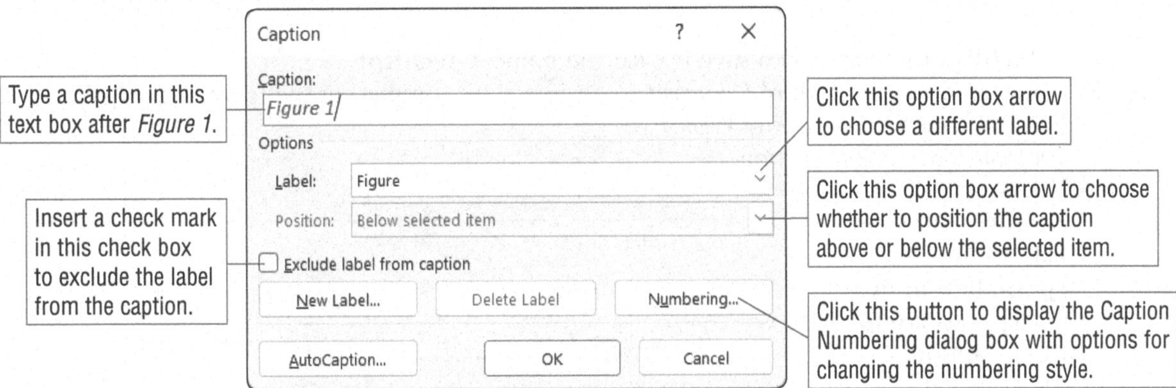

Inserting and Updating a Table of Figures

Quick Steps

Insert Table of Figures

1. Click References tab.
2. Click Insert Table of Figures button.
3. Select format.
4. Click OK.

Inserting a Table of Figures

After marking figures, images, tables, equations, and charts with captions in a document, insert the table of figures. A table of figures generally displays at the beginning of the document after the table of contents and on a separate page. To insert the table of figures, click the Insert Table of Figures button in the Captions group on the References tab. At the Table of Figures dialog box, shown in Figure 4.8, make any necessary changes and then click OK.

The options at the Table of Figures dialog box are similar to the options at the Table of Contents dialog box. They include choosing a format for the table of figures from the *Formats* option box, changing the alignment of the page numbers, and adding leaders before page numbers.

Figure 4.8 Table of Figures Dialog Box

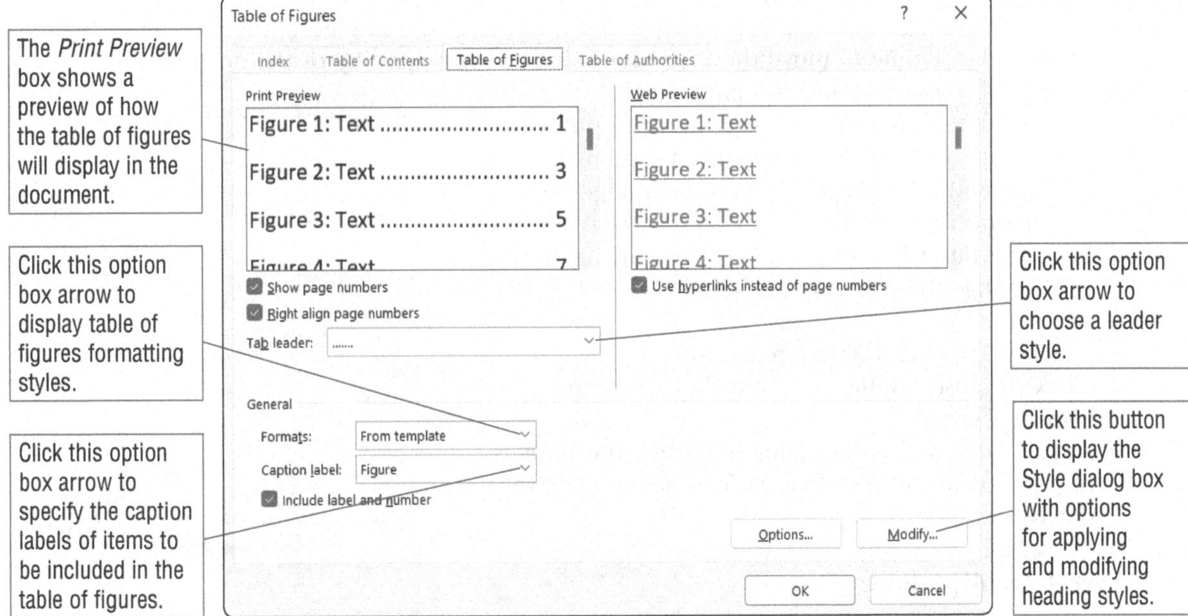

Activity 3a Creating a Table of Figures

Part 1 of 3

1. Open **TechRpt.docx** and then save it with the name **4-TechRpt**.
2. Add the caption *Figure 1 Word Document* to an image by completing the following steps:
   a. Click the screen image in the *WORD PROCESSING SOFTWARE* section.
   b. Click the References tab.
   c. Click the Insert Caption button in the Captions group.
   d. At the Caption dialog box with the insertion point positioned after *Figure 1* in the *Caption* text box, press the spacebar and then type Word Document.
   e. Click OK or press the Enter key.
   f. Press Ctrl + E to center the caption in the text box.

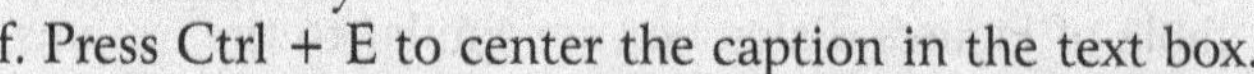

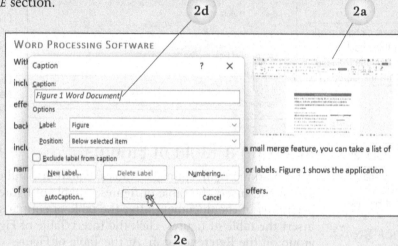

3. Complete steps similar to those in Step 2 to create and center the caption *Figure 2 Excel Worksheet* for the image in the *SPREADSHEET SOFTWARE* section.
4. Complete steps similar to those in Step 2 to create and center the caption *Figure 3 Monitor* for the image in the *MONITOR* section.
5. Complete steps similar to those in Step 2 to create and center the caption *Figure 4 Software Life Cycle* for the SmartArt graphic in the *Developing Software* section.
6. Insert a table of figures at the beginning of the document by completing the following steps:
   a. Press Ctrl + Home to move the insertion point to the beginning of the document.
   b. Press Ctrl + Enter to insert a page break.
   c. Press Ctrl + Home to move the insertion point back to the beginning of the document and then turn on bold formatting, change the paragraph alignment to center, and type the title TABLE OF FIGURES.
   d. Press the Enter key, turn off bold formatting, and then change the paragraph alignment back to left alignment.
   e. If necessary, click the References tab.
   f. Click the Insert Table of Figures button in the Captions group.
   g. At the Table of Figures dialog box, click the *Formats* option box arrow and then click *Formal* at the drop-down list.
   h. Click OK.
7. Save **4-TechRpt.docx**.

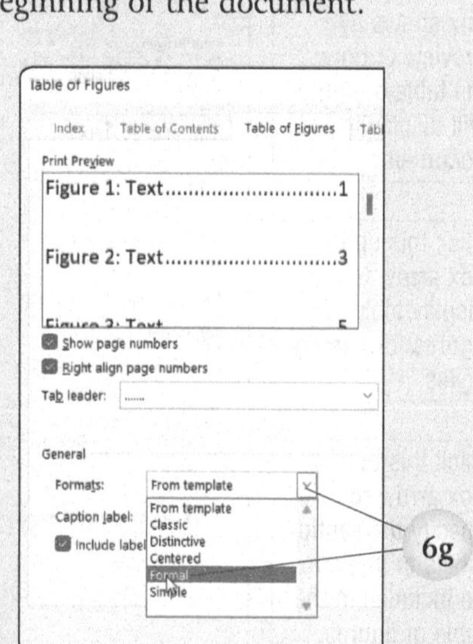

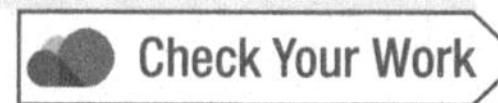

Updating or Deleting a Table of Figures

Quick Steps

Update Table of Figures
1. Click in table of figures.
2. Click References tab.
3. Click Update Table button or press F9.
4. Click OK.

Delete Table of Figures
1. Select entire table.
2. Press Delete key.

If changes are made to a document after a table of figures is inserted, update the table. To do this, click in the table of figures and then click the Update Table button in the Captions group on the References tab or press the F9 function key. At the Update Table of Figures dialog box, click *Update page numbers only* if changes were made only to the page numbers or click *Update entire table* if changes were made to the caption text. Click OK or press the Enter key to close the dialog box. To delete a table of figures, select the entire table using the mouse or keyboard and then press the Delete key.

Activity 3b Updating a Table of Figures

Part 2 of 3

1. With **4-TechRpt.docx** open, insert an image of a laser printer by completing the following steps:
   a. Move the insertion point to the beginning of the second paragraph of text in the *PRINTERS* section.
   b. Click the Insert tab, click the Pictures button in the Illustrations group, and then click *This Device* at the drop-down list.
   c. At the Insert Picture dialog box, navigate to your WL2C4 folder and then double-click the image file ***LaserPrinter.png***.
   d. Change the height of the image to 1.5".
   e. Change to square text wrapping.
2. Add the caption *Figure 4 Laser Printer* to the printer image and then center the caption.
3. Click in the table of figures.
4. Press the F9 function key.
5. At the Update Table of Figures dialog box, click the *Update entire table* option and then click OK.
6. Save, preview, and then close **4-TechRpt.docx**.

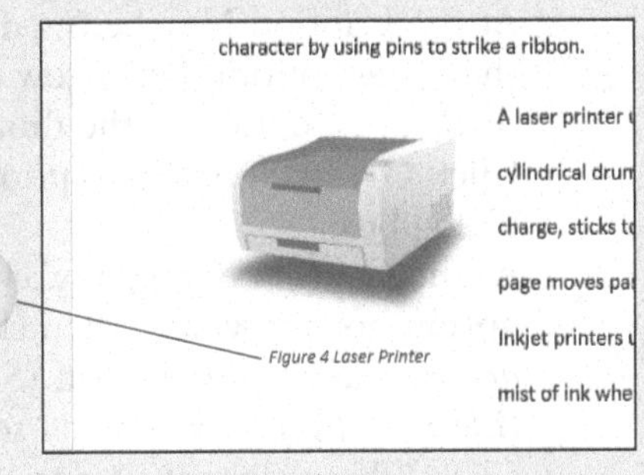

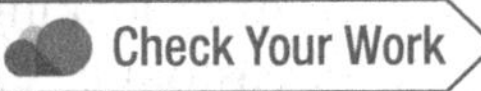

Check Your Work

Customizing a Caption

The Caption dialog box contains a number of options for customizing captions. These are shown in Figure 4.7 (on page 127). Click the *Label* option box arrow to specify the caption label. The default is *Figure*; it can be changed to *Equation* or *Table*. The caption is positioned below the selected item by default. Use the *Position* option to change the default position of the caption so it is above the selected item. A caption contains a label, such as *Figure*, *Table*, or *Equation*. To insert only a caption number and not a caption label, insert a check mark in the *Exclude label from caption* check box.

Click the New Label button and the Label dialog box displays. At this dialog box, type a custom label for the caption. Word automatically inserts an arabic number (*1*, *2*, *3*, and so on) after each caption label. To change the caption numbering style, click the Numbering button. At the Caption Numbering dialog box, click the *Format* option box arrow and then click a numbering style at the drop-down list. For example, caption numbering can be changed to uppercase or lowercase letters or to roman numerals.

If items such as tables are inserted in a document on a regular basis, captions can be inserted automatically with these items. To do this, click the AutoCaption button. At the AutoCaption dialog box, insert a check mark before the item (such as *Microsoft Word Table*) in the *Add caption when inserting* list box and then click OK. Each time a table is inserted in a document, Word inserts a caption above it.

Activity 3c Creating and Customizing Captions and Inserting a Table of Figures — Part 3 of 3

1. Open **BEA-ZA-Advs.docx** and then save it with the name **4-BEA-ZA-Advs**.
2. Insert a custom caption for the first table by completing the following steps:
   a. Click in any cell in the table.
   b. Click the References tab.
   c. Click the Insert Caption button in the Captions group.
   d. At the Caption dialog box, press the spacebar and then type Antarctic Zenith Adventures in the *Caption* text box.
   e. Remove the label (*Figure*) from the caption by clicking the *Exclude label from caption* check box to insert a check mark.
   f. Click the Numbering button.
   g. At the Caption Numbering dialog box, click the *Format* option box arrow and then click the *A, B, C, …* option at the drop-down list.
   h. Click OK to close the Caption Numbering dialog box.
   i. At the Caption dialog box, click the *Position* option box arrow and then click *Below selected item* at the drop-down list. (Skip this step if *Below selected item* is already selected.)
   j. Click OK to close the Caption dialog box.

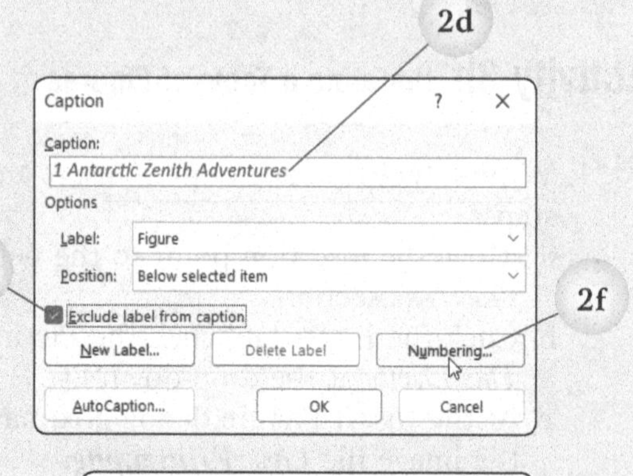

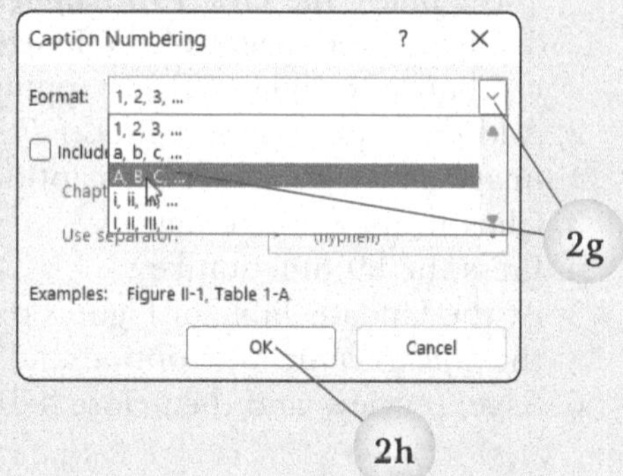

3. After looking at the caption, you decide to add a custom label and change the numbering. Do this by completing the following steps:
   a. Select the caption *A Antarctic Zenith Adventures*.
   b. Click the Insert Caption button.
   c. At the Caption dialog box, click the *Exclude label from caption* check box to remove the check mark.
   d. Click the New Label button.
   e. At the New Label dialog box, type Adventure and then click OK.
   f. Click OK to close the Caption dialog box.

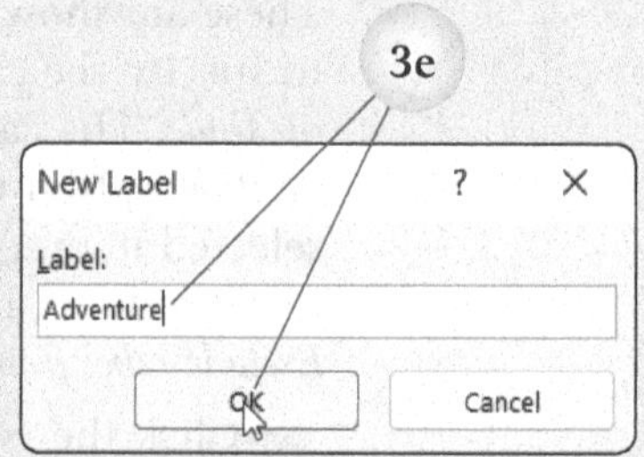

4. Format the caption by completing the following steps:
   a. Select the caption *Adventure 1 Antarctic Zenith Adventures*.
   b. Click the Home tab.
   c. Click the Font Color button arrow.
   d. Click the *Dark Blue* option (ninth color in the *Standard Colors* section).
   e. Click the Bold button.

5. Insert a custom caption for the second table by completing the following steps:
    a. Click in the second table.
    b. Click the References tab and then click the Insert Caption button.
    c. At the Caption dialog box, press the spacebar and then type Bicycle Adventures.
    d. Make sure *Below selected item* appears in the *Position* option box and then click OK to close the Caption dialog box.
6. Select the caption *Adventure 2 Bicycle Adventures*, apply the Dark Blue font color, and then apply bold formatting.
7. Insert a table of figures by completing the following steps:
    a. Press Ctrl + Home and then press Ctrl + Enter to insert a page break.
    b. Press Ctrl + Home to move the insertion point above the page break.
    c. Turn on bold formatting, type TABLES, turn off bold formatting, and then press the Enter key.
    d. Click the References tab and then click the Insert Table of Figures button in the Captions group.
    e. At the Table of Figures dialog box, click OK.
8. Save, preview, and then close **4-BEA-ZA-Advs.docx**.

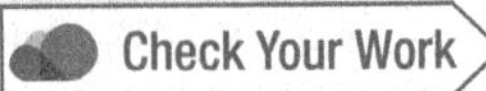

Activity 4 Navigate in a Computer Security and Viruses Report **6 Parts**

You will open a report on computer security and computer viruses, navigate using the Navigation pane, and then insert and navigate using bookmarks, hyperlinks, and cross-references.

Navigating in a Document

Word provides a number of features for navigating in a document. Navigate in a document using the Navigation pane or using bookmarks, hyperlinks, or cross-references.

Navigating Using the Navigation Pane

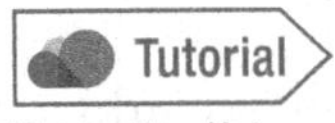

Navigating Using the Navigation Pane

Quick Steps

Display Navigation Pane

1. Click View tab.
2. Click *Navigation Pane* check box.

The Navigation pane can be used to navigate in a document by clicking the View tab and then clicking the *Navigation Pane* check box in the Show group to insert a check mark. The Navigation pane displays at the left side of the screen and includes a search text box and three tabs.

Click the first tab, Headings, and titles and headings with certain styles applied display in the Navigation pane. Click a title or heading and the insertion point moves to it. Click the Pages tab and a thumbnail of each page displays in the pane. Click a thumbnail to move the insertion point to that specific page. Click the Results tab to browse the current search results in the document.

Close the Navigation pane by clicking the *Navigation Pane* check box in the Show group on the View tab to remove the check mark. Another option is to click the Close button in the upper right corner of the pane.

Activity 4a Navigating Using the Navigation Pane

Part 1 of 6

1. Open **Security.docx** and then save it with the name **4-Security**.
2. Since this document has heading styles applied, you can easily navigate in it with the Navigation pane by completing the following steps:
   a. Click the View tab.
   b. Click the *Navigation Pane* check box in the Show group to insert a check mark. (This displays the Navigation pane at the left side of the screen.)
   c. With the Headings tab active, click the heading *CHAPTER 2: INFORMATION THEFT* in the Navigation pane.
   d. Click *CHAPTER 3: COMPUTER VIRUSES* in the Navigation pane.
   e. Click *Systems Failure* in the Navigation pane.

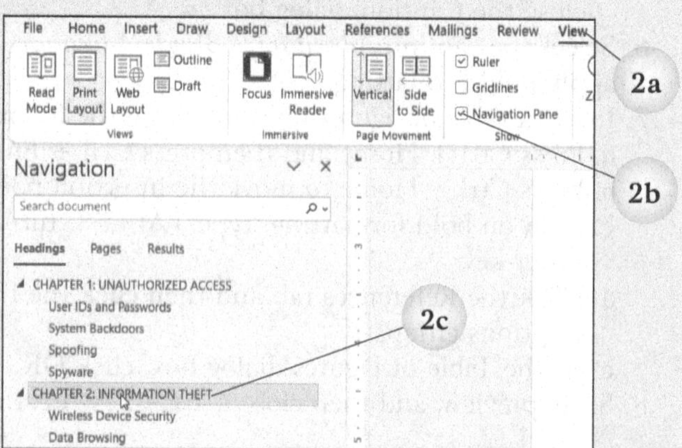

3. Navigate in the document using thumbnails by completing the following steps:
   a. Click the Pages tab in the Navigation pane. (This displays thumbnails of the pages in the pane.)
   b. Click the page 1 thumbnail in the Navigation pane. (You may need to scroll up the Navigation pane to display this thumbnail.)
   c. Click the page 3 thumbnail in the Navigation pane.
4. Close the Navigation pane by clicking the Close button in the upper right corner.
5. Save **4-Security.docx**.

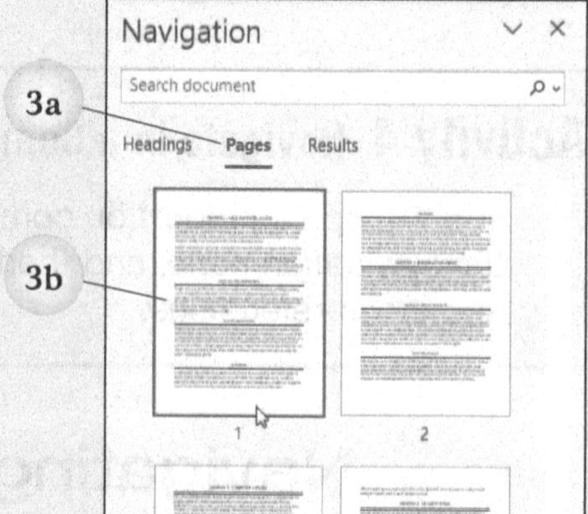

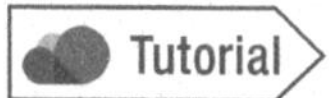

Inserting and Navigating with Bookmarks

Quick Steps

Insert Bookmark
1. Position insertion point at specific location.
2. Click Insert tab.
3. Click Bookmark button.
4. Type name for bookmark.
5. Click Add button.

Inserting and Navigating with Bookmarks

When working in a long document, marking a place in it with a bookmark may be useful for moving the insertion point to that specific location. Create bookmarks for locations in a document at the Bookmark dialog box.

To create a bookmark, position the insertion point at the specific location, click the Insert tab, and then click the Bookmark button in the Links group. This displays the Bookmark dialog box, as shown in Figure 4.9. Type a name for the bookmark in the *Bookmark name* text box and then click the Add button. Repeat these steps as many times as needed to insert additional bookmarks.

Give each bookmark a unique name. A bookmark name must begin with a letter and can contain numbers but not spaces. To separate words in a bookmark name, use the underscore character.

By default, the bookmarks inserted in a document are not visible. Turn on the display of bookmarks at the Word Options dialog box with *Advanced* selected. Display this dialog box by clicking the File tab and then clicking *Options*. At the Word Options dialog box, click *Advanced* in the left panel. Click the *Show bookmarks*

Figure 4.9 Bookmark Dialog Box

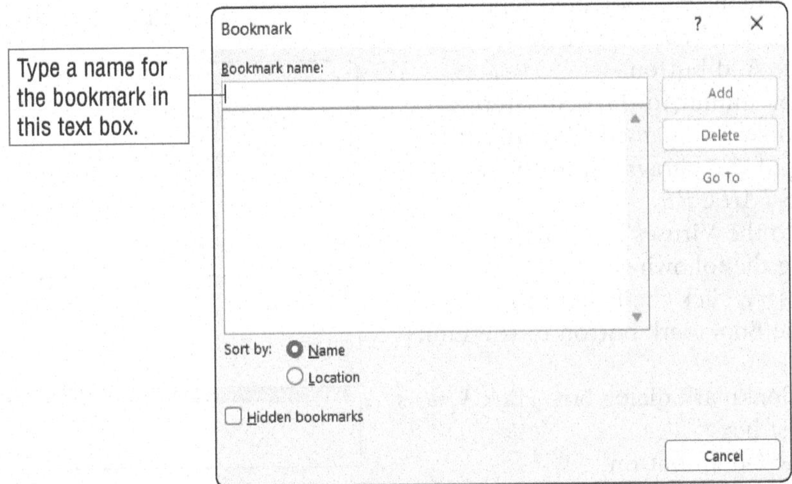

check box in the *Show document content* section to insert a check mark. Complete similar steps to turn off the display of bookmarks. A bookmark displays in the document as an I-beam marker.

Hint Bookmark brackets do not print.

A bookmark can be created for selected text. To do this, first select the text and then complete the steps to create a bookmark. A bookmark created with selected text displays a left bracket ([) indicating the beginning of the selected text and a right bracket (]) indicating the end of the selected text.

Quick Steps

Navigate with Bookmarks

1. Click Insert tab.
2. Click Bookmark button.
3. Double-click bookmark name.

Navigate in a document by moving the insertion point to a specific bookmark. To do this, display the Bookmark dialog box and then double-click the bookmark name or click the bookmark name and then click the Go To button. When Word stops at the location of the bookmark, click the Close button to close the dialog box. When moving to a bookmark created with selected text, Word moves the insertion point to the bookmark and then selects the text. Delete a bookmark in the Bookmark dialog box by clicking the bookmark name in the list box and then clicking the Delete button.

Activity 4b Inserting and Navigating with Bookmarks

Part 2 of 6

1. With **4-Security.docx** open, turn on the display of bookmarks by completing the following steps:
   a. Click the File tab and then click *Options*.
   b. At the Word Options dialog box, click *Advanced* in the left panel.
   c. Scroll down the dialog box and then click the *Show bookmarks* check box in the *Show document content* section to insert a check mark.
   d. Click OK to close the dialog box.
2. Insert a bookmark by completing the following steps:
   a. Move the insertion point to the beginning of the paragraph in the section *TYPES OF VIRUSES* (the paragraph that begins *Security experts categorize*).
   b. Click the Insert tab.
   c. Click the Bookmark button in the Links group.

d. At the Bookmark dialog box, type Viruses in the *Bookmark name* text box.
e. Click the Add button.
3. Using steps similar to those in Step 2, insert a bookmark named *Electrical* at the beginning of the paragraph in the section *SYSTEMS FAILURE*.
4. Navigate to the Viruses bookmark by completing the following steps:
a. If necessary, click the Insert tab.
b. Click the Bookmark button in the Links group.
c. At the Bookmark dialog box, click *Viruses* in the list box.
d. Click the Go To button.
5. With the Bookmark dialog box open, delete the Electrical bookmark by clicking *Electrical* in the list box and then clicking the Delete button.
6. Click the Close button to close the Bookmark dialog box.
7. Save **4-Security.docx**.

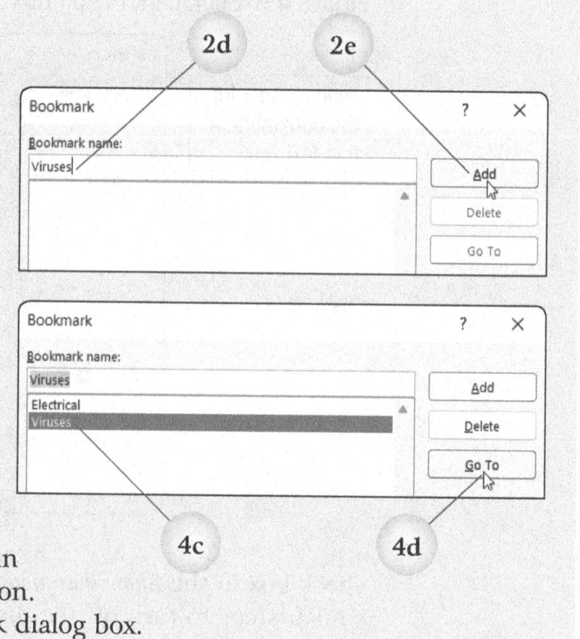

Inserting and Editing a Hyperlink

Inserting Hyperlinks

Hyperlinks can serve a number of purposes in a document. A hyperlink can be used to navigate to a specific location in a document, to display a different document, to open a file in a different program, to create a new document, and to link to an email address.

Insert a hyperlink by clicking the Link button in the Links group on the Insert tab. This displays the Insert Hyperlink dialog box, as shown in Figure 4.10. This dialog box can also be displayed by pressing Ctrl + K. At the Insert Hyperlink dialog box, identify what to link to and where to find the link. Click the ScreenTip button to customize the ScreenTip for the hyperlink.

Quick Steps

Insert Hyperlink
1. Click Insert tab.
2. Click Link button.
3. Make changes at Insert Hyperlink dialog box.
4. Click OK.

Figure 4.10 Insert Hyperlink Dialog Box

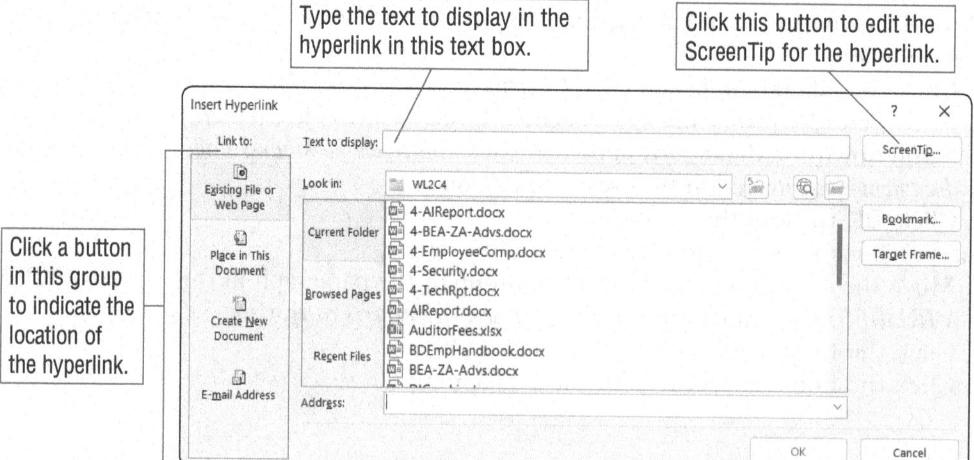

Linking to a Place in the Document To create a hyperlink to another location in the document, first mark the location by applying a heading style to the text or inserting a bookmark. To hyperlink to that heading or bookmark, display the Insert Hyperlink dialog box and then click the Place in This Document button in the *Link to* section. This displays text with heading styles applied and bookmarks in the *Select a place in this document* list box. Click the heading style or bookmark name and the heading or bookmark name displays in the *Text to display* text box. Leave the text as displayed or select the text and then type the text that will appear in the document.

Navigating Using Hyperlinks Navigate to a hyperlink by hovering the pointer over the hyperlink text, pressing and holding down the Ctrl key, clicking the left mouse button, and then releasing the Ctrl key. When hovering the pointer over the hyperlink text, a ScreenTip displays with the name of the heading or bookmark. To display specific information in the ScreenTip, click the ScreenTip button in the Insert Hyperlink dialog box, type the text in the Set Hyperlink ScreenTip dialog box, and then click OK.

Activity 4c Inserting and Navigating with Hyperlinks

Part 3 of 6

1. With **4-Security.docx** open, insert a hyperlink to a bookmark in the document by completing the following steps:
   a. Position the insertion point at the immediate right of the period that ends the first paragraph of text in the section *CHAPTER 4: SECURITY RISKS* (on page 4).
   b. Press the spacebar.
   c. If necessary, click the Insert tab.
   d. Click the Link button in the Links group.
   e. At the Insert Hyperlink dialog box, click the Place in This Document button in the *Link to* section.
   f. Scroll down the *Select a place in this document* list box and then click *Viruses,* which displays below *Bookmarks* in the list box.
   g. Select the text in the *Text to display* text box and then type Click to view types of viruses.
   h. Click the ScreenTip button in the upper right corner of the dialog box.
   i. At the Set Hyperlink ScreenTip dialog box, type View types of viruses and then click OK.
   j. Click OK to close the Insert Hyperlink dialog box.
2. Navigate to the hyperlinked location by hovering the pointer over the Click to view types of viruses hyperlink, pressing and holding down the Ctrl key, clicking the left mouse button, and then releasing the Ctrl key.

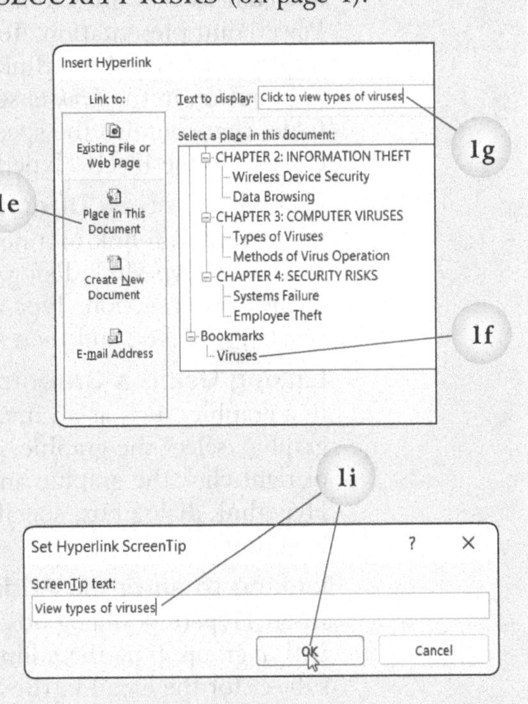

3. Insert a hyperlink to a heading in the document by completing the following steps:
   a. Press Ctrl + Home to move the insertion point to the beginning of the document.
   b. Move the insertion point to the immediate right of the period that ends the second paragraph in the document and then press the spacebar.
   c. Click the Link button on the Insert tab.
   d. At the Insert Hyperlink dialog box with the Place in This Document button active in the *Link to* section, click the *Methods of Virus Operation* heading in the *Select a place in this document* list box.
   e. Click OK to close the Insert Hyperlink dialog box.
4. Navigate to the hyperlinked heading by hovering the pointer over the Methods of Virus Operation hyperlink, pressing and holding down the Ctrl key, clicking the left mouse button, and then releasing the Ctrl key.
5. Save **4-Security.docx**.

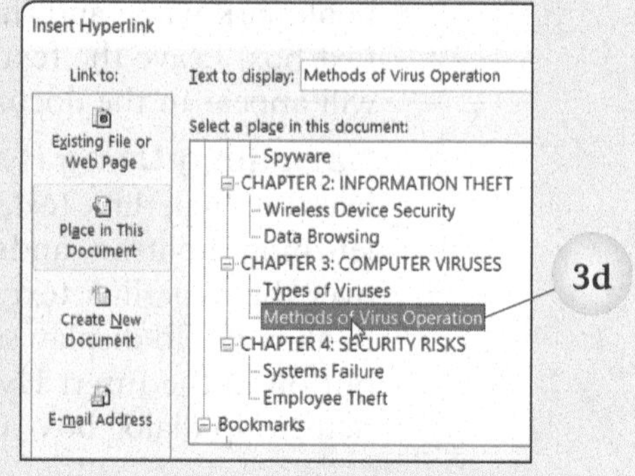

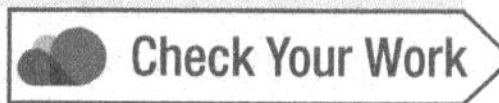

Linking to a File in Another Application A hyperlink can be inserted in a document that links to another Word document, an Excel worksheet, or a PowerPoint presentation. To link a Word document to a file in another application, display the Insert Hyperlink dialog box and then click the Existing File or Web Page button in the *Link to* section. Use the *Look in* option box to navigate to the folder that contains the specific file and then click the file name. Make other changes in the Insert Hyperlink dialog box as needed and then click OK.

Linking to a New Document In addition to linking to an existing document, a hyperlink can link to a new document. To insert this kind of hyperlink, display the Insert Hyperlink dialog box and then click the Create New Document button in the *Link to* section. Type a name for the new document in the *Name of new document* text box and then specify if the document will be edited now or later.

Linking Using a Graphic A hyperlink to a file or website can be inserted in a graphic, such as an image, table, or text box. To create a hyperlink with a graphic, select the graphic, click the Insert tab, and then click the Link button or right-click the graphic and then click *Link* at the shortcut menu. At the Insert Hyperlink dialog box, specify where to link to and what text to display in the hyperlink.

Linking to an Email Address Insert a hyperlink to an email address at the Insert Hyperlink dialog box. To do this, click the E-Mail Address button in the *Link to* group, type the address in the *E-mail address* text box, and then type a subject for the email in the *Subject* text box. Click in the *Text to display* text box and then type the text to display in the document. To use this feature, the email address must be set up in Outlook.

Activity 4d Inserting a Hyperlink to Another Program, to a New Document, and Using a Graphic

Part 4 of 6

1. The **4-Security.docx** document contains information used by Northland Security Systems. The company also has a PowerPoint presentation that contains similar information. Link the document with the presentation by completing the following steps:
   a. Move the insertion point to the immediate right of the period that ends the first paragraph in the section *CHAPTER 3: COMPUTER VIRUSES* and then press the spacebar.
   b. If necessary, click the Insert tab.
   c. Click the Link button in the Links group.
   d. At the Insert Hyperlink dialog box, click the Existing File or Web Page button in the *Link to* section.
   e. Click the *Look in* option box arrow. At the drop-down list that displays, navigate to your WL2C4 folder and then click the folder.
   f. Click the ***NSSPres.pptx*** PowerPoint file in the list box.
   g. Select the text in the *Text to display* text box and then type Computer Virus Presentation.
   h. Click OK to close the Insert Hyperlink dialog box.

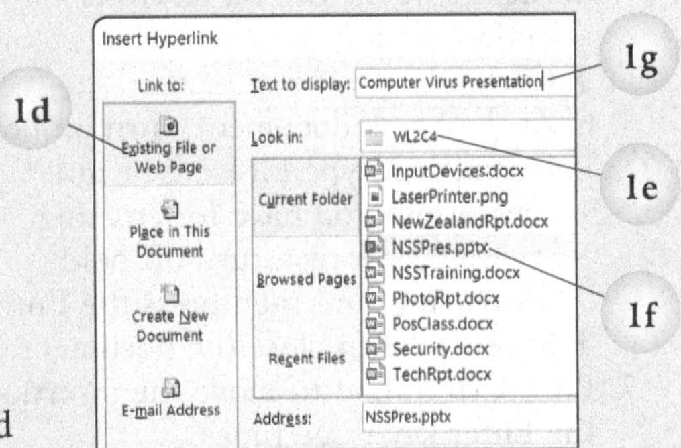

2. View the PowerPoint presentation by completing the following steps:
   a. Position the pointer over the Computer Virus Presentation hyperlink, press and hold down the Ctrl key, click the left mouse button, and then release the Ctrl key.
   b. At the PowerPoint presentation, click the Slide Show button in the view area on the Status bar.
   c. Click the left mouse button to advance each slide.
   d. Click the left mouse button at the black screen that displays the message *End of slide show, click to exit.*
   e. Close the presentation and PowerPoint by clicking the Close button (which contains an *X*) in the upper right corner of the screen.

2b

3. Insert a hyperlink with a graphic by completing the following steps:
   a. Press Ctrl + End to move the insertion point to the end of the document.
   b. Click the compass image to select it.
   c. Click the Link button on the Insert tab.
   d. At the Insert Hyperlink dialog box, make sure the Existing File or Web Page button is active in the *Link to* section.
   e. Navigate to your WL2C4 folder and then double-click ***NSSTraining.docx***. (This selects the document name and closes the dialog box.)
   f. Click outside the compass image to deselect it.
4. Navigate to **NSSTraining.docx** by hovering the pointer over the compass image, pressing and holding down the Ctrl key, clicking the left mouse button, and then releasing the Ctrl key.
5. Close the document by clicking the File tab and then clicking the *Close* option.

6. Insert a hyperlink to a new document by completing the following steps:
   a. Move the insertion point to the immediate right of the period that ends the paragraph in the section *USER IDS AND PASSWORDS* and then press the spacebar.
   b. Click the Link button on the Insert tab.
   c. Click the Create New Document button in the *Link to* section.
   d. In the *Name of new document* text box, type 4-PasswordSuggestions.
   e. Edit the text in the *Text to display* text box so it displays as *Password Suggestions*.
   f. Make sure the *Edit the new document now* option is selected.
   g. Click OK.
   h. At the blank document, turn on bold formatting, type Please type any suggestions you have for creating secure passwords:, turn off bold formatting, and then press the Enter key.
   i. Save and then close the document. 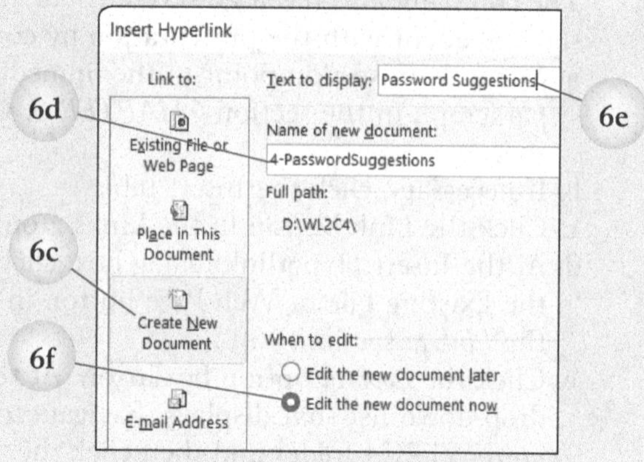
7. Press Ctrl + End to move the insertion point to the end of the document and then press the Enter key three times.
8. Insert a hyperlink to your email address or your instructor's email address by completing the following steps:
   a. Click the Link button.
   b. At the Insert Hyperlink dialog box, click the E-mail Address button in the *Link to* section.
   c. Type your email address or your instructor's email address in the *E-mail address* text box.
   d. Select the current text in the *Text to display* text box and then type Click to send an email.
   e. Click OK to close the dialog box.

   Optional: If you have Outlook set up, press and hold down the Ctrl key, click the Click to send an email hyperlink, release the Ctrl key, and then send a message indicating that you have completed inserting hyperlinks in 4-Security.docx.
9. Save **4-Security.docx**.

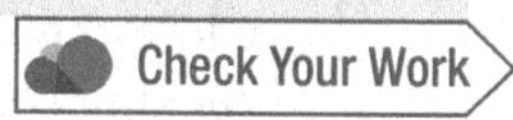

Editing a Hyperlink

The hyperlink or the hyperlink destination can be edited with options at the Edit Hyperlink dialog box. The Edit Hyperlink dialog box contains the same options as the Insert Hyperlink dialog box. Display the Edit Hyperlink dialog box by clicking the hyperlinked text and then clicking the Link button on the Insert tab or by right-clicking the hyperlinked text and then clicking *Edit Hyperlink* at the shortcut menu. Like the hyperlink, the hyperlinked text can be edited. For example, a different font, font size, text color, or text effect can be applied to the hyperlinked text. Remove a hyperlink from a document by right-clicking the hyperlinked text and then clicking *Remove Hyperlink* at the shortcut menu.

Activity 4e Editing and Removing a Hyperlink

Part 5 of 6

1. With **4-Security.docx** open, edit a hyperlink by completing the following steps:
   a. Display the hyperlink at the end of the paragraph below the title *CHAPTER 3: COMPUTER VIRUSES.*
   b. Right-click the Computer Virus Presentation hyperlink and then click *Edit Hyperlink* at the shortcut menu.

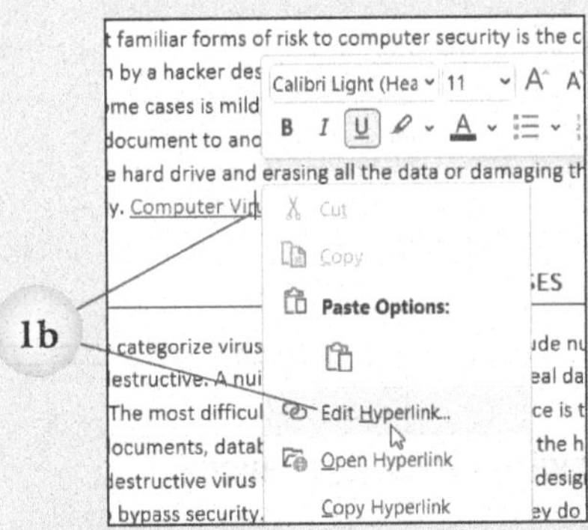

   c. At the Edit Hyperlink dialog box, select the text in the *Text to display* text box and then type Click to view a presentation on computer viruses.
   d. Click the ScreenTip button in the upper right corner of the dialog box.
   e. At the Set Hyperlink ScreenTip dialog box, type View the Computer Viruses PowerPoint presentation and then click OK.
   f. Click OK to close the Edit Hyperlink dialog box.
2. Remove a hyperlink by completing the following steps:
   a. Press Ctrl + Home to move the insertion point to the beginning of the document.
   b. Right-click the Methods of Virus Operation hyperlink at the end of the second paragraph below the title *CHAPTER 1: UNAUTHORIZED ACCESS.*
   c. At the shortcut menu, click the *Remove Hyperlink* option.
   d. Select and then delete the text *Methods of Virus Operation*.
3. Save **4-Security.docx**.

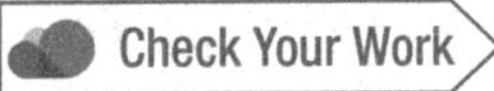

Check Your Work

Tutorial

Creating a Cross-Reference

Quick Steps

Insert Cross-Reference

1. Type text or position insertion point.
2. Click Insert tab.
3. Click Cross-reference button.
4. Identify reference type, location, and text.
5. Click Insert.
6. Click Close.

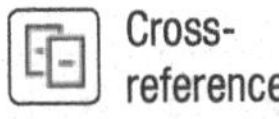

Cross-reference

Creating a Cross-Reference

A cross-reference in a Word document refers readers to another location within the document. Providing cross-references is useful in a long document or a document containing related items or sections of information. References to items such as headings, figures, and tables are helpful to readers. For example, a cross-reference can be inserted that refers readers to a location with more information about the topic, to a specific table, or to a specific page. Cross-references are inserted in a document as hyperlinks.

To insert a cross-reference, type introductory text or position the insertion point at a specific location, click the Insert tab, and then click the Cross-reference button in the Links group. This displays the Cross-reference dialog box, similar to the one shown in Figure 4.11. At the Cross-reference dialog box, identify the type of reference, the location to reference, and the specific text to reference.

The reference identified in the Cross-reference dialog box displays immediately after the introductory text. To move to the specified reference, press and hold down the Ctrl key, position the pointer over the text (the pointer turns into a hand), click the left mouse button, and then release the Ctrl key.

Figure 4.11 Cross-Reference Dialog Box

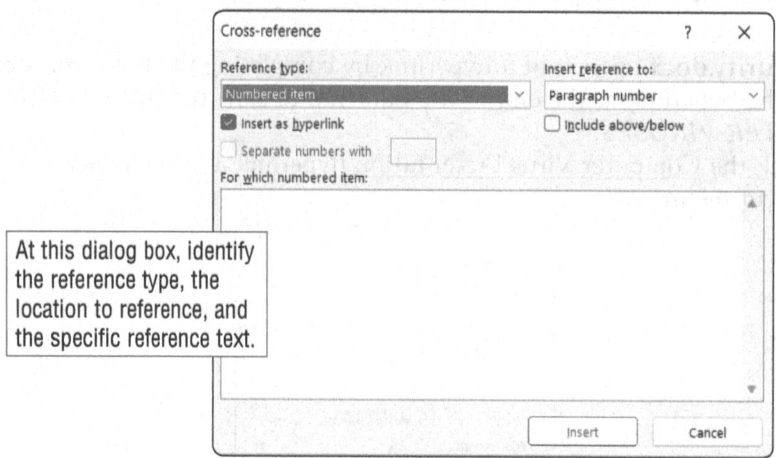

Activity 4f Inserting and Navigating with Cross-References

Part 6 of 6

1. With **4-Security.docx** open, insert a cross-reference in the document by completing the following steps:
   a. Move the insertion point immediately right of the period that ends the paragraph in the section *TYPES OF VIRUSES*.
   b. Press the spacebar and then type (For more information, refer to.
   c. Press the spacebar.
   d. If necessary, click the Insert tab.
   e. Click the Cross-reference button in the Links group.
   f. At the Cross-reference dialog box, click the *Reference type* option box arrow and then click *Heading* at the drop-down list.
   g. Click *Spyware* in the *For which heading* list box.
   h. Click the Insert button.
   i. Click the Close button to close the dialog box.
   j. At the document, type a period followed by a right parenthesis.
2. Move to the referenced text by pressing and holding down the Ctrl key, positioning the pointer over *Spyware* until the pointer turns into a hand, clicking the left mouse button, and then releasing the Ctrl key.
3. Save and then preview **4-Security.docx**.
4. Turn off the display of bookmarks by completing the following steps:
   a. Click the File tab and then click *Options*.
   b. At the Word Options dialog box, click *Advanced* in the left panel.
   c. Click the *Show bookmarks* check box in the *Show document content* section to remove the check mark.
   d. Click OK to close the dialog box.
5. Close **4-Security.docx**.

Chapter Summary

- Create a table of contents using the Table of Contents button in the Table of Contents group on the References tab. Creating a table of contents involves two steps: applying the appropriate styles to mark text that will be included and inserting the table of contents in the document.
- Identify the text to be included in a table of contents by applying a heading style, assigning a level, or marking text as a field entry.
- To insert a table of contents, position the insertion point where the table is to appear, click the References tab, click the Table of Contents button, and then click an option at the drop-down list.
- Generally, the pages containing the table of contents are numbered with lowercase roman numerals. Change the format of the page number at the Page Number Format dialog box.
- To separate the table of contents from the first page of the document, insert a section break that begins a new page.
- The headings in a table of contents are hyperlinks that connect to the headings where they appear in a document and can be used to navigate in a document.
- Customize a table of contents with options at the Table of Contents dialog box. Display this dialog box by clicking the Table of Contents button on the References tab and then clicking *Custom Table of Contents* at the drop-down list.
- If changes are made to a document after the table of contents is inserted, update the table of contents by clicking in the current table of contents and then clicking the Update Table button in the Table of Contents group on the References tab or by pressing the F9 function key.
- Remove a table of contents by clicking the Table of Contents button on the References tab and then clicking *Remove Table of Contents* at the drop-down list.
- To identify titles and/or headings for a table of contents without applying a style, mark each as a field entry at the Mark Table of Contents Entry dialog box. Display this dialog box by pressing Alt + Shift + O.
- When table of contents entries are marked as fields, the *Table entry fields* option needs to be activated when inserting a table of contents. Do this at the Table of Contents Options dialog box.
- Create a table of figures by marking specific text or images with captions and then using the caption names to create the table. Create a caption by selecting the figure text or image and then clicking the Insert Caption button in the Captions group on the References tab. This displays the Caption dialog box, where the figure name is typed.
- Insert a table of figures in a document by clicking the Insert Table of Figures button in the Captions group on the References tab. A table of figures generally appears at the beginning of the document after the table of contents on a separate page.
- Update a table of figures by clicking in the table of figures and then clicking the Update Table button in the Captions group on the References tab or by pressing the F9 function key. At the Update Table of Figures dialog box, specify if just page numbers are updated or the entire table.

- Customize a caption with options at the Captions dialog box. Display this dialog box by clicking the Insert Caption button in the Captions group on the References tab.
- To navigate in a document using the Navigation pane, click the View tab and then click the *Navigation Pane* check box in the Show group. The Navigation pane includes a search text box and three tabs: Headings, Pages, and Results.
- Navigate in a document using bookmarks, which move the insertion point to specific locations. Create bookmarks with options at the Bookmark dialog box.
- Insert hyperlinks in a document with options at the Insert Hyperlink dialog box. Insert a hyperlink to a location in the current document, to display a different document, to open a file in a different program, to create a new document, or to link to an email address. A graphic can also be used to link to a file or website. Edit the hyperlink or the hyperlink destination with options at the Edit Hyperlink dialog box.
- Create a cross-reference to another location within the same document with options at the Cross-reference dialog box.

Commands Review

FEATURE	RIBBON TAB, GROUP	BUTTON, OPTION	KEYBOARD SHORTCUT
Bookmark dialog box	Insert, Links		
Caption dialog box	References, Captions		
Cross-reference dialog box	Insert, Links		
Insert Hyperlink dialog box	Insert, Links		Ctrl + K
Mark Table of Contents Entry dialog box			Alt + Shift + O
Navigation pane	View, Show	*Navigation Pane*	
Remove table of contents	References, Table of Contents	, *Remove Table of Contents*	
Table of Contents dialog box	References, Table of Contents	, *Custom Table of Contents*	
Table of Contents Options dialog box	References, Table of Contents	, *Custom Table of Contents*, Options button	
Table of Figures dialog box	References, Captions		
update table of contents	References, Table of Contents		F9

CHAPTER 4

Review and Assessment

Skills Assessment

Assessment 1

Create and Update a Table of Contents for a Photography Report

1. Open **PhotoRpt.docx** and then save it with the name **4-PhotoRpt**.
2. Move the insertion point to the beginning of the heading *Photography* and then insert a section break that begins a new page.
3. With the insertion point positioned below the section break, insert a page number at the bottom center of each page and change the beginning number to *1*.
4. Press Ctrl + Home to move the insertion point to the beginning of the document (on the blank page) and then create a table of contents with the *Automatic Table 1* option at the Table of Contents button drop-down list.
5. Display the Table of Contents dialog box, change the *Formats* option to *Distinctive*, and make sure a *3* displays in the *Show levels* measurement box.
6. Change the page number format of the table of contents page to lowercase roman numerals.
7. Save and then preview the document.
8. Insert a page break at the beginning of the heading *Camera Basics*.
9. Update the table of contents.
10. Save, preview, and then close **4-PhotoRpt.docx**.

Assessment 2

Insert Captions and a Table of Figures in a Report

1. Open **InputDevices.docx** and then save it with the name **4-InputDevices**.
2. Insert a caption for each of the three images in the document that uses *Figure* as the label, uses an arabic number (1, 2, 3) as the figure number, and displays centered below the image. Use *Keyboard* for the first figure caption, *Mouse* for the second, and *Laptop* for the third.
3. Move the insertion point to the beginning of the title *Computer Input Devices* and then insert a section break that begins a new page.
4. Press Ctrl + Home, type Table of Figures, press the Enter key, and then insert a table of figures with the Formal format applied.
5. Apply the Heading 1 style to the title *Table of Figures*.
6. Move the insertion point to the title *Computer Input Devices*. Insert a page number at the bottom center of each page and change the starting number to *1*.
7. Move the insertion point to the title *Table of Figures* and then change the page numbering style to lowercase roman numerals.
8. Insert a page break at the beginning of the heading *Trackball*.
9. Update the table of figures.
10. Save, preview, and then close **4-InputDevices.docx**.

Assessment 3 Format and Navigate in a Corporate Report

1. Open **DIReport.docx** and then save it with the name **4-DIReport**.
2. Turn on the display of bookmarks.
3. Move the insertion point to the end of the third paragraph (the paragraph that begins *The audit committee selects*) and then insert a bookmark named *Audit*.
4. Move the insertion point to the end of the first paragraph in the section *FEES TO INDEPENDENT AUDITOR*, following the *(Excel worksheet)* text, and then insert a bookmark named *Audit_Fees*.
5. Move the insertion point to the end of the last paragraph and then insert a bookmark named *Compensation*.
6. Navigate in the document using the bookmarks.
7. Move the insertion point to the end of the first paragraph in the section *COMMITTEE RESPONSIBILITIES*, press the spacebar, and then insert a hyperlink to the Audit_Fees bookmark.
8. Select the text *(Excel worksheet)* at the end of the first paragraph in the section *FEES TO INDEPENDENT AUDITOR* and then insert a hyperlink to the Excel file **AuditorFees.xlsx**.
9. Move the insertion point to the end of the document, click the image, and then insert a hyperlink to the Word document **DIGraphic.docx**. At the Insert Hyperlink dialog box, create a ScreenTip with the text *Click to view a long-term incentives graphic*.
10. Press and hold down the Ctrl key, click the *(Excel worksheet)* hyperlink, and then release the Ctrl key.
11. Close the Excel program without saving the file.
12. Press and hold down the Ctrl key, click the image to display the Word document containing the graphic, and then release the Ctrl key. Close the graphic document.
13. Save, preview, and then close **4-DIReport.docx**.

Assessment 4 Customize a Table of Contents

1. Open **DIInformation.docx** and then save it with the name **4-DIInformation**.
2. By default, an automatic table of contents is created using text with the Heading 1, Heading 2, and Heading 3 styles applied. The **4-DIInformation.docx** document contains text with Heading 4 applied. Display the Table of Contents Options dialog box and determine how to specify that the table of contents should include text with the Heading 4 style applied. Replace the existing table of contents.
3. Save, preview, and then close **4-DIInformation.docx**.

Visual Benchmark

Create a Table of Contents and a Table of Figures

1. Open **NewZealandRpt.docx** and then save it with the name **4-NewZealandRpt**.
2. Format the document so it appears as shown in Figure 4.12 with the following specifications:
   a. Insert the captions for the figures as shown (see Page 3 of the figure). (You will need to expand the figure text box for the *Women Voting* figure so the figure text displays on one line.)

b. Insert the table of figures as shown (see Page 2 of the figure) using the *From template* format option with period leaders. Apply the Heading 1 style to the *FIGURES* heading.
c. Insert the table of contents as shown (see Page 1 of the figure) using the *From template* format option with period leaders. Apply the Heading 1 style to the *TABLE OF CONTENTS* heading.
d. Insert page numbers at the right margins as shown (see Pages 2, 3, and 4 of the figure).

3. Save, preview, and then close **4-NewZealandRpt.docx**.

Figure 4.12 Visual Benchmark

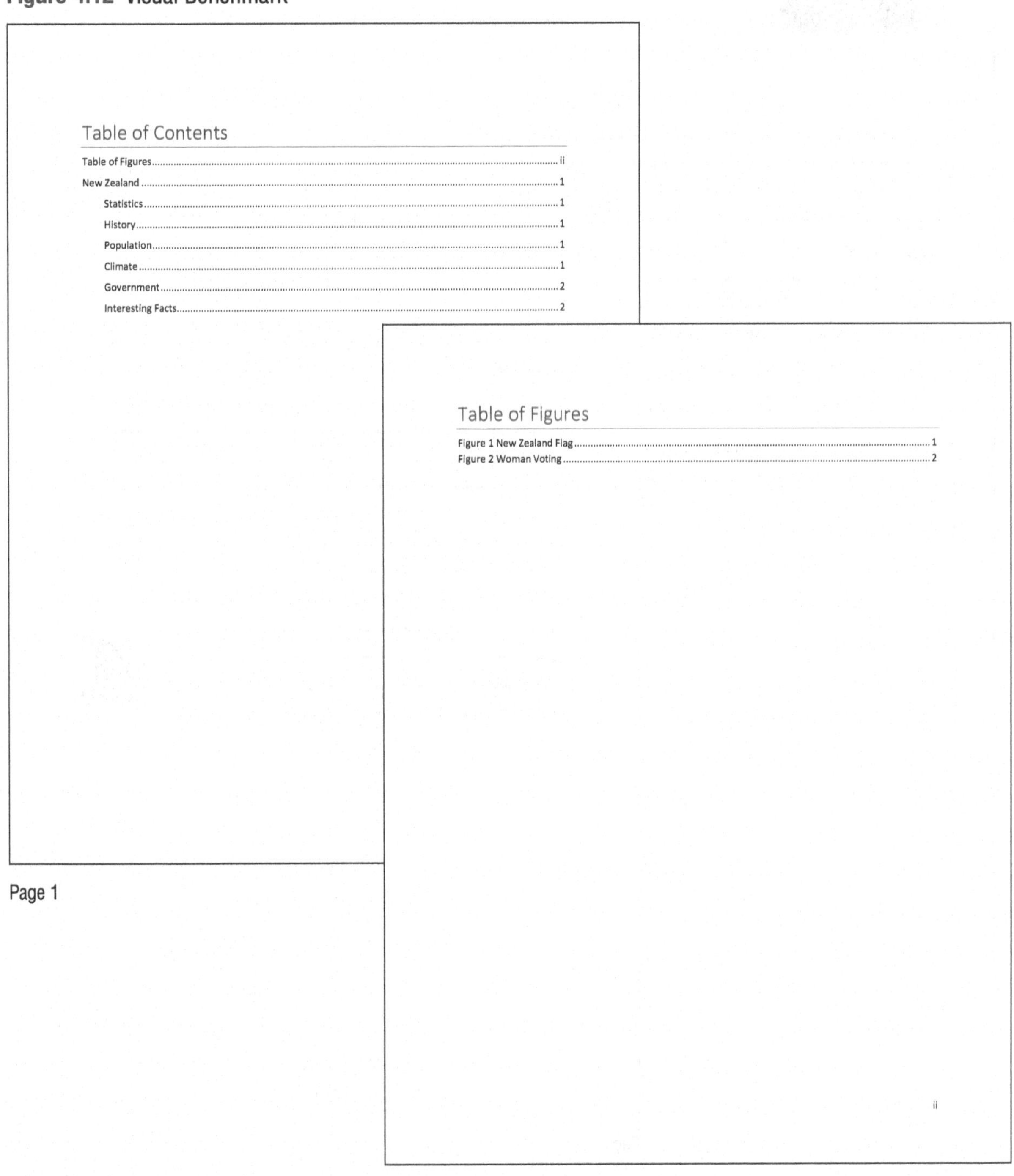

Table of Contents

Table of Figures.......... ii
New Zealand.......... 1
Statistics.......... 1
History.......... 1
Population.......... 1
Climate.......... 1
Government.......... 2
Interesting Facts.......... 2

Page 1

Table of Figures

Figure 1 New Zealand Flag.......... 1
Figure 2 Woman Voting.......... 2

ii

Page 2

Continues

Figure 4.12 Visual Benchmark—*Continued*

New Zealand

Statistics

New Zealand is a country in the southwestern section of the Pacific Ocean. The country consists of two main islands—the North Island and South Island. In addition to these two main islands, New Zealand contains more than 700 smaller islands and covers a total area of 103,500 squares miles. The country is approximately 1,200 miles east of Australia and 600 miles south of the islands of Fiji, Tonga, and New Caledonia. Wellington is the capital of New Zealand and Auckland is the most populous city.

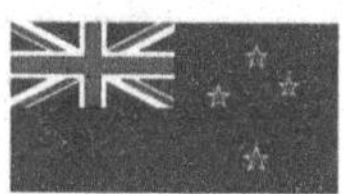

Figure 1 New Zealand Flag

History

Polynesians began settling in the islands between 1280 and 1350 A.D. and developed the Māori culture. In 1642, Abel Tasman, a Dutch explorer, is the first European to visit New Zealand. New Zealand became a colony within the British Empire in 1841 when representatives of the United Kingdom and Māori chiefs signed the Treaty of Waitangi. In 1907, New Zealand became a dominion of the British Empire and then gained full independence in 1947.

Population

Today, approximately five million people live in New Zealand, w

descent. Indigenous Māori are the largest minority population f

official languages in New Zealand are English, Māori, and New Z

Climate

Annual temperatures in New Zealand range from 10 degrees Ce

to 16 degrees Centigrade (61 degrees Fahrenheit) in the north.

83 days out of the year. The rainfall is high with the northern ar

rain in winter than in summer and the southern part having the

generally falls during the months of June through October. Mos

Page 3

Central Plateau in the north and the Southern Alps in the south. The coastal area of the country rarely receives snowfall.

Government

New Zealand has a parliamentary government based on the British model. The House of Representatives (Parliament) is the legislative power and members serve a three-year term. The political party that commands the majority in the House forms the government and, generally, the leader of the governing party becomes the prime minister. The British monarch is the formal head of state, and the monarch appoints a governor-general to represent the monarch. The governor-general has minimal authority but retains some residual powers to protect the constitution.

Interesting Facts

An interesting fact about New Zealand is that in 1893 it was the first country to approve the right for women to vote. Other interesting facts are that over thirty percent of the country is a national reserve, the country has more sheep than people, it has the most southerly capital in the world, and it is the last country in the world inhabited by humans.

Figure 2 Woman Voting

2

Page 4

Case Study

Part 1

You work in the Human Resources Department at Brennan Distributors and are responsible for preparing an employee handbook. Open **BDEmpHandbook.docx** and then save it with the name **4-BDEmpHandbook**. Apply the following specifications to the document:

- Insert a page break before the centered titles *Employee Categories*, *Probationary Periods*, *Employee Performance*, *Position Classification*, and *Compensation*.
- Apply the Heading 1 style to the centered titles and the Heading 2 style to the headings.
- Apply a style set of your choosing.
- Apply a theme that makes the handbook easy to read.
- Insert a table of contents.
- Insert appropriate page numbering. ***Hint: Insert a* Next Page *section break at the beginning of the title* Introduction.**
- Add any other elements that will improve the appearance of the document.

Save **4-BDEmpHandbook.docx**.

Part 2

After looking at the handbook document, you decide to add captions to the tables. With **4-BDEmpHandbook.docx** open, make the following changes to the document:

- Position the insertion point in the first table and then use the caption feature to create the caption *Table 1: Employee Categories* above the table.
- Position the insertion point in the second table and then create the caption *Table 2: Employee Appointments*.
- Insert a table of figures with the title Table of Figures on the page following the table of contents. (Apply the Heading 1 style to the heading *Table of Figures* and then update the table of contents to include a reference to the table of figures.)
- Check the page breaks in the document. If a heading displays at the bottom of a page and the paragraph of text that follows displays at the top of the next page, format the heading so it stays with the paragraph. ***Hint: Do this at the Paragraph dialog box with the Line and Page Breaks tab selected.***
- If necessary, update the table of contents and the table of figures.

Save, preview, and then close **4-BDEmpHandbook.docx**.

Part 3

Send an email to your instructor detailing the steps you followed to create the table captions. Attach **4-BDEmpHandbook.docx** to the email.

WORD LEVEL 2

Unit 1 Performance Assessment

Data Files

The data files for this unit work are in the WL2U1 folder that you downloaded at the beginning of this course.

Assessing Proficiency

In this unit, you have learned to apply advanced character formatting; insert symbols and special characters; find and replace formatting, special characters, styles, and using wildcard characters; manage, inspect, and proof documents; and insert custom headers, footers, and references. You have also learned to create a table of contents and a table of figures and to navigate in a document with the Navigation pane as well as bookmarks, hyperlinks, and cross-references.

Assessment 1 Apply Character Spacing and OpenType Features

1. Open **CVTakeoutMenu.docx** and then save it with the name **U1-CVTakeoutMenu**.
2. Select the title *Take Out Menu*, change the character spacing to Expanded by 1.5 points, turn on kerning, apply Stylistic Set 5, and use contextual alternates.
3. Select the heading *Soups*, change the font size to 22 points, change the character spacing to Expanded, turn on kerning, and apply Stylistic Set 5.
4. Apply the same formatting applied to the heading *Soups* in Step 3 to the other headings (*Salads*, *Main Dishes*, and *Desserts*).
5. Select the last sentence in the document (the sentence that begins *Enjoy the tastes*) and then turn on kerning and apply Stylistic Set 5.
6. Save, preview, and then close **U1-CVTakeoutMenu.docx**.

Assessment 2 Find and Replace Formatting and Use a Wildcard Character

1. Open **Agreement.docx** and then save it with the name **U1-Agreement**.
2. Find text set in the *+Headings* font and replace the font with Corbel.
3. Find text set in the *+Body* font and replace the font with Candara.
4. Using a wildcard character, find all occurrences of *Pin?h?rst?Mad?s?n Builders* and replace them with *Pinehurst-Madison Builders*. (Make sure you remove the formatting option from the *Find what* and *Replace with* text boxes.)

5. Using a wildcard character, find all occurrences of *?erry L?w?ndowsk?* and replace them with *Gerry Lewandowski*.
6. Save, preview, and then close **U1-Agreement.docx**.

Assessment 3 Sort Text

1. Open **SHSSort.docx** and then save it with the name **U1-SHSSort**.
2. Select the five clinic names, addresses, and telephone numbers below the heading *SUMMIT HEALTH SERVICES* and then sort the text alphabetically in ascending order by clinic name.
3. Sort the three columns of text below the heading *EXECUTIVE TEAM* by the extension number in ascending order.
4. Sort the text in the table in the *First Half Expenses* column numerically in descending order.
5. Save, preview, and then close **U1-SHSSort.docx**.

Assessment 4 Insert Document Properties and Inspect a Health Plan Document

1. Open **KLHPlan.docx** and then save it with the name **U1-KLHPlan**.
2. Display the Properties dialog box, type the following in the specified text boxes, and then close the dialog box:

Title	Key Life Health Plan
Subject	Company Health Plan
Author	(Insert your first and last names)
Category	Health Plan
Keywords	health, plan, network
Comments	This document describes highlights of the Key Life Health Plan.

3. Save the document and then print only the document properties.
4. Inspect the document and remove any hidden text.
5. Check the accessibility of the document. Type the alternate text Key Life Logo for the image (a key with *KEY LIFE* on the key) and the alternate text KLHP SmartArt including Compassion, Quality, and Commitment for the SmartArt diagram.
6. Save, preview, and then close **U1-KLHPlan.docx**.

Assessment 5 Proof and Insert Custom Footers for a Document

1. Open **NZ-Australia.docx** and then save it with the name **U1-NZ-Australia**.
2. Display the Word Options dialog box with *Proofing* selected in the left panel, remove the check mark in the *Ignore words in UPPERCASE* check box, insert a check mark in the *Show readability statistics* check box, and then close the dialog box.
3. Using the Editor, complete a spelling and grammar check on the document. (Proper names, except the country names, are spelled correctly.)
4. Create an odd page footer and type New Zealand and Australia at the left margin and insert the page number at the right margin. Create an even page footer and insert the page number at the left margin and type New Zealand and Australia at the right margin.
5. Display the Word Options dialog box with *Proofing* selected in the left panel, insert a check mark in the *Ignore words in UPPERCASE* check box, remove the check mark in the *Show readability statistics* check box, and then close the dialog box.
6. Save, preview, and then close **U1-NZ-Australia.docx**.

Assessment 6 Insert Footnotes in a Leadership Report

1. Open **LeadershipRpt.docx** and then save it with the name **U1-LeadershipRpt**.
2. Insert the first footnote shown in Figure U1.1 at the end of the second paragraph in the section *Basic Leadership Skills*.
3. Insert the second footnote shown in the figure at the end of the fourth paragraph in the section *Basic Leadership Skills*.
4. Insert the third footnote shown in the figure at the end of the second paragraph in the section *Essential Leadership Skills*.
5. Insert the fourth footnote shown in the figure at the end of the last paragraph in the document.
6. Save and then preview **U1-LeadershipRpt.docx**.
7. Select the entire document and then change the font to Constantia.
8. Select all the footnotes and then change the font to Constantia.
9. Delete the third footnote.
10. Save, preview, and then close **U1-LeadershipRpt.docx**.

Figure U1.1 Assessment 6

Laurie Fellers, *Effective Coaching Techniques* (Dallas: Cornwall & Lewis, 2024), 67-72.

Joel Moriarity, "Motivating Employees," *Leaderhip Development* (2024): 3-6.

Jin Loh, *Incentive Management Techniques* (Los Angeles: Monroe-Ackerman, 2024), 89-93.

Andrea Rushton, *Guide to Managing Employees* (Minneapolis: Aurora, 2024), 26-43.

Assessment 7 Create Citations and Prepare a Works Cited Page for a Report

1. Open **DesignWebsite.docx** and then save it with the name **U1-DesignWebsite**.
2. Format the title page to meet Modern Language Association (MLA) style requirements with the following changes:
   a. Make sure that MLA style is selected in the Citations & Bibliography group on the References tab.
   b. With the insertion point positioned at the beginning of the document, type your name, press the Enter key, type your instructor's name, press the Enter key, type the title of your course, press the Enter key, type the current date, and then press the Enter key. Type the title Designing a Website and then center the title.
   c. The text in the document is set in 12-point Cambria. Make this the default font for the document.
   d. Insert a header that displays your last name and the page number at the right margin.

3. Select and then delete the text *(Mercado)* in the second paragraph of text. With the insertion point positioned between the word *users* and the period that ends the sentence, press the spacebar and then insert the source information from a journal article using the following information:

Author	Claudia Mercado
Title	Connecting a Web Page
Journal Name	Connections
Year	2024
Pages	12-21
Volume	4

4. Select and then delete the text *(Holmes)* in the second paragraph of text. With the insertion point positioned between the word *routing* and the period that ends the sentence, press the spacebar and then insert the source information from a website using the following information:

Author	Brent Holmes
Name of Web Page	Hosting Your Web Page
Year	2023
Month	September
Day	20
Year Accessed	(type current year)
Month Accessed	(type current month)
Day Accessed	(type current day)
URL	https://ppi-edu.net/webhosting

5. Select and then delete the text *(Vukovich)* in the last paragraph of text. With the insertion point positioned between the word *hyperlinks"* and the period that ends the sentence, press the spacebar and then insert the source information from a book using the following information:

Author	Ivan Vukovich
Title	Computer Technology in the Business Environment
Year	2024
City	San Francisco
Publisher	Gold Coast

6. Insert thc page number *20* in the citation by Ivan Vukovich using the Edit Citation dialog box.
7. Edit the Ivan Vukovich source by changing the last name to *Vulkovich* in the *Master List* section of the Source Manager dialog box. Click Yes at the message asking about updating the source in both the *Master List* and the *Current List* sections.
8. Create a new source in the document using the Source Manager dialog box and include the following source information for a journal article:

Author	Sonia Jaquez
Title	Organizing a Web Page
Journal Name	Design Techniques
Year	2024
Pages	32-44
Volume	9

9. Type the following sentence at the end of the last paragraph in the document: Browsers look for pages with these names first when a specific file at a website is requested, and index pages display by default if no other page is specified.
10. Insert a citation for Sonia Jaquez at the end of the sentence you just typed.
11. Insert a citation for Claudia Mercado following the second sentence in the first paragraph of the document.

12. Insert a works cited page at the end of the document on a separate page.
13. Format the works cited page as follows to meet MLA requirements:
    a. Select the *Works Cited* title and all the entries and then click the *No Spacing* style.
    b. Change the line spacing to double spacing.
    c. Center the title *Works Cited*.
    d. Format the works cited entries with a hanging indent. ***Hint: Use Ctrl + T to create a hanging indent.***
14. Save and then preview **U1-DesignWebsite.docx**.
15. Change the document and works cited page from MLA style to APA style. Change the title *Works Cited* to *References*. Select the references in the list and then change the line spacing to double spacing with 0 points of spacing after paragraphs.
16. Save, preview, and then close **U1-DesignWebsite.docx**.

Assessment 8

Create Captions and Insert a Table of Figures in a Report

1. Open **SoftwareCareers.docx** and then save it with the name **U1-SoftwareCareers**.
2. Click in the first table and then insert the caption *Table 1 Software Development Careers* above the table. (Change the paragraph spacing after the caption to 3 points.)
3. Click in the second table and then insert the caption *Table 2 Application Development Careers* above the table. (Change the paragraph spacing after the caption to 3 points.)
4. Move the insertion point to the beginning of the heading *SOFTWARE DEVELOPMENT CAREERS* and then insert a next page section break.
5. With the insertion point below the section break, insert a page number at the bottom center of each page and change the starting page number to *1*.
6. Move the insertion point to the beginning of the document and then insert the *Automatic Table 1* table of contents.
7. Press Ctrl + Enter to insert a page break.
8. Type Tables, press the Enter key, and then insert a table of figures using the Formal format.
9. Apply the Heading 1 style to the title *Tables*.
10. Move the insertion point to the beginning of the document and then apply the Heading 1 style to the title CONTENTS.
11. With the insertion point at the beginning of the document, change the number format to lowercase roman numerals.
12. Update the entire table of contents.
13. Save, preview, and then close **U1-SoftwareCareers.docx**.

Writing Activities

Activity 1

Prepare an APA Guidelines Document

You work for a psychiatric medical facility and many of the psychiatrists and psychiatric nurses you work with submit papers to journals that require formatting in APA style. Your supervisor has asked you to prepare a document that describes the APA guidelines and provides the steps for formatting a Word document in APA style. Find a website that provides information on APA style and include the hyperlink in your document. (Consider websites for writing labs at colleges and universities.) Apply formatting to enhance the appearance of the document. Save the document with the name **U1-APA**. Preview and then close **U1-APA.docx**.

Activity 2

Create a Rental Form Template

You work in a real estate management company that manages rental houses. You decide to automate the standard rental form that is normally filled in by hand. Open **LeaseAgreement.docx** and then save the document with the name **U1-LeaseAgreement**. Look at the lease agreement document and determine how to automate it so it can be filled in using the Find and Replace feature in Word. Change the current *Lessor* and *Lessee* names to *LESSOR* and *LESSEE*. Save the document as a template named **LeaseForm.dotx** in your WL2U1 folder. Use File Explorer to open a document based on the **LeaseForm.dotx** template. Find and replace the following text (use your judgment about which occurrences should be changed and which should not):

DAY	22nd
MONTH	February
YEAR	2024
RENT	$1,250
DEPOSIT	$700
LESSOR	Samantha Herrera
LESSEE	Daniel Miller

Save the document with the name **U1-Lease1** and then close **U1-Lease1.docx**. Use File Explorer to open a document based on the **LeaseForm.dotx** template and then create another rental document. You determine the text to replace with the standard text. Save the completed rental document with the name **U1-Lease2**. Preview and then close **U1-Lease2.docx**.

Internet Research

Create a Job Search Report

Use a search engine to locate companies that offer jobs in a field in which you are interested in working. Locate at least three websites that identify employment opportunities and then create a report in Word that includes the following information about each site:

- Name and URL
- A brief description
- Employment opportunities available

Create a hyperlink from your report to each site and include any additional information pertinent to the site. Apply formatting to enhance the document. Save the document with the name **U1-JobSearch**. Preview and then close **U1-JobSearch.docx**.

WORD

LEVEL 2

Unit 2

Editing and Formatting Documents

WORD

CHAPTER 5

Customizing Objects, Using the Draw Feature, and Creating Charts

Performance Objectives

Upon successful completion of Chapter 5, you will be able to:

1 Insert, format, and customize images and text boxes

2 Group and ungroup objects

3 Edit points and wrap points in a shape

4 Link and unlink text boxes

5 Insert, format, and customize icons

6 Insert, format, and customize 3D models

7 Customize a document with options on the Draw tab

8 Insert and format charts

Objects such as images, shapes, text boxes, icons, and 3D models can be inserted in a Word document and then formatted with a variety of options. Use buttons on the object format tab and task pane to customize an object. An object can also be formatted with options at the Layout dialog box. The Draw tab contains options for drawing in a document, creating shapes, editing text, and selecting and highlighting text. In this chapter, you will learn how to customize objects, draw in a document, and how to present text visually in a chart and apply formatting to the chart.

Data Files

The data files for this chapter are in the WL2C5 folder that you downloaded at the beginning of this course.

Activity 1 Customize the Layout of an Adventure Agency Flyer **3 Parts**

You will open an adventure agency flyer describing sites and activities for adventures in Maui and improve the attractiveness of the layout by inserting and customizing images and a text box.

Customizing Objects

Word provides a number of methods for formatting and customizing objects, such as images, photographs, shapes and text boxes. Format images with buttons on the Picture Format tab and further customize images with options at the Format Picture task pane and the Layout dialog box. Use buttons on the Shape Format tab to format and customize shapes and text boxes and further customize shapes and text boxes with options at the Format Shape task pane and the Layout dialog box.

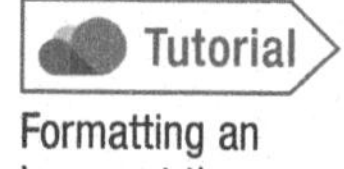

Formatting an Image at the Layout Dialog Box

Customizing Image Layout

Customize the layout of images with options at the Layout dialog box. Display the Layout dialog box by clicking the Size group dialog box launcher on the Picture Format tab. The Layout dialog box contains three tabs. Click the Position tab and the dialog box displays as shown in Figure 5.1.

Use options at the Layout dialog box with the Position tab selected to specify horizontal and vertical layout options. In the *Horizontal* section, choose the *Alignment* option to specify left, center, or right alignment relative to the margin, page, column, or character. Choose the *Book layout* option to align the image with

Figure 5.1 Layout Dialog Box with the Position Tab Selected

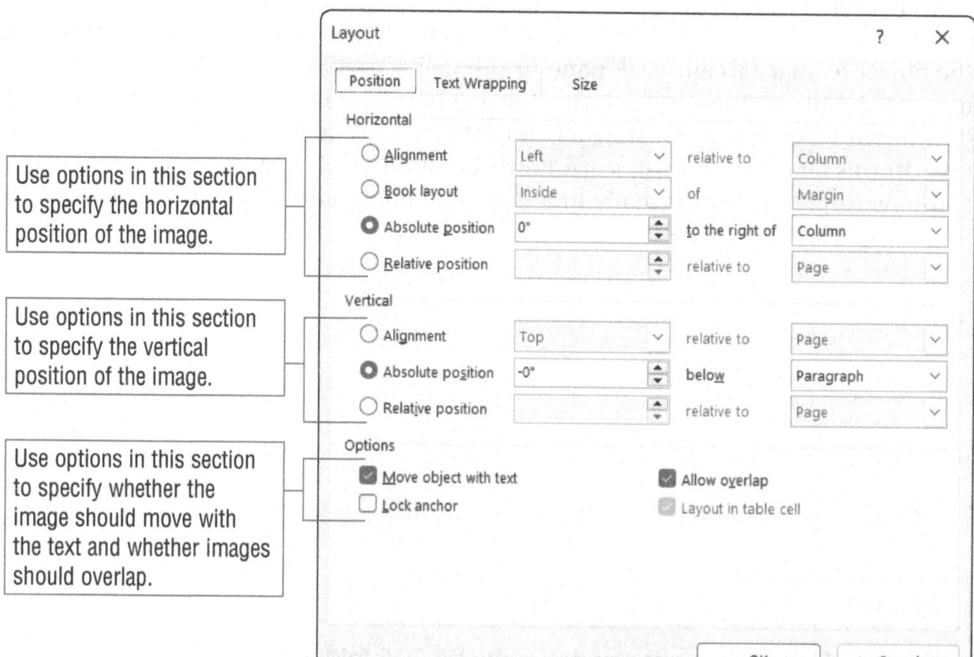

the inside or outside margin of the page. Use the *Absolute position* measurement box to align the image horizontally with the specified amount of space between the left edge of the image and the left edge of the page, column, left margin, or character. The *Relative position* measurement box uses a percentage to position an image relative to a specific location. For example, enter *50%* in the *Relative position* measurement box to align relative to the left margin and the image is positioned half way (50%) between the left edge of the page and the left margin.

In the *Vertical* section of the dialog box, use the *Alignment* option to align the image at the top, bottom, center, inside, or outside relative to the page, margin, or line. Use the *Absolute position* measurement box to align the image vertically with the specified amount of space relative to a specific location and use the *Relative position* measurement box to specify a percentage.

In the *Options* section, attach (anchor) the image to a paragraph so that the image and paragraph move together. Choose the *Move object with text* option to move the image up or down on the page with the paragraph to which it is anchored. Keep the image anchored in the same place on the page by choosing the *Lock anchor* option. Choose the *Allow overlap* option to overlap images with the same wrapping style.

Use options at the Layout dialog box with the Text Wrapping tab selected to specify the wrapping style for the image. Specify which sides of the image the text is to wrap around and the amounts of space between the text and the top, bottom, left, and right edges of the image.

Click the Size tab at the Layout dialog box to display options for specifying the height and width of the image relative to the margin, page, top margin, bottom margin, inside margin, or outside margin. Use the *Rotation* measurement box to rotate the image by degrees and use options in the *Scale* section to change the percentage of the height and width scales. By default, the *Lock aspect ratio* check box contains a check mark, which means that if a change is made to the height measurement of an image, the width measurement automatically changes to maintain the proportional relationship between the height and width. Change the width measurement and the height measurement automatically changes.

To change the height measurement of an image without changing the width or to change the width measurement without changing the height, remove the check mark from the *Lock aspect ratio* check box. To reset the image size, click the Reset button in the lower right corner of the dialog box.

Activity 1a Inserting and Customizing the Layout of an Image

Part 1 of 3

1. Open **BEAMaui.docx** and then save it with the name **5-BEAMaui**.
2. Insert an image by completing the following steps:
   a. Click the Insert tab.
   b. Click the Pictures button in the Illustrations group and then click *This Device* at the drop-down list.
   c. At the Insert Picture dialog box, navigate to your WL2C5 folder and then double-click the ***HawaiiBanner.png*** image file.
3. Select the current measurement in the *Shape Height* measurement box in the Size group on the Picture Format tab, type 2, and then press the Enter key.

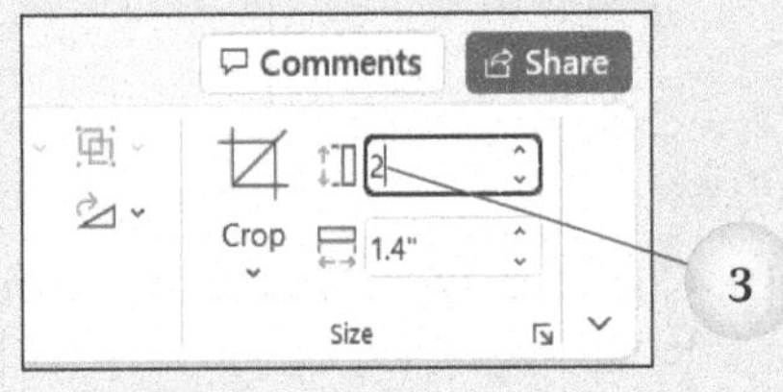

4. Click the *Beveled Matte, White* style in the Picture Styles group (second style from the left).

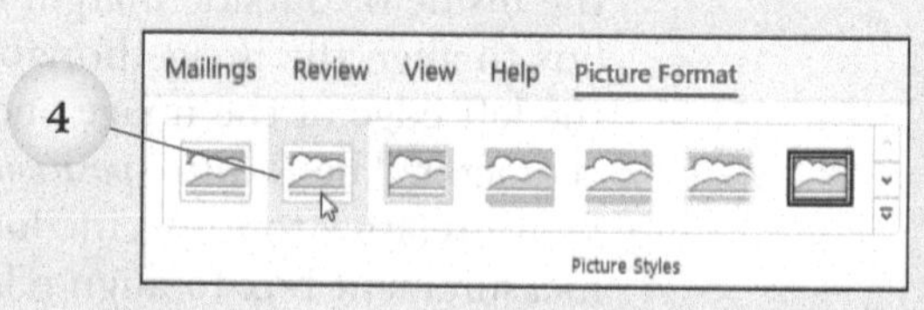

5. Click the Corrections button in the Adjust group and then click the *Brightness: –20% Contrast: +20%* option (second column, fourth row in the *Brightness/Contrast* section).
6. After looking at the image, you decide to reset it. Do this by clicking the Reset Picture button arrow in the Adjust group and then clicking *Reset Picture & Size* at the drop-down list.

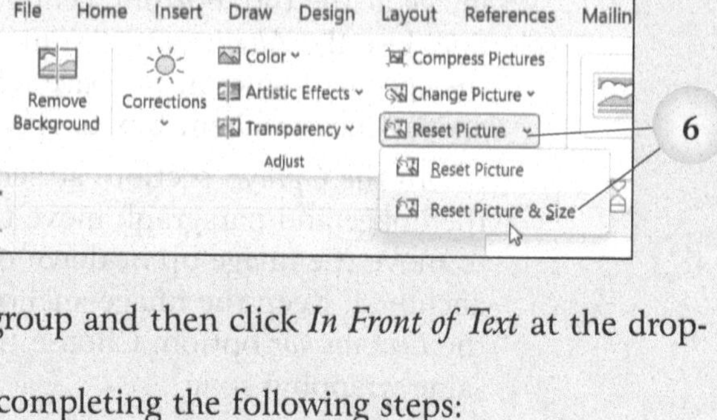

7. Select the current measurement in the *Shape Height* measurement box, type 1.3, and then press the Enter key.

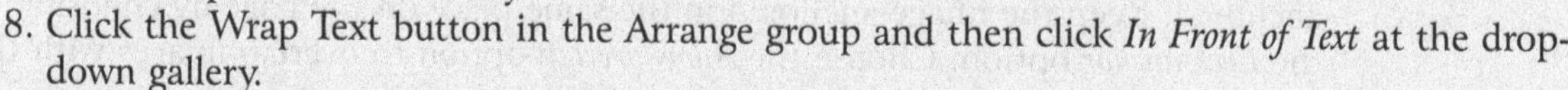

8. Click the Wrap Text button in the Arrange group and then click *In Front of Text* at the drop-down gallery.
9. Position the image precisely on the page by completing the following steps:
   a. With the image selected, click the Size group dialog box launcher.
   b. At the Layout dialog box, click the Position tab.
   c. Make sure the *Absolute position* option in the *Horizontal* section is selected.
   d. Press the Tab key two times and then type 6.2 in the *Absolute position* measurement box.
   e. Click the *to the right of* option box arrow and then click *Page* at the drop-down list.
   f. If necessary, click the *Absolute position* option in the *Vertical* section.
   g. Select the current measurement in the *Absolute position* measurement box and then type 2.
   h. Click the *below* option box arrow and then click *Page* at the drop-down list.
   i. Click OK to close the Layout dialog box.

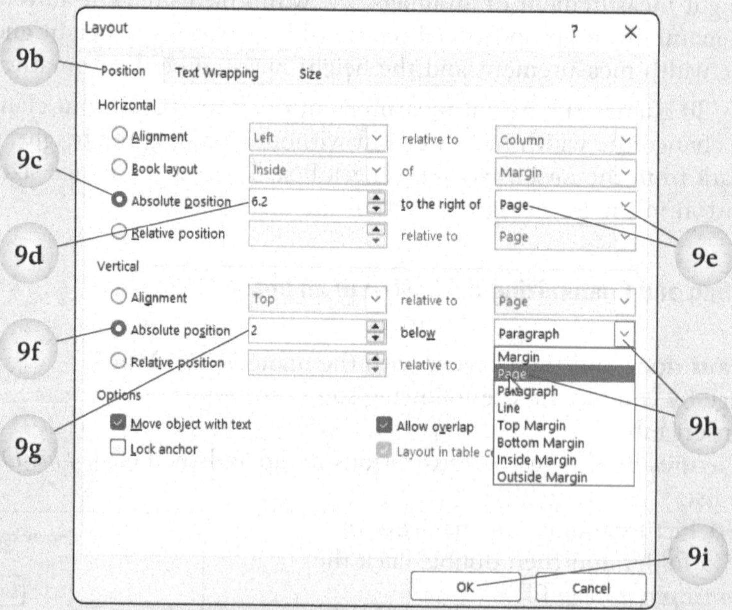

10. Click the *Drop Shadow Rectangle* style in the Picture Styles group (fourth style from the left).

11. Click the Color button in the Adjust group and then click the *Blue, Accent color 5 Dark* option (sixth column, second row in the *Recolor* section).
12. Compress the image by clicking the Compress Pictures button in the Adjust group and then clicking OK at the Compress Pictures dialog box.
13. Click outside the image to deselect it.
14. Save **5-BEAMaui.docx**.

Formatting an Image at the Format Picture Task Pane

Applying Formatting at the Format Picture Task Pane

Options for formatting an image are available at the Format Picture task pane, shown in Figure 5.2. Display this task pane by clicking the Picture Styles group task pane launcher on the Picture Format tab.

The options in the Format Picture task pane vary depending on the icon selected. The formatting options may need to be expanded within the icons. For example, click *Shadow* in the task pane with the Effects icon selected to display options for applying shadow effects to an image. Many of the options available at the Format Picture task pane are also available on the Picture Format tab. The task pane is a central location for formatting options and also includes some additional advanced formatting options.

Applying Artistic Effects to Images

Apply an artistic effect to a selected image with the Artistic Effects button in the Adjust group on the Picture Format tab. Click this button and a drop-down gallery displays with effect options. Hover the pointer over an option in the drop-down gallery to see the effect applied to the selected image. An artistic effect can also be applied to an image with options at the Format Picture task pane with the Effects icon selected.

Figure 5.2 Format Picture Task Pane

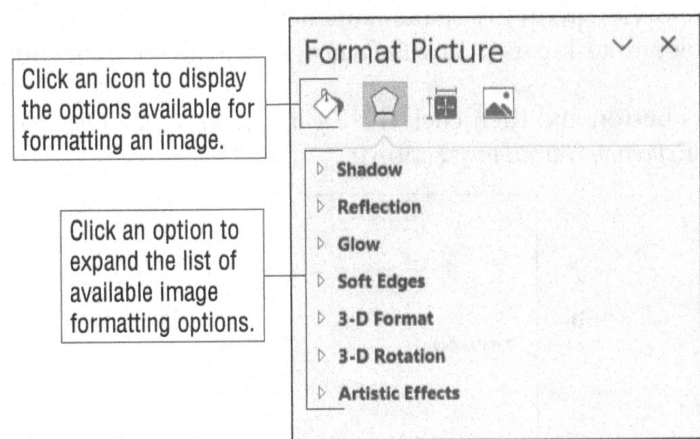

Activity 1b Inserting and Customizing a Photograph

1. With **5-BEAMaui.docx** open, press Ctrl + End to move the insertion point to the end of the document and then insert a photograph by completing the following steps:
   a. Click the Insert tab, click the Pictures button in the Illustrations group, and then click *This Device* at the drop-down list.
   b. At the Insert Picture dialog box, navigate to your WL2C5 folder and then double-click the ***Surfing.png*** image file.
2. With the surfing photograph selected, click the Picture Effects button in the Picture Styles group, point to *Bevel*, and then click the *Round* option (first column, first row in the *Bevel* section).
3. Click the Artistic Effects button in the Adjust group and then click the *Cutout* option (first column, bottom row).

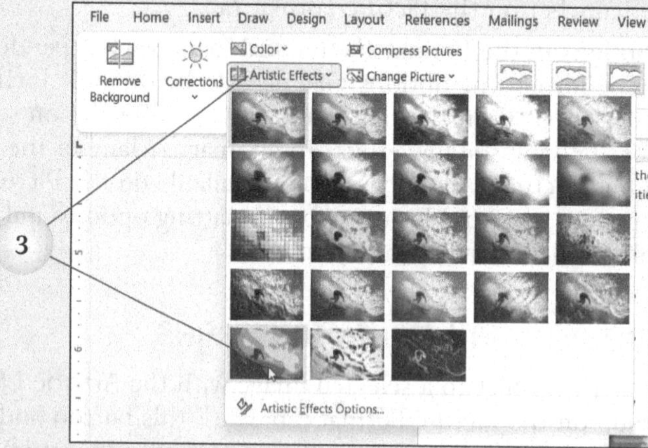

4. After looking at the formatting, you decide to remove it from the image by clicking the Reset Picture button in the Adjust group.
5. Select the current measurement in the *Shape Height* measurement box, type 1.4, and then press the Enter key.
6. Format the photograph by completing the following steps:
   a. Click the Picture Styles group task pane launcher.
   b. At the Format Picture task pane, click *Reflection* to expand the reflection options in the task pane.
   c. Click the Presets button and then click the *Tight Reflection: Touching* option (first column, first row in the *Reflection Variations* section).

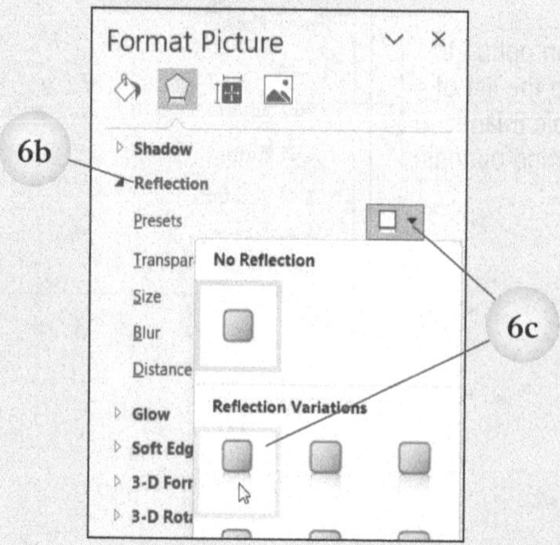

d. Decrease the size percentage of the reflection by selecting the current percentage in the *Size* measurement box and then typing 20%.

e. Click *Artistic Effects* in the task pane to expand the artistic effect options.

f. Click the Artistic Effects button and then click the *Paint Brush* option (third column, second row).

g. Close the task pane by clicking the Close button in the upper right corner.

7. Click the Wrap Text button in the Arrange group on the Picture Format tab and then click *Tight* at the drop-down list.
8. Position the photograph precisely on the page by completing the following steps:
   a. With the photograph selected, click the Position button in the Arrange group and then click *More Layout Options* at the bottom of the drop-down gallery.
   b. At the Layout dialog box with the Position tab selected, select the current measurement in the *Absolute position* measurement box in the *Horizontal* section and then type 5.3.
   c. Click the *to the right of* option box arrow and then click *Page* at the drop-down list.
   d. Click the *Absolute position* option in the *Vertical* section.
   e. Select the current measurement in the *Absolute position* measurement box and then type 6.8.
   f. Click the *below* option box arrow and then click *Page* at the drop-down list.
   g. Click OK to close the Layout dialog box.
9. Click outside the photograph to deselect it.
10. Save **5-BEAMaui.docx**.

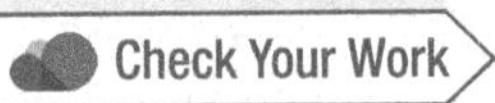

Customizing Colors, Text Boxes, and Shapes

When an object such as a text box or shape is inserted in a document, the Shape Format tab is active. Use options on this tab or the Format Shape task pane to apply custom colors at the Colors dialog box and apply formatting to customize a text box or shape.

Customizing Colors Apply color to text and objects with options at a Colors dialog box. The Colors dialog box contains two tabs—Standard and Custom. With the Standard tab active, colors display in a honeycomb. Choose a color by clicking the specific color in the honeycomb. Click the Custom tab and the dialog box displays a color box along with measurement boxes for specifying the red, green, and blue (RGB) values for a color ranging from 1 to 255. In addition to RGB values, colors can be represented by hue, saturation, and lightness (HSL). Change to HSL values by clicking the *Color model* option box arrow and then clicking *HSL* at the drop-down list. The *Hex* text box is available for entering a hexidecimal (six-digit) code representing a specific color. A hex code compresses the RGB values into one six-digit code that is a representation of color values in binary code. Hex codes are an integral part of HTML and web design for representing color formats digitally. The bar to the right of the color bar is a luminance scale. Drag the slider bar along the scale to make a color lighter or darker. Use the *Transparency* measurement box at the Colors dialog box to specify a percentage of color transparency.

Customizing a Text Box Click the Shape Styles group task pane launcher and the Format Shape task pane displays with three icons: Fill & Line, Effects, and Layout & Properties. Click the WordArt Styles group task pane launcher and the Format Shape task pane displays but with different icons. The task pane displays with *Text Options* selected and with three icons: Text Fill & Outline, Text Effects, and Layout & Properties.

Activity 1c Inserting and Customizing a Text Box

Part 3 of 3

1. With **5-BEAMaui.docx** open, insert a text box by completing the following steps:
   a. Click the Insert tab, click the Text Box button in the Text group, and then click the *Draw Text Box* option at the drop-down list.
   b. Click above the heading *MAUI SITES* and then type Hawaii, the Aloha State.
2. Select the text box by clicking its border. (This changes the text box border from a dashed line to a solid line.)
3. Press Ctrl + E to center the text in the text box.
4. Click the Text Direction button in the Text group on the Shapre Format tab and then click *Rotate all text 270°* at the drop-down list.

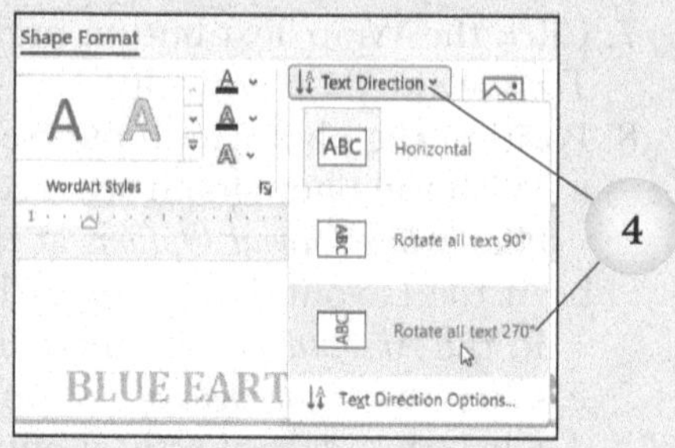

5. Select the current measurement in the *Shape Height* measurement box, type 5.7, and then press the Enter key.
6. Select the current measurement in the *Shape Width* measurement box, type 0.8, and then press the Enter key.
7. Format the text box by completing the following steps:
   a. Click the Shape Styles group task pane launcher.
   b. At the Format Shape task pane with the Fill & Line icon selected, click *Fill* to expand the options.
   c. Click the Fill Color button (displays at the right of the *Color* option) and then click the *More Colors* option.
   d. At the Colors dialog box, click the Custom tab.
   e. Select the number in the *Hex* text box and then type #8AB4F2.
   f. Select the percentage number in the *Transparency* text box, type 50, and then press the Enter key.
   g. Click the Effects icon and then click *Shadow* to expand the options.
   h. Click the Presets button and then click the *Offset: Bottom* option (second column, first row in the *Outer* section).

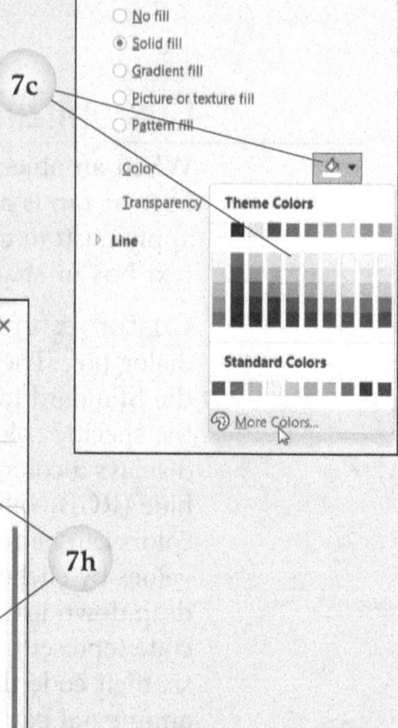

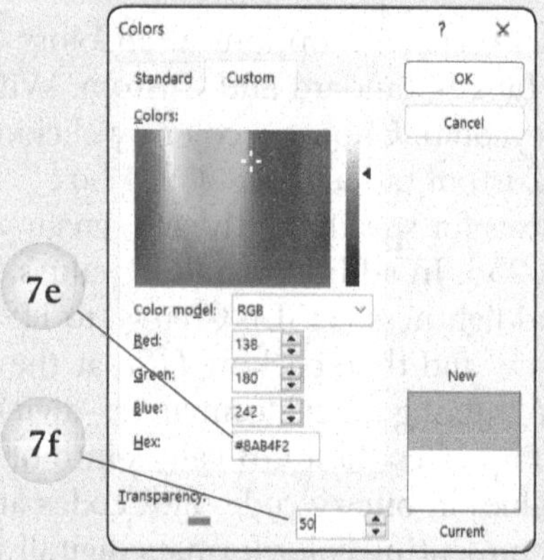

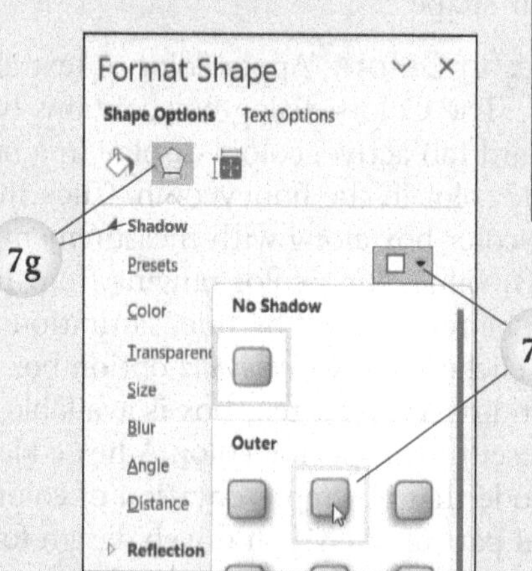

   i. Select the current point size in the *Distance* measurement box, type 5, and then press the Enter key.
   j. Close the Format Shape task pane by clicking the Close button in the upper right corner.

8. Click the More WordArt Styles button in the WordArt Styles group and then click the option in the fourth column, second row (white fill, blue outline).
9. Position the text box precisely on the page by completing the following steps:
   a. With the text box selected, click the Size group dialog box launcher.
   b. At the Layout dialog box, click the Position tab.
   c. Select the current measurement in the *Absolute position* measurement box in the *Horizontal* section and then type 1.
   d. Click the *to the right of* option box arrow and then click *Page* at the drop-down list.
   e. Select the current measurement in the *Absolute position* measurement box in the *Vertical* section and then type 2.7.
   f. Click the *below* option box arrow and then click *Page* at the drop-down list.
   g. Click OK to close the Layout dialog box.
10. Click the Home tab, click the *Font Size* option arrow, and then click *36* at the drop-down gallery.
11. Click outside the text box to deselect it.
12. Save, preview, and then close **5-BEAMaui.docx**.

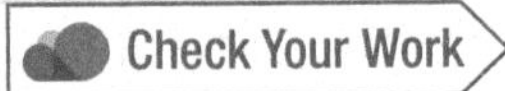

Activity 2 Customize Shapes and Link and Unlink Text Boxes in a Financial Services Flyer — 4 Parts

You will open a promotional flyer for a financial services group and customize the design. To do this, you will format, group, customize, ungroup, and edit points of a shape. You will also edit wrap points around an image and link and unlink text boxes.

Customizing Shapes Like a text box, a shape can be customized with buttons and options on the Shape Format tab or with options at the Format Shape task pane. Customize or format one shape or select multiple shapes and then customize and apply formatting to all the selected shapes. Display the Format Shape task pane for a shape by clicking the Shape Styles group task pane launcher. When a shape is selected, the WordArt Styles group task pane launcher is dimmed and unavailable.

Grouping and Ungrouping Objects

Group Objects
1. Select objects.
2. Click Picture Format tab (or Shape Format tab).
3. Click Group button.
4. Click *Group*.

Grouping and Ungrouping Objects Objects in a document, such as images, text boxes, or shapes, can be grouped so that they can be sized, moved, or formatted as one object. Text wrapping other than *In Line with Text* must be applied to each object to be grouped. To group objects, select the objects, click the Picture Format tab (or Shape Format tab), click the Group button in the Arrange group, and then click *Group* at the drop-down list. With the objects grouped, move, size, or apply formatting to all the objects in the group at once.

To select objects, click the first object, press and hold down the Shift key, click each remaining object to be included in the group, and then release the Shift key. Another method for grouping objects is to click the Select button in the Editing group on the Home tab, click the *Select Objects* option, and then use the mouse to draw a border around all the objects. Turn off selecting objects by clicking the Select button and then clicking the *Select Objects* option.

Hint Group multiple objects to work with them as if they are a single object.

Grouped objects can be sized, moved, and formatted as one object. However, an object within a group of objects can be sized, moved, or formatted individually. To do this, click the specific object and then make the changes to the individual object.

Hint A group can be created within a group.

To ungroup grouped objects, click the group to select it and then click the Picture Format tab (or Shape Format tab). Click the Group button in the Arrange group and then click the *Ungroup* option at the drop-down list.

Activity 2a Customizing and Formatting Shapes

Part 1 of 4

1. Open **Leland.docx** and then save it with the name **5-Leland.**
2. Rotate the middle arrow shape by completing the following steps:
   a. Scroll down the document and then click the middle arrow shape to select it (on the first page).
   b. Click the Shape Format tab.
   c. Click the Rotate button in the Arrange group and then click *Flip Horizontal* at the drop-down list.

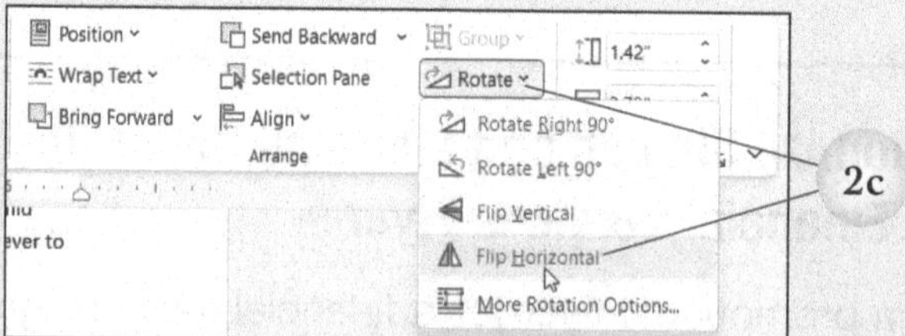

3. Align and format the arrow shapes by completing the following steps:
   a. With the middle arrow shape selected, press and hold down the Shift key.
   b. Click the top arrow shape, click the bottom arrow shape, and then release the Shift key.
   c. With all three arrow shapes selected, click the Align button in the Arrange group and then click *Align Left* at the drop-down list.
   d. Click the Shape Styles group task pane launcher.
   e. At the Format Shape task pane with the Fill & Line icon selected, click *Fill*, if necessary, to expand the fill options.
   f. Click the *Gradient fill* option.
   g. Click the Preset gradients button and then click the *Top Spotlight - Accent 2* option (second column, second row).

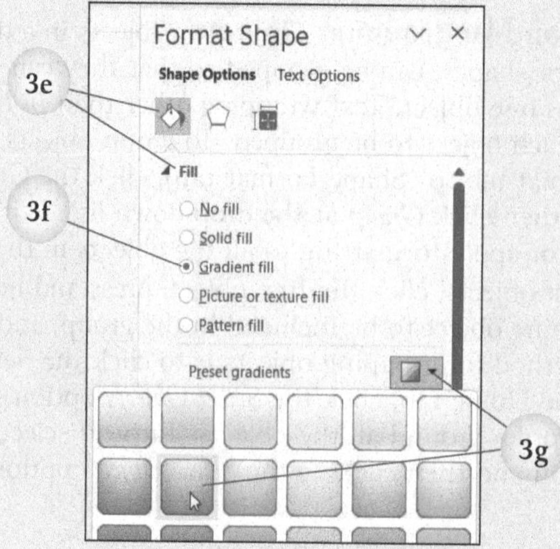

h. Scroll down the task pane and then click *Line* to expand the line options.
i. If necessary, scroll down the task pane and then click the *No line* option.
j. Click the Effects icon (at the top of the task pane).
k. If necessary, click *Shadow* to expand the shadow options.
l. Click the Presets button and then click the *Inside: Top Right* option (third column, first row in the *Inner* section).
m. Close the Format Shape task pane.

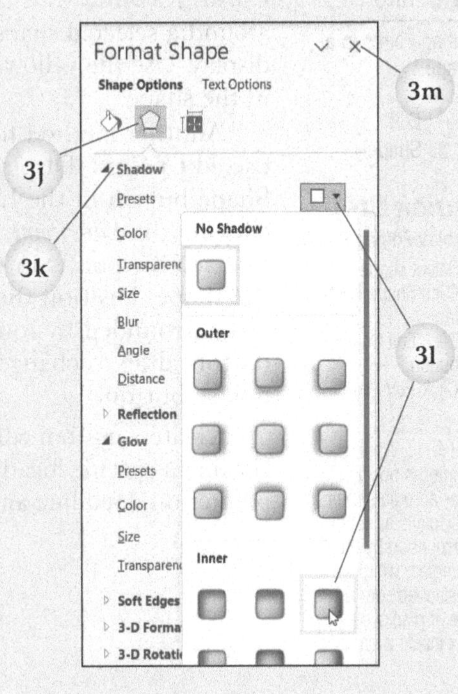

4. With the three arrow shapes still selected, group the shapes, size and move the group, and then ungroup the shapes by completing the following steps:
a. Click the Group button in the Arrange group and then click *Group* at the drop-down list.

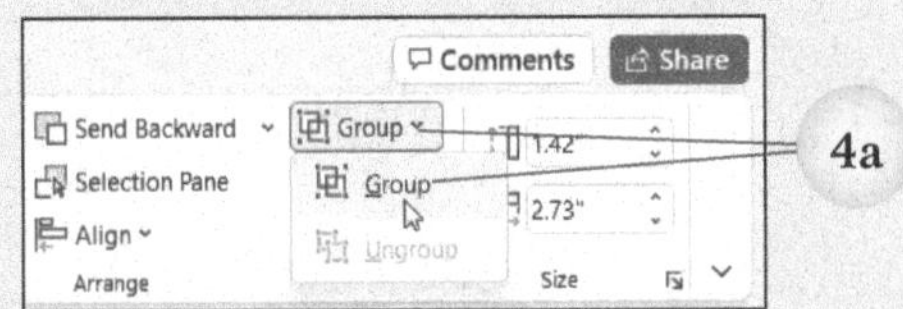

b. Click in the *Shape Height* measurement box and then type 6 in the Size group.
c. Click in the *Shape Width* measurement box in the Size group, type 3.7, and then press the Enter key.
d. Click the Position button in the Arrange group and then click the *Position in Bottom Center with Square Text Wrapping* option (second column, third row in the *With Text Wrapping* section).

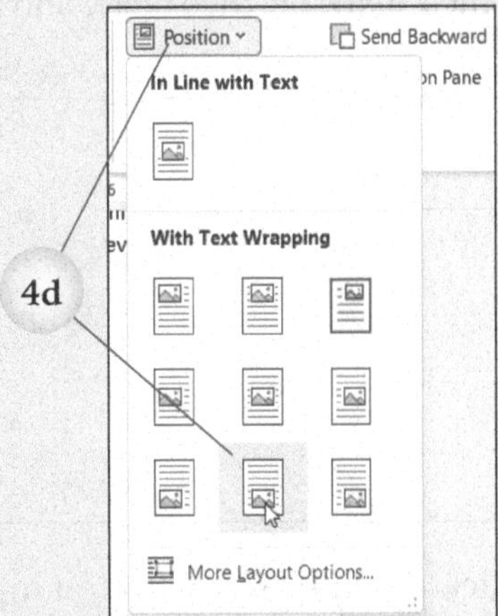

e. Click the Group button and then click *Ungroup* at the drop-down list.
f. Click outside the arrow shapes to deselect the shapes.
5. Delete the bottom arrow shape of the three arrow shapes by clicking the shape (make sure the border displays as a solid line) and then pressing the Delete key.
6. Save **5-Leland.docx**.

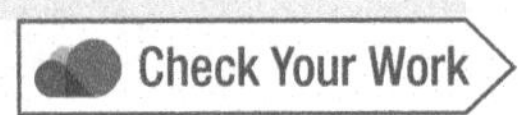

Editing Points in a Shape

Edit Shape

Quick Steps

Display Editing Points

1. Select shape.
2. Click Shape Format tab.
3. Click Edit Shape button.
4. Click *Edit Points*.

Hint When the pointer is positioned over an editing point, it displays as a box surrounded by four triangles; when positioned over a red line, it displays as a box inside a cross.

Editing Points in a Shape Sizing handles are small white circles that display around a selected shape. Depending on the shape, small yellow circles might also display. Use the yellow circles to change the width or height of a specific element in the shape.

Another method for customizing specific elements is to display and then use edit points. Display edit points by selecting the shape, clicking the Edit Shape button in the Insert Shapes group on the Shape Format tab, and then clicking the *Edit Points* option. Edit points display as small black squares at the intersecting points in the shape. A red line also displays between edit points in the shape. Position the pointer on an edit point and the pointer displays as a box surrounded by four triangles (✥). Click and hold down the left mouse button, drag to change the specific element in the shape, and then release the mouse button.

Create a custom editing point by pressing and holding down the Ctrl key, clicking a specific location on a red line, and then releasing the Ctrl key. Position the pointer on a red line and the pointer displays as a box inside a cross (✥).

Activity 2b Editing Points in a Shape

Part 2 of 4

1. With **5-Leland.docx** open, press Ctrl + End to move the insertion point to the end of the document (page 2).
2. Click the shape on the second page to select the shape.
3. With the shape selected, edit points by completing the following steps:
   a. Position the pointer on the top yellow circle, click and hold down the left mouse button, drag to the right approximately one-half inch (use the horizontal ruler as a guide and drag to approximately the 2.5-inch mark on the ruler), and then release the mouse button.

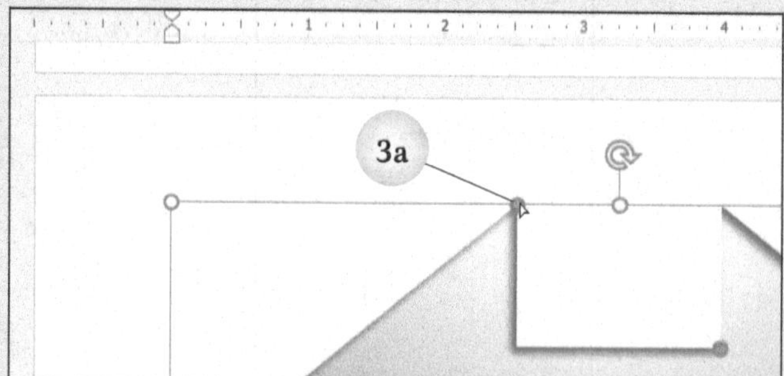

   b. Click the Shape Format tab, click the Edit Shape button in the Insert Shapes group, and then click *Edit Points* at the drop-down list.

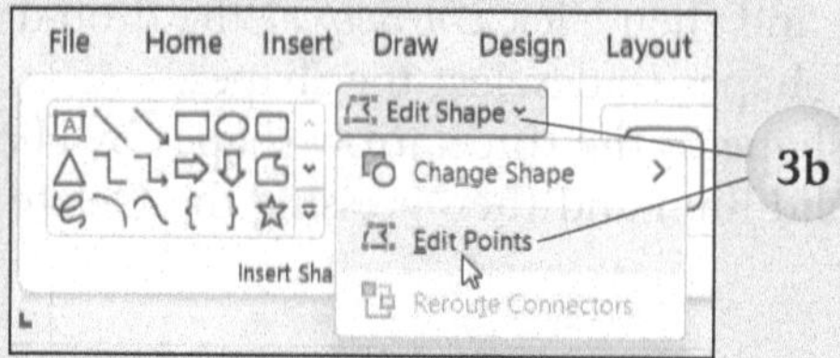

c. Position the pointer on the edit point that displays at the tip of the arrow at the right side of the shape. Click and hold down the left mouse button, drag to the left approximately 1 inch (use the horizontal ruler as a guide), and then release the mouse button. (The shape will move when you release the mouse button.)

d. Position the pointer on the edit point that displays at the tip of the arrow at the left side of the shape. Click and hold down the left mouse button, drag to the right approximately 1 inch (use the horizontal ruler as a guide), and then release the mouse button. (The shape will move when you release the mouse button.)

3c

4. Reposition the shape by clicking the Position button in the Arrange group and then clicking the *Position in Top Center with Square Text Wrapping* option (second column, first row in the *With Text Wrapping* section).
5. Insert and format text in the shape by completing the following steps:
   a. With the shape selected, type Free seminar!, press the Enter key, and then type 1-888-555-4588.
   b. Click the border of the shape to change the border to a solid line.
   c. Click the Text Fill button arrow in the WordArt Styles group and then click the *Orange, Accent 2, Darker 50%* color option (sixth column, bottom row in the *Theme Colors* section).
   d. Click the Home tab and then click the Bold button in the Font group.
   e. Click the *Font Size* option box arrow and then click *24* at the drop-down gallery.
6. Press Ctrl + Home to move the insertion point to the beginning of the document.
7. Save **5-Leland.docx**.

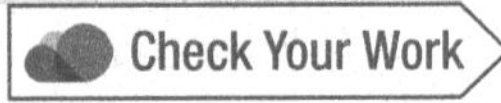

Editing Wrap Points in an Object

Quick Steps

Display Wrap Points for Object

1. Select object.
2. Click Picture Format tab (or Shape Format tab).
3. Click Wrap Text button.
4. Click *Edit Wrap Points.*

Editing Wrap Points in an Object When an object such as an image or shape is inserted in a document, a series of wrap points are defined around the object. These wrap points display in a manner similar to the editing points around an object. The difference between editing points and wrap points is that editing points change the shape of specific elements in an object while wrap points wrap text closer to or farther away from an object.

To display wrap points in a shape, select the shape, click the Shape Format tab, click the Wrap Text button in the Arrange group, and then click the *Edit Wrap Points* option. Display wrap points for an image in a similar manner except click the Wrap Text button on the Picture Format tab. Use wrap points to change how text or other data wraps around an object by dragging specific wrap points.

When wrap points are displayed in an object, red lines appear between wrap points. Create a custom wrap point by positioning the pointer on a location on a red line, pressing and holding down the left mouse button, dragging to a specific position, and then releasing the mouse button. Remove a wrap point by pressing and holding down the Ctrl key, clicking the wrap point, and then releasing the Ctrl key.

Activity 2c Editing Wrap Points in a Shape

Part 3 of 4

1. With **5-Leland.docx** open, click the border of the banner shape in the paragraph of text below the title.
2. Edit wrap points in the shape by completing the following steps:
   a. Click the Shape Format tab.
   b. Click the Wrap Text button in the Arrange group and then click *Edit Wrap Points* at the drop-down list.
   c. Drag the wrap point at the left side of the shape into the shape, as shown below.

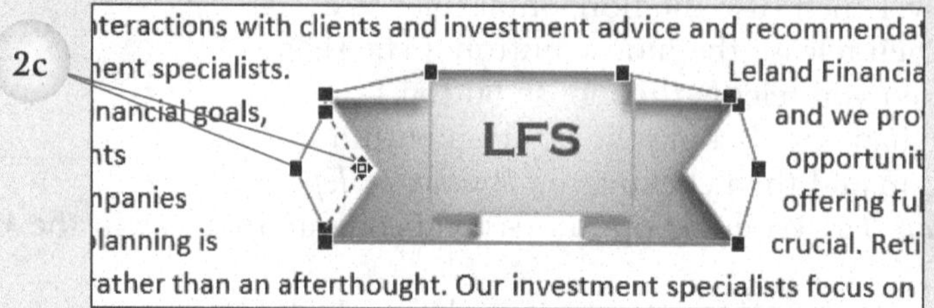

   d. Drag the wrap point at the right side of the shape into the shape, as shown below.

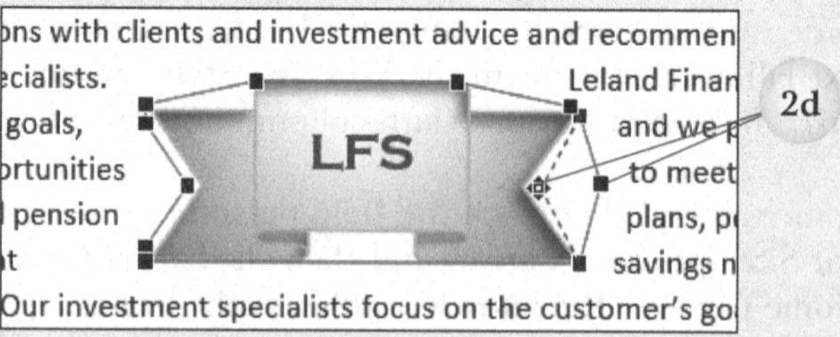

3. Click outside the shape to remove the wrap points.
4. Save **5-Leland.docx**.

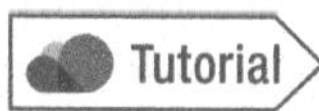

Linking and Unlinking Text Boxes

Quick Steps

Link Text Boxes
1. Select text box.
2. Click Shape Format tab.
3. Click Create Link button.
4. Click in another text box.

Hint Link text boxes to flow text in columns across multiple pages.

Inserting a Text Box on a Shape Not only can text be typed directly in a shape, but a text box can be drawn on a shape. When a text box is drawn on a shape, it is actually added as a layer on top of the shape. To format or move the text box with the shape, select or group the shape with the text box.

Linking and Unlinking Text Boxes Linking text boxes allows the text in them to flow from one box to another. To do this, draw the text boxes and then click in the first text box. Click the Create Link button in the Text group on the Shape Format tab and the pointer displays with a pouring jug icon (⧉) attached. Click an empty text box to link it with the selected text box. Type text in the first text box and the text will flow to the linked text box.

More than two text boxes can be linked. To link several text boxes, click the first text box, click the Create Link button on the Shape Format tab, and then click in the second text box. Select the second text box, click the Create Link button, and then click the third text box. Continue in this manner until all the text boxes are linked.

To break a link between two boxes, select the first text box in the link and then click the Break Link button in the Text group. When a link is broken, all the text is placed in the first text box.

Activity 2d Linking and Unlinking Text Boxes

1. With **5-Leland.docx** open, scroll down the document to display the first arrow shape on the first page.
2. Insert, size, and format a text box by completing the following steps:
   a. Click the Insert tab.
   b. Click the Text Box button in the Text group and then click *Draw Text Box* at the drop-down list.
   c. Click in the document near the first shape.
   d. With the text box selected, click in the *Shape Height* measurement box and then type 0.73.
   e. Click in the *Shape Width* measurement box and then type 2.
   f. Click the Shape Fill button arrow in the Shape Styles group and then click *No Fill* at the drop-down list.
   g. Drag the text box so it is positioned on the first arrow (see the image at the right).
   h. Copy the text box to the second arrow shape by pressing and holding down the Ctrl key, clicking the text box border and holding down the left mouse button, dragging the copy of the text box so that it is positioned on top of the second arrow shape, and then releasing the mouse button and the Ctrl key.

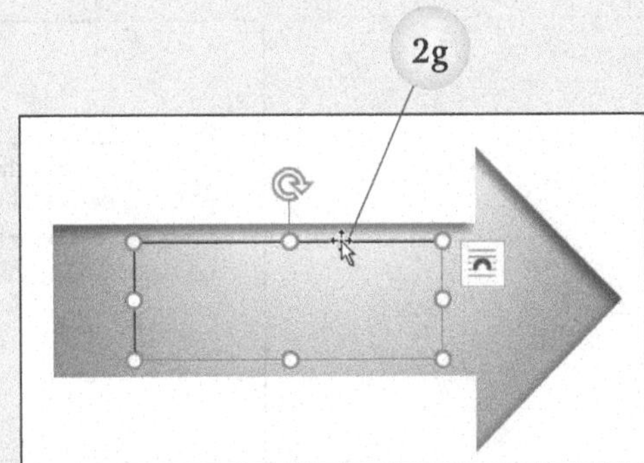

3. Link the text boxes by completing the following steps:
   a. Click the border of the text box on the first arrow shape to select the text box.
   b. Click the Create Link button in the Text group on the Shape Format tab.
   c. Click in the text box on the second arrow shape.

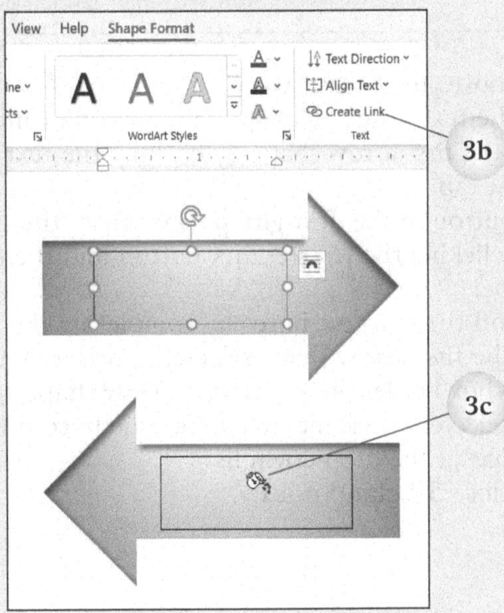

4. Insert text in the text box on the first arrow shape by completing the following steps:
   a. Click in the text box on the first arrow shape.
   b. Click the Home tab, change the font size to 12 points, apply the Orange, Accent 2, Darker 50% font color (sixth column, bottom row in the *Theme Colors* section), and then apply bold formatting.
   c. Click the Center button in the Paragraph group.
   d. Click the Line and Paragraph Spacing button in the Paragraph group and then click *Remove Space After Paragraph*.
   e. Click the Line and Paragraph Spacing button and then click *1.0*.
   f. Type Let Leland Financial Services help you plan for retirement and provide you with information to determine your financial direction. (The text will flow to the text box on the second arrow shape.)

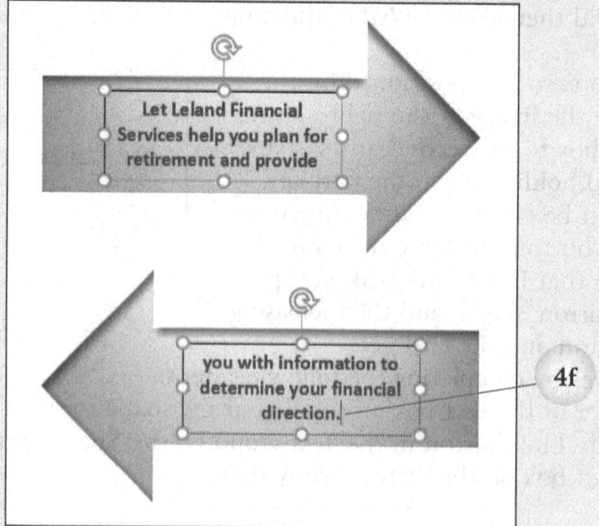

   g. Click outside the text boxes to deselect them.
5. Break the link between the text boxes by completing the following steps:
   a. Select the text box on the first arrow shape by clicking the text box border.
   b. Click the Shape Format tab.
   c. Click the Break Link button in the Text group (previously the Create Link button).
6. Relink the text boxes by clicking the Create Link button and then clicking in the text box on the second arrow shape.
7. Remove the outline around the two text boxes by completing the following steps:
   a. With the text box on the first arrow shape selected, press and hold down the Shift key and then click the text box border on the second arrow shape.
   b. With both text boxes selected, click the Shape Outline button in the Shape Styles group and then click *No Outline* at the drop-down list.
8. Save, preview, and then close **5-Leland.docx**.

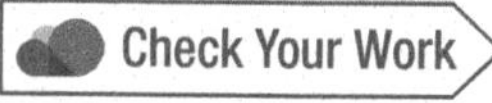

Activity 3 Insert an Icon and 3D Model in an Award Certificate — 3 Parts

You will open an award certificate document and then insert and customize a football icon and a 3D model of a lion.

Inserting and Customizing Icons

 Icons

Quick Steps

Insert Icon

1. Click Insert tab.
2. Click Icons button.
3. Double-click icon.

Hint Insert multiple icons at the same time by clicking each icon at the Insert Icons window and then clicking the Insert button.

Inserting and Customizing Icons

Use the Icons button in the Illustrations group on the Insert tab to insert an icon in a Word document. An icon is a graphical representation of something, such as an animal, weather, an emotion, or an element from nature. Click the Icons button on the Insert tab and the Icons window opens, as shown in Figure 5.3. At this window, scroll down the list box to view the various icons or click a category to display a specific category of icons. To insert an icon in a document, double-click the icon in the list box or click the icon and then click the Insert button.

When an icon is inserted and selected in a document, the Graphics Format tab is active, as shown in Figure 5.4. Use options on this tab to apply a graphic style, fill, outline, and effect; type alternate text for the icon; position, align, group, rotate, and size the icon; and apply text wrapping.

Icons, like other images, can be formatted with options at the Layout dialog box and with options at a task pane. Display the Layout dialog box by clicking the Size group dialog box launcher. Click the Graphics Styles group task pane launcher to display the Format Graphic task pane. The task pane contains the Fill & Line, Effects, Layout & Properties, and Picture icons. Use options at the Format Graphic task pane to format an icon in a manner similar to formatting an image, shape, or text box.

Figure 5.3 Icons Window

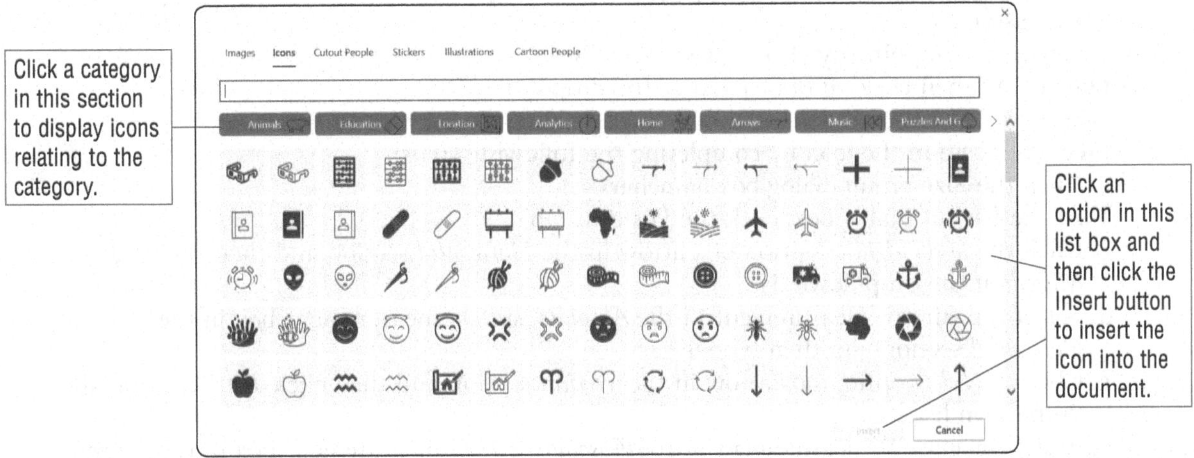

Figure 5.4 Graphics Format Tab

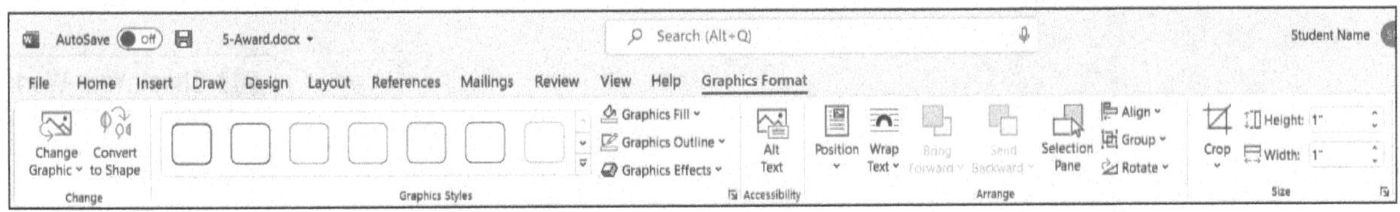

Activity 3a Inserting and Customizing an Icon

1. Open **Award.docx** and then save it with the name **5-Award.**
2. Insert an icon by completing the following steps:
   a. Click the Insert tab.
   b. Click the Icons button in the Illustrations group.
   c. At the Icons window, type football in the search text box.
   d. When football icons display, double-click the football icon shown at the right.
3. Increase the height of the football icon by clicking in the *Height* measurement box in the Size group, typing 2.7, and then pressing the Enter key.
4. Apply a style by clicking the *Light 1 Fill, Colored Outline - Accent 4* option (fifth style in the Graphics Styles gallery).

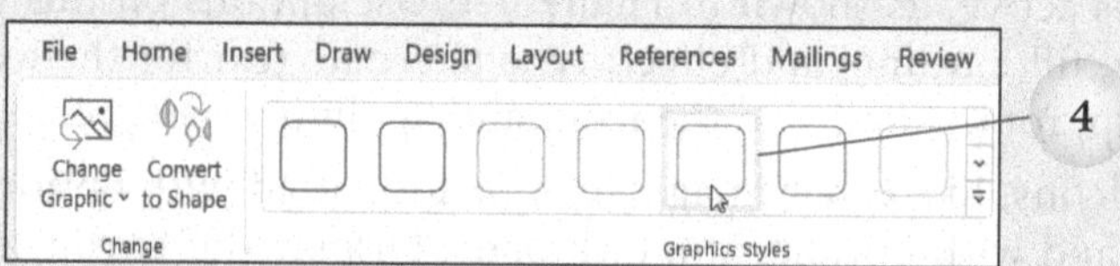

5. Change the width of the icon lines by completing the following steps:
   a. Click the Graphics Styles group task pane launcher.
   b. At the Format Graphic task pane, click *Line,* if necessary, to expand the line options.
   c. Click the *Width* measurement box up arrow two times. (This changes the width to *1.5 pt.*)
   d. Click the Close button in the upper right corner of the task pane.

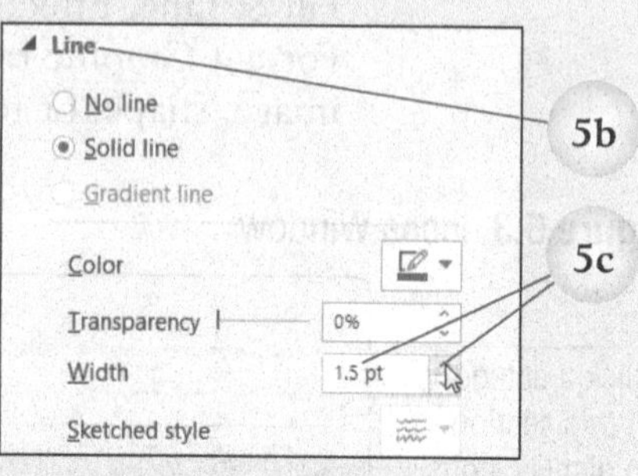

6. Change text wrapping by clicking the Wrap Text button and then clicking *Behind Text* at the drop-down gallery.
7. Precisely position the icon by completing the following steps:
   a. Click the Size group dialog box launcher.
   b. At the Layout dialog box, click the Position tab.
   c. Click the *to the right of* option box arrow in the *Horizontal* section and then click *Left Margin* at the drop-down list.
   d. Select the current measurement in the *Absolute position* measurement box in the *Horizontal* section and then type 4.15.
   e. Click the *below* option box arrow in the *Vertical* section and then click *Top Margin* at the drop-down list.
   f. Select the current measurement in the *Absolute position* measurement box in the *Vertical* section and then type 1.65.
   g. Click OK to close the Layout dialog box.
8. Save **5-Award.docx**.

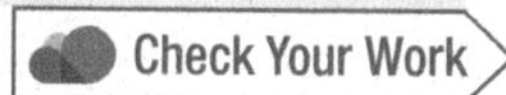

Inserting and Customizing 3D Models

 3D Models

Quick Steps

Insert 3D Model

1. Click Insert tab.
2. Click 3D Models button.
3. Click 3D model category.
4. Double-click 3D model.

Hint *3D* is an abbreviation for *three-dimensional*. It describes an object that has width, height, and depth.

Inserting and Customizing 3D Models

Word supports inserting 3D models into a document. A 3D model is a graphic file of an image shown in three dimensions. The model can be rotated or tilted to allow viewing from various angles or to display a specific portion or feature. Microsoft's 3D model gallery includes a collection of free 3D models that can be inserted in a document. Access these models by clicking the 3D Models button in the Illustrations group on the Insert tab. At the Online 3D Models window, as shown in Figure 5.5, click a category to view all the 3D models within the category or type one or more keywords in the search text box and then press the Enter key. Some 3D models include animation. These are identified with a "runner" badge (an icon of a runner in the lower left corner of the model). Insert a 3D model in a document by double-clicking the model or clicking the model and then clicking the Insert button.

When a 3D model is inserted in a document, the 3D Model tab is active. If the model is animated, the Play 3D group is available on the 3D Model tab. Click the Play button to play the animation and click the Scenes button to display a drop-down list of preset animations called *scenes*. Use buttons in the Adjust group to insert a different 3D model or to reset the selected model to its original size and position. The 3D Model Views group includes a gallery of preset views for the model. Click the Alt Text button in the Accessibility group and the Alt Text task pane displays where a description of the model can be added. Use options in the Arrange group to position the model, apply text wrapping, send the model forward or backward, and align the model. Change the height and width of the model with options in the Size group.

 Pan & Zoom

The Size group also contains the Pan & Zoom button. Click this button and a button (a magnifying glass with a plus symbol inside) displays at the right of the selected model. Position the pointer on this button, click and hold down the left mouse button, and then drag up to increase the size of the model (pan in) or drag down to decrease the size (pan out). To turn off the pan feature, click the Pan & Zoom button to deactivate it.

When a 3D model is selected, a Layout Options button displays outside the upper right corner. Click the Layout Options button and a side menu displays with text wrapping options. Click a text wrapping option and then click the side menu Close button.

Figure 5.5 Online 3D Models Window

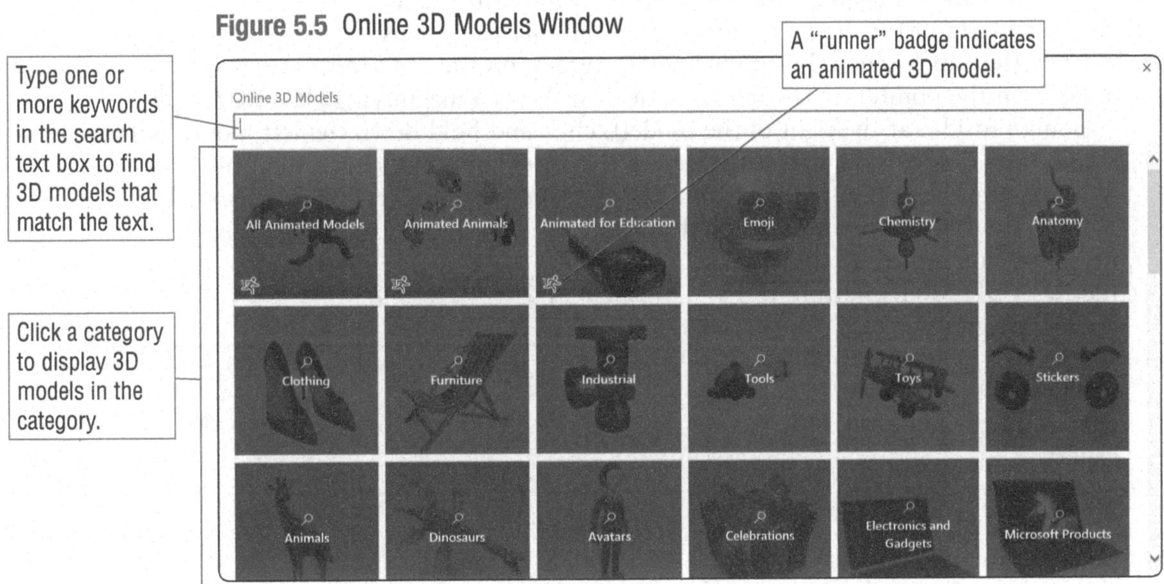

Use the 3D control in the middle of a selected 3D model to rotate or tilt the model. To use the 3D control, position the pointer on the control, click and hold down the left mouse button, and then drag with the mouse to rotate or tilt the model.

Advanced layout options are available at the Layout dialog box. Click the Size group dialog box launcher to display the dialog box. Use options at the Layout dialog box to specify the size, text wrapping, and position of the 3D model.

A 3D model saved to the computer's hard drive can be inserted in a document. Click the 3D Models button arrow and a drop-down list displays with the options *This Device* and *Stock 3D Models*. Click the *Stock 3D Models* option and the Online 3D Models window opens. Click the *This Device* option and the Insert 3D Model dialog box displays. At this dialog box, navigate to the folder containing the 3D model and then double-click the model to insert it in the document.

Activity 3b Inserting and Customizing a 3D Model

Part 2 of 3

1. With **5-Award.docx** open, press Ctrl + End to move the insertion point to the end of the document.
2. Insert a 3D model from the 3D model gallery by completing the following steps:
   a. Click the Insert tab.
   b. Click the 3D Models button in the Illustrations group.
   c. At the Online 3D Models window, type lion in the search text box and then press the Enter key.
   d. Double-click the lion model shown at the right.

   Note: If you do not have access to the Online 3D Models window, open Award3D.docx from your WL2C5 folder. This document contains the 3D lion model.

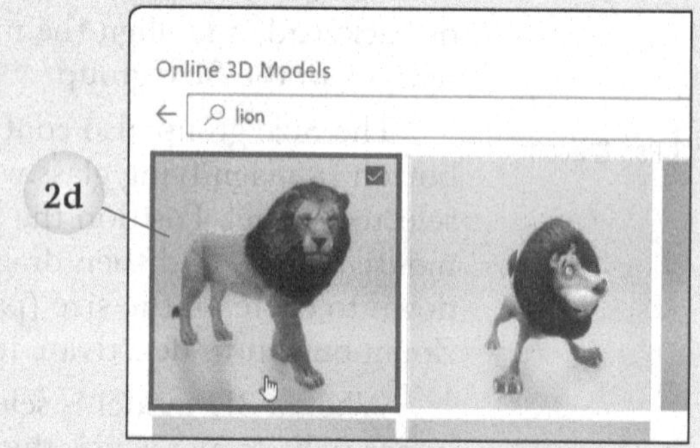

3. Experiment using the 3D control, which displays in the middle of the lion model, by positioning the pointer on the 3D control, clicking and holding down the left mouse button, and then dragging with the mouse to rotate the model.
4. Pan in and out of the model by completing the following steps:
   a. Click the Pan & Zoom button in the Size group on the 3D Model tab.
   b. Position the pointer on the button that displays as a magnifying glass with a plus symbol inside (at the right of the model), click and hold down the left mouse button, and then drag up to increase the size of the model and drag down to decrease the size. Make sure the lion displays within the placeholders after decreasing the size.
   c. Click the Pan & Zoom button to deactivate it.
5. Reset the lion model by clicking the Reset 3D Model button in the Adjust group.
6. Change the view of the model by clicking the *Left* view (second option) in the 3D Model Views gallery.

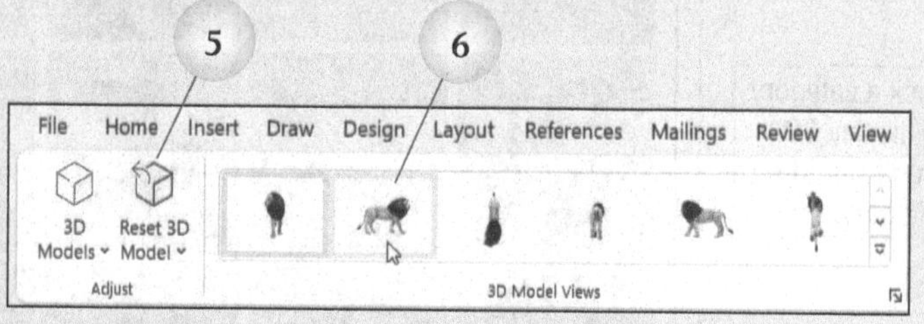

7. Using the 3D control, rotate the model so that it displays as shown at the right.
8. Change the height of the model by clicking in the *Height* measurement box, typing 3.7, and then pressing the Enter key.
9. Precisely position the lion model by completing the following steps:
   a. Click the Size group dialog box launcher.
   b. At the Layout dialog box, click the Position tab.
   c. Click the *to the right of* option box arrow in the *Horizontal* section and then click *Left Margin* at the drop-down list.

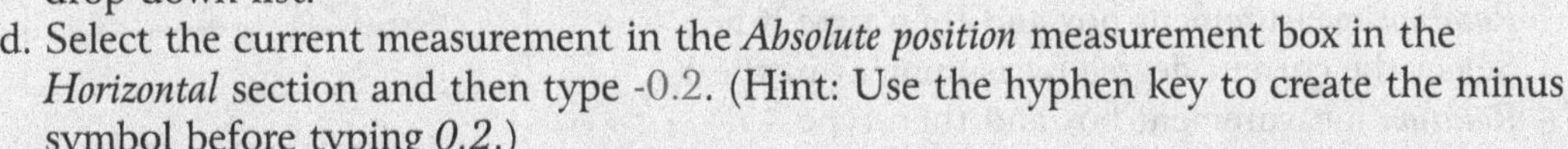

   d. Select the current measurement in the *Absolute position* measurement box in the *Horizontal* section and then type -0.2. (Hint: Use the hyphen key to create the minus symbol before typing *0.2*.)
   e. Click the *below* option box arrow in the *Vertical* section and then click *Page* at the drop-down list.
   f. Select the current measurement in the *Absolute position* measurement box in the *Vertical* section and then type 4.2.
   g. Click OK to close the Layout dialog box.
10. Check for alternative text for the lion model by completing the following steps:
    a. Click the Alt Text button in the Accessibility group.
    b. Notice that the description box in the Alt Text task pane contains the word *Lion*.

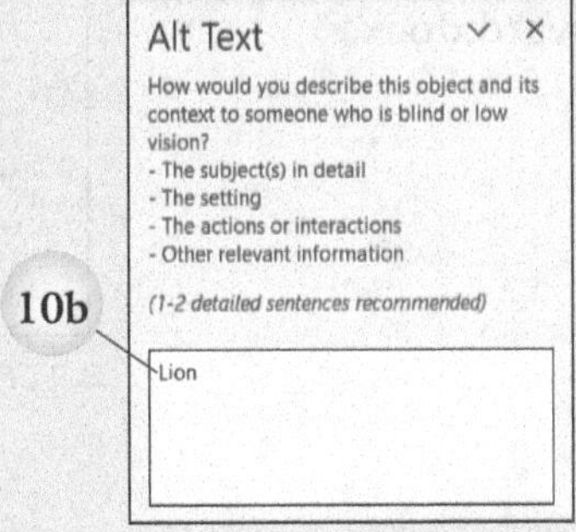

    c. Close the Alt Text task pane.
11. Save **5-Award.docx**.

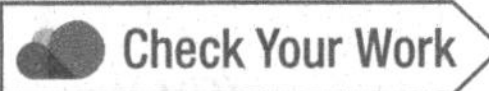

Options for formatting and customizing a 3D model are available at the Format 3D Model task pane. Display the task pane by clicking the 3D Model Views group task pane launcher. The task pane displays with four icons: Fill & Line, Effects, Layout & Properties, and 3D Model. The options in the task pane vary depending on the icon selected.

The task pane opens with the 3D Model icon selected and contains options for specifying a rotation and camera view. Click the Fill & Line icon to display options for formatting the border line and fill of the 3D model. Use options at the task pane with the Effects icon selected to apply formatting effects, such as shadow, reflection, glow, and soft edges, and to format and rotate the model. Click the Layout & Properties icon and the options in the task pane are dimmed and unavailable.

Activity 3c Formatting a 3D Model with Task Pane Options

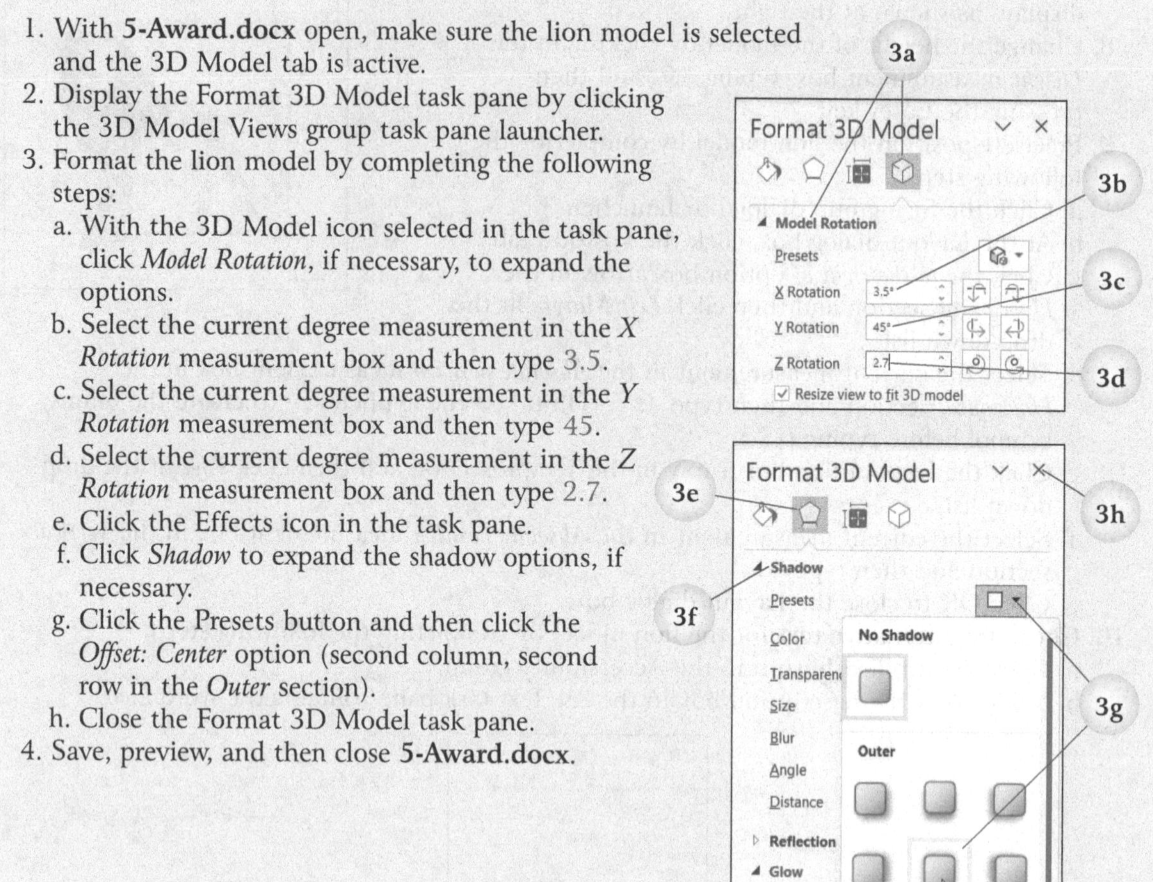

1. With **5-Award.docx** open, make sure the lion model is selected and the 3D Model tab is active.
2. Display the Format 3D Model task pane by clicking the 3D Model Views group task pane launcher.
3. Format the lion model by completing the following steps:
   a. With the 3D Model icon selected in the task pane, click *Model Rotation*, if necessary, to expand the options.
   b. Select the current degree measurement in the *X Rotation* measurement box and then type 3.5.
   c. Select the current degree measurement in the *Y Rotation* measurement box and then type 45.
   d. Select the current degree measurement in the *Z Rotation* measurement box and then type 2.7.
   e. Click the Effects icon in the task pane.
   f. Click *Shadow* to expand the shadow options, if necessary.
   g. Click the Presets button and then click the *Offset: Center* option (second column, second row in the *Outer* section).
   h. Close the Format 3D Model task pane.
4. Save, preview, and then close **5-Award.docx**.

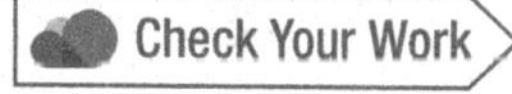

Activity 4 Use Options on the Draw Tab in a Produce Flyer

3 Parts

You will use options on the Draw tab to draw, select, convert, and format ink drawings, highlight text, and use editing features to edit a document.

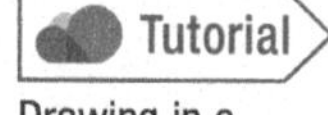

Drawing in a Document

Drawing in a Document

The Draw tab shown in Figure 5.6, contains buttons for drawing in a document, converting shapes, editing text, and selecting and highlighting text. If this tab is not visible, display the tab by right-clicking the ribbon and then clicking *Customize the Ribbon*. At the Word Options dialog box with *Customize Ribbon* selected in the left panel, click the *Draw* check box in the right list box to insert a check mark and then click OK. The Draw tab should display between the Insert and Design tabs. Use options on the Draw tab to draw using a mouse, finger, or digital pen.

Figure 5.6 Draw Tab

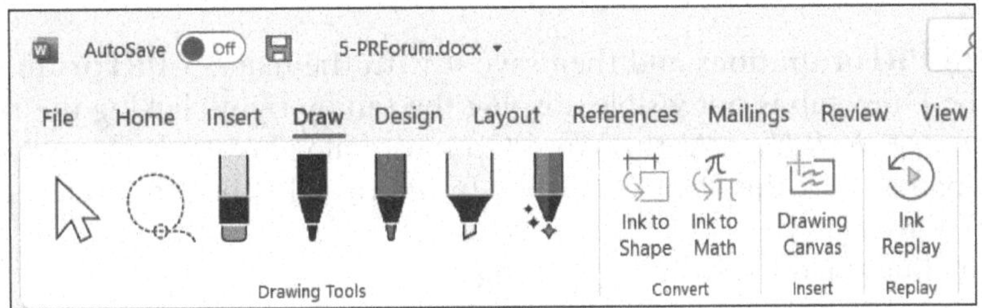

Using Pens to Draw and Highlight

The Drawing Tools group on the Draw tab contains buttons for selecting and erasing ink drawings as well as pens for drawing in a document, a highlighter pen for highlighting text, and an Action Pen for editing a document. Click a pen or highlighter button to select it and then use the mouse, a finger, or digital pen to draw in the document. A pen button stays active until a different button is selected. Click an active pen button and a drop-down list displays with options for changing the size, thickness, and color of the pen. Add additional pens to the Draw tab by right-clicking a pen and then clicking *Add Another Pen* at the shortcut menu. To remove a pen from the Draw tab, right-click the pen and then click *Delete Pen* at the shortcut menu.

Use the Highlighter pen to highlight specific text in a document. Click the Highlighter pen to activate it and then draw over text. The Highlighter pen button drop-down list contains the *Snap to Text* option. Click this option to turn it on and drawing with the Highlighter pen causes the highlighting to snap to the text. If this option is not turned on, drawing with the Highlighter pen is more freeform. Remove highlighting from text by drawing across the text again with the Highlighter pen active.

Selecting and Erasing Ink Drawings

Select an object such as an ink drawing or shape with the Select button in the Drawing Tools groups. Use the Lasso button to select ink drawings. To do this, click the Lasso button and then draw around the ink drawings.

Use the Eraser pen to erase ink drawn in the document. Click the Eraser button to activate it and then click the button again to display a drop-down list with options for specifying the width of the eraser. Choose the *Point Eraser* option at the drop-down list to precisely erase parts of an ink drawing.

Replaying Ink Drawings

Use the Ink Replay button in the Replay group on the Draw tab to show a replay of the most recent ink drawings. Click the Replay button and a replay bar displays along the bottom of the screen and any ink drawing is played in the document. Use buttons on the replay bar to rewind or play the ink drawings again. Remove the replay bar by clicking the Close button in the upper right corner of the bar or by clicking in the document outside the replay bar.

Activity 4a Using Pens to Draw and Highlight Text in a Document

1. Open **PRForum.docx** and then save it with the name **5-PRForum**.
2. If the Draw tab is not visible, display the tab by right-clicking the ribbon and then clicking *Customize the Ribbon*. At the Word Options dialog box with *Customize Ribbon* selected in the left panel, click the *Draw* check box in the right list box to insert a check mark and then click OK.
3. Draw lines below text by completing the following steps:
   a. Click the Draw tab to make it active.
   b. Click the left pen button (the first pen button after the Eraser button) to activate it.
   c. Click the left pen button again to display the drop-down list.
   d. Click the *1 mm* option in the *Thickness* section.
   e. Click the *Indigo* color in the *Colors* section (first column, second row).
   f. Using the mouse, draw a line below the text ***Date:*** *Wednesday, May 15, 2024.*
   g. Using the mouse, draw a line below the text *9:00 a.m. to 2:30 p.m.*

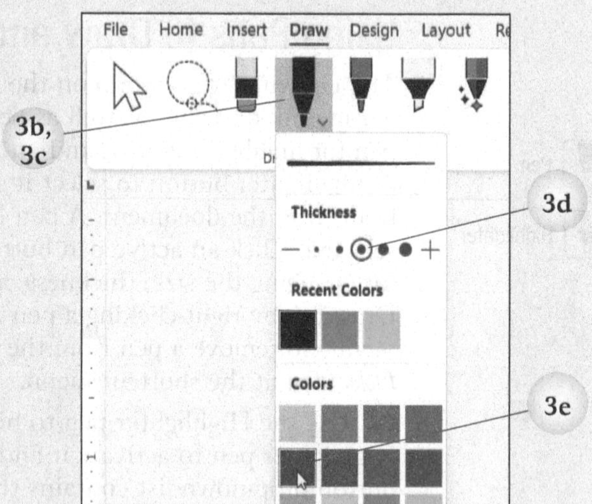

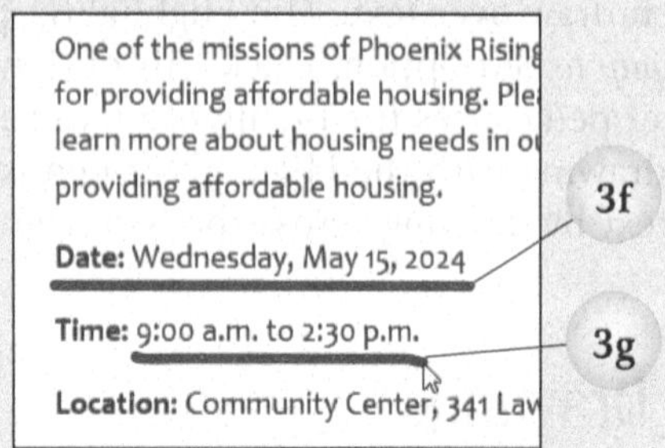

4. Replay the ink drawings you just made by clicking the Ink Replay button on the Draw tab.
5. Click in the document to remove the replay bar.
6. Erase the line below *9:00 a.m. to 2:30 p.m.* by completing the following steps:
   a. Click the Eraser button in the Drawing Tools group to activate it.
   b. Click the button again to display the drop-down list.
   c. At the drop-down list make sure *Eraser* is selected in the *Types* section.
   d. Click anywhere on the line below *9:00 a.m. to 2:30 p.m.*
7. Erase a portion of the line below ***Date:*** *Wednesday, May 15, 2024* by completing the following steps:
   a. Click the Eraser button and then click the *Point Eraser* option in the *Types* section.
   b. Using the mouse, remove the portion of the line below ***Date:*** by drawing along that portion of the line.

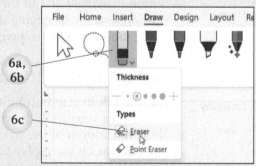

8. Highlight text by completing the following steps:
   a. Click the Highlighter button in the Drawing Tools group.
   b. Click the Highlighter button again to display the drop-down list.
   c. Click the *6 mm* option in the *Thickness* section.
   d. Click the *Pink* color in the *Colors* section (fourth column, first row).
   e. Click the *Snap to Text* option to insert a check mark before the option.
   f. Using the mouse, drag through the text *"With better understanding comes possibilities for solutions."*
   g. Using the mouse, drag through the text *"Opening doors to all."*
9. Remove highlighting by dragging through the text *"With better understanding comes possibilities for solutions."*
10. Save **5-PRForum.docx**.

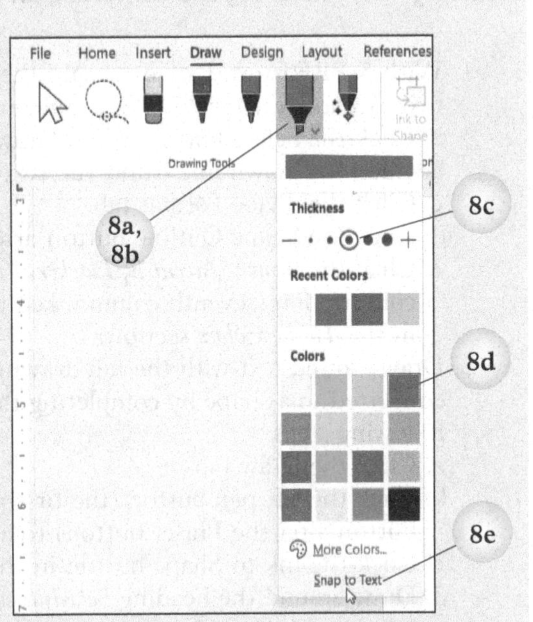

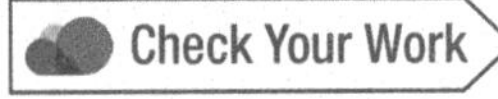

Converting an Ink Drawing

The Ink to Shape button will convert an ink drawing to a shape. To convert an ink drawing to a shape, choose a pen, click the Ink to Shape button to activate it, and then draw a shape in the document. The ink drawing is converted to the shape most similar to the ink drawing. For example, draw a box around text in a document and the ink drawing is converted to a square or rectangle. Draw a circle around text and the ink drawing is converted to a circle or oval.

Formatting an Ink Drawing and Converted Shape

Select an ink drawing and the Shape Format tab displays on the ribbon. Click this tab and options display for formatting the drawing. Some of the options on the Shape Format tab are dimmed and unavailable. If an ink drawing is converted to a shape and the shape is selected, most of the options on the Shape Format tab are available.

Activity 4b Formatting and Converting an Ink Drawing

Part 2 of 3

1. With **5-PRForum.docx** open and the Draw tab active, format the ink drawing below the text *Wednesday, May 15, 2024*, by completing the following steps:
   a. Click the Select button in the Drawing Tools group.
   b. Click the drawn line below the text *Wednesday, May 15, 2024* to select the line.
   c. Click the Shape Format tab.
   d. Click the Shape Outline button arrow.
   e. Click the *Brown, Accent 3, Darker 50%* color option (seventh column, last row in the *Theme Colors* section).
2. Draw around text with the ink drawing converted to a shape by completing the following steps:
   a. Click the Draw tab.
   b. Click the left pen button (the first pen button after the Eraser button) to activate it.
   c. Click the Ink to Shape button in the Convert group.
   d. Draw around the heading *Schedule of Events*. (When you release the mouse button, the ink drawing should convert to an oval shape. If this does not happen, undo the ink drawing and then try again.)

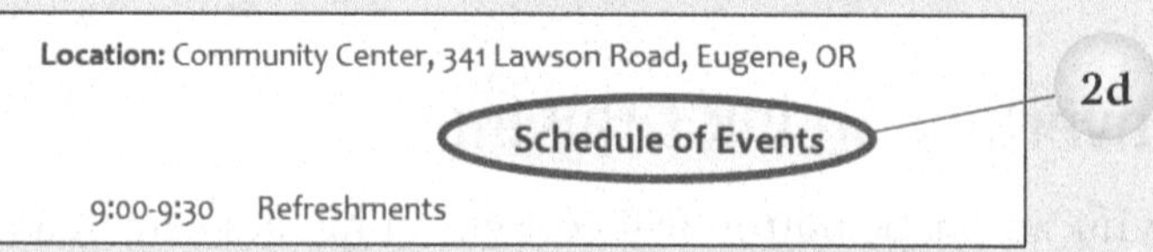

3. Format the converted shape by completing the following steps:
   a. Click the Select button in the Drawing Tools group.
   b. Click the shape around the heading *Schedule of Events*.
   c. Click the Shape Format tab.
   d. Click the Shape Outline button and then click the *Brown, Accent 3, Darker 50%* color option (seventh column, last row in the *Theme Colors* section).
   e. Click the Shape Effects button arrow, point to *Shadow*, and then click the *Offset: Bottom* option (second column, first row in the *Outer* section).
4. Save **5-PRForum.docx**.

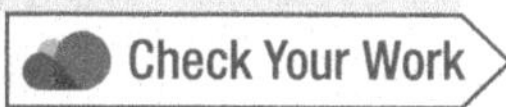

Editing with the Action Pen

Edit text in a document with the Action Pen on the Draw tab. Natural gestures can be used when editing with the Action Pen. Click the Action Pen button to select it and then click the button again to display a drop-down list with the options *Tracked Changes* and *Ink Gesture Help*. (You will learn about tracked changes in Chapter 8.) To see the gestures available for editing, click the *Ink Gesture Help* option and the Help task pane displays with a list of gestures and the result when using the gesture. For example, scribble through text to delete it, circle text to select it, and draw a line up or down to split or join text.

Activity 4c Editing a Document with the Action Pen

Part 3 of 3

1. With **5-PRForum.docx** open and the Draw tab active, click the left pen button.
2. Click the Action Pen button.
3. Click the Action Pen button again and then click *Ink Gesture Help* at the drop-down list. (This displays the Help task pane with information on gestures to use for editing.)

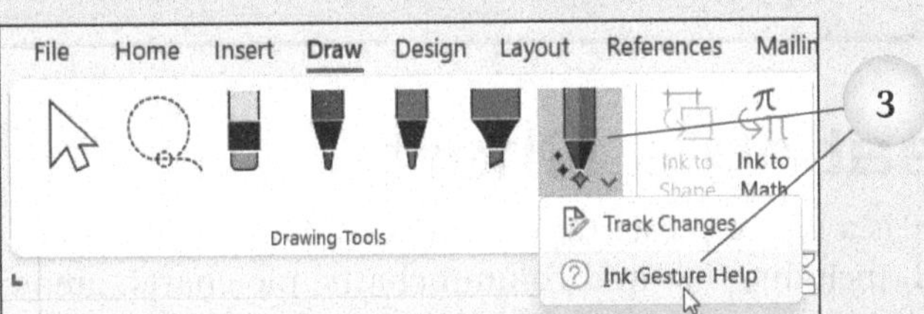

4. Using the mouse, scribble through the words *Reliable and* in the title. (This deletes the words.)

4

Opening Doors to Reliable and Affordable Housing

Affordable Housing Community Forum sponsored by PhoenixRising

5. Using the mouse, draw a line down between the letters *x* and *R* in *PhoenixRising* in the subtitle. (This inserts a space between the two letters.)
6. Using the mouse, draw a line up in the space between *Home* and *lessness* in the text after the *10:00 to 11:30* time to join the text.
7. Close the Help task pane.
8. Click the Select button in the Drawing Tools group on the Draw tab.
9. Click the Home tab.
10. Save, preview, and then close **5-PRForum.docx**.

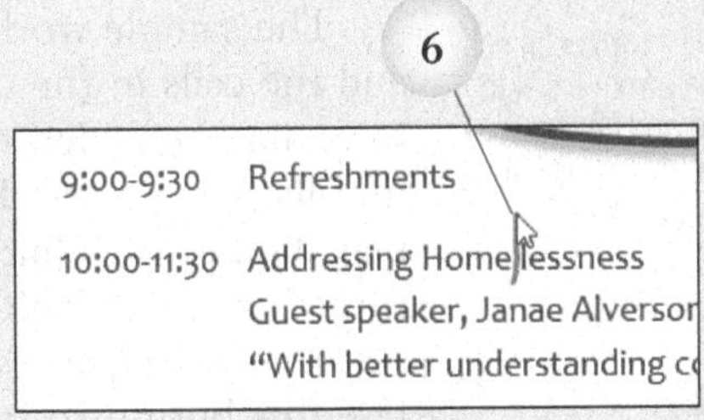

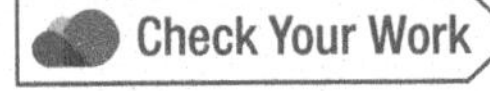

Activity 5 Create and Format a Column Chart and a Pie Chart — 5 Parts

You will use the Chart feature to create and format a column chart and then create and format a pie chart.

Creating a Chart

Chart

Quick Steps

Insert Chart

1. Click Insert tab.
2. Click Chart button.
3. Enter data in worksheet.
4. Close Excel.

Hint You can copy a chart from Excel to Word and embed it as static data or link it to the worksheet.

Creating a Chart

A chart is a visual presentation of data. In Word, a variety of charts can be created, including bar and column charts, pie charts, area charts, and many more. To create a chart, click the Insert tab and then click the Chart button in the Illustrations group. This displays the Insert Chart dialog box, as shown in Figure 5.7. At this dialog box, choose the chart type in the list at the left side, click the chart style, and then click OK.

Click OK at the Insert Chart dialog box and a chart is inserted in the document and a worksheet opens with sample data, as shown in Figure 5.8. Type specific data in the worksheet cells over the existing data. As data is typed in the worksheet, it appears in the chart in the Word document. To type data in the worksheet, click in a cell and type the data; then press the Tab key to make the next cell active, press Shift + Tab to make the previous cell active, or press the Enter key to make the cell below active.

The sample worksheet contains a data range of four columns and five rows and the cells in the data range display with a light fill color. More columns and rows may be added to the range as needed to create the chart. Simply type data in cells outside the data range and the data range expands and incorporates the new data in the chart. This occurs because the table AutoExpansion feature is turned on by default. If data is typed in a cell outside the data range, an AutoCorrect Options button displays in the lower right corner of the cell. Use this button to turn off AutoExpansion.

Figure 5.7 Insert Chart Dialog Box

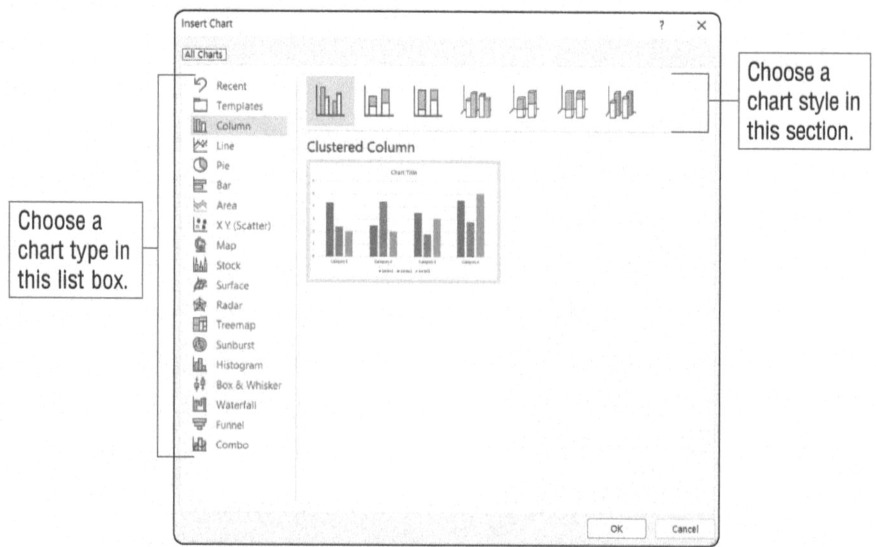

Figure 5.8 Sample Chart

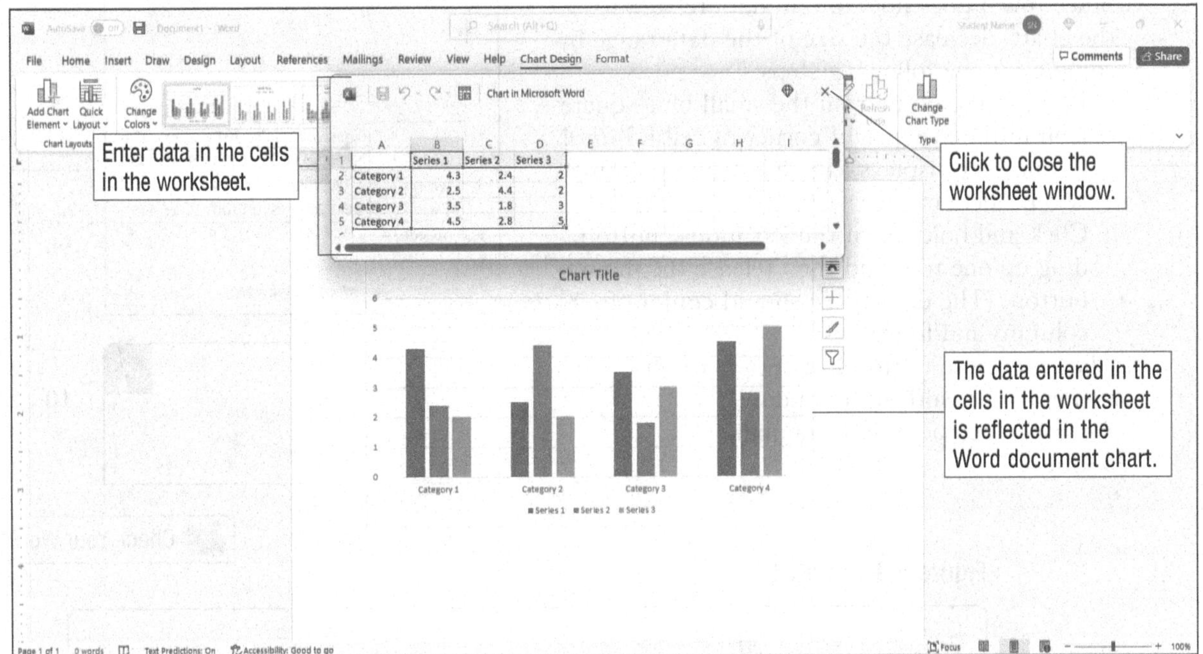

Enter data in the cells in the worksheet.
Click to close the worksheet window.
The data entered in the cells in the worksheet is reflected in the Word document chart.
Chart Title
Category 1
Category 2
Category 3
Category 4

If data is not typed in all four columns and five rows, decrease the size of the data range. To do this, position the pointer on the small blue square icon in the lower right corner of cell E5 until the pointer displays as a diagonally pointing two-headed arrow; then drag up to decrease the number of rows in the range and/or drag left to decrease the number of columns.

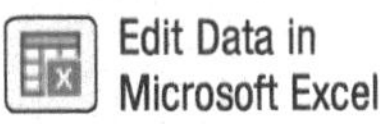

Edit Data in Microsoft Excel

Chart data can also be entered in Excel by clicking the Edit Data in Microsoft Excel button that displays in the worksheet window. When all the data is typed, click the Close button in the upper right corner of the worksheet. The worksheet window closes, the Word document window expands, and the chart displays in the document.

Activity 5a Creating a Column Chart

Part 1 of 5

1. At a blank document, click the Insert tab and then click the Chart button in the Illustrations group.
2. At the Insert Chart dialog box, click OK.
3. If necessary, drag the bottom border of the worksheet window down to display row 5 of the worksheet.
4. Click in cell B1 in the worksheet and then type Sales 2022.
5. Press the Tab key and then type Sales 2023 in cell C1.
6. Press the Tab key and then type Sales 2024 in cell D1.
7. Press the Tab key. (This makes cell A2 active.)
8. Continue typing the remaining data in cells, including dollar signs as shown in Figure 5.9. After typing the last entry, click in cell A1.

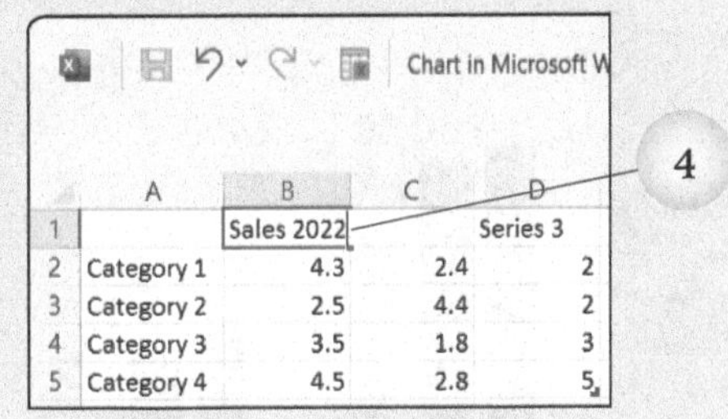

Chart in Microsoft W
4
Sales 2022
Series 3

	A	B	C	D
1		Sales 2022		Series 3
2	Category 1	4.3	2.4	2
3	Category 2	2.5	4.4	2
4	Category 3	3.5	1.8	3
5	Category 4	4.5	2.8	5

9. Since row 5 does not contain data related to the chart, decrease the size of the data range by completing the following steps:
   a. Position the pointer on the small blue square icon in the lower right corner of cell E5 until the pointer displays as a diagonally pointing two-headed arrow.
   b. Click and hold down the left mouse button, drag up one row, and then release the mouse button. (The data range should contain four columns and four rows.)
10. Click the Close button in the upper right corner of the worksheet window.
11. Save the document with the name **5-Charts**.

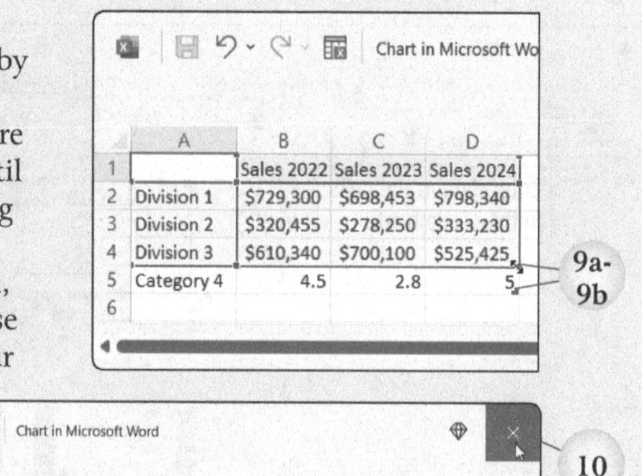

Check Your Work

Figure 5.9 Activity 5a

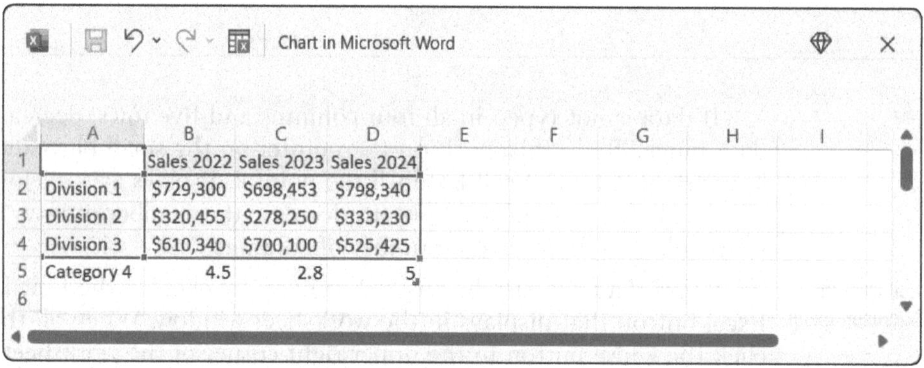

Chart in Microsoft Word

	A	B	C	D
1		Sales 2022	Sales 2023	Sales 2024
2	Division 1	$729,300	$698,453	$798,340
3	Division 2	$320,455	$278,250	$333,230
4	Division 3	$610,340	$700,100	$525,425
5	Category 4	4.5	2.8	5
6				

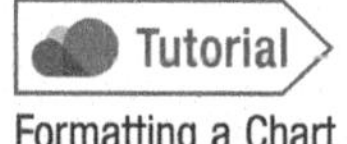

Formatting a Chart with Chart Buttons

Formatting with Chart Buttons

When a chart is inserted in a document, four buttons display at the right of the chart border, as shown in Figure 5.10. These buttons contain options for applying formatting to the chart.

Figure 5.10 Chart Buttons

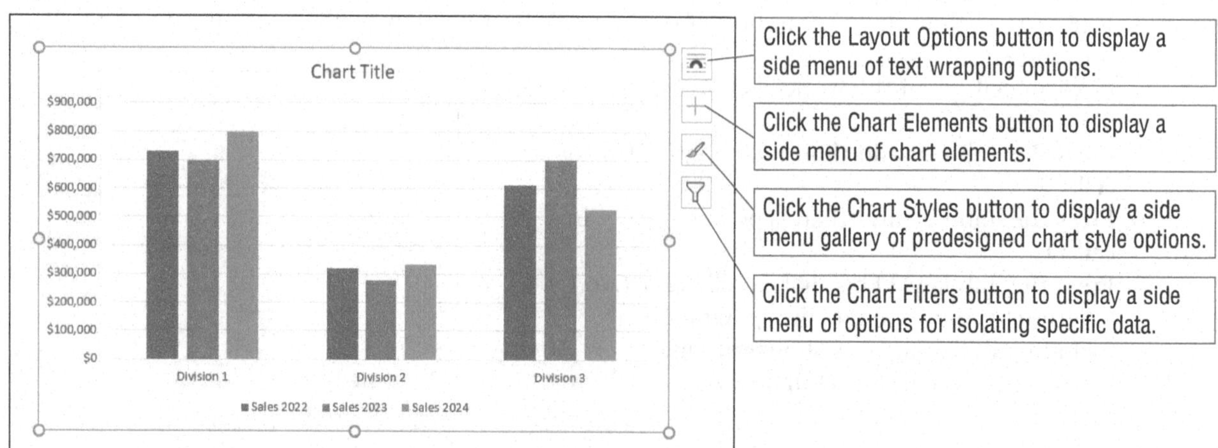

Click the top button, Layout Options, and a side menu displays with text wrapping options. Click the next button, Chart Elements, and a side menu displays with chart elements, such as axis title, chart title, data labels, data table, gridlines, and legend. Elements with check marks inserted in the check boxes are included in the chart. To include other elements, insert check marks in the check boxes for them.

Click the Chart Styles button at the right of the chart and a side menu gallery of styles displays. Scroll down the gallery and hover the pointer over an option and the style formatting is applied to the chart. In addition to providing options for chart styles, the Chart Styles button side menu gallery provides options for chart colors. Click the Chart Styles button, click the Color tab at the right of the Style tab, and then click a color option at the color palette that displays. Hover the pointer over a color option to view how the color change affects the elements in the chart.

Hint Use a pie chart if the data series you want to plot has seven categories or less and the categories represent parts of a whole.

Use the bottom button, Chart Filters, to isolate specific data in the chart. Click the button and a side menu displays. Specify the series or categories to display in the chart. To do this, remove the check marks in the check boxes for those elements that should not appear in the chart. After removing any check marks, click the Apply button in the lower left corner of the side menu. Click the Names tab at the Chart Filters button side menu and options display for turning on and off the display of column and row names.

Activity 5b Formatting with Chart Buttons

Part 2 of 5

1. With **5-Charts.docx** open, make sure the chart is selected.
2. Click the Layout Options button outside the upper right corner of the chart and then click the *Square* option in the side menu (first option in the *With Text Wrapping* section).
3. Remove and add chart elements by completing the following steps:
   a. Click the Chart Elements button below the Layout Options button outside the upper right side of the chart.
   b. At the side menu, click the *Chart Title* check box to remove the check mark.
   c. Click the *Data Table* check box to insert a check mark.

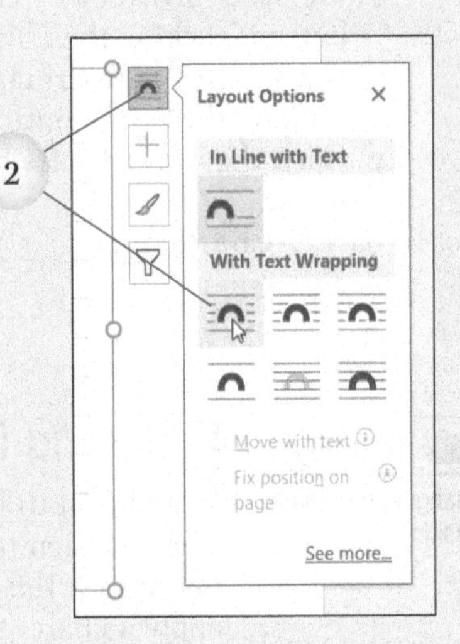

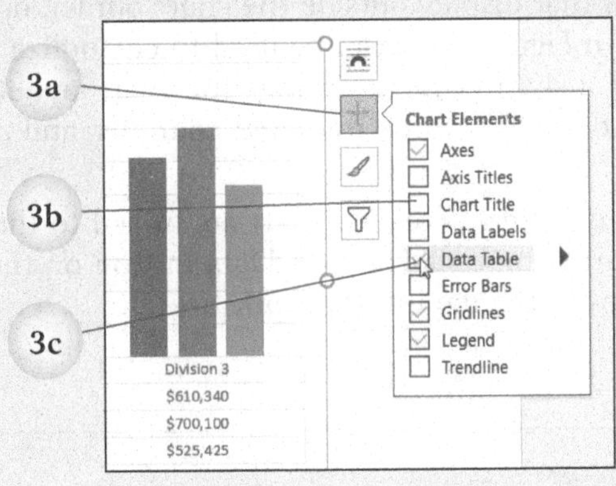

4. Apply a different chart style by completing the following steps:
   a. Click the Chart Styles button below the Chart Elements button.
   b. At the side menu gallery, click the *Style 3* option (third option in the gallery).
   c. Click the Color tab at the top of the side menu and then click the *Colorful Palette 4* option at the drop-down gallery (fourth row in the *Colorful* section).
   d. Click the Chart Styles button to close the side menu.
5. Display only Division 1 sales by completing the following steps:
   a. Click the Chart Filters button below the Chart Styles button.
   b. Click the *Division 2* check box in the *Categories* section to remove the check mark.
   c. Click the *Division 3* check box in the *Categories* section to remove the check mark.
   d. Click the Apply button in the lower left corner of the side menu.
   e. Click the Chart Filters button to close the side menu.
   f. After viewing only Division 1 sales, redisplay the other divisions by clicking the Chart Filters button, clicking the *Division 2* and *Division 3* check boxes to insert check marks, and then clicking the Apply button.
   g. Click the Chart Filters button to close the side menu.
6. Save **5-Charts.docx.**

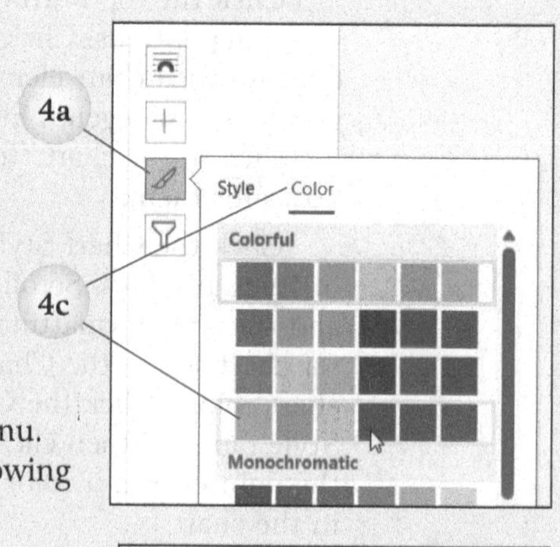

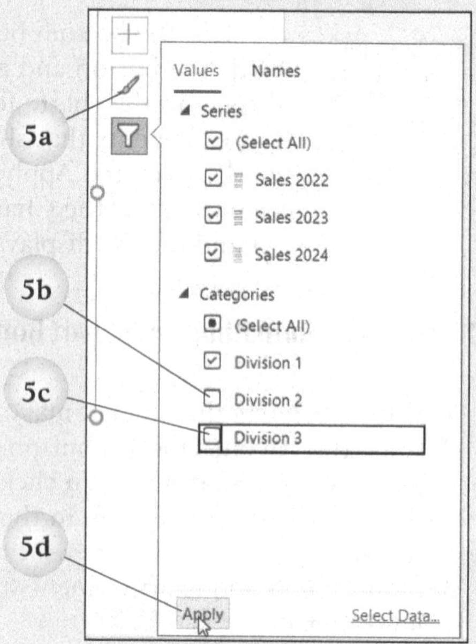

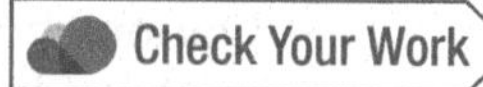

Changing the Chart Design

Changing the Chart Design

In addition to the buttons that display outside the chart border, options on the Chart Design tab, shown in Figure 5.11, can be used to customize a chart. Use options on this tab to add a chart element, change the chart layout and colors, apply a chart style, select data and switch rows and columns, and change the chart type.

The cells in a worksheet used to create a chart are linked to the chart in the document. To edit the chart data, click the Edit Data button on the Chart Design tab and then make changes to the data in the worksheet.

Figure 5.11 Chart Design Tab

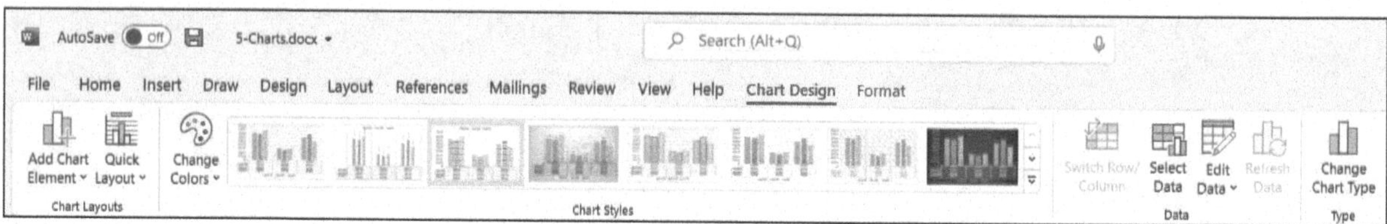

Activity 5c Changing the Chart Design

Part 3 of 5

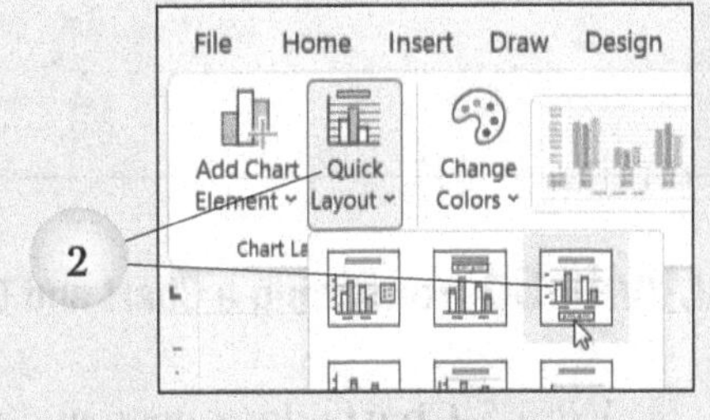

1. With **5-Charts.docx** open, make sure the chart is selected and the Chart Design tab is active.
2. Change to a different layout by clicking the Quick Layout button in the Chart Layouts group and then clicking the *Layout 3* option (third column, first row in the drop-down gallery).
3. Click the *Style 7* chart style in the Chart Styles group (seventh option from the left).
4. Click the Add Chart Element button in the Chart Layouts group, point to *Chart Title* at the drop-down list, and then click *Centered Overlay* at the side menu.

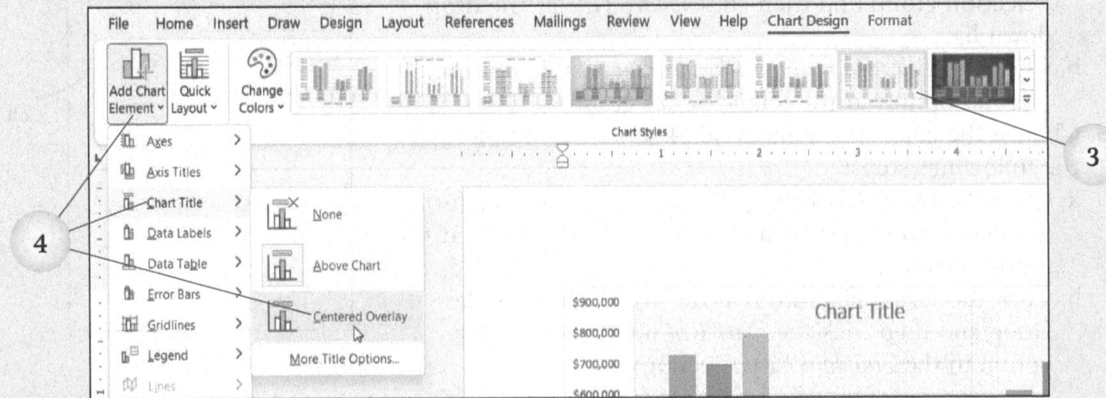

5. Type Regional Sales as the chart title.
6. Click the chart border to deselect the chart title.
7. Edit the data by completing the following steps:
   a. Click the Edit Data button in the Data group.
   b. Click in cell C3 in the worksheet.
   c. Type 375250. (Typing this text replaces the original amount, *$278,250*.)
   d. Click the Close button in the upper right corner of the worksheet.
8. Save **5-Charts.docx**.

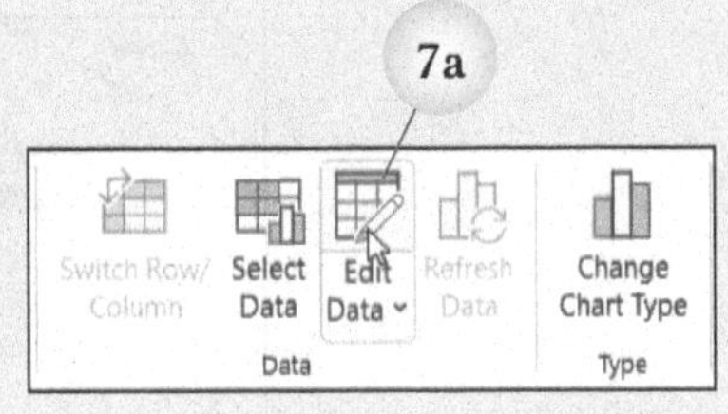

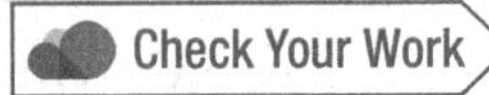

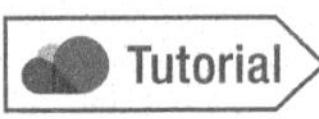

Changing Chart Formatting

Changing Chart Formatting

Use options and buttons on the Chart Format tab, shown in Figure 5.12, to format and customize a chart and chart elements. To format or modify a specific element in a chart, select the element. Do this by clicking the element or by clicking the *Chart Elements* option box in the Current Selection group and then clicking the element at the drop-down list. Use other options on the Chart Format tab to apply a shape style and WordArt style and to arrange and size the chart or chart element.

Figure 5.12 Chart Format tab

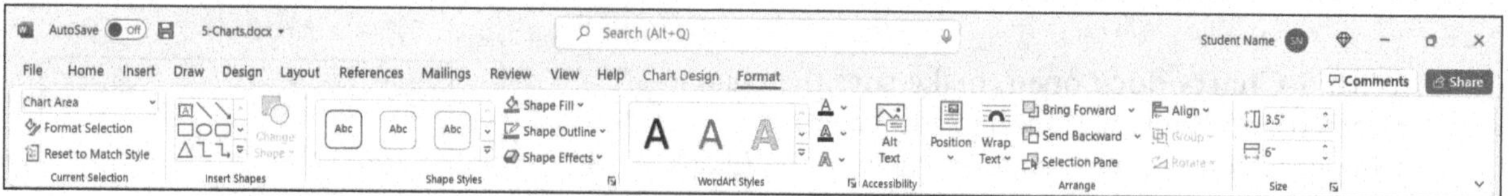

Activity 5d Formatting a Chart and Chart Elements

Part 4 of 5

1. With **5-Charts.docx** open and the chart selected, click the Chart Format tab.
2. Apply a shape style to the chart title by completing the following steps:
   a. Click the *Chart Elements* option box arrow in the Current Selection group and then click *Chart Title* at the drop-down list.
   b. Click the *Colored Outline - Blue, Accent 1* style option (second option in the Shape Styles group).
3. Change the color of the Sales 2024 series by completing the followings steps:
   a. Click the *Chart Elements* option box arrow in the Current Selection group and then click *Series "Sales 2024"* at the drop-down list.
   b. Click the Shape Fill button arrow in the Shape Styles group and then click the *Dark Red* option (first color option in the *Standard Colors* section).

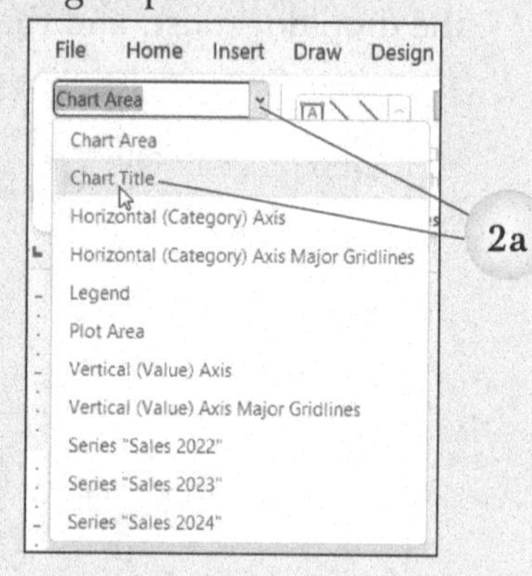

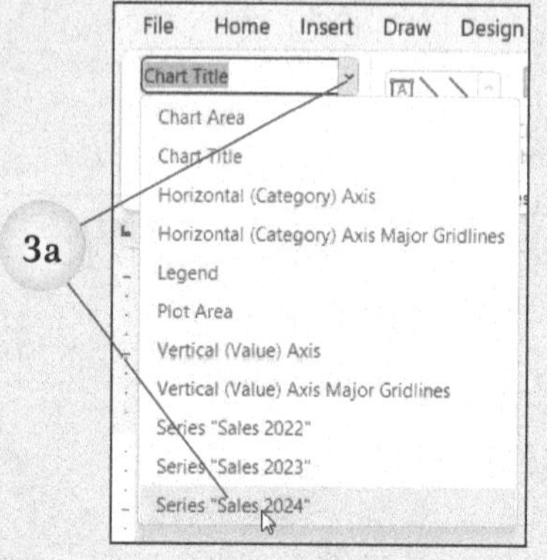

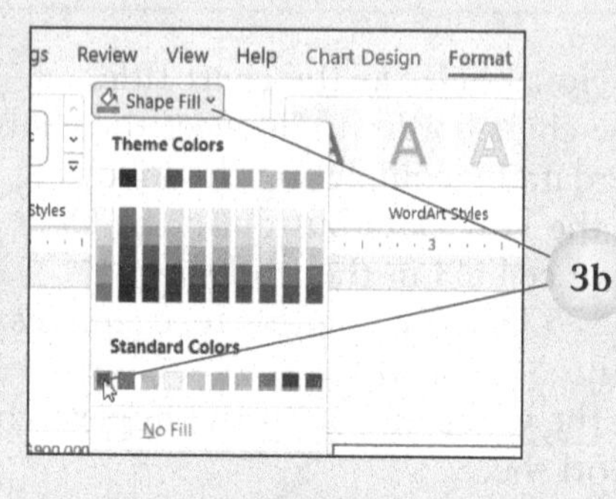

4. Apply a WordArt style to all the text in the chart by completing the following steps:
   a. Click the *Chart Elements* option box arrow.
   b. Click *Chart Area* at the drop-down list.
   c. Click the first WordArt style in the WordArt Styles group (black fill, shadow).

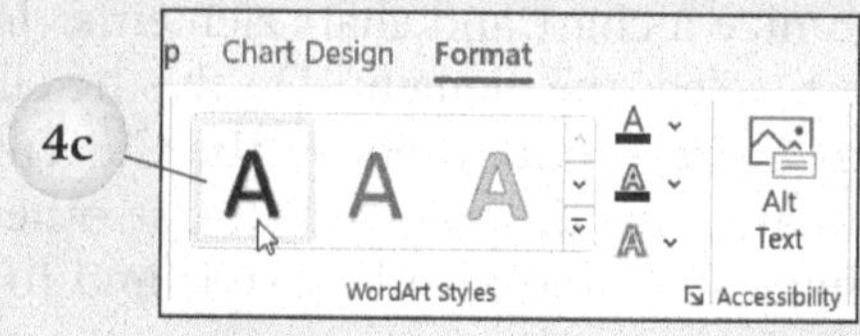

5. Change the size of the chart by completing the following steps:
   a. Click in the *Shape Height* measurement box and then type 3.
   b. Click in the *Shape Width* measurement box, type 5.5, and then press the Enter key.
6. With the chart selected (not a chart element), change its position by clicking the Position button in the Arrange group and then clicking the *Position in Top Center with Square Text Wrapping* option (second column, first row in the *With Text Wrapping* section).
7. Save and then preview **5-Charts.docx**.

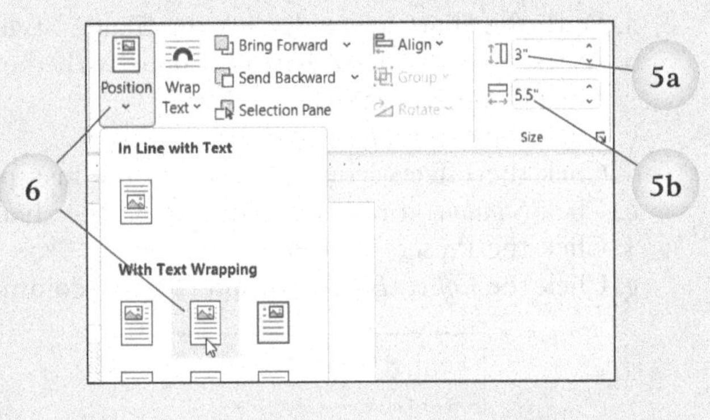

Formatting a Chart with Task Pane Options

Additional formatting options are available at various task panes. Display a task pane by clicking the Format Selection button in the Current Selection group on the Chart Format tab or a group task pane launcher. The Shape Styles and WordArt Styles groups on the Chart Format tab contain task pane launchers. Which task pane opens at the right side of the screen depends on which chart or chart element is selected.

Activity 5e Creating and Formatting a Pie Chart — Part 5 of 5

1. With **5-Charts.docx** open, press Ctrl + End (which deselects the chart) and then press the Enter key 12 times to move the insertion point below the chart.
2. Click the Insert tab and then click the Chart button in the Illustrations group.
3. At the Insert Chart dialog box, click *Pie* in the left panel and then click OK.
4. Type the data in the worksheet cells, including the percentage symbols as shown in Figure 5.13 (on page 193). After typing the last entry, click in cell A1.
5. Click the Close button in the upper right corner of the worksheet.
6. Click in the title *Percentage* and then type Investments.
7. Add data labels to the pie chart by completing the following steps:
   a. Click the Add Chart Element button in the Chart Layouts group on the Chart Design tab.
   b. Point to *Data Labels* at the drop-down list and then click *Inside End* at the side menu.
8. Click on the chart border to select the chart (not a chart element).
9. Click the Chart Format tab.

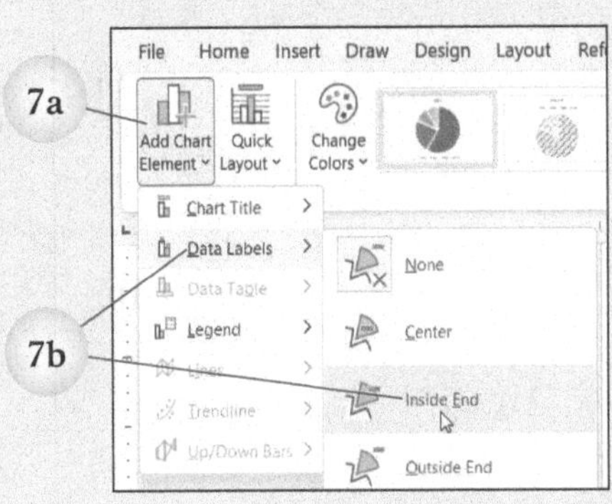

10. Apply formatting to the chart with options at the Format Chart Area task pane by completing the following steps:
    a. With the chart selected, click the Shape Styles group task pane launcher.
    b. At the Format Chart Area task pane with the Fill & Line icon selected, click *Fill* to expand the fill options.
    c. Click the *Gradient fill* option.
    d. Click the Effects icon at the top of the task pane.
    e. Click *Shadow*, if necessary, to expand the shadow options.
    f. Click the Presets button.
    g. Click the *Offset: Bottom* option (second column, first row in the *Outer* section).

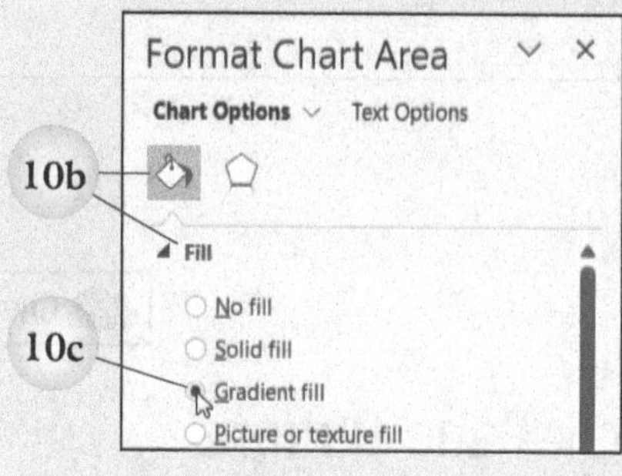

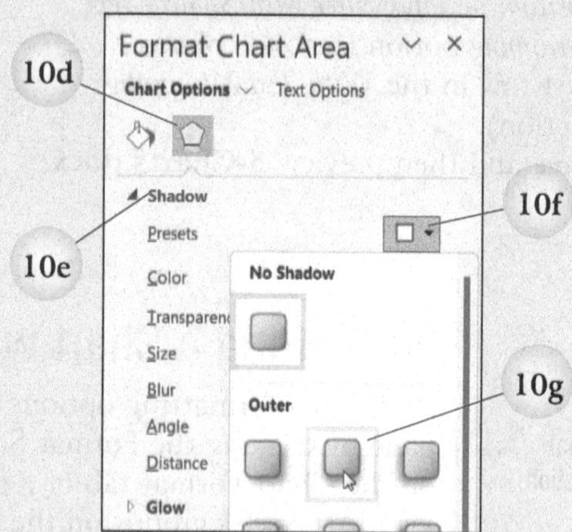

    h. Click the Text Options tab at the top of the task pane.
    i. Click *Text Outline*, if necessary, to expand the options.
    j. Click the *Solid line* option.
    k. Click the Color button and then click the *Blue, Accent 1, Darker 50%* option (fifth column, bottom row in the *Theme Colors* section).

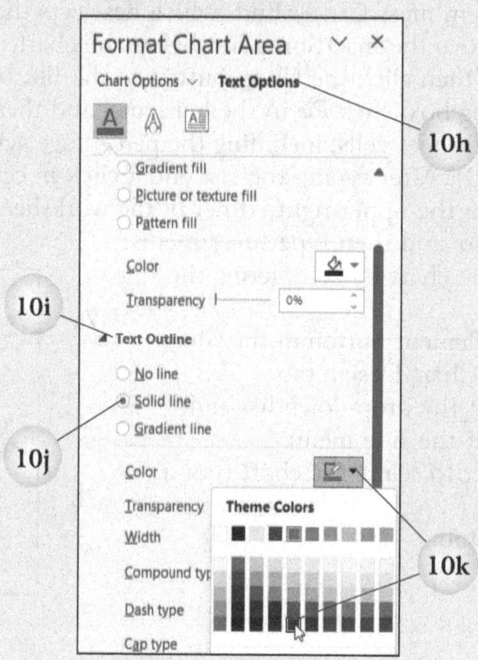

11. Format the pie chart by completing the following steps:
    a. Click in a blank area in any piece of the pie. (This selects all the pieces of the pie. Notice that the name of the task pane has changed to *Format Data Series*.)
    b. Click the Effects icon at the top of the task pane.
    c. Click *3-D Format* to expand the options.
    d. Click the Top bevel button and then click the *Soft Round* option at the drop-down gallery (second column, second row in the *Bevel* section).
    e. Close the task pane by clicking the Close button in the upper right corner.
12. Click the chart border to select the chart (not a chart element).
13. Change the size of the chart by completing the following steps:
    a. Click in the *Shape Height* measurement box and then type 3.
    b. Click in the *Shape Width* measurement box, type 5.5, and then press the Enter key.
14. Change the position of the chart by clicking the Position button in the Arrange group and then clicking the *Position in Bottom Center with Square Text Wrapping* option (second column, third row in the *With Text Wrapping* section).
15. Save, preview, and then close **5-Charts.docx**.

Check Your Work

Figure 5.13 Activity 5e

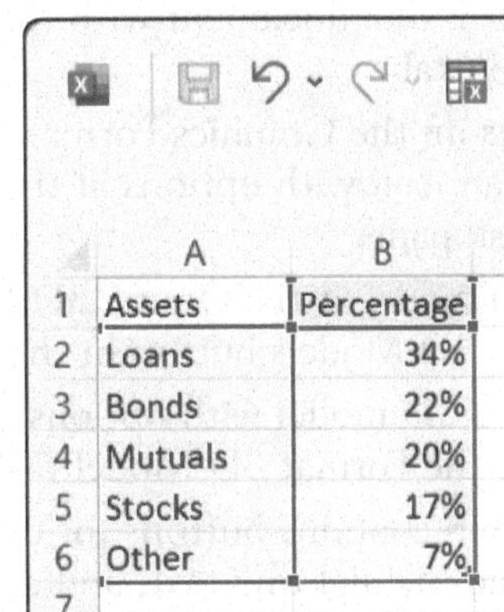

	A	B
1	Assets	Percentage
2	Loans	34%
3	Bonds	22%
4	Mutuals	20%
5	Stocks	17%
6	Other	7%
7		

Chapter Summary

- Customize the layout of images with options at the Layout dialog box. Display this dialog box by clicking the Size group dialog box launcher on the Picture Format tab.
- The Layout dialog box contains three tabs. Click the Position tab to specify the position of the image in the document, click the Text Wrapping tab to specify a wrapping style for the image, and click the Size tab to display options for specifying the height and width of the image.
- Format an image with options at the Format Picture task pane. Display this task pane by clicking the Picture Styles group task pane launcher on the Picture Format tab.
- Apply artistic effects to a selected image with the Artistic Effects button in the Adjust group on the Picture Format tab or with options at the Format Picture task pane with the Effects icon selected.
- Customize colors with options at the Colors dialog box with the Custom tab selected.
- Use the small yellow circles that display around certain selected shapes to change the width and height of a specific element in a shape.
- Use edit points to customize specific elements in a selected shape. Display edit points around a shape by clicking the Edit Shape button in the Insert Shapes group on the Shape Format tab and then clicking *Edit Points*.
- Display wrap points in a selected shape by clicking the Wrap Text button in the Arrange group on the Picture Format tab or the Shape Format tab and then clicking *Edit Wrap Points*. Use wrap points to wrap text closer to or father away from an object.
- Link text boxes with the Create Link button in the Text group on the Shape Format tab. Break a link with the Break Link button in the Text group.
- Insert an icon in a document with the Icons button in the Illustrations group on the Insert tab.
- Use options on the Graphics Format tab to customize an icon. Further customize an icon with options at the Layout dialog box and the Format Graphic task pane.
- Insert a 3D model at the Online 3D Models window. Display the window by clicking the 3D Models button in the Illustrations group on the Insert tab.
- Customize a 3D model with options on the 3D Model tab, at the Layout dialog box, and at the Format 3D Model task pane.
- The Draw tab contains buttons for drawing in a document, converting shapes, selecting and highlighting text, and editing text.
- The Drawing Tools group on the Draw tab contains buttons for selecting and erasing ink drawings and pens for drawing in a document and highlighting and editing text in a document.
- Click a pen button on the Draw tab to activate the pen and then click the button again to display a drop-down list with options for changing the size, thickness, and color of the pen.
- Use the Highlighter pen on the Draw tab to highlight text in a document. Click the Highlighter button to activate it and then click the button again to display a drop-down list with option for changing the size, thickness, and highlighting color as well as a feature to snap the highlighting to text.

- Use the Select button on the Draw tab to select an ink drawing and use the Lasso button to select multiple ink drawings. Use the Eraser pen to erase an ink drawing.
- Replay ink drawings in a document with the Ink Replay button in the Replay group on the Draw tab.
- Convert an ink drawing to a shape by activating a pen, clicking the Ink to Shape button, and then drawing in the document. The shape converts to the shape most similar to the ink drawing.
- Format an ink drawing or an ink drawing converted to a shape with options on the Shape Format tab.
- Edit text in a document with the Action Pen on the Draw tab. Click the Action pen button to activate it, click the button again to display the drop-down list, and then click *Ink Gesture Help* to display the Help task pane with information about editing gestures
- To present data visually, create a chart with the Chart button in the Illustrations group on the Insert tab. Choose a chart type at the Insert Chart dialog box and then enter chart data in a worksheet.
- Four buttons display at the right of a selected chart. Use the Layout Options button to apply text wrapping, the Chart Elements button to add or remove chart elements, the Chart Styles button to apply a predesigned chart style, and the Chart Filters button to isolate specific data in the chart.
- Modify a chart design with options and buttons on the Chart Design tab.
- The cells in a worksheet used to create a chart are linked to the chart in the document. To edit the chart data, click the Edit Data button in the Data group on the Chart Design tab and then make changes to the data in the worksheet.
- Customize the format of a chart and chart elements with options and buttons on the Chart Format tab. Select the chart or a specific chart element and then apply a style to a shape, apply a WordArt style to the text, and arrange and size the chart.
- Apply formatting to a chart with options in task panes. Display a task pane by clicking the Format Selection button in the Current Selection group on the Chart Format tab or a group task pane launcher. The options in the task pane vary depending on the chart or chart element selected.

Commands Review

FEATURE	RIBBON TAB, GROUP/OPTION	BUTTON, OPTION
edit points	Shape Format, Insert Shapes	, *Edit Points*
Format 3D Model task pane	3D Model, 3D Model Views	
Format Graphic task pane	Graphics Format, Graphics Styles	
Format Picture task pane	Picture Format, Picture Styles	
Format Shape task pane	Shape Format, Shape Styles	
group objects	Picture Format, Arrange OR Shape Format, Arrange	, *Group*
Icons window	Insert, Illustrations	
Insert Chart dialog box	Insert, Illustrations	
Layout dialog box	3D Model, Size OR Shape Format, Size OR Graphics Format, Size OR Picture Format, Size	
link text boxes	Shape Format, Text	
Online 3D Models window	Insert, Illustrations	
text box	Insert, Text	, *Draw Text Box*
ungroup objects	Picture Format, Arrange OR Shape Format, Arrange	, *Ungroup*
unlink text boxes	Shape Format, Text	
wrap points	Picture Format, Arrange OR Shape Format, Arrange	, *Edit Wrap Points*

Review and Assessment

CHAPTER 5

Skills Assessment

Assessment 1 Insert and Customize an Image and Text Box in a Timeline Document

1. Open **Au-Timeline.docx** and then save it with the name **5-Au-Timeline**.
2. Move the insertion point to the text that begins *1985*.
3. Display the Insert Picture dialog box, navigate to your WL2C5 folder, and then double-click the ***Uluru.png*** image file.
4. Customize the image so it appears as shown in Figure 5.14 by completing the following steps:
   a. Change the width of the image to 3 inches.
   b. Change the text wrapping to Square.
   c. Display the Layout dialog box with the Position tab selected.
   d. Precisely position the image on the page with an absolute horizontal measurement of 4.5 inches to the right of the left margin and an absolute vertical measurement of 5 inches below the page.
   e. Display the Format Picture task pane with the Effects icon active.
   f. Click *Shadow* to expand the shadow options.
   g. Apply the Offset: Top Left shadow effect (last option in the *Outer* section).
   h. Change the shadow color to Dark Blue (ninth option in the *Standard Colors* section). (Do this with the Color button in the *Shadow* section of the Format Picture task pane.)
   i. Click *Artistic Effects* to expand the options and then apply the Paint Brush artistic effect (third column, second row in the drop-down gallery). (Do this with the Artistic Effects button in the *Artistic Effects* section of the task pane.)
   j. Close the Format Picture task pane.
5. Insert the years *1908* and *1967* in text boxes as shown in Figure 5.14 with the following specifications:
   a. Insert a text box above the arrow line.
   b. Change the font size to 9 points, turn on bold formatting, and then type 1908 in the text box.
   c. Use the Text Direction button to rotate the text in the text box 270 degrees.
   d. Remove the outline from the text box. (Do this with the Shape Outline button in the Shape Styles group.)
   e. Change the text wrapping to Behind Text.
   f. Drag the text box so it is positioned as shown in Figure 5.14.
   g. Complete similar steps to create the text box with the year *1967* and position the text box as shown in the figure.
6. Save, preview, and then close **5-Au-Timeline.docx**.

Figure 5.14 Assessment 1

Australian History: 1900–2000 Timeline

1908: Female citizens in all Australian states gain the right to vote

1914–1918: World War I, over 330,000 Australians serve during the war

1917: Trans-Australian railway opens

1927: Federal parliament moves from Melbourne to Canberra

1939–1945: World War II, over 1,000,000 Australians serve during the war

1956: Olympic Games held in Melbourne

1960: Australia grants citizenship to Aboriginal people

1962: Aboriginal people gain the right to vote in federal elections

1967: Aboriginal people gain the right to vote in all Australian states

1972: "White Australia" immigration policy abandoned

1973: Sydney Opera House completed

1985: Uluru (Ayers Rock) and Kata Tjuta (The Olgas) returned to Aboriginal people

1993: Aboriginal lands recognized by government

1999: Referendum rejects prototype republic

2000: Olympic Games held in Sydney

Voting Rights Timeline

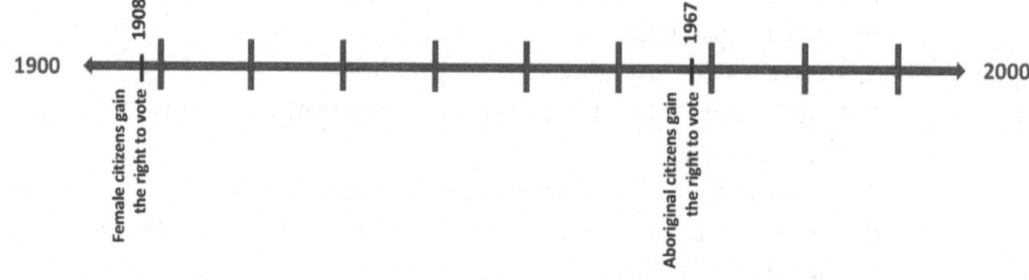

Assessment 2

Format a Shape and Edit Points and Wrap Points

1. Open **CedarMeadows.docx** and then save it with the name **5-CedarMeadows**.
2. Select the shape in the document, display the Format Shape task pane (click the Shape Styles group task pane launcher on the Shape Format tab), and then apply the following formatting:
   a. Apply the Bottom Spotlight - Accent 5 gradient fill (fifth column, fourth row).
   b. Apply the Inside: Bottom shadow effect (second column, third row in the *Inner* section).
   c. Close the Format Shape task pane.
3. Display editing points around the shape and then adjust the points so the shape displays in a manner similar to what is shown in Figure 5.15. (Click outside the shape after adjusting the editing points.)
4. Select the shape, display the wrap points, and then adjust the wrap points so text wraps around the shape in a manner similar to what is shown in Figure 5.15. (Click outside the shape after adjusting the wrap points.)
5. Save, preview, and then close **5-CedarMeadows.docx**.

Figure 5.15 Assessment 2

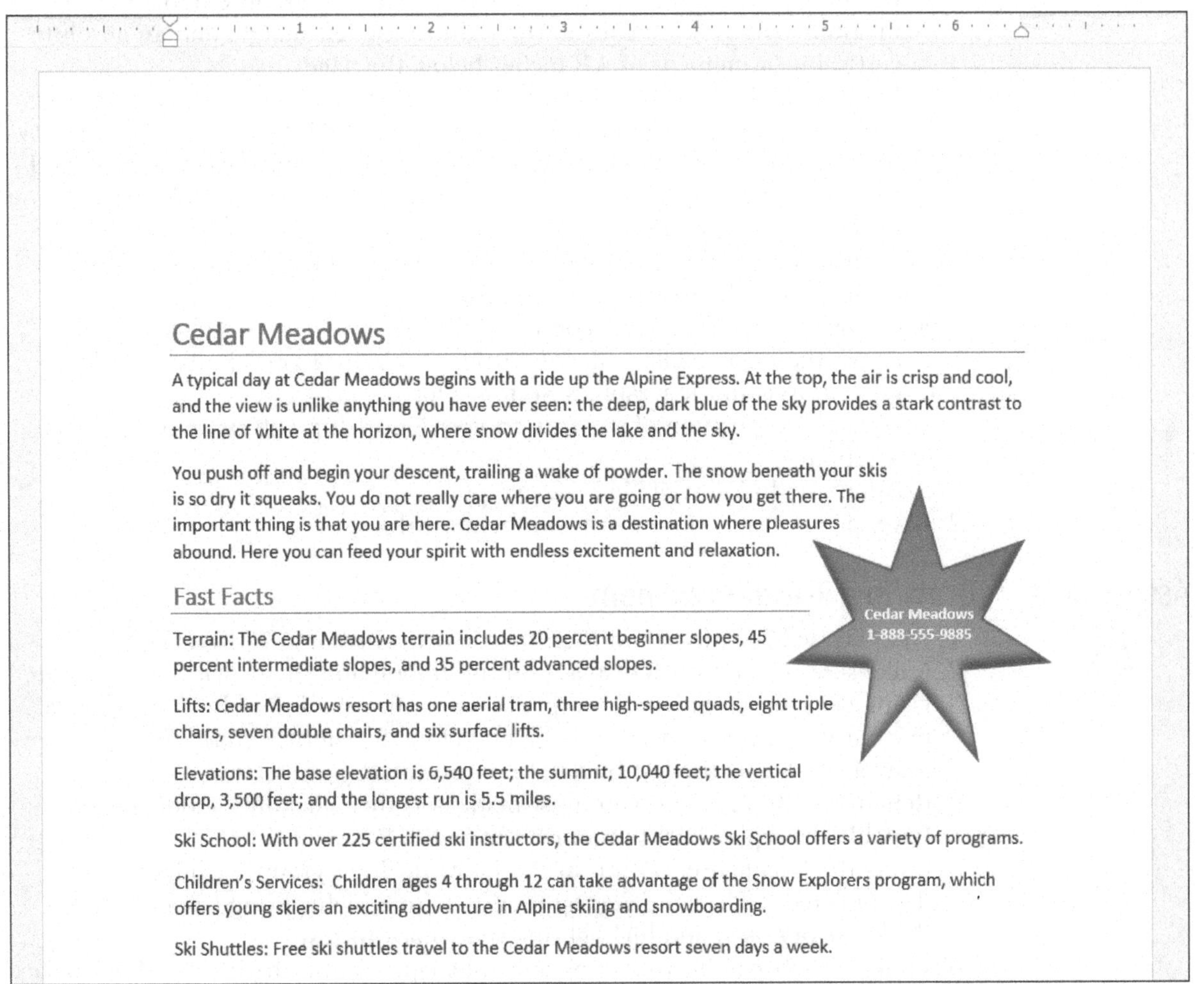

Cedar Meadows

A typical day at Cedar Meadows begins with a ride up the Alpine Express. At the top, the air is crisp and cool, and the view is unlike anything you have ever seen: the deep, dark blue of the sky provides a stark contrast to the line of white at the horizon, where snow divides the lake and the sky.

You push off and begin your descent, trailing a wake of powder. The snow beneath your skis is so dry it squeaks. You do not really care where you are going or how you get there. The important thing is that you are here. Cedar Meadows is a destination where pleasures abound. Here you can feed your spirit with endless excitement and relaxation.

Cedar Meadows
1-888-555-9885

Fast Facts

Terrain: The Cedar Meadows terrain includes 20 percent beginner slopes, 45 percent intermediate slopes, and 35 percent advanced slopes.

Lifts: Cedar Meadows resort has one aerial tram, three high-speed quads, eight triple chairs, seven double chairs, and six surface lifts.

Elevations: The base elevation is 6,540 feet; the summit, 10,040 feet; the vertical drop, 3,500 feet; and the longest run is 5.5 miles.

Ski School: With over 225 certified ski instructors, the Cedar Meadows Ski School offers a variety of programs.

Children's Services: Children ages 4 through 12 can take advantage of the Snow Explorers program, which offers young skiers an exciting adventure in Alpine skiing and snowboarding.

Ski Shuttles: Free ski shuttles travel to the Cedar Meadows resort seven days a week.

Assessment 3

Link Text Boxes

1. Open **ProtectIssues.docx** and then save it with the name **5-ProtectIssues.**
2. Select the text box at the left and link it to the text box at the right.
3. With the insertion point positioned in the text box at the left, insert the file named **ProIssues.docx**. ***Hint: Click the Insert tab, click the Object button arrow, and then click the*** **Text from File** ***option.***
4. Adjust the columns so all the text fits in the two columns by changing the height of both text boxes to 8.4 inches and the width of both to 3.1 inches.
5. Save, preview, and then close **5-ProtectIssues.docx**.

Assessment 4

Customize a 3D Model

1. Open **Announcement.docx** and then save it with the name **5-Announcement**.
2. Select the 3D model (a red square with a cross) and then apply the following formatting:
   a. Apply the Above Front Right 3D model view. (You will need to click the More 3D Model Views button in the 3D Model Views group to display additional views. The Above Front Right view is in the fifth column, second row.)
   b. Change the height of the model to 2.7 inches.
   c. Apply Tight text wrapping.
   d. Precisely position the model on the page with an absolute horizontal measurement of 4.7 inches to the right of the left margin and an absolute vertical measurement of 4.8 inches below the page.
   e. Display the Format 3D Model task pane and then apply the Perspective: Upper Right shadow effect. (To do this, click the Effects icon, click *Shadow* to expand the options, click the Presets button in the *Shadow* section, and then click the *Perspective: Upper Right* option, in the second column, first row in the *Perspective* section.)
3. Select the icon in the upper left corner of the document (a cross in a circle) and then apply the following formatting:
   a. Change the height of the icon to 1.7 inches.
   b. Apply the Light 1 Fill, Colored Outline - Accent 4 graphic style (fifth graphic style in the Graphics Styles gallery).
   c. Change the position of the icon to Position in Top Left with Square Text Wrapping.
   d. Apply the In Front of Text text wrapping.
4. Save, preview, and close **5-Announcement.docx**.

Assessment 5

Draw in a Travel Document

1. Open **TravelTips.docx** and then save it with the name **5-TravelTips**.
2. Make sure the Draw tab displays on the ribbon and then click the Draw tab.
3. Using the left pen button (first pen button after the Eraser button), draw a line with a thickness of *1 mm* in green below the subtitle *Travel Tips* and then draw a line below the last bulleted item in the *Baggage* section.
4. Replay the ink drawings you must made and then click in the document (outside the replay bar) to remove the bar.
5. Using the Highlighter button in the Drawing Tools group, highlight the first bulleted item in the *Baggage* section with a highlighting color of blue, a thickness of *6 mm*, and highlighting that snaps to text.
6. Using the left pen button, draw an oval shape around the last two lines of text that converts to a precise oval shape.

7. Erase the drawn line below the subtitle, *Travel Tips*.
8. Click the Select button in the Drawing Tools group and then make the Home tab active.
9. Save, preview, and then close **5-TravelTips.docx**.

Assessment 6

Create and Format a Column Chart and a Pie Chart

1. At a blank document, use the data in Figure 5.16 to create a column chart (using the default chart style at the Insert Chart dialog box) with the following specifications:
   a. Use the Chart Elements button outside the upper right border of the chart to add a data table and remove the legend.
   b. Apply the Style 4 chart style.
   c. Change the chart title to *Units Sold First Quarter*.
   d. Apply the first WordArt style to the chart area.
   e. Change the chart height to 4 inches.
   f. Change the position of the chart to Position in Top Center with Square Text Wrapping.
2. Move the insertion point to the end of the document, press the Enter key two times, and then create a pie chart (using the default pie chart style at the Insert Chart dialog box) with the data shown in Figure 5.17 and with the following specifications:
   a. Apply the Style 3 chart style.
   b. Move the data labels to the inside end of the pie pieces. ***Hint: Click the Chart Elements button that displays outside the upper right corner of the chart, click the arrow at the right of*** **Data Labels**, ***and then click*** **Inside End**.
   c. Change the chart title to *Expense Distribution*.

Figure 5.16 Assessment 6, Step 1, Data for Column Chart

Salesperson	January	February	March
Barnett	55	60	42
Carson	20	24	31
Fanning	15	30	13
Han	52	62	58
Mahoney	49	52	39

Figure 5.17 Assessment 6, Step 2, Data for Pie Chart

Category	Percentage
Salaries	67%
Travel	15%
Equipment	11%
Supplies	7%

d. Apply the Colored Outline - Orange, Accent 2 shape style to the title (third shape style).
e. Change the chart height to 3 inches and the width to 5.5 inches.
f. Change the position of the chart to Position in Bottom Center with Square Text Wrapping.

3. Save the document with the name **5-ColumnPieCharts**.
4. Preview and then close **5-ColumnPieCharts.docx**.

Assessment 7 — Insert a Horizontal Line in a Footer

1. Open a blank document and then insert a horizontal line by clicking the Borders button arrow in the Paragraph group on the Home tab and then clicking *Horizontal Line* at the drop-down list. Click the horizontal line to select it and then right-click the line. Click *Picture* at the shortcut menu and the Format Horizontal Line dialog box displays. Look at the formatting options that are available at the dialog box and then click the Cancel button to close the dialog box. Close the document without saving it.
2. Open **KECharityEvents.docx** and then save it with the name **5-KECharityEvents**.
3. Keep the Step 6 text at the bottom of the first page together with the paragraph that follows it.
4. Create a footer that contains a horizontal line in the standard green color (sixth color option in the *Standard Colors* section) with a height of 3 points.
5. Save, preview, and then close **5-KECharityEvents.docx**.

Visual Benchmark

Create a Company Chart

1. Open **Blueline.docx** and then save it with the name **5-Blueline**.
2. Select the gears icon and then customize the icon so it appears as shown in Figure 5.18 with the following specifications:
   - Flip the gears icon horizontally.
   - Apply the Colored Fill - Accent 1, Dark 1 Outline graphic style (second column, third row in the Graphics Styles group gallery).
   - Apply text wrapping that moves the icon behind text.
   - Size and move the gears icon so it is positioned as shown in Figure 5.18.
3. Create the column chart shown in Figure 5.18 with the following specifications:
   - Choose the 3-D Clustered Column Chart at the Insert Chart dialog box.
   - Use the information shown in the chart in the figure to create the data for the chart. (You will need to decrease the size of the data range by one column.)
   - Add a data table to the chart.
   - Change the color of the 2024 series to Dark Blue.
   - Make any other changes so your chart appears similar to the chart in the figure.
4. Save, preview, and then close **5-Blueline.docx**.

Figure 5.18 Visual Benchmark

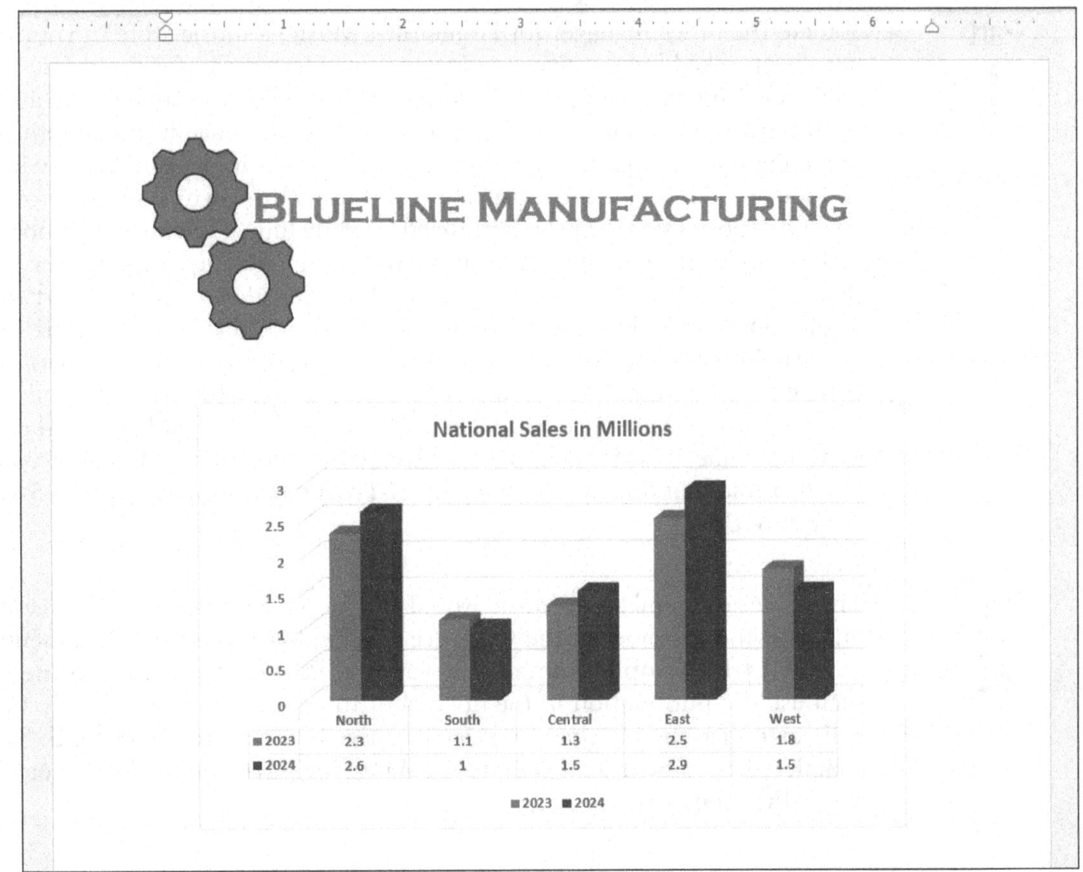

Case Study

Part 1

You are the office manager for Hometown Music, a music store in your town. You have been asked by the owner to create a new letterhead for the music store. Open a blank document, create a custom first page header, and then create a letterhead for the store in the First Page Header pane. Use an image in the letterhead. Some possible images are available in your WL2C5 folder and begin with *Music*. Include an address for the music store and use your town, state (or province), and zip code (postal code) in the letterhead; also include a telephone number. (The address and telephone number can be inserted in the First Page Footer pane rather than the First Page Header pane.) In the First Page Footer pane, insert three icons in the footer, including the eye icon (use the search text *eye*), the heart icon (use the search text *heart*), and the music note icon (use the search text *music note*). (These icons represent the saying "I love music.") Customize, size, and position the icons in the First Page Footer pane. Save the completed letterhead document with the name **5-HMLtrhd**. Save **5-HMLtrhd.docx** as a template in your WL2C5 folder and name the template **5-HMLtrhd-Template**. Close **5-HMLtrhd-Template.dotx**.

Part 2

The owner of Hometown Music would like to have a chart of the percentage breakdown of income for the year. Use File Explorer to open a document based on the **HMLtrhd-Template.dotx** you created in Part 1. Open **HMIncome.docx** and then use the information in the document to create a pie chart. Apply formatting and customize the pie chart so it is attractive and easy to understand. Save the completed document with the name **5-HMPieChart**. Preview and then close **5-HMPieChart.docx**.

Part 3

You have created an invitation for an upcoming piano recital at Hometown Music. You inserted a 3D model in the invitation and need to customize it so it has more visual impact. Open **HMPianoRecital.docx** and then save it with the name **5-HMPianoRecital**. Select the grand piano 3D model, rotate the image so that the keyboard is facing to the right, increase the size, apply a text wrapping option, and move the piano image into the lower left corner of the invitation. Save, preview, and then close **5-HMPianoRecital.docx**.

Part 4

The owner would like to have a flyer describing Hometown Music's instrument rental program that can be distributed at recitals and at local schools. Open **HMRentals.docx**, look at the information, and then create a flyer that includes some of the information in the document. Include visual interest in the flyer by inserting a photograph, picture, icon, and/or 3D model. Format the flyer so it appears similar to other Hometown Music documents you have created. Save the completed flyer with the name **5-HMRentalFlyer**. Preview and then close **5-HMRentalFlyer.docx**.

WORD

CHAPTER 6

Merging Documents

Performance Objectives

Upon successful completion of Chapter 6, you will be able to:

1. Create a data source file
2. Create a main document and merge it with a data source file
3. Preview a merge and check for errors before merging documents
4. Create an envelope, a label, and a directory main document and then merge it with a data source file
5. Edit a data source file
6. Select specific records for merging
7. Use the Mail Merge wizard to merge a letter main document with a data source file

---

Word includes a Mail Merge feature for creating customized letters, envelopes, labels, directories, and email messages. The Mail Merge feature is useful when the same letter is to be sent to a number of people and an envelope needs to be created for each letter. Use Mail Merge to create a main document that contains a letter, an envelope, or other data and then merge it with a data source file. In this chapter, you will use Mail Merge to create letters, envelopes, labels, and directories.

Data Files

The data files for this chapter are in the WL2C6 folder that you downloaded at the beginning of this course.

Activity 1 Merge Letters to Customers 3 Parts

You will create a data source file and a letter document and then merge the main document with the records in the data source file.

Completing a Merge

Start Mail Merge

Select Recipients

Use Word's mail merge feature to create multiple documents—such as letters, envelopes, and directories—with fixed or standard text along with variable text (text that changes with each document). Use buttons and options on the Mailings tab to complete a merge. A merge generally takes two files: the data source file and the main document. The main document contains the standard text along with fields identifying where variable information is inserted during the merge. The data source file contains the variable information that will be inserted in the main document.

Use the Start Mail Merge button in the Start Mail Merge group on the Mailings tab to identify the type of main document to be created and use the Select Recipients button to create a data source file or specify an existing data source file. The Mail Merge wizard is also available to provide guidance on the merge process.

Tutorial

Creating a Data Source File

Quick Steps

Create Data Source File

1. Click Mailings tab.
2. Click Select Recipients button.
3. Click *Type a New List* at drop-down list.
4. Type data in predesigned or custom fields.
5. Click OK.

Creating a Data Source File

Before creating a data source file, determine what type of correspondence will be created and what type of information is needed to insert in the correspondence. Word provides predesigned field names when creating the data source file. Use these field names if they represent the specific data. Variable information in a data source file is saved as a record. A record contains all the information for one unit (for example, a person, family, customer, client, or business). A series of fields makes one record and a series of records makes a data source file.

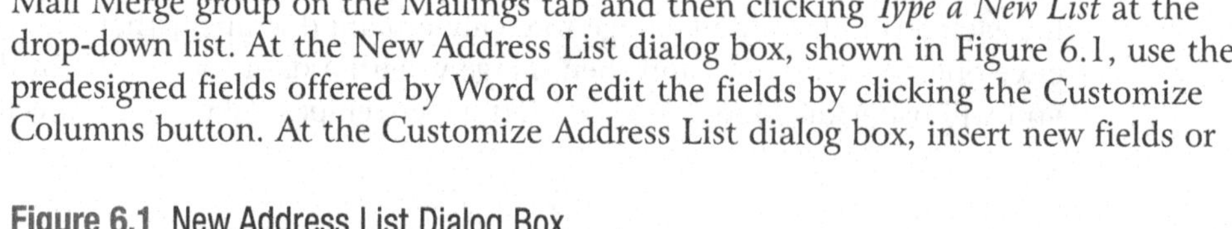

Create a data source file by clicking the Select Recipients button in the Start Mail Merge group on the Mailings tab and then clicking *Type a New List* at the drop-down list. At the New Address List dialog box, shown in Figure 6.1, use the predesigned fields offered by Word or edit the fields by clicking the Customize Columns button. At the Customize Address List dialog box, insert new fields or

Figure 6.1 New Address List Dialog Box

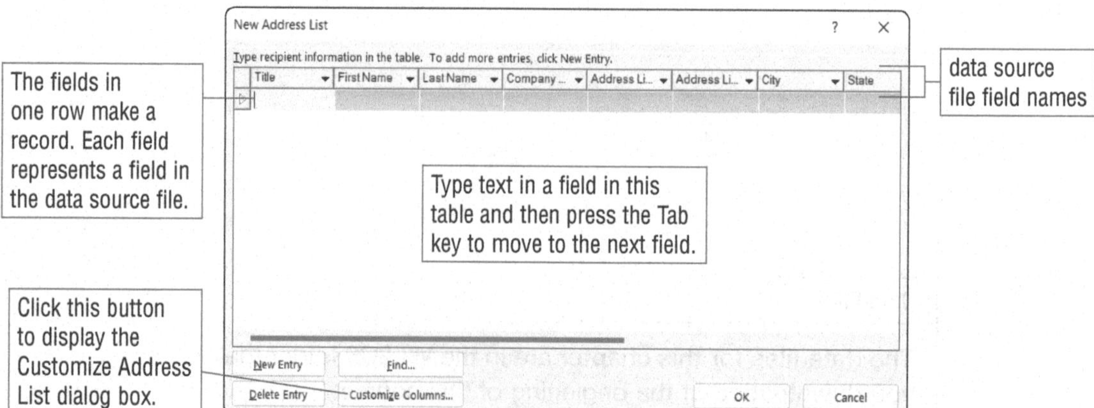

New Address List
Type recipient information in the table. To add more entries, click New Entry.
Title
First Name
Last Name
Company ...
Address Li...
Address Li...
City
State
New Entry
Find...
Delete Entry
Customize Columns...
OK
Cancel
The fields in one row make a record. Each field represents a field in the data source file.
data source file field names
Type text in a field in this table and then press the Tab key to move to the next field.
Click this button to display the Customize Address List dialog box.

delete existing fields and then click OK. With the fields established, type the required data. Note that fields in the main document correspond to the column headings in the data source file. When all the records have been entered, click OK. At the Save Address List dialog box, navigate to the desired folder, type a name for the data source file, and then click OK. Word saves a data source file as an Access database. Having Access on the computer is not required to complete a merge with a data source file.

Activity 1a Creating a Data Source File

Part 1 of 3

1. At a blank document, click the Mailings tab.
2. Click the Start Mail Merge button in the Start Mail Merge group and then click *Letters* at the drop-down list.
3. Click the Select Recipients button in the Start Mail Merge group and then click *Type a New List* at the drop-down list.

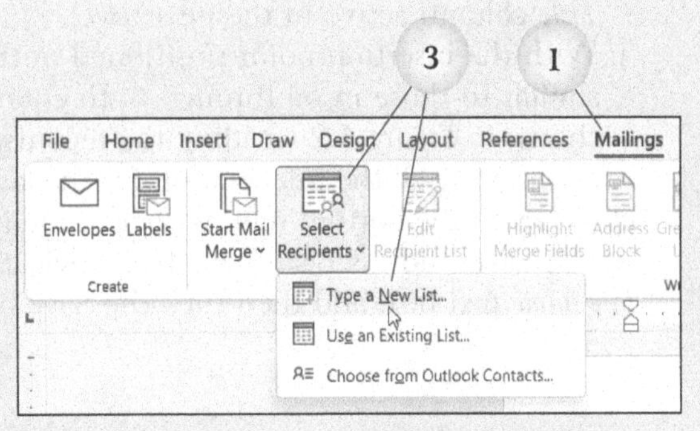

4. At the New Address List dialog box, Word provides a number of predesigned fields. Delete the fields you do not need by completing the following steps:
   a. Click the Customize Columns button.
   b. At the Customize Address List dialog box, click *Company Name* to select it and then click the Delete button.
   c. At the message that displays, click Yes.
   d. Complete steps similar to those in 4b and 4c to delete the following fields:
      Country or Region
      Home Phone
      Work Phone
      E-mail Address

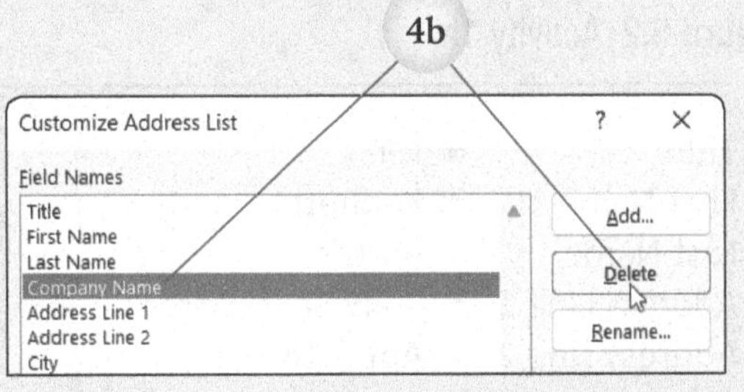

5. Insert a custom field by completing the following steps:
   a. With the *ZIP Code* field selected in the *Field Names* list box in the Customize Address List dialog box, click the Add button.
   b. At the Add Field dialog box, type Fund and then click OK.
   c. Click OK to close the Customize Address List dialog box.

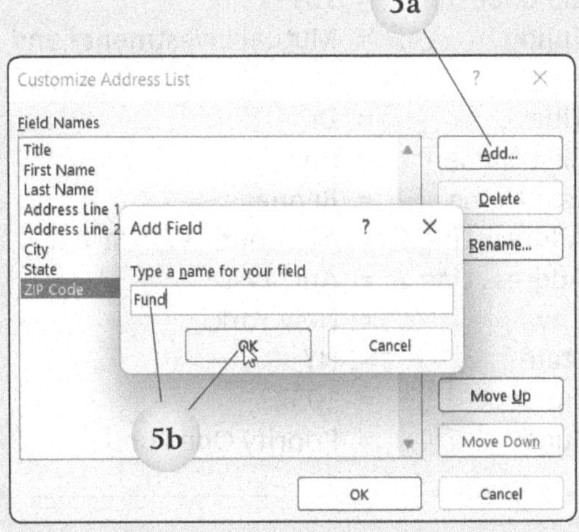

6. At the New Address List dialog box, enter the information for the first client shown in Figure 6.2 by completing the following steps:
   a. Type Mr. in the field in the *Title* column and then press the Tab key. (This moves the insertion point to the field in the *First Name* column. Pressing Shift + Tab will move the insertion point to the previous field. When typing text, do not press the spacebar after the last word in the field, and proofread all the entries to ensure the data is accurate.)
   b. Type Kenneth and then press the Tab key.
   c. Type Porter and then press the Tab key.

d. Type 7645 Tenth Street and then press the Tab key.

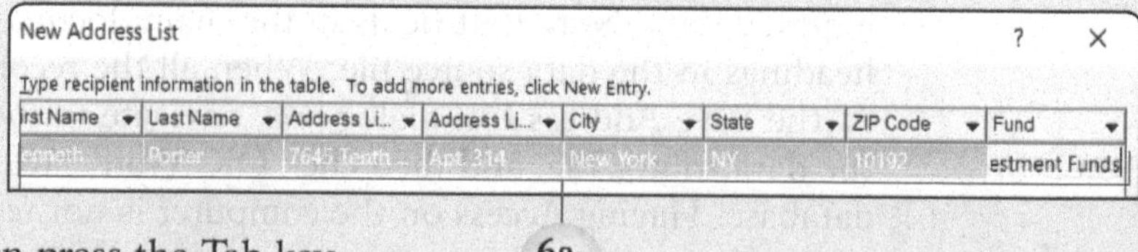

e. Type Apt. 314 and then press the Tab key.
f. Type New York and then press the Tab key.
g. Type NY and then press the Tab key.
h. Type 10192 and then press the Tab key.
i. Type Mutual Investment Fund and then press the Tab key. (This makes the field in the *Title* column active in the next row.)
j. With the insertion point positioned in the field in the *Title* column, complete steps similar to those in 6a through 6i to enter the information for the three other clients shown in Figure 6.2 (reading the records from left to right in each row).

7. After entering all the information for the last client in Figure 6.2 (Ms. Wanda Houston), click OK in the bottom right corner of the New Address List dialog box.
8. At the Save Address List dialog box, navigate to your WL2C6 folder, type 6-MFDS in the *File name* text box, and then click the Save button.

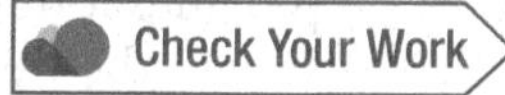

Figure 6.2 Activity 1a

Title	= Mr.	Title	= Ms.
First Name	= Kenneth	First Name	= Carolyn
Last Name	= Porter	Last Name	= Renquist
Address Line 1	= 7645 Tenth Street	Address Line 1	= 13255 Meridian Street
Address Line 2	= Apt. 314	Address Line 2	= (leave this blank)
City	= New York	City	= New York
State	= NY	State	= NY
Zip Code	= 10192	Zip Code	= 10435
Fund	= Mutual Investment Fund	Fund	= Quality Care Fund
Title	= Dr.	Title	= Ms.
First Name	= Amil	First Name	= Wanda
Last Name	= Ranna	Last Name	= Houston
Address Line 1	= 433 South 17th Street	Address Line 1	= 566 North 22nd Avenue
Address Line 2	= Apt. 17-D	Address Line 2	= (leave this blank)
City	= New York	City	= New York
State	= NY	State	= NY
Zip Code	= 10322	Zip Code	= 10634
Fund	= Priority One Fund	Fund	= Quality Care Fund

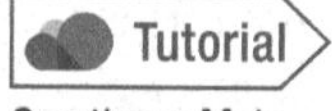

Creating a Main Document

Creating a Main Document

After creating and typing the records in the data source file, type the main document. Insert fields to identify where variable information will be added when the document is merged with the data source file. Use buttons in the Write & Insert Fields group to insert fields in the main document.

Quick Steps

Create Main Document

1. Click Mailings tab.
2. Click Start Mail Merge button.
3. Click document type at drop-down list.
4. Type main document text and insert fields as needed.

Address Block

Greeting Line

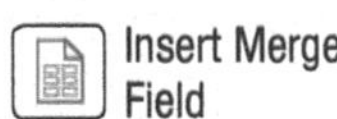
Insert Merge Field

Insert all the fields required for the inside address of a letter with the Address Block button in the Write & Insert Fields group. Click this button and the Insert Address Block dialog box displays with a preview of how the fields will be inserted in the document to create the inside address; the dialog box also contains buttons and options for customizing the fields. Click OK and the *«AddressBlock»* field is inserted in the document. The *«AddressBlock»* field is an example of a composite field, which groups a number of fields (such as *Title*, *First Name*, *Last Name*, *Address Line 1*, and so on).

Click the Greeting Line button and the Insert Greeting Line dialog box displays with options for customizing how the fields are inserted in the document to create the greeting line. Click OK at the dialog box and the *«GreetingLine»* composite field is inserted in the document.

To insert an individual field from the data source file, click the Insert Merge Field button. This displays the Insert Merge Field dialog box with a list of the fields from the data source file. Click the Insert Merge Field button arrow and a drop-down list displays containing the fields in the data source file.

A field or composite field is inserted in the main document surrounded by chevrons (« and »). The chevrons distinguish fields in the main document and do not display in the merged document. Formatting can be applied to merged data by formatting the merge field in the main document.

Activity 1b Creating a Main Document

Part 2 of 3

1. At the blank document, create the letter shown in Figure 6.3. Begin by clicking the *No Spacing* style in the styles gallery on the Home tab.
2. Press the Enter key six times and then type February 21, 2024.
3. Press the Enter key four times and then insert the *«AddressBlock»* composite field by completing the following steps:
   a. Click the Mailings tab and then click the Address Block button in the Write & Insert Fields group.
   b. At the Insert Address Block dialog box, click OK.
   c. Press the Enter key two times.
4. Insert the *«GreetingLine»* composite field by completing the following steps:
   a. Click the Greeting Line button in the Write & Insert Fields group.
   b. At the Insert Greeting Line dialog box, click the option box arrow for the option box containing the comma (the box at the right of the box containing *Mr. Randall*).
   c. At the drop-down list, click the colon.

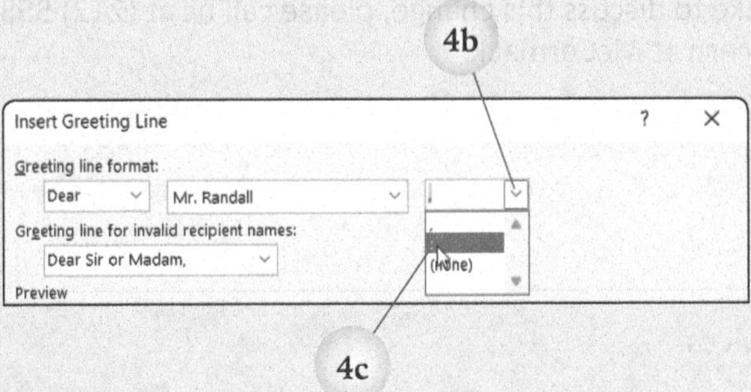

   d. Click OK to close the Insert Greeting Line dialog box.
   e. Press the Enter key two times.

5. Type the letter shown in Figure 6.3 to the point where *«Fund»* appears and then insert the *«Fund»* field by clicking the Insert Merge Field button arrow in the Write & Insert Fields group and then clicking *Fund* at the drop-down list.
6. Type the letter to the point where the *«Title»* field appears and then insert the *«Title»* field by clicking the Insert Merge Field button arrow and then clicking *Title* at the drop-down list.
7. Press the spacebar and then insert the *«Last_Name»* field by clicking the Insert Merge Field button arrow and then clicking *Last_Name* at the drop-down list.
8. Type the remainder of the letter shown in Figure 6.3. (Insert your initials instead of *XX* at the end of the letter.)
9. Save the document with the name **6-MFMD**.

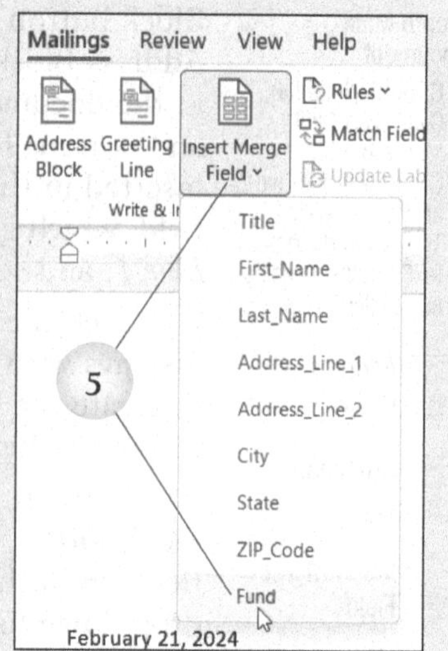

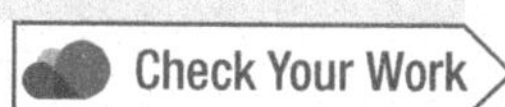

Figure 6.3 Activity 1b

February 21, 2024

«AddressBlock»

«GreetingLine»

McCormack Funds is lowering its expense charges beginning May 1, 2024. The reduction in expense charges means that more of your account investment performance in the «Fund» is returned to you, «Title» «Last_Name». The reductions are worth your attention because most of our competitors' fees have gone up.

Lowering expense charges is noteworthy because before the reduction, McCormack expense deductions were already among the lowest, far below most mutual funds and variable annuity accounts with similar objectives. At the same time, services for you, our client, will continue to expand. If you would like to discuss this change, please call us at (212) 555-2277. Your financial future is our main concern at McCormack.

Sincerely,

Jodie Langley
Director, Financial Services

XX
6-MFMD.docx

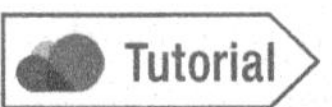

Previewing and Merging Documents

Previewing a Merge

To view how the main document will appear when merged with the first record in the data source file, click the Preview Results button in the Preview Results group on the Mailings tab. View the main document merged with other records by using the navigation buttons in the Preview Results group. This group contains the First Record, Previous Record, Next Record, and Last Record buttons and the *Go to Record* text box. Click the button that will display the main document merged with the specific record. Viewing the merged document before printing is helpful to ensure that the merged data is correct. To use the *Go to Record* text box, click in the text box, type the number of the record, and then press the Enter key. Turn off the preview feature by clicking the Preview Results button.

The Preview Results group on the Mailings tab also includes a Find Recipient button. To search for and preview merged documents with specific entries, click the Preview Results button and then click the Find Recipient button. At the Find Entry dialog box, type the specific field entry in the *Find* text box and then click the Find Next button. Continue clicking the Find Next button until Word displays a message indicating that there are no more entries that contain the typed text.

Checking for Errors

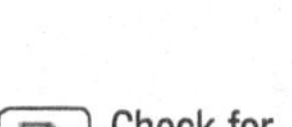

Before merging documents, check for errors using the Check for Errors button in the Preview Results group on the Mailings tab. Click this button and the Checking and Reporting Errors dialog box, shown in Figure 6.4, displays containing three options. Click the first option, *Simulate the merge and report errors in a new document,* and Word will test the merge, not make any changes, and report errors in a new document. Choose the second option, *Complete the merge, pausing to report each error as it occurs,* and Word will merge the documents and display errors as they occur during the merge. Choose the third option, *Complete the merge without pausing. Report errors in a new document,* and Word will complete the merge without pausing and insert any errors in a new document.

Merging Documents

To complete the merge, click the Finish & Merge button in the Finish group on the Mailings tab. At the drop-down list, merge the records and create a new document, send the merged documents directly to the printer, or send the merged documents by email.

Figure 6.4 Checking and Reporting Errors Dialog Box

Choose an option at this dialog box to tell Word to simulate the merge and then check for errors; complete the merge and then pause to report errors; or complete the merge and report errors without pausing.

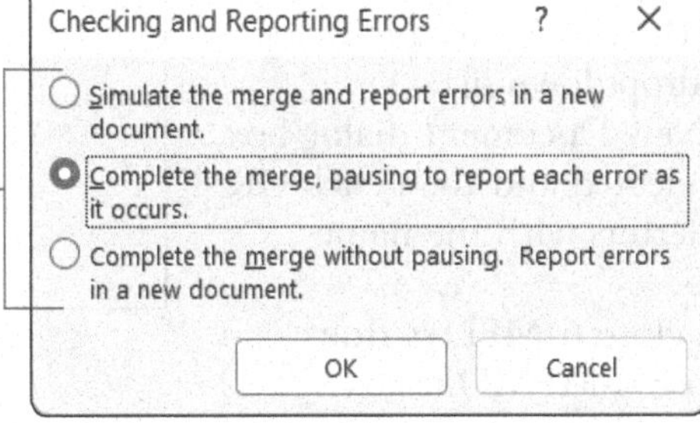

Quick Steps

Merge Documents

1. Click Finish & Merge button.
2. Click *Edit Individual Documents* at drop-down list.
3. Make sure *All* is selected in Merge to New Document dialog box.
4. Click OK.

Hint Press Alt + Shift + N to display the Merge to New Document dialog box and press Alt + Shift + M to display the Merge to Printer dialog box.

To merge the documents and create a new document with the merged records, click the Finish & Merge button and then click *Edit Individual Documents* at the drop-down list. At the Merge to New Document dialog box, make sure *All* is selected in the *Merge records* section and then click OK. This merges the records in the data source file with the main document and inserts the merged documents in a new document.

Identify specific records to be merged with options at the Merge to New Document dialog box. Display this dialog box by clicking the Finish & Merge button on the Mailings tab and then clicking the *Edit Individual Documents* option at the drop-down list. Click the *All* option in the Merge to New Document dialog box to merge all the records in the data source file and click the *Current record* option to merge only the current record. To merge specific adjacent records, click in the *From* text box, type the beginning record number, press the Tab key, and then type the ending record number in the *To* text box.

Activity 1c Merging the Main Document with the Data Source File — Part 3 of 3

1. With **6-MFMD.docx** open, preview the main document merged with the first record in the data source file by clicking the Preview Results button on the Mailings tab.
2. Click the Next Record button to view the main document merged with the second record in the data source file.
3. Click the Preview Results button to turn off the preview feature.
4. Automatically check for errors by completing the following steps:
   a. Click the Check for Errors button in the Preview Results group on the Mailings tab.
   b. At the Checking and Reporting Errors dialog box, click the first option, *Simulate the merge and report errors in a new document*.
   c. Click OK.
   d. If a new document displays with any errors, print the document, close it without saving it, and then correct the errors. If a message displays that no errors were found, click OK.
5. Click the Finish & Merge button in the Finish group and then click *Edit Individual Documents* at the drop-down list.
6. At the Merge to New Document dialog box, make sure *All* is selected and then click OK.
7. Save the merged letters with the name **6-MFLtrs**.
8. Preview and then close **6-MFLtrs.docx**.
9. Save and then close **6-MFMD.docx**.

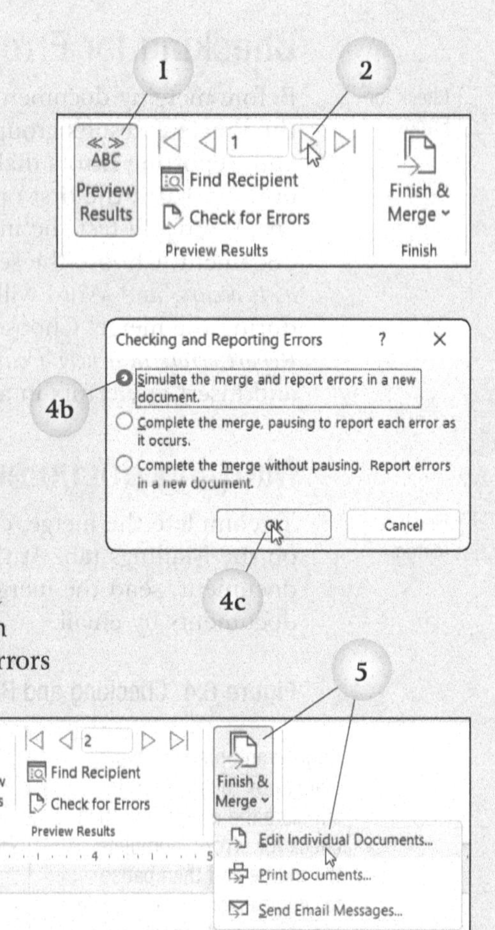

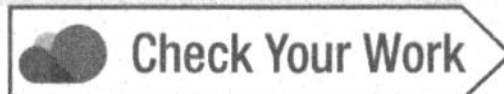

Activity 2 Merge Envelopes — 1 Part

You will use Mail Merge to prepare envelopes with customer names and addresses.

Merging with Other Main Documents

In addition to being merged with a letter, a data source file can be merged with an envelope, a label, or a directory main document. Create an envelope main document with the *Envelopes* option at the Start Mail Merge button drop-down list and create a label main document with the *Labels* option. Create a directory, which merges fields to the same page, with the *Directory* option at the Start Mail Merge button drop-down list.

Merging Envelopes

Merging Envelopes

To send out a letter created as a main document and then merged with a data source file will likely require creating properly addressed envelopes. To prepare an envelope main document that is merged with a data source file, click the Mailings tab, click the Start Mail Merge button, and then click *Envelopes* at the drop-down list. This displays the Envelope Options dialog box, as shown in Figure 6.5. At this dialog box, specify the envelope size, make any other changes, and then click OK.

The next step in the envelope merge process is to create the data source file or identify an existing data source file. To identify an existing data source file, click the Select Recipients button in the Start Mail Merge group and then click *Use an Existing List* at the drop-down list. At the Select Data Source dialog box, navigate to the folder containing the data source file and then double-click the file.

With the data source file attached to the envelope main document, the next step is to insert the appropriate fields. Click in the envelope in the approximate location the recipient's address will appear and a box with a dashed gray border displays. Click the Address Block button in the Write & Insert Fields group and then click OK at the Insert Address Block dialog box.

Figure 6.5 Envelope Options Dialog Box

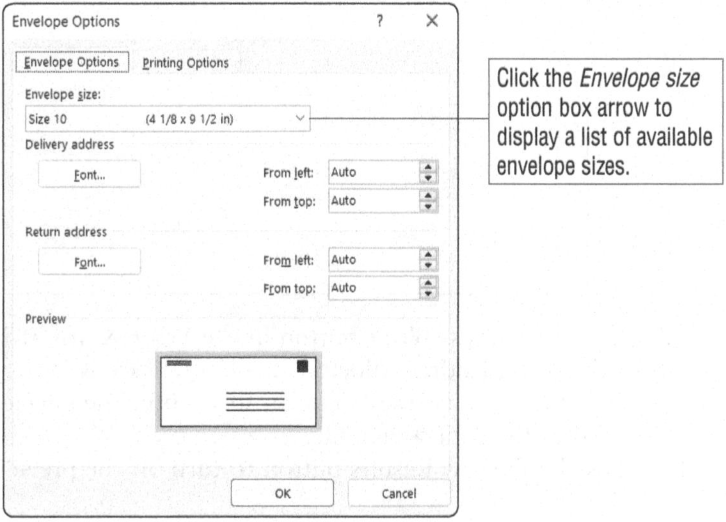

Activity 2 Merging Envelopes

Part 1 of 1

1. At a blank document, click the Mailings tab.
2. Click the Start Mail Merge button in the Start Mail Merge group and then click *Envelopes* at the drop-down list.

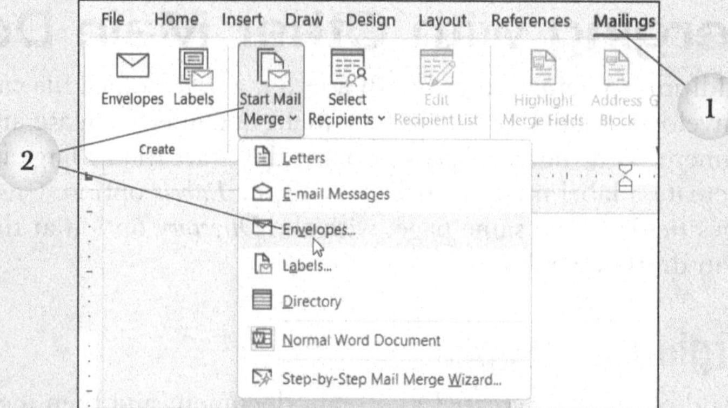

3. At the Envelope Options dialog box, make sure the envelope size is Size 10 and then click OK.
4. Click the Select Recipients button in the Start Mail Merge group and then click *Use an Existing List* at the drop-down list.
5. At the Select Data Source dialog box, navigate to your WL2C6 folder and then double-click the data source file named ***6-MFDS.mdb***. (Notice the Access icon that displays before the 6-MFDS.mdb file identifying it as an Access database file.)

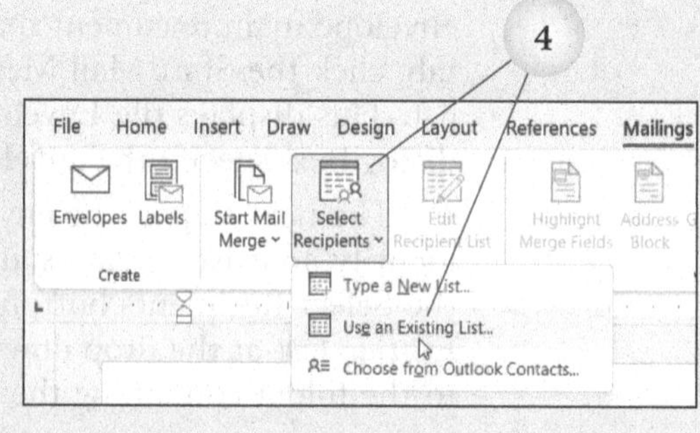

6. Click in the approximate location in the envelope document where the recipient's address will appear. (This causes a box with a dashed gray border to display. If you do not see this box, try clicking in a different location on the envelope.)

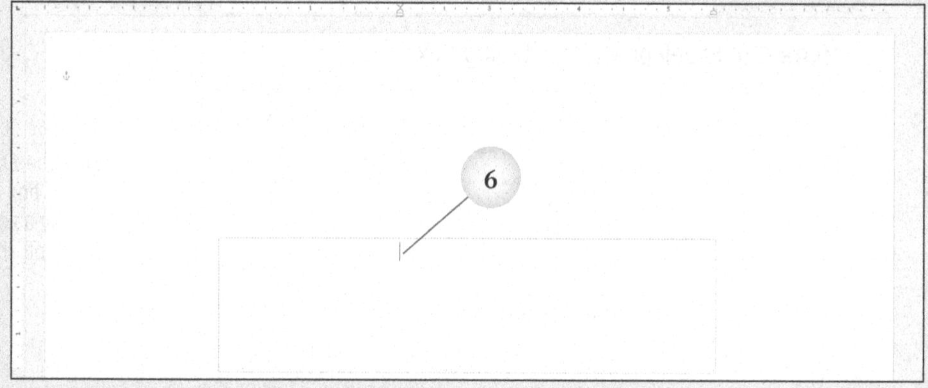

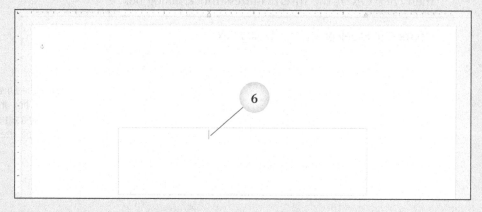

7. Click the Address Block button in the Write & Insert Fields group.
8. At the Insert Address Block dialog box, click OK.
9. Click the Preview Results button to see how the envelope appears merged with the first record in the data source file.
10. Click the Preview Results button to turn off the preview feature.

11. Click the Finish & Merge button in the Finish group and then click *Edit Individual Documents* at the drop-down list.
12. At the Merge to New Document dialog box, specify that you want only the first two records to merge by completing the following steps:
    a. Click in the *From* text box and then type 1.
    b. Click in the *To* text box and then type 2.
    c. Click OK. (This merges only the first two records and then opens a document with two merged envelopes.)
13. Save the merged envelopes with the name **6-MFEnvs**.
14. Preview and then close **6-MFEnvs.docx**.
15. Save the envelope main document with the name **6-EnvMD**.
16. Close **6-EnvMD.docx**.

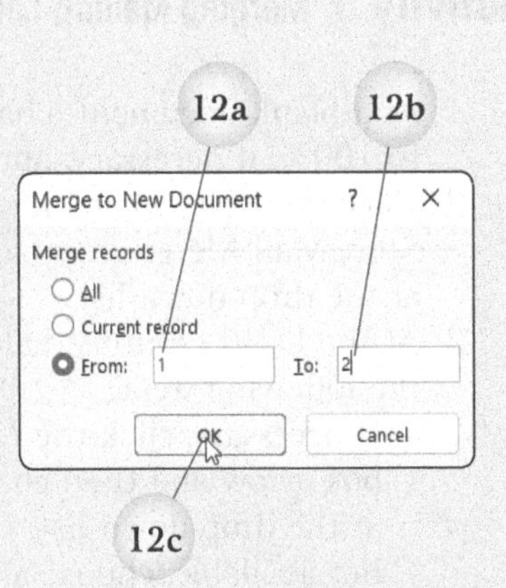

Activity 3 Merge Mailing Labels — 1 Part

You will use Mail Merge to prepare mailing labels with customer names and addresses.

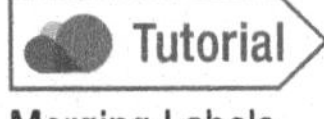

Merging Labels

Merging Labels

Mailing labels for records in a data source file are created in much the same way that envelopes are created. Click the Start Mail Merge button and then click *Labels* at the drop-down list. This displays the Label Options dialog box, as shown in Figure 6.6. Make sure the desired label is selected and then click OK to close the dialog box. The next step is to create the data source file or identify an existing data source file. With the data source file attached to the label main document, insert the appropriate fields and then complete the merge.

Figure 6.6 Label Options Dialog Box

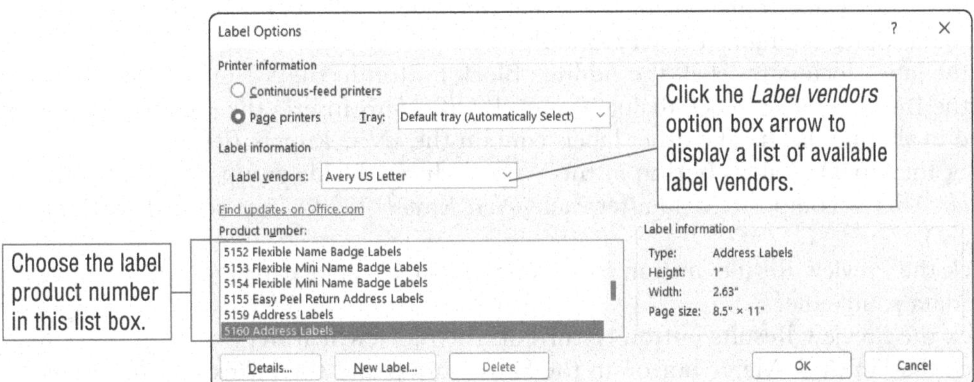

Activity 3 Merging Mailing Labels

Part 1 of 1

1. At a blank document, change the document zoom to 100%, if necessary, and then click the Mailings tab.
2. Click the Start Mail Merge button in the Start Mail Merge group and then click *Labels* at the drop-down list.

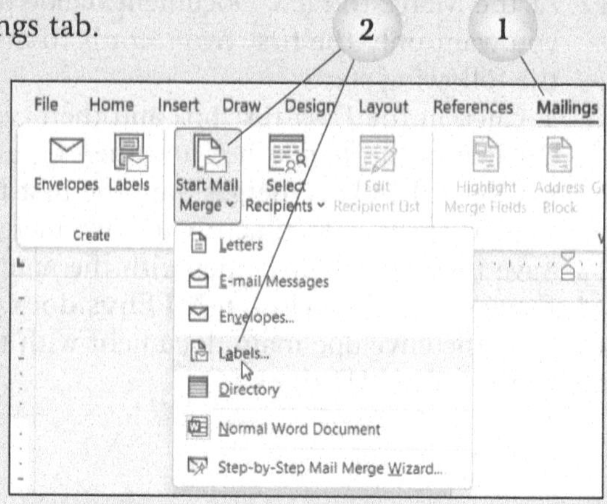

3. At the Label Options dialog box, complete the following steps:
   a. If necessary, click the *Label vendors* option box arrow and then click *Avery US Letter* at the drop-down list. (If this option is not available, choose a vendor that offers labels that print on a full page.)
   b. Scroll in the *Product number* list box and then, if necessary, click *5160 Address Labels*. (If this option is not available, choose a label number that prints labels in two or three columns down a full page.)
   c. Click OK to close the dialog box.

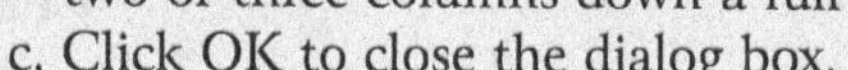

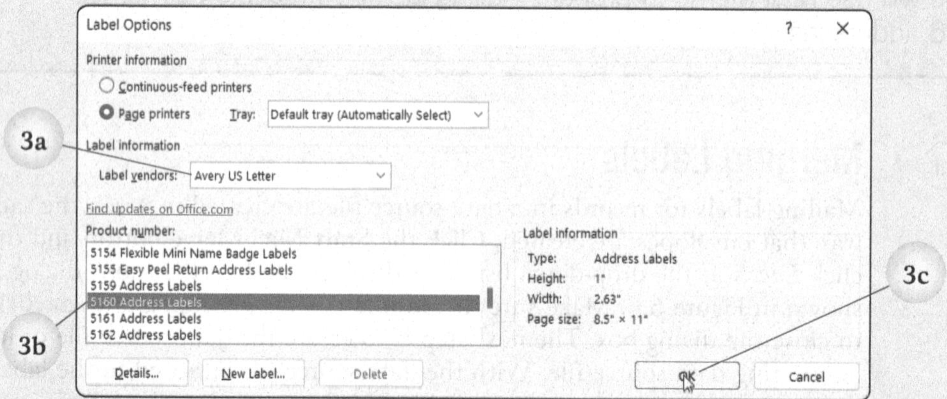

4. Click the Select Recipients button in the Start Mail Merge group and then click *Use an Existing List* at the drop-down list.
5. At the Select Data Source dialog box, navigate to your WL2C6 folder and then double-click the data source file named ***6-MFDS.mdb***.
6. At the label document, click the Address Block button in the Write & Insert Fields group.
7. At the Insert Address Block dialog box, click OK. (This inserts the *«AddressBlock»* composite field in the first label. The other labels contain the *«Next Record»* field.)
8. Click the Update Labels button in the Write & Insert Fields group. (This adds the *«AddressBlock»* composite field after each *«Next Record»* field in the second and subsequent labels.)
9. Click the Preview Results button to see how the labels appear merged with the records in the data source file.
10. Click the Preview Results button to turn off the preview feature.
11. Click the Finish & Merge button in the Finish group and then click *Edit Individual Documents* at the drop-down list.
12. At the Merge to New Document dialog box, make sure *All* is selected and then click OK.

13. Format the labels by completing the following steps:
    a. Click the Table Layout tab.
    b. Click the Select button in the Table group and then click the *Select Table* option.
    c. Click the Align Center Left button in the Alignment group.
    d. Click the Home tab and then click the Paragraph group dialog box launcher.
    e. At the Paragraph dialog box, click the *Before* measurement box up arrow to change the measurement to 0 points.
    f. Click the *After* measurement box up arrow to change the measurement to 0 points.
    g. Click the *Inside* measurement box up arrow three times to change the measurement to 0.3 inch.
    h. Click OK.
14. Save the merged labels with the name **6-MFLabels**.
15. Preview and then close **6-MFLabels.docx**.
16. Save the label main document with the name **6-LabelsMD**.
17. Close **6-LabelsMD.docx**.

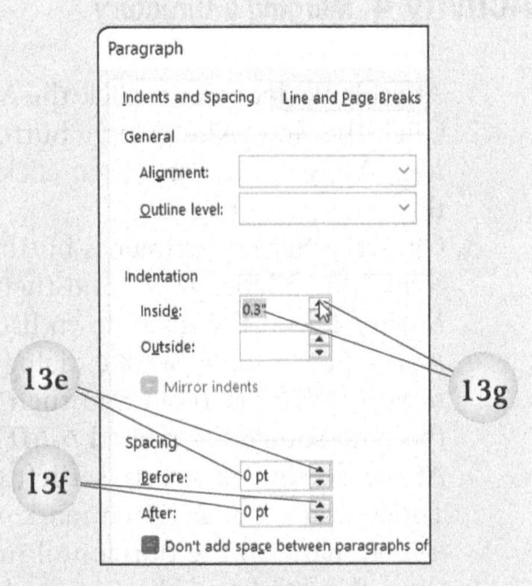

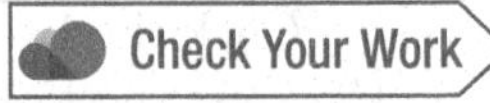

Activity 4 Merge a Directory **1 Part**

You will use Mail Merge to prepare a directory list containing customer names and types of financial investment funds.

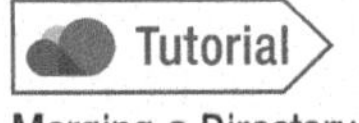

Merging a Directory

Merging a Directory

When merging letters, envelopes, or mailing labels, a new form is created for each record. For example, if the data source file merged with the letter contains eight records, eight letters are created, each on a separate page. In some situations, merged information should remain on the same page. This is useful, for example, when creating a list such as a directory or address list.

Begin creating a merged directory by clicking the Start Mail Merge button and then clicking *Directory* at the drop-down list. Create or identify an existing data source file and then insert the necessary fields in the directory document. To display the merged data in columns, set tabs for all the columns.

Activity 4 Merging a Directory

Part 1 of 1

1. At a blank document, click the Mailings tab.
2. Click the Start Mail Merge button in the Start Mail Merge group and then click *Directory* at the drop-down list.
3. Click the Select Recipients button in the Start Mail Merge group and then click *Use an Existing List* at the drop-down list.
4. At the Select Data Source dialog box, navigate to your WL2C6 folder and then double-click the data source file named ***6-MFDS.mdb***.
5. At the document screen, set left tabs at the 1-inch mark, the 2.5-inch mark, and the 4-inch mark on the horizontal ruler.
6. Press the Tab key. (This moves the insertion point to the tab set at the 1-inch mark.)
7. Click the Insert Merge Field button arrow and then click *Last_Name* at the drop-down list.
8. Press the Tab key to move the insertion point to the tab set at the 2.5-inch mark.
9. Click the Insert Merge Field button arrow and then click *First_Name* at the drop-down list.
10. Press the Tab key to move the insertion point to the tab set at the 4-inch mark.
11. Click the Insert Merge Field button arrow and then click *Fund* at the drop-down list.
12. Press the Enter key.
13. Click the Finish & Merge button in the Finish group and then click *Edit Individual Documents* at the drop-down list.
14. At the Merge to New Document dialog box, make sure *All* is selected and then click OK. (This merges the fields in the document.)
15. Press Ctrl + Home, press the Enter key, and then press the Up Arrow key.
16. Press the Tab key, turn on bold formatting, and then type Last Name.
17. Press the Tab key and then type First Name.
18. Press the Tab key and then type Fund.

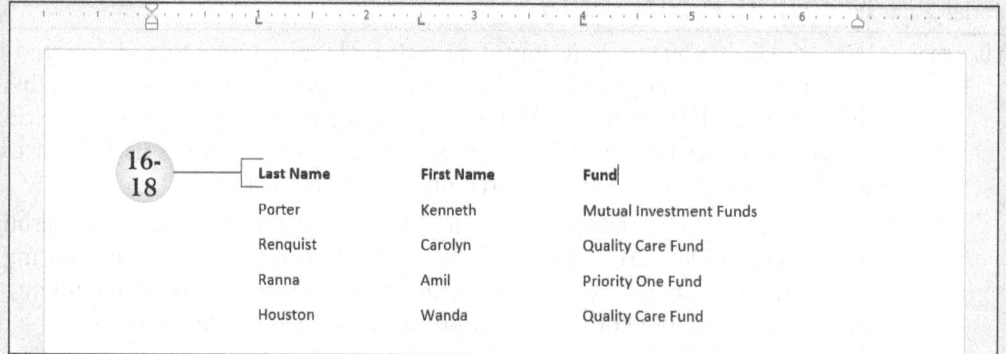

16-18
Last Name	First Name	Fund
Porter	Kenneth	Mutual Investment Funds
Renquist	Carolyn	Quality Care Fund
Ranna	Amil	Priority One Fund
Houston	Wanda	Quality Care Fund

19. Save the directory document with the name **6-Directory**.
20. Preview and then close **6-Directory.docx**.
21. Save the directory main document with the name **6-DirectoryMD** and then close the document.

Activity 5 Select Records and Merge Mailing Labels — 1 Part

You will use Mail Merge to prepare mailing labels with the names and addresses of customers living in Baltimore.

Editing a Data Source File

Edit Recipient List

Editing a Data Source File

Edit a main document in the normal manner. Open the document, make the required changes, and then save the document. Since a data source file is actually an Access database file, it cannot be opened in the normal manner. Open a data source file for editing using the Edit Recipient List button in the Start Mail Merge group on the Mailings tab. Click the Edit Recipient List button and the Mail Merge Recipients dialog box displays, as shown in Figure 6.7. Select or edit records at this dialog box.

Selecting Specific Records

Each record in the Mail Merge Recipients dialog box contains a check mark before the first field. To select specific records for merging, remove the check marks from those records that should not be included in a merge. This way, only certain records in the data source file will be merged with the main document.

Figure 6.7 Mail Merge Recipients Dialog Box

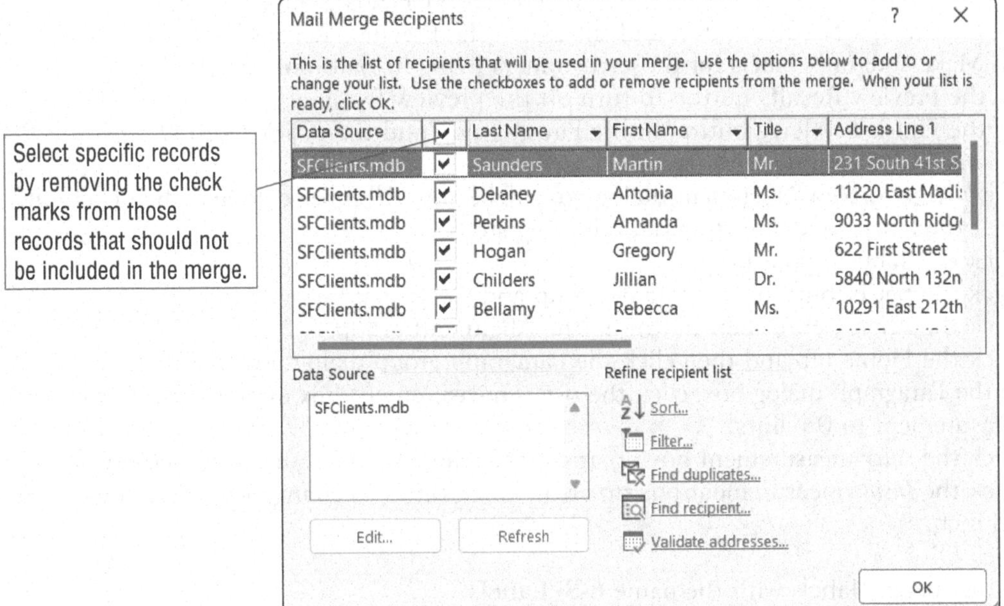

Activity 5 Selecting Records and Merging Mailing Labels

Part 1 of 1

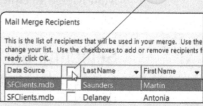

1. At a blank document, create mailing labels for customers living in Baltimore. Begin by clicking the Mailings tab.
2. Click the Start Mail Merge button in the Start Mail Merge group and then click *Labels* at the drop-down list.
3. At the Label Options dialog box, make sure *Avery US Letter* displays in the *Label vendors* option box and *5160 Address Labels* is selected in the *Product number* list box and then click OK.
4. Click the Select Recipients button in the Start Mail Merge group and then click *Use an Existing List* at the drop-down list.
5. At the Select Data Source dialog box, navigate to your WL2C6 folder and then double-click the data source file named ***SFClients.mdb***.
6. Click the Edit Recipient List button in the Start Mail Merge group.
7. At the Mail Merge Recipients dialog box, complete the following steps:
   a. Click the check box immediately left of the *Last Name* field column heading to remove the check mark. (This removes all the check marks from the check boxes.)
   b. Insert check marks by clicking the check box immediately left of each of the following last names: *Saunders*, *Perkins*, *Dutton*, *Fernandez*, and *Stahl*. (These are the customers who live in Baltimore.)
   c. Click OK to close the dialog box.

7a

Mail Merge Recipients

This is the list of recipients that will be used in your merge. Use the change your list. Use the checkboxes to add or remove recipients f ready, click OK.

Data Source		Last Name	First Name
SFClients.mdb		Saunders	Martin
SFClients.mdb		Delaney	Antonia

8. At the label document, click the Address Block button in the Write & Insert Fields group.
9. At the Insert Address Block dialog box, click OK.
10. Click the Update Labels button in the Write & Insert Fields group.
11. Click the Preview Results button and then click the Previous Record button to display each label. Make sure only labels for those customers living in Baltimore display.
12. Click the Preview Results button to turn off the preview feature.
13. Click the Finish & Merge button in the Finish group and then click *Edit Individual Documents* at the drop-down list.
14. At the Merge to New Document dialog box, make sure *All* is selected and then click OK.
15. Format the labels by completing the following steps:
    a. Click the Table Layout tab.
    b. Click the Select button in the Table group and then click *Select Table*.
    c. Click the Align Center Left button in the Alignment group.
    d. Click the Home tab and then click the Paragraph group dialog box launcher.
    e. At the Paragraph dialog box, click the *Before* measurement box up arrow to change the measurement to 0 points.
    f. Click the *After* measurement box up arrow to change the measurement to 0 points.
    g. Click the *Inside* measurement box up arrow three times to change the measurement to 0.3 inch.
    h. Click OK.
16. Save the merged labels with the name **6-SFLabels**.
17. Preview and then close **6-SFLabels.docx**.
18. Save the labels main document with the name **6-SFLabelsMD** and then close the document.

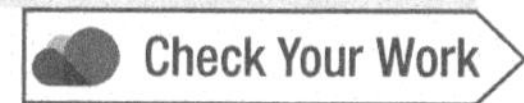

Check Your Work

Activity 6 Edit Records in a Data Source File 1 Part

You will edit records in a data source file and then use Mail Merge to prepare a directory with the edited records that contains customer names, telephone numbers, and cell phone numbers.

Editing Records

Quick Steps

Edit Data Source File

1. Open main document.
2. Click Mailings tab.
3. Click Edit Recipient List button.
4. Click data source file name in *Data Source* list box.
5. Click Edit button.
6. Make changes at Edit Data Source dialog box.
7. Click OK.
8. Click OK.

A data source file may need editing on a periodic basis to add or delete customer names, update fields, insert new fields, or delete existing fields. To edit a data source file, click the Edit Recipient List button in the Start Mail Merge group. At the Mail Merge Recipients dialog box, click the data source file name in the *Data Source* list box and then click the Edit button below the list box. This displays the Edit Data Source dialog box, as shown in Figure 6.8. At this dialog box, add a new entry, delete an entry, find a particular entry, and customize columns.

Figure 6.8 Edit Data Source Dialog Box

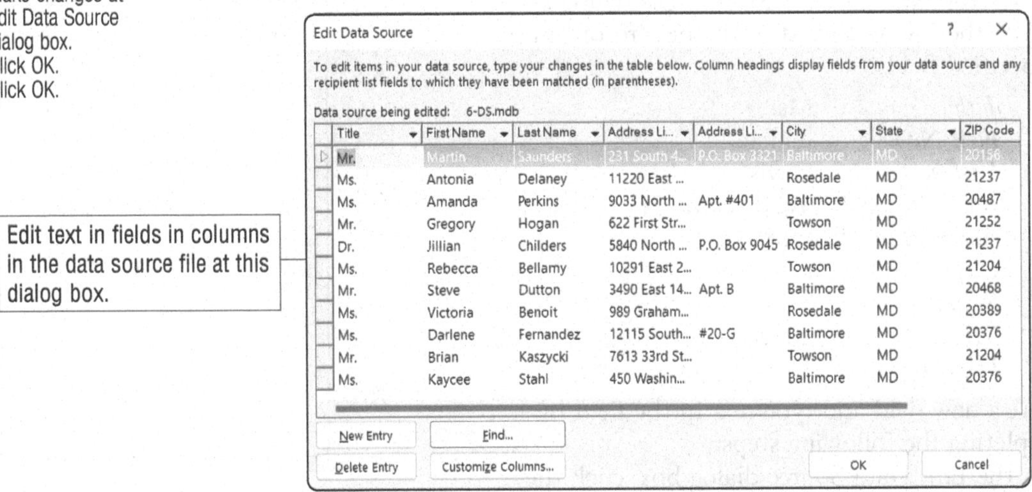

Activity 6 Editing Records in a Data Source File Part 1 of 1

1. Make a copy of the **SFClients.mdb** data source file by completing the following steps:
   a. Display the Open dialog box and make WL2C6 the active folder.
   b. If necessary, change the file type option to *All Files*.
   c. Right-click the ***SFClients.mdb*** data source file and then click *Copy* at the shortcut menu.
   d. Position the pointer in a white portion of the Open dialog box Content pane (outside any file name), click the right mouse button, and then click *Paste* at the shortcut menu. (This inserts a copy of the file in the dialog box Content pane and names the file **SFClients - Copy.mdb**.)
   e. Right-click ***SFClients - Copy.mdb*** and then click *Rename* at the shortcut menu.
   f. Type 6-DS and then press the Enter key.
   g. Close the Open dialog box.

2. At a blank document, click the Mailings tab.
3. Click the Select Recipients button and then click *Use an Existing List* from the drop-down list.
4. At the Select Data Source dialog box, navigate to your WL2C6 folder and then double-click the data source file named ***6-DS.mdb***.
5. Click the Edit Recipient List button in the Start Mail Merge group.
6. At the Mail Merge Recipients dialog box, click *6-DS.mdb* in the *Data Source* list box and then click the Edit button.

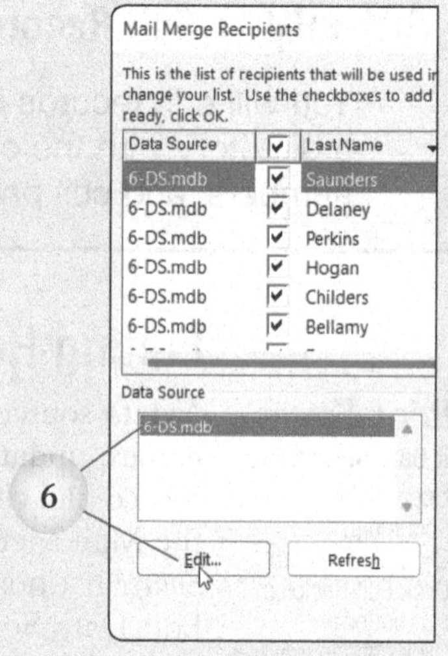

7. Delete the record for Steve Dutton by completing the following steps:
   a. Click the square at the beginning of the row for *Mr. Steve Dutton*.
   b. Click the Delete Entry button.
   c. At the message asking if you want to delete the entry, click Yes.

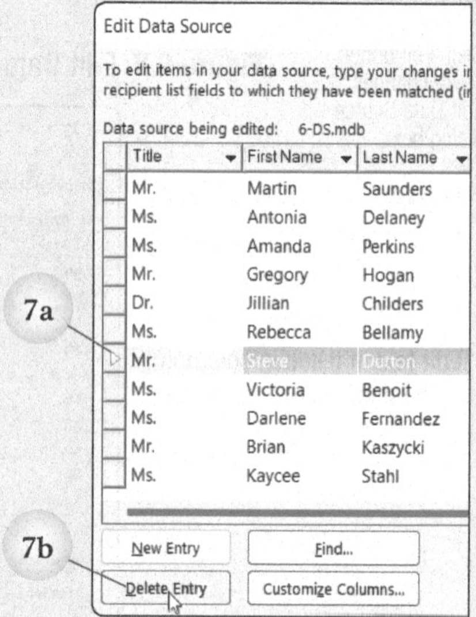

8. Insert a new record by completing the following steps:
   a. Click the New Entry button in the dialog box.
   b. Type the following text in the new record in the specified fields:

      Title Ms.
      First Name Jennae
      Last Name Davis
      Address Line 1 3120 South 21st
      Address Line 2 (none)
      City Rosedale
      State MD
      ZIP Code 20389
      Home Phone 410-555-5774

9. Insert a new field and type text in the field by completing the following steps:
   a. At the Edit Data Source dialog box, click the Customize Columns button.
   b. At the message asking if you want to save the changes made to the data source file, click Yes.
   c. At the Customize Address List dialog box, click *ZIP Code* in the *Field Names* list box. (You will insert a new field below this field.)
   d. Click the Add button.
   e. At the Add Field dialog box, type Cell Phone and then click OK.
   f. You decide that you want the *Cell Phone* field to display after the *Home Phone* field. To move the *Cell Phone* field, make sure it is selected and then click the Move Down button.
   g. Click OK to close the Customize Address List dialog box.

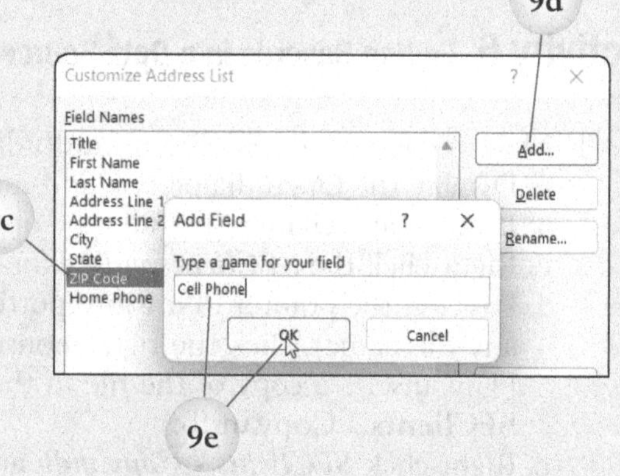

h. At the Edit Data Source dialog box, scroll right to display the *Cell Phone* field (the last field in the file) and then type the following cell phone numbers. (After typing each cell phone number except the last number, press the Down Arrow key to make the next field below active.)

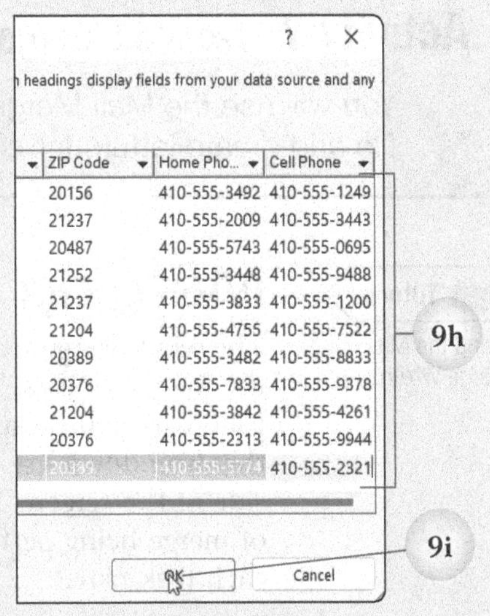

Record 1 410-555-1249
Record 2 410-555-3443
Record 3 410-555-0695
Record 4 410-555-9488
Record 5 410-555-1200
Record 6 410-555-7522
Record 7 410-555-8833
Record 8 410-555-9378
Record 9 410-555-4261
Record 10 410-555-9944
Record 11 410-555-2321

i. Click OK to close the Edit Data Source dialog box.
j. At the message asking if you want to update the recipient list and save changes, click Yes.
k. At the Mail Merge Recipients dialog box, click OK.

10. Create a directory by completing the following steps:
    a. Click the Start Mail Merge button and then click *Directory* at the drop-down list.
    b. At the blank document, set left tabs on the horizontal ruler at the 1-inch mark, the 3-inch mark, and the 4.5-inch mark.
    c. Press the Tab key. (This moves the insertion point to the first tab set at the 1-inch mark.)
    d. Click the Insert Merge Field button arrow and then click *Last_Name* at the drop-down list.
    e. Type a comma and then press the spacebar.
    f. Click the Insert Merge Field button arrow and then click *First_Name* at the drop-down list.
    g. Press the Tab key, click the Insert Merge Field button arrow, and then click *Home_Phone* at the drop-down list.
    h. Press the Tab key, click the Insert Merge Field button arrow, and then click *Cell_Phone* at the drop-down list.
    i. Press the Enter key.
    j. Click the Finish & Merge button and then click *Edit Individual Documents* at the drop-down list.
    k. At the Merge to New Document dialog box, make sure *All* is selected and then click OK.
11. Press Ctrl + Home, press the Enter key, and then press the Up Arrow key.
12. Press the Tab key, turn on bold formatting, and then type Name.
13. Press the Tab key and then type Home Phone.
14. Press the Tab key and then type Cell Phone.

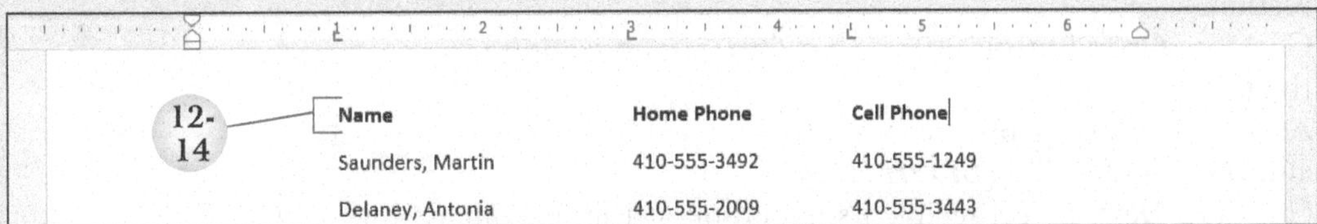

15. Save the directory document with the name **6-Directory-Act6**.
16. Preview and then close **6-Directory-Act6.docx**.
17. Save the directory main document with the name **6-Directory-Act6-MD** and then close the document.

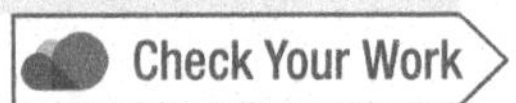

Activity 7 Use Mail Merge Wizard — 1 Part

You will use the Mail Merge wizard to merge a main document with a data source file and create letters for clients of Sorenson Funds.

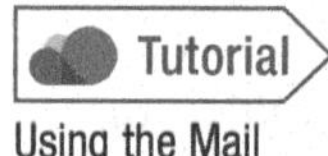

Using the Mail Merge Wizard

Merging Using the Mail Merge Wizard

The Mail Merge feature includes a Mail Merge wizard with steps for completing the merge process. To access the wizard, click the Mailings tab, click the Start Mail Merge button, and then click the *Step-by-Step Mail Merge Wizard* option at the drop-down list. The first of six Mail Merge task panes displays at the right side of the screen. The options in each task pane may vary depending on the type of merge being performed. Generally, one of the following steps is completed at each task pane:

- Step 1: Select the type of document to be created, such as a letter, email message, envelope, label, or directory.
- Step 2: Specify what is to be used to create the main document: the current document, a template, or an existing document.
- Step 3: Specify whether a new list will be created or an existing list or Outlook contacts list will be used.
- Step 4: Use the items in this task pane to help prepare the main document by performing tasks such as inserting fields.
- Step 5: Preview the merged documents.
- Step 6: Complete the merge.

Activity 7 Preparing Form Letters Using the Mail Merge Wizard — Part 1 of 1

1. At a blank document, click the Mailings tab, click the Start Mail Merge button in the Start Mail Merge group, and then click *Step-by-Step Mail Merge Wizard* at the drop-down list.
2. At the first Mail Merge task pane, make sure *Letters* is selected in the *Select document type* section and then click the Next: Starting document hyperlink at the bottom of the task pane.
3. At the second Mail Merge task pane, click the *Start from existing document* option in the *Select starting document* section.
4. Click the Open button in the *Start from existing* section of the task pane.
5. At the Open dialog box, navigate to your WL2C6 folder and then double-click ***SFLtrMD.docx***.
6. Click the Next: Select recipients hyperlink at the bottom of the task pane.

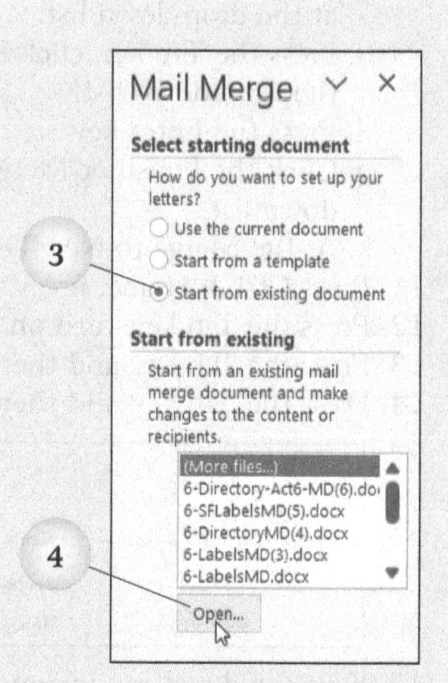

7. At the third Mail Merge task pane, click the Browse hyperlink in the *Use an existing list* section of the task pane.
8. At the Select Data Source dialog box, navigate to your WL2C6 folder and then double-click the ***SFClients.mdb*** data source file.
9. At the Mail Merge Recipients dialog box, click OK.
10. Click the Next: Write your letter hyperlink at the bottom of the task pane.
11. At the fourth Mail Merge task pane, enter fields in the form letter by completing the following steps:
    a. Position the insertion point a double space above the first paragraph of text in the letter.
    b. Click the Address block hyperlink in the *Write your letter* section of the task pane.
    c. At the Insert Address Block dialog box, click OK.
    d. Press the Enter key two times and then click the Greeting line hyperlink in the *Write your letter* section of the task pane.
    e. At the Insert Greeting Line dialog box, click the option box arrow at the right of the option box containing the comma (the box at the right of the box containing *Mr. Randall*).
    f. At the drop-down list, click the colon.
    g. Click OK to close the Insert Greeting Line dialog box.

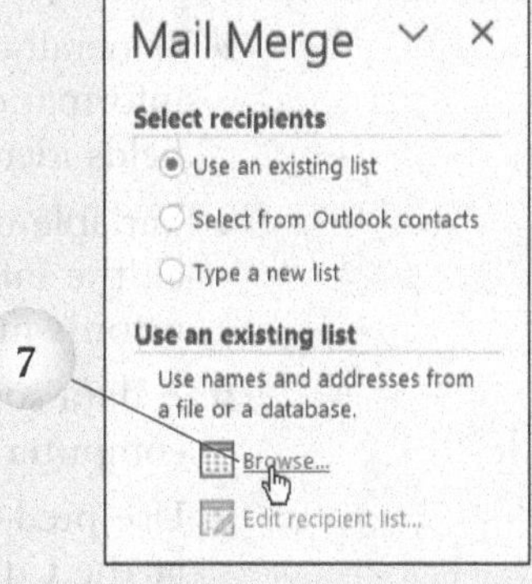

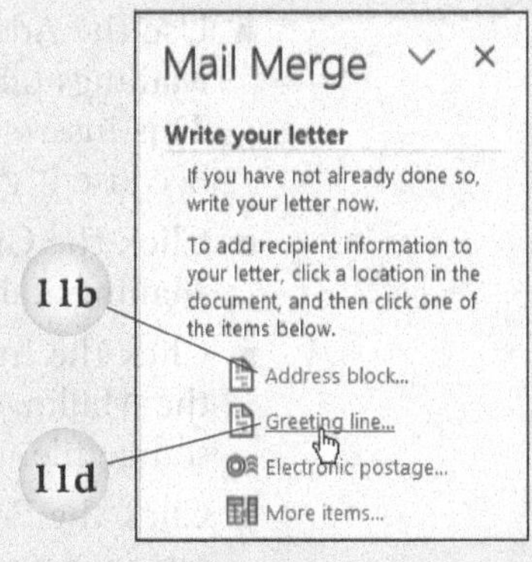

12. Click the Next: Preview your letters hyperlink at the bottom of the task pane.
13. At the fifth Mail Merge task pane, look over the letter in the document window and make sure the information is merged properly. If you want to see the letters for the other recipients, click the Next button (the button containing two right-pointing arrows) in the Mail Merge task pane.
14. Click the Preview Results button in the Preview Results group to turn off the preview feature.
15. Click the Next: Complete the merge hyperlink at the bottom of the task pane.
16. At the sixth Mail Merge task pane, click the Edit individual letters hyperlink in the *Merge* section of the task pane.
17. At the Merge to New Document dialog box, make sure *All* is selected and then click OK.
18. Save the merged letters document with the name **6-SFLtrs**.
19. Preview and then close **6-SFLtrs.docx**.
20. Save the main document with the name **6-SFLtrsMD** and then close the document.

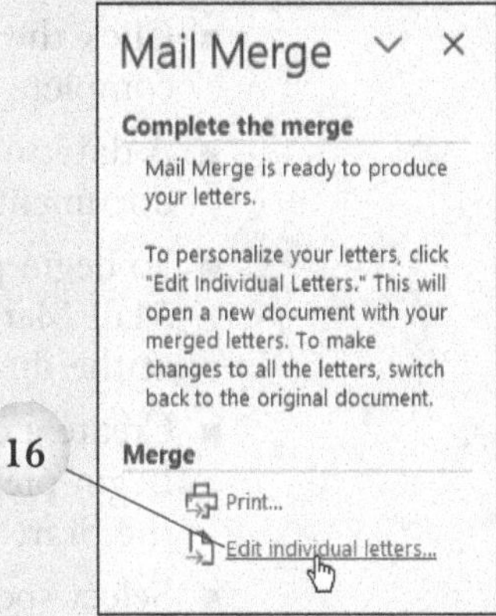

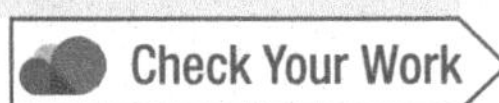

Chapter Summary

- Generally, a merge takes two files: the data source file containing the variable information and the main document containing the standard text along with fields identifying where variable information is inserted during the merge process.
- Variable information in a data source file is saved as a record. A record contains all the information for one unit. A series of fields makes a record and a series of records makes a data source file.
- A data source file is saved as an Access database, but having Access on the computer is not required to complete a merge with a data source file.
- Use predesigned fields when creating a data source file or create custom fields at the Customize Address List dialog box.
- Use the Address Block button in the Write & Insert Fields group on the Mailings tab to insert all the fields required for the inside address of a letter. This inserts the *«AddressBlock»* field, which is considered a composite field because it groups a number of fields.
- Click the Greeting Line button in the Write & Insert Fields group on the Mailings tab to insert the *«GreetingLine»* composite field in the document.
- Click the Insert Merge Field button arrow in the Write & Insert Fields group on the Mailings tab to display a drop-down list of the fields contained in the data source file.
- Click the Preview Results button in the Preview Results group on the Mailings tab to view the main document merged with the first record in the data source file. Use the navigation buttons in the Preview Results group on the Mailings tab to display the main document merged with specific records.
- Before merging documents, check for errors by clicking the Check for Errors button in the Preview Results group on the Mailings tab. This displays the Checking and Reporting Errors dialog box with three options for checking errors.
- Click the Finish & Merge button in the Finish group on the Mailings tab to complete the merge.
- A data source file can be merged with a letter, envelope, label, or directory main document.
- To begin preparing envelopes for merging, click the Mailings tab, click the Start Mail Merge button, and then click *Envelopes* at the drop-down list. Click *Labels* at the drop-down list to begin preparing labels for merging.
- Create a directory when merging records in a data source file on the same page. Begin preparing a directory for merging by clicking the Mailings tab, clicking the Start Mail Merge button, and then clicking *Directory* at the drop-down list.
- Select specific records for merging by inserting or removing check marks from the records in the Mail Merge Recipients dialog box. Display this dialog box by clicking the Edit Recipient List button in the Start Mail Merge group on the Mailings tab.
- Edit specific records in a data source file at the Edit Data Source dialog box. Display this dialog box by clicking the Edit Recipient List button on the Mailings tab, clicking the data source file name in the *Data Source* list box, and then clicking the Edit button.
- Word includes a Mail Merge wizard that provides guidance through the process of creating letters, envelopes, labels, directories, and email messages with personalized information.

Commands Review

FEATURE	RIBBON TAB, GROUP	BUTTON, OPTION
Address Block field	Mailings, Write & Insert Fields	
Checking and Reporting Errors dialog box	Mailings, Preview Results	
directory main document	Mailings, Start Mail Merge	, *Directory*
envelope main document	Mailings, Start Mail Merge	, *Envelopes*
finish merge	Mailings, Finish	
Greeting Line field	Mailings, Write & Insert Fields	
insert merge fields	Mailings, Write & Insert Fields	
label main document	Mailings, Start Mail Merge	, *Labels*
letter main document	Mailings, Start Mail Merge	, *Letters*
Mail Merge Recipients dialog box	Mailings, Start Mail Merge	
Mail Merge wizard	Mailings, Start Mail Merge	, *Step-by-Step Mail Merge Wizard*
New Address List dialog box	Mailings, Start Mail Merge	, *Type a New List*
preview merge results	Mailings, Preview Results	ABC

Review and Assessment

CHAPTER 6

Skills Assessment

Assessment 1

Create a Data Source File

1. At a blank document, display the New Address List dialog box and then display the Customize Address List dialog box. (To do this, click the Mailings tab, click the Select Recipients button, click the *Type a New List* option, and then click the Customize Columns button.)
2. At the Customize Address List dialog box, delete the following fields—*Company Name*, *Country or Region*, *Work Phone*, and *E-mail Address*—and then add a custom field named *Cell Phone*. (Position the *Cell Phone* field after the *Home Phone* field.)
3. Close the Customize Address List dialog box and then type the following information in the New Address List dialog box as the first record:

Title	Mr.
First Name	Tony
Last Name	Benedetti
Address Line 1	1315 Cordova Road
Address Line 2	Apt. 402
City	Santa Fe
State	NM
ZIP Code	87505
Home Phone	(505) 555-0489
Cell Phone	(505) 555-0551

4. Type the following information as the second record:

Title	Ms.
First Name	Theresa
Last Name	Dusek
Address Line 1	12044 Ridgeway Drive
Address Line 2	(leave blank)
City	Santa Fe
State	NM
ZIP Code	87504
Home Phone	(505) 555-1120
Cell Phone	(505) 555-6890

5. Type the following information as the third record:

Title	Ms.
First Name	Mary
Last Name	Arguello
Address Line 1	2554 Country Drive
Address Line 2	#105
City	Santa Fe
State	NM
ZIP Code	87504
Home Phone	(505) 555-7663
Cell Phone	(505) 555-5472

6. Type the following information as the fourth record:

Title	Mr.
First Name	Preston
Last Name	Miller
Address Line 1	120 Second Street
Address Line 2	(leave blank)
City	Santa Fe
State	NM
ZIP Code	87505
Home Phone	(505) 555-3551
Cell Phone	(505) 555-9630

7. Save the data source file with the name **6-CCDS**.
8. Close the blank document without saving changes.

Assessment 2 Create a Letter Main Document and Merge with a Data Source File

1. Open **CCVolunteerLtr.docx** and then save it with the name **6-CCMD**.
2. Select the **6-CCDS.mdb** data source file you created in Assessment 1.
3. Move the insertion point to the beginning of the first paragraph of text in the body of the letter, insert the *«AddressBlock»* field, and then press the Enter key two times.
4. Insert the *«GreetingLine»* field specifying a colon rather than a comma as the greeting line format and then press the Enter key two times.
5. Move the insertion point one space to the right of the period that ends the second paragraph of text in the body of the letter and then type the following text inserting the *«Title»*, *«Last_Name»*, *«Home_Phone»*, and *«Cell_Phone»* fields where indicated:

   Currently, *«Title» «Last_Name»*, our records indicate your home telephone number is *«Home_Phone»* and your cell phone number is *«Cell_Phone»*. If this information is not accurate, please contact our office with the correct numbers.

6. Merge the main document with all the records in the data source file.
7. Save the merged letters document with the name **6-CCLetters**.
8. Preview and then close **6-CCLetters.docx**.
9. Save and then close **6-CCMD.docx**.

Assessment 3 Create an Envelope Main Document and Merge with a Data Source File

1. Create an envelope main document using the Size 10 envelope size.
2. Select **6-CCDS.mdb** as the data source file.
3. Insert the *«AddressBlock»* field in the appropriate location in the envelope document.
4. Merge the envelope main document with all the records in the data source file.
5. Save the merged envelopes document with the name **6-CCEnvs**.
6. Preview and then close the envelopes document.
7. Save the envelope main document with the name **6-CCEnvsMD** and then close the document.

Assessment 4 Create a Label Main Document and Merge with a Data Source File

1. Create a label main document using the option *Avery US Letter 5160 Address Labels*.
2. Select **6-CCDS.mdb** as the data source file.
3. Insert the *«AddressBlock»* field.
4. Update the labels.
5. Merge the label main document with all the records in the data source file.
6. Save the merged labels document with the name **6-CCLabels**.
7. Preview and then close the labels document.
8. Save the label main document with the name **6-CCLabelsMD** and then close the document.

Assessment 5 Edit a Data Source File

1. Open **6-CCMD.docx**. (At the message asking if you want to continue, click Yes.) Save the main document with the name **6-CCMD-A5**.
2. Edit the **6-CCDS.mdb** data source file by making the following changes:
   a. Change the address for Ms. Theresa Dusek from *12044 Ridgeway Drive* to *1390 Fourth Avenue*.
   b. Delete the record for Ms. Mary Arguello.
   c. Insert a new record with the following information:
      Mr. Cesar Rivera
      3201 East Third Street
      Santa Fe, NM 87505
      Home Phone: (505) 555-6675
      Cell Phone: (505) 555-3528
3. Merge the main document with all the records in the data source file.
4. Save the merged letters document with the name **6-CCLtrsEdited**.
5. Preview and then close **6-CCLtrsEdited.docx**.
6. Save and then close **6-CCMD-A5.docx**.

Visual Benchmark

Prepare and Merge Letters

1. Open **FPLtrhd.docx** and then save it with the name **6-FPMD**.
2. Look at the information in Figure 6.9 and Figure 6.10 and then use Mail Merge to prepare four letters. (When creating the main document, as shown in Figure 6.10, insert the appropriate fields where you see the text *Title*; *First Name*; *Last Name*; *Street Address*; and *City, State ZIP*. Insert the appropriate fields where you see the text *Title* and *Last Name* in the first paragraph of text.) Create the data source file with customized field names using the information in Figure 6.9 and then save the file with the name **6-FPDS**.
3. Merge the **6-FPMD.docx** main document with the **6-FPDS.mdb** data source file and then save the merged letters document with the name **6-FPLtrs**.
4. Preview and then close **6-FPLtrs.docx**.
5. Save and then close **6-FPMD.docx**.

Figure 6.9 Visual Benchmark Data Source Records

Mr. Chris Gallagher
17034 234th Avenue
Newport, VT 05855

Ms. Heather Segarra
4103 Thompson Drive
Newport, VT 05855

Mr. Gene Goodrich
831 Cromwell Lane
Newport, VT 05855

Ms. Sonya Kraus
15933 Ninth Street
Newport, VT 05855

Figure 6.10 Visual Benchmark Main Document

FRONTLINE
PHOTOGRAPHY

Current Date

Title First Name Last Name
Street Address
City, State ZIP

Dear Title Last Name:

We have enjoyed being a part of the Newport business community for the past two years. Our success has been thanks to you, Title Last Name, and all our other loyal customers. Thank you for shopping at our store for all your photography equipment and supply needs.

To show our appreciation for your business, we are enclosing a coupon for 20 percent off any item in our store, including our incredibly low-priced clearance items. Through the end of the month, all camera accessories are on sale. Use your coupon and take advantage of additional savings on items such as camera lenses, tripods, cleaning supplies, and camera bags.

To accommodate our customers' schedules, we have extended our weekend hours. Our store will be open Saturdays until 7:00 p.m. and Sundays, until 5:00 p.m. Come by and let our sales associates find the right camera and accessories for you.

Sincerely,

Student Name

XX
6-FPMD.docx

Enclosure

559 Tenth Street, Suite A, Newport, VT 05855
802.555.4411 ◉ https://ppi-edu.net/frontline

Case Study

Part 1

You are the office manager for Freestyle Extreme, a sporting goods store that specializes in snowboarding and snow skiing equipment and supplies. The store has two branches: one on the east side of town and the other on the west side. One of your job responsibilities is to send letters to customers letting them know about sales, new equipment, and upcoming events. Next month, both stores are having a sale and all snowboarding and snow skiing supplies will be 15 percent off the last marked price.

Create a data source file that contains the following customer information: first name, last name, address, city, state, zip code, and branch. Add six customers to the data source file. Indicate that three usually shop at the East branch and three usually shop at the West branch.

Create a letter as a main document that includes information about the upcoming sale. The letter should contain at least two paragraphs and in addition to the information on the sale, it might include information about the store, snowboarding, and/or snow skiing.

Save the data source file with the name **6-FEDS**, save the main document with the name **6-FEMD**, and save the merged document with the name **6-FELtrs**. Create envelopes for the six merged letters and name the merged envelope document **6-FEEnvs**. Save the envelope main document with the name **6-FEEnvsMD**. Preview and then close the merged letters document and the merged envelopes document.

Part 2

A well-known extreme snowboarder will be visiting both branches of Freestyle Extreme to meet with customers and sign autographs. Use the Help feature to learn how to insert an *If...Then...Else...* merge field in a document and then create a letter that includes the name of the extreme snowboarder (you determine the name), the times of the visits to the two branches (1:00 p.m. to 4:30 p.m.), and any additional information that might interest customers. Also include in the letter an *If...Then...Else...* merge field that will insert *Wednesday, September 25* if the customer's branch is *East* and *Thursday, September 26* if the customer's branch is *West*. Add visual interest to the letter by inserting an image, WordArt, or other feature that will attract readers' attention. Save the letter main document with the name **6-SnowMD**. Merge the letter main document with the **6-FEDS.mdb** data source file. Save the merged letters document with the name **6-SnowLtrs**. Preview and then close the merged letters document.

Part 3

The owner of Freestyle Extreme wants to try selling short skis known as "snow blades" or "skiboards." He has asked you to research these skis and identify one type and model to sell only at the West branch of the store. If the model sells well, the owner will consider selling it at the East branch at a future time. Prepare a main document letter that describes the new snow blade or skiboard that the West branch is going to sell. Include information about pricing and tell customers that they can save 40 percent if they purchase the new item within the next week. Merge the letter main document with the **6-FEDS.mdb** data source file and include only those customers that shop at the West branch. Save the merged letters document with the name **6-SBLtrs**. Preview and then close the merged letters document. Save the letter main document with the name **6-SBMD**. Save and then close the main document.

WORD

Managing Building Blocks and Fields

CHAPTER 7

Performance Objectives

Upon successful completion of Chapter 7, you will be able to:

1 Insert and sort building blocks
2 Save content as building blocks in specific galleries
3 Edit building block properties
4 Insert and modify custom building blocks
5 Create a building block gallery and save building blocks in a different template
6 Delete building blocks
7 Insert document property placeholders from Quick Parts
8 Insert and update fields from Quick Parts

Word contains a number of predesigned blocks of text and formatting referred to as *building blocks*. Building blocks are available in galleries throughout Word, most of them on the Insert tab, where they can be quickly and easily inserted into any document. You have been inserting building blocks such as predesigned headers, footers, page numbers, text boxes, cover pages, and so on. Predesigned building blocks can be customized to meet specific needs, or a new building block can be created and then saved in a gallery. In this chapter, you will learn how to build a document using building blocks; how to create, save, and edit your own building blocks; and how to create a button on the Quick Access Toolbar for faster access to a gallery. You will also learn how to insert fields in a document and to format and customize fields.

Data Files

The data files for this chapter are in the WL2C7 folder that you downloaded at the beginning of this course.

Activity 1 Build a Document with Predesigned Building Blocks **1 Part**

You will open a document on home safety and then add elements to it by sorting and then inserting predesigned building blocks.

Managing Building Blocks

Word includes a variety of tools for inserting data such as text, fields, objects, and other items to help build a document. To view some of the tools available, click the Quick Parts button in the Text group on the Insert tab. This displays a drop-down list of choices for inserting document properties, fields, and building blocks. Word provides a number of predesigned building blocks that can be inserted in a document or custom building blocks can be created. Building blocks are pieces of predesigned document content that can be used over and over again to build a document.

Inserting and Sorting Building Blocks

Quick Steps

Insert Building Block

1. Click Insert tab.
2. Click Quick Parts button.
3. Click *Building Blocks Organizer*.
4. Click building block.
5. Click Insert button.
6. Click Close.

Inserting a Building Block

To insert a building block into a document, click the Insert tab, click the Quick Parts button in the Text group, and then click *Building Blocks Organizer* at the drop-down list. This displays the Building Blocks Organizer dialog box, shown in Figure 7.1. The dialog box contains columns of information about each building block, including its name, the gallery that contains it, the template in which it is stored, its behavior, and a brief description of it.

The Building Blocks Organizer dialog box is a central location for viewing all the predesigned building blocks available in Word. Some of the building blocks were used in previous chapters when a predesigned header or footer, cover page, page number, or watermark was inserted in a document. Other galleries in the Building Blocks Organizer dialog box contain predesigned building blocks such as bibliographies, equations, tables of contents, tables, and text boxes. The Building Blocks Organizer dialog box provides a convenient location for viewing and inserting building blocks.

Quick Steps

Sort Building Blocks

1. Click Insert tab.
2. Click Quick Parts button.
3. Click *Building Blocks Organizer*.
4. Click column heading.

Sorting Building Blocks

The Building Blocks Organizer dialog box displays the building blocks in the list box sorted by the *Gallery* column. The building blocks can be sorted by another column by clicking that column heading. For example, to sort the building blocks alphabetically by name, click the *Name* column heading.

Figure 7.1 Building Blocks Organizer Dialog Box

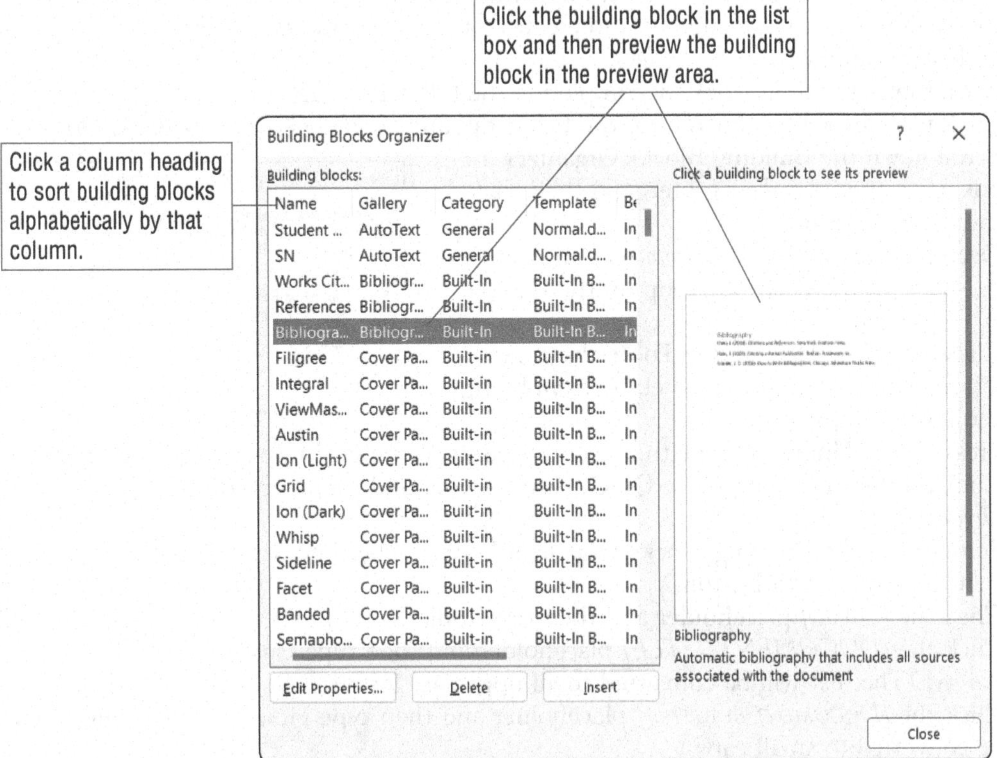

Activity 1 Sorting and Inserting Predesigned Building Blocks

Part 1 of 1

1. Open **HomeSafety.docx** and then save it with the name **7-HomeSafety**.
2. Sort the building blocks and then insert a table of contents building block by completing the following steps:
   a. Press Ctrl + Home to move the insertion point to the beginning of the document, press Ctrl + Enter to insert a page break, and then press Ctrl + Home again.
   b. Click the Insert tab, click the Quick Parts button in the Text group, and then click *Building Blocks Organizer* at the drop-down list.
   c. At the Building Blocks Organizer dialog box, notice the arrangement of building blocks in the list box. (The building blocks are most likely organized alphabetically by the *Gallery* column.)
   d. Click the *Name* column heading. (This sorts the building blocks alphabetically by name. However, some blank building blocks may display at the beginning of the list box.)
   e. Scroll down the list box and then click *Automatic Table 1*. (You may see only a portion of the name. Click the name and the full name as well as a description display in the dialog box below the preview of the table of contents building block.)

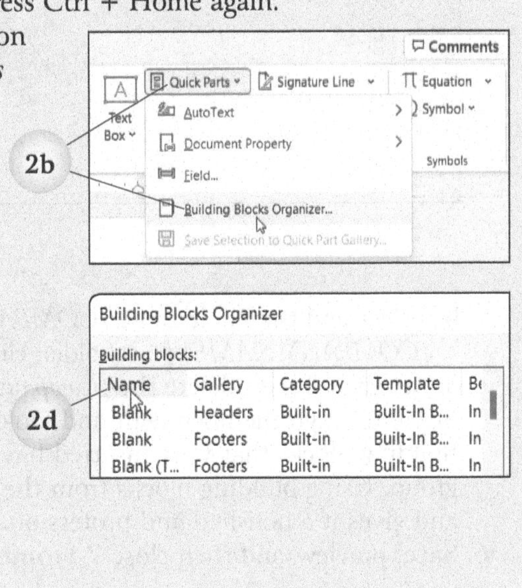

f. Click the Insert button at the bottom of the dialog box. (This inserts a contents page at the beginning of the document and creates a table of contents that includes the headings with styles applied.)

3. Insert a footer building block by completing the following steps:
   a. Click the Quick Parts button on the Insert tab and then click *Building Blocks Organizer*.
   b. Scroll down the Building Blocks Organizer list box, click the *Sempahore* footer, and then click the Insert button.
   c. Decrease the *Footer from Bottom* measurement to 0.3 inch (in the Position group on the Header & Footer tab).
   d. Click the Close Header and Footer button.
4. Insert a cover page building block by completing the following steps:
   a. Press Ctrl + Home to move the insertion point to the beginning of the document.
   b. Click the Insert tab, click the Quick Parts button, and then click *Building Blocks Organizer*.
   c. Scroll down the Building Blocks Organizer list box, click the *Semaphore* cover page, and then click the Insert button.
   d. Click the *[DATE]* placeholder and then type today's date.
   e. Click the *[DOCUMENT TITLE]* placeholder and then type Citizens for Consumer Safety. (The text will be converted to all uppercase letters.)
   f. Click the *[DOCUMENT SUBTITLE]* placeholder and then type Home Safety. (The text will be converted to small caps.)
   g. Select the name above the *[COMPANY NAME]* placeholder and then type your first and last names.

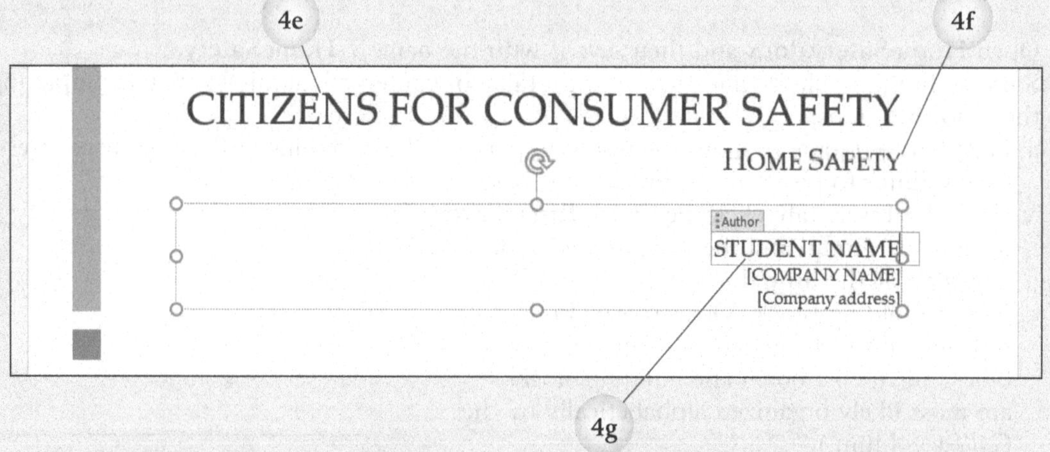

   h. Select and then delete the *[COMPANY NAME]* placeholder. (To do this, click in the *[COMPANY NAME]* placeholder, click the placeholder tab, and then press the Delete key.)
   i. Select and then delete the *[Company address]* placeholder.
5. Scroll through the document and look at each page. The Semaphore footer and cover page building blocks that were inserted have similar formatting and are part of the Semaphore group. Using building blocks from the same group provides consistency in the document and gives it a polished and professional appearance.
6. Save, preview, and then close **7-HomeSafety.docx**.

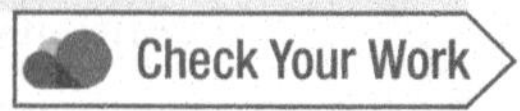

Activity 2 Create a Letter Document Using Custom Building Blocks 3 Parts

You will create custom building blocks and then use them to prepare a business letter.

Saving Content as a Building Block

Quick Steps

Save Content in Text Box Gallery

1. Select content.
2. Click Insert tab.
3. Click Text Box button.
4. Click *Save Selection to Text Box Gallery*.

Save Content in Header Gallery

1. Select content.
2. Click Insert tab.
3. Click Header button.
4. Click *Save Selection to Header Gallery*.

Save Content in Footer Gallery

1. Select content.
2. Click Insert tab.
3. Click Footer button.
4. Click *Save Selection to Footer Gallery*.

Hint When selecting content to save as a building block, turn on the display of nonprinting characters by clicking the Show/Hide ¶ button in the Paragraph group on the Home tab.

Saving Content as a Building Block

Consider saving data that is typed and formatted on a regular basis as a building block. Saving commonly created data as a building block saves time and reduces errors that might occur each time the data is typed or formatting is applied. The data can be saved as a building block in a specific gallery, such as the Text Box, Header, or Footer gallery, or saved in the AutoText gallery or Quick Part gallery.

Saving Content in a Specific Gallery To save content in a specific gallery, use the button for the gallery. For example, to save a text box in the Text Box gallery, use the Text Box button. To do this, select the text box, click the Insert tab, click the Text Box button, and then click the *Save Selection to Text Box Gallery* option at the drop-down gallery. At the Create New Building Block dialog box as shown in Figure 7.2, type a name for the text box building block, type a description of it, and then click OK.

To save content in the Header gallery, select the content, click the Insert tab, click the Header button, and then click the *Save Selection to Header Gallery* option at the drop-down gallery. This displays the Create New Building Block dialog box, as shown in Figure 7.2 (except *Headers* displays in the *Gallery* option box). Complete similar steps to save content in the Footer gallery and Cover Page gallery.

When data is saved as a building block, it is available in the Building Blocks Organizer dialog box. If content is saved as a building block in a specific gallery, the building block is available at both the Building Blocks Organizer dialog box and the gallery. For example, if a building block is saved in the Footer gallery, it is available when the Footer button on the Insert tab is clicked.

Figure 7.2 Create New Building Block Dialog Box

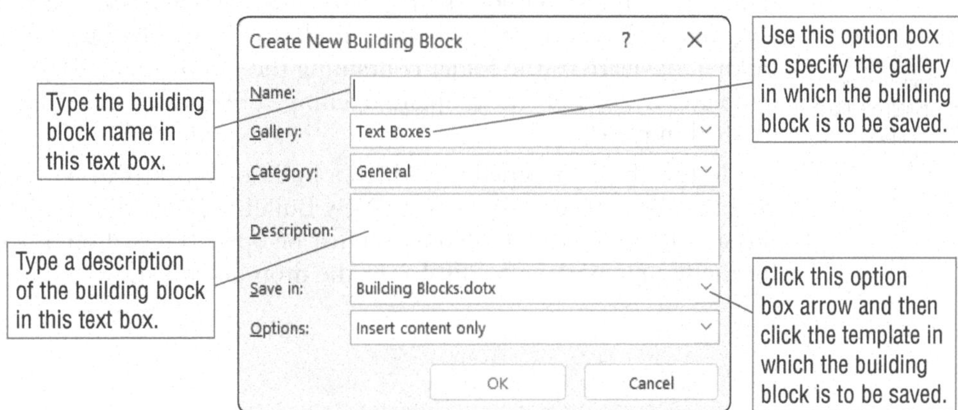

Quick Steps
Save Content in AutoText Gallery
1. Select content.
2. Click Insert tab.
3. Click Quick Parts button.
4. Point to *AutoText*.
5. Click *Save Selection to AutoText Gallery*.

Saving Content in the AutoText Gallery Content can be saved as a building block in the AutoText gallery. The building block can be inserted into a document by clicking the Insert tab, clicking the Quick Parts button, pointing to *AutoText*, and then clicking the AutoText building block at the side menu. To save content in the AutoText gallery, type and format the content and then select it. Click the Insert tab, click the Quick Parts button, point to *AutoText*, and then click the *Save Selection to AutoText Gallery* option at the side menu or use the keyboard shortcut Alt + F3. At the Create New Building Block dialog box, type a name for the building block, type a description of it, and then click OK.

Quick Steps
Save Content in Quick Part Gallery
1. Select content.
2. Click Insert tab.
3. Click Quick Parts button.
4. Click *Save Selection to Quick Part Gallery*.

Saving Content in the Quick Part Gallery Not only can content be saved in the AutoText gallery, but selected content can also be saved in the Quick Part gallery. To do this, select the content, click the Insert tab, click the Quick Parts button, and then click the *Save Selection to Quick Part Gallery* option at the drop-down gallery. This displays the Create New Building Block dialog box with *Quick Parts* specified in the *Gallery* option box and *Building Blocks.dotx* specified in the *Save in* option box. Type a name for the building block, type a description of it, and then click OK.

Quick Steps
Save as Template
1. Click File tab.
2. Click *Save As* option.
3. Click *Browse* option.
4. Click *Save as type* option.
5. Click *Word Template (*dotx)*.
6. Type name for template.
7. Click Save button.

Saving Building Blocks in a Specific Template By default, building block content is saved in one of two templates: *Building Blocks.dotx* or *Normal.dotm*. The template location depends on the gallery selected at the Create New Building Block dialog box. A building block saved in either of these templates is available each time a document is opened in Word. In a public environment, such as a school, saving to one of these templates may not be possible. To create a new personal template, display the Save As dialog box and then change the *Save as type* option to *Word Template (*.dotx)*. Choosing this option automatically selects the Custom Office Templates folder. Type a name for the template and then click the Save button; the template is saved in the Custom Office Templates folder.

Quick Steps
Open Document Based on Template
1. Click File tab.
2. Click *New* option.
3. Click *Personal* option.
4. Click template thumbnail.

OR

1. Click File Explorer icon on taskbar.
2. Navigate to folder containing template.
3. Double-click template.

To open a document based on a personal template, click the File tab and then click the *New* option. At the New backstage area, click the *Personal* option above the search text box. This displays thumbnails of the templates saved in the Custom Office Templates folder. Click the thumbnail of a specific template and a blank document opens based on the selected template.

Another option for opening a document based on a template is to save a template to a location other than the Custom Office Templates folder, such as the WL2C7 folder on your storage medium, and then use File Explorer to open a document based on the template. To do this, click the File Explorer icon on the taskbar, navigate to the folder containing the template, and then double-click the template. Instead of the template opening, a blank document opens that is based on the template.

To specify the template in which a building block is to be saved, click the *Save in* option box arrow in the Create New Building Block dialog box and then click the specific template. A document must be opened based on a personal template for the template name to display in the drop-down list.

Activity 2a Saving a Template and Saving Content in the Text Box, Footer, AutoText, and Quick Part Galleries

Part 1 of 3

1. Press Ctrl + N to display a blank document and then save the document as a template by completing the following steps:
   a. Press the F12 function key to display the Save As dialog box.
   b. At the Save As dialog box, type 7-QEATemplate in the *File name* text box.
   c. Click the *Save as type* option box and then click *Word Template (*.dotx)* at the drop-down list.
   d. Navigate to your WL2C7 folder.
   e. Click the Save button.
2. Close **7-QEATemplate.dotx**.
3. Open a document based on the template by completing the following steps:
   a. Click the File Explorer icon on the taskbar. (The taskbar displays along the bottom of the screen.)
   b. Navigate to your WL2C7 folder.
   c. Double-click ***7-QEATemplate.dotx***.
4. Insert the document named **QEAContent.docx** into the current document. (Do this by clicking the Object button arrow in the Text group on the Insert tab and then clicking *Text from File* at the drop-down list. This document is in your WL2C7 folder.)
5. Save the text box as a building block in the Text Box gallery by completing the following steps:
   a. Select the text box by clicking in it and then clicking its border.
   b. With the Insert tab active, click the Text Box button and then click *Save Selection to Text Box Gallery* at the drop-down list.
   c. At the Create New Building Block dialog box, type QEATextBox in the *Name* text box.
   d. Click the *Save in* option box arrow and then click *7-QEATemplate.dotx* at the drop-down list.
   e. Click OK to close the Create New Building Block dialog box.

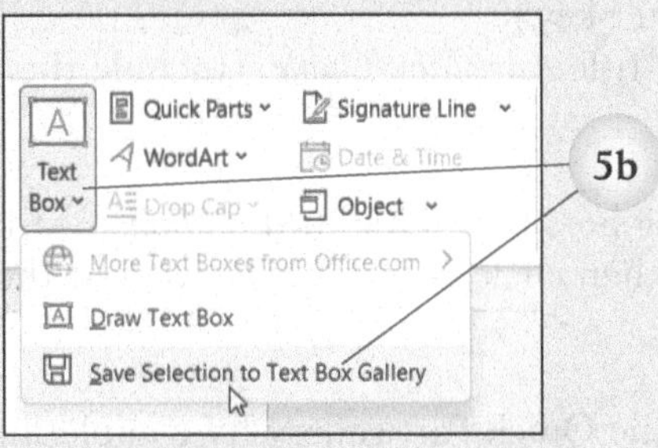

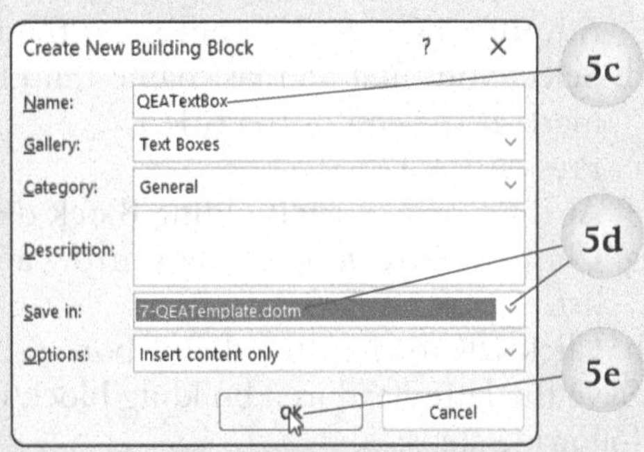

6. Save content as a building block in the Footer gallery by completing the following steps:
   a. Select the text *"Making your extreme adventure dreams a reality"* below the text box. (Be sure to select the paragraph mark at the end of the text. If necessary, click the Show/Hide ¶ button in the Paragraph group on the Home tab to display the paragraph mark.)
   b. Click the Footer button in the Header & Footer group on the Insert tab and then click *Save Selection to Footer Gallery* at the drop-down list.
   c. At the Create New Building Block dialog box, type QEAFooter in the *Name* text box.
   d. Click the *Save in* option box and then click *7-QEATemplate.dotx* at the drop-down list.
   e. Click OK to close the Create New Building Block dialog box.

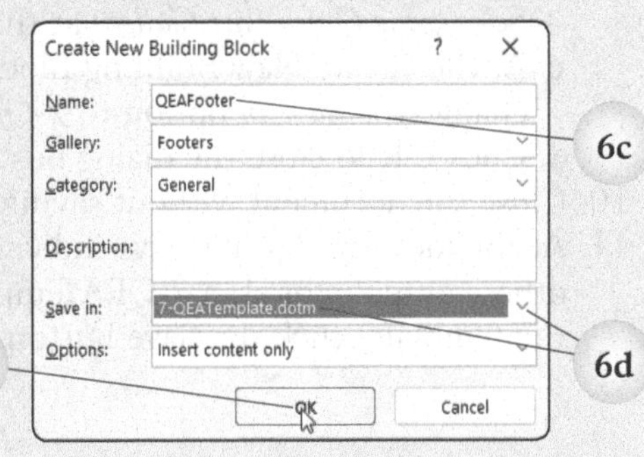

7. Save the company name *Southern Adventure Tours* and the address below it as a building block in the AutoText gallery by completing the following steps:
   a. Select the company name and address (the two lines below the company name). (Be sure to include the paragraph mark at the end of the last line of the address.)
   b. Click the Quick Parts button in the Text group on the Insert tab, point to *AutoText*, and then click *Save Selection to AutoText Gallery* at the side menu.

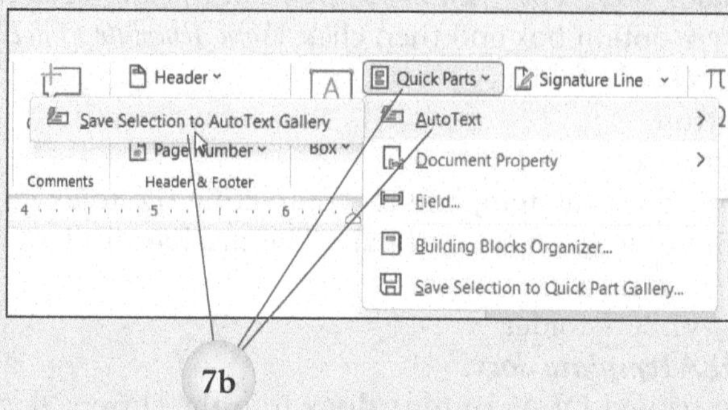

   c. At the Create New Building Block dialog box, type SAT in the *Name* text box.
   d. Click the *Save in* option box arrow and then click *7-QEATemplate.dotx* at the drop-down list.
   e. Click OK to close the dialog box.
8. Type your name and company title and then save the text as a building block in the AutoText gallery by completing the following steps:
   a. Move the insertion point two lines below the address for Southern Adventure Tours.
   b. Type your first and last names and then press the spacebar.
   c. Press the Down Arrow key to move the insertion point to the next line and then type Adventure Guide. (Do not press the Enter key.)
   d. Select your first and last names and the title *Adventure Guide*. (Include the paragraph mark at the end of the title.)
   e. Press Alt + F3.
   f. At the Create New Building Block dialog box, type Title in the *Name* text box.
   g. Click the *Save in* option box arrow and then click *7-QEATemplate.dotx* at the drop-down list.
   h. Click OK to close the dialog box.
9. Save the letterhead as a building block in the Quick Part gallery by completing the following steps:
   a. Select the letterhead text (the company name *QUEST EXTREME ADVENTURES*, the address and telephone number below the name, and the paragraph mark at the end of the address and telephone number).
   b. Click the Quick Parts button in the Text group on the Insert tab and then click *Save Selection to Quick Part Gallery* at the drop-down list.
   c. At the Create New Building Block dialog box, type QEA in the *Name* text box and then change the *Save in* option to *7-QEATemplate.dotx*.
   d. Click OK to close the dialog box.
10. Close the document without saving it.
11. At the message that displays indicating that you have modified styles, building blocks, or other content stored in 7-QEATemplate.dotx and asking if you want to save the changes to the template, click the Save button.

Editing Building Block Properties

Quick Steps

Edit Building Block

1. Click Insert tab.
2. Click Quick Parts button.
3. Click *Building Blocks Organizer*.
4. Click building block.
5. Click Edit Properties button.
6. Make changes.
7. Click OK.

OR

1. Click button.
2. Right-click custom building block.
3. Click *Edit Properties*.
4. Make changes.
5. Click OK.

Editing Building Block Properties

Changes can be made to the properties of a building block with options at the Modify Building Block dialog box. This dialog box contains the same options as the Create New Building Block dialog box.

Display the Modify Building Block dialog box by opening the Building Blocks Organizer dialog box, clicking the specific building block in the list box, and then clicking the Edit Properties button. The dialog box can also be displayed for a building block in the Quick Parts button drop-down gallery. To do this, click the Quick Parts button, right-click the building block in the drop-down gallery, and then click *Edit Properties* at the shortcut menu. Make changes to the Modify Building Block dialog box and then click OK. At the confirmation message, click Yes.

The dialog box can also be displayed for a custom building block in a button drop-down gallery by clicking the button, right-clicking the custom building block, and then clicking the *Edit Properties* option at the shortcut menu. For example, to modify a custom text box building block, click the Insert tab, click the Text Box button, and then scroll down the drop-down gallery to display the custom text box building block. Right-click the custom text box building block and then click *Edit Properties* at the shortcut menu.

Activity 2b **Editing Building Block Properties** — Part 2 of 3

1. Open a blank document based on your template **7-QEATemplate.dotx** by completing the following steps:
   a. Click the File Explorer icon on the taskbar.
   b. Navigate to your WL2C7 folder.
   c. Double-click ***7-QEATemplate.dotx***.
2. Edit the SAT building block by completing the following steps:
   a. Click the Insert tab, click the Quick Parts button, and then click *Building Blocks Organizer* at the drop-down list.
   b. At the Building Blocks Organizer dialog box, click the *Gallery* heading to sort the building blocks by gallery. (This displays the AutoText galleries at the beginning of the list.)
   c. Using the horizontal scroll bar at the bottom of the *Building blocks* list box, scroll to the right and notice that the SAT building block does not contain a description.
   d. Click the *SAT* building block in the list box.
   e. Click the Edit Properties button at the bottom of the dialog box.

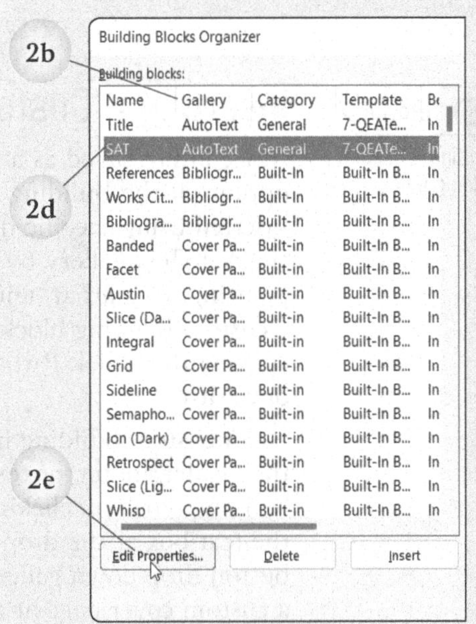

f. At the Modify Building Block dialog box, click in the *Name* text box and then type Address at the end of the name.

g. Click in the *Description* text box and then type Inserts the Southern Adventure Tours name and address.

h. Click OK to close the dialog box.

i. At the message asking if you want to redefine the building block entry, click Yes.

j. Close the Building Blocks Organizer dialog box.

3. Edit the letterhead building block by completing the following steps:

a. Click the Quick Parts button, right-click the *QEA* letterhead building block, and then click *Edit Properties* at the shortcut menu.

b. At the Modify Building Block dialog box, click in the *Name* text box and then type Letterhead at the end of the name.

c. Click in the *Description* text box and then type Inserts the Quest Extreme Adventures letterhead including the company name and address.

d. Click OK to close the dialog box.

e. At the message asking if you want to redefine the building block entry, click Yes.

4. Close the document.

5. At the message that displays, click the Save button.

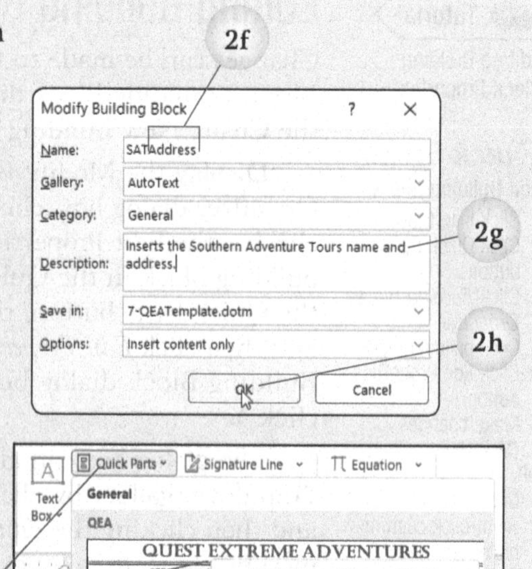

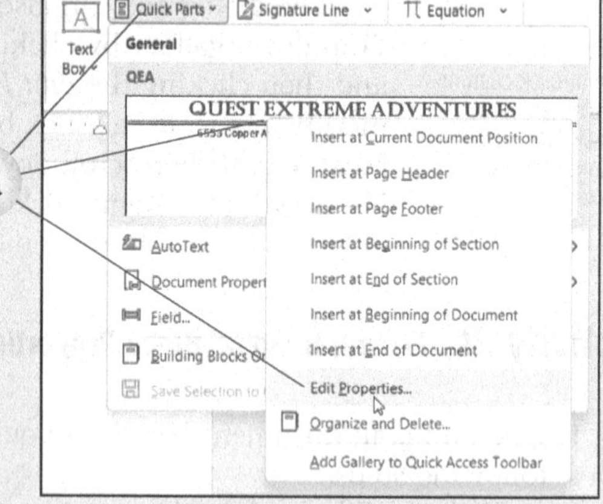

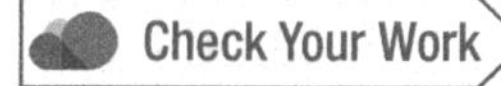

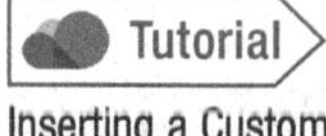

Inserting a Custom Building Block

Inserting a Custom Building Block

Any content saved as a building block can be inserted in a document using options at the Building Blocks Organizer dialog box. Some content can also be inserted using specific drop-down galleries. Insert a custom building block saved to the AutoText gallery by clicking the Insert tab, clicking the Quick Parts button, pointing to *AutoText*, and then clicking the building block at the side menu. Insert a custom building block saved to the Quick Part gallery by clicking the Insert tab, clicking the Quick Parts button, and then clicking the building block at the drop-down list.

A custom building block can also be inserted from a specific gallery such as the header, footer, or text box gallery. For example, insert a custom text box building block by clicking the Text Box button on the Insert tab and then clicking the text box at the drop-down gallery. Insert a custom header at the Header button drop-down gallery, a custom footer at the Footer button drop-down gallery, a custom cover page at the Cover Page button drop-down gallery, and so on.

Use the button drop-down gallery to specify where the custom building block content should be inserted in a document. To do this, display the button drop-down gallery, right-click the custom building block, and then click the location at the shortcut menu. For example, click the Insert tab, click the Quick Parts button, and then right-click the *QEALetterhead* building block and a shortcut menu displays, as shown in Figure 7.3.

Figure 7.3 Quick Parts Button Drop-Down Gallery Shortcut Menu

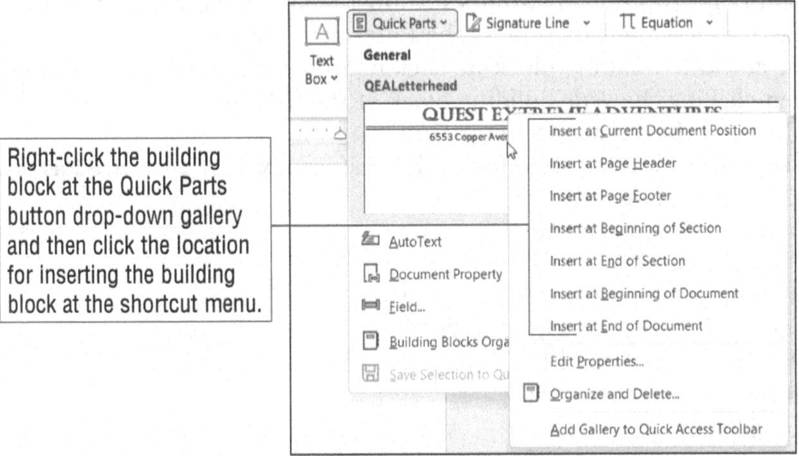

Activity 2c Inserting Custom Building Blocks

Part 3 of 3

1. Open File Explorer, navigate to your WL2C7 folder, and then double-click ***7-QEATemplate.dotx***.
2. At the blank document, click the *No Spacing* style in the Styles group on the Home tab.
3. Change the font to Candara.
4. Insert the letterhead building block as a header by completing the following steps:
   a. Click the Insert tab.
   b. Click the Quick Parts button, right-click the *QEALetterhead* building block, and then click the *Insert at Page Header* option at the shortcut menu.

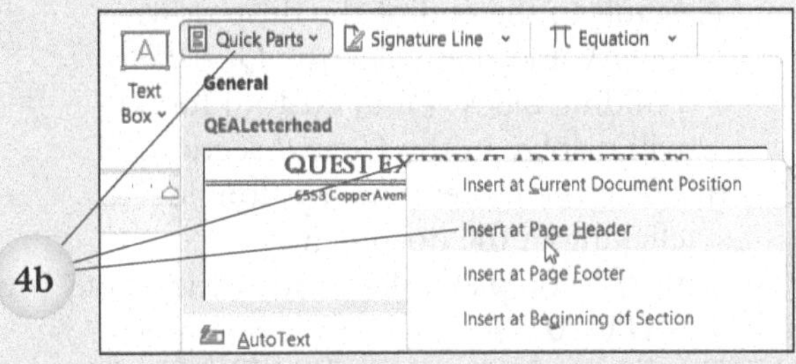

5. Press the Enter key two times, type the current date, and then press the Enter key five times.
6. Type Mr. Geraldo Vargas and then press the Enter key.
7. Insert the Southern Adventure Tours name and address building block by clicking the Quick Parts button, pointing to *AutoText*, and then clicking the *SATAddress* building block at the side menu.

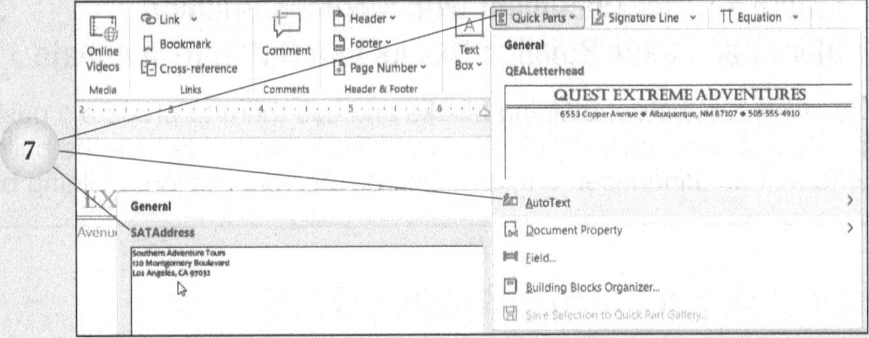

8. Press the Enter key and then insert a letter document by completing the following steps:
   a. Click the Object button arrow in the Text group on the Insert tab and then click *Text from File* at the drop-down list.
   b. At the Insert File dialog box, navigate to your WL2C7 folder and then double-click ***SATLetter01.docx***.

9. With the insertion point positioned two lines below the last paragraph of text in the body of the letter, type Sincerely, and then press the Enter key four times.
10. Insert your name and title building block by clicking the Quick Parts button, pointing to *AutoText*, and then clicking the *Title* building block at the side menu.
11. Press the Enter key and then type 7-SATLtr01.docx.
12. Press the Enter key five times and then insert the custom text box you saved as a building block by completing the following steps:
    a. Click the Text Box button in the Text group on the Insert tab.
    b. Scroll to the end of the drop-down gallery and then click the *QEATextBox* building block. (Your custom text box will display in the *General* section of the drop-down gallery.)
    c. Click in the document to deselect the text box.
13. Insert the custom footer you created by completing the following steps:
    a. Click the Insert tab.
    b. Click the Footer button in the Header & Footer group.
    c. Scroll to the end of the drop-down gallery and then click the *QEAFooter* building block. (Your custom footer will display in the *General* section.)
    d. Close the footer pane by double-clicking in the document.
14. Save the completed letter with the name **7-SATLtr01**.
15. Preview and then close **7-SATLtr01.docx**.

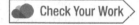

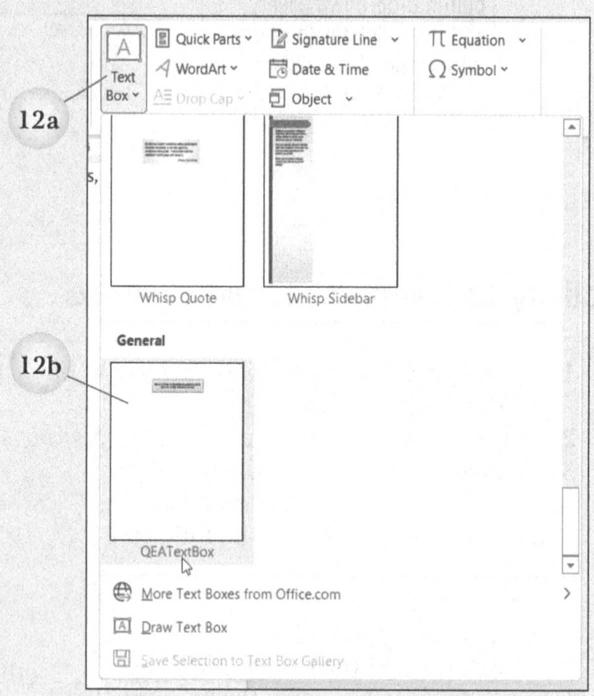

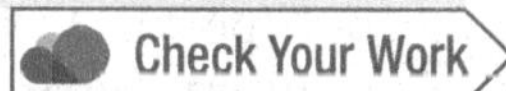

Activity 3 Create a Letter Document with Modified Building Blocks and Save Building Blocks to a Different Template — 3 Parts

You will modify your custom building blocks and use them to prepare a business letter. You will also save building blocks to a different template, use the building blocks to format an announcement, and then delete your custom building blocks.

Modifying and Deleting Building Blocks

Modifying a Custom Building Block

A building block can be inserted in a document, corrections or changes can be made to the building block, and then the building block can be saved with the same name or a different name. Save a building block with the same name when updating the building block to reflect any changes. Save the building block with a new name when using an existing building block as the foundation for creating a new building block.

To save a modified building block with the same name, insert the building block into the document and then make modifications. Select the building block data and then specify the gallery. At the Create New Building Block dialog box, type the original name and description and then click OK. At the confirmation message that displays, click Yes.

Adding a Building Block Gallery as a Button on the Quick Access Toolbar

Adding a Building Block Gallery as a Button on the Quick Access Toolbar

To make building blocks more accessible, add a building block gallery as a button on the Quick Access Toolbar. By default, the Quick Access Toolbar does not display. Turn on the display by clicking the Ribbon Display Options button (small button with down arrow) that displays at the right side of the ribbon and then click *Show Quick Access Toolbar* at the drop-down list.

Quick Steps

Add Building Block Gallery as Button on Quick Access Toolbar

1. Click specific button.
2. Right-click building block.
3. Click *Add Gallery to Quick Access Toolbar.*

To add a building block gallery as a button on the Quick Access Toolbar, display the toolbar, right-click a building block, and then click *Add Gallery to Quick Access Toolbar*. For example, to add the *Quick Part* gallery to the Quick Access Toolbar, click the Quick Parts button on the Insert tab, right-click a building block at the drop-down gallery, and then click *Add Gallery to Quick Access Toolbar*.

To remove a button from the Quick Access Toolbar, right-click the button and then click *Remove from Quick Access Toolbar* at the shortcut menu. Removing a button containing a building block gallery does not delete the building block. To turn off the display of the Quick Access Toolbar, click the Ribbon Display Options button and then click *Hide Quick Access Toolbar* at the drop-down list.

Activity 3a Modifying Building Blocks and Adding Custom Building Blocks as Buttons on the Quick Access Toolbar

Part 1 of 3

1. Open File Explorer, navigate to your WL2C7 folder, and then double-click *7-QEATemplate.dotx*.
2. Modify your name and title building block to reflect a title change by completing the following steps:
   a. At the blank document, click the Insert tab, click the Quick Parts button, point to *AutoText*, and then click the *Title* building block at the side menu.
   b. Edit your title so it displays as *Senior Adventure Guide*.
   c. Select your name and title, click the Quick Parts button, point to *AutoText*, and then click the *Save Selection to AutoText Gallery* option.
   d. At the Create New Building Block dialog box, type Title in the *Name* text box.
   e. Click the *Save in* option box arrow and then click *7-QEATemplate.dotx* at the drop-down list.
   f. Click OK.
   g. At the message asking if you want to redefine the building block entry, click Yes.
   h. With your name and title selected, press the Delete key to remove them from the document.

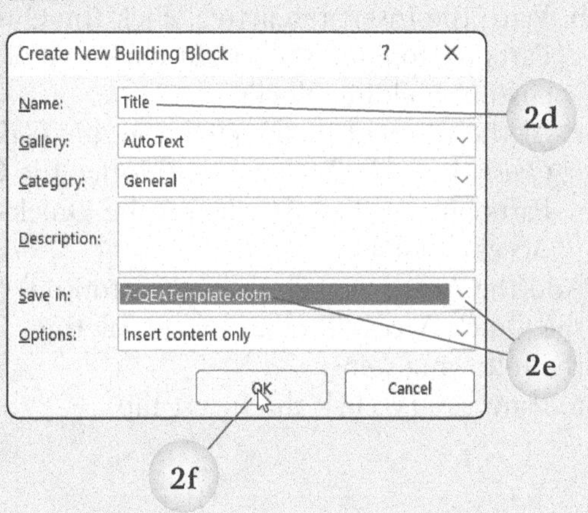

3. Since most of the correspondence you send to Southern Adventure Tours is addressed to Geraldo Vargas, you decide to include his name at the beginning of the company name and address by completing the following steps:
   a. With the Insert tab active, click the Quick Parts button, point to *AutoText*, and then click the *SATAddress* building block at the side menu.
   b. Type Mr. Geraldo Vargas above the name of the cruise line.
   c. Select the name, company name, and address.
   d. Click the Quick Parts button, point to *AutoText*, and then click the *Save Selection to AutoText Gallery* option.
   e. At the Create New Building Block dialog box, type SATAddress (the original name) in the *Name* text box.
   f. Click the *Save in* option box arrow and then click *7-QEATemplate.dotx* at the drop-down list.
   g. Click OK.
   h. At the message asking if you want to redefine the building block entry, click Yes.

3b

Mr. Geraldo Vargas
Southern Adventure Tours
120 Montgomery Boulevard
Los Angeles, CA 97032

4. Press Ctrl + End and then add the QEAFooter building block in the Quick Part gallery by completing the following steps:
   a. Click the Footer button on the Insert tab, scroll down the drop-down gallery, and then click the *QEAFooter* custom building block.
   b. Press the Down Arrow key to move the insertion point to the blank line below the text in the footer and then press the Backspace key to delete the extra space below the footer text.
   c. Press Ctrl + A to select the footer.
   d. Click the Insert tab, click the Quick Parts button, and then click *Save Selection to Quick Part Gallery*.
   e. At the Create New Building Block dialog box, type QEAFooter in the *Name* text box.
   f. Click the *Save in* option box arrow and then click *7-QEATemplate.dotx* at the drop-down list.
   g. Click OK to close the Create New Building Block dialog box. (You now have the footer saved in the Footer gallery and the Quick Part gallery.)
   h. Double-click in the document.
5. Add the Quick Part gallery as a button on the Quick Access Toolbar by completing the following steps:
   a. If the Quick Access Toolbar does not display, turn it on by clicking the Ribbon Display Options button at the right side of the ribbon and then clicking *Show Quick Access Toolbar* at the drop-down list.

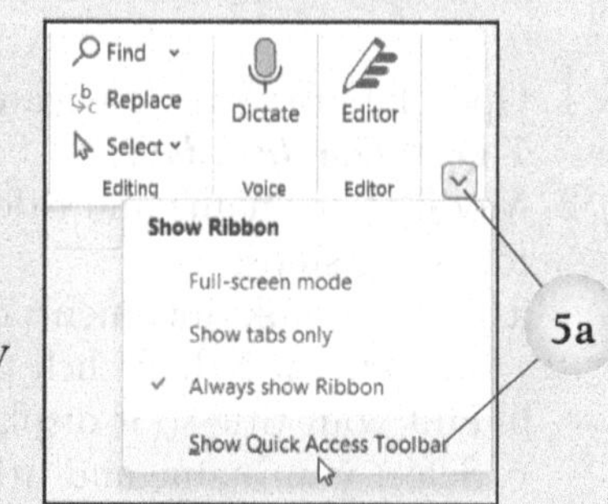

   b. With the Insert tab active, click the Quick Parts button and then right-click one of your custom building blocks.
   c. At the shortcut menu, click the *Add Gallery to Quick Access Toolbar* option. (Notice the Quick Parts button that appears on the Quick Access Toolbar.)
6. Add the AutoText gallery as a button on the Quick Access Toolbar by completing the following steps:
   a. If necessary, click the Insert tab.

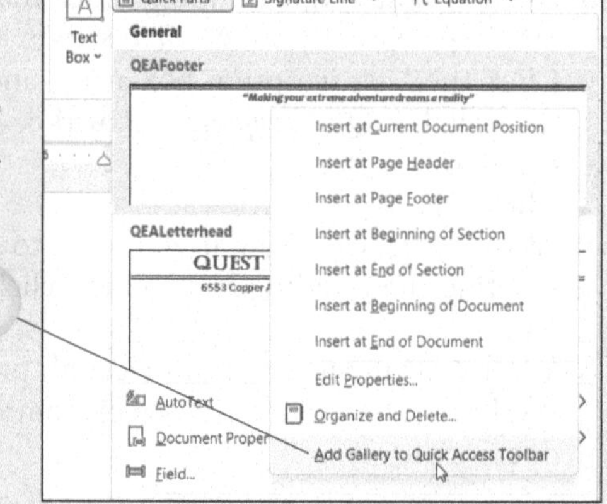

b. Click the Quick Parts button, point to *AutoText*, and then right-click one of your custom building blocks.
c. At the shortcut menu, click the *Add Gallery to Quick Access Toolbar* option. (Notice the AutoText button that appears on the Quick Access Toolbar.)

7. Close the document without saving it. At the message that displays indicating you have modified styles, building blocks, and other content, click the Save button.
8. Create a business letter by completing the following steps:
   a. Use File Explorer to open a blank document based on **7-QEATemplate.dotx** in your WL2C7 folder.
   b. Click the *No Spacing* style in the Styles group on the Home tab.
   c. Change the font to Candara.
   d. Insert the QEALetterhead building block as a page header.
   e. Press the Enter key two times, type today's date, and then press the Enter key four times.
   f. Insert the building block that includes the name Geraldo Vargas and the company name and address by clicking the AutoText button on the Quick Access Toolbar and then clicking the *SATAddress* building block at the drop-down list.
   g. Press the Enter key and then insert the file named **SATLetter02.docx** in your WL2C7 folder. ***Hint: Do this with the Object button arrow in the Text group on the Insert tab.***
   h. Type Sincerely, and then press the Enter key four times.
   i. Click the AutoText button on the Quick Access Toolbar and then click the *Title* building block.
   j. Press the Enter key and then type 7-SATLtr02.docx.
   k. Insert the footer building block by clicking the Quick Parts button on the Quick Access Toolbar, right-clicking *QEAFooter*, and then clicking *Insert at Page Footer* at the shortcut menu.

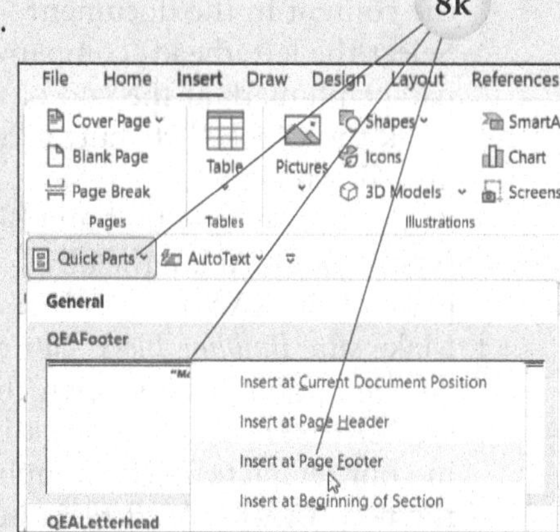

9. Save the completed letter with the name **7-SATLtr02**.
10. Preview and then close **7-SATLtr02.docx**.
11. Use File Explorer to open a blank document based on your template **7-QEATemplate.dotx**.
12. Click the AutoText button on the Quick Access Toolbar, press the Print Screen button on your keyboard, and then click in the document to remove the drop-down list.
13. At the blank document, click the Paste button. (This pastes the screen capture in your document.)
14. Save the document with the name **7-ScreenCapture**.
15. Preview and then close **7-ScreenCapture.docx**.
16. Remove the Quick Parts button you added to the Quick Access Toolbar by right-clicking the Quick Parts button and then clicking *Remove from Quick Access Toolbar* at the shortcut menu. Complete similar steps to remove the AutoText button from the Quick Access Toolbar. (The buttons will display dimmed if no documents are open.)
17. If necessary, turn off the display of the Quick Access Toolbar by clicking the Ribbon Display Options button and then clicking *Hide Quick Access Toolbar* at the drop-down list.

Check Your Work

Saving Building Blocks in a Different Template

Building blocks saved to a personal template are available only when a document is opened based on the template. To make building blocks available for all documents, save them in the Building Block.dotx template or Normal.dotm template. Use the *Save in* option at the Create New Building Block or Modify Building Block dialog box to save building blocks to one of these two templates.

If an existing building block in a personal template is modified and saved in the Normal.dotm or Building Block.dotx template, the building block is no longer available in the personal template. It is available only in documents based on the default template Normal.dotm. To keep a building block in a personal template and also make it available for other documents, insert the building block content in the document, select the content, and then create a new building block.

Activity 3b Saving Building Blocks in a Different Template — Part 2 of 3

1. Use File Explorer to open a blank document based on your template **7-QEATemplate.dotx**.
2. Create a new QEALetterhead building block and save it in the Building Blocks.dotx template so it is available for all documents by completing the following steps:
   a. Click the Insert tab.
   b. Click the Quick Parts button and then click the *QEALetterhead* building block to insert the content in the document.
   c. Select the letterhead (company name, address, and telephone number, including the paragraph mark at the end of the line containing the address and telephone number).
   d. Click the Quick Parts button and then click *Save Selection to Quick Part Gallery* at the drop-down list.
   e. At the Create New Building Block dialog box, type XXX-QEALetterhead. (Type your initials in place of the *XXX*.)
   f. Make sure *Building Blocks.dotx* displays in the *Save in* option box and then click OK. (The *QEALetterhead* building block is still available in your template 7-QEATemplate.dotx, and the new *XXX-QEALetterhead* building block is available in all documents, including documents based on your 7-QEATemplate.dotx template.)

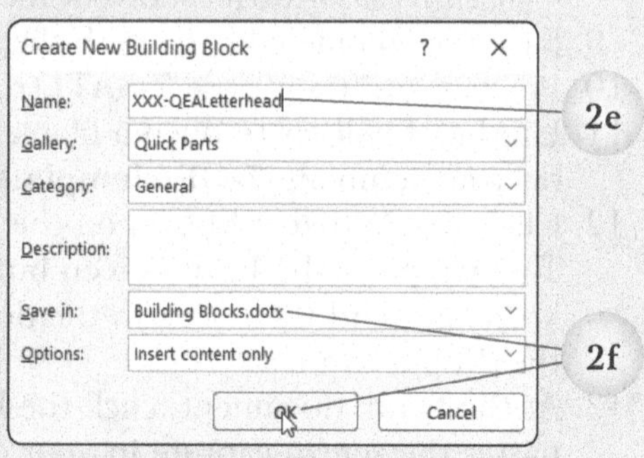

   g. Delete the selected letterhead text.
3. Create a new *QEAFooter* building block and then save it in the Building Blocks.dotx template so it is available for all documents by completing the following steps:
   a. Click the Quick Parts button and then click the *QEAFooter* building block to insert the content in the document.
   b. Select the footer text *"Making your extreme adventure dreams a reality"* (including the paragraph mark at the end of the text).
   c. Click the Quick Parts button and then click *Save Selection to Quick Part Gallery* at the drop-down list.
   d. At the Create New Building Block dialog box, type XXX-QEAFooter. (Type your initials in place of the *XXX*.)
   e. Make sure *Building Blocks.dotx* displays in the *Save in* option box and then click OK.
4. Close the document without saving it.

5. Open **QEAContent.docx.**
6. Create a new *QEATextBox* building block and save it in the *Building Blocks.dotx* template so it is available for all documents by completing the following steps:
   a. Select the text box by clicking the text box and then clicking the text box border.
   b. Click the Insert tab, click the Text Box button, and then click *Save Selection to Text Box Gallery* at the drop-down list.
   c. At the Create New Building Block dialog box, type XXX-QEATextBox. (Type your initials in place of the *XXX*.)
   d. Make sure *Building Blocks.dotx* displays in the *Save in* option box and then click OK.
7. Close **QEAContent.docx.**
8. Insert in a document the building blocks you created by completing the following steps:
   a. Open **SATAnnounce.docx** and then save it with the name **7-SATAnnounce.**
   b. Insert the *XXX-QEALetterhead* building block as a header by clicking the Insert tab, clicking the Quick Parts button, right-clicking *XXX-QEALetterhead* (where your initials display in place of the *XXX*), and then clicking *Insert at Page Header* at the shortcut menu.

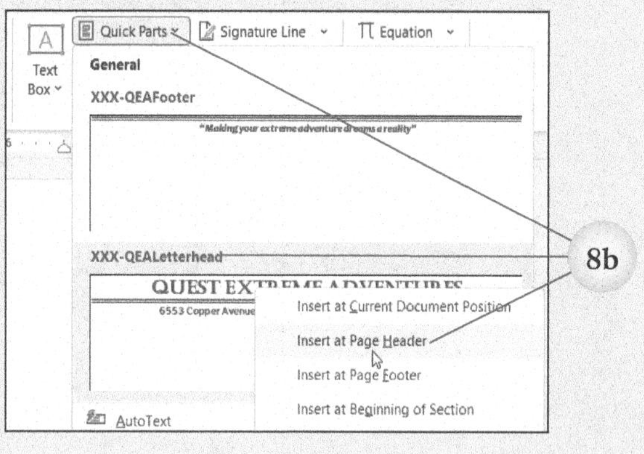

   c. Insert the *XXX-QEAFooter* building block by clicking the Quick Parts button, right-clicking *XXX-QEAFooter* (where your initials display in place of the *XXX*), and then clicking *Insert at Page Footer* at the shortcut menu.
   d. Press Ctrl + End to move the insertion point to the end of the document.
   e. Insert the *XXX-QEATextBox* building block by clicking the Text Box button, scrolling down the drop-down gallery, and then clicking *XXX-QEATextBox* (where your initials display in place of the *XXX*).
   f. Horizontally align the text box by clicking the Align button in the Arrange group on the Shape Format tab and then clicking *Distribute Horizontally* at the drop-down list.

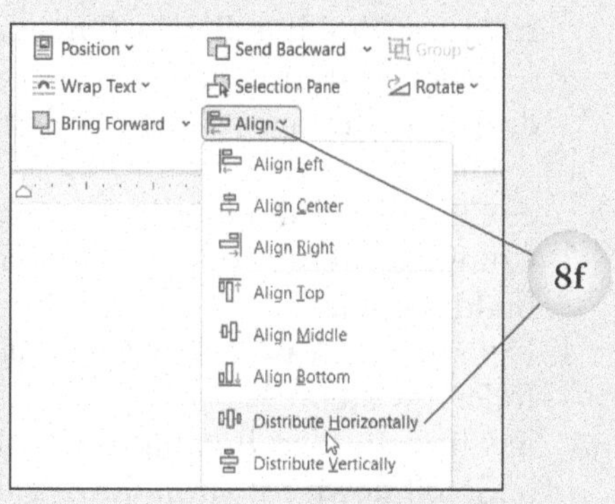

9. Save, preview, and then close **7-SATAnnounce.docx.**

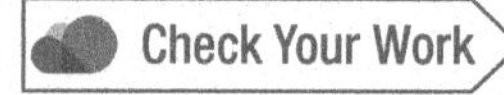

Quick Steps

Delete Building Block

1. Display Building Blocks Organizer dialog box.
2. Click building block.
3. Click Delete button.
4. Click Yes.

OR

1. Display button drop-down gallery.
2. Right-click building block.
3. Click *Organize and Delete* option.
4. Click Delete button.
5. Click Yes.

Deleting a Building Block

A custom building block that is no longer needed can be deleted by displaying the Building Blocks Organizer dialog box, clicking the building block, and then clicking the Delete button. At the confirmation message box, click Yes.

Another method for deleting a custom building block is to right-click the building block at the drop-down gallery and then click the *Organize and Delete* option at the shortcut menu. This displays the Building Blocks Organizer dialog box with the building block selected. Click the Delete button and then click Yes at the confirmation message box.

Activity 3c Deleting Building Blocks

Part 3 of 3

1. Press Ctrl + N to open a blank document.
2. Delete the *XXX-QEALetterhead* building block by completing the following steps:
   a. Click the Insert tab and then click the Quick Parts button in the Text group.
   b. Right-click the *XXX-QEALetterhead* building block and then click *Organize and Delete* at the shortcut menu.

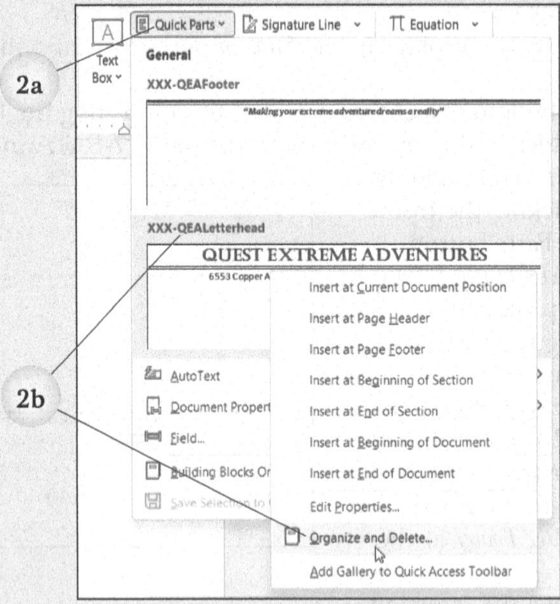

   c. At the Building Blocks Organizer dialog box with the building block selected, click the Delete button.
   d. At the message asking if you are sure you want to delete the selected building block, click Yes.
   e. Close the Building Blocks Organizer dialog box.
3. Complete steps similar to those in Steps 2a through 2e to delete the *XXXQEAFooter* building block.
4. Delete the *XXX-QEATextBox* building block (in the Text Box gallery) by completing the following steps:
   a. Click the Text Box button in the Text group on the Insert tab.
   b. Scroll down the drop-down gallery to display your custom text box.
   c. Right-click your text box and then click *Organize and Delete* at the shortcut menu.
   d. At the Building Blocks Organizer dialog box with the building block selected, click the Delete button.
   e. At the message asking if you are sure you want to delete the selected building block, click Yes.
   f. Close the Building Blocks Organizer dialog box.
5. Close the document without saving it.

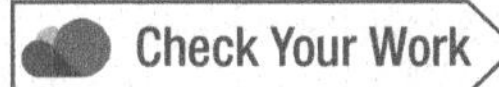

Activity 4 Insert Document Properties and Fields in a Testing Agreement Document — 2 Parts

You will open a testing agreement document and then insert and update document properties and fields.

Inserting a Document Property Placeholder

Inserting a Document Property Placeholder

Click the Quick Parts button on the Insert tab and then point to *Document Property* at the drop-down list and a side menu displays with document property options. Click an option at this side menu and a document property placeholder is inserted in the document. Text can be typed in the placeholder.

If a document property placeholder is inserted in multiple locations in a document, updating one occurrence of the placeholder will automatically update all occurrences of that placeholder in the document. For example, in Activity 4a, a Company document property placeholder is inserted in six locations in a document. The content of the first occurrence of the placeholder will be changed and the remaining placeholders will update to reflect the change.

Click the File tab and then click the *Info* option and the Info backstage area displays containing information about the document. Document properties display at the right side of the Info backstage area, including information such as the document size, number of pages, title, and comments.

Activity 4a Inserting Document Property Placeholders — Part 1 of 2

1. Open **TestAgrmnt.docx** and then save it with the name **7-TestAgrmnt**.
2. Select the first occurrence of *FP* in the document (in the first line of text after the title) and then insert a document property placeholder by completing the following steps:
   a. Click the Insert tab, click the Quick Parts button in the Text group, point to *Document Property*, and then click *Company* at the side menu.
   b. Type Frontier Productions in the company placeholder.
   c. Press the Right Arrow key to move the insertion point outside the company placeholder.
3. Select each remaining occurrence of *FP* in the document (it appears five more times) and insert the company document property placeholder. (The company name, *Frontier Productions,* will automatically be inserted in the placeholder.)

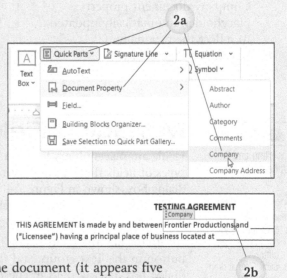

4. Press Ctrl + End to move the insertion point to the end of the document and then insert a comments document property placeholder by completing the following steps:
   a. Click the Quick Parts button, point to *Document Property*, and then click *Comments* at the side menu.
   b. Type First Draft in the comments placeholder.
   c. Press the Right Arrow key.
   d. Press Shift + Enter.
5. Click the File tab, click the *Info* option, and notice that the comment typed in the comments document property placeholder displays at the right side of the Info backstage area. Click the Back button to display the document.

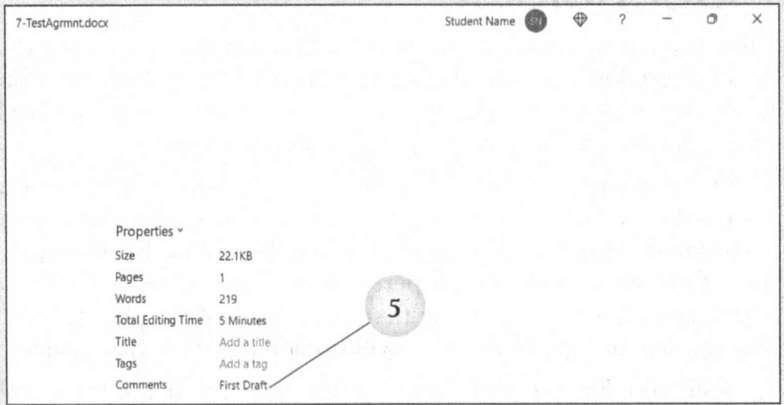

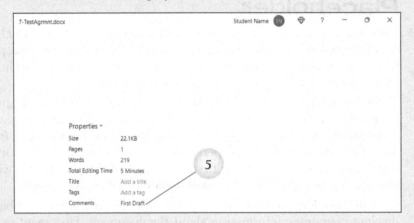

6. Save and then preview **7-TestAgrmnt.docx**.
7. Click in the first occurrence of the company name *Frontier Productions* and then click the company placeholder tab. (This selects the company placeholder.)
8. Type Frontier Video Productions.
9. Press the Right Arrow key. (Notice that the other occurrences of the Company document property placeholder automatically updated to reflect the new name.)
10. Save **7-TestAgrmnt.docx**.

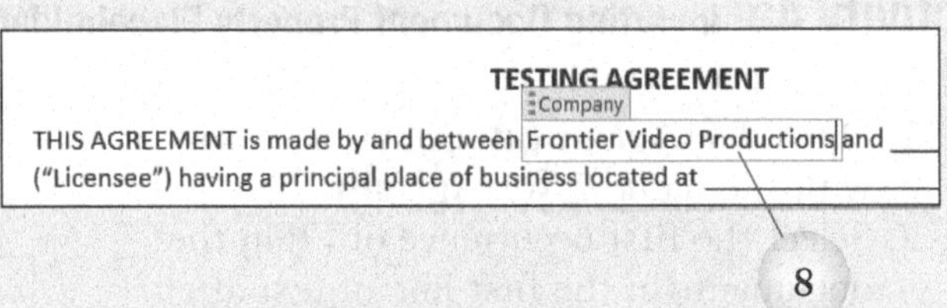

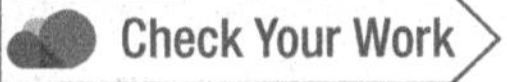

Inserting and Updating Fields

Quick Steps

Insert Field
1. Click Insert tab.
2. Click Quick Parts button.
3. Click *Field* at drop-down list.
4. Click field.
5. Click OK.

Managing Fields

Fields are placeholders for data that varies. Word provides buttons for many of the types of fields that can be inserted in a document as well as options at the Field dialog box, shown in Figure 7.4. This dialog box contains a list of all the available fields. Just as the Building Blocks Organizer dialog box is a central location for building blocks, the Field dialog box is a central location for fields.

To display the Field dialog box, click the Insert tab, click the Quick Parts button in the Text group, and then click *Field* at the drop-down list. At the Field dialog box, click a field in the *Field names* list box and then click OK.

Figure 7.4 Field Dialog Box

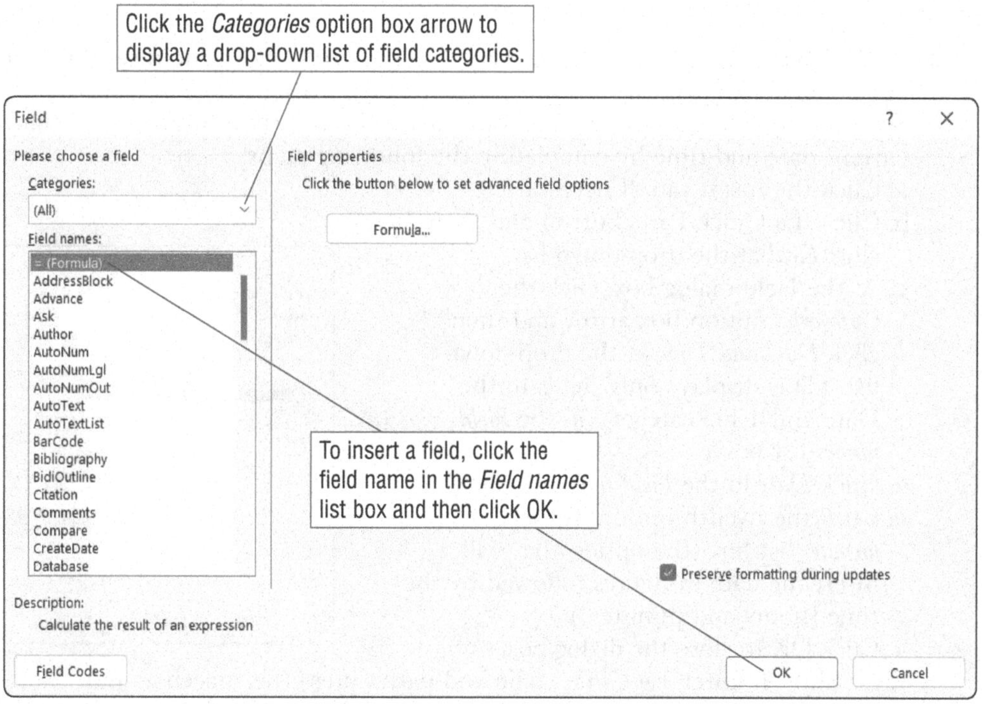

Choosing Field Categories

All the available fields display in the *Field names* list box at the Field dialog box. Narrow the list of fields to a specific category by clicking the *Categories* option box arrow and then clicking a specific category at the drop-down list. For example, to display only date and time fields, click the *Date and Time* category at the drop-down list.

Creating Custom Field Formats

Click a field in the *Field names* list box and a description of the field displays below the list box. Field properties related to the selected field also display in the dialog box. Custom field formats can be created for some fields. For example, click the *NumWords* field in the *Field names* list box and custom formatting options display in the *Format* list box and the *Numeric format* list box.

By default, the *Preserve formatting during updates* check box contains a check mark. With this option active, the custom formatting specified for a field will be preserved if the field is updated.

Updating Fields

Quick Steps

Update Field

1. Click field.
2. Click Update tab.

OR

1. Click field.
2. Press F9.

OR

1. Right-click field.
2. Click *Update Field.*

Some fields, such as the date and time field, update automatically when a document is opened. Other fields can be updated manually. A field can be updated manually by clicking the field and then clicking the Update tab; by clicking the field and then pressing the F9 function key; and by right-clicking the field and then clicking *Update Field* at the shortcut menu. Update all the fields in a document (except headers, footers, and text boxes) by pressing Ctrl + A to select the document and then pressing the F9 function key.

Activity 4b Inserting and Formatting Fields

Part 2 of 2

1. With **7-TestAgrmnt.docx** open, press Ctrl + End to move the insertion point to the end of the document.
2. Type Current date and time:, press the spacebar, and then insert a field that inserts the current date and time by completing the following steps:
   a. Click the Insert tab, if necessary.
   b. Click the Quick Parts button and then click *Field* at the drop-down list.
   c. At the Field dialog box, click the *Categories* option box arrow and then click *Date and Time* at the drop-down list. (This displays only fields in the Date and Time category in the *Field names* list box.)
   d. Click *Date* in the *Field names* list box.
   e. Click the twelfth option in the *Date formats* list box (the option that will insert the date in figures followed by the time [hours and minutes]).
   f. Click OK to close the dialog box.
3. Press Shift + Enter, type File name and path:, press the spacebar, and then insert a field for the current file name with custom field formatting by completing the following steps:
   a. With the Insert tab active, click the Quick Parts button and then click *Field* at the drop-down list.
   b. At the Field dialog box, click the *Categories* option box arrow and then click *Document Information* at the drop-down list.
   c. Click *FileName* in the *Field names* list box.
   d. Click the *Uppercase* option in the *Format* list box.
   e. Click the *Add path to filename* check box to insert a check mark.

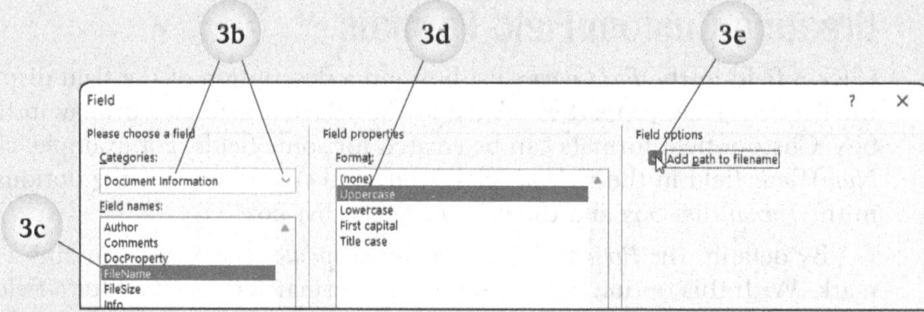

   f. Click OK to close the dialog box. (The current file name is inserted in the document in uppercase letters and includes the path to the file name.)
4. Insert a header and then insert a custom field in the header by completing the following steps:
   a. Click the Header button in the Header & Footer group and then click *Edit Header* at the drop-down list.
   b. In the Header pane, press the Tab key two times. (This moves the insertion point to the right tab at the right margin.)
   c. Click the Quick Parts button in the Insert group on the Header & Footer tab and then click *Field* at the drop-down list.

d. At the Field dialog box, click the *Categories* option box arrow and then click *Date and Time* at the drop-down list.
e. Click in the *Date formats* text box and then type MMMM yyyy. (This tells Word to insert the month as text followed by the four-digit year.)
f. Click OK to close the dialog box.
g. Double-click in the document.

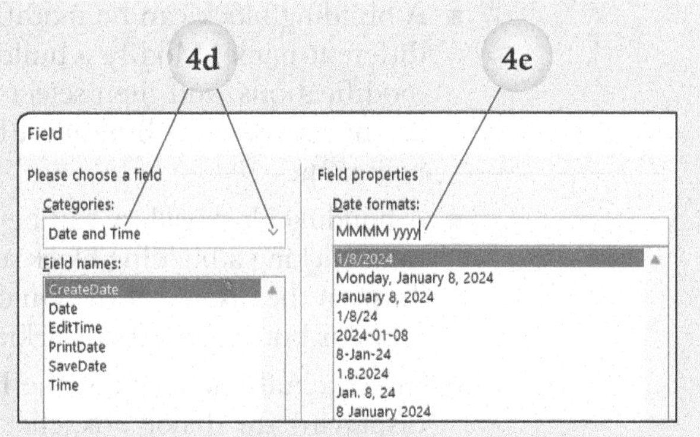

5. Update the time in the date and time field at the end of the document by clicking the date and time and then clicking the Update tab.
6. Save, preview, and then close **7-TestAgrmnt.docx**. (If a message displays asking if you want to save the changes to the template, click the Don't Save button.)

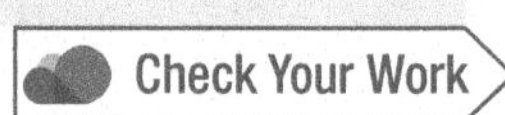

Chapter Summary

- Word provides a number of predesigned building blocks that can be used to help build a document.
- Insert building blocks at the Building Blocks Organizer dialog box. Display the dialog box by clicking the Quick Parts button in the Text group on the Insert tab and then clicking *Building Blocks Organizer* at the drop-down list.
- Sort building blocks at the Building Blocks Organizer dialog box by clicking the column heading.
- Content can be saved as building blocks in specific galleries, such as the Text Box, Header, Footer, and Cover Page galleries.
- Save content to the AutoText gallery by selecting the content, clicking the Insert tab, clicking the Quick Parts button, pointing to *AutoText*, and then clicking the *Save Selection to AutoText Gallery* option.
- Save content to the Quick Part gallery by selecting the content, clicking the Insert tab, clicking the Quick Parts button, and then clicking *Save Selection to Quick Part Gallery*.
- Building block content is saved, by default, to the *Building Blocks.dotx* template or the *Normal.dotm* template. The template location depends on the gallery selected at the Create New Building Block dialog box. A personal template can be created and saved to the Custom Office Templates folder and then building blocks can be saved to the personal template using the *Save in* option at the Create New Building Block dialog box.
- Open a personal template saved to the Custom Office Templates folder at the New backstage area with the *Personal* option selected.
- A personal template can be created and saved to a specific location other than the Custom Office Templates folder and then File Explorer can be used to open a document based on the template.
- Edit building block properties with options at the Modify Building Block dialog box. Display this dialog box by displaying the Building Blocks Organizer dialog box, clicking the specific building block in the list box, and then clicking the Edit Properties button.

- A building block can be modified and then saved with the same name or a different name. Modify a building block by inserting the building block, making modifications, and then select the building block data and specify the gallery. At the Create New Building Block dialog box, type the original name or type a new name.
- A building block gallery can be added as a button on the Quick Access Toolbar by right-clicking a building block and then clicking *Add Gallery to Quick Access Toolbar*. Turn on the display of the Quick Access Toolbar by clicking the Ribbon Display Options button and then clicking *Show Quick Access Toolbar* at the drop-down list.
- Insert a building block at the Building Blocks Organizer dialog box by displaying the dialog box, clicking the building block in the *Building blocks* list box, and then clicking the Insert button.
- Insert a custom building block saved to the AutoText gallery by clicking the Insert tab, clicking the Quick Parts button, pointing to *AutoText*, and then clicking the building block at the side menu.
- Insert a custom building block saved to the Quick Part gallery by clicking the Insert tab, clicking the Quick Parts button, and then clicking the building block at the drop-down list.
- Insert a custom building block from a specific drop-down gallery using a button by clicking the specific button (such as the Text Box, Header, Footer, or Cover Page button), scrolling down the drop-down gallery, and then clicking the custom building block at the gallery.
- Delete a building block at the Building Blocks Organizer dialog box by clicking the building block, clicking the Delete button, and then clicking Yes at the confirmation message.
- Insert a document property placeholder by clicking the Insert tab, clicking the Quick Parts button, pointing to *Document Property*, and then clicking the document property placeholder at the side menu.
- Fields are placeholders for data that varies. They can be inserted with options at the Field dialog box, which is a central location for all the fields provided by Word. Display the Field dialog box by clicking the Quick Parts button and then clicking *Field* at the drop-down list.
- A custom field format can be created for some fields by clicking the field in the *Field names* list box at the Field dialog box and then customizing formatting options.
- Some fields in a document update automatically when a document is opened. Other fields can be manually updated by clicking the field and then clicking the Update tab, by clicking the field and then pressing the F9 function key, or by right-clicking the field and then clicking *Update Field* at the shortcut menu.

Commands Review

FEATURE	RIBBON TAB, GROUP	BUTTON, OPTION	KEYBOARD SHORTCUT
Building Blocks Organizer dialog box	Insert, Text	*, Building Blocks Organizer*	
Create New Building Block dialog box	Insert, Text	*, Save Selection to Quick Part Gallery*	Alt + F3
Document Property side menu	Insert, Text	*, Document Property*	
Field dialog box	Insert, Text	*, Field*	

Review and Assessment

CHAPTER 7

Skills Assessment

Assessment 1: Create Building Blocks

1. Press Ctrl + N to open a blank document and then save the blank document as a template in your WL2C7 folder with the name **7-WLTemplate**. (Make sure to change the *Save as type* option at the Save As dialog box to *Word Template.dotx*.)
2. Close **7-WLTemplate.dotx**.
3. Use File Explorer to open a document based on **7-WLTemplate.dotx** in your WL2C7 folder.
4. Insert **WLFooter.docx** into the document. ***Hint: Use the Object button arrow on the Insert tab.***
5. Select the line of text containing the address and telephone number (including the nonprinting paragraph mark that ends the line). Save the selected text in a custom building block in the Footer gallery; name the building block *WLFooter* and save it in **7-WLTemplate.dotx**. ***Hint: Use the Footer button to save the content to the Footer gallery.***
6. Select the entire document, press the Delete key, and then insert **WLHeading.docx** into the current document. ***Hint: Use the Object button arrow on the Insert tab.***
7. Select the two lines of text (including the paragraph mark at the end of the second line). Save the selected text in a custom building block in the Quick Part gallery; name the building block *WLHeading* and save it in **7-WLTemplate.dotx**.
8. Select the entire document, press the Delete key, and then insert **WLFees.docx** into the current document. ***Hint: Use the Object button arrow on the Insert tab.***
9. Select the paragraph of text (including the paragraph mark at the end of the paragraph), save the selected text in a custom building block in the AutoText gallery and name the building block *WLFeesPara* and save it in **7-WLTemplate.dotx**.
10. Close the document without saving it. At the message asking if you want to save changes to the template, click the Save button.

Assessment 2: Use Building Blocks to Prepare an Agreement

1. Use File Explorer to open a blank document based on **7-WLTemplate.dotx** in your WL2C7 folder.
2. At the blank document, create an agreement with the following specifications:
   a. Insert the *WLHeading* custom building block in the Quick Part gallery.
   b. Press the Enter key and then insert the *WLFeesPara* custom building block in the AutoText gallery.
   c. Insert **WLRepAgrmnt.docx**. ***Hint: Use the Object button arrow on the Insert tab.***
   d. Insert the *WLFooter* custom building block. ***Hint: Do this with the Footer button.***

3. Click the Close Header and Footer button.
4. Save the completed agreement with the name **7-WLRepAgrmnt**.
5. Preview and then close **7-WLRepAgrmnt.docx**.
6. Use File Explorer to open a document based on **7-WLTemplate.dotx**.
7. Click the Insert tab, click the Quick Parts button, and then point to *AutoText*.
8. Press the Print Screen button on your keyboard and then click in the document.
9. At the blank document, click the Paste button.
10. Preview the document and then close it without saving it.

Assessment 3

Format a Report on the Writing Process

1. Open **WritingProcess.docx** and then save it with the name **7-WritingProcess**.
2. With the insertion point positioned at the beginning of the document, insert the *Automatic Table 2* table of contents building block.
3. Insert the *Banded* header building block, click the *[DOCUMENT TITLE]* placeholder and then type writing process.
4. Insert the *Banded* footer building block and then make the document active.
5. Press Ctrl + End to move the insertion point to the end of the document and then insert a field that will insert the file name (without any formatting).
6. Press Shift + Enter and then insert a field that will insert the current date and time (you choose the format).
7. Save, preview, and then close **7-WritingProcess.docx**.

Assessment 4

Insert an Equation Building Block

1. The Building Blocks Organizer dialog box contains a number of predesigned equations that you can insert in a document. At a blank document, display the Building Blocks Organizer dialog box and then insert one of the predesigned equations.
2. Select the equation and then click the Equation tab. Notice the groups of commands available for editing an equation.
3. Type the steps you followed to insert the equation and then type a list of the groups available on the Equation tab.
4. Save the document with the name **7-Equation**.
5. Preview and then close **7-Equation.docx**.

Visual Benchmark

Create an Agreement with Building Blocks and AutoCorrect Text

1. Use File Explorer to open a document based on **7-WLTemplate.dotx**.
2. Create the document shown in Figure 7.5 with the following specifications:
   a. Insert **WLAgreement.docx** into the open document.
   b. Display the AutoCorrect dialog box with the AutoCorrect tab selected and then create AutoCorrect entries for the text *Woodland Legal Services* (use *wls*) and *Till-Harris Management* (use *thm*).
   c. Press Ctrl + Home, press the Enter key, and then type the first two paragraphs of text shown in Figure 7.5 using the AutoCorrect entries you created.
   d. Move the insertion point to the beginning of the document and then insert the *WLHeading* building block and insert the *WLFooter* building block as a footer.
   e. Justify the six paragraphs of text in the document.

3. Save the completed document with the name **7-THMAgrmnt**.
4. Preview and then close **7-THMAgrmnt.docx**.
5. Display the AutoCorrect dialog box, delete the *wls* and *thm* entries, and then close the dialog box.

Figure 7.5 Visual Benchmark

REPRESENTATION AGREEMENT

Carlos Sawyer, Attorney at Law

This agreement is made between Carlos Sawyer of Woodland Legal Services and Till-Harris Management for legal services to be provided by Woodland Legal Services.

Legal Representation: Woodland Legal Services will perform the legal services required by Till-Harris Management, keep Till-Harris Management informed of progress and developments, and respond promptly to Till-Harris Management's inquiries and communications.

Attorney's Fees and Costs: Till-Harris Management will pay Woodland Legal Services for attorney's fees for legal services provided under this agreement at the hourly rate of the individuals providing the services. Under this agreement, Till-Harris Management will pay all costs incurred by Woodland Legal Services for representation of Till-Harris Management. Costs will be advanced by Woodland Legal Services and then billed to Till-Harris Management unless the costs can be met from deposits.

Deposit for Fees: Till-Harris Management will pay to Woodland Legal Services an initial deposit of $5,000, to be received by Woodland Legal Services on or before November 1. Twenty percent of the deposit is nonrefundable and will be applied against attorney's fees. The refundable portion will be deposited by Woodland Legal Services in an interest-bearing trust account. Till-Harris Management authorizes Woodland Legal Services to withdraw the principal from the trust account to pay attorney's fees in excess of the nonrefundable portion.

Statement and Payments: Woodland Legal Services will send Till-Harris Management monthly statements indicating attorney's fees and costs incurred, amounts applied from deposits, and current balance owed. If no attorney's fees or costs are incurred for a month, the statement may be held and combined with that for the following month. Any balance will be paid in full within 30 days after the statement is mailed.

Effective Date of Agreement: The effective date of this agreement will be the date when it is executed by both parties.

Client: ____________________________ Date: ______________

Attorney: ___________________________ Date: ______________

7110 FIFTH STREET ◆ SUITE 200 ◆ OMAHA NE 68207 ◆ 402-555-7110

Case Study

Part 1

You have been hired as the office manager for Highland Construction Company. The address of the company is 9025 Palmer Park Boulevard, Colorado Springs, CO 80904 and the telephone number is (719) 555-4575. You are responsible for designing business documents that have a consistent visual style and formatting. You decide that your first task is to create a letterhead document. Press Ctrl + N to open a blank document and then save the document as a template with the name **7-HCCTemplate.dotx** in your WL2C7 folder. Close the template document. Use File Explorer to open a document based on **7-HCCTemplate.dotx**. At the blank document based on the template, create a letterhead that includes the company name, address, and telephone number, along with an image and/or any other elements to add visual interest. Select the letterhead text and element(s) and then create a building block in the Quick Part gallery named **HCCLtrhd** that is saved in **7-HCCTemplate.dotx**. Create the following additional building blocks for your company. (You decide on the names and save the building blocks in **7-HCCTemplate.dotx**.)

- Create a building block footer that contains a border line (in a color matching the colors in the letterhead) and the company slogan:

  Colorado Business Since 1985

- Create the following complimentary close building block:

  Sincerely,

  Your Name
  Office Manager

- Create the following company name and address building block:

  Mr. Eric Rashad
  Roswell Industries
  1020 Wasatch Street
  Colorado Springs, CO 80902

- Create the following company name and address building block:

  Ms. Claudia Sanborn
  S & S Supplies
  537 Constitution Avenue
  Colorado Springs, CO 80911

Select and then delete the contents of the document. Close the document without saving it. At the message asking if you want to save changes to the template, click the Save button.

Part 2

Use File Explorer to open a document based on **7-HCCTemplate.dotx**. Apply the No Spacing style and then create a letter to Eric Rashad by inserting the Highland Construction Company letterhead (the *HCCLtrhd* building block). Press the Enter key, type today's date, press the Enter key four times, and then insert the *Eric Rashad* building block. Press the Enter key, type an appropriate salutation (such as *Dear Mr. Rashad:*), insert the file named **HCCLetter.docx**, and then insert your complimentary close building block. Finally, insert the footer building block you created for the company. Check the letter and modify the spacing as needed.

Save the letter with the name **7-RashadLtr**. Preview and then close the letter. Complete similar steps to create a letter to Claudia Sanborn. Save the completed letter with the name **7-SanbornLtr**. Preview and then close the letter.

Part 3

Use File Explorer to open a document based on **7-HCCTemplate.dotx**. Insert the Highland Construction Company letterhead building block you created in Part 1, type the title *Company Services*, and then insert a SmartArt graphic of your choosing that contains the following text:

Residential Construction
Commercial Construction
Design Consultation
Site Preparation

Apply a heading style to the *Company Services* title, insert the company footer building block, and then save the document with the name **7-CoServices**. Preview and then close **7-CoServices.docx**.

WORD

Managing Shared Documents

CHAPTER 8

Performance Objectives

Upon successful completion of Chapter 8, you will be able to:

1 Insert, edit, show, reply to, print, resolve, and delete comments
2 Navigate between comments
3 Distinguish comments from different users
4 Edit a document using the Track Changes feature
5 Display changes, show markups, display tracked changed information, and change user information
6 Lock the Track Changes feature and customize tracked changes options
7 Navigate to and accept/reject changes
8 Restrict and enforce formatting and editing in a document and protect a document with a password
9 Protect a document by marking it as final, encrypting it, restricting editing, and adding a digital signature
10 Open a document in different views
11 Share a document electronically
12 Manage document versions

In a workplace environment, you may need to share documents with coworkers and associates. You may be part of a workgroup, which is a networked collection of computers that share files, printers, and other resources. As a member of a workgroup, you can collaborate with other members and distribute documents for their review and/or revision. Workgroup activities include inserting and managing comments and tracking the changes made to a document. Managing shared document might also include restricting the formatting and editing changes users can make to a document and protecting a document with a password. In this chapter, you will learn how to manage shared documents as well as how to open a document in different views, share a document electronically, and manage document versions.

Data Files

The data files for this chapter are in the WL2C8 folder that you downloaded at the beginning of this course.

Activity 1 Insert Comments in a New Employees Document — 3 Parts

You will open a report containing company information for new employees and then insert and edit comments from multiple users.

Inserting and Managing Comments

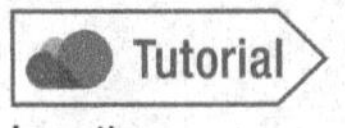

Inserting Comments

Quick Steps

Insert Comment

1. Select text.
2. Click Review tab.
3. Click New Comment button.
4. Type comment.

New Comment

Comments

Show Comments

Hint If your computer has a sound card and microphone, you can record voice comments.

Hint Ctrl + Enter is the keyboard shortcut to post a comment.

Use Word's comment feature to provide feedback on and suggest changes to a document that someone else has written. Similarly, get feedback on a document by distributing it electronically to others and having them insert comments in it or reply to comments. *Note: The functionality of the Comments feature is dependent on the version of Word you are using. Some of the information and steps in the textbook may vary from what you see on your screen.*

Inserting Comments

Insert a comment with the New Comment button in the Comments group on the Review tab or with the Comments button at the right side of the ribbon. Click the New Comment button on the Review tab and a comment box displays at the right side of the screen as shown in Figure 8.1. Type the comment in the comment box and then click the Post comment button. Click the Comments button at the right side of the ribbon and the Comments task pane displays. Click the New button in the task pane, type the comment, and then click the Post comment button.

Showing Comments

For a comment to display in a document, the *Display for Review* option box in the Tracking group needs to display either *Simple Markup* or *All Markup*. With either of the options displayed, the Show Comments button in the Comments group is active. If the *Display for Review* option box displays *No Markup* or *Original*, the Show Comments button is inactive and the comments do not display. To specify an option, click the *Display for Review* option box and then click either *Simple Markup* or *All Markup* at the drop-down list. If the Show Comments button is active, clicking the button will turn off the display of comments.

Figure 8.1 Sample Comment Box

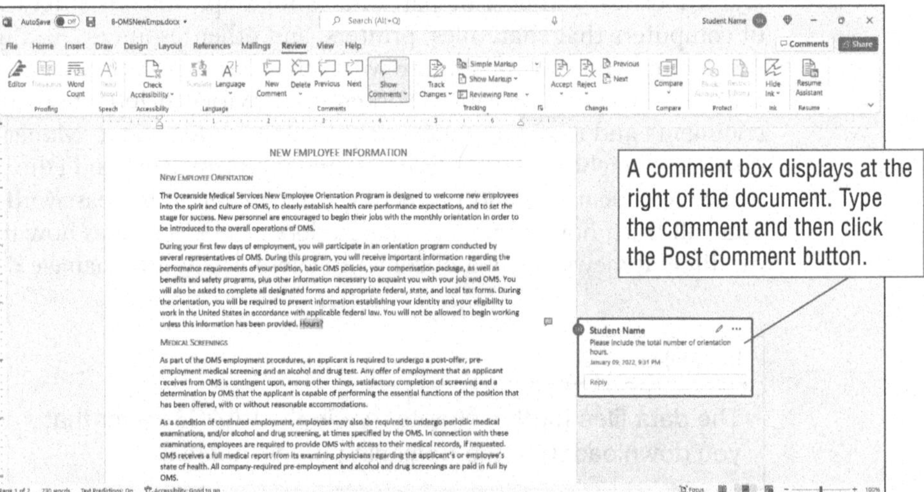
A comment box displays at the right of the document. Type the comment and then click the Post comment button.
NEW EMPLOYEE INFORMATION

Activity 1a Inserting Comments

Part 1 of 3

1. Open **OMSNewEmps.docx** and then save it with the name **8-OMSNewEmps.**
2. Insert a comment using the New Comment button on the Review tab by completing the following steps:
   a. Position the insertion point at the end of the second paragraph in the *New Employee Orientation* section.
   b. Press the spacebar and then type Hours?.
   c. Select *Hours?*.
   d. Click the Review tab.
   e. Make sure *Simple Markup* displays in the *Display for Review* option box. If not, click the *Display for Review* option box arrow and then click *Simple Markup* at the drop-down list.
   f. Click the New Comment button in the Comments group.
   g. Type Please include the total number of orientation hours. in the comment box.
   h. Click the Post comment button (right-pointing white arrow with blue background). (If your comment does not contain a Post comment button, click in the document to post the comment.)

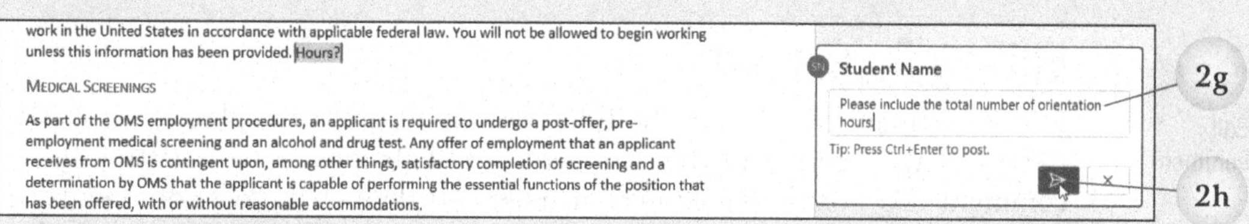

3. Insert a comment in the Comments task pane by completing the following steps:
   a. Move the insertion point to the end of the third (last) paragraph in the *Medical Screenings* section.
   b. Click the Comments button at the right side of the ribbon.
   c. Click the New button in the Comments task pane. (If a Comments task pane does not display, click the *New* option at the Comments button drop-down list.)

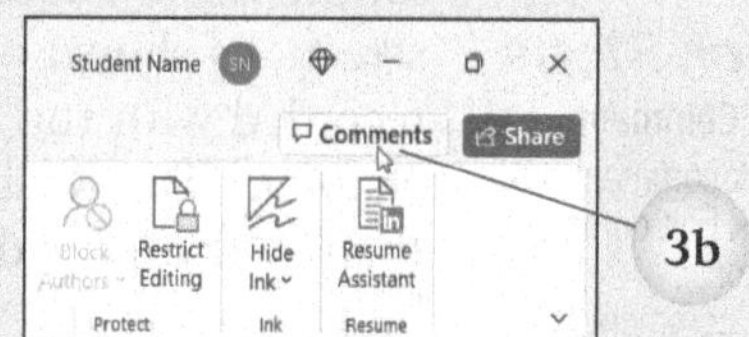

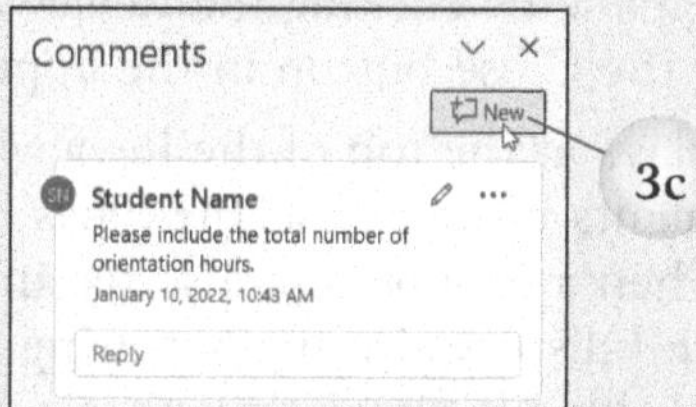

   d. Type Specify the locations where drug tests are administered. in the comment box. (Since you did not select any text before clicking the New button, Word selects the word immediately left of the insertion point.)
   e. Click the Post comment button. (If a Post comment button does not display, click in the document to post the comment.)
   f. Click in the document.

4. Insert another comment in the Comments task pane by completing the following steps:
   a. Move the insertion point to the end of the paragraph text in the *Introductory Period* section.
   b. Press the spacebar once, type Maximum?, and then select *Maximum?*.
   c. Click the New button in the Comments task pane.
   d. Type Please include in this section the maximum length of the probationary period. in the comment box.
   e. Click the Post comment button. (If a Post comment button does not display, click in the document to post the comment.)
   f. Click in the document.
   g. Close the Comments task pane by clicking the Close button in the upper right corner of the task pane.
5. Save **8-OMSNewEmps.docx**.

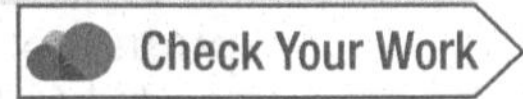

Managing Comments

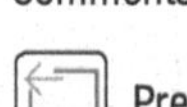

Previous

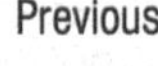

Next

Navigating between Comments

When working in a long document with many comments, use the Previous and Next buttons in the Comments group on the Review tab to move easily from comment to comment. Click the Next button to move the insertion point to the next comment in the document or click the Previous button to move the insertion point to the previous comment.

Editing Comments

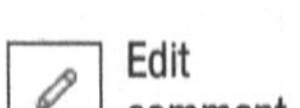

Edit a comment by clicking the Edit comment button (display as a pencil) in the upper right corner of the comment box. This moves the insertion into the comment text box. Make edits as needed and then click Post comment button (displays as a white check mark on a blue background) in the comment box.

A comment can also be edited in the Reviewing pane. Turn on the display of the Reviewing pane by clicking the Reviewing Pane button in the Tracking group on the Review tab. The Reviewing pane usually displays at the left side of the screen, as shown in Figure 8.2 and displays both inserted comments and changes recorded with the Track Changes feature. (Track Changes is covered later in this chapter.) The Reviewing pane might display along the bottom of the screen, rather than at the left side. To specify where the pane displays, click the Reviewing Pane button arrow and then click *Reviewing Pane Vertical* or *Reviewing Pane Horizontal*. Close the Reviewing pane by clicking the Reviewing Pane button in the Tracking group or by clicking the Close button in the upper right corner of the pane.

Quick Steps

Edit a Comment

1. Click comment box.
2. Click Edit comment button.
3. Edit comment text.
4. Click Post comment button in comment box.

OR

1. Click Reviewing Pane button.
2. Click in the comment text.
3. Edit comment text.

A summary displays at the top of the Reviewing pane and provides counts of the number of comments inserted and the types of changes that have been made to the document. When a comment is inserted in a document, the reviewer's name followed by *Commented* displays in the Reviewing pane. Edit a comment in the Reviewing pane by clicking in the comment text and then making the changes.

Figure 8.2 Vertical Reviewing Pane

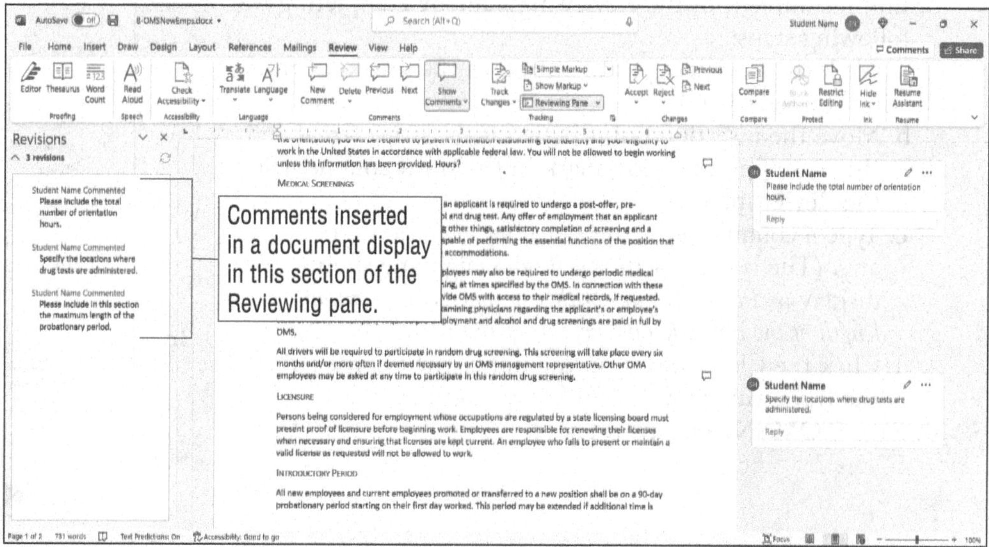

Activity 1b Editing Comments

Part 2 of 3

1. With **8-OMSNewEmps.docx** open, navigate from one comment to another by completing the following steps:
   a. Press Ctrl + Home to move the insertion point to the beginning of the document.
   b. If necessary, click the Review tab.
   c. Click the Next button in the Comments group. (This selects the first comment box.)
   d. Click the Next button to select the second comment box.
   e. Click the Next button to select the third comment box.
   f. Click the Previous button to select the second comment box.

2. Edit the second comment by completing the following steps:
   a. Click the Edit comment button (displays as a pencil) in the upper right corner of the comment box. (If an Edit comment button does not display, click in the comment text box.)

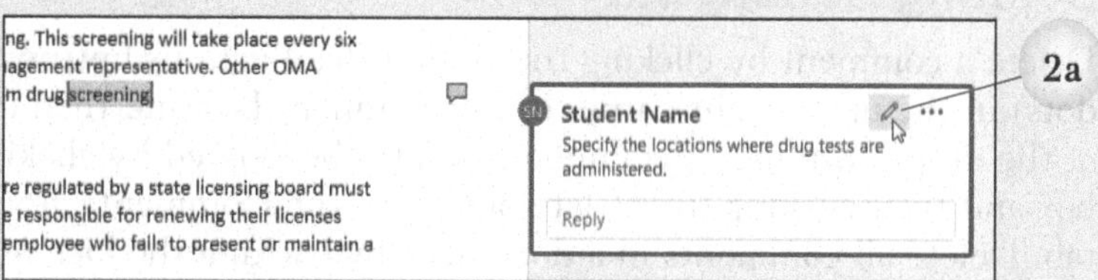

   b. Select the comment text and then type Specify the locations within OMS where drug tests are administered as well as any off-site locations.
   c. Click the Post comment button (white check mark on blue background) in the comment box. (If a Post comment button does not display, click in the document to post the comment.)

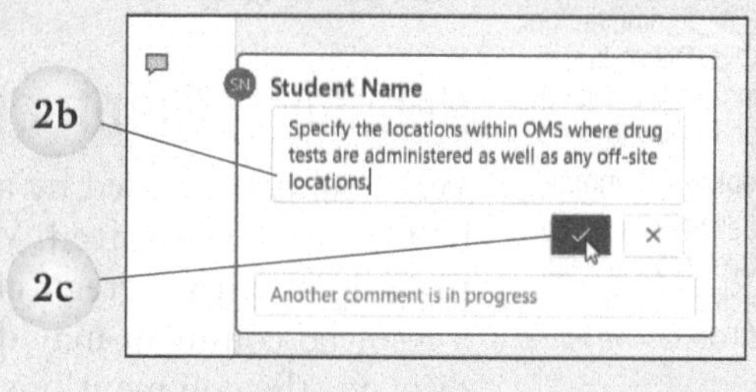

3. Edit a comment in the Reviewing pane by completing the following steps:
   a. Click the Reviewing Pane button in the Tracking group on the Review tab.
   b. Move the insertion point between the word *period* and the period puncutation mark in the third comment in the Reviewing pane.
   c. Type a comma, press the spacebar and then type if any. (The comment in the Reviewing pane should now display as *Please include in this section the maximum length of the probationary period, if any.*)
   d. Click the Close button in the upper right corner of the Reviewing pane.
4. Save **8-OMSNewEmps.docx**.

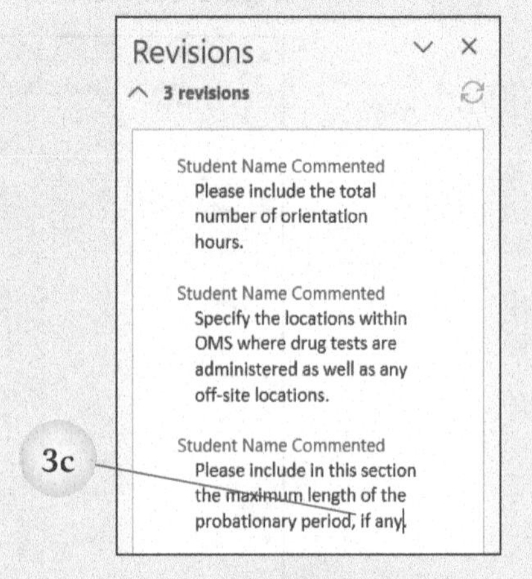

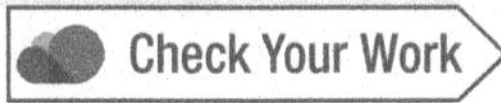

Replying to Comments

Quick Steps

Reply to Comment
1. Click in *Reply* text box.
2. Type reply.
3. Click Post reply button.

Print Document with Comments
1. Click File tab.
2. Click *Print* option.
3. Click first gallery in *Settings* category.
4. If necessary, click *Print Markup* to insert check mark.
5. Click Print button.

Print Only Comments
1. Click File tab.
2. Click *Print* option.
3. Click first gallery in *Settings* category.
4. Click *List of Markup*.
5. Click Print button.

Delete a Comment
1. Select comment box.
2. Click More thread actions button.
3. Click *Delete thread*.

OR
1. Select comment box.
2. Click Delete button in Comments group on Review tab.

Resolve a Comment
1. Select comment box.
2. Click More thread actions button.
3. Click *Resolve thread*.

More thread actions

During the review of a document, a reply can be made to a comment. To reply to a comment, click in the *Reply* text box in the comment box, type the reply, and then click the Post reply button (right-pointing white arrow on blue background).

Printing Comments

A document containing comments can be printed one of three ways: the document and the comments, the document without the comments, or only the comments. By default, a document will print with the comments. To print the document without the comments, display the Print backstage area and then click the first gallery in the *Settings* category (the gallery that contains the text *Print All Pages*). At the drop-down list, click the *Print Markup* option to remove the check mark, and then click the Print button. To print only the comments, display the Print backstage area, click the first gallery in the *Settings* category, and then click the *List of Markup* option at the drop-down list.

Deleting Comments

Delete a comment by clicking the More thread actions button (button with three dots) in the upper right corner of the comment box and then clicking *Delete thread* at the drop-down list. A comment can also be deleted by clicking the comment box and then clicking the Delete button in the Comments group on the Review tab. Delete all comments in a document by clicking the Delete button arrow and then clicking *Delete All Comments in Document* at the drop-down list.

Resolving Comments

When all issues raised by a comment have been addressed, the comment thread can by identified as resolved. When a comment is resolved, the comment box is reduced to an icon with a green check mark. (Depending on the version you are using, a resolved comment may display in a dimmed manner.) If the Comments task pane displays, the comment box displays in the task pane with *Resolved* at the top of the box preceded by a check mark. To resolve a comment, click the More thread actions button in the comment box and then click *Resolve thread* at the drop-down list. (Or, depending on your version, you may need to just click the Resolve button.) To delete all resolved comments, click the Delete button arrow in the Comments group and then click *Delete All Resolved Comments* at the drop-down list.

Distinguishing Comments from Different Users

More than one user can insert comments in the same document. Word uses different colors to distinguish comments inserted by different users, generally displaying the first user's comments in red and the second user's comments in blue. (These colors may vary.)

Change user name and initials at the Word Options dialog box with *General* selected, as shown in Figure 8.3. To change the user name, select the name that displays in the *User name* text box and then type the new name. Complete similar steps to change the user initials in the *Initials* text box. A check mark may need to be inserted in the *Always use these values regardless of sign in to Office* check box.

Figure 8.3 Word Options Dialog Box with *General* Selected

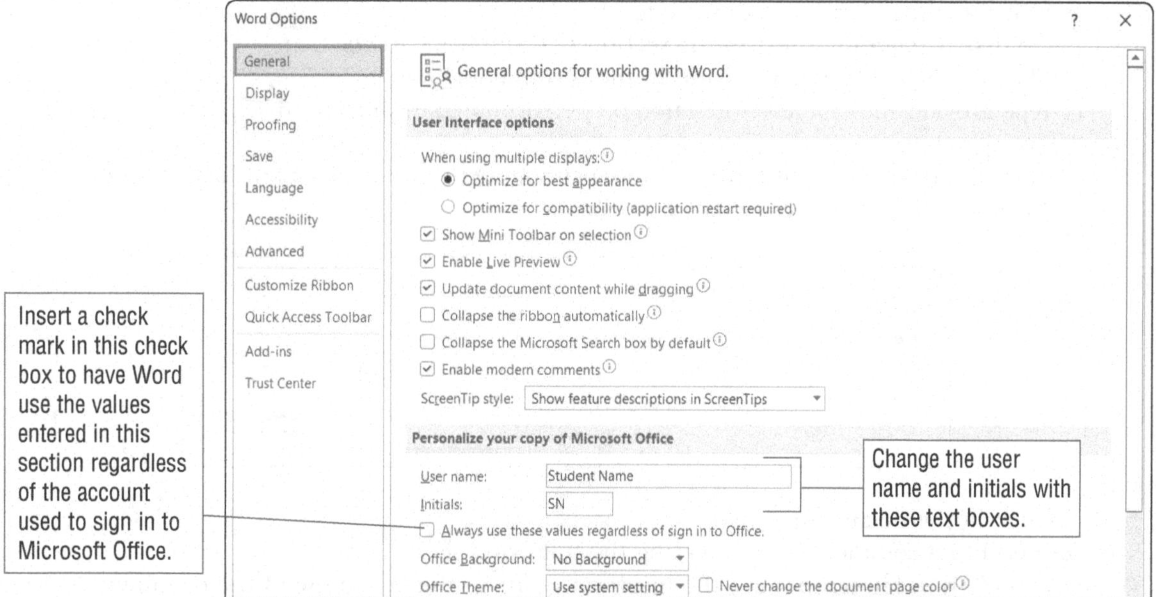

Activity 1c Changing User Information and Inserting, Resolving, and Deleting Comments Part 3 of 3

1. With **8-OMSNewEmps.docx** open, change the user information by completing the following steps:
   a. Click the File tab.
   b. Click *Options*.

c. At the Word Options dialog box, make sure *General* is selected in the left panel.
d. Make a note of the current name and initials in the *Personalize your copy of Microsoft Office* section.
e. Select the name displayed in the *User name* text box and then type Taylor Stanton.
f. Select the initials displayed in the *Initials* text box and then type TS.
g. Click the *Always use these values regardless of sign in to Office* check box to insert a check mark.
h. Click OK to close the Word Options dialog box.

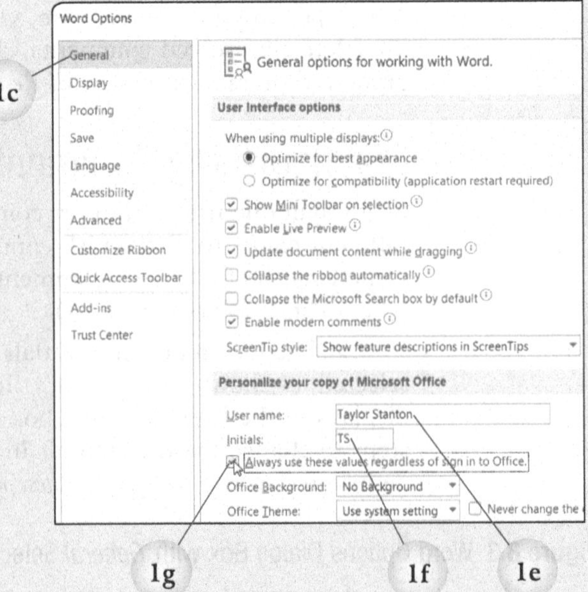

2. Insert a comment by completing the following steps:
   a. Move the insertion point to the end of the first paragraph of text in the section *Performance Review*.
   b. Click the New Comment button in the Comments group.
   c. Type Provide additional information on performance evaluation documentation. in the comment box.
   d. Click the Post comment button. (If a Post comment button does not display, click in the document to post the comment.)

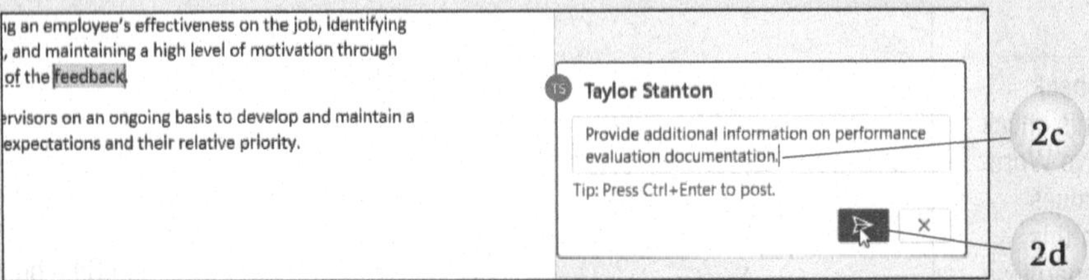

   e. Click in the document.
3. Respond to a comment by completing the following steps:
   a. Press Ctrl + Home to move the insertion point to the beginning of the document.
   b. Click the Next button in the Comments group. (This selects the first comment box.)
   c. Click in the *Reply* text box in the comment box.
   d. Type Check with Barb on the total number of orientation hours.
   e. Click the Post reply button. (If a Post reply button does not display, click in the document to post the reply.)

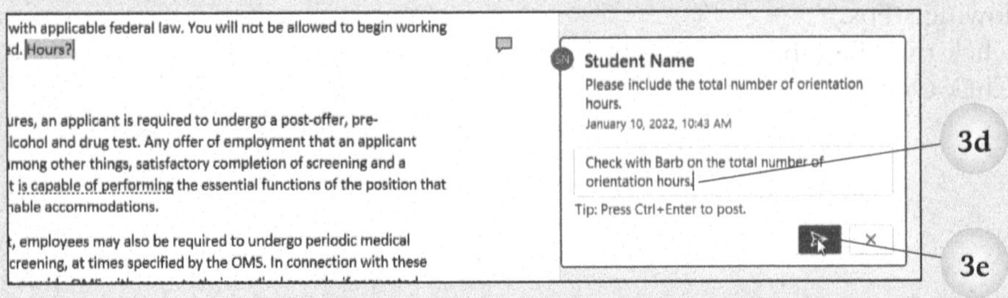

f. Click in the document.
4. Print only the comments by completing the following steps:
   a. Click the File tab and then click the *Print* option.
   b. At the Print backstage area, click the first gallery in the *Settings* category and then click *List of Markup* in the *Document Info* section of the drop-down list.
   c. Click the Print button.
5. Resolve and delete a comment by completing the following steps:
   a. Press Ctrl + Home.
   b. Click the Next button. (This selects the first comment box.)
   c. Click the More thread actions button.
   d. Click *Resolve thread* at the drop-down list. (The comment is reduced to an icon with a green check mark.) (Depending on your version, you may need to click the Resolve button and the resolved comment will display dimmed.)
   e. Click the Next button again.
   f. Click the Next button again. (This selects the third comment box.)
   g. Click the Delete button in the Comments group.

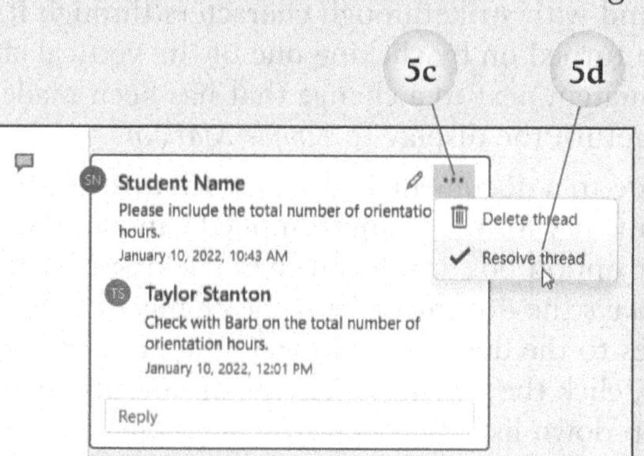

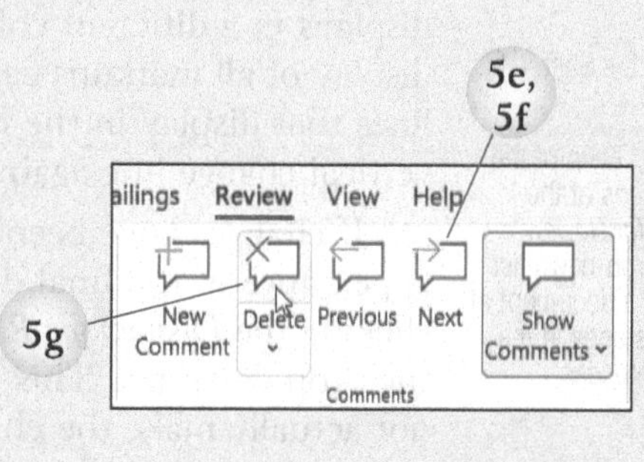

6. Print only the comments by completing Step 4.
7. Change the user information back to the default settings by completing the following steps:
   a. Click the File tab and then click *Options*.
   b. At the Word Options dialog box with *General* selected, select *Taylor Stanton* in the *User name* text box and then type the original name.
   c. Select the initials *TS* in the *Initials* text box and then type the original initials.
   d. Click the *Always use these values regardless of sign in to Office* check box to remove the check mark.
   e. Click OK to close the dialog box.
8. Save and then close **8-OMSNewEmps.docx**.

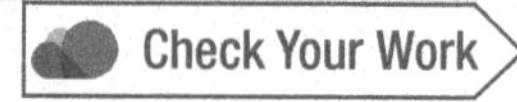

Activity 2 Track Changes in a Building Construction Agreement **4 Parts**

You will open a building construction agreement, turn on Track Changes, and then make changes to the document. You will also customize Track Changes and accept and reject changes.

Tracking Changes in a Document

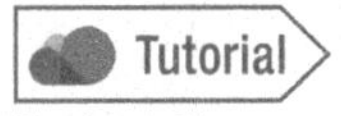

Tracking Changes in a Document

If more than one person in a workgroup needs to review and edit a document, consider using Word's Track Changes feature. When Track Changes is turned on, Word tracks each deletion, insertion, and formatting change made in a document. Turn on Track Changes by clicking the Review tab and then clicking the Track Changes button in the Tracking group or by using the keyboard shortcut Ctrl + Shift + E. Turn off Track Changes by completing the same steps.

Displaying Changes for Review

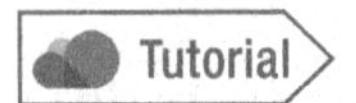

Displaying Changes for Review and Showing Markup

Quick Steps

Turn on Track Changes

1. Click Review tab.
2. Click Track Changes button.

OR

Press Ctrl + Shift + E.

Hint Each of the four options at the *Display for Review* option drop-down list displays a document at various stages in the editing process.

The *Display for Review* option box in the Tracking group on the Review tab has an original default setting of *Simple Markup*. With this setting applied, each change made to the document displays in it and a vertical change line displays in the left margin next to the line of text in which the change was made. To see the changes along with the original text, click the *Display for Review* option box arrow and then click the *All Markup* option.

With *All Markup* selected, all the changes display in the document along with the original text. For example, if text is deleted, it stays in the document but displays in a different color and with strikethrough characters through it. The display of all markups can be turned on by clicking one of the vertical change lines that display in the left margin next to a change that has been made. Click a vertical change line again to return the display to *Simple Markup*.

If changes have been made to a document with Track Changes turned on, the appearance of the final document with the changes applied can be previewed by clicking the *Display for Review* option box arrow and then clicking *No Markup* at the drop-down list. This displays the document with the changes made, but does not actually make the changes to the document. To view the original document without any changes marked, click the *Display for Review* option box arrow and then click *Original* at the drop-down list.

Showing Markups

With the display of all markups turned on, specify what tracking information displays in the body of the document with options at the Balloons side menu. To show all the changes in balloons in the right margin, click the Show Markup button, point to *Balloons*, and then click *Show Revisions in Balloons* at the side menu. Click *Show All Revisions Inline* to display all the changes in the document with vertical change lines in the left margin next to the affected lines of text. Click the *Show Only Formatting in Balloons* option at the side menu and insertions and deletions display in the text while formatting changes display in balloons in the right margin.

Activity 2a Tracking Changes in a Document

1. Open **Agreement.docx** and then save it with the name **8-Agreement.docx**.
2. Turn on Track Changes by clicking the Review tab and then clicking the Track Changes button in the Tracking group.

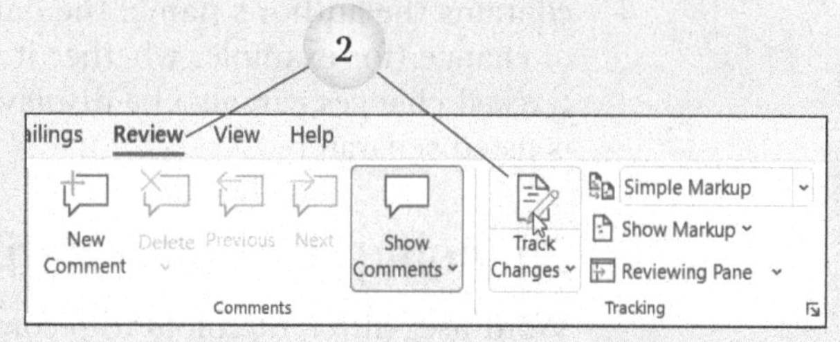

3. Type the word BUILDING between the words *THIS* and *AGREEMENT* in the first paragraph of the document.

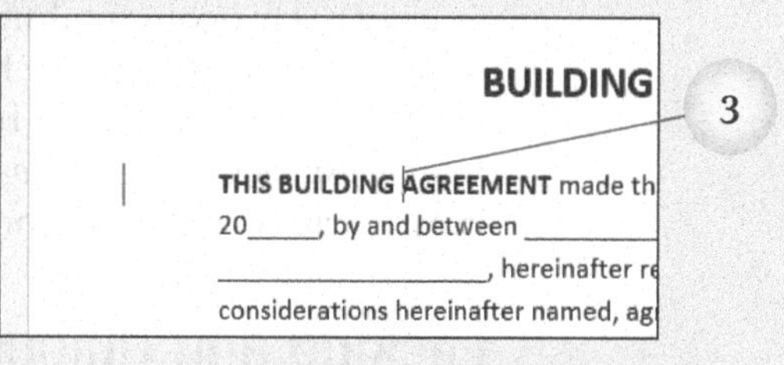

4. Show all markups by clicking the *Display for Review* option box arrow in the Tracking group and then clicking *All Markup* at the drop-down list. (Notice that the text *BUILDING* is underlined and displays in red in the document [the color may vary].)

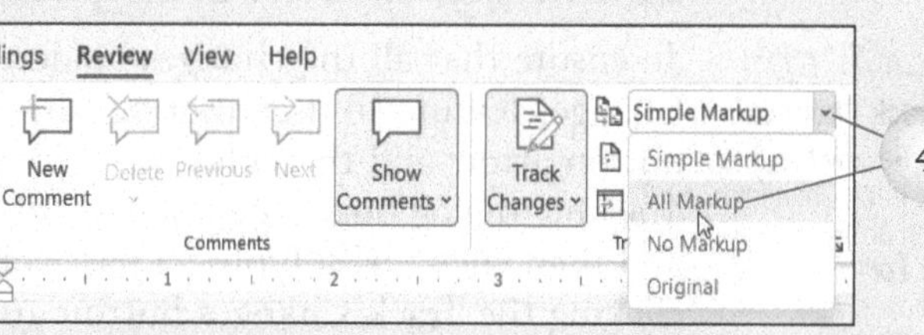

5. Click the Show Markup button, point to *Balloons*, and then click the *Show Only Formatting in Balloons* option. (Depending on your version, the option may display as *Show Only Comments and Formatting in Balloons*.)
6. Select and then delete *thirty (30)* in the second paragraph. (The deleted text displays in the document with strikethrough characters through it.)
7. Type sixty (60).

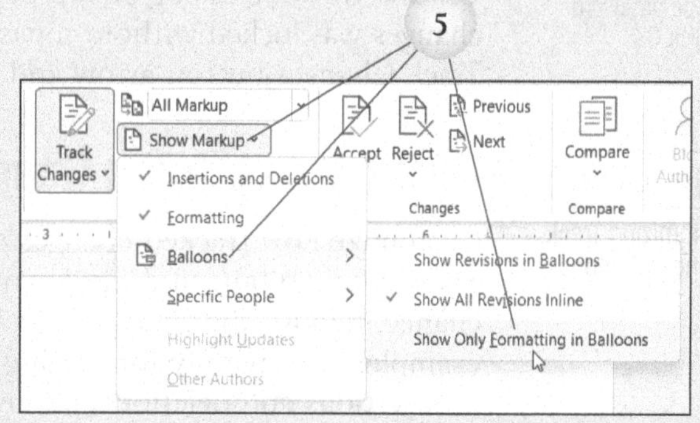

8. Move a paragraph of text by completing the following steps:
   a. Select the paragraph that begins *Supervision of Work* (including the paragraph mark that ends the paragraph).
   b. Press Ctrl + X to cut the text. (The text stays in the document and displays in red with strikethrough characters through it.)
   c. Position the insertion point immediately before the word *Start* (in the paragraph that begins *Start of Construction and Completion:*).
   d. Press Ctrl + V to paste the cut text in the new location. The inserted text displays in green and has a double underline below it. Notice that the text in the original location changes to green and has double-strikethrough characters through it.)
9. Turn off Track Changes by clicking the Track Changes button in the Tracking group.
10. Display revisions in balloons by clicking the Show Markup button, pointing to *Balloons*, and then clicking *Show Revisions in Balloons* at the side menu.
11. After looking at the revisions in balloons, click the Show Markup button, point to *Balloons*, and then click *Show All Revisions Inline* at the side menu.
12. Save **8-Agreement.docx**.

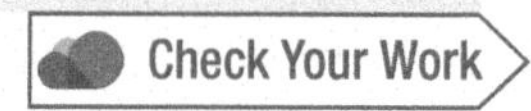

Displaying Information about Tracked Changes

Display information about a specific tracked change by hovering the pointer over it. After approximately one second, a box displays above the change that contains the author's name, the date and time the change was made, and the type of change (for example, whether it was a deletion or insertion). Information on tracked changes can also be displayed in the Reviewing pane, where each change is listed separately.

Changing User Information

Word uses different colors to record the changes made by different people (up to eight). This color coding allows anyone looking at the document to identify which users made which changes. How to change the user name and initials at the Word Options dialog box was covered earlier in the chapter (see the section *Distinguishing Comments from Different Users*). In Activity 2b, the user name and initials will be changed and then additional tracked changes will be made.

Locking and Unlocking Track Changes

Quick Steps

Lock Track Changes

1. Click Review tab.
2. Click Track Changes button arrow.
3. Click *Lock Tracking*.
4. Type password.
5. Press Tab.
6. Type password.
7. Click OK.

To ensure that all the changes made to a document will be tracked, lock the Track Changes feature so it cannot be turned off. To do this, click the Track Changes button arrow and then click *Lock Tracking* at the drop-down list. At the Lock Tracking dialog box, type a password, press the Tab key, type the password again, and then click OK. (Typing a password is optional.) Unlock Track Changes by clicking the Track Changes button arrow and then clicking *Lock Tracking*. At the Unlock Tracking dialog box, type the password and then click OK. If track changes was locked without a password, unlock track changes by clicking the Track Changes button arrow and then clicking *Lock Tracking* at the drop-down list.

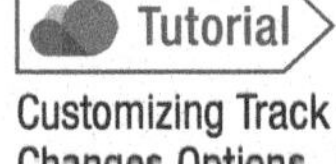

Customizing Track Changes Options

Customizing Track Changes Options

Customize how tracked changes display in a document with options at the Show Markup button drop-down list. To show only one particular type of tracked change, remove the check marks before all the options except the specific one. For example, to view only formatting changes and not other types of changes, such as insertions and deletions, remove the check mark before each option except *Formatting*. Another method of customizing the tracked changes display is to use options at the Track Changes Options dialog box, shown in Figure 8.4. Display this dialog box by clicking the Tracking group dialog box launcher.

Figure 8.4 Track Changes Options Dialog Box

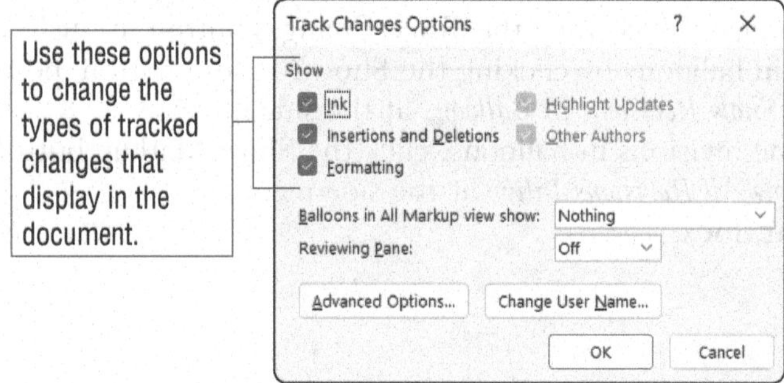

If the changes made by multiple reviewers have been tracked in a document, the changes made by a particular reviewer can be displayed. To do this, click the Show Markup button, point to *Specific People* at the drop-down list, and then click the *All Reviewers* check box to remove the check mark. Click the Show Markup button, point to *Reviewers*, and then click the check box of the specific reviewer.

Printing Markups

A document, by default, will print with all markups including comments, tracked changes, and changes to headers, footers, text boxes, footnotes and endnotes. To print a document without markups, display the Print backstage area, click the first gallery in the *Settings* category (contains the text *Print All Pages*) and then click the *Print Markup* option to remove the check mark. To print only the markups, display the Print backstage area, click the first gallery in the *Settings* category, and then click the *List of Markup* option at the drop-down list.

Activity 2b Changing User Information, Tracking Changes, and Locking Track Changes — Part 2 of 4

1. With **8-Agreement.docx** open, change the user information by completing the following steps:
   a. Click the File tab and then click *Options*.
   b. At the Word Options dialog box with *General* selected, select the current name in the *User name* text box and then type Julia Moore.
   c. Select the initials in the *Initials* text box and then type JM.
   d. Click the *Always use these values regardless of sign in to Office* check box to insert a check mark.
   e. Click OK to close the dialog box.
2. Make additional changes to the contract and track the changes by completing the following steps:
   a. Click the Track Changes button in the Tracking group to turn on tracking.
   b. Select the title *BUILDING CONSTRUCTION AGREEMENT* and then change the font size to 14 points.
   c. Delete the text *at their option* (located in the second sentence in the second paragraph).
   d. Delete the text *and Completion* (in the heading in the fourth paragraph).

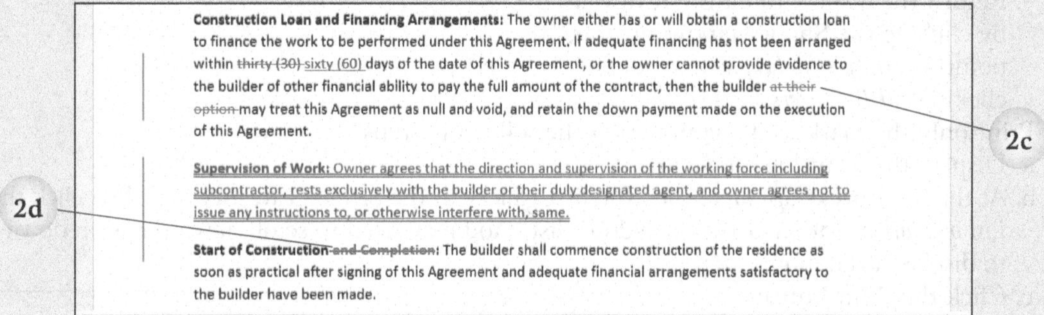

Construction Loan and Financing Arrangements: The owner either has or will obtain a construction loan to finance the work to be performed under this Agreement. If adequate financing has not been arranged within ~~thirty (30)~~ sixty (60) days of the date of this Agreement, or the owner cannot provide evidence to the builder of other financial ability to pay the full amount of the contract, then the builder ~~at their option~~ may treat this Agreement as null and void, and retain the down payment made on the execution of this Agreement.

Supervision of Work: Owner agrees that the direction and supervision of the working force including subcontractor, rests exclusively with the builder or their duly designated agent, and owner agrees not to issue any instructions to, or otherwise interfere with, same.

Start of Construction ~~and Completion~~: The builder shall commence construction of the residence as soon as practical after signing of this Agreement and adequate financial arrangements satisfactory to the builder have been made.

   e. Delete *thirty (30)* in the paragraph that begins *Builder's Right to Terminate the Contract:* (located on the second page).
   f. Type sixty (60).
   g. Select the text *IN WITNESS WHEREOF* (located near the bottom of the document) and then apply bold formatting.

3. Click the Review tab and then click the Track Changes button to turn off Track Changes.
4. Click the Reviewing Pane button to turn on the display of the Reviewing pane and then use the vertical scroll bar at the right of the Reviewing pane to review the changes.
5. View the changes in balloons by clicking the Show Markup button, pointing to *Balloons*, and then clicking *Show Revisions in Balloons*.
6. Click the Reviewing Pane button to turn off the display of the pane.
7. Scroll through the document and view the changes in the balloons.
8. Click the Show Markup button, point to *Balloons*, and then click *Show All Revisions Inline* at the side menu.
9. Change the user information back to the original information by completing the following steps:
   a. Click the File tab and then click *Options*.

   b. At the Word Options dialog box, select *Julia Moore* in the *User name* text box and then type the original name.
   c. Select the initials *JM* in the *Initials* text box and then type the original initials.
   d. Click the *Always use these values regardless of sign in to Office* check box to remove the check mark.
   e. Click OK to close the dialog box.
10. Display only those changes made by Julia Moore by completing the following steps:
    a. Click the Show Markup button in the Tracking group and then point to *Specific People* at the drop-down list.
    b. Click *All Reviewers* at the side menu.
    c. Click the Show Markup button, point to *Specific People*, and then click *Julia Moore*.
    d. Scroll through the document and notice that only changes made by Julia Moore display.
    e. Return the display to all the reviewers by clicking the Show Markup button, pointing to *Specific People*, and then clicking *All Reviewers*.

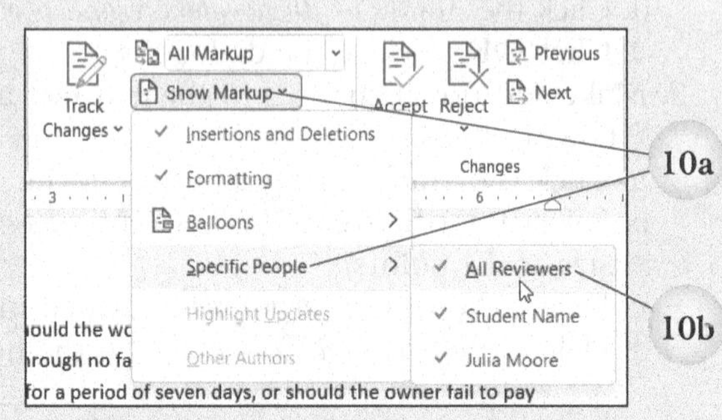

11. Print only the markups by completing the following steps:
    a. Display the Print backstage area.
    b. At the Print backstage area, click the first gallery in the *Settings* category and then click the *List of Markup* option at the drop-down list. (You may need to scroll down the drop-down list to display this option.)
    c. Click the Print button.
12. Lock track changes by completing the following steps:
    a. Click the Track Changes button arrow and then click *Lock Tracking* at the drop-down list.

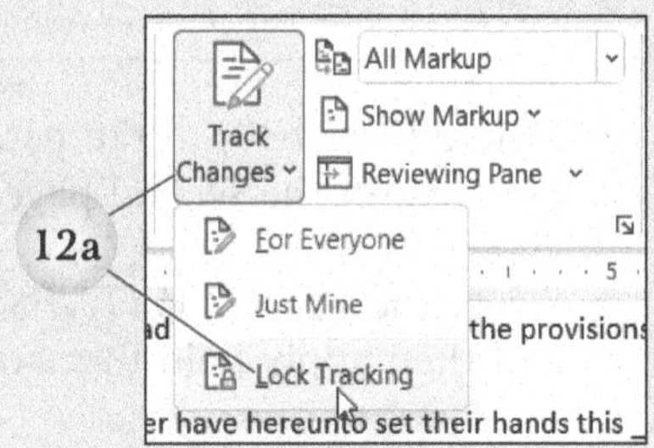

b. At the Lock Tracking dialog box, type agreement in the *Enter password (optional)* text box, press the Tab key, and then type agreement again in the *Reenter to confirm* text box.

c. Click OK.

13. Save **8-Agreement.docx.**

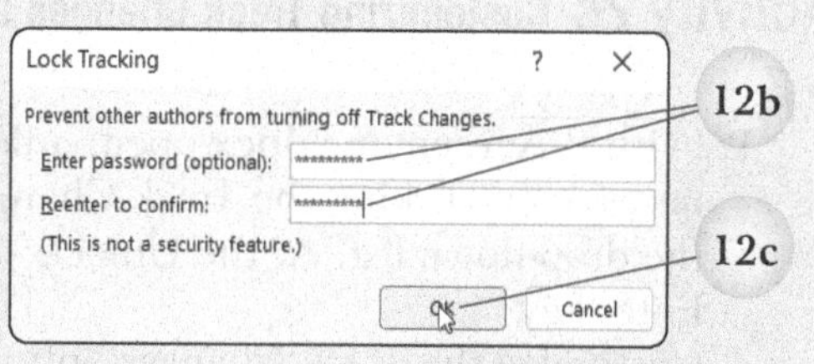

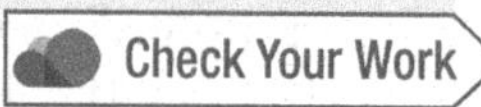

Customizing Advanced Track Changes Options

Customizing Advanced Track Changes Options

How tracked changes display in a document is determined by default settings. For example, with all the markups showing, inserted text displays in red with an underline below it and deleted text displays in red with strikethrough characters through it (these colors may vary). Moved text displays in the original location in green with double-strikethrough characters through it and in the new location in green with double-underlining below it.

Customize these options, along with others, at the Advanced Track Changes Options dialog box, shown in Figure 8.5. Use options at this dialog box to customize the display of markup text, moved text, table cell highlighting, formatting, and balloons. Display the dialog box by clicking the Tracking group dialog box launcher. At the Track Changes Options dialog box, click the Advanced Options button.

Figure 8.5 Advanced Track Changes Options Dialog Box

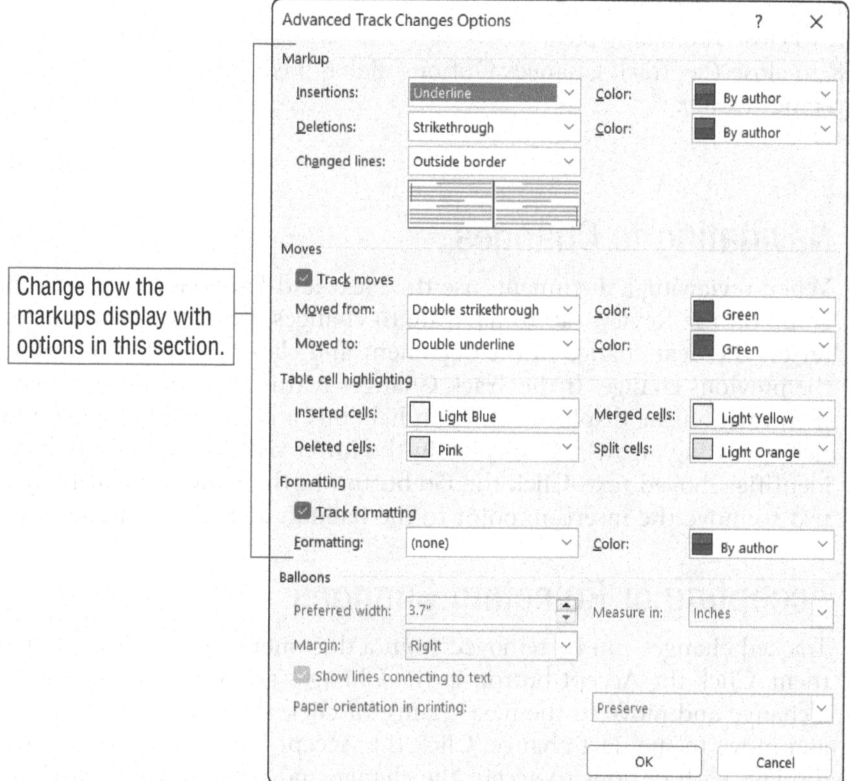

Activity 2c Customizing Track Changes Options

Part 3 of 4

1. With **8-Agreement.docx** open, unlock track changes by clicking the Review tab (if necessary), clicking the Track Changes button arrow, and then clicking *Lock Tracking* at the drop-down list. At the Unlock Tracking dialog box, type agreement and then press the Enter key.
2. Customize the Track Changes options by completing the following steps:
   a. If necessary, click the Review tab.
   b. Click the Tracking group dialog box launcher.
   c. Click the Advanced Options button at the Track Changes Options dialog box.
   d. At the Advanced Track Changes Options dialog box, click the *Insertions* option box arrow and then click *Double underline* at the drop-down list.
   e. Click the *Insertions Color* option box arrow and then click *Green* at the drop-down list. (You will need to scroll down the list to display this color.)
   f. Click the *Moved from Color* option box arrow and then click *Dark Blue* at the drop-down list.
   g. Click the *Moved to Color* option box arrow and then click *Violet* at the drop-down list. (You will need to scroll down the list to display this color.)
   h. Click OK to close the dialog box.
   i. Click OK to close the Track Changes Options dialog box.
3. Save **8-Agreement.docx**.

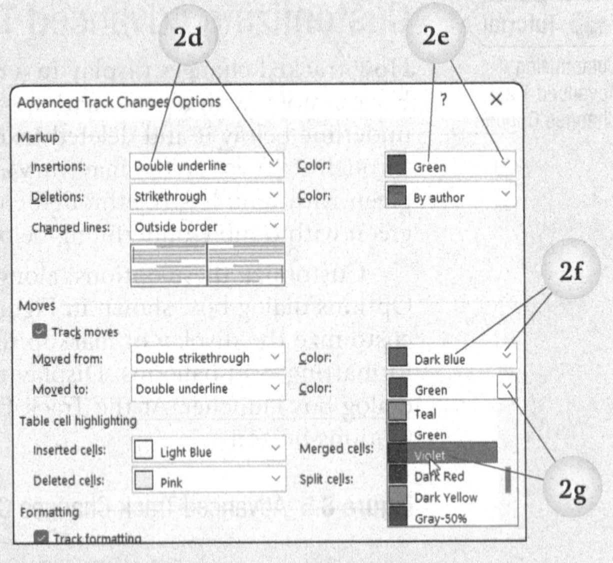

Check Your Work

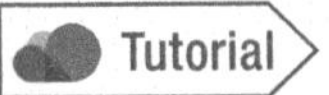

Navigating, Accepting, and Rejecting Tracked Changes

Navigating to Changes

When reviewing a document, use the Next and Previous buttons in the Changes group on the Review tab to navigate to changes. Click the Next button to review the next change in the document and click the Previous button to review the previous change. If the Track Changes feature is turned on, move text and then turn on the display of revision balloons and a small Go button (a blue right-pointing arrow) will display in the lower right corner of any balloon that identifies moved text. Click the Go button in the balloon identifying the original text to move the insertion point to the balloon identifying the moved text.

Accepting or Rejecting Changes

Reject

Tracked changes can be removed from a document only by accepting or rejecting them. Click the Accept button in the Changes group on the Review tab to accept a change and move to the next change or click the Reject button to reject a change and move to the next change. Click the Accept button arrow and a drop-down list displays with options to accept the change and move to the next change, accept the change, accept all the changes showing, and accept all the changes and stop tracking. Similar options are available at the Reject button drop-down list.

Activity 2d Accepting or Rejecting Changes

1. With **8-Agreement.docx** open, show all the tracked changes *except* formatting changes by completing the following steps:
   a. Click the Show Markup button in the Tracking group and then click *Formatting* at the drop-down list. (This removes the check mark before the option.)
   b. Scroll through the document and notice that the vertical change lines in the left margin next to the two formatting changes have been removed.
   c. Click the Show Markup button and then click *Formatting* at the drop-down list. (This inserts a check mark before the option.)
2. Navigate to review tracked changes by completing the following steps:
   a. Press Ctrl + Home to move the insertion point to the beginning of the document.
   b. Click the Next button in the Changes group to select the first change.
   c. Click the Next button again to select the second change.
   d. Click the Previous button to select the first change.
3. Navigate between the original and new locations of the moved text by completing the following steps:
   a. Press Ctrl + Home to move the insertion point to the beginning of the document.
   b. Click the Show Markup button, point to *Balloons*, and then click *Show Revisions in Balloons*.
   c. Click the Go button (a blue right-pointing arrow) in the lower right corner of the Moved balloon. (This selects the text in the *Moved up* balloon.)
   d. Click the Go button in the lower right corner of the *Moved up* balloon. (This selects the moved text in the document.)
   e. Click the Show Markup button, point to *Balloons*, and then click *Show All Revisions Inline*.

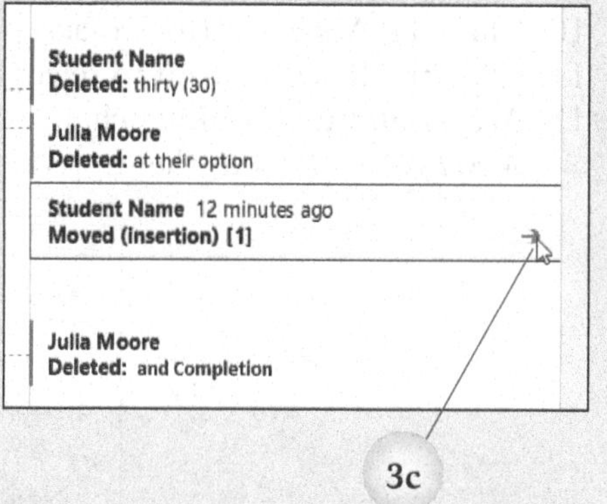

4. Press Ctrl + Home to move the insertion point to the beginning of the document.
5. Display and then accept only formatting changes by completing the following steps:
   a. Click the Tracking group dialog box launcher.
   b. At the Track Changes Options dialog box, click the *Ink* check box to remove the check mark.
   c. Click the *Insertions and Deletions* check box to remove the check mark.
   d. Make sure the *Formatting* check box contains a check mark. If it does not, click the *Formatting* check box to insert a check mark.
   e. Click OK to close the Track Changes Options dialog box.

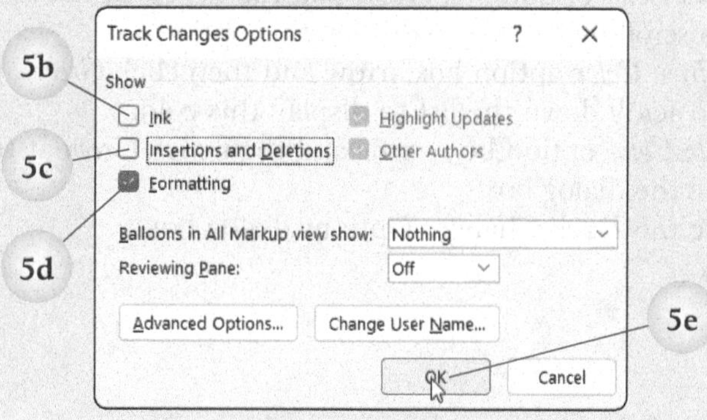

f. Click the Accept button arrow and then click *Accept All Changes Shown* at the drop-down list. (This accepts only the formatting changes in the document because those are the only changes showing.)

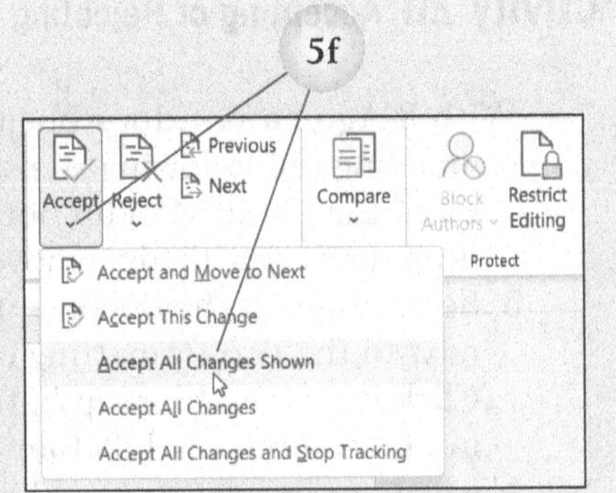

6. Redisplay all the changes by completing the following steps:
   a. Click the Tracking group dialog box launcher.
   b. Click the *Ink* check box to insert a check mark.
   c. Click the *Insertions and Deletions* check box to insert a check mark.
   d. Click OK to close the Track Changes Options dialog box.
7. Press Ctrl + Home to move the insertion point to the beginning of the document.
8. Reject the change that inserts the word *BUILDING* by clicking the Next button in the Changes group and then clicking the Reject button. (This rejects the change and moves to the next revision in the document.)

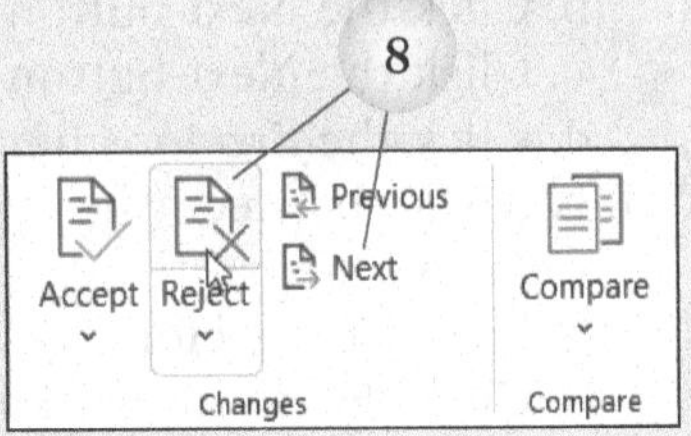

9. Click the Accept button to accept the change that deletes *thirty (30)*.
10. Click the Accept button to accept the change that inserts *sixty (60)*.
11. Click the Reject button to reject the change that deletes the words *at their option*.
12. Accept all the remaining changes by clicking the Accept button arrow and then clicking *Accept All Changes* at the drop-down list.

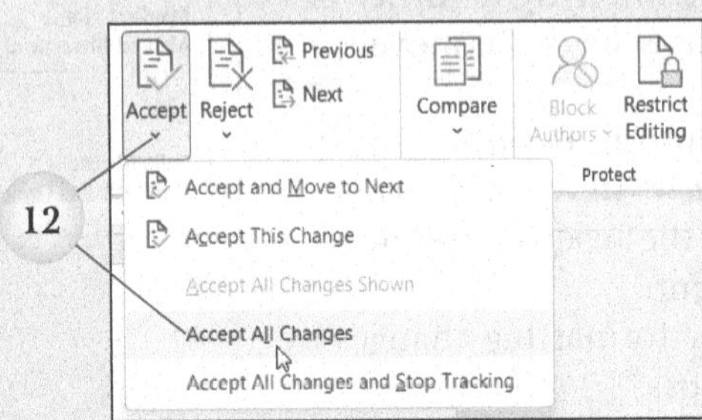

13. Return the track changes options to the default settings by completing the following steps:
    a. If necessary, click the Review tab.
    b. Click the Tracking group dialog box launcher.
    c. At the Track Changes Options dialog box, click the Advanced Options button.
    d. At the Advanced Track Changes Options dialog box, click the *Insertions* option box arrow and then click *Underline* at the drop-down list.
    e. Click the *Insertions Color* option box arrow and then click *By author* at the drop-down list. (You will need to scroll up the list to display this option.)
    f. Click the *Moved from Color* option box arrow and then click *Green* at the drop-down list. (You may need to scroll down the list to display this color.)
    g. Click the *Moved to Color* option box arrow and then click *Green* at the drop-down list.
    h. Click OK to close the dialog box.
    i. Click OK to close the Track Changes Options dialog box.

14. Check to make sure all the tracked changes are accepted or rejected by completing the following steps:
    a. Click the Reviewing Pane button in the Tracking group.
    b. Check the information at the top of the Reviewing pane and make sure that each option is followed by a 0. (You may need to click the up arrow at the right of *0 revisions* to show all the options.)
    c. Close the Reviewing pane.
15. Save, preview, and then close **8-Agreement.docx**.

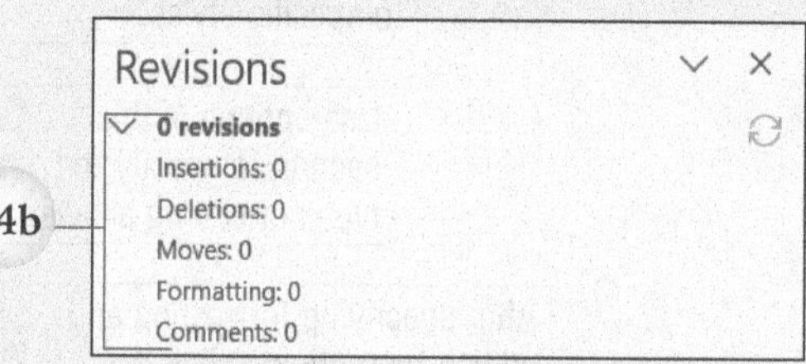

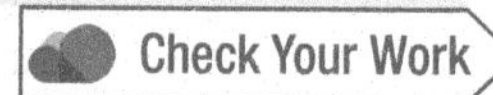

Activity 3 Restrict Formatting and Editing in a Company Report 4 Parts

You will open a company report document, restrict formatting and editing in the document, enforce protection, and protect the document with a password.

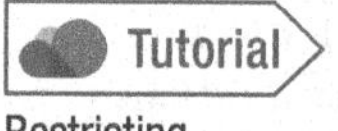

Restricting Formatting and Editing

Restricting a Document

Within an organization, copies of a document may be distributed among members of a group. In some situations, the document may need to be protected and the changes that can be made to it need to be limited. If a document contains sensitive, restricted, or private information, consider protecting it by saving it as a read-only document or securing it with a password.

Use options in the Restrict Editing task pane to limit what formatting and editing users can perform on a document. Limiting formatting and editing is especially useful in a workgroup environment, in which a number of people review and edit the same document.

For example, suppose a company's annual report is being prepared and it contains information from a variety of departments, such as Finance, Human Resources, and Sales and Marketing. Access to the report can be restricted so only certain employees are allowed to edit specific parts of the document. For instance, the part of the report pertaining to finance can be restricted to allow only someone in the Finance Department to make edits. Similarly, the part of the report on employees can be restricted so only someone in Human Resources can make edits. By limiting options for editing, the integrity of the document can be protected.

To protect a document, display the Restrict Editing task pane, shown in Figure 8.6, by clicking the Review tab and then clicking the Restrict Editing button in the Protect group. Use options in the *Formatting restrictions* section to limit formatting to specific styles and use options in the *Editing restrictions* section to specify the types of editing allowed in the document.

Figure 8.6 Restrict Editing Task Pane

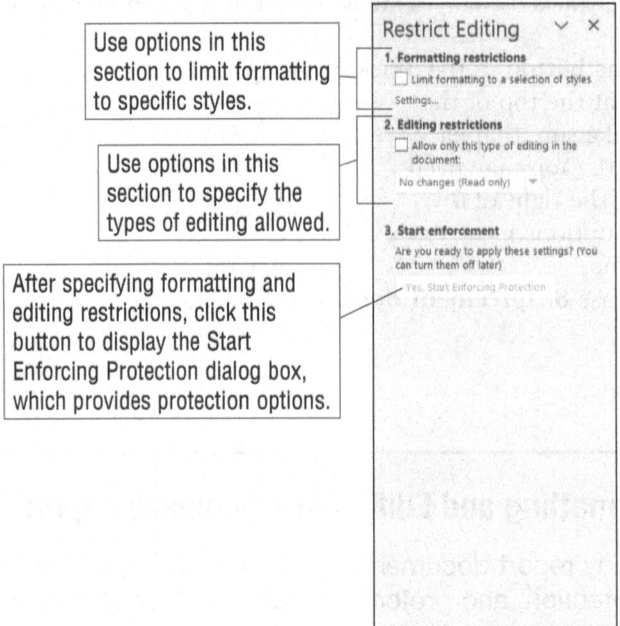
Use options in this section to limit formatting to specific styles.
Use options in this section to specify the types of editing allowed.
After specifying formatting and editing restrictions, click this button to display the Start Enforcing Protection dialog box, which provides protection options.
Restrict Editing
1. Formatting restrictions
Limit formatting to a selection of styles
Settings...
2. Editing restrictions
Allow only this type of editing in the document:
No changes (Read only)
3. Start enforcement
Are you ready to apply these settings? (You can turn them off later)
Yes, Start Enforcing Protection

The Protect group on the Review tab contains a Block Authors button when a document is saved to a Microsoft SharePoint site that supports workspaces. If the button is active, select the portion of the document to block from editing and then click the Block Authors button. To unblock authors, click in the locked section of the document and then click the Block Authors button.

Applying Formatting Restrictions

Quick Steps

Display Formatting Restrictions Dialog Box

1. Click Review tab.
2. Click Restrict Editing button.
3. Click Settings hyperlink.

Use options in the *Formatting restrictions* section of the Restrict Editing task pane to lock specific styles used in a document, thus allowing the use of only those styles and prohibiting users from making other formatting changes. Click the Settings hyperlink in the *Formatting restrictions* section and the Formatting Restrictions dialog box displays, as shown in Figure 8.7.

Insert a check mark in the *Limit formatting to a selection of styles* check box and the styles become available in the *Checked styles are currently allowed* list box. In this list box, insert check marks in the check boxes preceding the styles that are allowed and remove check marks from the check boxes preceding the styles that are not allowed. Limit formatting to a minimum number of styles by clicking the Recommended Minimum button. This allows formatting with styles that Word uses for certain features, such as bulleted and numbered lists. Click the None button to remove all the check marks and prevent all the styles from being used in the document. Click the All button to insert check marks in all the check boxes and allow all the styles to be used in the document.

Use options in the *Formatting* section of the dialog box to allow or not allow AutoFormat to make changes in a document. Also use options in this section of the dialog box to allow or not allow users to switch themes or style sets.

Figure 8.7 Formatting Restrictions Dialog Box

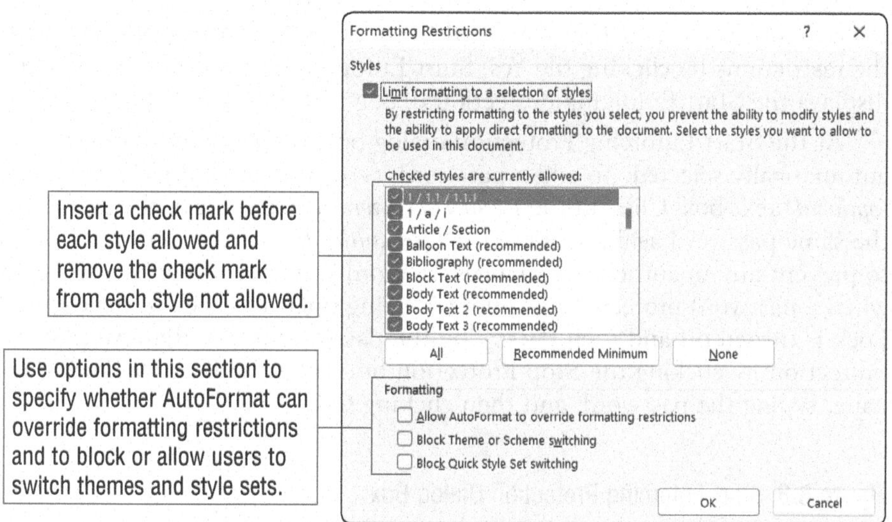

Activity 3a Restricting Formatting of a Document

Part 1 of 4

1. Open **TECRpt.docx** and then save it with the name **8-TECRpt**.
2. Restrict formatting to the Heading 1 and Heading 2 styles by completing the following steps:
   a. Click the Review tab.
   b. Click the Restrict Editing button in the Protect group.

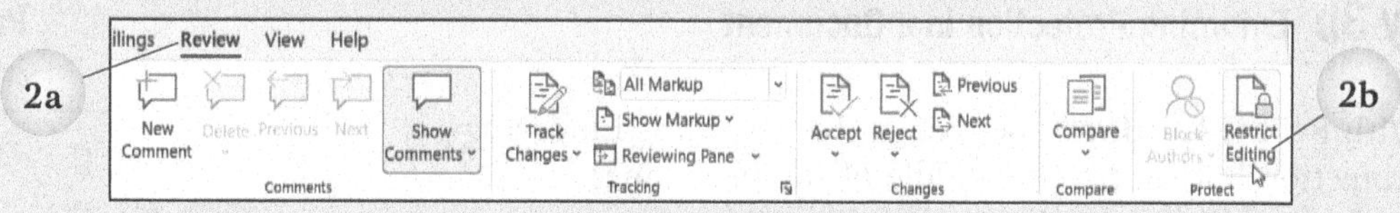

   c. At the Restrict Editing task pane, click the *Limit formatting to a selection of styles* check box to insert a check mark. (Skip this step if the check box already contains a check mark.)
   d. Click the Settings hyperlink.
   e. At the Formatting Restrictions dialog box, click the None button.
   f. Scroll down the *Checked styles are currently allowed* list box and then click to insert check marks in the *Heading 1* and *Heading 2* check boxes.
   g. Click OK.
   h. At the message stating that the document may contain formatting or styles that are not allowed and asking about removing them, click Yes.
3. Save **8-TECRpt.docx**.

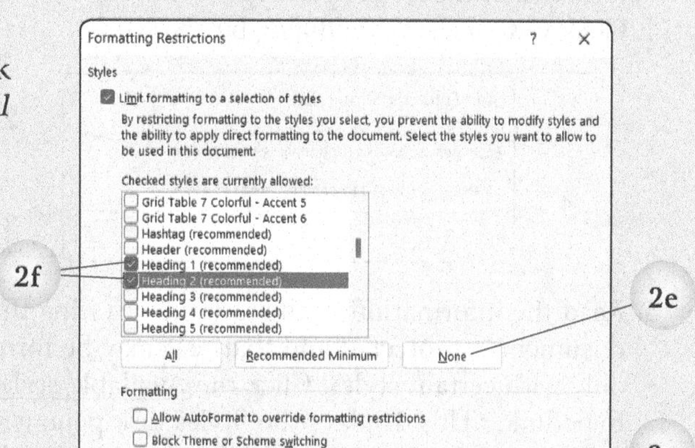

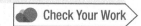

Check Your Work

Enforcing Protection

Quick Steps

Display Start Enforcing Protection Dialog Box

1. Click Review tab.
2. Click Restrict Editing button.
3. Specify formatting and/or editing options.
4. Click Yes, Start Enforcing Protection button.

When restrictions have been specified in the Restrict Editing task pane, enforce the restrictions by clicking the Yes, Start Enforcing Protection button. This displays the Start Enforcing Protection dialog box shown in Figure 8.8.

At the Start Enforcing Protection dialog box, the *Password* option is automatically selected. To add a password, type it in the *Enter new password (optional)* text box. Click in the *Reenter password to confirm* text box and then type the same password again. Choose the *User authentication* option to use encryption to prevent any unauthorized changes. If Word does not recognize the password when a password-protected document is being opened, check to make sure Caps Lock is turned off and then try typing the password again. Remove password protection by clicking the Stop Protection button at the Restrict Editing task pane, typing the password, and then clicking OK.

Figure 8.8 Start Enforcing Protection Dialog Box

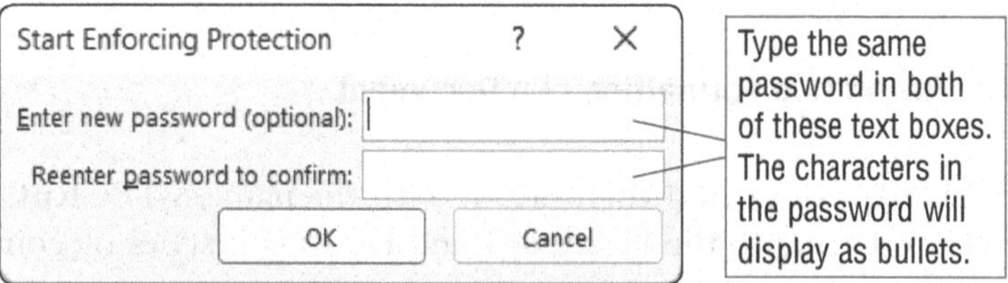

Activity 3b Enforcing Protection in a Document

Part 2 of 4

1. With **8-TECRpt.docx** open, click the Yes, Start Enforcing Protection button (in the middle of the task pane).
2. At the Start Enforcing Protection dialog box, type formatting in the *Enter new password (optional)* text box. (Bullets will display in the text box, rather than the letters you type.)
3. Press the Tab key (which moves the insertion point to the *Reenter password to confirm* text box) and then type formatting. (Again, bullets will display in the text box, rather than the letters you type.)
4. Click OK to close the dialog box.

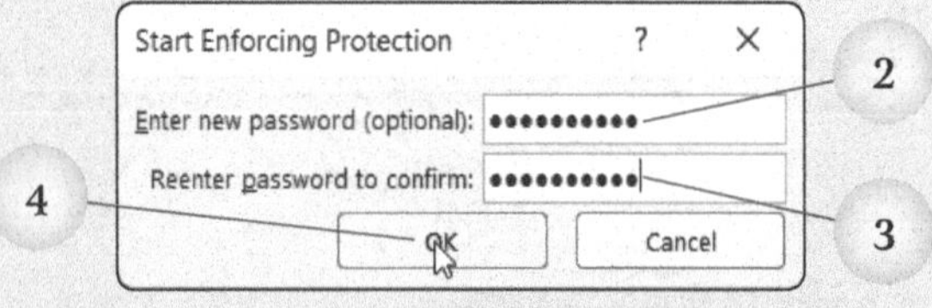

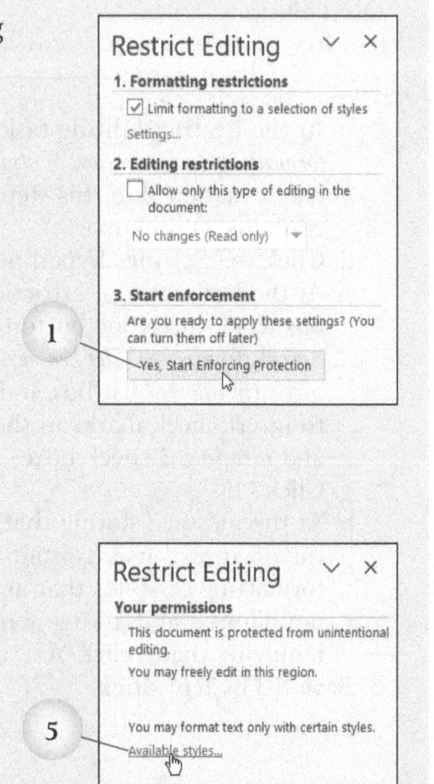

5. Read the information in the task pane stating that the document is protected and that text may be formatted only with certain styles. Click the Available styles hyperlink. (This displays the Styles task pane with four styles in the list box: *Clear All*, *Normal*, *Heading 1*, and *Heading 2*.)

6. Close the Styles task pane.
7. Apply the Heading 1 style to the title *TANDEM ENERGY CORPORATION* and apply the Heading 2 style to the following headings: *Overview*, *Research and Development*, *Manufacturing*, and *Sales and Marketing*.
8. Apply the Lines (Simple) style set. (This style set is in the Document Formatting group on the Design tab.)
9. At the message stating that some of the styles could not be updated, click OK.
10. Save the document.
11. Remove the password protection from the document by completing the following steps:
    a. Click the Stop Protection button at the bottom of the Restrict Editing task pane.
    b. At the Unprotect Document dialog box, type formatting in the *Password* text box.
    c. Click OK.
12. Save **8-TECRpt.docx**.

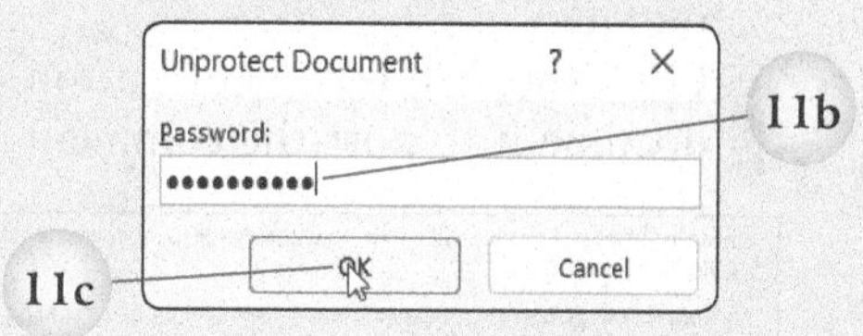

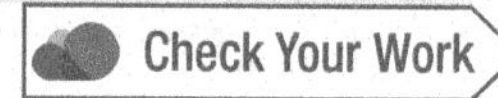

Applying Editing Restrictions

Use the *Editing restrictions* option in the Restrict Editing task pane to limit the types of changes users can make to a document. Insert a check mark in the *Allow only this type of editing in the document* check box and the drop-down list below the option becomes active. Click the option box arrow and the following options become available: *Tracked changes*, *Comments*, *Filling in forms*, and *No changes (Read only)*.

To restrict users from making changes to a document, choose the *No changes (Read only)* option. Choose the *Tracked changes* option to allow users to make tracked changes in a document and choose the *Comments* option to allow users to insert comments in a document. These two options are useful in a workgroup environment, in which a document is routed to various individuals for review. Choose the *Filling in forms* option and users will be able to fill in the fields in a form, but not make any other changes.

Activity 3c Restricting Editing of and Enforcing Protection in a Document — Part 3 of 4

1. With **8-TECRpt.docx** open, restrict editing to inserting comments by completing the following steps:
    a. Make sure the Restrict Editing task pane displays.
    b. Click the *Allow only this type of editing in the document* check box to insert a check mark.
    c. Click the option box arrow below *Allow only this type of editing in the document* and then click *Comments* at the drop-down list.
2. Click the Yes, Start Enforcing Protection button at the bottom of the task pane.
3. At the Start Enforcing Protection dialog box, click OK. (Adding a password is optional.)
4. Read the information in the task pane stating that the document is protected and that editing is restricted to inserting comments.

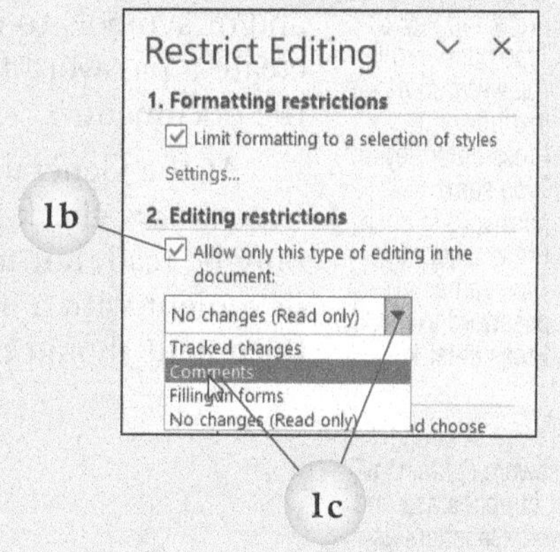

5. Click each ribbon tab and notice the buttons and options that are dimmed and unavailable.
6. Insert a comment by completing the following steps:
   a. Move the insertion point immediately to the right of the period that ends the last sentence in the second paragraph of the *Overview* section.
   b. Click the Review tab, if necessary; click the Show Markup button in the Tracking group; point to *Balloons*; and then click the *Show All Revisions Inline* option if necessary.
   c. Click the New Comment button in the Comments group on the Review tab.
   d. Type the following comment text: Include additional information on the impact of this purchase.
   e. Click the Post comment button. (If a Post comment button does not display, click in the document to post the comment.)

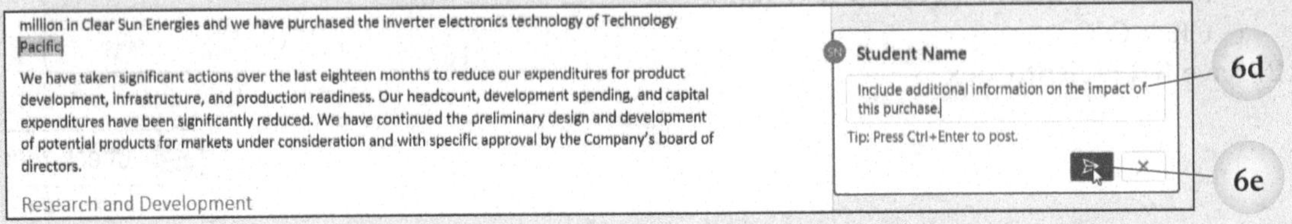

   f. Click the Stop Protection button at the bottom of the Restrict Editing task pane.
   g. Close the Restrict Editing task pane.
7. Save **8-TECRpt.docx**.

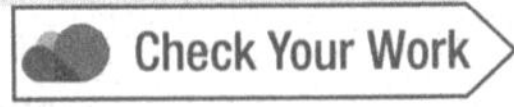

Protecting a Document with a Password

Quick Steps

Protect Document with Password

1. Press F12.
2. Click Tools button.
3. Click *General Options.*
4. Type password in *Password to open* text box.
5. Press Tab key.
6. Type password in *Password to modify* text box.
7. Press Enter key.
8. Type same password to open.
9. Press Enter key.
10. Type same password to modify.
11. Press Enter key.

Hint A strong password contains a mix of uppercase and lowercase letters as well as numbers and symbols.

Protecting a Document with a Password

In addition to protecting a document with a password using options at the Start Enforcing Protection dialog box, a document can be protected with a password using options at the General Options dialog box, shown in Figure 8.9. Display this dialog box by pressing the F12 function key to display the Save As dialog box, clicking the Tools button at the bottom of the dialog box next to the Save button, and then clicking *General Options* at the drop-down list.

Use options at the General Options dialog box to assign a password to open the document, modify the document, or both. To insert a password to open the document, click in the *Password to open* text box and then type the password. A password can contain up to 15 characters, should be at least 8 characters, and is case sensitive. Consider combining uppercase letters, lowercase letters, numbers, and/or symbols to make a password secure. Use the *Password to modify* option to create a password that someone must enter before being allowed to make edits to the document.

At the General Options dialog box, insert a check mark in the *Read-only recommended* check box to save a document as a read-only file. A read-only file can only be read, not modified. If changes are made, they must be saved into a new document with a new name. Use this option if the contents of the original document should not be changed.

Figure 8.9 General Options Dialog Box

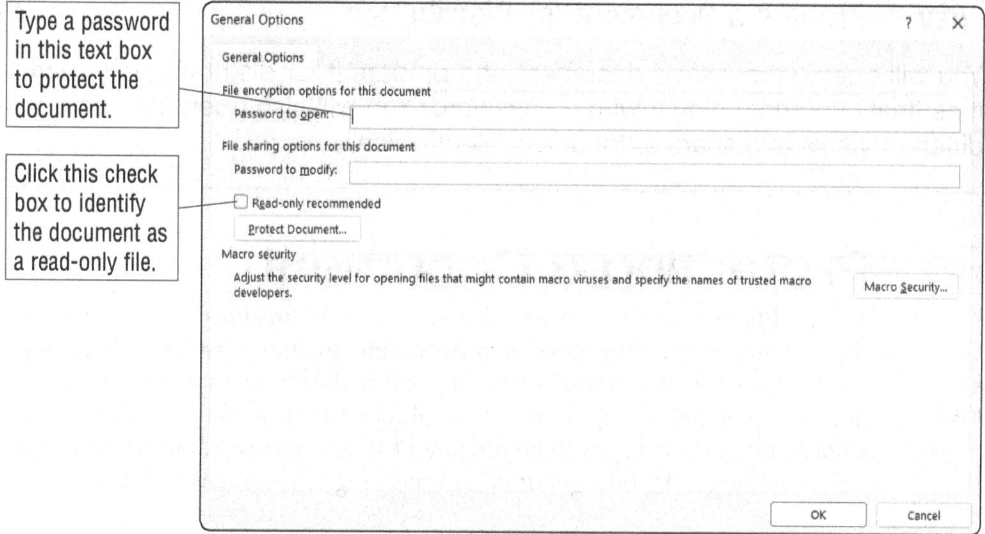

Activity 3d Protecting a Document with a Password

Part 4 of 4

1. With **8-TECRpt.docx** open, save the document and protect it with a password by completing the following steps:
   a. Press the F12 function key to display the Save As dialog box.
   b. Click the Tools button near the bottom of the dialog box (next to the Save button) and then click *General Options* at the drop-down list.
   c. At the General Options dialog box, type your first name in the *Password to open* text box. (If your name is longer than 15 characters, abbreviate it. You will not see your name; Word inserts bullets in place of the letters.)
   d. After typing your name, press the Enter key.
   e. At the Confirm Password dialog box, type your name again in the *Reenter password to open* text box. (Be sure to type it exactly as you did in the *Password to open* text box, including the same uppercase and lowercase letters.) Press the Enter key.
   f. Click the Save button at the Save As dialog box.
2. Close **8-TECRpt.docx**.
3. Open **8-TECRpt.docx** and type your password when prompted in the *Enter password to open file* text box and then press the Enter key.

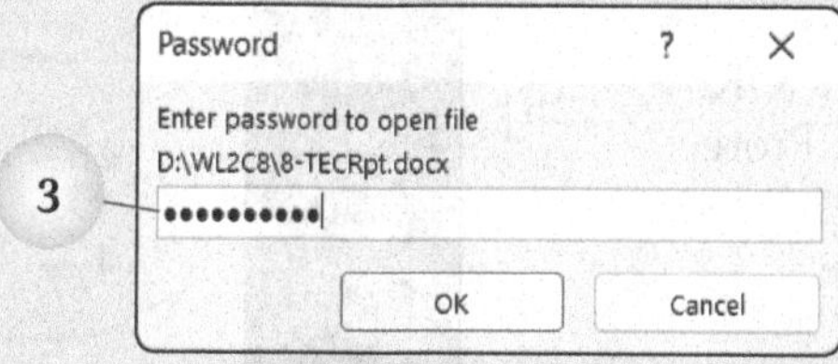

4. Close the document.

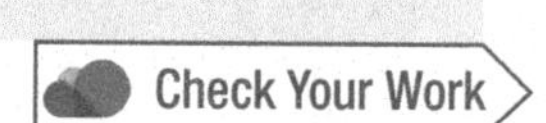

Activity 4 Prepare a Document for Distribution — 4 Parts

You will open a real estate document and prepare it for distribution by marking it as final and encrypting it with a password. You will also open the document in different views and share a document electronically.

Protecting a Document

Protecting a Document

The middle panel of the Info backstage area contains buttons for protecting a document, checking for issues in a document such as personal data and accessibility, and managing versions of a document. Click the Protect Document button in the middle panel and a drop-down list displays with options for opening a document as a read-only file, encrypting the document with a password, restricting editing and access, adding a digital signature, and marking a document as final.

Marking a Document as Final

Click the *Mark as Final* option at the Protect Document button drop-down list to save the document as a read-only document. Click this option and a message displays stating that the document will be marked and then saved. At this message, click OK. This displays another message stating that the document is the final version of the document. The message further states that when a document is marked as final, the status property is set to *Final*; typing, editing commands, and proofing marks are turned off. At this message, click OK. After a document is marked as final, the message *This document has been marked as final to discourage editing* displays at the right of the Protect Document button at the Info backstage area.

Activity 4a Marking a Document as Final — Part 1 of 4

1. Open **REAgrmnt.docx** and then save it with the name **8-REAgrmnt**.
2. Mark the document as final by completing the following steps:
   a. Click the File tab and then click the *Info* option.
   b. Click the Protect Document button at the Info backstage area and then click *Mark as Final* at the drop-down list.
   c. At the message stating that the document will be marked and saved, click OK.
   d. At the next message that displays, click OK. Notice the message at the right of the Protect Document button.
   e. Click the Back button to return to the document.

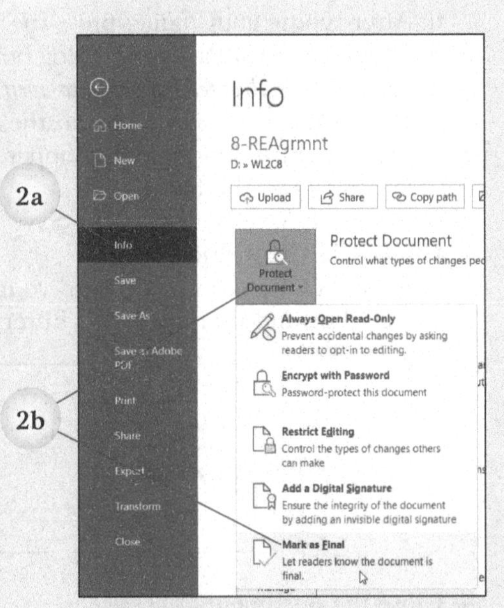

3. In the document window, notice the message bar at the top of the screen and then close the document.
4. Open **8-REAgrmnt.docx** and then click the Edit Anyway button on the yellow message bar.

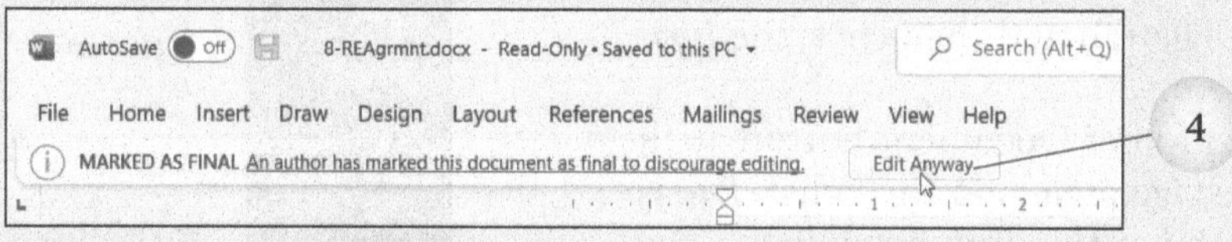

5. Save **8-REAgrmnt.docx**.

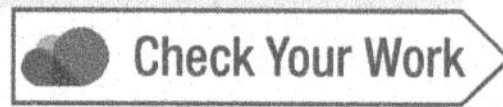

Opening as Read-Only

Click the *Always Open Read-Only* option at the Protect Document button drop-down list to identify a document that should be read and not edited. When a document is opened with this read-only option selected, a message displays indicating that the author of the document would like it to be opened as read-only, unless it needs editing. At this message, click Yes to open the document as read-only or click No if the document needs editing.

Encrypting a Document

Quick Steps

Encrypt Document
1. Click File tab.
2. Click *Info* option.
3. Click Protect Document button.
4. Click *Encrypt with Password.*
5. Type password and then press Enter key.
6. Type password again and then press Enter key.

Word provides a number of methods for protecting a document with a password. As previously discussed in this chapter, a document can be protected with a password using options at the Start Enforcing Protection dialog box and the General Options dialog box.

In addition to these two methods, a document can be protected with a password by clicking the Protect Document button at the Info backstage area and then clicking the *Encrypt with Password* option at the drop-down list. At the Encrypt Document dialog box, type a password in the text box (the text will display as bullets) and then press the Enter key or click OK. At the Confirm Password dialog box, type the password again (the text will display as bullets) and then press the Enter key or click OK. When a password is applied to a document, the message *A password is required to open this document* displays at the right of the Protect Document button.

Restricting Editing

Click the Protect Document button at the Info backstage area and then click the *Restrict Editing* option at the drop-down list and the document displays with the Restrict Editing task pane open. This is the same task pane discussed previously in this chapter.

Adding a Digital Signature

Use the *Add a Digital Signature* option at the Protect Document button drop-down list to insert an invisible digital signature in a document. A digital signature is an electronic stamp that verifies the authenticity of the document. Before a digital signature can be added, it must be obtained. A digital signature can be obtained from a commercial certification authority.

Activity 4b Encrypting a Document with a Password

Part 2 of 4

1. With **8-REAgrmnt.docx** open, encrypt the document with a password by completing the following steps:
   a. Click the File tab and then click the *Info* option.
   b. Click the Protect Document button at the Info backstage area, and then click *Encrypt with Password* at the drop-down list.
   c. At the Encrypt Document dialog box, type your initials in uppercase letters in the *Password* text box. (The text will display as bullets.)

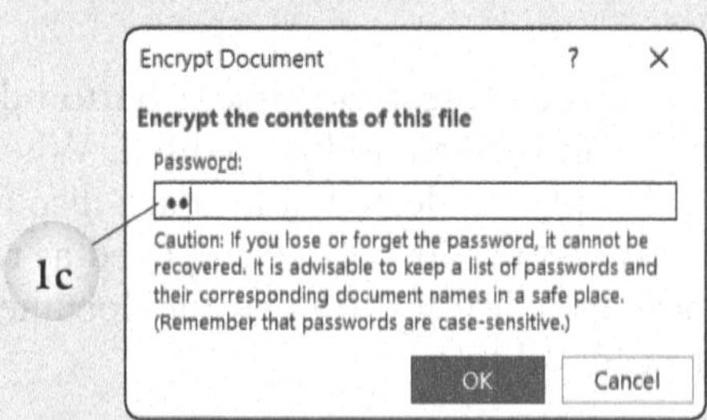

   d. Press the Enter key.
   e. At the Confirm Password dialog box, type your initials again in uppercase letters in the *Reenter password* text box (the text will display as bullets) and then press the Enter key.
2. Click the Back button to return to the document.
3. Save and then close the document.
4. Open **8-REAgrmnt.docx**.
5. At the Password dialog box, type your initials in uppercase letters in the *Enter password to open file* text box and then press the Enter key.
6. Save **8-REAgrmnt.docx**.
7. Remove the password from the document by completing the following steps:
   a. Click the File tab and then click the *Info* option.
   b. Click the Protect Document button and then click *Encrypt with Password*.
   c. Delete the circles in the *Password* text box.
   d. Click OK.
   e. Click the Back button to return to the document.
8. Save and then close **8-REAgrmnt.docx**.

Opening a Document in Different Views

Opening a Document in Different Views

Use the Open button at the Open dialog box to open a document in different views. At the Open dialog box, click the Open button arrow and a drop-down list of options displays. Click the *Open Read-Only* option and the document opens in Read-Only mode. In Read-Only mode, changes can be made to the document, but the document cannot be saved with the same name.

Quick Steps

Open Document in Different Views
1. Display Open dialog box.
2. Click document name.
3. Click Open button arrow.
4. Click option at drop-down list.

Click the *Open as Copy* option and a copy of the document opens with the text *Copy (1)* before the document name in the Title bar. Click the *Open in Protected View* option and the document opens with the text *(Protected View)* after the document name in the Title bar. A message bar displays above the document indicating that the file was opened in Protected view. To edit the document, click the Enable Editing button in the message bar. Open a document with the *Open and Repair* option and Word will open a new version of the document and attempt to resolve any issues.

Activity 4c Opening a Document in Different Views

Part 3 of 4

1. Open a document as a read-only document by completing the following steps:
   a. Press Ctrl + F12 to display the Open dialog box and then navigate to your WL2C8 folder.
   b. Click the document name ***8-REAgrmnt.docx***. (Click only one time.)
   c. Click the Open button arrow (in the bottom right corner of the dialog box) and then click *Open Read-Only* at the drop-down list.

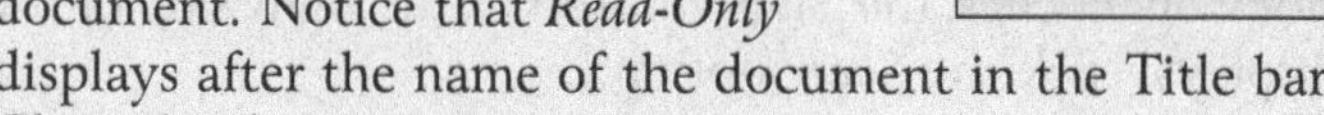

   d. The document opens as a read-only document. Notice that *Read-Only* displays after the name of the document in the Title bar.
   e. Close the document.
2. Open a document in protected view by completing the following steps:
   a. Press Ctrl + F12 to display the Open dialog box.
   b. Click the document name ***PremProduce.docx***.
   c. Click the Open button arrow and then click *Open in Protected View* at the drop-down list.
   d. Notice the message bar stating that the file was opened in Protected view.
   e. Click each tab and notice that most of the formatting options are dimmed.
   f. Click in the document and then click the Enable Editing button in the message bar. This removes *Protected View* after the document name in the Title bar and makes available the options on the tabs.

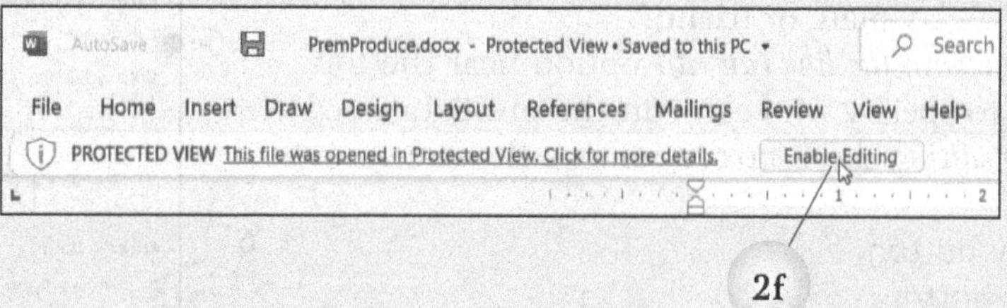

3. Close the document.

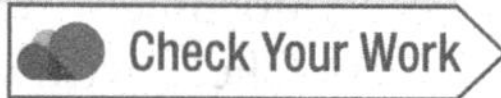

Sharing a Document Electronically

When collaborating with others in a workplace environment, being able to share files electronically may be useful. To share a document electronically with others, the document must be saved to a OneDrive account or a shared location such as a website. Share a document saved to a OneDrive account or other shared location by clicking the Share button in the upper right corner of the screen; clicking the File tab and then clicking the *Share* option; or by clicking the File tab, clicking the *Info* option, and then clicking the Share button below the document name.

At the Share window or task pane that displays, follow the instructions to send a link and invite others to view the document by typing in the email addresses of people to be invited. By default, anyone who is invited to view the document can also make edits to it. This option can be changed so that people can only view, but not edit, the document.

Activity 4d Sharing a Document Electronically

Part 4 of 4

Note: To complete this optional activity, you need to be connected to the internet and have a OneDrive account. Depending on your version of Word, the activity steps may vary. Activity 4d assumes that a Share window will display. If a Share task pane displays, check with your instructor to determine the steps to follow to share your document.

1. Open **8-REAgrmnt.docx**.
2. Save **8-REAgrmnt.docx** to your OneDrive account folder with the name **8-REAgrmnt-Shared** by completing the following steps:
   a. Click the File tab and then click the *Save As* option.
   b. Double-click the OneDrive account in the middle panel.
   c. At the Save As dialog box with the OneDrive account folder active, type 8-REAgrmnt-Shared in the *File name* text box and then click the Save button.
3. With **8-REAgrmnt-Shared.docx** open, click the Share button at the right side of the ribbon. (If a drop-down list displays, click the *Share* option.)

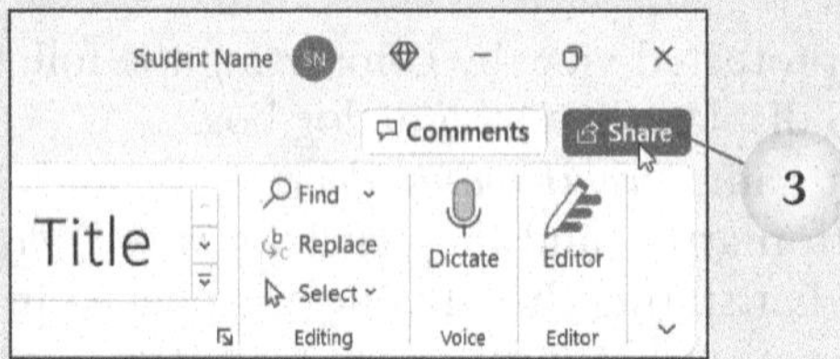

4. Click in the text box containing *To: Name, group or email* text box (displays above the blue line) in the Share window, type the email address for your instructor and/or the email of a classmate or friend.
5. Click the *Anyone with the link can edit* option near the top of the window to specify who can edit the presentation.
6. Click the *Allow editing* check box to remove the check mark.
7. Click the Apply button.
8. Click the Send button.
9. At the message that displays stating the link to the document was sent, click the Close button.
10. Check with your instructor, classmate, and/or friend to determine if he or she was able to open the email containing the link to your document.
11. Close **8-REAgrmnt-Shared.docx** saved to your OneDrive account folder.

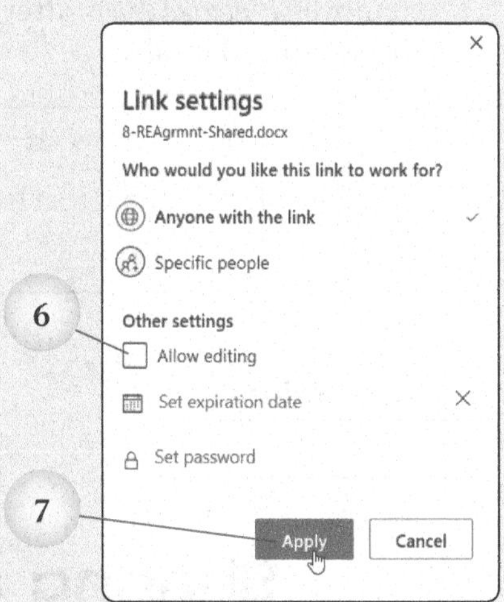

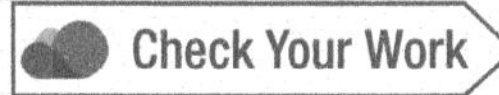

Activity 5 Manage Versions of a Document **1 Part**

You will decrease the autorecovery time to 1 minute, open a document containing an advertising flyer for a produce market, and make changes to it without saving the file. You will then review autorecovered versions of the document created automatically by Word.

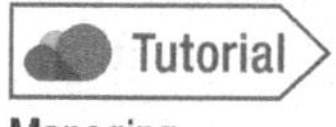

Managing Document Versions

Quick Steps

Display Unsaved Files Folder

1. Click File tab.
2. Click *Info* option.
3. Click Manage Document button.
4. Click *Recover Unsaved Documents*.

OR

1. Click File tab.
2. Click *Open* option.
3. Click Recover Unsaved Documents button.

Managing Document Versions

When working in an open document, Word automatically saves it every 10 minutes. This automatic backup feature can be very helpful if the document is closed accidentally without saving it or the power to the computer is disrupted. As backups of the open document are automatically saved, they are listed at the right of the Manage Document button at the Info backstage area, as shown in Figure 8.10. Each autorecovered document displays with *Today* followed by the time and *(autorecovery)*. When the document is saved and then closed, the autorecover backup documents are deleted.

To open an autorecover backup document, click the File tab, click the *Info* option, and then click the autorecover document. An autorecover document can also be opened by right-clicking the autorecover document at the Info backstage area and then clicking the *Open Version* option. When an autorecover document is opened, a message bar displays. What displays on the message bar depends on the Microsoft 365 update being used. The message bar may display a Save As button, a message indicating that a newer version is available, a Compare button, or a Compare and Restore button. Use the Restore button to save the original document and use the Compare button to compare the current version of the document with the autorecover document. If the hyperlink A new version is available displays on the message bar, click the hyperlink to display a message

Figure 8.10 Autorecover Documents at the Info Backstage Area

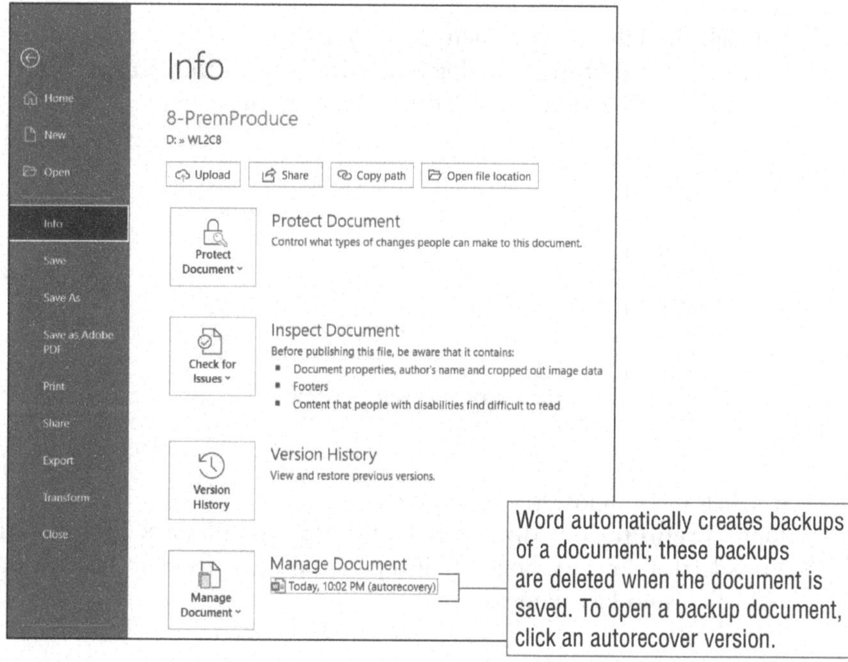

indicating that if you upload your file (to a OneDrive account, for example), Office will automatically save versions of your file as you work.

Quick Steps

Delete Autorecover Backup File
1. Click File tab.
2. Click *Info* option.
3. Right-click autorecover backup file.
4. Click *Delete This Version* at shortcut menu.

Delete All Unsaved Files
1. Click File tab.
2. Click *Info* option.
3. Click Manage Document button.
4. Click *Delete All Unsaved Documents*.
5. Click Yes.

Change AutoRecover Time
1. Click File tab.
2. Click *Options*.
3. Click *Save*.
4. Type minutes in *Save AutoRecover information every* measurement box.
5. Click OK.

When a document is saved, the autorecover backup documents are deleted. However, if a document is closed without being saved (after 10 minutes) or the power is disrupted, Word keeps the autorecover backup files in the UnsavedFiles folder on the hard drive. Access this folder by clicking the Manage Document button at the Info backstage area and then clicking *Recover Unsaved Documents*. At the Open dialog box, double-click the backup file to be opened. The UnsavedFiles folder can also be displayed by clicking the File tab, clicking the *Open* option, and then clicking the Recover Unsaved Documents button below the *Recent* option list. Files in the UnsavedFiles folder are kept for four days after a document is created. After that, they are automatically deleted.

Delete an autorecover backup file by displaying the Info backstage area, right-clicking the autorecover file (at the right of the Manage Document button), and then clicking *Delete This Version* at the shortcut menu. At the confirmation message, click the Yes button. To delete all unsaved files from the UnsavedFiles folder, display a blank document, click the File tab, click the *Info* option, click the Manage Document button, and then click the *Delete All Unsaved Documents* option at the drop-down list. At the confirmation message, click Yes.

As mentioned previously, Word automatically saves a backup of an unsaved document every 10 minutes. To change this default setting, click the File tab and then click *Options*. At the Word Options dialog box, click *Save* in the left panel. Notice that the *Save AutoRecover information every* measurement box is set at 10 minutes. To change this number, click the measurement box up arrow to increase the number of minutes between autorecovers or click the down arrow to decrease the number of minutes.

Activity 5 Opening and Deleting an Autorecover Document

Part 1 of 1

1. At a blank screen, decrease the autorecover time to 1 minute by completing the following steps:
   a. Click the File tab and then click *Options*.
   b. At the Word Options dialog box, click *Save* in the left panel.
   c. Click the *Save AutoRecover information every* measurement box down arrow until *1* displays.

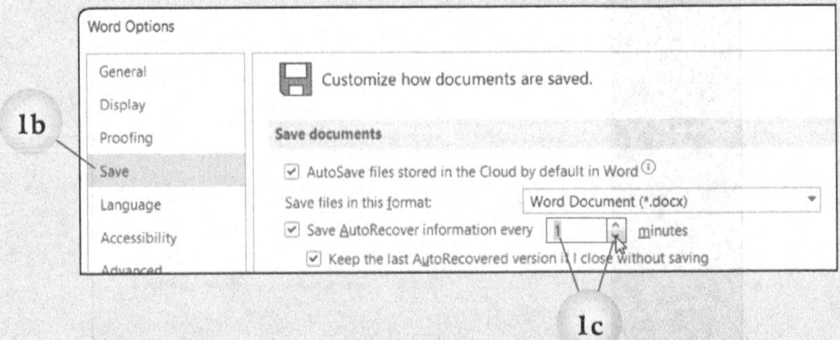

   d. Click OK to close the dialog box.
2. Open **PremProduce.docx** and save it with the name **8-PremProduce**.
3. Press Ctrl + End to move the insertion point to the end of the document and then type your first and last names.

4. Leave the document open for more than one minute without making any further changes. After at least one minute has passed, click the File tab and then click the *Info* option. Check to see if an autorecover document displays at the right of the Manage Document button. (If not, click the Back button to return to the document and wait a few more minutes.)
5. When an autorecover document displays at the Info backstage area, click the Back button to return to the document.
6. Select the SmartArt graphic at the end of the document, and then delete it.
7. Click the File tab, click the *Info* option, and then click the autorecover document at the right of the Manage Document button. If more than one autorecover document displays, click the one at the top of the list (the most recent autorecover document). This opens the autorecover document as a read-only file. Notice that the autorecover document contains the SmartArt graphic.

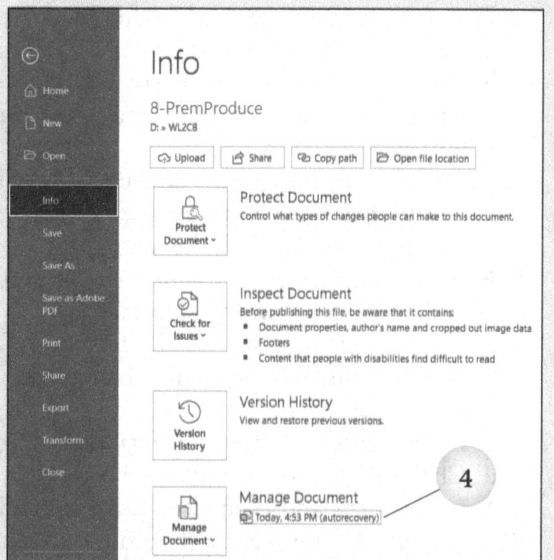

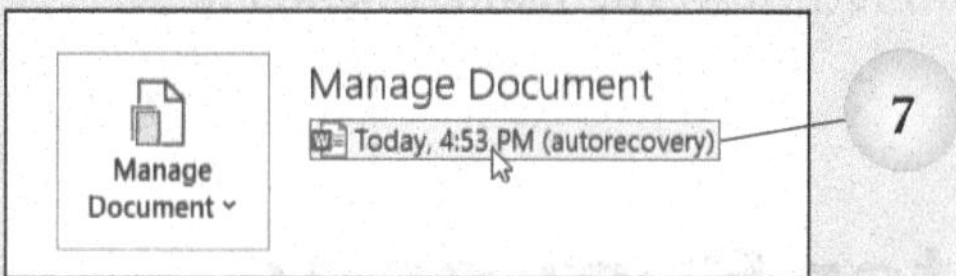

8. Instead of saving the autorecover document, close it without saving it.
9. Check to see what versions of previous documents Word has saved by completing the following steps:
   a. At the Info backstage area, click the Manage Document button and then click *Recover Unsaved Documents* at the drop-down list.
   b. At the Open dialog box, check the documents that display in the content pane.
   c. Click the Cancel button to close the Open dialog box.

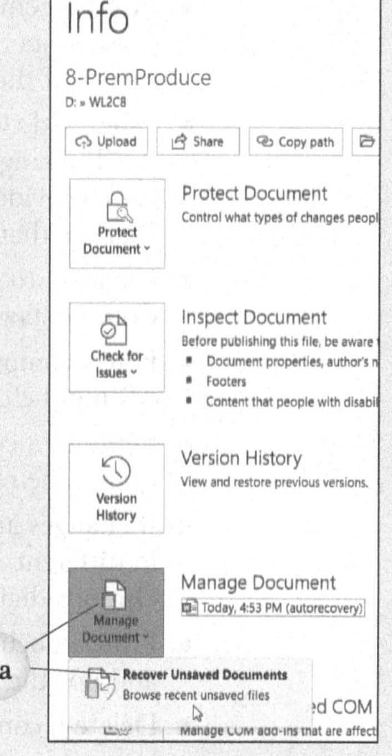

10. Delete an autorecover backup file by completing the following steps:
    a. Click the File tab and then click the *Info* option.
    b. Right-click the first autorecover backup file name at the right of the Manage Document button.
    c. Click *Delete This Version* at the shortcut menu.
    d. At the message asking whether to delete the selected version, click the Yes button.
11. Return the autorecovery time to 10 minutes by completing the following steps:
    a. At the backstage area, click *Options*.
    b. At the Word Options dialog box, click *Save* in the left panel.
    c. Click the *Save AutoRecover information every* measurement box up arrow until *10* displays.
    d. Click OK to close the dialog box.
12. Save, preview, and then close **8-PremProduce.docx**.
13. Delete all the unsaved backup files by completing the following steps:
    a. Press Ctrl + N to display a blank document.
    b. Click the File tab and then click the *Info* option.
    c. Click the Manage Document button and then click *Delete All Unsaved Documents*.
    d. At the message that displays, click Yes.
14. Click the Back button to return to the blank document.

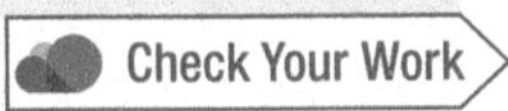

Chapter Summary

- Insert a comment in a document with the New Comment button in the Comments group on the Review tab or the Comment button in the upper right corner of the screen. A comment box opens and displays in the right margin.
- Open and close the Reviewing pane by clicking the Reviewing Pane button in the Tracking group on the Review tab. The summary section of the Reviewing pane provides counts of the number of comments inserted and the types of changes that have been made to the document.
- Navigate to review comments using the Previous and Next buttons in the Comments group on the Review tab.
- Edit a comment with the Edit comment button in the comment box. After editing the comment, click the Post comment button in the comment box.
- Reply to a comment by clicking in the *Reply* text box in the comment box, typing the reply, and then clicking the Post reply button.
- If changes are made to a document by different users, the changes display in different colors. The user name and initials can be changed at the Word Options dialog box with *General* selected.
- Print a document with or without the comments or print only the comments and not the document.
- Delete a comment with the *Delete thread* option at the More thread actions button drop-down list or with the Delete button in the Comments group on the Review tab.

- Use the Track Changes feature when more than one person is reviewing and editing a document. Turn on Track Changes by clicking the Track Changes button in the Tracking group on the Review tab.
- The *Display for Review* option box in the Tracking group on the Review tab has a default setting of *Simple Markup*, which shows changes in the document and a vertical change line at the left margin where the change was made. This setting can be changed to *All Markup*, showing all changes in the document along with the original text or *No Markup*, showing the document with all the changes applied.
- With the *Display for Review* option box set at *All Markup*, specify what tracking information displays in the document with options at the Balloons side menu. Display this side menu by clicking the Show Markup button in the Tracking group on the Review tab and then pointing to *Balloons*.
- Display information about tracked changes—such as the author's name, date and time, and type of change—by hovering the pointer over a change. After approximately one second, a box displays with the information. Another method for displaying information about tracked changes is to display the Reviewing pane.
- To ensure that all changes made to a document are tracked, lock the Track Changes feature by clicking the Track Changes button arrow in the Tracking group on the Review tab, clicking *Lock Tracking*, and then typing a password at the Lock Tracking dialog box.
- Customize what tracked changes display in a document with options at the Show Markup button drop-down list. At the drop-down list, remove check marks from those options that should not display and specify what reviewer changes should display.
- Change Track Changes default settings with options at the Advanced Track Changes Options dialog box. Display this dialog box by clicking the Tracking group dialog box launcher and then clicking the Advanced Options button at the Track Changes Options dialog box.
- When reviewing a document, move to the next change by clicking the Next button in the Changes group on the Review tab and move to the previous change by clicking the Previous button.
- Use the Accept and Reject buttons in the Changes group on the Review tab to accept and reject changes made in a document.
- Restrict formatting and editing in a document and apply a password to protect it with options in the Restrict Editing task pane. Display this task pane by clicking the Review tab and then clicking the Restrict Editing button in the Protect group.
- Apply formatting restrictions in a document by specifying what styles are and are not allowed at the Formatting Restrictions dialog box. Display this dialog box by clicking the Settings hyperlink in the *Formatting restrictions* section of the Restrict Editing task pane.
- Enforce restrictions to a document by clicking the Yes, Start Enforcing Protection button at the Restrict Editing task pane and then entering a password at the Start Enforcing Protection dialog box.
- Apply editing restrictions in a document using options in the *Editing restrictions* section of the Restrict Editing task pane.

- Mark a document as final, which saves it as a read-only document, by clicking the Protect Document button at the Info backstage area and then clicking *Mark as Final* at the drop-down list. Typing, editing commands, and proofing marks are turned off when a document is marked as final.
- Protect a document with a password by clicking the Protect Document button at the Info backstage area, clicking the *Encrypt with Password* option, and then specifying a password at the Encrypt Document dialog box.
- Another method for displaying the Restrict Editing task pane is to click the Protect Document button at the Info backstage area and then click *Restrict Editing* at the drop-down list.
- Open a document in different views with options at the Open button drop-down list at the Open dialog box.
- Share a document that has been saved to a OneDrive account or a shared location such as a website with options at the Share window or Share task pane. Use options at the Share window or task pane to identify who will receive the shared document and to specify whether or not the shared document can be viewed only or viewed and edited.
- By default, Word automatically saves a backup of an unsaved document every 10 minutes. A list of autorecover backup documents of an open document displays at the right of the Manage Document button at the Info backstage area. To open an autorecover backup document, click the File tab, click the Info option, and then click the autorecover document.
- When a document is saved, Word automatically deletes the autorecover backup documents. However, if a document is closed without saving it or the power to the computer is disrupted, Word keeps a backup document in the UnsavedFiles folder on the hard drive. Access this folder by clicking the Manage Document button at the Info backstage area and then clicking *Recover Unsaved Documents* at the drop-down list.
- Delete an autorecover backup file by displaying the Info backstage area, right-clicking the autorecover backup file, and then clicking *Delete This Version* at the shortcut menu.
- Delete all the unsaved documents from the UnsavedFiles folder by displaying a blank document, clicking the File tab, clicking the Manage Document button, and then clicking *Delete All Unsaved Documents*. At the message that displays, click Yes.
- Change the 10-minute autorecover default setting with the *Save AutoRecover information every* measurement at the Word Options dialog box with *Save* selected in the left panel.

Commands Review

FEATURE	RIBBON TAB, GROUP	BUTTON, OPTION	KEYBOARD SHORTCUT
accept changes	Review, Changes		
Advanced Track Changes Options dialog box	Review, Tracking	, Advanced Options	
balloons	Review, Tracking	, *Balloons*	
delete comment	Review, Comments		
display for review	Review, Tracking		
Encrypt Document dialog box	File, *Info*	, *Encrypt with Password*	
Formatting Restrictions dialog box	Review, Protect	, *Settings*	
new comment	Review, Comments		
next comment	Review, Comments		
next revision	Review, Changes		
previous comment	Review, Comments		
previous revision	Review, Changes		
reject changes	Review, Changes		
Restrict Editing task pane	Review, Protect		
Reviewing pane	Review, Tracking		
Share window			
show markup	Review, Tracking		
Track Changes	Review, Tracking		Ctrl + Shift + E
Track Changes Options dialog box	Review, Tracking		
UnsavedFiles folder	File, *Info*	, *Recover Unsaved Documents*	

Review and Assessment

CHAPTER 8

Skills Assessment

Assessment 1 — Insert Comments in a Country Report

1. Open **SingaporeRpt.docx** and then save it with the name **8-SingaporeRpt**.
2. Delete the only comment in the document.
3. Position the insertion point at the end of the first paragraph below the title *Singapore* and then insert a comment and type the following comment text: Please provide an image of the flag of the Republic of Singapore.
4. Position the insertion point at the end of the second paragraph below the heading *History* and then insert a comment and type the following comment text: Provide more information on the British East India company.
5. Position the insertion point at the end of the last paragraph below the heading *History* and insert a comment and type the following comment text: Describe the current government of the Republic of Singapore.
6. Save the document and then print only the comments.
7. Close **8-SingaporeRpt.docx**.

Assessment 2 — Track Changes in a Building Agreement Document

1. Open **BuildAgrmnt.docx** and then save it with the name **8-BuildAgrmnt**.
2. Turn on Track Changes and then make the following changes:
   a. Select and then bold the text *THIS AGREEMENT* at the beginning of the first paragraph below the title.
   b. Select and then delete the text *and Financing* that displays at the beginning of the second paragraph (the text in bold).
   c. Type either has or between *owner* and *will* in the first sentence in the *Construction Loan Arrangements* paragraph.
   d. Turn off Track Changes.
3. Display the Word Options dialog box with *General* selected and then change the user name to *Sandra Payne* and the initials to *SP*. Insert a check mark in the *Always use these values regardless of sign in to Office* check box.
4. Turn on Track Changes and then make the following changes:
   a. Select and then delete the last sentence in the *Changes and Alterations* paragraph (the sentence that begins *Where such change results*.)
   b. Move the *Exclusions* paragraph above the *Changes and Alterations* paragraph.
   c. Turn off Track Changes.
5. Display the Word Options dialog box with *General* selected. Change the user name back to the original name and the initials back to the original initials. Also remove the check mark from the *Always use these values regardless of sign in to Office* check box.
6. Preview the document with tracked changes displayed inline.
7. Accept all the changes in the document *except* the change deleting the last sentence in the *Changes and Alterations* paragraph; reject this change.
8. Save, preview, and then close **8-BuildAgrmnt.docx**.

Assessment 3

Restrict Formatting and Editing of a Writing Report

1. Open **WritingProcess.docx** and then save it with the name **8-WritingProcess**.
2. Display the Restrict Editing task pane and then restrict formatting to the Heading 2 and Heading 3 styles. (At the message asking about removing formatting or styles that are not allowed, click No.)
3. Enforce the protection and include the password *writing*.
4. Click the Available styles hyperlink.
5. Apply the Heading 2 style to the two titles *THE WRITING PROCESS* and *REFERENCES*.
6. Apply the Heading 3 style to the seven remaining headings in the document. (The Heading 3 style may not display until the Heading 2 style is applied to the first title.)
7. Close the Styles task pane and then close the Restrict Editing task pane.
8. Save, preview, and then close **8-WritingProcess.docx**.

Assessment 4

Insert Comments in a Software Life Cycle Document

1. Open **SoftwareCycle.docx** and then save it with the name **8-SoftwareCycle**.
2. Display the Restrict Editing task pane, restrict editing to comments only, and then start enforcing the protection. Do not include a password.
3. At the end of the first paragraph in the document, type the comment Create a SmartArt graphic that illustrates the software life cycle.
4. At the end of the paragraph in the *Design* section, type the comment Include the problem-solving steps.
5. At the end of the paragraph in the *Testing* section, type the comment Describe a typical beta testing cycle.
6. Print only the comments.
7. Close the Restrict Editing task pane.
8. Save, preview, and then close **8-SoftwareCycle.docx**.

Assessment 5

Track Changes in a Table

1. Open **SalesTable.docx** and then save it with the name **8-SalesTable**.
2. Make the Review tab active and then change the *Display for Review* option box setting to *All Markup*.
3. Display the Advanced Track Changes Options dialog box, look at the options for customizing tracked changes in a table, and then make the following changes:
   a. Change the color for inserted cells to Light Purple.
   b. Change the color for deleted cells to Light Green.
4. Turn on Track Changes and then make the following changes:
   a. Insert a new row at the beginning of the table.
   b. Merge the cells in the new row. (At the message stating that the action will not be marked as a change, click OK.)
   c. Type Clearline Manufacturing in the merged cell.
   d. Delete the *Fanning, Andrew* row.
   e. Insert a new row below *Barnet, Jacqueline* and then type Montano, Neil in the first cell, $530,678 in the second cell, and $550,377 in the third cell.
   f. Turn off Track Changes.
5. Save and then preview the document.
6. Accept all the changes.
7. Display the Advanced Track Changes Options dialog box and then return the color of the inserted cells to Light Blue and the color of the deleted cells to Pink.
8. Save, preview, and then close **8-SalesTable.docx**.

Visual Benchmark

Track Changes in an Employee Performance Document

1. Open **NSSEmpPerf.docx** and then save it with the name **8-NSSEmpPerf**.
2. Turn on Track Changes and then make the changes shown in Figure 8.11. (Make the editing changes before moving the *Employment Records* section after the *Performance Evaluation* section.)
3. Turn off Track Changes and then print only the list of markups. ***Hint: Do this by displaying the Print backstage area, clicking the first gallery in the Settings category, and then clicking the* List of Markup *option.***
4. Accept all the changes to the document.
5. Save, preview, and then close **8-NSSEmpPerf.docx**.

Figure 8.11 Visual Benchmark

N
Northland Security Systems
3200 North 22nd Street ✦ Springfield ✦ IL ✦ 62102

EMPLOYEE PERFORMANCE

Work Performance Standards

and/or behavior

cap

~~Some~~ work performance standards are written statements of the results expected of an employee when his or her job elements are satisfactorily performed under existing working conditions. Each employee in a permanent position must be provided with a current set of work performance standards for his or her position.

Employment Records

Your personnel file is maintained in the human resources department ~~at the main office of Northland Security Systems~~. The human resources department maintains a file with copies of the documentation in your specific department. Your file includes personnel action documents, mandatory employment forms, your performance evaluations, and documentation of disciplinary action. Your file may include letters of commendation, training certificates, or other work-related documents that your supervisor has requested to be included in your file.

working

Performance Evaluation

(full-time equivalent)

If you are serving a six-month probationary period, your supervisor will evaluate your performance at the end of the second and fifth months. If you are completing a one-year probationary period, your evaluations will be conducted at the end of the third, seventh, and eleventh month. You will receive a copy of each performance report. Once you have attained permanent employee status, your performance will be evaluated annually during the month prior to your pay progression date. Each evaluation will include a discussion between you and your supervisor to review and clarify goals and methods to achieve them. The evaluation will also include a report of your progress on the job. Evaluations will be made with reference to established work performance standards.

written

1-888-555-2200 ✦ https://ppi-edu.net/nss

Case Study

Part 1

You work for Premier Associates, a career development company that provides career placement, transition, and outplacement for clients. Some of the company's materials need formatting to reflect the company's brand. Open **PALtrhd.docx** and look at the first page header and first page footer. Notice the colors and shapes used in the header and footer and then close the document. Open **PAResume.docx** and then save it with the name **8-PAResume**. This document has been reviewed by your supervisor, who made her edits as tracked changes. Accept the editing changes to the document and turn off tracked changes. Look at the one comment in the document, make the change mentioned in the comment and then delete the comment. Format the document so it is attractive and easy to read. Consider using the **PAHead.png** image as a header and **PAFoot.png** as a footer. Add any additional information to the header or footer that you think is needed. Save, preview, and then close **8-PAResume.docx**.

Part 2

Your supervisor has given you another document that she has edited and wants you to format. Open **PAResumeStyles.docx** and then save it with the name **8-PAResumeStyles**. Accept or reject the edits made by your supervisor and then turn off tracked changes. (The document contains two edits that should be rejected.) Make the change suggested by her comment. Apply formatting to the document similar to what you applied to **8-PAResume.docx**. Save, preview, and then close **8-PAResumeStyles.docx**.

Part 3

Your company provides a sample chonological resume to clients. Your supervisor wants you to open the sample resume and apply formatting to the resume so it has the look and branding of the other Premier Associates documents. Open **PAChronoResume.docx** and then save it with the name **8-PAChronoResume**. Apply formatting so the document has the look of other Premier Associates documents. Save, preview, and then close **8-PAChronoResume.docx**.

Part 4

Your supervisor has asked you to search for a resume template and then download and print it to make it available for clients. Display the New backstage area and search for resumes. Download a resume that looks interesting to you. Apply formatting to the resume so it has the look of the other Premier Associates documents. Save the resume with the name **8-PAWordResume**. Preview and then close **8-PAWordResume.docx**.

WORD LEVEL 2

Unit 2 Performance Assessment

Data Files

The data files for this unit work are in the WL2U2 folder that you downloaded at the beginning of this course.

Assessing Proficiency

In this unit, you have learned to customize objects, create and format charts, merge documents, apply and customize building blocks, and insert and update fields. You have also learned to insert and manage comments, track changes, and restrict and protect documents.

Assessment 1

Insert and Format Objects

1. Open **HMConcert.docx** and then save it with the name **U2-HMConcert**.
2. The border is a drawn image that is positioned in the First Page Header pane. Double-click in the header, select the border image, apply the following formatting, and then close the First Page Header pane:
   - Apply the Light Gray, Background 2, Darker 10% shape fill (third column, second row in the *Theme Colors* section).
   - Apply the Offset: Center shape shadow effect (second column, second row in the *Outer* section).
3. Select the image of the music notes and then apply the following formatting:
   - Change the height of the image to 2.5 inches.
   - Precisely position the image on the page with an absolute horizontal measurement of 0.6 inch to the right of the left margin and an absolute vertical measurement of 0.65 inch below the page.
4. Click in the table cell immediately left of the telephone number 253.555.4500 (you may want to turn on the display of table gridlines), insert the telephone icon ☎ (use the search word *telephone* at the Icons window), and then apply the following formatting:
   - Change the height of the image to 0.3 inch.
   - Apply the Light 1 Fill, Colored Outline - Accent 3 graphic style (fourth style in the Graphic Styles gallery).

5. Click in the table cell immediately left of the email address, insert the envelope icon ✉ (use the search word *envelope* at the Icons window), and then apply the same formatting to the envelope icon that you applied to the telephone icon.
6. Save, preview, and then close **U2-HMConcert.docx**.

Assessment 2 Customize a 3D Model

1. Open **OpenHouse.docx** and then save it with the name **U2-OpenHouse**. (This document contains a 3D model of a person in a spacesuit.)
2. Select the 3D model of the person in a spacesuit and then apply the following formatting:
   - Apply the Above Front Right 3D model view (fifth column, second row in the 3D Model Views drop-down gallery).
   - Increase the height of the image to 4.4 inches.
   - Precisely position the model on the page with an absolute horizontal measurement of 5.2 inches to the right of the left margin and an absolute vertical measurement of 2.7 inches below the page.
3. Save, preview, and then close **U2-OpenHouse.docx**.

Assessment 3 Create and Format a Column Chart

1. At a blank document, use the data in Figure U2.1 to create a column chart with the following specifications:
   a. Choose the 3-D Clustered Column chart type.
   b. Apply the Layout 3 quick layout.
   c. Apply the Style 5 chart style.
   d. Change the chart title to *Yearly Sales*.
   e. Insert a data table with legend keys.
   f. Select the chart area, apply the Subtle Effect - Green, Accent 6 shape style (last column, fourth row in the *Theme Styles* section), and then apply the Offset: Bottom shadow shape effect (second column, first row in the *Outer* section).
   g. Select the series *Second Half* and then apply the standard dark red shape fill (first option in the *Standard Colors* section).
   h. Change the chart height to 4 inches and the chart width to 6.25 inches.
   i. Use the Position button in the Arrange group to position the chart in the middle center of the page with square text wrapping.
2. Save the document with the name **U2-SalesChart** and then preview the document.

Figure U2.1 Assessment 3

Salesperson	First Half	Second Half
Bratton	$235,500	$285,450
Daniels	$300,570	$250,700
Hughes	$170,200	$180,210
Marez	$308,520	$346,400

3. With the chart selected, display the Excel worksheet and then edit the data in the worksheet by changing the following:
   a. Change the amount in cell C2 from *$285,450* to *$302,500.*
   b. Change the amount in cell C4 from *$180,210* to *$190,150.*
4. Save, preview, and then close **U2-SalesChart.docx**.

Assessment 4 Create and Format a Pie Chart

1. At a blank document, use the data in Figure U2.2 to create a pie chart with the following specifications:
   a. Apply the Layout 6 quick layout.
   b. Apply the Style 3 chart style.
   c. Change the chart title to *District Expenditures*.
   d. Move the legend to the left side of the chart.
   e. Select the chart area, apply the Gold, Accent 4, Lighter 80% shape fill (eighth column, second row in the *Theme Colors* section), and then apply the Glow: 11 point; Gray, Accent color 3 glow shape effect (third column, third row in the *Glow Variations* section).
   f. Select the legend and apply the Blue color shape outline (eighth option in the *Standard Colors* section).
   g. Move the data labels to the inside ends of the pie pieces.
   h. Use the Position button to center the chart at the top of the page with square text wrapping.
2. Save the document with the name **U2-ExpendChart**.
3. Preview and then close **U2-ExpendChart.docx**.

Figure U2.2 Assessment 4

	Percentage
Basic Education	42%
Special Needs	20%
Support Services	19%
Vocational	11%
Compensatory	8%

Assessment 5

Merge and Preview Letters

1. Look at the information shown in Figure U2.3 and Figure U2.4. Use the Mail Merge feature to prepare six letters using the information shown in the figures. When creating the letter main document, open **SoundLtrhd.docx** and then save it with the name **U2-SoundMD**. (Change the punctuation in the greeting line from a comma to a colon.) Create the data source file with the text shown in Figure U2.3 and name the file **U2-SoundDS**. (When creating the data source, customize the columns to accommodate the text in the figure.)
2. Type the text in the main document as shown in Figure U2.4. Insert the *Title* and *Last_Name* fields in the last paragraph as indicated.
3. Merge the document with the **U2-SoundDS.mdb** data source file.
4. Save the merged letters document with the name **U2-SoundLtrs**.
5. Preview and then close **U2-SoundLtrs.docx**.
6. Save and then close the main document.

Figure U2.3 Assessment 5

Mr. Antonio Mercado
3241 Court G
Tampa, FL 33623

Ms. Kristina Vukovich
1120 South Monroe
Tampa, FL 33655

Ms. Alexandria Remick
909 Wheeler South
Tampa, FL 33620

Mr. Minh Vu
9302 Lawndale Southwest
Tampa, FL 33623

Mr. Curtis Iverson
10139 93rd Court South
Tampa, FL 33654

Ms. Holly Bernard
8904 Emerson Road
Tampa, FL 33620

Figure U2.4 Assessment 5

December 16, 2024

«AddressBlock»

«GreetingLine»

Sound Medical is switching hospital care in Tampa to Bayshore Hospital beginning January 1, 2025. As mentioned in last month's letter, Bayshore Hospital was selected because it meets our requirements for high-quality, patient-centered care that is also affordable and accessible. Our physicians look forward to caring for you in this new environment.

Over the past month, staff members at Sound Medical have been working to make this transition as smooth as possible. Surgeries planned after January 1 are being scheduled at Bayshore Hospital. Mothers delivering babies after January 1 are receiving information about delivery room tours and prenatal classes available at Bayshore Hospital. Your Sound Medical doctor will have privileges at Bayshore Hospital and will continue to care for you if you need to be hospitalized.

You are a very important part of our patient family, «Title» «Last_Name», and we hope this information is helpful. If you have any additional questions or concerns, please call our health coordinator at (813) 555-9886 between 8:00 a.m. and 4:30 p.m.

Sincerely,

Jody Tiemann
District Administrator

XX
U2-SoundMD.docx

Assessment 6 Merge and Preview Envelopes

1. Use the Mail Merge feature to prepare Size 10 envelopes for the letters created in Assessment 5.
2. Specify **U2-SoundDS.mdb** as the data source document.
3. Save the merged envelopes document with the name **U2-SoundEnvs**.
4. Preview and then close **U2-SoundEnvs.docx**.
5. Save the envelope main document with the name **U2-SoundEnvMD**.
6. Close **U2-SoundEnvMD.docx**.

Assessment 7 Create and Insert Custom Building Blocks

1. Using the Open dialog box in Word, open the template **CPTemplate.dotx** and then save it as a template with the name **U2-CPTemplate**.
2. This template contains three custom building blocks for Capital Properties. Add two more custom building blocks with the following specifications:
   a. Select the heading *Attorney's Fees* and the paragraph of text below the heading and then save the selected text in a custom building block in the Quick Part gallery with the name *Fees*.
   b. Select the image (the horizontal line and house with *Est. 1990*) and then save the image as a custom building block in the Footer gallery with the name *CPFooter*.
3. Select and then delete the entire document.
4. Save and then close **U2-CPTemplate.dotx**.
5. Use File Explorer to open a blank document based on **U2-CPTemplate.dotx**.
6. Build a real estate agreement by completing the following steps:
   a. Insert the *CPHeader* building block located in the Header gallery. Close the Header pane.
   b. Insert the *CPFooter* building block located in the Footer gallery. Close the Footer pane.
   c. Insert the *REAgreement* building block located in the Quick Part gallery.
7. Save the document with the name **U2-CPAgreement**.
8. Preview and then close **U2-CPAgreement.docx**.
9. Use File Explorer to open a blank document based on **U2-CPTemplate.dotx**.
10. Build a lease agreement by completing the following steps:
    a. Insert the *CPHeader* building block located in the Header gallery. Close the Header pane.
    b. Insert the *CPFooter* building block located in the Footer gallery. Close the Footer pane.
    c. Insert the *LeaseAgreement* building block located in the Quick Part gallery.
    d. Move the insertion point to the beginning of the heading *Use of Premises* and then insert the *Fees* building block in the Quick Part gallery. (If necessary, press the Enter key to start a new paragraph at the *Use of Premises* heading.)
11. Save the document with the name **U2-CPLease**.
12. Preview and then close **U2-CPLease.docx**.

Assessment 8

Insert Comments and Track Changes in an Orientation Document

1. Open **Orientation.docx** and then save it with the name **U2-Orientation**.
2. Move the insertion point to end of the first paragraph below the title and then insert a comment and type the following comment text: Specify that the orientation is required.
3. Move the insertion point to the end of the first paragraph in the *Medical Screenings* section and then insert a comment and type the following comment text: Provide specific information on the required medical screening.
4. Click the *Display for Review* option box arrow and then click *All Markup* at the drop-down list, if necessary.
5. Turn on Track Changes and then make the following changes:
   a. Move the insertion point to the beginning of the word *designed* in the first sentence in the first paragraph, type (VIS) and then press the spacebar.
   b. Select and then delete the words *As part of the employment procedures* and the comma and space that follow the words that display at the beginning of the first paragraph in the *Medical Screenings* section.
   c. Turn off Track Changes.
6. Display the Word Options dialog box with *General* selected and then type Trudy Holmes as the user name and TH as the user initials. (Make sure you insert a check mark in the *Always use these values regardless of sign in to Office* check box.)
7. Turn on Track Changes and then make the following changes:
   a. Select and then apply italic formatting to the words *New Employee Orientation Program* that display in the first paragraph below the title.
   b. Select and then delete the second paragraph in the *Identification Badges* section (located on page 2).
   c. Turn off Track Changes.
8. Print the document with markups.
9. Display the Word Options dialog box with *General* selected and then change the user name back to the original name and the initials back to the original initials. (Remove the check mark from the *Always use these values regardless of sign in to Office* check box.)
10. Accept all the changes in the document *except* reject the change deleting the last paragraph in the *Identification Badges* section. (Leave the comments in the document.)
11. Save, preview, and then close **U2-Orientation.docx**.

Assessment

Restrict Formatting in a Report

1. Open **CompPioneers.docx** and then save it with the name **U2-CompPioneers**.
2. Display the Restrict Editing task pane and then restrict formatting to the Heading 1 and Heading 2 styles. (At the message that displays asking if you want to remove formatting or styles that are not allowed, click No.)
3. Enforce the protection and include the password *report*.
4. Click the Available styles hyperlink in the Restrict Editing task pane.
5. Apply the Heading 1 style to the title of the report (*PIONEERS OF COMPUTING*) and apply the Heading 2 style to the two headings in the report (*Konrad Zuse* and *William Hewlett and David Packard*).
6. Close the Styles task pane.
7. Close the Restrict Editing task pane.
8. Save, preview, and then close **U2-CompPioneers.docx**.

Writing Activities

Activity 1

Create Building Blocks and Compose a Letter

You are the executive assistant to the vice president of Clearline Manufacturing. You are responsible for preparing company documents and decide to create building blocks to increase the efficiency of and consistency in the documents. Press Ctrl + N to open a blank document and then save the document as a template named **U2-CMTemplate.dotx** in your WL2U2 folder. Create the following building blocks in the template:

- Create a letterhead that includes the company name and any other enhancements to improve the appearance. Save the letterhead as a building block in the Header gallery.
- Create a building block footer that inserts the company address and telephone number. (You determine the address and telephone number.) Include a visual element in the footer, such as a border. Save the footer building block in the Footer gallery.
- You send documents to the board of directors and decide to include the board members' names and addresses as building blocks. Save each board member's name and address as a building block in the Quick Part gallery.

  Ms. Nancy Logan
  12301 132nd Avenue East
  Warminster, PA 18974

  Mr. Dion Jarvis
  567 Federal Street
  Philadelphia, PA 19093

  Dr. Tanner Svoboda
  9823 South 112th Street
  Norristown, PA 18974

- Create a complimentary close building block that includes *Sincerely yours,* your name, and the title *Executive Assistant*. Save the building block in the Quick Part gallery.

Delete the contents of **U2-CMTemplate.dotx** and then save the template. (This saves the building blocks you created in the template.)

At a blank document, write the body of a letter to a member of the board of directors and include at least the following information:

- Explain that the director of the Human Resources Department has created a new employee handbook and that it will be made available to all new employees. Also mention that the attorney for Clearline Manufacturing has reviewed the handbook and approved its content.
- Open **CMHandbook.docx** and then use the headings to summarize the contents of the handbook in a paragraph in the letter. Explain in the letter that a draft of the handbook is enclosed.
- Include any additional information you feel the directors may want to know.

Save the body of the letter as a separate document named **U2-CMLtr** and then close **U2-CMLtr.docx**. Use File Explorer to open a blank document based on **U2-CMTemplate.dotx** and then create a letter to Nancy Logan with the following specifications:

- Insert the letterhead building block you created for Clearline Manufacturing.
- Insert the footer building block.
- Insert the building block containing Nancy Logan's name and address.
- Insert into the document the file named **U2-CMLtr.docx**.

- Insert the complimentary close building block.
- Insert any other text or make any changes to complete the letter.

Save the completed letter with the name **U2-CMLtrNL**. Preview and then close **U2-CMLtrNL.docx**. Complete similar steps to create a letter to Dion Jarvis. Save the letter with the name **U2-CMLtrDJ**. Close the letter. Complete similar steps to create a letter to Tanner Svoboda. Save the letter with the name **U2-CMLtrTS**. Preview and then close **U2-CMLtrTS.docx**.

Activity 2

Create a Slogan Building Block

You decide to create a building block for the company slogan and save it in **U2-CMTemplate.dotx**. Open **U2-CMTemplate.dotx** from your WL2U2 folder. In the template, create a text box with the slogan *Where innovation and production come together.* inside the text box. Enhance the appearance of the text box by applying formatting similar to that applied to the company letterhead. After creating the text box, select it and then save it in the Text Box gallery with the name **CMSlogan**. After saving the text box as a building block, delete the text box and then save and close **U2-CMTemplate.dotx**. Use File Explorer to open a document based on **U2-CMTemplate.dotx**. Insert the letterhead header building block and the footer building block you created in Activity 1 and then insert the text box building block you created in this activity. Save the document with the name **U2-CMDocument**. Preview and then close **U2-CMDocument.docx**.

Internet Research

Create a Population Chart

Use a search engine to determine the population of the country in which you currently live for the years 1980, 1990, 2000, 2010, and 2020. Create a line chart with the information you find. Apply formatting to the chart to make the data easy to interpret and to improve the visual interest of the chart. Save the document with the name **U2-Population**. Preview and then close **U2-Population.docx**.

Job Study

Format a Guidelines Report

As a staff member of an electronics retailer, you are required to maintain cutting-edge technology skills, including being well versed in the use of new software applications, such as those in Microsoft 365. Recently, your supervisor asked you to develop and distribute a set of strategies for reading technical and computer manuals that staff members will use as they learn new applications. Use the concepts and techniques you learned in this textbook to edit the guidelines report as follows:

1. Open **Strategies.docx** and then save it with the name **U2-Strategies**.
2. Turn on Track Changes and then make the following changes:
   a. Change all the occurrences of *computer manuals* to *technical and computer manuals*.
   b. Format the document with appropriate heading styles.
   c. Turn off Track Changes.
   d. Insert at least two comments about the content and/or formatting of the document.
   e. Print the list of markups.
   f. Accept all the tracked changes.
3. Insert a table of contents.
4. Number the pages in the document.
5. Insert a cover page.
6. Save, preview, and then close **U2-Strategies.docx**.

INDEX

D

E

F

G

H

I

K

P

Q

R

S

T

U

V

W

Interior Photo Credits

All screen captures provided by the authors.

Preface

Page x: © LightField Studios/Shutterstock.com; **Page xii:** © Neyman Kseniya/Shutterstock.com; **Page xiv:** © Cameron Prins/Shutterstock.com; **Page xvii:** laptop © Kite_rin/Shutterstock.com, tablet © guteksk7/Shutterstock.com; **Page xviii:** © KucherAV/Shutterstock.com; **Page xix:** © Prostock-studio/Shutterstock.com

Chapter 2

Page 71: rainbow: publicdomainvectors.org

Chapter 4

Page 129: printer: publicdomainvectors.org; **Page 146:** flag: publicdomainvectors.org, voting icon: publicdomainvectors.org

Chapter 5

Page 196: photo © Kelly Rutkosky

Chapter 8

Page 305: compass: publicdomainvectors.org